10,000
GARDEN
QUESTIONS
ANSWERED BY 20 EXPERTS

10,000 GARDEN QUESTIONS

ANSWERED BY 20 EXPERTS

EDITED BY MARJORIE J. DIETZ
Fourth Edition

Originally edited by F. F. Rockwell
New drawings for the fourth edition
by Ray Skibinski

WINGS BOOKS
New York • Avenel, New Jersey

Copyright © 1944, 1959, 1974, 1982 by Doubleday Book & Music Clubs, Inc.

This 1995 edition is published by Wings Books,
distributed by Random House Value Publishing, Inc.,
40 Engelhard Avenue, Avenel, New Jersey 07001,
by arrangement with GuildAmerica® Books /Doubleday Book & Music Clubs, Inc.

GuildAmerica® Books is a registered trademark of Doubleday Book & Music Clubs, Inc.

Random House
New York • Toronto • London • Sydney • Auckland

Printed and bound in the United States of America

A CIP catalog record for this book is available from the Library of Congress

ISBN 0-517-12226-X

8 7 6 5 4 3 2 1

Contents

8. Annuals and Biennials 652

What Annuals To Grow • Propagation • General Culture • Specific Annual Plants • Biennials • Specific Biennial Plants

9. Lawns and Turf Areas 695

Grading • Preparation for Sowing • Lawn Grasses • Sowing Seed • Planting Lawns Vegetatively • Tending the Established Lawn • Mowers and Mowing • Lawn Irrigation • Lawn Fertilization • Lawn Weed and Pest Control • Moss Lawns

10. The Home Vegetable Garden 749

Planning the Garden • Soil Preparation • Seed Sowing • Maintenance • Exhibiting • Equipment • Miscellaneous • Pests and Diseases • Specific Vegetables

11. Home-grown Fruits 894

The Orchard • Specific Tree Fruits • Dwarf and Espalier Fruit Trees • Small Fruits • Cane Fruits • Nut Trees

12. House Plants 1000

General Culture • Decorating with House Plants • Miniature Gardens • Specific Flowering House Plants • Annuals and Biennials as House Plants • Foliage Plants • Gift Plants • Shrubs • Ferns • Vines for Indoors • Cacti • Succulents • Hardy Bulbs for Forcing • Hardy Spring Bulbs for Indoors • Tender Bulbs for Indoors

Introduction
to the Fourth Edition

GARDENERS ON ALL LEVELS of proficiency and of all ages will find this revised fourth edition of *10,000 Garden Questions Answered* as essential a tool as their trowel. Serving as *the* gardening "bible," *10,000 Garden Questions Answered* has been a primary source of information for generations of gardeners since the first edition appeared nearly 40 years ago. This edition has been prepared to equip gardeners with the practical knowledge as well as the inspiration needed for the challenges of a solar age in which, it seems reasonable to predict, gardening will be a more important part of our lives than ever before. At the same time it has been recognized by the contributing editors that many aspects of gardening never change. *10,000 Garden Questions Answered* remains a book for every season and for every age.

As with previous editions of *10,000 Garden Questions Answered,* the mountains of diversified gardening queries and their answers have been separated into 16 general sections, as follows:

1   Soils and Fertilizers
2   Planning and Landscaping
3   Ornamental Plants—Growing Techniques
     and Environmental Problems
4   Trees, Shrubs, and Vines
5   Bulbs, Tubers, and Corms
6   Roses
7   Perennials
8   Annuals and Biennials
9   Lawns and Turf Areas
10   The Home Vegetable Garden
11   Home-grown Fruits
12   House Plants
13   Plant Troubles and Their Control
14   Weeds
15   Regional Garden Problems
16   Sources for Further Information

The botanical names of plants, in this fourth edition, have been updated to conform as nearly as possible to the International Code for the Nomenclature of Cultivated Plants and *Hortus Third, A Concise Dictionary of Plants Cultivated in the United States and Canada.* Beginners who balk at the use of botanical plant names can take comfort from the prevalence of common names of plants which also appear. Unfortunately, there is no recognized authority for common plant names, but the editors have been as consistent as is possible in an area where such confusion abounds.

F. F. Rockwell, the dean of American garden writers and home gardeners *par excellence,* was the first editor of *10,000 Garden Questions Answered.* The following excerpts, which are from his original Introduction, are as relevant today as when he first wrote them and require no further embellishment or explanation:

"The preparation of *10,000 Garden Questions Answered* was originally undertaken in response to numerous requests from readers of *The Home Garden Magazine.* It seemed worthwhile to present, in some organized and permanent form, the wealth of information which the answers to these questions convey. Our purpose was to make these facts available in a form that would enable the reader to refer to it quickly, and find readily, all the information on any particular subject. The most practical method of obtaining this objective, it seemed to us, was to arrange this material in general categories or sections.

"For each of these sections an introduction which gives general information on the subject covered has been prepared. The introductions are based upon the questions most generally asked concerning the subject discussed. In other words, these questions, instead of being answered individually, have been answered in a composite reply that presents the general principles involved and provides a background for the more specific questions which follow.

"This treatment has two distinct advantages. In the first place, it enables the reader to get much more from the answers to the individual questions; in the second, it has saved a great amount of space. Actually, the answers to more than 13,000 questions are contained in the present volume.

"The advantages of having questions answered by experts widely experienced in many lines are obvious. Too often such answers are compiled from outdated reference books. The answers in this volume are by persons who are actually doing the things they write about. Many of them are recognized internationally as authorities in their respective fields. At the same time, with few exceptions, their daily work brings them into direct contact with the problems of home gardeners the country over.

"With so many different persons contributing information of one sort or another, it is inevitable that many differences of opinion have arisen. In so far as possible, the recommendations and suggestions made on any specific subject have been brought into harmony by correspondence or discussion. There are cases where this has not been possible. The result is honest differences of opinion such as would be forthcoming on almost any garden question that might be asked of any group of experts —differences similar to those that would be found in every field of human endeavor, in any science or art, and horticulture partakes of both.

"Our aim has been to present the home gardener with practical information in readily available form, concerning his or her own personal problems. To the extent that this has been accomplished, we will have succeeded in making the kind of book we set out to create."

Marjorie J. Dietz

What Is YOUR Question?

(Suggestions as to how to use this book most effectively)

To GET FROM THESE PAGES the information you wish, most completely and in the shortest time, read carefully the following paragraphs. They explain, first, how this book is put together; and, second, the definite steps to take in finding the answer to a specific problem, or to one so general in character that it might not be possible to locate it through the Index.

Organization Plan

There are 16 main divisions or sections, covering Soils and Fertilizers; Planning and Landscaping; Ornamental Plants—Growing Techniques and Environmental Problems; Trees, Shrubs, and Vines; Bulbs, Tubers, and Corms; Roses; Perennials; Annuals and Biennials; Lawns and Turf Areas; The Home Vegetable Garden; Home-grown Fruits; House Plants; Plant Troubles and Their Control; Weeds; Regional Garden Problems; and Sources for Further Information. The sources section covers Books, State Agricultural Experiment Stations, Horticultural and Special Plant Societies, Botanical Gardens, Arboreta and Public Gardens and Sources for Plants and Seeds.

Each of these sections is organized along the following lines:

1. A general introduction, giving basic information about the subject concerned. (The introduction for Soils and Fertilizers, for instance, describes the function of the soil in connection with plant growth, different types of soil, soil acidity, the various nutrients essential to plant growth, the part which humus plays in the soil, and so on.)

2. Following the introduction, the questions, in most sections, are arranged in the following order:

What to Grow	Winter Protection
Soils and Fertilizers	Propagation
Culture	Specific Plants
	(*In Alphabetical Order*)

Use of Index

In most instances any specific question can be located through the use of the Index.

1. Formulate your question in your own mind as definitely as possible.
2. Pick out the KEY WORD in the question. (For instance, it might be "How should I train *tomatoes?*" "How can I *graft* a good variety of apple on a wild tree?" or "What is a good *perennial* to grow in the *shade?*")
3. Then look up the key word ("tomato," "graft," "perennial," or "shade") in the Index. Under this item, in the Index, you will probably find several references. One of these (example: "tomato, staking") may indicate exactly what you are looking for, and you can then turn at once to the specific question you have in mind.

More General Questions

The question in your mind may, however, be of such a nature that you do not know what to look for in the Index to locate it. Suppose, for example, that you have seen somewhere, growing high on a wall, a vine-like plant with hydrangea-like flowers, and you would like to know what it is. A search through the section on "Vines—Perennial" should reveal that it is the climbing hydrangea (*Hydrangea anomala*).

It is recommended that, in looking up questions on any general subject—such as fertilizers, lawns, vegetables, fruits—the introduction be read in full first: Here you will find in text form the answers to many questions, some of which may not reappear in the questions and answers. Familiarity with the introduction will also help materially in augmenting the information to be gained from the answers to specific questions.

In the answers to some questions the reader is referred to his State Agricultural Experiment Station. A list of these stations, as well as a list of Botanical Gardens and other public gardens to visit, is given in Section 16. Also in that section is a list of books and bulletins that will guide the reader to full and detailed information on many different garden subjects.

The Editors of the Fourth Edition of 10,000 Garden Questions Answered

MARJORIE J. DIETZ is a former editor of *Flower Grower* and *The Home Garden* magazines and former associate editor of the Brooklyn Botanic Garden's publication, *Plants and Gardens*. She is the author of many articles for national magazines and several books, and was Editor of the Third Edition of *10,000 Garden Questions Answered* as well as this revision. Her interests include rhododendrons, daffodils, native plants, house plants, and flower and vegetable gardening. (Perennials; Annuals and Biennials)

GEORGE and KATY ABRAHAM are active in every phase of horticulture and are well known for their TV and radio programs, their syndicated garden columns, and the Green Thumb garden book series. Their 7-acre garden in Naples, New York, includes two greenhouses for research and demonstration. For their dedication to garden communication, they have received many national awards. (Ornamental Plants—Growing Techniques and Environmental Problems)

ARTHUR BING is a professor in Cornell University's Department of Floriculture and Ornamental Horticulture. He has taught courses in weed control at the State University, Farmingdale, New York, and is responsible for statewide weed control recommendations on turf, ornamentals, and greenhouse crops at the Long Island Horticultural Research Laboratory, Riverhead, New York. He includes gardening among his hobbies. (Weeds)

R. MILTON CARLETON has written many articles and several books on both the popular and technical aspects of horticulture. He has had flower, fruit, and vegetable gardens in Illinois, on an island off the Maine coast, and in Florida. For over 40 years he has visited annually every major horticultural research center in the United States. (Soils and Fertilizers; Regional Garden Problems)

BEVERLY R. DOBSON is an American Rose Society accredited judge and consulting Rosarian. She is the author of numerous articles about roses and is active in the Rose Hybridizers Association and Heritage Roses Group. Approximately 250 varieties of roses of all types grow in the Dobson garden in Irvington-on-Hudson, New York. (Roses)

DEREK FELL is former executive director of All-America Selections (the national seed trials) and the National Garden Bureau (an information office sponsored by the garden-seed industry). He has written several gardening books and contributes articles to national magazines. (The Home Vegetable Garden)

CHARLES MARDEN FITCH has written extensively on house plants and has studied and photographed them in their native habitats in Central and South America, Africa, Australia, New Zealand, New Guinea, Mexico, and Europe while working as an educational television specialist for the U.S. Department of State, the Organization of American States, and the Peace Corps. (House Plants)

ELIZABETH C. HALL is associated with the Library of The Horticultural Society of New York. She was formerly on the staff of the New York Botanical Garden, where she served as Librarian and Associate Curator of Education and Instructor in the children's gardencraft program. (Sources for Further Information)

BEBE MILES has contributed many articles to magazines on varied aspects of home gardening, with the major emphasis being on her favorite subjects: bulbs and native plants. Her latest book is *Bulbs for the Home Gardener*. (Bulbs, Tubers, and Corms)

ROBERT W. SCHERY is Director of The Lawn Institute, Marysville, Ohio. Major research projects have included tropical floristics and economic botany as well as subjects of interest to home gardeners. He is the author of *Lawn Keeping* and other books about lawns. (Lawns and Turf Areas)

ALICE UPHAM SMITH is a landscape architect who practices in Arkansas. She has written numerous articles and several books, including

Trees in a Winter Landscape. Because of the rock-strewn landscape of her region, she has become an enthusiastic rock gardener. (Planning and Landscaping)

ROGER D. WAY is Professor of Pomology at Cornell University's New York State Agricultural Experiment Station in Geneva, New York, where he spends full time on research in fruit tree breeding and fruit tree nursery techniques. He is responsible for the breeding and introduction of such apples as 'Empire', 'Jonagold', 'Jonamac', and 'Burgundy', the 'Ulster' and 'Hudson' sweet cherries, and 'York' elderberry. (Home-grown Fruits)

JOHN A. WEIDHAAS, JR., is Extension Specialist in Entomology at Virginia Polytechnic Institute and State University. He is the author of many articles on entomological subjects. He has been responsible for statewide insect-control recommendations for over 20 years, first in New York as Research-Extension Specialist at Cornell University, Ithaca, and now in Virginia. (Plant Troubles and Their Control)

DONALD WYMAN is Horticulturist Emeritus of the Arnold Arboretum, Harvard University. He has received many horticultural honors in this country and abroad. His many books include *Dwarf Shrubs* and *Wyman's Gardening Encyclopedia.* (Trees, Shrubs, and Vines)

*

The first edition of *10,000 Garden Questions Answered* was based on the knowledge and practical experience of 20 experts. Many of these original editors have remained as contributors to subsequent revisions, just as other experts have been added to the staff. Rather than 20 experts, it would be no exaggeration to state that *10,000 Garden Questions Answered* is the work of over 50 experts, a veritable hall of fame of distinguished horticulturists.

The following contributing editors assisted in the third edition revision: Margaret C. Ohlander, George L. Slate, Cynthia Westcott, and Helen Van Pelt Wilson.

Other horticultural authorities who helped in the preparation of the first and second editions of this book are the following: F. F. Rockwell, Montague Free, T. H. Everett, R. C. Allen, Robert S. Lemmon, P. J. McKenna, W. E. Thwing, Alex Laurie, C. H. Connors, T. A. Weston, Esther C. Grayson, Helen S. Hull, Louis Pyrenson, O. Wesley Davidson, Francis C. Coulter, Alex Cumming, Henry E. Downer, Kathleen

N. Marriage, John Melady, H. Dewey Mohr, H. Stuart Ortloff, Hildegard Schneider, P. J. Van Melle, Thomas A. Williams, Paul Work, and J. H. Clark.

Also John H. Beale, George A. Buchanan, George E. Burkhardt, L. C. Chadwick, A. S. Colby, Charles F. Doney, E. V. Hardenburg, D. C. Kiplinger, Stuart Longmuir, Harriet K. Morse, George D. Oberle, E. L. Reber, Roy P. Rogers, Kenneth D. Smith, Nancy Ruzicka Smith, John V. Watkins, Robert E. Weidner, Natalie Gomez, and John Wingert.

ARTISTS who have prepared illustrations for the first, second, and third editions are: George L. Hollrock, Pauline W. Kreutzfeldt, Helen Reddy, Carl Sigman, William Ward, Eva Melady, Tabea Hofmann, H. B. Raymore, Natalie Harlan Davis, Frederick Rockwell, Esther C. Grayson, Katherine Burton, and Reisie Lonette. New drawings for the fourth edition were prepared by Ray Skibinski.

10,000
GARDEN
QUESTIONS

ANSWERED BY 20 EXPERTS

1. Soils and Fertilizers

BEFORE TRYING TO understand soil, stop thinking in such outmoded terms as "the dirt under your feet" or "common as dirt." Far from being common, soil is perhaps the most complex substance with which we must work to stay alive. Without it, there would be no plants—the only source of the starches and sugars that are the fuels on which all living animals run.

The homeowner interested in gardening, unlike the farmer, does not make selection of soil his first concern, and few homes are purchased because they happen to have good soil under them. This vital substance for growing plants is not even considered until long after the purchase contract has been signed. It becomes of concern only when the owner becomes interested in gardening.

As a result, millions of prospective gardeners find themselves with stubborn clay or dry, porous sands rather than an ideal garden soil—a mellow loam rich in organic matter. One British authority described that ideal soil as one so loose and friable that an arm could be thrust into it up to the elbow. Most American gardeners would be happy with a soil into which they could thrust a hand up to the wrist!

A Test That Determines Soil Type

All too often, gardeners try to guess what is in their soil and—guess wrong. The only way to be sure is to make a wash test. Light sandy soils that contain little clay are easy to test. Heavier soils with a high clay content are difficult because of the strong electrical attraction of acid clay particles for lime. (There are alkaline clays but most are acid.) The bond between clay and lime can be broken by adding 2 tablespoons of a common fertilizer—nitrate of soda—to the test.

To make the test: Begin with a clean half-gallon Mason jar or other round glass container. Add half a cup of soil to the jar and pour in enough water to half fill it. Screw the lid on tightly and swirl the water around rapidly for about a minute. Let it settle. Repeat this swirling several times. Next, allow the water to stand until it is clear. Clay particles are extremely fine and may take a week to settle.

When the water has cleared, the various-sized particles will be in layers. On top will be the clay particles and on the bottom the larger bits of mineral matter such as sand and fine gravel. Between them, there is a layer of silt.

Importance of Organic Material

Since organic matter makes up less than 5 per cent of the volume of most soils, it is not conspicuous in wash tests, yet in comparison with the pure mineral components, it is far more important. Actually, no mixture of clay, sand, and silt can be called a true soil unless it contains some organic matter. In soils, organic matter has two important roles. The first of these is mechanical—as an absorbent and adsorbent agent to soak up solutions of plant nutrients such as nitrogen, phosphorus, and potash. It also serves as a reservoir for moisture, freeing the passageways between soil grains so air can enter freely.

By separating soil particles, organic matter helps form the desirable "crumb" structure that makes soil friable and easy to work. It also has an electrical attraction for the microscopically fine particles of clay, attracting them like flies to honey. This effect helps loosen heavy clay loam so it is more workable and able to contain the air vital to plant growth.

The second role of organic matter is to provide a home for the billions of microorganisms that exist in any true soil. Pick up a handful of loam from a garden and you will hold in your hand more living organisms than there are human beings on earth. Until the gardener understands that soil is alive, he cannot appreciate why he must add organic matter, why these tiny bits of matter are vital to proper feeding of plants, and why without them, the addition of fertilizer to soils would be all but wasted.

The most important function of these microorganisms is to attack the remains of plants such as roots and buried trash, as well as added organic substances, and break them down into simpler forms that living plants can use for food. Plants are no more capable of dining off the dead residues of last year's crop than they are of eating a hamburger.

Without teeth or a digestive system similar to that of animals, they can only absorb nutrients in the form of a soup—a solution of nutrients that have been predigested for them by bacteria.

This process of predigestion may take place in stages, with one species of soil organism doing the preliminary breaking down of plant protein, for example, into amino acids, with a third reducing them to ammonia. Since only acid-soil plants are able to use ammonia directly, this must be attacked by a fourth group which produces nitrate nitrogen, a compound most plants can absorb directly through their roots.

There is another way in which bacteria and other soil organisms enter into the nutritional aspect of growing plants. Most gardeners feel that when they add fertilizers to soil, these materials directly enter plant roots and are consumed completely. This might be true if root hairs filled practically every minute chink in the soil, but such is not the case. The roots of many plants are in contact with a small fraction of 1 per cent of the volume of soil through which they penetrate. If there is any free water between the grains of soil, fertilizers dissolved in this water are pulled downward by the force of gravity and are lost in drainage channels.

Bacteria, fungi, and other soil organisms, however, are plants that need the same food elements as do higher plants with green leaves. Instead of allowing excess fertilizer to escape, they absorb it and use it for their own growth. Since these soil organisms do not live long—at the most a few days—when they die the food they absorbed is released to feed plants that have already used up the fertilizer the gardener applied days before.

A gardener—faced with the problem of soil unsuited to growing most plants—has two alternatives. Both will call for the use of organic matter. The first solution is the more simple—adapt the plants to the soil by choosing those that can survive under existing conditions. For example, he may want to garden at a summer home where sandy soil makes certain plants impossible to grow. Yet there are hundreds of species that thrive near salt water, both in tropical and temperate climates. Away from the spray there are shrubs, trees, and vines that can grow in sandy soil. His one problem will be the constant addition of organic matter which disappears rapidly in sandy soils. Even these tolerant species of plants must somehow be provided with the elements it provides.

A second alternative is to adapt the soil to the plants that he really wants to grow; in short—produce topsoil. A great deal of nonsense is written about the aeons needed to build an inch or two of black loam.

True, in nature this is a slow process in which decaying leaves and plant wastes must work downward, with a slow accumulation of microorganisms, all modified by weather and other phenomena.

When, however, a gardener must work over a relatively small area, he or she can modify a heavy clay loam into an acceptable garden soil in a single year. Again, the solution is the incorporation of that magic ingredient of all good soils—organic matter. What can be used?

Provided it contains some fibrous material that has relative permanence in contact with soil, any form of organic matter will produce results. A substance such as dried blood, valuable as it is as the best organic fertilizer available, is worthless as a producer of the type of fibrous residue needed to build soil. Some substance such as lignin or cellulose is necessary to provide the long-lasting, porous remains that soil needs for aeration.

When the material applied is already partially decayed, then not only is time saved, but the chance of plant injury is reduced. When fresh plant wastes and green manures are turned under in the soil or added to the compost pile, there is a period when active fermentation takes place, releasing more carbon dioxide than roots can use if growing at the time, or than bacteria can tolerate in the compost pile. This is an important reason for composting, of which more is discussed later.

Even when it has gone through a preliminary decomposition, an application of organic matter can be improved by fertilizer additions in twice the amount recommended for the crops to be grown. Bacteria, working on plant wastes in soil, demand so much nitrogen, for example, that they often cause plants to turn yellow because of the lack of this vital growth element. Fertilizing prevents this.

A compost pile is little more than a huge culture of microorganisms. They begin the process by which organic wastes are converted to a long-lasting form that will improve soil for periods as long as half a century. Since these organisms are plants, they require the same foods as plants with green leaves. In addition, they must have an outside source of starches and sugars for energy, since they cannot make their own. Instead, they extract these from plant wastes.

Available Composting Materials

Peat moss: Peat moss derived from sphagnum bogs is perhaps the most universally available source of humus today. It is an excellent amendment for a variety of soils and kinds of plants and gardens. A neglected yet valid use for peat moss is adding it to the compost pile, not for further breakdown, which it doesn't need, but for the purpose of picking up soil organisms not present in peat bogs. At the same time, it helps aerate the compost pile. Peat moss has a low nutritive value, but it improves both clay and sandy soils and also serves as a home for soil organisms. Sphagnum peat, usually sold in 6-foot cubic bales, is an attractive brown in color, of a crumbly texture, and easy to handle. It is acid. Many domestic peats are derived from decayed reeds and sedges. They are fine-textured and dark to reddish-brown. For home gardeners who can buy it in bulk, sedge peat, while not as valuable as sphagnum peat moss, is useful as a soil amendment.

Sewage sludge: As a soil amendment, air-dried sewage sludge can be had for the hauling from most local treatment plants. Processed sludge has distinct disadvantages as a lawn fertilizer, for which purpose it is widely sold. Composting improves the processed form for lawn use. Raw sludge has one bad quality if used on the vegetable garden. It can carry the organisms of amoebic dysentery unless exposed to freezing for an entire winter. Composting also kills these organisms. In areas where heavy industry or service firms operate (if they are allowed to dump wastes into public sewers), sludge should not be used on vegetable gardens. It probably contains harmful chemicals. Check with your local utilities offices to find out if it is safe to use. It is still all right to use on ornamental plantings.

Ground corn cobs: These are higher in sugars than most composting materials, which means they will need extra nitrogen to use up this excess. Otherwise, corn cobs can cause a buildup of fungi, some of which can be harmful.

Spent mushroom manure: In some areas, mushroom growers will sell the worn-out mushroom soil, which contains more than half of decayed manure. Like peat moss, it is low in nutrients, since the mushrooms have used these as food, but otherwise it is an ideal soil amendment. An advantage is that composting for use in mushroom beds has destroyed weed seeds.

Fallen leaves: Fallen leaves are generally a poor source of nutrients but they do become a source of humus. (Forty bushels of leaves are equal in organic matter to 15 bushels of manure and supply a scattering of minerals.) Leaves are largely fiber, and for this reason improve soil. Leafmold, which results from the slow decay of fallen leaves, becomes more nutritive in the process because it contains the remains of dead microorganisms and other accumulated substances.

Weeds: Until they have set seeds, weeds are a good source of composting material. If you must compost weeds of high seed content, you had best make a separate pile and leave it for a year before using.

Lawn clippings: Lawn clippings are unusually rich in nutrients compared with other green matter because only the most active part, the growing tip of the blade, is removed in mowing. The clippings decay quite fast in the compost pile.

Animal manures: They were once the only source of fertility for gardens. This type of fertilizer has its advantages in that in addition to supplying some plant nutrients, humus and desirable bacteria are also added to the soil. The humus-forming value of manure is increased when it is combined with straw or a coarse grade of peat moss, often found with poultry manures.

The availability of animal manures today differs from region to region. In rural areas which often border suburban developments, there can be ample supplies of both cow and horse manures. Numerous riding stables exist today in both urban and suburban areas. One caution: Some riding stable proprietors, mostly in cities, heavily treat the manure with disinfectants and deodorizing chemicals, which are toxic to plants. Such treated manure should be composted in a separate pile before being applied to the soil. Test the composted manure before spreading by planting tomato seeds in it. If it is still toxic, the seeds may germinate, but will die quickly.

Green manure: The use of cover crops to be plowed under as green manure is often recommended, but it generally is impractical except in the vegetable plot. There, winter rye (the grain, not ryegrass) can be sown whenever an area becomes empty of crops. It will grow in fall and even in winter when temperatures are above freezing. After it has been tilled into the soil in spring (using additional fertilizer) a month must elapse. This limits green manuring to areas where late crops are to be sown or the areas that will lie fallow for a season.

Sawdust and wood chips: Not all that is written about the use of wood products as soil amendments can be taken as gospel. For example, soft woods such as pine, spruce, and fir are claimed to be unsuitable because they contain resins. Although their presence will slow up the process of reducing woody products to decayed organic matter, it will also mean that the resultant substance will last much longer once in the soil.

Sawdust and wood shavings in particular need treatment with added fertilizer (about a pint of a mixed fertilizer to a bushel of sawdust) and also about the same amount of lime added to the soil under the layer of sawdust or wood chips for each bushel spread out for tilling.

The Techniques of Composting

Although many homeowners find composting a nuisance, there are reasons why practicing this method of treating wastes is part of being a good citizen. In this age of consideration for the environment, a major problem is that of disposing of the millions of tons of solid waste engendered by the processes of living.

Plant wastes, table scraps, dust from the vacuum cleaner, and many other materials discarded into the garbage can can go onto the compost pile, where they will serve a useful purpose instead of contributing to the community's problem. The number of different materials that can be disposed of in this way is amazing. They include dead rats, bones, table wastes, lawn clippings, leaves, weeds, plants pulled from the garden, hair, wood shavings and sawdust, spoiled grain, clippings from woolen cloth, as well as countless other substances that came originally from a living organism.

Starchy and sugary products—spoiled cereals, jellies, potato peelings, and similar materials—do supply bacteria with the energy foods they need to do their work, but they lack nitrogen, which is also essential. Added fertilizer will make up for this.

A traditional prohibition has been against the addition to the pile of fats, greases, and waxes. The reason given was that these materials prevented the decay of organic matter. While it is true that large amounts of fatty materials could prevent breakdown of the entire mass of organic matter, smaller amounts only slow up the process slightly. Actually, waxes and fats are needed in a finished compost because they are essential to the formation of humus, perhaps the most valuable form of organic matter in gardening.

A soggy compost pile will not work. Choose a well-drained, level location in light shade. If located in a sunny spot, the heat in summer can go so high as to kill bacteria near the surface. As it is, the heat generated in decay can go as high as 150° F. inside the pile, so added sun heat is not needed. In arid regions, the pile can sit in a slight depression to save water, but should not be so deep that the bottom layer will drown.

Sprinkle the area where the compost is to be built with finely ground limestone, the grade used for topping driveways. Build the pile like a super "hero" sandwich out of alternate layers of organic materials and good garden soil, each about 4 inches thick. Sprinkle every other layer with a commercial fertilizer such as 5–10–5, about as thick as sugaring strawberries. The layer that doesn't get fertilizer should be sprinkled with finely ground limestone.

Purely organic fertilizers are not as useful for this purpose because they must themselves be broken down before they will provide the necessary nutrients. However, those who wish to use organic materials exclusively can use dried blood, fish emulsion, or urine.

If the amount of organic matter available is small, the area covered by the pile should be reduced, so several layers can be built up in a short period. A depth of 2 or 3 feet is necessary if the interior of the pile is to heat up properly. As each layer is placed, it should be sprinkled so that it will be moist but not soggy.

A month after it has been started (if the temperature is not below freezing) the pile should be turned over and over to mix thoroughly all the layers. This will release excess carbon dioxide that slows up bacterial action and will provide extra oxygen for the use of microorganisms. If the pile seems dry, moisten it. Turn again every month. Under ideal conditions, with outdoor temperatures above 70° F., the compost might be ready in three months, but over winter, it may take eight to ten.

What Is Humus?

The need for constantly replacing organic matter in soil lies in its vital role in building up the humus content. But what is humus?

Actually, nobody really knows. It is somehow tied up with lignin (a substance from wood), with protein and a colloidal complex—that about states what we know about it. The three or four lignin chemists who know more about it than anyone else differ and argue about its composition.

But what humus does is far from mysterious. It is so thirsty that it will absorb between 80 per cent and 90 per cent of the water in a saturated atmosphere. In comparison, the best clay can do is to absorb 20 per cent. It makes soil nutrients much more available. It breaks down slowly, releasing its protein in the form of nitrogen over a period of from five to fifty years. Thus, it is a "built-in" source of plant nutrients available even when other sources fail.

An important function of humus is to pull tiny soil particles such as clay into clumps or "crumbs," which make a heavy clay more porous, easier to work, and a better place in which to grow plants.

The breakdown of organic matter into humus is slower when fats and waxes are present, but the final release of the desirable elements in humus is correspondingly slowed up. Because of the more rapid destruction of humus in tropical and subtropical climates, it has little chance to accumulate. This means that organic matter is used up faster in such climates and must be replaced more often. Humus in warm climates is lighter in color; in northern soils it is often a deep blackish-brown.

Why pH Is Important

The term pH often confuses gardeners. Although the technical physics and chemistry behind the pH theory call for a college course or two, actually, in use, this scale is no more difficult to understand than a thermometer. It measures the hydrogen-ion concentration in a given substance on a scale of from 0 to 14. Since the hydrogen-ion concentration has a direct relation to the acidity or alkalinity of a substance, with a device for measuring that concentration, we can tell how "sour" or "sweet" a given soil may be. This measuring can be done in two ways: First, an electric bridge can measure this directly. Such a device is too expensive for the home gardener but most county agents have one, as do State Experiment Stations or any persons who make soil tests. Second, although not quite as hairline accurate, the small pH test kits sold in garden centers are adequate and usually give a reading within a tenth of a point or two. They are chemical and indicate pH by a change in color of test papers. For a small price, the gardener can determine one of the most important factors in gardening.

But why is pH important? First, it tells us what chemical nutrients can be available to a plant *if they are present*. A pH test does *not* tell you, for example, that phosphorus is present, but only if the soil is not too acid or too alkaline to allow phosphate to be released.

The point at which all elements are available to plants that do not require highly acid soil has its center at pH 6.5. On the pH scale, 7.0 is considered as neutral, where acidity and alkalinity balance out each other. Thus somewhere between 6.0 and 7.0 is perhaps the best point to strive for in altering soil acidity.

Acid-soil plants such as rhododendron, blueberry, mountain-laurel, and others are able to thrive in acid soil because they do not use nitrogen from the soil directly, but depend on a special type of fungus on their roots, called mycorrhiza, which is able to change ammonium nitrate into nitrate nitrogen. These plants also tolerate some free aluminum at their roots, an element which is released at a pH of 5.5 or lower.

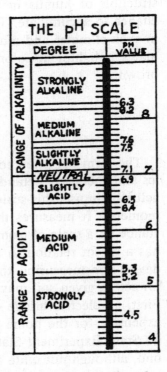

THE pH SCALE

DEGREE	pH VALUE

RANGE OF ALKALINITY

STRONGLY ALKALINE

MEDIUM ALKALINE

SLIGHTLY ALKALINE — 6.3 6.2 8

— 7.6 7.5

— 7.1 7

NEUTRAL — 6.9

SLIGHTLY ACID — 6.5 6.4

— 6

RANGE OF ACIDITY

MEDIUM ACID

— 5.3 5.2 5

STRONGLY ACID

— 4.5

— 4

The degree of acidity or alkalinity of the soil is indicated by the pH scale, which ranges from 1 to 14, with 7 as the neutral point. Practically all vegetables and a majority of other plants thrive in neutral to moderately acid soil (pH of 6 to 7).

Not only does acidity decrease the availability of elements directly, but it also reduces the activity of soil bacteria until at 4.0 such activity might cease entirely. Since organic matter is available to plants only after bacteria have digested it first, the effect on growth is obvious. Another effect of pH is the release of toxic elements such as aluminum, which is released at a low pH (below 5.5) and also at a high pH (8.5). The prevalence of disease is also affected by pH, both by acid and alkaline soils. Scab on potatoes, for example, occurs only at a pH above 7.0.

Modifying pH

To increase the pH reading of light sandy loams one full point (e.g., from 5.5 to 6.5), apply 35 pounds of ground limestone (agricultural limestone) to 1,000 square feet; on medium loam, 50 pounds; and on heavy clay loam, 70 pounds.

To reduce the pH of a light sandy loam one full point (e.g., from 6.0 to 5.0), apply 10 pounds of dusting sulfur to 1,000 square feet; on medium loam, 15 pounds will be needed, and on heavy clay loam, 20 pounds.

A word of caution is needed on a common recommendation—the use of aluminum sulfate for acidifying soils. This chemical is widely used in greenhouses for acidity for azaleas. However, as a pot plant, an azalea is intended to live only through the flowering period for which it was forced and then can be discarded. The permanent effect of aluminum on its roots means nothing. In garden soils, however, aluminum is a bad actor if a pH of 5.5 or lower is to be maintained, damaging roots and stunting plants. Ammonium sulfate can be used instead. Although not nearly as effective pound for pound as dusting sulfur, it has the added advantage of supplying nitrogen in ammonium form, which acid-loving plants can use. Use double the amount recommended for sulfur, but be sure to dissolve ammonium sulfate in water for applying.

Nutrient Elements

The "big three" in nutrient elements are nitrogen, phosphorus, and potash. They are the ones that must be declared on the bag of fertilizer you buy. The three figures, such as in a combination of 5–10–5, mean that the bag contains 5 per cent nitrogen, 10 per cent phosphorus, and 5 per cent potash.

These elements do not occur in pure form but as compounds with other materials. When they are elements in an organic fertilizer, they can be highly complex and are unavailable to plants until they have been digested or broken down into simpler forms by soil organisms. These organisms are partially dormant at temperatures below 60° F. and grow progressively more active up to about 90° F. Thus, organic fertilizers are not too effective in early spring on hardy crops. However, because they add organic matter, they have one value not possessed by pure chemical or mineral fertilizers.

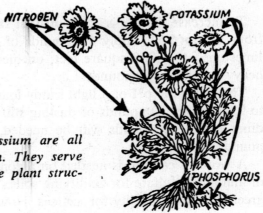

Nitrogen, phosphorus, and potassium are all essential to normal plant growth. They serve different purposes in building the plant structure.

One argument used against chemical fertilizers is that they "burn" foliage. This is true, but only when they are misapplied. If used in excess —if not watered in—many fertilizer salts are so "thirsty" that they will actually suck water out of leaves and roots. Water is a vital element in plant nutrition. In fact, some plants are 90 per cent water. The answer to burning is to water in any chemical fertilizer as soon as applied. Fertilizers in solution simply do not burn.

Whether applied in organic or chemical form, all plant nutrients must be broken down into near-elemental form before they can be taken up by roots. Plants cannot distinguish between nitrogen, phosphorus, or potash from the breakdown of organic matter and the same elements from a chemical source.

Nitrogen

Nitrogen is vital to the formation of all proteins. It is an essential element of chlorophyll, the green chemical that permits plants (and plants alone) to manufacture starches and sugars. Many of the compounds in plants—amino acids, aromatic compounds, etc.—must have nitrogen. It is the "grow" element, forcing soft, lush growth when used in excess. Because of the importance of nitrogen in plant growth, it is essential to have an available supply. Since nature cannot provide nitrogen in sufficient quantities, other sources are essential, namely, commercial fertilizers and manures. Nitrate of soda, sulfate of ammonia, dried blood, cottonseed meal, and the various manures are some of the materials used for supplying extra nitrogen when it is needed in greater amounts than the soil seems able to provide.

Phosphorus

Phosphorus also enters into the composition of proteins and amino acids. It is associated with cell division. It contributes to stiff stems that hold foliage to the sunlight. Flowering and seed formation must have this element. It is a difficult element to manage, since it locks up rapidly as soon as it touches soil and so must be applied in excess of actual use by plants. Many gardens that have been fertilized for years are practically low-grade phosphate mines, but this phosphorus is in an insoluble form that plants cannot use.

Superphosphate, mistakenly called acid phosphate—it is alkaline in reaction—is processed to delay this "fixing" process as long as possible. Phosphate rock, often recommended by organic garden enthusiasts, becomes slowly available as it is dissolved by soil acids. It is seldom of much use the first year it is applied and, weight for weight, is far less effective than superphosphate.

Perhaps one of the most sacred cows in gardening is bone meal. True, in Victorian England, bone meal *was* one of the few good fertilizers available, but it was a far different product from the dehydrated, devitalized product of today. Every dedicated gardener of that day had a bone grinder in his potting shed or garden house. Fresh, raw bone, with scraps of meat clinging to it, was ground and used immediately as a fertilizer. It included the marrow, blood, meat scraps, and valuable minor elements in addition to uncooked phosphorus. Today's bone, in my opinion, is all but worthless.

Although recommended for use on bulbs (which are actually injured in many cases by fertilizers), it is useful largely because it has no effect and gives the gardener something he thinks is doing good.

Potassium

Potassium—in the form of potassium hydroxide (potash)—has been neglected in plant nutrition. This is due to the fact that it is abundant in most American soils and when analyses are made for total nutrients it seems to be in adequate supply. Unfortunately, soil-bound potash is in a form that is difficult for plants to use. As a result, annual applications of potash in soluble form are essential, particularly if root crops are being grown. Potassium is an important catalyst in photosynthesis, is essential for starch formation and the movement of sugars in the plant, and is important to seed formation. It helps form stiff stems and is essential in formation of tubers and roots. It is a vital element in protein synthesis and in the utilization of nitrogen by plants.

Wood ashes, which also supply lime, are a convenient source of potassium. One point often overlooked in using wood ashes is that until the potash they contain has been dissolved and absorbed by the soil, a free lye solution is present. This can cause injury to roots for 2 or 3 days following application. It should be applied before planting and thoroughly mixed with the existing soil.

Muriate of potash and sulfate of potash are chemical salts that also need to be used carefully to avoid injury to plants.

The Minor Elements

Actually, these are minor in amounts used by the plants, not in their effects on growth. Of these, iron is the one most commonly in short supply. The rest are practically always present from decaying organic matter when this material is used freely, and when pH is held between 6.0 and 6.9.

A convenient way to apply iron is in the form of ferrous ammonium sulfate applied in solution. Four ounces of ferrous sulfate and 4 ounces of ammonium sulfate, dissolved in 3 gallons of water, form a solution that can be applied to soil directly, or even to a lawn if applied with a sprinkling can while walking at a moderate pace across the grass. If applied too liberally, it can turn grass a blackish-green for 2 or 3 weeks.

Iron deficiency shows up as a yellowing of the foliage and is particularly conspicuous on pin oaks.

Water and Plant Growth

Over vast areas of the United States, the growing of vegetables, for example, is practically impossible without some means of supplying water artificially. Elsewhere, the incorporation of large amounts of organic matter improves the water-holding capacity of soils to tide plants over periods when water is scarce.

Water is particularly important when mineral or chemical fertilizers are used. Since they are usually salts, they are hygroscopic and will actually pull water out of plant tissues unless they are in dilute solutions. Either they should be applied before soil is dug or tilled, or should be applied with a hose ready to water them in thoroughly as soon as applied.

Water in excess can cause problems. What is not commonly known is that roots are incapable of absorbing water and nutrients unless oxygen is also present in soil. A plant top can actually wilt for lack of water while its roots are completely submerged. The ideal soil is one that can absorb abundant water in its organic substances, but one in which the passages between the organic and mineral particles are filled with air.

On heavy soils, which are easy to overwater, the common recommendation of allowing plants to dry out between watering has some validity, but on most soils fit for growing plants, a much sounder policy is to keep the soil constantly moist to the root depth, without applying so much water that air passages are drowned out.

 Types of Soil

How do you recognize the value of natural soil? How do you improve it? The nutritional value of soil is hard to determine by casual inspection. A test must be made to determine it. However, dark soils usually have organic matter. A wash test as described in the Introduction will tell a great deal about a soil. Soil tests made by competent technicians at State Agricultural Stations are reliable guides. Home test kits, except for pH test kits, mean little without expert interpretation.

Are there special kinds of soil for different plants? Root crops require friable, light soils for best development. Crops with fine roots do better in coarse open soil, while coarse-rooted plants grow better in more dense soils composed of finer particles.

SANDY SOIL

We have a sandy lot and wish to enjoy good results. Should we put topsoil on? Yes. Extremely sandy soil needs loam but also plenty of organic matter.

What depth of topsoil should we use on sandy ground? Add 3 inches loam and spade to a depth of 6 inches. However, without additional organic matter, on very sandy soil loam is usually lost by being washed down into the sand.

My front yard is mostly sand. What flowers would be best to plant? Portulaca, California-poppy, annual phlox, calliopsis, cockscomb, morning-glory, anthemis, milkweed, aster, baby's-breath, liatris, yucca. To remedy the situation, add organic matter, such as peat moss, manure, or compost, and fertilizer.

How can we make a vegetable garden on pure sand? The only way this is possible is in raised beds made out of 2- by 12-inch planks for sides. Lay plastic and set the beds, usually 3 feet by 12 feet, on this base. Fill with a good loam. If soil is heavy, punch holes in the plastic. Another way to solve this problem is to dig out the entire garden to a depth of 12 inches, lay down plastic, and replace the soil. Either method slows up loss of fertility and water.

Our soil is sandy. How can we grow good roses? Add manure, compost, or peat moss. Keep soil fertilized and water heavily when necessary. Plenty of organic matter will be needed or roses will do poorly.

Our soil (on river front) is solid sand. Would surfacing it with a layer of topsoil be sufficient for planting fruit trees? No. A very large hole should be dug for each tree and filled with good soil in which to plant.

What would you suggest for a home garden at the seashore where there is a lot of sand? Additions of organic matter, such as manures, seaweed, peat moss, will help, although it would be better to mix some loam with the sand. Also dig under green-cover (see Introduction) crops.

I have a piece of very sandy land and wish to grow excellent corn. Can it be done? Yes, manure heavily or apply organic materials as recommended above; also apply a complete fertilizer several times during the growing season.

Our soil is all gravel. How can I adjust this for growing vegetables? Add a mixture of loam, peat moss, and/or manure to a depth of 3 inches and spade to a depth of 6 inches.

What is the best way of keeping land in shape for vegetables? The soil is light and sandy but well drained. Spade in manure or compost every fall. Keep well fertilized and properly cultivated.

Our soil is very sandy and is acid. What can we do so we can grow a vegetable garden? Increase the organic content of the soil by incorporating green-manure crops, farm manures, or other nonacid materials such as leaves, straw, plant refuse, or nonacid peat. Apply lime as needed to modify the acidity.

My ground is sandy. What is the best vegetable to plant? Any vegetable will grow in sandy soil if fertilized frequently. Apply fertilizer high in phosphorus and potash. (For sandy soil plant material, see also Section 3.)

CLAY SOIL

What makes clay so sticky? Clay is composed of very minute particles which have a large surface to absorb water. High water content causes the stickiness.

Why shouldn't clay soil be worked when wet? It puddles and hardens and makes a poor environment for roots. Digging too soon in the spring may make it practically useless for the season.

How much wood ashes is it safe to use on heavy clay soil? At least 10 pounds per 100 square feet.

My garden plot is heavy clay soil and produces well, but it is hard to work up. Would well-rotted manure and wood ashes be a benefit? Yes. Fine cinders would also be beneficial.

Can coal ashes be used to loosen clay soil? Only if they have been exposed to weather to leach out harmful substances. With coal once again being used, the supply of ashes should increase. Steam cinders from high-temperature boilers in electric-generating plants are also plentiful. They can be used up to one third the volume of clay to be treated. Break up or discard cinders more than ¼ inch in diameter.

What proportion of steam cinders should be mixed with clay to make it good for flowers? A 2-inch layer spaded in will be safe.

Are steam cinders in clay soil better than sand? Yes, they are of more help in opening it up and admitting air.

Does it make any difference what kind of sand is mixed with clay soil to lighten it? To what depth should the sand be spread on before spading in? Yes. Coarse or ungraded sands, containing a large proportion of $\frac{1}{16}$- to $\frac{1}{8}$-inch particles, will bring about the greatest improvement when added to a clay soil. Incorporate a 3-inch layer of such sand.

What shall I do to keep ground loosened? It gets sticky and lumpy. I mixed in sand and ashes but they did not help.   Probably too little sand was used. Manure and/or peat moss should improve such a soil.

My ground gets hard and dry on the surface, so that it is difficult for the young shoots to break through. It is soft enough beneath the surface. What can I do?   Incorporate sand and, if possible, well-rotted compost or peat moss in the upper surface. A layer of vermiculite $\frac{1}{2}$ inch deep at the surface will prevent crusting.

My garden soil is mostly clay. I dug under quite a few leaves in an effort to add humus to the soil. Will leaves tend to make the soil acid?   Usually not but it would be advisable in any case to test the soil for acidity.

Is chemical fertilizer harmful to clay soil?   The only chemical fertilizer which has a bad effect in clay is nitrate of soda. It causes the soil to become greasy and sticky. It is often necessary to furnish mineral elements so plants will grow. Ground limestone, a 2-inch layer, spaded into clay, will make it more workable. Gypsum is also recommended; consult your county extension agent concerning its use.

What can be added to a clay soil to increase root growth? It is slightly acid and in partial shade.   If wet, the soil must be drained by use of tile. Add organic matter or peat moss. Slight acidity is all right for vegetables and for most ornamental plants. (See Acidity, this section.)

What kind of fertilizer is best for inert clay soil?   Incorporation of organic matter and ground limestone will probably benefit such a soil. The fertilizer to apply will depend upon the crop to be grown.

How may I improve a heavy, extremely wet clay soil? Pine trees thrive on it.   The physical condition of an extremely wet clay soil can be improved by using 4-inch agricultural drain tile (see Drainage) and the incorporation of liberal amounts of screened cinders or sand. Add ground limestone, as necessary, to lower the acidity.

Will adding ashes and dry leaves to thin clay soil bring it to the consistency of loam?   Yes, if you add enough and wait long enough. Apply compost, peat moss, or both, to hasten the process.

The soil in the garden is very clayey and needs conditioning. How can I do that with all the shrubbery and perennials in?   Remove perennials after hard frost and spade in 3 inches of compost or peat moss and 2 to 3 inches of steam cinders or ground limestone. Replant perennials at once.

What are the best materials to mix with a heavy soil or blue clay? Peat moss, compost, and fine cinders. Avoid using sand. While often recommended, if it is not used in extremely heavy doses, it can make clay more difficult to work, not easier.

What crops would help to break up soil of blue clay? Shallow-rooted ones, such as rye and oats.

Is lime helpful to soil of blue clay? Have soil tested to determine if lime is needed; usually it is helpful. (See Lime, this section.)

How does gray clay differ from red clay? It depends on the kinds of minerals the clay is composed of and the amount of air present when the clay was formed. Red clay usually contains iron.

Is gray clay fertile? Yes, but it probably would be better for plants if it is fertilized.

What can be done with gray clay soil to make it produce? Add compost or peat moss first, then apply fertilizers as crop growth may indicate the need for them.

Is it best to grow a green-manure crop in gray clay soil over the winter, or dig it up in the fall and leave it so? Fertilize soil, grow a winter cover crop, and plow under in the spring.

What will darken light-colored (gray) clay soil? How many years will it take to make such soil black in color? Organic matter—manure, etc. It would require several years of constant applications, but it is not at all necessary to make the soil black in order to have it productive.

Is pipe-clay soil acid? Clay soils vary in their degree of acidity. To determine the reaction of the particular soil in mind, test it or send a sample to your state agricultural college. (See Acidity, this section.)

I have a patch of heavy red clay soil to condition. Is there an easy way to do it? I've used peat moss, sand, leafmold, and well-rotted manure. Use more of the same. Sorry, there's no easy way.

My tract of land has a heavy, tough, red clay base, with only a light topsoil covering. What is the best treatment? Grow cover crops of soybeans plowed under before beans are ripe. Follow with a crop of rye to be plowed under the following spring.

Will peat moss make a red clay soil heavier? No. It loosens it up and makes it easier to handle.

What green-manure crop is best for rocky clay soil, and when should it be sown? Grow soybeans planted in the spring and turn under before the beans are ripe. Follow with rye or oats, to be plowed under the following spring.

I have a rocky clay soil that has never been used except to grow

grass. Should it be exposed to the winter, or grown with cover crops?   For a small area, remove surface rocks, add 3 inches of peat moss or compost with some sand or ashes, and plow under. Do not disk or harrow until spring.

What does a white clay soil need when it becomes baked hard after a rain? In the early spring it is loose and mellow.   It needs organic matter in the form of peat moss, compost, or leafmold. Apply a 3-inch layer and spade in.

How can a very heavy yellow clay soil around the foundation of a house be improved so that plants will grow in it?   Incorporate 2 inches of steam cinders, screened through ¼-inch mesh, and 2 inches of compost, straw, or peat, preferably in the fall.

What is the best way to prepare heavy clay for fruit trees?   Drainage must be good for fruit trees in heavy soils. Spade or plow under a liberal quantity of compost or peat moss. Sod spaded under is likewise good. Be sure that the soil in planting holes can drain. If it has no outlet, water will stand around tree roots.

The soil of my garden consists mostly of clay. Would it be suitable for planting trees such as apples, pears, and cherries?   Yes, if well drained.

How can I prepare clay soil in full sun for growing lilies?   All varieties will grow in moderately heavy soil. Add 3 inches of well-rotted compost or peat moss and spade to a depth of 6 inches. Soil must be well drained for satisfactory results with lilies.

What ornamental plants will grow in clay soil?   If well prepared—organic matter added, well drained, fertilized—clay soils will support the growth of almost all plants.

What shrubs, flowers, and trees grow best in red clay soil?   If the soil is well drained, most shrubs and trees will grow. For flowers, add compost or peat moss along with fine cinders.

We have clay ground and must prepare it inexpensively. What vegetables will be successful?   Spade in a 3-inch layer of organic matter and expect any vegetable to grow. However, root crops will do better in lighter soils.

Is it practical to begin a vegetable garden on a rocky clay soil of poor color and texture?   Probably not, unless no other soil is available. Remove surface rocks and add large quantities of compost or peat moss each year. Fertilizer will also be needed.

Soil Problems

What kind of soil is most adaptable for general gardening? Any well-conditioned soil that would grow a crop of corn.

Is there any way to change the condition of a poor soil? Unless the soil condition is extremely unfavorable, it can be improved to the extent that it will produce good crops. The addition of plenty of organic matter is a basic need.

I am planning my first garden. How do I go about preparing the land for it? Add manure (600 pounds per 1,000 square feet); or 5 bales of peat moss (50 bushels per 1,000 square feet); fertilize it with a good complete garden fertilizer (30 pounds per 1,000 square feet); lime it (if test shows need).

Is it advisable to apply lime and commercial fertilizer during the winter on the snow for early melting and absorption? Lime and commercial fertilizers, for some crops, can be applied in the fall, but in most cases they are more economically applied in the spring. Chemical fertilizers leach out and are lost over the winter.

Are wood ashes as good or better than coal ashes for the garden? Under what conditions should each be used? Wood ashes and coal ashes serve two distinct purposes—the former adds potash, the latter improves the mechanical condition of soil.

If annuals are cut off at the ground in fall, instead of being pulled out, will the soil benefit by decomposition of the roots? Yes.

In clearing off my vegetable plot, I burned the old tomato vines. Does this in any way injure the soil for next year's crop? No. It really should be of benefit.

What can I do to improve tough, gummy, black virgin soil? I have added sand. Not enough has been added. Apply a 3-inch layer of compost or peat moss. Fertilizer will also help.

What is the best treatment for the soil that does not produce root crops? It probably is too heavy; lighten it with organic materials and cinders. It may lack phosphorus and potassium, which can be added in the form of superphosphate and potassium chloride. (See Introduction.)

Our soil is heavy black gumbo and bakes badly. Should I use manure, sand, sawdust, or peat moss? For long-lasting improvement, incorporate 2 to 3 inches of peat moss or a mixture of half peat moss and half coarse sawdust, plus a layer of fine gravel with no particles larger than $\frac{1}{16}$ to $\frac{1}{8}$ inch. This layer should be 2 to 3 inches thick and be worked in 6 to 8 inches deep.

How can I make a hard-packed, black alkaline soil friable and productive? (Nevada.) Sulfur must be added to neutralize the alkali. If not, soil must be drained by use of tile. Add compost or peat moss to loosen soil.

DEPLETED SOIL

What is the quickest way to bring an old used garden spot back into quick production? Spade in organic matter in the fall. In the spring apply superphosphate, hoe, rake, and plant. Add a complete fertilizer just before planting and again during the summer.

I have been raising flowers on the same ground for some time. What can I use to keep it in shape? Incorporate organic matter such as leaves or peat moss in the soil between the plants. Apply a good complete fertilizer in the spring.

I have planted flowers in the same spot for the last 15 years, using only a commercial fertilizer. My flowers do not have as large blossoms as they used to, but bloom very well. Should I add anything more, or do as I am doing? Unless the soil is very rich, it would be beneficial to add compost or peat moss, or some other form of organic matter.

ERODED SOIL

What causes erosion? Erosion—the washing away of soil on slopes by the runoff of surface water—results when the soil is left more or less bare and is so handled that it lacks humus to absorb moisture.

Please tell me how to handle a lot that is very sandy and slopes. The water washes the soil off as fast as it is replaced. I had thought of making about 3 different elevations (terraces). Is this too many for a garden about 50 feet deep? If the slope is not too steep, the trouble may be overcome by increasing the organic content of the soil through the use of green manures, strawy manure (if you can get it), compost, or peat moss. On steep slopes, handle the situation by strip-working the lot, or by terracing with railroad ties or stonework. Two terraces should be sufficient on a 50-foot lot unless the grade is very steep. On very steep slopes a ground cover such as crown vetch or Japanese honeysuckle may be necessary to help hold the soil.

What suggestions do you have for hillside soil that is mostly decomposed granite? Prepare small pockets of good soil by using compost or peat moss, and use plants which root as they spread. Crown vetch will hold such a hillside once it is established.

How can one improve clay soil on a hillside to make it good garden soil? Add compost, spade under, and plant ground covers (ornamental) to hold the soil in place. If wanted for vegetables, arrange the slope in terraces.

FOR FLOWERS

What type of soil is best for a mixed flower border? A sandy loam, slightly acid (pH 6.5) in reaction, with manure, compost, and/or peat moss worked in. You can hardly overdo the organic material when preparing the garden, as once planted it is difficult to work among the plants.

My annuals and perennials grow tall and spindly. Could this be due to overfertilization, lack of sun, or lack of some fertilizer element? The garden site receives sunlight half the day. The spindling growth of annuals and perennials may be due to lack of sunlight, improper fertilization, or other factors—or to any combination of them. Give as much sunlight as possible; improve the drainage and aeration of the soil; increase the phosphorus and potash in relation to nitrogen in the fertilizer used. A fertilizer low in nitrogen may be best for a few years.

Why do plants grow thin and scraggly? What is lacking in soils that produce such growth? Lack of balanced nutrition. Usually an addition of complete fertilizer will help. Drainage should be good. Calcium (lime or gypsum) may be needed to make good roots. Test your soil.

My flowers grow very poorly, and usually die before long. What causes this? The chances are that your soil lacks fertility, moisture-holding capacity, and aeration. Additions of humus and fertilizers should correct these handicaps.

How can you keep soil in good condition in the grimy atmosphere of big cities? Adequate drainage should be provided. A periodic soil test will determine the amount of lime necessary to maintain the correct soil reaction. However, where soot coats the foliage, no soil treatment will remedy the condition.

Do soil conditions cause double-flowered cosmos to be single? Doubling of flowers is a hereditary tendency. Soil conditions rarely have any effect. Improper selection of seed is the usual cause. Also, many flowers never come 100 per cent double from seed.

Are earthworms harmful or beneficial in the garden? I find that in a short time they eat all the humus in the soil the same as they do when they get into flowerpots. Earthworms are not harmful in outdoor soils, unless possibly on a lawn. In the greenhouse or in potted plants they are a nuisance, but can be controlled by watering the pots with lime water.

Would a garden plot laid out on the edge of a lake be satisfactory? And how would one get it in condition? Why not? Add compost or peat moss at the rate of 300 pounds per 1,000 square feet. The humus content is likely to be low.

NEGLECTED SOIL

Why is soil that has lain idle for years so deficient in plant food? When grass, weeds, leaves, etc., are continually decaying on it, wouldn't natural compost be made? Many cultivated plants are genetic weaklings which need fertility far beyond that which supports weeds. The weeds that grow on poor soils may not require the same proportions of elements for growth as do cultivated plants. When these weeds die down, they fail to change these proportions. Besides, insufficient aeration, due to lack of turning the land, may cause trouble.

How can I restore the fertility of an old garden? Soil is sand, with a clay subsoil. I've tried manure, lime, and commercial fertilizer. The predominance of sand seems to be the difficulty. Try heavy applications of organic matter, such as compost, manure, peat moss, straw, alfalfa, hay, or the use of green manure.

Last year was the first time my garden was plowed in 30 years. I think I need lime, as the ground showed green moss. How much should I use? The best way to tell lime need is to test your soil. Green moss is not an indication of acidity. More likely the drainage is poor, or nutrients are lacking.

I had a ½-acre vegetable garden last year; the plot had been uncultivated for 15 years. I applied a ton of lime after plowing and 2 truckloads of manure directly to the plants. I seeded the plot to rye and perennial ryegrass last fall and it looks all right. What, if anything, would you suggest adding this season before and after plowing? Apply 40 to 50 pounds of 20 per cent superphosphate per 1,000 square feet.

I recently bought a 171-acre farm which has not been worked for about 9 years. How can I determine what to plant? Have your soil tested. Ensure proper drainage. Consult your county agent.

I have just bought a 3-acre place which has not been worked for 4 years, but the annual crop of hay has been cut. Can I bring this into cultivation in a year? Yes. Plow in the fall. Fertilize heavily in the spring. Consult your county agent.

The plot I expect to use as a vegetable garden is a vacant lot infested with weeds. Will turning the weeds under be sufficient preparation of the soil? Such soil is loaded with weed seed. When the soil is disturbed they will germinate. Be prepared to fight them. The turning under of weeds will add organic matter to the soil. However, it may be too acid or alkaline; test for this. It may be poorly drained. It may need fertilization.

Our backyard is full of wild grass and weeds. Will the soil be suitable for anything after the condition is changed? Modern weedkillers, which destroy all vegetation but do not sterilize the soil, can be used to kill all weeds and are available from garden shops. Usually, a short wait is necessary before seed can be sown. By fertilizing heavily before spraying, soft growth is stimulated and kill is improved. As soon as vegetation is dead, it can be dug or tilled. The chances are good that the soil can be modified to produce the common vegetables and garden flowers satisfactorily.

If the soil produces a vigorous crop of weeds, is it a sign that it will grow desirable things well? Usually, yes. If the desired crops are adapted to the soil type supporting the weed growth, they should do well. However, plants will need help in competing with the more vigorous weeds that are certain to appear.

What is the best way to handle soil which has been allowed to grow with bracken and creeping berry vines and has lain idle for years?   Mow or cut off and remove all undesired plants. (They may be put into a compost heap.) Remove undesired woody material such as limbs and small trees. Plow or dig and leave in rough condition through the winter. In the spring, redig, fertilize heavily, and plant.

POOR SOIL

How can subsoil fill be converted so that vegetables can be grown? If organic matter can be worked in heavily, any subsoil other than pure clay can be made fit to grow crops. Allow 6 weeks to elapse, then test for fertility and pH. Many subsoils are rich in minerals but lack organic matter.

How can I build up soil that is mostly cinders?   In the upper 8 to 10 inches incorporate compost and haul in soil. The final proportion of cinders should not be more than one fourth of the total volume in the top 6 inches.

My garden plot is mostly brown soil and not too fertile. How can I make it fertile?   Apply compost and other organic matter and a complete fertilizer.

My soil is very poor. How can I improve it?   Add 3 inches of compost or peat moss; spade to a depth of 6 inches. Before raking, add a good complete garden fertilizer at 4 pounds per 100 square feet.

Are flowers or vegetables likely to grow in soil from which the top 18 inches have been removed?   Usually not. By manuring the subsoil and planting green-manure crops, the soil may be made fairly good after 2 or 3 years.

How much topsoil do you advise using over fill in order to grow flowers and vegetables?   At least 6 inches, preferably more. Keep in mind that practically any black soil you buy will be full of weed seed, no matter what the seller says.

I am planning to make a garden where the sod is rather heavy. How can I destroy this?   Till or spade in the fall or spring. Apply a complete fertilizer before spading to hasten decomposition. If infested with quackgrass, you might want to kill it with a weedkiller (consult your county extension agent) or with a black plastic mulch.

I have a brand-new home; the builder put in very little loam, and the

soil itself is very poor. How can I improve it? Without adding topsoil, the process of improvement will be very slow. Heavy additions of manure or other humus-forming materials would have to be substituted. This should be worked in in the fall or spring. The soil should be tested for acidity and proper corrections made. Fertilizers should be added, and green-manure crops planted—rye in the fall (2 to 3 pounds per 1,000 square feet), followed by soybeans the next spring (after plowing the rye under). After plowing the soybeans under, the soil should be in fair shape.

I bought topsoil to enrich my soil, but results were poor. How can I determine what is wrong? Topsoil can be worn-out and worthless. See the answer to the above question on how your original soil and the added topsoil can be improved.

What is the quickest, cheapest, and best way to rebuild "stripped" land, where loam was scraped off? See the answer to the above question.

Will it be necessary to add extra fertilizer to the topsoil we have just put on? Add a fertilizer high in phosphorus and potash.

STONY SOIL

To produce a good crop of the common vegetables, what fertilizer is best for shale ground that has not been farmed for several years? Any complete fertilizer, such as 4–12–4 or 5–10–5, applied at 4 pounds per 100 square feet, twice or three times a year.

Do stones continually work to the surface? If so, why? Yes, small ones do. Alternate freezing and thawing in the winter, digging and cultivation, and also wetting and drying in the spring, summer, and fall, will bring stones to the surface.

What shall I do for stony land? I continually rake stones off, but more appear. There is no remedy other than to keep removing surface rocks.

WET SOIL

Will you explain the terms "well-drained soil" and "waterlogged soil"? A well-drained soil is one in which surplus water runs off quickly and which dries out readily after a rain or watering. A waterlogged soil is the opposite and contains too much water and little air.

Can a low, wet area be used for general gardening? Only if it can be drained.

What vegetables will stand a wet, soggy soil best? Beets seem to like wet sour spots, but carrots won't even come up in these spots. No vegetables will grow well in soggy soil. If no other soil is available, raised beds made with 12-inch boards can be built and filled with a soil that drains well.

Our soil is in the shade and has too much moisture. What can we do for it? Improve the drainage by the installation of 3- to 4-inch agricultural tiles, 12 to 15 inches deep, with lines 12 to 15 feet apart, and incorporate liberal amounts of organic matter. Only shade-tolerant plants will grow, no matter how you improve the soil.

What can be done to eliminate excess water at the foot of a terraced hill? The water always stands in the garden at the foot of the hill. Provide a shallow grass-covered or stone-paved ditch to carry off the excess water or install a tile drain.

The earth in back of my home is wet and mossy. Is there anything I can do about fertilizing it for a garden? At present nothing will grow. The soil must be drained by use of agricultural tile. Apply 4–12–4 or 5–10–5 fertilizer at 4 pounds per 100 square feet.

My garden is on a slope and the lower end is wet, with heavy soil. Is there any simple way to drain this ground and loosen the soil? Incorporate steam cinders and organic matter. If this does not rectify the situation, install a tile drain.

My garden plot is low and level, the soil moist and heavy in the spring. Will leaves and grass cuttings help, or should I use sand? Soil should be drained by use of tile. The addition of humus will help the soil but will not correct poor drainage. Unless you can afford to apply one third as much sand as the amount of soil you treat, the sand may only make the soil less workable, e.g., a 2-inch layer to treat soil to a depth of 6 inches.

How much lime should be used to correct soil in wet condition? Lime is not a corrective for wet soils. Add lime only if the soil is too acid for crops to be grown. Improve drainage first.

A sewer pipe backed up last fall and overflowed in a small plot where vegetables were planted. What can I do to purify the ground? Dig it up, and leave it in a rough, open condition. In a very short time the ground will "purify" itself.

Will waste water from a sand-washing plant damage land where it settles? (Texas.) Since sand-washing plants differ greatly in their practices, this is a difficult question to answer. Have the soil tested for acidity, nitrogen, phosphorus, potash, soluble salts, and organic matter. Consult your county extension agent.

MOSSY SOIL

The soil turns green in one of my perennial garden beds. What is the best way to remedy this condition? As it is probably caused by poor drainage and lack of aeration, improve the drainage by one of the methods previously suggested. Moss usually also means a soil is low in fertility. Add organic matter and fertilizer.

What kind of fertilizer should be used when the soil is heavy and has a green top coating? See the answer to the above question.

Does green moss growing on the soil in the borders indicate an acid condition of the ground? No. It usually indicates poor drainage or lack of fertility. If it is a green scum (algae), excess nitrogen (especially if from organic sources) and poor aeration may be responsible.

How can I overcome excessive moss on a slope? Are you sure it is moss, which seldom grows on slopes? The usual reasons for the excessive growth of moss are poor underdrainage and infertile soil. Rake out as much moss as possible, apply compost or organic matter, and maintain fertility by applying fertilizer rich in nitrogen in the spring and fall.

What is the best type of fertilizer for soil which has not had previous nourishment and which contains a large percentage of clay? Although the area is sunny, the soil tends to become mossy. Tile drain the garden plot; incorporate compost or organic matter; add commercial fertilizer suitable to the crop to be grown.

I have a strip of soil a few feet wide where everything dies that is planted. Why? It may be due to packing of soil by constant walking. Try aerating by adding screened cinders or coarse sand. The trouble may also be caused by the application of some toxic weedkiller.

WOODLAND AND SHADED SOIL

What is the quickest, cheapest, and best way to convert a former wood lot into usable land? Remove stumps by hand, tractor, or dynamite, then work under compost or organic matter and fertilizer.

Does a garden of vegetables and flowers do well in soil which has just been cleared of hickory, oak, and wild cherry trees? There is a great deal of leafmold in the soil. It will do better in subsequent years, when aeration changes the structure of the soil. When well rotted, leafmold is a good soil conditioner.

Is acid woodland soil in any way beneficial as fertilizer? Woodland soil is not a fertilizer but may serve as a soil conditioner if it is high in leafmold. It is usually a good source of humus but not high in fertility. It can be used as a satisfactory mulch, containing a high percentage of organic matter, and later worked into the soil.

In red virgin soil under and near red-cedar, would oak leafmold and chicken fertilizer, mixed with sand, produce good vegetables? Only if the trees do not shade the garden spot. Check pH and add lime if the reading is less than 6.0.

What can I do with soil surrounded by fir trees to make it suitable for flowers? Deep spading and incorporation of a 2-inch layer of finely screened cinders should help. It is almost sure to be acid. Make a pH test.

What attention must be given to soil from which oak trees have been cleared? Through the years many layers of oak leaves have rotted and naturally form a part of this soil. Such a soil may be somewhat acid. It should be tested and, if necessary, lime applied. For most plants, a pH of 6.0 to 6.9 is best.

What is the best treatment of soil under pine trees for the growth of roses and old-fashioned annuals? If the shade is dense, despite soil preparation, neither will grow.

A willow tree shades my yard; the roots mat the soil for yards around. Is there any way to make flowers grow beneath it? Not satisfactorily.

My soil receives sun from noon on. The few things which grow taste like wood (tomatoes, strawberries, etc.). Why? The soil tested poor, but 5–10–5 was added, plus sheep manure. There is not enough sun. No fertilizer can substitute for sunlight.

How should I treat the ground where no sun ever shines? The ground packs. Besides ferns and shade-loving plants, nothing should be grown under such conditions. The packing of the ground may be reduced by working in leafmold or peat moss.

How can damp, cold, shady soil be fertilized to substitute for sunshine? There is no substitute for sunshine. Additions of nitrogen are helpful if trees take all the nourishment. Flowering plants and vegetables should not be planted in such localities.

What is deficient in the soil when plants tend to have slender stems

instead of branching? They may not have enough sun. Add a fertilizer low in nitrogen (2–10–10 or 0–12–12), 5 pounds per 100 square feet.

Soil Preparation

PLOWING AND DIGGING

When should soil be tilled or plowed? Any time of the year when it is not so wet as to roll in large clods, or so dry as to be a powdery dust.

Does it harm soil if I work it while it's wet? Yes, especially if the soil is heavy. Plowing compacts such soils, and clods and unbreakable lumps will result. Heavy soils will puddle and bake and will be difficult to work into a friable state.

What makes soil break up into large, hard lumps after it is plowed? The structure is bad—too clayey. Add compost, peat moss, and other organic materials, and cinders or sand. Do not till or dig while the soil is wet.

Is it better to plow gardens in the fall or spring? Fall plowing is better, especially when there is sod to be turned under. It reduces erosion, exposes heavy soils to frost, kills exposed insects, brings about decay of organic matter, and enables earlier planting. In the South, however, where little or no freezing occurs, fall plowing is apt to cause leaching.

I have a field that hasn't been plowed for years. I would like to have a vegetable garden. Is it best to plow in the fall? Fall plowing is best in such cases. See above.

We had land plowed which has not been cultivated for about 40 years. What is the best time to put lime and fertilizer on the soil? Plow early in the fall. Add lime at 2 pounds or more per 100 square feet (as test indicates) and a complete fertilizer at the same rate (or preferably a week or two later) and cultivate in. In the spring, hoe, apply fertilizer, rake, and seed.

Last year I made a new garden by filling in about 10 to 18 inches deep with loam. What should be done with this ground to put it in proper shape for this year's home garden? Add manure or compost and till or dig, preferably in the fall.

We plan to make a garden on a lot infested with poison-ivy, wild honeysuckle, and blackberry vines. Can you make any suggestions as to

how we can rid the soil of these? Will the roots from these vines ruin such root crops as potatoes? Kill woody plants with a chemical brush killer. Poison-ivy is dangerous, even when dead, so handle with care. Plant vegetables and remove, by frequent hand hoeing, the shoots of weeds that appear. Roots of the vines will decompose and not injure vegetables, once they have decayed, but poison-ivy roots are dangerous to handle until they have decomposed.

Should the ground be tilled or loosened up each year before planting, or only a little hole dug to put in bulbs or seeds? It is better to plow or spade the soil before planting each crop and easier in the long run.

Is it undesirable to leave soil barren after plowing, or after crops have been harvested? It should either be kept cultivated or mulched. If there is time (before the plot will be needed for future use), grow a green-manure crop.

Should I burn off the garden in the fall, or should the stalks be plowed under? If your old stalks are disease-free, it is better to plow under than to burn. Diseased material should be destroyed, but burning over land is prohibited in most regions.

In plowing cleared ground that had a growth of wild berries and brush, what should the procedure be? Spray with a brush killer. Burn off dead brush if you can get a permit, fertilize, and dig or till.

How can I loosen up hardpan soil on a 40-acre field? Use a subsoil plow.

How do you prepare soil in the fall for spring flower beds? Apply compost or peat moss. Dig and allow soil to weather over the winter. In the spring, apply a complete fertilizer at the recommended rate, then rake or till before planting.

After spading in the fall, how does one proceed in the spring? If manure is dug in at the time of spring spading, can lime also be used? How? See the above question. Add lime only if a pH test reads less than 6.0.

Soil is ready to be dug when a handful, firmly compressed, crumbles apart readily. If it remains in a sticky mass, with moisture on the surface, it is still too wet.

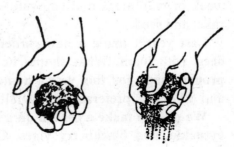

CULTIVATING

What is meant by the term "in good tilth"?   Soil that has a suitable crumbly structure, sufficient humus, and is well drained. To help secure good tilth, use compost or peat moss or grow a green-manure crop; tile if necessary.

How fine should soil be prepared for planting?   For seed beds, the soil should be fine enough so that few lumps remain, or else seed covering will be difficult. For large plants, coarse soil containing small lumps is satisfactory.

Relative composition of soil with good structure.

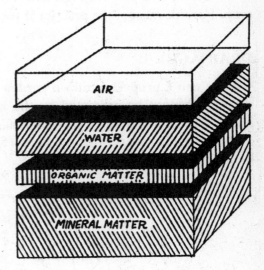

How can I know that my soil is right for growing vegetables and flowers?   If the structure is crumbly, the soil is dark; if compost, peat moss, and a complete fertilizer are added, good crops will grow. To make sure, have a soil test made.

Is cultivating—stirring the soil—necessary except to control weeds and grass in such crops as corn and potatoes?   Usually, mulching substitutes for cultivation. In some soils a fine dust mulch cuts off air movement between the soil and the atmosphere, which is hardly a desirable situation.

What is the best way to tell if soil is in condition to cultivate?   Put a clean trowel or spade into your soil. If, when you pull the tool out of the soil, many particles cling to the clean surface, the soil is too wet to be cultivated.

What is meant by a mud-pie test?   It tells if soil is in condition to work. Pick up a handful of soil and press it into a ball. If it forms a solid lump that does not crumble easily, it is too wet to dig or plow; if it holds its shape but is easy to break apart, it is just right. If it crumbles without forming a ball, it should be watered lightly before working.

What is meant by "fallow"?   Fallow means plowing the land and allowing it to stand idle with no crop. It may be spaded or tilled while fallow.

What is the purpose of fallowing?   It controls weeds by plowing them under. Soil standing idle one year stores moisture for next year's crop. For this reason, the practice is used mostly in arid regions.

DRAINAGE

How can I properly drain a garden that stays wet too long?   If the situation cannot be corrected by the incorporation of 3 to 4 inches of sand or cinders, install 3- or 4-inch agricultural drain tiles. Set the tiles 15 to 18 inches deep, with the lines 15 to 18 feet apart. Carry the lines to an open ditch or storm sewer.

Wet soils are improved by laying tiles to drain off excess water—a simple operation.

What is the best way to drain off a 1-acre garden that is too wet? Would some kind of furrow arrangement be sufficient? Would it be bet-

ter tiled, or drained to a storm-water sewer? Installation of tile drains would be more satisfactory and in the end more economical on such a large plot.

We have so much subsoil water that in winter our ground in spots is continually water-soaked. What can I do to counteract this in the spring? Tile drain the lot. (See the previous questions.)

How can we provide drainage economically at the low end of a lot? Water forms in a pool during heavy rains. If the situation cannot be corrected by slight modification of the grade, or shallow ditching, install 3- to 4-inch agricultural drain tiles.

Our lot is wide, but slopes. At this spot (at the end of the lot) we have "soggy" soil for days after a rain. Is there anything we can do about it? Tile drain the lower end of the lot. Carry the tile to an open ditch or storm sewer if possible. Drain into dry wells filled with coarse gravel if the water cannot be carried off.

I plan a combination vegetable garden and orchard on a very poor site. Since drainage would be expensive to install, would you advise against the project? Vegetables can be raised in beds above ground level made with 12-inch sides. No orchard trees will thrive with wet feet.

COAL ASHES

Can hard-coal stoker cinders be plowed into heavy soil to lighten it without bad effect? If weathered over the winter and broken down to ¼ inch or finer. Clinkers (the stonelike residue left by coal) make good subdrains if buried deeply.

The soil in my home vegetable garden packs hard when dry. Would coal ashes benefit this condition? Yes, use 1 inch incorporated into the top 6 inches of soil. Screen through a ¼-inch mesh before applying. Be sure they have been exposed outdoors over the winter before using.

What are the benefits from the fine siftings of coal ashes applied to a vegetable garden and mixed with the soil? The mechanical condition is improved, more air is admitted, bacteria work more efficiently, and roots grow faster.

Can coal ashes be used in the garden at the same time bone meal is worked into the soil? Yes, they can be used at the same time, but they should be fine enough to lighten the soil. (See comments on the lack of the fertilizing value of modern bone meal, however.)

Are coal ashes of any use as a chemical fertilizer?   Coal ashes have very little, if any, fertilizer value. They do improve the mechanical condition of most soils.

Do coal ashes help prevent cutworms?   To a degree. If a 1-inch layer is placed around the bases of plants, cutworms will have difficulty in attacking them.

A couple of years ago I noticed that an acquaintance had dumped his winter's coke ashes in a low spot in the back of his yard. In the spring he smoothed them out and set his tomato plants there, and they bore a heavy crop of fruit. Is there any plant food in coke ashes that is good for tomatoes? Or was it just an accident that the plants did so well in the ashes?   The coke ashes improved the soil aeration and thus helped produce better growth.

Are briquette ashes good for an entire garden?   Yes. They are good for the mechanical betterment of the soil and improving its texture.

Will ashes from a fireplace, in which some cannel coal has been used, be harmful in garden use?   Cannel-coal ashes contain a harmful oil unless completely burned.

Can the fine white ash of cannel coal be used to lighten a heavy soil?   Yes. (See the previous question.)

I understand cannel-coal ashes are strong in phosphorus and potash. Are they suitable to be added to flowers and a vegetable garden?   As mechanical aids mostly; they have only a little nutrient value.

Soil Acidity

pH

What is the meaning of the symbol pH?   See the Introduction.

I have several books on flower growing, but none gives the types of soils (acid or alkaline) in which all plants thrive best. Can you give me this information?   No *complete* list has ever been worked out. Of the vast number of plants grown, comparatively few show marked preferences for decidedly acid or alkaline soils. The vast majority exhibit a wide tolerance. (See the following questions.)

What plants grow well on acid soils of fair to good fertility (pH 5.0 to 5.5)?

Andromeda	Ferns	Pumpkin
Arbutus, Trailing-	Fir	Radish
Azalea	Hemlock	Raspberry
Beans	Huckleberry	Red-cedar
Bent Grasses	Hydrangea (Blue)	Red Top
Birch, White	Lily	Rhododendron
Blackberry	Lupine	Rye
Blueberry	Millet	Skimmia
Buckwheat	Mountain-laurel	Soybean
Camellia	Oak, Scrub	Spruce
Cedar, White	Oak, Red	Strawberry
Cineraria	Oats	Sweet Potato
Cowpea	Orchard Grass	Tobacco
Corn	Orchid	Turnip
Cranberry	Parsley	Vetch, Hairy
Cucumber	Pea	Violet
Cyclamen	Peanut	Watermelon
Daffodil	Pepper	Wintergreen
Dewberry	Pine	Wheat
Endive	Potato	Zinnia

What plants grow better on slightly acid or neutral soils (pH 5.6 to 6.5)?

Beans	Endive	Rye
Blackberry	Oats	Soybean
Brussels Sprouts	Orchard Grass	Squash
Buckwheat	Parsley	Strawberry
Carrot	Pea	Sweet Potato
Cabbage	Pepper	Tobacco
Clover, Crimson	Pumpkin	Tomato
Corn	Radish	Turnip
Cowpea	Red Top	Wintergreen
Cucumber	Rhubarb	Wheat

What plants do not grow well on strongly acid soils, but prefer slightly acid or slightly alkaline soils (pH 6.5 to 7.0)?

Alfalfa	Avens	Beets
Apple	Baby's-breath	Beggar Weed
Asparagus	Barley	Bluegrass
Aster	Balsam	Bokhara

Broccoli	Flax	Onion
Brome Grass	Foxglove	Pansy
Camomile	Foxtail	Parsnip
Candytuft	Gladiolus	Peach
Carnation	Gooseberry	Pear
Cauliflower	Grape	Peppermint
Celery	Helianthus	Petunia
Chard	Hemp	Phlox
Cherry	Horse-radish	Plum
Chicory	Hops	Poppy
Chrysanthemum	Hydrangea (Pink)	Quince, Orange
Clover, Alsike	Iris	Rape
Clover, Hungarian	Kale	Salsify
Clover, Japanese	Kohlrabi	Sorghum
Clover, Mammoth	Lady's Finger	Spearmint
Clover, Red	Larkspur	Spinach
Clover, White	Leek	Stock
Clover, Yellow	Lentil	Sunflower
Collards	Lettuce	Sweet-alyssum
Columbine	Linden, American	Sweet pea
Cosmos	Lobelia	Sweet Vernal
Cotton	Mangel Wurzels	Sweet William
Currant	Maple	Timothy
Dahlia	Marigold	Vetch
Delphinium	Meadow Grass	Walnut
Eggplant	Meadow Oat	Watercress
Elm, American	Mignonette	Willow
Everlasting Pea	Muskmelon	Wisteria
Fescue, Sheep's	Nasturtium	Witch-hazel
Fescue, Tall	Oak, White	Woodbine

What makes the soil acid?   Soil acidity is common in many regions where rainfall is sufficient to leach large proportions of calcium and magnesium out of the soil. Decay of organic matter releases carbon dioxide. Combined with soil water, this forms carbonic acid.

Soils also become acid due to the use of acid-forming fertilizers, such as sulfate of ammonia and ammonium phosphates. The following table shows the relative acidifying or alkalinizing power of various fertilizing, liming, or acidifying materials, rated in terms of commercial limestone (calcium carbonate) as 1.0:

Material	Acidifying	Alkalinizing
Dolomitic Limestone	—	1.1
Hydrated Lime (Calcite)	—	1.4
Hydrated Lime (Dolomitic)	—	1.7
Sodium Nitrate	—	0.3
Calcium Nitrate	—	0.2
Potassium Nitrate	—	0.2
Ammonium Nitrate	0.6	—
Ammonium Sulfate	1.1	—
Monoammonium Phosphate	0.6	—
Diammonium Phosphate	1.1	—
Urea	0.8	—
Sulfur	3.1	—
Ferrous Sulfate	0.4	—
Aluminum Sulfate	0.5	—

Where can soil be sent to have its acidity determined? To your State Agricultural Experiment Station, college, or university. (See list of stations in Section 16.) Also check with the Cooperative Extension Service listed under your county government.

What simple means can be used to detect acid soil? Soil-test kits for testing pH are available at most garden shops. They test both alkalinity or acidity.

Is moss an indication of acidity? No. Moss grows on either acid or alkaline soil. Usually it means low fertility and high moisture.

Are toadstools an indication of soil acidity? No, they are not.

What will an acid soil produce? Notable among the plants that do best in an acid soil are those of the Ericaceae, which includes such plants as azalea, rhododendron, leucothoe, pieris, mountain-laurel, blueberry, and others. (See the previous question under pH.)

How can an acid soil be neutralized? An acid soil can be neutralized by adding ground limestone. The amount required can be determined by a soil analysis. (See the Introduction.)

What is "sour" soil? A "sour" soil is a term sometimes used to denote the condition that develops in a poorly drained soil. More often, as the term is used, it is synonymous with an acid soil. If by "sour" soil is meant an acid soil, it can be sweetened by adding agricultural ground limestone or other forms of lime.

What can I do to counteract sour soil in seed boxes? The "sour" soil condition in seed flats can be prevented or corrected by providing sufficient drainage. Separate the boards on the bottom of the flat ¼ inch, or bore a few holes in the bottom. Raise the flats on bricks or wood strips. "Sourness," in these cases, generally does not mean acidity.

How can I improve a dry, acid, heavy clay soil?   Incorporate a liberal amount of peat moss, but first mix 10 to 15 pounds of pulverized limestone with each bale of peat before the latter is worked into the soil. Apply additional limestone to the soil if needed. Always test for pH after the soil settles, following treatment.

I am making a vegetable garden on a piece of lawn; the soil is very acid. Will it be worth trying?   Since most vegetables will do well on a slightly acid soil, this very acid soil could be changed without undue expense to grow vegetables by adding ground limestone.

What type of fertilizer is used in planting vegetables in acid soil?   If the soil is too acid to produce the vegetable crop in mind, apply lime. In addition, apply a fertilizer best suited to the particular crop.

My soil is neutral. Is there any chemical I can add to the soil to make it acid? I wish to try acorns from red oaks, and other things.   Finely ground sulfur or ammonium sulfate can be used to make the soil more acid. Red oaks, however, will do well on a neutral soil.

Can the soil in a garden in a limestone country be made permanently acid?   No. An acid soil made under such conditions can be maintained only by periodic treatment.

What use is sulfur for soil? How do you use it?   Sulfur is used to increase the acidity of the soil. (See the Introduction for amounts.)

What materials should be used in maintaining an acid-soil garden in a limestone country?   Acid peat moss or oak leafmold, sulfur, and ammonium sulfate.

What are the best kinds of leaves for producing an acid condition in the soil?   Leafmold from oak leaves has long been considered the ideal acidifying material for plants requiring an acid soil, such as rhododendrons, azaleas, and mountain-laurel. Recent experiments, however, indicate that this assumption is incorrect. Oak-leaf compost increased the pH temporarily, but after 45 days the pH value was higher (*less acid*) than before the application. However, there is no doubt that oak leafmold is beneficial to the growth of acid-loving plants. In soils high in humus, acid-soil plants can tolerate higher pH readings.

Will you please tell me how to prepare a soil mixture using oak leafmold for growing blueberries?   Dig a hole 3 to 4 feet wide for each plant; incorporate 3 inches of leafmold in the bottom; mix the soil for filling with one third its bulk of leafmold, and pack tightly around the roots. Keep the surface over the roots mulched heavily with the oak leafmold or with sawdust. Although aluminum sulfate is widely recommended for acidifying soil, don't use it. Over a long period it will destroy roots.

ALKALINITY

What is the best method for soil reconstruction? Our soil is of a lime structure (moderately alkaline). Our water is hard and slightly chlorinated. Compost at the rate of 1 pound to a square foot and 2½ pounds of superphosphate for each 100 square feet. This should be thoroughly mixed with the soil. Sow green-manure crops in the fall. Use an acid commercial fertilizer for plants.

What is the best way to counteract highly alkaline soil? Sulfur or ammonium sulfate is used for this purpose. A soil with pH 8.0 (alkaline) will require 4 pounds of sulfur to 100 square feet to make it slightly acid (pH 6.0), or 8 pounds of ammonium sulfate for the same area. Ammonium sulfate acts much more quickly than sulfur.

I would like to know what grows best in alkaline soil. What will counteract too much alkali? Very few plants do well in strongly alkaline soil. Use sulfur or ammonium sulfate for acidification.

We have alkaline soil. I succeed with most flowers but not with gladiolus. The bulbs rot. What is the reason? Gladiolus plants do better in slightly acid soil. Acidify it with sulfur and use acid-forming fertilizer.

Our soil has considerable alkali in it. For that reason I have hesitated about trying to raise lady's-slippers. What can I do to grow these? Leafmold acidified with sulfur will produce satisfactory growth. Acid peat moss mixed with leafmold will also do. It is doubtful, however, that an alkaline soil will remain fit for native orchids, if they are meant by "lady's-slipper." If you mean impatiens (a garden balsam), it will grow in slightly alkaline soil.

What vegetables will grow in alkali ground? No vegetables grow well in highly alkaline soil. The most tolerant of alkalinity are asparagus, beet, lima bean, cauliflower, muskmelon, parsnip, and spinach.

Can any chemical be used to correct alkali in soil? My soil is heavy and moist. The best methods of control for such conditions consist of (1) providing a soil mulch to retard evaporation and (2) applications of gypsum if the soil needs calcium; or sulfur if it needs to be acidified. True western alkali soils are almost impossible to fit for garden use.

I have had much difficulty in growing flowers and plants, as many turn yellow. (The soil has been diagnosed by a county agent as highly alkaline.) Why? Poor drainage may cause accumulation of alkaline salts. Apply iron sulfate at 1 to 2 pounds per 100 square feet. More than one application may be necessary. Or use dusting sulfur (see Introduction).

What can one add to alkali water to make it suitable for irrigation on a small garden plot? (Kansas.) Water may be acidified by sulfuric, phosphoric, or other acids. This should be done, however, only on the advice of your Agricultural Experiment Station or county extension agent. Treating alkaline water would probably be too costly for garden use.

LIME

What are the functions of lime in soil improvement? Lime furnishes calcium, which is needed for root development, strengthening of cell walls, and for formation of protoplasm and proteins; counteracts acidity; hastens decomposition of organic matter; aids in development of nitrogen-fixing bacteria; and reduces toxicity of certain compounds.

What type of lime should be used in the garden? Agricultural lime is the slowest but the most lasting. Several weeks may pass before its effect on soil is noticed. Hydrated and burned lime are much quicker in action, but tend to destroy humus. One hundred pounds of ground limestone is equivalent in action to 74 pounds of hydrated lime, or 56 pounds of burned lime. The amounts to use will vary with the acidity of the soil. Usually 2 pounds of agricultural limestone per 100 square feet is sufficient, unless soils are extremely acid.

What is raw ground limestone? Raw ground limestone is calcium carbonate, and is the material most commonly used for counteracting acidity. In urban areas, use fine crushed limestone for drives. Agricultural lime is identical.

What is hydrated lime? Hydrated or slaked lime is formed from burned or quicklime (calcium oxide) and water. Hydrated and burned or quicklime are quicker-acting than ground limestone (calcium carbonate). It is sometimes called slaked lime or quicklime.

Is lime the only material with which to sweeten an acid soil? Some form of lime is usually used to correct soil acidity. The most commonly used forms are ground limestone, dolomitic limestone, and hydrated lime. Other materials that may be used are calcium cyanamide and wood ashes. Calcium sulfate (gypsum), which is sometimes recommended for sweetening soil, is neutral (pH of 7.0) and of no value except as a source of calcium.

Can dry lime, left over from plastering a room, be used in any way as a fertilizer? It may be used to alkalize acid soil, but is apt to be too coarse and lumpy. If lime is needed, apply it in the fall.

Would lime, such as I can purchase at the hardware store, be good for acid soil? If it is hydrated lime, it can injure roots.

Can marl be used in place of lime, with the same, or as good, results? Marl (a natural deposit of calcium-bearing clay) is coarse, and its effect is very gradual and slow. Ordinarily, ground limestone is both less expensive and much more satisfactory.

What is "overliming" injury? Too much calcium (lime) in the soil causes the soil to become alkaline. Some elements such as boron, manganese, iron, zinc, etc., are not soluble in an alkaline solution, and because they are needed in small amounts by plants, poor growth develops. Usually the growth is chlorotic (yellow). Overliming can be corrected by applying sulfur to the soil at 1 pound per 100 square feet. More than one application may be necessary to bring about the desired acidity. Pin oaks are especially sensitive to overliming.

When and under what conditions should lime be added to the soil? Only when the soil is too acid for plants and when calcium is low.

When should lime be used around flowers and shrubs? Use lime only if the soil is so acid as to require correction. Use lime if calcium is lacking and the soil is acid. Use gypsum (calcium sulfate) when calcium is lacking and the soil is alkaline.

What is gypsum? A mineral composed of calcium sulfate which contains 2 molecules of water. Gypsum is used in horticulture to add needed calcium to the soil when it is not necessary to decrease acidity. It is also used to improve the physical condition of soils and, under some conditions, to improve drainage and soil aeration.

Is gypsum (plaster of Paris) a useful soil amendment? Gypsum is valuable as a source of calcium where the soil is already alkaline and a change in the pH of the soil is not desirable. Called land plaster in England, it has been used for over a century. It is not as effective in breaking up clay soils as ground limestone, however.

Is lime needed to improve a gravelly soil?   Have the soil tested; it may not need it.

How can lime benefit clay soil if the soil is originally composed of disintegrated limestone?   As stated by some authorities, benefit is obtained by cementing finer particles into larger ones. The flocculation (cementing of particles) of clay soils as a result of liming has been questioned. For cementing soil particles, humus is better than lime.

Should a garden be treated with lime in the fall or spring?   If ground limestone is used, it is best applied in the fall, but may be applied in the spring.

How much lime should be used (for one application)?   See Introduction under pH.

Is it necessary to put lime on the garden every year?   Lime should be used only on acid soils. If needed, apply agricultural lime in the fall. Usually 2 pounds per 100 square feet is sufficient.

Can lime be strewn over the ground in winter with the snow?   Yes, although it is better to apply early in the fall.

Why is it harmful to put commercial fertilizer and lime into the soil at the same time? What chemical reaction takes place?   If lime is allowed to come into contact with superphosphate or fertilizer, the solubility, and hence the availability, of the latter may be reduced, especially in a non-acid or slightly acid soil. In soils that are acid, there is no objection to the application of fertilizer and lime at the same time, providing they are well incorporated into the soil and the pH is not lower than 5.5.

When leaves are spaded in, in the fall, should lime be used in the spring?   Most leaves do not produce an acid reaction, so that liming is not necessary unless your soil is naturally acid.

What crops need lime in the soil, and which do better without it?   Legumes do better in neutral or slightly alkaline soils, hence lime additions are often necessary. Acid-tolerant plants like azaleas, rhododendrons, etc., need no lime although they need calcium. (See questions under pH.) For most plants, lime should be applied only when the soil is very acid, since they do best in slightly acid soil (6.0 to 6.9 pH).

Instead of sand, I put very fine limestone on my soil, which has a preponderance of gumbo. It has made the soil nice to work with. Will this small amount be apt to affect garden annuals and perennials? I have also added a great deal of barnyard fertilizer.   Small amounts of lime can do no harm. The change in the soil structure was probably due to the manure rather than to the lime.

In foundation planting, I assume it is possible that lime coming loose

from a building and washing into the soil may have a disastrous effect on such acid-loving plants as azaleas and rhododendrons. Is this so? There is rarely much lime in the soil from this source. However, any chunks of plaster should be removed. If the soil seems alkaline, apply dusting sulfur at 2 to 4 pounds per 100 square feet. Sulfur is an acidifying agent.

Should I sprinkle my lawn with lime in the fall? If soil needs lime, it will be most effective when applied in the fall. In acid soil areas, periodic applications of limestone are recommended.

Will lime put on a lawn on which oak and dogwood trees are growing injuriously affect such trees? Not unless excessive amounts are used. Have the soil tested and apply limestone only when needed.

My soil is covered with white pine needles from adjacent trees. Should this make additional liming or other treatment advisable? Pine needles produce acidity, hence constant use of lime may be required to counteract this condition.

Sewage sludge is very acid from aluminum sulfate. Is lime the proper neutralizer or does it leave the valuable plant and soil bacterial elements in a nondesirable form? Sewage sludge does not necessarily contain aluminum sulfate. If it does, lime is a good corrective; or superphosphate may be used.

When vegetable soil is too acid, as ascertained by a laboratory test, how much lime should be applied to overcome a state of hyperacidity? See Introduction under pH.

I am planning to plant a small vegetable plot. Can one add too much lime? Lime should not be added, unless a test shows it is needed. Decidedly, it can be overdone.

SOIL TESTING

What is the best method of determining the treatment a given soil requires? Test your soil, or have it tested. Your county agent or State Agricultural Experiment Station will do this for you.

What is the approximate cost of having soil analyzed? It varies. A few states make no charge.

Are the chemistry sets on the market practical? Sets that test for acidity only can be practical for home gardeners. Sets that test for nutrients can be useful but their results are best interpreted by a trained technician.

Can the true nature of the soil be learned from a test? Yes. A good soil-testing kit will give acidity, nitrates, phosphates, potassium, calcium, etc., but note the answer to the above question.

What size of soil sample is desired? If your soil varies in nature from place to place, don't mix soil for tests, as is often recommended. It can vary as much as 3 to 4 points in pH and nutrients in a few feet. A general mixture test is worthless. In such cases, send separate samples. Write your State Experiment Station for directions before sending your sample.

How can I obtain information on soil analysis without needing to take a course in chemistry? Write to your Agricultural Experiment Station for information on soil testing. Several stations have published bulletins on this subject.

After testing, how can I know what to add to soil, in what quantities, and when? Without experience in testing, one cannot tell from a soil test what kinds or quantities of fertilizers to use. Send your sample to your Agricultural Experiment Station. Along with the test results will come recommendations for improving your soil.

Which soil should I send for analysis—soil screened last fall and stored in a cellar, or fresh soil as soon as frost is out of it? Tests of cold soils are inaccurate. Wait until mid-June before taking samples in cool climates.

How can we determine what vegetable or fruit a soil is best suited to produce? The best procedure is to consult your local county extension agent.

Should untilled soil be analyzed to determine its fertility? Such tests are meaningless if you intend to use soil in tilled condition. Work the soil and allow organic matter to decompose before testing.

Should I have my soil tested to determine its acidity? If plants you grow do well, it is not necessary. It is desirable to have periodic tests of soils that are used to grow plants that require specific soil reactions, such as rhododendrons and azaleas. Home test kits will tell pH accurately enough and usually cost no more than a laboratory test. They can make many future tests without additional cost.

Can the soil condition be determined by what is found growing on it, such as wild blueberries and sour-grass? Can soil with fine shell stone be good? Yes. For example, blueberries indicate acid soil; dandelions sometimes indicate alkaline soil. Too much lime from shells may be detrimental to some plants.

Plant Nutrients

What are the various elements of plant nutrition and what are their uses? The three essential elements and their effect on plant growth are: *Nitrogen:* this element enters into the structure of protoplasm, chlorophyll, and various plant foods; it is needed for both the vegetative and reproductive stages of growth; its use is usually manifested by an increase in vegetative growth. *Phosphorus:* it is essential to cell division and for the formation of nucleoproteins; it aids root development; hastens maturity, or stiffens tissues; and stimulates flower and seed production. *Potash:* necessary for the manufacture and translocation of starches and sugar; it is a general conditioner, overcoming succulence and brittleness, hastening maturity and seed production, and aiding in root development.

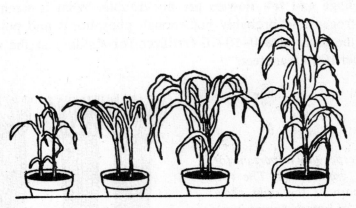

Nitrogen, phosphorus, and potassium are all needed for normal plant growth. Of the four pots of corn above, the first (left) lacked nitrogen; the second, phosphorus; the third, potassium. The one on the right was supplied with all three.

NITROGEN

How can I recognize nitrogen deficiency? The whole plant is dwarfed and the older leaves turn from green to yellow, and then to brown, and remain attached to the plant. Stalks are slender, and few new stalks develop.

How can nitrogen deficiency be corrected? Apply ammonium sulfate at ¾ pound or sodium nitrate at 1 pound per 100 square feet. Ammonium sulfate tends to make soil more acid; sodium nitrate makes it more alkaline. A complete fertilizer (4–12–4 or 4–10–5) will correct the deficiency of nitrogen as well as supply phosphorus and potash.

What is lacking in my garden soil, since the carrots I raise (although they are of good size) are almost tasteless and colorless? Nitrogen is lacking; a complete fertilizer (4–12–4 or 5–10–5) at 4 pounds per 100 square feet will correct this.

What causes yellowing of foliage? It may be due to poor drainage or to lack of nitrogen.

What shall I do for soil that grows annuals and perennials too large and weedy, but weak-stemmed? There is probably too much nitrogen in the soil and not enough phosphorus and potassium. Use a 0–10–10 fertilizer, or something similar, 2 pounds per 100 square feet for one or two applications. Excess nitrogen usually disappears rapidly.

All foliage and few flowers are my trouble. What is wrong? Too much nitrogen and probably not enough phosphorus and potash; add both in the form of a 0–10–10 fertilizer (or similar) at the rate of 2 pounds per 100 square feet.

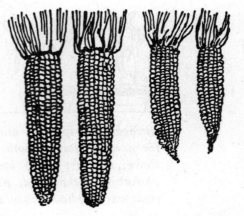

Potash is especially important for fruit and grain crops. The two ears of corn at the right show the result of potash (potassium) deficiency.

What causes an excess of nitrogen in the soil? I have added 10 pounds of bone meal in a 35-square-foot bed for annuals, and some dehydrated manure (100 pounds) for spring. Excess nitrogen, or the symptoms of excess nitrogen, may be brought about through the excessive use of nitrogenous fertilizers, high-nitrogen complete fertilizers, or a deficiency of phosphorus and potash. The amount of manure you have applied constitutes overfertilization. Bone meal usually is locked up in an insoluble form and has little effect on growth.

PHOSPHORUS

How can I recognize a phosphorus deficiency? The whole plant is dwarfed, but the foliage is a dark, dull green; the leaf stem (petiole) often turns purple. Areas between the veins on the leaf sometimes turn purple, and leaf margins often turn yellow. Loss of lower foliage follows.

How can a phosphorus deficiency be corrected? Apply treble superphosphate at 1 pound per 100 square feet or regular superphosphate at 5 pounds per 100 square feet.

POTASH

How can I recognize a potash (potassium) deficiency? Lower foliage begins to turn yellow at the leaf margin; leaves often become mottled yellow and green in between veins; margins of leaves turn brown and foliage drops from the plant; a plant generally becomes stunted.

How can a potash (potassium) deficiency be corrected? Apply muriate of potash or sulfate of potash, 1 pound per 100 square feet. Wood ashes will also add potash as well as lime.

What fertilizer should I use to encourage fruits and vegetable roots? Withhold nitrogen and increase the proportion of phosphorus and potash in the mixture. Use a 2–10–10 fertilizer for a few years, adding additional nitrogen only where and as needed.

Some soils tend to develop barren veins. What is lacking? This is usually the result of too little phosphorus and potash.

What does the soil lack if it produces an abundant crop of vegetables above ground, but no root vegetables (such as potatoes, beets, or turnips)? Phosphorus and potassium are probably deficient in this soil. (See previous questions.)

My garden is made of filled earth, has a large amount of street sweepings in it, and is high in leafmold. All root crops fail; beans and corn are the only crops that succeed. Why? Lack of phosphorus and potassium may cause the trouble. However, all fertilizer elements are lacking in leafmold. Try a complete fertilizer.

TRACE ELEMENTS

What are trace elements?   Elements (present in most soils) that are needed in very small amounts for plant nutrition. Some of these are present in such small quantities that they are known as trace elements (see discussion below).

What are the principal trace elements?   Boron, chlorine, copper, iron, manganese, zinc, and molybdenum.

Is boron a necessary ingredient in all types of soils?   A small amount of boron is essential for plant growth and to prevent various physiological disorders. It is present in most soils in sufficient quantity. It is most apt to be deficient in soils low in organic matter. If overused, it can be toxic to plants.

How should boron be used in the soil?   Boron is commonly applied in the form of borax, at the rate of 10 to 15 pounds *per acre*. This is only 4 to 5 ounces per 1,000 square feet.

How can I be sure that my soil will have enough sodium for a good growth of beets?   Use ½ to 1 pound nitrate of soda, or ½ pound table salt, per 100 square feet. Most mixed fertilizers contain enough sodium for beets, however.

My garden soil turns a red color on top when dry. Why?   The red color probably is due to a surface growth of red algae. These minute plants do no harm and are often found on moist soils. They go unnoticed until the soil surface dries and their red color is then apparent by contrast.

Are iron or steel filings beneficial in darkening colors of perennials, especially roses and lilacs?   No. Iron sulfate (copperas) is beneficial where iron in soil is low; it is chiefly useful in greening foliage, not darkening flower color.

HUMUS

What is humus?   For practical purposes, humus may be defined as the resultant brown or dark-brown substance that develops following the breakdown of organic materials by various soil organisms. Actually, no one knows the exact chemical composition, but a soil gel with lignin, a component, is as good a definition as any.

How does one recognize the different types of humus, such as peat, leafmold, muck, etc.?   *Peat:* soft, brown, spongy, semigranular material;

domestic peats, unless kiln dried, contain more water than the imported type. *Muck:* black, represents further state of decay than peat—not so useful. *Bacterized Peat:* supposedly treated; usually no better than muck. *Leafmold:* brownish-black material with some undecomposed leaves and twigs present; useful soil conditioner. *Wood Soil:* usually leafmold, but further decomposed; useless for most plants without additions of fertilizer.

In what forms is potential humus available to the average home gardener? See previous question. Manure, straw, peat moss, kitchen waste, seaweed, sawdust, decayed wood chips, pine needles, hay—all these must decompose before becoming humus. The compost pile is probably the best of all sources of humus for the home garden but look around your area—there may be more possibilities than you realize.

What is the function of humus in the soil? Among the important functions of humus are to effect granulation of the soil, thereby improving drainage and soil aeration; to increase its water-holding capacity; to increase the bacterial activity; to increase the percentage of such essential elements as nitrogen and sulfur; and to help in transforming essential elements from nonavailable to available forms.

Is humus important to soil fertility? Yes, by increasing moisture absorption and the activity of several of the essential elements, especially nitrogen.

How is humus incorporated into the soil? By spading or plowing.

Is spring or fall the best time to add humus to soil? Any time the soil can be worked. Humus does not injure growing plants.

Our soil is rich but hard to work. What is the best source of humus? Manure, peat moss, or a compost heap.

What method do you recommend to maintain humus and bacteria in soils? Keep soils aerated by the addition of compost and/or peat moss. Use green-manure crops wherever possible.

What is to be done when humus keeps the earth too moist? Incorporate sand or weathered steam cinders.

What would you recommend to keep a very rich black soil from caking? It forms a hard crust about an inch deep. Add humus—manure, peat, alfalfa hay. Incorporate fine steam cinders in the top 6 inches.

What causes soil to become very hard? Lack of organic matter.

A bog was dug up to make a lake; excellent humus was removed. How can this material be converted to garden use? The material should make an excellent mulch, or can be mixed with soil. Unless soil on which this is used is very acid, the acidity of the humus will have no detrimental effect. If the material is lumpy, place in small piles to dry; pulverize before applying.

Do commercial fertilizers supply humus?   The application of organic fertilizers such as soybean and cottonseed meals supplies a very small amount of humus. The inorganic or so-called commercial fertilizers do not supply humus.

PEAT MOSS

What is the difference in value between peat moss and peat? Between domestic and imported peat?   Peat moss is moss (usually sphagnum) in an advanced state of disintegration; peat is a product of some kind of vegetation (not necessarily moss) largely decomposed. Domestic peat is usually of sedge origin, although we have some sphagnum peat in this country. Imported peat is usually sphagnum peat. Unfortunately, the terms peat and peat moss are used interchangeably in garden centers. Sedge peat is of less value than that from sphagnum.

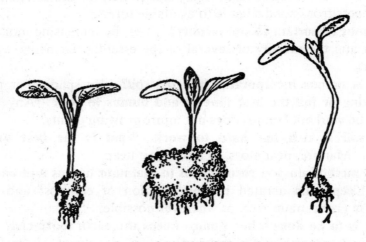

Humus in the soil absorbs and holds moisture, encouraging fibrous root growth. The center seedling above was grown in a half-soil, half-peat moss mixture; the other two were grown in very sandy and heavy clay soil lacking humus.

Does peat have any value as a fertilizer?   Yes, but it is very slowly available. Domestic sedge peat contains up to 3 per cent nitrogen. Sphagnum peat ("peat moss") contains less than 1 per cent nitrogen. It is slower in availability than sedge peat. Do not rely on peat or peat moss for fertility. Use it in conjunction with fertilizer.

Is peat moss good for flower gardens in general? Yes. When dug into the soil, it helps retain moisture and in other ways increases productiveness.

When is the best time to use peat moss—spring or autumn? Apply any time that the soil is being worked if humus is needed.

Is it true that peat moss worked into the soil will make a heavy soil lighter and will cause a light soil to hold more moisture? Yes. In this respect its action is similar to that of compost or manure or any other organic matter.

As a winter protection is peat moss considered as good as straw or leaves? No. Peat moss as a mulch can blow away or, at the opposite extreme, it can mat together, forming an impenetrable barrier against water. It is better used as a soil additive.

What is the best way to use peat moss in flower gardens? Work it into the bed.

I use peat moss as litter in my hen coop. Will I have to add anything to it for use in the vegetable garden? Yes. It is desirable to add superphosphate at the rate of 5 pounds per 100 square feet of ground.

What plants can tolerate peat moss? All acid-tolerant plants (azaleas, hydrangeas, oaks, coniferous and broad-leaved evergreens, etc.). Most other plants benefit through its use. Alkaline-loving plants are the exception. But adding lime (about a quart to a bushel) offsets acidity.

Why doesn't peat moss freeze? If sufficient moisture is present, peat moss freezes. If perfectly dry, its fluffiness provides an air cushion.

In the propagation of certain plants on a large scale, I need to have about one fourth of my soil mixture consist of peat moss. Is there any suitable substitute that could be found in the South Carolina low country? Well-rotted compost is best or you can use shredded sugarcane, shredded redwood bark, or decomposed pine needles.

What is the best substitute for peat moss? Sedge peat, bagasse (sugarcane pulp), leafmold, pine needles, shredded redwood bark, ground barks of most trees, compost, and sawdust used in smaller amounts than peat.

Manures

A local riding stable gives away manure for the hauling. How can it be used in the garden?   Although manure is a valuable soil amendment when composted, most riding stables spray their stalls with disinfectants, fly repellents, and other toxic chemicals. (See the Introduction for ways to handle this material.)

Is cow manure a good fertilizer for a vegetable garden?   Not if maximum production is wanted. It is not too rich in food elements, but is a valuable soil amendment. Allowing it to rot in a compost heap during the winter is the best way to prepare it for use.

Is manure worked into the garden this year of any value in future years?   Yes. Like all organic matter, manure becomes humus eventually and will continue to affect the soil for years.

How does poultry manure differ from other types? We are in a broiler-producing area and can get it for nothing.   Unless it is mixed with litter, it does not add much to the organic content of soil; it is of use largely as a source of nitrogen for immediate effect. Mixing it with superphosphate and wood ashes will not only make it more pleasant to handle, but will kill odors and increase its fertilizer value.

Is it necessary to use commercial fertilizer if I use the manure from our 200 hens?   Yes, if you want maximum production. A farm fertilizer such as a 2–10–10 would balance its high nitrogen. Or mix poultry manure with superphosphate and wood ashes; or use muriate of potash instead of wood ashes. The poultry manure should be aged until a strong odor of ammonia disappears before mixing with wood ashes.

We have a kennel and accumulate dog manure. Does it have any value as a fertilizer?   Dog manure, like poultry manure, is high in nitrogen. However, it and cat manure can contain intestinal worms and cysts. Composting the manures for six months or more will destroy them.

Would dumping cat litter and its manure on the compost pile hurt the compost?   On the contrary, it would improve the finished compost if allowed to age for six months or more. (See the previous question.)

Can the contents of a privy be used as compost?   Although there are aesthetic prejudices against such use, one of the famous English fertilizers, Clays, was nothing but artificially dried privy scrapings, used almost with reverence by gardeners until World War II. If aged for a year and perhaps applied only to soil in which ornamental plants grow, it would be a good use for material which is otherwise a nuisance. However, there is danger of dysentery if raw sludge is used on vegetable crops.

I planted a small vegetable garden of about 2,000 square feet. I plan to enrich the soil with a compost and dried cow manure this year. How much should be used? At least 100 pounds of dried cow manure should be used per 1,000 square feet. If you can afford it, triple the amount.

I am no longer able to get barnyard manure for my garden plot. Is there a substitute fertilizer that I can procure? "Commercial" (dried and ground) cow manure and sheep manure are available in most garden centers. Incorporate green manures and, in addition, apply a general-purpose fertilizer recommended for garden use.

Under what conditions can dried manure be used in place of rotted manure? It is useful as an ingredient in a compost heap or it can be mixed with soil in a flower or vegetable garden. Its drawback is its cost.

Can a garden have too much goat manure? Goat manure is reasonably strong in nitrogen. It should be used in about the same way as described for sheep manure.

Should goat manure and straw be put on frozen ground, or put in a compost heap until spring? Better in a compost heap, if mixed with other materials; otherwise, it would be better to spread the manure and straw on the ground. If left in a pile, some leaching will take place, not on the spot where wanted.

I procured fresh horse manure but find it difficult to keep it from "burning." Can leaves be mixed with it? When horse manure is "burned," it loses most of its nitrogen, but it is still good as a soil conditioner. Mixing peat or leaves or chopped straw with horse manure and keeping it wet will reduce "burning."

Will wood shavings harm horse manure? No. Apply to the soil in the fall.

Is horse manure harmful to roses and delphiniums? Much stable manure is treated to control flies and odors. Well-composted manure *may* be safe but test on tomato seedlings first. The seedlings, highly sensitive to possibly harmful chemicals in sewage, will give a quick, cheap indication.

LIQUID MANURE

Is there any fertilizer that can be used as a liquid for the small home garden?   Five teaspoons of a regular 5–10–5, 5–10–10, 7–7–7, or similar grade of complete fertilizer per gallon of water will make a satisfactory liquid fertilizer. Such fertilizers are about 75 per cent soluble. Do not use premium grades of fertilizers containing much organic materials. Apply 1 gallon to 5 square feet.

How can you make liquid fertilizer using chemical ingredients that are cheap to buy?   A liquid fertilizer containing 1 teaspoonful each of saltpeter (potassium nitrate), superphosphate (monocalcium phosphate), and Epsom salts (magnesium sulfate) is satisfactory.

Green-Manure Crops

What is a green-manure crop? A cover crop?   The term "green-manure crop" refers to any crop that may be turned into the soil in an undecomposed, green-tissue stage. In contrast, a cover crop refers to a more or less permanent crop used for the purpose of preventing erosion.

How are green-manure crops planted?   For small areas, seeds of the green-manure crops can be broadcast. For large areas, a row or drill is used. Seeds should not be covered too deeply—approximately twice their diameter is sufficient.

What are several good summer green-manure crops?   The crops most commonly used for summer green manure are alfalfa, cowpeas, crimson clover, red clover, sweet clover, crotalaria, lespedeza, soybeans, and Sudan grass.

What green-manure crop can be left growing in the ground over winter, to be turned under in the spring?   The most common winter green-manure crops are rye, perennial ryegrass, and oats.

What quantity of seed should be sown per 1,000 square feet of green-manure crops?   Alfalfa, ½ pound; cowpeas, 2½ to 3 pounds; crimson clover and red clover, ½ pound; sweet clover, ½ to ¾ pound; crotalaria, ½ to ¾ pound; lespedeza, ½ pound; soybeans, 2 to 3 pounds; Sudan grass, ½ to ¾ pound; rye, 2 to 3 pounds; ryegrass, 1 to 2 pounds; buckwheat, 1½ pounds. These are approximate amounts.

For thick and quick coverage on small areas, they can be increased up to double these quantities.

I cannot obtain cow manure. What do you suggest as a substitute? Old, partly rotted straw or hay, together with a complete fertilizer, can be used as substitutes. Turn under early in the fall and add a complete fertilizer at the same time. Or use a green-manure crop.

How tall should a green-manure crop be before it is turned under? In general, it is best to turn under green crops when their succulence is near the maximum, yet at a time when abundant tops have been produced. This stage occurs when they are about, or a little beyond, half mature. Always allow at least three weeks to elapse between turning under a green-manure crop and planting.

Are clover and buckwheat good for soil? Clover and buckwheat are good green-manure crops, but soybeans and rye are better and quicker. Sow soybeans in the spring and plow under in early fall. Sow rye in fall and plow under in the spring. Use 2 pounds per 1,000 square feet.

Where a green-manure crop is plowed under in the fall, is it advisable to follow with a winter crop? Only where there is a possibility of soil erosion.

What winter green-manure crops can be used following the turning under of red clover? Rye, ryegrass, or oats.

How soon after the summer green-manure crop is turned under can the fall crop be sown? It is advisable to delay the sowing of the second crop 3 weeks if possible; but follow the specific planting dates recommended for the winter crop used.

When should winter green-manure crops be sown? Late August or early September. Rye can be sown as late as the first week of October. If soil areas are available, sow at any time if the space is not needed for planting the same season.

If soil is respaded in spring, following the turning under of green manure (clover) in fall, will the crop come to the top? If the green-manure crop is turned under at the proper time, it will be sufficiently decomposed by spring so that respading can be done.

When land is cleared, and winter rye sown, what should be done in spring to prepare for vegetables? Plow the rye under in April. Apply a fertilizer recommended for vegetables at twice the recommended rate.

How can organics and nitrogen be supplied in city gardens without compost or chemical fertilizer? Peat moss and dried manures may be used. Soybean meal and cottonseed meal will add nitrogen.

Should turf and large roots be removed from virgin soil or turned

under to make humus? It is advisable to turn under as much organic matter as possible in preparing soil for planting. Turf and roots of annual and herbaceous plants should be turned under. Remove the large roots of woody plants.

Can a green-manure crop be planted which will raise the pH and sweeten the soil? No, green-manure crops in themselves exert very little influence on the degree of acidity of the soil.

When there is a shortage of animal fertilizer, what kind and proportion of other fertilizers are suggested for garden use? Incorporate green manures. Apply fertilizers made for vegetable gardens at twice the recommended rate. Always water well immediately after applying mineral fertilizers to prevent "burning" injury.

Do any plants, other than legumes and green-manure crops, supply any nutrients to soil? Any plant that is turned under supplies a certain amount of nutrients. The proportions vary with the type of plant.

Does planting rye in fall and plowing under in spring keep up the fertility of the soil? The use of rye as a green-manure crop will do little toward increasing the nitrogen content of the soil; in fact, it may even decrease it temporarily. It does, however, add humus, and thus helps to increase crop production.

Should green-manure crops such as rye be used every year? In gardens devoted to the production of vegetables or annual flowers, it is advisable to sow a winter green-manure crop each autumn, but this is seldom feasible.

At what stage should rye be turned under? As late as possible to produce more green growth, and up to within 3 weeks of planting time.

Should rye be completely covered when it is turned under? Yes, but the green-manure crop should be incorporated with the upper 8 to 12 inches of soil instead of being plowed or dug under in a layer. If a few of the stems are not covered, it is all right.

What is a legume? All leguminous plants belong to the *Leguminosae* family, recognizable by the formation of their flowers. Peas, beans, and clovers are legumes. They all attract bacteria which collect nitrogen and store it on the roots. The small nodules on the roots, when they decay, add nitrogen to the soil.

What is the special advantage of using a leguminous green-manure crop? The advantage of a legume is that the nitrogen content of the soil will be increased by the root-nodule organisms. However, the legume crops take longer to grow. For a small garden, rye or perennial ryegrass is usually more practical.

Are inoculant powders for use on legumes really helpful? Yes. These inoculant powders are listed under various trade names (such as Nitragen, Legume Aid) and are obtainable in local garden centers or from mail-order seed firms. They are used to assist in the development of nitrogen-fixing bacteria on the roots of leguminous plants. They are applied when seeds are planted. The mixtures vary with the crop to be planted, so the crop should always be considered when buying these products.

Is it advisable to try to grow alfalfa for soil improvement in the southern part of Maine? Yes. But plant early (mid-August) to avoid the roots heaving out of the soil from freezing, thawing, and winterkilling. Sow 12 to 15 pounds per acre. However, alfalfa is not a good one-season crop for soil improvement. It is valuable over a longer period because its roots penetrate deeply.

How is the land prepared for growing alfalfa? Same as for any other crop. It may be necessary to add lime.

When is it best to plant crimson clover and expect results from it in improving the soil for a garden? Crimson clover is usually seeded in July or August, or at least 6 weeks before the normal date of the first killing frost in fall. It may be turned under the following spring or early summer.

Do you plow crimson clover under when it is in bloom? It is best to turn it under when in bloom, or shortly after this stage. It can, however, be turned under at any stage; but the less growth that has been made, the less humus will be produced.

At what rate should soybeans be sown for a green-manure crop? Three pounds per 1,000 square feet.

Compost

What is "compost"? "Compost" is the term applied to organic matter—such as leaves, weeds, grass clippings—which has been sufficiently decayed to form a light, crumbly mold. In making compost in a compost heap, soil and manure are often mixed with the vegetable matter.

Should the average home gardener have a compost heap? Yes, by all means. It is about the only adequate substitute for well-rotted manure, which is less available than it used to be.

BUILDING

What materials are used in making a compost heap? Plant refuse: cornstalks, cabbage stems, dead foliage, and discarded vegetables; leaves, grass cuttings, garbage, soil, manure (in fact, any vegetable matter that will decay), plus lime and complete fertilizers. Weeds, even when seeding, may be used if the heap is to be remade at the end of each 3 months, turning it inside out so that every part of the heap is completely decomposed before use. A heap treated in this way is so well rotted that most seeds and insect eggs are destroyed.

How is a compost heap constructed? Heaps 4 feet wide and 6 feet long are a convenient size for a small place. Dig out this area to a depth of from 12 to 18 inches and throw the soil to one side. The bottom layer could be cornstalks, cabbage stems, and other coarse material, tamped down; or, lacking them, use whatever is available, even leaves. Over this, lay 2 or 3 inches of soil, and then 2 or 3 inches of manure, if available. Peat moss can be used if manure cannot be had. Sprinkle raw ground limestone over every other layer at the rate of a quart to a wheelbarrowload of compost material. On alternate layers apply a complete chemical fertilizer, about a quart to each alternate layer. Add layers of leaves, cuttings, weeds, etc., with a layer of soil, manure, or peat moss every 12 to 18 inches. Keep sides even by sloping very gradually inward toward the top. When all material has been placed in layers, soak thoroughly with a hose and cover entirely with 3 inches of soil, well firmed down. The top is left saucer-shaped to receive and absorb rainfall. Do not let heap dry out at any time. At the end of 3 months, remake the entire heap, turning inside out, if rapid decomposition is desired.

What length of time is required for a well-made compost heap to rot? Four months to a year, depending on its composition and whether or not ingredients have been added to hasten decay; usually about 9 months.

What is a good formula for making a compost pile break down quickly? I understand lime should not be used as it causes loss of nitrogen. Lime should be used but should not come in immediate contact with added fertilizer. Use it in alternate layers with organic matter between.

Is the use of a compost starter advisable? Most of those sold are only fertilizers plus limestone. Your own fertilizer will be much cheaper. Others are bacterial cultures. Or bacteria can be added with garden soil.

How often should a new compost heap be started?   To maintain a constant supply of compost, a new heap should be started every 6 months.

How is rotted compost used in gardening?   For a seed bed, it should be sieved through a coarse (1-inch) screen and then diluted with 3 or 4 parts of garden soil. It can be worked into the garden by applying a 1½-inch layer and cultivating it into the upper 6 inches of soil. For a lawn dressing, apply the sieved compost without dilution with soil.

How should decomposed compost be removed from the heap?   Cut sections down vertically with a spade, leaving straight, clean sides where it has been removed. Save coarse undecayed parts for a new compost heap.

Must I use compost in my garden? I have no space for a compost pile.   Unless you can afford to buy peat moss in large amounts or have access to other humus sources, compost is the only way to supply organic matter. For those with limited space, composting in the plastic bags used for disposing of lawn clippings and other wastes will solve the problem. Mix leaves, lawn clippings, or even garbage with about a handful of a good mixed fertilizer, plus a pint or two of good garden soil to each bushel. Dried leaves should be sprinkled enough to moisten them through but not make them soggy. Clippings and garbage will not need additional moisture. Seal the materials in a plastic bag and tie shut. Stack the bags in any convenient place (I have used a garage and a root cellar). At temperatures above 70° F., material will be ready for use in 3 to 4 months.

GARBAGE

Are these any good for the compost heap: orange peels, banana peels, and green corn shucks?   Yes, any vegetable refuse free of disease is all right. Even weeds with seeds are all right if properly fermented. Do not, however, use coffee grounds. Tests at the USDA show they are slightly toxic to plants. Tests have also shown that sunflower seed hulls inhibit plant growth. (See also Hickory Hulls, this section.)

Can fresh table refuse and garbage be applied to the garden? I have been putting everything through a meat chopper and this makes a fine lot of refuse. The problem is how to apply it. Are orange skins of much fertilizing value?   The materials mentioned, by themselves, do not constitute fertilizers, but when rotted in a compost pile they are valuable. They should be buried to put them in close contact with soil bacteria.

The refuse from my incinerator consists mostly of ashes and unburned garbage, such as grapefruit, orange peels, etc. Is this O.K. to bury in soil having a large clay content?   Yes, but better to make a compost heap with 6-inch alternate layers of soil, garbage, grass cuttings, etc. It would take a year to make a good compost, but it's worth the trouble.

After apples have been crushed and squeezed for cider, would it be advisable to use the apple pomace in the compost pile?   Yes, apple pomace is all right to add to compost; cover with soil.

What is the case for, and against, adding garbage to the compost heap?   Garbage is a most desirable source of compost. Each layer of garbage must, however, be immediately covered with soil to prevent odors. If dogs run loose in your community, unsorted table garbage will attract them unless the heap is fenced in. Garbage also attracts rodents. Garbage can be placed in a pit, at a distance from your house, each layer being sprinkled with a layer of soil and of raw ground limestone. When the contents of the pit are decomposed, it can be added in layers to a new compost heap when one is being built. In this way rodents are kept out of the compost heap and garbage is decomposed underground without odor.

GRASS CLIPPINGS

What good are grass cuttings? How fast do they decay?   Clippings make satisfactory compost. If layered with soil in thin layers (4 inches of soil and 2 inches of clippings), or added to a mixed heap, a compost will be ready in less than a year.

HICKORY HULLS

Do the hulls (not shells) from hickory nuts cause soil acidity? We have 3 hickory trees on a double lot and don't know whether to put the hulls into the compost pile or burn them.   Hickory and walnut hulls contain a chemical that is toxic to some plants, so they should not be added to the compost pile.

LEAVES

Should the leaves for compost be rotted? It is best to have them at least partly rotted before placing them in a compost heap. If not, it is likely to take a full year for them to decompose, unless manure or peat moss is also used in the compost pile.

Are elm leaves good to use on the compost heap? Yes.

How do you make fertilizer out of maple leaves? Add to compost heap in the same way as other leaves.

Should anything be used with leaves for compost? Compost or peat moss, lime, and complete fertilizers. Leaves are low in plant nutrients and must have added fertilizer to be of much use.

What can be added to accumulated leaves in the fall to hasten decomposition? Make a pile 4 feet wide and any desired length. Each layer of leaves 12 inches deep should be sprinkled with a complete commercial fertilizer at the rate of a pint per bushel of leaves.

Is soil put on the compost pile (made largely of leaves) to help decomposition? Yes. It adds the bacteria needed for decay.

Will this fall's leaves be fertilizer by next spring? Can anything be done to hurry the process? Not that soon. It will take about a year. Leaves saved from fall and composted in the spring may make good leafmold by fall.

Much has been said about the value of a compost of rotted leaves. I understand that some leaves, due to high acid content, have practically no value as manure. Which should be burned and which should be saved? Leafmold from most trees is only slightly, if at all, acid. This reference is to leaves of deciduous trees. Evergreens, however, will produce acid leafmold. The use of lime is an easy way to correct any such acidity. The value of leaves is for humus rather than a source of fertilizer. (See the following question.)

Are the ashes from burned leaves and grass cuttings of any benefit, or of as much benefit, as those same leaves and cuttings if they were permitted to decay? No. If leaves and clippings are made into a compost, they serve a much better purpose than when burned.

SPECIAL PROBLEMS

What can the home gardener make from refuse that will take the place of 5–10–5 and nitrate of soda? Make a compost pile of straw, weeds, grass clippings, leaves, and other plant parts. (See Compost, Introduction, this section.)

All the refuse from our lawns and vegetables and flower gardens has gone into our compost pile. This includes corn and dahlia stalks, peonies, etc. The entire pile has been covered with clay subsoil (topsoil being scarce). A little fertilizer has been added and some leaves. It is our intention to use this pile, accumulated during summer and fall, by digging it into the vegetable gardens. Is this a good practice? A better method would have been to make alternate layers of soil and refuse together, with a definite amount of commercial fertilizer and lime. The only thing to do now is to turn the pile several times, mixing all the ingredients together.

Will you give me an idea of the fertilizer value of compost, with inorganic chemicals added, as compared to that made of organic matter only? Organic fertilizers are less satisfactory to add to composts than inorganic fertilizers, largely because of their slower action. Once decomposed, there should be little difference between the two. Inorganic fertilizers and lime are added to the compost heap both to hasten decomposition and to supply nutrients otherwise low or lacking.

In making a compost pile, is it more advisable to pile up on top of the ground, or to dig a pit and gradually fill it in? In dry climates, a slight depression is best, but elsewhere a compost pile should be on level ground.

How do you keep a compost pile from smelling? If smelly ingredients are used (e.g., raw sewage sludge), using superphosphate on alternate layers instead of lime will kill odors.

What is a good substitute for city dwellers for the objectionable compost pile? Try making compost in plastic bags. Mix organic materials with fertilizers (1 quart to a bushel). Mixture should be slightly damp. Seal and store at 70° F. or higher. Don't use lime until compost is ready to use in 3 to 6 months.

Does the compost lose any of its elements when kept in the house all winter and dried up? The mechanical structure of such soils is affected more than its nutritional value. If stored inside, storing in plastic bags will keep it moist. Drying kills soil organisms vital to plant life.

Compost pits are sometimes thickly inhabited by very large, fat earthworms. Are these harmful, or should they be left in the decomposing material? Worms do no damage in the compost; in fact, they assist in the decomposition of vegetable matter.

PESTS AND DISEASES

In making a compost heap, how can we avoid carrying over diseases from the previous year, such as tomato and potato blight? Do not use diseased tops, vines, or fruits for composting, unless special care is taken in "turning" the heap. (See the next question.)

Some of the waste vegetable matter I put in my compost heap had a lot of aphids or similar insects on it. I put lime and superphosphate with the compost. Will the aphids be killed during the winter? The adults will probably die, but the eggs may carry over. At the time of making the compost, the vegetable matter should have been sprayed with malathion. However, if the heap is turned "inside out" every 3 months and if every part is thus thoroughly fermented, most insects and diseases will be destroyed.

Does it do any harm to put moldy fruit, vegetables, or mildewed shrubs and leaves into the compost? Any vegetable matter which is not infected with disease or infested with insects may be used safely for composting. Molds resulting from decay do no harm.

Please explain the chemistry of the compost heap. Would the pests it might harbor outweigh the advantages for a small (50 by 100 feet) garden? A compost heap is a mixture of soil, fertilizer, and organic matter. In decomposing, the combination does not always get rid of all diseases and pests. To save organic matter, a compost pile is worth having.

Organic Fertilizers

What is organic fertilizer? An organic fertilizer is one which is derived from organic materials—plant or animal substances. All are compounds of carbon. Some of these materials, such as cottonseed meal, bone meal, tankage, and castor pomace, may add small amounts of humus as well as nutrients to the soil. Others, such as urea or ureaform, may not add humus.

I am interested in organic gardening and would like some combinations of organic fertilizers I could mix for my vegetable garden. Here are a few: one pound of steamed bone meal; 9 pounds of wood ashes; 1¾ pounds of dried blood. Apply to 100 square feet. Or 1 pound of steamed bone meal; 7 pounds of wood ashes; 1¼ pounds of dried blood; 3 pounds of rock phosphate. Apply to 100 square feet.

What is best for a vegetable garden, compost or chemicals? Use both. They complement each other. Compost is organic but is not a balanced fertilizer, while a chemical fertilizer contains no organic matter to supply humus.

What fertilizers are best for loose soil? Loose soil will be benefited by the incorporation of organic matter to increase the humus. The use of commercial fertilizer does not depend upon the soil structure.

What causes soil to crack in dry weather? Heavy soils will crack unless sufficient organic matter is present to prevent cohesion of the fine particles.

Is bone meal a good fertilizer for all plants? Bone meal is a safe fertilizer to use, but it contains no potash and only a small amount of nitrogen. Although high in phosphorus, this element is released very slowly. Based on the amount of essential ingredients contained, it is more expensive than some chemical fertilizers. However, gardeners use it for many purposes. Superphosphate is a much better source of phosphorus at a fraction of the cost.

COTTONSEED MEAL

What nutrients does cottonseed meal contain? Cottonseed meal contains approximately 7 per cent nitrogen, 2.5 per cent phosphoric acid, and 1.5 per cent potash.

How long does it take for cottonseed meal to mix with soil? Part of the nitrogen and other essential elements of cottonseed meal are readily available; the remainder becomes available more slowly.

On what plants can cottonseed meal be used, and in combination with what other fertilizer? It can be used on nearly all plants as it contains about 7 per cent nitrogen, which becomes available slowly; also 3 per cent phosphorus and 2 per cent potash. It can be used with superphosphate. Cottonseed meal is especially recommended for use on rhododendrons and other ericaceous plants.

DRIED BLOOD

Is blood meal a fertilizer? Dried blood is high in nitrogen but low in both phosphorus and potash. Its greatest value is as a source of minor elements in soluble form. Unfortunately, it is too valuable as an industrial material to be economical as a fertilizer.

LEAFMOLD

In using leafmold as a fertilizer, should it be used liberally or sparingly? Leafmold is not a very high-grade fertilizer, but a good source of humus. It is a good soil conditioner and as such can be used liberally —a covering 4 inches deep is all right.

What effect do pine needles have on soil? They acidify it and help improve the soil's condition. They eventually add humus.

When should fallen leaves be used? As a mulch, use anytime. As a soil conditioner, apply when they are partially rotted.

Last fall I spaded my garden a foot deep and on the bottom I put a heavy layer of maple leaves. This was covered over with a foot of earth. Was this worthwhile? It would be better to spade leaves into the soil in the fall, or let them decay first and add to the soil later.

How do hard maple tree leaves affect the soil if they are left where they fall during the winter? It is better to compost them. They have little value if left on top of the soil.

Do large quantities of mixed leaves (elm, maple, oak, beech) make good fertilizer when rotted? They make a good soil conditioner but are of comparatively little fertilizer value; they are not nearly as effective as manures unless a heavy dosage of fertilizer is added in rotting them.

Is it true that the leaves of silver leaf and other poplars, spaded into the soil, are toxic to the growth of flowers? No.

Will oak leaves make the ground sour? No. When decomposed, they make an excellent soil conditioner. Used in quantity, they will make the ground acid but only temporarily. They are frequently employed for this purpose.

SLUDGE

The dried and pulverized sludge from sewage-disposal plants is used as a fertilizer not only for lawns and flowers but for vegetables as well. Therefore, is the liquid and sludge from septic tanks a good fertilizer, after it has passed from the first compartment and just before it passes into the third or final compartment? How would it compare with the liquid manure used by farmers? Such sludge should be satisfactory as a fertilizer. It should compare favorably with liquid manure. The one danger is that liquid raw sludge can carry the organism of amoebic dysentery, as well as other diseases.

The local sewage disposal sells sewage settlings. Nothing has been added to this. How does this compare in value with barnyard manure and with other commercial fertilizers for use on lawn and garden? (I have sandy soil.) Sewage sludge is actually an expensive fertilizer when fertilizer efficiency is considered. See the health hazard mentioned above. Also, if your town contains many industrial plants, there is danger from heavy metals and other chemicals in sewage. It would still be safe to use on ornamentals.

TANKAGE

What is tankage? Tankage is a by-product of slaughterhouses, which contains such refuse as lungs, intestines, bones, etc. These are processed, dried, and ground to produce a material used in stock feeds and for fertilizer.

What is the value of tankage? It contains about 4 to 10 per cent nitrogen and 7 to 14 per cent phosphoric acid. It is lacking in potash content.

How is tankage applied? About 4 pounds per 100 square feet; usually as a top- or side-dressing to growing plants, hoed or cultivated into the soil. It is often employed in place of nitrate of soda, which is quicker-acting. It must be kept *perfectly dry* in storage or it will quickly decay.

WOOD ASHES

Are wood or leaf ashes good for the garden? Yes. They contain potash and lime. However, they do not contain the humus-forming materials that were in the leaves and wood originally.

How do wood ashes affect manures? Wood ashes containing lime have a tendency to hasten the decomposition of manure.

Where can I use wood ashes and chicken manure to the best advantage? Do *not* use together if chicken manure is fresh. Otherwise the combination is good. Mix ashes and chicken manure at a 3 to 1 ratio.

What is the best way to apply wood ashes to lilies and roses? Since the majority of lilies do better in somewhat acid soils, wood ashes should not be used. Apply wood ashes to roses in the spring, about ½ to 1 pound around each plant.

What is the best way to use wood ashes in acid soil? Wood ashes tend to reduce acidity because of their lime content. Apply to the soil in the fall or spring, 4 to 6 pounds per 100 square feet. Fresh wood ashes will form lye when first applied. Do not use on plants in active growth.

What plants and trees benefit by an application of wood ashes? Almost all plants. Those that need potash—fruit trees, vegetable root crops, hydrangeas, carnations, roses, peonies, delphiniums, lawns, etc.—are especially benefited.

Will the action of wood ashes and cinders destroy alkali on irrigated land? (Washington State.) Neither wood ashes nor cinders would be useful: in fact, they would raise the soil pH. If the soil is alkaline, sulfur is needed.

Every year I burn a considerable amount of brush. Are the ashes good fertilizer? Wood ashes are especially good for their potash content.

Do oak wood ashes have any value as fertilizer for flowers or vegetables? Yes. They contain potash and are always safe to use.

If I put wood ashes from our fireplace on the vegetable and flower beds, will the oil from the coal ashes mixed with them harm the plants? Burned coal ashes do not contain oil. They contain toxic substances that must be leached out by weathering over the winter before being applied. Cannel coal, if incompletely consumed, contains oil.

Is there any value in wood coke from bonfires if applied to a garden in fall? Applied in fall, it would be partly wasted. Better to save it under cover and apply in the spring.

Should I spread the wood ashes from my fireplace around as they are available during the winter; or must I store and use them during the growing season? Store your ashes under cover to prevent the leaching of potash. Leached wood ashes contain little potash, although they are still of some value.

Are the ashes of burned leaves, twigs, and winter-killed dry stalks of vegetation of any material value if burned on the garden plot? Yes, but the ashes would have more value if stored under cover and scattered in the spring.

MISCELLANEOUS MATERIALS

Is crab meal a good fertilizer? Fresh crab contains 2 to 3 per cent nitrogen and 2 to 3 per cent phosphoric acid. Its immediate efficiency is relatively low. Mixed fertilizer made with dried and ground king crab may contain 9 to 12 per cent nitrogen.

Can crab meal be used on most garden plants with benefit?   Yes. Its cost will govern the extent of its use.

Is charcoal good to add to soil to help plants?   Yes, it adds a small amount of phosphorus and considerable potash and lime. These materials, however, as found in charcoal, become available very slowly.

Are rotted cranberries good as a fertilizer?   They would add a small amount of organic matter but very small quantities of the essential elements for plant growth.

How is soil affected by a daily application of coffee grounds?   Tests at the USDA indicate that coffee grounds are slightly toxic to plant growth. Small amounts added to compost are harmless but of little value.

Some people say that soapy water is beneficial to soil and growth of vegetation. Is this so?   Soapy water is not beneficial and is sometimes injurious if large amounts are poured in one spot, particularly where soap contains naphtha. Soapy water does contain small amounts of potash but is a poor source of that element. The words "soapy water" could refer to detergent-laden waste water, which could mean it might contain some phosphorus, which is a nutrient element, or one of the many alcohols, which are not.

What fertilizer value is there in eggshells?   Eggshells contain a considerable quantity of calcium and a very small amount of nitrogen. Crush or grind them.

What about burying fish trimmings deep in the earth?   Fish remains make an excellent fertilizer. Bury them just deep enough to avoid objectionable odors.

I'm burying all my garbage around the plants. Do you think this will be sufficient fertilizer?   No. Garbage at its best is a very low-grade fertilizer; it is a good idea to add humus, but this should be supplemented by a complete fertilizer.

Can leather dust be used as a garden fertilizer?   Leather dust contains some nitrogen, but it decomposes very slowly so that quick results should not be expected.

Is sawdust good to put on a garden?   It can be used to lighten soil and as a mulch. If applied with more than 1 inch, sawdust must have added nitrogen to decay.

I have some very fine sawdust of white pine. What would be its effect if worked into a soil in which vegetables or flowers are planted?   It should help lighten your soil if it's heavy. Do not use thicker than 1 inch.

How does one prepare kelp and other common seaweeds (which wash up on beaches along Long Island Sound) for fertilizer? If conditions are such that it can be done, the kelp can be handled as a green manure or plowed or spaded under. Otherwise, it can be composted and applied at an opportune time.

What value is sea kelp as a fertilizer? Sea kelp is high in potash and will compare favorably with farm manure in nitrogen, but it is low in phosphorus.

Where can I buy sea kelp in Iowa for fertilizer? Most of the sea kelp is processed for liquid fertilizer on the West or East coasts. In its natural state, it is too bulky to be shipped any distance. Most mail-order supply houses offer liquid seaweeds for fertilizing.

Can sea kelp be used immediately, or must it be stored? Sea kelp is used fresh as a green manure by farmers and gardeners near the seashore. For shipping, it is dried, then burned to an ash. In this state it can be used at once or stored. The ash contains about 30 per cent potash.

Are other seaweeds as valuable as a fertilizer as sea kelp? Seaweeds vary considerably in nutritive value. They are worth using if readily available.

Will you please tell me if seaweed is any good to use as a fertilizer. If so, how can I use it for best results, since I live on the seashore? I can get all the seaweed I need. Seaweed is a good fertilizer. For someone who can get the material fresh, it is best to use it as a green manure spread on the land and turned under. It need not be washed.

What soil-conditioning property does chimney soot have? When is it applied? Scotch soot from the peat-burning fireplaces was once an inexpensive source of nitrogen. Soot from stokers, etc., contains toxic substances. Oil-burner soot can be harmful. Soot from a fireplace in which only wood is burned is a valuable source of nitrogen.

Inorganic Fertilizers

What is inorganic fertilizer? An inorganic fertilizer is one derived from mineral or chemical substances, such as phosphate rock, potash salts, nitrate salts (nitrate of soda).

What is a chemical fertilizer? A chemical fertilizer is one derived from chemically processed or manufactured materials rather than from natural organic substances. The term is somewhat misleading in that organic fertilizers also may be treated with chemicals to increase their rate of availability. Many fertilizers contain both types of materials.

Are chemicals injurious to future plant growth? Not if they are used correctly. They do not, however, add humus to the soil.

Why don't we use stone dust as a natural fertilizer, which it really is? Pulverized granite (granite meal) is used as a source of potash in some areas. It contains about 5 to 10 per cent potash, along with a wide assortment of other elements. It is applied at rates of ½ to 2 tons per acre and lasts for a long time. On acid soils, pulverized phosphate rock is usually a satisfactory source of phosphate when used liberally. Some rocks are nearly devoid of fertilizer elements.

When preparing the soil in the spring for a garden of either flowers or vegetables, is it necessary to apply a chemical for better results? Usually additions of chemical fertilizers decidedly help production. They go to work at once, while organic fertilizers do not begin to feed plants until warm weather starts their decay.

What is the fertilizer value of calcium carbonate? Calcium carbonate in itself is of no value as a fertilizer, since it is insoluble in water. It must be converted into the bicarbonate form, or some other soluble calcium salt, before calcium becomes available to the plant. It may also beneficially modify the structure of the soil.

NITRATE OF SODA

For what purpose is nitrate of soda used? Nitrate of soda furnishes a readily available source of nitrogen. Nitrogen stimulates the vegetative growth of the plant and is also essential for the reproductive phases. If used in large amounts, it can cause greasy or pasty soils that are hard to work. Other sources of nitrogen are superior. Few garden centers offer nitrate of soda today.

What can we use in place of nitrate of soda? Ammonium sulfate, dried blood, cottonseed, soybean meal, or tankage.

SULFATE OF AMMONIA

What is sulfate of ammonia used for? This is used as a source of nitrogen. It contains about 20 per cent nitrogen.

When should sulfate of ammonia be used? How much? This is a good fertilizer to use when nitrogen is required. Apply about 5 to 10 pounds per 1,000 square feet.

When is a good time to spread ammonium sulfate on the ground? Ammonium sulfate is best applied after the soil is spaded and it should be raked into the upper 2 to 4 inches of the surface soil.

UREA

What is urea? Urea is a water-soluble organic compound containing 45 to 46 per cent nitrogen. It is a natural chemical found in urine. In soil, urea almost immediately decomposes to ammonium nitrogen and carbon dioxide.

Does urea leave an acid residue? Yes, but only a slight amount of acidity is left—about a third as much as would be left from a similar amount of nitrogen from sulfate of ammonia.

What is ureaform? To make ureaform (also spelled uraform), urea and formaldehyde are combined to form a soft plastic. This dissolves slowly, feeding nitrogen at a rate close to the rate of plant growth. A single application can feed all summer. Ureaform should be supplemented with other plant nutrients.

SUPERPHOSPHATE

Is there any way to add phosphorus to soil without using commercial fertilizer? Yes, in the form of pulverized phosphate rock, bone meal, or basic slag. All may take a year or more to become available to plants.

Are the effects of superphosphate somewhat similar to those of bone meal? Yes, the effects are similar. Bone meal contains a low percentage of nitrogen not found in superphosphate. The phosphorus in bone meal, however, is available only over a long period of time. It can "lock up" in completely insoluble form.

How should one use agricultural lime and superphosphate? They should not be mixed. If so, the phosphates are made unavailable to plant roots.

Is there any advantage in applying superphosphate to perennial borders or rock gardens? Many soils are deficient in phosphorus. If perennials or rock plants are planted in such a soil, they will be benefited by applications of superphosphate at the rate of 5 pounds per 100 square feet.

How should phosphate be used? I have some and do not know how to apply it to flowers.   You don't mention in what form you are using phosphorus. Assuming it is superphosphate, it is best applied when the flower beds are first prepared by working it into the upper 4 to 6 inches of soil. If plants are already in the bed, apply the phosphate between the plants and work it into the soil as deeply as possible (down 6 to 8 inches) without disturbing or injuring the roots. Apply 5 pounds per 100 square feet.

When and how often should superphosphate be applied to perennials and rock plants?   In addition to the use of superphosphate at the time the beds are prepared, yearly applications of phosphorus are advisable, especially in soils tending to be deficient in this element. Also apply a complete fertilizer such as 5–10–5 in the spring.

MURIATE OF POTASH

What is the best time and method to apply muriate of potash to a vegetable garden?   If the amount of potash applied in the complete fertilizer recommended for vegetable gardens is not sufficient, apply an additional quantity (1 pound per 100 square feet) and incorporate it into the surface 2 to 3 inches.

How often should muriate of potash be applied?   Usually one application a year is sufficient. Soil tests will show if additional quantities are needed.

My soil is deficient in phosphorus and potash. What shall I apply to correct this condition?   Apply commercial fertilizers such as 2–10–10 or 0–10–10 or superphosphate and muriate of potash.

Complete Fertilizers

What are the principles of fertilization?   Stated briefly, fertilization is practiced to supply the necessary essential elements to secure a normal growth of cultivated plants. A garden is an artificial environment designed to supply cultivated plants with more growth substances than they would find in the wild. In a garden the purpose is superior (not natural) growth.

What is commercial fertilizer?   The term "commercial fertilizer" applies to any carrier of essential nutrient elements that is sold (by itself or mixed with other such carriers) commercially.

Please explain what fertilizer formulas—such as 10–6–4 and 8–5–3—mean? Formulas such as 10–6–4, 8–5–3, etc., are used to express the percentages of the major ingredients in fertilizers: namely, nitrogen, phosphorus, and potash. A 10–6–4 fertilizer denotes 10 per cent nitrogen, 6 per cent phosphorus, and 4 per cent potash.

Do commercial fertilizers aid or destroy existing bacteria and humus in the soil? Commercial fertilizers aid the beneficial bacteria of the soil. At the same time they may hasten the decomposition of humus. They do not do harm unless applied at very high rates.

Does commercial fertilizer burn the minerals out of the ground? No, it adds essential minerals to the soil.

Will commercial fertilizer restore a worn-out soil? Commercial fertilizers will furnish the necessary essential elements and can restore the soil in this respect. To restore humus and to improve the physical condition of the soil, organic matter must be added.

What are some substitutes for fertilizer? There are no substitutes for fertilizer. Compost is used for its organic value, but there is little fertilizer value in it unless it is applied in very heavy quantities (at least 20 tons per acre). Small amounts of nitrogen are brought down in rainfall.

Is there a fertilizer that is generally good as an all-plant fertilizer for shrubs, perennials, vegetables, rhododendrons, trees, and grass lawns? There is no one fertilizer that would be considered best for all these groups of plants, although a formula such as 5–10–5 suits most plants. Most garden centers offer several types of fertilizers for special plants.

How can one tell just what kind of fertilizer is best to use? Soil tests will give a partial answer; the habit of growth of the plant is also a determining factor. Ornamental plants normally showing vigorous top growth respond best to a low-nitrogen fertilizer, and vice versa. Fleshy-rooted plants respond best to a fertilizer low in nitrogen, high in phosphorus and potash.

Can one add certain chemicals to the soil of a garden vegetable patch in order to get bigger and better crop yields? A 2–10–10 or similar analysis is listed for use on root crops. Use a general vegetable fertilizer for other vegetables. Side dressings of a nitrogen fertilizer may be advisable for leafy vegetables.

How long does it take for organic or inorganic fertilizers to become available to plants? Inorganic nitrogenous fertilizers are readily available. The insoluble organic nitrogenous fertilizers are slowly available. Phosphorus from superphosphate penetrates the soil slowly, but is readily available in the monocalcium form. Potash is readily available. A slowly available form of nitrogen is ureaform.

What is the best fertilizer for a new vegetable garden? In general, a 4–12–4 or 5–10–5 fertilizer. For root or tuber crops, a 2–10–10 is satisfactory. Exact analysis is not important as long as the proportions are approximately the same. Apply at the rate recommended on the container.

What fertilizers should be added to the soil to make vegetables yield bountifully? See the previous question. For leafy vegetables, follow the spring application with a side dressing of ammonium sulfate when the tops are half grown.

What is the best fertilizer to use in midsummer? For leafy crops, use ammonium sulfate. For other common crops, use a product specifically labeled for use on vegetables.

Is it possible to mix one's own fertilizer for a successful home garden? To make your own fertilizer, several separate ingredients are needed. It is usually much more convenient to buy a ready-mixed fertilizer. (For an organic fertilizer you can mix, see Organic Fertilizers.)

Are there garden fertilizers that are good and more reasonable in price than the highly advertised brands? In general, the regular 4–12–4, 5–10–5, and 7–7–7 farm fertilizers are the least expensive. They are good fertilizers.

Is a complete fertilizer enough to use for the garden? Or should something be used in the fall and left through the winter? A complete fertilizer should be sufficient in itself. Additional nitrogen may be required for some crops; if so, it should be applied in the spring or when its need is obvious. In addition, green manures or compost to supply humus are needed.

I have on hand a 100-pound bag of lawn fertilizer; also 100-pound bag of bone meal. Can these be used? In what proportions? Rather than attempt to mix these fertilizers, use the lawn fertilizer for the lawn and most flower and vegetable crops. Use the bone meal for plants with fleshy and tuberous roots. However, unless used at a very high rate, the bone meal will contribute little to plant growth.

Is 5–10–5 fertilizer comparable to fertilizers with special trade names? Trade-name fertilizers are usually somewhat better than commercial grades of similar analysis due to the use of better materials, better mixing, and sometimes the addition of trace elements. The standard-formula fertilizers, however, are used with success by both amateur and commercial growers.

Can a garden fertilizer recommended for vegetables and hydrated lime, nitrate of soda, etc., be kept several seasons? Which should be used during the season it is bought? Practically all garden fertilizers can be kept for several years if they are kept dry. Some, such as ammonium sulfate, cake while standing and should be crushed before being applied.

Are fertilizers in tablet form recommended? They are satisfactory for use on house plants. Liquid house-plant foods are more readily available and usually cheaper.

I have a plot 20 × 20 feet that is covered with 6 inches of sandy loam. What kind of fertilizer could I use to make good soil for raising different kinds of flowers? Incorporate 12 to 16 pounds of a good, mixed garden fertilizer in the upper 3 to 5 inches of the soil. In addition, add all the well-rotted compost you can, within reason.

What formula, in the commercial-type fertilizer, gives best results for the growth of annuals, perennials, and shrubs in a mixed border? Exact formulas are not too important as long as the product is balanced. Read the bag.

What type of fertilizer should be used on plants in the winter in order to have blooms and good color in foliage? The liquid house-plant foods, made by mixing a dry complete fertilizer with water or diluting an emulsion, used at half the rate recommended will do well. Most house plants are overfertilized. In winter it is important to reduce feeding to compensate for reduced growth due to weaker sunlight.

I would like some combinations of organic fertilizers I could mix up for my vegetable garden. See Organic Fertilizers.

What commercial fertilizers are suitable for fruit trees? Complete fertilizers; also ammonium sulfate, cyanamide, nitrate of soda, superphosphate, muriate of potash, and several others.

Applying Fertilizers

When should one fertilize the garden—fall or spring? For permanent plantings of shrubs, evergreens, and flowers, fertilizers may be applied in the fall or spring with equal success. It is best to apply fertilizers for annual crops (both flowers and vegetables) at, or just previous to, planting time.

Is it better to place fertilizer on the garden in the fall and turn it over in the spring? Or turn the soil first, and then apply the fertilizer? Commercial fertilizers for the most part are best applied after spading or plowing, a week or 10 days before planting, and raked into the upper 2 to 3 inches of the soil. Superphosphate may be spaded or tilled in during the fall or spring.

Should I plant first, and then fertilize? Or vice versa? Fertilizer can be applied and worked into the soil just before planting or at planting time. One or more subsequent applications may be necessary during the growing season.

For a new garden, do I have to fertilize the ground before I plant? Usually it is necessary to fertilize. A soil analysis will indicate what is needed.

Are better blooms obtained if a fertilizer is used when you set out your plants or when buds form? For best results, apply the fertilizer at the time the plants are set. Make a subsequent application at, or previous to, bud formation.

Do you advocate putting fertilizer in the rows under the seeds or between the rows? Recent experiments show that it is best to apply the fertilizer 2 to 3 inches to the side and 1 to 2 inches below the seed.

My soil is very rich but no fertilizer has been added since last fall. Is it necessary to apply any when the ground is so good? No. Except to make sure the soil is maintained in this condition.

What is the best fertilizer to use for soil that has been cleared of trees and in which you want to make a vegetable garden? Any good, mixed complete fertilizer designed for vegetables.

How do you fertilize plants such as peonies that remain in the same spot for many years? Apply the fertilizer between the plants and hoe it into the upper few inches of soil without disturbing or injuring the roots of the plants. If the soil is dry, water thoroughly.

How often during the season should a flower garden be fertilized? When? Once or twice a season. Apply fertilizer in the spring as growth starts and again in midsummer if growth is not satisfactory.

What kind of fertilizer is best for peat soil that is turning acid? Peat soils usually become less acid as they are cultivated. A soil test would be advisable. If the soil is acid, use a nonacid fertilizer. (See the Introduction to this section.)

Is it good practice to use a commercial fertilizer on acid-loving

plants? Yes, if it is needed. Use a fertilizer specifically recommended for acid-loving plants. They can use nitrogen in the form of ammonia, which other plants cannot. Be sure the product used is specifically recommended for acid-loving plants.

I am draining a cedar swamp for a garden. The soil is black swamp muck, highly nitrogenous, and about 2 feet thick; white sand is the subsoil. What fertilizer should be used? The fertilizer to apply will depend upon the nutrient test of the soil and the crops to be grown. A cedar swamp would be acid. For most crops, lime would be necessary.

How much water should be applied to a garden after fertilizing? The soil is sandy and both commercial and fresh manures are used. Water the garden when needed as indicated by the tendency of plants to wilt.

Soil Sterilization

What are the different ways to sterilize soil for seeds? Steam, very hot water, and chemicals, such as tear gas (chloropicrin), methyl bromide, and Vapam. Much easier, though, is to sow seeds in sterile soilless mixes (available at garden centers).

How does the gardener sterilize soil with steam? Make a soil pile 12 inches deep. Place 4 inches agricultural tile 2 feet apart in the center of the pile and running full length. Plug the tile at one end. Insert a steam pipe or hose in the other end. Cover the entire pile with building paper or canvas. Inject steam for 2 hours; remove the cloth; allow to cool. Remove tile and continue the process. Steam sterilization makes the structure better. Its effects are entirely beneficial. This is usually impractical for a gardener to do. Small quantities of soil for pot plants may be sterilized in a pressure cooker without closing the steam valve. After sterilization, clean compost should be added to the soil to replace the soil bacteria killed by steaming.

What is an easy and efficient method of sterilizing soil for growing seedlings in a small greenhouse where steam is not used? Boiling hot water should be poured over the soil and, in addition, the seeds should be dusted with Captan, Thiram, Terrachlor (PCNB), or similar compounds. Or use a sterile soilless mix as recommended in the first question in this section.

What is Larvacide? It is a gas that is packaged in bottles or cylinders as a liquid (chloropicrin, or tear gas) and is applied to the soil with a special applicator. The soil should be 60° F., or warmer, and medium moist. Three cc's of liquid (a small teaspoonful) is injected about 3 to 6 inches deep, at 10-inch intervals. A heavy watering is applied immediately. Follow with two other applications on successive days. The treatment controls soil diseases, insects, and weeds.

What chemicals can be used to sterilize small amounts of soil?   The most practical is Vapam, which requires no special equipment. Follow the simple directions.

How do you sterilize soil with formaldehyde?   Where steam is not available, formaldehyde may be used. Use commercial Formalin—1 gallon to 50 gallons of water. One gallon of the solution is used to 1 square foot of soil 6 inches deep. Pour the solution on, cover for 24 hours, then uncover and permit to dry for 2 weeks before using.

How do you sterilize soil for potted plants?   Use steam, hot water, or chemicals. A pressure cooker may be used satisfactorily.

How is sand, used as a rooting medium, best sterilized?   If small quantities are wanted, place sand in a shallow flat or box and pour boiling water through it.

How do you sterilize soil in a perennial bed?   This cannot be done satisfactorily unless chemicals are used—formaldehyde, chloropicrin, Vapam, or mercuric compounds. Beds must be free of plants before chemicals are applied.

Artificial Soils

What is "Cornell Mix"—used for starting seedlings?   It is mostly horticultural-grade vermiculite plus nutrients. To make a peck of the mix, use 4 quarts of vermiculite, 4 quarts shredded peat moss, 1 teaspoonful of 20 per cent superphosphate, 1 tablespoonful of ground limestone, plus 4 tablespoonfuls of a 5–10–5 or similar fertilizer. The limestone should be dolomite lime, not high calcium. If this is not available (it is found only in limited areas), add a level tablespoonful of finishing lime to a quart of water and wet the mix with this. Finishing lime is about 50 per cent magnesium. You can substitute 2 teaspoonfuls of Epsom salts for the lime.

A local greenhouse is growing plants in only a 50-50 mixture of peat moss and sand. Is this feasible for garden use?   Only under special conditions: liquid fertilizer in a weak solution must be used in place of water for irrigation. In a raised bed on desert sand, this mixture has been used for a vegetable garden in Arizona. Expensive, but better than no garden!

What is gravel culture? The commercial name, "slop culture," defines it. Plants are grown in gravel with slow drains. Nutrients are dissolved in water and slopped over the plants whenever they seem needed. Although not too scientific, it is easier to use than the practice of true hydroponics, which calls for highly accurate analyses of the nutrient solutions.

A gardening friend uses a mixture of half pet litter and half peat moss for house plants, starting seedlings, and rooting cuttings. I tried it, but it didn't work. What was wrong? Probably the type of pet litter you used. One type is nothing more than dried clay without any treatment. Mixed with peat moss, it forms a worthless, greasy mess. The type that really works (and is highly effective) is made of burned clay that forms grainy, porous particles. To test a given brand, soak in water for an hour. Swirl it around and if all the litter goes into suspension, it is plain clay and worthless. If still gritty, use it.

This mixture is good for seedlings up to the time they form the third leaf, but after that they need feeding. For house plants, use a house-plant fertilizer at one fourth the recommended rate, dissolved in water and used for watering plants every time they need moisture.

What is vermiculite? It is a form of mica that, when heated, explodes like popcorn. Treated to 2,500° F. in the process, it is then sterile, holds moisture, and, if not overwatered, allows air to reach the roots of plants. It contains a small percentage of potash, but no other plant food. It can be used as a mulch, as an artificial soil base, and is used commercially as a filler in fertilizers. Most lightweight fertilizers have a vermiculite base.

I have used vermiculite for rooting cuttings and starting seeds, but it gets soggy. What am I doing wrong? Watering too often. Vermiculite sops up about three to four times its volume in water, but then can't hold much more. Use a flat with a window-screen wire bottom and it will drain better.

How is ground sphagnum moss used? Is it mixed with soil? No, it is used as a bed in which to sow seeds so they can be exposed to light without drying out. It contains a natural biotic which prevents damping-off of seedlings. It is a highly valuable material. (It is especially recommended for the fine seeds of azaleas and rhododendrons and other ericaceous plants. It contains no nutrients so the seedlings must be fertilized or soon transplanted.)

Is cod-liver oil a good plant food for flowers?   No.

SOILLESS CULTURE

What is water culture?   Growth of plants in a watertight container filled with a weak solution of fertilizer salts.

What is sand culture?   Growth of plants in a container of sand through which a weak fertilizer solution either drips continually or is poured on at intervals.

What house plants can be grown in sand culture?   With care, almost any house plants.

What is gravel culture?   Growth of plants in a watertight container filled with some inert medium, preferably slightly acid, which is flooded, manually or mechanically, from below with a weak fertilizer solution.

What flowering crops may be grown in gravel culture if a greenhouse is available?   Any crop which can be grown in soil. Roses, carnations, chrysanthemums, snapdragons, calendula, annuals, and orchids are all successfully grown.

What vegetable crops may be grown by an amateur in gravel or water culture?   It is not practical to attempt to grow vegetables unless a greenhouse is available. Tomatoes, lettuce, cucumbers, radishes, spinach, kale, etc., can be grown.

What type of soilless culture is best suited for the home?   Sand culture; it requires less equipment than gravel culture and is more foolproof than water culture. The sensational advertising that promises fabulous results from home soilless culture is mostly moonshine.

What type of soilless culture is best suited for commercial use?   Gravel culture is less troublesome than water culture and requires less labor than sand culture. No type will accomplish any more than will normal soil culture.

Does chemical gardening (soilless culture) succeed commercially?   Yes, but good soil has many advantages over soilless culture, not the least of which is the former's adaptation to the use of large-scale equipment. Soilless culture can be a valuable research method.

Has the experiment with tank farming contributed much to general practices and knowledge in general gardening?   Tank farming (which is water culture) has not contributed much; but gravel and sand culture have been very helpful in the study of general garden problems, particularly from the standpoint of plant nutrition. However, much has been learned about the needs of minor elements from studies in water culture. What is lacking in soilless culture are microorganisms. We as yet don't understand the interactions between plant roots and these living organisms.

What is a "nutrient solution" for soilless gardens? It is composed of fertilizer elements completely soluble in water. Obtain chemicals from your druggist and use the following formula for water, sand, or gravel cultures:

Potassium nitrate	1.0 oz.
Monocalcium phosphate	0.5 oz.
Magnesium sulfate	1.75 oz.
Water	5 gals.
Iron sulfate	1 tsp.

Or you can usually buy hydroponic kits from garden-supply houses.

Soils for House Plants

House plants stop growing for me after a few months and finally die. What do I do wrong? Assuming that you have taken care of the basic needs—light, heat, air, water, and nutrition—soil condition would be the answer. The amount of soil in a flowerpot is so small that the mysterious "something" which is contributed by microorganisms is soon exhausted. That is why repotting with fresh soil at regular intervals is necessary, even though it does disturb root growth. Try to keep a supply of compost on hand and topdress the soil at intervals, replacing it regularly. When soil begins to dry out rapidly and shrink away from the sides of the pot, it's time to repot.

What is a good mixture of soil for pot plants? It is difficult to make definite recommendations without knowing what elements you have to work with. Mechanical requirements are: the soil should drain readily so that 50 per cent of the water applied will pass through within five minutes, leaving it thoroughly moist, but not sopping wet for long; it should have a high organic content to provide good conditions for soil organisms.

How should house plants be fertilized? Carefully. Most commercial products give recommendations worked out in a greenhouse, where growing conditions are much more favorable than in a house. As a result they recommend rates too high for home conditions. Try feeding at one fourth the rates given on the container, doubling this only if the lower rate does not give the desired results. And always keep in mind that in winter feeding should be adjusted for decreased sunlight, except for plants growing under artificial light.

How often should I repot house plants?   When the plant fills the pot with roots so that they form a white weblike pattern, plainly visible on the root ball.

2. Planning and Landscaping

GARDENS ARE FOR people—the people who own them. A beautiful garden does not just spring up overnight! This is especially true in the small gardens of today where space is so limited. New materials and techniques have broadened our horizons in garden-making. People today expect things of their gardens that their parents did not consider important at all.

Outdoor living has become a pleasurable way of life for most modern families. Planning for a patio or terrace, where one can have cookouts and entertain in the out-of-doors, is a "must" in almost every garden plan. Westerners have had a great influence on garden design all over the nation. Patios were seldom heard of (in the East at least) fifty years ago, but with the Spanish influence in Southern California, their popularity has swept the country from west to east. There are few homes being built today where a patio is not considered an important part of the overall plan.

The Japanese have also had an influence on our gardens, first on the Pacific coast, where thousands of Japanese have made their homes since the turn of the century. The deceptively simple gardens they prefer, often with small plants, and their techniques, such as those followed in the art of bonsai, have all influenced modern gardens from the West Coast to the East. During the past three quarters of a century, the plants native to Japan have become so popular in American gardens that today nearly half the plants in every garden are native to Japan.

Still other influences on garden design have come from trends in modern living, one result being gardens planned for the least possible maintenance. One way to reduce maintenance is to look at nature's own landscape efforts and then try to introduce similar natural effects. And the realization that our once-taken-for-granted energy sources are nonrenewable is bound to influence landscape design. Many homeowners have already discovered that using trees and shrubs to provide cool shade in summer is cheaper than running an air conditioner and that in winter the same plants can moderate winds, thus cutting back on fuel consumption.

You, the homeowner, must decide whether you should do your own landscaping or hire a landscape architect or designer. Landscape architects are trained to see potentialities of a property. They generally know from experience what can be done and will look well, and at the same time be functional. Often it pays in the long run to consult a reputable firm and let them study the situation and then present various possibilities to you.

On the other hand, you, in common with many of us, may be inhibited by a budget or just like to do things yourself. If you are in this group, you will enjoy landscaping your own property. Even so, you might consider going to a large local nursery that has landscape planners on its staff and ask them to draw up a rough plan of what they think might be best for you. The costs for such services vary, but are usually quite reasonable. Then, with that plan as a guide, you can start.

Planning the Outdoors

If you have just bought a place that is already landscaped, many of your problems are solved, but some problems remain. Is everything you want and need in a garden present? If not, which of the plants and features don't you like?

To start your plans, list the things you want of your garden. Are there small children who need an enclosed play area easily seen from the house? Do you want a vegetable garden, tennis court, swimming pool, general game area? Do you want flower beds to work in as a hobby, do you need hedges for protection or some kind of screening for privacy? Is your land on a slope where you might build a rock garden? Do you already have sufficient shade at the right places or should you plan for more?

The mood of the garden should reflect the taste and preference of its owners. The garden's outstanding features should dominate but not at the expense of the entire landscape. A beautiful garden results partially from proper basic design, but it also depends on the kinds of plant materials you select and how you use them. It is more interesting not to see all the garden at once from the front, the patio, or even from the rear of the house. Other areas can be artfully hidden by shrubs, trees, or by screening with some kind of fence.

Space for bulbs, annuals, and perennials should be planned if these are to be enjoyed and cut for arranging indoors. However, the flower beds should not be extensive unless this aspect of gardening is a major interest. Weeds do grow even though you can keep them in check pretty well with the right kind of mulching materials. Mulches save work and water and are beneficial to most plantings. They also look neat.

The Plan on Paper

On a large piece of graph paper, draw to scale (1 inch equaling 20 feet is a good one) the basic components of your property: house, driveway, garage, existing features such as trees, patio, walks, etc. Then indicate additions or changes you wish to make. Remember that in placing trees and flower beds about the area, one should always leave space for garden equipment to move about.

Proper screening in the garden is essential. The utility area, the children's sandbox, the vegetable garden, the street, objectionable views are all omnipresent in most gardens. Consider hedges of the proper kinds of trees or shrubs that grow just high enough but no higher and do not take monthly shearing. Or there are woven-sapling or board fences that are long-lasting and on which vines can be trained. In fact, there is a varied assortment of wood arbors, fencing, and walls that landscape architects are using the country over to provide privacy and shelter without detracting from beauty.

Selecting Trees and Shrubs

Pick out the right kinds of shrubs and trees. Elms are not considered dependable anymore and in addition they take a lot of care and space. Try smaller trees, like crab apples and dogwoods. These and many others go well with the smaller modern houses and require little attention. Take the same care with shrubs. Lilacs, for instance, need spraying and much pruning and even then are colorfully ornamental for a short two-week period during the entire year, whereas viburnums usually need no attention, have interesting flowers in the spring, colorful fruits in the fall, and autumn foliage color—some even have interesting trunk and branch formations which are of interest every season of the year.

In selecting shrubs, you might also think of those like leucothoe, mahonia, forsythia, cornelian-cherry (*Cornus mas*), and like plants, which have merit in cut arrangements indoors. There is nothing quite like the visual promise of spring when one forces a few branches of forsythia or cornelian-cherry into bloom in early February, when outside everything is cold and seemingly lifeless.

A beautiful garden is an interesting one in which hidden areas suddenly come into view as one walks around. Try an espaliered yew on the monotonous piece of fencing around the utility area in such a way that it cannot be seen from the house. Or a few evergreens off in a corner somewhere, hidden from the major viewing points but definitely evident as one comes upon them from the garden path.

Planting Near the House

Foundation plantings need careful thought. However, the new principle is not to have the house set in a "sea" of shrubbery, whether evergreen or deciduous, but to use a few plants for accent and connect them with plantings of ground covers, such as pachysandra, myrtle, or ajuga. Use plants that will not climb. Draw a sketch of the front of the house, and then decide which shapes and varieties of plants will be perfect for each place. It is true that some houses, both old and new, need special treatment to hide architectural defects. In such cases, bold, imaginative solutions are needed, and this can well be the time to seek professional help. (However, it should be kept in mind that not all nurserymen are landscaping authorities and often their sole objective is to sell as many plants as possible.) Sometimes the solution to a problem house does not lie solely in plantings anyway; the right color house paint and minor architectural renovations should be considered first.

It is difficult for beginners, sometimes, to pass up the inviting young coniferous evergreens advertised for foundation plantings and at such attractive prices. Most of these will actually grow into tall trees that will take a major amount of annual pruning to keep them in proper perspective. This does not help aesthetically or with the low-maintenance idea.

Rather, select plants like leucothoe, the new dwarf forms of mahonia, and truly dwarf needle evergreens that never grow above eye level. In this last group are many junipers and yews—and they are hardy over most of the country. There are deciduous shrubs in this category, too. Select a good reference book on shrubs and there will be found lists of the proper plants to use. When you know what you want, then start trying to find them in local nurseries or through mail-order sources.

The front entrance of your house should be given special thought. It should never be hidden, nor appear small and cramped because of inappropriate plantings. It should have grace and beauty achieved by planting soft-textured shrubs which seem to extend a gracious invitation to enter. An expansive lawn, unadorned with specimens or flower beds in its center, sets off the house to good advantage. Trees can be planted to the side or to frame the house. Unfortunately, many of us must use hedges for privacy in front, but even here, with a bit of careful planning, you should be able to come up with an interesting shrub border that might fit the situation better.

The Patio or Terrace

The patio (or terrace) is one of the most important adjuncts of houses today. Chances are, especially if you buy a new house, it already exists. If not, you will want to make the addition. Located next to the house, preferably outside the living room or dining area where sliding glass doors lead out to it, it is the transition between house and garden. The patio can be paved (there are many kinds of surfaces you can build) and sheltered from view of the neighbors or the street if necessary by a planting of evergreens or hedge, or sometimes by arbor-fence combinations (preferably of wood rather than plastic). Take advantage of any attractive views of your garden or distant hills—if you are fortunate enough to have them.

It should be furnished with tables and reclining chairs that are in keeping with the architecture of the house. There might be planters or containers with interesting plants (or herbs) in them, a hanging basket or two if you are prepared to keep them properly watered, and even a surrounding bed or two of flowers or herbs. These beds might be raised 2 to 3 feet above the ground level for easier viewing and weeding and—if herbs are planted—appreciation of their various scents.

There should be some shade on the patio, either from a large tree just outside its boundaries, or from a small dogwood (which has horizontal branches) planted within the patio itself. A pool might be provided for, or even a small fountain, and of course there should be a few discreetly placed lights for nighttime. If executed with thought and care, the patio is of interest throughout the entire year, always there to lure people to your out-of-doors.

The Sun Deck

In hilly areas, where houses are built on steep banks or hills, and in dunes and along the seashore—anywhere there is no room for a paved patio as such—the sun deck is an excellent substitute. It is a modern extension of the mid-Victorian porch, which was so firmly attached to the house and used extensively three quarters of a century ago. The modern deck starts at the house, but extends outward in all sorts of forms and heights—sometimes only a few feet above the rocky ground, in other places high above the bank below.

In other situations, it is on the roof or the top of the garage. It is usually built of wood boards with about a ¼-inch distance between them. Lounging chairs and a table or two are necessary, and in places where it is substituting for the patio, large tubs or pots of plants can be included. Of course, the larger the tubs, the less frequently they have to be watered.

Recreation Areas

So your family wants a swimming pool! It is probably the most popular property improvement in America today. There should be the proper place with planned screening, and most town ordinances call for fences around pools to prevent accidents. The pool should be a minimum of 34 × 14 feet (the larger the better), with a minimum of 8 feet under the diving board. But get a professional to build it for you, since amateurish mistakes in this area can prove costly and most discouraging. Avoid overhanging trees that drop their leaves.

The interests of some run to tennis, croquet, swings, ladder-trapezes, a basketball backboard, or volleyball, and if yours is one of these, plan for them rather than providing for them any old place on your property.

Lighting the garden at night can be a most desirable asset. Only a few spotlights are needed, and your electric company can tell you where to obtain them and how to install the underground weatherproof wiring system. With a few spare outlets, the lights can be moved from place to place in the garden as different plants come into bloom; or direct spotlights to trees, or for safety to steps along the garden walk. An arrangement of a few lights, most of which might be seen from the patio or living-room window, lengthens the time the out-of-doors can be enjoyed.

Growing plants need water, and fortunately with the easily laid plastic pipe available now, underground sprinkler systems and water outlets do not have to be the first things put in the garden. Admittedly, an 8-inch trench must be dug for the pipe, but this can often be done without too much disturbance to existing plants and turf. So it can be left until time and money are available, if necessary. Installing the system is one of the things you can do yourself, unless your property is very extensive.

Take all these things into consideration in planning a garden. Time spent in planning in the beginning will surely result in a beautiful garden that will add greatly to the value of your property as well as your enjoyment. Your garden is for pleasure and relaxation, a setting for your house, as well as a place of privacy for outdoor living.

 Planning the Landscape

DESIGN PRINCIPLES

What are the principles to consider in the design of a garden? Enclosure, emphasis, balance, unity, coherence, and proportion. For plants: texture, color, and scale. Use these as you plan to create lines and patterns of orderly beauty.

What are the essential things to keep in mind in the planning of a property? Grading comes first. All water must drain away from the house. Lay out areas to fit your needs: entrance walk and drive, service area, a place for entertaining with a patio or deck, room for recreation, play space for children, special gardens such as rose or vegetable, shade, privacy screening, movement of equipment over the area, and especially the need of beauty and interest in plants during every season of

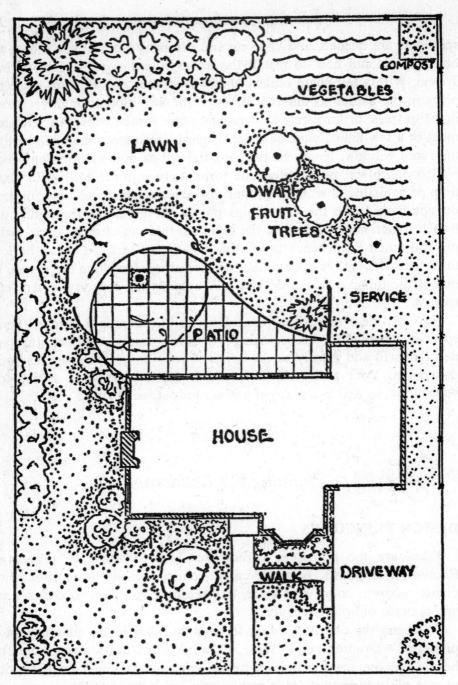

*A suburban property planned for privacy and outdoor living comfort.
It is enclosed on both sides by a hedge and fence and a mixed shrub
border at the rear. Dwarf fruit trees screen the vegetable garden.*

the year. The resulting plan should satisfy most of your needs as you now visualize them.

We have just bought a large suburban house, but the grounds have not been cared for properly and are overgrown. What is the best way to plan a renovation so we will not make mistakes? See a landscape architect. Tell him or her what you would like to have in the way of flowering trees, flower gardens, recreation area, etc. A landscape architect will submit a plan and give approximate costs of providing some or all of the things you want.

We have only a small garden and do not want to hire a landscape architect, but we need help. What should we do? Make a plan on graph paper of what you have, with trees, house, drive, and shrubs located. Possibly take a few pictures. Then go to a nursery that offers a planning service. Some of the larger nurseries have skilled landscape people on their payroll and they can give you much expert advice on the spot from your plan and pictures for a reasonable fee. Also, they might plant the garden for an additional fee when you order plants from them.

Is it necessary to make a plan of a garden? For any but the very simplest of gardens, a plan will be a great help in carrying out your intentions. Changes and rearrangements are more easily made on paper than in the garden itself. A plan is also most useful in estimating quantities; if the planting is not to be done all at once, it is essential.

Why should a garden be "balanced"? Balance, whether symmetrical or irregular, gives a garden picture a feeling of stability and restfulness. A garden that lacks it will be less pleasing, although it may not be immediately apparent what the trouble is, particularly in a naturalistic composition.

Our new house was erected on an overgrown lot. We spent so much money on the house that we will have to do the landscaping ourselves. How do we go about it? Make a list of all the shrubs and trees you have. Then on a piece of graph paper plot in one color those that you want to keep for one reason or another. Also plot what you would like to have in another color—trees for shade, flowers, or screening purposes; shrubs for beauty or screening; a flower garden; utility and game area, etc. Incorporate these with the plants you want to keep.

What is meant by the term "focal point"? A focal point is a point of highest interest in the development of the design, such as a garden pool or a group of particularly striking plants. It serves as a center around which the design can be built.

In a square garden, where should the focal point be? In the center, usually. In a square design, the important lines lead to or from the center.

What is a vista?   A vista is a narrow view framed between masses of foliage. It tends to concentrate the observer's attention rather than allowing it to spread over a wide panorama.

Must a garden be level?   A geometrical garden need not be level, but the slope should be away from the principal point from which the garden is seen, rather than from side to side. A naturalistic garden should have, if possible, a natural grade, irregular rather than level or smoothly sloping.

How do you decide on the size of a garden?   How well do you enjoy garden work? Plan as much as you can easily care for. The design should cover the entire lot, but the details might be simple. Instead of lawns, you might design areas of ground cover interspersed with sections of gravel over plastic and paving for patios and walks. Accent with shrubs that stay in scale. Fences with vines make good enclosures.

What is the rule for good proportion in the size of a garden?   There is no hard-and-fast rule. Oblong areas are most effective when they are about one and a half times as long as they are wide; but the method of treating them and the surrounding foliage masses affect this considerably. Generally an oblong is better than a square; and an oval (on account of perspective) is more effective than a circle.

How can you accent a planting?   Plantings made up of only one kind of plant, or of a few similar varieties, are likely to be monotonous and uninteresting. By using an occasional plant of a different sort, an accent is created that makes the planting more interesting.

What is the difference between a formal and a naturalistic garden?   Formal design uses straight lines and circular curves or arcs. Informal design uses long, free-flowing curves. Formality emphasizes *lines;* informality emphasizes *space,* a concept necessary today in low-maintenance landscaping.

What is required in a formal garden?   A formal garden is essentially a composition in geometric lines—squares, oblongs, circles, or parts thereof. It need not be large, elaborate, or filled with architectural embellishment.

Which is better suited to a small place, a formal or an informal garden?   Topography controls the type of design. On flat ground in proximity to buildings, the rectangular (formal) type of design is easier to adapt. On rough land, greater informality is desirable, particularly on slopes and in wooded areas.

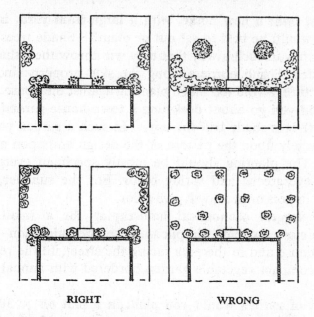

RIGHT   WRONG

Some mistakes to avoid in planting: (Top) Leave lawn areas open, free from beds or scattered borders in center of grass plots. (Below) Shrubs planted in unconnected polka-dot pattern increase maintenance and impede mowing operations. Better to mass them in borders or "islands" where they can be mulched together and increase their landscape effects.

What are the steps necessary to develop a small property? Rough grading; staking out walks, drives, and garden area; installation of utilities (water, gas, sewage, etc.); preparation of planting areas; planting trees, shrubs, and perennials, and making the lawn are all of importance.

Is there anything that can be done in advance of building on a lot that would improve the land or save time later on? The lot is 100 × 100 feet, with trees, bushes, weeds, etc. Clear out undesirable wild growths and trees where they are too thick. Confer with the builder to avoid destroying attractive native shrub masses in locations near the property lines where they may be valuable as part of future shrub borders.

We have a new home to landscape completely, and very little money to put into it. What do you advise concerning first plantings in our garden, to take away the bare, new look? Shade trees come first. Bareroot trees in spring are economical. Then front foundation plantings. Except for the doorway, begin with smallest-sized plants. Add framework and details later.

I have just built a new home, with a large front yard, in a country town. What would be best to set out or plant?   Shade trees are important. Plant a few in such a way that they will throw their shade where it is most needed. Shrub borders along the side property lines will help frame the picture. Avoid too much planting against the house.

How would you go about designing a town-house garden area about 18 × 25 feet? It is shady half the day.   In such a garden you will have to depend largely upon the pattern of the design and upon architectural accessories. The planting should be mostly specimen evergreens, perhaps dwarf evergreens and spring bulbs. For the summer, a few annuals, either in pots or beds, will give color.

Can you suggest economical landscaping for a small temporary home?   Maintain extreme simplicity. Use the minimum of planting next to the house and in the area facing the street. In the rear, if possible, have a compact vegetable garden bordered with annual and perennial flowers.

What sort of garden would you plant in a plot 60 × 30 feet?   An area of this sort is usually most effectively developed by having an open grass or gravel panel in the center, with flower borders along the sides backed by shrub borders or hedges, and a strong terminal feature (this could be a lily pool or patio).

I have read that a garden should not "compete with a view." Why? How is this prevented?   The intimate detail of a garden suffers by comparison with a wide view into the surrounding landscape. It is usually wiser to enclose the garden, shutting out the wide view and leaving an opening framed by trees or evergreens, so that the view becomes a focal point seen from the house or patio.

My house is surrounded by trees, and there is a fine view, but it is obscured by foliage. What should I do?   Do not hesitate to cut out trees to form a vista. Rather than cutting down the tree, it is often possible to cut branches higher in the tree in order to open holes through which the view will show.

Foundation Plantings and Entrances

(See also Foundation Material—Sections 3 and 4.)

What kind of shrubbery would you plant in front of a new house with a 30-foot frontage?   Use tall, upright-growing plants at the corners and low-growing, rounded masses between. Avoid too much planting. If the house foundation is low enough, leave some spaces bare to give the house the effect of standing solidly on the ground. Either deciduous or evergreen material is suitable.

We have large trees (oak, gray birch, maple, and ironwood). What should be planted near the house? The yard slopes toward the south and the house is new, so we are starting from scratch. Let the trees constitute the principal landscape feature. Use a minimum of planting near the house—ground covers along the foundation, a few shade-loving shrubs at the corners or at either side of the entrance.

What is the best method of foundation planting for an "unbalanced" house—one with the door not in the center? An unbalanced composition for a foundation planting can be made extremely attractive. The fact that the door is not in the center will make it even more interesting. Naturally the doorway should be the point of interest and your maximum height should begin on either side, tapering irregularly to the corners of the house where a specimen shrub or evergreen may go a little higher in order to break the sharp lines of the house corner. These corner accents need not be as tall as the main planting on either side of the doorway.

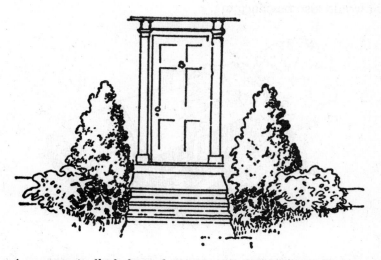

A symmetrically balanced entrance planting, especially suitable for a house of formal colonial design. Often the plantings at the door are all that are needed near the house.

What is best for planting around a small house on a small acreage? Everyone has evergreens. Can't we have simplicity and still be

different?   Deciduous shrubs can be just as interesting throughout much of the year although it is the evergreens which lend interest in the winter. Why not use deciduous shrubs with a few evergreens as a background?

Can I plant flowers along the base of our house?   Unless the house is an architectural jewel which should not be hidden, shrubs and ground covers with flowers planted in front of them give a better effect than flowers alone, which are apt to look too small and inadequate near a house foundation.

How shall I landscape the front of our Cape Cod house? It was built about 1810 and during the 6½ years we have owned it every minute has been spent in restoring the old pine paneling inside and developing the flower and vegetable gardens outside. There is the main house with a front door in the center, an ell, and a long shed-garage combination. What treatment all along the front would you suggest?   Planting for a Cape Cod house should be very simple, perhaps a boxwood, privet (pruned to a rounded form), or Japanese holly on each side of the door and clumps of lilacs at each corner of the house. Many colonial homes traditionally have two shade trees in the front lawn, one on each side of the door. A small dooryard garden enclosed by a low picket fence is an idea that would also be charming.

In most cases, the fewer plants close to the house, the better. Keep tall shrubs at the corners.

What can be done with a narrow front lawn between an old-fashioned house with a high porch and the street—which is lined with large old maples?   Instead of grass, which will not thrive in shade or under maples, try to establish a ground cover such as myrtle or pachysandra. However, the most practical solution may be gravel. Hide the porch foundation with a low hedge or informal grouping of yews or Japanese holly (*Ilex crenata*). Improve the soil with peat moss and fertilizer applications and water often during the growing season.

Could you tell me what kind of foundation planting I could use for an English-type home? The English style, being informal, calls for informal planting. Avoid symmetrically balanced groups of planting or too much planting. Accent the doorways and the corners, and leave the rest open. Vines are important to soften brickwork or stone.

Do you suggest landscaping around a farmhouse? Of course, a farm home needs planting. The same rules and options apply here. Use a few shrubs and small-flowering trees at the sides.

What sort of foundation planting is appropriate to a French chateau-type house? French architecture calls for a formal style of planting. Follow the lines of the house. Hold the planting to a minimum, using evergreens such as yew, boxwood, euonymus, and holly clipped into formal shapes.

A small house calls for simplicity of design in landscaping.

The doorway of my house is a reproduction of an old colonial door, with leaded side lights and fanlight. How should I plant this so as to enhance rather than detract from its beauty? For an elaborate doorway, which is sufficiently interesting in itself, elaborate planting is unnecessary. Possibly the most effective thing would be to plant a large lilac on either side of the door, or for a more formal effect, plant an Irish or cone-shaped yew on each side.

Should plantings on either side of the front door always be alike? Generally, yes. But if the house is in an informal or picturesque architectural style, the planting should also be informal and picturesque. Use a tall, dark plant on one side, with a few smaller things around its base, and on the other side use something lighter, more graceful, and spreading. Don't use too many kinds of plants and too many sorts of foliage. (See the following question.)

My colonial house seems to me to have a very plain doorway. How can I plant it to make it seem more important? Where the doorway is formal but very plain, interest must be created through the planting. Use identical groups on either side, but select the various plants carefully for form, texture, and foliage color. Evergreens give great dignity and are less likely to get too large in a short time. Tall masses to accent the lines of the doorway, with more spreading plants around them, usually make the most effective arrangement.

What plants should be used around a modern ranch-type house in front of a large rock outcrop? Make use of the natural rock by all means, planting rock plants and creeping junipers around it. Low yews and azaleas might be in the foundation planting with a dogwood or crab apples at the sides.

We have a cabin among trees and woodland. We would like to make the immediate grounds look much nicer than they now are. How could we go about it? Underplant the area with various kinds of native ferns and woodland wildflowers. Take a walk through your woodlands and select a few shrubs for transplanting. Avoid using exotic material.

How could a rather steep hillside, partly wooded, be planted to make it more attractive? Such a wooded hillside could be underplanted with native shrubs, evergreens, ferns, mountain-laurel, azaleas, rhododendrons, and woodland wildflowers. A system of trails leading through the area would add to its interest.

Screening

How can I disguise my chicken house and yard so that they will not injure the appearance of my property? If the wire of the chicken run is strong enough, you might plant a vine such as honeysuckle on it. The house itself can be made less conspicuous by planting a group of pines and hemlocks around it. Or the entire area can be hidden behind a dense hedge.

Would a mixture of plants with various-colored leaves or blossoms be satisfactory in an informal screening for enclosing a yard? Yes, if you plant them in groups of five, seven, or nine, depending on the length of the border. Accent the groups of shrubs at intervals with evergreens or flowering trees that are taller. Borders take up more room than hedges.

What are some fast-growing vines that would make good screens? Bower actinidia, Dutchman's-pipe, Virginia-creeper, fleece vine, and grape vines.

What type of shrubs make good informal screening for enclosing a yard? Your choice is determined by the size of the area to be enclosed and the height of objects to be "screened out." Persian lilac is excellent for areas of a quarter acre and larger. Smaller gardens may use *Rosa hugonis,* flowering quince, winged euonymus, *Euonymus kiautschovica* and rose-of-Sharon. A taller plant growing up to 12 feet high but excellent for a narrow screening hedge is *Rhamnus frangula* 'Columnaris' or 'Tallhedge', as it is often called.

Trees and Shrubs

Should trees be removed from gardens? Not necessarily. If the trees are fine old specimens, they should be left and the garden designed around them, using plants that will withstand shade; otherwise they should be taken out. Often trees form an important part of the garden's design.

Many American elms are being removed in our town because they have succumbed to the Dutch elm disease. What are some good large shade trees to use as substitutes? Maples, hackberry, yellow-wood, beech, ash, honey locust, especially the 'Moraine' and the yellow-leaved 'Sunburst' locusts, sweet-gum, cucumber tree, Amur cork tree, button-ball, Sargent cherry, various oaks, sophora, lindens, and zelkova.

Can shrubs and small trees be used in a flower garden? Yes, an occasional compact-growing tree or shrub in the garden relieves the monotony of perennial and annual plantings. The tree rose is especially suitable.

Some builders today try to retain the best of the existing growth, such as a tree or two. Such trees provide some shade and become an important part of the landscape design.

We plan to landscape a 3-acre tract. Will you name some flowering shrubs that give a succession of bloom throughout the year? For spring: azalea, forsythia, rhododendron, *Viburnum carlesii.* For summer: honeysuckle, hydrangea, buddleia, roses, abelia, heather, rose-of-Sharon. For fall: abelia, witch-hazel. For autumn color: *Euonymus alatus,* dogwood, enkianthus, viburnum, Japanese barberry, sumac, spice-bush, and blueberry.

Can you suggest hardy shrubbery for a small country home? Standard varieties of deciduous shrubs, such as spirea, lilac, deutzia, philadelphus, most of the viburnums, and weigela can always be relied upon to thrive with the minimum amount of care. Interest can be added to the planting by using some azaleas and rhododendrons and a few of the small-flowering trees, such as flowering crab, dogwood, and redbud.

Shade

(See also Shade—Section 3.)

There is no sun in my garden from September until May. What is the best way to treat a garden of this kind? Since the floral display in this garden will be effective only from late spring until early fall, make sure the garden background is interesting enough to make the garden attractive during the rest of the year. Use evergreen, berry-bearing shrubs and ones that have good fall color. For flowers, select only those plants that bloom during the time when sunlight is available.

What are some perennial flowering plants for shade? If you have a few hours of sun, you could expect flowers from monkshood (*Aconitum*) and hosta in summer and fall; from day-lilies (*Hemerocallis*) in summer; from ajuga, lily-of-the-valley, primroses, and wildflowers such as trilliums, sweet rocket (*Hesperis*), and violets (*Viola*) in spring to early summer. If your shade is dense, forget flowering plants and rely on ferns and such ground covers as English ivy, pachysandra, or paxistima.

What plants (tall, medium, low) may I use in a garden shaded by oak trees? What soil improvements should be made to overcome acidity from oaks? Your location should be ideal without treatment for all of your native wildflowers, such as cypripediums, ferns, May-apple, and Jack-in-the-pulpit. (See Woodland Wildflowers.) For taller plants, you have a wide choice from such shrubs as holly, mountain-laurel, azalea, blueberries, and rhododendron. The combination of these should be an attractive planting.

Please name a few evergreen shrubs that do well in light shade. Abelia, barberries, mahonia, mountain-laurel, leucothoe, privets, andromedas (*Pieris*), rhododendrons, evergreen azaleas, yews, arborvitaes, and certain viburnums.

Please name a few plants that will grow in dense shade, around the base of a large tree. Must I put them in pots on account of the roots of the tree? Few plants will subsist on what's left in the soil after the roots of a large tree have filled the surface and used all available food. Try digging out pockets, filling them with good loam, and planting one of the following: *Viola canadensis, Mahonia repens, Vinca minor,* Kenilworth-ivy, pachysandra. If these fail, you would be better off to spread crushed stone or a bark mulch over the area and to leave it bare of plants. Potted plants would be of only temporary value.

Which flower is the best to plant under a big maple tree where there are lots of roots and practically no sun? The altitude is 6,600 feet. Norway maple (*Acer platanoides*) foliage is so dense that few plants can survive both shade and the fight for root space and food. Deep watering of all maples encourages the development of deeper rooting, thus freeing the surface from this strangling network. Ground covers that accept the challenge of most maples are *Vinca minor, Mahonia repens,* pachysandra, *Sedum stoloniferum.*

Which plants would grow well along a shady wall? *Euonymus for-*

tunei vegetus, aquilegia, lady's-slipper, hepatica, *Epimedium niveum,* dicentra, digitalis, sanguinaria, ferns, mertensia, anemone, primroses, pulmonaria, aconitum, dodecatheon, thalictrum, *Anchusa myoso-tidiflora,* and day-lilies. Trees that provide shade for plants in nature also supply abundant humus in the soil from their decayed leaves. Shade plants in the garden appreciate humus, too.

Banks

(See also Section 3.)

Will you suggest some shrubs for the rocky bank in front of our house? Junipers are always good, both the shrubby types and the trailing types for over the rocks. The memorial rose (*Rosa wichuraiana*), *Stephanandra incisa* 'Crispa' and 'Arnold Dwarf' forsythia all root wherever their branches touch the soil and they are ideal for such situations. If vines would qualify, try the climbing hydrangea or the Virginia-creeper.

When a bank is too steep for good grass growth and its maintenance, plant a ground cover such as English ivy.

How should a sloping area (15 × 3 feet) along a driveway be planted? A fence or wall would be unsuitable. The location is sunny. Such a place is best treated by planting the slope with some easy-to-take-care-of, low, trailing shrub or perennial. *Phlox subulata, Teucrium chamaedrys, Juniperus chinensis sargentii, Stephanandra incisa* 'Crispa', or *Euonymus fortunei* 'Colorata' would be suitable.

How fast do memorial roses grow? How far apart should they be planted? This is one of the best shrubs for bank planting, rooting all along its stems, which can grow 4 feet a year. A new planting should have the plants spaced about 4 feet apart.

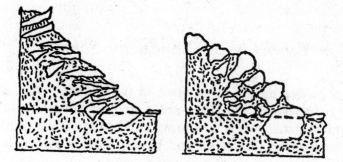

Methods of placing stones to hold a slope or a terrace without a formal wall. (Left) Using flat fieldstones. (Right) Using boulders. Either method can become the basis for a future rock garden.

Surface Drainage

What is a dry well, and what is it used for? A dry well is a pit dug 5 or 6 feet deep, filled with stones and gravel. A pipe or sewer leading either from the house or from a poorly drained area leads into this and provides drainage for difficult situations.

What can be done to prevent rain water from draining off the highway onto a sloping property, causing erosion? A low bank along the highway should be constructed, and at the lowest point in the gutter, a catch basin can be installed to gather the water and lead it through a pipe to a place where it will do no harm. Such a catch basin can be simply two 18-inch sewer tiles, one on top of the other, with a grating fitted into the top and a 4-inch side outlet about 1 foot below the top. If there is a great deal of water, it may have to be a brick, concrete, or stone basin.

Our lot slopes to one side and also out to the street. How do we stop erosion? Use one or two retaining walls starting at the front of the house and curving or angling them until they eventually blend with the existing slope. Plant low-spreading junipers or flowers along the tops of the walls. At the lower corner of the house, curve a level space 5 to 6 feet wide around the end, leading into a walk along the side. Plant on the outside of the level area, using the tallest shrub or evergreen as a focal point for balance at the corner.

Lawns in the Landscape Scheme

Should a garden have a lawn space in the middle? Not all gardens should be so designed, but there are many advantages to this type of layout. A grass panel serves as a foreground to the floral displays in the beds and as a space for chairs and tables. Such a garden is easier to maintain than one made up of many small beds.

A lawn can provide background for the house and trees, shrubs, and other features that make up the landscape.

How would you grade a front lawn where the house is small and is several feet below the highway level? A gradual slope from the house up to the street is usually more pleasing than abrupt terraces. To prevent water from draining toward the house, however, the grade should be carried down from the house slightly, to a low point from which the water can drain off to the sides before the slope up to the street begins. (See Section 9, Lawn and Turf Areas.)

Fences, Gates, and Walls

Is a wattle fence appropriate for the home garden? Yes, it is excellent for screening of a small garden utility area and provides privacy. Wattle fences are made of thin split saplings and are quite durable.

I have a horizontal clapboard fence but it looks rather monotonous in design. What can I do to make it more interesting? Since it is of wood, clinging vines would not prove satisfactory. Why not espalier a pyracantha, yew, or fruit tree against it?

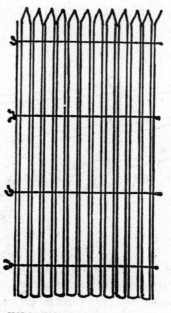

WOODEN-SAPLING FENCE

Where can I get a design for a picket fence? There are many designs for an old-fashioned picket fence. To select the right one, consult a general garden book.

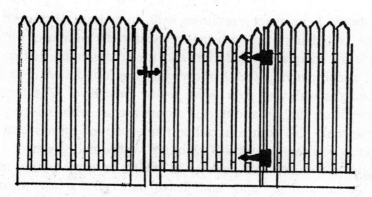

PICKET FENCE

What sort of fence is best for use along the road in front of a modified colonial house where something elaborate would be out-of-place? A simple post-and-rail fence, such as the one in the accompanying sketch, has proved very satisfactory. It can be painted white, or, if made of chestnut, cypress, or redwood, left unpainted to weather. If it is meant to keep out small animals, chicken wire can be attached to the inside.

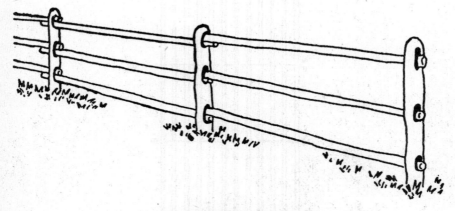

POST-AND-RAIL FENCE
This kind of fence makes excellent support for climbing roses or vines such as clematis.

I need a moderate-priced fence to shut out the view of the street from my front lawn. What shall I use? A fence of palings made of 1 × 4-inch redwood, 5 feet 6 inches high, will answer your purpose. Or a stockade-type fence which comes already built in sections of varying heights.

How should I construct a retaining wall, to be built of stones? Since it may be called upon to withstand considerable pressure, a dry wall must have an adequate foundation and the stones must be firmly bedded. The accompanying sketch shows that the foundation is as wide or wider than the wall and goes down below frost level. The face of the wall slopes back slightly and all the stones are set with the long dimension horizontal. Use squarish rather than rounded stones and use as large ones as you can get. Avoid "chinking" with small stones.

How do you make soil pockets in which to grow plants in a dry wall? As the wall is being laid, leave gaps all the way through it, about 4 inches in diameter. Be sure these openings slope downward to-

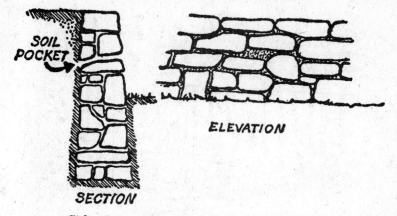

*Side view and cross section of a dry stone
wall with soil pockets left for rock plants.*

ward the back of the wall to keep soil and plants from being washed
out. See that the soil is continuous from the face of the wall to the soil
back of the wall so that moisture can penetrate evenly. Fill the holes
with rich soil. Be sure the stones above them make solid bridges over
the holes. (See Wall Gardens, this section.)

What kind of gate is best to use with a clipped privet hedge?   A
well-designed gate of stained, weathered, or painted wood, or wrought
iron.

Do you recommend wire gates for gardens?   Wire gates are not usually as decorative as wooden or iron gates. They are suitable for vegetable areas or dog runs.

**To be correct, must the planting on either side of a garden gate or en-
trance be the same?**   A symmetrically balanced arrangement is the
usual thing, but it is often less interesting than an unsymmetrical treatment such as the one in the following sketch. Here a ceramic container
planted with a shrub is balanced by the tall, dark evergreen on the other
side. Such a treatment is easier to arrange when the position of the entrance, or conditions of shade, etc., make a symmetrical arrangement
difficult. It is more lively and striking.

**We have a picket fence but have difficulty with visitors who don't
close the gate. How do you construct one that is self-closing?**   The old
method used in colonial times was simple enough. Merely place a heavy
metal ball on a chain. Attach one end of the chain to a sturdy post
about 4 feet high, the other end to the gate. In this way the weight of
the ball closes the open gate.

*A board-on-board fence is not difficult to construct, once the
necessary upright posts are securely positioned and the horizontal boards, top and bottom, have been fastened to them.
Such a fence makes an attractive background for temporary or
more permanent plantings. Redwood is long-lasting.*

Espalier Plant Forms

What is an espalier? Popularly it is a plant that has been trained by
special pruning to grow all in one plane, against a wall or fence. This
old-world practice is now returning as a popular hobby and is an easy
way of making dull, monotonous walls look most interesting.

What are some plants that can be espaliered? Pyracantha, forsythia,
Cotoneaster horizontalis, fruit trees, crab apples, yews, mock-oranges,
Japanese quince, *Jasminum* species, magnolias, and *Tamarix* species, to
name a few.

Is training espaliers time-consuming? Not necessarily. Shearing or
clipping to the right form at the start, then about twice a year, is all that
is necessary. Bending and tying young twigs in place should be done
when they are young and pliable—in the spring. They should be tied to
wires firmly, but not so tightly that the wires will girdle the twigs. Such
wires should be loosened or changed periodically.

What are some of the forms used in training espaliers? Fan shapes
with 3 to 7 main leaders from the base; horizontal branches on either
side of one central leader; curved fan types; horizontal cordon, oblique
cordon, U-shaped forms, and gridirons of various shapes.

What is more important in pruning espaliers, the time of pruning or the shape? The shape must always be kept in mind. Even taking off a single wrong bud may retard the final shaping for a year or more. Never prune off any buds or twigs without having a mental picture of the final shape desired.

Driveways

What material do you recommend for building a driveway? Many materials make satisfactory driveways, but much depends on whether the drive is straight or curved, flat or sloping, in cold country or warm. A good, cheap driveway for a level drive in the New York area can be made of either cinders mixed with loam and sand or bank-run gravel. Either can be finished with grits or bluestone screenings. If there are curves or grades, crushed stone with a tar binder is practically mandatory.

How would you build a driveway on a steep slope to prevent washing? What material should be used? For a short driveway on a steep slope, granite paving blocks set in sand make an ideal material. They are rough enough to give good traction in icy weather; they need no maintenance and are good-looking. For a long driveway, they may be too uneven for comfortable riding, and concrete, heavily scored to provide traction, may be better. But it is a hard, uncompromising-looking material.

I am building a driveway for my home. What sort of parking space

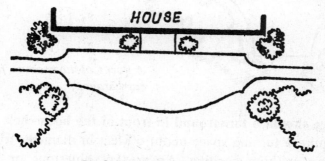

Parking space at an entrance that does not block the passage of other cars.

for visiting cars do you recommend, and where should it be located? Parking space for at least one guest car should be provided right at the front door or the path leading to it, arranged so that the use of the driveway by other cars is not prevented. (See the next question.) Parking for a larger number of cars should be located at a distance from the front entrance of the house. It should be constructed of the same material as the driveway.

When guests come to the house and leave their cars before the front door, it is impossible for anyone else to use the driveway from the garage to the street. How can I avoid this situation? Construct a pass court in front of the door wide enough so that a car can stand at the door and another pass it on the outside. The court should be about 30 feet long and 16 feet wide. Any interesting shape can make it a pleasing part of the landscape picture.

What is the most practical shape for a turn court at the garage on a small property? The so-called Y-turn takes up the least space and yet provides for easy turning, either for your own car coming out of the garage or for other cars using the driveway. The radius of the curves in the accompanying sketch should be 15 feet to 20 feet, and it is important that the space into which the cars back be at least 14 feet wide.

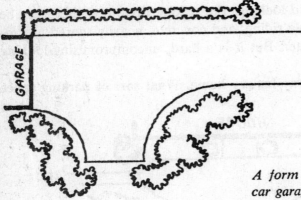

A form of turn court for a single-car garage.

How large should a turnaround in front of the house be? The largest cars require a turning space about 60 feet in diameter for making a complete turn without backing. An area of bluestone or gravel that large is often out of proportion to the house. It can be broken up with a grass island (but this should not have anything else planted in it). To

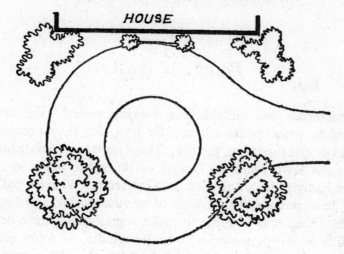

Turnaround for a car.

make arrival at the house door easy, it is wise to distort the shape of the turnaround somewhat, making it more of an apple shape instead of a true circle.

Would you recommend brick or stone edging for a driveway or path? For a driveway, brick edging is somewhat too fragile unless the bricks are set in a heavy foundation of concrete. Then they are unsightly. Try the new plastic driveway edging. It looks better because it does not show, is strong, and installs easily. For pathways, brick is ideal. Small rounded stones are useless for either purpose and never are aesthetically pleasing.

What sort of edging should I use for a brick walk or driveway? There are three standard patterns of edging: sawtooth, rowlock, and stretcher. For garden paths where there are no grass edges, sawtooth looks good, and it uses less brick than does rowlock. Against a lawn or grass edge, rowlock is better because the mower can be run up on it and there is less hand clipping. Stretcher edging uses the least brick of all, but since the bricks do not go down into the ground any farther than the bricks of the walk itself, it provides less stability for the walk.

What can I use to edge a driveway that will look good, but will also make a strong, permanent edge? There is a brown plastic edging on the market that is strong, neat, and unobtrusive. It is 6 inches deep with a rounded top, and comes in 25-foot lengths. Keep it level with the drive and lawn for easy mowing.

Paths and Walks

What materials are suitable for making paths? For an average flower garden, grass paths are usually best, for they present a green foreground for the garden picture. They need no maintenance other than what the lawn receives. Gravel or bluestone paths in the flower garden are likely to be a nuisance to take care of. Where a path must be dry, or at least passable in all sorts of weather, brick and flagstone are serviceable. Often it is possible to make a grass path more practical by laying a line of stepping-stones down its middle, or along either edge.

Should a path be laid out in a straight line or with a curve? Generally speaking, a path should be as direct as possible, because the purpose of it is to provide a passage between two points. However, a natural-looking path should follow the contour of the garden, curving around trees or shrubs that are in a direct line. Sharp curves and all unnecessary turns should be avoided. When a curve is to be made, it should have a long, gentle sweep. For very small paths, a straight line with no curves at all is advisable.

How should I construct a brick walk? Brick walks look best when laid in sand rather than cement mortar. Provide a gravel or cinder bed about 6 inches thick; then put down a layer of fine sand, set the edge courses, and fill in the field brick in whatever pattern you wish. Fill the cracks between the bricks with fine sand, wash it well, and tamp thoroughly. In tamping, lay a heavy board on the walk and pound that rather than the bricks themselves. The walk will be smoother if you do this and you will break fewer bricks.

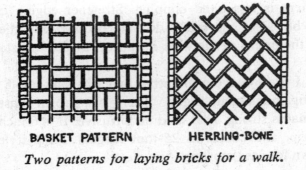

BASKET PATTERN   HERRING-BONE

Two patterns for laying bricks for a walk.

What pattern should be used in laying a brick walk?   There are two standard patterns: basket and herringbone. Either may be varied somewhat according to taste. The basket pattern is more economical since there is no cutting of brick. The accompanying sketch shows basket pattern with a rowlock edge and herringbone with a sawtooth edge. In laying out the walk, set only one edge course first. Lay out a section of the field to see how the pattern is working out, then set the other edge. Do not decide on a predetermined width for the walk and then try to fit the pattern into it.

I have been thinking of putting in a gravel path. Is it commonly used in the garden?   Gravel paths are often used. They are inclined to look a bit formal and cold, however, and they are not as comfortable to walk upon as grass. Also, in the winter in cold climates, the stones and snow stick to the soles of shoes and so can be brought into the house.

What sort of stones are suitable for a path of stepping-stones?   Water-washed flat stones with rounded edges are the most effective. If these are unobtainable, other flat stones or random slates or flagstones that are thick enough to bear the weight of traffic can be used. Discarded, broken-up sections of concrete paving can also be used.

Are sections of tree trunks as practical and longlasting as stepping-stones?   Yes, the chain saw has made it simple and inexpensive to cut flat cross sections of any size tree trunk, 4–6 inches thick. These should be treated with wood preservative and can be expected to have a long life. Fish net stretched over the top will keep them from being slippery in wet weather.

Is it possible to encourage the growth of moss? I want to put some between stepping stones.   Moss can be started only by transplanting sods of it from some place where it naturally grows. Find a variety that is growing under similar conditions of sun or shade. Probably you will get better results by using plants of *Arenaria verna,* the moss sandwort, which can be purchased.

Will you suggest some plants to place between stepping stones? Various thymes, sedums, *Cerastium tomentosum, Euonymus fortunei* 'Kewensis', *Mazus reptans, Potentilla tridentata, Sagina subulata, Veronica repens, Tunica saxifraga,* and *Viola arenaria.*

Can you recommend a substitute for tanbark to use on our woodland garden path?   Wood chips should be suitable, if you live in an area where they are available. They are often available for a slight charge from utility companies and should last for three or four years before they decay. Another substance—if your path is not too extensive—is pine bark, usually available from garden centers. A third material, but of much finer texture than the others, is sawdust, a practical solution if you live in a lumbering region.

Garden steps should be safe for the user as well as attractive. These steps combine bricks and railroad ties.

Of what shall I build my garden steps?   Steps of stone with brick or flagstone treads harmonize well in many gardens. All-brick steps often look too harsh and formal. Fieldstone is all right if you can find enough flat ones. Concrete is much too unyielding. Grass steps held in place by steel bands imbedded in the turf are beautiful but hard to make and to maintain. For very informal situations, sod, gravel, or tanbark steps held up by fieldstone or log risers are most effective. Sometimes the steps themselves are made of squared sections of cypress, black locust logs, or railroad ties.

Patios and Terraces

(See also Roof Gardens, Container Gardening and Window-Box Gardens, this section.)

What is the difference between a patio and a terrace?   In popular thinking, not much. The terms are used interchangeably. Actually, the patio originated with the Spanish and we have come to associate terra-cotta pottery and tiles with it. A terrace is a raised platform supported by a wall or bank, while a patio nowadays is any paved outdoor living area.

Where should the patio be located? Immediately outside the living room or dining room, where it is easily accessible and can be seen from indoors. Be sure to plan the patio and plant it so that it is most attractive from indoors. The use of sliding glass doors adds a picture-window effect.

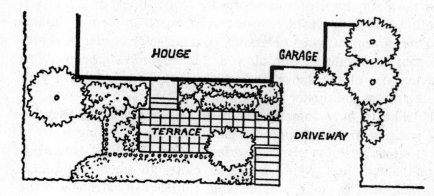

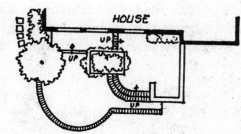

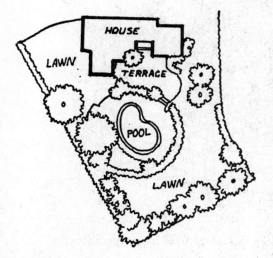

A terrace can be constructed in a variety of shapes and styles, as shown by the three examples here. They should harmonize with the house and not appear as tacked-on additions lacking any connection with the rest of the landscaping. The plan at the left shows how terrace areas can be extended to include a swimming pool.

What is the best material for paving a patio?   It depends on your likes and dislikes. The material should go well with the house or its foundation, or the chimney. Tile, gravel, paving stones, bricks, even redwood planks are all possibilities.

I want to build a partially enclosed patio. With what do you suggest I enclose it?   If there is a good view, be certain to take full advantage of it. Shield the patio from prevailing winds. A low brick or stone wall with small openings; louvered redwood or redwood to form a "board-on-board" arrangement; glass or plastic; or a hedge or border of shrubbery are some possibilities. Consult your lumberyard salespeople. The principal purpose of the above-mentioned alternatives is to give your patio some privacy and shelter from winds.

I would like to have some flower beds on my patio. Do they belong?   Certainly, and you might consider raised beds, using walls of brick or stone to raise the planting surface 2 feet above the ground. If herbs are planted, they would be much closer to smell and touch. Weeding such beds is not a backbreaking chore, as it might be if the beds were at ground level.

How do I provide shade for the patio?   If a large tree is not already there, plant a dogwood, crab apple, magnolia, or some other small tree. Dogwood is ideal because it has horizontal branching and one can sit

Outdoor furniture should be in harmony with its surroundings.

under it. A larger tree, like a hemlock, pine, oak, or maple, just outside the patio walls, would do the same trick, but place it where one can take fullest advantage of its shade at the right time of day.

Is there any special furniture for the patio that is best?   It certainly should be weatherproof. Chairs and tables might be of metal and heavy enough so they would not be blown around. Lounging chairs should be of a type to go well with the architecture of the house and the type of patio constructed.

Should pots for plants on a patio be large or small?   The larger pots are more decorative and usually in keeping with the patio idea. Even more important, they do not dry out as fast. Don't eliminate large wooden tubs as possibilities on the patio. Some of these, well-planted, make excellent ornaments for display.

Is there any reason why a sandbox for our two small children should not be placed in one corner of our patio?   No. It would be an excellent place if it is in the shade and easily seen from the house. Incorporate it into the design and use it as a planter later.

Which flowers will grow on a very windy terrace?   Creeping phlox, dianthus, *Gypsophila repens,* hemerocallis (day-lilies), evergreen candytuft, lavender, marigolds, geraniums, low-growing zinnias, sweet-alyssum.

How should I construct a flag terrace, and the steps down from it to the lawn?   The flagstone, about 2 inches thick, can be laid on a bed of cinders or gravel covered with a thin layer of fine sand. No mortar is needed if the flags are heavy enough to stay in place. Slate cannot be used as easily. Brick can be substituted for flag. Steps should have treads with at least a 1-inch overhang, and there should be a solid concrete foundation under them. Ramps, parapets, or wing walls should be substantial and have copings with the same overhang as the step treads. Steps and walls should be laid in cement mortar.

Will you suggest a plant giving a long period of bloom for the narrow border around my flagged terrace?   Lantana. Purchase young blossoming plants from a florist or garden center and plant 18 inches apart. They will grow into sturdy shrubs by midsummer and are not winter hardy. Try an edging of lobelia on the inside. A more economical substitute for the lantana would be dwarf marigolds.

Which plants are suitable for a patio?   In the Northeast or North, a patio might include a permanent planting of broad-leaved evergreens, an espaliered fruit tree (if there is a sunny wall), and a wisteria vine. Potted foliage plants (monstera, *Nephthytis afzellii,* dracaena, dieffen-

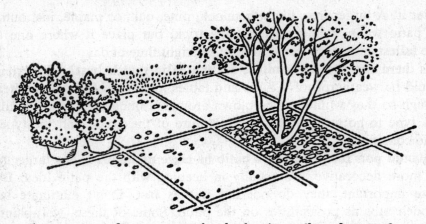

A terrace can become a garden by leaving soil pockets in the pavement for trees and other plants. Seasonal color can be provided by plants in pots.

bachia, etc.) and potted geraniums, fuchsias, lantanas, begonias, and caladiums; crown-of-thorns and other succulents (such as crassulas) could be set out in warm weather. Patios in warm climates have a wider choice of plants, including such shrubs as oleanders, camellias, and gardenias; also bougainvillea and vines and other semitropical plant material.

I would like to have a patio garden. Would this be suitable with a colonial house? Patio gardens are usually made within a courtyard or similar enclosure. Although they are of Spanish origin and suited to this type of dwelling, the idea can be adapted to any style of architecture today. If you have or can arrange a suitable protected terrace or courtyard adjacent to your colonial house, you can use flat stones or flagging to pave the area, put potted plants in white containers, and by using colonial ornaments and furniture, arrange a fitting outdoor living area which would serve the same purpose as a patio.

Are sun decks recent additions to outdoor living? Actually no, they are adapted from the mid-Victorian porch of the nineteenth century, which was firmly attached to the house. They now are built over slopes, in the trees, over the garage, and many other places, giving opportunity for the sun-loving people of today to enjoy outdoor relaxation. Building a redwood sun deck over the edge of a steep bank makes it possible to have outdoor living where there is no room for the standard patio or terrace. Usually more exposed to the elements, there is opportunity for outdoor entertainment and gardening by growing plants in tubs or planters.

I want to screen one side of our patio from the view of the road, but I don't like the idea of a wall. What do you suggest? Landscape architects have come up with all sorts of beautiful screening ideas—actually walls made of wood but with the boards cut and put together in interesting ways so that the "wall" is actually a thing of beauty when viewed from either side. Cedar, redwood, translucent glass, or plastic, louvered slats of redwood, etc.—all have been used effectively. The salespeople in your local lumberyard will have suggestions. Look through general gardening books for specific suggestions.

Garden Lighting

Is garden lighting costly to maintain? No. The lights are turned on for such a short time that the cost of electricity is negligible. Initially the installation of weatherproof lights, wiring, and sockets might seem expensive, but the results of being able to illuminate parts of the garden and its paths at night adds a new appreciation of the garden.

Should lights be directed up to or down on foliage in the garden at night? Both. Varying this direction brings about diversification of interest—a few flowers in bloom by the walk, and at another place a spotlight on tree branches from below.

Are garden lights set out permanently in one situation? Not necessarily. The initial installation of underground wiring might include a series of weatherproof plugs so that lights of various types could be changed from place to place as different plants come into bloom.

Are there special lamps for garden lighting? Yes. Your electrical contractors can recommend fixtures of different types and will do the initial installation. A diversified series of lights, illuminating plants to show both flowers and form as well as steps and walks, brings a new enjoyment to the garden at night.

Garden Pools and Water Gardens

How should a small pool be constructed? The accompanying sketch shows a simple concrete pool and the necessary plumbing connections. For the successful growing of aquatics, the deep part of the pool should be 1½ feet, and if it is to be used at all by birds, some part of it should be shallow enough for them. They do not like water more than 2 inches deep.

How shall I go about building a small pool?   Excavate the ground about 6 inches deeper on the bottom and wider at the sides than you wish the pool to be. Insert drainage if the pool is to be large enough to require it (see accompanying sketch); if it is very small, this will not be necessary. Fill the hole with a gravel layer, tamp down firmly, or line with chicken wire. Pour cement, 1 part cement to 3 parts mixed sand and gravel. Add water, enough so that the mixture will spread evenly. The layer should be about 4 or 5 inches thick. Next day, finish with a coat of cement mortar, 1 part cement to 2 parts sand, applied with a trowel.

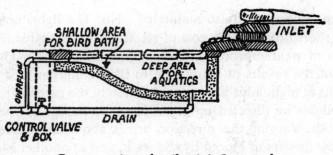

Cross section detail of inflow and overflow for a garden pool.

How thick should the concrete walls of a garden pool be?   The thickness of the walls of a pool depends on its size. A large pool naturally has to have thicker walls. For the average small pool (6 feet or so in diameter), walls 6 inches thick are sufficient. Some reinforcement in the form of wire or steel rods should be used.

How soon after finishing the construction of a small pool can plants be put in?   If the pool is concrete, paint the surface with one of the special preparations available from lumberyards. Or leave the pool filled with water for about 2 weeks, flushing occasionally, then add plants and fish.

Are plastic pools practical? I do not want to go to the expense of putting in a concrete pool, but would like to have a small pool for a few years' trial.   Plastic molded pools are available in small sizes but are not necessarily inexpensive when compared with concrete pools. Various types are frequently advertised in the garden magazines. They can be installed by any gardener. The most inexpensive pool is made with heavy polyethylene.

What shape should a small pool be? It depends on your location and general garden design. If your garden is informal, an informally shaped pool would be best. This should be "kidney-" or "egg-shaped" with gently curving, irregular contours. By using the garden hose to lay out the shape of the pool, good curves may be attained. Avoid sharp curves and too many irregularities. Simplicity is the keynote.

I want to build a small informal pool. About what size should I make it? A good-looking small pool might be about 25 square feet but smaller sizes can be successful.

I want to build a small formal pool with a fountain and statue at the back. What shape would be best for the pool? A round or oblong formal pool is always good. If your garden is very formal, you could have a rectangular pool.

Will goldfish live in my pool during the winter? That depends on how deep and how large the pool is and on your winter temperatures. Goldfish can live in large pools that do not freeze solid in the winter, but will not live through the winter in small pools that either freeze solid or have only a few inches of water under the ice in winter. Under such conditions the fish actually smother to death.

I understand pools take time to clean and it may be too much for me but I'd like to try one for a while without going to the labor and expense of constructing a concrete pool. What do you suggest? By all means, try a pool temporarily. Line a depression with heavy polyethylene film, the edges tucked in the soil at the sides, rocks at the edges as for other pools. You can even purchase a small circulating pump and install a fountain. In this way, with little expense you can have a pool for a trial run. It will last longer than you think!

Do you recommend putting a fountain into a small home garden? Elaborate fountains throwing large streams of water are rather expensive to maintain and too impressive for a small garden. A small fountain which drips water slowly over a shallow basin or a wall fountain that runs a tiny stream into a bowl are pleasing and in scale.

I want water at various places in my garden for a pool, for sprinklers, for a fountain, and for watering plants during dry spells. Can I put in a simple water system myself? Yes, by using plastic pipe. It is easily laid about 8 inches deep in a V-shaped trench in lawn or garden. Outlets and connections are available, as are drain plugs, so the system can be drained before winter. It is less expensive than metal pipe.

Prefabricated Fiberglas pools are available from water-gardening specialists. When skillfully surrounded by plants, they look very natural.

We want a small pool for a few fish and water plants but I don't want to go to all the trouble of building one out of concrete. Can't I buy one? Yes. Various types of small pools are now available made out of Fiberglas and plastics that are extremely durable and long-lasting. Heavy-duty polyethylene film can also be easily used. Even the smallest garden can feature an aquatic display.

What background materials should I use for my small informal pool? Small evergreens, yew, arborvitae, cedar, hemlock, azalea, mountain-laurel, rhododendron, leucothoe, euonymus, cotoneaster, daphne.

I want a formal-looking clipped hedge around the sides of my formal pool, which is at the rear of my garden. What would you suggest? Yew, hemlock, barberry, box (for sheltered positions), privet.

Can I have a successful fish pond in a plot about 9 × 15 feet? How can something this small be landscaped? Yes. Miniature Fiberglas pools are available. Why not pave the area with flagstones, leaving wide cracks between the stones? These could be planted with small rock plants. The pool would be the central feature.

Have you any planting suggestions for the rim of a pool? Astilbe, cardinal-flower, Japanese iris, loosestrife, marsh-marigold, rosemallow, Siberian iris, and *Primula japonica*.

I have a rocky ledge by my pool. What evergreen might be grown over it? Depending on the size of the ledge and the pool, one of the creeping junipers might be used. For larger pools, there is nothing quite as graceful as a dwarf weeping Canada hemlock planted with its branches hanging down over the rocks, but other dwarf conifers would also be suitable.

Which flowering plants can be grown in a pool other than water-lilies? Floating-heart (*Nymphoides peltatum*); true forget-me-not; water-hyacinth (*Eichornia*); water-poppy (*Hydrocleis*); water-snowflake (*Nymphoides indicum*). The last three are not winter-hardy in the North.

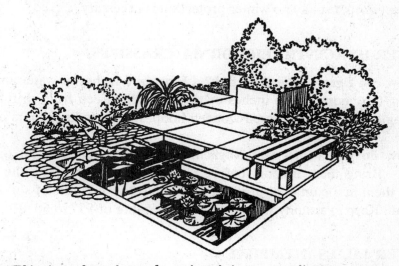

This formal pool can be enjoyed from an adjacent terrace. Water-lilies need full sunshine.

What can be used to break the monotonous flatness of a lily pool? Tall-growing water plants, such as American and Hindu lotus; calla; cattails (if pool is large); flowering rush; yellow and blue flags; taro; water-plantain.

With what flowers shall I border an informal pool 6 × 10 feet? *Filipendula vulgaris* 'Flore-pleno', *Iris ochroleuca*, *Trollius ledebouri*, *Lythrum salicaria*, *Hemerocallis*, *Liatris pycnostachya*, *Myosotis scorpioides semperflorens*, *Primula japonica*.

I have a hillside rock garden with an uneven 6-foot diameter pool. Will you give me advice as to plants for inside the pool and for outside to hold up the soil, which seems to wash away with each rain? Plant *Nymphoides peltatum* inside the pool. *Caltha palustris* (marsh-marigold) along the edge; also *Primula rosea, Trollius europaeus,* and 2 or 3 *Lobelia cardinalis* (cardinal-flower). To hold the soil beyond the pool, plant a low-creeping juniper.

HINDU LOTUS

Which is the best way to keep sacred lotus (Nelumbo nucifera) through the winter? If growing in a pond that is drained during the winter, cover the roots with a sufficient depth of leaves to prevent the frost from penetrating to the tubers. When this plant is grown in water 2 or 3 feet deep, usually no winter protection is necessary.

WATER-HYACINTH (EICHORNIA CRASSIPES)

How can I grow water-hyacinth? Float in 6 inches of water above a box or tub containing 6 inches or more of soil. Keep from drifting by confining within an anchored wooden hoop. Bring plants indoors before frost.

How do you winter water-hyacinths that have been in an outside pool? Bring them indoors before the leaves are injured by the cold. Float them in a container of water which has 3 or 4 inches of soil in the bottom. Keep in a sunny window in a temperature of 55° to 60° F.

WATER LILIES (NYMPHAEA)

What is the proper soil for water-lilies? Use a rich, heavy soil (3 parts loam, 1 part sand). A soil mixture containing too much organic matter, such as peat moss, will cloud the water.

What shall I use to make water-lilies bloom better? Possibly your plants are starved. Divide and replant in the soil recommended above, adding a 5-inch potful of bone meal to each bushel of soil. Water-lilies need full sun all day for best results.

How large should containers be for water-lilies? It depends on the variety. Small-growing kinds can be grown in boxes 15 × 15 × 10 inches, while the tropical varieties can be grown to advantage in sizes up to 4 × 4 × 1 feet.

In a small concrete pool, is it better to cover the bottom with soil or use separate boxes for water-lilies? The plants are better off if the bottom is covered with soil, but it is easier to avoid muddying the water in the pool if the soil is confined in wooden boxes or similar containers.

How deep should the water be over water-lilies? Six inches to 3 feet. Preferably 1 foot for tropical varieties, 1 to 2 feet for hardy varieties, provided this is enough to prevent roots from freezing in the winter.

What is the most practical way to care for a water-lily pool in the winter? If the pool is small enough to be bridged by boards, do so and then cover with a sufficient thickness of straw or leaves to prevent the water from freezing. If the pool is drained and the water-lilies are growing in tubs, move the tubs together and cover around and over them with leaves held in place with wire netting or something similar.

What if the mud is not sufficiently deep to support the growth of water-lilies? Plant them in rich soil in plastic baskets or wooden tubs with openings sufficiently wide to allow roots to emerge, then gently slide the planted container into the pond.

How often should water-lilies be divided? Whenever the container becomes so crowded that growth is poor—usually after 3 or 4 years.

Would colored water-lilies grow where wild white ones grow in a lake with a muddy bottom? Yes.

Which water-lily can be grown in a pool fed from an underground stream? The water is cold the year round and is in dense shade. Water-lilies will not grow in such a location. They need full sun.

How can I plant hardy water-lilies in a natural pond? If the pond has a rich mud bottom, merely tie a heavy sod or half brick to the tuber or rhizome and drop it in the pond where the water is between 1 and 3 feet deep.

When is the best time to plant hardy water-lilies? When ice has left the pond in the spring, but they may be planted successfully up until mid-June.

Should hardy water-lilies be left outside in the pool through the winter? (New York.) Yes, if they are growing in water so deep that there is no danger of the roots freezing—18 inches should be enough in your locality.

How early can tropical water-lilies be set out? Not until all danger of frost is past and the water has become warm—about the second week in June in the vicinity of New York.

How are tropical water-lilies planted? Pot-grown plants are commonly used. A hole is scooped in the soil of the container deep enough to receive the ball of earth around the roots, then the roots are covered with soil, taking care not to bury the crown of the plant.

Can tropical water-lilies be kept through the winter? It is difficult to carry over tropical water-lilies unless one has a sunny greenhouse. When it is possible to find small tubers around the crown of the old plant, these may be gathered in the fall, stored in sand, protected from mice, and started in an aquarium in a sunny window in April.

During the past 2 summers some sort of leafminer has eaten the leaves (making marks like Chinese ideographs) of my water-lilies. Consequently the leaves soon die. What are they and how may I get rid of them without injuring the fish in the pond? The larvae of a midge—*Chirononus modestus*. Water-lily foliage is sensitive to insecticidal sprays, so it is best, whenever possible, to use mechanical means to get rid of pests; therefore, pick them off infested leaves as fast as they appear and destroy them by burning, which will ultimately eliminate the miner.

We have an old pond on our place but now it is almost one solid growth of water-lilies. How can these be eradicated? The aquatic herbicides are difficult to use properly, especially when you are using them on a large area of water. A slight overdose can cause considerable problems, so it would be best for you to consult with your Cooperative Extension Service agent, who can tell you the safest and best way to cope with the problem.

Game Areas

Can I utilize a flat, paved driveway for games? Yes, you can play shuffleboard on a drive if it is long enough. The official size is 52 × 6 feet, but that can be modified. You can also put up a basketball backboard at the side on a free-standing post.

We cannot afford a tennis court. What other game can be played on a lawn? Volleyball is an excellent lawn game requiring little more than a ball and net. Most home sets use 20-foot nets and a playing area 20 × 40 feet. Sets containing balls, nets, and supporting posts are available in a wide range of prices.

How can I lay out a badminton court? Allow about 30 × 60 feet of level lawn space for a badminton court.

I want to make part of my garden into an area for a bowling green and for horseshoe pitching. How much room is necessary? For a bowling green, you should have a smooth grass area at least 60 feet long. A gutter of sand 1½ feet wide and about 6 inches deep should surround this strip. For horseshoes, you will need an area 10 × 50 feet. The sand pit at either end should be 6 square feet, with a stout wooden or iron stake in the center.

How much room does a croquet lawn require?   About 30 × 60 feet. A level, well-mowed area is essential for this game. (See Lawns.)

What games or equipment would be suitable for a children's game area?   A wading pool, sandbox or sand pit, swings, seesaw, sliding board, ball court.

My children want a tennis court. What is the most practical type?   The surface choices are clay, grass, asphalt, or all-weather. It depends on your individual preferences, local conditions, and budget. It should not be a do-it-yourself project, but one for the contractors, who have had experience in building them.

What is the simplest means of fencing in a pool to keep out animals and small children?   Probably a simple wire fence, 4 feet high. This could be augmented by a shrub planting on the outside to hide the pool as well as to give protection from winds. A yew hedge would be ideal and would eliminate the leaf problem in the fall.

What are the things to keep in mind in planning for a swimming pool?   Situation, size, and shape. Also plan for the necessary maintenance, for a flat area around the pool (usually paved), for sunbathing and relaxing in general, and for fencing in the pool to keep out animals and small children. Have a small camouflaged space for the filtering equipment. Drainage of the pool is also very important. Consult a reliable contractor.

Would a rectangular or informally shaped swimming pool be best?   This depends on your wishes and your budget. The latter is more expensive to build.

Where should I locate a swimming pool?   Preferably on flat land, in the sun, and away from overhanging tree branches, but nevertheless in a protected area if possible, out of windy areas.

What is the minimum size of a swimming pool if one wants to really swim?   Probably 34 feet × 14 feet, and if there is a diving board, a depth of at least 8 feet where the diver hits the water. Of course, the larger the pool, the more room to swim!

We want to provide a play area for two very small children. What do you suggest?   First, a sandbox, at least 6 × 6 feet, with arrangements for covering it with canvas to keep out rain and prevent dogs and cats from digging in it. This should be located where there is some shade and preferably screened with shrubs to prevent youngsters from wandering too much. Second, a swing-ladder-trapeze affair of either steel or wood, easily seen from the house. Several types are readily available. A shallow wading pool might be included.

Tool Houses and Utility Areas

I want to fix up some space in my garage as a tool house and potting shed. How can I arrange this? Build a long bench, at a convenient height for standing, to be used for potting plants, mixing sprays, etc. Under this, have drawers or shelves for pots, labels, and baskets, and bins for fertilizers and soil materials. Over the bench, racks may be built for holding vases, and a peg board will be a convenient holder for small tools such as trowels, dibbers, and hand cultivators. A space against one wall should be left for the wheelbarrow and lawn mower. Wooden racks for rakes, hoes, and other long-handled tools (which are hung handle-down) can be made by nailing a strip of wood on the wall about 6 feet above the floor. Pairs of nails protruding from this hold the tools. The garden hose needs a special rack where it will not be damaged by sharp tools. A stout 2-foot bracket jutting out from the wall will be convenient for this purpose.

Where and how can I provide a convenient storage place for my vegetable-garden tools and equipment? A small addition to the garage, opening out into the vegetable garden, makes an ideal tool house. If the garden is fairly large and the garage not conveniently near, a small separate building, disguised as a garden house, will serve. On a sloping lot, enclosed space under a rear deck often makes a good place for this equipment. Also, the large mail-order houses have small prefabricated tool houses available that are easily erected in a concealed part of the garden.

Where should the utility area be located? Preferably near the kitchen door. Here would be space for garbage and trash cans, propane-gas cylinders, if used, storage space for fireplace wood, and possibly even space for clothes drying.

How large an area should I plan for clothes drying? It depends on the amount of clothes to be dried at one time. With electric dryers so wasteful of energy, many homeowners are using them only on rare occasions. A portable aluminum umbrella-type dryer can be set in a prepared hole in the ground, or a few lines can be run across the utility area.

How high should the screening around the utility area be? About 6½ feet.

How about garbage cans in the utility area? The best choice is the sunken metal type in the ground, with a foot pedal for lifting the lid. Trash cans or polyethylene barrels should have lids and might be enclosed (except for the front) within a wood-storage closet.

How can I best screen a small utility area? By planting a tight hedge of narrow evergreens; by a split sapling, woven-slat, or tight, rustic fence; or simply by a tall board fence over which interesting vines like English ivy, Dutchman's-pipe, honeysuckle, or climbing hydrangea are used. Another way is to erect a tight-fitting red-cedar sapling fence, which in itself is interesting, and on the outside train a few espaliered yews or pyracanthas.

Garden Features and Accessories

What type of bird bath is good for the small garden? Containers of concrete, clay, lead, wood, or stone are suitable, as long as they are well designed and unobtrusive. Select a design which fits your garden plan. Homemade cement-and-fieldstone bird baths must be carefully constructed to be aesthetically pleasing. For a small garden, a height of 2½ feet is about right.

Are the bird baths which are set on the ground without a pedestal practical? Yes, they are very effective if well designed. Handmade ceramic or metal basins are interesting, or a hollowed stone may be used. They are usually placed in a sheltered spot surrounded by plantings to give the birds protection.

How often should bird baths be cleaned? As often as they look dirty or stained, which is usually 2 times a week at least in warm weather. It will help to have a special scrubbing brush for the bird bath for removing scum around the edges.

What can be used to remove algae from a bird bath? Usually water or soapy water and a scrubbing brush are all that is necessary. Borax may be added or a bleaching disinfectant. However, these must be well rinsed off before filling the bath with water for the birds.

I want to have an arbor. Shall I buy one or make one? First, decide on why you need an arbor—for ornament, for screening, for shade? There are all sorts available: metal, white-painted wood, rustic types, those made of redwood or cedar. Decide what fits into your garden or patio scheme best. Consult a good picture reference book for possible designs and suggested materials. An arbor is a rather permanent garden fixture and one should be certain it fits in well with the garden scheme.

What is a pergola?   A pergola is a passageway covered by an arbor which supports grape vines or large flowering vines. The structure is usually somewhat elaborate, with decorative columns and crosspieces. It is of Latin origin and is suitable for only a limited number of American gardens.

Is a pergola recommended for the small garden?   The old-fashioned white-painted wood pergola, used so much in gardens years ago, is now out of place in most American gardens. In its place have come arbors built of thick planks and of rather heavy structure, supplying some slight shade but also support for ornamental vines to give additional shade over walks, patios, or terraces.

I want to have some statuary in my garden. Can you suggest some types?   In the small garden, care must be taken not to overdo the use of statuary. One well-designed piece, not too large and used as a center of interest, is sufficient. A statue is usually placed at the end of a vista or in a niche formed of evergreens. It needs a background of green plant material to fit it into the garden picture. Avoid use of pottery figures of gnomes, ducks, etc., and other novelties as being too conspicuous and artificial.

Is a bench practical in a small modern garden?   Yes. One always wants to sit down in the garden when a permanent, well-placed bench is present. It can be of metal, wood, or cement or a combination of materials.

Should weather vanes be used on small properties?   The use of weather vanes is sometimes overdone. They are best used in the country, on barns, tool sheds, or other outbuildings. For a small place, get a simple style, not too large, to be used on the garage or garden house.

Do you recommend using a sundial in the garden?   A sundial is very effective in the right setting as the center of interest in a rose or herb garden, or formal garden. It must, of course, be placed where the sun will hit it all day.

What is topiary work?   Pruning of hedges, shrubs, or trees in specific shapes, as of animals, houses, balls, spools, figures, or geometric forms, used in formal gardens and primarily associated with medieval landscape design. Boxwood, yew, and privet are employed for this purpose. Also, English ivy growing over prearranged wire frames. Good examples of this garden art can be seen at Disney World in Orlando, Florida.

Special Types of Gardens

HERB GARDENS—WHAT TO GROW

Which herbs are annuals and which are perennials? I am confused about which ones will come up a second year. The annual herbs most widely used are anise, basil, dill, summer savory, fennel, coriander, and borage. The perennial herbs include chives, thyme, lavender, lemon-balm, winter savory, pot marjoram, sage, horehound, mint, tarragon, and bee balm. Parsley, angelica, and caraway are technically biennials, but are grown as annuals. All of these grow in full sun and like a well-drained garden soil. Sow annuals as early in the spring as the weather permits, either in rows or broadcast.

Will you list 6 annual herbs for the kitchen garden? Basil, borage, chervil, parsley (really biennial but treated as an annual), summer savory, and sweet marjoram.

Sweet Marjoram

Summer Savory

Which 6 perennial herbs do you suggest for the kitchen herb garden? Chives, horse-radish, mint, sage, tarragon, and thyme.

Which herbs do you suggest for a fragrant herb garden? Bergamot, lavender, lemon-verbena, rosemary, scented geraniums, southernwood, sweet wormwood, lovage, valerian, lemon-balm, sweet Cicely, thyme, and costmary.

What herbs may be grown successfully at home, and preserved for winter use? Try mints (care must be taken to prevent the plants from overrunning their space), sage, thyme, parsley, caraway, dill, and anise.

What are the best combinations of herbs for tea (as a beverage)?   For flavoring tea, try mints or lemon-verbena. Sage and camomile, each used alone, make tasty beverages. (Never use a metal container for making tea.)

I like the idea of having a few large pots of herbs set around on our terrace. Is this practicable?   Absolutely! Several herbs have interesting foliage and flowers. They withstand dry sunny situations and their fragrance is an addition to the pleasure of terrace or patio living. (See Herbs in Pots.)

I only have a very small garden but I do want to grow a few herbs. What would you suggest?   A few could be grown in large clay pots or wooden tubs on the sunny part of a terrace or patio. A small corner of the garden (in sun) could be used to advantage, or a spot in front of a fence, by the garage, or near the kitchen door. A few could be selected to border a walk or simply be added to the flower or vegetable garden.

Which are the most ornamental herbs?   Hyssop, thyme, lavender, winter savory, the artemisias, borage, rue, calendula, and the sweet-scented geraniums are a few.

What are the best ones with gray foliage?   Lavender, santolina, the artemisias, borage, sweet marjoram, rue, sage, and thyme.

What is a knot garden?   A garden of low-growing plants or hedges planted in a formal, intricate design. Knot gardens were common to medieval landscape design, when colored sand was often used to form the paths or sections which outlined the beds. They are now used in parks, herb gardens, and formal gardens.

In a knot garden, what material do you put between the miniature herb hedges?   Such things as marble chips, pea coal, broken clay pots,

A knot garden pattern. Suggested herb plants: 1. Gray santolina; 2. Green santolina; 3. Lavender; 4. Germander (Teucrium).

sandstone chips, finely chipped gray gravel, and redwood bark are a few colorful materials that make an excellent background for the plants.

Can you clip the plants in a knot garden anytime? Woody plants such as santolina and lavender should not be clipped after mid-July, otherwise a late clipping might force out young growth that would not have sufficient time to mature properly before freezing weather.

How should I start a small herb garden with a half-dozen varieties of herbs? Plant informally in little groups, taller plants more or less in back.

Can you give some information on herbs—some to eat and some to smell? Good herbs for flavoring: basil (sweet) for salads, soups, and tomato sauces; chives for salads, sour cream, and pot cheese; dill for fish, shellfish, and pickles; fennel to eat like celery, or cooked; sweet marjoram, seasoning for stuffings, etc.; mints for teas and sauces; rosemary for seasoning roasts and chicken; sage for dressing; savory (summer) for flavoring vegetables, particularly snap beans; thyme, seasoning for foods, salads, and sauces; tarragon to flavor vinegar and in chicken dishes. Herbs for scent: bee balm, lavender, lemon-verbena, mints, and scented geraniums.

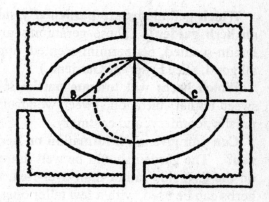

Method of laying out ellipses for a small herb garden. String is secured to stakes at B and C.

Which herbs grow successfully in the house? Basil, dittany of Crete, lemon-verbena, parsley, rosemary, sweet marjoram, tarragon, and perhaps peppermint, if the room is cool and has plenty of light.

Which herbs are attractive enough to grow in a flower garden—the only space I have for them? Lavender, bee balm, calendula, rosemary, rue, sage, thyme, hyssop, and the gray artemisias.

Which herbs are particularly attractive to bees? Thyme, lavender, germander, bee balm, lovage, hyssop, lemon-balm, sweet Cicely, borage, and marjoram.

Can you name some herbs suitable for low hedges? Hyssop, lavender, santolina, germander, southernwood, and rue. In fairly mild climates, rosemary.

Can you suggest herbs for a usable kitchen garden for the beginner? Where can I get information as to their culture, preservation, and use? The following are particularly good for a beginner's garden: sage, tarragon, parsley, chives, shallots, basil, dill, rosemary, some of the thymes, and sweet marjoram. For further information write The Herb Society of America, 300 Massachusetts Ave., Boston, Massachusetts 02115.

Parsley

Chives

Which geraniums are particularly suited for planting (in summer) in an herb garden? These geraniums are botanically *Pelargonium*. The lemon-scented, peppermint-scented, apple-scented, and rose-scented are all good. (See Fragrant Gardens.)

Which herbs will tolerate partial shade? Balm, bee balm, chervil, sweet fennel, tarragon, sweet woodruff, mints, angelica, sweet Cicely, parsley, comfrey, and costmary.

Can you give me information on herbs suitable for an herb rock garden? The garden should be well drained and sunny; the soil should be on the lean side rather than over-rich. Almost any of the lower-growing herbs can be used, with a few taller ones for accents.

Can I plant herbs in among my vegetables? Herbs, such as chives or parsley, make decorative edgings for vegetable-garden paths. Use thyme as a ground cover around bolder plants of sage or scented geraniums (*Pelargonium*) for a focal point or at each side of an entrance. Dill will grow and show off among squash, but it is reputed to inhibit the growth of tomatoes. A few calendula plants would add color and are said to repel asparagus beetles.

I dislike the old formal design of herb gardens. Why not a simple informal border planting? Of course, this can be charming if you study carefully the individual habits of the herbs you are going to use and place them to look well in the final planting. Usually one should not position individual plants with large spaces in between. Plan to allow the plants to grow together. They are being grown to be clipped!

What materials should I use in making raised beds? It depends on the patio, terrace, walks, or house foundation. Use whatever goes well with what you have—brick, fieldstone, or concrete, or raised beds of redwood or cypress. If an herb bed is to be placed along a brick walk, just a simple edging of raised bricks might prove satisfactory.

How large a space do I need for my herb garden? Actually an area only 4 feet × 8 feet is sufficient for all the herbs one normally needs, but one large clay pot can hold several plants—sufficient for most culinary needs.

I would like to edge a brick walk with a few herbs. Which are the best for this purpose? Basil, thyme, santolina, winter savory, and dwarf lavender. In mild climates, where it is hardy, rosemary can also be used.

HERBS IN POTS

What types of containers other than clay pots might be used for herbs set out on the terrace or sun deck? Wooden tubs of various descriptions are used: an old butter tub, if you can get one, or various types of redwood tubs or square containers. Plastic pots do not break and do not get disfigured outside with chemical deposits or plant growth and they stay moist longer than clay pots. Buckets: old wooden sap buckets have a special appeal.

Should I leave my potted herbs out on the terrace during the winter? (New York.) No. Replant them in the open ground for the winter, and possibly give them some winter protection with a good mulch.

Is there any special soil treatment for the growing of herbs in containers? For drainage, place a layer of cinders, gravel, or pieces of broken clay pots on the bottom. Use light, well-drained sandy soil with a little humus added. Only a very small amount of dried manure or bone meal should be added to the mixture, for these plants should not be forced into overvigorous growth. It is not advisable to leave plants in pots or tubs during the winter in the North. Rather take them out of the containers and plant in the ground during the winter months.

What are a few herbs for growing in pots? Lavender, dill, sage,

A clay strawberry jar is an ideal container for different kinds of herb plants. Suitable ones include basil, thyme, chives, summer savory, sweet marjoram. In shade, try different kinds of mint.

basil, santolina, the artemisias, and fragrant-leaved geraniums. These might be clipped once or twice a season to keep them looking well.

HERB CULTURE

What general type of soil is preferred by herbs?   Ordinary well-drained garden soil, lean rather than rich, and not too acid, suits the majority. Mints prefer a fairly rich, moist soil, although less-than-ideal soils serve and prevent the plants from becoming rampant.

Do herbs thrive in sandy soils?   The great majority of herbs do very well in sandy soil if some humus is added and moisture is supplied in very dry weather.

I understand that most herbs need dry soil conditions. Can you suggest some for a moist, but not waterlogged, place?   Angelica, bergamont, sweet Cicely, sweet flag, yellow-stripe sweet flag, lovage, mints, parsley, English pennyroyal, snakeroot, valerian (*Valeriana officinalis*), and violets.

What is the best exposure for an herb garden?   A southeast exposure is ideal, but any location that gets full sunshine during the growing season will do.

What are the general cultural requirements for herbs?   A rather poor, well-drained, slightly acid or neutral soil, warmth, sunlight, and free circulation of air. Space the plants adequately, according to type.

What is the most practical arrangement of annual and perennial herbs —to interplant them, or to keep them separate?   Plant the perennial kinds together and the annual kinds together. The area devoted to annuals can then readily be prepared afresh each spring and the perennial area is disturbed only every few years when replanting becomes necessary. To avoid a jumbled effect, plant the same kind of herb in blocks or groups.

Is it necessary to make more than one sowing of the various annual herbs each season? Only for quick-maturing kinds such as dill, chervil, and anise.

Is watering important in an herb garden? A few herbs (such as mints) need generous supplies of moisture, but the majority develop their fragrances and flavors best when they are subjected to rather dry conditions; therefore, apply water with discrimination. Newly transplanted herbs and young plants need more attention in this respect than established plantings.

Should herbs be fertilized during the summer? The majority of true herbs require no fertilization. Feeding induces rank growth but does not favor the production of the essential oils which give them their flavor and fragrance.

Can any nonhardy herbs be kept successfully over the winter in a cold frame? Thyme, lavender, sage, and other "hardy" herbs that are often susceptible to winterkill can be kept during the winter in a cold frame. Very tender subjects, like rosemary, pineapple sage, scented geraniums, and lemon-verbena, must be kept in a temperature safely above freezing.

HARVESTING, CURING, AND STORING

Should herbs be washed before drying? What is a safe insecticide to use on these plants? Washing is not needed unless foliage is mud-spattered. A rotenone or pyrethrum insecticide is recommended.

How shall I cure herbs properly in order to retain their flavor? Dry as quickly as possible in a warm, airy, well-ventilated place, *without exposure to sun.*

How does one cure herb leaves for drying? Pick them just before the plants begin to flower, any time during the day after the dew has disappeared. Tie in bundles, each of a dozen stems or so. Hang in an airy, warm, but not sunny place. When they are completely dry and crisp, strip off their leaves and put in tight jars. The leaves may also be stripped fresh, right after cutting, and placed in shallow screen-bottomed trays until dry.

When should herb seeds be harvested?   When they have matured, and before they fall naturally from the plants.

How should herb seeds be dried?   Collect the heads or seed pods and spread them in a tray made of screening, or in a thin layer on a cloth in a warm, well-ventilated room. Turn them frequently. At the end of a week or so, they will be dry enough for threshing.

What is the best method of storing dried herbs?   In airtight containers.

How can seeds in quantity, such as caraway, be best separated from stems and chaff?   Remove as much of the stems as possible. Rub the heads or pods between the palms of the hands. If possible, do this outdoors where a breeze will help carry away the chaff. A kitchen strainer or screen is useful in the final cleaning.

What are "simples"?   Herbs that possess, or are supposed to possess, medicinal virtues.

What is the "Doctrine of Signatures"?   This was an ancient belief that plants, by the shape or form of their parts, indicated to man their medicinal uses. The spotted leaves of the lungwort showed that this plant was a cure for diseases of the lungs; the "seal" on the roots of Solomon's-seal promised the virtue of sealing or closing broken bones and wounds; and so on.

POTPOURRIS

What leaves and petals can be used for making potpourri?   Any leaves or petals that have a pleasing fragrance may be used. Some of the best are rose, lavender, lemon-verbena, jasmine, marigold, stock, mignonette, heliotrope, violet, geranium, rosemary, lemon-balm, mint, southernwood, santolina, pink, wallflower, and thyme.

I want to make a potpourri of rose petals from my garden. How can I do this?   Pick the rose petals (red holds its color best) when the flowers are in full bud but not completely blown. Spread them carefully on sheets of paper or strips of cheesecloth in a dry, airy room, away from the sun. Turn daily. Let them dry completely. This will take from a few days to a week. To each quart of petals, add 1 ounce of orrisroot. Spices such as cloves, cinnamon, coriander, and mace may be added, if desired, ½ teaspoon of each. Keep in an airtight earthen jar.

What is "wet potpourri" and how is it made?   Potpourri made by the wet method contains rose petals and the petals of any other fragrant flowers that are available. These are spread on cloths or papers to dry out partially. They are then packed in an earthenware jar with layers of table salt or coarse salt between. Add a layer of petals, then a sprinkling of salt, until the jar is filled. One ounce of orrisroot or violet powder is added, and, if desired, some cloves, allspice, and cinnamon. Put a weight on the petals and let them stand in the jar, covered, for several weeks before mixing. In addition to rose petals, lavender, lemon-verbena leaves, and geranium leaves are the most commonly used ingredients.

What is a "fixative," and for what is it used in potpourris? A fixative is used to retain the natural scent of leaves or petals and aids in preserving them. Orrisroot, violet powder, ambergris, and gum storax are common fixatives.

In making a sweet jar of flower petals, what can be used to keep the natural color of such flowers as delphinium, pansy, aconitum, and other colorful blooms? If the flowers are carefully dried, out of direct sunlight, they partially retain their color naturally. Orrisroot also seems to have a color-fixing effect.

HERB WHEELS

I would like to put plants around the spokes of an old wagon wheel that I have. How would you suggest doing this? A wagon wheel or oxcart wheel can be made the central feature of a small, formal herb garden. Select a level, sunny spot in the garden with enriched, well-prepared soil. Place the hub down into the ground and put a few plants

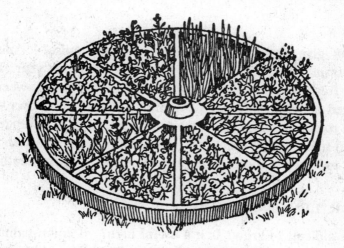

WHEEL GARDEN OF HERBS

of each variety in between the spokes. A narrow path edged with thyme can surround the wheel. Low-growing, compact plants are better for a wheel-planting than tall, straggly ones.

What culinary herbs would be best in a "wheel garden"? Thyme, chives, sage, parsley, mint, lemon-balm, French tarragon, winter savory, sweet basil, sweet marjoram, chervil. Or the wheel can be planted exclusively with low-growing varieties of thyme.

Would you suggest some fragrant herbs that would look well planted in an oxcart wheel? Lemon-verbena, mint, rosemary, rose geranium, sweet Cicely, lavender, and summer savory.

Specific Herbs

ANGELICA

How do you grow angelica and what is it used for? Sow in the summer as soon as the seed is ripe; thin out seedlings and transplant the following spring. The soil should be moist and fairly rich. Light shade is beneficial. The seeds are slow to germinate. The plant is biennial under some conditions, so it is better to sow a few seeds each year to maintain a supply. The stems and leafstalks are used for salads and candied to decorate confections; the seeds are used for flavoring and for oil. The plants tend to self-sow and the resulting seedlings can be transplanted.

ANISE

Can you give some information on growing anise? Anise (*Pimpinella anisum*) is an annual, so it must be sown each year. The seeds should be fresh because old seed will not germinate. Sow when the soil has warmed a little (about the beginning of May) in rows where the plants are to stand (anise does not transplant readily). Prepare the soil deeply and make it very fine. Sow in rows 15 inches apart and thin the plants out to 9 inches apart in the rows. Water in very dry weather.

BALM OR LEMON-BALM

Is balm difficult to grow? Is it a useful herb? Lemon-balm (*Melissa officinalis*) is a hardy perennial of easy culture. It can be grown from seeds sown in prepared soil in July or August; the seedlings are transplanted, when large enough, to their flowering quarters. It can be propagated by division in the spring, but this is hardly necessary as it self-sows prodigiously. Any ordinary garden soil is satisfactory. The leaves are used for seasoning, particularly in liqueurs. They are also used for salads and for potpourris.

BASIL (OCIMUM)

Can you give me information on growing basil? When should I sow the seeds? Seeds are sown outdoors after settled warm weather has arrived; or they are started indoors in April and the seedlings are transplanted outdoors later. Allow 12 inches between plants. Basil yields abundantly. When cut, it repeatedly sends out new growth. Plants can be lifted in the fall and potted for winter use if desired. Grow under lights or in a sunny window.

Sweet Basil

BORAGE (BORAGO OFFICINALIS)

Is borage annual or perennial? Can it be grown from seed? It is an annual, easily grown from seed in any good garden soil. Sow in the spring when all danger of frost is past. The seedlings can be transplanted if care is exercised, but the plants are better if grown undisturbed. About 15 inches should be allowed between plants.

CAMOMILE

Is Anthemis nobilis useful as an herb? Yes, indeed. This is the old-fashioned Roman camomile, with finely cut fragrant leaves and white daisy-like flowers, which are used in making a medicinal tea. It is also used as a ground cover.

CARAWAY (CARUM CARVI)

How is caraway grown?   From seeds sown outdoors in late May in rows 2 feet apart. The plants are thinned to about 9 inches apart. The first year low-growing plants are formed; the second year seeds are produced; then the plants die. Seed is most abundantly produced if the soil is not too rich. Do not water much, as this tends to keep the stems soft and causes the blossoms to fall before setting seed. Dry, sunny weather favors this crop.

CHERVIL (ANTHRISCUS CEREFOLIUM)

How is chervil grown?   From seeds sown in the spring where the plants are to grow. Thin plants to stand 9 inches apart. Light shade is beneficial. Chervil is an annual. A second sowing can be made in early summer.

CHIVES (ALLIUM SCHOENOPRASUM)

Can chives be grown from seeds or must I buy plants?   They can be grown from seeds sown outdoors early in the spring (but buying a plant is much easier). Thin the little plants to about ½ inch apart. They are hardy perennials, multiply rapidly, and need little attention. Divide every second year. They like a moderately moist soil.

CLARY

Is clary difficult to grow?   Clary (*Salvia sclarea*) is a biennial and dies after flowering. Sow seeds in early spring; thin to 6 inches apart; as the plants develop, pull out every other one. Those removed can be dried. The plants bloom and set seeds the second year. A rich soil is advantageous.

CORIANDER (CORIANDRUM SATIVUM)

Is it easy to grow coriander seed?   Yes. Sow (thinly) in the spring in well-drained, average soil and in a sunny position. Thin to stand 9 or 10 inches apart. Plants and fresh seeds are unpleasantly scented, but ripe seeds become very fragrant as they dry.

COSTMARY

How is costmary grown? Propagate it from seeds or by root division. Plant in full sun or very light shade. Space plants about 3 feet apart. Lift and replant every third year. A freely drained soil is needed. (The botanical name is *Chrysanthemum balsamita.*)

Dill

DILL (ANETHUM GRAVEOLENS)

How do you grow dill? Dill is a fast-growing annual that matures in about 70 days. Sow in early spring in well-prepared soil, in rows 2 feet apart, where the plants are to remain. The plants grow about 3 feet tall and make a good-sized bush. Thin out the seedlings to 3 or 4 inches apart at first; later give a final thinning so that they stand a foot apart. Later sowings can be made.

DITTANY OF CRETE

What is dittany of Crete and how is it grown in the herb garden? It is *Origanum dictamnus.* Increase it by seeds or cuttings. It is not hardy where winters are cold and must be wintered indoors in pots. A sandy soil, perfect drainage, and full sun are needed.

FENNEL

Is there a perennial fennel that grows 10 feet tall? The common fennel (*Foeniculum vulgare*) has escaped to the wild in the South and grows 8 feet in height. In colder climates, fennel is less tall, rarely reaching 4 feet, and is usually grown as an annual.

How is Florence fennel grown?   As an annual. Seeds are sown in the spring where the plants are to mature. The seedlings are thinned out to 6 inches apart. The plants mature in about 60 days.

FOXGLOVE (DIGITALIS PURPURIA)

Is the foxglove a perennial?   No, a biennial, although occasionally a plant will persist for 3 years. Sow seeds each spring. They need a well-drained soil that is deep and fairly moist.

Can foxglove be grown in partial shade?   Yes, if you are growing it for its decorative effect; but when raised commercially for drug purposes, it must be grown in full sun, as the valuable alkaloid does not develop satisfactorily in shade-grown plants.

GARLIC (ALLIUM SATIVUM)

Will garlic live over the winter?   It is often treated as an annual since it is the young bulblets at the base of the plant that are used in cooking. If the winters are not too severe, and if winter cover is given properly, garlic can be treated as a perennial.

GINGER

Can ginger root be grown in New York State?   Common ginger (*Zingiber officinale*) is a tropical plant adapted for culture only in warm climates, or in pots as a house plant in the North. The wild-ginger (*Asarum canadense*) is a native of our own rich northern woodlands. It responds to cultivation if given a rich, rather moist soil. There is also *Asarum europaeum,* a good ground cover because of its evergreen foliage.

HYSSOP (HYSSOPUS OFFICINALIS)

What are the cultural requirements of hyssop?   Give this perennial full sun or light shade, and a warm, freely drained well-limed soil. Allow about a foot between plants. Trim plants back after flowering. Hyssop is easily propagated by seeds, cuttings, or root division.

LAVENDER (LAVANDULA)

What is the care and use of lavender? Lavender grows well in any well-drained soil that is not too acid and in a dry, sunny place. Protect in winter with evergreen boughs; but, even with protection, plants 3 years old or more have a way of dying back in winter. Cut dead branches back in the spring after new growth near the base is fairly strong. It is best propagated from cuttings of the season's growth taken in the late fall or early spring. The plants are grown for ornament and fragrance. The flowers are used in perfumes, aromatic vinegar, sachets, and are tied into bundles for use in linen closets, etc.

How can I make lavender plants bloom? They give much more prolific bloom, with better fragrance, if grown in a light, well-drained soil that is high in lime content. Rich or heavy soils encourage foliage growth rather than bloom.

When should lavender flowers be harvested? Just as soon as they are fully open.

Can lavender grow and live over winter as far north as Boston? *Lavandula angustifolia* should, if given good winter protection.

Do you have to protect thyme and lavender in winter, and how? The true lavender, *Lavandula angustifolia,* is hardier than others of its kind. However, it prefers a sheltered spot. Both lavender and thyme die during the winter because of excessive moisture rather than cold. Marsh hay or evergreen boughs are good mulches. It is safer, if there is any question about the drainage, to winter both of these plants, in the North, in a cold frame.

How can I start lavender from seed? Seeds are rather slow to germinate and the tiny plants grow slowly. Start seeds indoors in early spring and set out the new plants after all danger of frost is past. Do not allow them to bloom the first year by cutting off buds as soon as they appear. Protect them through their first winter by placing them in a cold frame, if possible. A well-drained soil is essential to success.

Can I propagate lavender from cuttings? Take 2-inch shoots off the main stems and branches in late fall or early spring, each with a "heel" (or portion of older wood) attached to its base. Cut the heel clean. Remove lower leaves for about 1 inch from the base. Insert in well-packed sand, and keep the sand moist. Slight bottom heat will help rooting. While roots are not more than ½ inch long, put in small pots in a mixture of half sand and half soil. Keep in a cool greenhouse for the winter if they are fall-made cuttings, or in a cold frame if they are spring-made cuttings.

LEMON-BALM. See Balm.

LEMON-VERBENA

How is lemon-verbena grown? Lemon-verbena (*Aloysia triphylla*) is a tender shrub which in cold climates must be taken in for the winter. Cut plants back in the fall; water just enough to keep them from drying out. In February, bring into the light, in a cool temperature. Repot and set out again in the garden when the danger of frost is past.

When should cuttings of lemon-verbena be made? In the fall when the plants are trimmed back before being brought inside; or in the spring when new growth is made. Give the same treatment as advised for cuttings of lavender.

LOVAGE (LEVISTICUM OFFICINALE)

Is lovage suitable for a tiny herb garden? Hardly. It is a perennial 6 or 7 feet tall, and plants need to be spaced about a yard apart.

What soil and culture is needed to grow the herb lovage that has the flavor of celery? Propagate by seeds sown in early fall, or by root division in the spring. Provide a rich, moist soil in full sun or light shade.

MARJORAM

Can you grow in the house over the winter a plant of marjoram dug from an herb garden? If you refer to sweet marjoram (*Origanum majorana*), this is the only way to keep it for another year in cold climates. It is a tender perennial, sensitive to frost. Pot the plant in September, before there is any danger of frost, and let it get accustomed to its new quarters before bringing it indoors. Cuttings can be rooted in September, keeping the young plants indoors also. It is often grown as an annual.

In what soil and situation, and how far apart, should sweet marjoram plants be set? Give light, well-drained soil, slightly acid or neutral; full sun; space 9 or 10 inches apart. This is a tender perennial that may be grown as an annual. Sow seed in the spring. Seeds are slow to germinate.

Is there any hardy marjoram? Yes, what is known as wild marjoram, *Origanum vulgare,* a hardy perennial native of Europe and sometimes a weed in eastern North America. It has long been used as an essential plant in the herb garden, having aromatic leaves.

MINT (MENTHA)

What are the best culinary mints? Is there a market for them? The most common culinary mint is spearmint (*Mentha spicata*), but perhaps the most refreshingly flavorful is peppermint (*Mentha piperita*). *Mentha requienii* is a creeping, tiny-leaved mint with a powerful mint flavor that is used to flavor the liqueur *crème de menthe.* It is not winter-hardy in most northern regions. Apple mint (*Mentha suaveolens*) has hairy foliage and is especially decorative in its variety 'Variegata', sometimes listed as pineapple mint. For information on commercial growing, see the following question. You might also write the Herb Society of America, 300 Massachusetts Avenue, Boston, Massachusetts 02115.

What is the culture of peppermint? How is oil extracted from it? Peppermint grows best in deep, rich, humus-rich soil which is open and well drained. The runners are planted in spring, 2 to 3 feet apart, in shallow trenches. Keep well cultivated and free from weeds. When in full bloom the plants are cut and cured like hay. The oil is extracted by distillation with steam. For information concerning commercial cultivation write the Superintendent of Documents, U.S. Government Printing Office, Washington, D.C. 20402 for bulletins of the U.S. Department of Agriculture.

PARSLEY (PETROSELINUM CRISPUM)

Can parsley be dug in the fall and potted for winter use in the home? Yes. Usually a biennial, it is propagated by seed, best sown in early spring in a pot indoors on a warm window sill. Seed is very slow to germinate.

POT-MARIGOLD (CALENDULA)

What is pot-marigold? What is it used for? Is it hard to grow? *Calendula officinalis*—one of our most useful decorative annuals. As an herb, the flower heads were used for seasoning and coloring butter. It thrives best in cool weather. Sow outdoors in early spring. Transplant or thin 12 inches apart. Sow again about July 1 for a fall crop. The plants from this sowing will grow on into late fall and will survive light frost. The plants and flowers do best in cool weather and tend to sulk in midsummer in very hot, muggy climates.

Rosemary

ROSEMARY (ROSMARINUS OFFICINALIS)

What is the best way to grow rosemary? Rosemary is a tender shrub, not hardy in the North; but as a pot subject, it may be plunged outdoors in a sunny, sheltered spot during the summer, and kept during the winter in a cool, light room. Pot in well-drained soil to which a sprinkling of lime has been added. Propagate by cuttings.

What is the best protection for rosemary in this location? (Illinois.) It is a tender shrub and must be brought in for the winter in cold climates. If there is not space for so large a plant, make a few cuttings, which will root readily in moist sand and be ready to set out in the spring.

RUE

Is rue hardy in northern gardens? Could you give its culture? Rue (*Ruta graveolens*) is hardy to Long Island, New York. It will not winter over outdoors in very severe climates, so it is much safer to keep it indoors during the winter. It is easily grown from cuttings or seeds sown early in the spring in rows 18 inches apart. Thin seedlings to 8 inches apart and remove every other one. Keep the soil well cultivated. The leaves can be used whenever they are large enough. Any ordinary garden soil is satisfactory.

SAGE

Which kind of sage is used for culinary use? *Salvia officinalis*.

I have been unsuccessful in growing sage. What are its needs? Sage enjoys a sweet, well-drained, light sandy soil. Sow seeds in very early spring or in August; or set out good-sized plants in early spring. Sage is not difficult. Give very little water and cultivate during the early part of the season. In spring, give a light dressing of bone meal. Cut back the previous season's growth. Sage is easily propagated by means of cuttings.

Can sage planted from seed be used and dried the first year it is planted? Yes. Don't strip the whole plant bare, however. Take only the largest leaves, or a branch here and there.

When is the best time to "pick" sage; and what is the best method of curing it? Harvest in late summer. Cut shoots before they bloom, tie into bundles, and hang up; or strip leaves and place loosely in shallow trays in a warm, airy place, not exposed to the sun.

SALAD BURNET (POTERIUM SANGUISORBA)

Is salad burnet a good herb for the herb garden? Yes, it is easily grown and is often a weed. Usually perennial in habit, frequently found in dry, gravelly fields or pastures, it is used in salads or iced drinks. Salad burnet is propagated by seeds or division of the plant. Its leaves have a cucumber flavor.

SAVORY

What kind of soil and culture does savory need? There are two kinds of savory: summer savory (annual; *Satureja hortensis*) and winter savory (perennial; *S. montana*). Both grow best in a rather poor but well-limed soil, in an exposed sunny site. The annual kind is considered better than the perennial. The seeds are very small and are best sown indoors in pots and barely covered. Watering is done by immersing the pot in water, as the seeds wash out easily. Seedlings are set out when all danger of frost is over. Set seedlings in rows, 8 inches between plants, 15 inches between rows. The perennial sort can be handled in the same way.

SWEET CICELY (MYRRHIS ODORATA)

What are the garden requirements for growing sweet Cicely? Sow seed in early fall, in well-drained average soil, and in light shade. When plants are mature, they should stand 18 to 20 inches apart. It is a hardy perennial and may be increased by root division.

SWEET FLAG

I want to grow sweet flag in my herb garden. Does it need full sun? Full sun is not necessary for *Acorus calamus,* but it must have moist soil. It is really a waterside plant and is propagated by division of rhizomes.

SWEET WOODRUFF

What conditions in the garden does sweet woodruff (Asperula odorata) need? An open, rather moist soil, where drainage is good, and shade or partial shade. It is a fine perennial ground-cover plant in the right location. The leaves are used to give May wine its special flavor.

TARRAGON (ARTEMISIA DRACUNCULUS)

What soil does tarragon need? Shade or sun? Almost any well-drained garden soil. Sun preferred, but it will endure light shade.

Will you give me information in order to grow tarragon? Tarragon, a hardy perennial, needs a well-drained soil, moderately rich, with considerable lime. It does best in a lightly shaded location. This plant is propagated by stem or root cuttings, or by division. Stem cuttings are taken any time during the summer, rooted in sand, and planted out. Root cuttings or divisions can be set out in early spring, 12 inches apart. Do not use chemical fertilizer to force growth, as the quality of the leaves is affected by a too-rich diet.

THYME (THYMUS)

I would like to grow thyme for seasoning. Will it stand our severe winters? (Western New York.) There are many varieties of the common thyme that may be used in the herb garden. The greatest menace to thyme during the winter is not so much cold as wetness. Wet crowns, caused by snow, will winter-kill. One of the means of preventing this is to grow thyme on rather poor soil, containing gravel or screened cinders. Do not feed in summer to force growth, and do not cut tops after September 1. A cold frame is an excellent place to keep thyme over the winter, where it will be dry. Otherwise, covering the plants with boxes to keep the snow off will help. Be certain their position is well drained.

How can I grow common thyme? What soil? Shade? Sun? (Massachusetts.) It is best grown on a light, well-drained soil. If the soil tends to be heavy, work in screened cinders or gravel. Seeds can be sown in early spring outdoors, or earlier in pots indoors. Transplant seedlings 6 inches apart. When growth is advanced, do not water much; omit fertilizer, as this tends to force soft growth that will winter-kill. Do not cut foliage after September 1, as this depletes vitality. Winter protection is given by covering with light evergreen boughs, or by using brushwood with a light covering of marsh or salt hay. Lift and divide every 2 or 3 years. Grow in full sun.

Will you name several creeping thymes for planting in steps and paths? Mother-of-thyme (*Thymus serpyllum*); caraway thyme (*T. herba-barona*); woolly thyme (*T. pseudolanuginosus*); common thyme (*T. vulgaris*).

WATERCRESS (NASTURTIUM OFFICINALE)

How could I grow watercress for table use in my home garden that has no water? Watercress is a plant of running water, growing in the edge of clear, fresh streams. It may be grown in a moist spot in the garden, and the plants will last for a time in such a location if it is shady, but they will not live through the winter unless covered with water. They become true perennials only when grown in running water. As an alternative, you can grow the garden cress, or pepper-grass, *Lepidium virginicum*. This is an annual and furnishes salad in 3 to 4 weeks. Sow seed thickly in shallow drills, 12 inches apart. Make 2 sowings, 2 weeks apart in the spring, and 2 sowings in August. Another cress is the winter or upland cress (*Barbarea verna*), a biennial with leaves similar in appearance and flavor to watercress.

Rock Gardens

PLANNING

We are undecided about whether to build a rock garden. What do you think?   Can you fit this kind of garden properly into your home landscape without the effect being unnatural? Is there a bank or slope that could be utilized in making the garden? Have you access to natural rock material that could be used? If the area is all level, is there a section where low, natural rock outcroppings could be simulated? The extent of the garden will be determined by the time, labor, and money that can be spent on it. A rock garden is costly to build and usually time-consuming to maintain. These are the facts that need to be considered in deciding to build—or not to build.

Will I have as much color in a rock garden as in other kinds of gardens?   The floral display will be concentrated between early spring and mid-June. From then on your enjoyment will come mostly from pleasing mats and mounds and spreading foliage effects; these are decidedly worthwhile.

How can I best fit a rock garden into my property?   Use, if you have it, a somewhat steep slope, not overhung by foliage. A natural ledge of porous rock, of acceptable weathered appearance and provided with deep fissures, is ideal. Where such a ledge lies buried, it pays to expose and use it.

What exposure is best for a rock garden?   For easy-to-grow, sun-loving plants, such as many sedums, pinks, and rock-cresses, any exposure but a northern one. For gardens containing more finicky, choicer plants, and if it is along a building or a fence, an eastern exposure; otherwise, an open slope facing east or northeast. If you're deciding between southern and northern slopes, choose the latter.

Is there a rock-garden organization?   Yes, the American Rock Garden Society, Box 183, Hales Corners, Wisconsin 53130.

SOIL AND FERTILIZER

Should the rock-garden soil mixture be acid or alkaline? Some rock plants insist upon acid soil; others insist on alkaline. But most will do with an approximately neutral soil; therefore, it is best to provide this kind of mixture throughout, and then to acidify or alkalize special areas for particular plants.

Do all rock-garden plants need a specially prepared soil? No. Many robust, easy-to-grow plants, such as most sedums, pinks, and rock-cresses, will thrive in soil that would suit other garden plants. But in sharply drained places even these will be helped by an addition of some peat moss to help retain moisture in the summer.

What is a good average rock-garden mixture? Approximately 1 part each of good garden loam, leafmold, peat moss, sand, and fine gravel (preferably ⅛-inch screen). The mixture should be gritty. It should let surface water penetrate promptly, but should be retentive enough to hold a reasonable supply of moisture.

What depth of prepared soil is desirable in a rock garden? About 1 foot. For gardens made above the surrounding grade, there should be, underneath, another foot of a coarse mixture of rubble and retentive ingredients, such as peat moss, to act as a sponge.

In a rock garden is it necessary to provide the great depth of drainage that I read about in books? For gardens laid above the grade—no. In sunken gardens or in low-lying parts, unfailing provision must be made to prevent stagnant moisture below. In a dry summer climate, we must think of drainage in reverse as well—of retaining some moisture below, which later will find its way back to the surface.

I have a rock garden at the side of my house and would like to rearrange it. Can you make any suggestions concerning soil preparation and enrichment? It should be deeply dug and a liberal amount of peat moss should be added. Also, incorporate cinders or coarse pebbles or rubble, leafmold, well-rotted manure or compost, and a little bone meal or superphosphate.

What is the best fertilizer to use for rock-garden plants, and when should I put it on? The majority of rock-garden plants should not be heavily fed; rich feeding causes soft growth, which invites disease and leaves the plants subject to winterkill. Mix in bone meal or superphosphate and leafmold with the soil when preparing it, and in early spring add to established plantings a topdressing containing superphosphate or bone meal mixed with soil and leafmold.

CONSTRUCTION

What type of rock is best for rock gardens? Any porous, weathered rock that will look natural in place. It is all the better if it is deep-fissured. Use only one kind of rock throughout the garden.

What about tufa rock? No rock is more acceptable to a wide diversity of plants than a soft, porous grade of tufa. But because of its glaring, bony color in sunny places, it is not an attractive-looking material. In shade, and moisture, it quickly accumulates mosses and then becomes very beautiful.

Are large rocks desirable, or will small ones do as well? Construction should simulate nature. Therefore, in gardens, large or small, use rocks as large as you can handle; or match smaller ones together in such manner that they will create an effect of large masses.

Can you give me a few pointers on the placing of rocks? Embed the rockwork deeply enough to create an effect of natural outcroppings. Leave no lower edges exposed to betray superficial placing. Have the several rock masses extend in parallel directions and carry out this principle even with the lesser rocks. Match joints and stratifications carefully. Try to get the rhythm of natural ledges and outcroppings.

How shall I build a rockery in a corner of my level lawn? In the foreground of corner shrubbery, create the effect of a smoothish, shelved outcropping with several broad, low shelves. Push this arrangement back far enough for the shrubs to mask the sheer drop behind.

How should I arrange a rock garden and pool in the center of a small lawn without a natural elevation of rock? Create the effect of one large, flattish, or somewhat humped rock, broken, so as to provide two or more broad crevices for planting. Locate the pool, somewhat off center, immediately against this rock effect.

What is featherock? This is a pumice rock quarried in California and only about one eighth the weight of native stone. It is often used in rock gardens or on patios, and is easily cut and even hollowed out to make soil pockets for small rock plants. Some garden centers have it or can obtain it from California.

PLANTING AND CULTURE

When is the best time to plant rock gardens? If pot-grown plants are available and you can arrange to water and shade them carefully, planting may be done almost any time from the spring to early autumn. Spring is a proper season everywhere. In moderately cold climates (as in lower New York State), September and October are also good months.

What rock-garden plants should one set out in early spring? Any of the sedums, pinks (dianthus), dwarf phlox, primroses, bellflowers, and saponarias as well as most any other rock plants.

I am planting a rock garden. What distance between the plants will be necessary? Much will depend upon the kind of plants you are using. If they are spreading kinds, such as cerastium, phlox, helianthemum, the sedums, thyme, and dianthus, set the plants about 12 inches apart. Plants that spread more slowly, such as primula, sempervivum, saxifraga, candytuft, arenaria, aubrieta, douglasia, *Anemone pulsatilla,* and the dwarf achilleas, plant 6 to 8 inches apart.

How deep should rock plants be set in the ground? Most form a spreading top that either roots as it spreads or grows directly from a central root system. The crown of the plant must not be covered. Dig a hole with a trowel; gather the loose tops in your hand; hold the plant at the side of the hole, the crown resting on the surface, the roots extending into the hole while held in position; firm the soil around the roots. When the hole is filled, the crown should be resting on the surface. A good watering will then help establish it.

The soil on the slopes in my rock garden keeps washing out, especially after planting. How can I prevent this? If a considerable stretch is exposed, set in a few good-sized rocks at irregular intervals and tilt them so that their upper surfaces slope downward into the hill. Into the surface 2 inches deep, incorporate screened cinders mixed with peat or leafmold. Set the plants in groups 9 to 12 inches apart (depending on their size) and cover the spaces between the groups with peat or leafmold until the plants effect a covering.

What are the main items of upkeep in a rock garden? Weeding; thinning; repressing too-rampant growths; removal of old flower stalks; occasional division of robust plants; watering; winter covering. For the choicer, high-mountain plants, maintain a gravel mulch about their base and topdress with compost on steep slopes each spring.

When is the best time to trim and thin plants that begin to overrun a rock garden?   Cut back the running kinds any time during their growing period and especially after flowering.

Will you please discuss spring work in a rock garden?   Remove winter covering when all danger of frost is over. If there is danger of cold winds and some plants have started to grow, uncover gradually. Firm back into the soil any plants that have been loosened. Replant as may be necessary. Topdress with a mixture of 3 parts good soil, 1 part old, rotted manure or compost, leafmold, or peat moss, and 1 part coarse sand, with a 6-inch potful of bone meal added to each wheelbarrow load. When topdressing, work this down around the crowns of the plants and over the roots of spreading kinds by hand. If a dry spell occurs in the spring, give plants a good watering.

How should the rock garden be watered and how often?   With a fine sprinkler, so as to avoid washing the soil off the roots. The frequency of watering depends upon the type of soil, amount of slope, kind of plants, and whether they are established or are newly planted, the amount of shade, exposure, and of course weather. If dry spells occur in the spring and early autumn, watering should be done in a very thorough fashion; toward late summer, unless a very prolonged dry spell occurs, watering should be confined to such plants as primroses, globeflowers, and other moisture-lovers. Ripening and hardening of most rock plants are necessary if they are to winter over properly.

What is the best winter cover? When applied and when removed?   A single thickness of pine boughs or any narrow-leaved evergreen that will hold its leaves all winter after being cut. It is more quickly applied and removed than marsh hay. Apply after the surface has frozen solid. It is needed, not as a protection against frost, but against thawing of the soil. Remove when danger of very hard frost seems past. Just when is always something of a gamble.

Is marsh hay a good winter cover?   Yes, but it is not quickly removable in the spring. Use it lightly so that you don't invite mice and kindred vermin.

WHAT TO GROW

Will you please name a dozen foolproof rock-garden plants, stating flower color and season?   *Aurinia saxatilis* 'Citrinum' (lemon-yellow; May), *Arabis caucasica* (double-flowered, white; April to May), *Arabis procurrens* (white, April to May), *Campanula carpatica* (blue; May),

Ceratostigma plumbaginoides (blue; September to October), *Dianthus plumarius* (white and varicolored; June), *Phlox subulata* varieties (white, rose, dark rose, pink; May), *Sedum sieboldii* (rose; September to October), *Sedum album* (white; June), *Sedum kamtschaticum* (yellow; July), *Thymus serpyllum* 'Coccineus' (deep rose; July), and *T.s.* 'Albus' (white; June to July).

What are the best plants for a rockery for spring and midsummer bloom? For early spring: *Tulipa kaufmanniana* varieties, *Crocus* species, snowdrops, *Scilla sibirica,* and grape-hyacinths. Nonbulbous plants: *Arabis caucasica, Aubrieta deltoidea, Primula, Anemone pulsatilla, Armeria caespitosa, Aurinia saxatilis,* draba, epimedium, *Erysimum pulchellum,* and *Phlox subulata.* For midsummer bloom: *Dianthus plumarius, Campanula carpatica, Bellium bellidioides, Campanula cochleariifolia, Carlina acaulis, Globularia cordifolia, Lotus corniculatus, Dianthus knappii, Linum alpinum, Linaria alpina, Nierembergia caerulea,* penstemon, *Rosa chinensis* 'Minima,' *Santolina virens,* and *Ceratostigma plumbaginoides.*

Can you name 12 good perennials that will bloom in my rock garden at different periods? Creeping or moss phlox (*Phlox subulata* varieties), April to May; rock cress (*Arabis alpina*), May; basket of gold or yellow alyssum (*Aurinia saxatilis*), May; primroses (*Primula* species and varieties), April to June; cottage or grass pink (*Dianthus plumarius*), June; tussock bellflower (*Campanula carpatica*), June; speedwell (*Veronica incana* and *V. spicata*), June to July; *Allium senescens,* July; thyme (*Thymus serpyllum*), July; astilbe (*Astilbe chinensis* 'Pumila'), August; heather (*Calluna vulgaris* varieties), August to September; plumbago (*Ceratostigma plumbaginoides*), September to October. If you want a baker's dozen, add the heaths (*Erica* species and varieties), November to August.

Will you list late-flowering rock plants? *Ceratostigma plumbaginoides, Allium pulchellum, A. flavum, Calluna vulgaris* and its varieties, *Chrysogonum virginianum,* colchicums, autumn crocuses, *Saxifraga cortusifolia,* and *Sedum sieboldii.*

What are the fastest-growing plants for a rock garden? *Cerastium tomentosum, Ajuga reptans, Thymus serpyllum* and its varieties, *Lamium maculatum, L. m.* 'Album,' *Phlox subulata* and its varieties, *Arabis caucasica,* sedums, *Saponaria ocymoides, Lotus corniculatus, Campanula carpatica,* and *Asperula odorata.*

Should I try to fill my new rock garden quickly with fast-growing plants, or do it gradually, with smaller plants? By all means the latter.

Most people come to regret their first impatience, and wind up by rooting out the rampant growers and replacing them with choicer, small plants; they are so much more delightful.

Which flowers are best to plant in a small rock garden?   Such plants as the drabas, *Aubrieta deltoidea*, *Gypsophila repens*, *Myosotis alpestris*, *Nierembergia repens*, *N. hippomanica*, *Primula vulgaris*, *Armeria caespitosa*, *Veronica prostrata*, *Androsace sarmentosa*, *A. villosa*, and *Rosa chinensis* 'Minima'. Avoid the use of coarse creeping plants; they will overrun the garden.

Can you suggest some plants for a very steep rock garden?   *Thymus serpyllum* and its varieties, *Cerastium tomentosum*, *Sedum spurium*, *S. hybridum*, *Phlox subulata*, sempervivums, *Lotus corniculatus*, *Ceratostigma plumbaginoides*, *Muehlenbeckia axillaris*, and *Campanula carpatica*.

Which plants can I use for a very exposed location in a rock garden?   *Arabis caucasica*, *Anemone pulsatilla*, *Phlox subulata* varieties, *Veronica prostrata*, *Cerastium tomentosum*, *Dianthus deltoides*, *D. plumarius*, *Lamium maculatum*, *Aquilegia canadensis*, *A. vulgaris*, *Campanula carpatica*, and *Dicentra eximia*.

Can you suggest a few small, decorative plants to fill small crevices in rocks and tiny pockets? My garden is in full sun.   *Draba aizodes*, *Globularia repens*, *Sedum dasyphyllum*, *Sedum acre* 'Minus,' *Sedum anglicum*, and sempervivums (the tiny kinds).

Which are some good plants for shady corners in my rock garden for spring flowers?   *Anemone nemorosa* (several kinds), *Brunnera macrophylla*, *Chrysogonum virginianum*, *Epimedium niveum*, *Iris cristata*, *Phlox divaricata laphamii*, *Phlox stolonifera*, *Pulmonaria saccharata*, and *Saxifraga umbrosa*.

Which perennials, not over 10 inches in height, bloom between June 15 and September 15, and are suitable for a rock garden in shade?   *Chrysogonum virginianum*, *Corydalis lutea*, *Mitchella repens*, *Myosotis scorpioides*, *Sedum ternatum*, *S. nevii*, *Allium moly*, *Saxifraga cortusifolia*, *Arenaria montana*, *Gentiana asclepiadea*, *Cymbalaria muralis*, *Scilla chinensis*, and *Dicentra formosa* 'Alba.'

Which are some small summer-blooming plants for the shady rock garden?   *Astilbe chinensis* 'Pumila,' dwarf *Aster* varieties, *Chrysogonum virginianum*, *Cotula squalida*, *Mitchella repens*, *Sedum ternatum*, and *S. nevii*.

Which are the most hardy rock-garden plants that will grow in semishade?   Many primroses, epimediums, aubrietas, aquilegias, *Phlox di-*

varicata laphamii, Chrysogonum virginianum, Viola odorata, V. sororia, Vinca minor, Lysimachia nummularia, Sedum ternatum, Ceratostigma plumbaginoides, Asperula odorata, trilliums, erythroniums, and dodecatheons.

Will you name rock plants that will grow and bloom in the shade of a large oak tree? *Phlox divaricata laphamii, Dicentra eximia, Chrysogonum virginianum, Asperula odorata,* erythroniums, trilliums, *Gaultheria procumbens, Mitchella repens, Vinca minor, Lysimachia nummularia,* and *Primula veris.* Also many ferns would be suitable.

Can you name several plants which will grow between rocks of a patio in very sandy soil; preferably fast growers? *Arenaria verna, Thymus serpyllum* and its varieties, *Sedum acre, Dianthus deltoides, Muehlenbeckia axillaris, Mazus reptans,* and *Ajuga reptans.* Keep the soil reasonably moist.

Which rock plants require acid soil? Dwarf rhododendrons, azaleas, pieris, shinleaf, partridge-berry, lady's-slipper (*Cypripedium acaule*), erythroniums, galax, and shortia.

Will you name a dozen or so of the choicest and most unusual plants that I might grow in my rock garden? *Androsace lanuginosa, Androsace sarmentosa, Armeria juniperifolia, Campanula cochleariifolia* 'Alba', *Dianthus gratianopolitanus, D. pavonius, Saxifraga burseriana, S. irvingii,* and many, many others.

Will all kinds of rock-garden plants grow successfully in a garden without rocks? Yes, although many of them look better against or between rocks. Many can be grown in the foreground of a flower garden.

ALPINES

What is the best site for alpines? A gentle slope facing northeast or northwest.

What soil is best for alpines? One that is not too rich. A neutral, porous soil, well drained, and with grit and cinders to lighten it, will be satisfactory for most alpine plants.

Should I know a lot about alpines to have a good rock garden? No. You may use, more or less exclusively, plants from high, intermediate, or low altitudes. A good rock garden need not be filled with "highbrow" plants. It should afford a happy glimpse of nature's play with rocks and plants—whether it's in a moraine or on a roadside ledge.

Why are alpine plants so difficult to grow? Because the conditions prevailing in lowland rock gardens are so utterly different from those at or above timberline: the heavy winter pack of snow; the short summer; pure, crisp air; and chilly baths of mountain mist. One must learn gradually to devise acceptable equivalents or approximations to these conditions.

Can you name a few alpine plants that are not too difficult for a beginner to grow? The following high-mountain plants (not all strictly alpines) are suggested: *Armeria juniperifolia, Androsace lanuginosa, A. sarmentosa, Campanula cochleariifolia, Dianthus alpinus, Douglasia vitaliana, Gentiana acaulis,* and saxifragas.

What are the best alpine campanulas for the rock garden? *Campanula allionii, alpina, cochleariifolia, elatines, fragilis, lasiocarpa, portenschlagiana, poscharskyana, pulla, raineri,* and *tommasiniana.*

What winter care should be given to alpines? Cover lightly with evergreen boughs or salt hay after the ground is frozen, usually in December.

MORAINE GARDEN

Can you explain what a moraine garden is? How is it made? A moraine is constructed for the purpose of growing certain alpine plants from high altitudes. The garden contains little or no soil, the growing medium being mostly stone chips and shale. The important factor is water. The most complete moraines have cool water circulating below the growing medium so that the roots of the plants are in a cool, moist medium much as are alpines in their native habitats. A moraine can be built in a watertight basin 2 feet deep and of any length and breadth. A foot-thick layer of stones is laid in the bottom. The remaining space is filled with a mixture of 5 parts crushed stone (½ inch), 1 part sand, and 1 part leafmold. Water is supplied during the growing season through a pipe at the upper end and the surplus is drawn off by a pipe at the other end, 12 inches below the surface.

Will you give me a list of plants suitable for a moraine garden? Aethionema, androsace, *Arenaria montana, Dianthus sylvestris, Campanula glomerata, Silene acaulis,* and saxifragas. For others, consult *Rock Gardening* by H. Lincoln Foster, Houghton Mifflin Co., and *Rock Gardens* by George Schenk, Lane Book Company, Menlo Park, California.

PAVEMENT PLANTING

How are plants grown between the flagstones in a pavement? For the plants to succeed, the stones should be laid on sand overlying several inches of soil. Watering during hot, dry weather is very helpful.

How are plants planted between flagstones? Planting is first done as the flat stones are laid. When the spot for a plant is selected, the plant is set so that when the surface is leveled for the next flagstone, the top of the plant is resting at the correct level. You can also try sowing seeds between the stones in early spring or late fall.

Which plants are suitable for planting in a flagged walk? Those that will withstand much walking are *Festuca ovina glauca, Sagina subulata,* and *Tunica saxifraga.* Others to use are *Thymus serpyllum* varieties, *Alyssum montanum, Erinus alpinus, Veronica repens,* and *Lysimachia nummularia.*

WALL GARDENS

What exposure should a wall garden have? Eastern exposure. However, shade-loving plants such as ramonda, haberlea, *Saxifraga stolonifera,* English ivies, and certain ferns should have a northern exposure.

What is the best type of rock for a wall garden? For an informal effect, any natural, porous rock with a good facing surface; squarish pieces, such as one might use for an ordinary dry wall, are best. A good wall garden can be made of bricks.

How does one make a wall garden? Much like a dry retaining wall, but the joints are packed with prepared soil and the stones are tilted backward to keep the soil from washing out and to direct the rainwater toward the plant roots. To prevent squashing of roots, chink the horizontal joints with small pieces of stone. Place plants in position as the laying up proceeds and firm the soil well at the back of the wall.

What special upkeep does a wall garden need? Upkeep is reduced by using suitably compact, small, rock-hugging plants. Remove all old flower stalks. Pull out weeds and excess seedlings. Prune and thin so as to maintain a balanced distribution of planting effect. On top of the wall, provide a watering trench or trough and use it freely to prevent drying out in the summer.

How are plants planted in a wall? In a wall garden, building and planting are done at the same time. If the plants are located at the joints, the soil is packed in, the plant set, a little extra soil added, and then the stones are placed. Chips placed between the stones near the plants prevent them from sinking and squeezing the plants. If planting has to be done after building, the job is more difficult. The roots must somehow be spread out in a narrow space and the soil must be rammed in with a piece of stick. Don't plant fast-growing plants near slow-growing ones or the latter will be smothered.

In planting a retaining wall, place the plants irregularly, imitating the way they would grow among rocks in the mountains.

What summer upkeep is necessary for a rock wall?   Keep plants well watered and weeded. Spray if necessary.

Can you tell me what spring care should be given to a rockery made in an old stone wall?   Trim dead pieces off plants; fill washed-out cracks with new soil. Push heaved-out plants into the soil or take them out altogether and replant.

What winter cover should a wall garden have?   Stick a row of pine boughs into the ground thickly enough to provide shade from the brightest sun of winter. Or place a row of two-by-fours, slanting against the wall, and over them stretch a burlap cover. The pine boughs will be better-looking.

Which plants are particularly suitable for use in a rock wall?   All the sempervivums, *Sedum hybridum, coccineum, nevii,* and *sieboldii, Nepeta hederacea, Campanula carpatica, cochleariifolia,* and *rotundifolia, Silene caroliniana, Phlox stolonifera, Achillea ageratifolia,* and *Mazus reptans.*

Are wall gardens easy to maintain?   They are at their best in moist climates (England) where there are not long drought periods. If left unwatered in long summer droughts, many of the plants will die. They require more attention than other types of gardens, especially care in watering.

BULBS FOR A ROCK GARDEN

How should chionodoxa (glory-of-the-snow) be used in a rock garden?   Scatter the bulbs in groups of 2 dozen or more in various places among low ground covers. They may also be used effectively beneath shrubs that may form a background to the garden.

Will you give a list of crocuses suitable for a rock garden?   Spring-flowering: *Crocus flavus, biflorus, chrysanthus* and its varieties, *imperati, angustifolius, tomasinianus.* For autumn: *cancellatus, longiflorus, pulchellus, speciosus* and its varieties, *kotschyanus.*

Can you suggest some good daffodils for a rock garden?   The best kinds are the small species and their varieties, such as *Narcissus asturiensis, cyclamineus, triandrus* (angel's tears), *bulbocodium* (hoop-petticoat daffodil). The sweet jonquils and campernelles can also be used, such as *Narcissus jonquilla* and *N. odorus.*

Can you tell me kinds of tulips to plant in a rock garden and what conditions they need?   The best are the tulip species and their hybrids. These need well-drained soil and sunshine. Plant them about 6 or 7 inches deep. The following are among the best: *kaufmanniana, acuminata, clusiana* (lady tulip), *dasystemon, greigii, praecox, praestans, fosterana,* and *sylvestris.*

Which spring-flowering bulbs are suitable for a rock garden?   Squills, glory-of-the-snow, snowdrops, spring-snowflakes, crocuses, grape-hyacinths, miniature daffodils, dogtooth-violets, fritillaries, calochortuses, brodiaeas, and *Iris reticulata.*

When are small spring-flowering bulbs planted in a rock garden?   In late summer plant snowdrops, winter-aconites, autumn-flowering crocuses, and colchicums. Plant the small daffodils and crocuses in September and October.

I wish to plant a number of small bulbs in my rock garden. Should I dig up the other plants before planting the bulbs? How deep must I plant the bulbs?   Unless the soil needs improving, it is not necessary to remove the plants. Use a bulb trowel (a tool with a narrow concave blade), push it into the soil through the mat of plants, pull the handle toward you, and then push the bulb into the soil and smooth the plants back again. Plant these small bulbs in groups and closely together. The depth at which they are set should be roughly 3 times the depth of the bulb.

EVERGREENS IN A ROCK GARDEN

Which are some dwarf evergreens that can be used effectively in a rock garden? *Juniperus horizontalis* 'Wiltonii'; *Chamaecyparis obtusa* 'Nana'; *Buxus sempervirens* 'Suffruticosa'; *Chamaecyparis pisifera* 'Plumosa Aurea Nana'; *Calluna vulgaris* vars.; *Gaylussacia brachycera; Ilex crenata* 'Helleri'; *Pinus strobus* 'Nana'; *Tsuga canadensis* 'Cole'; *Erica* species and varieties, to name a few.

Can you tell me some evergreens for a rock garden which will withstand severe winter exposure? *Arctostaphylos uva-ursi; Chamaecyparis obtusa* 'Nana'; *Taxus cuspidata* vars.; *Juniperus communis* vars.; *Juniperus horizontalis* vars.; *Chamaecyparis pisifera* 'Filifera Nana'; *Picea abies* vars.; *Picea pungens* 'Glauca Procumbens'; *Pinus sylvestris* 'Pygmaea'; *Pinus mugo; Ilex glabra* 'Compacta'.

What soil does Daphne cneorum require? This is a much-debated question! Its success seems to depend mostly upon climate. It does better in cold climates (with a winter covering) than in warmer climates. Plant in a well-drained soil to which peat moss or some form of humus has been added, and away from the fiercest sun.

SHRUBS

Will you suggest some shrubs to use in a rock garden? *Rhododendron impeditum; Leucothoe fontanesiana* 'Nana'; *Berberis thunbergii* 'Crimson Pygmy'; *Calluna vulgaris* vars.; *Cotoneaster adpressa* 'Park Carpet'; *Cytisus procumbens; Euonymus fortunei* 'Gracilis'; *Ilex crenata* 'Green Cushion'; *Juniperus communis* 'Compressa'; *Lavandula officinalis; Pieris japonica* 'Pygmaea'; *Spiraea japonica* 'Alpina'; *Tsuga canadensis* 'Minima'.

Will you name a few small shrubs that look well in a small rock garden? *Spiraea decumbens, S. bullata, Cotoneaster microphylla, Berberis verruculosa, Ilex crenata* 'Helleri'. In part shade and an acid, humusy soil, 'Gumpo' azaleas, *Rhododendron kiusianum* and its varieties, and *R. racemosum* and its forms and hybrids should be satisfactory.

Which shrubby plants would make a good background for our rock garden along the side of the garage? In east to northeast exposures: rhododendrons, azaleas, mountain-laurel, pieris, Japanese holly, and *Mahonia aquifolium.* In sunnier exposures: *Berberis koreana, Symphoricarpos chenaultii,* and perhaps an upright yew.

SPECIFIC ROCK-GARDEN PLANTS

What is the proper treatment of a basket of gold alyssum which has grown "leggy"? It is best to raise new plants from seed. This plant does not usually last much longer than 2 to 3 years. It is inclined to rot away during hot summers. After flowering, cut off the fading flowers to prevent seeds from forming. Or let some seeds self-sow around the old plants. This plant's nomenclature has been changed from *Alyssum saxatile* to *Aurinia saxatilis.*

Does aubrieta remain in bloom for a long period? No. Its blooming season is short. However, it flowers in very early spring and is worthy of a place in the garden.

Are the plants called cinquefoils suitable for a rock garden? Can you suggest a few? Many cinquefoils (potentilla) are excellent; others are worthless weeds. *Potentilla nepalensis, tridentata,* and *villosa* are worth trying. Give them full sun and well-drained, gritty soil.

What is the best method to grow pinks in a rock garden? Dianthuses do best in a well-drained, sunny position. Do not make the soil very rich (most seem to do best in a slightly acid to near-neutral soil) and do not overwater them. They are good on gentle slopes, planted so that they can spread over the top of a rock, or in flat, well-drained pockets. Start with young, pot-grown plants if possible, and plant them out at about 9 inches apart. Some kinds die after a while, so it is best to keep raising a few fresh plants each year.

What kinds of dianthus do you suggest for a rock garden? *Dianthus deltoides* (maiden-pink), *plumarius* (grass-pink), *gratianopolitanus* (cheddar-pink), and *pavonius* (glacier-pink).

What can I do to make the bottle gentian, Gentiana andrewsii, grow? It appreciates a moist, semishaded situation, preferably on the edge of a pond, and a deep, humus-rich soil. Topdress in the spring with peat moss mixed with a little dried cow manure or compost.

Which irises are suitable for a rock garden? *Iris reticulata, gracilipes, pumila* (in many varieties), *dichotoma, cristata, cristata* 'Alba', *lacustris, tectorum,* and its cultivar 'Alba'.

What conditions do primroses need in a rock garden?   A rich, moist soil and a shady or semishady situation. Some, like *Primula pulverulenta*, grow best in almost boggy conditions along the sides of streams. Practically all need plenty of moisture. If very moist conditions cannot be given, grow them in the shade.

Will you suggest some primroses for a rock garden?   *Primula polyantha, veris* (the cowslip), *bulleyana, denticulata, frondisa,* and *japonica.*

What care should be given leontopodium raised from seeds?   The edelweiss likes a well-drained, limy soil, full of sun in the spring, semishade in the summer, and light protection in the winter. Either evergreen boughs or salt hay should be used, as leaves pack too hard and keep the plant waterlogged, which may result in rotting. From seed, they should bloom well the second year. Carry the plants over in a cold frame, in pots, the first year.

Will you name a few penstemons that would grow in my rock garden? Are they difficult to grow?   *Penstemon alpinus, heterophyllus, rupicola,* and *unilateralis.* These are not difficult. They require gritty soil and do not like a position that becomes sodden in the winter. They are not long-lived plants and in order to maintain them it is best to raise a few each year.

What soil is suitable for Phlox subulata?   Any light, well-drained garden soil.

Where does Phlox subulata grow wild?   In the eastern, western, and southern parts of the United States, on dry banks and in fields.

Do most of the western species of phlox require loose, rocky conditions in the eastern states?   Yes, they seem to do better under such conditions in the East.

What are some good kinds of phlox for a rock garden?   Some of the most suitable kinds, besides the various varieties of *Phlox subulata,* are *Phlox amoena, divaricata* (and its variety *laphamii*), *douglasii,* and *stolonifera.*

What is the best place in the rock garden for saxifragas? What kind of soil?   A partially shady situation facing east or west. The soil should be gritty, open, and well drained. Mix garden soil, leafmold, and stone chips, or screened cinders, in about equal proportion, and have a foot depth of this in which to plant. Limestone chips are also beneficial.

Which saxifragas are not too difficult to grow?   *Saxifraga paniculata, apiculata, cochlearis, rosacea* (a mossy type, requiring partial shade), *hostii, macnabiana,* and *moschata.*

How many species and varieties of rock-garden sedums are there? Approximately 200, but far fewer distinct and useful kinds are available in nurseries.

Which are the best sedums? *Sedum album, anglicum, brevifolium, caeruleum* (annual), *dasyphyllum, ewersii, kamtschaticum, lydium, nevii, oreganum, populifolium, pilosum, rupestre, sexangulare, sieboldii, spurium, ternatum, stoloniferum, hybridum,* and the self-sowing biennial *nuttallianum.*

I need information regarding the culture of sedums. Most are easily propagated from cuttings taken in the fall or spring. They root best in sand, either in flats or directly in cold frames. When well rooted, transfer them into small pots or put them directly into their permanent places in the garden. The location should ordinarily be sunny, the soil sandy and well drained. Western-America sedums prefer a semishaded position.

Are the sunroses (Helianthemum) hardy? Do they require much care? They are not very hardy; they thrive fairly well in the vicinity of New York but farther north they are doubtful subjects. They need no more care than ordinary rock-garden plants. Give them a well-drained soil in a sunny location. Protect them in winter with hay or evergreen boughs, and cut them back to within a few inches of their crowns in the spring to encourage fresh growth.

Wildflower Gardens

WOODLAND

What is the best location for a wildflower garden? This depends on the type of flowers to be grown. Some wildflowers grow naturally in woodlands, and others in a sunny meadow. Try to make the condition of your garden most like the one which the particular plants came from.

Should a wildflower garden be attempted in an ordinary backyard garden? Certainly. An informal sort of garden can be made, using the more common type of either woodland flowers or meadow flowers.

How can a woodland garden be planned and arranged? A woodland garden made for native plants should simulate natural wild conditions. There should be shade and semishade formed by trees that grow in the woods. The soil for most woodland plants should be rich with leafmold and slightly damp. The plants are best placed in natural-looking clumps around the base of the trees. A few rocks may be used as focal points and plants placed around them. If shade is too dense, lower branches of trees can be removed.

How does one go about starting a wildflower garden beginning with a piece of wild woodland in Vermont? It's just a small patch about ¼ acre. How do you get cardinal-flowers to grow in such a garden? You probably have a wildflower garden already in existence! Start by gradually replacing and replanting under and around trees, along paths, but you should go through one growing season to see what is worth keeping. Cardinal-flower (*Lobelia cardinalis*) likes the stream sides and will grow in partial shade almost in the water, although it sometimes thrives when transplanted to garden soil with less moisture.

Will bloodroot, trillium, and columbine grow under pine trees? If not, what will grow there? The plants mentioned grow well under oak trees. They will grow under pine trees if the shade is not too great, lower branches are removed, and the soil is loamy. Why not try partridge-berry for ground cover and also the club mosses? Plant Christmas fern and shield fern. Pipsissewa and shinleaf (*Pyrola elliptica*) will be dainty but difficult additions, as well as wintergreen (*Gaultheria procumbens*), lady's-slipper (*Cypripedium acaule*), and bunchberry (*Cornus canadensis*). Many worthy native plants are present and you will need a wildflower guide book (such as *A Field Guide to Wildflowers* by Peterson and McKenny; Houghton Mifflin Company) to help you identify them.

What are the best methods of growing wild plants under shady conditions? Try to create the conditions in which the plants grow naturally. The amount of shade, moisture, and kind of soil are all important. If under oak trees, you may plant most of the early spring flowers, such as bloodroots, Dutchman's-breeches, partridge-berry, hepatica, bishop's cap, violets, shinleaf, wood-betony, and many ferns and club mosses, such as shield fern, polypody, Christmas fern, spleenworts. The club mosses include ground-cedar, running-pine, and staghorn. The last, however, are very difficult to transplant.

What mulching materials are suitable for woodland wild plants? Fallen leaves, leafmold, wood chips, and evergreen boughs.

What soil and fertilizer should be used for wildflower planting? Generally speaking, the soil should approximate that in which the plants grow naturally. Woodland plants thrive in rich leafmold.

Many prefer slightly acid soil. No artificial fertilizer should be used; well-rotted compost is next best to natural leafmold.

Should the soil around wildflowers be cultivated? The weeds should be kept out, but the soil does not need cultivating.

What plants go well with mertensia, bloodroot, and Dutchman's-breeches, to fill in when their foliage dies down in late spring? Use Christmas fern or evergreen wood fern with mertensia and bloodroot; use spleenworts and grape ferns among the Dutchman's-breeches. These ferns do not have crowding habits and are almost evergreen. Their colors are good with the flowers mentioned.

Which wildflowers and trees can be established in dry, sandy, stony soil? Trees for dry, stony soil are the red-cedar (*Juniperus virginiana*) shadblow (*Amelanchier*), and the locust (*Robinia pseudoacacia*). Many shrubs will grow, such as bayberry, barberry, scrub oak, raspberries and blackberries, sumacs, blueberries. The blackhaw may assume the stature of a tree. Flowers include many of the flowers of the open field—daisies, asters, black-eyed Susans, pearly everlasting.

Do woodland wildflowers require any special care in planting? They need the same careful planting as do all flowers. Put them in well-prepared soil with enough room for the roots and do not crowd them. Tamp the soil firmly around them. Water. Mulch with leaves to duplicate their forest conditions.

My property is a gray birch grove. Which wildflowers can I plant in among the birches? Under your gray birches, you can grow speed-well (*Veronica officinalis*), violets, wild strawberries, pearly everlasting, pipsissewa, shinleaf, *Phlox divaricata,* rue and wood anemones, mertensia. Ferns: Christmas fern, spleenwort, and polypody; the lycopodiums (club mosses).

Can you suggest a group of native American wildflowers for planting in a wooded lot on home grounds? *Aralia nudicaulis, A. racemosa,* trilliums, *Dicentra eximia, Gillenia trifoliata, Shortia galacifolia, Tiarella cordifolia, Actaea pachypoda,* and *A. rubra.*

Which wildflowers will grow in a beech grove? Spring beauty (claytonia), wild columbine, harebells, hepatica, violets, mertensia, *Phlox divaricata, Trillium grandiflorum,* Jack-in-the-pulpit, red baneberry, the anemones, yellow lady's-slipper (if moist), Solomon's-seal, false Solomon's-seal, bloodroot. Ferns: among ferns, there are the walking and woods ferns.

Which wildflowers will grow in a woodland where there are hemlocks and oaks? A few are pink lady's-slipper, painted trillium, wood lily

(*L. philadelphicum*), trailing-arbutus, bellwort, *Iris verna,* wintergreen, purple-fringed orchis, wood anemone, partridge-berry, wood aster. Shrubs: rhododendron, azalea, and mountain-laurel.

MEADOW WILDFLOWER GARDEN

Can you give me some pointers on planning and setting out a meadow wild garden? The meadow where wildflowers are to be grown should be open, sunny, and preferably fenced with either a rustic fence or rock wall. The soil for common meadow flowers should be dry, porous, and preferably a little sandy. Most meadow flowers are easily grown from seed and then transplanted. Weeds should be kept away from the plants so that they are not choked out. Room should be allowed for them to reseed themselves and form natural-looking patches.

What are the general cultural requirements for growing meadow wildflowers in the garden? The conditions should be as much like those of a meadow as possible: full sun, plenty of room for the plants, and undisturbed conditions. The soil should be porous and loamy except for moist meadow plants.

What sun-loving wildflowers are suitable for rural garden planting to give color and succession of bloom? Crested iris and verbena (April to May); daisies and coreopsis (May and June); wild roses, penstemons, and California-poppy (June to July); butterfly-weed, harebell (*Campanula rotundifolia*) and blackberry-lily (July to August); purple cone flower and black-eyed Susan (August to September); blazing star, goldenrod, and many wild asters (September and October).

Which wild plants will grow well in a sunny meadow? Daisies, black-eyed Susans, the goldenrods, butterfly-weed, phlox, Joe-Pye-weed, hawkweed (devil's-paint-brush), yarrow, thistles, ironweed, lupine, pearly and sweet everlastings, tansy, chicory; New England, smooth, and New York asters, trumpet creeper and bush honeysuckle, Queen Anne's lace, wild sweet pea.

BOG GARDEN

What conditions are necessary for a bog garden? Is it different from water gardening? Generally a swampy piece of ground, not under water, but where at all times there is plenty of moisture, and it is usually too soft to walk upon. In water gardens, the plants are immersed or floating. In bog gardens, the plants grow free above the soil.

What is the most practical way I can simulate bog-garden conditions in my home garden so I can grow sundews (Drosera sp.), pitcher-plant (Sarracenia purpurea), bog orchids, marsh-marigold, and other wetland plants? Pick a sunny area about 6 feet long and 3 to 4 feet wide, excavate about 2 feet deep, and line with heavy-duty polyethylene. You can make a few perforations for drainage, but usually the plastic is severed soon enough by rodents, tree roots, and general wear and tear. Replace about a quarter of the soil; the remainder is to be sphagnum peat moss. Mix the two together thoroughly, tamp solidly, and water thoroughly. Other methods for making bog gardens include the conversion of leaky fish ponds by filling with a soil-peat-moss mixture and burying various discarded containers such as washtubs or bathtubs (and for a quite small bog garden, even a dishpan) to their rims.

Which plants grow in wet marshland? Swamp milkweed, marsh-marigold, Joe-Pye-weed, yellow flag, blue flag, cardinal-flower, loose-strife, forget-me-not, sedges, marshmallow, water-plantain, yellow- and white-fringed orchids, and many more.

Are tall-growing wildflowers, such as hibiscus, cardinal-flower, and lobelia, suitable for the wild garden? Yes. They are best grown in the bog garden or in a moist border.

Which wildflowers are suitable for planting near a naturalistic pool in sun and shade? *Iris pseudacorus, Iris prismatica, Aruncus sylvestris, Vernonia noveboracensis, Anemone canadensis, Asclepias incarnata, Calla palustris, Caltha palustris, Chelone glabra, Gentiana andrewsii, Hypoxis hirsuta, Lilium superbum, Parnassia glauca.*

Which wildflowers do you suggest for the edge of a slow-moving, shaded stream? Cardinal-flower, boneset, turtle-head, great lobelia, fringed and bottle gentians, forget-me-not, monkey-flower, mertensia, blue flag (iris), marsh-marigold, American globeflower. A little distance from the stream, but where they profit by some of the moisture, you can grow yellow lady's-slipper, trilliums, yellow adders-tongue, fringed polygala, Solomon's-seal, false Solomon's-seal, foamflower, Jack-in-the-pulpit, white violet, rue anemone (*Anemonella thalictroides*).

PROPAGATION OF WILDFLOWERS

Is it best to grow wildflowers from seed, or to buy the plants? Choice plants may be started from seed. Plants of many kinds may be purchased.

Which wild native plants may be started from seed and how is this

done?   Practically all of the field flowers, such as asters, milkweeds, goldenrods. Also columbine, pale corydalis, climbing fumitory (vine), celandine-poppy, bloodroot, early saxifrage, bishop's cap, foamflower, and painted cup. The seeds are best started in flats, in a cold frame, or in a protected part of the garden. Sow in early winter or spring, using a light, sandy leafmold or peat-moss mixture.

What is a good all-around soil mixture in which to sow wildflower seeds?   One half ordinary garden soil, ¼ leafmold or peat moss, and ¼ coarse sand, thoroughly mixed.

How long can wildflower seeds be kept before planting?   Much depends on what kind they are. Some, such as trillium, bloodroot, and others that are produced in a more or less pulpy berry or pod, should be sown immediately before they dry at all; many other harder and thinner kinds can be kept for 5 or 6 months. A good general rule is to sow as soon as the seed is ripe, regardless of the time of the year. Germination is often erratic.

Which kinds of wildflower seeds can be sown in a cold frame late in the fall?   Practically all of the perennial kinds, especially those which flower in midsummer or later.

I want to have thousands of beautiful wildflowers all over my meadow. Can't I get them by strewing handfuls of seed in all directions —a "wildflower mixture," you know, like I see advertised in the catalogs?   You can try—and some success can result, depending on the quality of the seed, its freshness, soil conditions in your meadow, and the weather—but most likely, only the commonest, such as daisies and goldenrod, will catch hold and grow. Raise the kinds you want from seed sown in a place where they won't be overrun, and set the plants out in the meadow when they're big enough to hold their own.

What wildflowers self-sow so quickly that they become pests if planted in a garden?   Goldenrod, cattails, wild carrot, jewel-weed, ironweed, black-eyed Susan, sunflower, asters, golden ragwort, mullein, daisy, and many others.

I am not a botanist but like to identify wildflowers. Can you give me one or two references of well-illustrated books that would help me identify wildflowers from illustrations?   Consult such regional wildflower guides as *A Field Guide to Wildflowers,* by Roger Tory Peterson and Margaret McKenny (Houghton Mifflin Co.); *Kansas Wild Flowers,* by W. C. Stevens (University of Kansas Press).

COLLECTING WILDFLOWER PLANTS

Which wildflowers cannot be collected from the wild without breaking the conservation laws? Nearly every state has its own list of native plants under conservation, so a complete list of all protected species is impossible. Some of the more important kinds are trilliums, trailing-arbutus, mountain-laurel, all native orchids, anemone, lilies, dodecatheon, fringed gentian, cardinal-flower, birdsfoot violet, bluebells, wild pink. However, it is only sensible conservation to collect plants from lands about to be bulldozed for highways and building.

Where can wildflowers be obtained? There are special dealers in wildflowers throughout the country who carry all types of these plants.

How do you start a wildflower preserve? Start a wildflower preserve by acquiring a spot that already has enough trees and flowers and beauty to suggest preserving. Gradually bring in groups of plants which you wish to include and see that they are planted in situations like those in nature. This involves a good working knowledge of the soil and other conditions which the plants prefer and matching these conditions in the places you plant them.

May a flower preserve be joined with an arboretum? It should be a splendid addition to an arboretum.

Specific Wildflowers

ANEMONES

I have tried several times to transplant rue anemone (Anemonella thalictroides) from the woods, without success. What could be wrong? They should be dug with a large ball of soil right after flowering, before the leaves die down. Take enough of the soil in which they are found to establish them in their new location. Plant in light shade. They require light, moist soil and are indifferent to acidity. The wood anemone (*A. quinquefolia*) requires moderate acidity.

What are the soil conditions required by the wood anemone (A. quinquefolia)? It enjoys a moist, open woodland, and the borders of streams. It must have moderately acid soil. Dig with a large ball of soil just after flowering.

ARBUTUS, TRAILING-

What is the botanical name for trailing-arbutus or mayflower? *Epigaea repens.*

How can I grow trailing-arbutus? Get pot-grown plants from a nursery since they more easily adapt themselves to changed soil conditions. Where plants grow in abundance in nature, there is usually a sandy base to the soil, often old sandy riverbeds, or they may live along a shoreline. The soil should be light, strongly acid, and rich in organic matter, with good drainage. Plants can be propagated from cuttings in the summer. Insert cuttings in a sand-peat-moss mixture in a flat. Water. Cover with a tent of polyethylene stretched over wire hoops.

BLOODROOT (SANGUINARIA CANADENSIS)

How is bloodroot transplanted? Take care to get the whole root. Set it carefully in a well-dug soil in light shade in early spring. Bloodroot is indifferent to soil acidity.

How may one germinate bloodroot seed? Collect the seed capsules just before they burst open. When seeds have ripened, they may be planted immediately in a prepared spot in the garden where they are to stay.

Dogtooth-violet (left) and bloodroot, two favorite native spring flowers.

BLUETS (HOUSTONIA)

I should like to have a large patch of bluets (or quaker lady or inno-cence, as they are called). How can this be done? They are best in a rather moist, acid soil, in full sun. If you get them from nature, put them in a place as much like the one they were in as possible. They should reseed themselves and form a patch.

What kinds of bluets are there besides the common quaker lady? Only one, if you are thinking of kinds that are worth planting. This one is the creeping bluet (*Houstonia serpyllifolia*), from the southern Appalachians. It is a mat-forming, rather short-lived perennial that flowers profusely for about 3 weeks in May. It will usually self-sow freely.

BUTTERFLY-WEED

Is butterfly-weed difficult to transplant from the field to the garden? Yes, since *Asclepias tuberosa* is, as its scientific name implies, tuberous-rooted. In moving a mature specimen, a very large, thick ball of earth must be dug with it in order not to break the tubers. It can be transplanted in the fall. Butterfly-weed is one of the last plants to appear above ground in the spring.

Can I grow butterfly-weed from seed? Yes. Sow in the fall or spring —preferably the latter. Transplant seedlings to a place where they are to grow when they are about 6 inches tall. Be careful not to break their very long taproots. Give them full sun and well-drained soil.

CARDINAL-FLOWER (LOBELIA CARDINALIS)

Is cardinal-flower suitable for wild plantings? Yes, if you have soil that retains some moisture. It is ideal for the edge of a stream or natu-ralistic pool in sun or partial shade.

How can cardinal-flower be propagated? By late-fall or early-spring sowing of fresh seed; by dividing large plants; and by pinning down a strong stalk on wet sand in August and half covering it with more sand until young plants start where the leaves join the main stem.

COLUMBINE

I have heard that wild columbine (Aquilegia canadensis) grows much taller and fuller in good garden soil than in the wild. Is this true?   Yes, but the improvement is limited to the stems and foliage; the flowers remain the same size. The result is a plant devoid of most of the grace and charm which make it so attractive in the wild. We recommend retaining its natural characteristics by giving it a rather poor, dryish soil.

What causes wild columbine to rot off at the crown when other plants flourish around it?   Columbine is used to thin, poor soil. Perhaps your soil is too moist, or the roots may be burned by too much fertilizer.

CREEPING JENNY (LYSIMACHIA NUMMULARIA)

Where can I plant creeping Jenny?   In a low, damp, pasturelike location in the sun.

DUTCHMAN'S-BREECHES

What is the botanical name for Dutchman's-breeches? In what climate do they thrive?   *Dicentra cucullaria*. The plant grows in thin woods and on rocky slopes, from New England south to North Carolina and west to South Dakota and Missouri. It prefers neutral soil.

FERNS

Which wild ferns can I plant in my woodland wildflower garden?   Those that grow in your locality in wooded sections. Give them conditions as nearly as possible like those in which you find them. Among the best possibilities are evergreen wood fern, Christmas fern or sword fern, sensitive fern, ostrich fern, interrupted fern, royal fern. (The last three need very moist situations.)

Why can't I grow walking fern successfully in my rocky woodland? I give it just the kind of place it likes, but the leaves turn yellowish and just barely stay alive.   It sounds as if the soil is acid, as is likely to be the case in a region where the rock ledges and outcrops are granite. Walking fern appears to be a lime-lover, so we suggest having your soil tested for acidity.

In what section of the United States is the climbing fern native?   The climbing fern, *Lygodium palmatum*, strangely enough is native to fields in which shrubs are abundant, often in old riverbeds. It is found sporadically along the East Coast and abundantly in the Pine Barrens of New Jersey.

GENTIANS

Is there any way to start or plant blue gentians? Fringed gentians (*Gentianopsis crinita*) need a very moist situation in the sun. Turn the soil, sow absolutely fresh seed on the surface in autumn, press it in, and cover with cheesecloth to prevent washing. Remove cheesecloth in the spring as soon as the frost is out of the ground. Or, if you prefer, sow the seeds in pots.

Is bottle gentian a biennial? Is it hard to grow? Bottle or closed gentian (*Gentianopsis andrewsii*) is definitely a hardy perennial. It is easy to grow in rather heavy, dampish soil that does not dry out during droughts. Light shade is preferred.

HEPATICA

What sort of soil is preferred by hepaticas? Can they be placed in a wildflower garden? There are two native hepaticas: *Hepatica acutiloba,* with pointed 3-lobed leaves, and *H. americana,* with rounded 3-lobed leaves. Hepaticas are common near the Atlantic seaboard. Either can be planted in the home garden in shaded locations, near rocks, if the soil is suitable. A neutral soil is preferred, though *H. americana* is tolerant of slightly acid soils.

IRIS

Which wild irises can be used in the garden? *Iris cristata,* which needs a protected, moist situation and is indifferent to soil acidity; *I. verna,* wooded hills, very acid soil; *I. versicolor,* marshes, wet meadows, thickets, needs some sun; *I. prismatica,* marshes, swamps, full sun.

JACK-IN-THE-PULPIT (ARISAEMA TRIPHYLLUM)

Can Jack-in-the-pulpit be grown in a wild garden? Yes. Give them a deeply prepared soil. If they are transplanted from the woods, take care to get all of the roots and tubers.

LYCOPODIUM (CLUB MOSS)

When is the best time to transplant such things as princess-pine? Transplant running-pine and other lycopodiums early in the spring before new growth starts. All club mosses are difficult to establish if conditions are not very close to their native habitats. They may be moved anytime if the place is damp enough.

MARSH-MARIGOLD (CALTHA PALUSTRIS)

Is it difficult to transplant marsh-marigolds? No, it is very easy. Dig or pull the plants gently from their position in the marsh or stream. Do not let the roots dry out. Replant promptly in a similar situation on the edge of a stream or naturalistic pool.

How can I propagate marsh-marigolds? The simplest way is to divide the clumps in the spring, right after flowering. Wash the mud away from around the roots so you can see what you're doing, and separate the numerous small crowns (with their roots and leaves) with your fingers. Replant at once in a bog garden or on the edge of a slow-moving stream or near the outlet of a naturalistic pool.

MERTENSIA

Is mertensia easy to grow in the garden? Yes. Though *Mertensia virginica* is found in very moist situations—chiefly along the edges of slow-moving streams—it is adaptable to partly shaded positions in the average garden.

How can I keep rabbits from eating my mertensia plants? The only way we know of is to get rid of the rabbits, by fair means or foul. Mertensia seems to be a special favorite of theirs in some localities.

ORCHIDS

How can I get wild orchids without breaking the conservation laws? Purchase them from a wildflower specialist.

How many native American cypripediums (lady's-slippers) are there? Which of these are suitable for use in the garden? There are about 10 native cypripediums, of which the following are the best for naturalistic gardening (none are suitable for gardens in the ordinary sense—they need special soil and care): *Cypripedium acaule* (pink); *C. montanum* (white); *C. calceolus pubescens* (yellow); *C. reginae,* (white and rose); *C. candidum* (white).

Can lady's-slippers be transplanted to a semi-wild garden successfully? When should transplanting be done? Yellow and pink lady's-slippers are transplanted with less risk than most other types. It is best to do this in late summer or fall, but it can be accomplished in the spring if a firm root ball is taken to prevent injury or disturbance to the roots. Be sure to include an ample amount of the surrounding soil.

Which of our native cypripediums are perennial? How deep should their roots be set? All are perennial. The roots should be set so that the growing bud, formed in the fall, is just under the surface. Use rich woods soil, the surface kept from drying with a thin layer of oak leaves. Whenever you transplant these cypripediums, take as much as possible of the soil in which they have been growing.

Can you tell me what to do with a moccasin plant after it is through blooming? If by moccasin plant you mean the native pink lady's-slipper, *Cypripedium acaule,* and if it is planted in a suitable place, you need do nothing after it blooms. An oak-leaf mulch in the fall is desirable.

Does showy lady's-slipper (Cypripedium reginae) require a neutral soil? (Minnesota.) It generally is found in the wild where the soil is boggy and acid but it tolerates neutral soil.

Where will I find the showy orchis? The showy orchis (*Orchis spectabilis*) and the pink lady's-slipper (*Cypripedium acaule*) inhabit rich, moist woods from Maine to Georgia, especially oak woods and hemlock groves. The showy orchis, however, is tolerant of nearly neutral soil, if it is rich enough.

Where will the purple-fringed orchis grow? This native orchis (*Habenaria psycodes*) grows in woods, swamps, meadows, or locations in the garden which simulate such conditions.

Where can I plant the white-fringed orchis (Habenaria nivea) in my garden? If you have a bog garden, plant it there. It is native to swamps and bogs.

Can I grow the yellow-fringed orchis (Habenaris ciliaris) in my garden? Perhaps, if you have a strongly acid, continuously moist wild garden. It is generally not very long-lived.

PARTRIDGE-BERRY

Can partridge-berry (Mitchella repens) be grown in the wild garden? Yes, especially if it is damp. It requires an acid, rich woods soil.

PHLOX DIVARICATA

How can I get wild blue phlox (Phlox divaricata) and what are its uses? It can be purchased from many nurseries, especially those which deal in wild plants. Its uses are innumerable. Plant in the open shade of deciduous trees. It blends well with mertensia, trilliums, and other plants of the open woodland. Wild blue phlox self-sows. It can also be grown with tulips and candytuft in a flower garden.

PITCHER-PLANT

Can pitcher-plant (Sarracenia purpurea) be grown in the wild garden? Yes. This is a good bog-garden subject.

SHOOTING-STAR

Is shooting-star a good wild-garden subject? Yes. *Dodecatheon meadia* is a showy wildflower suitable for woodland planting in slightly acid or neutral soil.

SPRING BEAUTY (CLAYTONIA)

What are the cultural requirements of spring beauty (Claytonia)? Damp, leafmold soil and full shade in the summer.

TRILLIUM

Which trilliums are best for the wild garden? *Trillium grandiflorum* (large-flowering white trillium); *T. nivale* (small white, earliest); *T. viride luteum* (yellow); *T. ovatum* (sessile type in white or red).

Can trilliums be purchased? Yes, specialists in wild plants and some other nurseries list them.

How can trilliums best be propagated from seed? The best way to propagate trilliums is by division of old, large clumps. Absolutely fresh seed, sown before it has a chance to dry, may germinate the following spring, but growth is very slow and all conditions have to be just right.

VIOLETS (VIOLA)

Are violets dug from the woods suitable for planting in the wild garden? Yes. They are easily transplanted.

What sort of conditions does birdsfoot violet need? Give a dryish, well-drained, sandy, very acid soil in full sun.

WINTERGREEN

Will you please name and describe some of the native plants called wintergreen? Spotted wintergreen (*Chimaphila maculata*) with white-veined lanceolate evergreen leaves; showy white flowers, very fragrant. Pipsissewa (*Chimaphila umbellata*), rather like the above but with wedge-shaped unmarked evergreen leaves and smaller flowers, sometimes blush pink. Shinleaf (*Pyrola elliptica*), oval basal leaves, persistent but not evergreen; white flowers on 5- to 10-inch stalks, in racemes. Creeping wintergreen (*Gaultheria procumbens*), evergreen, blunt, aromatic leaves; creeping subterranean stems; blush flowers in leaf axils; edible red berries; 2 to 6 inches tall. Flowering wintergreen or fringed polygala (*Polygala paucifolia*), evergreen leaves; rose-purple, fringed flowers or, sometimes, white; low-growing and spreading.

How is pipsissewa (Chimaphila umbellata) propagated? By cuttings of new growth taken the first half of July and rooted in sand and peat moss in a seed flat.

Gardens of Other Types

CHILDREN'S GARDENS

What would be a good location to give a child for a garden? A spot that has full sun all day, where the ground is in good condition and easily workable. Children are easily discouraged if their garden does not produce, so do not select any unfit "leftover" area.

Which plants would be suitable for a child to grow in his own garden? Bright, easily grown annuals, which can be raised from seed:

zinnia, marigold, sweet-alyssum, and portulaca. These give a child the opportunity to learn how seeds are planted and what the plants look like as they come up. If a fence encloses the garden, morning-glories can be used to cover it.

Will you list some easy vegetables that a child might grow from seed?   Carrots, beets, leaf lettuce, beans, radishes, and summer squash.

I am very much interested in planning a garden that will interest my children. Just what arrangement would you suggest? I have in mind something to go along with their own yard and playhouse.   Any garden for children should be scaled down to their size. They like simple patterns and odd plants. Paths should be narrow and all plants should be relatively small. Choose varieties that will stand the maximum amount of abuse. Allow plenty of play space.

GARDENS TO ATTRACT BIRDS

Which flowers attract birds?   Birds (except for hummingbirds) are attracted by the seed of the plants, and then only seed-eating birds. Sunflowers, *Eryngium amethystinum,* rudbeckia, coreopsis, pokeweed, lily-of-the-valley, shrub roses, partridge-berry, wild strawberry, wintergreen, cosmos, bittersweet.

Which flowers and shrubs can I plant that are most attractive to hummingbirds?   Aquilegia, delphinium, monarda, phlox, penstemon, physostegia, tritoma, flowering tobacco, flowering currant, quince.

Which vines attract birds?   Vines that produce seeds or berries: bearberry, bittersweet, cranberry, dewberry, the grapes, the honeysuckles, Virginia-creeper, morning-glories.

Which evergreens attract birds?   Red-cedar, fir, hemlock, the pines, yew, the junipers, arborvitae, hollies.

Which shrubs encourage birds?   Most of the berried shrubs. Some are bayberry, benzoin, blueberry, winterberry, blackberry, chokeberry, elderberry, hawthorn, holly, mulberry, shadbush, snowberry, the viburnums.

Which deciduous trees shall I plant to attract birds?   Alders, white ash, linden, beech, the birches, hackberry, hornbeam, larch, black locust, the maples, mountain-ash, wild cherry, crabapples, oriental cherries, hawthorns.

BONSAI

What are Bonsai?   These are woody trees and shrubs, painstakingly dwarfed by meticulous pruning techniques and by being grown in root-restricting pots.

Is it possible to have a garden of Bonsai?   Yes. Before you enter into it wholeheartedly, be certain you understand that this takes much patience and time. It should not be undertaken in areas of hot, dry summers, unless one establishes complete control of the humidity and moisture requirements of these plants.

Can Bonsai be grown and cared for in the open ground?   Probably no, unless they are sunken in pots during the winter. It is the restraining characteristics of the small pots that aid in causing the dwarfing. Look for books on Bonsai at your public library.

CONTAINER GARDENING

How large should a concrete container be for a small tree?   The larger the better. Small containers dry out more easily in the summer, and winter cold penetrates to the root system more quickly in the winter. Look around in your area and see what are the sizes of containers in which trees live during the winter.

What particular care should trees which grow in containers on city streets receive?   In many northern towns such containers are taken into a cool building for the winter. Mulching the soil is helpful; watering well before the first soil freeze is almost essential.

What are some of the best plants to be grown in concrete containers along the streets of our town?   In southern areas there are many plants suitable for this purpose. In the North, yew, pines, andromedas, crab apples, and junipers are a few possibilities.

I have some woody shrubs and herbs in large containers on my patio. Is it safe to leave them out during the winter?   Probably not, unless you have no choice. Either the containers might crack from freezing soil or the plant roots might be killed by winter cold. Better take them into a cool garage or cellar during the winter, but do not let the soil dry out. If the plants must be left outside, mulch them heavily. Push the containers together so they can protect each other. Water when the soil is dry.

Our garden club wants to supply a lot of "planters" or concrete tubs

Three different shapes of wooden containers that can be constructed from redwood (best for permanence), drift wood, or scraps that are handy. The bottom container can be fastened to a wall. The container above it (right) has holes in each end for hanging. Screws, rather than nails, should be used to fasten the wood together.

for growing trees in the shopping area of the town. Is this practical? (New Hampshire.)   Probably not in your area. The roots of plants do not withstand the very low temperatures the tops can withstand. The tops of American holly can withstand temperatures of 20° F. *below* zero, but the roots are hardy only to 20° F. *above* zero. In a tub or planter set on the sidewalk, the soil inside the tub often approximates the air temperature. If planters are used, they should be removed in the fall to a barn or other building where temperatures do not go as low as outside. Why not plant the containers with the annuals for the summer?

What shrubs do well in containers?   Many shrubs will do well in good-sized containers. Trimmed in espaliered or topiary forms, they can be very decorative on a patio or at either side of steps. There are tree forms of lilac, euonymus, and cotoneaster. You can use privet, boxwood, euonymus, pyracantha, cotoneaster, lilac, camellia, forsythia, quince, and the viburnums.

Do trees and plants in large containers that are left outside during the

winter survive? It depends on the size of the container, type of plant, and the winter temperatures. Many survive if winter temperatures (of the soil in the container) do not go below 25° F. The larger the container, the better the chances for survival.

FRAGRANT GARDENS

I would like some fragrant annuals in my garden. What do you suggest? Nicotiana, nasturtium, sweet-alyssum, petunia, marigold, stock, heliotrope (tender shrub), mignonette, sweet pea.

Will you name some bulbs for a fragrant garden? *Crocus versicolor* and *C. biflorus; Endymion hispanicus; Fritillaria imperialis;* hyacinths; lily-of-the-valley; *Lycoris squamigera;* daffodils; many lilies; day-lilies; tuberose.

What are some fragrant hardy flowers? *Arabis; Dianthus* species and scented bearded iris; lily-of-the-valley; *Viola odorata* and varieties; *Lavandula officinalis;* hemerocallis; buddleia; primula; clematis; sweet William; monarda; phlox; peony; roses; salvia; *Campanula lactiflora;* sweet-alyssum; wallflower.

Will you tell me which geraniums to buy for fragrance? *Pelargonium tomentosum* (mint); *P. graveolens* (rose); *P. limoneum* (lemon); *P. odoratissimum* (nutmeg).

What will give fragrance in the late summer garden? Chrysanthemums and sweet autumn clematis on a trellis.

Which shrubs shall I plant for fragrance? *Skimmia japonica;* many viburnums; crab apples; pink and swamp azalea; *Jasminum nudiflorum* and *J. primulinum;* benzoin; summersweet (*Clethra*); magnolia; flowering almond; lilac; honeysuckle; daphne; roses; mock-orange; strawberry-shrub; English hawthorn; wisteria; witch-hazel. Tender (not winter-hardy in cold climates): lemon-verbena; rosemary; heliotrope.

ROOF GARDENS

What soil mixture should be used to fill the boxes on a roof garden? A good, friable loam is ideal. Avoid heavy clay or very sandy soil. Be sure that the roof is strong enough to support the boxes. If in doubt, use the soilless mixes, which are lightweight.

What are the proportions of a typical soilless growing medium? I would like to mix my own to save money. One bushel of vermiculite; one bushel of peat moss; 1¼ cup of ground limestone (preferably dolomitic); ½ cup of 20 per cent superphosphate; one cup of 5–10–5 fertilizer. Mix thoroughly before using.

What kind of fertilizer should I use for the plants on my roof garden? Dried manure, a complete commercial fertilizer, or a liquid fertilizer.

Should one use a mulch on the soil in roof-garden boxes? Yes, a mulch will help prevent sudden drying out of the soil from the wind and sun on the roof. Peat moss, rotted manure, leafmold, or black polyethylene plastic film with a few holes punched in could be used.

Can one grow vegetables successfully on a roof? Yes, with full sun and good soil, quite a few can be grown. In boxes about 8 inches deep, grow lettuce, parsley, radishes, bush beans, endive, onions (from sets), New Zealand spinach, summer squash and cucumbers, Swiss chard, and small-size tomatoes such as 'Tiny Tim'. Try stump-rooted carrots and beets. Standard tomatoes planted in deeper boxes, staked and sheltered so that they will not blow over, will thrive.

I would like to grow some herbs on my roof garden. Do you think they would be successful? Yes. Herbs are a good choice for the shallow boxes usually used on a roof. Try thyme, chives, parsley, mint, sage, and basil. (See Herbs for soil and culture.)

Will you give a list of annual flowers for growing on a roof? Marigolds, zinnias, ageratum, petunias, calendulas, sweet-alyssum, lobelia, portulaca, celosia, iberis, forget-me-nots, salvia, coreopsis, aster, scabiosa.

I am planning to make the boxes for plants on my roof garden. Can you give me some suggestions? Your boxes should be made deep enough to hold 8 to 12 inches of growing medium. They can be as wide as you like. Use cypress or redwood. Provide drainage holes in the bottom of each box. The inside of the boxes can be painted with asphaltum to protect the wood, and the outside with several coats of durable outdoor paint.

I want to grow some vines on my roof. How could I effectively support them? Make an arbor over part of the roof if the winds are not too strong. This would not only be a good support for your vines but would also supply shade and some shelter on the terrace. Otherwise, use a trellis against the side of the building, or put vine supports along the side of the building on which to tie the vines.

I want to have a roof garden that is good-looking but will not be expensive. Will you make some suggestions? Edge the railing or wall with planters painted dark green or any color which fits your scheme.

Grow such plants as petunia, ageratum, geranium, sweet-alyssum, marigold, and calendula. Some potted plants can be arranged around the roof. If you can get some large tubs or barrels, try a few shrubs, such as privet or forsythia, or trees, such as junipers or yews, for a background. Train vines against the wall or building. Ivy, honeysuckle, or morning-glories would do well.

What can be done on a flat roof, approximately 10 × 10 feet, on the west side of an apartment? Can soil be put on the roof to sufficient depth to raise anything successfully? Six to 8 inches of soil will successfully grow many flowers or even a few vegetables. Check with your superintendent before putting this considerable weight on the roof. Otherwise, confine your efforts to a few boxes filled with a soilless mix.

I have some large roof-garden boxes. How can I tell if the soil is suitable? How can I fertilize the earth before we plant? If in doubt, have a soil test made. For most plants, add ground limestone every two years. Bone meal or superphosphate and dried cow manure are excellent fertilizers or use any complete commercial fertilizer. Add lime in the fall or very early spring and fertilizer at planting time.

SUNKEN GARDENS

I have a natural spot for making a sunken garden. How can I plan this? The sunken garden is viewed from above and the basic layout is very important because of this. An informal or untidy effect would spoil it. A formal garden, with a path running through the center and a focal point at the end, would probably work out well. If your garden is well drained, you might plan a formal rose garden or an herb garden with thyme-planted steps and borders of fragrant plants around the four sides of the area in front of the walls. Leave the center in turf.

There is an old foundation on our property where a house burned down. Would this make a good place for a sunken garden? Yes, it should be excellent. You may have to provide drainage, if water collects in the foundation. Build steps down into the garden of the same kind of material as the foundation. Perennials of doubtful hardiness and shrubs which need much protection from cold winds can be incorporated in your planting plan.

WINDOW-BOX GARDENS

What special problems are involved in window-box gardening? First, provide appropriate boxes with holes in the bottom for drainage. Put in 2 or 3 inches of cinders or broken brick and fill with rich, porous soil, or use a soilless mix according to the directions on the bag. Plant with appropriate material in the spring. Regular attention to watering is of prime importance. Fertilize two or three times a season.

Can you give some pointers on making window boxes? Make the box fit your window space, but if the length is in excess of 3 feet, the box should be in two sections. For good results, a window box should be not less than 8 inches deep and 10 inches wide. Use cypress or white pine at least 1 inch thick. Bore ½-inch holes, 6 inches apart, in the bottom for drainage.

What is the best soil for window boxes? One that is rich, with plenty of humus to retain moisture. Use 2 parts loam, 1 part dried manure or peat moss, with a 5-inch pot of superphosphate mixed with each bushel. Or you can use the soilless mixes available from garden centers.

Are the metal "self-watering" boxes satisfactory? Yes, but don't place too much reliance on the "self-watering" feature.

Is there any flowering plant suitable for window boxes which will last all summer and be colorful? Lantana. Get potted plants in May; usually then in flower, they will bloom until the frost. They stand heat, drought, and city conditions, but are at their best when well watered and pruned occasionally to restrain lanky growth. Lantanas stand partial shade, but prefer full sun. Petunias and dwarf marigolds are also good.

Which flowers grow in window boxes? Among the most satisfactory are begonias, geraniums, fuchsias, ageratum, petunias, dwarf marigolds, torenias, pansies, sweet-alyssum, morning-glory, vinca, sedum, balsam, portulaca, lobelia.

Is there a blooming plant that will grow in window boxes under an awning? (West Virginia.) None that you can be sure of. Try *Begonia semperflorens* varieties, petunias, and *Lobelia erinus* varieties.

What would you suggest for flowers (not tuberous begonias) for window boxes that are very shaded? I would like plenty of color. You will probably have difficulty with any flowering plant if the shade is heavy and continuous. Fuchsias, *Begonia semperflorens*, impatiens, torenias, and lobelias will stand as much shade as any.

What shall I plant in a window box with a northern exposure? (Washington.) Flowering plants: tuberous begonias, fuchsias, lobelias, torenias. Foliage plants: aucuba, boxwood, Japanese holly, dwarf yew, arborvitae, privet, English ivy, vinca, Kenilworth-ivy.

What could we plant in front-stoop window boxes that will survive New York City's winter climate? Among the most satisfactory plants are small yew, arborvitae, Japanese holly, privet, and English ivy. All suffer, however, when the soil is frozen solid. Make sure that the soil is well soaked in the fall. *Sedum acre* and *S. spectabile* will survive year in, year out.

What can be put in a window box (southern exposure) during the winter months? (Virginia.) Small evergreens, boxwood, arborvitae, junipers, spruces, with English ivy and trailing myrtle to droop over the edge. This material cannot be expected to thrive permanently, however, because of poor environment.

Is it necessary to put ivy and myrtle grown in window boxes into the ground for the winter? If the soil about their roots freezes solid, they cannot take up water to replace that lost by their leaves, and the plants die. Place boxes on the ground, pack leaves or straw well about them, and cover with burlap or a light layer of straw.

How early can pansies be planted in outdoor window boxes? (North Carolina.) Pansies are much hardier than most people realize. The established plants can be put in an outdoor window box as soon as the severe portion of winter is past. Plants grown indoors should be hardened off by gradually exposing them to cooler temperatures before setting them in the outdoor boxes. March 15, or even earlier in your locality, might be about right.

Are hanging baskets made of wire practical? Yes, provided they are made right with plenty of moss on the outside of the soil and are never allowed to dry out.

3. Ornamental Plants

—Growing Techniques and Enviromental Problems

MOST OF OUR leading garden plants have their origin in wildflowers, but a few have been cultivated for so long that the original species is unknown or uncertain. They have been greatly changed by domestication, so they are quite different from the wild prototypes. Hybridizing and selection have improved the form, size, color, and garden value. Taken as a whole, the number of different kinds and varieties of garden flowers available to the home gardener is staggering.

Many flower-lovers prefer to specialize in one or a few groups and become experts in growing roses, irises, dahlias, chrysanthemums, or rhododendrons. There is much to recommend the practice, because the gardener comes to know his or her particular plants thoroughly. Those who are familiar with the interesting habits of their plants get the most fun from gardening. Most of the leading horticulturists of the country have been specialists to a certain degree, and have then in turn mastered the culture of many groups.

Plants as Garden Material

The real gardener is interested not only in the plants themselves, but also in the garden pictures that can be created with them.

Floriculture is a combination of both science and art. Each complements the other. To be able to grow good flowers without the skill to use them artistically gives only part of the enjoyment from them that is possible. Merely using plants and flowers for decorative purposes, without understanding their culture, is an empty form of art.

Joining a garden club or special plant society or taking a course at a community college is an asset. Gardening organizations are dedicated to the improvement of horticulture or to promoting the culture and development of a particular flower. Besides furnishing helpful information through their meetings and publications, they give an opportunity to become acquainted with other gardening hobbyists. The friendships and sociability encouraged by horticultural organizations are by no means a minor factor in making the world a better place in which to live.

The gardener who knows something of plant structure and ecology (the relation of plants to their environment) finds such knowledge helpful in dealing with problems of plant culture. Furthermore, a smattering of general botany adds greatly to the pleasure and interest which come from gardening.

Structure of the Plant. All of us know that the function of the *roots* is to anchor the plant in place and to absorb water containing dissolved nutrients from the soil. The botanists can tell us, in addition, that roots of most plants, in order to remain healthy, require air. They also need water. Over 98 per cent of the water is supplied by roots, which pump the fluids up the stems. The "fuel" for these pumps is oxygen, which is why cultivation ("stirring" the soil), which admits air to the roots, is important. Without oxygen, plants grow poorly. Modern gardeners save labor by less cultivation and prevention of oxygen starvation by adding certain materials to the soil, such as organic matter: compost, peat moss, rotted leaves, sawdust, wood chips, and whatever is available.

Knowing the need for air around roots, we can avoid overwatering and poor drainage by using these materials to provide air "stations" between soil particles, where they can take on oxygen for normal growth.

Water, with its dissolved minerals, is absorbed mainly near the root tips; this indicates to us that fertilizers should be applied to that area where the roots are actively growing, and not in close proximity to the stem or trunk, where there are few if any actively "feeding" roots.

Plant stems, in addition to supporting the leaves and flowers, provide a connecting link which distributes water (with the dissolved nutrients absorbed by the roots and the food materials manufactured in the leaves) between the roots and other parts of the plant. The internal structure of the stem has an important part to play in some aspects of plant culture. For example, in those plants which have two or more seed leaves the stem contains a layer of actively growing cells between the bark and wood: this is the *cambium layer*. It is essential for the gardener engaged in grafting or budding to be aware of this because the cambium layer of the understock must be brought into close contact with that of scion or bud to be grafted on it; otherwise union cannot take place.

The leaves are the factories of the plant where water, containing dissolved minerals absorbed from the soil, and carbon dioxide, taken in by the leaves, are combined to form complex food substances which are then transferred by the sap to other parts of the plant where they are needed. When we realize the importance of the leaves we can readily understand the necessity of keeping them healthy and why we should never remove too many of them. If the work of leaves were more widely understood, there would be fewer beginners expecting a harvest of edible roots from young beets from which all the leaves have been cut for use as "greens." The function of leaves is recognized in the oft-repeated advice to leave plenty of foliage when cutting such flowers as gladioli, peonies, or tulips, and thus avoid weakening the underground parts.

The flowers produce seeds and thus provide a means of reproduction. Commonly they are "perfect": that is, the male and the female elements are contained in a single flower—as in a rose, or a sweet pea. But sometimes they are "monoecious"—that is, with stamens and pistils in separate flowers on the same plant; for example, corn, squash, and oak. In some cases the male and female flowers are "dioecious" (pronounced dye-ee-shus) and are produced on separate plants, as in holly and willow. While, contrary to a widespread impression, it is never necessary to have plants of both sexes growing in proximity for flowers to be produced, fruits are possible on dioecious plants only when both sexes are growing fairly close together. Also many varieties of fruits, such as apple, pear, plum, and cherry, although their flowers are "perfect," require another variety of the same kind growing near by to provide cross-pollination, because their own pollen is incapable of securing a good "set" of fruit.

Environment Is Important

Often it is helpful to the gardener to know the kind of surroundings in which the plants thrive in the wild state. The study of such environment is known as plant ecology. Some plants are found always growing in the shade; others revel in hot, dry situations. They must, in most cases, be accorded similar conditions when we grow them in our gardens. Again, some plants are more perfectly at home in heavy clay soils, while some thrive in sand. There are those which have to be grown in water, and others which languish if their feet are too wet. Some plants demand a soil with an acid reaction; some prefer a soil which is abundantly supplied with lime; and others—many of them—seem almost indifferent to the chemical reaction of the soil. It is obvious that the right kind of soil and its proper preparation are among the most important factors in plant culture.

Other things also have to be considered, such as shelter and exposure to wind. Climate, of course, has a very important bearing. In some regions the extreme cold of winter prohibits us from growing some plants outdoors throughout the year. Plants in windy situations are especially vulnerable. Prevailing winds can also reduce the size and number of blooms and crop yields by as much as 50 per cent. A planting of evergreens or dense deciduous plants can cut wind speeds by 75 per cent or more for a distance of 10 times their own height. Hedges will also diminish the blowing of soil. Regular additions of organic matter (compost, manure, sawdust, wood chips) will make it less apt to blow, as will the planting of a cover crop (see Section 1, Soils).

To other plants the heat of summer may be inimical. Many plants are adapted to dry air; and in this group we find a large proportion which are successful as house plants. The polluted air of large cities is fatal to many plants, but there are some which can endure it; these, of course, are of special interest to those whose gardening has to be conducted in urban surroundings.

Competition for food, light, and air among themselves, and from other plants, is another environmental factor which affects growth. In order to secure room for adequate development it is necessary for us either to thin or transplant the seedlings which we raise; and it is also necessary to ensure that they are not starved, smothered, or crowded by weeds.

Information bearing on these environmental factors can be obtained from observation, from books, and from the experience of friends. But sometimes if the gardener's special bent is the cultivation of rare and unusual plants, he may have to experiment for himself before he is able to discover a location and conditions in which his plants will thrive. A knowledge of the natural environment is always helpful, but there are isolated cases where plants seem to thrive better under garden conditions when their usual environment is changed. An example is our native cardinal-flower, which grows naturally in wet places, usually in shade, but which, in our garden, we find does better in the rich soil of the perennial border where it gets sun for most of the day. The wise gardener first selects plants which are adapted to the environment of his garden. If he is ambitious to grow other kinds, he must change the environment to suit them if that is possible.

Propagation of Plants

Starting new plants is an absorbing garden operation which never loses its thrill. Even experienced gardeners still get a kick out of watching seeds germinate and from inserting cuttings with the expectation of getting roots on them.

Nature increases plants by means of seeds, spores, bulbils, tubers, rhizomes, runners, offsets, suckers, and stolons. The gardener uses all these methods and in addition makes cuttings of stems, leaves, and roots. He also increases plants by division, by layering, and by budding and grafting.

PROPAGATING PLANTS BY CUTTINGS
Many plants are easily propagated by means of cuttings. Most commonly used for house plants, perennials, tender annuals, and some shrubs are softwood cuttings. In (1), such a cutting is being made; (2) shows it trimmed, ready for (3) inserting in sand or sand and peat moss to root. (4) Cutting properly inserted in rooting medium. (5) Hardwood cutting of rose, showing callus formed at the bottom.

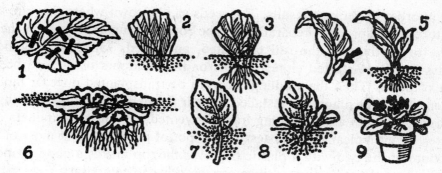

LEAF CUTTINGS

Some kinds of plants are propagated by leaf cuttings: (1) and (6)
show begonia leaf cut across main ribs and laid flat on moist sand,
with new plants starting from cuts; (2) and (3) show triangular leaf
cutting of begonia; (4) and (5), leaf cutting with bud; and (7), (8),
and (9) leaf cutting of African-violet and young plant developed
from it.

Modern propagation methods include the use of polyethylene and
such rooting media as perlite, vermiculite, shredded styrofoam, and
mixtures of these, often with peat moss and sphagnum moss. Professionals and some home gardeners use mist under plastic film for many
hard-to-root cuttings. These mixtures are referred to as soilless mixes or
"instant" soils.

The advent of fluorescent lights has made it possible for indoor gardeners to start both seeds and cuttings in the absence of natural light.
This is a great advantage where window space is limited or nonexistent
as well as during the winter months when light duration and intensity
are usually inadequate. Many garden catalogs and stores have special
units employing fluorescent tubes with a reflector.

Gardeners can use their ingenuity in strategically placing mirrors or
other reflectors to bring more outdoor light inside or for intensifying
artificial light. Growing trays lined with perlite or aluminum foil help
reflect light onto the plants from below. House overhangs painted white
are good reflectors for windows directly below them.

Keeping Plants Well and Happy

The Art of Transplanting. The gardener's job is not finished when he
has started or purchased his young plants. They must be properly cared

for in order to get best results. The seeds can be sown where they are to mature (after proper preparation of the soil, of course), and then they have to be thinned, the soil cultivated, and weeds suppressed. Sometimes seeds are started either in pots or trays indoors or in seed beds out of doors. Then the seedlings have to be transplanted once or more often before the plants are installed in their permanent location. Cuttings can be started in a propagating frame, a vented terrarium, containers of water, or even clear plastic bags. A clay pot of perlite or peat moss or a mixture of the two with a plastic bag over the top makes a good propagator. Transplanting the cuttings can be done in temporary rows outdoors, or to pots, preliminary to their final shift to the garden. In some cases, however, the rooted cuttings can be transferred directly to the garden.

Today gardeners are fortunate to find a wide selection of annual seedlings (and some biennials and perennials) sold in garden centers. These are generally in small trays containing from six to twelve plants, or in individual peat or plastic pots. The plants are usually small, but sometimes they have buds or even flowers.

Plants can easily be removed from a tray or flat by running a putty knife between the plants (through the soil and root mass) in two directions (just as you would cut a pan of fudge), or you can remove the whole block of plants and "tease" them apart with your fingers.

Then each plant is carefully lifted and set immediately into a prepared hole in the ground. (If dry, water the growing medium before removing plants.) Plants, once they have been removed from the flat, should never be exposed to the air or sun for more than a few seconds or they will dry out and be damaged or killed. Plants grown in peat pots or peat pellets (Jiffy-7's) should be set so that the top of the pot is *below* soil level. If left exposed, it will act as a wick and draw water from the soil. With Jiffy-7's, it helps to cut or tear the outer nylon net before planting. Most gardeners have found that it is a good idea to break the root ball slightly to help roots establish quick contact with the soil into which they are being transplanted. Water transplants well to eliminate air pockets and assure intimate contact of soil and roots. If plants should exhibit excessive wilting (especially noticeable when young seedlings from indoors are planted outdoors), cover with upturned baskets or pots for a few days during the sunny hours. After that, they should be able to take the sun without wilting.

Some growers find it helpful to use a transplanting solution to lessen shock and help plants become established sooner. One can also use almost any quick-dissolving type fertilizer, according to the directions given for transplanting.

Transplanting is an important operation. It must be done at the right season for best results, and care must be taken to avoid undue injury to the root system. Usually trees and shrubs are transplanted when they are more or less dormant, provided the ground is unfrozen. Most of them can be moved either in spring or fall, but for best results some require spring transplanting. (However, container-grown plants can be set out any time the soil is workable because there is no root disturbance involved.) Frequent transplanting (every year or two), when the trees are young, produces roots that make transplanting possible, even when they are of large size, with little injury. Each transplanting inevitably shortens the wide-spreading roots, and this causes the remaining roots to branch freely. Thus the plant produces a compact mass of fibrous roots which enables it to be transplanted easily. For this reason plants obtained from a nursery (where regular transplanting is practiced) can be moved with greater success than those which are dug from the wild.

Seedlings, and young plants in general, can be transplanted when they are actively growing because it is possible to move them with the root system almost intact. There are some exceptions among those plants which produce a deep taproot. Carrots and annual poppies, for example, cannot be transplanted with good results. Occasionally, transplanting is done to promote fruitfulness, as with dwarf fruit trees that are growing in rich ground and making excessive branch and leaf growth at the expense of flowers. The loss of roots brought about by transplanting often results in checking such vegetative growth and promoting the formation of flower buds.

Benefits of Cultivation and Mulching. Cultivation is the term applied to the loosening of the surface soil. It aids in the aeration of the soil, enables rain to penetrate more easily, and, perhaps most important, it helps keep down weeds.

Cultivation is accomplished in many ways, and a variety of tools is involved. In pots or flats a pointed stick or an old dinner fork can be used. For cultivating soil in crowded areas, there are various types of hand cultivators. In flower borders the scuffle hoe is the most useful tool, while in the vegetable garden either the scuffle hoe or draw hoe can be brought into action. In large areas, where the crops are grown in rows, power tillers or cultivators, either ridden or walked, are useful.

Cultivation can be reduced to a minimum by covering the soil with a mulch of black plastic (biodegradable plastic is available), sawdust, wood chips, peat moss, leafmold, bark nuggets, newspapers, or whatever is available.

Mulches can be put on at the time of planting or you can apply them around established plants. Before applying any mulch, it's a good idea to wet the ground, as this traps moisture inside. Black plastic is preferable to clear plastic since light cannot enter and weeds cannot grow under it. Organic mulches should be applied about 2 or 3 inches thick. These can be worked into the soil at the end of the growing season to add humus.

If you want to use a hoe or cultivator to loosen up the soil, wait until after the soil has dried off. Never cultivate immediately after a rain as this may cause soil to become lumpy or compacted. Beans should never be worked while the leaves are wet, as such a practice may spread diseases such as anthracnose.

Power equipment has lessened maintenance time for owners of large gardens and extensive lawn areas. Gardeners with small properties can manage with only a few tools. Before buying gardening equipment, decide which tools are really needed so that the cellar, garage, or tool house doesn't become a repository for useless gadgets.

Labor Saving

Mulching the soil surface as a means of controlling weeds is a major labor-saver. Among the organic materials that can be used for mulching are: buckwheat hulls, peat moss, ground corn cobs, shredded sugarcane (bagasse) sold as chicken litter, salt-meadow or marsh hay, grass clippings, sawdust, wood chips, bark, and newspaper. Most of these serve a triple purpose—that of making it easier to control weeds; conserving soil moisture by checking evaporation; and adding organic matter. Naturally there are some drawbacks to the wide use of mulches. Among them are the possibility of an increase in the slug population and the temporary depletion of available nitrogen in the soil. Fortunately these drawbacks can be counteracted by putting out slug bait containing metaldehyde or beer in saucers, and by keeping a close watch on the plants and applying quick-acting nitrogen in the form of nitrate of soda, fish emulsion, or sulfate of ammonia at the first sign of yellowing foliage.

The ready availability of bedding plants at local outlets or even by mail has eliminated the labor of sowing seeds for those who either don't have the time or don't enjoy this phase of gardening. Today one can achieve a completely planted garden (sometimes in bud or even in bloom) in a matter of hours, even in midsummer, if necessary.

There is also a trend toward making greater use of trees and shrubs that, once planted, take care of themselves. Ground-covering plants, which serve somewhat the same purpose in the landscape as rugs and carpets do indoors, do not require mowing, as does a lawn, and also crowd out weeds.

Watering. Plant physiologists tell us that the plant nutrients in the soil can be absorbed by the roots only when they are in solution. The necessity for ample moisture is therefore obvious.

In addition to conserving the moisture already in the soil it is often necessary to *supplement* the rainfall. This is accomplished by irrigation, or by watering with the aid of a hose or watering pot. When watering is done, *it should be thorough,* so that the soil is wet, if possible, to a depth of 6 to 8 inches. Do not water again until the soil begins to get dry. Always water newly set plants. It settles the soil around the roots and gives them moisture to keep the plants' top growth fresh.

With regard to potted plants, it is not a good idea to let the soil ball get "bone-dry." Soil shrinks away from the wall of the pot and water then rushes down the sides of the pot without wetting the soil, giving the illusion that the plant has been watered when actually no moisture has even touched the roots.

Pruning. In a reaction against the plant butchering which went under the name of " pruning," many gardeners have come to look on all cutting back of plants as a practice to be avoided. Actually, however, pruning is not altogether bad. By pruning it is possible to aid the rejuvenation of sickly plants and assist in the control of insect pests and fungus diseases. Pruning can be used to correct faulty habits of growth, to promote interesting branch formations, and to bring about earlier blossoming. In certain cases it is possible to develop larger flowers on longer stems by pruning to reduce the number of flowering shoots. The complete removal of dead and dying branches is an operation that can be safely performed at any time.

There are several principles which are helpful to the would-be pruner:

(1) Severe pruning *when the plant is dormant* stimulates the production of strong, leafy shoots; contrariwise, pruning *when the plant is actively growing* tends to check exuberant growth and helps bring about the formation of blossom buds.

(2) Trees and shrubs which *blossom early,* in the spring, ordinarily should be pruned immediately after they flower; while those which bloom in summer or autumn, on shoots of the current season's growth, can be pruned in the spring.

(3) In general, the aim of the pruner should be to maintain the natural habit of growth of the tree or shrub. Sometimes, however, when plants of definite outline are required (as, for instance, privet hedges, or shrubs or small evergreens used as accent points in a formal garden), "shearing" or light surface pruning is practiced. This alters and controls the plant's habit of growth.

(4) Pruning, limited to *pinching out the tips* of the growing shoots (called "pinching back"), stimulates branching and develops a plant of compact habit. Chrysanthemums are commonly thus treated. The same principle is sometimes followed with woody plants, with the same purpose in view.

(5) In pruning, *no stubs should be left* that will die and decay. The cuts should be made close to the supporting branch or trunk, or just above a bud—preferably one which is pointed in the direction it is wished to have the bush or tree develop.

(6) Wounds should not be painted with a protective covering. It is liable to pull away and make crevices for insects and diseases. It is better to leave it exposed to the air, as fruit growers do in their orchards.

(7) Be a barber, not a butcher.

(8) Follow the old saying: "Prune any time shears are sharp."

Winter Protection. Northern gardeners commonly grow plants which are not able to survive the winter without help. In some cases this requires that the plants should be dug up and stored in a frost-free place, such as a greenhouse, cellar, cold frame, or garage. Often sufficient protection is afforded merely by placing a mulch of insulating material on the soil over the roots. Sometimes the tops have to be enclosed in burlap to protect them from the effects of drying winds and winter sunshine, but never use plastic. There are also antidesiccants available that are sprayed on the plants one or more times through the winter to prevent excessive loss of moisture through evergreen leaves.

Plant Supports. Some of the most useful decorative plants have twining or climbing habits. To be effectively displayed, such plants usually have to be provided with supports. These may be walls, fences, pergolas, arches, trellises, or poles stuck in the ground.

There are other plants that are not climbers but which, under garden conditions, have weak stems likely to be toppled over as a result of heavy rains or strong winds. These can be held upright by staking and tying, or by pushing twigs in between and around the clump before the plants have attained their full height.

Plant Enemies. In addition to all these operations, plants have to be protected from the various insect pests and plant diseases to which they are subject. Insect-eating birds are a help in controlling the insect population, while birds that prefer seeds and berries add life and movement to a garden all year. All kinds of birds are drawn to gardens that provide water, nesting sites, fruiting trees, and shrubs, and shelter in evergreens, hedges, and windbreaks. In keeping the garden free from pests, sanitation must be practiced. This involves getting rid of diseased plants immediately—and also those that become too badly infested with insects —by sealing them in plastic bags, ready for the dump. Leaves and other plant parts that are not diseased or loaded with insects can be put on the compost pile. Inspect fruit trees, shade trees, and shrubs, and cut out and destroy all dead wood with tissues showing evidence of disease. Remove and destroy old fallen fruits or shriveled dry fruit left on fruit trees. Rake and destroy any leaves showing evidence of leaf-spotting diseases.

Close observation is important to note any departure from the normal so that remedial measures (fully discussed in Section 13) can be put into effect before much damage has been done. The wise gardener also tries to avoid growing plants known to be particularly prone to insects and diseases. Such information may have to be learned the hard way by first growing a plant and then having the fortitude to discard it if the maintenance time is beyond what one cares to provide.

 Problems of Environment

CITY CONDITIONS

What are the best varieties of annual flowers for a small, sunny, city backyard garden? Sweet-alyssum, China-aster, balsam, calliopsis, candytuft, celosia, cynoglossum, dianthus, impatiens, lobelia, dwarf marigold, annual phlox, portulaca, salvia, verbena, dwarf zinnia, and four-o'clock.

Which annuals would you advise for a very small half-shaded city garden?   Balsam, begonia, calliopsis, campanula, celosia, cleome, impatiens, lobelia, nicotiana, petunia, torenia, vinca, viola.

Which annuals and potted plants stand shade in a city garden?   Very few. Browallia, coleus, impatiens, lobelia, nicotiana, and torenia thrive in partial shade. Begonia, fuchsia, and lantana are good. Potted plants include begonia, caladium, calla, fuchsia, balsam.

How can I grow sweet peas?   As a rule, they do not succeed in or around large cities. Sweet peas should be planted either in late fall or *very* early spring (mid-March if possible) in full sun. They need cool weather to come to perfection. The soil is prepared 18 inches deep, rotted or dehydrated manure or enriched compost being mixed in. Seeds are planted 2 inches deep in a 4-inch furrow. As the plants grow, the trench is filled in and supports are provided for vines to climb on—twiggy branches, chicken wire, or stakes. There are also low-growing varieties that do not require support.

Which are the best varieties of perennial flowers for a small city backyard garden?   Ajuga, basket-of-gold, forget-me-not, columbine, artemisia 'Silver King', astilbe, hardy aster, campanula, chrysanthemum, coreopsis, day-lily, sweet William, bleedingheart (both tall and dwarf), *Eupatorium coelestinum,* gaillardia, heuchera, hosta (plantain-lily), tall bearded iris, lily-of-the-valley, mertensia, *Phlox divaricata,* platycodon, plumbago, sedum, and sempervivum in variety, tradescantia, viola.

Are there any other bulbs which furnish bloom in a city garden besides daffodils and other spring bulbs?   Calla, caladium (colored leaves), gloxinia, tuberose for very late bloom, lilies that are listed as easy of culture and tolerant of partial shade, gladiolus for sunny, well-drained situations, and small-flowered dahlia.

How can we grow evergreen trees successfully in the city?   Select only ones that are known to be smoke- and pollution-resistant. Give them good soil, occasional fertilizer, plenty of water, and protect them from dogs. The trick is to select resistant species such as Austrian pine, *Pinus nigra;* Japanese black pine, *P. thunbergiana;* and American holly. But don't be too disappointed if they fail. None will survive in closed-in shaded places, except, possibly, Japanese yew.

Which evergreens are suitable for a shady city garden?   Broad-leaf evergreens such as andromeda, azalea, *Ilex crenata, I. glabra,* kalmia, leucothoe, mahonia, rhododendron, wintercreeper, abelia, pyracantha (the last two, semi-evergreen), and varieties of yew, which are narrow-leaf evergreens.

How shall I care for evergreens in the city? Soil should be prepared to a depth of 18 to 24 inches, incorporating peat moss and dehydrated manure. Transplant only in early fall or spring, except for container-grown plants. Never allow roots to dry out, and wash foliage frequently with fine but strong spray from hose. Both narrow and broad-leaf evergreens require acid soil.

We don't want a paved area in our city garden, and it is too shady for a lawn. What ground covers are best? English ivy, suitable for formal as well as informal gardens; and vinca (common periwinkle), which has blue flowers in the spring. A pleasing effect is achieved with ajuga, either green or bronze-leaved, which has blue flowers in spring, good foliage all season, and is very hardy.

How can I have a good lawn in the city? This is difficult unless the area gets at least 6 hours of direct sunshine. The soil should be rich and deep (at least 8 inches) with good drainage. Prepare the soil and sow a good grade of lawn seed in early September. Sod will make the quickest lawn.

What can I plant in a shady city rock garden? If you furnish proper soil, rich in leafmold, you can have an attractive planting of ferns, small-leaved ivies, and native woodland wildflowers, with small bulbs—such as chionodoxa, snowdrop, Siberian squill (*Scilla siberica*), and crocus—for spring bloom.

Can roses be successfully grown in a city garden? Yes, providing there is abundant sunshine, deep, rich soil, and the garden is outside of congested metropolitan areas. Roses can also be grown in deep containers and planters.

What deciduous shrubs tolerate shade in a city garden? Aralia; calycanthus (sweet-shrub); deutzia; *Euonymus alatus;* rose-of-Sharon; hydrangea; kerria; privet; clethra (sweet-pepper bush); rhodotypos (jetbead); stephanandra; viburnum in variety.

Can you recommend any distinctive shrubs for a city garden? We don't want only privet and forsythia! If your soil is good, the following will succeed: *Abelia* x *grandiflora; Acanthopanax sieboldianus; Berberis julianae; Euonymus alatus* (brilliant red foliage in fall); *Pyracantha coccinea* (firethorn), transplant only when young, preferably potted; stephanandra; tamarix.

Which small ornamental and flowering trees can you recommend for a city garden? *Aralia spinosa* (devil's-walking-stick); flowering crab, peach, plum, Japanese cherry; flowering dogwood (only for more open situations and good, deep soil); hawthorn; honey locust; *Magnolia* x *soulangiana* and *M. stellata;* Russian-olive; umbrella catalpa; weeping mulberry.

Would a pink hawthorn or a mountain-ash grow in a city garden?   Hawthorns do very well, but mountain-ash is completely intolerant of urban conditions.

What good-sized trees stand city life? We don't want ailanthus.   Catalpa, ginkgo, London plane, *Magnolia* x *soulangiana,* Norway maple, paper mulberry, pin oak, willow oak, and willow.

Do trees on our property help purify the air? If so, how can we calculate the beneficial effect?   The Louisiana Forestry Association gives this tip for measuring the air-purifying capacity of trees: the age of the tree times 4 equals pounds of carbon dioxide absorbed per year. Also, the age of a tree times 3 equals pounds of oxygen released per year.

We've heard a windbreak can cut down on our fuel bill. What kind of windbreak should we plant?   A well-placed windbreak can save 15 to 30 per cent on fuel costs once full size is reached. As a general rule, it should be between 40 and 50 feet away, on the prevailing wind side. If tall trees (evergreens especially) are too near the house, they may shade it during winter and cut down on solar radiation, thus increasing costs. Small property owners may have to resort to shrubs and fences to cut down on wind. Privet is a good candidate for this situation. For large properties, windbreaks might include Amur maple, red maple, European hornbeam, hawthorn, green ash, Osage-orange, Norway spruce, Serbian spruce, Austrian or white pine, Douglas fir, and blackhaw viburnum.

We cannot build new fences for our city garden and would like vines which would cover the old ones within a year or so. What can you recommend?   The fastest-growing and most tolerant perennial vines are fleece-flower (*Polygonum aubertii*); Hall's honeysuckle; kudzu vine (dies to the ground in winter in the North but grows rapidly every summer—can be weedy); Virginia-creeper for shade particularly. Try hyacinth-bean, or morning-glories, if annuals are preferred.

What is the fastest-growing vine to cover an old brick wall in the city?   Either Virginia-creeper or Boston-ivy.

It is difficult to maintain the humus supply in our city garden because everything has to be carried through the house. Could I grow "green" manure?   Yes. Plant winter rye seed in late September in bare places, and dig under in spring. You can also make compost from kitchen wastes in large plastic bags. (See Soils, Section 1.)

What locations and conditions in an average city house are suitable for starting seeds in flats? South or southeast window, with sunshine available for the major part of the day; fresh air without direct drafts or chilling; even temperature not exceeding 65° F. during daytime, 10° lower at night; humidity, provided by syringing, pans of water, or humidifiers; freedom from cooking or heating gas fumes. Fluorescent lights can be used when window light is insufficient.

The only place we have to grow vegetables is in a spot in our front yard, near a busy thoroughfare. We have heard that lead from automobile exhaust affects the quality of vegetables? Is this possible? Gardens along high-traffic areas can absorb lead from exhaust fumes. Lime is reputed to help cancel out or tie up lead in the soil: hence, adding lime to your garden soil can mean less lead absorption than if the soil is acid. In high-lead-level soils, keep the soil pH around 6.5 and 7, which is about neutral or mildly acid. Consult your Cooperative Extension Service for information.

Our neighbor recently spilled weedkiller near our lawn and shrubs. We tried to get up as much as possible. Already it appears to be affecting clover in our lawn and some of the shrubs. Will the effects linger? What can be done to eliminate them? Weedkillers can cause a lot of trouble when used carelessly. Windblown vapors have even caused lawsuits. Weedkillers applied in excess or contrary to directions on container can have a lingering effect which can injure plants for weeks, months, or even years. About the only thing you can do is to apply some activated charcoal as a dry dust or as a wet slurry (as with a sprinkling can). Apply it as quickly as possible to those areas affected. Try to cultivate the charcoal into the contaminated soil.

How can we keep dogs away from plants? If the dogs belong to you, fence off a small exercise yard for them; it is an aid in training the dogs. If they do not, low wire fencing or special curved-wire guards can be placed around shrubs or borders. Spraying individual plants with a solution of 40 per cent nicotine sulfate, 2 teaspoons to 1 gallon of water, is sometimes effective, as are proprietary preparations sold by garden-supply dealers. Spraying must be renewed at intervals. There is also a specially treated rope that repels dogs and can be used to encircle shrubs and garden beds.

Small Gardens (Mini-gardens) for Small Properties

We would like to raise a few vegetables but have only the space among our evergreens in front of our house. Could you name some that would be ornamental as well as edible? The following vegetables can be planted in the ground or in containers placed at entranceways or corners, but must receive sun: patio-type tomatoes; eggplants; peppers; red okra; flowering cabbage and kale (no flowers, but beautiful edible foliage in the fall); beans and cucumbers grown up trellises on a terrace; bush squash; Swiss chard; and lettuce, especially the frilly, red leaved ones that are heat resistant.

Would herbs do well in our foundation planting? Herbs can be planted among evergreens and other shrubs as you would annual flowers, or plant them in pots or window boxes. Parsley and basil (both ornamental and green) can be very attractive in pots on patios or at front entrances. Ornamental basil makes a good border around flower beds and the purple-leaved variety also lends color in a window box.

Can I use wooden or metal barrels for growing plants on my terrace? They work fine. Just make sure the barrel is free from harmful chemical residue. Also make sure that there are drainage holes in the bottom of the container. A deep layer of pebbles in the bottom of the barrel helps drainage but makes the containers heavier to move.

Is it enough to just add pebbles or broken pots in the bottom of a container? No. Pebbles, sand, or broken pieces of pots will do no good if the soil mixture itself is not well drained. That is why it is important to add perlite or sand to the soil mixture. Some people add polystyrene balls (size of buck shot) to soil mixture. In fact, there is a trend away from using drainage material, especially with the light soilless mixes.

We have just a small spot in the backyard and would like to grow fruits, flowers, and vegetables in containers only. Is this possible? Yes, container gardening is an old idea that simply has been revived. Pictured in the tombs of the Pharaohs of Egypt are edible plants growing in tubs and pots, much as we do today. Historic pictures show fruits as well as vegetables.

Does it make any difference to plant growth as to what kind of containers we use? The type of container you use depends on whatever is available. Many people use the gutter pipe or eaves trough, especially the modern square or "K" type. Just solder the end caps on the desired length, drill several holes in the bottom, and fill with soil.

We do not have room for an ordinary garden but have many nooks and crannies around our property where we could grow vegetables in containers. What types of containers would you recommend? Let your imagination and ingenuity be your guide. Herbs grow well in cement blocks, with holes facing the sky, and filled with soil. Wooden barrels cut in half; oil drums (thoroughly cleaned) split in half; hot water tanks split lengthwise; wastepaper cans; mop pails; fruit boxes; hanging baskets and old wheelbarrows, as well as large planters and window boxes are just some of the ideas for containers. Be sure that metal containers and plastic ones have well-drained soil and ample holes in the bottom. Wooden barrels should have at least 3 holes in the bottom and clay pots should have 1 hole. Clay pots (unglazed) lose moisture much faster than all the other containers because water evaporates through the porous sides of the pots.

What are "vertical gardens"? Are they practical? Vertical gardens are proving a boon for the space-restricted city gardener as well as others who want to grow vegetables and flowers on balconies, terraces, patios, and rooftops. They can also be used along property lines, against foundation walls, and small hanging gardens can be suspended from house overhangs. They can be any shape—cylindrical, oblong, or conical. They can be made with fencing wire and sisal craft paper, wooden slats, Fiberglas, or plastic. You can make your own or buy various types from garden centers. Some even come with automatic watering devices. Whichever type you decide on, remember that no neglect is tolerated as they will take more watering and feeding than even a conventional container because there are more plants and roots concentrated in one spot. The exception to this would be a wall garden against a foundation wall. It would be planted on one side only and the moisture would be retained because of its proximity to the wall. It is possible to get unusual yields from vertical gardens provided they are taken care of.

Are there vertical gardens in which plants can be grown hydroponically? Yes, they are made of trays suspended on racks. Most that are made commercially are for growing plants with the aid of artificial lights. There are also types that are made from pipes in which plants are "plugged" into a solution of plant food and water. Pipes may run horizontally or vertically. Salad greens and herbs can be adapted to these methods, and they are used in some hotel kitchens specifically for these plants.

What soil mixture do you use for various containers?   A good mixture for flowers, fruits, and vegetables is equal parts of sand, peat moss, loam (which is simply the upper 8 inches of your garden soil), and perlite.

Are "soilless mixes" or synthetic soil mixes suitable for hanging baskets, tubs, and pots?   Yes, but they dry out faster, lack "body," and need to be fed more often, once the initial nutrients have been used up. You can add some extra loam or rotted compost to the mixture.

Are there dwarf vegetables for people who have no room to garden except in containers?   Most seed catalogs now include listings for bush squash, bush cucumbers, bush pumpkins, compact tomato plants and eggplants, and even midget melons. (See Section 10, Vegetables.)

What are the space needs of various vegetables when they are grown in containers or small spaces?   Container-grown plants will need more frequent feeding and watering, but they tolerate more crowding. Here is an approximate number of seeds that can be planted in limited spaces: bush beans, 3 plants per square foot; pole beans, 2 plants per 12-inch pot; beets, sow 3 inches apart (beets have compound seeds), then thin to 12 seedlings per square foot; carrots, sow 3 or 4 seeds per inch and thin to ¾ inch; Swiss chard, sow 1 to 2 seeds per inch, thin to 4 inches apart; cole crops (cabbage, etc.), allow 8 to 10 square inches per plant; cucumbers, allow 8 to 10 square inches per plant; eggplants, allow 1 square foot per plant; lettuce, sow 2 or 3 seeds per inch, thin to 5 inches apart for leaf lettuce, 6 inches apart for semihead; muskmelon, allow 1 square foot per plant; scallions, sow seeds ½ inch apart; mature onions, thin to 2 or 3 inches apart; peas, sow about 15 seeds per square foot; peppers, allow 1 plant per 8 or 10 inches; pumpkins (midget), allow 2 square feet per plant; radishes, sow 2 or 3 seeds per inch, thin to 1 inch apart; spinach, 2 or 3 seeds per inch, thin to about 6 square inches per plant; squash (summer and bush winter), sow seed 2 or 3 per square foot, thin to 1 per square foot; tomatoes, allow 1 plant per square foot, one dwarf plant per 10-inch pot; turnip, sow 3 seeds per inch, thin to 2 to 3 inches apart.

In summer we have a low water supply. Is it safe to use dish or bath water for grapes, roses, and flowers growing in borders, tubs, and pots?   It is safe to use wash water for your crops if you dilute it about ⅓ to be sure that strong detergent solutions will not affect the plants. Rinse water can be used without any problem. Actually, most laundry products contain nutrients beneficial to plants if the amounts are not too concentrated.

We have a very small garden and wish we could grow enough vegetables for our family. Can you tell us something about the French Intensive Method for gardening? This system, also called "intensive gardening," is simple. First, the soil is spaded and a layer of rotted horse or cow manure or compost is spread (about a foot deep) over a small area, then worked in. Rotted leaves can also be used, along with or without manure, then dug in. The vegetables are spaced close together so that the plants practically touch as they mature. This enables the plants' leaves to shade the soil, and also conserves moisture, keeps soil temperatures more uniform, and crowds out weed growth.

In short, the method stresses close spacing in a soil high in organic matter and fertility. It includes successive planting (planting again after harvesting) and interplanting to keep the area filled with plants at all times. If your spot gets 6 hours of sun daily, good air circulation, and ample water, you can practice intensive gardening.

We have a small backyard and cannot grow pumpkins because they ramble all over. Is it true that you can grow pumpkins on bushes? Yes, 'Cinderella' produces a 10-inch pumpkin on a bush. You can also grow good winter squash on bush varieties, which take up only a small space (4 × 4 feet).

Is it possible to grow crops on a wire fence? Will the crops burn because of the hot sun's reflection on the wire? Fences on a property line can be used for growing cucumbers, gourds, tomatoes, and other climbing or twining plants. Set your plants next to the base of the fence after the danger of frost is over, or you can sow seed directly into the ground. There is no truth to the idea that a wire fence will burn the vines of cucumbers and other crops.

We like herbs but have only a small space to grow them. Would cement blocks work for this? Yes, fill the openings with an equal mixture of sand, peat moss, loam, and perlite and insert the seeds or plants directly into the holes. For green onions, 6 to a hole; carrots, 6 to a hole; radishes, 8 to a hole; beans, 1 seed per hole; chives, parsley, peppers, oregano, and dozens of other plants, 1 per hole. On hot days, the blocks should be watered well.

Why is it that our flowers and vegetables do not resemble the pictures and descriptions in the catalogs? Weather plays an important role in the way trees, shrubs, flowers, and vegetables turn out, so don't blame your seed company if they do not look like the pictures in the catalog.

Weather works in subtle ways to change the appearance of a given variety. Carrots are a good example. The 'Chantenay' carrot should be fairly blocky and 4 to 5 inches long. In hot weather it forms a small globe which resembles a beet rather than a carrot.

Seed taken from the same packet and grown at 50° to 60° F. will produce a carrot 6 or 7 inches long. To produce an average-sized carrot, a temperature range between 60° to 70° F. is necessary. Radishes get hot and tangy in dry soils. Lettuce may get bitter in hot spells. Corn does not fill out well in dry weather as the silk is cooked, preventing pollination. Peppers form "all bush" and no fruit because hot, searing winds can prevent fruit set, as will low temperature. Winters kill flower buds of shrubs, preventing bloom. Hot sun will cause flowers on annuals to change colors or wilt.

Is it true that the size of vegetable transplants you grow or buy depends on the size or type of container? There is some connection. If you use a pot that is too small, the plants will not grow as they would in a larger pot. A container that is too small will limit the amount of nutrients (due to small soil volume), and the roots may become pot-bound. Usually the containers that commercial growers use are large enough to give good temporary growth to seedlings until you set them in your garden.

Our hanging baskets start out fine in late spring but by early summer they start to look ragged. What makes this happen? Summer can be hard on plants swinging in hanging baskets. Here are some tips to help:

(1) Water daily, soaking thoroughly. The sun, plus swinging in the breeze, dries out the soil, especially the artificial mixes. Most tend to dry out quicker than humus-rich soils.

(2) Give the plants a liquid feeding (diluted according to directions) every 3 or 4 weeks.

(3) Snip off seed pods and spent blooms to generate new growth.

(4) If growth seems poor, take a spike and loosen up the soil carefully to let air get to the roots. Avoid breaking roots, although a few broken ones will not do any harm.

(5) If the hanging basket gets bone dry, take it down and soak it thoroughly in a bucket of water for at least 20 minutes. Do not try to water a neglected basket the conventional way since the soil ball is not apt to become saturated.

(6) If the plant is wilted, even though the soil is moist, suspect overwatering. Also, check the soil for grubs, mealybugs, and aphids around the roots. If present, drench with Sevin, malathion, or nicotine sulfate.

(7) Do not count on rainwater to keep plants growing. But make sure the plants are not in a spot where they can be deluged by rainwater.

(8) Yellowed foliage can be due to overwatering, spider mites, or a lack of nitrogen. A lot of plants confined in a small space use up nitrogen, the nutrient that gives green color to leaves.

(9) Hanging baskets should have removable saucers to prevent fertilizer salts from building up. Those with saucers attached permanently can get root burn.

Does it make any difference what time of day you water your plants? It makes little difference, but there is less evaporation if you water early in the morning. Do not worry about the sun burning the foliage if you water in midday, or about disease if you water the plants at night. Pour water all around the soil surface, not just in one spot, because water does not move sideways, as many people believe. Apply a gentle flow rather than a blast of water, which will wash the soil.

What type of containers dry out the quickest? Plastic and metal containers are the most water-retentive, followed by concrete, glazed ceramic, wood, and clay containers in that order. Watch out for overwatering plants in containers that drain poorly or lose water more slowly. Water plants often if they are in drying winds or blazing sun.

Is it true that night temperature affects the fruit set of tomatoes in hanging baskets? Yes, night temperatures (59° F. or below) can prevent a good fruit set on tomatoes, whether in the garden, in tubs, or hanging baskets. It seems to reduce fruit set by affecting pollen formation. If the tomato plants are in the bud stage, a drop in night temperature might injure the plants' ability to form pollen and ovules. You can spray tomato plants with hormones to offset the effects of cold nights and this seems to increase fruit set. As the season advances and the weather gets warmer, later flowers are not affected too adversely by low night temperatures and your plants should produce plenty of tomatoes.

Foundation Material for Problem Areas

(See also Sections 2 and 4.)

We have a new house with a foundation planting of little pointed evergreens that our neighbor says are hemlocks. He says they will soon grow tall and cover our windows. How can we keep them low? You can't. Hemlocks (*Tsuga canadensis*) naturally grow tall and will also spread too much for a foundation. Transplant them in early spring or fall to the boundaries of your property where they will have space to grow naturally. (There are a few dwarf hemlocks but these are expensive and not suitable for most foundations.) Replace with compact, low-growing evergreens, such as yews, Japanese hollies, one by each side of your entrance. Fill in with ground covers.

We do not have a lot of room for our foundation planting since our house is close to the street. Since our shrubs and trees must compete for space, how often should we feed them? Should we use a granular or a liquid fertilizer? There is some argument as to whether a liquid or a granular feed is more economical for trees and shrubs, but roughly speaking the cost is about the same. Whereas granular fertilizer lasts a bit longer in the soil, a liquid feed is more quickly available to the plants. It is usually more convenient to apply granular (or dry) fertilizers.

We want to set out some container-grown plants. Can you give us some tips? When planting, remove the root ball from the container (some are metal, fiber, peat, etc.). If roots are a tangled mass, take your fingers and disentangle the twisted roots. Some root balls are so tightly interwoven that nurserymen advise cutting or clipping the surface of the container ball, using a knife or clippers, to get the roots loose. If the plants are not tightly root-bound inside the container, such rough treatment is not needed—just those that have a solid mass of roots. If you plant a shrub or tree that has a mass of entwined roots, without disturbing or disentangling the roots, it is likely that the plant will die because the roots are so entangled that they never grow into the new surrounding soil.

What is a good evergreen or deciduous shrub to use for foundation concealment—one that will not grow more than 2 or 3 feet high and will not be too bushy? Most dwarf shrubs tend to be broader than tall. The following are slow-growing and can easily be kept at 3 feet by careful pruning: *Berberis thunbergii* 'Erecta', *Picea glauca* 'Conica'; *Taxus canadensis* 'Stricta', and *Taxus media* 'Hatfieldii' (yews); *Thuja occidentalis* 'Rosenthalii'.

What would be a good thing to plant between two windows to fill a blank wall on the south side of a house in full sun? There is only 4 feet from the house to the lot line and the ground is sandy from excavating the cellar. Most plants die from the heat. The house is Cape Cod style. *Juniperus chinensis* 'Columnaris', or *Juniperus virginiana* 'Cannaertii'. Remove the poor soil and replace with good, light, loamy soil enriched with about ⅕ part leafmold or peat moss.

Which shrubs would be best to plant along a house that has a very high foundation? These shrubs average around 4 or 5 feet in height: coral-berry, *Cotoneaster apiculatus,* fragrant sumac, mapleleaf viburnum, *Physocarpus intermedius,* hydrangea, sweet-pepper bush, Vanhoutte spirea.

What is a suitable planting on the west side of a house along the foundation; there is about 6 feet of space from the house to the driveway? Deciduous materials: *Cotoneaster apiculatus,* flowering quince, *Physocarpus monogynus,* rose-of-Sharon, rugosa rose, slender deutzia. Evergreen kinds: dwarf hemlock varieties, spiny Greek juniper, *Taxus cuspidata* 'Nana' (if kept pruned), also *Taxus media* 'Brownii', 'Hatfieldii', or 'Hicksii' (yews).

Which is the best evergreen for a corner? I want a tall one that is graceful and smooth and not too spreading because my yard is small. (D.C.) Arborvitae, Chinese column juniper, red-cedar cultivars.

What would be suitable foundation plantings for an old (1792) farmhouse in southern New England that is in excellent condition? Very few plants are necessary if you wish to retain the 1792 look. When these houses were built, little if any foundation material was used. Sometimes a dooryard garden, enclosed by a picket fence, was planted, but usually not at the front entrance. You might consider: boxwood (Korean box is hardier than common boxwood) or Japanese holly at each side of the front door, a lilac at a corner of the house, and nothing else but a low ground cover, such as vinca, in a border along the rest of the foundation. Such a simple planting would also be suitable for a modern house built along colonial lines or even a ranch-type dwelling.

What can be done with 3 feet of space under eaves which do not get any natural moisture in summer? This space is always barren, and nothing seems to grow even though watered with the hose. Such a spot should be watered with unfailing regularity. Occasional neglect may be ruinous. Improve soil by working in leafmold or peat moss. If this is done, try *Symphoricarpos* x *chenaultii, Berberis thunbergii* 'Erecta' (truehedge columnberry), spirea 'Anthony Waterer'. These will grow about 3 to 4 feet high. You may want to apply bark chips or a stone mulch.

How can one grow shrubbery about a house that has eaves projecting 3 feet without excessive watering? A 6-inch layer of rich compost or leafmold and peat moss at the base of roots and a generous amount of it mixed in planting soil would reduce artificial watering. There are available plastic or canvas soaker hoses that can be run the length of the shrub planting and left in place all summer. To water, all one does is attach a regular hose at the end of soaker hose (or attach at faucet if possible) and allow water to run for a few hours at a time when needed.

We have a very small front yard. How close to the foundation can we plant shrubs and evergreens? The planting should be no closer than 3 feet from the foundation. If your space is very limited, you may be better off using a low ground cover rather than an extensive shrub planting around your foundation.

Does close foundation planting (3 feet away) affect the walls of a house in any way—possibly causing dampness on the inside walls? Probably not. While the planting keeps sun and air from the walls, it also sheds rain and the roots absorb much water.

We planted two shade trees, one on each side of our house, four years ago. Because our soil is very sandy, we planted them a foot deeper than they were at the nursery, thinking it would anchor them better. Now they are beginning to look sickly and we wonder if it is because of the deep planting. It could be. The effects of planting too deep are slow to appear but a lot of trees have died because of deep planting. Dead branches may occur in the top of a tree as soon as 2 or 3 years after planting if the soil is clay-like and wet. It may take longer in a sandy soil.

Sometimes a tree will overcome this problem by throwing out a new root just below the surface. Usually, however, the tree finally dies. A seven-year study at the University of Massachusetts shows that growth of maples decreased as the depths of planting increased. Tree roots and the trunk exchange gases with the outside atmosphere. The cells use oxygen and give off carbon dioxide. Root tissues can stand lower oxygen levels than the trunk can. Roots can be smothered or "drowned" if left in a soil saturated with water too long. However, the roots may be smothered by soil alone if the tree is either surrounded by earth fill or is planted too deep. When you plant a tree, set it in at the same depth it was in formerly.

We have several flowering shrubs in our foundation planting but they have never bloomed. Our soil is very poor and we are wondering if a lack of nutrients will affect blooming. A shortage of phosphorus and potassium may inhibit blooming but this can be corrected by adding a balanced plant food. Often shrubs and trees which prefer a sunny location will fail to bloom in shade. They need light for bud formation.

Even shade-tolerant plants bloom more profusely in a well-lighted situation. Also, don't overlook competition from adjacent trees and shrubs. Their roots may rob moisture and nutrients from your plants. Cold weather can freeze buds and prevent formation, as in the case of the French hydrangea. Likewise, a dry summer may be responsible for nonblooming the following year.

FOUNDATION MATERIAL FOR SHADE

Which flowering plants would bloom in a location next to a garage wall where very little sun reaches the ground except in late afternoon? Bugbane, columbine, coral-bells, meadow-rue, monkshood, hosta. These are all perennials. Among annuals, impatiens would be the most reliable bloomer under your conditions. Painting the wall white and adding a white stone mulch will add reflected light.

What would give me a profusion of color, or at least green, on a narrow strip (about 10 inches wide) on my driveway and against my house? The strip is on the north side and therefore sunless. Ferns, goutweed (*Aegopodium podagraria* 'Variegatum'), Japanese spurge (*Pachysandra*), *Vinca minor,* lily-of-the-valley, plantain-lilies and other hosta.

What are good perennials for the shady north side of a house? This is on the front side of my property. There is a space approximately 3 × 14 feet between the house and the walk around the house. Astilbe in variety, ferns in variety, balloon-flower, columbine, coral-bells, day-lily, *Eupatorium coelestinum,* plantain-lily (hosta), *Anemone japonica.*

What can I plant in the shade of a building under oaks, on a sandy ridge? Nothing worth trying, unless you prepare the ground thoroughly, mixing in abundant humus, leafmold, and some very old or dehydrated manure. Having prepared an acid mixture of this sort, try rhododendrons, mountain-laurel, and *Skimmia japonica,* and English ivy, vinca, or pachysandra as ground covers.

Can azaleas and rhododendrons be used in foundation plantings about the house? Yes, if you choose from among the small-leaved rhododendrons that remain within bounds and don't grow and spread too much. Although highly touted for the purpose, the majority of rhododendrons are not suitable for plantings near the house, as they simply grow too large. A secondary problem is that if the foundation of the house contains cement, and it usually does, rain falling against this washes a certain amount of lime into the soil in which the rhododendrons are growing, frequently causing it to become too alkaline.

Can I safely put in a foundation planting of evergreen trees where the outer branches of the street maples reach? Probably only the native yew would thrive. The Japanese yew might survive, but would not thrive. Both the shade overhead and the roots below would trouble evergreen trees. Why not use ground covers such as ivy or pachysandra?

Which plants for foundation plantings are best suited for northern New England? Especially for the shady north side of a house? Evergreens would be best, especially the broad-leaved types, such as mountain-laurel, mountain andromeda (*Pieris floribunda*), and yews (*Taxus*). Avoid hemlocks. Although they will grow in the shade, they are much too big for foundations.

Can you advise if there is any flowering shrub which will grow in a totally shady place in the front of the house—the north side? (New York.) Few, if any, shrubs will bloom satisfactorily in complete shade. *Rhododendron* hybrids, mountain-laurel, and jet-bead (*Rhodotypus scandens*) are worth trying. Among the best foliage shrubs for northern exposures, totally shaded by the house (not overhung by trees), are *Euonymus fortunei* 'Sarcoxie' and *Skimmia japonica*.

What can be planted, to grow successfully, on the north side of a house? The ground is covered with fine green moss. Prepare the ground deeply, mixing in a liberal supply of leafmold or peat moss and rotted or dehydrated manure. Then you may safely try *Euonymus kiautschovicus, Symphoricarpos orbiculatus, S. albus laevigatus,* honeysuckle (*Lonicera*) of various kinds. If you prepare an acid soil, such a situation may do for rhododendrons, mountain-laurel, azalea, andromeda (*Pieris*), *Skimmia japonica*.

Which shrubbery is best for foundation planting in a very shaded spot facing west? Deciduous shrubs: *Symphoricarpos* x *chenaultii, Rhodotypos scandens, Physocarpus monogynus, Lonicera morrowii.* Evergreen shrubs (for acid soil): *Mahonia aquifolium, Pieris floribunda, P. japonica,* mountain-laurel, and skimmia.

Which inexpensive ground and foundation plants can be used to fill in a north-side foundation? Low to medium-height shrubs: *Skimmia japonica, S. reevesiana, Viburnum wrightii, Berberis triacanthophora* and *B. verruculosa, Mahonia aquifolium, Symphoricarpos orbiculatus.* Taller shrubs: *Lonicera tatarica, L. morrowii,* regel privet. Ground covers: *Pachysandra terminalis, Vinca minor, Hedera helix* (English ivy).

Which shrub can be used beside a house for a sort of hedge, to grow 5 feet high? Not much sun hits the spot, and the soil is not too good. I don't want barberries. Try Amur river privet, five-leaved aralia, gray dogwood, Siberian pea-tree. Hills of snow hydrangea grows 4 feet tall and tolerates some shade.

Ground Covers for Problem Areas

I want an all-purpose ground cover that doesn't need mowing, grows in poor soil, grows fast, yet does not get out of bounds. It should be able to take sun or shade and wet spots because our property has all those conditions. There is no such thing as a perfect ground cover. Grass is the best ground cover you can get if you select varieties that tolerate the conditions you mention. No property is self-maintaining so you must use a particular plant for each situation and you may have to incorporate a mulch of bark, gravel, or wood chips where plants do not grow well.

We would like a ground cover that does not attract snakes. What do you suggest? Garden snakes prefer tall growth, hence a mowed lawn or short-growing ground cover is not attractive to them. Weeds and piles of stones around the property provide good hiding places for snakes.

Is it harmful for ground-ivy to grow over ground where flowers (perennials and annuals) grow? If the other plants are small, the ground-ivy (*Nepeta hederacea*) may smother them. A better choice might be a bark mulch.

What ground-cover flowering plants are suitable for a steep bank with northeast exposure. *Ajuga reptans,* Japanese honeysuckle, moneywort (*Lysimachia nummularia*), *Vinca minor,* English ivy, some sedums, and thyme.

What can I use for ground cover between sidewalk and curb, on a 2-foot bank, 3½ feet wide, with some shade? *Vinca minor* 'Bowles Variety', pachysandra, or English ivy.

We have a small, steep terrace shaded by trees. It is next to impossible to grow grass on it. Last year I planted ivy (Hedera helix 'Gracilis'), which seemed to grow only fairly well. Was our selection wise? *Hedera helix* 'Gracilis' is a well-recommended plant for dry banks and will probably do much better when it has become established. Try giving it a mulch of leafmold or well-rotted cow manure this winter.

What is the best coverage to plant where there is full sun on a hill? Grass and weeds make it hard to cut.   Honeysuckles are good, so are trailing roses and any number of creeping junipers.

What is the most beautiful flowering ground cover for regal lilies in a perennial border?   *Myosotis sylvatica* (forget-me-not) should please you.

Which evergreen euonymus vine would grow well as a ground cover for a narrow strip between our house and driveway?   Purple-leaf euonymus (*Euonymus fortunei* 'Colorata').

What is a good ground cover to plant along a house wall? The space is about 4 feet wide, running north and south, with a stepping-stone path in center. The strip gets rain but not dew. I would like something deep-rooted, short, and not viny.   *Arenaria montana* (mountain sandwort), *A. verna* (moss sandwort). Both of these are very low, tufted-growing grass substitutes; they are the best plants available for planting between flagstones in a walk.

Which ground cover do you suggest to border a stream?   Moneywort (*Lysimachia nummularia*), which is also known as creeping Jenny or creeping Charlie—(take your choice!)—is an excellent semi-evergreen ground cover which might be used near the stream. Also, watercress would be attractive as well as edible. Forget-me-nots (*Myosotis sylvatica*) will add a touch of blue and self-sow freely.

What is a good ground cover for my tulips?   Pansies or violas may be selected to flower with the tulips, also forget-me-nots, especially to underplant yellow tulips. To follow these, petunias would give a good display until the frost comes.

Will it be harmful to bulbs left in the ground if they are overplanted with annuals for summer bloom?   Not if the bulbs are planted at the proper depth and the soil is enriched annually. Any kind can be used—from sweet-alyssum to zinnia—that will conform to the situation.

Are there annuals that can be sown in fall to cover a bed of spring-flowering bulbs?   Yes, sweet-alyssum, California-poppy, annual candytuft, calliopsis, nigella, portulaca, and annual baby's-breath are good for this purpose.

I have a triangular bed of tulips in the front lawn. What fairly low-growing plants can I place between the tulips after the foliage dies down? The bed is partially shaded in the morning.   For color and profusion of bloom nothing will outdo petunias for the purpose, particularly those of the bedding type. Other good dwarfs are ageratum, sweet-alyssum, portulaca, verbena, marigold, lobelia, and dwarf impatiens.

What can I do to get grass to grow under oak trees? If trees are low-headed and dense, remove lower branches and thin top to admit more light and air. Better, perhaps, use a shade-enduring ground cover, such as ferns, pachysandra, ivy, vinca, ajuga, or gill-over-the-ground, or try shade-tolerant grass such as fescue.

Grass will not grow on terraced ground which is quite shady. What is the best ground cover for such a location? The terrace is about a 45° slope. Japanese pachysandra, English ivy, Hall's honeysuckle, *Ajuga reptans,* ferns, *Vinca minor, Paxistima canbyi.*

We have just planted a flowering cherry tree in our back lawn. Will you tell us what to grow around the tree? We prefer something that blooms in early spring to late fall and spreads around to cover the earth under the tree. Only annuals would give you flowers from summer into autumn—petunias, for instance. For a permanent ground cover, try the evergreen periwinkle or Japanese spurge. The former has blue flowers in the spring; the latter has no appreciable flower at all. You can plant daffodil bulbs among the ground covers for spring bloom.

Which ground cover might be used under large elm trees? *Ajuga reptans,* Canada yew, English ivy, *Euonymus fortunei,* ferns, yellow-root (*Xanthorhiza simplicissima*). Best of all, *Pachysandra terminalis,* the Japanese spurge.

What would be a good ground cover under large plantings of 3-year-old lilacs? *Veronica prostrata,* lily-of-the-valley, *Phlox divaricata,* and *P. stolonifera, Ajuga reptans.*

What will really grow under maple trees as a substitute for grass? *Pachysandra terminalis,* especially under Norway maples. If this will not grow, nothing will; you might as well save time and money and stop further experimentation. Maples cast dense shade and their roots are very near the surface. Better settle for a pebble or bark-chip mulch.

Is there a low-growing or creeping plant that would form a carpet for a shady pine grove? The pines are young and do not shed enough needles to cover the ground. Partridge-berry; blueberries—the smooth-leaf low-bush blueberry; yellow-root (easily propagated by root division). As the pines increase in size, they can be expected to kill everything beneath them.

How can I plant English ivy from cuttings for low cover under a tree? Root the cuttings first in a propagating frame, then prepare the soil well with leafmold, peat moss, rotted or dehydrated manure. Plant rooted cuttings 6 to 8 inches apart in early spring and keep watered until they are established.

Is Japanese spurge (pachysandra) better than creeping myrtle for a ground cover in the shade?   Yes.

What fertilizer or special care is needed to maintain healthy pachysandra plants?   Pachysandra prefers partial shade. Dig the soil 8 inches to 1 foot and incorporate manure, compost, or leafmold before planting. If the foliage of established plants is not deep green, spread a ¼-inch layer of dehydrated manure or compost on the surface of the soil in the fall.

Does pachysandra grow better in acid or alkaline soil?   It is reasonably tolerant. If the soil is quite acid, plant pachysandra; if alkaline, use English ivy.

Plants for Sandy Soil

Which annuals grow best in very light, sandy soil?   Sweet-alyssum (*Lobularia maritima*), arctotis, calendula, California-poppy, castor-bean, geranium, lantana (a tender shrub treated as an annual), marigold, nasturtium, petunia, *Phlox drummondii,* portulaca, *Cleome spinosa,* statice, verbena, zinnia, *Sanvitalia procumbens.*

Which perennials grow best in sandy loam soil?   *Penstemon barbatus,* butterfly-weed (*Asclepias tuberosa*), *Nepeta* x *faassenii,* false-indigo, *Anthemis tinctoria, Phlox subulata,* and lupines. *Achillea; Anchusa azurea; Arabis caucasica; Arenaria montana; Armeria; Artemisia abrotanum* (old-man); *A. stelleriana* (old-woman); *Cerastium tomentosum; Dianthus deltoides;* globe-thistle; Oriental poppy; balloon-flower; *Salvia azurea; Santolina chamaecyparissus;* sedums; yucca.

Which shrubs and trees are suitable for a sandy soil in a sunny location?   With proper, ordinary care in planting and after care until established, the following commend themselves: medium to tall shrubs—*Elaeagnus umbellata;* hydrangea (various); hypericum; *Hippophae rhamnoides* (sea-buckthorn); *Lespedeza thunbergii;* bayberry; *Rosa rugosa; R. setigera; Robinia hispida* (rose-acacia); *Vitex agnus-castus;* tamarix. Tall-growing—Siberian pea-tree; *Elaeagnus angustifolia;* golden-rain-tree (*Koelreuteria*).

Which edging plants, preferably flowering kinds, will do well in dry,

sandy soil? Several kinds of statice (armeria); *Sedum hybridum, S. ellacombianum,* and *S. spurium;* 'Silver Mound' artemisia, lavender.

Plants for the Seashore

Which annuals are suitable for planting near the ocean? Sweet-alyssum (*Lobularia maritima*); California-poppy; geranium; lantana (tender shrub treated as annual); petunia; *Phlox drummondii;* portulaca; nasturtium; *Cleome spinosa;* verbena. If a sufficient depth of topsoil (6 to 8 inches) is provided, and sufficient water in dry periods, practically all annuals that grow successfully inland will be suitable provided the low-growing types are selected if the garden is not protected from the wind.

Which perennials endure salt spray and high winds? Tall-growing kinds will require staking in windy places. Among perennials able to withstand salt spray and shore conditions are Carpathian bellflower (*Campanula carpatica*); *Allium schoenoprasum* (chives); day-lily; echinops; *Erigeron speciosus;* eryngium (sea-holly); gaillardia; bearded iris; coral-bells; perennial flax; asters; pinks; rudbeckia; sedums; *Armeria maritima; Limonium* (sea-lavender); veronica; *Yucca filamentosa,* goldenrod, especially *Solidago sempervirens.*

Are there any shrubs which will grow near the shore exposed to salt-laden air? Yes, but immature leaves are damaged by salt-laden fogs in the spring. This also applies to native shrubs. The following are good choices: arrow-wood, bayberry, beach plum, chokeberry, coral-berry, groundsel-bush, highbush blueberry, inkberry (*Ilex glabra*), Japanese barberry, *Rosa rugosa, R. humilis, R. lucida,* Russian-olive, sea-buckthorn, shadbush, sumac, winterberry, shore juniper, and tamarisk in several varieties.

Which deciduous trees are most suitable for seashore planting? Birch; blackjack oak (*Quercus marilandica*), but it does not transplant well; Siberian elm does fairly well; hawthorn; pepperidge (*Nyssa sylvatica*), but it does not transplant well; red maple; sassafras; white poplar; white willow; mulberry; shadblow.

Which evergreen trees resist salt air? American holly, best broad-leaved evergreen; Austrian pine; Japanese black pine—best; red-cedar, especially good.

Which northern evergreens will grow best near salt water in spite of

the danger of water occasionally reaching their roots? No evergreen tree will *thrive* where salt water reaches the roots occasionally. Red-cedar and Japanese black pine are best bets among tall evergreens, the shore juniper (*Juniperus conferta*) among low-growing evergreens.

Will you suggest protective planting for a sloping shore bank, about 18 feet, which is inclined to wash, due to wind, rain, and high water? Study the vegetation of similar situations and plant that material closely on your own bank. Beach-grass, bearberry, elaeagnus, goldenrod, poverty-grass, sand blackberry, sumac, Virginia-creeper, wild grape (fox or frost grape), and wild roses are good, especially *Rosa rugosa*.

Which fertilizers are best for sandy seashore gardens? Seashore soils usually are benefited by heavy applications of humus (rotted leaves, peat moss, seaweed, grass, or other vegetation) and well-rotted barnyard manure. This is largely to improve their physical condition. Moderate applications of commercial fertilizer will help build up the nutrient content of the soil. Applications should be small but frequent.

Plants for Slopes and Banks

(See also Ground Covers.)

I have a steep bank at the end of my lawn which extends to the street. Can you advise me what the best plants are to keep the soil from washing away? Cover it with plants that make a dense mat, or tangle of growth: Japanese barberry, Japanese honeysuckle (especially in shade), *Juniperus horizontalis,* matrimony-vine, *Rosa wichuraiana,* yellow-root (especially in shade). If low-growing plants are desired, Japanese spurge or trailing myrtle.

We have a slope behind our house and would like to plant some evergreen-bittersweet. Do you think it will do well in this situation? There are several creeping or trailing forms of *Euonymus fortunei* that should be suitable. *E. f. radicans,* wintercreeper, is one of the best—and very hardy. You might also consider Hall's honeysuckle, a fast grower for hillside plantings, but eventually weedy. For dense shade you can use pachysandra. If you want a shrub that weeps over the bank, try forsythia. It will tolerate some shade, but does best in full sun. English ivy makes a natural blanket of glossy green leaves, and is suitable for covering terraces, banks, and other places where grass is not practical.

What would you suggest to plant on a bank across the front of our yard, about 4 feet high off the highway and about 375 feet long? Akebia, English ivy, Japanese honeysuckle, Japanese spurge (if shaded), memorial rose (*Rosa wichuraiana*), *Vinca minor,* or crown vetch.

What can I plant on a sunny south slope now covered with tufted grass? Coral-berry, five-leaved aralia, fragrant sumac, gray dogwood, jet-bead, rose-acacia, Scotch broom, crown vetch.

What can I plant on a dry, sunny slope (southern exposure, formal surroundings) on which it is impossible to grow any grass? Japanese barberry, box barberry, Chenault coral-berry, Tibet honeysuckle.

What can best be planted on a sandy slope that will cover well, look well, and keep sand from blowing? *Arenaria montana, Cerastium tomentosum, Dianthus deltoides,* and *D. plumarius* (cottage pink). Or mix equal parts of seed of domestic ryegrass and Chewings' fescue grass, and add 1 part of the seed to 10 parts of soil by bulk, and broadcast this. If your home is near the seashore, dig up the roots of wild perennials, mostly weeds and grasses, that are growing above the high-water mark, divide them, and plant them on your property; surround the plants with a little soil when setting them.

What are good plants for the south slope of a gravel hill? The soil is loose and sandy. Try beach plum, Scotch broom, crown vetch.

What can be used for fast coverage of a steep bank, with heavy clay soil? We now have bearberries, but after 2 years they are not covering very quickly, and deep gorges are being cut in the bank. Keep the bearberries but also plant clumps of Hall's honeysuckle or bittersweet. Fill gullies with brush to catch and hold the soil. Mulch the slope with coarse compost or straw to check washing.

Which flowering plants can be planted on a sandy, rocky bank? *Phlox subulata, Gypsophila repens,* and day-lilies are suitable perennials; use a good half pailful of soil in each planting hole. Buy seed of single mixed portulaca, mix it with screened soil (1 part of seed to 10 parts of soil); broadcast the mixture.

Planting in Shade

(See also Foundation Material in this section and Section 2.)

In a shaded location, which flowers will bloom in each month of the season?   The month of bloom may vary with the degree of shade and the geographical location, but one can depend upon the following plants to flower in the broader seasonal divisions of spring, summer, and fall. Spring: barrenwort (epimedium), bleedingheart, *Ajuga reptans, Pulmonaria saccharata,* spring bulbs (chionodoxa, muscari, scilla, etc.), Mertensia virginica. Summer: day-lily, foxglove, fringed bleedingheart (*Dicentra eximia*), monkshood, plantain-lily and other hosta. Fall: *Aconitum autumnale, Eupatorium coelestinum,* and *E. urticaefolium, Anemone japonica.*

Which low-growing flowering plants thrive best in the shade?   Epimedium, *Ajuga genevensis* and *A. reptans, Dicentra eximia, Iris cristata,* lily-of-the-valley, *Pulmonaria saccharata, Lysimachia nummularia, Vinca minor,* primrose.

Which flowering plants will grow in an area that receives only about 2 or 3 hours of strong sun daily?   Day-lily, bleedingheart, primrose, hosta.

Due to many trees adjacent to the entire length of the south side of my yard, my garden stretch is damp and shady all day. What type of planting would you suggest?   A mixture of shrubs and a few perennials, including the following: arrow-wood, bee balm (*Monarda didyma*), five-leaf aralia, cornelian-cherry (*Cornus mas*), mountain-laurel, plantain-lily, spice-bush (*Lindera benzoin*), and ferns.

What low-growing plants can I grow to cover a small space under a cluster of oak trees?   Barrenwort (epimedium), fringed bleedingheart, *Iris cristata,* and ferns. Or evergreen shrubs, in not-too-heavy shade, in acid, humus soil: *Leucothoe, Pieris, Paxistima canbyi,* and rhododendrons.

I have had no success with shade-loving plants put near some trees. I have enriched the soil but the trees take all the moisture. Would a mulch be of use? I can use grass clippings and rotted grain straw. A garden hose is not available.   If your trees are maples or elms, your problem is a difficult one. Try *Pachysandra terminalis* (Japanese spurge), planting it in the spring while the ground is moist—after first spading and raking the ground—then apply a mulch as well. This plant will often succeed where nothing else will. Grow plants in boxes or tubs to prevent competition from tree roots.

Which flowers grow the best in tubs on a terrace that is shaded very heavily from a tree that is in the center?   You will have to bring into bloom elsewhere, and use for temporary effects on the shaded terrace, any flowering plant that lends itself to pot culture, such as hydrangea, lantana, geraniums, calla, caladiums, and coleus (for colored foliage), and annuals such as begonias, impatiens, and lobelia.

I have a row of Lombardy poplar trees. Can I plant flowers in front or back, or in between spaces?   Yes, particularly on the sunny side: *Aquilegia canadensis, Iberis sempervirens, Digitalis purpurea,* rose 'Paul's Scarlet' climber, *Anemone japonica,* day-lilies.

What could one plant in the shade of a mulberry tree?   If a mere ground cover is wanted, prepare the area, working in leafmold or peat moss, compost or dehydrated manure, and plant either Japanese spurge or periwinkle; the former 6 to 9 inches apart, the latter 8 to 12 inches, depending upon size of plants. If shade is not very dense, the following shrubs may, with proper preparation, be used: *Symphoricarpos* (any), *Clethra alnifolia,* Morrow honeysuckle (about 7 feet tall). In an acid, humus soil: *Rhododendron roseum* and *R. calendulaceum;* also try hills of snow hydrangea (*Hydrangea arborescens*).

Which annuals grow best in a shady location?   In general, annuals must have sunlight to grow satisfactorily. There are a few, however, which get along fairly well in the shade (the less dense, the better): *Begonia semperflorens,* impatiens, balsam, *Torenia fournieri,* coleus, browallia, flowering tobacco (*Nicotiana*), *Lobelia erinus, Catharanthus roseus* (syn. *Vinca rosea*), monkey-flower (*Mimulus*).

What are the best annuals for partial shade and all-summer flowers?   Balsam, flowering tobacco, lobelia, *Catharanthus roseus* (syn. *Vinca rosea*), impatiens, petunia, begonias (both tuberous and wax), and browallia.

I have a semishady spot in my perennial border in which I have been able to grow only wild violets. Can you give me some other suggestions? The ground in this spot is inclined to remain damp.   Astilbe in variety, bee balm, bugbane, bugle (*Ajuga reptans*), buttercup, cardinal-flower, ferns, great blue lobelia, plantain-lily and other forms of hosta.

Which perennials can be grown in a dry, shady place?   Bugle, *Aquilegia canadensis,* moneywort, red baneberry, white snakeroot, *Aster ericoides.*

Which perennials should I plant on slopes in the shade of immense forest trees high up the hill?   Day-lilies, ferns, foxglove, epimedium.

What can I plant in a damp place in the shade of a neighbor's garage?   Hardy primroses are good for spring, along with lily-of-the-valley. Pachysandra and English ivy are good ground covers. Foxglove, hosta, forget-me-not, ground-ivy, and periwinkle. Tuberous-rooted begonias may be planted every spring if soil is well drained.

Which shrubs will grow in a shaded place?   Andromeda (*Pieris floribunda*), arrow-wood (*Viburnum dentatum*), cornelian cherry, five-leaf aralia, jet-bead, mountain-laurel, rhododendrons, spice-bush (*Lindera benzoin*), *Clethra alnifolia,* yellow-root (*Xanthorhiza simplicissima*), American yew.

Which shrubs can be planted near the front of a house shaded by tall maple trees?   If the soil is full of tree roots, very few plants will get along well; try five-leaf aralia in tubs.

What kind of shrubs will grow the best along the west side of a house in the almost constant shade of large oak trees?   If you will prepare a deep, humus-rich, acid soil and remove lower tree branches, this would seem fine for rhododendron, skimmia, mahonia, azalea, mountain-laurel, leucothoe, and pieris.

Will shrubs do well near evergreen trees?   Near—yes; not *under* them, unless the evergreens are tall conifers, such as pines, with their lower branches removed.

Plants for Dry, Sunny Areas

Which shrubs will thrive along the south side of a brick house in full sun?   In deeply prepared, enriched, well-drained soil, kept sufficiently moist in summer, your choice is almost unlimited. Within the limits of permissible ultimate height and width, select from catalogs any good shrubs which require no special conditions or shade. Avoid rhododendron, evergreen azalea, and, generally, evergreen shrubs.

Are there any annuals that can be grown in some sunny, dry areas where we must depend on rainfall only?   Try arctotis, cornflower (*Centaurea*), coreopsis, California-poppy, *Phlox drummondii,* portulaca, marigolds, and the creeping-zinnia (*Sanvitalia procumbens*).

Are there any showy perennials that will grow in the same situation?   Gloriosa daisy (*Rudbeckia*) is a dandy. Oriental poppy, once it is established, does well, as do *Gaillardia* (blanket flower), and day-lilies. Many perennial asters and goldenrod thrive in dry, sunny spots.

Which shrub would suit an open, sunny, enclosed corner atop a retaining wall? Whatever you plant, prepare the soil 18 inches deep with leafmold, old manure, or some peat moss. See that the place does not dry out in summer. Usually, for a situation like this, a shrub that will drape its branches somewhat over the wall is best. You might plant any of these: *Cotoneaster racemiflorus, Lespedeza thunbergii, Rosa hugonis, Spiraea* x *arguta* or *S. thunbergii, Forsythia suspensa.*

What would you suggest as a fairly low, long-blooming flower for about a 2-foot space between a brick house and the sidewalk, on the south side of the house? Dwarf marigolds would be excellent. Or dwarf zinnia, or the little blue *Torenia fournieri* (wishbone-flower).

Can you suggest an edging for a 24-inch-wide border between a house and driveway, where it is dry and sunny? Germander, *Teucrium chamaedrys.* This may need some pruning, which can be done in the spring by thrusting a spade in the soil alongside the row to check its lateral growth, using shears to trim the top growth. Creeping thyme would also grow well here.

Planting in Wet Ground

(See also Bog Garden, Section 2.)

Are there any flowers or flowering shrubs that like wet ground throughout the year? Perennials: cardinal-flower, loosestrife (*Lythrum salicaria*), rose-mallow. Shrubs: *Viburnum dentatum, Cephalanthus occidentalis, Aronia arbutifolia,* swamp azalea (*Rhododendron viscosum*), *Clethra alnifolia.*

The boundary line of my property is quite low and wet. I have put up a 5-foot fence. Which vines would grow in such soil (clay)? Which shrubs or hedges could I plant there as a screen? Vines: porcelain-vine (*Ampelopsis brevipedunculata*), Dutchman's-pipe, bittersweet, Japanese honeysuckle. Screen: *Clethra alnifolia, Viburnum cassinoides, Ilex verticillata, Lindera benzoin, Aronia arbutifolia.*

Our lot is about 1 foot lower than the lot next door. Consequently, after a rain, water stands in one spot for some time. The space is 3 × 6 feet. I would like the names of low-growing shrubs that would not interfere with the grass. The spot receives sun all day long. Do you have any other suggestion as to what to plant on the spot? *Aronia arbutifolia,* dwarf willow (*Salix purpurea* 'Gracilis'), *Ilex glabra, I. verticillata,* snowberry (*Symphoricarpos*), *Itea virginica.* Pruning may be necessary to keep them low.

What shall we plant on a space which is liable to be flooded during bad storms?   Rose-mallow, Japanese iris, *Lythrum salicaria.*

How should the sides of a stream be treated or built up to prevent caving in? The stream, which meanders for 210 feet, is about 1 foot deep and 18 inches wide; it is completely dried out in the dry season.   Set some large rocks in the bank, at 10 to 15 feet apart. Plants mentioned in preceding question should hold the bank once they are established.

Which annuals grow best in wet soil in the shade?   Jewel-weed (*Impatiens capensis*), *Myosotis,* monkey-flower (*Mimulus*), and the perennial turtle-head (*Chelone*).

Which perennials will thrive in wet soil?   Bee balm, boneset, cardinal-flower, *Iris pseudacorus,* Japanese iris, Joe-Pye-weed, *Lythrum salicaria,* marsh-marigold, rose-mallow, starwort (*Boltonia asteroides*).

What planting is suitable for the sides of a small stream which becomes a full storm sewer after a rainfall?   *Myosotis scorpioides, Lysimachia nummularia, Iris pseudacorus, Lythrum salicaria.*

Which shrubs will thrive in wet soil?   Buttonbush (*Cephalanthus occidentalis*), *Aronia arbutifolia* and *A. melanocarpa,* highbush blueberry, *Lindera benzoin,* Siberian dogwood, *Clethra alnifolia, Calycanthus floridus,* swamp azalea (*Rhododendron viscosum*), winterberry (*Ilex verticillata*), and inkberry (*I. glabra*).

Which trees will thrive in wet soil?   Pin oak, red maple, swamp white oak, sycamore, sour gum (*Nyssa sylvatica*), weeping willow, *Oxydendrum arboreum, Lindera benzoin.*

Which flowering plants will grow in a boglike spot?   Japanese iris, Siberian iris, astilbe, flowering-rush, marsh-marigold, cardinal-flower, *Primula japonica* and *P. pulverulenta,* trollius, *Myosotis scorpioides,* loosestrife, Jack-in-the-pulpit, bottle gentian.

Aspects of Culture

(*For soils and fertilizers in general, see also Section 1; for individual plants, see under Trees and Shrubs, Roses, Perennials, Annuals and Biennials, this section. For plant material for special decorative effects, see also Planning and Landscaping, Section 2.*)

CULTIVATION

What are the reasons for cultivating the surface soil? To kill weeds and maintain a loose surface that is readily penetrated by rain. It also helps in soil aeration in those cases where a crust forms on the surface.

In cultivation, should the soil be left level or mounded around the plants? Generally, level cultivation is best, because it exposes less surface from which soil moisture can evaporate. When it is desirable to get rid of excess soil moisture, hilling or ridging is sometimes practiced. Corn and similar crops are mounded with soil to help them stay erect; potatoes, to prevent "greening" of the tubers.

How soon after a rain should one hoe the soil? When it has dried to such an extent that it no longer sticks to the hoe.

Is it desirable to cultivate the surface every week? No. Cultivate according to the circumstances rather than by the calendar. Hoe after rains to prevent the formation of a crust and to kill weeds when the surface has dried somewhat. Never work in a garden when plants are wet. If no more rain falls, hoe only to kill weeds.

How deep should the surface soil be cultivated? This depends on the character of the soil, the time of year, and the root formation of the plants cultivated. It may be desirable in some soils to cultivate deeply— 3 to 4 inches—early in the season to dry the surface. Later, shallow cultivation, 1 inch deep, is preferable to avoid injury to crop roots. The modern tendency is toward shallow cultivation.

My soil forms a crust after every rain. What shall I do? Cultivate with a hoe or cultivating tool to break the crust, or use a mulch of organic matter. (See Mulches.) Improve the soil by adding bulky organic material—strawy manure, partly decayed leaves, sedge peat, peat moss, etc.—annually until the condition is cured.

Does a dust mulch really conserve soil water? Probably not in most soils, if the soil is stirred to a depth of more than 1 or 2 inches. Moisture in the loosened soil is quickly lost by evaporation and the dust mulch is likely to absorb all the water from light showers before it has a chance to reach the soil occupied by roots.

MULCHES AND OTHER SOIL AMENDMENTS (See also Perennials, Trees and Shrubs, etc.)

What is meant by mulching? The application of various materials— usually organic—to the soil surface to hold moisture in the soil, to prevent weed growth, and in some cases to help keep the ground cool, or to warm it, accomplished by laying black plastic.

Once a mulch has been put on, is it necessary to do anything further about it? Not much; just keep it loose. Peat moss must be watched because it is likely to pack down after a heavy rain, forming a felted surface when dry that sheds water like a roof.

Mulches are put on to conserve water in the soil. Don't they also work in the opposite direction by absorbing rain which otherwise would reach crop roots? Yes, to some extent. However, some mulch material —buckwheat hulls and cranberry tops, for example—allows easy penetration of water and does not absorb a great deal. Examination of the soil after rain will show whether or not the mulch is too thick. Peat moss is not the best mulching material because it crusts over and becomes impervious to water, but when mixed with leafmold, rotted manure, and compost, it can be a satisfactory mulch. However, peat moss's best use is as an additive to the soil to increase humus content.

Essential hand tools—shovel, hoe, iron rake, trowel, and spading fork.

What can I use to mulch my perennial border? I want something not unsightly. Peat moss, leafmold, buckwheat hulls, shredded sugarcane (bagasse), pine needles, coconut-fiber refuse, compost, grass clippings, and bark chips.

Of what value, if any, are grass cuttings for garden beds, and how should they be used? They are of use as a water-conserving mulch, and if incorporated with the soil after they are partly decayed they add to its humus content. They should be spread in a layer of 1 to 2 inches thick.

Can newspapers be used as a mulch? Many gardeners use papers as a mulch for strawberries, raspberries, etc., as well as in the vegetable garden. Wet 4 or 5 thicknesses and apply between rows. Cover with

Mulching the flower or vegetable garden, as well as around shrubs and other plantings, helps retain soil moisture and suppress weed growth.

soil. In fall, the papers can be incorporated into the ground with a power tiller. Newspapers are made from wood; they help loosen up a clay soil and tighten a sandy one. Add a little extra plant food high in nitrogen in fall or spring. Papers add extra minerals to the soil and the black ink used in printing is not harmful.

Are leaves just as good as rotted manure for the garden? Yes. They are both good and you should stockpile both if available. About 40 bushels of leaves mixed into the soil are equal to 15 bushels of manure. Even chicken or turkey manure is all right if it is well rotted. These materials contain very few seeds because the digestive system of poultry is tougher on them than that of cattle.

Our soil is full of clay which bakes hard as a rock. Is there any way to change this? If your soil is hard and clayey, don't despair. Add a 6-inch or more layer of organic matter—grass clippings, leaves, peat moss, sawdust, manure, etc.—every fall and you will notice an improvement.

How can we help leaves break down into leafmold? As with any organic matter, soil organisms that break it down need extra nitrogen. Sprinkle a liquid plant food on leaves or use a general garden fertilizer (5–10–5) at the rate of 2 pounds for each bushel of packed leaves. Leaf compost will not break down rapidly during cold weather, but will speed up when warm weather arrives. Lime or wood ashes added to the leaves help correct acidity and build up the finished product so your plants can take up more nutrients.

Is black plastic a good material to use as a mulch?   It is best used in the vegetable garden where it can easily be laid between rows. It warms the soil, so it is good for melons and squash.

Can black plastic be used to mulch newly planted shrubs?   Yes. Cut off a square of 3 or 4 feet, slit to a little beyond the center, put it in place, and anchor it by covering each corner with soil. It is desirable to punch a few holes in the plastic so that water can get in over the entire space.

My cottage is on a saltwater beach; is it beneficial or injurious to mulch with seaweed that is washed up in abundance on the shores? Could the presence of salt kill the plants?   Seaweed makes an excellent mulch. The amount of salt present should do no damage and it is unnecessary to wash the seaweed before use.

We like the looks of bark as a mulch but have heard that it attracts grubs, moles, and mice. Is this true? Is it as good as peat moss or sawdust?   It's very doubtful if any organic mulch will attract enough grubs, mice, moles, or ants to be bothersome. Mulching is an age-old technique practiced by gardeners for centuries. The various bark mulches, including wood chips, are attractive in appearance and practical. Peat moss will dry out and is hard to wet once it becomes dry. Sawdust crusts over and sheds water. If peat and sawdust are not stirred, they make a poor mulch because the soil underneath remains dry.

What plants would be benefited by mulching with pine needles?   Pine needles are especially good for cone-bearing evergreens and acid-soil plants such as rhododendrons, but they can be used on all plants.

We want to use bark for a mulch in our flower and vegetable garden. What sizes or grades does bark come in?   Bark comes in different grades: a coarse grind with particles up to 3 inches, a medium grind with particles up to 2 inches, and a fine grind with sizes up to 1 inch. There is also a screened bark with particles less than 1 inch. These are best applied in 2- to 4-inch layers. Weed control is better at the 4-inch level. Tests show that the fine bark holds more moisture, followed by the medium and coarse bark. Soil tests show that these mulches caused an increase in calcium, magnesium, and potassium, with no difference in the nitrogen and phosphate amounts or any change in soil reaction (pH).

How about the use of well-rotted sawdust around plants and on lawns as a mulch?   Sawdust makes a satisfactory mulch during the summer. Do not apply deeper than 1 inch unless it is mixed with sulfate of ammonia at the rate of 1 pound to 100 square feet or nitrate of soda, 1½ pounds per 100 square feet.

Mulching between vegetable rows prevents weed growth and conserves moisture. Mulching materials include leaves, marsh hay, seaweed, straw, and partially decomposed compost.

I mulched my kitchen garden with wood chips and sawdust. The crops did not grow at all well. The foliage looked peaked and yellowish. I presume this was caused by acid soil as a result of the mulch. Is there anything I can do to counteract this? It is doubtful if this condition is caused by acid soil. More likely it is due to the depletion of nitrogen caused by the microorganisms which bring about the breakdown of the organic matter in the mulch. Apply sulfate of ammonia—1 pound to 100 square feet; or nitrate of soda at 1½ pounds. You should test the soil and, if it shows a reaction of less than pH 5.5, pulverized limestone should be applied—the amount is contingent upon the degree of acidity plus the character of the soil (more will be needed if it is a heavy clay). Your county extension agent should be consulted on this matter.

Is it true that when undecayed organic materials are put in or on the soil that it is necessary to add chemical fertilizer to supply food for bacteria that cause its decay? How much and what kind of fertilizer should I use? Chemical fertilizer is not absolutely necessary but it is usually more convenient to obtain than organic fertilizer. Nitrogen is the element that is most likely to be lacking; this can be provided by sulfate of ammonia at 1 pound to 100 square feet or 1½ pounds of nitrate of soda. Phosphorus can be added by superphosphate at 5 pounds to the same area. Organic fertilizers such as poultry manure can be used at 5 pounds to 100 square feet or sheep manure at the rate of about 10 pounds. It is important to watch the behavior of the plants and if they become yellow, indicating nitrogen deficiency, use quick-acting nitrogen such as nitrate of soda or sulfate of ammonia, either liquid or dry and watered in.

We have not limed our garden soil for 3 or 4 years and would like to do so now. How can we find out how much lime to add? The best way to find out how much lime to add, and to see if any is needed, is to have a simple pH (acidity) test. The right pH is important for best plant growth and efficient use of nutrients. (See Introduction to Section 1, Soils and Fertilizers.)

How can we tell if our soil has traces of herbicide (weedkiller) in it? If you think your soil has herbicide traces, a simple test will prove it. Sow bean seeds 1 inch deep in pots of the suspect soil. Keep the soil moist and warm (65° to 70° F.). Within one week the seed should be germinated. Allow plants to grow until the second set of true leaves is well developed. If weedkiller is present, seeds may not germinate, and those that do will produce distorted leaves. Tomato seed can also be used for testing for weedkillers. Young growth will be curled or cupped. Do not use a contaminated soil for house plants or for starting seed.

Can a weedkiller or herbicide move in soils? Our neighbor used some in his garden and our trees developed symptoms which make us believe that they got some of the chemicals. Yes, herbicides will travel in the soil. Heavy rains can carry some of the materials to lower levels of the soil, affecting roots of nearby plants. Damage may possibly result when weedkiller-fertilizer doses have been made on lawns during dry spells. If the dry spell is broken by a heavy rain, weedkillers may be moved downward in the soil and contact tree or shrub roots. Watch out for products containing herbicides and fertilizers. People often use these to feed flowers, trees, and shrubs—with disastrous results. They are for lawns only. Never apply a weedkiller on a windy day because particles or droplets may drift onto nearby plants. Vapor or fumes may also damage nearby plants, even after application.

How close can we use a weed-and-feed fertilizer to shade trees? Do not use them within 10 feet of the drip line of branches and do not apply on slopes where heavy rains can wash them down into flower beds, food crop areas, or root zones of trees or shrubs. Weed-and-feed applications are for lawns only!

Our lawn was treated with herbicides. Can we use the grass clippings on our compost or garden? Grass clippings may contain enough residues of weedkillers to be injurious. Put them on the compost and let the microorganisms in the pile deactivate the residues for a year or so. Do not mulch fruit trees with weed-and-feed clippings as it can totally defoliate them.

We have a compost pile in our backyard and everything goes into it, even diseased plants. Is this harmful? The usual recommendation is that diseased plant parts should be sealed in a plastic bag and discarded. If put on the compost pile, there is a possibility that the parts will fall to the outside of the pile and diseases could be carried over another year. However, many gardeners put diseased plants and almost everything else on the compost pile. Great heat is generated in a pile, 180° F. or higher, enough to kill weed seeds and diseases, as well as insects. Use organic items such as tea leaves, banana and orange peels, fluff from the vacuum cleaner, eggshells, dead flowers, potato and apple peelings, shredded newspapers, lawn clippings, and hedge trimmings.

I saved the shells from sunflower seeds that were rejected by birds. The hulls were used as a mulch and the plants made very poor growth. Is there a reason? The sunflower has a built-in weedkiller or toxin which may have been passed along in the hulls. When one plant is poisoned by another plant it is called allelopathy. There are other plants besides the sunflower which "do their own weeding," including the Jerusalem-artichoke, oats, black walnut trees, some varieties of cherry and cucumber, and some wild plants.

In tests, extracts of sunflower plants inhibited the growth of many common weeds by 50 to 75 per cent. We may get safer herbicides from the chemicals of these plants. However, not all plants are affected by these natural toxins.

WATERING

How should one water flowers? Water well at planting time. When growth is active, and soil is really dry, water before the plants wilt. Mere surface sprinkling does no good. Give enough to wet the soil 6 inches down.

Are there any objections to spraying or watering plants in the evening? Some authorities believe that if the foliage is wet when the temperature is falling, the plants are more susceptible to attacks by disease organisms. Under outdoor conditions this is probably not important, but in a greenhouse or hotbed it is wise to spray or water early in the day.

Is it harmful to water plants when the sun is shining on them? It is better to water in early morning or in evening, so that water has a chance to penetrate the soil before much is lost by evaporation. If you must water in hot sun, avoid hitting the foliage. Apply water directly on the soil. There will be much less evaporation; it gets quickly to the roots, where it will do the most good; it may "burn" foliage by droplets of water acting like a magnifying glass. Tender new leaves are more susceptible to this. We have seen large portions of bean leaves turn black and shrivel as a result of watering in hot sun.

When watering newly set annuals, should water be applied to the soil or over all by sprinkling? If water is in limited supply, leave a depression around each stem and fill it with water. If ample, sprinkle the whole bed, making sure the water penetrates several inches.

We live in a water-short area. Can you give us some tips for saving and using waste water? The best way to save water is to use a mulch around trees and shrubs and in between garden rows. Use either organic materials or black plastic. First, make sure the soil gets a good soaking. If you must water, do so infrequently but deeply to encourage deep rooting and greater tolerance to dry spells. Water early in the day to reduce evaporation. Avoid overhead sprinkling since one third of the water evaporates before it has a chance to hit the ground. Avoid unnecessary hoeing and cultivation. Use bath or dishwater. Soaps, detergents, and ammonia are not generally harmful and may actually provide some nutrients. Add fresh water occasionally to wash out any heavy accumulation.

Does it matter when we spray flowers and shrubs outdoors? Do not spray pesticides on a hot day. Spray in the morning if possible, between 6 and 10 A.M. This will give the moisture time to dry off before evening. Also, when the air or plant tissue temperature is about 90° F. or higher, damage is likely to occur. On bright sunny days, leaf tissue temperatures may be 5° to 15° F. higher than the surrounding air, thus increasing the chance of injury. Avoid temperature extremes outdoors, either high or low, since slow-growing plants (due to cool weather) are more likely to be damaged. Never spray plants when they are in need of water. Wilted or dry plants are very sensitive to spray injury. Wettable powders are usually safer for plants than emulsions because they do not contain emulsifiers and solvents. Dusts may leave an objectionable residue on the leaves, especially on ornamentals. If you use aerosol spray cans, apply at temperatures lower than 75° F. The spray may damage plants when applied above 85° F. Be sure to hold the can at least 18 inches away from the plants.

PRUNING (See also under Trees, Shrubs, Evergreens, etc.)

What is the difference between shearing and pruning? Shearing is a form of pruning in which all young shoots extending beyond a definite line are cut off. Pruning proper involves cutting individual shoots or branches with a view to improving the tree or shrub.

Last year our shrubs did not flower. Could pruning have caused this? This could be due to many factors. Pruning at the wrong time of year will remove flower buds, thus preventing flowering. If pruning is needed, do the job right after the blooming period and you will be safe. Another cause might be excessive nitrogenous fertilizer which encourages leaf growth at the expense of floral development. You can reduce the amount of nutrients being taken up in the soil by root pruning. To do this, insert a spade vertically into the soil at various places in a circle around the plant within the outer perimeter of the branches. About one third of the roots should be severed. This does not seriously harm the plant.

When is the best time to trim trees? If the purpose is to check growth, it is better to prune trees when they are actively growing. Ordinarily, however, trees are pruned when they are dormant, in the fall or late winter. This stimulates strong shoot growth; however, pruning can be done any month of the year.

What is meant by "dormant"? Plants are said to be dormant when they are not actively growing. In deciduous trees and shrubs it is a period between leaf fall and starting into growth the following year. Evergreens are never fully dormant.

Is it all right to trim trees in winter? Yes. However, from the standpoint of comfort for the operator and the danger of breaking surrounding branches when they are brittle from frost, it is desirable not to prune when it is extremely cold. It is preferable to wait until late fall or winter.

How can I avoid tearing the bark on a tree trunk when I cut off large limbs? Make the first cut from underneath the branch, cutting upward until the saw binds. Then cut from above, which results in the removal of the branch. The stub may now be cut off with safety by sustaining it with one hand while the few last cuts with the saw are being made.

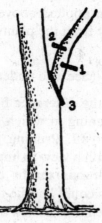

*Proper way to cut off a large limb.
(1) Make an "under cut" near the
trunk; (2) saw off the limb, leaving
a stub; (3) saw off the stub as close
to the trunk as possible.*

Is there any special rule to follow when making the cuts in pruning? Yes; branches should always be cut off flush with the branch from which they spring. When shoots are shortened, the cut should be made just above a growth bud, pointing in the direction you wish to have the tree develop.

Should a single or double leader be developed? Generally speaking, a single leader is preferable, especially for those trees which naturally grow with a single trunk. Some trees, and all shrubs, have a diffuse habit and cannot well be restricted to a single leader.

Does pruning help make a tree bushy? Yes, if it is limited to cutting off the tips of the leading shoots. It can be done during the growing season if the tree is too vigorous; if not, at any time of year.

Is it better to use hedge shears or pruning shears when trimming trees into globes, squares, etc.? If the leaves are large, as in linden, or evergreen, as in cherry-laurel, it is better to use pruning shears because the use of hedge shears results in obviously marred leaves. In the case of small-leaved trees, hedge shears can be used.

I have heard that one should paint a tree dressing on a wound where a limb was cut off. Is this true? The latest thinking is that dressings are not needed on tree wounds. Quite often the dressing applied does more harm than good because some break away from the wood, leaving a space in which insects, fungi, and bacteria work. In most cases, tree wounds will become closed by a natural callus, without any aid. You'll notice that apple growers who prune both huge limbs and small ones never treat the wounds. Exposure to air seems to favor callusing. The USDA made a thorough study of wound dressings. Tests included more than 400 wounds deliberately made on shade trees. After 5 years it was found that the wound dressings had no effect on the rate of healing, and the dressings failed to prevent infection by wood decay fungi. In fact, the least decay occurred in the *untreated* wounds. Their tests seem to point out the fallacy that dressings protect against wood-inhabiting microorganisms.

Is pruning of any help in the case of trees infested with scale insects? Yes. Branches dying as a result of attack by scale insects should be cut off. This will tend to strengthen the rest of the tree. The cut-off branches should be destroyed by burning, and spraying measures taken to kill the insects remaining.

Is pruning sometimes used as an aid in controlling plant disease? Yes; for example, canker on roses, and fire blight on trees and shrubs of the apple family. The affected limbs must be cut off well below the point of injury, and the tool used should be disinfected after every cut, using 1 part household bleach to 9 parts water.

We have a young tree with the center broken off; will it grow into a tree or should we dispose of it? If there is a strong side shoot near the break, it could be trained to take the place of the broken leader. Tie a stout stake securely below the break, and let it project 2 or 3 feet above it; then tie the side shoot to this.

We have some tree roots which stick up above the ground. Would it be advisable to chop the roots off or will it hurt the tree? Take a sharp ax and chop the troublesome roots off. Get below the soil level, and after the roots are chopped, cover with soil and sprinkle grass seed on top. Cutting the root off is not going to injure the tree.

I'm interested in evergreen sculpturing of Japanese yew and would like to trim them into animal shapes. How do you do it? Clipping and training shrubs into ornamental or grotesque forms is called topiary. The clever topiary work at Disney World in Florida has generated interest in this art form. If you want to learn topiary, study books that include pictures showing sculptured animals and birds, etc., trimmed by specialists. One such book is *The Art of Shaping Shrubs, Trees and Other Plants* by Iatsuo and Kiyoko Ishimoto (Crown Publishers, Inc., New York).

How can I keep tree wounds from bleeding? Maples and birches, if pruned in spring, will bleed, but this is temporary. Another form of bleeding is caused by "slime flux," and this is often very difficult to control and may cause the bark to decay if it persists for a considerable time. Sometimes a short length of pipe is inserted to carry off the flux.

What tools are necessary for pruning? For close work on trees, a narrow-bladed pruning saw is desirable. In some cases it is helpful to have one attached to a long pole to get at branches which otherwise would be difficult to reach. To cut branches ½ inch in diameter or less, sharp hand pruners should be used, or a pruning knife. In pruning old, overgrown shrubs, long-handled loppers are useful. Small power saws, electric or gasoline, are a good investment where extensive pruning is to be done. The cut limbs can easily be cut into firewood. However, cutting large trees can be hazardous, especially if they are near buildings, so it can be more sensible to call in a tree expert.

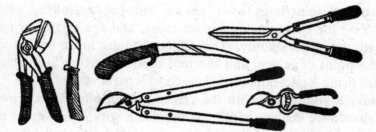

Types of pruning equipment for trees and shrubs.

DISBUDDING AND PINCHING

What is meant by disbudding?   Disbudding is the removal of some flower buds while they are still small, so that those remaining will develop into flowers of larger size. Plants on which disbudding is commonly practiced include carnation, chrysanthemum, dahlia, peony, rose.

When are plants disbudded?   As soon as the buds to be removed are large enough to handle, usually about the size of a pea or bean.

How often should plants be pinched to force blooms? Should they be kept pinched as long as they bloom?   Pinching a plant delays blooming instead of forcing it, but results in a bigger, stockier plant. Some plants, such as snapdragon, give good, bushy plants with only one pinching. Others, such as chrysanthemum, may be pinched 3 or 4 times until late July. A plant such as geranium, after the first pinching (soon after rooting), may be pinched just beyond each flower bud as it appears.

What plants should I pinch, and when?   These are a few examples: coleus, carnation, chrysanthemum, dahlia, fuchsia, heliotrope, iresine, salvia, and the garden geranium. One pinching, when the plants are a few inches high, may be sufficient, but in the case of coleus and chrysanthemum, pinching may be repeated more than once if extra-large

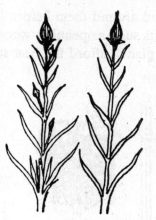

Disbudding—pinching out most of the buds in order to secure fewer but larger blooms—is often practiced with some plants, such as carnation, dahlia, chrysanthemum, and rose. The carnation at the left shows buds along the stem; the one on the right shows the stem after disbudding.

plants are desired. Some woody plants are pinched back during the growing season to make them more compact.

What is meant by "terminal bud"? The topmost bud on a shoot.

ROOT-PRUNING

What are the reasons for root-pruning? To promote formation of fibrous roots, to make transplanting easier, to induce blossoming, and to check excessive shoot and leaf growth.

Can I, by root-pruning ahead of time, make it possible to move some shrubs with greater safety? Yes. In the spring, thrust a sharp spade into the ground to its full depth all around the shrub, a few inches inside the digging circle. This will induce the formation of fibrous roots which will enable it to be easily moved the following fall or spring.

Is there any simple method of dwarfing plants? It is helpful to start off with naturally dwarf varieties. Restrict the roots by growing the plants in comparatively small containers, or by root-pruning if in the open ground. Prune the top at frequent intervals during the growing season by shortening new growth. In the case of fruit trees, the use of a dwarfing understock is indicated.

SUPPORTS

What is the best method of staking perennials and annuals? The type of support varies with the subject. Those with only comparatively few slender stems (delphinium, for example) should have individual slender stakes to which the stems are loosely tied. Low, bushy plants can be supported by twigs stuck in the ground around them before they have completed their growth. For other plants such as peonies, wood or metal hoops, on 3 or 4 legs placed over the plants, afford the best solution.

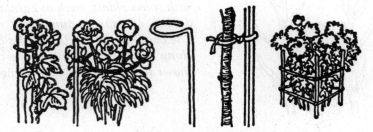

Many flowers require support. Devices for this can be homemade or purchased in garden centers. Detail drawing (second from right) shows a method of securing a plant stem to a stake: String is first tied tight around the stake; then the ends are tied in a loose loop around the stem.

Do you have any pointers on staking plants? Always maintain the natural habit of growth. Don't tie stems in a bundle and fasten to a broomstick, for example. (See answer to the preceding question.)

How can one obtain twiggy shoots for staking perennials? Save all suitable material from shrub-pruning. Keep one or more privet bushes solely for this purpose—cutting off the twigs early in the fall so that they will dry up and not grow when stuck in the ground. Gray birch twigs are ideal, if available.

I want to use espaliered trees to enclose a small flower garden. How can I support them? If in a continuous row, use galvanized wire stretched tightly on posts or a wood fence with horizontal members. Isolated specimens are best supported on wooden trellises.

How are espaliered trees or shrubs supported on walls? Sometimes by fastening directly to the wall, but this is considered undesirable where exposed to full sun in regions having hot summers. They can be fastened to wires strung on brackets 6 inches or more from a wall or on wood trellises, thus allowing circulation of air between plant and wall.

How can I attach trained shrubs directly to a wall? Use broad tape; or use cloth or leather (old gloves) cut into strips ½ inch wide, 3 to 6 inches long, passed around branches and fastened to the wall with

Delphinium and its annual relative larkspur are among the flowers that may require support for each flowering stem.

stubby nails. Also special wall nails are obtainable from firms dealing in garden supplies.

I want to use vines for "accent points" in my flower garden. What is best for holding them up? Use red-cedar posts, sunk 2 to 3 feet in the ground and wrapped with chicken wire, or a "tepee" support.

Plant Propagation

(See also Propagation under Plant Groups.)

What are the various methods of plant propagation? Seeds, spores, bulbils, cormels, tubers, rhizomes, runners, offsets, suckers, stolons, layers, division, cutting, grafting.

SEEDS

What are the main factors in seed germination? Quality and freshness in seed. Correct temperature (most seeds like a 68° to 72° F. temperature day and night for good germination), uniform moisture supply, and sufficient air. Some seeds must never be allowed to become really dry (usually these are stratified in a moist medium); some must be sown as soon as they are ripe; some wait a year or more before germinating; and some require an "after-ripening" period at low temperatures. However, these special treatments are necessary more often for tree and shrub seeds than for annuals, perennials, and biennials.

We started seeds of petunias, snapdragons, tomatoes, and peppers and they came up fine, but then died off. Why? Your trouble is due to "damping off" caused by various fungi in the soil. Usually the newly emerged seedlings rot off at the soil line, as if mowed down by a scythe. Certain conditions favor damping off: too much water; low soil temperature during germination (below 65° F.); high soil temperature after sprouting (78° to 80° F.); overcrowded seedlings and improper sprouting medium.

Can you give us some good tips on how to start seeds?

1. Sow in milled sphagnum moss, peat moss, or in one of the soilless mixes such as Jiffy Mix, which commercial growers use. Or you can mix your own growing medium with one part each of peat moss, vermiculite, and medium or fine perlite.

A homemade tamper is useful for firming and smoothing the growing medium in flats before sowing seeds, transplanting seedlings, or inserting cuttings.

2. Fill boxes or flats and level off with medium that has been moistened in a plastic bag.

3. Scatter seeds thinly, 6 to 12 seeds per square inch, depending on size of seeds, or sow in rows marked with a dowel about ¼ inch deep (⅜ inch for larger seeds).

4. If seeds want light to germinate, press lightly with a dowel to ensure contact with soil. Other seeds should be covered lightly with the medium, using your hands or a sieve or a flour sifter.

5. Water (mist or sprinkle gently—don't splash!) top of the seed box or set box in a pan of water.

6. If you sprinkle the medium, slip it into a clear plastic bag; if you subirrigate in a pan, lay a piece of plastic or glass over the top of the box.

7. Keep seed box at 68° to 72° F. If the room temperature drops below this, invest in an inexpensive heating cable from a garden center or mail-order seed firm.

8. Once the seedlings have become visible, remove the plastic or glass cover.

9. Keep the seedlings in a bright window or 4 inches below a fluorescent light. They can stand a temperature down to 65° F. once they have germinated.

10. Once seedlings get their first set of true leaves, they can be transplanted into pots or boxes.

11. Note: a few seeds prefer cool temperatures to germinate (e.g., parsley and verbena), so consult seed catalogs.

Is it difficult to start seeds at home? We have no greenhouse. Seeds will germinate well under the conditions mentioned above. However, in most houses adequate light is a problem after seedlings are up. Even with a sunny window, seedlings are apt to become spindly during short cloudy days of winter and early spring. But fluorescent lights are a great boon and can be used to augment daylight. Another precaution: seed-

TRANSPLANTING SEEDLINGS
(Top left) Dig hole wide and deep enough for roots (left). (Top center) Remove only a few seedlings at a time from the flat so the roots don't dry out. (Top right) If soil is very dry, pour water into the hole to lessen transplanting shock. (Bottom left) Use a trowel to set the plant in the hole; water at once with the transplanting solution. (Bottom center) Firm the soil around the plant with your fingers. (Bottom right) A paper bag or other container such as a plastic milk or cider jug with its bottom cut off can protect the plant from frost, wind, or bright sun for a week or so.

lings may react unfavorably to any leaking gas fumes from heating or cooking elements.

How can germination be hastened in hard-shell seeds?   Soak in warm water overnight, or longer, to soften shell; or you can scarify them by nicking the hard shell of large seeds with a sharp knife. Sometimes seeds are treated with acids, but this is not recommended for beginners.

What is meant by "stratification" of seeds?   It is the term applied to the practice of storing seeds over winter, or longer, in moist material such as sand or peat moss. Seeds which lose their vitality if allowed to become dry (oak, chestnut, etc.) and "2-year seeds" (hawthorn, dogwood) are commonly so treated.

Should seeds be treated with a disinfectant before planting?   Yes, if trouble has been experienced in the past with seed-borne diseases.

We saved some of our seeds left over from last year. Is it true that the older the seed, the stronger the plants that are produced?   It is true that the best seeds at harvesttime will keep the longest in storage, but their vigor *never* increases. Vegetable and flower seeds are at their prime as soon as they reach maximum dry weight on the mother plant.

We always have seed left over. Is there any safe way to keep it for another year?   There is no reason why you cannot keep excess seed for another year as long as it is stored in a dry place. One way to keep the vigor and longevity of leftover seeds is as follows: unfold and lay out a stack of 4 facial tissues. Place two heaping tablespoons of powdered milk on one corner (the dry milk must be from a freshly opened box to guarantee dryness). Fold and roll the facial tissue to make a small pouch. Secure with tape or a rubber band. Place the pouch in a widemouth fruit jar and immediately drop in packets of leftover seeds. The tissues will prevent seed packets from touching the desiccant (powdered milk). Seal the jar tightly, using a rubber ring to shut out moist air. Store the jar in the refrigerator, *not in the freezer*. Recap the jar any time you remove the seed packets.

BULBS, CORMS, AND TUBERS

What is the usual method of propagating bulbs?   By digging them up when dormant and taking off small bulbs formed around the mother bulb. They should be planted separately.

Is there any way of inducing bulbs to form offsets for propagating purposes?   Planting shallower than normal is supposed to be helpful. Commercial growers, in the case of hyacinths, either scoop out the base

STARTING SEEDS INDOORS

(1) First moisten growing medium (soilless mix or milled sphagnum moss) in a plastic bag by adding warm water. (2) If using sphagnum moss, squeezing the moss in the bag helps it absorb water. (3) Put the moistened medium into a flat. (4) Firm the growing medium in the flat. (5) Open the seed packet. (6) Sow the seeds in shallow rows or scatter over the medium. (7) Cover the seeds with a very thin layer of moist medium. Small seeds in sphagnum moss need not be covered. Water well with gentle water spray. To retain moisture until seeds germinate, slip the flat into a plastic bag and keep in warmth but out of direct sun. Remove the bag as soon as the seeds germinate and put the flat under fluorescent lights.

of the bulb or cut into it in several directions to induce the formation of bulbils. Special after-treatment is necessary.

What are offsets? Shoots with short stems with a miniature plant at the end—sometimes applied to the small bulbs produced around the mother bulb. Typical offsets are produced by houseleeks. They may be taken off and used to start new plants.

How are plants propagated by tubers? By separating or cutting, and planting. Sometimes, as in the potato, the tuber may be cut into several pieces, each having an "eye" or growth bud.

CUTTINGS

What is meant by softwood cuttings? These are made from shoots that are still actively growing and are taken from hardy shrubs during May and early June. Sometimes suitable plants are placed in greenhouses to force young growth for cuttings.

What is meant by half-ripe wood cuttings? Cuttings of half-ripe wood are taken when the shoots of woody plants have finished their growth but are not yet mature. July and August are suitable months.

What are hardwood cuttings? Hardwood cuttings are made from fully matured shoots, generally of the current year's growth. These are taken after there have been a few frosts, packed in moist sand or peat moss, stored at a temperature of 35° to 40° F., and planted out the following spring.

How does one propagate softwood (begonia) and hardwood (forsythia) plants? This depends entirely upon the plant under consideration. In most cases, softwood plants may be increased by stem cuttings, and many of the hardwood plants may be increased in the same way; but there are innumerable exceptions in both groups.

What is the best and surest way to root cuttings? I have a cold room in a cellar with no heat. It faces east and has two small windows. I also have a dark closet behind the burner where it is always warm. The dark closet behind the burner is most unsuitable. Probably you could root most of the common shrubs and house plants in the cellar room if the cuttings were placed near the window. You could also install a fluorescent light unit.

What is the best way to propagate plants from cuttings without a greenhouse or hotbed? Many shrubs, some trees, most of the plants used for summer bedding, herbaceous perennials, many rock-garden plants, and several house plants can be propagated during the summer almost as readily in a cold frame as in a greenhouse or hotbed.

What is polyethylene? Polyethylene is the name given to a plastic film which has the properties of permitting the passage of gases and retaining water vapor.

How is polyethylene used in plant propagation? It is used in the same way as glass. Among the advantages as compared with glass are: its light weight; it usually eliminates any need for additional watering. It is also used to enclose the moist sphagnum moss when air-layering is practiced or to enclose flats of cuttings and seeds to create a moist atmosphere. The plastic is stretched over a wire frame, giving the flat the look of a flat-topped tent or miniature greenhouse.

How can I make a propagating frame? An ordinary cold frame is satisfactory; or you can use a box 10 to 12 inches deep covered tightly with a pane of glass. Make ½-inch drainage holes in the bottom; cover with 1 inch of peat moss, and put in 4 inches of some rooting medium (such as sand or sand and peat moss) packed down firmly. (See also the above question.)

What are the essentials in using polyethylene in rooting cuttings? Thoroughly soaking the rooting medium and completely enclosing the cuttings. When only a few cuttings are to be rooted, they are put in a flowerpot which is then put in a polyethylene bag and the open end is tightly closed. Or, on a slightly larger scale, a shallow wooden box (flat) can be used. In this case, some kind of support is needed to keep the film from contact with the cuttings. It can be wire coat hangers. After the cuttings are inserted and have been thoroughly watered, the whole is wrapped in plastic, taking care that no opening is left to permit the escape of moisture. The best way to do this is to drape the plastic over the flat and then tuck the sides and ends underneath it. The plastic can be stapled to the flat.

What is the after-treatment? The cuttings are put in a well-lighted place where they can be shaded from direct sun. In six weeks or so they should be examined, and if they are rooted, gradually inure them to the outside air by gradually loosening the cover.

What is meant by the "constant mist" system of propagation? This is a method in which cuttings are rooted by keeping their leaves constantly moist by subjecting them to a fine mistlike spray. Special nozzles are sold for this purpose and usually emit the mists in timed intermittent spurts rather than constantly.

I am interested in the possibilities, on a small scale, of rooting cut-

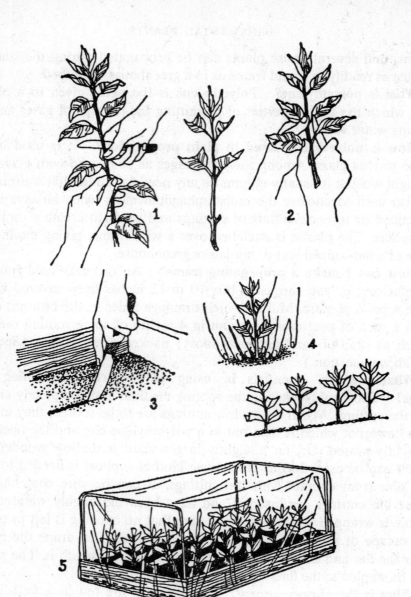

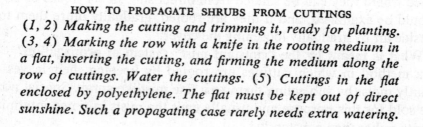

HOW TO PROPAGATE SHRUBS FROM CUTTINGS

(1, 2) *Making the cutting and trimming it, ready for planting.*
(3, 4) *Marking the row with a knife in the rooting medium in*
a flat, inserting the cutting, and firming the medium along the
row of cuttings. Water the cuttings. (5) Cuttings in the flat
enclosed by polyethylene. The flat must be kept out of direct
sunshine. Such a propagating case rarely needs extra watering.

tings by mist. How does one go about it? You will need a nozzle that will deliver about 1½ gallons of water per hour, and water pressure of 30 to 50 pounds. This should be sufficient to cover an area of about one square yard. The site should be in the open in full sun; if in a windy location a windbreak, which may be a sheet of plastic fastened to a wooden frame (about 3 × 4 feet), may be necessary. There must be free drainage; therefore the rooting medium should be coarse sand or perlite, and the pots or flats should be placed on a platform of galvanized hardware cloth raised an inch or two above the ground.

Is it necessary to keep the spray going all the time? No, it is not —although no great harm will accrue if it is left on night and day. It is considered desirable, however, to have an intermittent mist. This may be accomplished by the installation of an electronic leaf which automatically shuts off the water when it is wet and turns it on when it is dry.

What are the advantages of rooting cuttings by mist? It enables us to root larger cuttings than is possible by conventional means; and cuttings usually considered difficult often can be rooted with ease. It is especially useful in the propagation of rhododendrons and other broad-leaved evergreens.

Will you please tell me something about air-layering by using plastic film? This is a method that can be used successfully outdoors on a large number of different trees and shrubs. It also works for large indoor plants such as rubber plant (*Ficus*), dieffenbachia, and others. With a sharp knife, cut a slit in a stem at the point where it is desired to have roots form. (Other ways of wounding the stem are to cut a small notch in the stem or to remove a cylinder of bark about an inch long.) The wound is wrapped with a wad of moist sphagnum moss, which is tied in place with twine preparatory to covering it with the plastic film, which should be between 2 and 4 thousandths of an inch thick.

When is the best time to make a layer? Probably early spring for outdoor plants.

Is it a foolproof method? It is not. Care must be taken to avoid getting the medium too wet. This involves squeezing out as much of the water as possible prior to applying the moss; also, in putting on the wrap it is essential to ensure that no water gets in. Be careful to have the overlap on the under side; and see that the ties, both top and bottom, are made watertight by taping them spirally so that the rain cannot seep in.

How does one know when to remove the layer? When roots are visible through the plastic. The removal of the layer is probably the most critical period. The layers, when they are rooted, should be treated for a time as though they were unrooted cuttings, by potting them, keeping them in a closed and shaded cold frame, or enclosing them in plastic and gradually hardening them off.

What is the best material in which to root cuttings? Sand has been most commonly used, but a half-and-half mixture of peat moss and sand has become popular for almost all kinds of cuttings. Sphagnum moss, vermiculite, and perlite are other materials used and are often mixed with the sand and peat-moss mixture.

Is there any special trick in inserting cuttings? Make individual holes with a pointed stick; or make a narrow trench by drawing a blunt knife or label through the rooting medium. It is important to be sure that the bases of the cuttings touch the rooting medium and that it is well firmed about them.

Is there any reason for removing leaves when inserting cuttings in the rooting medium? The reason for removing leaves is to prevent undue loss of moisture from the plant tissues by transpiration. Its value has been questioned by some propagators in recent years, and it is probably necessary only in the case of cuttings with very large leaves. However, removing lower leaves that will be buried in medium prevents them from rotting.

A bulb pan or a flowerpot, enclosed in a polyethylene bag, makes an excellent miniature propagating case. In it, cuttings can readily be rooted.

Why do professional growers use a powder when planting cuttings? Is this powder a talc or some special powder? A root stimulant is used for the purpose of obtaining a higher percentage of rooting, to shorten the time required for the production of roots, and, in many instances, to obtain a bigger root system. Talc is sometimes the carrier with which small amounts of active chemical substances are mixed. Most soft cuttings such as geraniums do not need a rooting hormone. It works best on woody cuttings such as roses and evergreens.

Which chemicals are used as stimulants for cuttings? Many chemicals have been tried—indoleacetic acid, indolebutyric acid, naphthaleneacetic acid, etc.—and others are always under trial. This is a rapidly changing field and new materials and techniques appear constantly, especially for the professional gardener and nursery owner.

Why are acids used, and what kinds, to promote good cuttings? Most cuttings root better in an acid than in a neutral or alkaline medium. Old-time propagators frequently added vinegar to water applied to cutting beds. (See answer to preceding question.) The acid cuts or checks the growth of bacteria and fungi. Some rooting hormones now contain a fungicide that suppresses fungus growth.

Can anyone use root-inducing chemicals? As prepared for general use, these can be readily applied by anyone. The most popular are in powder form. The bases of the cuttings are merely dipped into this before being inserted in the rooting medium. They are sold in garden centers or by mail-order supply firms.

How do you treat cuttings started with the aid of chemical stimulants? The treatment of cuttings after the application of the root-inducing stimulant is the same as for untreated cuttings.

What about the use of Vitamin B_1 and hormones in rooting plants? Vitamin B_1 is probably present in sufficient quantities in any soil reasonably well supplied with humus, so that the addition of this substance is unnecessary. If by hormones you mean the substances now on the market for facilitating the rooting of cuttings, there is little doubt that they are a definite aid to propagation, especially for woody cuttings.

What is the general treatment of cuttings after they have been placed in a propagating frame? Keep the rooting medium moist and the frame closed until roots have formed, then gradually increase ventilation to harden cuttings. The frame must be in a shady location or shaded by a double thickness of cheesecloth on sash. Maintain a temperature of 70° F., if possible.

How can one know when a cutting has developed roots and is ready to be transplanted? When it is judged that sufficient time has elapsed

Cuttings of various house plants, including two leaf cuttings of African-violet, in a propagating box. Each cutting is inserted in its own peat pot. When roots grow through the peat pots, it is time to set the cutting and pot in a larger container.

for roots to have developed, gently pull on one or two cuttings, and if they offer resistance it is a good indication that they have rooted. Most of the plants commonly rooted in the summer produce a good root system in from 6 to 10 weeks. Many conifers, however, require as many months.

How are cuttings treated after rooting? Those rooting early (July, August) are potted and the pots plunged in sand, peat moss, or ashes in a cold frame, to be planted the following spring. Late rooters may be left in the rooting medium. Both kinds should be protected by scattering marsh hay, or similar litter, among them after the first severe frost.

ROOT AND LEAF CUTTINGS

When are root cuttings usually made? Usually late in autumn for hardy plants. They should be planted ½ to 1 inch deep in sandy soil and kept in a cool greenhouse; or the flats may be stored in a cold but frost-free place. They can be made any time for indoor plants.

Does it make any difference which end of a root cutting is inserted in the soil? Yes. In order to be certain that the right end will be uppermost, it is customary to make a straight cut across the upper end of the cutting and a sloping cut at the basal end. However, with thin cuttings (such as phlox), both ends are cut straight across and the cuttings are laid flat.

Do plants made from cuttings always resemble the parent exactly? Yes, in most cases. This type of increase is called vegetative propagation, in contrast to "sexual" propagation, as in the case of seed.

How many kinds of root cuttings are usually made? When true roots, as distinguished from underground stems, are being dealt with, there is only one type of root cutting. Such cuttings are usually from 1 to 3 inches long, depending upon their thickness.

How are cuttings of fine, stringy roots made? Cut them into lengths of an inch or a little more and lay them flat in the container in which they are to grow.

Are root cuttings more likely to succeed than stem cuttings? This depends entirely upon the plant to be propagated. The roots of all plants do not produce buds, and in these cases it is useless to attempt to reproduce them by root cuttings. In those instances where past experience has shown that a plant will produce buds on severed root pieces, this method is generally a little less trouble than stem cuttings.

What type of plant is usually propagated by root cuttings? Many plants can be raised from root cuttings. These include rose, blackberry, horse-radish, phlox, trumpet creeper, daphne, bouvardia, Oriental poppy, and many others. It must be understood, however, that if root cuttings are made of grafted or budded plants, it will be the understock that is propagated.

Are any indoor plants propagated by root cuttings? Not many of the more familiar house plants are propagated from root cuttings, but sansevieria, dracaena, and bouvardia are sometimes increased in this way.

Will leaves make new plants if treated in the same way as stem cuttings? In some cases, yes. Among the plants commonly propagated in this way are African-violet, gloxinia, rex begonia, pick-a-back plant, and many succulents, such as the sedums.

CLONING AND TISSUE CULTURE

What is cloning? Is it practical for the home gardener? Cloning is a form of tissue culture and has been done for thousands of years. A tip cutting or root cutting produces a clone of the parent plant that is almost always identical. The difference between taking a tip cutting and using only a few cells is merely a laboratory technique and the fewer the cells, the less space they take up in the propagation process. The amateur will not have much luck propagating plants by tissue culture, but he can still resort to cuttings or division with good success.

What is tissue culture?   Plants identical with a parent plant are reproduced by taking a cell or a few cells from the parent and putting them into a special agar solution that contains all the nutrients necessary to life. These cells continue to grow, divide, and split into complete plants, free from disease. Cloning by tissue culture has been around for many years but has gained new impetus. A plant that is threatened by a virus, and consequently may become extinct, can be propagated by tissue culture and produce plants free from the disease. Cells are taken from the meristematic tissue (that which is at the very tip of the growing stem, or root) and placed in the agar solution. By this process, one can produce thousands of plants in the time and space it would take to produce only a few hundred by the "cutting" method. Commercial growers have had great success with tissue culture in producing chrysanthemums, orchids, and foliage plants.

LAYERING

What is meant by layering?   Layering means bringing a shoot of the plant into contact with the earth with the object of having it form roots. Such shoots are slit with an upward cut, twisted, or girdled, either by having a ring of bark removed, or by encircling them with a tight wire, in order to induce the formation of roots at the injured part. This injured part must be covered with soil and kept moist. Many plants naturally form layers, especially when lower branches remain in contact with a moist mulch.

How long before layers are ready to transplant?   Many herbaceous plants will form roots in a few weeks. Shrubs layered in the spring will usually have a satisfactory root system by the end of the growing season. Some shrubs, such as rhododendrons and others that form roots slowly, require 2 years. After new roots form, the layers may be severed from the parent plant to become new plants on their own roots.

How many kinds of layering are there?   Layering may be broadly divided into two classes: (a) layering in the ground and (b) air layering. Class (a) may be divided into simple layering, serpentine layering, continuous layering, and mound layering. In all these ways it is necessary to bring the branches to ground level. Air layering (b) refers to rooting stems at points above the ground by means of "layering pots" filled with soil or by wrapping moist moss around the stem, then tying a piece of plastic around it to retain moisture.

When is layering done? Spring is the best time, as in most cases a good root system will then be developed before winter. It may be done at any time, however, but in the colder parts of the country the roots may be torn off the layers due to winter heaving if plants are layered at a later period.

Some plants, such as the strawberry-begonia or strawberry-geranium (Saxifraga stolonifera), multiply themselves by runners, which are easily rooted in pots while still attached to the parent plant.

What is the best kind of wood for layering? If shrubs are to be layered, stout 1-year-old shoots are preferred, as they form a root system much more readily than older wood.

Is there a limit to the size of branch used in layering? For practical purposes, yes. The younger they are, the more readily they may be expected to root. However, layering frequently takes place when large branches, many years old, come in contact with the ground, but it may take many years before they form a root system sufficiently large to support them independently.

SUCKERS, STOLONS, AND RUNNERS

How are plants propagated by suckers? If the plant is not grafted and is a type that produces suckers (lilac, for instance), rooted suckers can be dug up, cut back, and planted to produce new plants.

What is a stolon? A branch which grows downward and roots at the tip, where it comes into contact with the soil. When rooted, it can be detached from the parent, dug up, and planted to lead an independent existence. Forsythia and matrimony-vine commonly produce stolons.

How are plants propagated by runners? Merely by digging up the runners when rooted. In special cases, to avoid root disturbance, small flowerpots may be filled with earth and the developing runner fastened to the soil with a hairpin.

Propagating a rhododendron by layering. After a good root system has formed, the new plant can be severed from its parent and replanted.

GRAFTING

What is meant by a "graft"? A graft is the union of parts of two plants in such a manner that they will grow together to form one plant. It consists of two parts: the *understock* and the *scion*. The union of these two, by grafting, results in a new plant having the roots of one plant and the branches, leaves, flowers, and fruit of the plant from which the scion was taken.

What is double grafting? This refers to the practice of first grafting onto the understock a scion that will unite readily with it, and later grafting onto the first scion a second one of a kind that will unite with it but will not unite satisfactorily with the understock when grafted directly upon it.

Can any plant be grafted on any other plant? Only those plants that are closely related can be grafted.

What is a scion (cion)? A scion is one of the two parts necessary when making a graft, and consists of a short portion of stem of the plant that is to be duplicated. It usually contains two or more buds, and the base is cut in such manner that the cambium, a layer of actively growing tissue between bark and wood, or a part of it, will come in direct contact with the corresponding layer of the understock, which is cut to fit the scion.

What is meant by understock? The understock is the part that constitutes the root system of a grafted or budded plant. Seedlings, or pieces of root, or rooted cuttings, are generally used as understocks. It is the part to which the scion or bud is attached that is to become the new plant.

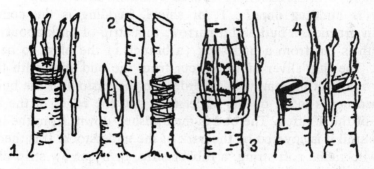

Grafting is an interesting operation that, with a little practice, any gardener can accomplish. Above are shown (1) bark grafting; (2) whip or tongue grafting; (3) bridge grafting; (4) cleft grafting. In each case, the detail sketch shows how the scion (or bud wood) is cut.

When is grafting done? Grafting is usually practiced in the spring, either in the open or in greenhouses, just as the understocks are beginning to break dormancy. The understocks should be beginning growth while the scions must still be dormant. For this reason the scions are buried in the ground or kept on ice until required for grafting. Summer grafting of some ornamental trees and shrubs is also practiced.

Why are plants grafted? To propagate horticultural varieties (cultivars) which do not "come true" from seed; to increase plants which are difficult to propagate by other vegetative means, such as cuttings or divisions; to modify the growth of scion by use of dwarfing understocks, etc.; to hasten flowering; and to produce plants of special form as when "weeping" trees (mulberry, elm, etc.) are "worked" on a tall understock.

How are ornamental trees grafted? In several ways, depending upon the plant being grafted. Splice, whip, veneer, and side graft are probably more commonly used than others, but saddle grafting and grafting are other forms frequently employed.

What sort of roots are ornamental trees grafted on? Can any root be used?   The kind of root that an ornamental tree is grafted on must be very closely related to it. Oaks cannot be grafted on elms, for example, nor beech on ash. Even in a group as large as the oaks, not all oaks can be grafted on just one kind of oak.

What is meant by budding?   Budding is a form of grafting by means of which a single bud and a portion of its surrounding bark are brought into contact with the cambium layer of a suitable understock.

How is budding done?   T, or shield, budding is the commonest form. In practice, a bud and a narrow, thin strip of bark about ¾ inch in length is cut from a bud stick (a branch of the plant to be propagated). The thin sliver of wood, cut from the bud stick with the bud, may or may not be removed, according to the custom of the budder. A T-shaped cut is made on the understock and the edges of the bark on the leg of the T lifted. The bud is then pushed down, from the top, into the cut until it is covered by the bark of the understock. It is then tied in place with raffia, soft string, a rubber strip, or a narrow strip of plastic film.

What is a bud stick?   A bud stick is a shoot, usually of the current year's growth, from which buds are cut for budding.

Why is budding practiced in preference to grafting?   Because only one bud is required to produce a new plant, consequently a given amount of scion wood will furnish more buds than scions for grafting, as each scion would require about four buds. In the case of stone fruits, budding ensures a better union than grafting. Also, since less time is consumed in budding than in grafting, it is preferred where suitable.

When is budding done?   Budding is usually a summer operation, as it can be done only when the sap is running and the bark lifts easily from the wood. June, July, and August are the usual months in the North.

How does grafting differ from budding?   The principal differences are in the time of year when each is performed and the amount of scion or budwood required. A graft consists of an understock and a scion, i.e., a short length of shoot containing two or more buds. In budding, an understock is also required, but in place of a scion a single bud is inserted on the understock.

Does the plant on which the bud is placed (understock) have any influence on the budded portion?   Very definitely in many cases. Weak-growing garden roses are much more vigorous when budded on a suitable understock than when on their own roots. Dwarf fruit trees are good examples. Such trees are dwarf because they have been budded or grafted on understocks that cause dwarfing.

What is bark grafting?   The tree is prepared as for cleft grafting, but the branches are not split. Instead, a slit is made in the bark, about 1½ inches long, from the stub down. The scions are prepared by making a sloping cut at their bases, but a shoulder is cut at the top of the slope so that the lower part of the scion, which is to be pushed under the bark, is quite thin. Several scions may be placed on one stub, depending upon its size. On large stubs the scions may be secured with brads; on smaller ones they are tied in. All must be covered with grafting wax.

What is the purpose of bridge grafting?   This form of grafting is confined to the repair of tree trunks (particularly fruit trees) which have been entirely or largely girdled by rodents. Its purpose is to maintain a connection between the top and the roots. Unless the girdled portion is bridged in this way, the tree will shortly die.

How is bridge grafting done?   Trim away ragged bark. Make longitudinal slits above and below the wound and loosen the bark. Cut scions (from the tree being operated on) of one-year-old wood about 3 inches longer than the wound. Bevel each end with cuts ½ to 1 inch long; bend the scion in the middle; insert under the slit bark; fasten with small brads. Cover the points of insertion with grafting wax. Scions should be placed every 2 inches around the trunk.

What is cleft grafting?   Cleft grafting is one of the simpler forms and involves the insertion of scions cut to a long wedge shape in a cleft of the understock. It is chiefly used in "making over" fruit trees and in grafting certain herbaceous plants.

What is the purpose of cleft grafting?   The particular value of this form of grafting is in the conversion of unsuitable kinds of apples, pears, and sometimes such stone fruits as cherries and plums, to the production of fruit of better quality or greater productiveness.

How is cleft grafting done?   Cut back all branches to be grafted to leave a shapely tree; smooth over the cut faces; split each cut end with a grafting chisel. Cut scions with a wedge-shaped base about 1½ inches long. Open the cleft with the end of the chisel and insert scions, two in each cleft. See that the inner edges of bark on the scions and stock are in contact. Tie in the scions on small branches; on the thicker ones this will be unnecessary. Cover the scions and all parts of the cleft with grafting wax. If both scions unite, the weaker one may be cut off level with the stump the following spring. At least one branch should be left to be grafted the second year, otherwise there will be an enormous growth of water sprouts.

When is cleft grafting carried out? In the spring, as soon as the buds show the first indication of swelling. The scions must be completely dormant.

What is whip grafting? The base of the scion is cut across with a downward, long, sloping cut, about 1¼ inches long; then an upward cut ½ inch long is made on this face, commencing about ½ inch from the lower end of the first cut. The understock is cut in a similar way. Press the tongue of the scion into the cut in the understock until the one face covers the other. Tie together with raffia or soft string and cover the union with grafting wax; or pack in moist material and treat the same as hardwood cuttings.

What is the procedure in whip grafting if the understock is much thicker than the scion? The first cut should be straight across. Then on one side of the understock, and near the top, cut off a strip of the same length and width as the cut face of the scion. Cut a tongue in it as previously described; tie; wax. Where the scion and the understock are not exactly the same width, it is most important that the inner edges of the bark of the scion and understock *come in contact on one side* of the joint; otherwise they will not unite.

Cold Frames and Hotbeds

COLD FRAMES

How can I make a simple cold frame? Use a 12-inch plank for the back, a 6-inch one for the front. Make ends of one 6-inch plank and half a 6-inch plank cut diagonally lengthwise (to allow for slope from back to front) cleated together. A standard sash is 6 × 3 feet, so the width of the frame should be 6 feet and the length made up of units of 3 feet plus about 1¼-inch allowance between each sash to accommodate cross ties, usually 1 inch thick. The above specifications do not allow much headroom—a height of 9 to 12 inches in front and 15 to 18 inches in back is preferable.

Are the ready-made self-ventilating cold frames offered in nursery and seed catalogs practical? Yes, but they are expensive compared to a cold frame you could construct yourself with Fiberglas or polyethylene instead of glass. If you wish to make a frame with the self-venting feature (very practical for those who may be away during the day), you can buy a solar-powered ventilator designed for the purpose (some are made for greenhouses).

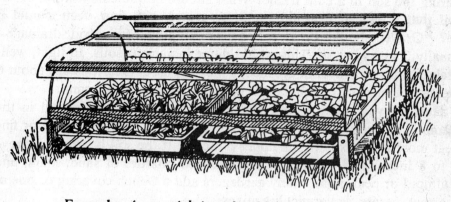

Example of a prefabricated cold frame with acrylic cover and walls and a thermostatic solar device that raises or lowers the top automatically according to the temperature.

What are the advantages and uses of a cold frame? Basically, it provides a protected area for sowing seeds, growing young seedlings, and rooting cuttings. In the spring the additional warmth provided by the enclosed structure makes it possible to sow seeds several weeks earlier than could safely be done in the open ground. In addition, the seed bed can be protected from heavy rains, which could wash out the seed. It also helps deter animals from digging in the seed bed. In the winter it can be used for holding over tender perennials, rooting shrub cuttings, or giving a cold treatment to seeds or bulbs requiring such conditions.

Can I make a cold frame in December? I have a large, dry cellar where I can thaw out the soil. It is possible to construct a cold frame of wood in December and get the soil in place ready for spring planting.

I have been informed that plants will not do so well in a cold frame constructed with concrete walls instead of wood. Is this true? No, it is not true. In fact, concrete frames can be kept more sanitary.

Since a glass sash is so heavy, can I use plastic or Fiberglas for the cover? Yes, both are satisfactory. Although its cost is minimal, the plastic will have a useful life of only a year or two. Light weight is an advantage when it comes to lifting or storing the plastic sash but it is a disadvantage in high winds unless some means of anchoring it is provided.

Should a layer of crushed stone or coarse gravel be used when preparing the soil in a cold frame? What should be the composition of the soil that is placed over the stone or gravel, and how deep should it be? Gravel should be deep enough to allow for good drainage—usually 3 inches or so. This would differ in various soils. In light, well-drained soil, no gravel or crushed stones are used. Over this use about 6 inches of a mixture of equal parts humus, garden soil, and sand.

How do you make a seed bed in a cold frame? If the soil in the frame is a sandy loam, spread a 2-inch layer of sifted leafmold or fine peat moss and mix with the upper 6 inches. If the soil is clayey, remove 6 to 8 inches and replace with a screened mixture of sand, loam, and leafmold or peat moss. Many gardeners add a 2-inch covering of one of the peat, perlite, or vermiculite mixes.

What should be added to the cold frame each year, and at which season should this addition be made? Well-rotted manure, compost, or leafmold shortly before plants are to be set or seed sown.

How do I go about starting plants in a cold frame? In March and April, depending on your region, seeds of annuals and vegetables that can be transplanted may be sown, either in flats or directly in a bed of good, friable (loose) soil. Seeds of perennials can also be sown at this time. In June greenwood cuttings of some shrubs can be rooted in a few weeks if kept under rather close conditions and shaded from bright sun. In August seeds of pansy, forget-me-not, and English daisy can be sown for early-spring bloom outdoors.

What is the best way to use cold frames (of which I have quite a few) to obtain maximum year-round efficiency? Seeds of perennials and biennials can be sown in cold frames in the summer and the seedlings transplanted and wintered over in them. A cold frame is also a convenient place in which to root greenwood cuttings of certain shrubs inserted in sandy soil in June and July and kept there for a few weeks until rooted. A frame provides good conditions for seed flats of certain woody plants, such as dogwood, during the winter; also to winter stock plants of chrysanthemums and other perennials not reliably hardy. With the approach of spring, sow certain annual flowers and vegetables for early planting outdoors. In April and May a frame is useful to harden off indoor or greenhouse-grown plants for a short time before planting out. Any vacant space in the summer could be utilized for the growing of tomatoes, melons, and cucumbers.

Is it possible to get early blooms from bulbs and other spring plants in a cold frame? Pansies and forget-me-nots from August-sown seeds flower well in a cold frame in early spring. Good divisions of polyanthus primrose planted at the same time would also reward you with nice flowers. The chaste flowers of Christmas-rose open to perfection under cold-frame protection. Potted bulbs of daffodil, tulip, scilla, and snowdrop can be put in the frame in October to be brought out early in the year for flowering indoors if need be, or planted directly in the frame to flower in place. Leave the sash off until freezing weather threatens and ventilate on all warm days during the winter. In very severe weather it would help to have the frames banked outside with leaves and the sash covered with mats or similar material.

Can violets be grown in cold frames for flowering in spring? Yes. Plant strong, field-grown plants in early September. Cover with a sash for a few days to help them recover, keep moist but admit some air, and shade lightly from bright sun. When established, give all light possible and plenty of air until hard freezing weather. Put mats or some other covering over the sash on very cold nights, and ventilate on every warm day in winter.

Will you tell me how to operate a cold frame with plants in pots and flats? Provide a bed of sifted ashes or gravel 4 to 6 inches deep on which to stand plants during early spring. If they are to be kept in the frame throughout the year, the pots should be buried to their rims to conserve moisture in summer and help prevent breakage from frost in winter. (See answers to preceding questions for general management.)

Why do I have such a hard time growing plants from seeds in cold frames, even though care and thought have been used? Plants grown in frames require more careful attention than when grown in the open. Correct soil, temperature, watering, and *especially* ventilation, all are of utmost importance. Attention to these should produce satisfactory results. If the cold frame has no source of heat (manure, light bulbs, heating cable, etc.), low night temperatures may cause the seeds to rot.

What is meant by "hardening-off"? This is the process whereby plants are gradually inured to a change in environment. For example, when moving seedlings from indoors to outdoors, they are first put in a protected frame for a few days to ease the transition to stronger light and temperature change. If one lacks a frame, the plants can be put in a somewhat protected spot for a few hours each day. If they wilt, the transition is probably being made too rapidly. When for some reason hardening-off is not possible, it helps to spray the plants with an antidesiccant, such as Wilt-Pruf, before setting plants outdoors.

Is it necessary to "harden off" plants before they are moved from a cold frame, greenhouse, or hotbed to open ground? Yes. A sudden change to more intense sunlight, lower humidity, and exposure to wind is injurious to them.

I have a cold frame. When the soil freezes do I fill it in with marsh hay and close it for the winter, or do I have to give it ventilation on warm days? A light covering of marsh hay or straw put on plants when the soil freezes will give added protection. Ventilate on warm days. If the frame is vacant, a covering of hay or leaves will keep out some frost but is hardly necessary.

How would you manage a small cold frame containing little perennial seedlings and some very choice perennial cuttings during winter? See that the soil is moist before hard freezing. After this, lightly cover the plants with clean litter, such as hay or pine needles. Provide ventilation on warm days.

When plants are stored in a cold frame during the winter, what protection should be provided? Cover with a mulch and then use a mat over the sash. Put a mulch around the outside of the frame.

Is commercial fertilizer good to put in a cold frame to give added heat? Commercial fertilizers are of no value in this respect. (See Hotbeds.)

HOTBEDS

What is the difference between a hotbed and a cold frame? A cold frame has no other heat than that provided by the sun. A hotbed is heated by fermenting material, such as fresh manure, electricity, steam, hot water, or light bulbs.

How can I make a medium-size, manure-heated hotbed to start early tomato plants? Assuming you have the frame complete, a pit should be made 2½ feet below ground level and the same size as the frame. Then mix 2 parts fresh stable (horse) manure with 1 part unrotted leaves. Turn two or three times at about 4-day intervals and moisten if dry. When well heated, place mixture in the pit in 6-inch layers, each one well packed, until there is a solid 2-foot bed, or a little more. Finish off to ground level with 4 to 6 inches of good, fine soil in which to grow the plants.

The solar-pod hotbed has a Fiberglas-arched cover and a 30-gallon drum (painted black) filled with water to store heat. In cold climates in the middle of winter, Hotkaps provide added protection to plants as does a layer of straw. The outer walls of the frame must be well insulated.

Can you tell us what the "solar pod" hotbed is? The solar-pod hotbed was designed to replace the manure (the source of heat) and glass sash of the nineteenth-century hotbed with solar energy and Fiberglas. Solar energy is available free everywhere, even in the city. The "pod" is a new kind of hotbed made of a double layer of translucent Fiberglas which has been arched in a frame over a planting bed. Fiberglas is cheaper and easier to handle than glass. In the planting bed lies a 30-gallon drum filled with water that provides heat storage. Also, the walls have to be well insulated to help the earth retain heat. The bed can be used to start seeds in spring and as a year-round tool for growing plants.

Is it necessary to line a hotbed pit? If the soil holds together, and if only a temporary hotbed is required, then the answer is no. Permanent hotbed pits are usually lined with concrete blocks, boards, or styrofoam.

I am planning to raise flower and vegetable plants for sale to gardeners. What is the best way to heat my garden beds? Each is 6 × 17 feet. If this is a more or less permanent proposition, the installation of an electric heating cable or of electric bulbs, arranged in series, would be the best. A mixture of 2 parts fresh stable manure and 1 part leaves from the previous fall would be the best fermenting material. You can, however, raise good flower and vegetable plants for home gardens in just sun-heated frames.

I expect to start a hotbed on March 1. Manure is available on February 15 and March 15. How can I store the February manure so I can make use of it later? The manure you gather in February can be left piled, either indoors or out, for hotbed use in March.

When is the best time to start a hotbed in the northeast U.S.? Late March is soon enough. Put the sash on the frames before snowfall, so they do not have to be emptied of snow.

Does the depth of manure in a hotbed depend on climate? Yes, to some extent. Around New York City, 2 feet is the usual depth. Farther north, 2 feet 6 inches is desirable; in the South, 18 inches or less is enough.

How much soil should be put over the manure in an outdoor hotbed? If seeds are to be sown directly in the bed, about 6 inches of good, friable soil is sufficient. If seeds are to be sown in flats, then 1 inch or so of soil over the manure will do.

How does one know when a manure-heated hotbed is ready for sowing seeds? Stick a soil thermometer (available from most mail-order seed firms) in the manure and close the frame. When the temperature recedes to 90° F. (it will go higher at first), it is safe to sow the seeds.

Does the manure in a manure-heated hotbed have to be changed every year? Yes, it will not heat up a second time. Clear it out after the plants are removed and use it in the compost pile or garden.

What can be used for hotbeds in place of manure besides electricity? Under certain conditions, such as where the frames are close to a greenhouse, it is possible to heat them with steam or hot water piped from the greenhouse system. Or a pipe may be run from the house heater if the frame adjoins the house.

Is there anything besides leaves that is suitable to mix with manure in the making of a hotbed? If obtainable, tanbark and spent hops give good results in prolonging the period of heat in a hotbed. Chopped cornstalks can also be used.

How, or in what way, are cornstalks used for a hotbed in order to take the place of manure for heating in the hotbed? Cut the stalks into 1- or 2-inch lengths, wet thoroughly, pack in 2-inch layers to a total depth of 6 inches in excess of the depth when manure is used. Sprinkle each layer of 18 square feet (area of a standard hotbed sash) with ½ pound of cottonseed meal, ½ pound of ground limestone, and 3 ounces of superphosphate. This increases heat and improves the fertilizing value of cornstalks when rotted.

Can one raise hotbed plants without manure? Yes, with electric heating cable or ordinary light bulbs, arranged in series, with thermostatic control. The installation is good for some years, and the disagreeable features of the old-time hotbed procedure are eliminated.

When and how can a hotbed be prepared to supply a small garden in town? Use special electric heating cable obtainable from a garden-supply outlet. Where spring is slow to arrive, the last half of March would be soon enough to start. Sun heat alone would do for an early start in the frame, as compared to outdoor sowing.

Is it necessary to ventilate hotbeds? Yes, every day except in severe weather. Tilt the sash on the side or the end opposite to the direction from which the wind is blowing. Automatic venting is possible with solar-powered ventilators.

Are any special precautions necessary when watering seedlings in a hotbed? Yes, because of humid air, seedlings are especially vulnerable to attack by "damping-off" fungi. Water in the morning so that the leaves dry more readily. Water only when the soil begins to get dry. If possible, use warm water.

Do hotbeds need any special protection during cold spells? When especially cold nights are anticipated, the sashes are covered with plastic sheets, thermal blankets, mats, or boards as an additional protection.

What is the best way to make a hotbed for seeds that will be left outdoors all year round if the seedlings will have to stay 2 or more years? In this case a cold frame will serve the purpose better than a hotbed. Depending on kinds, the seeds could be sown in the fall or spring, and the seedlings could be transplanted in the bed of the frame until ready to be planted outside.

Do you sow seeds directly into the hotbed or do you sow them in boxes or "flats"? In early spring, if you want to grow lettuce, radishes, or onions, sow directly into the soil. However, if you want to raise tomatoes, peppers, and annuals such as petunias, coleus, marigolds, or zinnias, sow in boxes ("flats") and transplant when first pair of true leaves appears. Or you can sow individually in peat pots, Jiffy-7 pellets, plastic or clay pots.

I have built a manure-heated hotbed. Will it be possible to grow any vegetables in it during the winter months? If temperatures in your area drop to 0° F. or below, you will probably want to add some incandescent light bulbs, which can be attached to the frame. You could use eight 25-watt bulbs, for a 3- × 6-foot hotbed, mounted on the inside of the frame after having been attached to another board. Placing them at equal distances apart is best. If 50- or 60-watt bulbs are used, you will need only half as many. On very cold nights, put a blanket over the frame. Also, remember the wind-chill factor. A windy night makes it much more difficult to heat the bed than if the wind were not blowing. A ten-mile-per-hour wind blowing with an outside temperature of 10° F. would be equivalent to −9° F. Be sure to install the light bulbs in porcelain sockets and use waterproof electric wire and cable. A small thermometer laid on top of the soil bed will be necessary to determine how well your hotbed retains heat during cold weather. You can take readings for a week or so before planting crops. Lettuce, endive, small kinds of turnips, spinach, radishes, and onions do well in cold temperatures. You may want to sow the seeds indoors for quicker germination and transplant seedlings into the bed, since plants will tolerate 40° F. temperatures, but seeds are difficult to germinate at those temperatures.

The Home Greenhouse

CONSTRUCTION AND ENERGY-SAVING IDEAS

We want to put up a small greenhouse. Which is better—glass, Fiberglas, or plastic?   You can make one out of polyethylene, rigid plastic, or glass. Glass is probably more aesthetic, but with its high price, the rigid plastic Fiberglas makes sense. It is available in flat or corrugated forms. The Fiberglas should be translucent yet it provides privacy within the greenhouse. Some people prefer the flat sheets to the corrugated ones, but the corrugations add structural strength so that less framing is needed.

Which greenhouse loses heat faster—one made of glass, plastic, or Fiberglas?   Corrugation increases the surface area of the greenhouse, allowing greater heat loss. However, because there are fewer laps with the Fiberglas (over glass panels), you get less heat loss. Polyethylene is so airtight you get no, or little, heat loss.

Which type of greenhouse shuts out more light for plants?   Don't worry about light not getting to plants with any types. Fiberglas transmits between 70 to 90 per cent of the light that strikes it, which is enough for all plants. Most of the light is diffused, providing a soft, even light. So, although it may not look sunny inside a Fiberglas house, it gets almost as much light as a glass house. Also, the sun's rays are less apt to burn plants in a Fiberglas house, which does not require shading in the summer as does a glass house.

Is it true that some Fiberglas is treated to last 20 years? Yes, Fiberglas can be purchased which is treated with a material called Tedlar, a plastic foam bonded molecularly to the rigid sheet. It costs more than the untreated but does prolong the life of a Fiberglas construction.

Is it true you can get a sunburn inside a Fiberglas house but not inside a glass house? Yes. Glass shuts out the ultraviolet rays.

We have a small glass greenhouse and want to cut down on heating costs by using a plastic sheet. Do you put the plastic on the inside or on the outside? Commercial growers use the plastic in two ways: outside over the glass and also inside. The advantages of placing the plastic *over* the glass are that it is easier to install and it will deflate and allow snow to melt if it is overloaded. A fuel saving of 30 per cent can be realized in a tight glass house, and as much as a 50 per cent loss if the greenhouse is poorly glazed or full of leaks. Commercial growers who apply plastic over their greenhouses say that it results in more uniform temperatures in the greenhouse and also keeps the glass in place. One disadvantage is that plastic sheets applied on the outside are apt to whip and tear in the wind.

We have a small greenhouse that gets a lot of wind. Could we cut down on heat loss by putting up a windbreak of some sort? Yes, put up a windbreak of trees (which could be expensive) or a temporary wind barrier such as a commercial snow fence of 1-inch slats. The fence should be 10 to 12 feet high for the typical greenhouse, with a ridge height of 11 to 14 feet, and it should be located 40 to 50 feet to the windward side of the greenhouse. A shelter belt of trees and shrubs will give permanent protection. Use a 4- or 5-foot row of evergreens. You could plant small evergreens and use the fence until the trees mature. Trees around properties cut home heating costs up to 20 or 30 per cent.

We want to run our greenhouse during the winter but the cost of fuel is so high. Do you have suggestions for growing plants while using less fuel? One of the best ways is to cut down the heat for plants that do not need it at night. Many plants need a high temperature only as seedlings. As they mature, they often require a night temperature that is lower than during the day.

According to tests at the Connecticut Agricultural Experiment Station and elsewhere it was shown that following cloudy days, *lower* night temperatures favor best growth. For example, while 77° F. was the best night temperature for the growing of greenhouse tomatoes, following a day of full sunshine, 46° F. was the favored temperature following a cloudy day with only 8 per cent sun. In other words, climate helps determine night temperature. Cloudy days mean that you should have lower night temperatures.

Are the crops grown at lower night temperatures as good as those produced at higher night temperatures? Yes. For instance, you can produce just as good a crop of petunias at a lower night temperature as with a higher one. Lower night temperatures do cause a 2- to 3-week delay in flowering, which is not serious when you consider winter fuel savings.

One suggestion to try: use a temperature of 60° F. for the first few hours after sunset, followed by 45° F. for the remainder of the night. Most processes for growth can be sufficiently completed in the first few hours of darkness at a warm temperature. However, don't try to grow tropical plants in low temperatures.

Does the temperature of water used for plants have an effect on growth? Yes, warm water increases the number of blooms, the weight of the pot plants, and the length of stems of certain flowers such as snapdragons. In winter try to use water at or near the temperature of your greenhouse (or house). Water temperature for seeds you are trying to sprout is very important. In winter (and spring) tap water can run close to 35° F. or even lower. To get good germination of seed, the medium or starter should be 72° F. or higher. If you water seeds with 42° F. tap water, it reduces the soil temperature to 45° F. and it takes one day for the temperature to get back up to 70° F.

We are considering a sun-heated "pit house" and wonder how practical it is? A pit house or underground greenhouse is built by excavating in a suitable location, with the walls below ground and the glass, Fiberglas, or plastic roof built above ground. This permits the sun's rays to heat inside the structure, which also makes use of the heat below ground. A small knoll or accessible hillside is an ideal place to build an underground greenhouse because this allows a convenient entrance from the outside without having to walk down steps. It is also less expensive to construct because there is no added excavation needed for entranceway and steps. If you dig down 6 feet or more and have the roof nearly flush with the soil surface, there will be very little heat loss at night during the winter months. During daylight hours the sun is allowed to enter and at night the glass is covered to retain heat. Usually this type of greenhouse needs very little auxiliary heat to keep it above freezing. It is a fine place to grow spring-flowering bulbs, alpine plants, perennials, cool-crop vegetables, shrubs such as camellias and azaleas, and flowering plants that can be sown in the fall.

Do you need a wall to make a pit house? Yes, side walls should be of cement blocks and the structure built in a well-drained spot so it will not collect water during a rainy spell. Leave earthen floors, but they can be covered with gravel or crushed stone. In fact, stones help store heat to help with nighttime temperatures.

What is a solar greenhouse? A pit house could be considered a type of solar greenhouse. Actually all greenhouses (and cold frames and hotbeds) are solar-heated to a degree. The sun furnishes heat during the day, even in the coldest weather. However, methods of retaining the heat add to the true concept of solar structure. Double panes, made of Fiberglas or glass in tight-fitting frames with no air spaces, are important. Plastic over the outside or used as a liner inside helps to create dead air space for insulation. Bubble plastic attached to glass also aids in heat retention.

We have a small greenhouse and want to insulate it with a material called "air-cap bubble insulation." How effective is it? Air-cap bubble insulation has been used in recent years by commercial growers to insulate the side walls and gable ends of greenhouses. With this material there is about 50 per cent less heat loss through the side walls. It comes in 16-inch, 24-inch, and 48-inch widths, in both 100-foot- and 300-foot-length rolls. It is very effective in cutting down on your fuel bill. A sheet of plastic placed inside your greenhouse is very effective in cutting down on heat loss, especially if you cover the north side. Use the clear material so light can penetrate.

What are some methods for cutting down on heat loss in our greenhouse in winter? (1) Keep glass or plastic clean to let sunlight in. (2) Fill plastic jugs with stones and paint the outside of the jugs black. Store these where they can heat up from the sun's rays during the day. (3) Line the outside of your greenhouse with polyethylene sheets to cut down on heat loss. Put two plastic sheets up inside and use a fan to blow air in between the layers. Some use styrofoam beads between the two sheets for extra insulation. (4) Place aluminum sheets or aluminized material on inside walls to reflect heat. (5) Compartmentalize part of your greenhouse so you do not have to heat all of it. Do this by hanging drapes or plastic sheets in areas to be sealed off. (6) Use the bubble-cap insulation sheets that fasten to the glass.

WHAT TO GROW

Which flowers are suitable for a beginner to grow in a small greenhouse for winter bloom?   Among the easiest are calendula, stock, snapdragon, forget-me-not, daffodil, tulip, freesia, chrysanthemum, and buddleia. All of these grow in a night temperature of 45° to 50° F.

We have a small greenhouse and want to grow vegetables for winter salads. Please name some easy ones that will stand cool temperatures.   Here are some suggestions for the cool, energy-saving greenhouse (night temperature 50° F. or below): cress (curly and upland types): sow every 2 to 3 weeks in shallow box. Lettuce ('Salad Bowl', 'Buttercrunch', and other butterhead types): start in Jiffy pots and thin after seedlings are up. Parsley: grow in 5-inch pots or hanging baskets. Radishes ('Cherry Belle', 'Sparkler'): sow every 2 to 3 weeks, ready in a month. Kale and spinach: sow in a bench (a raised growing area) from early fall to early winter for long spring harvest. Swiss chard: sow in bench or 6-inch pots. Beets: sow in fall for greens; roots take longer to mature. Carrots: sow in early fall for harvest in late winter; grow in bench or containers 6 inches deep. Celtuce, chicory, endive—same as for lettuce. Chinese cabbage—same as for lettuce. Annual herbs: anise, basil, chervil, coriander, dill, lemon-balm (dig up plants from garden), sweet marjoram, summer savory and others: sow periodically for continuous supply; grow in 4-inch pots. Perennial herbs: burnet, chives, mints, oregano, sage, thyme, and others—obtain plants or dig from garden and pot. Peas, edible-podded: sow in fall for winter harvest; resow in January for early spring. Vines need support—wire, string, or trellis.

I have constructed a glass-covered frame over the cellar well which is outside our home on the southeast side. Please mention some plants that can be brought inside to flower during the winter months.   Annual carnations, petunias, marigolds, begonias (wax), geraniums, and even dwarf salvia can be cut back and potted up to flower later on during the winter.

I am building a small greenhouse so I can start seeds of flowers and vegetables that can be transplanted later into a garden in my backyard. What plants should be started early and what dates should I start them?   Eggplants, peppers, tomatoes, melons, and members of the cabbage family are those most commonly started indoors since they require a long growing season. To have flowers in bloom by Memorial Day or soon after, you should start petunias, impatiens, begonias, pansies, asters, lobelia, browallia, snapdragon, and marigolds indoors. Coleus and dusty miller also should be started early. Since all of the above require different starting dates, it is best to consult a seed catalog or a good complete book on greenhouse gardening. Sowing information is also usually on seed packets.

What are some books on greenhouse gardening? *Greenhouse Gardening for Fun* by Claire L. Blake (M. Barrows Co.); *Gardening Under Glass* by Jerome A. Eaton (Macmillan Co.); *Organic Gardening Under Glass* by Doc and Katy Abraham (Rodale Press); *The Complete Greenhouse Book—Building and Using Greenhouses from Cold Frames to Solar Structures* by Peter Clegg and Derry Watkins (Garden Way Publishing). (See also Section 16.)

Which plants, other than the little English daisy and blue forget-me-not, would be suitable to raise in a small greenhouse for small corsages? Baby's-breath, candytuft, cornflower, lily-of-the-valley, miniature roses, gardenia, and miniature cymbidiums.

I have a practically unheated lean-to greenhouse that seldom goes below freezing. Could I keep perennials during the winter in it and also sow seeds of pansies for early spring bloom? Strong specimens of various early-flowering hardy perennials could be dug in fall and planted inside to flower in advance of season. Chrysanthemum plants could be stored, so that early cuttings can be made in spring. Hardy bulbs could be planted. Snapdragons, calendula, stock, larkspur, clarkia, nigella, and pansies could be planted in fall, as well as seeds of rock-garden plants and other perennials. Lettuce and spinach could be grown in early spring or late winter.

I am unable to heat my greenhouse. What practical use can be made of it? If it is span-roofed and fully exposed, perhaps it is best to wait until March, and then sow seeds of flowers and vegetables that can be transplanted for an early start outdoors. If there are benches of soil, such plants as radish, beet, lettuce, romaine, chicory, mustard, and carrot could be sown and grown inside until big enough to use. During summer, chrysanthemums could be grown to finish before winter really starts. Hardy, early-flowering plants dug and planted in fall would give earlier blooms than those left outdoors. You might also try such shrubs as camellia and azalea.

We have a 10- × 6-foot greenhouse and would like to grow house plants from seeds. What are some foolproof ones? Try the Arabian coffee tree, a fast-growing shrub with shiny dark foliage. Polka dot plant (*Hypoestes*) has bright green leaves splashed with pink. Many cacti are easily seed-started. Some seed houses sell a mixture of 10 or 12 varieties, all ready to germinate in 3 weeks. Slower in results are primroses, cineraria, and cyclamen.

Is there a good all-purpose soil mixture that can be used for most plants one might grow in a greenhouse? Yes, most plants are not so fussy that they need special mixes. Exceptions are orchids and azaleas. Azaleas and other acid-loving plants are potted in humus-rich soil with high peat-moss content. For most other plants, a soil mix of 1 part each of garden loam, peat moss, perlite, and sand will do a fine job. Some gardeners like to add some rotted manure or compost for extra humus.

TEMPERATURES

What temperature should be maintained in a small greenhouse? It depends on what is grown. A minimum night temperature of 50° to 55° F. will suit a large variety of plants commonly grown.

At what temperature should a small greenhouse be kept in order to germinate seeds and at the same time keep seedlings at the right temperature? For the usual run of annuals and vegetables, a night temperature of 50° to 55° F. with a rise of 5° to 10° in daytime is about right. Seed pots or flats should be kept in propagating cases having higher temperatures (68° to 70° F.) until they germinate, or they should be placed near heating pipes until seeds *start* to sprout.

What is the minimum night temperature for a small greenhouse growing sweet pea, stock, snapdragon, calendula, and begonia during the winter? Fifty degrees. The sweet pea, stock, and calendula would do better at 45° F., the begonia at 55° F.

Is a temperature of 65° to 70° F., maintained by hot-water heat, correct in a flower conservatory? It depends upon what is to be grown. For most kinds of plants, maintain a night temperature of 50° to 55° F. It should be vented if day temperatures go much above 70° F.

We are keeping a coal furnace going in our one-wing greenhouse. How low can the temperature drop at night without harming the plants? It depends on what is being grown. Azalea, calceolaria, camellia, cineraria, cyclamen, erica, genista, hydrangea, primula, violet, and many others can endure 45° F. without injury.

Do most house plants need the same night temperature as they do during the day? Most plants prefer to have a lower night temperature, but keep in mind that tropical plants such as African-violets do not like a lower night temperature (not below 55° F.). Greenhouse operators have found that bright, clear days followed by very cold nights can cause a dwarfing of these plants, as there is no chance for movement of starch. It's also noted that stretching of leaves stops when the soil temperature is around 54° F. That's why you shouldn't water plants with very cold water. However, petunias, calceolaria, cineraria, chrysanthemums, and cyclamen actually prefer cool night temperatures down to 50° or 55° F. and will not bloom as well if night temperatures are higher.

Potted plants that I place on my sunny terrace during the summer have their leaves scorched when they're transferred from the greenhouse. Is there any way of overcoming this? Ventilate the greenhouse as freely as possible for a week before they are moved. Keep them in a partially shaded location outdoors for a week or so before putting them on the terrace.

How does one harden off plants which have to be moved from a greenhouse into the open? By transferring them first to a cold frame, where they are gradually exposed to outdoor conditions by progressively increasing the amount of ventilation until, at the expiration of 10 days or so, the sash is entirely removed.

Is bottom heat more important than the temperature around the plants? It is, under certain conditions of plant propagation, and for the growing of some plants under glass. For general culture it will not take the place of air temperature.

WATERING, SOILS, AND GENERAL CARE

What is the proper soil mixture that will avoid damping-off for flower seeds sown in a small greenhouse? Regardless of type or size of greenhouse, the best seed-sowing medium is either pure milled sphagnum peat moss or one of the sterile soilless mixes available in garden centers. If you want to make your own soilless mix you can use one part each of sphagnum peat moss, medium or fine perlite, and vermiculite. You will also have to apply a liquid fertilizer according to directions on the container. (If the medium has been lying around in an open bag and you are in doubt as to its sterility, you can bake it in an oven for a half hour at 180° F.)

How is it possible to tell when the soil in pots is dry? If the soil is in a clay pot you can tell by sight, touch, and hearing. If the soil looks dry, feels dry, and the pot "rings" when tapped with your knuckle or a stick, watering is necessary, provided the plant is in active growth. Plastic pots are more difficult. A good moisture meter available from mail-order gardening supply firms is helpful, or a pointed wooden probe can be carefully inserted into the pot. If the soil is moist, the probe will be moist, as indicated by a darker color and particles of soil clinging to the wood.

Do you think it is a good idea to invest in a moisture meter for use on plants in a greenhouse?   Most people can tell if a plant is dry or not by using their fingers, but this is not always accurate. For example, if you have a schefflera growing in a metal or plastic container, the surface soil may seem dry to the touch. But actually the center or lower part of the soil may have ample moisture even though the top is dry. If you insert the probe of a soil meter into the soil ball, it will read moist and alert you not to pour on water. Most professionals have little faith in the accuracy of these gadgets, but for some they may be a help.

Is there any harm in setting potted plants in a saucer of water?   There is no reason why you cannot place *shallow* saucers under your plants. This results in a saving of water and plant nutrients. The water that is normally lost through the bottom of the pot is caught in the saucer where it is quickly used by the plant.

How often should I water plants in our greenhouse and in our home?   Here are some factors to consider. *Dry air:* too much ventilation. *Light:* more sunlight means more water. *Type of pot:* clay pots lose 50 per cent of water applied. Plastic or glazed containers do not breathe and lose little water, so require less. *Size of plant:* large plants need more water than smaller ones. *Location:* plants in full sun, or near a window, radiator, or television set usually need more water than those farther away. *Soil mix:* a well-drained, loose soil needs more water than a tight, poorly drained one.

What is the procedure for watering newly potted plants?   Be sure the ball of soil is thoroughly moist at potting time. Water well immediately after potting, then wait until the soil is dry on surface. It is very easy to overwater newly potted plants. If they tend to wilt, syringing the foliage once or twice a day will be beneficial.

Is the amount of watering influenced by weather?   Yes, on cloudy, moist days little is needed, especially if temperature is low. When it is sunny and dry, especially in winter when artificial heat is used, much more water must be applied to keep the air moist and plants from wilting.

Is there any way to cut down on the need for frequently watering pot

plants?   Bury the pots to their rims. Outdoors: in earth, ashes, sand, or peat moss. Indoors: in cinders, pebbles, peat moss, or sphagnum. If this is done, great care must be taken to avoid overwatering in damp, cloudy weather, and when plants are not actively growing. Also, you can use mat-watering and wick-watering methods available from mail-order gardening supply houses.

Please describe the capillary mat system for watering plants. We want to use it in our greenhouse.   Capillary mats are soft mats that are kept damp and pots are placed on them. The mats are watered once or twice a week and this helps to keep your plants cool during the summer and humid during the winter. The big benefit is the extra humidity around the plants. Many believe these mats are the answer to carefree plants (especially African-violets) and they have an advantage over wicks in pots. The mats can be made of pieces of indoor-outdoor carpeting, acrylic blankets, cotton flannel, or you can buy matting from any greenhouse supply company.

How is the wick method of watering plants accomplished?   Wicks can be made of nylon or acrylic yarn. Do not use Orlon or wool as they rot very fast. Nylon stockings and used pantyhose can be cut in very thin strips. The wicks should be thin in order to conduct a large amount of water. If the wicks are too thick, they are apt to invite rot.

How do you prepare the wicks?   Cut the wicks just long enough to reach the bottom of the reservoir container (which can be a margarine tub, butter tub, cottage-cheese container, etc.). It should be long enough to make one circle in the bottom of the pot, plus enough length to reach the reservoir container. Thread the wick into a hole in the bottom before planting the plant. Then place a small layer of coarse perlite in the hole to cover the wick. After that, the plant is set in, using a loose soil mixture. Plants already in pots can be adapted by using tweezers to insert the wick. Water the plant thoroughly (including wick) and let the plant sit until well drained before putting the other end of the wick into the reservoir.

How often and when should greenhouse plants be sprayed or misted with water?   Tropical foliage plants can be sprayed every sunny day. This is an excellent prophylactic measure against insect pests. Generally, plants in bloom should not be sprayed because of the danger of marring flowers. Spraying should be done in the morning, after plants have been watered.

How can humidity be controlled in a greenhouse?   By careful attention to heating, ventilating, and wetting down of the paths and other interior surfaces, and the balancing of these factors to produce the desired result. A wet-bulb thermometer is useful to indicate the relative humidity. Special humidifiers are sold for this purpose.

Is it necessary to sprinkle frequently to keep the air humid in a greenhouse? It depends on what is grown. Cacti and succulents get along in dry air. Most cool-house plants—primroses, cyclamens, stocks, house plants, etc.—get along with moderate humidity, provided by sprinkling the walks once or twice on dry, sunny days. Tropical plants from moist climates can require the sprinkling of walls, floors, and benches three or four times a day in sunny weather.

I have a small greenhouse heated by a kerosene room heater, supplemented by a thermostatically controlled electric heater. A large bucket of water is kept on top of the heater to supply plenty of humidity. The temperature is kept at 55° to 60° F. Geranium growth is good, but the leaves turn brown and fall off. There is some progress in the plants' size, but in time the same thing happens. What is wrong? It could be fumes from the kerosene heater. Otherwise your problem is probably insufficient humidity. Wet down the floors once or twice a day. Install a humidifier sold for greenhouse use.

What direct effect, if any, does coal gas have on greenhouse plants? I'm thinking of a small greenhouse heated by a small stove. Even minute quantities of coal gas will seriously injure or kill plants. If you have in mind placing a stove *inside* the greenhouse, make sure it is properly vented.

What is meant by "acclimatizing" your plants? We want to put ours outdoors for the summer months. Acclimatizing means adjusting your plants gradually to a different environment. Foliage growers in Florida and elsewhere accomplish this for plants grown under high humidity and intense light conditions. If sent north and brought into interiors before they are acclimatized, the leaves turn brown or fall off. This is why northern growers try to acclimatize southern plants by using a special greenhouse to toughen them up before they are sold.

What should we do with our greenhouse-grown plants that need to go outdoors? If you are going to set your plants outdoors for the summer, do not expose them to direct sun immediately. Gradually adjust them to their new location. Plants growing indoors usually have larger leaves than those in full sun. Also, they are thinner in cross section, enabling the plant to make maximum use of light. If a shaded plant is placed in full sun for even a short period of time, its leaves will become bleached because of cell death from high temperature.

REPOTTING

When do plants need repotting? For plants that are rapidly increasing in size, whenever the roots get crowded in the pots and available plant nutrients are exhausted. For plants which have "settled down" and slowly increase in size, at the end of the resting season—usually midwinter or late winter. Also when, because of poor drainage, overwatering, or unsuitable soil, the roots are unhealthy.

How does one repot a plant? Prepare a new pot by cleaning it and putting broken pots, small pebbles, or something similar in the bottom for drainage—from ½ inch to 2 inches, depending on the size of the pot and the plant's need for quick drainage. Cover with ½ inch of moss or fibrous loam. Remove the plant from the old pot by turning it upside down and tapping the rim of the pot on a bench or table. Place in a new

REPOTTING A PLANT

Removing a plant from a pot. The rim of the pot (1) is rapped sharply on the edge of a bench or table to remove the root ball; (2) the root ball is loosened up to remove some of the old earth; (3) the crock (drainage material) and more earth are removed from the bottom of the root ball. The plant is now ready for repotting.

The plant is then placed in a larger pot, partly filled with fresh soil, and (4) more soil filled in around it. Cross section of pot (5) with crock over drainage hole. Soil is tamped in firmly (6) around the old root ball. Water well.

pot at the correct depth; fill around with new soil; tamp the soil firmly with a potting stick—a small piece of lath will do. The surface soil should be a sufficient distance below the rim for convenience in watering.

VENTILATION

What about ventilation in a small greenhouse? Open the ventilator daily, even if it is only a crack, for a short time. Avoid drafts by opening on the side opposite to that from which wind is blowing. When air outside is warm and still, ventilate freely except when plants requiring high humidity are grown, when it is necessary to exercise discretion to maintain air moisture. If you must be away for most of the day or don't want to give time to ventilating, an automatic ventilating device is your answer. These are available from greenhouse suppliers.

REST

How are plants "rested"? By lowering the temperature and reducing the supply of water to their roots. Northern plants become more or less dormant in winter; some (certain bulbs) in summer, as a means of tiding themselves over during summer drought. Certain tropical plants almost completely suspend activities during the dry season.

How can I tell when my greenhouse plants need rest? By close observation and by reading about the culture of specific plants. When a plant has grown actively for 6 to 9 months it can indicate its need for rest by yellowing and dropping leaves—for example, the poinsettia.

For how long should plants be rested? It varies with the subject: amaryllis, October to January; poinsettia, January to May; tulips, May to November. These are approximate resting periods of some commonly grown plants.

INSECTS

What are the most common insects found in a greenhouse and how are they controlled? Whiteflies, aphids, woolly aphids, mealybugs, nematodes, red spider mites, scales, slugs, and snails. Malathion will control aphids (including woolly) and whiteflies. Special baits are sold for controlling slugs and snails. Some gardeners get good results with shallow saucers of beer placed at intervals on the plant bench. The slugs and snails apparently drink the beer and drown. There are materials sold for controlling nematodes, but their use is somewhat dangerous, so in small home greenhouses it's generally safer to discard any infested plant. Red spider mites can be controlled with Kelthane. For whiteflies, resmethrin is recommended, but even that is not effective in some instances. Many amateur growers are finding that spider mites can be controlled by spraying with a buttermilk-wheat flour solution: 1 tablespoon buttermilk, ½ cup flour in 2½ quarts water. Mix well and strain before putting into sprayer. For whiteflies, persistent spraying with detergent water: 1 tablespoon liquid detergent to 2 quarts water. This kills adult flies only, so it must be sprayed underneath leaves as well as on top and must be repeated every 3 or 4 days to get new adult stages as they hatch. For scale and mealybugs, many use a spray of rubbing alcohol (2 parts) mixed with water (1 part). Commercial growers are resorting to stronger and stronger chemicals and still losing the battle.

Does it matter if your water is soft or hard when you use a pesticide for a greenhouse or outdoor plants? Yes, acidity of the water used in mixing a spray has a lot to do with its effectiveness. For example, Sevin (carbaryl) is a relatively safe and common pesticide. When mixed with water for spraying, it loses half its strength in from 100 to 150 days where the pH (acidity) is 6 (slightly acid); in 24 to 30 days where the pH is 7 (neutral); in 2 to 3 days where the water is 8 (alkaline), and in 1 day where the pH is 9 (very alkaline). The more alkaline the water is, the more the pesticide loses its effectiveness.

For years we have been using a household bleach as a drench to kill springtails and other insects in the soil of plants. Our water was from a well. Now we use tap water and I tried the same bleach solution. It killed the plants. I used only 1 tablespoon of household bleach to 1 quart of water. What happened? If your water source (city water) is highly chlorinated, it no doubt added to your unhappy experience. Chlorine in the water plus the chlorine in your drench solution made too strong a solution for your tender plants, especially the young ones. If you still want to use household bleach in a drench, draw off a pail of tap water and let it sit overnight so the chlorine can dissipate. In fact, it's a good idea to let water stand overnight before watering plants.

DISEASES

The leaves on some of my plants have a powdery substance on the surface. What is this and how do I get rid of it? This is powdery mildew, a fungus disease. Karathane is generally effective when sprayed according to the manufacturer's directions.

In cloudy weather the leaves of some of my plants develop a gray mold that I have been told is botrytis fungus. How can this be controlled?   Use captan or any material recommended for the purpose.

Our foliage plants have a dull look on them. What causes this?   Leaves of foliage plants often become coated with dust and soil, plus pesticide residues. Not only are these leaves unsightly, but the debris can clog the leaves' stomata (openings) and pose a problem. Wash off foliage, using a few drops of detergent in a gallon of lukewarm water. Just moisten a soft cloth and rub the leaves without bending them.

I'm confused about the claims made for various types of lights. Which are the best?   There have been many claims made for various kinds of fluorescent lights, but generally speaking most of them work about the same.

Books tell us that certain plants need so many "foot candles" for best growth. What does this term mean?   Generally speaking, plants are divided into 3 general light-need groups: low light (50 to 500 foot candles); medium light (500 to 3,000 foot candles); and high light (3,000 to 8,000 foot candles).

We are using a water softener and wonder if it will affect our plants?   In most cases water passing through a softener does have a harmful effect on plant growth. Softening water does this: the calcium (harmless) is exchanged for sodium (harmful). Sodium is harmful because it tends to puddle a soil (make it sticky) and sodium can be toxic to plants that are sensitive. However, if you have a water softener don't worry because there's a simple trick to eliminate the sodium hazard. Since the softener takes the calcium out, why not add calcium back to the water to restore that which was present before softening removed it? This simply nullifies the effect of the sodium added in the softening process. Here's all you do: go to your garden center or farm store and buy some gypsum (calcium sulfate), a very cheap and harmless form of calcium. It has low solubility yet can be dissolved to treat softened water. One-half level teaspoon is added to a gallon of softened water or a tablespoon per 6 gallons of water is enough to supply the necessary calcium to change the softened water back to the "unsoftened" water. Pelleted gypsum works even faster.

Every year our greenhouse tomatoes have a brownish leathery spot on the bottom. What causes this?   A dry soil for a period of as little as

30 minutes when the fruits are one third to one half mature size can trigger this disorder because of a lack of calcium (found in lime). Lack of water causes a lack of calcium and the cell walls collapse. Lime applied to the soil helps control this blossom-end rot.

We sprayed our greenhouse foliage plants with an aerosol spray and it burned the leaves of my schefflera. Are aerosols safe? Some are and some are not. Try the aerosol spray on just a few leaves several days before treating the entire plant. Be sure to read the label instructions, and do not treat plants that are in an extremely hot environment or in a wilted condition. Be sure to hold the can at least 18 inches from the plant.

We were given some old clay pots but we are afraid to use them because of disease. Can they be salvaged? Yes, a good soaking in household bleach will kill most disease organisms. Mix a solution of household bleach, 1 part bleach to 9 parts of water. Soak for an hour or so and then scrub with a wire brush. This gets rid of the white crusty formations on the outside of the pot. If you have a swimming pool, use the "liquid pool chlorine," mixed at the rate of 1 part to 20 parts of water to get a similar concentration.

We grew many plants from seed in our greenhouse and at the time of transplanting the stems were darkened and constricted. What causes this? The plants probably have rhizoctonia, a fungus that causes the stems to darken, become constricted, and look like a wire at the soil line. Rhizoctonia may attack all plant parts, and it causes diseases of seedlings. Although rhizoctonia is not commonly spread by airborne spores, it very frequently makes its appearance in growing media where it can rapidly spread itself through the soil. To control it try a soil drench of household bleach, or Benlate, 1 tablespoon to a gallon of water. Commercial growers use PCNB (Terrachlor) but it has to be used with care as plant damage may result.

SPECIFIC GREENHOUSE PLANTS

Are abutilons easy to grow in a small greenhouse? Yes. Take cuttings from outdoor plants in September or from greenhouse plants in February. Pot in ordinary soil. Pinch the tips of the shoots occasionally to induce bushiness. They like sunshine and a temperature about 50° F. at night. They can also be raised from seeds.

Can small plants of yellow-flowered "mimosa" (acacia) be grown in pots? Several kinds are well adapted for growing in pots in a cool greenhouse (night temperature, 40° to 45° F.). Try *Acacia armata, A. pubescens, A. drummondii,* and *A. longifolia.*

What is the correct treatment for an acacia plant grown in a tub in a greenhouse?   Cut old flowering branches back to a length of 6 inches. Retub or topdress as necessary, using light, porous, peaty soil. Spray the tops to encourage new growth. After the danger of frost has passed, place the plant outdoors, with the tub buried nearly to the rim. Bring inside before freezing weather, in the fall. Keep cool. At all times give plenty of sun. Beware of dryness at the root. Feed established plants during the summer.

What is the proper way to winter an allspice tree?   The allspice tree (*Pimenta dioica*) is not suited to outdoor growing where freezing temperatures occur. If the plant is in a tub, it could be wintered in a cool greenhouse or other suitable well-lighted place under cover where the temperature range is between 40° and 50° F. Water only enough to keep the soil from getting bone dry.

How shall I plant and care for bulbs of amaryllis in a greenhouse?   Pot bulbs firmly in porous loam enriched with dried cow manure and superphosphate, using pots 4 inches to 6 inches, according to the size of the bulbs. Leave the top half of a bulb out of the soil. Keep nearly dry until roots form, then gradually increase the water supply. Spray the foliage with clear water on bright days. Provide a temperature of 60° to 65° F. at night, 70° to 75° F. by day. Give full sunlight until flowers appear, then light shade. (See also under Tender Bulbs, Section 5.)

I would like to grow anemone from seed for blooming in my greenhouse. How is it done?   Sow the seeds in April or May. Transplant them individually into 2½-inch pots. Grow in the summer in a cool, shaded cold frame or a greenhouse (pots buried to their rims in sand or ashes). Repot into 4-inch pots or plant 6 inches apart in benches in September. Grow in cool temperature.

Will anthuriums thrive in a greenhouse where cattleya orchids grow well?   Indeed they will. Both need a humid atmosphere and a 60° F. temperature at night. Pot the anthuriums in a mixture of orchid bark, sphagnum, and charcoal. Keep moist at all times.

What greenhouse conditions best suit antirrhinum (snapdragons)?   Night temperature 45° to 50° F.; full sunshine; free air circulation; light but rich soil; 9 inches to 1 foot between plants in benches, or 4-inch to 6-inch pots; judicious feeding when in vigorous growth. Avoid wetting leaves. Pinch plants in their early stages to encourage branching. Propagate by seeds or cuttings.

When should snapdragon seed be sown for fall flowering? For early-spring flowering (in a greenhouse)? From the middle to the end of May for fall. Late August or early September for spring.

I saw the beautiful flowering vine Aristolochia elegans growing at the Brooklyn Botanic Garden. I would like to grow it in my own greenhouse. Can you tell me how? It is very easy to grow. Sow seeds in light soil in the spring and grow seedlings in a sunny greenhouse where there is a night temperature of 55° F. Prune plants back each spring and topdress or repot as necessary. Unlike some *Aristolochia* species, this one is not evil-smelling.

Can you give me instructions for forcing astilbe for Easter blooming in a greenhouse? Plant strong clumps in the fall in pots just large enough to hold them; sink pots in soil up to their rims in a cold frame; bring indoors in January or later; give plenty of water and grow in a well-lighted position. They need from 10 to 14 weeks in a temperature of 55° to 60° F. to bring them into bloom.

What treatment should be accorded greenhouse azaleas that are kept from year to year? After flowering, trim the plants back lightly, repot if necessary (using an acid, peaty soil), and grow in a temperature of about 60° F.; spray frequently to encourage new growth. Sink pots in soil up to their rims outdoors, in a sunny or partially shaded place from June to September, then bring into a cool house in a light position. Never let plants suffer from lack of moisture in the soil.

I am greatly interested in the begonia and, having acquired a small lean-to greenhouse, would like to grow a collection. Can you give me some instructions? Maintain a night temperature of 55° F., rising 5° to 10° during the daytime. Shade lightly during March, April, and September, more heavily from May to August. Ventilate to keep the atmosphere buoyant rather than stagnant; damp down sufficiently to keep the air fairly humid. Be sure to keep the house clean at all times. (See also Begonia, Section 12.)

How can I grow bouvardia? Propagate by stem or root cuttings in spring. Grow in sweet (slightly alkaline) soil that is well supplied with humus, yet is porous. Give plenty of water during active growing periods. Plenty of sunlight is needed and a greenhouse temperature of about 55° F. Keep plants pinched freely during early growth to make them bushy.

What soil does a bougainvillea (grown under glass) require? If in a pot, a rich but porous soil is needed. If planted in a ground bed, a less rich soil is preferable. Good drainage is essential, and the soil should be coarse (not sifted) and loamy.

How can I grow the winter-blooming buddleia in my green-house? There are two types—*B. asiatica* (white) and *B. farquharii* (light pink). Root the cuttings in the spring; pinch out the tips of young growing plants to encourage bushiness; sink the pots in soil outdoors in the summer; use good, rich soil; feed when pot-bound. Bring the pots into the greenhouse before the winter frost and keep cool; give the plants plenty of sun and air. Never let your plants suffer from dryness.

I would like to have a succession of bulbs for my greenhouse. Which bulbs shall I buy, and when do I plant them? Paper-white narcissus can be planted at 2-week intervals, from October 1 to January 1. Roman hyacinths, at 3-week intervals, from September 1 to December 1. Calla-lilies are constant bloomers. Plant amaryllis in November. Lachenalia planted in September will bloom for Christmas. Try veltheimia, also. Plant tulips in November. (See also Tender Bulbs.)

Please give instructions on raising calceolaria from seeds. Sow in shallow well-drained pans, using a prepared seed-sowing medium or a mix of sand, leafmold, peat moss, and loam in equal parts sifted through a ¼-inch sieve. Firm the soil, make it level, sow the seeds, and gently press them in with a tamper. Moisten by standing the pan in a vessel of water for a half hour. Cover with a pane of glass; shade with newspaper. When seeds germinate, tilt the glass; remove entirely after a few days. Keep cool.

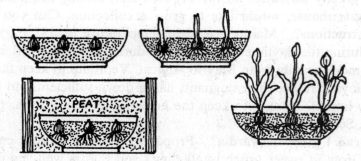

Tulips for indoor bloom: Bulbs are planted with tips level with the soil's surface; stored in a cold frame, pit, or cool cellar for several weeks to form roots; brought indoors to a cool temperature to start top growth; and then given higher temperature, sunshine, and abundant water to develop their flowers.

What conditions are needed to grow calceolarias in the green-house?   A well-drained soil that contains a liberal amount of humus, together with some dehydrated manure and bone meal or superphosphate. Give free circulation of air and shade from strong sunshine; provide a cool, moist atmosphere, uniform moisture, and a night temperature of 50° F.

How is it possible to force calceolarias into bloom early?   By using fluorescent light to provide supplemental illumination for about 5 hours each evening from November on.

I would like to grow calendula for winter flowering in my greenhouse. Can you tell me how?   Sow the seed of a good greenhouse strain in early August. Transplant the seedlings into small pots and later set them out in benches (14 or 15 inches apart) or put them in 5-inch pots. Use rich soil. Grow in full sun with a night temperature of 45° to 50° F. Good air circulation is necessary.

Is it possible for me to grow carnations for winter bloom, along with other greenhouse plants?   Yes, if the other kinds are chosen so that their needs are similar; however, carnations are usually at their best when grown in a house by themselves. They need full sunlight, free ventilation, and a night temperature of 45° to 55° F. The soil must be sweet, fertile, and porous. It is usually advisable for the home gardener to buy young plants rather than attempt to propagate his or her own.

When should carnation cuttings be made?   Late November, December, or January. Select strong growths from near the base of the flowering shoots and remove with a slight side twist. Insert in moist sand, perlite, or vermiculite in a greenhouse where the night temperature is 50° F. Shade with cheesecloth or newspaper for a week or two.

What causes carnations to split?   Splitting is caused by overfeeding and especially by a too-high temperature, which induces rapid development. Carnations are cool-temperature plants, so growth must be gradual and the temperature at night kept evenly at about 45° to 55° F.

What are important points for a home gardener with a small greenhouse to bear in mind when growing indoor chrysanthemums in pots?   Secure healthy stock. Keep plants repotted as they grow (without permitting them to become pot-bound) until they are in their flowering pots. Feed after the flower buds have set. Keep the greenhouse cool (a night temperature of 40° to 45° F.). Full sunshine is necessary.

What kind of soil is best for growing chrysanthemums in pots?   A rich mixture containing plenty of mellow, fibrous loam, rotted manure, or rich compost, a good sprinkling of bone meal or superphosphate, a generous dash of wood ashes, and sufficient coarse sand to keep the mixture porous. A sandier mixture, without manure or fertilizer, is preferred for the first potting of cuttings.

Can greenhouse chrysanthemums be planted in a vegetable garden in the summer and then be dug up in fall and transplanted to soil beds in a greenhouse? Yes. Plant them in fertile soil. Dig them up carefully before a severe frost (keeping as much soil on the roots as possible), replant, and then water thoroughly. Shade from bright sunshine for a few days.

Can large chrysanthemums be grown in a greenhouse, and at what temperature? Cool (40° to 50° F.) greenhouse culture is best for large-flowered chrysanthemums. (See previous questions for culture.)

How does one propagate greenhouse chrysanthemums? After blooming, old plants are cut back close to the ground and stored in a light place (just above freezing). In January or February they are placed in a temperature of about 45° F., and young shoots, which soon appear, are made into cuttings when about 2 inches long. These are inserted in sand, perlite, or vermiculite in a propagating bench.

How do I make chrysanthemums flower from September until March in my greenhouse? Catalogs list blooming dates of each variety. They also give helpful information about how to give plants extra light so they will bloom later than normal, or how to shade them so they will bloom earlier than normal. Chrysanthemums are affected by day length (photoperiodism), hence their blooming time can be manipulated.

Why does my Christmas cactus bloom so early in the fall? There are three kinds of holiday cacti—Thanksgiving, Christmas, and Easter. The Thanksgiving cactus (*Schlumbergera* [syn. *Zygocactus*] *truncata*) and its hybrids bloom any time from November until Christmas. Your plant is a Thanksgiving rather than a Christmas cactus. People get this cactus confused with the true Christmas cactus (*S.* x *buckleyi*). Usually you can tell Thanksgiving cacti by the sawtooth points on the leaf segments, making them clawlike. Christmas cacti lack points and have rounded leaf segments. (See also Section 12, House Plants.)

What culture is required for cineraria? Sow seed from June to September. Transplant to flats, later to small pots. Keep repotting as the plants grow, using rich, porous soil containing a fair amount of humus. Grow in full sunshine during winter weather and stand the pots on a cool, moist bed of pebbles. Keep moist. Grow cool (night temperature of 40° to 45° F.).

Do cineraria plants need much feeding? They are heavy feeders; therefore provide rich soil (but do not use liquid fertilizers until they are well rooted in their flowering pots), then feed once or twice a week until the flowers are open. Cease feeding after the flowers open.

How is the fragrant, yellow-flowered cytisus handled in the greenhouse? Its full name is *Cytisus racemosus*. After blooming, shear the plants and repot them, using sandy, peaty, fertile soil. Spray with clear water to encourage new growth and grow in a cool, sunny greenhouse. Sink the pots in soil outdoors in a sunny place through the summer and bring them in again in the fall. Provide a night temperature of 40° to 45° F. Propagate by cuttings in the spring.

Can bleedingheart (Dicentra spectabilis) be forced into bloom early in a small greenhouse? Yes. Plant strong roots in the fall or winter in pots just large enough to hold them. Bury the pots up to their rims in a cold frame; about February bring them into a light greenhouse (temperature of 45° to 50° F.). Keep the soil moist.

What soil and culture are required for Eucharis grandiflora (Amazon- or Eucharis-lily)? It needs tropical greenhouse conditions. The soil should be rich, medium, and well-drained. Bulbs must be partially dried off for a month or 6 weeks twice a year to induce blooming. Feed generously with organic fertilizer when the plants are growing.

How can I grow the tender maidenhair fern in my small greenhouse? Adiantums are easily grown in a temperature of 60° to 65° F. if the atmosphere is kept humid. Pot in a sand-peat soil. Avoid wetting the foliage, but keep the soil evenly moist (except that plants can be rested by partially drying off for a couple of months in the winter). Propagate by division in early spring.

Can I grow ferns in a conservatory? What is the best temperature? Ferns do well in a conservatory. Keep the temperature above 55° F. and the house shaded in the summer. *Adiantum, Pteris, Davallia, Nephrolepis* (Boston forms) are good kinds to grow.

When should I sow forget-me-nots (Myosotis) for blooming in a greenhouse? What are some tips on culture? Sow in May or June. Select a variety recommended for greenhouse culture. Transplant seedlings 3 inches apart in flats. Later, pot or plant in benches. Grow in cool, airy conditions. Shade from strong sunshine. Keep the soil always moist.

What causes geraniums (pelargoniums) suddenly to turn yellow and then die? Gas in the air, poor drainage, overwatering, underwatering, or disease might cause this.

What is the best way to propagate geraniums that damp off or rot before rooting? Expose cuttings to the sun for one day before setting in a rooting medium. Water after planting, and keep moist but not soggy until roots are formed.

I have gerbera plants that were raised from seed in my greenhouse; the potted plants are now nearly a year old, but have never bloomed. Why? Gerberas need rich, well-drained soil. Crowns should be just above the soil level. Feed with liquid fertilizer as the blooming period approaches. Gerberas should be grown in a cool house (a night temperature of 50° F.).

Can you give me advice on how to raise and grow hydrangea for blooming in a greenhouse? Propagate by cuttings from February to May. Grow in light, well-drained loam in a temperature of 50° F. and full sun. Pinch once or twice before June. Keep in a cold frame, water freely, and spray the foliage with water during the summer. From September on, keep drier and just above freezing. Provide a temperature of 45° F. in January or February.

How is the leopard-plant grown? The correct name is *Ligularia tussilaginea*. Ordinary greenhouse culture or conditions that suit ferns or saintpaulia (temperature around 60° F.), shade, and high humidity; but avoid wetting the leaves too much.

What is Russian statice? Can I grow it in my small greenhouse? This is *Psylliostachys* (syn. *Limonium*) *suworowii*. Sow seeds in September in a sandy soil. Transplant seedlings into well-drained flats and later pot singly into 4-inch pots. Grow in full sun, in a temperature of 50° to 55° F. Be careful with watering and watch out for aphids.

I have a breadfruit plant, so-called. Will you tell me more about this plant, and how to care for it? Probably it is Mexican breadfruit (not related to real breadfruit) or ceriman—*Monstera deliciosa;* it is often sold as philodendron. Its fruits are edible. Mexican breadfruit prefers a warm, moist atmosphere, but will grow almost anywhere provided the temperature does not fall below 50° F. When planted in good soil, it is a vigorous grower, climbing high on tree trunks by means of its stem roots. It succeeds well as a pot plant.

What treatment do calanthe orchids require? Pot in spring in a mixture of fibrous loam, sand, and old cow manure, or use the mixture given below for lady's-slipper and other terrestrial orchids, being sure drainage is perfect. Water with extreme care at first; more generously as roots take possession of soil. Shade spring and summer. Grow in warm temperatures. Reduce water supply when foliage begins to die away in fall. After blooming, keep dormant pseudobulbs in a warm, dry place until spring.

What kind of soil should I use for potting a cattleya orchid? Soil (in the ordinary sense) is not used for epiphytic orchids such as cattleyas. Previously they were potted in osmunda fiber (the wiry roots of osmunda fern). Osmunda fiber is difficult to use and becoming scarce, but good substitutes are various kinds of bark chips and perlite. A formula for cattleyas is: 3 parts Douglas fir bark; 1 part coarse perlite; 1 part redwood chips; and 1 part coarse hardwood charcoal (½ inch to 1½ inches in diameter). For the lady's-slipper (*Paphiopedilum*) or other terrestrial orchids, use the following: 3 parts Douglas fir bark (fine, ¼ inch to ¾ inch in diameter); 1 part coarse perlite; 1 part tree fern, chopped fine. Orchids require good drainage, and that is why bark plus coarse perlite works so well. A pencil-sized stick is a helpful tool to use for pushing the medium in and around roots when potting orchids.

Is a beginner likely to succeed in raising orchids from seed? Not likely. The raising of orchids from seed calls for specialized skill and closely controlled environment. Consult a book on orchid culture. (See Section 12.)

I have some palm tree seeds. Can you tell me how to plant these? Plant them in sandy, well-drained soil in 4-inch flowerpots (in flats, if quantity is large). Space seeds about 1 inch apart and cover about ½ inch deep. Keep moist in temperature of about 70° F.

How are pansies grown for flowering during the winter in a greenhouse? Seeds are sown in July, and resulting plants are grown in a cold frame until October, when they are planted in benches or in pans of light, fertile soil. They are grown in a light, cool greenhouse, and flowers are picked promptly to prevent seed forming.

Which primrose would you recommend for growing in a small home greenhouse (temperature of 45° to 50° F. minimum)? *Primula malacoides* (white, lavender, pink, red); *P. sinensis* (same color range); *P. kewensis* (yellow). It may be well to avoid *P. obconica* because it causes severe dermatitis in some people.

Will you give some pointers on growing greenhouse primroses? Soil should be medium loam with plenty of humus; grow in cool temperature; keep pots standing on a layer of moist pebbles; shade in the summertime; keep the soil moist at all times but not waterlogged; feed with a diluted liquid fertilizer when the final pots are filled with roots.

Can you tell me how to grow greenhouse ranunculus from

seeds? Treat exactly as greenhouse anemones from seed. Both like a porous soil that is well supplied with humus.

Can I force climbing roses into bloom early in my greenhouse? Obtain strong plants in November and set in pots just big enough to contain roots easily. Use medium-heavy, fertile soil. Bury pots to their rims in a deep cold frame. Bring inside in January to a temperature at first 45°, later 55° F. Spray with clear water to encourage growth. Water freely.

How should roses be pruned when they are potted in fall for spring forcing in the greenhouse? Tall-growing ramblers and climbers not at all, other than removing any dead or broken growths. Dwarf polyantha, hybrid tea, hybrid perpetual, etc.: cut back to within 9 or 10 inches of their base. Leave strong shoots longer than weak shoots.

Which classes of roses are best for blooming in a tiny greenhouse during early spring? Polyanthas and all miniature varieties would be suitable.

Would it be practical for me to grow roses for cut flowers in a very small greenhouse in which I want to grow a good many other kinds of plants? Hardly. To grow cut-flower roses with even moderate success demands fair space and rather exacting conditions, but you could try a few plants in pots. 'Sonia' is a fine coral-colored greenhouse rose.

What makes the leaves turn yellow and fall off my miniature rose plant? Poor drainage in the pot; not enough light; too much water; too rich a soil; too high a temperature; red-spider infestation; black-spot disease—one or more of these may be responsible.

I would like to grow salpiglossis in pots for spring blooming in the greenhouse. Is this possible? Quite practicable. Sow seeds in sandy soil in August; transplant seedlings; later pot them individually. Beware of burying plants too low in the soil. Water with care. Provide full sunlight and grow in a temperature of 50° F. Fumigate if aphids appear.

Would it be possible to grow a bird-of-paradise flower (Strelitzia) in a greenhouse built against my house? It should be. Healthy specimens need a large pot or tub, good drainage, medium-heavy soil, plenty of water, and feeding when pot-bound. They like abundant light and a night temperature of 50° to 55° F.

Can you tell me how to grow in winter the feathery stevia that used to be mixed with cut flowers? Propagate by cuttings taken from January to March. Keep plants repotted as one does chrysanthemums. Take pots outdoors from May to September, then bring into cool greenhouse (temperature of 45° to 50° F.). Water well at all times. Feed when pot-bound. Also grows from seed—if you can find a source.

Are stocks good flowering plants for the home greenhouse? Yes. They can be grown either in pots or in benches. Sow seeds August to January, using rich soil. Then transplant into 4- to 6-inch pots. If planted in benches, set branching types 6 to 8 inches apart, nonbranching types closer. Grow in full sun and a night temperature of 40° to 45° F. Avoid a highly acid soil.

Can you give instructions for growing sweet peas in a greenhouse that has scarcely any artificial heat? Sow in October in moderately fertile soil, preferably in a ground bed. Rows should be 3 feet apart. Thin plants to 6 inches apart. Ventilate freely, and avoid encouraging too much growth until February. Provide strings or other means of support. Feed when flower buds form. They need full sunshine. They can also be grown in 10-inch pots (though not so well), using brush-wood for support.

Which vegetables can I grow in a greenhouse? See What to Grow, in this section.

4. *Trees, Shrubs, and Vines*

TREES AND SHRUBS are the backbone of any garden plan. It is they that frame the house, give it an interesting background to show it off to good advantage. They screen objectionable views and give privacy and shade where they are needed. They bring beauty and color into the garden, and if chosen carefully, they can make a beautiful setting that is of colorful interest every season of the year.

Gardeners today can obtain plants that have been introduced from all parts of the world. Nurseries have been so busy propagating plants that there is a bewildering number available. How does one select from the many different crab apples, the different lilacs, and the different varieties of mock-orange—let alone all the other trees and shrubs available today?

Fortunately, there are arboretums and botanical gardens about the country where one can go to see plants growing together and labeled. Also there are books available in which one can find listed the better varieties—more important—and why they are better. Then it is always possible to visit a nursery or garden center to see what special types of plants are offered locally. Just walking around any suburb of a large metropolitan area will provide some ideas, for in this way one can see what plants other people have bought and how they have used them in their own plantings. There is also an opportunity here to learn from others' mistakes!

With houses and gardens being considerably smaller than they were fifty years ago, there is a demand for smaller plants. Why plant an eventual 100-foot oak if a 25-foot crab apple will suffice? The smaller tree is attractive in all seasons, easier to care for, to spray and prune if it is necessary, and considerably cheaper to remove if that becomes a problem.

The difficult task of pruning is reduced if plants are purchased that will not grow quickly above the height wanted. The person who wants a lilac near the terrace, and has in mind a plant not over 3 feet tall, covered with bloom, can easily be dismayed when that plant continually tries to grow 15 to 20 feet and causes all kinds of pruning work each spring. Much better would have been to plant a 'Dwarf Snowflake', which will never get much above 3 feet.

It pays also to learn about the susceptibility of some plants to disease and insect attacks. Why plant a European snowball, for instance, when it is known that the plants become covered with plant lice in the spring and need considerable spraying to keep them anywhere near good condition? The Japanese snowball would be much better, for it is not nearly so susceptible.

Also it is advisable to pick out the trees and shrubs that you know in advance will grow under your conditions. Why fuss around with azaleas and rhododendrons if they are not hardy in your area or if you know your soil is alkaline?

When to Buy

Spring is traditionally the most popular time to buy plants, for, after a long winter indoors for gardeners over a large part of the country, the urge is to go out and see things grow. Actually, in many parts of the United States, spring *is* the best time to plant deciduous, dormant woody plants. Certainly if the plant is known to be difficult to move, it is safest to plant in the spring. Then you can purchase a plant from the nursery or garden center and plant it immediately, before it has time to dry out. If set in the ground in the early spring, the plant gets off to a good start, with a long growing season ahead to adjust to its new location.

On the other hand, if it were planted in the fall, it might have sufficient time to get its roots established, but it would have to suffer through the cold winter with trying winds and freezing and thawing soil. Many plants, especially in the colder parts of the United States, fail to survive the first winter. Early planting and a mulch aid trees and shrubs set out in the fall.

Such rugged, deciduous plants as forsythia, privet, spirea, lilac, maple, many of the oaks and crab apples can be planted in the fall in the North, as well as in the spring. It is the more difficult plants like the brooms, birches, and magnolias that might best be left for spring transplanting if there is any question about their survival in the North.

In milder parts of the South, fall planting of dormant nursery stock is just as good as spring planting. It really depends on the area, whether the fall plantings will be exposed to vicious winter winds, and whether one has taken the time to properly plant, water, and mulch the plants early in the fall.

Evergreens, both narrow-leaved and broad-leaved, are best planted in the very early fall in the North. They are always dug with a ball of soil about the roots, and planting in early September gives them time to get their roots established before the soil freezes, especially if they are mulched. The theory behind this is good to keep in mind. Evergreens always have their leaves and these give off water all the time, more on hot days than on cold days. They will lose a certain amount of water the first winter. However, if planted in the spring, their old leaves and the new growth also would lose much more—the reason why in some areas they have a difficult time staying alive. Even in the South, it is safer to plant evergreens in the early fall than in the spring—chiefly because they are not in active growth.

Container-grown plants are being widely offered by nurseries and garden centers throughout the country. This innovation makes it possible to plant almost any time—in the spring, summer, or fall and during winter in mild climates. It is still a good practice, though, to plant as early as possible.

There is one condition to watch for in container-grown plants. Sometimes they are grown too long in the containers, so their roots have become a solid ball. If planted out in this condition, the roots can easily strangle themselves as they grow and the plant will severely suffer. In the first place, such plants should be avoided. However, if purchased, remove the plant from its container and open up the ball of roots carefully, cutting back especially deformed roots so the ball can be placed in the planting hole in a fairly loose condition. While unnecessary fussing around with the roots of certain plants can have harmful results, some breaking up of the roots of container-bound plants has proved to be a good gardening practice.

Planting

It is at planting time that one should take the greatest care with the young tree or shrub. If the soil is poor, it should be replaced with good soil, possibly mixed with peat moss or well-rotted manure or compost. The hole itself should be ample to receive the roots, which in the case of bare-root stock, should be spread out in their normal growing condition, and not jammed into a small, tight mass.

In handling balled, as opposed to bare-root, stock, one should be very careful not to break the ball by dropping it, for then many of the young feeding roots in the ball will be broken. If it is possible to remove the burlap without breaking the ball, do so, or place the ball in the hole and then cut the strings and push the burlap down the sides of the hole, where it will eventually rot. If the plant was wrapped in polyethylene film, this must be removed.

Fill in good soil around the roots, tamping in well, and leave a small depression about the plant to catch water and prevent it from running off. Water thoroughly so the entire root area is wet; then, if rains fail, keep it watered at regular intervals to prevent the roots from drying out the first year or two. Also, it is excellent practice to mulch the newly transplanted tree or shrub, for this aids in conserving soil moisture and also keeps the weeds in check.

General Pruning

Pruning is always a dwarfing process, merely because in cutting off branches one removes so many of the food-manufacturing organs—the leaves. Therefore, if the plant is to flourish and grow as fast as possible, keep the pruning to a minimum. It is always a good idea to consider carefully why each pruning operation is to be done. There are good reasons.

In the first place one prunes at transplanting time to compensate for the number of roots that have been cut in the digging operation. It is impossible to dig all the roots, and it is unreasonable to expect a smaller proportion of roots to support the same amount of top growth with water and fertilizer. So, with deciduous bare-rooted plants, it is always safest to plan on removing at least one third of the branches at the time of transplanting. Admittedly this is hard to do, for one winds up with a much smaller plant than one has paid for! Experiments have shown that plants pruned this way at transplanting recover much faster than do unpruned plants, which sometimes die because of too much leaf area for the roots to support. (Many nurseries ship properly pruned plants.)

With evergreens and other plants that are balled and burlapped, the pruning need not be so severe nor is it necessary. Container-grown plants are another exception. If they have been growing in containers for some time, removal of branches is not necessary. Sometimes, though, plants are dug and forced into containers immediately for quick sale, and so are actually merely "held" for a week or so. Such plants should also be pruned at transplanting time.

One prunes to remove dead or diseased wood, to correct bad crotches on young trees, to preserve a single leader in certain trees and so prevent several leaders from taking over. Suckers are cut out at the base of some plants, such as lilacs, and certainly all suckers are cut off below the union of grafted plants.

Old shrubs can be rejuvenated, either by cutting them to the ground (in early spring), or by thinning out the older branches at the base, and then possibly reducing the height of those remaining. This is the way to prune many lilacs, mock-oranges, spireas, and deutzias. Hedges, of course, are pruned for a purpose, and sometimes it is necessary to cut off a few limbs from a tree to give it a better shape. Girdling roots must be cut when they are noticed. When there is no good reason for pruning —don't! The plant will grow better without it.

Watering

Soils differ in the amount of water they retain, but the more humus or decaying organic matter in the soil the more water it will retain. Newly transplanted trees and shrubs need water to bring them through the summer droughts. It is essential that you keep track of their needs the first year or two by checking their foliage for wilting or by digging in the soil to see how dry it is. Trees have most of their feeding roots in the upper 18 inches of soil, and many shrubs, such as rhododendrons, have all their feeding roots in this area. It is essential that this soil not dry out the first growing season.

Water should be applied slowly, possibly with a soil soaker, so that it sinks gradually into the soil. Applying water from the garden hose with its high pressure does little good if one hurries away to the next spot as soon as the surface soil looks "wet." If a slight depression is left around the newly transplanted shrub or tree, this helps trap the water and keeps it from running off. Checking, by digging in the soil a bit, gives an indication of how far down the water has gone. Leaving a pan out under the sprinkler gives an idea of how much water has been applied, and once you check the depth to which a certain amount of water has penetrated, it is a simple matter to repeat the timed operation the next time.

It is much better to give trees and shrubs a thorough soaking once a week during drought periods than to sprinkle them lightly each evening. Also, if it is an evergreen, don't forget to sprinkle the foliage, too, in the evening, for in this way it will take in much needed water through its leaves. Deciduous plants will benefit from having their leaves sprinkled, too. The cool of the evening is an ideal time as the plants have all night to absorb the moisture. This is also true of watering the soil.

Mulching

Mulching is provided chiefly to keep the soil from losing a lot of water by surface evaporation. It also prevents weed growth around the base of the plants. In autumn it tends to keep the soil from freezing a little longer and thus gives the roots more time to elongate before winter arrives and the soil freezes hard. After the soil has frozen, a mulch tends to keep it frozen and prevents the disastrous "heaving" of the soil caused by freezing and thawing of late winter and early spring as temperatures moderate. Such alternate freezing and thawing causes young plants to be raised out of the soil and they can die by having their roots exposed to the elements.

In most areas of the United States mulching has beneficial results when used on all trees and shrubs, especially newly transplanted ones. There are some, like rhododendrons, that benefit from a mulch all the time, because their feeding roots are close to the surface and they thrive in the additional moisture and cooler soil thus provided.

Many things can be used as mulching material: peat moss, compost, ground corn cobs, ground sugarcane, leafmold, peanut shells, buckwheat hulls, ground bark, wood chips, cocoa shells, pine needles, marsh hay, seaweed, black polyethylene film, even crushed stone. Most should not be put on over 2 to 3 inches deep. The applying of a mulch to any newly transplanted woody plant is an excellent practice, and it is a good idea to keep the mulch annually replenished for several years until the plant becomes thoroughly established.

Fertilizing

There are many kinds of fertilizers used in the feeding of trees and shrubs. Usually it is not necessary or even advisable to fertilize a tree or shrub at transplanting time, especially if pains have been taken to provide good soil, compost, or well-rotted manure in the planting hole. It is best to let the newly transplanted tree or shrub get acclimated to its new situation for a year before it is forced into additional growth with fertilizer.

Years ago, well-rotted manure was advocated for everything. It is still an excellent source of humus and of nutritive value, but not always plentiful in all regions. As a substitute, there is the dried and granulated form readily available in bags at most garden centers. Many kinds of commercial fertilizers are available, the most common being a 5–10–5 combination. This is a general, all-purpose type.

The best time for application is in the early spring, before the plants start growing. It can be "broadcast" (by far the easier way) around the plants, or for trees growing in a lawn it might be applied by the crowbar, punch-hole method to prevent the burning of the grass, which sometimes occurs when it is broadcast over the lawn under the trees. Approximate amounts of this fertilizer might be:

deciduous trees: 2–4 pounds per inch in diameter of tree trunk measured breast high

evergreen trees: 2 pounds per inch in diameter of tree trunk measured breast high

deciduous shrubs: 3–6 pounds per 100 square feet

evergreen shrubs (exclusive of ericaceous plants): 3–6 pounds per 100 square feet

Fertilizers for ericaceous shrubs, that is, azalea, rhododendron, mountain-laurel, heath and heather and the like, are special in nature and one might refer to the section on broad-leaved evergreen shrubs for specific questions and answers dealing with this point. Several of the large fertilizer-manufacturing companies make fertilizers especially for broad-leaved evergreens and ericaceous plants, and where these are available from the nursery or garden center they are recommended at the rates given on the bags.

The above fertilizer recommendations are based on a 5–10–5 analysis.

Actually, the amount of fertilizer applied depends on the kind and age of the plants, the type of soil, and the kind of fertilizer used. One would apply a 10–6–4 fertilizer at only one half the rate of a 5–10–5 in order to apply the same amount of nitrogen. If one were interested in obtaining more flowers on a plant that flowered poorly but grew well, one would apply a high-phosphorous-type fertilizer with little or no nitrogen, such as superphosphate.

When commercial fertilizers are applied, they should be watered in immediately, making certain that all the fertilizer has been washed off the foliage of any plants it has clung to.

Fertilizing Trees

Draw a circle on the soil under the outside limits of the branches, then another circle two thirds of the way toward the trunk. It is the area between these two circles that is to be fertilized. With a crowbar, punch 8- to 10-inch holes in the soil, making the holes 2 feet apart. Divide the fertilizer (see approximate amounts of fertilizer to use above) evenly among the holes, fill in with soil, and water well. Or if you are very fussy, remove a plug of soil where each hole is to be made, punch the hole, apply the fertilizer, fill to within 1½ inches of the top with soil, then replace the plug of turf. Water in thoroughly and you probably will not notice where the holes have been punched.

It is always best, when contemplating fertilizing trees and shrubs, if you are not familiar with the process and the fertilizers, to write the State Experiment Station for their recommendations. In this way you obtain the best information available for your area, and possibly save yourself much trouble from applying the wrong fertilizer in the wrong amount. Recommendations on the fertilizer bags or containers can also be followed.

The questions in this section have been divided into five general groups:

Deciduous Trees and Shrubs
Narrow-leaved Evergreens
Broad-leaved Evergreens
Vines
Hedges

This segregation might be kept in mind when trying to locate answers for specific problems with specific plants.

Deciduous Trees and Shrubs

GENERAL

What is meant by "deciduous" trees and shrubs?   Those which shed their foliage in the autumn. Some, which retain their dry leaves, all or partly, through the winter, like beech and some oaks, are commonly included in "deciduous" trees.

Is it possible that a chain or a peg fastened to a tree at a certain distance from the ground will ever be further from the ground, no matter how old the tree?   No, there will be no elevation of anything driven into a tree at a given point.

SOIL AND FERTILIZERS

How should I prepare the ground for planting trees and shrubs?   Over a well-drained subsoil there should be, throughout the area, a foot of good topsoil. Beyond this, prepare individual planting holes for trees to a depth somewhat in excess of the depth of root balls or root systems. Remove any excavated soil of poor quality and improve the remainder with leafmold and rotted manure or compost.

Most trees and shrubs seem to grow poorly in my soil, which is very sandy. What can I do?   Select kinds especially suited for light, very sandy soil. For any others, work in, around their root spread, a liberal quantity of peat moss, leafmold, compost, rotted manure, commercial fertilizers, or seaweed (available from beaches if you live near the coast).

My soil, though well drained, is heavy and clayish. It bakes and cracks in the summer. Is it all right for trees and shrubs?   You should lighten it by mixing into all planting areas, about a foot deep, a liberal quantity of fine cinders (not fine ashes) or coarse sand. At the same time work in some humus matter (leafmold, peat moss, rotted manure).

Trees offer more than just shade. Many show interesting bark patterns, two being the sycamore (left) and gray-birch (right). The striped maple's green bark is striped with white.

Few trees and shrubs succeed on my property, which adjoins a swampy tract. What can I do about this? The only cure for lack of drainage is to provide it. Either raise the level of your ground considerably or limit your selection to those trees or shrubs which will accept the condition. Among these are aronia, swamp azalea, winterberry, buttonbush, pussy willow, tupelo, weeping willow, red maple, clethra, blueberry.

My soil is shallow, with hardpan beneath. Should I take any special precautions when planting trees and shrubs? Before investing heavily in planting, break up the hardpan so that it will let water through. For the run of ordinary shrubs, there should be a depth of about a foot of good soil; for trees, about 2 feet. Neglect of these conditions may greatly limit your success.

What does the term "hardpan" mean and how does one overcome it? This is a condition in some clay soils where the clay particles are so packed together that they do not allow water to drain through properly. Before planting, one must break through this, either by digging, laying drains, or by using dynamite. Sometimes gypsum can be used to mix with the soil particles and so break up the clay, and thus allow water to drain through properly.

What should I plant in front of an apartment house where the soil is "sour" (of yellow clay) and the spot is shady? I've tried several types of

evergreens. This is an unpromising condition. In amply prepared pockets, try untrimmed privet, bush honeysuckle, or *Euonymus kiautschovica*. Or, in an elaborately prepared and improved bed with acid, humusy soil, try dwarf rhododendrons and mountain-laurel. If tree roots intrude, the prospects of success are poor.

Homeowners can profit from the way landscape architects choose—and judge—trees before deciding which ones to plant. (Top row) The many forms of deciduous (leaf-losing) trees, including those of very narrow and weeping habits. (Second row from top) The shapes of conifers, of importance because these trees are evergreen. (Third row from top) Trees as canopies, either as single specimens or in pairs (left); and trees as walls and hedges (right). (Bottom row) The width of trees, either singly or in combination, must be considered when screening is the objective.

What do I use to make soil acid? See Acidity in Soils, Section 1. A 3- to 6-inch layer of oak leafmold, rotted pine needles, or peat moss is one way of acidifying soil. Aluminum sulfate (applied 4 ounces to 12 ounces per square yard, depending upon the alkalinity of the soil and the degree of acidity required) is another method, but it is generally less satisfactory. Flowers of sulfur can also be used, making the initial application at the rate of 6 ounces per square yard.

Our soil is rich but moist and acid. What tree do you advise—something with good autumn color? Sweet-gum (liquidambar) would be a tree for you. The fall color is crimson. Red maple, sourwood, flowering dogwood, and tupelo (*Nyssa sylvatica*) are also appropriate.

What is the best commercial fertilizer to use for deciduous trees and shrubs? A 10–6–4 fertilizer, or something similar, if they are making weak, short growth; or a 0–12–4 fertilizer if blooms are scant.

Are commercial dry pulverized manure and peat moss as beneficial for trees and shrubs as rotted cow or horse manure are for mulching? Just about, provided the soil is not made too acid thereby.

Which of these shrubs thrive in a soil with lime? Barberry, Japanese quince, mock-orange, Irish juniper, crape-myrtle, nandina, and roses? Any of them will grow in a slight to moderately alkaline soil. Roses seem to do best in a slightly acid soil, however.

How shall I feed an old tree which seems to be weakening? The easiest way in areas without clayey soils is to broadcast a complete chemical fertilizer (10–6–4, 5–10–5, or some equivalent) on the ground and wash it in thoroughly with a hose. The amount could be 2 to 4 pounds of fertilizer per inch in diameter of a tree trunk measured breast high, spread evenly under the branches of the tree. Another way is to dig 18-inch-deep holes with a crowbar, the holes 2 feet apart over the same area; then divide the fertilizer equally among the holes, afterward filling them with soil. This second method does not burn the grass as much as the first. Water in thoroughly when complete. This is done in early spring or early fall.

How and when do I apply fertilizers to my shrubs? Spring is probably the best time, although October is also satisfactory. Use a commercial fertilizer (10–6–4 or 5–10–5) and merely spread it on the ground before the leaf buds open. Use the 5–10–5 fertilizer at a rate of about 3 to 6 pounds per 100 square feet and water it in well.

TRANSPLANTING

When is the best time to transplant deciduous trees and shrubs?　Either fall or spring, but the transplanting of all shrubs which are recognized as difficult to move, and such trees as birch, dogwood, redbud, magnolia, yellow-wood, and all tender types, had best be planted in the spring in the central and northern parts of the United States. Plants grown in containers can be transplanted any time. Transplant before the trees or shrubs begin to leaf. In the fall, transplant as soon as most of the leaves drop.

How about evergreens?　The best time for transplanting these is early in September. (See also under Evergreens, this section.)

What is your opinion of winter planting?　By this you probably mean moving in the depth of winter with a frozen ball of earth around the roots. This method is often used successfully by professional tree movers. For the average gardener, it should be avoided, except of course with very small specimens, because specialized equipment is needed to do the job successfully.

What is the advantage to be gained from a mass of fibrous roots?　Ease of transplanting. At good nurseries, trees and shrubs are transplanted regularly, thus inducing fibrous root growth. Or the stock is root-pruned by means of a U-shaped blade which is dragged beneath the soil of the rows, thus severing wide-spreading and deep-penetrating roots. Home gardeners can root-prune trees and shrubs several months before transplanting them by inserting a spade around the plant.

Can all deciduous trees be moved with bare roots?　No. Experience shows that some kinds, especially in large sizes—birch, dogwood, magnolia, oak, tupelo, and all evergreens, for example—are best transplanted with a ball of earth.

How large a tree can be transplanted?　It depends upon the kind of tree. Fibrous-rooted, easily transplanted kinds, with trunks up to 1 foot in diameter if proper machinery and equipment are available, but many professional tree movers can move very large trees successfully.

I have a shade tree 10 feet high, which was planted in the wrong place 3 years ago, that I want to transplant. How do I dig it up?　Dig a trench around it 18 inches deep. If many thick roots are encountered, keep farther away from the trunk. With a digging fork, carefully pick away the soil from the roots. Making a ball of soil about the roots, held together by tightly wrapping burlap around it and tying with rope, carefully remove the ball without breaking it and transplant to a new site before the roots dry out. Either remove the burlap without breaking the ball, or push the burlap to the bottom of the hole. Fill in with good soil and water thoroughly.

Can I dig a 6-foot hemlock in the woods and transplant it to my garden with reasonable success? Possibly. Dig a circular trench 3 feet in diameter all around the tree with a spade in early spring. This is to cut the roots. Watch the tree during the spring and summer. If it survives this treatment, dig it carefully in early September. Keep all the roots in a tight ball by tying burlap tightly around the ball and do not let this dry out. Move as quickly as possible.

When planting trees is it best to mound the soil around them or should I leave a pocket to hold moisture to soak down to the roots? Do not mound the soil. Have it flush with the grade when planting is completed. It will then probably settle a couple of inches below the grade, which is proper. A slight, saucerlike depression is advisable to facilitate watering.

Is it necessary to cut back trees and shrubs when they are transplanted? If so, how much? Usually by about one third. If the roots are scant in relation to the top, reduce the lateral growths in the crown, leaving the leader unpruned.

Is it desirable to wrap the stems of newly planted trees with burlap? How long does one keep the wrappings on the tree? Certain thin-barked trees like birch and yellow-wood and even beech benefit from this treatment. Leave it on for a year or two. Also, spraying the trunk with a chemical material like Wilt-Pruf gives just as good results.

Is it necessary to support the trunk of a newly planted young tree? In windswept places, and where schoolchildren pass—yes. Before setting the tree, drive a stout stake into the center of the hole and snuggle the tree up to it. Fasten it by means of nonabrasive tape crossed between the stake and the tree. Large trees are usually held firm by securing them with wires to 3 or 4 pegs driven into the ground around the tree, several feet from it.

What should be done in the spring for fall-transplanted shade trees? Do what necessary pruning may have been deferred in the fall planting. Check over fastenings and prevent chafing of the bark. Replenish the mulch if necessary. Water during drought.

How can I help my newly transplanted trees (large) to form a new and strong root system? If planted in proper soil, do not overfeed or overwater your trees. Keep a mulch at the base. Prevent drying out of the soil.

When you transplant trees, why do suckers shoot from the ground instead of the branches?   When suckers appear at the base and no growth develops in the top, there is trouble. It is probably due to root injury and failure to prune the top sufficiently at transplanting time.

Is it correct, in pruning newly fall-set shade trees of 5 to 8 feet in height, to cut back the whip or leader one third or more as most garden books recommend?   Do not cut the leader back unless absolutely necessary. When necessary, reduce competing branches to prevent the development of future crotches.

When planting trees in the fall of the year, when is the best time to prune them?   Immediately after planting.

I want to plant a double row of mixed flowering shrubs between my lawn and garden, using tall and medium varieties. How far apart should they be planted in order to avoid either a sparse or a crowded appearance?   As you do not give the names of the shrubs you intend to use for your border, exact directions cannot be given. As a general rule, 4 to 5 feet should be a sufficient distance between plants in the front row, about 6 to 8 feet between those in the back row.

Can most flowering shrubs and berry bushes be set out in the fall and winter, instead of waiting until spring?   Shrubs (with some exceptions) and berry bushes may be safely set out in the fall, but the work should be undertaken while there is still sufficient warmth in the soil to develop new root growth. It is impossible to plant satisfactorily when the soil is largely composed of frozen lumps.

Could I transplant between December 15 and the end of March the following: common lilac, French pussy willow, forsythia, deutzia, mockorange, snowball, hydrangea, and bridalwreath?   Do the transplanting in late March rather than in December in the colder parts of the country. In the warmer parts of the Pacific Coast and the South, transplanting can be done during the winter months.

Is the fall the best time of year to plant trees and shrubs in a climate as cold as that of central Vermont?   No, early spring is better.

How does one go about digging up shrubs for transplanting?   If they are small, thrust a spade to its full depth in a continuous circle at a sufficient distance from the center to avoid undue root injury and pry out. Roots are likely to extend at least as far as the spread of the branches.

Is it necessary to cut back shrubs when they are transplanted? If so,

how much? Balled-and-burlapped specimens need not be pruned heavily after planting. Vigorous young shrubs of quick-growing kinds are best pruned to about half the length of their main stems. Older, bare-rooted shrubs, with poor root systems and large tops, are best pruned back to from two thirds to one half their length.

What is the reason for cutting back trees and shrubs when they are transplanted? It reduces the plant to a size more easily supported by a disturbed root system; it reduces the area exposed to the drying effect of wind and sun and divides the vigor of the new growth over a smaller number of growing points. (See also Pruning.)

How low should fall-planted barberry, Vanhouttei spirea, and rose-of-Sharon be pruned? With the barberry and spirea, cut out, at about ground level, half of the older stems; reduce the remainder about half their length. If the rose-of-Sharon is on a single stem, it must not be cut to the ground. Cut out some of the branches at a point where they fork, and shorten the remaining ones to one third their length.

Why do shrubs bloom well some years and bloom poorly other years? Last spring my forsythia and flowering crab had only a few blooms. For two reasons. Some winters are cold enough to kill the flower buds of plants such as forsythia. Then too, many flowering and fruiting ornamentals, such as some crab apples, bear alternately (that is, they have profuse flowers and fruits one year and only a few the next year). There is little the homeowner can do to change this sequence.

I bought some small shrubs grown in cans. On dumping them out, I found a tight ball of roots. Should I plant them anyway? Sometimes plants are grown too long in cans and when this happens the roots grow into a tight ball. Carefully open them, unwind them, even cut some roots where necessary, and spread them out normally in the prepared hole. If planted in a tight ball, the roots might choke themselves as they enlarge and the plant would suffer seriously.

What is meant by "heeling in"? The *temporary* planting of trees or plants close together in a trench or hole, with at least the roots covered and properly watered. It serves to tide plants over an interval between their arrival and permanent planting. If kept like this during the winter, they should be set in a little deeper (usually at an angle of 45°) and covered overall with a thick layer of straw, leaves, or other mulch.

We heeled in 150 tree seedlings in November, and the weather prevented us from planting them. Will they be ruined, or can they be planted in the spring? It depends upon the kinds of trees and on the severity of the winter. If the seedlings were deciduous and great care was taken to cover all the roots thoroughly with soil and then mulch afterward, the chances are that they will come through the winter in good condition.

CARE

How can I stimulate the growth of newly planted flowering trees? If the planting hole was well prepared, no special stimulant should be needed until the trees are well established. However, it is good practice to put a mulch of peat moss, compost, or decaying leaves on the soil over the roots in the fall.

Three years ago I started a grove of various shade trees on a plot 100 by 250 feet. There are approximately 100 trees. I am keeping the place very clean of any weeds with a small power cultivator, thereby also loosening the soil for better penetration of rain. The trees seem to do well. But am I right in keeping the plot scrupulously clean? The longer you keep the plot cultivated, the more vigorously you may expect the trees to grow; but as it is an ornamental planting and the trees are now well established and growing to your satisfaction, you can sow it down to grass. This would slow the rate of growth a little but otherwise not be injurious.

What is the procedure to follow when watering trees and shrubs? Give them a thorough soaking so that the soil is moist to a depth of 18 inches. If necessary, loosen the topsoil with a spading fork to facilitate the penetration of water. Or use a tool (obtainable from horticultural supply houses) designed to deliver water below the surface by means of a hollow, pointed rod.

The grade has to be changed around my house, necessitating a "fill" averaging 2 feet around a large oak tree. Will this harm the tree? It will probably kill it. (See the following question.)

Can anything be done to help trees survive when the grade over their roots has to be raised? Build a "well" of rocks around the trunk, keeping it at least a foot away from the trunk. Spread a 6-inch layer of coarse gravel on the soil. Lay agricultural tiles in rows, radiating from the well to the outer spread of the roots, at the end of each line; then raise the grade. The purpose of all this is to admit air to the soil in which roots are growing. Unless the soil is exceptionally well drained, it might be wise to install drain tiles, 2 feet below the original grade, to prevent roots from suffering from too much water.

How high can the grade over the roots of trees be raised safely? It depends on the kind of tree and the soil in which it is growing. Six inches probably would not harm surface rooters, such as elms and maples, especially if the soil and fill is porous. Willows and ash can endure even more fill than this. The statement has been made that trees can survive a fill of 8 to 10 feet if protected by a properly built dry well. (See above question.)

What can we do to stop a tree from "bleeding"? This depends upon the kind of tree and the cause of the bleeding. If it is merely bleeding due to pruning in the spring, such trees (for example, maples and birches) should be pruned in the summer. The bleeding soon stops. If it is due to "slime flux disease," it may be exceedingly difficult to control.

What is used to treat a decayed hole in a tree? The best thing to do is to clean out all the rotten wood carefully with a chisel.

Should I fill the cavity in our maple tree with cement? Usually no. This would not stop the rotting, nor would it give any strength to the tree. After cleaning it out carefully and painting (see the above question), you could tack over some tin to keep out the rain and insects, then paint the tin a neutral color. In this way you could inspect the cavity every year or so, giving it another coat of paint when needed.

Will the roots of trees affect a garden? The roots of some trees are very objectionable. For instance, maples root right up to the surface of the ground, and elms are nearly as bad. Oaks and hickories are deep-rooting and cause less interference with other plants. But the most serious objection to trees is to the amount of moisture they take out of the soil—and with it any soluble plant food in the vicinity.

Does smoke from a smelter damage trees and shrubs? Yes. Trees growing near a smelter may be seriously injured or killed, particularly if growing in such a position that the smoke is constantly carried to them by the prevailing wind.

Is anyone making studies of what trees and shrubs are most affected by air pollution? Yes. There is a Center for Air Environment Studies at the Pennsylvania State University, University Park, Pennsylvania 16802. Write them for their most recent literature on the subject.

What is used to whitewash yard trees? Lime and water. But why whitewash them? Its only value is for the destruction of lichens, as its use as an insecticide is now recognized as negligible.

What is a girdling root? Sometimes one can see, just at the base of the trunk of a tree, one large root crossing another. As they both enlarge, they tend to choke each other, often with serious effects to the tree. The best way to cure this situation is to cut one of the roots where the constriction occurs, thus leaving one root to enlarge normally.

How can I prevent seed formation on trees and shrubs?   By cutting off the dead flowers, but of course this is feasible only on young or small plants.

PRUNING DECIDUOUS TREES AND SHRUBS

Why should trees and shrubs be pruned?   Trees should be pruned only to remove dead or diseased branches, crossed limbs, weak crotches, to aid single-leader tree types in growing a sturdy central leader, and in some cases to "shape up" the tree. Some shrubs need pruning or thinning to keep them from becoming too dense and over-grown, and to promote flowering, as well as to cut out dead branches. Many trees and shrubs do well with no pruning.

Should all shrubs and trees be pruned? How does one know which to prune?   It is not necessary to prune all of them. Some are benefited by pruning—such as most varieties of roses and certain flowering shrubs whose branches become crowded and cluttered with worn-out wood which does not bloom freely. Generally speaking, if a shrub does not give satisfaction, it is worthwhile to try the effect of pruning. Prune only where necessary to keep plants within their allotted space and to keep them at the highest level of effectiveness.

Is it better to prune flowering shrubs in the spring or fall?   Few, if any, should be pruned in the fall in northern climates. Generally, shrubs which blossom on old wood (forsythia, for example) should be pruned in the spring immediately after flowering. Those whose blossoms are produced on shoots of the current season can be pruned in the spring before growth starts.

Which shrubs should be pruned in the fall? (South Carolina.)   Where severe winters are experienced, it is desirable to defer pruning until the worst of the winter has passed. In your area of the country, fall pruning might be permissible for those shrubs which produce their blooms on young shoots of the current season. Examples are hybrid tea roses, peegee hydrangea, and late-blooming tamarisks.

When is the best time to prune a hedge?   Hedges are best pruned when their young shoots are nearing the completion of their growth. With many hedges, one trimming at this time is sufficient; with others, a second trimming can be necessary in late summer. In order to keep a fast-growing privet hedge in shipshape condition, trimming has to be done several times in a season. (See Hedges.)

What is the reason behind the recommendation to avoid, during the dormant season, the pruning of shrubs which blossom on the old wood? Because such pruning results in the loss of branches which would produce flowers the following spring. Sometimes exceptional circumstances make it desirable to sacrifice flowering wood to attain a definite purpose, as, for example, when old, scraggly lilacs are cut back to rejuvenate them, reduce their height, and make a more compact bush.

Why are some shrubs pruned back every spring to mere stubs? This is done in the case of some shrubs which, though pruned back short, will flower on the new growth made after pruning. It affords a method of keeping them within limited proportions without sacrifice of blossom. It is done with hills of snow hydrangea, vitex, abelia, spirea 'Anthony Waterer', and rose-of-Sharon.

Should you remove dead flowers from shrubs? Yes—if you want to increase the bloom of plants such as lilacs and rhododendrons the next year. No—if you wish the plants to produce fruits, such as berrying viburnums.

Should shrubs, such as mock-orange, hills-of-snow hydrangea, weigela, roses, and beauty-bush, be pruned the first fall after the spring planting? Shrubs usually require little if any pruning the first year after planting—certainly not in the fall. In the spring, hills-of-snow hydrangea and rose-of-Sharon can have the growth of the preceding year cut back two thirds.

When is the proper time for, and what is the correct method of, thinning out shrubs that have not been cared for properly for years? Should they be cut to the ground and allowed to grow up again? Indiscriminate cutting to the ground can upset the balance between the root and the top. Thinning out crowded branches can be done during the late fall or winter. Those shrubs which normally are pruned by shortening the shoots of the preceding year in the spring should be so treated. Any large, overgrown specimens can be cut back one third to one half, but this is done by cutting out one third to one half of the older stems at the base of the plant, possibly shortening the rest.

How many branches should be left when shrubs are espaliered against a wall? Enough should be left so that the wall is well covered when the branches are clothed with leaves and shoots during the growing season.

Can narrow-leaved evergreen trees be trimmed as drastically as deciduous trees?   No. One should be very careful in removing a branch, especially near the base of a tree, since new ones are seldom grown. They do not "break" as readily with new shoots. Hence, a slight pruning of the tips is about all one can do to make them thicken. This is best done in late June.

How about evergreen shrubs like yews and junipers?   These are easier to prune for they usually are dense-growing. If needles and branchlets are below the cut, the chances are that they will send out new growth.

My rhododendrons and mountain-laurel are very tall and overgrown. Can I cut them off at the base as I do privet and forsythia?   Absolutely not! Pruning rhododendrons properly (unless it is just a snipping off of the young shoots) is a difficult thing to do right, partly because there are so many different kinds with varying growth habits. In order to make sure that they "break," always be certain that there are some dormant leaf buds left *below* the cut. The best time for pruning broad-leaved rhododendrons is in early spring. Mountain-laurel, cut back to the ground in the spring, usually produces new basal growth.

My linden tree is lopsided. Can I prune it to become a nice pyramidal tree like my neighbor's?   Yes. In the early spring remove those branches or parts of them that are "out of line." Study the form of the tree carefully, taking out only the branches that make the tree appear ungainly.

WINTER PROTECTION

Are leaves good for mulching shrubs in the fall?   Yes, where a mulch is desirable. Oak leaves are especially valuable around rhododendrons and should be left in place, finally to rot down.

I have read that maple leaves are not the right kind to use for a winter covering. Is this true?   It all depends on what is being covered. They could be safely used as a mulch among shrubs. They are not so good as a cover for many perennials, since they tend to make a sodden mass with a smothering effect.

What is "salt" hay?   It is hay from salt marshes cut and dried the same as ordinary hay. (It is often called marsh hay.) It is used for covering plants in the winter as protection. It is obtained from dealers in horticultural supplies or from nurseries in your vicinity; or collect your own if you live near the coast.

Do shrubs have to be mulched for the winter with leaves or marsh hay after their first winter? No, but it always aids root growth.

When is the proper time to remove mulching around shrubs? It is not always necessary, especially in the case of rhododendrons and related plants where a perpetual mulch is desirable. If necessary to remove, do it in the spring.

How can I keep the leaves of my rhododendron from turning brown in winter? This is caused by either poor soil or too much exposure to winter winds. Correct the soil (see Soils) and place a windscreen of cut evergreen branches or burlap around the plant in winter.

KILLING TREE ROOTS

How can you kill tree roots growing in the sewers? Dissolve 1 pound or more copper sulfate crystals (poisonous) in hot water and pour it down the drain. If the pipe is badly matted, it must be cleared by a plumber. The copper sulfate treatment will tend to prevent the return of tree roots, but the only sure remedy is to eliminate offending trees or install rootproof pipes.

Can you tell me a sure way to stop the roots of a large buttonball tree from growing? I have girdled the tree and filled holes bored into it with copper sulfate. It should be unnecessary to do anything more to the tree.

Is there any way to prevent elm tree feeder roots from spreading all over the lawn? I have heard that the United States Government recommends trenching the grass plot 12 × 36 inches deep and lining both the sides and the bottom of the trench with tar paper. Will that work? This will work for a time. It would be better to sink a concrete trench into the ground. The deeper it is, the less the opportunity for the roots to grow underneath it and up to the surface on the other side. It may be necessary to dig down beside such a barrier every 4 or 5 years and cut all the roots growing around it.

How can I prevent the roots from shrubs in a neighbor's yard from taking over in my seeding bed? They have become a very thick mat, stopping growth and preventing even the digging of dahlia tubers. Dig a trench 2 feet deep along the boundary and install a barrier below the soil's surface. This may be a narrow concrete wall, sheet metal, or asphalt-impregnated roofing material, which comes in rolls.

How can one combat shrub roots where shrubs and flowers are in the same bed? Chop off roots annually in the spring with a spade or a lawn edger, or install a barrier as described in the previous question.

What season is best for ridding property of wild cherry trees and elderberry bushes, and what is the best method? If possible, grub them out by the roots with a mattock, or pull them up with a tractor in the early fall. If cutting down is the only practicable method for you, do so in the summer and chop off sprouts as soon as they appear. This will starve the roots. There are also chemical sprays available for killing foliage as well as roots, easily done in the fall or spring.

How can I remove a wild cherry tree without having some shoots appear later? This tree is on a lawn. Cut down the tree and spray the stump with chemicals recommended at the garden center or by your State Agricultural Experiment Station. Any suckers that appear will be cut off when the lawn is mowed. The remaining roots will soon die if no foliage is allowed to grow to nourish them.

What can I use to kill a large lilac bush? This can be done by applying commercial weed killers to the foliage, then cutting off the tops when they are thoroughly dead.

I cut a hickory tree down to about 20 feet from the ground. The tree is a foot in diameter. I would like to put a large birdhouse on the part that remains. What can I use to prevent the tree from sprouting from what remains and still have a strong pole for the birdhouse? Cut off a ring of bark at the base of the tree or, better still, take off all the bark; the stump will then last longer.

What can you do when a neighbor to the south plants poplar trees and shuts off all sunlight along the entire lot line? Dig a 3-foot-deep trench along the lot line, cut off all roots encountered, install a barrier of asphalt roofing material, and plant shade-loving plants. Cut off branches projecting over your boundary.

What is the best way to kill a sycamore tree that is growing so fast that it shades our perennial garden? It is about 8 or 9 years old. Is there any chemical that can be used? If so, how? The safest way to kill the tree would be by cutting off a ring of bark about 6 inches wide all the way around the trunk. Any chemical you might use on the roots would also kill any other plants near it. Why not take it out?

What is the best method to get rid of alder and alder roots so that we may enlarge our vegetable garden? If there is much ground to clear, spraying with chemicals, and when they are dead pulling them out with a tractor would be the cheapest. If there are only a few, then grub them out. Subsequent plowing would cut up the smaller roots. Also consult your county agent on the use of chemical brush killers.

How can old roots of large trees be removed from the ground when other trees are growing? If you attempt to take out the old roots, there is sure to be some injury to the roots of the growing trees. The extent of the injury will depend upon how greatly the roots are intermixed. If the old roots must come out, dig them out with a grubbing ax. But it will do no harm to the growing trees if the old roots are left to decay.

Is there anything you can put on tree stumps to make them rot quicker? Drill holes in the stump with an auger, fill with saltpeter, sulfuric or nitric acid, or Ammate, then place stoppers in the holes. Use with care, as the acid will burn clothes or flesh when it comes in contact with them.

PROPAGATION

How should I store oak and maple seeds during the winter? It is better to sow as soon as ripe. This is particularly necessary with many maples and white oaks. Maple and some oak seeds can be kept until spring by mixing them with moist sand in a box (this process is called stratification) and covering them with 6 inches of soil outdoors. Or wrap the filled box in polyethylene and store in a refrigerator until sowing time.

Can trees be started from cuttings? The percentage of rooting of many kinds is so small as to make this method impractical.

What general procedure is followed in making cuttings of shrubs? Softwood cuttings are usually from 3 to 5 inches long. Softwood cuttings must be rooted in a close, humid atmosphere such as that provided by a hotbed or polyethylene-film-covered box and taken in late spring or early summer just when growth elongation is nearly complete. Hardwood cuttings are taken in the late fall, after there have been a few frosts, stored in moist sand in a cool cellar (or buried in the earth) until early spring, when they are set in the open ground. (See also Mist Propagation.)

When making cuttings of shrubs, is the time of year or the condition of the wood the determining factor? Probably the condition of the wood is the more important, but as the most desirable condition occurs only at a particular time of year, there is a rather narrow range during which the best results can be obtained.

How can I propagate leucothoe? If the plant is a large clump merely dividing the clump with a spade or even an ax in the early spring is sufficient. Cuttings can be taken, both softwood and hardwood, and rooted in a greenhouse bench with some bottom heat or in a polyethylene-film-covered box.

Can boxwood and Japanese holly be rooted from cuttings? Easily —both by hardwood and softwood cuttings, taken either in late June (softwood) or early fall (hardwood) and placed in a sand medium in the greenhouse with some bottom heat and plenty of moisture or in a polyethylene-film-covered box.

Generally speaking, when should I take cuttings from hardy shrubs? The majority root most readily during July and early August. Lilac and beauty-bush are two notable exceptions. The latter part of May, while the shoots are still growing, is the best time for a lilac, and mid-June for a beauty-bush.

How are cuttings from hardy shrubs rooted? By placing them under preserving jars or in an electric hotbed in a shady place. Sand, or a mixture of sand and peat moss, forms the best rooting medium. Also, one can use a polyethylene-film-covered box, plastic breadbox, or flat filled with sand and peat moss. All should have a little bottom heat, about 75° F., except in the summer.

What procedure should be followed after cuttings taken from hardy shrubs have rooted? (Wisconsin.) They can be potted up singly or planted in boxes. In the northern states it is exceedingly risky to plant them in the open ground late in the fall. The pots or boxes should be stored in a cool place, such as a garage or cold cellar, where they will not be subjected to hard freezing. In the spring they should be planted in the open ground. The rooting medium should not be allowed to dry out. (See also Propagation, Cuttings, this section.)

Are there any shrubs that can be increased by division? Yes. Some types of boxwood, hydrangea, rose, spirea, forsythia, kerria, etc.

I have heard about a plant propagation box covered with polyethylene film. What is it? An easy method of rooting many kinds of cuttings in the home garden is to take a greenhouse flat or wooden grocery box and fill it with a mixture of moist sand and peat moss (half and half). Make a wire support above it 8 inches high. Place the cuttings, moisten the rooting medium, and wrap a clear piece of polyethylene (without holes) above and below. This keeps in the moisture. It may be necessary to moisten the mixture only occasionally. Do not let it get soggy, just keep it moist. Keep it in a warm room with not too much direct sunlight. It is easy to care for and if cuttings are taken at the right time you'll be surprised how many cuttings will root.

Can rhododendrons and evergreen azaleas be propagated by cuttings? Yes. See section about Broad-leaved Evergreens.

TREES FOR SPECIAL PURPOSES

What trees have interesting bark besides birch? Beech and yellow-wood (gray), white poplar (white), Scots pine (reddish), several species of cherries, lace-bark pine, stewartia, sycamore and cornelian-cherry (*Cornus mas*) (exfoliating), halesia and shadblow (striated).

We want some very narrow trees (not Lombardy poplar) to screen out an objectionable view at the rear of our property. Are there such trees? Yes. Included would be the columnar Norway maple, Temple's upright maple, the fastigiate European beech, *Liriodendron tulipifera* 'Fastigiatum', columnar English oak, red-cedar, *Juniperus chinensis* 'Mas', and arborvitae.

How can I start an arboretum? Professor Sargent, first director of the world-famous Arnold Arboretum, used to say that in order to start an arboretum one should have a thousand acres of land and a million dollars' endowment. The best advice would be to consult some recognized arboretum authority to ascertain what can best be grown in the proposed locality, how much it will cost to plant and care for it, what future purpose will be best fulfilled by the arboretum, and how this can be accomplished most economically. (See *Wyman's Gardening Encyclopedia* by Donald Wyman, Macmillan.)

Which trees are undesirable on home grounds because of their spreading greedy roots? Maple, elm, and poplar.

Which food plants (shrubs or trees) can be used on a lawn of less than 1 acre without detracting from the ornamental aspects? For beautiful blossoms, any of the fruit trees. For added beauty of fruit, any of the showy-fruited apples and crab apples. If the soil is acid, blueberries for autumn color; for early-spring blossom and good jelly fruit, the flowering quinces. Hickories and black walnuts are very acceptable as ornamental trees.

Which tree would be a good companion for a magnolia in front of a house? If it is a star magnolia, the Arnold crab apple might do well. If it is a saucer magnolia, a fringetree could be used.

Which trees can you plant close to a house without having their roots get into the drains? The kinds will depend upon the soil and the amount of space you can sacrifice for shade. Avoid the following: elms, maples, willows, and poplars.

We live in the country. Our driveway is on the north side of the house and unprotected. The driveway runs east and west. On which side of the drive should trees and shrubs be planted to avoid snowdrifts?   On the side away from the house, providing the winds causing those drifts come from a northerly direction.

How near a house is it safe for an oak or elm to grow?   An elm could grow nearer than an oak (say 10 feet), for the elm has high, wide-spreading branches and would eventually top the house. The oak, on the other hand, would have wide-spreading branches nearer the ground and might have to be twice the distance from the house so that its branches would not interfere with the building. However, planting an American elm is risky because of Dutch elm disease.

Will maidenhair (ginkgo) and laburnum grow in the Northeast?   Yes.

Is the Douglas-fir a good ornamental tree for the Portland-Seattle area?   Yes, one of the very best! It is native there.

What tree can I get whose leaves have a silvery effect?   White willow, 30 to 80 feet; white poplar, 30 to 70 feet; Russian-olive, 20 feet; silver linden, 50 to 90 feet.

We are going to buy a few more trees with handsome foliage. We already have a hedge maple and an American beech. What else can we buy?   Black oak, corktree, fernleaf beech, honey locust, especially the 'Moraine' and/or the 'Sunburst' varieties, tupelo, pin oak.

We do not like dense-leaved, heavy-looking trees such as Norway maples. We prefer airy, delicate foliage. What do you suggest?   Birch, poplar, honey locust, willow.

Are there any trees with distinctively tinted spring foliage?   Here are a few: Katsura-tree (*Cercidiphyllum japonicum*); flowering cherries (*Prunus serrulata*); sourwood (*Oxydendrum arboreum*); some Japanese maple varieties; 'Crimson King' maple, purple smoketree (*Cotinus coggygria* 'Purpureus').

I would like to plant a few small trees with good autumn foliage. Will you name a few?   *Cornus florida*, dogwood, and its cultivars; *Cercidiphyllum japonicum*, Katsura-tree; *Crataegus phaenopyrum*, Washington thorn; *Oxydendrum arboreum*, sourwood.

We would like to plant a good shade tree that will grow quickly. Which of the following do you suggest: green ash, Siberian elm, silver

maple, or rock maple? Siberian elm is the fastest, with the silver maple a close second (but it is a poor ornamental), and green ash.

Can you give me some idea of a fast-growing shade tree for about a 61 × 50-foot backyard? The Siberian elm, *Ulmus pumila*. However, it grows so fast that proper steps should be taken to prune it regularly and vigorously each year to keep it at the height you prefer. Green ash would be a better tree.

Will you name some fast-growing trees for southern New England? Red maple, silver maple, Scots and white pines, red oak, oriental cherries, and American and green ash, as well as the sycamore.

Which tree of rapid growth is best to plant for shade around a new home? Golden-rain-tree, flowering dogwood, Washington thorn, crab apple, if the house is small; red oak, sugar maple, and 'Moraine' locust.

What kind of shade tree should I plant that has rapid growth, is well shaped, is comparatively clean during the summer, will not require spraying, and whose lower limbs, when mature, will not be less than 15 feet from the ground? Tulip tree (*Liriodendron tulipifera*) and sweetgum (*Liquidambar styraciflua*) are favorites. Other good ones: sycamore, scarlet oak, and pin oak.

Which small ornamental flowering trees would you recommend besides fruit trees and dogwoods? Laburnum, silverbell (*Halesia*), redbud, magnolia, golden-rain-tree, crab apples, flowering cherries, sourwood.

What is a good tree to use on a small place—one which will not have a too wide root spread? Crab apple, magnolia, flowering cherry.

What type of trees should be planted on the front of a lot for decorative purposes where large trees are not desired because of their effect on the lawn? Are dogwoods, flowering cherries, etc., suitable? Dogwoods and crab apples are both superior to flowering cherries for this purpose.

What kinds of trees can be planted in a Wisconsin pasture used by hogs (that they will not root out or eat)? Hawthorn.

Can you name a few small trees with decorative fruit? *Cornus florida* (dogwood); *Crataegus phaenopyrum* (Washington thorn); and *C. mollis* (downy hawthorn); *Sorbus aucuparia* (European mountain-ash); siebold viburnum (*Viburnum sieboldii*).

Which trees provide food for birds? Cherries, mulberry, mountain-ash, hawthorn, small-fruited flowering crab apple, flowering dogwood, hollies, fringetree, tree viburnums.

Which are the best deciduous trees for specimen lawn planting? Flowering cherry, weeping willow, Norway maple, dogwood, beech, and 'Moraine' locust. Among the fruits, apple is best, although crab apple is more often used.

Will you name some lawn trees good for the windy southern New England coast?　Red maple, red oak, poplar (especially white poplar and quaking aspen), sassafras, white willow, sour gum.

Can you suggest a shade tree for a backyard?　Canoe birch, yellow-wood, red oak.

What are the best deciduous trees to plant for shade on landscaped grounds?　Maple, apple, red oak, birch, buttonball; lindens are good.

How does one identify the sex of shade trees?　The only certain way is to study the flower when open. Those with flowers having both stamens and pistils are bisexual. Most trees, especially fruits, are of this type. Then there are trees like the hollies, ginkgo, willows, and mulberries which have only pistillate or fruiting flowers on one tree—these are the female or fruit-bearing trees. Staminate (male) flowers are produced on a separate tree. These latter are the male or nonfruiting trees.

Specific Trees

AILANTHUS (TREE-OF-HEAVEN)

Of what special value is the ailanthus tree?　It is useful in city backyards, where it grows rapidly and endures almost any soil conditions, smoke, and dust.

Why do some ailanthus trees give off a disagreeable odor when in flower?　These are the male, or staminate, trees. The female, or pistillate, plants are inoffensive.

What is the ultimate height of the tree-of-heaven (ailanthus)?　Sixty feet.

BIRCH (BETULA)

What is the difference between the paper birch and the gray birch?　Paper birch (*Betula papyrifera*) bark peels off in shreds; gray birch (*B. populifolia*) does not. Paper birch has horizontal black marks on its bark; gray birch has triangular black patches. Gray birch has softer wood, is subject to fungus disease, and is comparatively short-lived (20 to 30 years), while paper birch survives more than twice that long.

Which species of birch have white bark and several stems that come from the ground? Gray birch (*Betula populifolia*).

I bought some white birch trees and when they came the bark was gray instead of white. Did they send the wrong trees? Probably not. When very young the bark is gray; it turns white later.

Would a weeping birch make a good tree to plant in front of a house? No. This is a variety of the European birch, all of which are susceptible to the pernicious bronze birch borer. The best birch is the canoe or paper birch, native all over New England, and a splendid ornamental which is very resistant to the bronze birch borer.

Are birch and sycamore trees suitable for shade on a small property? Birch trees would be better because they are considerably smaller. The sycamore takes a great deal of room.

At what time of the year should weeping white birch trees be planted? (Missouri.) In the spring is best. In the case of large specimens, balled, burlapped, and platformed, autumn or winter should be safe in your climate.

When is the proper time for transplanting birches? (New York.) In the spring, before growth starts. In the milder parts of the state, balled-and-burlapped trees may be moved in the fall.

Is it practical to plant white birch in this locality (25 miles east of Pittsburgh, Pennsylvania)? Please give me directions for the type of soil and any special care necessary to keep it healthy. Yes, it can be planted. All it needs is a good, well-drained soil, preferably on the sandy side. White birch is susceptible to serious infestations of leaf-miners, which can be kept in check by a systemic insecticide.

Last spring we planted a 14-foot paper birch tree (it was balled in burlap). It did not fully leaf out and was attacked by aphids, for which we sprayed. The tree did not seem to do well. Is there anything we can do for it this spring to make it healthier? Birch trees do not transplant too readily, but if yours was properly balled it should survive. Try placing a mulch of old or dried manure, leafmold, or compost over the surface of the soil occupied by the roots. Put this on in May after the soil has had time to absorb some warmth. Do not let the soil become too dry.

What is the life span of birch trees? Can they be planted near fruit trees? Yes, the birch tree—especially the paper or canoe birch (*Betula* *papyrifera*)—will live to be 50 to 75 years old or more. These trees do not send up suckers, nor do they harm fruit trees in any way.

Vandals have removed a cylinder of bark 6 or 8 inches wide from my canoe birch. Will it harm the tree?   Yes, but only if the inner bark has been removed. The leaves may start into growth because the sap passes up through the wood to the branches, but the roots will ultimately die of starvation because the food which nourishes them passes downward through the bark. If the injury is discovered early enough, it can sometimes be repaired by bridge grafting.

If a young white birch tree is pruned, do the branches need to be treated where pruned?   It is unnecessary when the wounds are less than ½ to 1 inch in diameter. Large wounds may be covered with tree paint or something similar to keep out moisture and spores of disease organisms, although many authorities feel that applying tree paint is unnecessary.

Can white birch be raised from cuttings?   It is next to impossible to root white birch from cuttings.

BLACK TUPELO   See Sour gum.

BUCKEYE   See Horse-chestnut.

BUTTONBALL   See Sycamore.

CATALPA

What is the origin of the umbrella tree?   This is a dwarf form of catalpa (*Catalpa bignonioides* 'Nana'), usually grafted or budded, at a height of 6 feet or so, on straight, single-stemmed plants of *C. bignonioides*.

I have 2 catalpa trees; the bark is becoming loose and part of one top looks rather dead. Can I save these trees?   Your description suggests root trouble, possibly due to poor drainage or frost injury. Cut out all dead branches and note whether the wood below the loose bark is also dead, for if it is you may have difficulty saving the trees. If the grade has been changed, this may have produced conditions unfavorable to the trees.

How do you prune an umbrella (catalpa) tree?   It is the practice to cut it back annually if a formal effect is desired. Prune in the spring just before growth starts. It may, however, be left unpruned; then the head will present a more natural appearance and increase considerably in size over pruned specimens.

Should all the branches of the umbrella tree be cut away in the fall? It is the usual practice to cut them in the fall, but this leaves an ugly stubby knob. If pruning has to be done, delay it until just before growth starts in the spring. (See preceding question.)

Is there any special way of trimming a catalpa tree if it has branched out too close to the ground? Mine is about 2 feet from the ground and the leaves are so heavy that they smother the grass underneath. The lower branches may be cut off to raise the head of the tree. It should be done gradually, taking not more than 1 or 2 in any one year.

CORKTREE (PHELLODENDRON)

What does a Chinese corktree (Phellodendron amurense) look like? It is a round-headed, wide-spreading tree. The leaves are compound, with 7 to 13 leaflets, aromatic and handsome.

ELM (ULMUS AMERICANA)

Should I plant an American elm? Many have been lost in our town from the Dutch elm disease. Unfortunately it is better not to plant American elms now. There are many other trees that make good substitutes. (See below.)

What is the best time to plant American elms? Either in early spring or in autumn, after the leaves drop.

At what season should elm trees be trimmed? During the growing season, if it is desired to check growth. Otherwise pruning can be done in fall or late winter.

Our elm was killed by Dutch elm disease. Should I plant another elm? No. Select a good substitute like sugar maple, Katsura-tree, yellow-wood, beech, 'Moraine' locust, sweet-gum, oak, linden, or zelkova 'Village Green'.

ELM, SIBERIAN (ULMUS PUMILA)

How far apart and how close to the house should Siberian elms be planted? How close to a septic tank and drainage bed? Keep them some 25 feet away from drains. If you have in mind a row of them, plant no closer than 25 feet apart and at least 20 feet from the house.

What is wrong when a Siberian elm does not thrive? It is impossible to give a definite answer without more information. The soil may be at fault, but more probably you have not had it long enough for it to become established. Or it may have Dutch elm disease.

When and how should I prune a Siberian elm, now about 10 feet high and very bushy, with the lowest branch about 3 feet from the ground? Growing V-shape on top. If a high-headed tree is required, prune by removing 1 or 2 of the lowermost branches every year. This can be done in early spring before growth starts. It might be desirable to eliminate the "V," because of the danger of splitting, by removing the weaker of the 2 branches forming it.

Will you give suggestions for pruning (not trimming) Siberian elms to a globe shape and a square shape? When trees are trimmed to formal shape by shearing them, usually no further pruning is necessary.

I planted two Siberian elms which have grown along entirely different lines. One grew very rapidly, with spreading, upright branches and sparse foliage. The other grew slower, with dense foliage, and has a tendency to droop, very similar to a weeping maple. Since I prefer the second, could you tell me whether there are two varieties, and the name of the second? There are many variations in the Siberian elms, unnamed as yet.

Is the Siberian elm considered a good ornamental today? No. It is susceptible to Dutch elm disease like all other elms.

EUONYMUS

Can you tell me why euonymus does not have berries in the fall? It has white blossoms in the spring and is supposed to have berries in the fall. Euonymus species frequently perform in this fashion. They are probably alternate-bearing, like fruit trees. It may also have been that weather conditions were such that when the pollen was ripe it was not distributed properly by wind or insects. Fertilize with a complete fertilizer containing ample amounts of available phosphorus and potash. This could be done in the very early spring.

GINKGO

For what special uses is the ginkgo suitable? The ginkgo, or maidenhair, is quick growing and useful as a city tree. It is picturesque and erratic in its habit of growth and is remarkably insect- and disease-resistant. Autumn foliage color is clear yellow.

Will you tell me about the history of the ginkgo tree? How long has it been grown in this country? The ginkgo, since ancient times, has grown around temples in China. It is the sole survivor of a large group of plants with a long geological ancestry, perhaps unchanged for a million years. It is probably more ancient than any other tree except the dawn-redwood, *Metasequoia glyptostroboides*. The ginkgo was introduced into this country in the early nineteenth century.

When and how shall I transplant two 5-foot ginkgo trees, standing 4 inches apart, with roots intertwined? Transplant them in the spring before growth starts. Try to untangle the roots carefully without breaking them. If you can do no better, save the roots of one intact and cut those of the other if necessary. Set as deeply as they stood. Water them well. Mulch the base and prevent the soil from drying.

GOLDEN-CHAIN See Laburnum.

HONEY LOCUST (GLEDITSIA)

Is the honey locust good for a small property? I have recently seen one without thorns. The thornless honey locust (*Gleditsia triacanthos* 'Inermis') is a very desirable, lacy-leaved tree. It can, however, grow too tall for a small property. It is more slender than the common honey locust, which is undesirable under certain conditions because of the vicious thorns on trunk and branches and its habit of suckering freely.

HORNBEAM (CARPINUS)

What is the difference between the American and the European hornbeam? The native tree reaches a height of about 30 feet while the European one grows to 50 feet and is more vigorous when young. The European is more treelike; the American tree is hardier in the North.

HORSE-CHESTNUT (BUCKEYE)

What is the difference between the horse-chestnut and the buckeye? Generally speaking, the horse-chestnut has five to seven leaflets in a cluster, while the buckeye has only five. Also the horse-chestnut attains greater height, and the fruits, flowers, and leaves are larger. We commonly think of *Aesculus hippocastanum* as "the" horse-chestnut. This is a native of Europe. The members of the *Aesculus* genus that are native to America we commonly consider buckeyes.

Is the horse-chestnut a good lawn tree? It is not considered so anymore for it is rather untidy and too large for today's small properties. There are many better lawn trees available, such as crab apples, mountain-ash, and dogwoods.

How long will it take for a 35-foot horse-chestnut tree to re-establish after being transplanted? It is about 10 inches in diameter at the base. If successfully moved into a suitably moist, well-drained soil, it will probably take two years for the tree to resume approximately normal growth.

JAPANESE PAGODA TREE   See Sophora.

LARCH

We have a tree which looks like a pyramidal evergreen but loses its foliage in winter. What is it? A larch; probably the European larch (*Larix decidua*).

Is the larch a desirable lawn tree? Yes. The European larch is best for lawns, while the American larch (commonly known as tamarack and hackmatack) is best in low, moist places.

Would a larch tree make good growth in rather heavy clay soil? (Ohio.) Yes, it might grow well in a heavy clay soil, but it prefers a cool, rather moist atmosphere such as that of the lower mountainous regions of the northern and northeastern United States.

How and when should a larch be transplanted? (New Jersey.) In the fall or spring, with a ball of earth.

LINDEN

Are lindens good lawn trees? Yes indeed, and one, the littleleaf European linden (*Tilia cordata*), is excellent for urban-street tree planting. The dense pyramidal habit and fragrant flowers in early July are outstanding. Other specimen trees are the pendant silver linden (*T. petiolaris*) and the silver linden (*T. tomentosa*).

LIQUIDAMBAR (SWEET-GUM)

In the late fall I purchased from an Ohio nursery a sweet-gum or liquidambar tree 10 feet high. It was covered with bright red leaves— beautiful fall coloring. Here it has not shown any fall coloring, only a drab yellow. Why? (Pennsylvania.) It should have a western exposure and plenty of available nitrogen to make vigorous growth. Often it takes several years after being transplanted for it to really "reach its stride." Soil conditions often affect coloring.

Is the sweet-gum a good ornamental for the Pacific coastal area? Yes. The cool, moist climate should suit them very well. 'Palo Alto' is a form known for its superior autumn foliage.

MAPLE (ACER)

I would like to have a maple tree but haven't much room. What shall I select? The Amur maple is comparatively small, its leaves are handsome, turning brilliant scarlet in the fall, but it casts a rather heavy shade.

What kind of hard maple has reddish or purplish leaves all summer? The Schwedler maple has a reddish tinge to the foliage throughout the season. 'Crimson King' is an improvement on Schwedler, with red leaves throughout the summer.

What kind of maple is Acer negundo? Commonly called box-elder or ash-leaved maple, this is a large, rapid-growing tree which withstands cold, dryness, and strong winds, but has very weak wood and splits easily. It is best used only in dry areas where other maples will not grow.

Is the box-elder a good type to try in the dry areas of the Southwest? Yes, this and one or two of the poplars are the best. If these will not grow, few other trees will.

Will you please tell me the common names of the following maples: Acer circinatam, A. macrophyllum, A. barbatum, and A. grandidentatum? 1. Vine maple; 2. bigleaf maple; 3. Florida maple; 4. bigtooth maple.

In what kind of soil and location do hard maples thrive? In any soil of fair quality that is not completely sandy, not too acid, and is well drained.

I have a maple tree facing northwest which gets a lot of wind. The branches are very short and high up. Can you advise me how to get a

fuller and shadier tree? It is probable that on the windy side the branches will always be shortest. You might try feeding it with a good tree food or mulching the ground under the branches with dried manure or compost.

What is the best time to transplant maple trees about 12 to 15 feet high? In the spring, before growth has started, or in the autumn, after the leaves have dropped.

My maple grows very thick and casts too dense a shade. How can I overcome this? Thin out superfluous branches during the summer months. Do this in such a way that the tree has a pleasing branch pattern. In some instances you may find it necessary to cut branches up to 10 feet long. Always make the cuts close to the parent branch.

How can the top 6 inches of soil be kept clear of the roots from a 3-year-old hard maple? This is a surface-rooting tree, and there is no means of preventing the roots coming to the surface without injuring the tree in the attempt.

How hardy is Japanese red maple? What sub-zero temperatures can it endure? It probably cannot live through consistently sub-zero winters. Many varieties are grown in the Pacific Northwest.

What location and what kind of soil should the Japanese maple (the cut-leaved variety) have? A well-drained, open situation and a light loam of fair quality, but not necessarily rich. Mulch the soil around newly planted trees.

Would you recommend covering with burlap my Japanese red maple tree? (New York.) If you do not mind the appearance, this is a good idea. Japanese maples are subject to winter injury. They may stand uninjured for a number of years, and then some abnormal winter condition will cause one side of the tree to die.

My Japanese maple has unsightly, withered leaf edges. I am told that the soil isn't right. Is that so? The condition is probably caused by sun-scorch during the period of soft spring growth, at which time the leaves are extremely sensitive. All you can do is provide some slight protection from the brightest sun in the spring.

How can one root cuttings of Japanese maple? Take cuttings in June and place them in a shaded cold frame or polyethylene-covered box. Unless you have had some experience with the propagation of plants, you may not be very successful. It is usually propagated by grafting or seeds.

What is the Norway maple like? A large, massive, quick-growing tree with big, dark-green foliage. It creates a dense shade and its roots are so greedy that practically nothing can be made to grow under it. This is not a good choice for most suburban properties.

When is the best time to cut large lower limbs on Norway maples? Should cuts be painted? If so, with what? As soon as the leaves have fallen or in the summer. When the wound has dried, paint with asphalt tree-wound paint or white lead and linseed oil.

Why does a red maple tree turn green in the summer? This is quite normal.

When is the proper time of year to prune an ornamental red maple tree? In the spring. If it is a matter of promoting bushiness and checking growth, shoots can be shortened during the growing season.

I have a silver maple tree on which the leaves dry up before fall. One other silver maple tree on the same place is all green. What can be the reason? Probably a difference in soil or moisture conditions. However, it can be due to a leaf blight.

I should like to transplant some soft maples. How much should they be pruned? It would depend upon the relative proportions of roots and tops. If roots are scant and coarse, reduce the length of side branches by as much as one half, leaving the leader intact.

What causes the bark on a large soft maple tree to split and hang in tatters? Apparently the tree is otherwise healthy. It is natural for the bark on old soft maples to peel off; this need cause no alarm, provided the bark immediately below that which is peeling is in good condition.

When and how does one plant and care for sugar maple trees? Where can they be bought? Sugar maples can be purchased (by that name) from many nurseries. Plant in the spring before growth has started or in the autumn after the leaves have dropped. They require no special care or coddling and will thrive in any well-drained soil of fair quality.

MOUNTAIN-ASH

What can be done to make mountain-ash produce more berries? Does it need a special soil? Mountain-ash or rowan-tree (*Sorbus aucuparia*) will grow well in any reasonably good garden soil. However, if your trees have reached the age where they can be expected to fruit heavily and fail to do so, they could be in need of fertilizer.

Would the mountain-ash be hardy here where dogwood trees are not? (Northern Maine.) Yes.

How close to my house can I plant a mountain-ash tree? I want its shade to fall on our terrace. As close as is consistent with comfort and convenience. As close, if you wish, as 5 or 10 feet, but it would develop more perfectly if set at least 15 feet away.

Is a mountain-ash 6 feet high easily transplanted in the fall? (New Jersey.)   In New Jersey—yes.

I have a 3-year-old mountain-ash. Would moving harm the tree? When is the best time to move it?   Move it in the spring with a good root ball. Have the hole large enough to accommodate it in a natural position. Water well and place a mulch about the base.

Why doesn't my mountain-ash (5 years old) bloom?   If your tree is healthy, it should bloom within the next year or two. When the growth is very vigorous, blooming is sometimes delayed; but it is too early to worry about that on a 5-year-old tree.

What treatment will encourage bloom on young mountain-ash trees?   As they get older they should flower more freely, but there is no treatment that will ensure equally free flowering every year. Whatever the age of the tree, in some years it will flower more profusely than in others. Make sure the supplies of phosphates and potash in the soil are adequate.

Why does my mountain-ash have a tree full of blossoms but only about 10 clusters of red berries in the fall? The tree is 6 years old.   Weather conditions at the flowering time may have been too cold or too wet, so that only partial pollination took place.

My mountain-ash is weak. It bloomed with a heavy crop of seeds, but then became thin. When should I prune it? Some branches are weak and broken. It is in an open northeast location.   The production of a heavy crop of seeds is a severe drain upon the resources of a tree and may account for the appearance of thinness. Feed it at least after every heavy fruiting. Cut out the broken branches immediately. Any other pruning should be done in the spring before growth starts. Have you looked for borers at the base of the trunk? (See Section 13.)

I planted a small mountain-ash tree this summer. The branches are long and growing more perpendicular than I like. Would pruning help? If so, when should it be done?   Shorten the young shoots about one half in late winter. If, during the growing season, any shoots show excessive vigor, pinch out their tips.

I know that the berries of mountain-ash are bright orange, but what are the blooms like?   Broad clusters of small creamy-white flowers in midspring.

OAK (QUERCUS)

Which are the fastest-growing oaks?   Red oak and pin oak.

How can I identify the different oaks?   Black (*Quercus velutina*), bark very dark brown; inner bark orange; leaves to 10 inches long, 7 to 9 inches broad toothed lobes, shining dark green above. White (*Q. alba*), very light bark; leaves to 9 inches long; 5 to 9 rounded lobes. Red (*Q. rubra*), leaves to 9 inches long; 7 to 11 pointed lobes, indented halfway to middle; pale beneath. Scarlet (*Q. coccinea*), leaves to 6 inches long; 7 to 9 very deep pointed lobes; bright green. Pin (*Q. palustris*), pyramidal form; lower branches drooping; leaves to 5 inches long; 5 to 7 oblong pointed lobes; bright green.

When is the best time to transplant oak trees?   In the spring, before growth starts.

Why must a pin oak be transplanted in the spring only?   Practice indicates that bare-rooted pin oaks are better planted in the spring only. Balled, burlapped, and platformed trees can be moved successfully in the fall.

When and how should a small oak, grown from seed, be transplanted?   In the spring, before growth commences. Dig out the whole root system. Have the hole wide enough to accommodate it; water the soil thoroughly; place a mulch at the base and see that the roots do not lack moisture at any time.

In transplanting red oak trees, is it wise to cut the tap root?   When transplanting oak trees not previously transplanted, it is inevitable. Young trees can survive it, but old trees will resent it.

How should I feed a pin oak?   See under Soils and Fertilizers in this section.

What does my soil need to make white oak leaves turn red in the fall instead of just drying up? Also, my pin oak leaves turned brown with very little of the normal red.   White oak leaves seldom turn red—usually purplish—in the fall. Pin oak leaves should turn a brilliant red some seasons when climatic conditions are just right. If your tree has a full western exposure, has plenty of nitrogenous fertilizer, and the weather is just right, it should turn the desired red. But the reasons vary considerably from year to year, some years resulting in "good" color and other years being decidedly "poor."

PEPPERIDGE   See Sour gum.

PLANE   See Sycamore.

POPLAR (POPULUS)

During heavy, wet, unseasonable snow, when leaves were on the trees, several bolleana poplars with trunks over 4 inches in diameter broke off and had to be trimmed. What trimming shall I do on upright branches from low side branches? Paint wounds; leave upright branches to develop.

What time of year should Lombardy poplars be topped? Ordinarily Lombardy poplars are not planted in situations where it is necessary to cut off their tops. If it has to be done, they can be cut back at any time without injury. Cutting back during the growing season checks growth; during the dormant season it promotes strong, leafy shoots.

How can I choose new leaders for some Lombardy poplars which lost their tops due to a severe wind and rain storm? Select the strongest shoot near to the top and center of the tree to make a new leader. Cut off the splintered stub just above the shoot. Make a slanting cut, which will shed rain, and paint the wound.

SASSAFRAS

Is it easy to transplant sassafras trees from the wild? No, it is very difficult. This interesting tree, with large, various-shaped leaves which turn brilliant yellow, rose, and scarlet, is not easily transplanted. Choose trees not more than 6 to 8 feet high—the smaller the better.

My yard has numerous sassafras trees growing. Do they have any ill effect on the soil? No. They are desirable trees, especially when they reach maturity. They are picturesque in winter because of their gnarled branches and are very wind-resistant.

SOPHORA (JAPANESE PAGODA TREE)

What is the Japanese pagoda tree like? What is its scientific name? *Sophora japonica* is called Japanese pagoda tree or Chinese scholar tree. It has a rounded top with foliage which suggests the locust and casts a light shade. In summer it has small, yellowish-white, pealike flowers in large panicles. It is hardy as far north as Massachusetts. Although it can attain a height of 60 feet, it remains small for many years.

SOUR GUM (NYSSA SYLVATICA)

I am told that a sour gum (also known as black gum, black tupelo, and pepperidge) would be appropriate for a place with poor drainage. What is this tree like? In silhouette when young, a little like pin oak. Slow-growing, moisture-loving, attaining a great height; very hardy; distinguished tree; noted for scarlet and crimson foliage in autumn; difficult to transplant. The foliage is a dark glossy green.

SWEET-GUM See Liquidambar.

SYCAMORE (PLANE, BUTTONBALL)

Sycamore, plane tree, or buttonball tree—which is the correct name? All three common names are used for sycamore.

What is the best plane tree for city streets? London plane (*Platanus acerifolia*).

What is the difference in appearance between the bark of the American plane and the bark of the London plane? When the bark is shed, the trunk of the American is white; the London plane is yellowish.

What is the rate of growth of a plane tree? When young, it averages about 2 or 3 feet of growth in height each good growing season.

Does London plane prefer spring or fall planting? What are the best soil conditions? Plant in early spring or in the fall. It will grow well in any good soil.

Does the plane tree shed its bark untidily? Yes, but the white or yellowish inner bark thus disclosed is definitely decorative.

Can a sycamore root about 3 inches in diameter growing out of a slope be removed without harming the tree? If the tree is well provided with roots on the side away from the slope, cutting off the root should not hurt the tree. As soon as the cut surface is dry, paint it with a good tree paint.

When is the best time to cut large lower limbs on a sycamore? This can be done in late winter or early spring, before growth begins. It is not advisable to cut off more than 1 or 2 limbs at one time because of the danger of promoting excessive sappy growth.

TULIP TREE (LIRIODENDRON TULIPIFERA)

Which tree grows tall and stately and has cream, green, and orange tulip-shaped flowers in June? In autumn the coloring is yellow. The tulip tree (*Liriodendron tulipifera*). It does not flower, however, until it has attained good size—probably 10 years or more after being planted.

Is it possible to grow tulip trees in northern New York State? Near Rochester and Buffalo—yes. In the upper Adirondacks—no.

How shall I prune a tulip tree that was transplanted this spring with three or four new shoots at the base? The original tree died. Before growth starts in the spring, remove all shoots but the strongest. Avoid leaving any stubs which might decay.

TUPELO, BLACK   See Sour gum.

WILLOW

What is a good willow (not weeping)? White willow (*Salix alba*).
When is the best time to move a willow tree? In the spring, before growth starts.
Can a 4-year-old weeping willow be moved from one side of a lawn to the other side without injuring its roots? It can be moved safely, but not without cutting some of the roots. This will not be serious. Willows move easily in moist soils.

How far should a weeping willow tree be planted from a sewer? Are their roots a particular menace to sewer pipes? At least 25 to 30 feet away. Their roots are very likely to be troublesome.

Will the roots of willow trees damage concrete pits, septic tanks, or drilled wells? I am anxious to plant a pair near these things and have been told that the roots damage underground constructions. The roots of willows will enter the tiniest crevices where they can obtain moisture, and unless all pipe joints are screw joints or are filled with lead, you may have considerable trouble in a few years.

Is a weeping willow tree self-pruning? I notice all the small limbs have dropped off. Is this caused by a disease? Many willows shed some of their twigs annually by the development of what the botanist calls "abscission layers." Probably this is what your tree has been doing. This is not a disease, but it certainly is not a neat habit.

Decorative Flowering Trees

CHERRY

Are there flowering cherry trees whose leaves unfold reddish and then turn green? Yes. Among these are Sargent cherry with single pink blossoms, and Kwanzan cherry with double pink ones.

Which flowering cherry trees have white and pale pink flowers? Try two beauties, 'Naden' with semidouble fragrant blossoms in pink and white, and 'Shirotae' with double white flowers.

I once saw a cherry tree blooming in autumn. What was it? It must have been autumn cherry (*Prunus subhirtella* 'Autumnalis'), pink, which blooms in the spring and again sparingly in the fall.

What is the best way to propagate Nanking cherry (Prunus tomentosa)? Either from seeds, which should be stored cool, 40° to 50° F., in moist sand during the winter; or from cuttings taken in July and placed under a bell jar or in a polyethylene-enclosed flat; or in a cold frame kept closed until roots are formed.

Is there a narrow or columnar Japanese cherry? Yes, a beauty named 'Amanogawa', with semidouble pink flowers, 1¾ inches in diameter.

CRAB APPLE, FLOWERING

I have a sunny space alongside my house about 10 feet wide. Will you recommend a flowering tree that will not spread too much and will not grow over 20 feet tall? Any one of 20 different kinds of crab apples, especially 'Dorothea' crab apple.

Would you advise spring planting of flowering crab? Yes.

What is the best way to move flowering crab apple trees 3 inches in diameter, about 8 feet high? Balled, burlapped, and platformed—preferably in the spring, but safe enough in the autumn after the leaves have dropped.

Can you recommend a few decorative crab apple trees? Arnold crab (*Malus arnoldiana*) with single pink and white blossoms; carmine crab (*M. atrosanguinea*), deep pink blossoms and red fruits; 'Dorothea' with double pink blossoms, 2 inches in diameter, and yellow fruits; and the cherry crab (*M.* x *robusta*) with white flowers and red and yellow fruits. There are nearly 100 others being offered by nurseries in the United States.

Is the Bechtel crab apple still a popular ornamental?   No. Although it has double pink flowers, the fruits are only green and not ornamental. There are many much better Oriental crab apples with both good flowers and ornamental fruits.

Do crab apples make the same type of growth as apples?   In some cases, but most make a much finer texture, are dense and rounded in habit, and can be grown with branches touching the ground on all sides. 'Van Eseltine' is narrow and upright in habit; the tea crab is vase-shaped; 'Red Jade' has pendulous branches.

I live in Wisconsin. Are crab apples hardy here?   Yes, they can be grown wherever there are apple trees.

What care does the dolgo crab apple tree need in winter?   No more care is needed than would be given an apple tree. A mulch of rotted manure or compost spread around in the fall would be helpful.

Is there any way of preventing a flowering crab apple from increasing in size too rapidly, without loss of the flower display?   Yes. Shorten young shoots each season, about ½ when they are ⅔ grown.

DOGWOOD (CORNUS)

Does the flowering dogwood tree come in any color other than white?   Yes, there are pink or rose forms.

What is the Japanese flowering dogwood like?   It is similar to our native flowering dogwood, but the flowers (bracts) are pointed instead of blunt. The Japanese species (*Cornus kousa*) blooms a few weeks later. The berries grow together in a head and appear to resemble large raspberries.

Should the soil for a dogwood tree be acid or alkaline?   It grows well in both, if not extreme. Slightly acid soil is preferred.

What is the best fertilizer for dogwoods? How should it be applied and when?   Flowering dogwood (*Cornus florida*) is usually planted in the spring. In such cases, mix a 10–6–4 fertilizer with a good compost at the rate of a 4-inch potful to a wheelbarrow of soil and use this to fill around the ball of soil. Thereafter, if necessary, apply a 10–6–4 fertilizer in the fall. A 4-inch tree (diameter of the trunk) will need 10 pounds applied over the area covered by the spread of the branches and a little beyond.

I have been told that white flowering dogwood (Cornus florida) will not bloom if it is planted in an unprotected place, only if it is in a wooded place. Is this true? (Michigan.) This may be true in the colder parts of Michigan where the wooded areas give it winter protection and prevent its buds from winterkill from too severe cold. Farther south, the dogwood will do well either in the open or in wooded areas.

When is the best time to move a dogwood tree from a woods to a garden? In the spring only, before growth starts.

Should pink dogwoods be planted at a different time than white dogwoods? (Kentucky.) Both white and pink dogwoods can be planted at the same time. Transplant with a ball of earth—not bare root, unless plants are very young.

Are dogwood trees, 3 to 4 feet, hardy in northern New York? In Rochester and Buffalo—yes; but in the Adirondacks these trees are frequently subjected to such low temperatures that winterkill results.

How soon after transplanting wild dogwood trees do they bloom? From 1 to 5 years, depending on the size and age of the plant and the growing conditions.

What would cause a white dogwood to show only 2 bracts to a flower, every flower, every season? Winter injury—the outside bracts being killed or stunted by severe weather. Also, there may be individuals in which this is characteristic. Such specimens should be replaced with normal plants.

What makes all the buds fall from my white dogwood in the spring? They set perfectly in the fall, but just drop off. They are frequently killed by severe winters. This is especially true in central to northern New England.

Can dogwood be grown in this state? Our soil is alkaline. My tree had about 6 leaves all summer. (Utah.) Give it the best garden soil you have available. Mix acid leafmold with it. Chances are that the summers are too hot and the winters are too cold for flowering dogwood (*Cornus florida*) to amount to very much in many sections of Utah.

I have a white dogwood tree that is 5 or 6 years old. It appears to be very healthy, but it does not blossom. What should be done? Have patience; work superphosphate into the soil around the roots. (See below.)

My pink dogwood has faded to a dirty white. Is there anything I can fertilize it with to bring back its original lovely pink color? Possibly a heavy application of a nitrogenous fertilizer would help. It might be that the pink-flowering part has died and you now have the white-flowering understock left in its place, since pink dogwoods are usually grafted plants. If this is the case and only the understock remains, it will never have pink flowers.

What is the treatment to ensure the blooming of red dogwood? Every well-established flowering dogwood should bloom if the soil is normal. If it does not, a 3-foot ditch 18 inches deep could be dug around the tree several feet from the base. Superphosphate should be mixed with the soil as it is returned to the ditch. This treatment frequently results in aiding the flowering of dogwoods and wisterias.

A transplanted twin (2-stemmed) wild dogwood bloomed for the first time this year. When is the proper time to cut the shoot or twin, which does not bloom? Anytime, preferably just after flowering. However, both branches will bloom eventually.

When is the best time to prune and transplant a dogwood tree? Ours has small flowers and is getting too large. The branches have fallen over the ground and rooted themselves. Can I use these in any way? Dogwoods are best pruned in the spring after flowering and are most easily moved in early spring. The branches that have rooted can be cut off and transplanted, and in this way might make separate plants.

What winter protection should be provided for very young dogwood trees? Mulching the roots with leaves, rotted manure, or compost would help the first year or two.

Is it true that there are 2 kinds of dogwood trees—male and female? No. Dogwood flowers are "perfect," having both stamens and pistil in the same flower. They are borne in clusters and form the center of what commonly is considered the dogwood "flower." The large "petals" are really bracts or modified leaves surrounding the clusters of the tiny *true* flowers.

Is it difficult to grow dogwoods from seed? (North Carolina.) No. Sow 1 inch deep in late fall, protect carefully from mice, and leave outdoors all winter to freeze. Germination will begin in the spring and may continue for a year. Transplant when 4 inches high.

Will pink dogwood tree seedlings bloom true? Probably not. They should be propagated either by grafts or budding to ensure the young plants having the identical characteristics of the parents. These are termed asexual methods of propagation. Propagation by seed is the sexual method.

The Pacific dogwood (Cornus nuttallii) is so beautiful in Portland

and Seattle. Can it be grown on the East Coast?   It does not do at all well in the eastern United States, although some specimens have been known to persist and bloom.

FRANKLINIA and GORDONIA

What is Franklinia alatamaha?   A beautiful shrub or small tree originally from Georgia, it was introduced to cultivation in 1790 by John Bartram, who discovered it on one of his plant-collecting trips to the South; it has since never been found in the wild. It has handsome, glossy, bright green leaves about 5 inches long. In autumn its foliage turns orange-red and it bears cup-shaped, fragrant white flowers to 3 inches across with handsome golden anthers. A large specimen in Bartram's Garden near Philadelphia was long supposed to be the only living specimen. All other specimens in cultivation are believed to have been propagated from the Bartram tree, which is now dead. Its common names include Franklin-tree and gordonia, the last probably because it has been shunted back and forth between two genera, *Franklinia* and *Gordonia.*

Does the "lost tree" (Franklinia) have any special requirements? Mine does not grow well.   It prefers a moist but well-drained soil. It is not reliably hardy inland far north of New York City.

Does the Franklin-tree require an acid or alkaline soil?   There is a conflict of opinion on this point. Usually it is considered that an acid soil is preferred, but some have found that it responds to an application of lime.

Is loblolly bay (Gordonia lasianthus) hardy in Pennsylvania?   Probably not. It is native from Virginia to Florida. *Franklinia alatamaha,* its close relative (see previous questions), if sheltered, sometimes can be grown in southeastern Massachusetts.

FRINGETREE (CHIONANTHUS)

Is the fringetree native? What is it like?   Yes. This tree or large shrub bears loose, shredlike tassels of fragrant green-white flowers in May or June and has glossy, tapering leaves. The male plant has larger flower trusses, but the female has plumlike fruits in September.

GOLDEN-RAIN-TREE (KOELREUTERIA)

Is there any tree I can get that has yellow flowers?   Golden-rain-tree and laburnum.

I want to try an uncommon flowering tree. What do you advise?   The golden-rain-tree (*Koelreuteria paniculata*) is a small, decorative tree with a rounded top. Large panicles of small yellow flowers bloom in July or August. In September it has papery pods and the foliage turns bright yellow.

Would a golden-rain-tree be appropriate for a small informal place? We like yellow blossoms. (Mid-New England.)   Excellent, if given a sheltered location; otherwise the branches can be killed back during severe winters. It likes full sun.

HAWTHORN (CRATAEGUS)

What color are the flowers and berries of the hawthorns?   To choose a few popular kinds—Washington thorn and cockspur thorn have white flowers; English hawthorn has several varieties, single and double, varying in color from white to scarlet. These all have red berries, the Washington thorn bearing the most decorative ones.

What is a "May Day tree"?   Perhaps you mean the May-tree of England, also called English hawthorn, which is a hawthorn, *Crataegus laevigata* (*oxyacantha*).

Do you need two trees to make hawthorns bloom?   No.

I transplanted a hawthorn tree in November. Is it natural that the leaves should die in a few days? I cut back all the tips of the branches at the time of transplanting.   If planted with bare roots (which would not be advisable), any leaves left on the tree would promptly wither. But this would not be harmful so late in the season.

Why will a very flourishing pink hawthorn tree start to shed its leaves in early August and have new leaves and even blossoms in September? Can this condition be corrected?   The fact that the hawthorn sheds its leaves in August suggests that the tree has been attacked by spider mites or by a leaf blight. For the spider mites, use diluted miscible oil as a dormant spray; for the blight, use Bordeaux mixture. (See also Section 13.)

When should red hawthorn trained on a wall be pruned?   It should be pruned after flowering by shortening new shoots as they are produced during the summer. The following spring, before growth begins, thin out some of the weakest shoots if they appear to be crowded.

How shall I prune my Paul's double-scarlet hawthorn? If it is growing vigorously and you wish to keep it within bounds, shorten the leading shoots in July. If growth is weak, cut out branches in late winter, having in mind the desirability of maintaining its interesting branch pattern.

LABURNUM (GOLDEN-CHAIN TREE)

I saw in June a small tree that had flowers like wisteria but they were yellow. What was it? Golden-chain laburnum (*Laburnum anagyroides*).

How hardy is the Laburnum x watereri? This is probably the hardiest of the laburnums. However, it is not reliably hardy much farther than 50 miles north of New York City and southeastern Massachusetts.

Will you describe the necessary soil, exposure, etc., and give any other suggestions for the culture of "golden tree," which I understand is a variety of laburnum? (Massachusetts.) These trees prefer a sandy soil, not too acid, which must be well drained. Protection from cold winds is also necessary.

Will you give some advice on the culture of Laburnum x watereri? I have had difficulty growing this tree. This should not present any difficulties provided it is growing in a well-drained position. (See the previous question.) Do aphids attack it? If so, spray with malathion or nicotine whenever they are present; otherwise they can completely ruin the new growth.

MAGNOLIA

Are Magnolia fraseri, macrophylla, kobus, and x soulangiana 'Lennei' hardy in Pennsylvania? Yes. All these should be hardy in Pennsylvania except in the very coldest areas.

Are the following kinds of magnolias satisfactory in Seattle: M. virginiana (sweet bay), M. acuminata (cucumber tree), and M. hypoleuca (whiteleaf Japanese magnolia)? Yes.

Are any magnolia trees hardy north of New York City? Would their leaves be evergreen? Their leaves would not be evergreen. The cucumber tree, the saucer magnolia, the star magnolia, and the sweet bay (or swamp magnolia) are hardy in Boston.

Will a magnolia tree grow around Woodbridge, New York? Certainly. The star magnolia, the cucumber tree (*Magnolia acuminata*), or any one of several selections of the beautiful saucer magnolia should all do well.

Should the soil for magnolias be sweet or acid? Slightly acid, pH 6.5.

When is the best time to transplant magnolias? In the spring, even during or immediately after the flowering period. Move with as good a ball of fibrous roots as it is possible to obtain.

Should a small, potted magnolia tree be kept growing in the house in a sunny window for the winter, then planted outdoors in the spring? Do not attempt to keep the magnolia growing through the winter as it requires a rest at that time. Keep it in a cool cellar or garage, but do not allow the soil to become entirely dry. It should be planted in the garden in the spring.

When can I move magnolia trees from the woods to a garden, and what treatment should be given? In the spring. The cucumber tree (*Magnolia acuminata*) is not easily transplanted from the wild. Get as many of the fibrous root ends as possible. Have the hole wide enough to accommodate them. Mulch the soil over the roots. Wrap the trunk with burlap and spray the tops with Wilt-Pruf *before digging.*

Would you give me some suggestions for growing magnolias? Magnolias require a moist rich soil, therefore the addition of rotted cow manure or compost and peat moss is advisable. While they require a moist soil for best results, it is equally important that it be well drained. For most, a position with full exposure to the sun is desirable.

What kind of year-around treatment will be best for the growth of Magnolia soulangiana in my area (particularly the establishment of young trees)? (Pennsylvania.) Once the plants begin to grow satisfactorily after they are planted in the garden, they require little in the way of extra attention. A mulch over the roots, particularly a mulch of rotted cow manure or compost, will feed them and keep the roots cool in the summer.

How can I get results with a magnolia in this area? (Pennsylvania.) The star magnolia is the easiest to grow and is also the hardiest. If it is given a good soil, it should do well. The many varieties of the saucer magnolia (*Magnolia* x *soulangiana*) can also be grown with no particular attention other than the supplying of good soil.

Our Magnolia x soulangiana, planted in October, had scant bloom and very few leaves the following spring and summer. Will it survive?

We mulched with cow manure in the fall. What else can be done? Magnolias frequently make very little growth during the year after they are transplanted. Mulching is beneficial. For the first winter at least, protect from the sun and wind with a screen of burlap, evergreen branches, or boards. It should make good growth after the first year.

What can I do to make a magnolia bloom? I have had the tree for 5 years and it is 7 feet high, grows well, but has never bloomed. It is possible that you have a seedling of one of the tree magnolias, in which case it might be several years more before the tree blooms. As the growth is satisfactory, do not worry. Some tree types take nearly 20 years to bear their first flowers. However, 'Merrill', a hybrid with large, double white flowers, will bloom only 3 to 4 years after it is grafted. Star and the saucer magnolias usually bloom a year or so after transplanting.

I have a Magnolia x soulangiana which was in bloom when I bought it from the nursery; it bloomed the next season but hasn't bloomed for two seasons. What should be done? Magnolias resent being moved and sometimes take a few years to become established after being transplanted. If it is planted in good soil in a well-drained position, it will soon resume its flowering. If you have any doubt about the quality of the soil, topdress it with cow manure or rich compost.

How do you cut back a Magnolia virginiana (6 to 7 feet tall) when transplanting? Reduce the main stems to about two thirds. If it appears to be making good growth, do not cut it.

My young magnolia produced many sucker shoots this summer. Should they be cut or left on? If the shoots originate from below the ground line, they probably come from the understock on which the magnolia is grafted and should be cut off. However, if they come from *above* the ground line, they may be left, provided they are not too crowded, do not spoil the looks of the tree, and are not understock.

How should I protect magnolias, planted in spring, during the first winter? (Michigan.) Sometimes it is advisable to wrap the trunks in burlap, especially for the first winter. If the plants are small, you might build a burlap screen around them for the winter and even partly fill it with leaves, which would aid in protecting the roots from too-severe winter cold.

Do young magnolia plants (4 to 5 years) need winter protection? The magnolias commonly grown should not need protection at that age unless your garden is so situated as to be exposed to northwest winds. If that is the case, erect a screen on that side of the plants.

Can you start a new magnolia from cuttings from an old tree? If so, how can it be done? Some of the magnolias may be rooted in early summer from softwood cuttings, but they are very difficult. Side shoots, about 5 inches long, are generally the most successful. Cut very close to the branch so that a little of the old wood is also taken. They must be kept in close, humid conditions until rooted. A cold frame or polyethylene-covered box in a place out of the sun would be required. *Magnolia stellata* (and possibly others) can be easily rooted by the "mist" method, commonly used by plant nurseries.

A branch was broken from my young magnolia bush. It has one bud on it. I placed it in a bottle of water and it started blooming. How can I grow roots on it? You can't! (See answer to preceding question.)

Where and how should magnolia seeds be planted? Soak in water until the fleshy covering can be removed. Plant seeds at once before they dry out, a half inch deep in the soil of a cold frame or in a cool place during the winter. They will germinate the following spring.

PEACH, FLOWERING (PRUNUS PERSICA)

When is the best time to transplant a flowering peach? (New Jersey.) In early fall or in spring.

PEAR

What is the 'Bradford' pear? It is a hybrid, a fast-growing seedling of *Pyrus calleryana*, selected by the U.S. Department of Agriculture, that is proving to be a good street and garden tree in the vicinity of Washington, D.C., although it is perfectly hardy north to Boston. It is a standard tree, 50 feet tall, with white flowers and brilliant scarlet autumn foliage. The small fruits, only a half inch long, have no economic value. This plant is resistant to fire blight.

PLUM

How and when shall I prune the Pissard or purpleleaf plum (Prunus cerasifera 'Atropurpurea')? Severe pruning of trees related to plums and the stone fruits generally is to be avoided. Unless there is some urgent reason to the contrary, pruning of the Pissard plum should be restricted to shortening "wild" (too energetic) shoots during the growing season.

REDBUD (CERCIS)

Which other native tree would make a good companion to the white-flowered dogwood? The redbud; it flowers simultaneously and likes a similar environment.

What does redbud look like? In open places it has a wide crown and grows 15 or more feet high. In shaded and crowded quarters it will grow taller and slimmer. It has deep pink, pea-shaped flowers which grow in clusters along the stems. Its leaves are large and roundish, turning bright yellow in the fall.

Can redbud be successfully moved in fall? Redbud is not one of the easiest shrubs to move, and spring is much safer than fall for the operation. Move it with a ball of earth, held by burlap, and unless the ball is very firm, do not attempt to remove the burlap when the plant is in its new position.

This is the second year for a redbud tree. Will it bloom this spring if I move it quite early? Do not expect redbuds to flower much the first spring after being transplanted. Do not transplant them unless necessary. They are not very good-natured about being moved.

Why does my redbud tree not bloom freely? It has grown nicely but has very few blossoms. Redbuds, dogwoods, and some other flowering trees often fail to produce flowers during periods of vigorous growth. Do not feed your tree with nitrogenous fertilizers.

RUSSIAN-OLIVE (ELAEAGNUS)   See Shrubs.

SHADBLOW (AMELANCHIER)

What is a good small flowering tree for a light woodland? Serviceberry (*Amelanchier canadensis*), also called shadblow or shadbush. It has delicate white flowers in the spring and red fruits in the summer.

Does the serviceberry grow well near the salt water's edge? Yes. Thicket serviceberry, *Amelanchier canadensis,* endures salt-laden winds.

SILVERBELL (HALESIA)

Is the silverbell a desirable small tree? Yes. Its main attraction is in the spring when the dainty white flowers are produced, but its striated bark can be of interest in all seasons.

Where would the silverbell be attractive?   On the edge of woodland in company with a ground cover of Virginia bluebells, violets, and other woodland flowers. On a small property it can be planted as a shade tree.

SMOKETREE (COTINUS)

What gives the smoketree its name?   When the seed pods form in June, they produce whorls of gray-lavender hairs. As they become full blown, the bush seems enveloped in a whorl of smoke.

Why doesn't my young smoketree grow taller? I have had it for 6 years and it is the same height as when I bought it.   Either it is being recurrently injured by cold winters or the soil is not to its liking. Fertilize with well-rotted manure or rich compost in the fall, *after* digging it up, examining the roots, and transplanting it to some new place which you know has fertile soil.

Why does my smoketree blossom but not set any seeds? The blossom stems wither and drop off. It is more than 20 years old.   The sexes are sometimes on separate individuals and this particular plant is probably the male or staminate type, which never bears fruits.

I have a smoketree 6 years old and more than 10 feet high. Why doesn't it bloom? It gets leaves, but no flower buds.   You may have the native smoketree (*Cotinus obovatus*), which blooms sparingly. The European (*Cotinus coggygria*) type is more floriferous.

How should a smoketree be trimmed to tree form instead of a bush?   No attempt should be made to change the common smoketree (*Cotinus coggygria*) to tree form—it naturally forms a bush. The American smoketree is occasionally seen as a tree. This form can be encouraged by the gradual removal of the lower branches, starting when the tree is young.

YELLOW-WOOD (CLADRASTIS)

What tree has white flowers resembling wisteria and a sweet perfume? I saw it at night and it was beautiful.   It was probably yellow-wood, *Cladrastis lutea* or the black locust, *Robinia pseudoacacia*. Both bloom in late spring.

Will yellow-wood resist high winds?   No. The wood is inclined to be brittle.

Deciduous Shrubs

WHAT TO GROW

Can you give me a list of uncommon but worthwhile hardy shrubs? *Berberis mentorensis, Buddleia alternifolia, Corylopsis glabrescens, Cotoneaster divaricatus, Euonymus alata* and *E. europaeus, Kerria japonica* 'Variegata', *Rhododendron schlippenbachii, Rubus deliciosus* (thimbleberry), *Symphoricarpus orbiculatus* (coral-berry), *Viburnum burkwoodii, V. carlcephalum.*

Could you suggest good shrubs with an interesting winter habit? Flowers are not essential. Regel privet, five-leaf aralia, shrub dogwoods with colored branches, cork bark or winged euonymus, and several varieties of Japanese barberry.

We have a steep bank between the house and sidewalk, filled with boulders. It is impossible to grow grass between them and keep it looking neat. What do you suggest? The best shrubs would include the Arnold dwarf forsythia and *Stephanandra incisa* 'Crispa'. Both are deciduous, about 3 feet tall, and root wherever their branches touch moist soil. *Juniperus horizontalis* varieties (evergreen) would also be good. The memorial rose (*Rosa wichuraiana*) has long been used for this purpose and it is semi-evergreen.

Will you name a few pretty shrubs, besides lilacs and forsythia, that grow rather heavy and would make a "wall" for an out-of-door room? Beauty-bush (*Kolkwitzea amabilis*), gray dogwood (*Cornus racemosa*), bush honeysuckle, *Viburnum dilatatum.*

Which shrubs will give us bloom in the garden from spring until fall? We have a narrow strip on one side of our house. March–February —daphne (*D. mezereum*); April—*Corylopsis spicata,* forsythia, *Abeliophyllum distichum;* May—*Spiraea prunifolia, S. x arguta,* Vanhoutte spirea, *Viburnum carlcephalum,* lilacs; June—mock-orange, beauty-bush, various shrub roses; July—snowhill hydrangea, clethra, vitex; August—peegee hydrangea, rose-of-Sharon, buddleia; September— firethorn (orange berries). You didn't say how wide your "narrow strip" is. Consult a book like *Shrubs and Vines for American Gardens,* by Donald Wyman, for detailed information on these and other shrubs.

Will you list some dwarf shrubs? *Deutzia gracilis, Juniperus pro-*

cumbens 'Nana', *Ilex crenata* 'Helleri', dwarf boxwood, *Spiraea bu-malda, Spiraea japonica* 'Alpina', Rhododendron 'Veesprite', several dwarf yews, heaths and heathers, *Daphne cneorum,* 'Gumpo' azaleas, *Leiophyllum buxifolium* (sand-myrtle).

Will you name some shrubs that can be trained against a wall in espalier fashion? (Oregon.) *Abeliophyllum distichum, Kerria japon-ica,* firethorn (*Pyracantha coccinea*), *Forsythia suspensa,* yew, *Co-toneaster horizontalis* and others, flowering almond, *Jasminum nudiflorum,* privet, peach, golden-chain (*Laburnum anagyroides*).

Which shrub can be planted near a window as a screen and be trimmed? If by trimming you mean close shearing, privet will take it. As an irregular bush that will tolerate removal of some growths and still flower, try forsythia; but prune out old growths right after blooming.

BERRIES

In order to have a continuous succession of colorful berries along a long drive, which shrubs should be planted? The drive has very little sun in the summer. To provide fruits throughout late summer, fall, and winter, use the following: barberries, cornelian cherry (*Cornus mas*), red-stemmed dogwood, gray-stemmed dogwood, many viburnums in-cluding *Viburnum wrightii, V. dilatatum, V. sieboldii, V. acerifolium, V. trilobum.*

Will you name a few shrubs with outstandingly bright fruit? *Aronia arbutifolia, Berberis thunbergii, B. koreana,* callicarpa, *Cotoneaster dielsiana, C. franchetti, Euonymus europaea, Ilex verticillata, Lonicera tatarica, Rosa rugosa, R. eglanteria, Symplocos paniculata,* and nan-dina.

Are there any shrubs with decorative fruit colors other than the usual bright reds? Asiatic sweetleaf (*Symplocos paniculata*), turquoise; yel-lowberry flowering dogwood; gray dogwood, white berries on red stalks; jetbead (*Rhodotypos scandens*), black; privet, black; Chenault coral-berry (*Symphoricarpos chenaultii*), pink; beautyberry (*Callicarpa ja-ponica*), metallic purple; *Viburnum cassinoides,* berries first white, then pink, finally black.

What are some of the best berried shrubs? Aronia, mahonia, bar-berry, viburnum, shrubby dogwood, cotoneaster, Asiatic sweetleaf, pyracantha, holly, and privet. (For others, see Evergreens.)

BIRDS

Which shrubs, easily grown in partial shade, will attract birds? Blueberry (*Vaccinium* species); buckthorn (*Rhamnus cathartica*); fragrant thimbleberry (*Rubus odoratus*); red (*R. strigosus*) and blackcap (*R. orientalis*) raspberries; red-berried elder (*Sambucus pubens*); *Viburnum* species; shadblow (*Amelanchier canadensis*); chokeberry (*Aronia arbutifolia*); *Cornus alba, C. mas,* and *C. racemosa; Ilex glabra; Lonicera tatarica.*

What shrubs should I plant to attract birds to my garden? (Vermont.) Bush honeysuckle, chokeberry, cotoneaster, honeysuckle, shadbush, spice-bush, wild roses, and most other berry-bearing shrubs. (See above.)

BLOOM IN ABUNDANCE

We would like a succession of bloom in our shrub border. Our place is informal and we like native plants. Can you help us? February and March—vernal witch-hazel; April—spice-bush, cornelian cherry, shadblow, redbud; May—pinkshell azalea, dogwood, rose-acacia, red chokeberry, rhododendron, viburnum (various); June—silky dogwood and gray dogwood, mountain-laurel, snow azalea, rhododendron, prairie rose, flowering raspberry; July—Jersey-tea (*Ceanothus americanus*), showy cinquefoil, summersweet (*Clethra alnifolia*); August, September, and October—colored foliage and pods and berries, witch-hazel (*Hamamelis virginiana*).

What shrubs can be planted to bloom from early spring until late fall? To obtain a succession of bloom one must plant several plants which bloom in sequence rather than looking for everblooming shrubs. *Hamamelis mollis* (earliest); *Abelia grandiflora,* 12 to 15 weeks; *Potentilla fruticosa,* 10 to 12 weeks; *Spiraea bumalda* 'Anthony Waterer', 8 to 10 weeks; forsythia in variety, 3 to 4 weeks; vitex, 8 to 10 weeks; *Hibiscus syriacus,* 8 to 10 weeks; azaleas; lilacs; rhododendrons; roses; hydrangeas; rose-of-Sharon; common witch-hazel (latest). (See the preceding question.)

Can you name some shrubs with fragrant flowers? Honeysuckle (*Lonicera fragrantissima*); mock-orange (*Philadelphus coronarius* and *P. x virginalis* cultivars); *Viburnum carlesii;* clethra; common lilac; *Daphne cneorum;* strawberry-bush (*Calycanthus floridus*); shrub roses;

Natal-plum (*Carissa grandiflora*); Mexican-orange (*Choisya ternata*).

We are planting an old-fashioned summer cottage with old-time shrubs. Can you remind us of a few blooming from June to September? June—rose-acacia, mock-orange, sweet azalea, shrub roses, *Spiraea* x *bumalda*, lilacs, hydrangea;. July—strawberry-bush, smoke-bush, hydrangea; August—summersweet, rose-of-Sharon.

Will you name 5 deciduous shrubs desirable for flowers, berries, and foliage color? *Aronia arbutifolia, Berberis koreana, Viburnum prunifolium, Vaccinium corymbosum, Cornus alba* 'Gouchaultii'.

FOLIAGE

Which shrubs have distinctive autumn color, other than the brilliant reds and orange shades? Here are a few: *Abelia* x *grandiflora* (reddish-bronze); *Cotoneaster divaricata* (purplish); *Mahonia aquifolium* (chestnut and bronze tints); *Viburnum carlesii* (purplish-red); *V. plicatum tomentosum* (purplish).

Can you name some shrubs with outstandingly bright autumn foliage? *Berberis koreana, B. vernae, B. thunbergii; Cotoneaster adpressa; Enkianthus campanulatus; Euonymus alata* and *E. alata* 'Compacta'; *Fothergilla; Franklinia alatamaha; Itea virginica; Rhododendron arborescens, R. schlippenbachii,* and *R. kaempferi; Rhus aromatica; Stephanandra incisa; Vaccinium corymbosum; Xanthorhiza simplicissima.*

I am partial to shrubs with foliage of a fine, lacy quality. Can you mention a few? *Acer palmatum* 'Dissectum'; *Abelia* x *grandiflora; Cotoneaster dielsianus; Neillia sinensis; Rosa hugonis* and *R. eglanteria; Spiraea* x *arguta; S. thunbergii; Symphoricarpos chenaultii;* tamarisk; *Stephanandra incisa* 'Crispa'.

Will you name a few shrubs with aromatic foliage? *Calycanthus floridus, Comptonia asplenifolia, Cotinus* species, *Elsholtzia stauntonii, Lindera aestivale, Rhus aromatica, Rosa eglanteria,* bayberry, lavender.

Specific Shrubs

ABELIA, GLOSSY

How would abelias harmonize with broad-leaved evergreens? Very well; they like peaty soil as the evergreens do, but not too much shade. And abelias are semi-evergreen.

Are Abelia x grandiflora and the crape-myrtle hardy in the Pittsburgh, Pennsylvania, areas? *Abelia* x *grandiflora* is hardy in Pittsburgh, but the crape-myrtle may not prove completely hardy. Certainly it should be tried only in the most protected areas.

How long is the blooming season of Abelia x grandiflora? From June or July to late October or even November, making it one of the few everblooming shrubs. However, the best display comes early.

ABELIOPHYLLUM

Is there such a plant as "white forsythia"? *Abeliophyllum distichum* is often called that although it is not a true forsythia. It is a shrub from Korea, growing 5 feet tall with dense clusters of white flowers, especially conspicuous because they are borne in early spring before the leaves appear, just before forsythia blooms. The flower buds are not reliably hardy much north of southern Connecticut.

ALMOND (PRUNUS TRILOBA)

How do you prune a flowering almond? The flowers are produced on the shoots made the preceding year; therefore, as soon as the flowers fade, cut back the flowering shoots to within 2 inches of the point of origin. Also, when necessary, prune out the older branches at the base.

Can I root cuttings of an almond? Yes. The cuttings must be taken in July and placed in a cold frame or plastic-covered box in order to have the requisite moist, humid conditions to induce rooting.

AMORPHA

What is the indigobush? Is it hardy in northern Ohio? Indigobush (*Amorpha fruticosa*) is somewhat weedy, with purplish flowers, in spikes, during June and July. It will grow in poor soil and should be hardy in northern Ohio.

ARALIA, FIVE-LEAF (ACANTHOPANAX)

A nursery owner recommends Acanthopanax sieboldianus for planting in the shade. Is it any good? Yes! Its flowers and fruits are negligible but this shrub has beautiful 5-part, lacy leaves and is fast-growing. It will grow under trees, in any shaded place, or in full sun, and is drought-resistant. Its height is about 5 feet.

AZALEA, DECIDUOUS (RHODODENDRON)

Why do I have trouble growing azaleas dug from the woods when those purchased from the nursery do very well? Most plants growing in the woods have considerably longer but fewer roots than if they were grown in the nursery, where they are periodically root-pruned. In digging azaleas in the woods, usually much of the root system is cut off.

I have two plants of pinxterbloom and two of roseshell azalea. They have been in the ground for 3 years and both of the former have bloomed each year, but the latter never have. Why? What degree of temperature is the minimum under which the pinxterbloom will bloom? Both these azalea species need acid soil, and if grown in identical conditions the one should bloom if the other does. Pinxterbloom will bloom even though temperatures fall considerably below zero.

I have a wild azalea. How can it be made to bloom? If collected in Massachusetts, this is probably pinxterbloom (*Rhododendron nudiflorum*). If given acid soil, plenty of water, and a mulch of pine needles, oak leaves, or peat moss and compost, it will undoubtedly bloom well in two years' time.

What can you combine with azaleas for summer and fall bloom? The soil is part clay. I have put oak-leaf mulch around the azaleas, but nothing else seems to thrive. For a midsummer shrub, try *Clethra alnifolia*. For autumn flower, try the low, matting, blue-flowered ceratostigma. For both of these, the clay soil should be lightened with compost and peat moss. (For questions on soil and care of azaleas, see Broad-leaved Evergreens.)

What conditions are necessary for the growth of Ghent azaleas? These deciduous hybrid azaleas need a fairly open situation and deep-drained acid soil. At least one third of it should be humus-forming oak leafmold or peat moss.

Where and in what soil should I plant roseshell azalea (Rhododendron prinophyllum syn. roseum)? Light shade, such as that given by a thin woodland. Provide a deep, moist soil with plenty of humus.

When is the best time to set our azaleas? (Georgia.) In your region, only late summer and fall planting are preferable. Most varieties of azaleas, however, can be transplanted in full bloom if they are carefully dug and immediately replanted.

At what season of the year should a wild azalea be transplanted? It can be transplanted either in the fall after its leaves have dropped or in the early spring, before new growth starts. Spring is the preferred season. It should be carefully dug to preserve all roots, with soil adhering to them. The roots should not be allowed to dry out while the plant is being moved.

What types of deciduous (or leaf-losing) azaleas would be hardy for this section of the country? The temperature often goes to 20° F. below, but not for any great length of time. (New York.) Many azaleas can be grown in northern New York and New England and in fact grow in the woods as natives. Some are flame, torch, pinxterbloom, roseshell, pinkshell, royal, sweet, and swamp. Many of the Exbury, Knaphill, and Ghent hybrids are also worth a trial and will grow and bloom even when temperatures drop as low as −20° F.

What are the best varieties of azaleas to plant in southern New York State? Practically any of the azaleas except the evergreen Kurume and the Indian varieties. Many of the colorful Exbury and Knaphill hybrids are hardy even as far north as central Maine.

How can I lengthen the period of bloom for azaleas? By selecting types which bloom successively. The following species should ensure two months of continuous flowers from early April to late August: Korean, pinkshell, pinxterbloom, flame, sweet, swamp.

Are there any azaleas that will grow in swampy places? Swamp azalea grows naturally in swampy ground. Pinkshell (*Rhododendron vaseyi*) is also satisfactory.

Are the Exbury and Knaphill azaleas really superior to our native azaleas, such as the flame azalea (R. calendulaceum) and pinxterbloom (R. nudiflorum)? No easy answer is possible. Perhaps it's all a matter of personal taste. The clarity of colors and their range and the size of each floret are spectacular in the Exbury, Knaphill, and other deciduous hybrid azaleas. Yet the natives, several of which have been used in the breeding which has achieved the hybrids, have undeniable beauty and grace, especially when grown informally in an open woodland.

What are those big-flowered azaleas, with flowers nearly 2 inches across, that I saw in some Georgia gardens last spring? These are varieties of either the Kurume or the Indian azaleas. They are evergreen, but not hardy north of southern Virginia, except in protected places in Washington, D.C. They are well worth growing in the warmer parts of this country.

BARBERRY (BERBERIS)

What is Korean barberry? A very decorative shrub (*Berberis koreana*) growing 6 to 7 feet high, erect when young and then spreading and arching. Thick, broad, wedge-shaped leaves turning orange-red in autumn. Small but showy yellow flowers in the spring, followed by scarlet berries in the fall.

Is there a barberry suitable for a very low hedge? Yes. Box barberry (*Berberis thunbergii* 'Minor'), just like a miniature of the well-known Japanese barberry. There is also a variety called truehedge columnberry. It grows narrower and more erect but can be kept low by merely cutting off the top. It is good for its fine autumn color. The dwarf red-leaved variety 'Crimson Pygmy', not over 2 feet high, is an excellent choice.

Why is the common barberry (Berberis vulgaris) no longer grown? It serves as an alternate host for the black stem rust of wheat, and government regulations severely restrict its growth in most areas. Check with your county extension agent for local regulations—if they exist.

When shall I transplant a barberry bush that is 3 years old? How far apart? When should I prune it? Barberry bushes that lose their leaves every fall can be transplanted in the spring or fall while they are leafless. Evergreen kinds are better transplanted in the spring. If they are to be planted in a shrub border where every plant is to be allowed enough room for normal development, the smaller kinds can be allowed 4 to 5 feet and the taller ones at least 6 to 7 feet. Pruning should be done immediately after they are transplanted.

When shall I prune barberry? Barberry ordinarily requires little if any pruning except in those cases when a special shape is desired, as in hedges or in a formal garden. Then the practice is to shear it when the new shoots have almost completed their growth in late spring.

If Japanese barberry is trimmed to the ground in December, is it possible to transplant it in the spring in another spot in the garden? If any small part of the stems is left above ground, you may safely move it in the spring. If cut clear to the ground, then wait until new growth starts.

How can a truehedge columnberry barberry be raised from seed? This plant is a "cultivar." It will not reproduce itself from seed.

How can I best propagate Japanese barberry? The simplest method is from seeds, which should be stored in a cool place in moist sand during the winter and sown very early in the spring. Or they may be rooted from cuttings taken in July and kept in a closed hotbed or polyethylene-covered box (see Propagation) until rooted.

BAYBERRY (MYRICA)

When is the proper time to transplant bayberry bushes? (New Jersey.) Spring; or in New Jersey, early autumn.

Wild bayberries were planted on the north side of my house. Will these grow? This is not a good situation. Wild bayberries prefer open situations and will take only very light, partial shade.

What is the proper cultivation of bayberry? Where may it be obtained? It is by nature a shrub of open, sunny, sandy coastal tracts. Therefore, in cultivation it should be kept out of the shade. It is a poor-soil shrub. Plant it, balled-and-burlapped, in the spring in nonalkaline soil. Few nurseries grow it. One may have to obtain it from dealers in native plants.

BEARBERRY (ARCTOSTAPHYLOS)

Is bearberry (Arctostaphylos uva-ursi) a good ground cover to plant just behind a dry retaining wall? Yes, one of the best if there's plenty of sun and the soil is well drained and sandy. Be sure to get only pot-grown plants from a reliable nursery; wild plants are *very* difficult to transplant.

What conditions are necessary for the growth of bearberry? Full sun or light shade, well-drained and aerated, very sandy soil, and acid.

Where can bearberry be grown? In the northern United States, from coast to coast.

BEAUTY-BUSH (KOLKWITZIA)

I've heard about kolkwitzia. What is it like? Beauty-bush is top-ranking. It suggests weiglea, but is much finer. Its flowers are smaller, more abundant, and pale pink with a yellow throat in early June. It is slow-growing. Its ultimate height of 9 feet (and nearly as broad) makes it ultimately a very large shrub.

Last year I planted a beauty-bush. It has not bloomed and has

thrown out only one new shoot. It gets morning sun and careful attention. Shouldn't it have flowered? Next spring, prune back the one shoot. It will probably branch out and begin to form a solid shrub. It might flower the following spring. The beauty-bush often doesn't flower at an early age.

What kind of fertilizer should be used on a beauty-bush to get it to bloom? There is no need for a special fertilizer. This shrub often does not flower at an early age. It is worth waiting for.

Should a beauty-bush (Kolkwitzia amabilis) be pruned? If so, when? If the bush is crowded, cut away the oldest flowering branches to the ground immediately after the flowers have faded. Otherwise, little or no pruning is required.

How can I start new plants from my beauty-bush? Either from seeds, which take several years to reach the flowering stage, or from cuttings. Cuttings must be of soft wood, i.e., taken from the tips of the shoots while they are still growing actively. If taken at a later stage, they will form a large callus but generally fail to form roots. Softwood cuttings can be rooted only in a shaded cold frame or polyethylene-enclosed box.

BENZOIN (SPICE-BUSH)

At approximately what age does Lindera benzoin (spice-bush) flower? Does it make a good screening shrub? How far apart should it be planted for that effect? Is it thoroughly winter-hardy in Connecticut? It begins to flower when it is 5 to 8 years old. In New England it grows to about 8 to 10 feet tall. It makes a fair screen, with plants set 5 to 6 feet apart. It is relatively pest-free, requires no special attention, and should be thoroughly hardy in Connecticut, where it is native. The sexes are separate.

BLUEBERRY (VACCINIUM)

I want to grow blueberries for their ornamental foliage. Are there any special soil requirements? Make the soil acid by mixing in rotted oak leaves, rotted pine needles, or peat moss. Maintaining a 2- to 3-inch layer of oak leaves or wood chips on soil over roots is a good plan to help keep the soil moist.

BROOM (CYTISUS)

What is the scientific name of the shrub called "Scotch broom"? It has yellow flowers similar to sweet peas, with the seed borne in a pod like peas. Does it have commercial possibilities? *Cytisus scoparius.* There are probably no commercial possibilities except as an ornamental. It is used in a limited way for making brooms, in basketry, for thatching, etc., mostly in Europe.

What soil is best for Scotch broom? It succeeds well in many places in poor, almost barren sand dunes, roadsides, and embankments. It prefers a light, sandy, nonalkaline soil. The admixture of a little peat moss will be helpful. Plant in well-drained, open places. Start with small plants—pot-grown, if you can get them. It is difficult to transplant except from pots or cans.

Has the Scotch broom become naturalized in this country? Yes, in many regions including parts of coastal New England and Long Island, New York, to southern Virginia and in the Pacific Northwest.

BUTTERFLY-BUSH (BUDDLEIA)

Which kinds of buddleia bloom in late summer? There are several, but the varieties of *Buddleia davidii* with flowers ranging from mauve to deep purple are the best.

Which buddleia is the most reliably hardy? *Buddleia alternifolia,* which has short, dense clusters of fragrant blue flowers in May.

Where would be the best place to plant buddleia? In a sunny place or shady place? It makes its best growth in full sun.

How should buddleias be planted? Buddleia, dug from a nursery, should be planted in the spring. Probably the roots will have been roughly pruned when the plant is received, but before being planted they should have any ragged ends cut clean. Plant an inch or two deeper than previously and pack the soil carefully between the roots. Cut the stems back to 2 inches from the point where growth started the previous spring. Give full sun.

Is it too late to prune branches of buddleia in April? I understand they should be cut late in November. Spring is the correct time to prune buddleias. They should not be cut back in the fall because of the danger that a severe winter will injure them and necessitate still more pruning in the spring.

Is it advisable to debud the first spikes of buddleias?   There is no particular advantage to be gained from this practice.

Should butterfly-bush be cut down every year in Pennsylvania?   In your area of the country the effects of winter are almost certain to make pruning necessary. Wait until the buds begin to grow in the spring, then cut the top down to vigorous shoots.

Is Buddleia alternifolia pruned in the same way as the butterfly-bush buddleia?   No. Its flowers are produced on old wood; therefore, pruning should be done immediately *after* flowering, merely thinning out crowded shoots and shaping up the bush.

What care should be given buddleia (butterfly-bush or summer-lilac) for winter protection?   A mulch of littery material around the base is all that may be needed. It is advisable not to cut the tops back until spring.

Can butterfly-bushes be grown from cuttings? If so, how is it done? When are cuttings made?   Yes. The cuttings, 4 to 5 inches long, are made in July or August from side shoots. Cut off the bottom pair of leaves and make a clean cut through the stem just below the joint from which the leaves were cut. Insert one third of their length in sand in a propagating case.

CARYOPTERIS (BLUEBEARD)

What is caryopteris like?   The one commonly grown (*Caryopteris incana*) is a shrub bearing bluish flowers. It is not fully hardy in the North, where it is treated as a perennial, with new above-ground growth appearing each spring.

How should one prune caryopteris, and when?   Wait until the buds swell in the spring and then cut back each branch to a strong-growing bud. If winter-killed to the ground, remove dead stalks in early spring.

CHASTE-TREE (VITEX)

Is chaste-tree really a tree? Mine is more like a shrub.   It may develop into a small tree in a favorable climate. In the North its young branches often are killed by low temperatures, which make it assume a shrubby habit.

Does chaste-tree (Vitex agnus-castus) require acid soil?   It appears to reach its best development in sandy peat. This would indicate a preference for a nonalkaline but not highly acid soil. It grows readily enough in average, light garden soil.

How and when is the proper time to prune chaste-tree (Vitex agnus-castus)? This blossoms on shoots of the current season and should be cut back in the spring. Wait until growth begins (it is a late starter) and cut back the branches to strong-growing buds.

COTONEASTER

What are some of the best cotoneasters for border planting? *Cotoneaster hupehensis*, 6 feet high; *C. salicifolius floccosus*, 10 feet; *C. zabelii miniatus*, 6 to 8 feet.

We are looking for a cotoneaster which is lower-growing than Cotoneaster horizontalis. What do you suggest? *C. adpressa* grows only 9 to 12 inches high; it has glossy berries in fall like *C. horizontalis* but it is hardier. Also *C. microphyllus thymifolius*, 1 to 2 feet; *C. dammeri*, 1 foot; and *C. congestus*, 3 feet.

How can I grow cotoneasters successfully? Give them a sunny position in well-drained soil. Protect young plants from rabbits in rural districts.

CRAPE-MYRTLE (LAGERSTROEMIA)

What kind of soil does crape-myrtle need? It has no special requirements and will thrive in any ordinary garden soil.

What is the proper care of crape-myrtle in regard to fertilizer, trimming, watering, and winter protection? (Maryland.) Fertilize by mulching with compost or rotted manure in the fall, which will also help protect the roots against winter injury. If in an exposed location, cover the top with evergreen branches. Shorten the shoots of the preceding year one half to two thirds in the spring. Cut back flowering shoots when the blossoms have faded. Water only during droughts.

Can you advise why my crape-myrtle shrubs do not bloom? I have had these shrubs for 4 years and protect them each winter. They bloomed only the first year after planting. (New York.) Winter injury and not enough heat during the growing season could be the reason. Crape-myrtle shrubs bloom freely about once in 10 years as far north as this. Grow them in the warmest, sunniest situation; cut back in the spring to strong-growing shoots.

Why did my 8-year-old crape-myrtle fail to bloom the past summer?

Two of them have always bloomed beautifully until last season. (Kentucky.) The chances are that they were injured by a very severe winter.

The crape-myrtle, an old bush that is very tall and is located about 10 feet from an oak, is thrifty as to foliage but has no blooms. We have a stratum of clay soil but have put in many tons of topsoil and plenty of fertilizer. What is wrong? The proximity of the oak may be a factor in the failure of the crape-myrtle to bloom. Omit nitrogenous fertilizers and try the effect of an application of superphosphate to the soil over the roots at the rate of 6 ounces per square yard. Maybe the soil is too acid and would be helped by an application of ground limestone.

Can a crape-myrtle be protected sufficiently to winter safely outdoors in a climate where the temperature falls to −10° to −15° F.? No.

How do I care for crape-myrtle? Do the plants need pruning? (California.) Crape-myrtle is not satisfactory in Southern California. Pruning consists of cutting back the shoots immediately after flowering to encourage new growth and further flowering.

DAPHNE

What is the name of the daphne that blooms very early? February daphne (*D. mazereum*). It is valued for its early blooming and lilac-purple fragrant flowers. Its height may reach 3 feet; it is stiff, erect, and deciduous.

Why do the leaves of a Daphne mezereum turn yellow and drop off during the months of August and September? It is characteristic of this species to shed its leaves during droughts in late summer.

DEUTZIA

Are there any low-growing deutzias? If so, when do they bloom? *Deutzia gracilis,* with white flowers in May; *Deutzia x rosea* has pinkish flowers, otherwise it resembles the preceding.

What are the advantages of the tall deutzias? Are their branch patterns attractive in winter? Their flowers are showy; otherwise their foliage and their branch pattern are uninteresting.

When should I transplant deutzias? In the spring or early fall.

When is the proper time to trim deutzias? They should be pruned by cutting out worn-out and crowded flowering shoots immediately after the blossoms have faded.

DOGWOOD (CORNUS) (See also under Decorative Flowering Trees.)

Which dogwood shrubs have colored twigs in winter? *Cornus alba* (Tatarian d.), bright red twigs; *Cornus sericea* (red Osier d.), deep red; *Cornus* 'Flaviramea' (golden-twig d.), yellow; *Cornus racemosa* (gray d.), gray; *Cornus sanguinea* (blood-twig d.), dark blood-red; *Cornus sanguinea* 'Viridissima' (green-twig d.), green.

What color are the berries of dogwood shrubs? Tatarian dogwood, whitish; silky dogwood, pale blue; blood-twig dogwood, black; red Osier dogwood, white or bluish; gray dogwood, white.

How are shrubby dogwoods used to best advantage? In masses as open woodland border or as an informal hedgerow planting of mixed shrubs.

Enkianthus bears drooping clusters of yellow bell-shaped flowers in the spring. Its foliage turns bright red and orange in the fall.

I have had a Cornus mas (cornelian cherry) for 3 years, but it has not grown. What do you suggest? It takes a few years to become established. If you have given it good soil, fertilized it occasionally with well-rotted manure, compost, or a complete commercial fertilizer, and given it plenty of water, you have done the best you can for it.

ELAEAGNUS See Russian-Olive.

ENKIANTHUS

What is Enkianthus campanulatus like?   A graceful, upright shrub with an ultimate height of 12 to 15 feet but slow-growing. In May and June it bears drooping clusters of yellowish bell-shaped flowers similar to blueberry flowers. Its chief value is in its foliage, which turns brilliant orange and scarlet in the fall, and in its gray bark.

What deciduous shrub with good autumn color can we put in among the evergreens at the east and west side of our house?   *Enkianthus perulatus,* which grows to 6 feet, would be a good choice because, like the broad-leaved evergreens, it prefers acid soil. Use *E. campanulatus* if a taller shrub is required.

EUONYMUS

I have seen a shrub which has curious corky-flanged bark on its branches. Its leaves turn deep rose in the autumn. What is it?   Winged euonymus (*E. alata*). It is sometimes called burning-bush.

FORSYTHIA

What different kinds of forsythia are there?   About 5 species and several varieties. Among the best are: *F. intermedia* 'Spectabilis', urn-like in form; F. suspensa, which is fountainlike (or drooping); and the heavily flowered variety 'Karl Sax'.

There is such a difference in the number of flowers on forsythias that I wonder if it is due to soil or location; or is there more than one kind of plant? (Arkansas.)   There are several kinds of forsythia. *Forsythia intermedia* 'Spectabilis' is a very showy one.

What is the hardiest forsythia?   A species called *F. ovata* is the earliest to bloom; its flowers, however, are less effective and more amber in color.

When is the best time to transplant forsythia? Does it require cultivation?   This shrub may be safely transplanted in the spring or fall, any time that it is leafless. Cultivation to remove weeds around newly transplanted shrubs for a period of 1 or 2 years is decidedly beneficial.

Our forsythia had a late fall bloom this year. Will that impair the spring bloom?   Yes, for the flower buds are formed in the summer, and if some open, then the bloom the following spring will be much reduced.

Why do forsythias bloom around the bottom of bushes only? Because in cold areas the flower buds—present all winter long—are killed by low temperatures except where they are protected by a blanket of snow or fallen leaves or mulch.

I have forsythia that is about 6 years old on the southwest corner of our house. It used to bloom in the spring, but now blooms in October and November. Why? The chances are that the autumns have been unusually mild in this particular location.

Why doesn't my forsythia bloom? The buds seem to dry up. They have been killed by winter cold. Try *Forsythia ovata*. This is the most hardy of all the forsythias.

How and when should forsythia be pruned? Cut out some of the oldest branches annually, making the cut not far from the base of the bush. This can be done in February; the cut branches can be brought indoors and placed in water to force them into bloom. Or wait until the bush has flowered and prune it immediately after the flowers have faded.

How do you prune forsythia when it has grown too high? Thin out some of the older stems a few inches above the ground level. Sometimes by removing a major number of the taller older stems, those left will be much lower. If not, reduce those that remain to the desired height but never cut them off in a horizontal line, for this disfigures the bush.

How can I keep forsythia bushes from getting straggly? Make them more compact by pinching out the tips of strong-growing shoots during late spring and early summer. Comparatively compact varieties, such as *F. viridissima* and *F. ovata,* are preferable if there is an objection to a straggling habit.

Can forsythia, or goldenbells, be pruned in the fall as well as in the spring? Usually the shrub gets very awkward after the spring pruning. Forsythia produces its flowers on the preceding year's growth, and any cutting back during the time it is dormant results in a diminution of the floral display in the spring. Try pinching out the tips of strong-growing shoots during the growing season.

When is the proper time to trim weeping forsythia? The beauty of this variety is in its long, trailing growth. It should not be trimmed in the usual sense of cutting back the tips. Thinning out crowded branches is permissible in the spring immediately after the flowers have faded.

HAZELNUT (CORYLUS)

Are there any garden forms of the European hazelnut that are grown for their beauty rather than for the production of nuts? There are two outstanding ones. One is a variety of the filbert (*Corylus maxima* 'Purpurea'). The other is the European hazel (*Corylus avellana* 'Contorta'), which is interesting rather than beautiful. The leaves of 'Purpurea' are dark purple, especially in early spring; and in 'Contorta' the stems are twisted and curled in a way that makes it an excellent example of living sculpture.

HONEYSUCKLE (LONICERA)

Are the fruits of the honeysuckle ornamental? Yes, they are small round berries that are blue, red, or yellow. It is the red and yellow ones on such plants as the Amur, Tatarian, and fragrant honeysuckles that make a display and are most attractive to the birds. There are some yellow-fruited varieties also.

Can you mention a few desirable honeysuckle shrubs? Fragrant honeysuckle—April, white; Morrow honeysuckle—May, cream-yellow; blueleaf honeysuckle—May, pink; Amur honeysuckle—May, white; and Tatarian honeysuckle—May, rose and white.

How can I best propagate honeysuckle? In order to have plants of a uniform kind, it is best to root the plants from cuttings. Many of them root quite readily from hardwood cuttings and this is the simplest way. Or they can be raised from cuttings taken in July and kept in a closed polyethylene-covered flat until rooted.

HYDRANGEA

Will you tell me what is the real name of the hydrangea with pink or blue flowers? Bigleaf or French hydrangea (*Hydrangea macrophylla*). There are many varieties of this species, both with blue flowers and with pink flowers. 'Rosea' is a popular variety with pink flowers.

What are some hydrangeas other than the peegee and snow hill? Try panicle hydrangea, the parent of peegee, with flowers more opened out, not so "top-heavy"; climbing hydrangea (*H. anomala petiolaris*), as vine or shrub; oakleaf hydrangea, with interesting foliage.

What exposure to sun should hydrangeas have? The common species do best in full sun, although they will stand slight shade.

Do oakleaf hydrangeas need a shady or sunny location? Partial shade.

What plant food do hydrangeas need and when? They require no special fertilizer treatment. The use of well-rotted manure or compost or a mixed commercial fertilizer in the spring is satisfactory.

Can a hydrangea be transplanted in my state in the month of October or November? (New York.) Yes.

Would transplanting a large hydrangea into another section of the garden cause injury to the plant? No, not permanently, if properly done. Transplant in early spring.

When is the best time to move hydrangeas? Either fall or early spring for very hardy types; spring in the case of French hydrangeas.

Should a potted hydrangea with a large beautiful blue flower which came from a greenhouse be transplanted to the outdoors? (Kansas.) It probably would not live through the winter but you could try it in a protected area. (See below.)

My mother gave us a 4-year-old hydrangea to plant in our garden. Could you tell me what to do to make it bloom next year? Protect canes from winter injury by covering them in the fall with a bushel basket or leaves held in place by chicken wire or something similar. Do not cut back the canes in the spring any more than is necessary to remove injured tips.

Does peegee hydrangea require any special care? I don't seem to be able to grow it. It is one of the easiest shrubs to grow. It needs no special care.

Why do the leaves on my pink hydrangeas appear yellow and mottled? The soil is too sweet, or alkaline. Have it tested and add aluminum sulfate to reduce the pH value to 6.8 or lower.

What would cause a hydrangea to stop flowering after having bloomed beautifully for 3 seasons? Too much shade, poor soil, overfertilization, improper pruning, and winter injury (see below) are some of the more important factors that affect the flowering of hydrangeas.

Why do my French hydrangeas bloom some years and not others? (New York.) Cold injury to the flower buds is the most common reason for failure to flower. The flower buds are formed in the fall, and if the winter is severe they may be killed even though the plant is not seriously injured.

Why has my French hydrangea plant not bloomed for 15 years,

even though it grows well and is kept pruned? (Massachusetts.)
Undoubtedly the flower buds which form in the fall are killed during the winter. Give more winter protection by covering with leaves held in place by chicken wire, etc. Pruning at the wrong time of year (each spring or fall) will prevent flowering by removing the flower buds. Prune immediately *after* blooming (late July).

After blooming, should the old flowers be cut from hydrangeas? Not necessarily, unless they are unsightly.

Do hydrangeas bloom on old or new wood? Some common species, such as *Hydrangea paniculata* 'Grandiflora' and the hills-of-snow type, bloom on new wood and can be pruned in the early spring. On a few other types, particularly the common greenhouse or French (*Hydrangea macrophylla*) varieties, the buds originate near the tips of the canes formed the preceding year and should be pruned *after* flowering or not at all.

How near to the ground do you prune hydrangeas? This depends on the species. *Hydrangea arborescens* can be cut off at the ground each year. (See the preceding answer.)

What is the best way to prune a snowhill hydrangea? Since round, uniform tops are desired, all branches should be cut back so that only 2 or 3 buds are left at the base of each old stem. Pruning should be done on this type in the early spring.

How should peegee hydrangeas be pruned? This is the strong-growing shrubby type which sometimes attains almost the dimensions of a small tree. It blossoms on the shoots of the current season, and if large blooms are desired, the shoots of the preceding year should be cut back to one bud in the spring.

When should the oakleaf hydrangea be pruned? Immediately after flowering. This is another species, like the French type, in which the flower buds form in the fall. Since the buds are likely to be injured during severe winters, the plants should be protected by mulching.

Why do my hydrangeas have so many leaves and so few flowers? Too much nitrogenous fertilizer and improper pruning can encourage the growth of foliage instead of flowers. In warm climates the common French hydrangeas may not set flower buds in the fall because of high temperatures.

What care should be given blue hydrangeas in an eastern exposure for the winter? Wrap in burlap or straw and mulch the soil heavily with leaves.

Can blue hydrangeas be propagated? Yes, by cuttings. However, the flowers may have a pink coloration when grown under different soil conditions.

What causes pink hydrangeas to turn blue? Experiments have conclusively demonstrated that the presence of aluminum in the tissue of hydrangea flowers causes the blue coloration.

Can all kinds of hydrangeas be made to produce blue flowers? No. Only the pink varieties of the common greenhouse or French hydrangea (*Hydrangea macrophylla*) will turn blue.

Will my hydrangeas be blue if I plant them in an acid soil? Pink varieties of the common greenhouse or French hydrangea produce blue flowers when grown in acid soil (pH 5.5 or below). Soil acidity is an indirect factor in the production of blue flowers because of its relationship to the solubility of aluminum in the soil. The aluminum is soluble and can be absorbed by the plants when the soil is acid (pH 5.5 or below). In neutral or slightly alkaline soil, the aluminum is insoluble.

Can dry aluminum sulfate be mixed with the soil to produce blue hydrangea flowers? Dry aluminum sulfate can be used in the spring at the rate of 1 pound for each square yard of ground area. It may be necessary to repeat the treatment for several years. Aluminum sulfate can also be mixed with the soil when it is prepared. The soil should be tested to determine its reaction (pH). If the soil is neutral, mix in thoroughly ½ pound for each bushel.

How does one make hydrangeas growing in pots have blue flowers? Water 5 to 8 times, at weekly intervals, with a 2½ per cent solution of aluminum sulfate (1 pound to 5 gallons of water). Use 1 gallon for each plant.

If rusty nails are put in the soil, will a hydrangea produce blue flowers? Rusty nails or any other form of metallic iron has no effect upon flower color. Potassium alum (common alum), however, will induce blue coloration.

How can I make a blue-flowering hydrangea produce pink flowers? The soil should be made neutral or very slightly alkaline (pH 6.7 to 7.2) by the addition of lime. Too much lime will cause mottling of the leaves as the result of a lack of iron. The required amount of lime should be deeply and thoroughly mixed with the soil. It is best to lift the plants in the fall, shake off as much soil as possible, and replant them in the specially prepared lime soil.

How can one prevent the discoloring of hydrangea flowers? Flowers of intermediate hues between pink and blue are produced when the soil reaction is between pH 6 and 6.5. If pure blue flowers are desired, add aluminum sulfate to make the soil more acid (pH 5.5). For pink flowers, add lime to bring the soil reaction to pH 6.8 or 7.0.

KERRIA

What is Kerria japonica?   This shrub grows 4 to 8 feet high and produces bright yellow flowers. The variety 'Pleniflora' is double and more vigorous. Both have green stems. It is a shrub of easy culture and does well in partial shade. There are also varieties with variegated foliage.

I have an old kerria shrub. Only one or two branches bloom. How can I treat or prune it?   Winter injury or crowded branches can be responsible for its failure to bloom. Cut out weak shoots in the spring and remove flowering branches as soon as the flowers have faded.

What is the best way to propagate Kerria japonica 'Pleniflora'?   Either by means of cuttings in July, which must be kept in close, humid, shady conditions until rooted, or by hardwood cuttings taken in late fall, buried in the soil during the winter, and set in the garden in early spring.

LILAC (SYRINGA)

What are the best lilacs (French hybrids) in each color?   White— 'Marie Legray', 'Mme. Lemoine'; violet—'De Miribel'; blue—'Bleautre', 'Firmament'; pink—'Alice Eastwood', 'Lucie Baltet'; purple—'Sunset', 'Ludwig Spaeth'; two-tone—'Sensation'.

Are there everblooming lilac bushes?   No.

What are so-called own-root lilacs?   Those lilacs that are propagated so that the roots and tops are from one continuous piece of plant. i.e., not grafted with two pieces grown together as one. Hence, they are not susceptible to the serious graft-blight disease. "Own-root" lilacs are the best kind to buy.

Would you consider a Syringa reticulata (Japanese tree lilac) a good lawn specimen tree? How tall does it grow?   Yes. It may grow 40 feet high and more but usually is under 20 feet and is comparatively slow-growing.

What is the difference between lilac species and the other, or common, lilacs?   Lilac species are the wild lilacs of the world found growing in uninhabited places. The "common" lilacs are usually considered either natural hybrids, which have appeared in gardens, or (more frequently) the direct results of hybridizing efforts, mostly of *Syringa vulgaris*.

Why are French hybrid lilacs so called? Because hybridizers in France have had much to do with their production.

What kind of soil and nourishment are best for lilacs? Any fair, not too heavy, well-drained, alkaline or slightly acid garden soil. If needed, every other year apply a 3-inch mulch of rotted cow manure or compost alternated with a dose of limestone. Do not feed them unless the need is indicated so they don't grow too tall and have to be cut back.

Please advise when to plant a lilac bush—spring or fall? Either. Lilacs are among the easiest of plants to transplant and will grow under almost any conditions.

I planted a lilac at the end of November. Was that too late? Probably; but if the ground didn't freeze until late December, this date for planting should have been satisfactory.

Can a large lilac bush be moved and continue blooming—that is, without waiting several more years? Yes, if moved with a large ball of soil about the roots, and if a few of the older branches are pruned back to near the ground in the operation.

How long do lilacs have to be planted before blooming? This depends on many things, such as soil, skill of transplanting in the soil, etc. Some plants, grown properly, will bloom profusely when they are only 4 feet tall. Others may take years before they will start to bloom.

I transplanted a lilac bush. Should the leaves be stripped at the bottom in the spring or left alone? Always prune off some of the branches when transplanting; approximately one third of the total branches is a good average. Stripping off the leaves is not a good practice in this case.

What is the ultimate height of French lilacs? It depends on the variety; 10 to 25 feet.

Which lilacs, if any, will thrive with only forenoon sunshine? All lilacs need sunshine. The less sunshine they have, the fewer the flowers.

Will you give me information pertaining to the culture, pruning, and general care of own-root, French hybrid lilacs for specimen bloom? I have a collection of young plants comprising 12 varieties. The general care of these lilacs is no different than that of any others. For specimen blooms, cutting out a few of the weakest flowering shoots in the winter is helpful. Read other questions and answers.

Why do the leaves on new lilac bushes turn brown? Transplanting injury, lack of sufficient water, too much fertilizer, or air pollution.

We have lilacs of different species, some more than 10 years old. The foliage always looks clean, but the plants never have any buds or flowers. Neighbors have flowers on their lilacs. Why not ours? When lilacs fail to bloom, 4 things can be tried, since every lilac should bloom if grown properly: 1. Thin out some of the branches at the base of the plant. 2. Root-prune by digging a 2-foot ditch around the plants. 3. When the soil is removed from the ditch, mix with it a generous amount of superphosphate (about 8 ounces to every 3 feet of ditch) and return the soil to the ditch. 4. Apply limestone if the soil is acid. One of these methods, or a combination of all, should force the plant to bloom. Some lilacs, like many other plants, are alternate-blooming, flowering profusely one year and sparsely or not at all the next. This, unfortunately, is to be expected.

Why do lilacs fail to bloom even though flower buds are formed? This may be due to a severe drought in the late summer after the buds have been formed.

We have old-fashioned lilacs, large clumps that are 8 or 10 years old, which have only 5 or 6 blossoms each year. Why don't they bloom freely? There are too many young suckers at the base, most likely. Cut out most of these and you probably will be repaid with good blooms.

I have some Persian lilacs, also French lilacs, none of which seem to do well. What kind of soil and conditions do they require? They need a good alkaline soil with sufficient moisture throughout the summer. Try applying limestone in the spring and a 3-inch mulch of manure or compost in the fall to see if they help.

How does one prune lilacs to keep them a decent height and still have blooms? Do not give all the pruning in one year, but over a period of several years. Do not allow them to become too dense, for this forces them to grow high. Allow each branch room to grow. Thin out older branches by cutting them off at the base of the plant. Remove all but a few suckers.

Should lilacs be pruned? Yes, prune out most of the young suckers and all of the dead or diseased wood. Some of the older branches could be cut out to allow more light to reach the branches in the center of the plant. Prune just *after* blooming.

My lilacs are 10 feet tall. How can I bring them down to eye-level height? In 2 ways: 1. Cut them down to within a foot of the ground and start entirely new plants. 2. If this is too drastic, do the same thing but over a period of 3 years, hence thinning out only one third of the branches each year and allowing for continuous bloom.

Will severe pruning force old-fashioned lilacs to give more bloom? Yes, it may; but do not expect flowers for a year or two.

What is the best way to cut back very old, tall, uncared-for lilac bushes? Cut them down nearly to the ground.

What is the best way to start growth again on lilac bushes? All the growth seems to be at the top, leaving the lower part very unsightly. Cut back to within a foot of the ground and start all over again.

Should any suckers be allowed on French hybrid lilacs? Yes, if they have been propagated on their own roots. However, if they have been grafted, the suckers from the understock may prove to be either California privet or some very different lilac. Therefore, *all* should be cut out of grafted plants.

My French hybrid lilacs were propagated by cuttings and are growing on their "own roots." Can I allow suckers to grow? Yes, to some extent. A few of these can be allowed to grow to replace the older branches which are cut out or to allow the bush to increase in size. Do not allow them all to grow, however, as the bush will become too dense and flower formation will be decreased.

Is it necessary or better for the bushes if I cut off dead flowers from lilacs before they bloom again? Yes. Cut them off as soon as they are finished blooming. This prevents seed formation and allows more nourishment to go to the flower buds for the next year.

What is the proper time and method of root-pruning lilacs to bring them into bloom? Dig a 2-foot trench in the spring slightly within the outside limit of the branches, in this way cutting all the roots encountered.

How can you stop lilacs from spreading into your neighbor's yard? Sink a concrete barrier down in the soil or continually dig and cut the roots on that side of the plant.

How do you start new bushes from an old lilac bush? The best method is to raise a new stock from cuttings; or if it is not a grafted plant, rooted suckers may be dug up, tops cut back by one half, and planted.

I have a lilac bush 'President Grevy'; one branch has flowers of a different color, pale pink with a yellow center. How can I propagate this variation? It is not from the rootstock, as it appears on a bush 10 feet high. Either by cuttings or by grafting or budding it on California privet. This privet is not recommended as an understock, but in order to work up a stock of the "sport," or mutant, that has occurred on your lilac, you would be justified in using it until you could obtain enough plants on their own roots.

When should lilac cuttings be made? While the shoots are still growing, usually about the middle of May. Make cuttings 5 to 6 inches long; remove bottom leaves; make a clean cut through the stem, ¼ inch below the place where the leaves were attached. However, lilacs are sometimes raised from hardwood cuttings (taken in early winter) which are planted in boxes of sand and kept in cool but frostproof sheds until spring when rooting takes place.

How is lilac best rooted from cuttings—outdoors, cold frame, or greenhouse? Either in propagating cases in a greenhouse or in a shaded hotbed. The cuttings are placed in sand and kept in a close, humid atmosphere until rooted. (See the preceding question.)

How is Persian lilac propagated? Either from seeds sown in the spring or from cuttings in May. Also from suckers.

The leaves of my lilacs are a gray-green instead of a true shade. What is the remedy? The chances are that they have mildew. This happens especially in the late summer or during a moist season. It is not serious and can be ignored. Dusting with powdered sulfur as soon as mildew appears is one remedy.

What is lilac "graft blight"? This is a disease occurring on plants which have been grafted on California privet understock. A plant which has this disease will look sickly, have yellowish leaves, and may die even in good growing weather. The only remedy is to dig up and destroy such a plant.

How can one eliminate chlorosis in lilacs? This is not well understood. Chlorosis occurs even on healthy plants growing in normal soil during dry seasons. During the following year, the same chlorotic plants may appear healthy. About all one can do is to see that they have some fertilizer and lime, and water thoroughly during dry spells.

MIMOSA (ALBIZIA JULIBRISSIN)

Will a mimosa tree survive a Michigan winter? The hardiest mimosa—*Albizia julibrissin* 'Rosea'—might be tried in southern Michigan. This proves fairly hardy in Boston, Massachusetts. The mimosa of the South (*Acacia*) will not be hardy.

Are you supposed to prune mimosa (Albizia) trees? Yes, when they require it to make them shapely. Where they grow rapidly, they tend to be too flexible and "weak-backed" unless pruned.

MOCK-ORANGE (PHILADELPHUS)

Which are some of the best mock-oranges? The old-fashioned sweet mock-orange (*Philadelphus coronarius*); 'Avalanche' with single very fragrant flowers and gracefully arching branches; 'Conquête', 'Mont Blanc' with single flowers 1¼ inches in diameter; double-flowered varieties like 'Albâtre', 'Argentine', 'Bannière', 'Girandole', 'Minnesota Snowflake' with 2-inch flowers and able to withstand temperatures to −30° F., and the ever-popular 'Virginal', all of which are fragrant.

Will you give me information on the comparative merits (ease of growth, hardiness, floriferousness, fragrance, shape, and height) of the following hybrid mock-oranges: 'Bannière', nivalis, 'Norma', 'Pavillon Blanc', 'Pyramidale', and 'Voie Lactée'? These are all of approximately equal hardiness—not reliably hardy north of Philadelphia—but they are being grown as far north as Boston. They are all about 5 to 7 feet tall, equally easy to grow, but vary in beauty and the amount of flowers and fragrance. Using another hybrid, 'Avalanche', as a basis for good flower, and the old-fashioned fragrant *P. coronarius* as best for fragrance, and rating these both at 10 points, the varieties could be rated as follows: 'Bannière'—flower, 5; fragrance, 4; *nivalis*—flower, 3; fragrance, 6; 'Norma'—flower, 6; fragrance, 4; 'Pavillon Blanc'—flower, 2; fragrance, 0; 'Pyramidale'—flower, 3; fragrance, 0; 'Voie Lactée'—flower, 2; fragrance, 2.

I once saw some mock-oranges with large double flowers. What might they have been? 'Virginal', or perhaps 'Argentine'; they are beautiful, with flowers 2 inches across. There are several others of equal size also available.

Why don't my mock-oranges, planted last spring, bloom? They have so much brush in them. They need a year or two in order to recuperate from the shock of being transplanted. Thin out a few of the branches if they are too crowded.

Although pruned, why does mock-orange 'Virginal' not bush out, but grow only lanky shoots at the top? This variety is naturally gawky. It can be made a little more compact by pinching out the tips of lanky shoots when they are actively growing.

How should I trim an overgrown mock-orange bush? Thin it out during the winter by cutting the oldest branches as near the ground line as possible. Shorten those remaining about one third if it seems necessary. This drastic treatment will result in few, if any, flowers the following spring.

When and how is the best way to prune a mock-orange shrub? Immediately after flowering by cutting out the oldest and weakest shoots, making the cuts as near the ground line as possible.

PRIVET (LIGUSTRUM)   (See also Hedges, this section.)

If a privet is not pruned, what kind of flowers and berries does it have? It has cream-white flowers in small panicles somewhat like lilacs, but with a sweet (but to some distressing) odor in midsummer. Its berries are black.

What is the name of a privet which forms a broad bush? Regel privet—*Ligustrum obtusifolium regelianum.*

What is the best time to prune Amur privet? When grown as a bush, it needs no pruning. As a hedge, it should be sheared when new growth is 6 to 8 inches long. Repeat shearing in August.

QUINCE, FLOWERING (CHAENOMELES SPECIOSA)

What colors of flowering quinces are there? When do they bloom? Today many nurseries offer their own varieties, often grown from seed. They are hybrids or varieties of the species *Chaenomeles speciosa* and range in color of flower from pure white through pink to deep red. Single- and double-flowered varieties are available. They bloom in early May. Flowering quince has been variously known as *Cydonia japonica, Chaenomeles japonica,* but the current classification is *Chaenomeles speciosa.* The designation *Chaenomeles japonica* is reserved for the Japanese quince, a low-growing species which flowers in the spring before the leaves develop. (See the following question and answer.) *Cydonia* is the fruiting quince grown for jelly.

What kinds of flowering quince bushes are there? Are some varieties taller than others? The tall shrub *Chaenomeles speciosa* grows to about 6 feet high. The dwarf species (*C. japonica*) is a broad, low shrub, growing to 3 feet high. A still lower variety (*C. j. alpina*) spreads into a low patch seldom over 1½ feet high.

I have a flowering quince (red) that does not bloom, although the

plant is 6 years old. The sprout was taken from a beautiful bush which blooms each year. This plant has never bloomed and it's planted beside 2 other quinces that bloom each year. Why? It may well be that the original plant was a grafted plant and the understock was the common quince, which blooms only after reaching some size. Check their foliage. If they differ, discard yours. If they do not differ, check them again when the parent is in flower next spring.

The blossoms of my flowering quince are produced toward the center of the bush and are not well displayed. Can this be avoided? Yes. Prune the bush by shortening the new shoots as they are produced throughout the summer. This will cause the formation of flower spurs near the tips of the branches.

I have a shrub in my garden that I have been told is a variety of flowering quince. It has never bloomed and I was wondering what could be done to force it to bloom. Would pruning help? Summer pruning will help, as described in the preceding answer. The incorporation of superphosphate in the soil over the roots, at the rate of 6 ounces per square yard, may be helpful. Root-pruning should be resorted to if these measures fail.

How can I propagate my flowering quince? The flowering quince can be treated in the same manner as the flowering almond.

Is the fruit of the so-called burning bush, or Chaenomeles speciosa, edible? It is very sour but can be used in making jellies. Incidentally, "burning bush" is a misnomer as an English name for this shrub. It is more correctly applied to the wahoo, or strawberry-bush, Euonymus americana or to E. alata.

ROSE-ACACIA (ROBINIA)

What is a rose-acacia? A hardy shrub (Robinia hispida) native to the Allegheny Mountains. It grows to 3 feet, with dark, rich green foliage and racemes of rose-colored, pealike blossoms in late spring.

Where shall I plant a rose-acacia shrub? In a spot protected from heavy winds, in light soil. It is good for dry banks and as a screen. It suckers freely and, if neglected, forms a dense thicket.

Do rose-acacia shrubs have to be grafted stock to bloom or can they be taken from old plants? No. If the old plants spread from year to year by suckers, it is a simple matter to dig up and replant some of the suckers, and so form new plants. However, rose-acacia is sometimes grafted high to form "standards," in which case any growth taken from the base would merely increase the understock, probably black locust (*Robinia pseudoacacia*).

ROSE-OF-SHARON (HIBISCUS SYRIACUS)

What colors does the rose-of-Sharon come in?   White, pink, purple, red, and blue, both single- and double-flowered varieties.

The most beautiful rose-of-Sharon I have seen has single lavender-blue flowers with carmine eye. What is its name?   'Coelestis', an old favorite. A newer blue-flowered variety is 'Blue Bird'.

What is shrub-althea?   Same as rose-of-Sharon, *Hibiscus syriacus*.

What kind of soil does rose-of-Sharon thrive in? Mine was doing poorly. I put lime around it and it died.   It needs a deep soil which has plenty of water. A complete fertilizer and water would possibly have saved your plant.

Can rose-of-Sharon shrubs or trees be transplanted in the fall?   They can be safely transplanted in the fall except in places subjected to high, cold winds during the winter.

What is the correct care of rose-of-Sharon? (Maine.)   There are many places in Maine where the rose-of-Sharon simply will not grow because of winter cold. Where it will survive, cut back the last year's shoots to about 4 buds early in the spring. This heavy pruning usually results in heavy flower production—providing, of course, that it has good soil.

What is the cause of my rose-of-Sharon buds falling off before they open?   This is partly a varietal characteristic. Other factors might be insufficient phosphorus or potash in the soil, too little soil moisture, or attack by aphids.

When and how should rose-of-Sharon (Hibiscus syriacus) be pruned?   Blossoms are produced on shoots of the current season, so the shoots of the preceding year can be cut back to within 3 to 4 buds at their point of origin in the spring with no loss of blooms. However, this heavy pruning makes an ungainly bush, and many gardeners prefer to prune them lightly or let them go unpruned.

What are the best conditions for rose-of-Sharon? Can it be budded or grafted?   Rose-of-Sharon will grow quite well in any reasonably good garden soil. It may be budded or grafted, but this hardly seems justified since most of the varieties root very readily from cuttings taken in the summer.

RUSSIAN-OLIVE (ELAEAGNUS)

What shrub would give a distinct silvery effect? Russian-olive (*Elaeagnus angustifolia*), with narrow leaves, silvery on reverse side, a shrub to 20 feet high; silverberry (*E. commutata*)—bushy, to 12 feet, leaves silver on both sides, fast-growing; cherry elaeagnus (*E. multiflora*), leaves silvery beneath, grows 4 to 9 feet.

Does elaeagnus have flowers or fruits? Flowers are inconspicuous but strongly fragrant in *E. angustifolia,* silverberry, and *E. umbellata.* There are small, yellow-silvery berries on silverberry; brown-red berries on *E. umbellata.*

In what manner and how severely should Russian-olive (Elaeagnus angustifolia) be pruned if it is 3 years old and about 15 feet high? It usually needs no pruning when growing in a poor, dry soil and a sunny location to which it is adapted. Yours evidently is in rich ground and should be pruned by shortening lanky growths about midsummer.

SNOWBERRY (SYMPHORICARPOS)

How and when should the snowberry bush (Symphoricarpos rivularis) be trimmed? If it is behaving itself by producing plenty of fruits on a shapely bush, leave it alone. If not, cut it down to the ground in late winter.

SPIREA (SPIRAEA)

I would like to know if I should snip the tips of bridalwreaths? If so, when? Do not snip off the tips, as this spoils the grace of the bush. Instead, cut out some of the old shoots at the base as soon as the blossoms have faded.

Is it possible to trim and drastically reduce bridalwreath (Spiraea prunifolia) in size? Yes, cut back all flowering shoots immediately after the flowers have faded. Shorten those remaining, if necessary, to reduce to the height required.

How should spirea 'Anthony Waterer' be pruned? This is a late bloomer, producing its flowers on shoots of the current season; therefore, it may be cut back about one half in the spring, just as growth begins.

We have a number of spirea plants on an old lot which are much too large and tall for our present building lot. How drastically can these shrubs be pruned so we can transplant them? Spireas in general can withstand severe pruning. It may be done in late winter, but this results (in the case of early-blooming varieties) in no blooms the following season. They can be cut to within a few inches of the ground.

STEPHANANDRA

What is stephanandra? The cutleaf stephanandra has finely cut leaves and terminal spikes of small, greenish-white flowers 2 inches long in June. It is from Japan. It grows about 7 feet tall in a graceful arching manner.

Is stephanandra a good ornamental shrub for my garden? (Connecticut.) Probably only mediocre, but its recent variety 'Crispa' has become extremely popular, especially for planting on banks or in rocky areas. Only about 3 to 5 feet tall, it roots vigorously wherever its branches touch the soil. It is easily propagated by merely digging up the rooted branches, preferably in the spring. Don't plant in the rock garden as it quickly outgrows its space and can become a pest.

SUMAC

Can fragrant sumac be closely trimmed, down to about 4 inches? When? Yes, in the spring, before growth starts. But better leave it a little longer than 4 inches.

SWEET-SHRUB (CALYCANTHUS)

What color are the flowers of sweet-shrub (Calycanthus)? When does it bloom? Reddish or purplish brown. It blooms in June and July. This shrub, *Calycanthus floridus,* is also called strawberry shrub and Carolina allspice.

Is calycanthus a difficult shrub to grow? We planted one, pruned it, and gave it plenty of water, but it slowly died after having come out in full leaf. Calycanthus should not present any great difficulty, though it is sometimes slow to start into vigorous growth after being moved. The treatment you gave your plant appears to be correct. If you make another attempt, cut out at least half of the older stems at the ground level and reduce the remainder about half their length. Be careful not to give too much water.

A sweet-shrub bush which formerly produced very fragrant flowers now continues to have lovely blooms but they have no scent. Is there anything that can be done? No, unless you wish to try fertilizing it heavily with well-rotted manure or some complete commercial fertilizer. Sometimes increased vigor produced in this manner will make the flowers more fragrant. It is a good idea to smell the flowers of this shrub before you purchase it, as apparently some scentless forms have been propagated.

TAMARISK

What does a tamarisk (Tamarix) look like? It is a handsome picturesque shrub with a plumy effect. Its leaves resemble heather. Its flowers are pink and white. Two of the hardiest (to southern New England) are *Tamarix parviflora* and *T. ramossima* syn. *odessana*.

I have been told that tamarisks can stand ocean spray and wind. Is that true? (Massachusetts.) Yes. It is one of the finest of all shrubs for shore planting and thrives in sandy soil.

When and how is a tamarisk pruned? We have one which has 6 or 7 long branches which begin at the ground level and sprawl. Pruning depends on the group to which it belongs. Some bloom early on old wood, while others flower on wood of the current season. The first type should be cut back severely after flowering; the latter in the spring. In both cases, the (approximately) 1-year-old shoots should be cut back one half to two thirds.

VIBURNUM

Which viburnums do you recommend for autumn coloring and fruiting? Linden viburnum (*V. dilatatum*); witherod (*V. cassinoides*); Wright or Oriental (*V. wrightii*); mapleleaf (*V. acerifolium*); blackhaw (*V. prunifolium*); Siebold (*V. sieboldii*).

Which viburnums have the most effective flowers? Double-file viburnum (*V. plicatum tomentosum*); Japanese snowball (*V. plicatum*). The former has flat flower heads which lie along the top of the horizontal branches.

Which viburnum would lend itself best to foundation plant-

ing? None, except possibly *Viburnum plicatum* 'Mariesii' because of its horizontal branching and good flowers and fruits; and then the house must be a large one. About the only location for it would be at a corner. The low-growing *V. opulus* 'Nanum' could be used as a hedge under a bay or picture window.

Which viburnum will stand the most shade for woodland planting? Mapleleaf viburnum, also called dockmackie (*V. acerifolium*).

Is there a low, compact viburnum? Yes; dwarf cranberry-bush (*V. opulus* 'Nanum'), to 2½ feet high, and *V. opulus* 'Globosum', about 5 feet high.

Does Viburnum carlesii prefer a neutral soil? It will grow well enough in any approximately neutral garden soil of good quality, not likely to become parched.

Why is Viburnum carlesii so difficult to grow on its own roots, and Viburnum burkwoodii so easy, when the plants are practically identical? This is one of nature's many as-yet-unanswered questions. In fact, *V. carlesii* is one of the parents of *V.* x *burkwoodii*—which only makes the answer more difficult.

Why did my Viburnum dilatatum fail to produce berries? It may have been that a cool rainy spell predominated just when the pollen was ripe. This would have prevented insect activity and wind from disseminating the pollen at the proper time. Also, with this species it is essential to plant two to three plants—all grown from seeds (not grown from cuttings of the same plant) to ensure fruiting.

Can you suggest reasons why three Japanese snowballs (Viburnum plicatum tomentosum) that I planted died? The European snowball (V. opulus 'Roseum') and American cranberry-bush (V. trilobum) lived. They were possibly killed by a harsh winter. The Japanese snowball is not as hardy as the European.

When and how can I prune my snowball bush, which has grown too high and too shaggy? You might take a chance on cutting it back immediately after flowering, or in early spring if you are prepared to sacrifice the season's crop of bloom, but often snowball bushes do not respond well to severe pruning.

I have a snowball bush 5 or 6 years old that has never bloomed. What is wrong with it? The flower buds have probably been killed by winter cold or lack of nutrients in the soil.

WEIGELA

Is there a weigela with very showy blooms? Yes, variety 'Bristol Ruby', with red blossoms; or 'Eva Rathke' or 'Vanicek', both of which have a tendency to recurrent bloom from June to August.

What is the best way to treat a weigela bush that is very old and produces very few flowers? Thin out the bush by removing some of the oldest branches during the winter. Cut them as near as possible to the ground line. Annual pruning should consist of the removal of worn-out flowering branches as soon as the blossoms have faded.

WILLOW, PUSSY (SALIX)

Will a pussy willow do well in dry soil? Pussy willow (*Salix discolor*) adapts itself to a dry soil but prefers it moist. In dry soil it may become quite susceptible to diseases, and it will grow more slowly and remain smaller.

Why does my pussy willow burst forth in December and not in spring? (Massachusetts.) Mild winter days frequently force pussy willows into premature growth, especially if the tree is growing in a protected spot.

When is the best time to prune pussy willows? If it is desired to have the "pussies" develop on long, wandlike shoots, the tree should be pruned severely before growth starts by cutting back all of the shoots made the preceding year to 1 or 2 buds. Otherwise, no pruning is necessary.

Is it best to let a pussy willow grow in a bush or in a tree form? How tall should it grow? It is best to keep it in bush form by pruning out any central leader that may appear. The height depends upon conditions, varying from 10 to 20 feet.

The florist sells long branches of pussy willows. What are these? These are the so-called French pussy willows (*Salix caprea*) with larger flowers than our native *S. discolor*. Long shoots are grown by heavily fertilizing the plants and cutting the branches back severely each spring, thus forcing vigorous growth.

How can I start pussy willows in the ground, and at what time of year? As soon as the frost is out of the ground in the spring, make cuttings 8 to 10 inches long. Place three fourths of the cutting in the ground. Or root the shoots indoors in water, then plant them.

WINTERBERRY (ILEX VERTICILLATA)

I have seen a shrub in the wild which, in the fall, has shining scarlet berries close to the stem after the leaves are gone. What is it?   Probably winterberry (*Ilex verticillata*), a deciduous holly.

How can winterberry or black-alder be used?   In a shrub border, preferably in moist soil. It grows somewhat lank, so plant it in back of lower shrubs as, for instance, inkberry (*Ilex glabra*), an evergreen relative.

Does winterberry require "wet feet" or does it grow in spite of the water?   Winterberry is a shrub often found in the wild state in swampy ground. However, it grows quite successfully in any good garden soil, provided it is not too dry.

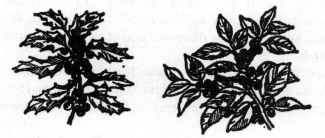

Two native plants for autumn and winter color— American holly (left) and its relative, the winter- berry. The latter is much hardier, but it is not evergreen.

Will you tell me the best way to move, transplant, and grow the winterberry holly?   Dig it carefully in the very early spring, with or without a ball of earth about the roots. Place it in a good garden loam, slightly on the moist side if possible. Prune back one third. Water well. Remember, the sexes are separate and both should be grown to ensure fruiting of the female plant.

WITCH-HAZEL (HAMAMELIS)

Where would you plant a witch-hazel?   In the woodland, in the rear of a shrub border, or near a window of the house so the blossoms may be enjoyed from indoors at close range. They are not showy, but they are valued for their late winter or late fall bloom.

What is the ultimate height of a witch-hazel? The tallest witch-hazel I have seen was an old specimen of the native *H. virginiana*, some 40 feet high. That is exceptional. Another native species, *H. vernalis,* usually remains less than 8 feet high.

When do witch-hazels bloom? October or November—native witch-hazel; February or March—Japanese, Chinese, and vernal.

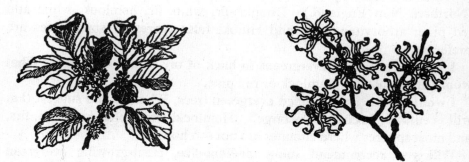

The native witch-hazel (Hamamelis virginiana) (left) *has yellow flowers in late fall that blend with the bright yellow foliage. The Chinese witch-hazel* (H. mollis) (right) *has yellow flowers in the winter that close tight on the coldest days but unfurl as the temperature rises.*

Will witch-hazel grow in half shade? Is it worth growing? Witch-hazels are eminently suited for planting as undershrubs in wooded places. Their unseasonal flowers are more interesting than spectacular. The showiest in flower is the Chinese (*H. mollis*). Where open woodland situations are to be planted, the witch-hazels are well worthwhile.

Narrow-Leaved Evergreens

WHAT TO GROW

What does coniferous mean? It means cone-bearing. Among the cone-bearing trees are fir, spruce, pine, Douglas-fir, and hemlock.

I have recently bought a new property of several acres and think that there will be space for me to plant many coniferous evergreens—both the dwarf and standard kinds. Can you recommend any books on this subject? *Manual of Cultivated Conifers,* by P. den Ouden (Marinus Nyhoff, The Hague, The Netherlands); *Dwarf Conifers, A Complete*

Guide, by H. J. Welch (Charles T. Branford Co., Newton, Massachusetts); *Handbook on Conifers* (Brooklyn Botanic Garden, Brooklyn, New York); *Evergreen Garden Trees and Shrubs,* by Denis Hardwicke and Alan R. Toogood (Macmillan).

What are retinosporas?   Formerly this was the name of the genus we now call *Chamaecyparis,* or false-cypress.

What are the best evergreen trees for specimen lawn planting? (Northern New England.)   Douglas-fir, white fir, hemlock, white and red pine; arborvitae, yew, and Hinoki false-cypress if small trees are preferred.

I want to put some evergreens in back of my white birch trees. What would harmonize?   Hemlock or red pine.

I would like a few dignified evergreen trees. What do you suggest that will eventually become very large?   Hemlock, white pine, red pine, firs, and most spruces where climates are not too hot.

Will you recommend some medium-size, erect-growing evergreen trees?   Arborvitae (*Thuja occidentalis*); red-cedar (*Juniperus virginiana*); Chinese juniper (*J. chinensis*); upright yew (*Taxus cuspidata* and *T. media* varieties).

Can you suggest some drooping evergreen trees to plant beside our garden pool?   Weeping hemlock, weeping Norway spruce.

We are planting a wildflower sanctuary in our woodland. Which evergreens would be the best to introduce there?   Hemlock, rhododendrons, Canada yew, white pine (if not too shady).

What is the fastest-growing evergreen?   In the northern United States this is probably the hemlock, although the white pine might grow faster if it is in good soil.

Are there any evergreen trees with berries?   Red-cedars and other junipers have blue-gray berries; hollies and yews have red berries. The sexes of both groups are separate, and both male and female plants must be grown to ensure the fruiting of the female plants.

What are some evergreens that can be grown for Christmas decorations?   Hollies, all kinds, both deciduous and evergreen; pine, spruce, fir, hemlock, arborvitae, juniper, yew, mountain andromeda, Japanese andromeda, mountain-laurel. Spruce and hemlock quickly drop their needles when cut unless they stand in water.

I wish to set out 50 or 75 evergreens for use later as cut Christmas trees. What kind of trees would you recommend for western Pennsylvania?   Douglas-fir (*Pseudotsuga menziesii*) and Scots pine. Balsam fir is best if it will grow in your region.

LOW-GROWING EVERGREENS

What evergreens, 4 to 6 feet high, are spreading in habit? Common and Pfitzer juniper, some varieties of Japanese yew, Sargent weeping hemlock.

Which low evergreens could be used to edge our terrace in a sunny, dry location? *Juniperus conferta*, *J. communis* varieties, and *J. horizontalis* varieties.

Junipers are available in many forms. The spreading or prostrate varieties are useful for ground covers, especially on banks.

Which formal evergreen would be suitable for each side of our sunny front door? *Picea glauca* 'Conica', the dwarf Alberta spruce.

Is there a dwarf evergreen with red berries in winter? Yes, dwarf forms of Japanese yew.

Are there any evergreens that will remain low—not more than 2 feet? *Chamaecyparis obtusa* 'Nana' and 'Pygmaea', several varieties of *Ilex crenata*, *Juniperus procumbens* 'Nana', and 'Cole' dwarf hemlock. All will remain under 2 feet tall.

Are there low-growing conifers suitable for a rock garden? Spreading English yew, dwarf Japanese yew, dwarf Hinoki false-cypress, 'Andorra' juniper, 'Bar Harbor' juniper, dwarf forms of Norway spruce.

Dwarf conifers (mugo pine, left, and false-cypress, right) are slow-growing and suitable for rock gardens and Oriental-style gardens.

Which evergreens would make a suitable foundation planting for the four sides of a large farmhouse? Are fruit-bearing bushes practical for such use? Evergreens would be selected from the rhododendrons (for shady areas), yews, arborvitaes, and junipers. Yes, fruit-bearing shrubs, such as the blueberry, viburnum, and cotoneaster, would be assets in such a planting.

CULTURE

What kind of soil is best for evergreens? A soil suitable for most kinds is a good loam, well drained, but somewhat retentive of moisture. On such a soil, additional nourishment can be supplied for yews, which like a rather rich diet. Junipers, pines, and Douglas-fir should not require it. Most broad-leaved evergreens need an acid soil.

For foundation plantings, choose low-growing evergreens that stay low (such as Pfitzer juniper). Dwarf Alberta spruce (right) is a very slow-growing conifer especially desirable as an accent in the rock garden or among other dwarf evergreens.

Can good results be expected from evergreen trees planted on land stripped of its topsoil? Such land is not suited for the intensive cultivation of evergreen trees, but pockets can be prepared for occasional trees. In a clayish subsoil, prepare these pockets by mixing in cinders and peat moss; in sandy soil, work in plenty of peat moss.

Our soil is dry. Would pines and junipers be advisable? Yes, most pines and junipers tolerate dry soil.

What is the best fertilizer for dwarf evergreens? Some, including dwarf junipers and pines, will require none unless the soil is very poor. Arborvitae, yews, and chamaecyparis like some fertilizer. The best way to apply nourishment to established plants is by applying a topdressing of leafmold or peat moss mixed with old manure or dried manure or compost before the snow falls.

Do evergreens need a leaf-and-manure fertilizer? In planting—depending upon the quality of the soil—mix leafmold and old manure or compost with the planting soil. For established evergreens in good soil, nothing more than a topdressing of the same is necessary. Yews like a topdressing of dried manure or compost.

Can evergreens be fed in winter? A rich mulch of compost or a mixture of dried manure and peat moss, applied in the fall, is satisfactory. It is unwise to spread commercial fertilizers on the ground in the winter in the North, as melting snows or rain will take it away without its penetrating the soil. The best time is October or very early spring.

How often should bone meal be placed around evergreens? Do not use bone meal. Use somewhat acid artificial fertilizers; or still better, topdressings of leafmold or compost or old manure. (See previous questions.)

TRANSPLANTING

How are evergreens transplanted? Small specimens are moved with a ball of earth around their roots, held in place by burlap. Large specimens should be moved with a ball of earth attached to a platform beneath them, installed by someone with experience.

When is it best to transplant small evergreens and how? Either early September or early spring. Dig a hole twice as wide and twice as deep as the root system of the plant; have plenty of good soil available; be certain that there is drainage at the bottom of the hole. Set in the plant carefully—no deeper in the soil than it formerly grew—untie the burlap and remove it (if possible without the root ball collapsing; otherwise tuck it in between the side of the hole and the root ball), fill in the soil, make it firm, and water thoroughly. Leave a slight depression in the soil around the plant so that it will receive plenty of water until it becomes well established.

I would like to change several small evergreens to another location. When and how do I go about it? If the plants are small, dig them in the spring with the best possible root ball. Plant in a friable soil mixed with leafmold, compost, or dried manure. Water thoroughly; mulch the base to prevent drying out. If they are large trees, transplant in the spring or in early autumn.

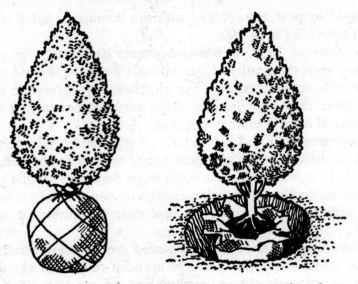

Planting balled-and-burlapped evergreen. After the root ball is positioned in a hole at the correct depth, untie and loosen the burlap, as shown, before packing soil around the ball. More and more shrubs are being sold in containers. Such plants are often root-bound. Before planting, loosen the outer roots of the ball.

When is the best time of the year to plant small evergreens (seedlings)?   In the spring, when the ground has dried and warmed so that it is friable, and before the evergreens have started growth.

When is the best time to transplant evergreens?   For well-grown nursery grades, transplant in the spring before growth has started, or in early autumn from September 1 on. For plants that have not been transplanted recently, the spring is the best. Large trees, properly balled and platformed, can be moved in the spring or as late into the autumn as the ground can be dug.

Evergreens planted with the burlap on do not grow for me, although I have raised beautiful evergreens. Should I remove burlap instead of slitting it?   Unless it might break a weak root ball, remove the burlap; at least open the knots, spread it out in the bottom of the hole, or cut it off close to the base of the ball.

How early in the spring can evergreens be transplanted?   Wait until all the frost is out of the ground and the soil has dried off and warmed up, so that it is thoroughly workable. Transplant evergreens before they have started their growth.

When does the fall planting season for evergreens begin? Generally, as soon as the early summer growth has become hardened. In the case of pines, spruces, and firs, this means as soon as the annual growth has been completed and has hardened and the terminal buds are firmly "set." In dry seasons, one usually waits for a favorable moist spell of weather. Usually all this occurs around September 1.

In New York, what are the best months for planting evergreens? What months in spring and fall are the deadlines for planting? Plant preferably in early September (first choice) or March to April (second choice).

Which evergreens could be planted in December? In lower New York State and similar climates, large specimens of the hardy kinds could be planted, if properly balled, platformed, and moved by professionals. December is late for smaller evergreens and one might best wait until early spring.

Is it O.K. to move evergreens in midwinter, as long as the ground is not frozen, although it may freeze up any time after the planting? It is safe enough for large trees, dug with solid fibrous root balls, carefully planted, well watered, mulched, and moved by professionals. It is not advisable for small evergreens and unsafe for trees that have not been previously transplanted.

Why do I lose so many evergreens, purchased with solid-looking balls and tightly burlapped? Possibly because these good-looking trees had been dug and kept out of the ground for some time prior to your purchase without being watered as needed. Freshly dug trees, promptly planted, stand a far better chance of succeeding than "pre-dug" stock.

I often find roots of dead evergreens packed hard in a dry ball, despite repeated soakings. Why? Root balls dug in clayish soil, or puddled in clay, when planted in a lighter soil may easily become caked hard, so that water cannot penetrate them. Loosen the surface of hard-looking balls before planting.

Why do so many evergreen trees die after being transplanted? There are many possible causes. The trees may not have had fibrous root systems; they may have been dug with inadequate root balls or planted at the wrong season; they may have perished from drought or they may have been tender kinds.

Will oak sawdust, if it is put in the ground while transplanting evergreens, help or harm the trees? On a soil deficient in humus, rotted (not fresh) hardwood sawdust may be helpful. Or use leafmold, peat moss, or old manure.

Our water supply comes from a deep well and is quite hard. We have planted many seedling evergreens. Will it be harmful to use well water on them; will the foliage be injured if water gets on it?   Alkaline water is definitely harmful to all broad-leaved evergreens and might injure some narrow-leaved ones, such as pines, hemlocks, spruce, fir, false-cypress. The foliage will be injured through damage done to the whole plant by introducing alkali into the soil, not by contact of water with the leaves.

Should one cultivate around evergreens?   Cultivation at the base of established evergreens can disturb surface roots and do more harm than good. Keep the soil from caking by means of a mulch or leafmold or compost, with perhaps a little old or dried manure.

Should one keep a mulch around the base of evergreen trees at all times?   Mulch all newly planted evergreens. While a mulch will be helpful to many established evergreens, not all kinds require it if planted in a suitable soil.

Why do evergreens such as pyramidal arborvitae or Scots pines turn rusty brown and lose their needles?   This may represent only a normal shedding of old foliage. Drought and soil exhaustion may cause premature shedding. Vigorous growth and proper sanitation tend to reduce it.

My arborvitae has many brown leaves. I have dusted it with sulfur. Can you give me any advice?   Prevent the soil from caking and see that the roots do not lack water. Just before the ground freezes, give it a very thorough soaking. Keep a mulch of leafmold or compost around the base.

I have poor luck with mugo pine and Koster blue spruce. I lost two mugos and the spruce doesn't look well. What is wrong?   Both kinds, unless transplanted frequently in the nursery, make coarse roots, which mean great risk in transplanting. Most losses are due to this. Secure transplanted, fibrous-rooted plants. These will usually grow well in any fair soil if planted where they get sun.

Will the exhaust from autos, blowing into evergreens, cause their death?   Repeated and protracted exposure to these gases can cause the death of evergreens, especially hot exhaust gas on a cold winter day.

Should healthy evergreen trees turn yellowish?   No. A yellowish discoloring may indicate any of several causes of trouble: poor drainage, overwatering, or a poor quality of soil.

In the planting around our house, one corner plant died 6 months after being planted. A reset did the same. The soil was examined and no lime pocket or sign of insect trouble was found. All other plants are doing well. What may have been the trouble? Corner plants often suffer from a strong draft of air. This can be fatal to newly planted trees. A windscreen might prevent the trouble.

I have red-cedars and Pfitzer junipers that were planted 2 years ago. They are not growing and look dry, although I have tried to treat them right. I hoe around them and water them thoroughly. They are on the west side of a terrace (not very close to the terrace) and pretty far apart. What do they need? Examine them for spider mites. If these are found, spray promptly and repeatedly with malathion. The ground may be hard and poor. Cultivate shallowly and apply a mulch.

Do evergreen trees need shade or sun? Nearly all prefer an open situation. The native yew prefers shade. Balsam fir and hemlock prefer a situation open overhead, but some partial protection from the brightest winter sun.

When is the best time to apply a dormant oil spray to evergreens (in central Pennsylvania)? What should the temperature be? Early spring; but this kind of spray should always be used on evergreens most carefully, for if too strong it will quickly burn the foliage and possibly kill the plant. It will remove "bloom" from types such as blue spruce. The temperature should be under 65° F.

How can I straighten spruce and other evergreens bent from snowstorms? Pull them back into position. Light trees may be held in place by stakes; larger ones by guy wires or ropes fastened to pegs in the ground or to overhead points. After a snowstorm, go over your evergreens and brush off the snow with a broom or the back of a rake.

PRUNING

When and how should an evergreen be trimmed to make it bushy instead of tall? Different kinds can be trimmed at different times, but the season which will suit all is in late June or July. In upright growing kinds, trim both the top and side branches to avoid a chopped-off effect. See that those trees with a rich soil, such as yews and chamaecyparis, are kept supplied with a nourishing topdressing. Don't grow them in the shade.

Can evergreen trees, which have been allowed to grow too tall near the house, be trimmed back? It can be done with the kinds that will "break" readily from the old wood, but not with pines, firs, spruce, hemlock, or Douglas-fir. Trimming back, however, can leave large evergreens in an unsightly condition. Most tall-growing evergreens should not be planted near the house and never in a foundation grouping.

Can evergreen trees be kept low by cutting the tops?   Yes, but a radical "topping" will spoil the appearance and natural beauty of most—especially pines, spruces, and firs, which will not "break" from the old wood and will remain stunted. An exception is when evergreens are used as a hedge.

Is it advisable to heavily prune small evergreens to control their shape?   With the exception of erect-growing pines, spruces, firs, and Douglas-fir (which are best left with a minimum of pruning), most young evergreens will be benefited by pruning uneven shoots so that they will eventually make more solid and compact plants.

Does it harm a spruce or pine to cut branches from it for indoor purposes?   It may not threaten the life of a large tree, but it can spoil its appearance if overdone.

WINTER PROTECTION

Will you outline the winter care of untransplanted seedling evergreens and of once- or twice-transplanted ones?   For seedlings and once-transplanted trees, a covering with dry leaves (not maples) in late autumn; for twice-transplanted trees a mulch over the ground and light branches (not necessarily evergreen) laid over the rows or beds. Water the plants thoroughly just before the winter frost and previous to applying a mulch.

How should pines and junipers be cared for during the winter?   If well established, no special winter protection is needed. In the case of newly set plants, a mulch of leaves or other littery material, applied as the ground is about to freeze, might be helpful and would certainly do no harm.

How should I care for Douglas-fir, Serbian spruce, Austrian pine, and mugo pine in the winter? (New York.)   The evergreens mentioned are quite hardy in New York and need no special winter protection.

Is it true that I shouldn't mulch with oak leaves around my small firs?   There is nothing harmful to firs in oak leaves; but in a planting near the house, for instance, the leaves may be too loose to be the best mulching material. If you have access to wood chips, you can mix them with the leaves.

What is the proper procedure to protect low evergreen shrubs and trees in the winter (located at the seashore with only the house to pro-

tect them)? If the soil is dry, give a good watering before the ground freezes, then put on a mulch of leaves or litter several inches deep. Protection from the wind is probably important, and this may be afforded by sticking evergreen boughs in the ground around them. In some cases it may be advisable to erect a temporary windbreak made of boards or burlap.

Will it be worthwhile to cover the bases of evergreens with partly decayed leaves now (January) after the ground has been covered with snow for some time? The trees were planted in October. If the snow is likely to remain all winter, there is no need for a mulch at this time; but if a midwinter thaw occurs, then it would be advisable to spread leaves to curtail the bad effect of alternate freezing and thawing.

Is there any way to prevent windburn on evergreen trees? The injury referred to is probably the scorched appearance of foliage sometimes noted in the spring, especially on firs. This is caused by the sun in winter and can be prevented largely by placing trees so that they will have some slight protection from the brightest sun in winter.

How shall I take care of evergreens in winter, when they cannot be watered? There is not much to be done in this case. In some cases, such as small specimens in a foundation planting or in a very exposed position, evergreen boughs could be stuck in the ground around them to give some protection from winter sun and wind.

PROPAGATION: SEED AND CUTTINGS

Is it possible for an amateur to raise evergreens from seeds? Yes, providing one has reasonable patience and is prepared to give careful attention to the seeds and seedlings. (See the following questions.)

How can I grow evergreens from seed? Sow fall-collected seed in the spring in shallow boxes filled with light, well-drained soil. Cover, to about the diameter of the seed, with sifted soil. Place the flats in a cool, shaded cold frame and keep evenly moist. When watering, avoid disturbing the surface of the soil. Transplant when large enough to handle.

How do you keep seeds of evergreens until planting time? Store in tins, jars, or tight paper bags that are nearly airtight in a cool, dry place.

When should evergreen tree seed be planted, and how old should the seed be? Seed collected in the fall should be sown in the spring. Older seed, kept under proper conditions, will germinate, but viability becomes progressively less with each passing year.

Can evergreens be propagated by using the clippings for cuttings?

(Wisconsin.) Most of the yews, junipers, false-cypresses (chamaecyparis), arborvitaes, and some of the spruces can be propagated by means of clippings. These can be taken in late August, but as a rule many of them do not form roots before winter; therefore, a greenhouse is desirable, particularly in your climate. If you have a greenhouse (night temperature, 50° to 55° F.), you could also take cuttings in November and December.

What is the best temperature to root pines and spruces from cuttings in hothouse beds? The percentage of pine cuttings that can be rooted is so small as to make this method almost valueless. A very few of the spruces can be rooted and for these a greenhouse with a night temperature of 50° to 55° F. is required.

Will you describe the simplest way to start cuttings of arborvitaes and junipers? Take the cuttings in the latter part of August and set them out, about 1½ inches apart, in boxes of sand. The boxes should not be more than 4 inches deep, but any convenient size; the sand must be made firm before the cuttings are put in. Cover the box and cuttings with polyethylene film after watering thoroughly. Keep them in a hotbed until there is the possibility of the sand freezing, then place them in a cool, frostproof storage for the winter. If covered tightly with polyethylene film, they may need water only once a week or even less often.

Should boxes filled with sharp sand and leafmold, containing cuttings of yew and boxwood, be placed in deep shade or in semishade for best results? The important thing is that the cuttings must not be directly exposed to the sun, except possibly very early in the morning or late in the afternoon.

Specific Narrow-Leaved Evergreens

ARBORVITAE (THUJA)   (See also Hedges.)

Which arborvitae would be best in our northern climate to serve as a boundary-line screen? Pyramidal arborvitae, *Thuja occidentalis* 'Fastigiata'.

Would an arborvitae stand city conditions? Not very well, but it will grow in the city if conditions are not too severe. It needs good moist soil and sunshine for at least half of the day.

Will golden arborvitae do as well in shade as in sun? No. All "colored" evergreens require full sun to bring out their peculiar coloring.

When is the best time to plant arborvitae? What kind of soil should it have? Plant in early fall, up to October 1; small plants a foot or so tall, only in the spring. Dig them with a solid root ball. Set as deeply as they formerly stood. Fill around the ball with friable soil enriched with compost or peat moss and water this down well. When settled, add more soil, leaving a slight depression around the plant to catch rain water. Mulch the base and in dry weather administer occasional soakings.

Why are arborvitaes so hard to grow? They are by nature lovers of open situations and moist soils. Their use in foundation plantings, which is rarely suitable, is highly artificial and unnatural. (See previous questions.)

Can an arborvitae be pruned if the tree becomes too tall and thin? When is the proper pruning time? This can be done effectively in the case of quite young plants. Pruning and topping will do little good to old plants. Pruning should be done during the period of soft spring growth. To improve the denseness of old plants, apply a nutritious topdressing of leafmold and rotted manure or compost.

When and how is the best time to trim arborvitae? During the period of soft spring growth, shear the outer surface slightly, trimming the extremities of the soft growths. Close shearing results in a dense, formal appearance; light shearing, in a less formal appearance.

CEDAR (CEDRUS)

Could I grow a cedar-of-Lebanon here? What is its botanical name? (Southern Pennsylvania.) *Cedrus libani* would probably grow for you, but it is not hardy much farther north, though a hardy strain of the cedar-of-Lebanon (*stenocoma*) has been introduced by the Arnold Arboretum near Boston and has been growing there since 1903.

CRYPTOMERIA

What is the cryptomeria like? The Japanese temple-cedar or cryptomeria is a rapid-growing evergreen tree with tufted branches. It reaches a height of 125 feet in Japan. It is not hardy much above Zone VI (average minimum temperatures of $-5°$ to $5°$ F.). In this country it is handsome when young but it soon becomes scrawny.

FALSE-CYPRESS (CHAMAECYPARIS)

I have a tiny dwarf tree which has frondlike foliage, seems very tolerant and hardy, and looks very well in the rock garden. What is it?   It is probably dwarf Hinoki-cypress (*Chamaecyparis obtusa* 'Nana'), or one of this species' many other dwarf forms.

FIR (ABIES)

What does the Nikko fir (Abies homolepis) look like?   It is a large, broadly pyramidal evergreen tree with spreading upturned branches and glossy dark-green leaves. Needles spread upward, forming a V over the twig. Identify it by its grooved branchlets.

What is a good fir as a specimen tree? (New Hampshire.)   White fir (*Abies concolor*).

Which of the evergreens is very dark in color, of pyramidal form, tall, and with pendulous branches?   This is probably the Douglas-fir (*Pseudotsuga menziesii*), one of the best.

Will you suggest some good fir trees?   Douglas-fir, white fir, Nikko fir, Nordmann fir, Veitch fir, Fraser fir.

Can we grow fir trees in a dry, rather hot part of the East?   Probably not; they require a cool, somewhat humid climate. But if you must try one, the white fir would probably do best.

Can one grow a balsam fir in New Jersey?   Probably not. It does best north of Connecticut, or in the mountains south of Virginia.

Do fir trees grow well in a fairly sandy soil? How early in spring can they be planted?   Yes, in a somewhat sandy soil, enriched with leafmold, peat moss, or other humus matter. The best time to plant them is in the early fall.

How can I grow Christmas trees in Massachusetts?   In New England the "Christmas tree" is usually the balsam fir (*Abies balsamea*), which requires the cool, moist climate of the mountains. It has a difficult time in the warmer areas about Boston and on Cape Cod. If the climate is right, young trees 6 to 18 inches high can be set out in any field and be expected to begin to yield suitable Christmas trees in from 7 to 10 years. However, because of the time element involved, only marginal land should be used for this purpose. Write your local State Experiment Station for the most recent bulletin on the subject.

Is it practical to buy a tubbed fir Christmas tree and then, on a mild day after the holidays, plant it outdoors (the hole having been previously dug and filled with leaves)? From a viewpoint of gardening economy, better buy proper kinds and grades of trees for ornamental use, in the proper seasons, and avoid the inflated prices of evergreen trees at Christmas. However, many living Christmas trees are successfully set out after the holidays, following the method you mention.

How does one plant trees used indoors as Christmas trees? Prepare the planting hole in advance. Fill and heap it over with leaves. Have planting soil ready indoors. Keep the tree moist; remove it promptly after use to a cool place. Plant on a frost-free day and water thoroughly. Apply a thick mulch and place a burlap screen around it.

How can I prune a fir tree which is growing too tall and narrow? Does it need fertilizing? The soil is very poor. Many fir trees grow naturally tall and narrow. It is not practicable to prune back a fir tree after it has reached any great size. In poor soil apply a nutritious mulch of leafmold and compost at the base.

HEATHS AND HEATHERS (ERICA AND CALLUNA)

I want to plant a little "sheet" of heath. What kind of soil does it need? Choose a well-drained, acid soil and sunny situation. Prepare a cushion, a foot deep, made up of about half garden loam and half peat moss. (If your soil is heavy clay, add sand and more peat moss.)

Can heather (Calluna vulgaris) be satisfactorily grown out of doors in the vicinity of New York? Heather grows quite well in acid soils, along the eastern seacoast. The plants often kill back during very cold and windy winters so they should be mulched with evergreen boughs or marsh hay. Apply the hay lightly so the plants aren't smothered.

Should heather be pruned? Early-blooming varieties should be cut back to the *base* of the flowering shoots as soon as the blossoms have faded. In regions where heather suffers from winter injury, pruning should be done in early spring just as growth is beginning. Such yearly pruning (technically, "shearing") keeps the plants shapely and floriferous.

Which is more hardy—the heaths (Erica) or the heathers (Calluna vulgaris)? Which would be more likely to survive in Ithaca, New York? Generally, there are more winter-hardy forms of *Erica carnea*, such as the well-known 'Springwood Pink', than there are among the many varieties of *Calluna vulgaris*. (However, there are other species of *Erica*, such as *E. hyemalis*, which are not hardy in northern regions and can be grown only as pot plants there.) In Ithaca most of the varieties of *E. carnea* should be winter-hardy, especially with a good snow cover for protection.

Does heather bloom in winter?   No. Heather (*Calluna vulgaris* and its varieties) blooms in the summer. You are thinking of heath, probably varieties of *Erica carnea,* which often start flowering around Thanksgiving and Christmas. However, their major flower display is usually in early spring.

Can I divide heaths and heathers?   Not too well, although sometimes the plants form layers, which when removed make new plants fairly quickly—depending on the variety.

I would like to make a small heath and heather garden, but the only sunny area I have directly adjoins our terrace. Would the plants look all right there?   Yes, it sounds like an excellent location and as you relax on the terrace you will be able to look down on the intricate patterns of the plants. Try to keep your access areas to the terrace obvious enough so that guests and family members won't trample the plants.

Are heaths and heathers hard to grow?   No, if consideration is given to soil, mulching, and pruning, as mentioned in the first three questions at the beginning of this section.

I am planning a heath and heather garden. What other plants can I use with them? (Seattle, Washington.)   Many dwarf conifers, such as *Juniperus communis* 'Compressa'; dwarf small-leaved rhododendrons, such as *Rhododendron impeditum* and *R. intricatum;* and the evergreen azaleas such as the 'Gumpo' varieties. Larger-leaved and taller-growing rhododendrons and azaleas can be introduced as background plantings to your garden.

HEMLOCK (TSUGA)

We have an extremely shady garden. Would any evergreens do well for us?   Hemlocks and the native yew only (*Taxus canadensis*).

Which evergreen trees obtained in ordinary woods would be best to put around a home?   If by "around a home" you mean along the foundation, avoid naturally tall-growing evergreens such as hemlocks. Eventually no pruning will keep them in bounds. However, hemlocks can be used on the grounds as a hedge and their growth somewhat restrained by trimming or clipping their new growth once or twice a year, in the early summer and late summer or early fall.

What type of soil is best for young hemlocks? Do they require much

water? A light loam, rich in humus. In an ordinary garden soil, up to 25 per cent of leafmold or other humus can be worked in; in a light, sandy soil, twice this amount. Hemlocks should not be permitted to suffer for lack of water, but do not keep the soil drenched.

When is the best time to transplant hemlocks? (New York.) In early autumn, during favorable moist weather, up to about October 15 in much of the North.

What conditions and methods are advocated for most successful transplanting of hemlocks from the woods? (New York.) The safest method is to root-prune the tree a year in advance of moving. When actually transplanting, the roots should all be carefully dug in a tight ball of earth and not allowed to dry out while the plant is being moved from one place to the other.

Can a 25-foot hemlock, once transplanted, regain new needles on branches that are now bare? If the bare branches do not develop new leaves during the spring following transplanting, they never will. In that case, remove the dead branches.

What is the proper care of hemlock trees? They prefer a situation sheltered from strong winds and a soil very rich in humus. They revel in leafmold. Use lots of it or peat moss when planting, and apply a leaf mulch about the base. Do not let them get dry and in dry autumns soak the soil thoroughly just before winter. If set in a sun-scorched place, partial shade will be helpful in establishing seedling trees.

Why do hemlocks die back soon after planting? They should not. The trouble can be due to one or more of several causes: lack of a good, solid, fibrous root ball when transplanted; improper planting; lack of humus in the soil; lack of water; or windy exposure.

How would you propagate hemlock from cuttings? Do they need heat? Propagating by cuttings is difficult but it can be done with a very small percentage of rooting. Take softwood cuttings in early July, place them in a mixture of sand and peat moss in a greenhouse bench with bottom heat or under mist.

JUNIPER

Which juniper would grow tall, compact, and narrow? Canaert redcedar. Or one of the Chinese junipers, such as *Juniperus chinensis* 'Columnaris', would be good.

Are Irish junipers of the same genus as red-cedar trees? Can they be safely planted near apple trees? Yes, they both belong to the genus

Juniperus. They serve as alternate hosts for the cedar-apple rust and should not be grown within several hundred yards of apple trees.

Will Irish junipers do well in an east foundation planting? Mine don't look very good. Red spider might be the trouble, as they were not sprayed this year. A northeast exposure would be better. This juniper is subject to winter burn on the sunny side. Spider mites are often injurious, but the effect would spread over the entire tree, not merely on the sunny side.

How can I keep my Irish juniper from turning brown each spring? Keep the brightest sun in the winter from the foliage, either by locating the junipers in a northeast exposure or by means of a burlap screen or other protection.

Are cedar and red-cedar the same? No. The word "cedar," when correctly used, applies to the genus *Cedrus*—a group of trees native in North Africa and southwest Asia. These are quite different from our native "red-cedar" (*Juniperus virginiana*) of the eastern United States.

What is the best time of year to transplant red-cedar from a field? Trees over 7 feet high should be root-pruned in September and moved a year later. This will ensure a fibrous root system, which is necessary to successful transplanting.

What can be done to improve the appearance of red-cedar trees planted in front of a house? Examine them for the presence of spider mites. If these are present, spray promptly and repeatedly. Cultivate the surface lightly, without disturbing any roots. Mulch with leafmold or rich compost. See that there is no lack of moisture. Red-cedars should not be used in a foundation planting since they grow too tall.

What time of year should I plant a spreading juniper? Spring, after the ground has become thoroughly workable, before growth has started, or early autumn; in lower New York State, up to about November 1. During dry autumns, take advantage of any wet spells that come along.

What fertilizer do spreading junipers need? Established, thriving plants, in soil of fair quality, need none. In poor soil, apply a topdressing of leafmold or peat moss mixed with compost. Avoid alkaline fertilizers.

What winter and summer care does an erect juniper, 2 to 3 feet high, require? Is it possible to prevent dead branches at the base? Is this due to dogs? Examine branches for spider mites. If found, spray promptly. See that the soil does not cake. Apply a mulch. Dogs may be responsible for injury to lower branches.

When are junipers pruned? The principal annual pruning is done during the period of soft spring growth. If a formal appearance is desired, a second, lighter pruning can be given about September 1 to upright-growing kinds like the red-cedar.

Can I cut about 27 inches off the top of a Meyer juniper without damaging the tree for summer growth? Our tree is too tall. Yes, you can reduce the height by cutting back. It will produce new growth below the cut, which will eventually cover the stubbed effect.

Please tell me the right way to trim Savin junipers. Can the long branches be trimmed back? For proper development, Savin junipers should be pruned rather heavily in their young stages. This will make them bushy. When old branches are pruned back, they can be slow in producing new growth and the effect can be unsightly.

After the top is broken off a silver juniper, Juniperus virginiana 'Glauca', will it ever be a nicely shaped tree? It will readily develop a new leader of acceptable appearance within 2 or 3 years. The process may be helped by staking up the new leader and pruning back competing growths.

How long does it take for juniper berries to ripen; when is the time to pick them? Some junipers will never have berries. Only the female (pistillate-flowering) trees bear fruit. The Rocky Mountain juniper (*Juniperus scopulorum*) and several other junipers take 2 years to mature their fruits. These could be picked in the late summer or early fall of the second year. The female trees of *J. virginiana* should bear fruit every year if weather conditions are just right.

How do nurserymen increase junipers? I have done it by slicing a branch and burying it until it roots, but there must be a quicker way. Either by cuttings or grafting. Cuttings are placed in the greenhouse in summer or early winter. Cuttings of some junipers will remain alive and in good condition for more than 2 years without rooting. Grafting is done early in the year.

Can I start Pfitzer junipers from cuttings? It is possible but this juniper does not root too readily. Make cuttings, about 5 inches long, in the latter half of August and place in a greenhouse bench with bottom heat. (See Propagation, this section.)

PINE (PINUS)

Which is the more satisfactory—red pine or Austrian pine? They are similar, but the former is less susceptible to insect pests in some areas.

We like pine trees, but our soil is moist. Would any of them do well? White pine (*Pinus strobus*) and pitch pine (*P. rigida*) are occasionally found growing wild in swamps in New Jersey. In the South, longleaf pine (*P. palustris*) could be planted.

We were advised to buy pine trees for our garden near the windy seashore. Is Scots pine a good choice? Yes. Japanese black pine is most resistant to wind and salt spray, however.

I would like to plant a pine tree which is not coarse in texture. What do you suggest? Use either white pine or Japanese red pine.

How can I tell the principal pine trees apart? Many of them by the length of their "needles," and the number in each cluster (fascicle). White pine—5 in a cluster, 5 inches long (soft bluish); Austrian pine—2 in a cluster, 6½ inches long (stiff); Scots pine—2 in a cluster, 3 inches long (twisted); red pine—2 in a cluster, 6 inches long (glossy); Japanese black pine—2 in a cluster, 4½ inches long (sharp-pointed).

What is the best fertilizer to keep a pine tree healthy and growing? Is bone meal O.K.? Bone meal (superphosphate is better) when transplanting, but it is not a complete fertilizer, which can be applied later on. However, if the soil is of good quality and the tree healthy, no feeding will be required. At the slightest sign of soil exhaustion, apply a topdressing of leafmold or peat moss mixed with rotted manure or compost.

Can pine trees be planted all year round? No. Not during the period of soft growth, from May to August, unless they are in containers.

I have some fine 4-year-old white pine and Norway pine. When is the best time to transplant them? Should they be in full sun or partial shade? (Wisconsin.) Transplant in early spring before growth starts. Mulch the surface. An open situation is best, but some temporary shading would be desirable.

When is the best time to transplant pine trees? (New York.) In New York City, fibrous-rooted trees can be transplanted either in the spring or in the autumn (between August 1 and November 1). Pines not previously transplanted had better be planted in the spring only, with as good a root ball as possible.

How should pine trees be transplanted? Untransplanted trees over 6 feet high should be root-pruned in September and moved a year later. Transplanted trees with fibrous root systems can be dug with a ball of roots, burlapped, in the spring or in early autumn. Water down the filling soil. Fill the hole flush with the grade. Mulch soil over the roots.

Is it too late to transplant pine trees that were set out as seedlings and

are now about 10 feet tall? No. Root-prune them in September; move them a year later or in the spring of the second year. They should then have developed sufficient fibrous roots to facilitate successful transplanting.

Should grass be kept away from the ground around young pines? Yes.

When and how does one prune mugo pines? When the candlelike spring growths have about reached their full length, but before the leaves have spread out, cut these "candles" back partly. When they are reduced to ¼ or ⅓ their length each year, a mugo pine will form a dense, cushionlike plant.

I have a matched pair of mugo pines. One is getting larger than the other. Is it possible to trim them back? Yes. In the annual pruning of the candlelike spring growths, cut those on the larger plant a little farther back than those on the smaller plant. In a year or two this will tend to even the two plants up. Do not prune into the old wood.

What can be done to save young pine trees badly browned by the heat from burning brush? If the scorched branches produce new leaves in the spring following injury, no harm will have been done. If not, nothing can restore the damage; cut off the burned parts.

Will you please tell me what makes our pines have brown edges and be so thin-looking? Probably unsuitable environment, such as inadequate underdrainage, too dry soil, or too much shade.

Are new pine trees started by seeds or cuttings? Pine trees are started from seeds sown in the spring. Some varieties are grafted. Most species and varieties are exceedingly difficult to raise from cuttings.

Can pine trees be grown from seed? Yes. Seed ripens from September to November, the cones that produce the seed being 2 or 3 years old. Collect the cones before the seed has shed and place them in shallow boxes in a warm, dry place. (See answers to other inquiries.)

Is there any disease that pine trees catch from fruit trees? No, but the white-pine blister rust lives for part of its life on gooseberry and currant bushes. This is a very serious disease.

RED-CEDAR See Juniper.

SPRUCE (PICEA)

Which are some of the outstanding spruce trees? Oriental spruce

(*Picea orientalis*); Serbian spruce (*P. omorika*); Colorado spruce (*P. pungens*)—some varieties of this are bluish in tone.

What is the best fertilizer for blue spruce? An occasional topdressing of leafmold or peat moss with compost mixed into it. When planting, mix leafmold and some rotted manure or compost or a little complete chemical fertilizer with the planting soil.

I have planted spruce trees in oyster shell. I was advised to use sulfate of ammonia and pine needles to make the soil acid. Was it wrong? Oyster shell is not suitable for evergreens. Add a large quantity of acid humus material, such as peat moss, hemlock or pine-needle leafmold.

What type of soil is suitable for spruce trees? A good loam, enriched with humus. Untransplanted trees over 6 feet high should be root-pruned in September and moved a year later. Trees previously transplanted should be dug with a good ball, either in the spring or in early autumn. Water the soil after planting. Fill flush with the grade. Mulch.

Should the ground be frozen in order to remove spruce and pine from woods to lawns? Not necessarily. The main thing is to secure an adequate, solid ball of fibrous roots and earth. Large trees are sometimes most conveniently moved with frozen balls.

How much space should be available in front of a house to plant a blue spruce? It should have an area 20 feet or more in diameter in which to grow.

In a blue spruce, successfully transplanted last year, the old foliage has lost its bright color. Will it return? This often happens when in transplanting or transit a blue spruce is tied in tightly or crowded. The blue, waxy coat of the foliage rubs off and does not renew itself. Subsequent new growth will eventually cover the dull inner foliage. The color rubs off most readily on the soft new growth.

I have had little success with blue spruces. Will you give information on their culture? Be sure to procure transplanted, fibrous-rooted plants. Plant in a well-drained, sunny place in any fair, loamy soil. Plant in the spring before growth starts, or shortly after August 1 during suitable damp weather. Water plentifully; mulch the base. Keep the roots moist, but not too wet, and in dry autumns soak thoroughly just before winter.

What is the proper care for Norway spruce and blue spruce seedlings, now 1½ inches high? Assuming that they were planted in well-prepared planting beds, keep under lath shades and maintain soil moisture with a light, fine surface mulch. Transplant or root-prune every two years until they are the proper size for permanent planting.

Can you prune and shape a blue spruce? If so, when is the proper time? Yes. Prune only during the period of soft spring growth. The shaping process can sometimes be aided by tying in misdirected branches and staking a crooked leader.

How shall I trim the sides of a Colorado blue spruce that has grown too close to my driveway? If this involves cutting into old wood, it will not be found practicable. Better move the whole tree back from the drive, if possible, or cut it down and start over with a new tree properly set back from your driveway.

I have a blue spruce that is growing lopsided. How shall I trim it? If the leader is crooked, stake it. If any branches can be tied into place, do this before you use the pruning shears. If it is a matter of one or more protruding branches in an otherwise well-balanced plant, then reduce these branches as necessary.

How does one prune blue spruces to prevent them from growing too large? They are by nature tall-growing trees. They can be restrained artificially by means of annual prunings or shearings during their period of soft growth in the spring. This involves the snipping off of the extremities of the shoots.

In two spruce trees that serve as windbreaks the lower branches are dying. How can I improve their appearance and discourage any great increase in height? Once the lower branches have died, nothing will bring them back to life, and no new growth will replace them. To prevent further loss of the lower branches, remove all crowding nearby growths which shut out light. Keep a mulch about the base; eventually cut off top shoots if necessary.

Can I get information about propagating blue spruce? Can they be increased by cuttings? They can be rooted from cuttings, but not very readily. Use the shoots of one year's growth with a very small "heel" of old wood inserted in January in a propagating case in a warm greenhouse. For detailed information consult *Wyman's Gardening Encyclopedia* by Donald Wyman (Macmillan) and *Plant Propagation in Pictures* by Montague Free, revised and edited by Marjorie J. Dietz (Doubleday & Company).

How can Moerheim blue spruce be propagated? It is usually propagated by grafting.

How, when, and where should one plant seeds of Norway spruce and Colorado blue spruce? Sow ¼ inch deep in a bed of fine soil, shaded by lath screens, until the seeds have germinated, or in flats in a cold frame in the spring.

Will handling spruce and red-cedar Christmas trees, after they have been in the house, cause a bad case of poison on the hands and face? Such a difficulty is not common. Some individuals might be allergic to the resins in these trees, but cases of poisoning are rare. Sometimes handling needle-leaved evergreens causes a temporary irritation to the skin on your hands, but it soon disappears. Could you have had a potted plant of *Primula obconica* in the house at the same time? This primrose causes a severe skin poisoning, similar to that of poison-ivy, on those who are allergic to it.

YEW (TAXUS)

Which yews grow in tree form? English yew and the single-stem Japanese yew, but they rarely attain a great height in this country except in the Pacific Northwest.

Which yews make narrow upright growth? Hatfield, Hicks, and Irish yew (where winters are not severe); also Japanese upright yew and the variety 'Stovekenii'.

Do dwarf yews prefer an acid soil? No, they will grow well in either acid or alkaline soils.

When is the best time to move yews? Either in spring, before growth starts, or in early September.

Should dwarf Japanese yews be fed? If so, what and when? Not necessarily. If their color is good, leave them alone. Dwarf Japanese yews always grow slowly. Well-rotted manure makes a good fertilizer when needed, or use commercial fertilizers according to directions.

I have two Japanese yews. One has retained its dark-green color, but the other has a slight yellow cast. Why? Frequently Japanese yews are grown from seed; there are wide differences in the resulting plants. Height, shape, and color of foliage are all variables in such instances.

My Japanese yew is dying. I have given it plenty of water and fertilizer and sprayed the foliage, all to no avail. What is the trouble with it? The roots of this plant are probably being attacked by the grubs of the strawberry root weevil. Consult your county agent for local recommendations to correct this condition.

I planted two yews four years ago. One seems to be dying. It has been this way for two seasons. The foliage is green but very thin. There are no grubs around the roots. This is a condition frequently related to finding aphids on the roots. If this is not the case, the explanation could be in some peculiar soil condition. Dig the plant, remove the soil from around the roots, and transplant it in some other situation.

When is the best time to trim Japanese yew?   Just after growth has been completed, in late June or early July.

Should yew trees be trimmed in August or are they prettier left untrimmed?   Usually they are prettier untrimmed when grown as specimens, but some years a small amount of trimming (which really can be done any time) is necessary to keep certain branches from growing too much out of proportion to the rest of the plant.

Should low-spreading yews in foundation plantings be pruned?   Not if they stay low and do not grow out of proportion to the other plants.

Should the branches of Taxus cuspidata be tied for winter protection or supported in some way? The branches break easily.   This might be done if they are growing in situations where the snow and ice will accumulate on them, as under the eaves of the house.

How can I best propagate Japanese yew for a hedge?   Take cuttings 6 to 7 inches long at the end of June, place them in sand in an electric hotbed (temperature about 75° F.), keep them watered and shaded, and they should be rooted by fall. Pot them and keep in a cool place (not freezing) over winter, then plant out after all danger of frost is over.

Can you advise how to grow Japanese yew from seeds?   Clean the fleshy pulp from the seed, stratify by placing alternate layers of moist peat moss and seeds in a box, keep at a temperature of 30° to 40° F., possibly in a refrigerator, and sow in the early spring. Some seeds may not germinate for a full year, so don't be discouraged if they all do not come up the first year.

How can I raise seedlings from berries on a Hicks yew?   This can be done (see preceding question), but Hicks yew is a hybrid and seedlings of it will not all have the characteristic upright shape of the Hicks yew. A better method would be to propagate by cuttings taken in early summer.

Why do some yews fruit and others do not?   The sexes are separate and both should be planted (one male to about ten females) to ensure the fruiting of female plants.

Broad-Leaved Evergreens

CULTURE

What does "ericaceous" mean? This term is applied to the plant family Ericaceae, consisting mainly of shrubs, some very small plants, and mostly small trees which require a sandy, peaty, acid soil. Among the Ericaceae are the following genera: *Andromeda* (bog-rosemary); *Arbutus; Arctostaphylos; Calluna* (heather); *Enkianthus; Erica* (heath); *Kalmia* (mountain-laurel); *Pieris,* and *Rhododendron* (including azaleas). Some are evergreen; others, deciduous.

What fertilizer ingredients, in what formula, would you suggest for feeding ericaceous plants and at the same time maintain acidity in the soil? Tankage or cottonseed meal applied at the rate of 5 pounds per 100 square feet is satisfactory for small plants. For large plants use 6–10–6 fertilizer in which cottonseed or soybean meal is used to supply one fourth to one half of the nitrogen. Apply at the rate of 2 to 3 pounds per 100 square feet of bed area. If the soil is sufficiently acid, 7½ pounds of nitrate of soda, 10 pounds of superphosphate, and 2½ pounds of sulfate of potash could be used to approximate the above formula. (See also Azalea and Rhododendron.)

What kinds of native shrubs, besides azaleas, need acid soil? Rhododendrons and all other broad-leaved evergreens; blueberries, huckleberries, and bayberries. As a general rule, provide acid soil conditions for all kinds that grow naturally in oak or evergreen woods.

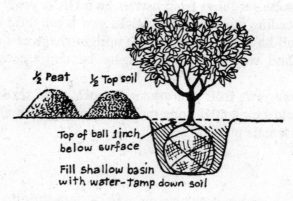

½ Peat   ½ Top soil

Top of ball 1 inch below surface

Fill shallow basin with water—tamp down soil

PLANTING A BROAD-LEAVED EVERGREEN

Which broad-leaved evergreens will grow best in New York City? Japanese holly (*Ilex crenata*); inkberry (*Ilex glabra*); drooping leucothoe (*Leucothoe fontanesiana*); Oregon holly-grape (*Mahonia aquifolium*); *Pieris floribunda* and *japonica,* and *Rhododendron obtusum* 'Amoenum'.

What soil is best for mountain-laurel? Soil that is moist, acid, and bountifully supplied with humus. It grows well in rhododendron soils.

Do rhododendrons, mountain-laurel, etc., require special soil? Yes. A well-drained subsoil beneath and 12 to 18 inches of topsoil containing up to 50 per cent acid humus matter. A totally uncongenial soil should be removed and replaced with a suitable mixture. For acid humus, use pine, spruce, hemlock, or oak leafmold, or peat moss. Peat moss, mixed with well-rotted manure or compost and added to soil, makes a good medium for plants of this type. The soil acidity should be 4.5 to 6.5 pH.

Can I condition my alkaline soil for rhododendrons? Yes, but it can be a long, tedious, and sometimes unsuccessful process. Sulfur is the safest way. (See Introduction to Soils, Part 1, for directions.)

My soil is very acid, but rhododendrons do not grow well. Why? The soil may be *too* acid and poorly drained. Bring it up to pH 5.5 by adding pulverized dolomitic limestone (a soil test will indicate how much lime you need). Dig out the bed to a depth of 18 inches, put in 6 inches of cinders, and return the soil mixed with limestone and peat moss.

How can I be certain that a soil is acid? Send samples to your county extension agent or to a State Agricultural Experiment Station for testing, or buy one of several soil-testing kits available for just this purpose. (See Acidity in Section 1.)

Our soil is definitely alkaline, but I want to grow azaleas and rhododendrons. What should I do? The best way is to excavate the soil in the area for planting to an approximate depth of 2½ feet. Place in the excavation only acid soil rich in humus. Sphagnum peat moss is an acceptable source of humus. (See questions above and below.)

With a soil only slightly alkaline, how does one make it acid with a minimum amount of trouble? The second best way of acquiring an acid soil is to apply aluminum sulfate to the soil in question at rates depending on the alkalinity or the pH. The following figures indicate the soil reaction at the start and the amount of aluminum sulfate per square yard: pH 5.5 to 6.0, ¼ pound; pH 6.5 to 7.0, ½ pound; pH 7.0

to 8.0, ¾ pound. This should be well watered in and the soil tested again at the end of 2 weeks. If the soil has not reached the desired acidity, to a depth of 6 to 12 inches, apply sulfur at one sixth of the rate given above.

How acid should soil be for azaleas and rhododendrons? For most of them, pH 5 to 6.

Should a soil in which azaleas and rhododendrons are growing be tested more than once a year? Only if the plants fail to grow well.

Will coffee and tea grounds sprinkled around azaleas help to acidify the soil? Would this practice be harmful? No, it would not acidify the soil to any marked degree. If too deep, it might be harmful.

What is the best time of year to feed azaleas? They can be fed either in early spring or fall.

We use cottonseed meal for fertilizer a great deal down here. Can this be used on azaleas? (South Carolina.) Yes. A mixture of 2 pounds of cottonseed meal and 1 pound of ammonium sulfate, used at the rate of 1 to 2 pounds per 100 square feet, makes a very good acid fertilizer. (See also under Rhododendron.)

I would like to grow rhododendrons here. How can I make the soil acid? (Illinois.) See under Azaleas for method of making soil acid. In Illinois, especially the northwestern part, the summers are very hot and dry and the winters very cold, which is extremely hard on rhododendrons. Precautions should be taken to give the foliage and roots plenty of moisture in the summer; also to give winter protection, especially in exposed situations.

My soil is very dry and some of my rhododendrons have died. What should I do? Mix decomposed vegetable matter (rotted manure, rotted oak leaves or pine needles, compost, and peat moss) with the soil. Then apply a mulch of rotting oak leaves, pine needles, or peat moss mixed with compost about the base of the plants. All these help to conserve moisture.

What fertilizer should one give rhododendrons that are growing in a poor, sandy soil? Add decaying vegetable material, such as rotted manure, decaying oak leaves, pine needles, and peat moss. Chemical fertilizers alone added to a poor, sandy soil would not be sufficient.

Is flowers of sulfur a desirable fertilizer for azaleas and rhododendrons? It acts as a fertilizer, for in making the soil more acid it releases certain materials which were not formerly available to the plant.

What summer and winter care do evergreen azaleas need? Water thoroughly during a drought in the summer. Mulch with oak leaves, pine needles, or peat moss to maintain acidity and to protect roots in the winter. Tender varieties should have evergreen boughs or burlap screens placed around them.

Is it possible to grow rhododendrons and azaleas successfully in Ohio? What are the soil requirements? Yes. Evergreen azaleas are easier to grow than evergreen rhododendrons, but both can be grown if they have acid soil, plenty of moisture, and not too severe winter temperatures.

What is the proper treatment for azaleas the year round? Our bushes are not blooming. (Minnesota.) Many azaleas, especially in the colder parts of the United States, have their flower buds killed by very low temperatures. Plant only the hardiest deciduous kinds in cold areas, such as the pinkshell azalea, pinxterbloom, and some of the Ghent hybrids.

How can I grow azaleas (which come from West Virginia) between lakes Ontario and Seneca in soil that is not naturally acid? First make the soil acid. Practically anything which is hardy in the mountains of West Virginia will prove hardy in central New York.

How do you pinch back evergreen azaleas? Merely pinch off the end of growing twigs in the spring. This will force several side buds to grow and will result in a bushier shrub.

How should azaleas be pruned? Cut out diseased or dying branches from the base of the plant. Often it is advisable to cut off a few twigs here and there to force thick growth. Otherwise they need little pruning.

Should seed pods be pruned from azaleas? Cut off dead flowers before seed pods form, then more strength will go into flower-bud formation for the next year. However, this may be too much of a chore where many plants are involved.

For what should azaleas be sprayed? Lacebug and red spider are the most serious pests of azaleas.

Will rhododendrons grow in full sun? Yes, if you mean the small-leaved kinds, but partial shade is best for the large-leaved types.

Are there any particular requirements, as to sun or shade, for rhododendrons? Rhododendrons bloom most profusely in the full sun, but if grown in partial shade they will bloom sufficiently well to be attractive. In deep shade most varieties bloom very little.

Do rhododendrons and azaleas need the same growing condi-

tions? Yes, except that large-leaved rhododendrons will grow better in shaded situations protected from the wind.

When should rhododendrons be planted? Preferably in spring, then in late summer or early fall.

Where should rhododendrons be planted? Where they get some shade and some filtered sunlight. Also, they should be protected from high winter winds. Their roots should not be allowed to dry out at any time.

My place is exposed to the wind from the ocean. Will rhododendrons thrive? No. In any case, they need shelter from strong wind—especially in winter.

How old must rhododendrons be to bloom? Mine are five years old and growing well in prepared acid soil and partial shade, but they do not bloom. Many rhododendrons bloom when they are about five years old. This particular plant may be growing too fast vegetatively. Root-pruning might be practiced by pushing a spade into the soil around the base of the plant, not too near the stem. Or you might try superphosphate (15 to 20 per cent) applied beneath the mulch at the rate of 4 ounces per square yard. Some varieties and species bloom at earlier ages than others. Too much shade hinders blooming.

Can you tell me why my rhododendron did not bloom although it has healthy foliage and growing conditions (acid) are favorable? Is it receiving too much shade? Or it may have been that the flower buds were killed by an unusually cold winter. Also, rhododendrons are like many other ornamentals in that some bloom profusely one year and very little the next. There is little that the amateur can do about this "alternate-bearing" habit of some kinds.

How is Rhododendron maximum made to bloom better? This species does best only in the shade. Ornamentally it is not so good as the earlier-flowering hybrids because the flowers appear after the new growth has started and this frequently hides the flowers. Plenty of moisture, acid soil, and an acid mulch are helpful aids.

Are all broad-leaved evergreens transplanted with a ball of soil about their roots? Absolutely, yes! This applies specifically to boxwood, daphne, holly, inkberry, and all azaleas and rhododendrons. The idea is to dig as many of the fibrous feeding roots as possible, enclosed in a tight burlapped ball of soil so the ball does not break up. If this happens, many fibrous roots are broken and the plant may fail to survive. Handle the ball as carefully as possible and do not let it dry out!

Do I take the wrapping material off the ball at transplanting

time? Yes, if you can do it without breaking the ball. If you can't, set the ball in the prepared hole, cut all tied strings and ropes, carefully roll back the wrapping material, and push to the bottom of the hole without breaking the ball.

I have heard that the Portland-Seattle area is probably the best in this country for growing rhododendrons. It this true? Yes, because of good soil, temperate (and often cloudy) climate, and considerable humidity.

WINTER PROTECTION

Do azaleas and rhododendrons need winter protection in the vicinity of New York? How is this best provided? Only the more tender evergreen sorts need the kind of protection provided by a burlap screen or pine boughs that are placed around the plant to protect it from high winds and sun. All azaleas will do better if provided with a mulch of some acid material (oak leaves, pine needles, or compost) around their roots in the winter.

Should broad-leaved evergreens be covered completely for the winter? If by this is meant the complete covering of the leaves, the answer is, No! But if a mere shading of the plant is meant, this proves helpful when tender varieties are being grown.

Should young azaleas be protected for the winter if they are not sheltered by shrubs? The evergreen varieties might well be mulched since these are the least hardy. The mulching material should be light, allowing air circulation. Use evergreen boughs, marsh hay, or oak leaves.

How can potted azaleas purchased at the florist and full of buds and flowers be taken care of so as to bloom again? Most of the florists' potted azaleas are Kurume azaleas and are not hardy north of Philadelphia, Pennsylvania. They will grow out-of-doors the first summer but will be killed by winter cold in most northern regions. In the South such plants can be planted out-of-doors in acid soil, protected the first winter, and usually come through in fine shape. In the North such potted plants can be summered outdoors by plunging the pot to its rim in soil. Bring indoors before winter.

Should azaleas and rhododendrons have a mulch about their roots? Why? Yes. Because their roots are shallow and grow best when the soil is cool and moist. In the winter a mulch protects the roots against extremely low temperatures.

Is it good to mulch azaleas and rhododendrons with manure? Not if it is fresh. Well-rotted manure can be used without injury to the plants.

When should a mulch be applied to azaleas and rhododendrons? It is advisable to put a mulch over the roots after planting. This mulch, a few inches deep, can be left on permanently and replaced as it decays.

What makes a good mulching material for azaleas and rhododendrons and other broad-leaved evergreens? Oak leaves, pine needles, and peat moss mixed with compost. Upon decomposition, all these are beneficial to the growth of this type of plant.

I have no oak leaves but plenty of maple leaves. Could I use these as a mulch? It would be better to use peat moss mixed with compost. Maple leaves tend to pack closely when wet, thus keeping air from the plant roots. When very tightly packed, they frequently "cake" and have been known to kill azaleas for this reason. Also, maple leaves are alkaline when decomposed.

Would it be helpful or harmful to tie burlap sacks around the branches of my camellia and to cover the buds in winter? It would be harmful. Air must circulate around these plants in the winter, and wrapping stems and branches would not permit this. It is far better to build a screen of burlap around them, open at the top to permit free air circulation at all times but also giving a screening and shading protection.

What is the best protection for rhododendrons exposed to strong winds? Burlap screens, or screens of evergreen boughs, designed and placed to give protection from winds and some shade during winter months—especially February and March. Snow fencing can also be used.

When should leafmold mulch be applied to rhododendrons? Any time, especially after planting. Renew as necessary.

PROPAGATION

Can azaleas, rhododendrons, and other ericaceous plants be propagated by seed? Yes, depending upon the kind and the purpose for which they are needed. Any of the wild forms, native or exotic, can be raised from seeds, and unless natural hybridization has taken place, the seedlings will reproduce the characteristics of the parent. Hybrid forms and sports (natural deviations from a species or cultivar) should not be reproduced from seeds but by cuttings.

How can I start ericaceous plants from seed? Collect seed pods in late fall when they are ready to open. Keep dry, and in late fall shake the seeds out on milled or ground sphagnum moss 1 inch deep on top of acid soil well firmed in pots or flats. Keep the moss moist, preferably by using a fine mist spray from time to time, or enclose pots in polyethylene. In several months seedlings should be the right size to transplant into flats or small pots. They develop well under fluorescent lights.

Can azaleas be propagated by cuttings? It is exceedingly difficult to root cuttings of deciduous azaleas, but the evergreen varieties can be rooted with great success in July. The cuttings should be about 3 inches long, taken (just after new growth is completed) from the tips of the shoots and placed in a rooting mixture of sand and peat moss, vermiculite, or a mixture of vermiculite and perlite. After being thoroughly watered, the cuttings should be kept in a flat that is tightly enclosed by polyethylene. Keep the flat out of direct sun.

What is the type of graft used on rhododendrons? The veneer graft is most commonly used. The understock is not cut back at the time of grafting. A downward, slanting cut is made on the stem of the understock about 1½ inches long and about one third of the way through the stem. A second cut into the stem (at the base of the first) removes the piece of bark and attached wood. The base of the scion is cut to correspond to the cuts on the understock. Few rhododendrons are grafted today.

How should rhododendrons be separated? Rhododendrons as a rule should not be "separated" in the same sense that one thinks of separating perennials. They grow as individual plants, often in clumps. Any attempt to divide these clumps would probably prove disastrous. However, some of the native deciduous azalea clumps can be divided successfully.

Specific Broad-Leaved Evergreens

AZALEAS, EVERGREEN (RHODODENDRON)

How can I grow evergreen azaleas? They need much the same conditions as rhododendrons. (See questions and answers on Culture, above.) Most of them are not reliably hardy north of New York City; they are at their best southward and in the Pacific Northwest.

A group of Hinodegiri azaleas have become too large. Can they be clipped rather severely, after their next bloom, without injury or serious loss of future bloom? Yes, they withstand heavy pruning.

Will you discuss winter protection for azaleas in this region? Mine fail

to blossom in the spring. Most of the leaves are brown and new growth is slow to start. During the summer they grow well. (Northern New York.)   The evergreen types are not hardy in northern New York. If you build a screen of burlap or pine boughs, this might help to bring them through in better condition; but if the flower buds are killed even with this protection, then switch to a hardier type. *Rhododendron calendulaceum, R. nudiflorum,* and *R. viscosum* are among the hardiest of the deciduous azaleas.

What are the Glenn Dale hybrid azaleas? Would they be hardy in Connecticut near the coast?   The Glenn Dale hybrids are the breeding results of B. Y. Morrison, formerly head of the Division of Plant Exploration and Introduction of the USDA at Glenn Dale, Maryland. The breeding aim was to obtain evergreen azaleas hardy in the Middle Atlantic states that would bloom from April to June. Of the 400 or so named varieties introduced in 1940 and for several years thereafter, most are probably not available now from commercial nurseries. Many of the Glenn Dales would be hardy in your region but the problem is finding a source. A few are listed by nurseries that specialize in rhododendrons and azaleas.

BOXWOOD (BUXUS)

I have heard about Korean box; what is it like?   It does not grow more than 3 feet high, resembles dwarf box, and is the hardiest of all the boxwoods, but the foliage often burns brownish in winter.

In making an English box garden in a space 50 × 75 feet, what should the spacing be?   This depends on the height at which the box bushes will be kept. If a height of 3 to 4 feet is desired, then the plants could be spaced 18 inches apart for a hedge. Single specimens, if allowed to grow unclipped, should be allowed a space at least 5 feet in diameter.

What fertilizer should I use on boxwood?   Well-rotted manure or rich compost is best. Commercially prepared chemical fertilizers should be used with discretion, as they sometimes burn the foliage.

What is the best time of year to move large boxwoods?   Commercial tree movers transplant them at any time of the year. The home gardener might best do it in early spring or very early fall.

Would small boxwood plants, of which we have a number to be transplanted, do well along a cemented parkway around a building? How far apart and when should these be planted?   These would grow satisfactorily if given good soil and sufficient room. They should be set 15 inches apart if this is the dwarf variety, *Buxus sempervirens* 'Suffruticosa', and the plants are not over a foot tall. Transplant in early spring.

Should boxwood be covered for a time after being transplanted? If the weather is very hot, shading with a burlap screen will help cut down the water loss. Also syringing the foliage during the evenings of hot days will aid young boxwoods in pulling through. Covering such young plants the first winter is a good practice.

What winter and summer care do boxwoods require? A thick mulch of leaves or straw on the soil for the winter; plenty of water during hot, dry summer weather.

Many of the leaves of my boxwood drop off in midsummer and the plants become unsightly. What causes this? Probably the boxwood leafminer, the most serious of boxwood pests. The tiny maggots tunnel within the leaves, causing irregular swellings or blisters in the leaf. Spray with methoxychlor, diazinon, or malathion in early spring.

When should I spray my boxwoods for boxwood leafminer? Timing is most important. Keep a close watch on the undersides of the leaves during April and early May. When the pupae begin to get active, it is necessary to spray right away with malathion. A better way to determine the timing is to open some of the blisters and if the pupae have black heads it is time to spray. When the infestation is heavy, one spraying is not sufficient, so spray with malathion again early in the summer. Follow the directions on the container and observe all precautions.

When is the best time to trim boxwood? Late June.

Can boxwood be trimmed close to the ground in order to thicken the growth at the base of the plant, where many of the limbs are very lanky? In the case of old plants with very thick trunks and branches, it is practically impossible to coax new growth from the base. In young plants, this may be feasible, but cutting heavy branches back severely should be avoided.

How shall I protect old, very large, and dense boxwood during the winter? Prune out any dead or diseased branches. Thoroughly water, if the ground is dry. This is frequently necessary, for winter injury may result if they enter the winter with dry roots. Cover with burlap supported on wood frames if injured by winter in previous years.

What makes some boxwood turn reddish brown in winter? Is there any remedy? Either too low temperatures or too much bright, warm sun while the ground is still frozen. The remedy is to protect the box-wood with a screen of wood, burlap, or pine boughs.

What makes boxwood growth die in winter? Many complex physio-logical factors. The chief cause of winterkill is bright, warm sunshine in early spring while the ground remains frozen. Another cause is low tem-perature.

Is the true dwarf boxwood hardy in Boston? It will survive with protection, but is not reliably hardy there.

How can I root cuttings of boxwood? Put them in polyethylene-enclosed boxes of sharp sand or a mixture of sand and peat moss in July or August. Remove to a frost-proof building during the winter months.

CAMELLIA (See also Regional Section and Specific Tender Shrubs, this section.)

In a southern garden I saw an evergreen shrub in which I became very interested. The owner called it Camellia japonica. It had a double flower like a rose and was as large. Please tell me where I can buy this shrub. (Pennsylvania.) Camellias in many beautiful forms and colors can be obtained from southern nurseries. *C. sasanqua* and possibly *C. japonica* will be hardy for you in Pennsylvania if you live in the moder-ate areas. They probably would not survive in the western part of the state and certainly not in the mountains. Pick as protected a location as you have with some shade in the winter and summer. Some camellias are being successfully grown in New Jersey, on Long Island, and on Cape Cod, but they are mainly shrubs for mild climates.

DAPHNE

I have tried Daphne cneorum (rose daphne) many times and had no luck. I tried full sun, half shade, shade in sandy soil enriched with fertil-izer, wet soil, dry soil, and also clay soil. Can you advise? As a matter of fact, it grows in *both* acid and alkaline types of soil. More important, the soil should be a sandy loam and well drained. Shade has little to do with it. Such successive failures as indicated above would point to the possibility that the acidity or alkalinity of the soil might be at fault and the soil should be made more neutral.

Is it possible to transplant a daphne which has been in one place for 5 years? (Michigan.) If the daphne is growing satisfactorily in its present position, it would be better not to attempt to move it. If it must be moved, transplant in the spring with a ball of earth—as large as possible —around the roots.

What is the proper method of pruning Daphne cneorum? My plants sprawl all over the place. It is the nature of this species to be wide-spreading. Pinching out the tips of the growing shoots will help keep it more compact.

Can Daphne odora be pruned? Daphnes tend to resent severe pruning. You can keep them compact by pinching out the tips of the growing shoots.

Should a daphne plant receive special protection during the winter? Generally it seems desirable to protect *Daphne cneorum* from winter sun and wind, though some plants come through perfectly without any protection, even when exposed to morning sun. A loosely arranged overcoat of pine branches is sufficient.

How can an amateur best propagate the dwarf daphne? The rose daphne can be rooted from cuttings, but with difficulty by usual means. Under constant mist, 100 per cent rooting can be expected. Shoots can be layered in the usual way. Another method (mound layering) is to place sandy soil in among the shoots in the form of a mound, leaving only a few inches of the ends of the shoots protruding. At the end of the season, the earth is drawn away and rooted shoots are cut off and potted singly. The great objection to the latter method is that the resulting plants are rather spindly.

ELAEAGNUS

I recently encountered in the fall (on Long Island, New York) a beautiful evergreen shrub trained against a wall with small white flowers with a haunting fragrance. I was told that it was an elaeagnus. Is there a fall-blooming evergreen elaeagnus? You probably saw *Elaeagnus pungens,* the thorny elaeagnus, which does flower in October and is famous for its fragrance. It is quite common in the South but Long Island is a bit north of its range. Probably the wall helps to protect it during cold winters.

EUONYMUS (WINTERCREEPER)

Which evergreen euonymus does not climb but remains a shrub? *Euonymus japonica,* not reliably hardy north of Washington,

D.C., and varieties of *E. fortunei*. One is the cultivar 'Carrierei'. Another is *E. fortunei vegeta,* but this will climb if near a wall.

HOLLY (ILEX)

What is the difference between Osmanthus aquifolium and holly?   Osmanthus is often mistaken for holly because of the similarity of the foliage, but they are easily distinguished by the opposite leaves of osmanthus and the alternate leaves of holly. There is no close botanical relationship between the two.

What is the hardiest kind of holly? We have a "Christmas garden" and would like to add this to it. (Massachusetts.)   The American holly (*Ilex opaca*) might grow near the coast, if protected; English holly probably would not, except in very sheltered locations. *I. pedunculosa* and the native inkberry, *I. glabra,* are the hardiest, but they do not look like the Christmas holly. The deciduous winterberry (*I. verticillata*) is also very hardy and has beautiful Christmas-red berries.

Does the American holly grow low or high?   Both the American and English hollies are trees, growing eventually to 50 feet or more in height.

What kind of soil does the American holly prefer?   A light, sandy soil containing some decaying leafmold. Heavy clay soils should be avoided in planting hollies.

What fertilizer shall I use for American holly?   If it is growing well, do not apply any fertilizer. Well-rotted leafmold, worked well into the soil, is about the best material that can be applied. Rotted manure or compost can be applied in the late fall as a mulch. Hollies prefer a light, sandy soil.

When is the best time to plant a holly tree?   In early September or early April, just as the new leaf buds begin to open.

When and how is it best to transplant holly, especially in a hedge?   In areas where the climate is moist, either spring or very early fall. In the eastern United States, very early spring is usually best. The plants should be dug carefully with a ball of earth around the roots. If planted as a hedge, space 2 feet apart.

How can I most successfully transplant hollies?   The safest way is to move them with a ball of earth around the roots. If they are to be dug up in the woods, sizable trees should be root-pruned a year in advance of transplanting.

Is it possible to raise holly that is used for Christmas decorations in

Maine, or is that too far north? Maine is too far north. The northernmost limit for American holly is Cape Cod. English holly can be grown very little in the northeast except on Cape Cod and Long Island and farther south near the coast.

Can I get holly to grow in my garden? (Michigan.) It is doubtful if either the American or the English holly will grow in Michigan except in extremely well-protected situations.

Is it true that in Ohio holly should be planted where the winter sun will not hit it? It is not the winter sun so much as the high, dry winds of late winter which injure holly trees. If these are prevalent, it will pay to protect the holly trees from such winds.

Where is the beautiful English holly grown commercially? In the moist regions of Oregon and Washington.

I have set out native American hollies, using leafmold and soil from the woods as a fill around their roots. How should I fertilize and care for them from now on? You have done the best possible. Keep the soil moist, sprinkle the tops in the evening of hot days throughout the first summer. If you have good soil, do not fertilize until one year after transplanting.

How shall I care for small holly trees? Water well, especially through the first summer after transplanting. Apply a mulch of well-rotted leafmold in the fall and place a protective screening of burlap or pine boughs around them the first few winters

Why do some English holly trees have no berries? The male, or pollen-bearing, trees never have berries. Only the trees with the female, or pistillate, flowers will fruit.

I have a thriving grafted English holly which produces a good berry crop each year. When the berries are half formed, they all drop. I have tried less water, more water, and fertilizer—with no results. Why? This sounds very much as if the female flowers had not been properly fertilized with pollen. A male tree should be nearby to make certain that pollination occurs.

We have a female English holly which flowers, but no berries set. I have tried grafting male cuttings, but none took. Would you suggest that I try budding instead? If so, what type of bud, and when and where on the limbs should I do the budding? English hollies can easily be budded. Use the shield bud, commonly used in propagating peaches. Insert buds in August or very early September. Be certain that only the pointed leaf buds found on the more vigorous shoots are used. Insert buds only on the current year's growth. (See Propagation.)

What is the matter with a holly tree that has stopped producing berries, even though male trees are present?   Such incidents are difficult to explain. Some trees are alternate in their bearing habit, having a large crop of fruits one year and very few fruits the next. Sometimes a cold, rainy season, just when the pollen is ripe, prevents its distribution by wind and insects.

A holly tree purchased three years ago, which then had berries, has failed to produce them since. The pH of the soil is 5.4, and there is a male tree within 70 feet. Why does it fail to bear?   It may be recuperating from the shock of being transplanted. Fertilize and water well. Berries will soon be formed if the nearby tree flowers and really is a male.

When and to what extent should holly trees be pruned?   Pruning, especially of fruiting plants, might be done just before Christmas, by cutting short branches for decoration. Other pruning should be limited to taking out dead or diseased wood and crossed branches. Slight trimming, to make the tree dense and compact in habit, can be done during early spring before growth starts.

How can one tell the sex of a lone holly plant? I want to buy more but don't know which sex is needed.   Observe the flowers, which are very small, inconspicuous, and appear in late spring. The pistillate, or fruiting, flowers have a well-developed pistil in the center and undeveloped stamens. In the male flowers, the pistil is small and undeveloped, and the stamens bear pollen.

Should you plant more than one Burford holly for it to produce berries?   No, the Chinese holly (*Ilex cornuta,* of which the Burford holly is a variety) is unique among the hollies in this respect. The fruiting plants will bear fruits even though their flowers do not receive pollen from male plants.

How is English or American holly propagated from cuttings?   In a greenhouse, either in sand or a mixture of sand and peat; or vermiculite or a mixture of vermiculite and perlite have proved satisfactory. Use cuttings 4 to 5 inches long taken in August or September. Shade with cheesecloth and keep the bottom at a temperature of 75° F.

Does inkberry (Ilex glabra) have attractive fruits? If not, why is it popular?   While the inconspicuous flowers are small, the female plants have attractive black berries and glossy leaves, somewhat like boxwood. It is hardy, shade-enduring, and able to withstand city growing conditions.

Recently I admired an evergreen hedge which the owner said was a holly. It had rather small, glistening leaves without the "points" found

on holly foliage. **Could this have been a holly?** Yes, probably a form of Japanese holly (*Ilex crenata*), and possibly the form known as 'Convexa', which has foliage resembling boxwood. The Japanese holly is a superior evergreen shrub, quite hardy, and with many named forms. (Not all hollies have prickly foliage, nor are they all evergreens.)

LEUCOTHOE

What is Leucothoe fontanesiana? How is it used? This is an evergreen with arching stems clothed with handsome long racemes of small fragrant white flowers and long, oval leathery leaves. Provide acid soil and partial shade. It is good for woodland plantings with rhododendron, mountain-laurel, and hemlock, and excellent in foundation plantings.

MAGNOLIA (See also Flowering Trees.)

Is Magnolia grandiflora hardy in the North? There is a large specimen growing in a sheltered spot in Brooklyn, New York, but it is not usually reliably hardy north of Washington, D.C.

MAHONIA (HOLLY-GRAPE)

Is Oregon holly-grape the low-growing shrub with leaflets something like holly? This is *Mahonia aquifolium* (Oregon holly-grape), but the leaves are compound and not simple as are those of holly. The leaves vary from deep green to rich purple-red. If its environment is suitable and not too exposed, it has clusters of small yellow flowers followed by little grapelike bunches of bluish-black berries. It prefers half shade.

Which kind of mahonia is used as a ground cover? *Mahonia repens.*

What exposure suits the mahonia? A northeast exposure, where it gets enough winter sun to bring out the bronzy colors in the foliage but not enough sun and wind to scorch the leaves.

Is mahonia (Oregon holly-grape) hardy at sub-zero temperatures? Yes, it will withstand temperatures of 5° to 10° F. below zero. Persistent temperatures any lower than this will probably cause injury.

How and when shall I trim mahonia planted on the north side of my house? Some of it grows upright, but part of it lies almost on the ground. I thought there was only one kind of mahonia, but I seem to have two different kinds. There are several kinds, two of which are commonly grown in the East. One is upright and shrubby (*Mahonia aquifolium*) and another is really a ground cover (*M. repens*). They can best be pruned in the spring. *M. bealei* is dubiously hardy in most northern areas but is excellent in the southern states.

MOUNTAIN-LAUREL (KALMIA LATIFOLIA)

When does mountain-laurel bloom and what color are the blossoms? Will it stand shade?   Deep pink buds and pink-white flower clusters, in early June. Sun or shade.

What are some uses for mountain-laurel?   Mass plantings in woodland or as occasional accents among azalea, rhododendron, leucothoe, ferns, hemlock.

When is the proper time to transplant the wild mountain-laurel?   In the early spring, before the buds have started growth.

Is mountain-laurel hardy in Cleveland, Ohio, without any protective covering?   Yes, but be certain the soil in which it is planted is acid.

In transplanting mountain-laurel from woods, I have been generally unsuccessful, even with the utmost care. Any specific reasons?   There might be soil trouble. Perhaps by bringing in considerable leafmold and soil from the woods you could succeed in growing it. Add peat moss to your soil, also.

Will you give culture instructions for Kalmia latifolia? Mine is seven or eight years old and has never bloomed, although it seems to be healthy.   If the plant is healthy, this shows that it is growing in good soil. You might try the effect of superphosphate (15 to 20 per cent), applied beneath the mulch, at the rate of 4 ounces per square yard. Perhaps the shade is too dense.

OSMANTHUS   See Holly.

PIERIS (ANDROMEDA)

When do the "andromedas" bloom? What are the blossoms like?   Mountain andromeda (*Pieris floribunda*) has erect panicles of small cream-colored waxy bells in May. Japanese andromeda (*P. japonica*) has drooping panicles slightly longer than on the mountain andromeda. The flowers appear in the spring.

Would Japanese andromeda be hardy in northern New England?   No, but our native mountain andromeda might be.

What is the difference between our native mountain andromeda and the Japanese species?   The native mountain andromeda (*Pieris flori-*

bunda), has upright flower clusters and dull leaves, whereas *P. japonica* has graceful drooping flower clusters and lustrous leaves. The latter is better suited to formal plantings and the former to woodlands.

Which andromeda has leaves that turn reddish bronze in winter and has new spring leaves with a rose-colored cast? Japanese andromeda.

What soil is required by the andromedas? Moist, peaty, or sandy soil. Partial shade is desirable.

Would Pieris japonica survive the winter if planted on a north or west exposure with a leafmold mulch? (New York.) Yes, there should be no problem if the winter winds are not too high.

Is there any insect that attacks the leaves of pieris? The lacebug is the most serious pest of pieris foliage. This is a small insect with lace-like wings that appears on the under surface of the leaves. It appears in May and June; a second infestation follows later in the summer. Control by spraying with malathion.

When should pieris be sprayed to control the lacebug? What material should be used? Spray as soon as the insects appear, usually in June. Several materials are available for control. Use diazinon, Cygon, or malathion according to directions. Spray forcibly on the *under* surfaces of the foliage on a cloudy day when the temperature does not exceed 80° F. Spraying in full, hot sunshine will burn the foliage. Lacebug infestations disappear when pieris plants are moved into a more shady location.

PYRACANTHA (FIRETHORN)

Are any of the pyracanthas hardy? Yes. *Pyracantha coccinea,* or firethorn, is hardy in the Middle Atlantic states. It sometimes is killed by harsh winters in the vicinity of New York City, but it is grown in protected places north to Boston. The varieties 'Lalandei' and 'Kasan' are hardiest.

I would like to plant two pyracanthas, one on either side of my large living-room window, to grow against the house. However, there are three small oak trees, about 9 to 12 feet away, on the front lawn. Would their shade cause the pyracanthas not to fruit? Planting where you suggest would not be advisable. For an abundance of berries, full light is needed. Though the oaks may not be very big at present, it is probable that in a few years they would cast a shade too dense for the pyracanthas to fruit satisfactorily.

When is the best time to transplant Pyracantha coccinea 'Lalan-

dei'? This is a difficult plant to move successfully, particularly if it has attained any size. Spring is the most suitable season and it must be moved with a ball of earth. Do not attempt to remove the burlap when replanting.

What can one do to make pyracantha bushes have more berries? Keep them in good health and growing vigorously. They frequently bear good crops only in alternate years. A fertilizer rich in superphosphate, combined with root-pruning if the bush is growing vigorously, might aid in increasing fruit production. Full sunshine, or at least uninterrupted light, is a requisite.

Firethorn—one of the most colorful of berried shrubs for autumn.

How should pyracanthas be treated when dead branches appear? Pyracanthas are susceptible to fire blight, a serious disease of apples and pears, their close relatives. When this appears, cut out the branches immediately and burn them. The cut should be made considerably below the injured part.

Last year my pyracantha was full of berries. This year it had none. Why? How can I keep it from growing so tall? Most berried shrubs are alternate in their bearing, producing heavy crops one year and light crops the next. Pyracantha can be restrained at any height by pruning, preferably in the summer.

How are pyracantha cuttings rooted? Take the cuttings in July and place them in 3 to 4 inches of sand in a fairly deep box. Enclose the box with polyethylene and keep it in a position out of the sun but with good light; or root them in a greenhouse bench with a bottom heat of about 75° F.

RHODODENDRON

Which types of rhododendrons are the hardiest and the most satisfactory for growth in northern New England as mass planting, not as

specimen plants? The giant rosebay (*Rhododendron maximum*) is the hardiest of all the rhododendrons. It is not as colorful as some of the hybrids, but it can be used for massing where there is sufficient space. It is definitely not suitable for small properties.

What color are the flowers of different native rhododendrons? Carolina rhododendron, pink; Catawba rhododendron, rosy-purple; rosebay (*Rhododendron maximum*), pale pink.

How tall does the Carolina rhododendron grow? Six to 8 feet is the maximum height, usually less under cultivation.

What are some of the hardiest rhododendron species for the Boston area? *Rhododendron catawbiense; R. carolinianum; R. maximum; R. mucronulatum; R. smirnowii; R. racemosum; R. laetevirens;* and, in most areas, *R. yakusimanum.*

The foliage of many of my rhododendron plants folds tightly in the winter. Will this do harm? On the contrary, this is a natural phenomenon which occurs with many rhododendrons when the weather is cold (below freezing) and dry. The curling or folding reduces the exposed leaf surfaces and conserves moisture.

What are some of the hardiest rhododendron hybrids? 'Album grandiflorum', white; 'Atrosanguineum', red; 'Charles Dickens', red; 'Mrs. C. S. Sargent', persian rose; 'Purpureum Elegans', violet; 'Purpureum Grandiflorum', purple; 'Lady Armstrong', pink.

Please suggest some rhododendron hybrids that are not magenta-colored and that are hardy. 'Boule de Neige', white; 'Nova Zembla', red; 'County of York', white; 'Caroline', fragrant, mauve; 'Vernus', early, pink; 'Ramapo', violet; 'Windbeam', pink; 'Wyanokie', white; 'Scintillation', pink; 'Catawbiense Album', white; 'Ignatius Sargent', red.

I have recently become interested in rhododendrons. Where can I find detailed information on these plants? In *Rhododendrons of the World,* by David Leach (Charles Scribner's Sons, New York); *Rhododendrons and Their Relatives, a Handbook* (Brooklyn Botanic Garden, Brooklyn, New York); *Rhododendrons in America,* by Ted Van Veen (Sweeney, Krist & Dimm, Inc., Portland, Oregon). Also join the American Rhododendron Society (see Sources for Further Information, Plant Societies).

Is there a rhododendron with fragrant flowers? Yes. There are several species with fragrant flowers and many hybrids of these species have inherited this desirable characteristic. Some are hardy only in the benign climates of the Pacific Northwest, but one very hardy hybrid, suitable for colder climates, is 'Caroline'. Its pale mauve flowers have a delicious perfume. There are others, some of the hardier hybrids being derived from *Rhododendron fortunei*.

Can I successfully propagate rhododendrons from cuttings?   Once considered nearly impossible for the home gardener, with the advent of polyethylene and root-inducing hormone powders, such propagation is possible for the amateur. Take the cuttings from the new growth in late summer, remove all but three or four leaves, and after dipping the end of the stem in the rooting powder (available from garden centers and seed houses), insert the cutting in a half-and-half mixture of sand and peat moss in a flat or pot. Water thoroughly. Then enclose the flat or pot in a tent of polyethylene, stretching it over a flat-topped wire frame. The polyethylene should be stapled or fastened securely so that a humid atmosphere exists within the flat. Keep the flat out of direct sunshine but somewhere that it can receive light and give it a bottom heat of about 75° F. For faster rooting and growth, the flat can be kept in a frost-free room during the winter with the temperature of the sand-peat moss mixture at about 70° F. Rhododendrons and evergreen azaleas respond well to fluorescent lights.

SKIMMIA

Would you recommend growing Skimmia japonica as far north as Long Island, New York?   Yes. This evergreen appears to be more hardy than once believed, but it should be in the shade and protected from strong winds.

I have had a skimmia for two years, and while it always flowers, it never produces berries. What is wrong?   You must be growing the male plant. As with some hollies, both a female and male plant are necessary for the fruiting of *Skimmia japonica*. (See the next question.)

I have heard that there is a skimmia species in which both female and male flowers and berries are borne on the same plant. What is it?   This is true. The plant is *Skimmia reevesiana* and it is similar to *S. japonica* but seldom reaches over 1½ feet in height.

VIBURNUM, EVERGREEN

Is there a good evergreen viburnum?   Yes, the leatherleaf viburnum (*Viburnum rhytidophyllum*), with long, oval, leathery wrinkled leaves. Protect it from too much winter sun. It is not reliably hardy north of

New York. The popular evergreen viburnums are used in southern gardens and in the Pacific Northwest where the climate is mild, namely the sweet viburnum (*V. odoratissimum*) and laurestinus (*V. tinus*).

Specific Tender Shrubs

ACACIA (MIMOSA)

Where can I get plants of the acacia with small yellow blossoms? Can it be grown in the garden? (Missouri.) Many California nurseries can supply acacias. They are either trees or shrubs. They are not hardy where winter temperatures drop below 20° F. In the North, they are grown in greenhouses.

BAY TREE (LAURUS)

How hardy is bay tree or sweet bay and when is the best time to trim it to formal shape? It is not really hardy north of Philadelphia, Pennsylvania. Trim when the new shoots have almost completed their growth. A second trimming may be necessary if the first stimulates the production of new shoots.

CAMELLIA

At what pH do camellias grow best? Will they do better at 5.7 to 6.2 or from 6 to 7? Camellias are less particular in this regard than gardenias and some other plants. They should thrive in either of the soils mentioned, providing it is physically in good condition and is fertile.

What soil preparation is necessary for camellias? (California.) Make the soil rich and friable to a depth of at least a foot, or better still, 2 feet. Mix with it very generous amounts of leafmold or peat moss and very old rotted manure. Good compost can also be used.

What is the best fertilizer for camellias? When should it be applied? Old cow manure (or dehydrated manure or cottonseed meal, plus compost) applied as a mulch at the beginning of the growing season, followed a few weeks later by a light dressing of any complete fertilizer.

What is the best way to start and grow camellias?   For outdoor culture, prepare the ground so that it is rich and well drained but retentive of moisture. Select a lightly shaded position. Obtain good plants. If possible, visit gardens and nurseries where camellias are grown and familiarize yourself with their needs.

When is the best time to move Camellia japonica?   During the dormant season, in winter or in early spring.

Can camellias be forced to bloom earlier? If so, how?   They can be encouraged to bloom early by planting them in sheltered locations; a more certain method is to grow them in pots, tubs, or planted out in ground beds in a cool, airy greenhouse.

What causes few blossoms, rather than many, on a well-fertilized camellia bush?   Possibly the plant is in too dense shade. Some protection from strong sunlight is helpful, but lack of sufficient light is harmful. Also overfertilization may result in too vigorous growth at the expense of flower production.

What is it that eats holes in camellia leaves? I have never found anything on them and no spray that I have used seems to do any good.   Probably the Asiatic beetle or the black vine weevil. Before specific advice can be given, a surer diagnosis is desirable. Send specimens to your State Agricultural Experiment Station.

What causes my camellia leaves to fall off?   Damage to roots due to careless transplanting; waterlogged soil; lack of sufficient water, particularly during the growing season; or spray damage.

What causes the leaves of an apparently healthy camellia plant to turn brown just before coming into blossom?   This can be due to very cold weather, disease, or extreme drought. Spray injury could also be responsible.

My camellia has a rusty coat on its buds and they do not open in the spring. What should I do? (Texas.)   You seemingly have a variety unsuited to outdoor conditions. There are some kinds that are satisfactory in greenhouses but not outdoors. Replace the plant with a variety recommended by a local nursery.

Will frequent sprinkling of camellias cause their buds to rot and drop off? I understand they should be sprinkled during hot weather.   Spraying of the foliage during hot weather is beneficial. Make sure, however, that the ground is kept moist to a good depth. Do not be deceived by merely wetting the soil surface.

Why do many full buds fall off my red camellias late in the season? They are planted on the east side of my house and have only the morn-

ing sun. Should they be moved? The most common reason for buds dropping is lack of sufficient moisture at the roots of the plant. This is particularly true of secondary buds that develop if a late frost has killed early growth. Certain diseases also cause buds to drop.

Can I increase my favorite camellia by layering? Yes, in June or July, nick a low branch with a knife, bend it to the ground, hollow out a little trench, and lay the branch in this. Cover with sandy soil and use a brick or other heavy object to prevent motion. Be sure that the layer is kept constantly moist.

How and when can we start camellias from cuttings? July. Select firm, young growths, 3 or 4 inches long; cut away lower leaves and cut the stem horizontally below the joint with a sharp knife. Plant firmly in sand, or sand and peat moss. Keep lightly shaded, moist, and in a humid atmosphere. A slight bottom heat helps rooting.

What makes the buds on my 'Soeur Therese' camellia turn brown on the edges of its petals? This can be due to flower-blight disease. Send specimens to your Agricultural Experiment Station for examination.

What is the scurfy white substance on the underside of my camellia leaves? This is tea scale and must be controlled by carefully spraying with a white-oil emulsion or Cygon after flowering.

The leaves on one of my camellias have large dark spots and drop off the tree. What causes this? Possibly black mold disease, which is often associated with another infection called spot disease. Grow your plants under pines or in light shade.

GARDENIA   (See also House Plants, Section 12.)

I know cape-jasmine (gardenia) requires acid soil. I have fed it copperas (ferrous sulfate) and aluminum sulfate, but still the leaves are yellow and smutty and there are no blooms. Can anything be done? Use more natural methods of acidifying the soil. Mix oak leafmold, rotted pine needles, or peat moss with the soil in a proportion of 1 to 3. The smutty appearance is indicative of the presence of scale insects. Spray with malathion to get rid of them.

When is the best time to transplant a gardenia that is crowded in its present location? At the very beginning of the growing season, when new shoots and leaves are starting to grow.

Can gardenia plants remain outside in a garden all year-round? (New York.) Even with protection, gardenias are not hardy in New York.

Southeastern Virginia is about as far north as *Gardenia jasminoides* can be successfully grown outdoors.

How can I make gardenias bloom in my yard?   The cape-jasmine, or *Gardenia jasminoides,* needs a sheltered, sunny position, a moist (not waterlogged) acid soil, and protection from frost.

Is it necessary to protect small gardenia plants by building a frame around them and wrapping with sacks?   They need protection of this kind if there is danger that they will encounter frost.

JASMINE

Which jasmines are hardy in the North?   None reliably hardy, though *Jasminum nudiflorum* (a good wall shrub), blooming very early before leaves appear, can be grown in the vicinity of New York City if given a southern exposure with the protection of a sheltering wall. *J. humile,* an erect evergreen to 20 feet with yellow flowers, and *J. officinale,* climbing, with white flowers, are grown near the seaboard in the Middle Atlantic states.

Can jasmine (the flowers of which are used for tea) be grown as far north as Cleveland, Ohio?   Not very well. In a protected spot it might live through the winter; normally one would expect it not to be hardy.

OLEANDER (NERIUM)

Are oleanders easy to grow?   Yes, in the Deep South and in Southern California. There are nearly fifty varieties offered commercially. Bamboolike in habit—with flowers of white, purple, pink, red, and yellow, single or double—they do well in hot, dry areas. They are often used as hedges or as tub plants. The leaves are toxic and can cause dermatitis.

Will you tell me how to start cuttings of oleanders?   Cuttings taken in July and August root readily in sand if kept in close, humid surroundings such as a hotbed or polyethylene-covered box. Or shoots may be kept in water until rooted, and then potted in soil.

POMEGRANATE (PUNICA)

What soil is best for pomegranate?   A heavy, deep loam. They are suited only to tropical and subtropical climates, or for the greenhouse or indoor garden in the North.

When should a pomegranate (flowering) be pruned? Shorten strong-growing shoots about one third when they have attained almost their full length.

Hedges

WHAT TO GROW

What would be the best kind of hedge to set out on the north side of a lot? This depends on the height. For under 6 feet a yew hedge would be good, but expensive. For over 6 feet a hemlock or white pine hedge would be suitable. These are evergreens and so would give protection 365 days a year. Evergreen hedges cost more, but they are worth it for their winter protection.

Which flowering hedge would look well around a vegetable garden? It should be low so that it will not shade the vegetables. Spirea 'Anthony Waterer', with its flat-topped, deep rose-red flowers, would give color to the area. Prune back after it has bloomed and more blossoms should follow. Also *Berberis thunbergii* 'Minor' would be good. Why don't you select something attractive but more practical? For example, a blueberry or raspberry hedge, kept pruned to about 4 to 5 feet.

Which flowering shrubs would make good hedge plants, even if unpruned? Barberry, especially upright-growing types; *Abelia grandiflora;* Siberian pea tree (*Caragana*); Japanese quince, especially the 'Spitfire'; deutzia; hydrangea; bush honeysuckle; spirea; common lilac; many of the viburnums. Unpruned California privet makes a good tall hedge or screen and Regel privet makes a good low hedge (4 to 5 feet) if unpruned.

What are the beautiful hedges made of that one sees in England? Can they be grown here? (Maryland.) Many different species are used. Perhaps you refer to the English hawthorn and English holly combination. This could be done here by substituting American holly for the less-hardy English species where the latter is not hardy. However, the English hawthorn has too many pests in America to make it the best choice in a hedge here.

What would be a good low deciduous hedge, not over 2 feet high, to put around a sunken garden? One of the dwarf barberries (*Berberis* *thunbergii* 'Minor'), slender deutzia, the dwarf cranberry-bush viburnum (*Viburnum opulus* 'Nanum').

What would be good as a fairly high deciduous hedge for screening? Acanthopanax, corkbark or winged euonymus, rose-of-Sharon, privet, buckthorn, Vanhoutte's spirea, various lilacs.

Could you suggest some good deciduous trees that would screen our garage driveway from our terrace—something natural-looking for an informal place where there is plenty of room? (Massachusetts.) Tallhedge or alder buckthorn (*Rhamnus frangula* 'Columnaris') is vigorous, tall, and narrow; it grows 12 feet tall and needs no clipping. Also consider Amur maple, cornelian cherry (*Cornus mas*), Washington hawthorn, and the littleleaf European linden.

What is a hedge plant that will grow at least 6 feet tall? I do not want privet or barberry. The one I have in mind has dark berries on it. The American cranberry-bush with red berries (*Viburnum trilobum*) or the glossy buckthorn with red and black berries (*Rhamnus frangula*).

What is the difference between buckthorn (Rhamnus cathartica) and alder buckthorn (R. frangula)? Which is better for a hedge? (Maine.) The former (for Maine), because it is hardier than alder buckthorn. The latter has pointed glossy leaves, while the former has dull rounded ones.

What is the best fast-growing hedge for screening (not privet)? (North Carolina.) Myrtle (*Myrtus communis*), cherry-laurel (*Prunus laurocerasus*), Portuguese cherry-laurel (*Prunus lusitanica*).

Is a flower border or a shrub border better to screen a vegetable garden from view? Either kind of border would be proper; shrubs would be more permanent. Why not plant a yew hedge, which would not take up more than 2½ to 3 feet of width, or a single, informal row of *Spiraea* x *vanhouttei,* or bush fruits, such as blueberries or gooseberries?

What hedges are recommended for the lazy gardener who prefers not to have to clip them every week? Truehedge columnberry, the upright privet, true dwarf box, dwarf winged euonymus, the dwarf hedge yew, and other similar plants would be ideal. They need practically no clipping. At most, this need be done only once every other year.

What hedge would be best for city property—one that would need least attention? One of the best would be the five-leaved aralia (*Acanthopanax sieboldianus*). Japanese barberry hedges are also good under adverse conditions; and privet, of course—but this needs some attention eventually.

Can you suggest a neat, small, broad-leaved evergreen shrub to use at the edge of a terrace? (We want to have the plants untrimmed, but not more than a few feet high.) English ivy trained on a frame, any one of several dwarf forms of the Japanese holly (*Ilex crenata*), dwarf box, *Euonymus fortunei vegeta,* warty barberry (*Berberis verruculosa*), germander (*Teucrium*).

What is the rate of growth of a Canadian hemlock hedge? Which low shrubs would go well in front of it? A well-established young hemlock hedge in good soil will average at least 18 inches a year. Such a hedge is very beautiful, but if shrubs have to be placed in front of it, some low-growing types—coral-berry (*Symphoricarpos*), slender deutzia, roses, Oriental quinces, and the like—might be used, but not too close!

What kind of evergreen can I grow for a hedge, not more than 6 feet high, that will keep a neat shape without needing to be sheared? Hicks yew will do this, although it will take quite a few years for it to grow 6 feet high if small plants are purchased. Farther south the Irish yew would be ideal. Another would be the glossy abelia.

What could be used for a low evergreen hedge (not box) between a vegetable garden and lawn? A yew called *Taxus canadensis* 'Stricta' or *Ilex crenata* 'Helleri' (commonly called the Heller Japanese holly).

Will spruce trees make good hedges? (New Hampshire.) Yes. Norway spruce (*Picea abies*), either trimmed or untrimmed; also various forms of white spruce (*P. glauca*). A hemlock hedge would be even better.

Are there any evergreen barberries for hedge purposes? Yes. Juliana barberry, with black berries, grows to about 5 feet. *Berberis verruculosa,* with tiny holly-like leaves, growing about half as tall, is also suitable, as well as Chenault barberry, about the same height.

What hedge material will give a soft, blue-gray tone? Moss retinospora (*Chamaecyparis pisifera* 'Squarrosa').

Which evergreens can we grow across the front of our property to form a hedge that people can neither see over nor through? Either *Ilex crenata,* red-cedar, American arborvitae, or hemlock (all are evergreen).

Can we have an evergreen hedge, unclipped, which will have berries? Yes, firethorn (*Pyracantha*) or *Taxus cuspidata* 'Nana'.

Which evergreen will make a handsome hedge that, without trimming, will never exceed 6 feet—preferably less? Dwarf Hinoki-cypress

(*Chamaecyparis obtusa* 'Compacta'). Also, other dwarf forms of this evergreen, as well as the glossy abelia and the dwarf Japanese yew.

Which trees, other than native hemlock, make a good hedge? The trees would have a northern exposure and semiclay soil. The hedge is wanted for beauty as well as to serve as a windbreak. White pine, red pine, red-cedar, Serbian spruce. Hemlock would be the most ornamental.

Which tall evergreen—not too expensive—would you suggest for use as a fence along a boundary line? Hemlock or white pine.

FERTILIZERS AND PLANTING

What is a good fertilizer for hedges? Any complete commercial fertilizer. For instance, 5–10–5 might be applied at the rate of 5 to 10 pounds per 100 square feet of hedge, depending on the size of the plants.

How shall I plan a hedge? Decide whether you want it low or high, thorny or flowering, evergreen or deciduous. Decide why you want a hedge and select the best plant material to fit the need. (See above.)

How does one plant a hedge? Dig a trench 2 feet wide, 1 to 2 feet deep, close to property lines, but at a safe distance away from the sidewalk or street, so the hedge will have plenty of space to expand up to the size at which it is to be permanently maintained. Put well-rotted manure or compost on the bottom of the trench, then some good soil, and tamp firmly. Space the plants 1 to 3 feet apart (depending on size), filling in soil about their roots. Make firm, and water well. Cut back severely if a deciduous shrub is being used.

How far apart (approximately) should 6- to 8-foot shrubs be planted for screening purposes? It depends upon the kinds used and on how quickly you want a solid screen. For instance, rose-of-Sharon might be set 6 to 7 feet apart; the Morrow honeysuckle, 8 to 10 feet apart; and the tallhedge (*Rhamnus frangula* 'Columnaris'), only 4 feet apart.

When is the best time to move a hedge of flowering shrubs? Should they be cut back? We want to keep them as large as possible for a screen. They can be moved after the leaves have fallen in the autumn, or in the early spring. In transplanting, cut their tops back about one third for best results.

TRIMMING AND TRAINING

What is the best way to prune hedges? Different sorts of plants used as hedges demand different treatments. Large plants like white pine and spruce should be allowed to retain approximately their outline. Hemlock hedges should always be much wider at the bottom than at the top. Large privet hedges should also be somewhat wider at the bottom, although smaller ones can be trimmed with the sides vertical. Regel privet and other shrubs of that sort should be allowed to grow as naturally as possible. Hedges of dwarf yew should be broader than they are high. Dwarf boxwood and other edging plants can be trimmed to a rectangular shape.

How should one prune a deciduous hedge the first year? Cut back to within 6 to 12 inches of the ground at planting time. Lightly shear whenever new shoots reach a height of 10 to 12 inches if a close, compact hedge is needed.

Should hedges be trimmed to any special shape? Wider at the bottom, preferably with a rounded top.

Do all hedge plants have to be trimmed several times in the season? No. Most evergreens can be kept tidy with one shearing. The same is true of such deciduous shrubs as barberry, buckthorn, and spirea.

Should hedges be trimmed during the winter? This can be done with no injury to deciduous hedges. It is best to let it go until spring, however.

How shall I cut a hedge in order to make it grow? Cutting or pruning never makes a hedge "grow." Good soil, fertilizer, and plenty of water for the roots make a hedge grow.

I have heard that constant trimming devitalizes a hedge. Is this true? Yes, to some extent. Privet, for example, sheared every 3 weeks is more likely to succumb to the effect of a severe winter than one sheared only 2 or 3 times during the growing season.

Are electric hedge shears satisfactory? Yes, a good type will do the work in about one fourth the time required with hand shears.

Is it necessary to cultivate the soil along a hedge? Yes. Primarily to keep out weeds that might grow and choke the lower branches of a hedge, especially when it is small. Or you may apply a mulch to suppress the weeds.

Specific Hedge Plants

ARBORVITAE (THUJA)

How shall I plant an arborvitae hedge? (The topsoil is rather poor and only 9 inches deep.)   Dig a trench 2 feet wide and 1½ feet deep. Put topsoil on one side. Either remove 9 inches of subsoil and replace with good soil or take out 3 inches and fork in 4 to 5 inches of rotted manure, compost, or peat moss and make firm by tramping. Return the topsoil and proceed with planting. The young trees should be set from 18 inches to 3 feet apart, according to their size.

When and how should an arborvitae hedge, about 18 inches high, be trimmed?   Top it evenly, during the period of spring growth, to about 1 foot high. Thereafter, if you want a solid hedge, permit it to gain each year not more than 6 inches until the desired height has been reached. From then on, keep it closely sheared.

BARBERRY (BERBERIS)

What is the best treatment to produce a thriving barberry hedge?   Give it good soil to grow in from the start. Fertilize with rotted manure or commercial fertilizers once a year if needed. Keep watered during very dry spells. In trimming, keep the hedge slightly wider at the base than at the top.

When and in what manner should barberry and privet hedges be trimmed?   Always trim hedges so that they are wider at the base than the top, thus giving the lower branches plenty of exposure. Trimming might best be done when the young shoots are half grown or nearly full grown in late spring. However, trimming can be done without injury at practically any time.

BOXWOOD (BUXUS)

What time of year is best for planting a boxwood hedge?   Either early spring or early fall.

CARAGANA (PEA-SHRUB)

At what season should a caragana hedge be trimmed for the first time? At the time it is planted; not again until the very early spring of the next year.

CYPRESS, MONTEREY (CUPRESSUS)

What is the cause of scant foliage on the lower part of a Monterey cypress hedge? (California.) There is not sufficient room at the base. Hedges should be *wider* at the base than the top; this gives the lower branches plenty of sunlight and exposure. When hedges are clipped perpendicularly, or narrower at the base than at the top, the lower branches can be expected to become sickly and die.

ELM, SIBERIAN (ULMUS PUMILA)

To make Siberian elms form a thick hedge, what procedure should be followed? Cut them back hard. Any plants up to 3 inches in diameter at the base (and possibly larger) could be cut back to within 6 inches of the ground. Then a trimming before active growth has stopped, and another trimming a month later, will aid in forcing bushy growth.

HEMLOCK (TSUGA)

What is the best way to grow a thick hemlock hedge and yet not stop its upward growth too much? Allow it to elongate upward a full year untrimmed, then merely trim off the terminal buds of the branches several times during the next season. If it thickens up well in that year, allow it to grow with little trimming the next, and so on. This would be true of most evergreen hedges.

Will a hemlock hedge thrive in a northwestern exposure without protection from sweeping winds? It depends on the area. If in the Middle Atlantic states, or in the South, yes. If in the extreme northern parts of Minnesota, Illinois, or Wisconsin, where winds are high and extremely cold, some "burning" might result in the winter. If in the Midwest, where winds are very hot and dry in the summer, the answer is, No!

In planting 18-inch hemlock bushes for a hedge, should their spacing be 2 feet or less? The best spacing would be 18 inches apart.

When do you shear a hemlock hedge? Shorten new growth about the end of June.

LAUREL, CHERRY- (PRUNUS LAUROCERASUS)

When is the best time to prune a cherry-laurel hedge? This can be pruned at any time. The best time (i.e., when one trimming would do the most good) is when the new shoots have nearly completed their growth for the current year. To avoid cutting the leaves, use pruning shears rather than hedge shears.

LILAC (SYRINGA)

What is your opinion of having purple lilac for a hedge? It makes a splendid tall hedge, but you must remember that the more it is clipped, the more flower buds are removed. Also, in many places it must be sprayed annually for bad infestations of lilac scale.

PINE, WHITE (PINUS STROBUS)

How does one trim white pine into a compact hedge, solid from the ground up? Trim during the period of soft growth, reducing the new, candlelike growth, but not pruning into old wood. Permit only a slight annual gain in height. Shape the hedge so that it tapers up from a wide base to a narrower, rounded top. Keep the base free from weeds.

PRIVET (LIGUSTRUM)

I want to plant a waxleaf privet hedge. Please tell me how tall this privet grows? How far apart should I set the plants? What kind of soil do they need? (New Jersey.) This privet (*Ligustrum lucidum*), untrimmed, can grow up to 30 feet in height. For a hedge, space 18 to 36 inches apart and keep trimmed to the height desired. Privets grow well in either acid or alkaline soil, but this species would be hardy only from southern New Jersey southward.

In the first warm spell can I spread bone meal around my California privet hedge so that it can get a quick start in the spring? I planted the hedge last May. You can, but the "early start" would be doubtful, for bone meal is very slow in taking effect. You might better use a commercial fertilizer, such as 5–10–5.

How low should a privet hedge be cut when it is planted? Shorten all branches at least two thirds.

What is the procedure for trimming a newly planted privet hedge in order to make it bushy? Shear it whenever the new shoots attain a length of about 1 foot, cutting them back one half.

What should I do with an old overgrown privet hedge? Cut it off 6 inches above the ground in the early spring and in this way force it to start anew.

How often is it necessary to shear a privet hedge? About 3 times during the growing season, giving the last clipping early in the fall. It is better to shear every few weeks if a very trim hedge is required.

I was unable to trim and shape my privet hedge last fall. Now it is unsightly. When is the earliest time to trim? A privet hedge can be trimmed any time of the year.

What makes a privet hedge die from the roots? The common privet (*Ligustrum vulgare*) is subject to a serious blight which kills the plants and for which there is no known cure. Better use some other kind; they all do well in normal soils.

When is the time to make cuttings of privet hedges? How do you go about doing it? Late spring or early summer is best. Take 6-inch cuttings of the new wood and place them in sand in a hotbed, with some bottom heat if possible. Keep moist but not wet; shade; they should be rooted in 4 weeks or less.

ROSA MULTIFLORA (LIVING FENCE ROSE)

Do you approve the use of Rosa multiflora as a hedge plant? It grows much too large for use on small properties but is satisfactory for a country property or farm. A 3-year-old hedge can be 8 feet high and 12 feet across.

SPIREA (SPIRAEA)

At what time of the year should a spirea hedge be trimmed? Just after it has flowered. Then one gets the full benefit of the flowers.

How can you get a hedge of spirea in which the plants are set 2½ feet apart to grow together at the bottom? The best plan would be to cut it down to the ground and thus force it to make bushy new growth. If it doesn't grow together then, reset the plants 18 inches apart—as they should have been set in the first place.

SPRUCE (PICEA)

I planted a hedge of 6- to 8-foot Norway spruces 3 feet apart. How should I trim them so that they will stay thick and rich at their base? Top in the spring to 5½ or 6 feet. Thereafter, in the annual shearing, allow only a little gain in height. Trim the sides no more than necessary for an even appearance. Shape the hedge so that it tapers from a wide base to a narrow, rounded top.

TAMARISK (TAMARIX)

Can tamarisk be used for a hedge? It makes an excellent informal hedge. If it is a late-blooming species, cut it back in the spring. If it is a May- or June-flowering species, cut it back when the flowers have faded.

WILLOW (SALIX)

Can you tell me whether a golden willow hedge is suitable for a boundary around a farm building? (Iowa.) If a tall, quick-growing hedge is required and there is plenty of room, the willow would be quite suitable, but it would always require a lot of shearing.

YEW (TAXUS)

What distance apart should Japanese yew (2 to 3 feet) be planted for a straight borderline hedge? Eighteen inches is best, but if this costs too much, 24 to 30 inches would do. It would take the hedge a longer time to grow together in the second instance.

When is the best time to trim a yew hedge? It can be trimmed almost any time. Trim "wild" shoots in the spring; major shearing should be at the end of June.

Windbreaks

For how great a distance is a windbreak effective? About 20 times its height. To get the maximum benefit, you need several shrubs or trees planted together.

Which trees are suitable for use as windbreaks? If the soil is sandy, red pine and Scots pine. For sandy loam, white pine, Douglas-fir, spruce. For heavy soil, arborvitae, balsam fir, white spruce.

We need a windbreak on the west line of our property. The spot is quite shaded. Would Scots or Jack pine thrive there? No, not in the shade. Use hemlock if height is needed; or Japanese yew for upright form.

Which evergreens are best to use for a windbreak? We get heavy windstorms from the southwest and the garden is on a hill sloping to the south. Red pine.

What can I plant for a hedge and windbreak—something that will grow fast? There is a strong north wind all summer and there is ample space. The Siberian elm is one of the fastest-growing trees we have. Plant it thickly, about 5 feet apart, if the hedge is to be over 20 feet high; about 3 feet apart if the hedge is to be about 10 feet high. If elms are not wanted because of susceptibility to the Dutch elm disease, consider osage-orange, red oak, glossy buckthorn, lilacs, littleleaf linden, and the Norway maple.

I haven't much room on my property but I would like a windbreak on the north and west side. Any suggestions? Plant arborvitae, red-cedar, an upright form of Japanese yew, or white pine. Keep in bounds by annual pruning.

What would make a good windbreak for a garden that is exposed on all sides? Closely set evergreens, such as red-cedar, hemlock, or arborvitae, are good. A 6-foot paling fence or a storm fence might also help.

Vines and Their Culture

How do different vines climb? By clinging rootlets, such as English ivy, trumpet creeper, euonymus; by adhesive disks, such as Boston-ivy; by coiling tendrils, as balloon-vine, *Cobaea scandens,* sweet pea; by stems which twine, such as wisteria, bittersweet.

Is any special preparation needed before planting vines to grow on a house? Make sure there is sufficient depth (1½ feet) and width (2 feet) of good soil. All too often the planting area next to a foundation is filled with builder's rubbish.

WHAT TO GROW   (See also Landscaping.)

I have a partially shaded backyard in the city. Which flowering vines can be grown on the fence?   Cinnamon-vine (*Dioscorea batatas*); silver fleece-vine (*Polygonum aubertii*); wisteria. The last will bloom only if it can climb to where there is sun. All these vines need a trellis or have to be supported in some way.

Which flowering vines will look well growing over a stone wall? We would like to see the flowers from our terrace, 100 feet away.   Perennial pea, wisteria, clematis, hyacinth-bean, trumpet vine, rambler roses, climbing hydrangea.

Which flowering vines will cling, without support, to the wall of our garage?   Trumpet creeper, climbing hydrangea, Boston-ivy.

Which vines shall I grow on our clapboard house, which will need painting occasionally?   Do *not* use clinging vines, such as the ivies, climbing hydrangea, or trumpet creeper; nor wisteria, which will thrust strong stems between the clapboards, sometimes destroying them. Honeysuckle, silver fleece-vine, clematis, akebia should do well. A trellis hinged at the bottom would be advisable so you can lay it (with the vine) down at painting time.

Which hardy flowering vines will stand the winter in southwestern Massachusetts (elevation 1,800 feet)?   Bittersweet, trumpet creeper, sweet autumn clematis.

Which vines would you suggest for growing on stone walls, chimneys, and house walls?   *Euonymus fortunei;* ivy (*Hedera*), small-leaved varieties; Boston-ivy.

Which vines will grow and climb in the shade of an oak?   Virginia-creeper, wild grape, bittersweet.

Which are the best climbing vines for this area (southeast New York)?   Clematis, bittersweet, silver fleece-vine, and wisteria.

Which vines will thrive in water in the North?   None, in the northern United States.

What kind of a flowering vine or climber will grow every year to a height of 15 or 20 feet on the north side of a house, where it would get the early morning and late-afternoon sun?   Sweet autumn clematis, silver fleece-vine, and *Cobaea scandens,* an annual.

Which vine can be planted on top of a ledge where the soil is very shallow and dry in ordinary years? Foliage is desired to keep dust from the house.   Very few vines would do well under such circumstances, but bittersweet and sweet autumn clematis might be tried. Virginia-creeper is another possibility.

Which flowering vines are satisfactory for use on the north side of a house, in the shade during most of the day?   It is improbable that any flowering vine will thrive very well, but you might try trumpet honey-suckle, climbing hydrangea, or silver fleece-vine. *Cobaea scandens,* annual, and mountain fringe (*Adlumia*), a biennial, might do well.

What are some of the easiest-grown and most beautiful flowering perennial vines?   Wisteria, honeysuckles, trumpet creeper, silver fleece-vine, clematis.

I have a terrace 13 × 14 feet which is sunny most of the day. I want to "grow a roof." What would you suggest that will grow quickly, give protection in the summer, and be decorative and useful as a more permanent screen. How about a grape vine? How long would it take to provide a screen, and how many should I plant? The soil is sandy.   Grape vines would serve well. Plant 4 on each of two opposite sides. It will take at least 3 to 4 years to cover this area. The kudzu-vine might cover the areas in a shorter time—but it has no grapes!

Which woody vines are good for screening purposes?   Kudzu-vine is probably the best, for it is the fastest-growing. Dutchman's-pipe makes a very dense screen with its large rounded leaves. The bower actinidia, Virginia-creeper, and grapes are also possibilities, although the last ones have rather coarse foliage. None are evergreen.

Which vine grows the quickest as a trellis at a window for shade?   Kudzu-vine grows the fastest (and the most!) of any of our "perennial" vines. Where it is not hardy, bittersweet, the five-leaf akebia, or the bower actinidia might be used. All these are rapid-growing vines and have smaller and more interesting leaves than the large, coarse-leaved *Vitis coignetiae,* which is about the fastest-growing of the grapes.

Which flowering vine would be pretty to cover the top of a cave, the end and sides of which will be planted as a rock garden?   Sweet autumn clematis or rambler roses.

Is there an evergreen vine that will cling to a wall in the shade?   English ivy (*Hedera helix*); wintercreeper (*Euonymus fortunei radicans*).

Which evergreen vine do you recommend to hang down from the top of a driveway wall?   Wintercreeper or English ivy, where hardy.

What is the best creeping vine for walls of stucco?   *Euonymus for-*

tunei, or one of its varieties, is very good. Boston-ivy usually adheres well.

Which ivy can I plant by a doorway and hang down from the top of a place that is shaded most of the time? Either Boston-ivy or English ivy, the latter being evergreen. Give both good soil in which to grow; keep moist during dry weather.

Is there some small-leaved vine that will cling to rocks? I would like something besides ivy and euonymus. (Delaware.) Creeping fig (*Ficus pumila*). Its small leaves lie flat. It is not reliably hardy north of Baltimore, although it has been known to survive 80 miles north of New York City.

Annual Vines

We have rented a summer cottage and would like to grow some annual vines to cover a lattice. What would be appropriate, easy to grow, and have attractive flowers? Morning-glory, moonflower, scarlet runner bean, hyacinth-bean (*Dolichos*), cup-and-saucer vine (*Cobaea scandens*).

Which vine can be grown over a poultry fence to provide shade and concealment? I have tried 'Heavenly Blue' morning-glory, but my chickens eat it. Is there any annual vine distasteful to poultry? Try climbing nasturtiums, hyacinth-bean, wild cucumber, Japanese hop (humulus), scarlet runner bean, and cardinal-climber. Mix the seeds together, sow quite thickly along the bottom of your fence on the outside. Chickens may eat some seeds and leave enough of others that will grow.

Can you suggest vines—annuals—that will grow in a place that has shade three fourths of the day? Try cup-and-saucer vine (*Cobaea scandens*), hyacinth-bean, morning-glory, and cardinal-climber.

Will you give the correct information about how to grow Adlumia fungosa, or mountain fringe, from seed? I have not been at all successful. Reproduce the conditions natural to this native plant of the northeast United States. Give it a cool, damp situation, as it would have in a woodland, protected from sun and wind, with shrubs to climb on. It is a biennial, sometimes grown as an annual.

What does the scarlet runner bean look like? It resembles in leaf and habit the pole beans we grow in our vegetable gardens, but the blossoms are larger and scarlet in color. The pods and green beans are edible.

I saw a beautiful vine twining on strings to cover a cellar window wall. It had purple sweet-pea-like flowers in late summer, and then broad, flat, red-purple beans. What was it? Hyacinth-bean (*Dolichos*).

Is the cup-and-saucer vine (Cobaea scandens) a satisfactory annual? Yes, if started indoors 6 weeks before the ground warms up. Plant individual seeds in peat pots or Jiffy-7 peat pots so the roots won't be disturbed at planting time. Set out at tomato-planting time. The vine grows to the top of a 3-story house in one season. It has lovely foliage and showy buds, flowers, and seed pods in late summer and autumn. The foliage is red-purple in light frosts. The vine continues to grow until a hard freeze.

Is moonflower a good annual vine? Yes. It has large leaves and beautiful, fragrant, night-blooming flowers in late summer and autumn. Give it something to climb high on. Start indoors. (See cup-and-saucer vine.)

What is the proper procedure in propagating moonflowers? Sow seeds. Proceed as suggested for morning-glories (below) or start seeds in individual peat pots indoors in early April (as suggested above for the cup-and-saucer vine).

Is there a variety of moonflower which climbs and has colored flowers? Moonflower is a twining night-bloomer with white flowers. There are also pink varieties. Twining day-bloomers are morning-glories.

Which large-flowered morning-glories are best? 'Heavenly Blue', 'Scarlett O'Hara'—crimson; 'Pearly Gates'—a white "sport" of 'Heavenly Blue'. Start indoors in peat pots under fluorescent lights for early bloom in the North.

I would like some morning-glories (not the large-flowered varieties) for a window box. What do you suggest? You want the Japanese type (*Ipomoea nil*), in white, crimson, purple, blue, and other colors. They grow 2 to 8 feet high, while 'Heavenly Blue' grows 10 to 20 feet. Then there are the dwarf morning-glories, which grow only about a foot high.

Should I plant morning-glories in the same place a second time? Theoretically this is wrong, but practically there is little objection. Dig the soil deeply and work in decayed manure or compost; if after a few seasons the morning-glories seem to be doing less well, sow instead hyacinth-bean, *Cobaea scandens,* or tall nasturtiums.

Will you tell me how to make 'Heavenly Blue' morning-glories grow? Dig the soil 1 foot deep, mixing superphosphate with it, ¼ pound per square yard. Sow seeds about ½ inch deep and 2 inches apart after soaking in water overnight. Thin out to 6 inches from plant to plant. Make your sowings at the base of a fence, trellis, or some similar support.

Do morning-glories require a rich soil? Soil of average quality is good enough. If it is too high in nitrogen, you may have large plants with small flowers; if you work in a balanced fertilizer, however, they should have large flowers and remain in bloom for a longer period each day.

I had some 'Heavenly Blue' morning-glories and watched for seed, with no success. Shouldn't they have formed seeds? They grow readily from seeds. It is possible that fertile seeds cannot be collected in your part of the country. Seeds are produced in large quantities for the trade in Southern California.

Is there any known way to keep morning-glories open longer in the morning? No.

When picking morning-glories, how do you keep them open in the house in a container? Cut buds at sunset, selecting those ready to open. Keep in water up to their necks in a cool cellar overnight. Clip the stems and place them in position in the morning. Moonflowers cut in late afternoon will open in containers indoors.

How tall will climbing nasturtiums grow? How do they cling? To 6 feet. They climb by means of coiling leaf stalks.

SWEET PEA   See Annual Flowers, Section 8.

Woody Vines

AKEBIA

What do you recommend to mask an ugly leader pipe near our front entrance? *Akebia quinata* deserves such a place where one can view it closely. It has dainty oval leaves, five to a group, and a decorative manner of growth. It will festoon itself around any upright support. The vine will have to be tied up at intervals along a leader pipe. Sun or shade suits akebia.

Is there any vine, except English ivy, that remains green during the winter and that is suitable for covering the side of a frame building? The five-leaf akebia (*Akebia quinata*) is worthy of a trial. It climbs by twining and would have to be supplied with wire for support. It is not completely evergreen, but leaves remain on the vine long into the winter. Another evergreen vine, *Euonymus fortunei radicans,* would satisfy these requirements but it is susceptible to serious infestations of scale.

Does akebia have flowers? It has small rose-purple waxy flowers, neither conspicuous nor numerous, but very interesting at close range and fragrant.

AMPELOPSIS AND PARTHENOCISSUS

I have cement blocks about 4 feet high on the 3 sides of my porch and would like to know what will grow up and cling to these blocks so they will not be conspicuous. The porch faces north, so there is not much sun. Wintercreeper or St. Paul Virginia-creeper (*Parthenocissus quinquefolia* 'Saint-Paulii').

What plant will cover a stone wall where the location has a hot, dry southern exposure? The ordinary ivy which flourishes on the north wall does not thrive here. Boston-ivy or St. Paul Virginia-creeper.

Which deciduous ivy is the best to cover a stone wall? What kind of soil is needed? Should the soil be covered by a mulch for the winter? The Boston-ivy, St. Paul Virginia-creeper, or even the Virginia-creeper could be used to cover a stone wall. These do not need any special soil, simply a good garden loam. No winter mulch is required.

How shall I order an "ivy" that has deeply cut leaves and berries that turn lilac to bright blue? This is porcelain ampelopsis (*Ampelopsis brevipedunculata*).

Which deciduous "ivy" has the best autumn coloring? Virginia-creeper (not a true ivy) has the most brilliant crimson foliage in autumn, together with the Boston-ivy (*Parthenocissus tricuspidata*).

Where will Virginia-creeper grow? In the woods, on the ground, up a tree, in the sun or shade, along a wall, or on sand dunes. It is very hardy and adaptable.

What kinds of deciduous clinging vines are there? Among them are Virginia-creeper and its several smaller-leaved varieties. Then there is

Boston-ivy and its small-leaved varieties, trumpet creeper, and climbing hydrangea.

BITTERSWEET (CELASTRUS)

I have heard that the Oriental species of bittersweet is better than our native kind. Is that so?   It is more vigorous and has better foliage, but the fruits are about the same.

How will bittersweet look growing on a trellis by the front door?   As it is rather rampant, we doubt if you would like it there. Its chief charm is in its dark bare stems with their clinging berries in the fall and winter. A clematis would be much better.

If bittersweet seeds are planted, how long will it take before the vine produces berries? Does bittersweet prefer acid soil?   About 3 years. They grow well in either acid or alkaline soil. The sexes are separate and a male plant is needed to ensure the fruiting of the female plant.

At what time of year can bittersweet be planted?   Spring or fall.

Will bittersweet climb on a stone chimney?   No. It is a *twining* vine, not a *clinging* one.

How can I make my small patch of bittersweet larger?   Allow some of the shoots to touch the ground, cover portions of them with soil, and they will soon take root, especially if you cut partway through the vine on the underside of the portion to be covered with soil.

What causes blossoms to fall from the stems at the base of a bittersweet vine?   Probably the male flower blossoms, which never have any fruits and fall off the plant after the pollen has been dispersed.

I have several bittersweet vines on trellises. The clusters that I gather in fall are usually small and imperfect. Is there anything I can do so that these vines will produce clusters like I see in florist shops in the fall?   Be certain that 1 or 2 strong male, or pollen-bearing, plants are close by, preferably growing in with the fruiting vines. Another method is to note when they bloom in June, obtain cut branches of male flowers from some distant plant, put in a bottle of water, and tie up in your fruiting vine. Leave there for 2 weeks and the pollen distributed by insects and winds will fertilize the pistillate, or fruit-bearing, flowers, ensuring a good crop of fruits.

Should bittersweet be pruned while it grows? Mine grows 4 or 5 feet high and then starts long runners 7 or 8 feet long and there is no trellis for them.   Yes, it can be pruned while growing.

I have a bittersweet vine. When should the berries be picked for winter bouquets? Any time in the early fall just before the leaves drop.

I have read that only the female plants of bittersweet have berries. How can you sort the seedlings to discard male plants? They can't be sorted as seedlings. It is necessary to wait until they are old enough to bloom.

CLEMATIS

I am interested in clematis. Which species or variety is best in bloom and easy to care for? *Clematis paniculata,* the sweet autumn clematis, is one of the easiest of all to grow. The Jackman clematis can be grown fairly easily if the soil is alkaline.

Which clematis is it that one sees in a woodland? Rock clematis, *Clematis occidentalis,* blooming in May or June; or virgin's-bower, *C. virginiana,* with white flowers in August to September. It must climb into the sunlight to bloom well.

Could you tell us the name of a clematis with rosy-pink flowers about 2 inches across? There are 4 petals and yellow stamens. It blooms in May. It is probably pink anemone clematis (*C. montana rubens*).

Is there any clematis with red flowers that is easier to grow than the big-flowered hybrids? Scarlet clematis (*C. texensis*) is a native of Texas. It grows to about 6 feet with flowers about 1 inch long; it blooms from July to September.

Can you tell me of a yellow clematis that will grow in Maine? I saw a beautiful small variety (on the ground) in Canada but could not find its name. *Clematis tangutica,* the golden clematis, is certainly worthy of a trial. It is the best of the yellow-flowered species, a native of China. It will need winter protection.

What is the best exposure for Jackman clematis? (Illinois.) As protected a situation as possible, but not complete shade. All clematis bloom better where the vines reach full sun, but they like shade at their bases.

What fertilizer does clematis need? Should one cultivate around it or are the roots near the surface of the ground? Most clematis varieties require lime and a cool, moist soil, best supplied by a mulch of leaf-mold. The roots are very near the surface.

Is it always necessary to shade the roots and lower stem portions of clematis? This is necessary on most of the many large-flowered hybrids, but it is not necessary on our native clematis types nor on the sweet autumn clematis.

What type of trellis is best for clematis? Chicken-wire netting supported in a rigidly upright position on a light frame.

Will different varieties of clematis, planted very close together, "cross," thus spoiling the species? No, this will not change the plants or flowers. Seeds from the flowers might yield seedlings of mixed parentage.

How can I grow large-flowered clematis? They do well for 6 months or a year and then die. Unfortunately, many large-flowered clematis are susceptible to a rather serious disease which kills them during the summer months. No manure should be applied, nor should water be allowed to stand at the base of the plants. If the disease occurs, spray with wettable sulfur at once and again in a week or ten days.

How and when should one prune clematis? Those which bloom on old wood (such as *C. florida, montana,* and *patens*) need little or no pruning beyond the removal of dead or diseased wood. The *lanuginosa, jackmanii,* and *viticella* types bloom on wood of the current season and may be cut back in the spring before growth begins.

A white clematis, planted in the fall, grew about 10 or 12 feet the following summer, but did not flower. Should I have pinched it back after it was 3 or 4 feet high? No. Let it grow and gain nourishment; it will bloom the second or third year.

When and how should Clematis paniculata be pruned? In many places in New England this clematis will be killed to the ground by winter cold. In such places it should be pruned back in early spring to just above where the buds break. In situations where it does not kill to the ground, merely cutting out some of the older wood is all that is necessary.

Should clematis be pruned in the fall or summer? I notice that some people cut them down to the ground, but I have never cut mine and yet I have lovely vines. What is the best preventive for aphids? If you have lovely vines, continue the same treatment. Cutting them down does not help. (See preceding questions.) Aphids can be controlled by spraying with malathion or diazinon.

Should a Clematis jackmanii be trimmed or pruned in the springtime? Yes, but only if the vine is cluttered up with a mass of unproductive or dead shoots.

Can you start clematis from cuttings? Clematis is rather difficult to propagate. This can be done either by cuttings or seeds. For the amateur, sowing the seed in the fall is the easier method. Many large-flowered hybrids must be propagated by cuttings or by grafting.

DUTCHMAN'S-PIPE (ARISTOLOCHIA MACROPHYLLA)

Which vine would make a good solid screen to hide a compost pile? Please describe Dutchman's-pipe. Dutchman's-pipe would be fine if grown on a series of vertical cords or slats. The big roundish leaves, 10 inches in diameter, overlap each other. Flowers, nondescript in color, resemble a Dutchman's-pipe.

EUONYMUS FORTUNEI (WINTERCREEPER, EVERGREEN-BITTERSWEET)

Which one of the wintercreeper vines has berries like bitter-sweet? The best of the berried varieties is the big-leaf wintercreeper (*Euonymus fortunei vegeta*).

Our wintercreeper is distinctive because of its leaves, which are variegated, sometimes with white or pinkish tones. What variety could it be? Silver-edge wintercreeper (*Euonymus fortunei* 'Gracilis').

Which euonymus vine has very tiny leaves? Baby wintercreeper (*Euonymus fortunei* 'Minima').

Which is the hardiest of all evergreen vines that will cling to a stone wall? Wintercreeper (*Euonymus fortunei*) and its varieties.

Is Euonymus fortunei the new name for what we used to call Euonymus radicans? Yes. It is now *Euonymus fortunei radicans* (until the botanists decide to change it again).

I have a euonymus that I thought would climb on a wall, but it remains a bush. What is the trouble? It must be the variety called glossy wintercreeper (*Euonymus fortunei* 'Carrierei'), which is shrubby and nonclimbing. There is another variety which remains shrubby unless planted near a wall (*E. fortunei vegeta*), the big-leaf wintercreeper.

GRAPE See Fruits—Section 11.

HONEYSUCKLE (LONICERA)

Which honeysuckle has flowers that are yellowish on the inside and rose-purple on the outside? Everblooming honeysuckle (*Lonicera heckrottii*).

Please describe the scarlet trumpet honeysuckle (Lonicera semper-virens). I believe it used to grow in gardens long ago. Yes, it has been in cultivation for a long time. It has orange-scarlet flowers with long tubes, yellow inside, produced from May to August.

What low-growing variety of honeysuckle would you recommend for a northern exposure with semishade? Hall's honeysuckle. But watch out: it is a pernicious weed if it gets out of bounds.

What low vine may one plant under the shade of a large maple tree but unprotected from the wind; one which will grow with myrtle, where grass will not? You might try Hall's honeysuckle, but it is very difficult to coax anything to grow under most maples.

Our honeysuckle vine (2 years old this past spring) had only one spray of bloom. Why? The foliage is beautiful and healthy-looking. It needs time to become well established before it will bloom properly.

My honeysuckle lost all its leaves in midsummer, then bore leaves and blooms and seeds at one time. What should be done this year? Give it more water. This was probably due to unusually dry weather.

Does Japanese honeysuckle eventually work its way into water drains? Should it be planted near them? Like the roots of most plants, it probably will, but usually the roots won't do much damage in this respect.

How does one trim out honeysuckle which is very thick and about 12 feet high? If there is too much wood, it may be necessary to cut it off at the base and start all over again.

Will you tell me whether honeysuckle vine can be pruned and at what time of the year? Prune it in the early spring when the buds are breaking. Unless the vine is to be restrained within a limited area, it is necessary to prune out only dead or diseased wood.

What is the proper way to prune a honeysuckle for profuse blooming? Mine is a cutting about 3 years old, with very few flowers. Is a trellis necessary? Don't prune; allow it to grow profusely on some support. If good soil, plenty of water, and sunshine are available, it will soon bloom well.

HYDRANGEA

How tall does the climbing hydrangea grow? How does it climb? *Hydrangea anomala petiolaris* can grow 50 feet or more in time, but it is a slow grower. It clings to a wall without support, sends out branches at right angles to the wall, and blooms in June.

What kind of flowers does the climbing hydrangea have? Its flowers are white, in round, flat, open clusters, resembling some of the viburnum flowers; it has small fertile flowers in the center and large sterile flowers on the perimeter of the cluster.

IVY (HEDERA)

How can one tell whether an ivy is a variety that will be hardy if placed outdoors? We want to plant some on a new cottage chimney. Try several. The hardiest evergreen variety is the Baltic ivy (*Hedera helix* 'Baltica'). If this dies in the winter, no English ivy will grow there. You might also try the varieties 'Bulgaria' and 'Taconic'.

What does Baltic ivy look like? Its leaves are slightly smaller than those of the typical English ivy, and the white veins are often more prominent.

Which evergreen vine can I plant on the north side of a brick house? English ivy, if a tall-growing kind is required; otherwise, use wintercreeper, which is hardier.

Which vine is suitable for planting on a west slope, to cover the ground and stay green all year-round—one that won't spread too much? Baltic ivy.

WISTERIA

I have had a wisteria for several years that has not flowered. What can I do? Root-prune around the plant (use a sharp spade, inserting it deeply in a circle around the stem, as though you were going to transplant); then make a shallow trench into which superphosphate (use 3 to 4 pounds for each inch in trunk diameter) is poured and then mixed in the soil, after which the trench is filled with soil; and finally, prune back vigorous vegetative shoot growth. The pruning can be done in the summer and perhaps again in the fall or winter.

How do I prune a wisteria? The objective in pruning a wisteria is to keep the growth restricted to force spurlike shoots which produce flowers. In the summer, cut back the shoots at about the seventh leaf; in the winter, the shoots are further shortened—to within 1 to 3 inches of their base. At this time the future flowers will be readily apparent in the bud stage.

I have grown several wisteria plants from seed, but they have not flowered. Why?   It's better to buy grafted or wisteria vines grown from cuttings from a specialist. Some species are slow to come into flower and seed-grown plants are known to be even slower. However, you might try root-pruning, drastic top-pruning, and adding superphosphate, as recommended above.

I would like to grow a wisteria plant on an oak tree. Will the vine hurt the tree?   Yes. Wisteria is a twining vine and eventually its heavy trunk can strangle the tree.

Should wisterias be grown in rich or lean soil?   Probably a soil on the lean side is to be preferred, as too rich a soil can stimulate vegetative growth at the expense of flower production. However, if the space in which the wisteria grows is at all restricted, such as might be the case near a house, yearly fertilizer applications in the spring might be necessary, especially if the vine is flowering abundantly.

Can I grow a wisteria in a large tub on my terrace?   Yes. Start with a fairly rich soil mixture (see above question). A wisteria trained in tree formation would also be satisfactory.

5. Bulbs, Tubers, and Corms

NO FLOWERS ARE more rewarding for the time and room required for their culture than the various bulbs and other bulblike plants—those which form tubers and corms instead of true bulbs. A considerable number produce flowers very early in spring when our spirits—and our gardens—need their gaiety. Others add brilliant color to the garden scene all summer. A few extend the bulb-flowering season well into the fall.

There are still many gardens, however, where one looks in vain for any sight of bulbs other than a few daffodils, perhaps a planting of that ubiquitous tulip, 'Red Emperor', and a dahlia or two. The owners of such gardens are overlooking a wide range of easily grown plants which could provide them with beautiful and interesting flowers, very literally from one end of the year to the other, for there are a number of bulbs and corms that may readily be flowered indoors too. The most easily obtained and grown of these are commented on in the following pages. You can add to your store of garden pleasures by becoming acquainted with them.

National organizations made up of specialists and devoted amateur growers have developed for some of the very popular types of bulbs. Many of these publish bulletins, have annual conventions, and sponsor seasonal shows. Many also have regional and local affiliates. Dues are usually nominal. A local garden club or agricultural and horticultural schools and societies will be able to provide current addresses. If you are enthusiastic about a particular genus, you'll find kindred company in the following: American Begonia Society, American Daffodil Society, American Dahlia Society, North American Gladiolus Council, American Gloxinia and Gesneriad Society, or North American Lily Society.

Hardy Bulbs

WHAT TO GROW

Which hardy bulbs are the most reliable for permanent plantings, such as in the foreground of a shrub border?   Daffodils rank first, but if your region is rodent-free, hyacinths, hybrid lilies, various alliums, and the little bulbs such as chionodoxa, snowdrop, crocus, colchicum, grape-hyacinth, and scilla should flourish for years. Tulips, if not eaten by rodents, will give several years of bloom before the bulbs split and need replanting, especially if planted deep (about 8 to 10 inches).

Which bulbs can be left in the ground the year-round in the North?   All hardy bulbs (see above, as well as the rest of this section for other kinds).

We have spring-flowering bulbs. Which hardy bulbs shall I plant for summer bloom?   Hybrid lilies and flowering onions. You might also want to consider lycoris for late summer, and fall crocus and colchicum for fall.

CULTURE

What kind of soil is best for spring-flowering bulbs?   Average garden soils, well-drained and slightly acid, are best. Superphosphate is a good fertilizer.

Bulbs do not multiply readily in the soil in my garden. Tulips do not last over 3 years. What element in the soil is lacking?   Possibly your soil is not suitable, but this is not unusual for tulips. Most bulbs prefer a loose, fertile soil that has been well worked to a depth of 10 or 12 inches.

Does well-rotted manure or a rich compost above, but not touching, the bulbs rot them?   No. But it is much better to spade the manure and other organic material under before planting so that it is well below the bulbs but not in direct contact with them.

How deep should bulbs be planted?   No general rule can be applied to all bulbs. Some lilies should be planted 8 or 9 inches deep, others 2 inches deep. If possible, obtain specific information for each kind before planting. Otherwise, a rough rule that can be followed in the case of the hardy spring-flowering bulbs is to cover them with soil equal in depth to 2 or 3 times the diameter of the bulb.

How late in the fall can bulbs in the North be planted? Bulbs planted in December will grow and thrive, and instances are known of January-planted bulbs succeeding. But much earlier planting is recommended.

I just received some early-flowering bulbs. We are currently having sub-zero weather and snow. How can I take care of the bulbs during the winter and when can I plant them? They are winter-aconites, scillas, and tulips. Keep them in a cool, dry place until the ground thaws and then plant them. Or plant the bulbs in pots or flats of soil (if you have some stored) and cover with a 6-inch layer of sand or soil and leave outdoors. They cannot be kept all winter out of the soil.

How can I tell which end goes up when planting a bulb? Generally there will be vestiges of roots at the bottom of the bulb. The top is usually more tapered, and a shoot or eye may be visible as a clue. Tubers often show "eyes" on the top.

Can you plant bulbs in the spring that call for planting in fall? Certain hardy, summer-flowering bulbs can be held in cold storage and planted in the spring as, for instance, lilies; but fall planting is better. Spring-flowering bulbs must be planted in the fall.

Can I plant bulbs of all kinds in the spring? Only summer- and fall-blooming kinds can be planted at that time.

When should I order and plant autumn-flowering bulbs, such as fall crocus, sternbergia, and colchicum? Order as early in the summer as possible and plant immediately on arrival.

Can you take up daffodil bulbs, separate, then replant them as soon as the leaves die down? Yes.

Should bulbs be watered after being planted? This is usually not necessary if the soil is moist, but in case of a long, dry spell after planting, a thorough watering is beneficial.

What can be done with spring-blooming bulbs which come through the ground in winter due to a warm spell? If planted very shallowly, cover with a layer of soil or whatever plant litter is available. However, some bulbs, such as madonna lilies and grape-hyacinths, make early foliage naturally.

If true bulbs have their flower buds within them, do they need full sunshine in order to bloom? Yes, they need sunshine and moisture to bring the blooms to maturity.

Does it inhibit next year's bloom to pick flowers of bulbous plants?   No, not if most of the foliage is left. This is needed to manufacture food that feeds the bulb and produces the next year's bloom. Removal of flower heads before they set seed aids the bulb.

What can I do with the unsightly foliage of my spring-flowering bulbs after their blooming is over?   Removal of foliage before it has matured (turned yellow and wilted) is sure to prevent normal bloom the following year, as the maturing foliage provides nutrients for the flowers to come. Water in dry spells to keep foliage growing as long as possible. Place later-flowering plants in front of and around bulbs to detract from the maturing foliage. An example would be Christmas ferns among naturalized daffodils.

Do spring-flowering bulbs need fertilizer after they are planted?   An application of a complete plant food should be applied and gently raked into the surface each spring. In light, sandy soil a second application in late spring after bloom is over is also advisable.

Do you advise the use of a summer mulch on bulb beds?   Yes, by all means. A mulch of shredded bark, pine needles, buckwheat hulls, shredded sugarcane, or other similar material may be applied early in the spring after weeding and fertilizing is done. If the bed is later overplanted with annuals, the mulch remaining on the bed will help to control weeds and retain moisture through the summer heat.

What causes bulbs to disappear in the soil? Hardy bulbs such as daffodils, tulips, lilies, and iris are examples.   Unsuitable soil or poor drainage; cutting the flowers without leaving sufficient foliage to make food to fatten up the bulbs; cutting of leaves before they wither naturally; and disease or the depredations of rodents.

How short a rest period should bulbs have after being lifted from the soil?   This varies with the kind of bulb. Colchicums and lilies, for example, should be replanted with the least possible delay, as should daffodils. Tulips can be stored out of the ground for 3 months or more without harm.

Should tulips, daffodils, and hyacinths have mulch (leaves) over them in the fall in the North? When should they be uncovered?   It is not necessary except in extremely cold sections, unless you are in an area subject to frequent alternate freezing and thawing. Damage is then from the "heaving" of the roots and bulbs from the soil. Under these conditions, cover *after* the ground has frozen hard, with leaves, compost, and marsh hay. This keeps the ground uniformly cool and prevents damage to roots by heaving. Uncover gradually when growth appears in the spring.

RODENTS

I have had trouble losing lily and tulip bulbs in the winter. Some rodent makes burrows 3 inches below the surface of the ground. I have used wire baskets in planting (to no avail) as well as poison and traps. What can I do? You may have to encircle the whole bed with fine mesh wire netting, 12 inches wide, buried vertically and extending 2 to 3 inches above the ground surface. Do not mulch bed until the ground is well frozen.

Do moles eat bulbs? No, moles are carniverous, but mice use mole runs and destroy many bulbs. Consult your county agent for regional suggestions to combat rodents. If it is any consolation to you, there are "on" and "off" years for these pests!

We have heavy populations of both field and pine mice. Are there any spring bulbs that they will not destroy? All rodents love tulips and crocus but will not touch any of the many kinds of daffodil bulbs.

Rabbits eat my tulip buds and devour crocus plants, flowers and all. What can I do? Dried blood sprinkled heavily around the plants can give temporary protection. Try covering your plantings loosely with boughs cut from your Christmas tree. Leave them on the tulips until their stems are a foot tall. Don't remove them from your crocus until the clover is in leaf. A cat or dog can help, too!

What can I do about deer eating my tulips and lilies? Ordinarily deer will not touch daffodils, so use these for open areas and keep tulips, crocus, and lilies closer to dwellings. Double the number of susceptible bulbs you plant—some for you and some for the "critters"!

Specific Hardy Bulbs

ALLIUM

Do flowering alliums possess an unpleasant onion odor? No—unless the stems or leaves are crushed or bruised. In fact, flowers of many alliums are decidedly pleasant to smell.

What are the best flowering onions for outdoor gardens? Many species of *Allium* are excellent for planting in borders. Among the best are *Allium neapolitanum* (white); *caeruleum* (blue); *flavum* (yellow); *aflatunense* and *rosenbachianum* (purple lilac); and *christophii* (violet). Shorter kinds that are ideal for rock gardens and foreground planting are *A. karataviense* (silvery lilac); *moly* (yellow); *roseum grandiflorum* (rose); *stellatum* (pink); and *schoenoprasum* (rosy purple). *A. giganteum* bears large violet flower heads as high as 4 feet in early summer. *A. senescens* (rose-violet) blooms a little later.

What soil and treatment do summer-flowering onions require?   A rather light, well-drained loam is best, although they will thrive in most garden soils, providing drainage is good. *Allium moly* flourishes in partial shade, but full sunshine is preferred by most species. Divide and transplant whenever crowded, either in the fall or in early spring. Most are very easy to grow.

ANEMONE

Will anemone tubers survive the winter in New York if they are planted in the fall? Will they bloom if planted in the spring? If so, when should they be planted in the vicinity of New York?   Rock-garden tuberous-rooted kinds (such as *apennina, blanda, ranunculoides, quinquefolia,* and *nemorosa*) are hardy and should be planted in the fall. The florists' tuberous-rooted kinds are not hardy. You might try storing them in a cool place (40°F.) during the winter and planting them in the spring, or order from a spring catalog and plant them on their arrival.

How should one plant tuberous anemones, such as Anemone nemorosa, blanda, etc.?   Plant in early fall in porous soil containing a generous proportion of humus. Set tubers 2 or 3 inches apart and cover about 2 inches deep. Light woodland shade is needed.

ARUM

I have a lily-like plant which produces a flower, dark purplish in color (almost black), on a stem 8 inches tall, with leaves 5 × 3 inches. It seems to be hardy since it survives our occasional frosts. It becomes dormant in summer. Could you please identify it?   It is probably black-calla (*Arum palaestinum*), which needs a winter mulch in the North.

BELAMCANDA

Can you tell me something about a plant called black-berry-lily? *Belamcanda chinensis,* a hardy iris relative from the Orient, is now naturalized in many parts of this country. It is easily grown in the sun or light shade and is propagated by seeds or division. Orange summer flowers, spotted with purple-brown, are followed by blackberry-like fruits much prized for dried arrangements.

BRODIAEA (TRITELEIA and DICHELOSTEMMA)

What treatment do brodiaeas need in the garden? Plant in the fall in gritty soil in full sun. Set bulbs about 2 inches apart and cover 3 or 4 inches deep. Protect with a light winter covering of marsh hay or similar material. The same applies for *Triteleia* and *Dichelostemma.*

Can you tell me the name of the floral firecracker plant? *Brodiaea coccinea* (now botanically *Dichelostemma ida-maia*) is native to the western United States. The flowers bear a close resemblance to a gaily colored bunch of firecrackers.

CALOCHORTUS

Can calochortus (or mariposa-tulip) be successfully grown in the Middle Atlantic states? Yes, but they are not very easy to keep from year to year. Plant at twice their own depth, late in the fall, in specially prepared, very gritty soil. Mulch well to prevent heaving. Water freely when growing, but keep the bed as dry as possible in late summer and fall. They need sunshine and demand perfect drainage.

CAMASSIA

Will you tell me something about camassias and their care? They thrive in any good garden soil that is not too dry. Camassias prefer full sun or light shade; they bloom in May (flowers are blue or white), then die down. Plant in early fall so that the bulbs are 4 inches below the surface and 7 or 8 inches apart. Do not transplant as long as they bloom well.

Are camassias good garden flowers? Very good indeed, and worthy of being more widely planted. Most of them are native to the United

States and are easily cared for. Apart from their garden value, their spires of starry flowers are excellent for cutting purposes.

CHIONODOXA

Does the bulb glory-of-the-snow (chionodoxa) need any special care? This is one of the easiest and loveliest of hardy spring-flowering bulbs. Plant in the fall in any fairly good soil, 3 inches deep, 2 or 3 inches apart. Do not disturb for many years. Topdress every 2 or 3 years with fertilized soil. They increase and improve with the passing years. They are excellent for planting in low-growing ground covers such as vinca or bearberry. Good pink and white forms exist as well as many blues.

COLCHICUM

How deep should colchicum be planted and how often should it be divided? Cover the tops of the bulbs with not more than 3 inches of soil. Divide every third or fourth year.

What soil and situation are best for colchicums and when should they be planted? The soil should be rich and reasonably moist (but not wet). Provide with light shade. Plant in early August. They often self-sow.

Why does my colchicum have no leaves with its flowers? This is normal. Colchicum foliage is produced in the spring. A low ground cover such as vinca or thyme sets off the early fall flowers admirably. American colonists called them "naked ladies."

CONVALLARIA (LILY-OF-THE-VALLEY)

Can lilies-of-the-valley be grown in an absolutely shady place? Yes. They will grow in dense shade if the soil is fairly good, but will probably not bloom as freely as when they are in partial shade.

How can I grow lily-of-the-valley? What kind of soil does it need? A moist but not wet soil that contains generous amounts of humus. Improve the soil by spading in rotted manure, leafmold, and peat moss before planting. Lily-of-the-valley prefers light shade. Plant in the spring. Each year in early spring, the bed may be topdressed with leafmold, compost, or rotted manure. Do not allow the plants to become overcrowded.

The garden in which I have very fine clumps of giant lilies-of-the-valley has been okayed as to soil, sunshine, and shade; the plants have splendid foliage. Why don't they multiply? Why do they produce only a few stems that bloom? The soil is basically clay, although it has been enriched. If the soil is very rich, the foliage will be good, but flowers will be scarce. Let the plants become firmly established, then they will flower when the excess nutrients are used up.

Is there any difference in the size of lilies-of-the-valley? How can they be grown to be a good size? The largest-flowered variety is named 'Fortunei'. Old, worn-out plantings usually produce few small flowers. Lift, separate, and replant in newly fertilized soil every 3 or 4 years. Make sure that shade is not too dense.

How do you grow clumps of lily-of-the-valley for forcing for cut blossoms? Plant clumps in very rich, sandy loam. When pips are ¼ to ⅜ inch thick and ⅞ to 1 inch long, cut away from clumps with as much root as possible. Wrap in bundles and place in cold storage, 28° to 32° F., for at least 3 months. Best results, however, are obtained from specially prepared pips from commercial sources.

Are the roots of lily-of-the-valley poisonous? Yes. The druggists' convallaria, which is used as a heart tonic, is made from lily-of-the-valley roots. Red fall berries are toxic, too.

CROCUS

When should I plant crocus and how? Spring-flowering kinds should be planted in September and October. Plant in light, fertile soil in a sunny place. If among grass, plant only where the grass can remain uncut until the leaves have died away in late spring. Plant 2 or 3 inches apart and about 3 inches deep. Fall-blooming kinds should be planted in July or August.

Should crocus be planted in beds or with grass in order to look natural? They appear best when planted among some low ground cover, such as creeping thyme, creeping phlox, or vinca. Without the competition of grass roots, crocus thrive and multiply, so in a few years a planting will make a bright splash of color in the foreground of a garden, even without an underplanting. Fall types, however, look much better with a ground cover; clove pinks are ideal. Other garden situations for crocus groupings include those within or near stone steps or walls, in soil spaces in rock gardens, between steppingstones on terraces, and under shrubs and small trees such as forsythia, cornelian cherry, and birch.

DAFFODILS (NARCISSUS)

Many of the early spring-blooming plants would not be worth a second glance if it were not for the fact that they are harbingers of spring. Daffodils, on the other hand, would be important even if they bloomed in June or August.

The daffodils belong to the genus *Narcissus,* and the two names are used interchangeably. One species (*N. jonquilla*) and its hybrids are often called jonquils, but they are still daffodils. Over 10,000 varieties have been introduced. The color range of the group is largely yellow, orange, and white, but hybridizing has produced good cultivars with apricot and pink tones as well as some with green markings.

Daffodils have much to recommend them. While a given species or variety may not succeed in all parts of the country, there are types that do well in warm climates and others that thrive where winters are severe. They are highly prized in rock gardens, borders, and in small intimate gardens, and they may be naturalized in woodlands and meadows. They are also fine as cut flowers. Many are very fragrant.

What type of soil is needed to grow daffodils?   Any garden soil is suitable, providing it is deep, well drained, and reasonably fertile. Avoid planting in hot, barren soils or where the soil remains wet for long periods. They will not survive in wet soils.

What is the correct preparation of soil for planting daffodils?   Elaborate preparation is unnecessary, although some specialists might go to the trouble of spading the soil 12 inches deep and placing rich compost or rotted manure in the bottom of the trench or area. The homeowner can either spade the area to be planted and incorporate about 3 to 5 pounds of a complete fertilizer such as 5–10–5 to 100 square feet in the soil; or place the bulbs where he or she wishes them to grow and dig individual holes for each bulb. Mixing about the same amount of superphosphate in the soil before planting is also recommended, especially in sandy soils. A quick way to prepare the soil for daffodils, especially in large plantings and naturalized groupings, is to rototill the soil to a depth of 8 to 10 inches.

Can you tell me how to prepare the bed in which to grow daffodils for exhibition?   The classic recommendation is to excavate a trench 18 inches deep, dig into the bottom a 6-inch layer of well-rotted manure or

Daffodils can be planted in an informal way under trees. The major above-ground growth of the bulbs comes before the leaves on the trees unfurl or reach maturity, so they do not cause much shade.

rich compost, and on this spread a generous sprinkling of bone meal or superphosphate. Cover with 6 inches of good topsoil (without manure), set bulbs on this, and cover with any fairly good soil.

How should one fertilize daffodils that do not need lifting and replanting? Topdress in early fall with superphosphate and in early spring with a complete fertilizer and compost or old, well-rotted manure.

Is superphosphate a safe fertilizer to use on daffodil beds? Yes. It may be forked in at planting time.

With what can I feed my daffodils to increase the size of their blooms for exhibition? A dilute liquid fertilizer, applied when flower scapes appear, helps immensely. Avoid high-nitrogen fertilizers. Keep beds well watered. If reduction in size and quantity of bloom is caused by overcrowding of bulbs, fertilizer does not help. When foliage becomes crowded and bloom falls off (4 to 6 years after planting), dig after the foliage matures, separate bulbs, and replant.

What type of situation is best adapted for daffodils? A slight slope, sheltered from drying winds, with deep and well-drained soil.

Can daffodils be naturalized among trees? A light deciduous woodland affords an ideal location for daffodils which, under such conditions, thrive and increase abundantly. Plant them on the fringes of the tree branches, but never to the north of a tree and never under evergreens in deep shade.

When is the best time to plant daffodils? August, September, or October, with preference for the earlier dates. If bulbs do not arrive until November—then plant them then.

The daffodil bulbs I order from a seedsman usually do not arrive until fall, yet I am told to transplant those that are in my garden in July. Why? Bulbs in storage remain dormant for some considerable time after those in the garden have developed new roots. Bulbs are harmed by being moved after root growth is far advanced. Early planting is always advisable.

Can daffodil bulbs be planted as late as December? Yes, dormant bulbs can be planted any time before the ground freezes solid. Well-stored bulbs have been planted with success as late as February. Earlier planting, however, is much preferred.

Is it true that if you transplant daffodils in the spring, they will not bloom? If so, why? It is scarcely possible for them to bloom satisfactorily if removed from the soil during peak growth. By spring the bulbs have a fully developed root system and the disturbance of transplanting causes a serious setback. If taken up in clumps of soil with their roots intact, they probably will bloom fairly well.

About what distance should be left between full-sized daffodil bulbs when planting? It depends upon the effect desired and also upon the variety, because bulb sizes vary considerably. A minimum distance of from 3 to 6 inches should be allowed. For colonizing, the bulbs should be set in a pleasingly informal pattern rather than evenly spaced.

How deep should daffodils be planted? In light soils large bulbs are set with their bases 6 to 8 inches deep; in heavier soils, 5 to 7 inches deep. Small bulbs should be planted shallower than those of larger size.

Does deep planting encourage daffodils to multiply? No. On the contrary, it checks rapid division. Shallow planting induces rapid multiplication. Deep planting tends to build up strong-flowering bulbs and lengthens the years between transplantings.

Can daffodils be interplanted with tulips to produce early flowers and thus extend the blooming season of the planting? Yes. This is an entirely satisfactory combination—especially in small gardens.

How are daffodils cared for? Plant in good deep soil. Water during dry weather, especially after flowering, to keep foliage green as long as possible. Remove faded flowers. Fertilize yearly. Give at least a half day of sun.

What are the moisture requirements of daffodils grown outdoors? They need ample supplies during the growing season, particularly in the spring when the flower scapes and foliage are developing.

When should daffodils be lifted in order to store them through the summer? Or is it better to leave them in the ground all year? Summer storage is not necessary for daffodils. If they must be dug, July is the best time. Store in a dry place, as cool as possible down to 50° F.

Daffodils left in one place too long (right) produce excessive foliage and few flowers. Dividing old clumps and replanting will result in blooms like those at the left.

What time of the year should daffodils be separated? June or July is the best time; wait until the foliage has fully matured, so the bulbs are dormant. If you dig when the leaves are just browning, you can trace the bulbs best and avoid slicing into any with the fork. After separation, replant at once. However, bulbs can be transplanted earlier—even in bloom, if they are replanted at once and watered.

Do daffodil bulbs naturalized among trees have to be dug and replanted at intervals? Yes, whenever they become so crowded that the quantity and quality of the blooms have deteriorated. This may be as often as every third year, or as infrequently as every 5 or 10 years. Remember, growing trees cast increasing shade each year, so conditions gradually change. Move bulbs out to the periphery of branches.

Will daffodils bloom the spring after they have been divided and reset? Yes, if of blooming size: 1½ to 2 inches diameter for trumpet varieties; 1 to 1½ inches for smaller varieties; and ⅝ to 1 inch for the *triandrus, cyclamineus,* and *jonquilla* types.

What should be done with clumps of daffodils that won't bloom? After the foliage has died down, dig them up, separate the bulbs, fertilize the soil, and replant. Avoid very shady locations.

How can I get miniature daffodils to bloom every spring? Plant in a sheltered place in moist, but not waterlogged, soil. Water freely during dry periods whenever foliage is present. Dig up, separate, and replant every 3 years. Miniature hybrids are easier than true species.

Can daffodil bulbs that have bloomed indoors in pots be stored after blooming, to be used next year? Not for forcing again. If kept well watered until the ground is in satisfactory condition, they may be planted outdoors and will bloom in future years.

I have heard that it is harmful to cut the foliage off daffodils when they have finished blooming. Is this so?   Yes, the leaves are needed to produce food to plump up the bulbs in readiness for next season's flowering. Never remove foliage until it has died down, or at least turned yellow. Encourage it to grow as long as possible by watering during dry spells.

Is it harmful to "braid" daffodil foliage after flowering?   Generally, yes. The leaves can be bruised and fewer surfaces will be available to catch sunlight and manufacture food. Next year's flowers depend on this year's foliage.

Daffodils planted at the end of September are now (late October) through the ground. Will they survive?   Probably. Throw an additional 2 inches of soil over them. They were planted too shallowly.

Can you tell me why double daffodils do not mature their blooms? Hundreds of stems come up with empty cases at the tops.   They are overcrowded and are robbing each other of nutrients and moisture. Dig up the bulbs, separate them, enrich the bed, and replant. Water thoroughly during dry weather in the spring.

What is the simplest way for a home gardener to increase a limited stock of a choice daffodil?   Plant bulbs shallowly (about 4 inches deep) in a well-prepared bed—preferably in a cold frame. Give good cultural care and lift, divide, and replant every second year.

Is there any rapid method of vegetatively propagating daffodils?   In summer large bulbs can be sliced vertically into many sections (each containing a small portion of the basal plate). The sections are then planted in peat moss and sand. Mild bottom heat stimulates production of new bulblets.

How are daffodils raised from seeds?   Sow in late August in rows 6 inches apart in a well-prepared seed bed in a cold frame. Cover seeds ¾ inch deep. Shade the bed, keep uniformly moist, weeded, and covered with marsh hay or other protection during the winter. Allow seedlings two summers' growth, then lift and replant with wider spacing. Expect at least 7 years before blooming.

Why can't I get daffodil seeds to come up?   It is possible that the seeds are not fertile, or perhaps your cultural care is incorrect. Hand pollination of the flowers should result in fertile seed. Some hybrids are sterile, however. (See the previous question.)

Are daffodils subject to pests and diseases?   Several diseases and some insect pests may be troublesome, but these usually do not appear in garden plantings. If trouble is suspected, remove affected bulbs and send samples to your State Agricultural Experiment Station for diagnosis and advice.

Is hot-water treatment of daffodil bulbs effective? Yes, as a control for eelworms, bulb flies, and mites. The treatment consists of soaking for 4 hours in water maintained at 110° to 111.5° F. One pint of formalin to each 25 gallons of water is added if basal rot is present. Bulbs must not be treated too early or too late in the season. There are now many new chemical miticides on the market.

What is the difference between a daffodil and a narcissus? These names are interchangeable, although "daffodil" is applied particularly (but not exclusively) to those kinds that have large, well-developed trumpets. *Narcissus* is the botanical name for the entire group.

What is a jonquil? A jonquil hybrid? The true jonquil is *Narcissus jonquilla,* a species that has slender, rushlike foliage and sweet-scented flowers in clusters. Jonquil hybrids are horticultural developments of this species, usually with larger flowers.

How do I decide what daffodils to choose from in catalog listings? The various species are usually italicized as *N. cyclamineus.* Most varieties in the trade are hybrids and labeled *N.* 'February Gold'. These are usually showier and easier to grow than true species. Large bulb firms group their offerings according to divisions developed by the American Daffodil Society. These classifications indicate the bloodlines of a daffodil hybrid. More important, they make it easier to select your daffodils. By planting clumps from different classes, you will obtain a longer season of bloom and a wider color range, and enjoy flowers of quite varied form and size.

Can you recommend some good daffodils in each of the various classes? Reasonably priced varieties in the current catalog of a reputable dealer are a reliable source. Local chapters of the American Daffodil Society have up-to-date advice on good varieties for specific areas and they often sponsor spring shows where you can see for yourself. *The Complete Book of Bulbs* (revised edition, Doubleday) lists many standard varieties.

What determines the division or class of a daffodil? It can be its parentage. Thus, *Narcissus cyclamineus, triandrus, jonquilla, tazetta,* and *poeticus* hybrids all exhibit clearly the distinguishing characteristics of their particular parent.

Doesn't size have anything to do with classification? Yes, and so does form. Any double flower belongs in the double division. The size of its cup or trumpet in relation to the length of its outer petal segments (perianth) determines whether a daffodil is listed as a trumpet, a large-cup, or a small-cup.

I want something other than yellow daffodils. What can I choose? Most of the daffodils with bright-colored cups are either large-cups (Div. II) or small-cups (Div. III). Colors of cups range from red-orange to apricot and pink. Outer petals of these are generally yellow or white. There are pure whites in almost every class from big trumpets to dainty *triandrus* hybrids.

Are cluster-flowered (tazetta) daffodils less hardy? They do not do well in the northernmost states, but they are perfectly hardy in the Middle Atlantic region, for example.

What is a split daffodil? Through irradiation and selective breeding a race of daffodils has been developed which does not have a center cup. Instead, the trumpet has been "split" into petal segments which lie more or less flat against the outer perianth.

What daffodils are outstandingly fragrant? Choose hybrids that are listed as *jonquilla, tazetta* (cluster-flowered), or *poeticus* types. One cut specimen of the easy-to-grow species, *N. jonquilla* 'Simplex', perfumes a whole room.

What are some early-flowering daffodils? Choose hybrids from catalog descriptions of the following types: *triandrus, jonquilla, poeticus, tazetta,* and white small-cups. A touch of afternoon shade prolongs their flowering.

Are there good double daffodils? 'Cheerfulness' and 'Yellow Cheerfulness' are charming and very fragrant. Try also the larger-flowered 'White Lion', 'Texas', and 'White Marvel'. Mulch to keep clean in rainy weather.

ENDYMION (WOOD-HYACINTH, ENGLISH BLUEBELL)

Which scillas are best adapted to planting in a shaded situation in soil containing lots of leafmold? The scillas you ask about are now listed in the genus *Endymion,* although bulb catalogs continue to list them as *Scilla.* They are the Spanish bluebell (*E. hispanicus*) and the wood-hyacinth or English bluebell (*E. non-scriptus*). The latter is still listed in most catalogs as *Scilla campanulata.* It is much larger than the true scilla (*Scilla siberica*) and blooms in May at the same time as tulips.

The potatolike tubers should be planted 5 inches deep. Endymions are available in blue-, pink-, and white-flowered forms.

ERANTHIS (WINTER-ACONITE)

I have not had success with winter-aconites, although I planted them in a favorable situation early in October. Can you suggest why this happened? Your planting was done too late. They should have been planted as soon as available. They quickly deteriorate when kept out of the ground.

What conditions do winter-aconites (eranthis) need? A woodsy, moist soil in light shade. They often do well on gentle slopes and once planted should be left undisturbed. Set tubers 3 inches deep and about the same distance apart. Water well once immediately after planting.

EREMURUS

Are foxtail-lilies hardy? These stately (5- to 12-foot) members of the lily family produce star-shaped, fibrous rootstocks, rosettes of narrow leaves which send up blooming stalks bearing heavy racemes of bell-shaped white, pink, yellow, or orange flowers in late spring. They are hardy to Zone 4 if heavily mulched after the ground freezes hard. Do not remove mulch until late spring frosts are past, as early spring growth may be frost-nipped. For this reason, a northern exposure is desirable. Handle brittle tubers carefully.

ERYTHRONIUM (DOGTOOTH-VIOLET, TROUT-LILY)

What are the habits and culture of dogtooth-violets? Erythroniums are woodland plants which like humusy soil and partial shade. Many prefer a moist situation. European varieties are usually offered by color. Native American species vary greatly and are offered by specialists in wildflowers.

What is the proper depth for planting dogtooth-violet bulbs and how late can they be planted for spring blooming? Plant with the top of the bulb 3 inches below the surface. September is the latest month for planting. The bulbs quickly deteriorate if they are kept out of the soil long.

Are the trout-lilies, or dogtooth-violets, easily grown in gardens? They are among the loveliest of plants for lightly shaded places where the soil is deep, humusy, and moist. Unfortunately, many plants gradually deteriorate when planted in eastern gardens, but they are well worth replanting from time to time.

FRITILLARIA

What is the guinea hen flower? *Fritillaria meleagris,* a good rock-garden subject. The speckled, pendant blooms are more curious than beautiful. Sources in the western United States offer several other good native species.

What is the culture for crown imperial? *Fritillaria imperialis,* like many others of its genus, is capricious—sometimes doing well and other times failing to thrive. Plant in early fall in deep rich soil and in light shade. Leave undisturbed as long as it continues to thrive.

GALANTHUS (SNOWDROP)

I am very fond of snowdrops. Where and how shall I plant them? Plant in early fall, setting bulbs 3 to 4 inches deep and about 3 inches apart. If possible, choose a porous soil that contains a fair amount of humus and provide a lightly shaded position. Snowdrops multiply fairly rapidly, if congenially located. Try *Galanthus elwesii* for earliest flowers.

How often should snowdrops (Galanthus nivalis) be lifted and transplanted? Do not disturb unless absolutely necessary; they do best when left alone. If transplanting is imperative, do it after foliage dies down. Do not keep bulbs out of the ground longer than necessary.

HYACINTH

Can hyacinth bulbs be planted outside in November for spring flowers? Yes, but a month earlier is preferable.

Can I plant hyacinth bulbs in the spring? If so, will they bloom the first summer? Only the so-called summer-hyacinth (*Galtonia candicans*) can be planted at this time. It blooms the first summer. Spring-flowering hyacinths are planted in the fall and bloom in the spring.

Will hyacinths be injured if they are moved after the leaves show? Yes, they will suffer somewhat. If absolutely necessary, take care to keep a large ball of soil intact around the roots.

Are there miniature hyacinths? Roman hyacinths (*Hyacinthus* *orientalis albulus*), sometimes called French Roman hyacinths, are considerably smaller than either exhibition-size or bedding hyacinths and might be called "miniatures." Other so-called miniature hyacinths have been placed in other genera. They are *H. amethystinus,* now *Brimeura amethystina,* that blooms at the end of May and early June and takes light shade; very early *H. azureus,* now *Muscari azureum,* whose bulbs should be planted in the fall, 3 to 4 inches deep. The wood-hyacinth is *Endymion non-scriptus.* (See under Endymion, Wood-hyacinth.)

HYPOXIS HIRSUTA

What is the little lily-like yellow flower with grasslike foliage that blooms so long? A native American, *Hypoxis hirsuta,* is often called gold star-grass. It blooms from May to November in much of the Northeast. Order from wildflower specialists. Plant in humusy soil and half shade. It is in the amaryllis family.

LEUCOCRINUM (STAR-LILY)

Are star-lilies annuals or perennials? I have had them in the house during the summer and winter but they increase so fast that I won't have room for them all during the winter. Will they stand the winter in the flower bed? Star-lilies or sand-lilies (*Leucocrinum*) are hardy perennials. They are native from Nebraska to the Pacific coast.

LEUCOJUM (SNOWFLAKE)

A friend gave me a clump of leucojum which I greatly admired in her garden 2 years ago. They have never bloomed in mine. Why? This plant dislikes root disturbance and being transplanted may have caused it to stop blooming for a couple of years. Leucojums enjoy a soil rich in leafmold and a sunny or very lightly shaded position.

I bought bulbs of Leucojum vernum, which books say grows 6 inches tall. Mine grew 2½ feet. Was the soil too rich? The plant often sold as *Leucojum vernum* (spring snowflake) is the later-blooming and much taller *L. aestivum* (summer snowflake). The former has only 2 flowers on each stem; the latter usually has 4 to 6.

LILIES

Today's gardener is luckier than his forebears, for he has at his command new races of lilies for which growth success is almost guaranteed. Lilies have been called both the most fascinating and the most exasperating of all garden flowers: fascinating because of their beauty of form and coloring; exasperating because of frequent failures and disappointments. Now with the new hybrids available, no one need temporize about planting lilies. Few ornamental bulbs have as great decorative value or are better adapted to modern gardens. Because they are closely linked with art and religion, they are interesting for aesthetic reasons, too.

In nature different species are found under the most diverse conditions: some grow at high altitudes, others at low; some inhabit the desert, while others are found in damp meadows. They come from both dry and humid climates, and from cold and warm regions. Is it any wonder that as a group they used to appear capricious when included in a garden planting?

While lilies have been cultivated in gardens for a long time, it is only in this century that they have really been domesticated. Previous efforts to hybridize the wild species had proved almost futile. Once a few hybrids were obtained, however, these intercrossed readily. The result has been new races or groups of man-made lilies which are infinitely easier to grow in gardens than were their progenitors. Today lilies have become flowers for every garden. Flower forms and colors are unbelievably diverse, and bloom is spread from June to September. Most of the first hybrids were quite tall, but lower-growing selections are now on the market, too.

How should soil be treated before planting lilies? Well-drained garden soil that is in good condition requires no special treatment. Spade it well, allow it to settle, and plant the bulbs. It is desirable to mix some peat moss or other humus into most soils before planting.

Do lilies require "sweet" or acid soil? Most hybrid lilies prefer soil slightly on the acid side, but the madonna lily (*L. candidum*) needs some limestone. The foliage of a few kinds becomes chlorotic or yellowish in alkaline soil. *Lilium hansonii, speciosum, canadense,* and *superbum* are some of these; add generous amounts of peat moss when planting them. *L. philadelphicum* demands highly acid soil.

What kind of fertilizer is best for lilies? A good garden fertilizer, or almost any complete fertilizer that is relatively high in potash. One good formula is 5–10–10. Manure should not be used since it may encourage losses from basal rot.

Can bone meal and cottonseed meal be used in the ground where lily bulbs are to be planted?   Yes, they are satisfactory, but superphosphate would be more efficient than bone meal.

When is the best time to fertilize lilies?   Early spring.

How should hardy lily bulbs be planted?   The ground should be deeply dug and compost or peat moss added. Small bulbs should go 3 to 4 inches deep; 5 to 6 inches is about right for large bulbs. Madonna and chalcedonicum lilies and their hybrids should be covered 1 to 2 inches. The shallower figure is for heavy soils; the deeper figure is for light sandy types.

When is the best time to plant most lilies?   As early in fall as you can obtain the bulbs. If necessary, mulch the spot well with thick newspapers and leaves to prevent freezing until the bulbs arrive. Then plant them immediately. Bulb suppliers have improved storage techniques, so it is now possible to get some good American bulbs in the spring as well; but the selection is not nearly as complete as in the fall.

When is the best time to divide and transplant various kinds of lilies?   When the tops begin to die. Somewhat-earlier or somewhat-later lifting will not materially affect the performance of the plants the following year. Lilies are never completely dormant; don't leave the bulbs out of the ground, even overnight.

How often should lilies be divided and reset?   Only when the number of stems indicates that the plants are becoming crowded. Lilies often resent being moved. Plant far enough apart so they can remain undisturbed for some years. Never set closer than 6 inches; a foot is better for vigorous hybrids.

Can you tell me how to take up lilies? The leaves often stay green until cold weather. Also, how about the roots? I was always afraid to cut off the roots, so I just took the plants up and set them in a new place, although I wanted to ship them.   If necessary to replant, do so in the fall, about a month before the ground freezes hard. Ship with roots intact.

Should lilies be moved in the spring? How deep should they be planted?   They may be moved if taken up early with considerable soil around their roots. Plant at the same depth in the new site as they were before being moved. Fall, however, is much wiser.

Why are the American hybrid lilies so much better than the old spe-

cies for gardens?   Many are grown from seed and are thus disease-free; extreme care is exercised to keep propagating areas clean by the American growers. These lilies also have built-in hybrid vigor and resistance to disease. Many of the old bulb species came from foreign sources, which meant long shipping delays as well.

What should a beginner look for when purchasing lily bulbs?   Buy reasonably priced hybrids from American-grown sources. These are lilies which have proved themselves.

What is a "stem-rooting" lily?   Many garden lilies are stem-rooting; that is, they produce most of their roots from the stem that grows upward from the bulb.

Why do lilies become spindly after a season or two?   Some lilies fail to bloom because they become crowded; others don't bloom because of disease or frost injury to the growing point. Trees or shrubbery may provide too much competition for sunshine or soil moisture. Most lilies need sun on the leaves most of the day but need shade to keep their roots cool; use mulch or a ground cover.

Examples of modern lilies: Aurelian hybrids.

Does Lilium speciosum 'Rubrum' bloom in August? Can it be planted in the spring?   It blooms in late August or September. It may be planted in the spring. Try the hybrid speciosums such as Jamboree Strain or Imperial Crimson Strain.

I have been unsuccessful growing auratum lilies. What do they need?   They usually fail because they become infected with mosaic disease. Try again with mosaic-free bulbs, planted away from other lilies, in ground that has not grown lilies recently. A surer bet is one of the new hybrid auratums such as 'Imperial Gold'.

If different kinds of lily bulbs are planted in the same bed, will the

different species "mix"? They will not "mix," if "mixing" means that the pollen of one kind will influence adjoining plants so that their flowers change. However, any seed that formed would be a mixture of all the different kinds.

Hybrid speciosum lilies: The Imperial Crimson strain.

Should Easter lily bulbs be taken up and dried before replanting? No. If it is necessary to move them, take them up late in the season and replant promptly.

I planted lilies 4 years ago. Should I have taken them out since and transplanted them? Lilies that are doing well need not be transplanted until they become crowded, when there are numerous short, weak stems.

Why do lilies "run out" in this area? (Pennsylvania.) Because of their susceptibility to obscure virus diseases, certain lilies, such as *Lilium auratum*, are not long-lived in many areas of the country. Others, such as the tiger lily, thrive despite the diseases. Try some of the new hybrids in a fresh spot.

How shall I plant and care for lilies of various kinds? Plant madonna lilies in late August or September and all others when bulbs are received, usually in late fall. Madonna lilies are covered 1 to 2 inches deep, to the top of the bulb; most others are covered 3 to 6 inches, depending on the size of the bulb and the kind of soil (see under Planting). In cold parts of the country, mulch for winter with straw or marsh hay or leaves weighed down with branches after the ground freezes. During the growing season, mulch with shredded pine bark or other porous material, especially in warmer areas. Remove weeds, fertilize with a complete fertilizer, and water if the season is dry.

Will you give me some information about growing madonna lilies? Mine have always failed. Deep planting is a common cause of failure. The top of the bulb should not be more than 2 inches from the surface of the ground. Any good garden soil, well drained, and a sunny site are suitable. Use organic fertilizer and a sprinkle of lime, but no manure or peat moss near the bulbs. Spray, if necessary, against botrytis blight. Unfortunately, many stocks of madonna lilies are badly infected with disease. Buy only American-grown bulbs from a reputable dealer. Unhappily, too, madonna lilies have proved more difficult to hybridize even for such a miracle worker as Jan de Graaff, the father of many of the modern hybrids.

What are the cultural requirements of most lilies? What ground cover shall I use over them? Any good, well-drained garden soil in full sun or light afternoon shade. Low-growing, shallow-rooted plants, such as pansies, violas, Scotch pinks, arabis, and low-growing ferns, are the best ground covers for lilies.

Can the ground where lilies are growing be cultivated? Yes, but with extreme care. Many lilies appear late in the spring and careless hoeing may result in chopping the shoots off below the ground. Lily roots are near the surface and are damaged by deep hoeing. A summer mulch of leafmold, lawn mowings, or shredded bark or bagasse will eliminate the necessity for much cultivation.

What sort of mulch should be used around madonna lilies? Marble chips, shredded bark, buckwheat hulls. They do not want anything highly acid.

Does it harm lily bulbs to cut the flowers? Unfortunately, yes. One can scarcely avoid removing a considerable proportion of the foliage together with the blooms, and these leaves are needed to manufacture food to build up the bulbs for the next season's growth. Some kinds can be cut every second year without serious damage.

How do you get long stems on lilies? Long stems are produced on well-grown plants that are free from disease. Cultural requirements are a fertile soil well supplied with organic matter, mulching to conserve moisture, and the annual application of a complete commercial fertilizer. Old plants with numerous stems should be divided and the bulbs should be replaced in enriched soil.

Should lily blooms be left on the plants or should they be picked off before seeding? Remove flowers as they fade. This favors the development of larger plants the following year.

Should lily stems, after they have dried up and died, be left on the

plants or should they be cut or pulled off? They should be removed in case they harbor disease. They can be pulled up gently, if desired, to save the bulblets which are found at the bases of the stems of certain species; otherwise they should be cut off.

At what time of year should lily bulbs be dug? Do not dig unless it is necessary to move them to another location or divide them. Take them up when the tops begin to die.

Do we cover lilies because they are not quite hardy or to prevent freezing and thawing? Lilies are mulched to prevent damage to the bulbs from low temperatures and to prevent injury to the roots from alternate freezing and thawing.

At what temperature should lily bulbs be kept during the winter? They are hardy and should be left in the ground during the winter. In cold regions, protect with a 6- or 8-inch straw mulch. (See the next question.)

My lily bulbs arrived too late to plant outside. I have buried them in sand in a cold fruit cellar. Will they be all right? Yes, if the temperature is kept just above freezing. It would have been better, however, to have potted them before storing them in the cellar. Knock them gently from their pots and plant them outside in the spring at the proper depth.

Can lily species be grown from seed? Seeds of such lilies as *Lilium regale, pumilum, amabile, concolor, formosanum, henryi,* and *davidii willmottiae* germinate promptly. Plant in early spring in flats of good soil, and leave in a cold frame under lath shades for 2 seasons. Water and weed regularly, and mulch or cover the flats with boards during the winter. At the end of the second summer, plant the seedlings in nursery beds for another year or two, mulching the beds for winter. Plant seeds of *L. auratum, speciosum, martagon,* and native American lilies in the spring. They will not send up leaves until the following spring. If the flats are stacked during the first summer, no weeding and only occasional watering will be necessary. At the end of the third season, the plants should be large enough for the nursery bed. Hybrid lilies will not ordinarily breed true from seed, but you may get some interesting variations.

What is the most successful way to propagate regal lilies? How long before blossoms may be expected from seed? By seed. The larger seedlings should bloom during their third season.

Our madonna lily set seed after it bloomed. Could I plant the seed this winter in a box in the house? Madonna lily seeds can be started in flats in the house any time during the winter.

When and how should lily bulblets be planted?   Remove bulblets borne at the bases of the stems when the stems are cut down in the fall. Plant them in a nursery row for a year or two until they are large enough to be transplanted to the garden. Bulbils borne in the axils of leaves of some varieties may be planted about 1 inch deep as soon as they begin to drop from the plants.

How can I propagate the gold-banded lily (Lilium auratum)?   Remove the bulblets from the bases of the stems in the fall and plant them in a nursery for a year or two until they are large enough for the garden. This is often a difficult lily to grow.

I have three madonna lily bulbs grown from scales I took from large bulbs last August. What should I do with them until next August? I have them potted in the house now.   Keep them growing in the pots until next August, when they may be planted in the garden.

Can small bulbs of lilies that appear almost on top of the ground be separated from the main plant and be planted deeper to increase the stock?   Yes. To prevent crowding, bulblets which form near the surface of the ground on the bases of the stems should be removed every year or two and planted elsewhere.

How do you separate lily bulbs when you wish to start new plants?   Dig and break up the clumps in late fall. The small bulbs on the bases of the stems may also be saved. Lilies which do not increase by bulb division or by stem bulblets may be propagated by removing a few of the scales from the bulbs as soon as the flowers fade and planting these an inch deep in a light soil. These vegetative ways of propagating work for both hybrid and lily species.

What is the best way to avoid mosaic disease in lilies?   Plant only bulbs known, or guaranteed, to be free from mosaic. Your best bet is American-grown hybrids. Or grow the bulbs from seed away from all lilies and other bulbous plants. When you see any sign of disease, dig up the plant and burn it at once.

What is the treatment for basal rot in madonna lilies?   It is caused by a fungus. If detected before the bulbs have rotted much, remove decayed tissue, dip the bulb for 20 minutes in 1 part formaldehyde to 50 parts water, and replant in a new location.

What is the recommended treatment for botrytis blight of lilies?   Destroy diseased leaves and bulbs. Spray remaining bulbs at weekly intervals with Bordeaux mixture. This disease is most serious in wet seasons and where air circulation is bad.

How can I prevent mice from destroying lily bulbs?   Plant the bulbs in cages of wire netting with a large enough mesh to let the stems grow through. Or mix generous quantities of pebbles or gravel in the soil on top of the bulbs. Neither method is foolproof.

Is it true that L. philippinense and tiger lilies are disease carriers and should be removed from the garden? They may or may not have mosaic disease. Foreign stock, often vegetatively produced, is more likely to carry disease than seed-grown American bulbs. Our lily growers also use new acreage, which is less likely to harbor disease microorganisms.

How can I decide which of the hundreds of new hybrids to buy? Preferences for color, height, and blooming season should be your guides when studying catalogs. Attend one of the shows sponsored by the North American Lily Society or its local affiliates and see some of them for yourself.

Please tell me what new hybrid lilies to choose for my garden. June—Mid-Century Hybrids, Martagon Hybrids, Del Norte Hybrids; July—Harlequin Hybrids, Fiesta Hybrids, Bellingham Hybrids, Aurelian Hybrids; August—Potomac Hybrids, Jamboree Hybrids, Imperial Hybrids.

What lilies are long-lived? Healthy bulbs give long life. Buy only American-grown bulbs from a reliable dealer.

What is the difference between a strain of lilies and a named hybrid clone? Hybrid strains are developed by crossing two different lilies. Often grown directly from seed, a general strain will show some color variation, but selected strains will be generally of the same hue. For example, Pink Perfection Strain, Golden Splendor Strain, and Green Magic Strain are all selections of Aurelian Hybrids. A clone is a named variety selected for its outstanding characteristics. It is vegetatively produced and all bulbs sold under the name give identical flowers. Examples are 'Enchantment', 'Shuksan', 'American Eagle'.

What is the botanical name of the commonly used Easter lily? *Lilium longiflorum*. Several improved varieties of this lily have shorter, stocky stems for pot growing. They are not reliably hardy outside in the North, however.

Can lilies be forced to bloom indoors? In addition to the well-known Easter lily, several hybrids are excellent for forcing during the winter. Try any of the Mid-Century Hybrids such as 'Enchantment', 'Cinnebar', 'Harmony', and 'Joan Evans'. The pink and ivory 'Corsage' and 'Red Carpet' are reported excellent, too.

LYCORIS SQUAMIGERA (RESURRECTION-LILY)

Which lily is it that shows its leaves in the spring, then dies, and in August sends up stalks which have a pink-lavender bloom? *Lycoris squamigera,* sometimes sold as *Amaryllis hallii.* It is not a lily and is a member of the amaryllis family.

How shall I care for Lycoris squamigera? Plant in September in light, loose soil, either in full sun or light woodland shade. Set bulbs so that the tops are 5 inches deep and spaced 5 or 6 inches apart. Leave undisturbed for many years. Ferns make a good companion planting.

Why has my Lycoris squamigera failed to bloom since it was transplanted two years ago? It is in a sunny, well-drained location. The bulbs multiplied but sent up no flower stems. It often happens that transplanted bulbs of this species refuse to bloom for 2 or 3 years after being transplanted.

I have 2 lycoris bulbs that are now 4 years old. They come up in the spring and the leaves are healthy and long; they die down in July but never bloom. Can you help me? Maybe you planted small bulbs. If in a suitable soil (deep, light, well drained) and location (full sun or light shade), they should grow and eventually flower.

When do you dig Lycoris squamigera? Some say after the foliage dies and before they bloom; others say after they bloom. The best time for transplanting is immediately after the foliage dies.

MUSCARI (GRAPE-HYACINTH)

How late can grape-hyacinth (muscari) bulbs be planted? They can be planted any time before the ground freezes hard; but it is better to plant them in early fall.

Do grape-hyacinths multiply? If so, when can one transplant them? Yes, they multiply freely. Self-sown seedlings come up in great numbers. Lift the bulbs as soon as the foliage has died down and transplant them immediately.

Can I keep grape-hyacinth bulbs, without planting them, until next spring? No. If you cannot plant them in open ground, plant them closely together in shallow boxes of soil. Stand outdoors and cover with leaves or hay during the winter.

When should grape-hyacinth, which have been undisturbed for years, be reset? To what depth? They can be lifted and replanted when the foliage has died and become completely brown. Plant 2 inches apart and cover the tops of the bulbs with 3 inches of soil.

I have 2 kinds of muscari; one sends up top growth in the fall. Which variety is it? How do I care for them during the winter? *Muscari armeniacum* and its named varieties, of which there are several, produce foliage in the fall. They are quite hardy and require no special winter attention.

ORNITHOGALUM

Can you give me some information about ornithogalums? (Texas.) More than 100 kinds exist. They are natives of Europe, Asia, and particularly Africa, belonging to the lily family. Many kinds should be hardy in Texas. They need a fertile, sandy soil. The article in Bailey's *Standard Cyclopedia of Horticulture,* available in most libraries, although written many years ago, would be of interest and help to you.

Is the very fragrant Ornithogalum arabicum hardy in the vicinity of New York City? Not generally so, although it will winter and bloom if given a very sheltered position, porous soil, and winter protection. *Ornithogalum nutans* is hardier, and *O. umbellatum* (star-of-Bethlehem) has become a weed in parts of the East.

PUSCHKINIA

Will you give me directions for growing a scilla-like bulbous plant called puschkinia? Plant in early fall about 3 inches deep and the same distance apart in light, well-drained, fertile soil, either in full sun or very light shade. It is a fine, hardy, early-blooming bulb which increases well into colonies if left undisturbed. It has attractive light blue flowers which appear about the time forsythia blooms.

SCILLA (SIBERIAN SQUILL)

What is the best way to plant and care for the blue scilla? Plant *Scilla sibirica* in the fall 3 inches deep in loose soil that is fairly fertile. It thrives for years without disturbance. Do not remove foliage until it has completely died down. Another species, *S. bifolia,* is one of the earliest spring bulbs. (See also *Endymion* for other species once classified as *Scilla.*)

STERNBERGIA

What is the name of the rich golden-yellow flower that looks like a crocus (but more substantial) and blooms in September? *Sternbergia lutea.* Plant bulbs 4 or 5 inches deep in August in quite porous soil and a sheltered situation where snow seldom lies long. Mulch with shredded pine bark. Sternbergia must have winter sun on its foliage and resents root disturbance. Overplant with annual sweet-alyssum since it flowers before the leaves develop much. They die down naturally every June.

TULIPS

The spring garden would indeed be dull without tulips. They are one of the "musts" of the mixed flower garden because they are unsurpassed in their wide array of harmonious colors and stately forms. The range of hues covers the entire spectrum and all its tints and shades except pure blue. What artist would not revel in tubes of tulip colors as a medium for painting garden pictures?

For generations tulips grew in the fields and gardens near Constantinople before they found their way to Holland in 1571. Few plants have been molded to such an extent into the economic and social life of a nation. Even though grown in all the temperate regions, they are still thought of as Dutch.

In the course of history tulips have had their ups and downs. Soon after their introduction into Holland they reached a peak of popularity never before or since achieved by any plant. Men speculated and gambled with them as is done today in cotton, corn, and oil. The prices of new varieties soared to staggering heights. A single bulb of the variety 'Semper Augustus' once sold for 13,000 florins, the equivalent of $6,500. Then came the crash; and the economic and financial structure of the entire nation was threatened. The popularity of tulips vanished, and for years they were hidden in the small home gardens of the poorer people of Holland, only to rise again and become a leading industry.

Tulips are valuable in many kinds of garden planting. Their best use is in the border, where they combine beautifully with other spring-flowering plants. Do not line them up in rows like soldiers. In small groups of a single kind they offer friendliness and charm whether you plant early dwarfs in a warm niche or dramatic Darwins as a focal point.

They are also useful for formal beds where they take on an appropriate quality of elegance and constraint. In swaths of a single color they will lead the eye however the designer fancies. Early-flowering types are the easiest to force for winter enjoyment inside. Finally, for flower arrangements their form is distinctive and their coloring delightful.

Hybridization in the last few decades has produced new groups of tulips ideal for home gardeners. The Fosteriana 'Red Emperor' was perhaps the most famous of these man-made wonders, but it has been joined by a wide range of others. Earliest are the Kaufmanniana hybrids. They are followed by the Fosteriana hybrids, the Greigi hybrids, and the Darwin hybrids. The season ends with the traditional tall Darwins. By planting groups of the various kinds of hybrids plus some of the true species, which are charmers, too, it is possible to have almost three months of tulip bloom.

What kind of soil suits tulips best? A fertile, well-drained, light loam, at least 12 inches deep. They will grow satisfactorily, however, in a wide variety of soils.

Will tulips grow well in a position that is located in a wet spot in my garden? No. Good subsurface drainage is of the utmost importance in growing tulips. The bulbs will quickly rot in a waterlogged soil.

Is it necessary to change the soil yearly in beds where tulips are planted? It is easier for most gardeners to change the location in the garden than to move all that soil. In fact, tulips can be planted in the same ground for many years before diseases become a problem.

What can I add to my garden soil to make my tulip bulbs grow larger? Superphosphate and commercial fertilizer, mixed with the soil at planting time, and rich compost or well-rotted manure, set 2 inches under the bulb with a soil separation layer between the bases of the bulbs and the organic matter, will aid.

Is it worthwhile to put commercial fertilizer on a tulip planting in late fall? Yes, but it is better in the spring. Apply and water it in immediately.

What is the best fertilizer for tulips? Complete commercial fertilizers, of low-nitrogen content, and superphosphate are satisfactory. Avoid all fresh manures.

Is it all right to put manure on my tulip bed? Manure is practically wasted when put on the surface. It should be used only in the bottom of the bed. The best winter covers for tulip beds are marsh hay, clean straw, pine bark, and rough compost.

When is the best time to plant tulips? October 15 to November 1, except where a short growing season makes earlier planting necessary.

How late can one plant tulips and still hope for fair results? (Ohio.) December 15 in your area of the country. Their stems will be shorter and their blooms will not be as large as those of earlier-planted bulbs.

How can I save tulip bulbs which are not in the ground at the time of the first hard freeze? Build a fire over the frozen ground and thaw it out, or else chop through the crust and plant. Tulips cannot be held a full year out of the ground.

Could tulip bulbs be planted in January or February if the weather permits? Yes, if sound and well preserved. By February the flower buds contained in the bulbs are usually dead. However, this procedure may result in saving the bulbs so that they will flower the following year.

How does one obtain even results from tulip plantings—flowers all the same height and all of one kind blooming together with flowers of the same size? By planting good-quality, even-sized bulbs of one variety at the correct season and setting them all at the same depth. Professional gardeners accomplish this by removing soil from the bed, placing the bulbs, and then refilling with soil. For the very best results, new bulbs of the same variety or the same type should be planted each fall.

Is it true that tulip bulbs do better when planted 10 or 12 inches deep, as stated by some bulb growers? Deep planting retards tulips splitting up and saves the task of digging and separating them every 2 to 3 years. Large bulbs may do well planted with their bases at this depth, but shallower planting is usually more advisable if bulbs are small. Perfect drainage is a must for deep planting, however. A high water table in a wet year will wreak havoc.

Do you agree that if tulips are planted 9 inches deep they'll never have to be moved? No, but they will need replanting less frequently than shallowly planted bulbs.

What happens if you plant tulip bulbs too deeply or too shallowly? If planted too deeply, small bulbs will waste their strength pushing through to the ground level. If too shallowly, they may heave out of the ground or freeze completely.

What do you think of treating tulips as annuals (that is, plant new bulbs every fall, enjoy the flowers in the spring, and then pull the plants

and discard)? This is a great waste. Healthy tulips planted fairly deep in well-drained loam often increase to delightful clumps before having to be separated because of crowding.

In planting 1,000 tulips in beds 36 inches wide, should I remove the soil to a depth of 6 or 8 inches and replace it after setting the bulbs? I want to plant annuals without lifting the tulips. Your method is quite satisfactory, but it is quicker to prepare the bed and then sink the bulbs into the ground, using a long-shanked trowel. Annuals can be planted over bulbs planted 6 or more inches deep.

How can I get larger tulip blooms? I plant only top-size bulbs obtained from a reputable dealer. Fertilize each September with 5 pounds of a 4–8–4 fertilizer to each 100 square feet of bed. Water freely during dry periods in the spring. Do not remove leaves when cutting flowers. Remove faded flower heads to prevent seed production. Never remove leaves or dig bulbs until the tops have dried completely. However, you always have the largest tulip flowers the first spring after planting. Thereafter, the flowers tend to get smaller as the bulbs split.

Will tulips bloom as well the second year after being planted as they do the first year? Generally, no. However, if the soil is well prepared, moisture is provided during the growing season, and the flowers are removed immediately after blooming (but the foliage is left intact), there often is little difference between the quality of the first and second year's blooms. Some varieties deteriorate quickly, though, after one year.

Could tulips be satisfactorily grown in a planter 5 feet long, 15 inches wide, and a foot deep, with a northwest exposure? Possibly—for one spring's bloom. Drainage must be adequate and boxes shouldn't freeze solid. Pack and mulch with straw or marsh hay.

Can tulip bulbs which have been forced be made to produce flowers outside? If so, how? They can be planted outside if the soil is well fertilized, but the number of flowers as well as their size may be disappointingly small for several years. If you intend to try this, be sure to keep the forced plants watered and growing so that they retain their foliage as long as possible. It's really not worth the trouble.

Can tulips be left in year after year? I have some that have been in for some years and they look very good. As long as the bulbs continue producing satisfactory blooms, keep them in the ground. Cut the flowers off as soon as they fade. Keep watering the bed in dry weather until the foliage has completely died down. Fertilize in the spring.

If all that comes up from a tulip bulb is one large leaf and no bloom

stalk, will that bulb, or the increase from it, ever bloom? This indicates either the need for digging and separation or immaturity. First-year bulblets produce only one big leaf. Both the bulb and its increase can eventually bloom if planted in enriched soil. This "growing on," however, may prove tiresome, and for practical purposes it is often better to discard such weakened bulbs and start afresh with new stock.

Last year I lost about 1,000 tulips. Do they run out? One bed was replanted after the bulbs were lifted and separated, but many died. Would a lack of snow affect them this way? (Minnesota.)   No. Losses may be caused by disease, rodents, or too much water. In your area of the country, shallowly planted bulbs need the protection of a winter mulch.

What is the best method of producing tulips from bulbs which have bloomed 2 years and now show only leaves?   Dig the bulbs in July or early August. Replant only those having a diameter of 1 inch or more in fresh soil. Set small bulbs in rows, in a vegetable garden or elsewhere, to grow, or discard entirely.

Is it advisable to prevent small tulip bulbs from blooming the first year in order to obtain larger bulbs for the next year?   Yes, but do not remove buds until they show color.

Tulips border a brick walk. Sow seeds of annuals (or use transplants) among the tulips to provide summer color. Good annuals for this purpose are sweet-alyssum and petunia.

Can tulips be lifted and packed in soil until the tops are dry in order to save the bulbs; or should they be planted deeper so I can plant gladiolus above them?   Tulips can be lifted, carefully "heeled in" in a shallow trench, and watered frequently until their tops are fully dried. They may then be separated, stored, and replanted in the fall. It would be easier to discard them and start with fresh bulbs in the fall.

Is it all right to dig tulips in the fall for transplanting? Tulips can be dug and transplanted as late as October 1. An earlier date is better, however, as vigorous new root growth begins in October and continues until there is a hard freeze.

Can tulips be moved in the spring before blooming? No, it is impractical and very likely will prevent the bulbs from blooming. It is also dangerous to the future welfare of the bulbs.

Do tulips need to be cured in the sun after digging? They should not be exposed to the sun; even a 30-minute exposure to full sunshine may crack the coats on the bulbs. Cure them by storing them in a cool, dry place protected from sunlight.

What is the best way to store tulip bulbs through the summer? Dry them thoroughly, dust well with sulfur, and hang them in ventilated bags from the rafters of a cool, dry cellar, shed, or garage.

How can I keep tulips during the winter in order to plant them in the spring? This is not a good practice. If it must be done, store at 34° to 40° F., but not for periods longer than 6 to 8 months.

When do you reset tulip bulbs that have been lifted and stored through the summer? No sooner than mid-September, but a month later is better if the bulbs are storing well.

What should be done with small tulip bulbs taken up in the spring but not planted the following fall? They are hardly worth bothering with. Small bulbs will have wasted most of their substance by being stored so long.

Is it important to cover the ground after planting tulip bulbs when the weather is freezing? In very cold sections of the country it is wise to cover tulip plantings with marsh hay or leaves. Apply this after the ground is frozen.

How is the breeding of tulips accomplished by the home gardener? By the same methods used for most other flowers. Ripe pollen is transferred, with a camel's-hair brush, from the stamens of the male parent to the receptive stigma of the seed-bearing parent. All stamens are removed from the female parent before they ripen and shed pollen, and the flower is covered with a paper or plastic bag to prevent accidental pollination from other plants.

Is it true that it takes 7 years to flower tulips from seeds? During this

time is there any top growth? No. Tulips often produce blooms in 3 years from seed. Top growth appears on the young seedlings.

Could you give detailed directions for growing tulips from seeds? Seeds should be planted in light, well-drained soil in a cold frame in the summer. Dig the bulblets the following year when the foliage has died down and plant them 3 or 4 inches deep in nursery beds in the fall. The soil should be enriched for the young bulbs. It is a tedious process that appeals only to the most interested amateurs and to breeders of new varieties.

How do tulip bulbs multiply? By offsets (young bulbs), which grow from the base of the mother bulb. These are separated and are grown on to flowering size in specially prepared nursery beds.

How can small tulip bulbs be taken care of so that they can produce full-size bulbs that will flower? When tulip bulbs are dug up, there are so many small ones. Immediately replant the small bulbs 3 to 4 inches deep in good soil; or they may be stored in a cool place in a mixture of *slightly* moist peat moss and sand, to be replanted in the fall. Small bulbs are often immature when dug. They have high water content and little stored food. Loss of water causes withering, so do not store them dry. Allow flower buds (if any) to develop the next spring after planting until they show color, then nip them off. Encourage the foliage to grow as long as possible. Have soil well enriched at all times.

What are the major tulip diseases? Tulip diseases include fire blight, gray bulb rot, shanking, root rot, and mosaic. For all of the above, destruction of infected stock and a change of soil or sterilization of the infected soil are the only effective remedies.

Last year some of my tulips had small greenish spots on the leaves; the spots grew larger and many of the leaves turned yellow. Some buds failed to open. What was the trouble and what can I do? Fire blight (botrytis). Remove and burn infected leaves; dig bulbs each year and burn all that show infection. Replant in a new location where no tulips have been grown for several years.

What causes new colors and varieties to appear in tulip beds after a few years? Do the bulbils, or offshoots, produce other varieties? Are the new forms seedlings? A change of color is usually due to mosaic disease. Infected plants should be removed or the virus will spread through the entire planting. It is unlikely that there would be any self-sown seedlings.

Do moles eat tulip bulbs during the winter or early spring? Moles are carniverous and therefore do not eat bulbs, but mice and other pests can follow the mole runs and destroy the bulbs. However, mice exist without the help of moles and are very destructive among tulip plantings. Some years they are worse than other years. Their prevalence in a region can be a reason for treating tulips as annuals.

What can I do to keep pocket gophers from eating my tulip bulbs? (Idaho.) Use commercial rodent repellents, poisons, or cyanogas in the form of dust forced through a special air pump made for the purpose. Plant the bulbs nearer your house.

How do you prevent mice and squirrels from eating tulip bulbs? There is no easy way. You can try planting the bulbs in wire-mesh baskets, experiment with rodent repellents, keep cats—and plant so many tulips that some will be overlooked by the pests.

What tulip types are generally available? What are their characteristics? *Species or "Botanical" Tulips and Their Hybrids:* Many of them low-growing and very early; a few like the Fosterianas ('Red Emperor' was the first) are very large. Hybrids of species like the Kaufmanniana, Fosteriana, and Greigii are among the most spectacular for early color. *Darwin Hybrids:* Contain some of the largest tulips known and bloom later than the Fosteriana hybrids but earlier than the regular Darwins. *Single Early Tulips:* Bloom just after early species. There are many fine yellow and orange varieties in this group and many are fragrant. They are 10 to 16 inches in height. *Double Early Tulips:* Double form of Single Early class; they are long-lasting, especially when cut, and good for massing. *Late Doubles:* Often called peony-flowered and are also long-lasting but taller. *Cottage:* Tulips with tall, flexible stems and oval flowers. *Darwin:* The largest group, with big, globular flowers on very tall stems; colors range from white, yellow, and orange through pinks, salmons, and reds to lavenders and deep purples. *Parrot:* Late-flowering with laciniated and twisted petals; they are excellent for arrangements. *Fringed or Crystal Tulips:* Finely cut petal edges but no twisting. *Lily-flowering:* Bloom late with graceful, goblet-shaped blooms with pointed, recurved petals.

What types of tulips give the earliest bloom? Two fine species (*T. pulchella 'Violacea'* and *T. turkestanica*) usually bloom in March in much of the Northeast. The many water-lily tulip hybrids (Kaufmanniana) are also very early.

What tulips are best for midseason bloom? Select your favorite colors from among those listed as Darwin hybrids, Mendel, Triumph, and Greigii hybrids.

What are bouquet tulips? Also known as branching or multiflowered tulips, they produce from 3 to 11 flowers on one main stem from one bulb. In a small garden, a few bulbs will make a good splash of color.

What tulips are good for flower arrangements?   All tulips are excellent in bouquets. For unusual effects, grow some from the following groups: fringed, viridiflora, broken (Rembrandt), and parrot.

How shall I select late-flowering varieties of tulips?   From the catalog of a reputable dealer, select kinds that appeal and that are within your price limit (the highest-priced varieties are usually the newest). Make your selection from the Darwin, cottage, and lily sections. If possible, visit tulip plantings in May and make your selections then.

Are the early-single and early-double types of tulips satisfactory for spring bedding?   Yes. They are lower-growing and earlier-flowering than the Darwins and cottage tulips. Try also Kaufmanniana and Greigii hybrids in groups of a single variety for mass effects.

Which of the "botanical" tulips are most satisfactory for the average garden?   *Tulipa kaufmanniana* (the water-lily tulip); *clusiana* (the lady tulip); *sylvestris* (the Florentine tulip); *praestans*, red; *tarda* (*dasystemon*), yellow; *pulchella*, purple-red; *turkestanica*, cream.

Tender Bulbs, Corms, Tubers

(See also House Plants)

GENERAL

How often should bulbs be watered when being forced in a dark, cool room?   Until growth starts, just enough to keep the soil moist. All forced bulbs, while in active growth, require constant supplies of moisture and should never be allowed to dry out.

Do the following need to be placed in the dark in order to form roots: freesias, St. Brigid anemone, ranunculus?   Freesias, no. Anemone and ranunculus preferably, but not necessarily. All should be started in cool temperatures.

How long a rest period must bulbs that have been forced in pots have before being replanted?   Hardy bulbs, such as daffodils, tulips, hyacinths, etc., that have been forced in winter and early spring must have their foliage ripened naturally for later outdoor planting, which means keeping the pots in good light and watering as necessary. This can be a nuisance and most people discard the bulbs, although hyacinths and daffodils may be worth the effort. Tender bulbs, such as amaryllis, blood-lily (*Haemanthus*), lachenalia, and others should be rested from the time the leaves have died away naturally and completely until they show evidence of starting into growth again. They can then be repotted, if necessary.

Can I store bulbs in a cellar that is damp? If too damp, many bulbs will rot. We suggest you make provisions for better ventilation, which might result in drier conditions.

ACHIMENES

How are achimenes grown? Pot rhizomes about 1 inch apart and ½ inch deep in flats of sandy, humusy soil early in the spring. Water sparingly, then place pots or flats in plastic bags in temperatures between 60° and 70° F. out of direct sun. When growth begins, remove from the bags and water as necessary. Allow about a dozen rhizomes or plants to an 8-inch pot; 5 to a 12-inch hanging container. Shade from strong sun; feed with fish emulsion when actively growing. Gradually dry off at the end of the growing season and store when dormant. Achimenes increase prodigiously each season.

My achimenes leaves developed brown blotches and spots. Is this a disease? This sounds like spotting caused by water remaining on the foliage. Try to keep the leaves dry and out of bright sun; this combination is responsible for the browning of leaves of achimenes as well as its relatives, such as African-violet and gloxinia.

ACIDANTHERA

Is it true that I can grow acidanthera outdoors, like gladiolus? Yes, except in far northern states where it is better to start early by planting several bulbs together in good soil in large pots or tubs indoors; grow them outside during the summer and bring them into a cool situation indoors before the frost; after blooming, dry them off and let them rest. In other sections of the country, plant acidanthera outdoors in a sunny garden in soil rich in humus after all danger of frost is past. Treat as for gladiolus.

AGAPANTHUS (AFRICAN-LILY)

Is the blue African-lily hardy, or must it be protected (in New Jersey)?   Agapanthus is not hardy where more than very light frosts are experienced. In New Jersey and similar climates, it should be wintered in a light, cool, frostproof cellar or some similar situation.

ALSTROEMERIA

Is alstroemeria hardy in New York? How is it grown?   *A. aurantiaca* survives on Long Island when it is established; however, most kinds need the protection of a cold frame, or may be grown by planting out in the spring, lifting, and storing in a cool cellar through the winter. They need an abundance of moisture (but not soggy soil) during the growing season.

AMARYLLIS (HIPPEASTRUM)

What is an amaryllis?   *Amaryllis belladonna* of South Africa is the only plant to which the name *Amaryllis* truly belongs. It is tender north of Washington, D.C., and requires deep planting and full sun. The name is commonly applied to *Hippeastrum,* which hails from South America, as well as to *Sprekelia* (Mexico), *Lycoris* (Asia), sometimes to *Vallota* (South Africa), and occasionally to *Crinum* and other genera.

Will red and white amaryllis (Hippeastrum) bulbs bloom in a summer garden?   The florists' amaryllis or, as it is more correctly named, *Hippeastrum,* cannot be successfully grown as a garden plant except in warm regions, such as Florida and California.

Is there a way to have amaryllis bloom at a more desirable time?   They are typically winter and spring bloomers. The exact time of flowering can be controlled to some extent by varying the temperature in which they are grown, by the methods employed to ripen them off in the fall, and by delaying their restarting.

Do amaryllis bulbs absolutely need to rest?   Yes. However, some individual bulbs exhibit much less of a tendency to go completely dormant and lose all of their foliage during the rest period. Withholding water in late summer is a good way to force dormancy.

During the past summer my older amaryllis bulbs have grown some new bulbs. I will soon have to reset the large bulbs. How can I save the

small ones? Would it be safe to separate them?   Rest young bulbs with the older bulbs and separate at potting time. Plant young bulbs individually in small pots of sandy soil and give them the same treatment as the older specimens. These bulbs prefer to be pot-bound.

AMORPHOPHALLUS (SNAKE-PALM, HYDROSME)

Can snake-palm—the type bulb that has a flower like a big purplish calla-lily and a huge, finely cut umbrella leaf—be grown outdoors in summer?   Yes, its foliage is both distinctive and decorative. Plant the bulb in a large pot of rich soil after the weather has warmed, at which time it grows quickly. Keep in partial shade on a terrace protected from strong winds. The huge flower is evil-smelling and appears before leaf growth. Only large bulbs will bloom.

BABIANA

I have a bulb called babiana. Will you please tell me how to care for it?   Use exactly the same treatment as for freesia.

BEGONIA (TUBEROUS-ROOTED)

Are tuberous-rooted begonias annuals?   They are tender tuberous perennials. They bloom the first season if seed is sown very early indoors.

Do tuberous-rooted begonias need any special attention except shade? The stems on mine seemed so brittle, the flowers fell off almost before they were open, and the tubers diminished considerably in size.   They need a loose, woodsy soil containing plenty of humus, even moisture, good drainage, and shelter from strong winds and hard rain. They like well-rotted manure; if not available, fertilize with a fish emulsion. They need good light—not total shade—to flower properly and can stand filtered sunshine. Careful staking, especially of potted plants, is usually needed.

Where can I plant, and how can I start and care for, tuberous-rooted begonias?   Purchase tubers in early spring. Plant in pots or flats of light soil indoors for 6 to 8 weeks before the plants are to be set outside. Set the plants in open ground when all danger of cold weather has passed. A sheltered, partly shaded position is necessary, and soil enriched liberally with humus. Keep moist but not soggy throughout the summer.

What is the proper soil mixture for tuberous begonias to grow in planters placed on the ground outside?   One part good garden soil, 1 part coarse sand or vermiculite, 1½ parts flaky leafmold or peat moss. Add superphosphate, 1 pint to a bushel of the mixture. You may vary this mixture, but the result should be a rich but porous, humusy soil. Well-rotted manure or rich compost can also be added. Or use a soilless mix according to the directions on the container.

Will growing plants or tuberous-rooted begonias set out in May or June do as well as the tubers?   Well-established plants set out from pots after the weather has become warm and settled should do as well as, and will produce earlier flowers than, tubers set in the open ground.

Should tuberous begonias be lifted before or after the first hard frost?   Before the first killing frost. A light frost that just touches the foliage will not harm them.

What should be done to tuberous begonias in the fall? (Outdoor grown.)   Lift them before severe frost and spread them out in flats (leaving soil adhering to the roots). Put in a sunny, airy place and allow to ripen. When the stems and leaves have died, clean and store the tubers in dry sand, soil, or peat moss, or in plastic bags, in a temperature of 40° to 50° F.

My tuberous-rooted begonias "run out." Is there a way to grow them so they will bloom year after year?   Too heavy a soil, strong competition from the roots of other plants, lack of fertility, too much shade, or any other factor that discourages growth may account for this. If grown under favorable conditions, the tubers will increase in size and will last for many years.

How can I grow tuberous-rooted begonias indoors?   Start tubers in flats of leafmold or peat moss in a temperature of 60° to 70° F. The saucer-shaped tubers should be just below the surface. When growth is 2 or 3 inches high, pot into 4-inch pots, using loose, rich soil or one of the soilless mixes. Later, pot into larger pots as needed, but avoid overpotting. Keep moist at all times; feed established plants; shade from bright sunshine. They do well under fluorescent lights.

Can tuberous begonias be grown in the house when taken from a garden?   No, at least not the same year. After a season's growth in the garden, they need a winter's rest. They may be started into growth again the following spring.

Do tuberous begonias grown as house plants need a rest period?

Yes, indeed. They must be dried off and completely rested during the winter. At the end of the summer, plants begin dying back naturally.

How can one propagate tuberous begonias? From seed, by rooting cuttings made from the young growths, or by carefully cutting the tuber into pieces. This last operation is done in the spring just after growth has started. Be sure that each piece of tuber retains a growing sprout. Dust cut surfaces with fine sulfur before potting up.

Will a cutting from a tuberous-rooted begonia grow a bulb or tuberous root, and will it bloom? Cuttings taken in early spring (they are made from very young shoots) and inserted in a moist, warm, sand propagating bed or in individual pots should bloom well the first season. They will form tubers that may be stored in the usual way through the winter.

CALADIUM

I bought a beautiful potted plant of fancy-leaved caladium, but it began to die in the fall. What did I do wrong? It is natural for this plant to lose its foliage in the fall, remain dormant through the winter, then start into growth again in the spring.

Can I grow caladiums in the open ground rather than in pots? Yes. Select a partially shaded location. Prepare the soil well and incorporate humus (peat moss, rotted manure or compost, and/or leafmold) with it. Plant tubers after the ground has warmed up. Water freely in dry weather.

How can I care for tubers of caladiums that have been dormant during the winter in pots of soil in which they grew last season? To start into new growth, remove tubers from old soil and place in shallow boxes of leafmold or peat moss, just covering the tubers. Keep moist and in a temperature of 70° to 80° F. When growth has started, pot up again, using a light, rich, humusy soil.

CANNA

I was given some very large canna tubers. How do I divide them? Use a sharp knife and cut so that each division consists of one good eye on a substantial piece of rootstock. Allow to dry overnight before planting.

How early should cannas be started? They can be started indoors as early as February 1 and then potted into 4-inch pots. For tubers that are to be planted outdoors without potting, start in large flats of peat moss 4 to 6 weeks before planting (after the danger of frost).

What is the best soil for cannas, and how deep should they be planted? Any ordinary soil. Plant so that the eye is less than 2 inches below the surface.

How shall I care for canna roots during the winter? Dry thoroughly after digging. Dust lightly with sulfur and cover with clean sand or peat moss kept slightly moist, or keep in plastic bags. Store in a cool dark place and inspect occasionally to see if drying occurs. If too dry, sprinkle the sand or soil with water. Plastic bags eliminate this problem.

Are there any cannas suitable for a small garden? There are "dwarf" cannas in several colors which seldom grow over 30 inches. A few good ones are 'Rigoletto', 'Halloween', and 'Stadt Fellbach'.

How should canna roots be divided before storing for the winter? Do not divide in the fall. Store whole, and cut in the spring. (See above.)

The cannas I planted last year grew large and healthy, but very few developed flowers; they were small and poor. Why? Poor, run-out planting stock is most likely responsible. Too much nitrogen could also be the cause. Cannas need fertilizer containing a high phosphoric content. Lack of sunshine may also be responsible.

Is it a good plan to dig cannas and store the roots over the winter? (Georgia.) No. In the lower South it is a good practice to allow cannas to grow without being moved until the clumps become very matted. Every 3 or 4 years dig the clumps sometime during the winter, separate the roots, and set the divisions in new beds of well-enriched soil.

CLIVIA

Will you please tell how to grow clivias in pots? Pot in rich, well-drained soil. Do not repot more often than absolutely necessary. Water to keep the soil always moist; shade from the sun; feed when growing actively. Give winter temperature of 50° to 60° F. In the summer keep outdoors in the shade.

COLOCASIA (ELEPHANT'S EAR)

Is the elephant's-ear a kind of caladium? How do you grow it? It is often sold as *Caladium esculentum,* but the correct genus is *Colocasia.*

Plant tubers in pots indoors in the spring. After all danger of frost has passed, set outdoors in moist, rich soil. After the first frost, lift, dry off, and store in a cellar or similar frost-free place.

DAHLIAS

Few flowers have attained—and maintained—such wide popularity as the dahlia. Yielding readily to the handiwork of plant breeders, innumerable forms and colors have been introduced. In the early days the breeding work was aimed at increasing the size of bloom. When flowers were obtained as large as dinner plates, the gardening public began to feel they were coarse and too big to be artistic. The hybridizers were not disheartened but proceeded to develop miniature types. Today the size of different varieties varies from ½ to 15 inches in diameter, and the plants are from 18 inches to 7 feet in height!

The colors, clear and rich, include all the hues except clear blue. The petals have a crystalline texture which gives a luminous or translucent quality to the color. In addition to the pure spectrum hues, they embrace the rich, warm tones of the sunrise and the soft, full tints of the sunset. There are flower forms to suit any fancy. Some varieties are dense, full, and formal; others are loose, shaggy, and carefree. There are ball-shaped types, singles, and some even mimic the forms of other flowers, such as the peony, orchid, and anemone.

The dahlia hails from Mexico, where it may be found growing at altitudes from 4,000 to 8,000 feet, among the broken rocks of lava beds and where the temperature is moderate and rains are frequent. As with other plants, its native habitat provides an indication of its cultural needs: good drainage, plenty of moisture, cool temperatures.

In garden plantings the lower-growing dahlias are not combined with other plants to the extent they might well be. Many gardeners feel that they are difficult to use except by themselves in mass plantings. Yet when placed in the perennial border or among annuals, or in front of shrub plantings, they give a magnificent effect. Dahlias should be more generously used in the flower gardens of America to give added color in the late summer and fall.

Even gardeners who do not want the bother of storing tubers over the winter can enjoy dahlias quite inexpensively. Fine varieties, both single and double, are available through seed. Started early in the house, the seedlings develop quickly into bushy plants in the garden. Needing no staking, these lower-growing types are perfect for bedding and yield cut flowers until frost. The tubers they form, of course, can be gathered in the fall by the provident gardener, or they can be discarded.

What type of soil do dahlias need?   They will grow in a wide variety of soil. Important points are porosity for free drainage, reasonable humus content, and sufficient moisture retentiveness so that the plants do not become bone dry. Any good vegetable garden soil is satisfactory.

Will you suggest a fertilizing program for dahlias?   At planting time broadcast 5 pounds bone meal or superphosphate mixed with 1 pound muriate of potash to each 100 square feet of ground, or divide among 10 hills. About July 10 give each plant a handful of a complete fertilizer (5–10–10 or 5–10–5). Finally, about August 25, when buds appear, mix 3 pounds of superphosphate, 4 pounds of dried manure, and ½ pound of muriate of potash together and rake this amount into every 10 hills. Do not apply closer than 6 inches or more than 18 inches away from stems.

I have saved wood ashes from my fireplace. Should I use them on my dahlia bed?   Yes. They are a valuable source of potash. Be sure to store in a dry place, then either dig the ashes into the ground at planting time, using up to 10 to 15 pounds per 100 square feet, or apply them as a topdressing in early September.

Is liquid fertilizer good for dahlias?   Excellent. A diluted solution, made from either cow manure or chicken manure or a fish emulsion used according to container directions and applied at weekly intervals while the flower buds are developing, increases both size and quality.

What is the best location for dahlias?   They need free circulation of air, direct sunlight for at least 6 to 7 hours each day, freedom from competition with roots of large trees or dense shrubbery, and a fertile, well-drained soil.

In planting dahlias, should they be kept a certain distance from other flowers?   Not more than is necessary to permit both the dahlias and the other flowers to grow and develop satisfactorily. Dahlias should not be crowded. Set the taller kinds from 3 to 4 feet apart; somewhat less for the miniatures and pompons.

How soon can dahlias be planted in pots indoors before they are transplanted outdoors?   For May planting outdoors in most northern regions, pot during April.

What is the proper planting time for dahlias?   After all danger of frost has passed, usually about May 15 in the vicinity of New York City and much of the North.

Can the tubers formed by the dahlia that one buys in pots and sets out in late spring be held over and used the following year? Yes.

Which is better—to leave dahlias in bunches or to plant the tubers separately? I have mine put away in bunches for the winter. Leave in bunches to store, but always divide the clumps before planting.

If the necks of dahlia tubers are injured, will the plants bloom? No. Dahlia tubers with broken necks will not grow.

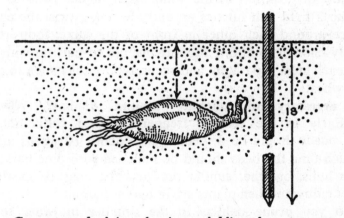

Correct method for planting a dahlia tuber, one root with a strong "eye," cut from a clump.

Can dwarf or bedding dahlias be started indoors under fluorescent lights? Yes. Start seed, sowing in flats or bulb pans, indoors in March. Or sow one or two seeds in a peat pot, pinching off the smaller plant in each pot after germination. As plants enlarge, transplant them into pots of suitable size, and set out in open garden beds when all danger of frost is over and the ground has warmed up.

Dahlia catalogs list the plants as well as the roots of certain varieties. I would like to try some plants next season. How do you handle them? When received, remove from their carton but leave in the pots. Soak in shallow water to freshen. Set out in the late afternoon or on a cloudy day. Dig holes 6 inches deep; remove the plants from their pots; set so that the root balls are just covered with soil; leave the finished surface around the plants 3 inches below the grade. If the following day is sunny, shade the plants. They will take hold in a few days. Gradually fill the holes with soil as the plants grow.

How are dahlia tubers of the exhibition types planted after clumps have been divided? First, set stout stakes in place; at the base of each stake, dig a wide hole 6 inches deep; loosen up the soil. Lay each tuber horizontally, with its neck near the stake and with its eye pointing upward. Cover with soil so that the tuber is just hidden. As the eye grows, keep filling in the soil so that the bulb is kept just covered until the surface grade is reached. (Small types need no staking.)

I think that my method of tying up dahlias is not very successful. They are always damaged in storms. What do you suggest?   Plant in a position not too exposed to the wind. Sisal binder twine is good for tying. Make 2 tight half hitches around the stake; twist the ends of the twine twice around each other in front of the stake; loop around the stem tightly enough to afford support but not to cut; tie with a square knot. Tie each stem separately and securely; do not bunch together like a sheaf of wheat!

Is it necessary to cultivate around dahlias? What about mulch?   Early in the season, frequent surface cultivation is very beneficial, but it should be dispensed with about 10 weeks after planting, at which time the beds should be mulched with pine bark, bagasse, buckwheat hulls, or other similar products that may be locally available. Do not cultivate when plants are in bud or bloom.

How do you prune dahlias in the summer in order to get fall blooms?   Allow only one main stalk to grow. When plants reach about 10 inches in height, pinch out their centers just above the second pair of leaves. Side branches that develop should also be pinched. Remove any flower buds that appear before August 1.

How much water do dahlias require?   Unless the weather is very dry, they need none until they start to bloom. Then water thoroughly, soaking the ground every week or 10 days, whenever rainfall is insufficient.

How are dahlias disbudded so that they have large blooms?   When the buds appear (usually in clusters of three), pinch out all except the central one of each group. New lateral shoots will appear. All of these below the remaining bud, except the two shoots nearest to the main stalk, should be pinched out. This will not only produce large blooms but will keep the plants low and bushy and will encourage the development of long stems.

What is the proper method to produce strong-stemmed dahlias that will support large blooms when cut?   Remove all but 1 stalk from each plant. After 3 sets of leaves develop on this, pinch out its tip. Laterals will soon grow and eventually become main branches. All laterals and sublaterals other than the 4 main branches should be pinched out except for the 2 sublaterals that develop near the base of each flowering stem.

How many days should one allow from planting time for blooms of giant dahlias to develop for show? From 80 to 120 days, depending on the variety. A hot, dry season may cause blooms to mature from 10 to 15 days later than normal.

When and how do you cut dahlia flowers for exhibition? After sunset on the evening before the show. Cut with long stems, trim off any leaves that are not needed, and immediately stand the stems in water. Carry indoors and then trim the base of each stem by cutting it slantwise under water. Keep in a cool, dark place until they are packed for transportation.

How do I dig and divide dahlia tubers? After the first frost, dig up clumps carefully with a fork. Turn upside down and allow them to dry in the sun for 4 to 5 hours. Let some soil cling to the clumps to guard the necks from breaking and to prevent excessive drying during storage. Do not divide until some months later (March or April).

What care do you suggest if part of the dahlia tuber is injured in lifting? Remove injured tubers with a sharp knife or pruning shears. Sprinkle the cut surface with sulfur.

How shall I store dahlia tubers? In a cool (45° to 55° F.) cellar or in barrels or boxes lined with newspaper and placed where the temperature is not more than 55° nor less than 40°. Examine periodically to see that they are not becoming mildewed or dried up.

Should dahlia roots be wrapped in paper or packed in earth for winter storage? Either. Allow the soil to cling to the clumps to prevent excessive drying. Peat moss makes a good material in which to store them.

Can dahlias be stored outdoors if buried below the frost line? Yes, if well below the frost line. They will not survive if the tubers are frozen.

What makes dahlia roots rot after they are dug? We put ours in the garage and in about 3 weeks they had all rotted. Probably they had not dried sufficiently before you stored them. There are also several rot organisms which affect stored dahlia roots.

A short time after digging my dahlias, the roots shriveled and became soft. What was the reason? They were dug after the first frost. You probably kept them in a warm place and thus dried them out too fast.

Why do my dahlia tubers sprout after being stored? They were put away in peat moss in the cellar. The storage place is too warm. See that they are not near a heater. The temperature during storage should not be above 55° F.

My dahlia tubers in storage are beginning to sprout. I have them packed in sand. Will this harm them? Not if it happens in the spring when planting time is approaching. Sprouting in winter weakens roots and should be prevented by storage at 40° to 55° F.

What causes large dahlias to wilt as soon as they are cut? Large-flowered dahlias always wilt if cut during the day. Cut in late evening, well after the sun is down, or *very* early in the morning. Dipping the ends of the stems in boiling water for 1 or 2 minutes has a tendency to keep the flowers fresh.

We have dahlias which never bloom. Does their age have anything to do with it? Not if they are healthy. Dahlia "stunt," a virus disease, and tarnished plant bug often prevent flowering.

Why do dahlias with large flowers have very thin stems? The excess buds were pinched out. Some varieties naturally have weak stems. Excess nitrogen and too little potash also cause this condition.

My dahlia garden is between two buildings. I get very good plants but the frost kills the buds before they bloom. Is there any way to speed the blooming of dahlias? Your plants may not receive sufficient sun. Plants in the shade tend to become soft and to bloom late. Possibly you have late-flowering varieties. These should be planted early.

Why do my dahlias have so many leaves and so few flowers? Probably because of too much shade or too much fertilizer. Attention to pruning and disbudding may help.

Why do some dahlias (of varieties supposed to be tall) stay low? Very possibly because they are infected with mosaic disease or "stunt." Check with a skilled grower or with your State Agricultural Experiment Station. Destroy diseased plants.

My dahlias have good growth and lots of flowers but never form tubers. What can I do to encourage the plants to grow large, plump tubers that will keep during the winter? Probably you use an unbalanced fertilizer. Excess nitrogen will cause the condition you describe. Try more potash and phosphate. There are some dahlias, particularly choice varieties, that are very poor tuber producers. If the plant was grown from a cutting made *between* the joints, it would bloom but not form tubers.

How can I stop my dahlias from growing 9 feet tall, with very little bloom? Probably too much shade, or fertilizer containing too much nitrogen caused this condition. Allow only one main stalk to grow from each plant, disbranch, and disbud as described in other answers.

Why do my dahlias refuse to bloom? They have plenty of water and fertilizer and are planted in good garden soil. They have a southern exposure. The plants grow strongly but have few, poor blooms. Is the air circulation good? Dahlias should not be planted along the side of a house or close to a hedge. They may be infested with insects such as thrips, leafhoppers, earwigs, borers, or tarnished plant bug; or infected with mosaic or "stunt." Try a change of stock. Dahlias planted in the same soil year after year sometimes deteriorate.

I have a dahlia that grows about 8 feet tall and has lots of flower buds, but they never open up. Why? It grows lots of tubers. These symptoms are suggestive of tarnished plant bug injury. (See above.)

What causes imperfect dahlia blooms? Diseases, such as "stunt"; pests, such as leafhoppers, tarnished plant bug, earwigs, and thrips; unfavorable weather conditions.

Has anyone discovered the cause of the variation in color in some bicolored dahlias? The exact cause is not definitely known. Bicolored cultivars seem to be particularly unstable and tend to run back to solid colors.

I have heard that dahlia tubers were used as a food. Is there any reason why they should not be so used; are they habit-forming or harmful in some way? According to the authoritative Sturtevant's *Notes on Edible Plants*, "It was first cultivated for its tubers, but these were found to be uneatable." Ancient Mexicans are said to have used them for food, however.

How are dahlias propagated? By division of the clumps of roots; by cuttings; by seeds; and, much more rarely, by grafting.

How are dahlias increased by cuttings? Undivided clumps are planted in a cool greenhouse in January or February. Cuttings, each with a sliver of tuber attached at the base, are prepared when shoots are about 3 inches long and are inserted in a propagating bench (bottom heat, 65° F.; atmosphere, 5° lower) or in a flat. Shade and a "close" atmosphere are supplied. When the roots are an inch long, cuttings are potted up individually. Ordinary stem cuttings may also be used, but the basal cut should be made just below a node. It is scarcely practical to use this method unless a greenhouse is available.

What types of dahlias bloom the first year from seed? All types, but the dwarf hybrids that are grown chiefly for mass-color effects in the garden, rather than for perfection of their individual blooms, are the kinds most commonly raised from seeds.

Dahlia tuber in moist peat moss to force sprouts. When cut from the tuber, the sprout is handled as a cutting and will root to produce another plant. This method of propagation is most practical in a greenhouse.

How can I save the seeds from my dahlias?   After the petals have fallen, allow the flower head to dry on the plant. Gather the heads before the killing frost comes and place them in a dry place until they have fully dried out. It is unlikely that they will exactly reproduce their parents. The best seeds are produced in California, where the growing season is long.

How should dahlia seeds be started?   Sow them in pots or flats of light, sandy soil, February to March, in a temperature of 60° F. Transplant seedlings (when the second pairs of leaves have developed) individually into small pots. Grow in a sunny location or under lights, with a temperature of 55°. When roots crowd the small pots, replant into 4-inch pots or into open ground if it is already warm enough.

Is it necessary to remove the tubers from seedling dahlias, and when?   No, the small tubers must be left on and set out with the seedling plants.

How can I hybridize dahlias?   Most hybridizers use hand pollination, which involves using a camel's-hair brush to transfer the pollen of one variety to the pistil of another.

How were the giant dahlias developed from smaller ones? By systematic breeding, based on hand cross-pollination, and by carefully selecting the most promising seedlings. This work has been going on for a long time. The Aztecs were doing it in Mexico when the Europeans arrived.

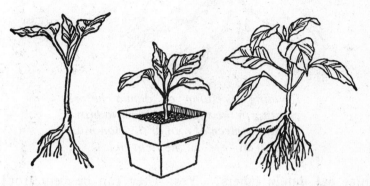

Left: Dahlia cutting rooted, ready to be potted (center). Right: Dahlia seedling, ready to be transplanted. Note the small tuber already forming.

Can dahlias be divided immediately after they are dug in the fall or must they wait until spring when they are sprouted? It is better to wait until spring, when their eyes (buds) are visible.

How should dahlia clumps be divided? By using a sharp knife and pruning shears. Each division of a clump should include a portion of the old stem attached to the neck of a tuber; on each should be a visible eye capable of developing into a sprout. After being divided, let the tubers air dry overnight before being planted.

How can I divide dahlia tubers when absolutely no eyes are visible? Do *not* divide until eyes appear. If the clumps are slow in "eying up," put them in a flat with damp peat moss and place in a warmer, well-ventilated spot. This will cause eyes to develop in a few days. If eyes fail to appear, the stock is "blind" and will not produce plants. Discard and start over with new, fresh tubers.

Are dahlia tubers that shrivel up after division any good? They will probably produce weak plants. After dahlia roots are divided, they should be kept in slightly damp peat moss until planting time.

How can I know a live dahlia tuber from one that will not grow when

dividing for spring planting?   Roots that will grow possess eyes (buds) which usually appear on part of the stalk or old stem of the clump. Many clumps produce "blind" roots. These should not be planted.

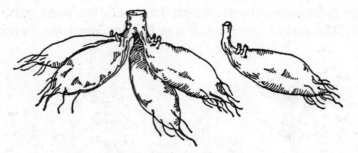

*Dividing a clump of dahlia before
planting in the spring. In order to grow,
each new piece of root or division must
contain an "eye" at the stem end.*

Do mice eat dahlia tubers?   Yes. They can be very troublesome. Wire-mesh baskets, as recommended for tulips, around the tubers, can help (leave room at the top for a sprout to come through). Keep weeds down; mice do not like to cross open areas. They can also get into stored tubers; inspect frequently and set traps if necessary.

Do rabbits eat dahlias?   They can level a bed of new shoots but seldom bother established plants. If rabbits are a problem in your area, at planting time protect each tuber site with a circle of chicken wire, pushed into the soil or anchored by stakes, which can be removed later. Or cut the bottoms off cardboard milk containers and push these into the soil a few inches when shoots appear; the container also acts as a wind screen to protect tender new shoots until they harden off. Dried blood applied around the shoots is often an effective temporary deterrent against rabbits.

My dahlias are not growing well. I suspect mosaic disease. What are the symptoms?   The plants are usually dwarfed; the leaves are smaller than normal and show a yellowish mosaic or spotting. Pale-green bands are often developed along the midribs and larger secondary veins.

Is there any cure for mosaic disease of dahlias?   No. Dig out and destroy the affected plants. Under no circumstances should you propagate from them. Spray to control aphids, as they transmit the disease from plant to plant.

What is the cause of dahlia "stunt"?   A temporary dwarfing, not carried over from year to year, may result from attacks of such insects as tarnished plant bugs, leafhoppers, thrips, and aphids. Virus diseases may cause real stunting, which is not curable. Virus-infected plants should be promptly destroyed.

What is the recommended treatment for dahlia wilt disease? Two wilts attack dahlias—one caused by a fungus, the other by a bacterium. Destroy all affected plants. Use only healthy tubers for propagation. Move dahlias to new ground.

How can I recognize and control red spider mite on dahlias? It is most common in hot, dry weather. The leaves become yellowish or pale brown. The tiny insects, usually covered with a fine web, can be seen crawling on the undersides of the leaves. Forcible spraying with clear water to wash them off is helpful.

My dahlias are attacked by small bugs that jump off the leaves when disturbed. The leaves are turning yellow and becoming brittle. No holes appear in the leaves. What is it, and what remedy do you suggest? This is a leafhopper. Spray at weekly intervals with an all-purpose spray that contains carbaryl or malathion. Destroy all weeds in the vicinity.

I have had a lot of trouble with corn borers in dahlias. How can I check their ravages? Spray or dust twice a week with rotenone or carbaryl from August to October. Cut off infested blooms and stalks. Burn the old stalks at the end of the season.

Does more than one kind of borer attack dahlias? Yes. The common stalk borer hatches in May, eats a hole in the stem, and usually remains until August. Watch for holes in stems and probe with fine wire to kill borers. Destroy all coarse weeds in the vicinity.

I have found large shell-less snails eating my dahlia flowers. Can I do anything other than hand-pick them off? Clean up all rubbish and debris. Slugs hide under stones, bricks, boards, etc., during the day. Spread metaldehyde around, according to directions, or use alcohol or beer poured into a shallow container that the slugs can climb into.

How can I control earwigs, which eat dahlia flowers? They operate mostly at night, hence are hard to hand-pick. Try Sevin (carbaryl) dusted on the ground around the plants. An alternative is to spray foliage with malathion. During daylight, earwigs congregate under stones and boards where you may be able to kill them.

How can I learn more about dahlia growing and exhibiting? Join one of the numerous local societies devoted to dahlias; there are also several regional groups and the parent American Dahlia Society. Watch in your local paper for notices of dahlia shows in autumn.

How important are the classifications of dahlias made by the A.D.S.? These divisions are used in all shows sponsored by the A.D.S. For the casual gardener, these groupings offer quick ways to pick varieties by size, flower form, and color from the catalogs. Very extensive collections will have a key as an aid.

What is the meaning of initials like FD, SC, etc., after the names of dahlias in catalogs? These identify flower forms. FD = formal decorative; SC = semi-cactus; M = miniature; BA = large ball-shaped; POM = small ball-shaped, etc. Look for a key in the catalog or consult A.D.S. lists for complete descriptions.

What is the difference between cactus-type and decorative dahlias? Cactus types have more or less tubular petals, while petals of decorative types are more flat than tubular.

What are the round ball-like dahlias called in catalogs? These may be listed as ball or pompon, depending on their size.

What are some good dahlias for cutting? Those classed as pompons and miniatures are particularly good for bouquets.

What are the easiest dahlias to grow? The small-flowering dwarfs, because they require less space and less attention in regard to disbranching, disbudding, and staking. In many ways they are more useful than the large-flowering types both in the garden and as cut flowers. They are usually listed in catalogs as miniature or dwarf bedding dahlias. Pompons are excellent, too, but many will grow up to 5 feet.

EUCHARIS (AMAZON-LILY)

Will you give me the recommended method of growing the Amazon-lily? *Eucharis grandiflora* bulbs should be planted, several together, in large pots containing rich, well-drained, fibrous soil. Avoid repotting unless necessary. Give a temperature of 65° to 75° F., plenty of moisture when growing, and shade from bright sun. The foliage is evergreen, so the plants should never be dried off completely. Eucharis sometimes blooms twice a year, outside in the summer and inside in late winter. A month after any flowering, begin to reduce water until the foliage almost wilts. Continue this regimen for 4 to 6 weeks, then resume regular watering and fertilizing.

FREESIA

What conditions are necessary for growing freesias successfully? Well-drained but fertile soil; strict care in regard to watering; cool (45° to 55° F.), airy growing conditions; and the fullest possible exposure to sunshine. Sound, healthy corms of fair size are a prerequisite.

What is the secret of watering freesias? When first potted, give a thorough soaking, place in a cool situation, and cover with several inches of leafmold or coarse compost. When growth starts, remove the mulch and water to keep the soil only just moist. Freesias abhor too much water during their early stages of growth. Gradually increase the supply of water as leaves develop, and water generously when well rooted and in full growth. After blooming, water freely until the foliage begins to fade, then gradually reduce, and finally withhold water entirely.

Do freesias need a high temperature? Quite the contrary. They thrive best where the night temperature does not exceed 45° or 50° F., with a daytime rise of 5° to 10° permitted.

How shall I fertilize freesias grown in pots during the winter? Mix superphosphate with potting soil. When flower buds begin to show, feed at weekly intervals with dilute liquid fertilizer.

Is it possible to grow freesias outdoors? Specially prepared bulbs are now available through spring bulb catalogs.

GLADIOLUS

The gladiolus species, from which the modern garden varieties have been developed, grow wild along the shores of the Mediterranean Sea and in South Africa. The true species are of little significance as garden plants, although a few are offered for fall planting. In areas where winters are not too severe they bloom in May and June. While the flowers are small and the colors limited, they do add an interesting note to the late spring garden.

It is a far cry from any of the wildlings to the glorious flowers we know today as gladiolus. They are available in heights from a few feet to giants taller than the average person, although such giants should be considered novelties rather than legitimate garden subjects. Every color of the rainbow is represented, even green. The individual florets of modern cultivars are set closely together along the spike with most having flaring open petals. An increasing number are frilled or ruffled. Many have contrasting color in the throats.

All-America Gladiolus Selections, sponsored by the North American Gladiolus Council, are announced every year. These winners have been tested in gardens around the country and represent outstanding new varieties.

Mirroring today's smaller homes and gardens, many of the newer gladiolus are smaller than the huge florist's spikes once so popular. These miniatures average about 30 inches in height, seldom need staking, and should increase the gladiolus's popularity with modern gardeners. Of late many All-America winners are in this class, and flower arrangers are delighted with their daintier spikes.

The ease with which gladiolus can be grown anywhere in the United States undoubtedly contributes to their popularity. They are not particular in their soil requirements. They do well in warm exposures. While they tolerate neglect better than many other plants, they also respond to good treatment. Of upright growth, they require little room, so that large quantities of flowers can be produced in a limited area.

Usually they are grown in beds or in rows in the cutting garden. However, if combined with other plants in the flower border they will add much color interest and a good vertical line. Gladiolus, however, are more important as cut flowers than as decorative garden plants. They keep exceptionally well, and the form of the spike is especially well adapted for use in various types of arrangements.

Do gladiolus exhaust the soil? I have 20 acres on which gladiolus have been planted for the last 2 years, but the soil has been fertilized each time they were planted. Gladiolus do not exhaust the soil, particularly if fertilizer is used, but repeated growing in the same soil can result in an increase in disease and this may make the corms unsalable.

I am interested in raising gladiolus. Does the soil have to be very fertile for best results? Fertile, but not excessively rich.

Which fertilizer shall I use when I plant gladiolus in my flower border? Providing the soil is in good condition, almost any complete fertilizer will be satisfactory. Bone meal or superphosphate, and unleached wood ashes are excellent. Avoid fresh manure; leafmold or peat moss and commercial fertilizers are satisfactory.

What type of soil should gladiolus have to be most successful? A well-drained, sandy loam in which gladiolus have not been grown for the past 3 years.

Will gladiolus grow in sandy soil?   Fine specimens can be grown in sandy soil if enough moisture is supplied. Better mix peat moss in the soil before planting, though, to help retain moisture and nutrients.

How am I to pick out the right kind of gladiolus corms to plant?   Best for planting are clean No. I corms 1½ inches or more in diameter with small scars, which proves they were grown from small corms. Very large, flat corms are less desirable than moderate-sized ones with greater depth.

Do gladiolus prefer sun all day or partial shade?   Full sun, although they can be grown in partial shade.

How early can gladiolus be set out?   As soon as frost is out of the ground. Little is gained by extra-early planting, and sometimes later plantings bloom first. Many catalogs list early, midseason, and late varieties to help stretch the flowering period. If you have a favorite, successive plantings will allow you to have it in bloom over a long period of time.

When is the best time to plant gladiolus; and how deep?   Make the first planting about May 1 and follow with successive plantings up to early July. Set corms 4 to 6 inches deep. In warmer climates, planting times are earlier.

When should I plant gladiolus for them to bloom in September and mid-October?   Between June 15 and July 1.

Will the flowers of late gladiolus be as large as if the corms were planted early?   Late flowers should be larger than early ones of the same variety because cool nights produce larger flowers and better color in gladiolus.

How deep do you advise planting gladiolus; and how far apart in rows?   Four inches deep in heavy soil and 5 to 6 inches in light, sandy soil. Three inches apart is close enough in the rows for good spikes. Space rows 18 to 30 inches apart.

What is the best method for planting gladiolus?   In rows, like vegetables, for cutting. They can then be given better care and will produce better spikes. In the garden, use clumps of a single variety for focal points.

Can gladiolus corms be planted too closely to each other?   The old rule is to plant the diameter of the corms apart, but small sizes (at least) should be given more room.

How deep should the cormels (young corms) be planted?   About 2 inches deep.

The gladiolus corms that I planted along the borders of my shrubbery

failed to grow well. What is wrong?   Gladiolus are not able to compete successfully with the roots of strong-growing trees and shrubs. Try planting in well-prepared soil away from the competition of roots.

Can gladiolus corms be used after not having been planted one year?   Gladiolus corms are of little use the second year; but bulblets or cormels are still good the second year, and those of hard-to-sprout varieties grow better then. Soak them in tepid water for 2 or 3 days first.

What is the best way of supporting gladiolus so they do not fall over?   Tie to individual slender stakes or place the stakes at intervals along both sides of the rows and stretch strings from stake to stake.

Do gladiolus need much watering?   The soil must be well drained, but they need an abundance of moisture, and if the season is at all dry they should be watered liberally, particularly after the sixth or seventh leaf begins to develop.

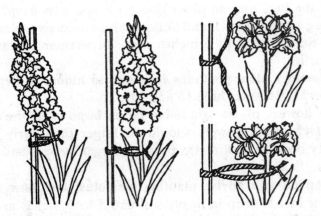

Method of staking a gladiolus spike to prevent injury by wind. Left: Incorrect. Center: Correct. Right: Tie twine first around the stake, then loop around the stem.

How are gladiolus corms grown to such mammoth sizes as 4 to 5 inches in diameter?   Some varieties under good conditions make 4- and 5-inch corms, but a good, thick 1½-inch corm is more satisfactory.

Do gladiolus corms need to be taken up every year?   They are killed by freezing, and so should be dug and stored in a cool, dry cellar or frost-free place during the winter.

How can I keep my late gladiolus from sprouting?   To keep your corms from sprouting, store them in a cool, dry, dark place in slatted or screen-bottom trays. The temperature should be evenly maintained, as near 40° F. as possible.

What can I do with gladiolus that I failed to take up last fall? Are they ruined? (Kentucky.) Gladiolus are only half-hardy and ordinarily will freeze and rot if left in the ground during the winter unless they are in a well-drained soil and are covered with a heavy layer of protective mulch.

When should gladiolus corms be taken up in the fall? When the leaves start to turn brown. A good new corm is formed 6 weeks after blooming.

Should gladiolus corms be trimmed before storing? The tops should be cut off close to the corm at digging time. The husk should never be removed while in storage, as it helps the corm to retain its moisture.

How can I store gladiolus corms to keep them from shrinking and drying out in the winter? If stored in a cool cellar, they will not shrink or dry out. The ideal temperature is 40° F. Never allow them to freeze. Try hanging them in bags made from the legs of discarded nylon hose.

Will a light frost on gladiolus corms ruin them; and how can I tell if they are still all right? A light frost will not harm the corms. If the frost is severe, they will dry out and become very light in weight.

Why do gladiolus corms produce large blooms one year and none or very poor ones the next? Possibly your corms were dug too soon after blooming, or perhaps you cut the stems too low when picking flowers. Corm diseases, thrips, or poor growing conditions may be factors.

Why do my gladiolus corms exhaust themselves within 2 or 3 years and produce inferior blooms? Varieties vary greatly in this respect; some will produce good spikes for a number of years, others for only a single season. Gladiolus scab is often responsible.

What makes my gladiolus flower stems develop crooked necks? Not all varieties of gladiolus "crook," but those that do should be planted so that they bloom in the cool weather of fall.

I have 200 gladiolus seeds planted. They have grown 8 inches tall and have fallen over. They look healthy. Will they be all right? Gladiolus, the first year from seed, look like grass. They should form small, mature corms in about 12 weeks.

Why don't gladiolus bloom all at one time? The blooming time varies according to the size of the corms and the variety. Larger corms bloom the soonest. Catalogs of gladiolus specialists often list the number of growing days necessary before planting. It may vary from 60 to 150 days.

What makes gladiolus of different colors gradually change to one color after a few years? Many people think that gladiolus change color. What actually happens is that the more robust-growing varieties in a mixture outlive and outmultiply the weaker-growing ones.

My gladiolus corms end up with a growth on the bottom. Is this natural or is it a disease? If so, what is the treatment? Gladiolus, when growing, form new corms on the tops of the old ones. The old corms remain attached to the bases of the new ones; they are easily removed 3 or 4 weeks after lifting in the fall. Often a cluster of tiny cormels grow from the base of the new corm and are a means of propagation.

What is the best way to increase gladiolus? By saving and planting the small bulblets or cormels that form around the large corms.

How are gladiolus corms raised from the many small corms that develop on each large one? The small corms are dusted with malathion, stored through the winter in a cool, dry place, and are then planted in rows in well-prepared soil like larger corms (except that they are not set so deeply). They are then grown on to flowering size.

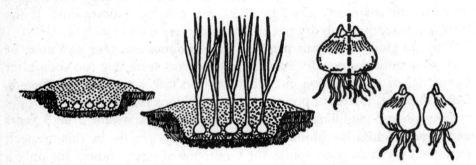

Gladiolus cormels, planted early in the spring, like seeds of peas, produce small corms by fall, some of which will flower the following year. Right: Mature corms, with more than one sprout or bud, can be cut apart before planting to increase stock of a favorite variety.

What is the best way to get gladiolus cormels to sprout quickly and evenly? Soak them in tepid water for 2 or 3 days before planting them. Plant them as closely together as 20 per foot, as they seem to like company.

How are new varieties of gladiolus developed? They are raised from seeds. Most improvements are obtained from seeds collected from hand-pollinated flowers.

How can gladiolus be raised from seeds? Plant them in a light, friable soil in an outdoor bed early in the spring while the ground is still cool. Sow the seeds rather thinly in shallow drills, spaced so that a cultivator can be used between them. Cover about ¼ inch deep. Corms the size of a pea or smaller should develop the first year, and most of these will bloom the second year.

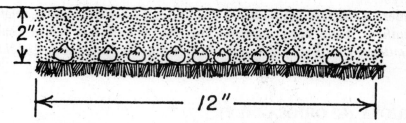

Small gladiolus corms can be planted very close together in rows about 2 inches deep.

Should gladiolus corms be treated before planting? Certain fungus and bacterial diseases or thrips are sometimes carried on the corms. If these are suspected, dust the corms just minutes before they are planted in a mixture of malathion and captan. Many mail-order nurseries list a special gladiolus dust for this purpose.

What should be done to stop wireworms from damaging gladiolus corms? Wireworms are usually bad only in newly made gardens or where trash is allowed to accumulate. Spray or dust the soil with diazinon.

How can I check the ravages of cutworms among my gladiolus? Clean the ground of all weeds and other unwanted growth. For large plantings, dust diazinon on the soil.

What is the most satisfactory method of combating gladiolus thrips? In the fall, after corms are dug, dust with malathion and again before planting. During the growing season, if thrips or aphids appear, spray with malathion or Meta-Systox-R, following the directions on the label carefully. Keep the weeds cut down nearby as a sanitary measure.

How can I obtain good gladiolus varieties? Look for listings of gladiolus in garden catalogs; order several spring editions through advertisements in any of the garden magazines. Corms are often available locally through garden centers in the spring. Choose colors to harmonize with the color scheme inside your home since gladiolus make wonderful cut flowers. Plant at least 10 of a kind so you'll have enough for bouquets.

What are the uses of miniature gladiolus? Please name a few varieties. Miniatures are generally useful in mixed border plantings and especially as cut flowers. They are more informal than the standard varieties and the spikes are more graceful for use in arrangements. Also, they seldom need staking. All-America miniatures are excellent choices. Some catalogs also list such smaller-sized varieties as 'Butterfly' and baby hybrids.

Is there a fragrant gladiolus?   Yes and no! *Gladiolus* and a relative, *Acidanthera,* have been crossed. The progeny of this union (called *Glad-anthera*) look like gladiolus but retain the fragrance of *Acidanthera.*

GLORIOSA (GLORIOSA-LILY)

Can gloriosa be grown outdoors in summer?   Yes. Plant strong tubers in pots of light, humusy soil in March or April and grow as container plants outside on the terrace or patio after the weather warms up. Or start plants in a sunny border after all danger of frost has passed. Lift the tubers before frost comes and store in dry sand or peat moss through the winter in temperatures between 50° and 60° F. Container plants may be rested dry in the same pot, but replace soil every year before beginning its growth cycle. This is one of the rare vining tubers. The plants climb by means of barbed tendrils at the ends of the leaves, so place a cord or wood trellis for support.

HAEMANTHUS (BLOOD-LILY)

Are haemanthus bulbs adapted for growing indoors?   They are both interesting and beautiful as house plants or greenhouse plants and bloom in the summer and the fall. Some of the best are *Haemanthus katharinae, coccineus, multiflorus,* and *albiflos,* but finding a source for all of these may be difficult.

How should I care for blood-lilies (haemanthus)?   Water freely when leaves are in evidence; keep dry at other times. Give full sunshine, well-drained soil, and repot every 3 or 4 years at the beginning of the growing season. Fertilize (follow directions on container) when in active leaf growth. Provide a temperature of 50° to 60° F. This is a relative of amaryllis and bulbs should be planted the same way.

HEDYCHIUM (GINGER-LILY)

Is the ginger-lily (hedychium) adaptable for growing outdoors in the North?   Only in sheltered, warm situations, and then the roots must be lifted in the fall and stored in sand in a frostproof cellar or room during winter. Plant outdoors after all danger of frost has passed and give an abundance of water when growing.

HYMENOCALLIS (PERUVIAN-DAFFODIL, ISMENE)

How can I raise Hymenocallis narcissiflora? Plant out after ground is warm, the weather is settled, and absolutely all danger of frost has passed, in a sunny, well-drained border in fertile soil. Cover to a depth about 3 times the diameter of the bulb. Dig up before the first frost; do not remove foliage, but allow it to dry on the bulb and store with fleshy basal roots intact at a temperature of about 60° F. Leave some soil on the roots for the winter.

I planted Peruvian-daffodils—bulbs as large as those of amaryllis. On taking them up this November, the bulbs were much smaller. Why was this? Unsatisfactory cultural conditions. The soil was perhaps too heavy, or not fertile enough, or there was not enough sun. They probably will not bloom as well next year.

Should Hymenocallis be stored in dry sand during the winter or be left spread out? Either way is satisfactory. Leave the roots on.

IXIA

Will you give me cultural directions for ixia and sparaxis? Read the answers under Freesia. Ixia and sparaxis need exactly the same treatment.

LACHENALIA (CAPE-COWSLIP)

Will you give me the cultural needs of lachenalia (capecowslip)? Plant bulbs close together in early fall, in pots or hanging baskets containing light soil. Treat the same as freesias.

Which varieties of lachenalia would you recommend to a beginner? *Lachenalia bulbiferum* syn. *pendula* (red and yellow) and 'Aurea' (golden yellow) are the easiest to find.

LEUCOCORYNE (GLORY-OF-THE-SUN)

What is glory-of-the-sun and how is it grown? A tender, bulbous plant from the uplands of Chile named *Leucocoryne ixioides*. It is handled indoors like freesias. Avoid high temperatures and grow in a sunny, airy situation. It blooms in late winter and in the spring.

LYCORIS RADIATA (SPIDER-LILY)

I have 3 bulbs of Lycoris radiata in a pot in my house. They have been potted since September. Why haven't they bloomed? Is there anything I can do to encourage bloom? *Lycoris radiata* often passes its bloom season. July and August are the best months to plant these. Work a tablespoonful of superphosphate for each bulb into the surface soil.

OXALIS

How should one grow the tender kinds of oxalis bulbs? Pot during August (or when received from the seller) in light, fertile soil. Space the bulbs 2 or 3 inches apart, just below the surface. Water carefully at first; water freely when growth has developed. Give plenty of sunshine and a temperature of 50° to 60° F. Feed when the pots are filled with roots. After flowering, gradually reduce water, and finally let dry completely and rest for a few months. Some species, *Oxalis regnellii,* are virtually everblooming, although an occasional rest is beneficial.

POLIANTHES (TUBEROSE)

Will you give me some information on tuberoses? (Washington, D.C.) Purchase good bulbs of tuberose (*Polianthes tuberosa*), plant outdoors in full sun and light and fertile soil after the ground has warmed up. Lift in the fall and store dry in a temperature of 60° F.

RANUNCULUS

Ranunculus bulbs sent from California arrived after the ground was frozen. Can I successfully plant them in the spring? How should I treat them during the winter? Store in dry sand or peat moss in a cool but frostproof place. Plant 2 inches deep, 6 inches apart, as soon as the ground can be worked in the spring. Make the soil friable with plenty of peat moss and sand. The position should be moist and lightly shaded. Tuberous-rooted varieties, *Ranunculus asiaticus,* are dug and stored through the winter in the North.

SPREKELIA (JACOBEAN-LILY)

In California I saw a lily called a Jacobean-lily that looked like a curious crimson orchid. What is it? How can one grow it? *Sprekelia formosissima* (sometimes sold as *Amaryllis formosissima*). Plant the bulbs 6 inches deep in light, fertile loam in a sunny position after all danger of frost is over. Water freely when foliage is above the ground, and fertilize while in active growth with any complete fertilizer. In cold climates lift after the first frost and store the bulbs above freezing through the winter; remove the tops but leave the roots on. Sprekelia also makes an interesting pot plant for indoors and is usually offered for such use in fall catalogs.

TIGRIDIA

What soil and situation do tigerflowers (tigridias) prefer? A warm, well-drained soil and a sunny situation. Plant the same time as gladiolus. Take up and store in the same way.

TRITONIA (MONTBRETIA)

Will you describe the culture of tritonia? It needs essentially the same care as gladiolus. The corms are, however, rather hardier and in mild climates may be left in the ground over the winter if given a very heavy mulch. *Crocosmia* is similar.

TUBEROSE   See Polianthes.

OTHER BULBS

I understand that there are a number of South African bulbs that need to be treated like freesias. Will you please list some of these? Ixia, sparaxis, babiana, tritonia, crocosmia, lapeirousia, ornithogalum, and lachenalia.

What is the best way of propagating ixia, sparaxis, tritonia, veltheimia, and similar South African or "Cape" bulbs? They all multiply quickly by offsets. These can be removed and planted in bulb pans, about an inch apart, at potting time. They are also very readily raised from seed.

6. Roses

ROSES ARE SO closely associated with the painting, literature, music, and even the politics of the world that they have for many centuries been an integral part of our culture. The rose is the very symbol of beauty and loveliness. Since the dawn of history it has been admired, appreciated, and linked with all kinds of human activities. It would be difficult to find an individual who could not recognize a rose—the best known and most loved of all our cultivated plants, and truly the "queen of flowers." Its majestic form, gorgeous colorings, and delightful perfume are unsurpassed. Even the thorns command respect. It is the standard of perfection by which all other flowers are judged.

Contrary to widely held opinions, roses are not difficult to grow. Their presence around long-deserted houses is evidence of their tenacity.

Many new homeowners harbor the mistaken idea that roses are specialists' plants, and that the beginning gardener, with very limited space at his disposal, would do well not to attempt growing them—except, of course, for the ubiquitous climber or two at the front door or along a fence.

It is quite true that such roses are better than none at all, but no true flower lover will—or should—be content until he has in his garden at least a half dozen or so of the modern bush roses to provide flowers for enjoyment both in the garden and as cut-flower decoration indoors.

The often-heard argument that roses "require so much care" scarcely seems to hold when one considers that the modern garden varieties give flowers almost continuously from late spring until frost, while most other hardy flowers are in bloom for little more than two or three weeks. And many of the splendid new varieties developed during the last decade or two, in Hybrid Tea, Floribunda and Grandiflora groups, have remarkable vigor and hardiness. The development of improved "all-purpose" controls for insect pests and diseases has greatly simplified rose culture and gone far to assure success even to the least experienced beginner, so we have really reached the day when there should be roses in *every* garden.

Roses give more in proportion to time spent than most other flowers. They respond to every bit of attention but they do survive some neglect, given a good start in life. Modern roses provide about seven months of bloom in the Middle Atlantic states and even more in warmer climates. They are versatile enough for many landscape purposes, as they vary from tall shrubs suitable for accent or background planting to dwarf polyanthas and tiny miniatures for edging, rock gardens, and pots. They can be used as boundary hedges or to line a driveway or walk. They climb over fences and walls and sprawl as ground covers. They can be planted in small groups through the perennial border as well as grown by themselves in formal beds. More and more roses are now being grown in tubs on patios or penthouse terraces and the many Mini-Rose Shows in February and March attest to the popularity of miniature roses grown indoors under lights.

The recent rise of interest and enthusiasm during the past several years in the old garden roses, species, and shrub roses, resulting in the formation of the Heritage Roses Group, has shown that many people want more variety in their rose gardens than is provided by modern roses, and that they also want roses that are hardy and disease-free without a great deal of care. The fact that many of these roses have only one seasonal bloom is compensated for by the display of rose hips in the fall, and by the presence in the garden of at least a few of the everblooming modern varieties as well.

More than 10,000 worldwide rose cultivars (varieties) are registered with the International Registration Authority, and the *Handbook for Selecting Roses,* published by the American Rose Society, lists over 1,000 varieties as currently available in this country. Truly, there are roses for everyone and for every garden situation.

Selecting Plants

What are the main types or classes of roses?

HYBRID TEA, HT.   Derived from crossing tea roses with hybrid perpetuals. Flowers produced singly and intermittently through the season are one to a stem and in small clusters.

GRANDIFLORA, Gr.   Derived from crossing hybrid teas with floribundas. Flowers with the form of small hybrid teas are borne one to a stem and in small clusters. Plants are usually larger and more vigorous than either parent group. Generally more floriferous than hybrid teas.

FLORIBUNDA, F.   A hybrid between the polyantha and the hybrid tea, hardy, with large clusters of single or semidouble flowers. A little later coming into bloom than hybrid teas, but much more floriferous during the entire growing season. Plants are generally not as tall as hybrid teas but more spreading in habit. More recently developed floribundas begin to take on the flower form of the hybrid tea, and to bloom one to a stem and in small clusters.

POLYANTHA, Pol.   Usually a small plant bearing large clusters of small flowers, hardy, recurrent.

MINIATURE, Min.   Fairy roses, flowers less than 1 inch across, single or in clusters; plants seldom more than 12 inches high. Miniatures introduced more recently tend to be rather larger than those introduced in past years, so that some miniature roses are now being described as "micro-minis" or "macro-minis." Climbing minis and miniature moss roses are also recent developments.

LARGE-FLOWERED CLIMBER.   Large flowers in clusters, produced on old wood. Usually one annual bloom. This class does not include the climbing sports of hybrid teas, grandifloras, or floribundas, which are included in the classes for the bush roses of those varieties.

RAMBLER, R.   Usually one annual bloom of small flowers in large clusters.

OLD GARDEN ROSES, OGR.   Includes all classes in existence before 1867, the date of introduction of the first hybrid tea, La France. Some of these are species of wild roses, gallicas, damasks, albas, centifolia and moss roses, china and tea roses, bourbons and hybrid perpetuals.

SHRUB, S. This class includes modern species hybrids such as the hybrid rugosas, the hybrid musks, and the kordesii climbers. In a sense it is a catchall class, containing some roses of highly mixed parentage. Tree or standard roses are manufactured by budding a hybrid tea or other type at the top of a straight trunk.

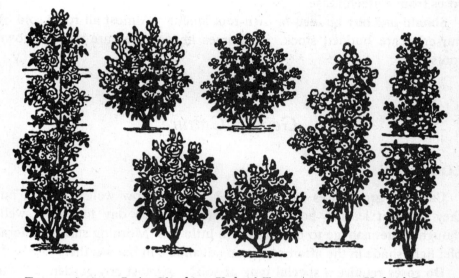

Types of roses. Left: Climbing Hybrid Tea; center top, Hybrid Perpetual and Polyantha; center bottom, Hybrid Tea and Floribunda; right, Large-flowered Climber and Rambler.

What are the major categories of rose colors? The American Rose Society has established the following groups: w, white or near white; my, medium yellow; dy, deep yellow; yb, yellow blend; lp, light pink; mp, medium pink; dp, deep pink; pb, pink blend; mr, medium red; dr, dark red; rb, red blend; ab, apricot blend; ob, orange and orange blend; o-r, orange-red; m, mauve; r, russet.

You will notice there is no color class for light yellow or light red. Light-yellow roses are usually classed as white or near white, and sometimes as medium yellow. Light-red roses are classed as deep pink. There are deep shades of purple among the old garden roses, and they are usually classed as dark red, red blend, or mauve.

What are the standard rose grades? No. 1, three or more strong canes; No. 1½, two or more strong canes; No. 2, two or more canes; No. 3, one cane. The best grades will have longer canes but these are usually cut back before they are mailed from the nursery.

What age plants should be purchased? Two-year-old field-grown plants, with the No. 1 grade, usually give the best results.

Are inexpensive roses offered by nurseries a good investment? No, you get what you pay for. The original cost of a good rose is small compared to later care. Cheap roses may be poor grade or outworn bench roses from a greenhouse.

Should one buy budded or own-root stock? Almost all roses sold by nurseries are budded stock. Sometimes hedge roses are on their own roots.

General Culture

LOCATION

Can you grow roses in semishade? Roses grow well in shade, but they need at least 6 hours of full sunlight each day to bloom well, though some manage to bloom with a little less. Morning sun is preferable; light shade in the afternoon is an advantage in hot weather.

Do roses require a special type of soil? Almost any garden soil can be amended to grow roses. The ideal type is a well-aerated, slightly acid, medium-heavy loam containing an abundance of organic matter. Sandy soils and clay soils can both be improved by plenty of organic matter—peat moss, leafmold, well-rotted manure, or compost.

Do roses like wet or dry feet? Roses require good drainage. Dig a hole 18 inches deep; fill it with water. If this does not soak away in a few hours, choose another location or have tile drains installed.

SOIL PREPARATION

How deep should the soil be prepared for a rose bed? The old rule was 2 to 3 feet; now we find that 18 inches is sufficient, even though the roots may go much deeper.

How do you prepare a new rose bed? The standard method has been as follows: Remove the soil to a depth of approximately 18 inches, keeping the topsoil and subsoil separate. Next, put back a 6-inch layer of the topsoil in the bottom of the bed. Add 3 inches of compost, peat moss, or other type of organic matter; fork it in thoroughly. Shovel

in another 6-inch layer and work in more organic matter; lastly, fill the
bed with the subsoil mixed with more organic matter.

Is there a short cut?   Yes, you can take out the first spade depth and
then improve the second 9 inches of soil in place. Fork it thoroughly,
incorporating plenty of peat moss, some dehydrated manure or rotted
manure, and superphosphate, about 3 pounds per 100 square feet.
Work in more of the same as you replace the topsoil.

Should you use lime as you prepare the bed?   Only if a soil test
shows a pH value of 5 or lower. Use ground limestone or common agricultural lime (not hydrated lime) at the rate of 3 to 6 pounds per 100
square feet of ground area, depending on the degree of acidity. If you
want a similar soil conditioner that will not change the pH, you may use
gypsum.

Why will roses not do well in a sweet or alkaline soil?   The iron in
an alkaline soil is insoluble, and thus unavailable to plants. All garden
plants require iron to form chlorophyll (the green coloring matter in the
leaves); absorption of iron is interfered with in a lightly alkaline soil.

**What is the appearance of rose plants when the soil is too alka-
line?**   The veins of the leaves become dark green and the area between
becomes mottled with yellow. In severe cases, the leaves may become
almost pure white.

How do you acidify the soil for roses?   The soil may be made
slightly acid by mixing in finely powdered sulfur, 1 to 3 pounds per 100
square feet.

Can aluminum sulfate be used to acidify the soil for roses?   Aluminum sulfate is less desirable than powdered sulfur. It is more expensive, less easy to obtain, and more has to be used. In large quantities, it
may be harmful, but it is quick-acting.

Will peat moss, used in preparing the bed, acidify the soil?   Peat
moss, if used in large enough quantities, will temporarily increase soil
acidity. Its effect is not permanent and the peat moss-soil mixture gradually returns to nearly the pH value of the original soil. It is highly important as a source of humus and in improving the mechanical condition of the soil, and is readily available.

**What special treatments do roses growing in a sandy soil re-
quire?**   Working into the soil an abundance of organic material; watering during dry periods; and 2 or 3 applications of a mixed commercial
fertilizer during the growing season.

Is it necessary to have a clay soil for success with roses?   Not at all.
Some of the best rose gardens are found in regions where the soil is

light and sandy. Almost any type of soil can be improved for roses by proper treatment.

How much peat moss should be used?   On very heavy clay soils, as much as 50 per cent by volume may be incorporated. Ordinarily, 25 per cent by volume is satisfactory. This means 1 bushel of peat to each 3 bushels of soil.

How should peat moss be used in preparing the soil for roses?   It is best to mix it thoroughly with the soil if a new bed is being prepared. Where individual plants are set in to replace those that have died, mix the peat moss with the soil that is used to fill in around the plant.

Should the peat moss be moistened before it is mixed with the soil?   It is not necessary, but a thorough soaking of the soil and added ingredients is necessary after planting.

What kind of peat moss is best?   Any of the commonly available brands of peat moss (sphagnum moss peat) are satisfactory. It should be fibrous and thoroughly granulated. The more thoroughly decomposed sedge and muck peats are less beneficial.

Can both peat moss and manure be used?   Yes, they make an excellent combination. A mixture of 1 bushel of well-rotted manure, 2 bushels of peat moss, and 10 bushels of soil is ideal.

What kinds of organic material can be used in preparing rose soil, other than peat moss and manure?   Leafmold is satisfactory and can be used at the rate of 1 bushel to 5 bushels of soil. Compost, muck, seaweed, and various commercial organic materials can be used.

I have access to chicken manure. Can it be used on roses? If so, when?   It is a satisfactory fertilizer if it has been composted to become well rotted before using. It is advisable to put it on in the late fall or very early spring; or mix with soil at planting time.

How much chicken manure can be used on roses?   One bushel for each 100 square feet can be used with safety.

PLANTING

What is the best time to plant roses?   It depends on where you live. Spring planting is safest in Minnesota; winter planting, mid-December to mid-February, is best in California and much of the South. November planting is sometimes recommended for winter blooms in Florida. For the temperate states, November planting allows first choice of varieties from the nursery and the bushes are out of the ground a very short time, but in many nurseries the roses are not hardened off enough to ship in the fall before your ground becomes frozen. Spring planting is therefore somewhat safer.

How can roses be kept if they arrive before planting time? Nurseries try to ship plants for arrival at your correct planting time; set them out immediately if you can. If you must wait a few days, keep the unopened package in a cool place. (See also the next question.)

Should rose plants be heeled in if planting is delayed too long? Yes. Dig a trench about 12 inches deep; pack the plants closely in the trench, at an angle, and cover the roots and part of the canes with soil. Plant within 3 weeks.

What do I do when I'm ready to plant the roses? Unpack the box in the shade and away from wind; trim off broken roots or canes, then put in a pail of water. You can plant immediately or let soak for a few hours, but not longer than overnight.

How may one prepare the soil for individual plants set in to fill out a bed? Dig a hole large enough to accommodate the plant. Mix the required amount of peat moss with the soil that was removed and use the mixture to fill in around the plant.

How deep should roses be planted? In most areas the bud union (a "bump" at the top of the roots) should be at ground level. If this "bump" is exposed to the sun, there will be more basal breaks. In very cold climates the bush is sometimes set an inch or two deeper, but it is better to set it at ground level and provide winter protection. If it is set more deeply it is important each spring to scoop out the soil around the bud union, exposing it to sun and air.

How far apart should roses be planted? In favorable climates where they make vigorous growth, they should be farther apart than in cold areas. An average would be 2 feet apart for most hybrid tea and floribunda varieties, 3 to 4 feet for many old garden roses and shrubs, 6 to 8 feet for climbers, but about 1 foot for miniatures.

How large a hole should be dug for a rose plant? It depends on the size of the root system, but if the roots are too long, they should be cut off and not coiled around in the hole. You may need a hole about 18 inches across and 12 or more inches deep.

Should the roots be placed straight downward or spread out horizontally? Usually you make a soil mound in the hole and spread the roots out and down over this.

Is it necessary to firm the soil when planting rosebushes? Yes, as you add the soil, firm it in with your fingers and then, when the hole is two thirds full, step around the bush so that no air space is left. Fill the hole with water and let it soak away before you add the rest of the soil, which should be left loose. After that, mound the soil around the canes to about 8 inches.

After planting a rose bush, tramp around it firmly to be sure that the roots and soil are in close contact.

Why do you mound the soil around newly planted bushes in the spring? To keep the canes from drying out while the root system becomes established. This is very important in giving the roses a good start in life. Remove this extra soil in a couple of weeks in a spring planting. Leave it on all winter after the fall planting.

Are potted roses satisfactory and how late in the season can they be planted? Rose plants grown in large plastic or fiber pots are available from many rose growers and at local garden centers. If you cannot plant dormant, bare-root roses early in the season, it is wise to buy potted roses. There is a better selection in May and June, but they can be planted as long as they are available. Even if they are advertised as potted in biodegradable containers which may be planted as is, it is important to carefully remove the pot without breaking the root ball when planting.

How should potted roses be planted? Dig a large hole, cut off the bottom of the pot, and set the pot in the hole. Slit the container down the side and carefully remove it without breaking the root ball. Fill in around the ball with earth mixed with peat moss. The bud union should be at ground level, as with other roses, but you do not mound after planting a potted rose—which is usually in full growth and even in flower.

Are the roses sold at supermarkets and garden centers in cardboard containers good plants? The roots of these roses have been cruelly pruned and compressed into the rather small cardboard containers, but if they are purchased when they are first brought in, they will grow and become satisfactory plants. Never buy roses that have started to put out white shoots, or that have canes that look shriveled and dry. Even though the container is advertised as biodegradable, and the instructions say to plant it, it is important to remove it, and spread the roots out as much as possible in planting. With proper care, these roses can recover and become satisfactory plants, but it is better to buy regular dormant bare-root roses or nursery-potted roses.

TRANSPLANTING

Should rosebushes be moved periodically? No. Once a rose is established, it is best not to move it.

Can old rosebushes be transplanted? Transplanting old bushes (10 to 15 years) is advisable only on a limited scale. Old plants do not send out new roots readily and it can take them several years to become reestablished. Transplant when the bush is dormant, pruning to keep the top and the roots in proportion. For insurance, propagate new plants from cuttings the year before you move the old rosebush.

How can I move a large climbing rose without the danger of losing it? Do not try to move the plant without drastic pruning. Cut out all but 4 or 5 young, vigorous canes. Lift the plant carefully with a ball of soil.

Is it better to move an old rosebush than to buy a new one? Not unless it is an old favorite and a substitute is no longer available.

Can roses be transplanted after the ground begins to freeze or should they be stored during the winter in the basement in case it is necessary to move them? Move to the new location even if the ground is somewhat frozen. If you know they must be moved, mulch the new location with straw or leaves to keep it from freezing. After transplanting, mound the soil as high as possible around the canes. If it is possible, wait until very early spring, as soon as the soil can be worked, and transplant while the bush is still dormant.

PRUNING

Do you prune new bushes when planting? They are usually pruned sufficiently in the nursery. Wait until they start to grow and then some limited pruning may be required. If so, cut back to the new shoots.

Is it better to prune in the fall or in the spring? Always in the spring. In autumn you may cut back extra-tall canes that might whip in the wind or not fit under plastic rose cones for winter.

Does severe pruning result in more vigorous plants? Not usually.

Exhibitors may prune and feed their plants rather heavily, but for long-lived, vigorous bushes, you need plenty of foliage to manufacture food. Moderate pruning allows more flowers that are still of excellent size.

How far back do you cut hybrid tea roses in the spring? That depends on the amount of winter injury. Cut back to sound wood, preferably the size of a lead pencil, remove diseased or weak growth, branches that cross each other in the center of the bush, and any candelabra type of growth.

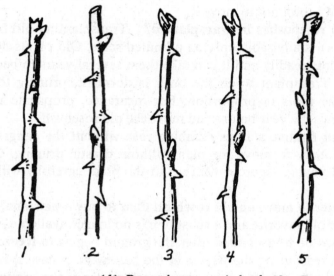

How to prune a rose: (1) Ragged cut, won't heal. (2) Cut too far above the bud. (3) Cut too close to the bud. (4) Cut too slanting, comes below the bud. (5) Right: Slight slant about ¼ inch above the bud.

How far above a bud should a cut be made? Make a slanting cut in the direction of the bud and as close to it as is safe—leaving not more than a ¼-inch stub.

Is it always necessary to make the cut where a bud points outward? Not always, but it helps to keep the interior of the bush open. It is more important to cut above a sound bud that is starting to grow. With a sprawling variety like 'Crimson Glory', cutting to some inside buds keeps the bush more upright.

Should roses be pruned with a knife or pruning shears? Use pruning shears rather than a knife. A good pair of sharp, pruning, curved-edge shears are fine and less apt to injure canes than the straight-cut type of pruning shears. For old heavy canes, you may need lopping shears, and you may find a small, curved, narrow-bladed saw helpful.

Do you prune grandifloras the same way as hybrid tea roses? Essentially. Some, like 'Queen Elizabeth', are rather tall and might be pruned somewhat higher.

How do you prune polyanthas and floribundas? Remove all the dead and injured wood; but for masses of color display, cut back less than hybrid tea roses.

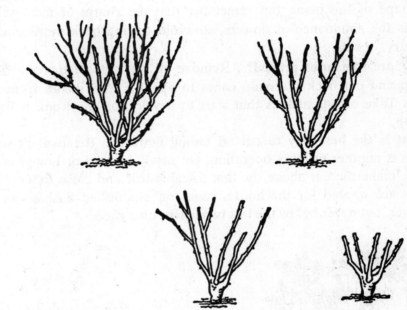

Pruning hybrid tea roses. Top left: After one year of growth. Top right: Weak and dead wood thinned out. Bottom left: Cut back moderately for large number of flowers. Bottom right: Pruned hard for bigger blooms on longer stems.

Are the large-flowered climbers pruned any differently from the ramblers? Yes. Old-fashioned ramblers, such as 'Dorothy Perkins', usually bloom on canes produced during the previous summer. Hence, after the June bloom, some of the old canes are removed at ground level and the new ones tied to supports.

The large-flowered climbers bloom on older wood. Clean out dead wood in the spring and prune as necessary for the space. Most varieties will bloom more abundantly if the main canes are trained horizontally.

If it is a large-flowered climber rather than a rambler, do you still cut

out everything but new basal shoots?   Keep some of the older canes but prune the laterals (side growth) back to within a foot of the cane.

How should shrub roses be pruned?   A few of the older canes should be cut back to the ground each spring to encourage the growth of new basal shoots. This helps keep the plant young and vigorous. Cut out any crossing branches that rub against each other. It is always correct to remove any dead or diseased wood. Beyond this, you may cut back any thin twiggy branches, or any that extend far beyond the general shape of the plant, but remember that the charm of most shrub roses is the abundance of flowers, so avoid cutting back more than is necessary.

How are tree roses pruned?   Remove all weak or dead wood from the top and cut back the main canes to about 6 to 8 inches from the crown. Take off all suckers that start to develop on the trunk or from the base.

What is the best way to cut off fading flowers?   Removal of dead blooms is another pruning operation. On newly planted or low-growing bushes, make the cut above the first 5-leaflet leaf and close to it. If the flowers are wanted for the house, canes on established bushes can be cut lower, but never below the last two leaves on a cane.

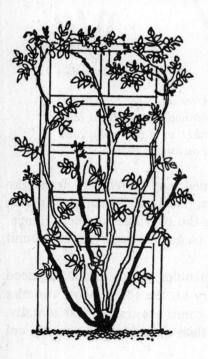

Climbing roses of the rambler type, which flower on new wood of the current season's growth, are pruned just after flowering, by cutting old canes back to the ground (as indicated by the lighter canes in the sketch), thus leaving room for the husky new canes.

How do you summer-prune large-flowered climbers? If the variety repeats its bloom through the summer, cut off the fading flowers, as for hybrid teas, and shorten the lateral canes as necessary to prevent too vigorous growth. If the climber is a once-bloomer, leave the dead flowers to produce attractive hips (seeds) in the fall.

FERTILIZING

When is the best time to fertilize roses? Feed established roses soon after pruning, but wait several months before feeding newly planted bushes.

Are commercial fertilizers good for roses? A mixed commercial fertilizer, 5–10–5 or comparable grade, is satisfactory. Apply one to two trowelfuls per bush, lightly worked into the soil but not touching the canes. Mixing this with dehydrated cow manure is helpful, or you may prefer a special rose food with an organic base.

How often do roses need fertilizer? One rule has been a ground feeding in early spring, another about the time of heavy June bloom, and a third in early August. Some rosarians make lighter feedings more often.

How can one tell when roses need fertilizer? The leaves are a light yellowish-green; the plants fail to make lush, vigorous growth.

How do roses look when they are overfertilized? Usually the growth is stunted; the stems are short; the flowers are small. New shoots fail to develop promptly after the first blooming period; midsummer and fall bloom is reduced. The tips of the feeding roots, normally white, appear brown.

What can be done if roses have been overfertilized? Very heavy watering on several days in succession will leach out some of the excess nutrients.

Can manure be used as a fertilizer? Well-rotted manure is an excellent source of organic matter in the soil and a rather weak fertilizer. Use it in conjunction with a complete commercial fertilizer.

Is horse manure satisfactory for roses? Yes. If well-rotted, it can be applied as a mulch or mixed with the soil at planting time.

Is there any danger in using bone meal on roses? Bone meal contains a large portion of lime, which tends to "sweeten" the soil. If the soil is already neutral or alkaline, bone meal might make the pH too high for best growth. However, bone meal is usually applied to supply phosphorus, but for this purpose it is too slow-acting. Superphosphate is better. Bone meal is also very expensive. However, rosarians in acid-soil areas recommend it for miniature roses, which should not be over-fertilized, and some rosarians like to include it in planting all their roses, simply because it is safe and slow-acting.

Is there anything better than bone meal as a fertilizer for roses? Superphosphate is quicker-acting and more effective as a source of phosphorus. It can be used at the rate of 3 pounds per 100 square feet. It is best used in the initial preparation of a bed; thereafter the "complete" commercial fertilizer should supply sufficient phosphorus.

Are wood ashes good for roses? Yes, if the soil is acid; they contain potash and lime. Use at the rate of 4 to 5 ounces per square yard. If the soil is neutral, the ashes might make it too alkaline.

Are there any roses that should not be fertilized? Yes, the shrub rose *Rosa hugonis* does best in poor soil; it can die if fed. Other rose species are not artificially fertilized in native or wild areas, and should be only lightly fertilized under cultivation. Miniature roses should be only lightly fertilized or they may lose their miniature characteristics.

Can cottonseed meal be used as a rose fertilizer without making the soil too acid? Yes, unless the soil already has a low pH. It is often used as a base in special rose foods.

MULCHING

Is it better to cultivate or to mulch rose beds? Mulching is preferable because it reduces the amount of labor, helps to retain soil moisture, keeps the soil cool, and does not disturb the roots. If there is no mulch, there should be *very shallow* cultivation every week or so. This is sometimes referred to as a dust mulch.

What materials are best for mulching? Whatever is readily available in your area: buckwheat hulls, cocoa shells, bagasse (sugarcane refuse), ground corn cobs, wood chips, pine needles, or sometimes partially decayed leaves.

Is peat moss a good mulch? Peat moss is far better incorporated into the soil and not used on top. As a mulch, it cakes readily so that water flows off the bed rather than down into it.

When do you apply the mulch? In the spring, after pruning and fertilizing. Cultivate the soil first, to remove all weeds. If no winter protection is required, the mulch may be left in place all year, adding a little more as it decomposes.

Can mulches be worked into the soil to increase the organic content?   Some can, but buckwheat hulls can be slightly injurious to plant growth in the soil. They are best left on top and not used too deep; about an inch of mulch is sufficient.

WATERING

Is it a good plan to water roses in dry weather?   Roses like plenty of water. They will make more growth and produce more flowers if they are *thoroughly* watered about once a week, unless there is sufficient rainfall.

What is the best way to water roses?   To be most effective, the soil should be soaked to a depth of at least 5 or 6 inches. A light sprinkling on top does more harm than good. It is best not to wet the foliage because this spreads black-spot disease; but if you must use an overhead sprinkler, water in the morning so that the foliage can dry off before evening.

How can roses be watered without wetting the foliage?   Use a soil-soaker hose (a hose perforated with holes) or a Waterwand; or let a gentle stream of water from the hose flow over a board into the bed. Some ardent rosarians install subirrigation systems.

What happens in a prolonged drought when water is restricted?   The roses will survive but go into semidormancy, producing few new flowers. Never fertilize unless you can also water. Mulching helps conserve soil moisture.

PEST CONTROL   (For more detailed information see Section 13, Plant Troubles and Their Control.)

What are the most common and harmful rose pests?   The more common insects include aphids, leafhoppers, rose slugs, rose chafers, Japanese beetles, and thrips; sometimes borers, rose scale, rose midge, rose curculio, budworms, and leaf tiers. Red spiders (mites, not true insects) are almost always present. Black spot is the most devastating rose disease, causing defoliation and occasionally death if uncontrolled. Powdery mildew, more common in late summer, is conspicuous with its powdery white coating over the foliage and may deform buds and flowers, but it is not lethal. Rust and cankers are occasional problems.

What is the best way to keep roses healthy?   Start at time of spring pruning by cutting back to white pith. Brown pith in the center of the cane is a sign of winter damage. Cut below the work of pith borers and remove cankered canes. Then, beginning when the leaves are fully out, spray weekly with a mixture containing fungicides to protect against black spot and mildew, the most common diseases of roses. Include an insecticide only when necessary to bring under control large populations of sucking or chewing insects. Take the precaution of wearing protective clothing when spraying, never spray on a windy day, and always read labels carefully and thoroughly.

Some common diseases of roses. Left to right: Black spot, mildew, and canker.

In these days of increased environmental awareness, many products which have been used in the past are now being removed from the market. You can get information about products that rosarians in your area are using by asking the American Rose Society, P.O. Box 30,000, Shreveport, Louisiana 71130 for a list of the ARS-appointed Consulting Rosarians near you. They are always happy to provide information about growing roses, and there is no cost or obligation.

Does spraying give better control of rose pests than dusting? It is somewhat more effective, but either will do if the pesticide is applied often enough and the undersides of the foliage are protected. It is rather important to dust early in the morning before the dew has evaporated so that the dust will adhere.

Are there any roses that don't require spraying? Yes, there are some that survive for years without being sprayed—despite visitations by an occasional pest. Most of the old garden roses are highly disease-resistant. The rugosa species and many of the rugosa hybrids are practically immune. Unfortunately, the tendency for black spot was inadvertently bred into our modern roses around the beginning of this century, but some modern roses are quite resistant. Most catalogs mention disease resistance in descriptions of new roses. You can find out about other varieties by checking the "Proof-of-the-Pudding" reports in the

Rose Annual published each year by the American Rose Society (address above).

Can I grow healthy roses without spraying? I want to grow varieties that appeal to me, not just immune types. Yes, you can. It is very important to have nearly ideal conditions, good location in your garden, and to follow good cultural practices. Feed and water lavishly. Keep bushes clean by removing any diseased foliage as soon as you see it. Don't practice monoculture. Alternate your roses with other garden plants. Keep clean of insects by hand-picking, and by washing bushes with a strong stream from the garden hose early on sunny days only. Some ARS Consulting Rosarians are organic gardeners, or can put you in touch with someone who is. You can get many good tips from them.

How can mice be controlled in the rose garden? At frequent intervals poisoned grain should be placed under the mulch in small containers (with an accessible opening) that will keep the grain from becoming wet. A jelly tumbler laid on its side and covered with a piece of board serves the purpose. (Ask your county extension agent about poisons that are licensed in your state.) However, mice populations fluctuate from year to year. Some years they do very little damage. A cat or two is a help and caring for the cat(s) is less tedious than preparing the poison grain.

SUMMER CARE AND PROBLEMS

Should roses be disbudded? Yes, if cut roses are desired for the home or exhibition. For garden display, there can be partial disbudding of hybrid teas but not of grandifloras and floribundas, buds of which are left to produce an abundance of flowers.

How does one disbud roses? Just as soon as the secondary buds become visible, pinch them out, leaving the largest or top one to flower.

How do I recognize a sucker? A sucker is a rose shoot arising from the rootstock of a budded or grafted plant. It will come from below the bud union and the foliage will differ from that of the good rose. Multiflora understock has dull, light-green foliage and, if allowed to bloom, small white flowers. 'Dr. Huey' understock has reddish foliage and red flowers.

How do I get rid of suckers? Cut them out just as soon as you notice them, but be sure you don't confuse them with basal breaks of the budded rose.

Do all suckers have 7 leaflets to a leaf? Not all; some understocks have 5 leaflets and some hybrid teas and climbers can produce leaves with 7 leaflets. You must note the type of foliage rather than the number of leaflets to be sure that a new shoot is understock rather than a good basal break.

Can roses revert to a wild form? No. If you see flowers of a different type and color from the variety purchased, it means that the growth from the understock has overpowered and killed the budded rose. Discard and order another plant.

Should I keep tree roses on which the top has died but which are sending up new shoots from the base? No, these are understock and the plant is worthless.

What causes roses to be lighter-colored at some seasons than at others? The more foliage on the plant, the brighter and more intense the coloring. Cool weather increases the color because less of the food from which the pigment is manufactured is used up in respiration. Rose blooms are always paler and smaller in the summer heat and sun.

Will iron or rusty cans have any effect in changing the color or shading of a rose? No.

Why are my 'Talisman' roses pale yellow instead of their real color? Perhaps the plant was incorrectly labeled; perhaps the sun was too bright.

Some of the shoots on my new hybrid tea did not develop into flower buds. Why? No one knows for sure the reason for these blind shoots. It happens more frequently on new bushes and some varieties are more apt to have blind shoots than others. Usually, if you cut the shoot back a few inches it will later produce a flower.

Is it necessary to rake up and destroy fallen rose leaves in the fall? Keeping the rose bed clean of fallen leaves is good garden practice. If you maintain a spray program right up to the first hard frost, and remove all fallen leaves, you will cut down considerably on the chance of overwintering disease spores in your garden.

WINTER PROTECTION

Is winter protection necessary? Definitely *yes* in Minnesota, Maine, and other cold states; definitely *not* in the South and California, and probably not in many other areas. A lot depends on your microclimate, but in many cases too much winter protection has been found to be more harmful than none at all. The best defense against winter damage is to grow varieties that are hardy. Most old garden roses are extremely hardy. Information about hardy modern varieties may be found in the ARS Proof-of-the-Pudding reports in the *Rose Annual,* published yearly.

Summer treatment is the key to winter safety. A rose without plenty of food reserve in its canes, depleted by repeated defoliation from black spot, may die no matter how well it is protected for the winter.

If protection is necessary, what is the best method? Mounding (hilling) has been the standard method. Hoeing up the soil from between the plants can disturb or expose roots; bring it in from the vegetable garden, the annual garden, or compost pile. Pour about a pailful into the center of each bush, making a natural hill about 8 inches high. In temperate climates do not add straw or salt hay; this encourages field or pine mice and is too difficult to remove in the spring.

When should the soil be mounded? After frost, but before the ground freezes hard—November in southern New York.

Can leaves be used for winter protection? In regions where there is alternate freezing and thawing, leaves keep the canes too wet and encourage canker fungi. However, pine needles and oak leaves allow good drainage and may be used. Never use maple leaves or similar leaves that pack together and retain moisture.

Is manure satisfactory for mounding around roses? Not for mounding. It should never touch the canes, but rotted manure can be applied to the valleys between the soil mounds after the ground freezes.

Is it all right to use peat moss around roses for winter protection? Peat moss retains too much moisture and increases canker diseases. It is much better to put it into the soil when the bed is prepared.

Should plant collars be placed around rose plants to hold the soil high around the stems? Yes, as long as drainage is good.

Is it all right to cut hybrid teas to about 8 inches from the ground before protecting for the winter? No. Prune as little as possible in autumn. If you are using rose cones (see the next question) instead of mounding, you may have to cut back to 12 to 18 inches, depending on the height of the cone.

What are rose cones? Lightweight cone-shaped covers made of plastic or styrofoam, with a lid on top that can be opened for air when it is too warm. The cone is used in place of a soil mound, but the cone has to be held in place with earth or stones. Cones are mostly used by ardent rose exhibitors. They generally discard the tops and replace them with two bricks, which help to hold down the cones and can be placed close together on cold days and moved farther apart on any unseasona-

bly warm winter day. Cones are not placed over the roses until after
they are fully dormant. A fungicide is used inside the cones in powdered
form or the rose canes are sprayed just before the cones are put in
place.

**Is it all right to cover rosebushes with peach baskets during the
winter?** If the temperature goes very low, mound up the bushes with
soil before putting on the basket.

How do I winter roses in Minnesota? Some rosarians in your state
have adopted what they call the Minnesota tip method. They dig
trenches between the rows of roses, loosen the roots on one side of a
bush, tip it into the trench, and cover with more soil.

How should climbing roses be protected? When the temperature
does not drop below 0° F., no protection is needed for the hardy varieties. Where temperatures between 0° and 10° below can be expected,
mound the soil over the base of the plants. In more severe climates,
remove the canes from their support and pin them close to the ground,
then cover with soil.

How can tree roses be protected in cold climates? Remove the
stake, loosen one side of the earth ball, lay the rose down on the ground
or into a trench, and cover the top, trunk, and exposed roots with soil.

**Is wrapping with burlap sufficient protection for tree roses in New
York State?** Not unless the winter is very mild and the plants are in a
sheltered situation. It is safer to tip them into a trench and cover them
with soil or dig them up and bury them.

Do miniature roses require special protection? Miniatures are very
hardy. If floribundas winter without protection in your area, so will
miniatures. I never cover them near New York City. A miniature rose
grower near Boston, Massachusetts, rakes several inches of oak leaves
into the mini beds for the winter.

Can miniatures be potted up for indoor winter bloom? This was
recommended in the past, but rosarians have found that pests and diseases were brought inside. It is so easy to root stem cuttings of minis
that this is preferred. Remember not to propagate patented varieties
while the patent is in effect. Minis will bloom well all winter if enough
light is provided. Sometimes a sunny window is enough, but more certain success can be obtained by growing them under lights. They are a
special delight during the winter months.

**How shall I treat a rosebush that has been growing on the patio all
summer in a tub?** Move it into an unheated garage. If the tub is very
large, so that the roots cannot freeze, it might be left outside in a shel-

tered location. A gardener who grows floribundas and climbers on a New York City terrace reports that they winter there safely without protection. But the minimum size of container is 14 inches in all dimensions, and preferably larger.

DISPLAYING ROSES

What time of day should roses be cut, either for the house or for exhibition?   Late afternoon is best; early morning is the next choice.

How long a stem should be taken?   Only as long as actually needed, with a little leeway for later trimming. The less foliage removed from the plant, the better. Be sure to leave at least two leaves above where the stem joins the main cane. Cut just above a leaf, without leaving any stub.

Should you plunge cut rose stems into cold water?   Contrary to former advice, it is best to place cut stems into warm water immediately; it rises faster in the stem. If water is not available when the roses are cut, and they start to wilt, they can be revived. Bring a shallow pan of water to boiling, turn off the heat, and insert the lower inch of stem while you count to 10.

How to cut a rose: (1) Cut pointed buds when they are fairly tight.
(2) Cut varieties with globular flowers when they are partly open.
(3) When cutting a rose, leave two sets of leaflets and eyes on the
remaining stem. These will develop into new buds.

What further conditioning is done?   Keep containers in a cool, dark place away from drafts. If they must be held for exhibition more than overnight, keep in a refrigerator at about 35° F.

Are the flower preservatives satisfactory for keeping roses?   Yes, they do prolong the life of cut roses. Sugar may be just as effective.

Can you time rose blooming for a show by pruning?   Hard pruning in the spring means bloom about a week later than moderate pruning. For a fall show, roses are pruned back a little about 40 to 55 days before the show, the number of days depending on the variety.

How are roses judged? Points are given for form, color, substance, stem and foliage, balance and proportion, and size, with emphasis on form.

What is meant by form? When judged, the rose should be at the most perfect stage of possible beauty. For heavy-petaled hybrid teas, this means two thirds to three fourths open, with petals unfurling in a circular pattern around a well-defined center. Roses with fewer petals are at their best when one half to two thirds open.

Is disbudding obligatory? For rose shows, single specimen, one-bloom-to-a-stem exhibits of hybrid teas, grandifloras, floribundas (if the schedule provides a class for them), hybrid perpetuals, teas, and noisettes must be grown disbudded. There are also classes in most standard rose shows for hybrid tea sprays as well as grandiflora and floribunda sprays. Polyanthas, old garden roses, shrubs, large-flowered climbers and ramblers are shown "naturally grown," without disbudding, although unwanted side growth may be removed at the exhibitor's discretion. Single hybrid teas, with one row of petals, may also be shown naturally grown. Climbing sports of hybrid teas, grandifloras, and floribundas are shown in the same classes as the bush varieties, and follow the same rules. There is a place in a rose show for every type of rose, and it is an education for any rose lover to examine all the diverse varieties on display.

How do you select the right color class in a show? You must know the name of the variety and then look up the color class in the *Handbook for Selecting Roses,* published annually by the American Rose Society.

Propagation

GENERAL

What different methods can be used to propagate roses? Rose varieties can be propagated by budding, grafting, cuttings, and layering.

Are own-root rose plants propagated at home as satisfactory as budded stock? They are much slower in getting started, but will usually develop into equally good plants. Some gardeners consider them longer-lived and more productive.

What is the "union" of a rose plant?   The place where the bud of the desired variety was inserted on the understock in the propagation of the plant. It can usually be seen as a jointlike swollen area 2 or 3 inches above the roots. It is just below the region from which all main branches of the plant arise.

BUDDING

Are roses propagated by budding or grafting?   Most outdoor roses are budded.

What is meant by budding?   Budding is a method of vegetative propagation. It means to graft by inserting a bud of one variety into the bark of another.

Why are outdoor roses budded instead of grafted?   It is the simpler method for large-scale production and requires less greenhouse space and equipment.

What is the best time to bud roses?   As soon as the petals fall from the first flowers, the canes are sufficiently mature to take cuttings or budwood. This is usually from the middle of June through July in the metropolitan New York area. The best dormant buds will be found in the leaf axils on the center portion of the stem of a truly fine bloom that has just shattered (dropped its petals).

How do you bud roses?   Grow or procure an understock of *Rosa multiflora* (sometimes called "the living fence") or some similar species. Make a T-shaped slit in the bark just at the ground level. From the stem of the desired variety, cut out a well-developed bud with the petiole of the leaf attached. Pick out the wood attached to the bark. Open the slit on the understock and insert the bud so that the bark fits close to the wood of the understock. Wrap firmly with raffia or soft twine, but be careful not to injure the shoot bud. After 3 or 4 weeks, remove the binding.

Should a home gardener try to bud roses?   Yes. It is fun to do. Do not be discouraged if you are unsuccessful at the first attempt. Some enjoy it as a hobby and some use it to get roses no longer available commercially. But it is an infringement of the Federal Plant Patent Act to reproduce patented roses while the patent is in force.

CUTTINGS

Can roses be grown from cuttings or "slips"?   Yes.

When is the best time to root rose cuttings?   Rose stems will root best about the time the petals fall.

Where can one find the best cuttings on a rosebush?   The flower stems make the best cuttings.

How long should a rose cutting be?   Four to five inches is the right length. It should contain 3 nodes.

Will a slip from a grafted plant be like the variety or the understock?   It will be the same as the variety.

Will all varieties of roses root readily?   Most rose varieties will root easily, but some varieties will root more easily than others. No rose variety will root as easily as a geranium, and some knowledge of how to do it is essential. It is also important to remember that a few varieties will not grow as well on their own roots as they will when budded onto a rootstock.

Should the leaves be removed from rose cuttings?   Leaves that will be below the surface of the rooting medium (usually sand) in which the cuttings are placed should be removed; others should be left on.

Should the blossom be left on a rose cutting?   Never. The middle and lower part of the stem make better cuttings.

What is the best material for rooting rose cuttings?   Clean, sharp, medium coarse sand or a mixture of sand and peat moss.

What conditions are necessary for rooting rose cuttings?   Keep the rooting medium moist. Shade during the first few days with newspaper or cheesecloth. Take out any cuttings that appear to be rotting and any leaves that fall off. For a high percentage of success, use mist propagation. You will need a misting nozzle, clear plastic sheeting to make a "tent," and a timing device of some sort to turn the mist on for a few seconds each hour. Cuttings will root in a few weeks.

Are root-growth substances helpful in rooting roses?   Yes. They usually cause cuttings to root more quickly and to produce a better root system. With a razor or sharp knife, make quarter-inch-long vertical cuts, removing tiny strips of bark at four equidistant points around the base of the prepared cutting before dipping it, first in water, then in the rooting hormone. This provides more surface for root formation. Insert cuttings in planting medium carefully so as not to brush off hormone powder. Firm well, and water in.

Can rose cuttings be rooted in soil under a glass jar? Yes, if only a few plants are needed.

What special precautions need to be taken in rooting cuttings under a fruit jar? Select a place where the jar is shaded during the hot part of the day. Keep the soil moist at all times. Do not put more than 3 cuttings under a single jar.

How long before cuttings rooted under a jar can be moved? If the cuttings are taken early in the summer, they are usually large enough to move by fall. They will need to be protected by mounding soil over them.

How does one go about removing the glass jar? Don't let too much growth develop before removing it. Select a cloudy day. Remove the jar. If the sun comes out, shade the cuttings with newspaper for a few days.

Can cuttings be rooted in a cold frame? Yes. The soil should be removed and clean, sharp, medium coarse sand put in to a depth of 4 inches or so. It may be necessary to keep the cuttings shaded with cheesecloth.

New rose plants from cuttings. Left: Two hardwood cuttings, the second with a "heel" for setting out in the spring to induce rooting. Center: Typical softwood cutting. Right: A time-honored method when only a few cuttings are involved is to place each cutting in the open ground under a glass jar to induce rooting.

Can seed flats filled with sand be used for rooting rose cuttings? Yes, but they must be watched very carefully to make sure the sand doesn't dry out. Enclosing the flat in polyethylene should help.

Will spring rose cuttings withstand the winter if left in the garden? Yes, if completely covered with soil and if they are in a place where the drainage is good.

How should rose cuttings rooted during the winter be cared for? Plant out-of-doors in the early spring in good soil. Keep them well watered.

Where should one transplant rose cuttings after they are rooted? They can be planted in their permanent location or in a nursery bed or cold frame.

How long before a cutting from a climbing rose will bloom? Ordinarily some flowers can be expected the second year after the cutting was rooted.

Can a new shoot which has come up about a foot from the original plant of variety 'Blaze' be moved? If possible, this shoot should be allowed to bloom before it is transplanted to make certain it is the same variety and not a sucker from the understock. Cut the root connection between it and the main plant the spring before it is moved. It will then develop a good root system of its own and will transplant easily.

GRAFTING

What does grafting mean? Grafting is a method of vegetative propagation by which a piece of the stem of the variety is made to grow on another plant. (See Section 3, Grafting.)

LAYERING

How are roses layered? A branch is cut a little more than halfway through. It is then bent down and the portion of the stem where the cut was made is buried in the soil. When the branch appears to be rooted, it is severed from the plant. After a year, it can be moved where desired.

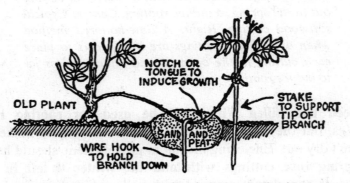

Propagating a rose by layering. Climbing roses are well suited to this method.

SEEDS

Do roses come true from seed? Only rose species that have not cross hybridized with other roses. Named varieties are hybrid plants and every seedling will be different.

How can roses be made to set seeds? Some varieties are comparatively sterile and will set little or no seed. Try putting pollen from other varieties on the stigmas.

How does one germinate rose seed? Place the seed in small, unstoppered bottles in moist peat moss and store in a refrigerator for 3 months at 41° F. Plant the seeds in soil containing one third peat moss, one third sand, and one third soil. Keep moist and at a temperature of about 68° F. Sometimes seed planted in a protected cold frame in the fall will germinate the following spring and summer.

HYBRIDIZING

How do you "cross" roses? While the flower is still in the bud stage, carefully remove all stamens before the pollen is shed. Cover the emasculated flower with a cellophane or paper bag. When stigmas have developed, place some pollen of the plant selected for the male parent on them. It is desirable to repeat the pollination on several successive days. Remove the paper bag when the seed pod starts to develop. More information on hybridizing can be obtained from the Rose Hybridizers Association, which distributes a *Quarterly Newsletter* to members. For information, write to the American Rose Society, P.O. Box 30,000, Shreveport, Louisiana 71130.

UNDERSTOCKS

What is meant by a rose understock? Garden roses are not grown on their own roots but are budded on the stem of a wild rose grown for the purpose. The stem, upon which the rose is budded or grafted, is called the understock. (See Budding and Grafting above.)

How can you propagate your own understocks? Make hardwood cuttings 6 to 8 inches long of smooth 1-year-old shoots of *Rosa multiflora* or other species. Remove the 2 lower eyes to prevent suckering. Insert in moist peat moss or sand at 45° F. where calluses form prior to root appearance. Plant out-of-doors in the early spring, or root inside and plant out later. Bud during July or early August.

Where may understocks be obtained? Few rose growers offer them except in large quantities. Try rose-growing firms.

What understocks are used for tree roses? *Rosa rugosa, Rosa canina,* and occasionally *Rosa multiflora.* Sometimes 'Dr. Huey' with 'De la Grifferaie' for stem portion.

Roses for Every Purpose

AUSTRIAN BRIAR

Are Austrian briars considered old-fashioned roses? Yes, they are hardy, bright-colored, once-blooming old garden roses. The species is *Rosa foetida,* the Austrian briar, also called Austrian yellow. Its color sport, *Rosa foetida* 'Bicolor', Austrian copper, is brilliant orange-scarlet, with yellow petal reverse. As are all species of wild roses, these are single, with five petals. Persian yellow or 'Persiana' is the semidouble form used by Pernet-Ducher at the beginning of this century to bring strong yellows and better reds into the hybrid tea class. Unfortunately, susceptibility to black spot was inadvertently "bred in" at the same time, and hybridizers are still trying to breed it out again.

BLACK ROSE

Is the so-called black rose really black? There is no truly black rose. Dark maroon 'Nigrette', 'Dame de Coeur', and 'Zulu Queen' have been called black.

BLUE ROSE

Is a blue rose possible? The chemical substance which produces the true blue color in delphiniums, violas, forget-me-nots, and other flowers does not exist in roses; therefore, unless genetic changes take place, a true blue rose is unlikely. Roses you see advertised as blue will be shades of mauve. Perhaps the closest to blue occurs in some of the old garden roses, such as the deep purple 'Cardinal de Richelieu', a gallica rose.

BROWN ROSE

Is there a brown rose? The so-called brown roses, or pansy-colored roses, are really very unusual shades of yellow blend and pink blend, and could just as well be classed as such instead of russet, which is their official ARS color class. Hybridizers are trying to breed better, more distinctive shades in this color class, which is very popular with arrangers. Some of the best so far are 'Brownie', 'Tom Brown', 'Amberlight', 'Cafe', and 'Fantan'.

BORDERS

Which rose is best to border a walk? Almost any floribunda would do beautifully. Repeat-blooming hybrid rugosas would be good, such as 'Frau Dagmar Hartopp' with single pink flowers, or the species rugosas, with white or pink flowers continuously produced. These would have the advantage of not needing to be sprayed.

What is available for low borders? Low-growing floribundas, polyanthas, and miniature roses. The polyanthas are especially recommended since they do not require spraying for fungus diseases. In poor locations they may be susceptible to mildew.

Besides miniature roses, what can be used to border rose beds? Ageratum, lobelia, sweet-alyssum, or dwarf marigolds. Pansies, violas, or Johnny jump-ups are delightful. These are only a few suggestions; many more small plants can be used. Rosarians who do not spray have used strawberry plants successfully. They respond very well to the richly fertilized soil. Plants that require poor soil to bloom well, or those that need a higher pH, should not be used in the same beds as roses.

CABBAGE

Can you give me any information about the cabbage rose? Is it suitable for a garden? The cabbage rose (*Rosa centifolia*), along with its sport, the moss rose, is an excellent garden plant—fragrant, hardy, and producing quantities of bloom during June. Its growth habit is open, with gaunt, thorny canes, which can best be controlled by training to a small trellis or by pegging down. A few varieties make fairly dense free-standing bushes about 5 feet high and wide.

CLIMBERS

Can I have climbers that bloom every month like hybrid tea roses? (Northern New York.)   There are several large-flowered climbers that are hardy and repeat during the summer. White—'Colonial White', 'Pax' (a semiclimbing hybrid musk); yellow—'Golden Showers'; pink—'Blossomtime', 'New Dawn', 'Rhonda'; red—'Blaze', 'Don Juan'.

What climbing roses are recommended for northern Vermont?   Any of the above should do if properly protected by removing the canes from their support and pinning them close to the ground for winter. Most ramblers and the older large-flowered climbers are very hardy. Even though they do not repeat bloom, they are very beautiful. Try them in protected locations with no special winter protection.

What is the red climbing rose, somewhat like 'Paul's Scarlet' climber, that blooms in the fall?   'Blaze', the improved form, blooms profusely in June and repeats all season.

What is the difference between a rambler and a large-flowered climber?   Any tall-growing roses that require the support of an arbor, trellis, or similar structure, or can be trained to one, can be classed as climbing roses. A rambler is one type of climber and is distinguished by its long, slender canes, produced the previous season, and dense clusters of small flowers. The varieties 'Dorothy Perkins' and 'Crimson Rambler' are typical but they tend to mildew very badly. 'Chevy Chase' is a much-improved 'Crimson Rambler' that seldom mildews, but it is now hard to find. Ramblers bloom only once; they do not repeat.

Most large-flowered climbers are much hardier than climbing hybrid teas, grandifloras, and floribundas, and are more vigorous, more supple, and easier to train. Many of them bloom only once, and have decorative hips in the fall. Examples are light pink 'Dr. W. Van Fleet', white 'City of York', yellow 'Lawrence Johnston' and 'Elegance', red 'Gladiator' and 'Paul's Scarlet Climber'.

DAMASK

Can you give me some information about the damask rose?   The damask rose (*Rosa damascena*), together with its repeat flowering form, the autumn damask (*Rosa damascena* 'Semperflorens') is an ancient rose. Grown by the Romans, it was kept in cultivation in the monasteries during the Dark Ages, and resurged into popularity in

Europe and England during the sixteenth century. Intensely fragrant, it makes a delightful though thorny garden plant. The bright-red fall hips are long and tubular.

How tall do damask roses grow and are they hardy? They are very hardy and grow to about 5 feet.

Is York and Lancaster a damask rose? Yes, it has pink and white petals, usually mixed in the same bloom, which is called parti-colored. Sometimes one flower will be all pink or all white. It is not a very vigorous plant, and is grown mainly as a curiosity.

Is there a white damask? 'Mme. Hardy' has large, very full, very fragrant white flowers, occasionally tinged flesh-pink, in clusters.

EARLY BLOOMERS

What are the earliest roses to bloom? The shrub species are the earliest, followed by their hybrids. Some of the old garden roses begin blooming next, and continue at peak bloom for 4 to 6 weeks, depending on weather conditions. Hybrid teas and grandifloras are next, followed by floribundas. Polyanthas are usually the last to bloom, but are then never out of bloom until hard frost. Miniatures usually begin before the hybrid teas, and most of them continue in constant bloom. Late spring and early summer bloom is most profuse for all groups. Late summer bloom will continue for everblooming types only if culture is optimum. Fall is the second-best blooming season, and though it is more sparse than early summer bloom, it is extravagantly welcomed by rose lovers.

FLORIBUNDA

What are floribunda roses? Technically, they are hybrid or large-flowered polyanthas. They originated through hybridizing polyanthas with hybrid teas. The flowers are larger than those of the polyantha group but in growth and flowering habit are much like them. Because of the cluster form and repeat habit, they are very colorful all season.

What are some good floribunda roses? White—'Ivory Fashion', 'Iceberg', 'Saratoga'; yellow—'Spanish Sun', 'Sunsprite'; yellow blend—'Golden Slippers', 'Redgold'; pink—'Betty Prior', 'Cherish', 'Gene Boerner', 'Gruss an Aachen'; pink blend—'Fabergé', 'Fashion', 'Rose Parade'; orange blend—'Orangeade', 'Anabell'; orange-red—'Fire King', 'First Edition', 'Sarabande', 'Spartan'; red—'Europeana', 'Frensham', 'Red Pinocchio'; mauve—'Angel Face', 'Lilac Charm', 'Lavender Pinocchio'.

Do floribundas have a longer blooming period than hybrid tea roses? Not by the calendar. Hybrid teas usually come into bloom a week or more ahead of floribundas, but the latter produce more flowers during the summer.

Are there floribundas that are especially good for corsages? Yes. Any of the floribundas with hybrid tea form are especially good for corsages.

Can floribundas be used with other flowers? Many gardeners use them for accents in the flower border, choosing those of medium height and grouping two or three together. The advantages are that they provide continual bloom in the desired color, and mixing them with other plants avoids the dangers of monoculture. Spraying can be minimized or eliminated.

FRAGRANCE

Is it true that modern roses have lost their fragrance? No. A few popular modern roses, like 'Peace', have little or no fragrance, but there are many with some fragrance and an increasing number that are outstandingly fragrant. The American Rose Foundation has awarded the Gamble Fragrance Medal to the hybridizers of 'Crimson Glory', 'Chrysler Imperial', 'Sutter's Gold', 'Tiffany', 'Granada', and 'Fragrant Cloud'.

What are some fragrant roses? In addition to those noted above, 'Candy Stripe', 'Christian Dior', 'Electron', 'Lemon Spice', 'Mr. Lincoln', 'Oklahoma', 'Pink Peace', 'Sweet Afton', and 'Tropicana' among hybrid teas have a delightful scent. Grandiflora 'Apricot Nectar' is very fragrant and so are climbers 'Don Juan' and 'Clair Matin'. 'City of York', a once-blooming climber, is so fragrant that it scents an entire yard, but it is now hard to find in nurseries.

FRENCH ROSES

Will you please name some old-fashioned French roses? These are the gallica roses. They include the deep pink *Rosa gallica* 'Officinalis', the apothecary rose, an almost single rose with bright golden stamens, and its sport 'Rosa Mundi' or *Rosa gallica* 'Versicolor', striped deep pink on a blush ground, with the same spectacular stamens. Other fuller petaled gallica roses include the deep purple 'Cardinal de Richelieu'; mauve 'Belle de Crecy'; mauve and blush-striped 'Camaieus'; two-toned

'President de Seize', mauve with a paler edge on the outer petals of most blooms; and deep rich red 'Charles de Mills', with mauve overtones. The rich, varied pinks and purples are typical of the gallica roses.

Gallica roses are hardy plants of good upright habit, about 2½ or 3 feet high. On their own roots they will quickly make a small, dense thicket, so it's best to purchase them budded onto an understock if this is a consideration in your garden. They bloom once, for 4 to 6 weeks, and most of them have attractive though not spectacular hips in the fall.

GRANDIFLORAS

What are grandiflora roses? A relatively new class of roses with the free-flowering habit of the floribundas and the perfection of flower form of hybrid teas. Some are taller than hybrid teas, with more vigor; the flowers are borne singly as well as in sprays. Pink 'Queen Elizabeth' was the first rose to be named in this class, in 1954, and it remains one of the best.

What are some outstanding grandifloras? 'Queen Elizabeth', 'Sonia', 'Camelot', and 'Pink Parfait', pink; 'Carrousel', 'John S. Armstrong', and 'Scarlet Knight', red; 'Arizona' and 'Montezuma', orange-red; 'Granada', red blend; 'Mt. Shasta', white.

What are the flora-tea roses? The flora-tea roses, like the grandifloras, represent a merging of the hybrid tea and floribunda classes. They are shorter plants than the grandifloras, and tend to have smaller blooms, which are borne singly and in small clusters. Like the grandifloras, the blooms have the hybrid tea shape. They are officially classed as floribundas. In England, where the grandiflora class is not recognized, all these roses are generally classed as floribunda/hybrid tea type.

GREEN ROSE

I have been told that there is a rose called the "green rose." What is it like? The green rose (*Rosa chinensis viridiflora*) originated in about 1855 and is still available as a novelty, but it is certainly not a beauty. The petals are just narrow green leaves, so the flower is very disappointing. It is sometimes used in flower arrangements before the buds open, as the foliage has a tint of bronze.

Is the green rose a climber? No. It belongs to the group of China roses (see above). Aside from its interest as a curiosity, it is of no garden value.

GREENHOUSE ROSES

How do you grow roses in a small greenhouse?   Plant in a bench in good soil. Keep moist, but not soaked. Keep the temperature as near 60° F. at night and 68° F. during the day as possible. Use plants propagated for greenhouse culture rather than those for out-of-doors, because the former are budded on *Rosa noisettiana* 'Manettii' understock and are better adapted for growing in a greenhouse. Potted miniature roses, on their own roots, should do very well in a greenhouse.

GROUND COVERS

What rose is satisfactory for planting as a ground cover?   A number of ground-cover roses are being introduced by W. Kordes' Sohne in West Germany and by Dickson Nurseries in North Ireland. New miniature ground-cover roses are also being offered by the miniature-rose nurseries. An important consideration is the need for spraying. Roses formerly recommended, *Rosa* x *paulii, Rosa wichuraiana*, 'Max Graf', and 'Mermaid', which did not need spraying, are now hard to find. Still available from many nurseries is the everblooming disease-free 'Sea Foam'.

HEDGES

What is the rose often advertised as a living fence?   This is *Rosa multiflora*, which has small, blackberry-like flowers. It is a prolific grower and does make an impenetrable hedge, but it is suited to the farm and large properties rather than suburban lots. It may grow 10 feet wide and keeping it trimmed is a thorny, impossible task.

What roses can be planted as a hedge?   The richly fragrant *Rosa rugosa*, mauve pink, and its color sports *R. rugosa* 'Alba', white, and *R. rugosa* 'Rubra', a very deep pink or red, are highly recommended for hedges because their attractive dark-green rugose foliage is disease-free. Also, they flower continually, even after the bright hips, resembling cherry tomatoes, form. They will make a medium-sized dense hedge which will be about as wide as it is high and can actually be sheared.

Some of the rugosa hybrids have double flowers, but make much bigger plants, and they are not all equally hardy and disease-free. Larger, less dense hedges can be made of closely planted hybrid musk roses, which are like semiclimbers, with sweetly scented flowers that bloom continually in full sun. If you are willing to spray, floribundas make excellent continuously flowering hedges. Climbing roses make gorgeous hedges trained to a post and wire fence, which is soon densely covered if the canes are trained horizontally, a treatment that also produces a wealth of bloom.

HYBRID PERPETUALS

How do hybrid perpetuals differ from hybrid teas?   The hybrid perpetuals were the progenitors of the hybrid teas and in their heyday ranked first in popularity. They have a decided Victorian quality in the largeness, fullness, and boldness of their blooms, but lack the refinement in form of hybrid teas. The colors include purest white, deepest crimson, and the innumerable hues linking these two extremes. The plants are vigorous, rather coarse, and quite hardy. There is profuse June bloom and some varieties have recurrent bloom.

What are a few of the best hybrid perpetuals?   'Frau Karl Druschki' is considered by many rosarians to be unsurpassed by any other white rose in the hybrid perpetual or hybrid tea classes. It has large, pure white flowers of hybrid tea form that are produced repeatedly. 'Henry Nevard' has very large, fragrant, crimson-scarlet blooms and also repeats. 'General Jacqueminot' has recurrent, very fragrant clear red flowers. 'Mrs. John Laing' and 'Baroness Rothschild' have huge, clear pink flowers.

Can hybrid perpetuals be planted in a bed with hybrid teas?   It is better to keep them separated. They take more room and those that do not repeat rather spoil a rose bed in the summer. Use them as shrubs. However, if space is a problem, there is no reason why the two kinds can't be combined in one large bed or border.

HYBRID TEAS

What are hybrid tea roses?   As a class, they are moderately vigorous and hardy, requiring some protection in colder states. Their chief merit is their frequency of bloom. In variety, richness, and delicacy of their coloring, and their perfection of form, they are not equaled by any other type.

What are some of the best hybrid teas? The following are highly rated hybrid teas, presently available, grouped according to color class.

White or near white—'Blanche Mallerin', 'Garden Party', 'John F. Kennedy', 'Matterhorn', 'Pascali', 'White Masterpiece'.

Yellow or yellow blend—'Eclipse', 'Irish Gold', 'King's Ransom', 'Oregold', 'Peace'.

Pink—'Charlotte Armstrong', 'Electron', 'Miss All-American Beauty', 'Pink Favorite', 'Royal Highness', 'South Seas', 'Swarthmore'.

Pink blend—'Chicago Peace', 'Confidence', 'First Prize', 'Helen Traubel', 'Portrait', 'Tiffany'.

Apricot blend—'Medallion'.

Orange-red—'Fragrant Cloud', 'Tropicana', 'Simon Bolivar'.

Red—'Crimson Glory', 'Christian Dior', 'Chrysler Imperial', 'Gypsy', 'Mr. Lincoln', 'Oklahoma', 'Proud Land'.

Mauve—'Blue Moon', 'Lady X'. 'Sterling Silver' has beautiful flowers but the plant does better in a greenhouse.

What varieties of single hybrid teas are worthwhile? 'Dainty Bess', with 5 pink petals and maroon stamens, is most desirable and is still offered by many nurseries. White 'White Wings', yellow 'Cecil', and 'Irish Fireflame' are sometimes available. There are also many lovely single floribundas, such as 'Betty Prior', 'Nearly Wild', 'Dainty Maid' in pink, 'Dairy Maid' in yellow, and 'Lilac Charm' in mauve.

Are the new varieties of hybrid teas as hardy and strong as the older ones? Yes, many of them may be somewhat more hardy.

Where does one purchase older varieties? A list of rose nurseries may be obtained by writing to the American Rose Society, P.O. Box 30,000, Shreveport, Louisiana 71130.

I know nothing about hybrid tea roses, but wish to have a rose garden. What are the best varieties to purchase as a beginner? (Nebraska.) Try some of the old garden roses and shrubs. Most of them are rock-hardy. If you want to provide winter protection for modern roses, start out with just a few, and add more if you find your pleasure in them makes the extra effort worthwhile.

I have only a few hours a week to spend in my garden, but I want some roses. Can I grow hybrid teas? Yes. Start with a few and then add more as you see how little time they take. Once a routine has been established, many rose lovers have found it takes very little more time to care for 50 plants rather than a dozen, for 200 plants rather than 50. This is how rose lovers get carried away and turn into rosarians.

IMPORTING ROSES

How do I go about importing roses? To import roses from overseas countries, you must request import permit application forms from the Permit Unit, USDA, PPQ, Federal Building, Room 638, Hyattsville, Maryland 20782. After you complete the application forms and return them, the USDA will send you an import permit, which you must send to the nursery from which you are ordering the roses. Then, when you receive the shipment, you are required to plant the roses in a separate bed, away from other plantings in your garden. During the next two years, agents from the USDA will inspect them regularly. It is essential to have your roses shipped by air mail. No import permit is required for roses ordered from Canadian nurseries.

MINIATURE ROSES

What are "fairy roses"? Another name for the miniature roses that are forms of *Rosa chinensis* 'Minima'.

What are miniature roses? They are naturally dwarf, growing from 5 to 15 inches tall, with flowers an inch or less across. They are like tiny hybrid teas, with the plant, foliage, buds, and flowers in perfect scale, but the pleasure they give is immeasurable. Many gardeners grow these miniature roses indoors under fluorescent lights, but the plants are hardy outdoors, wintering better than do hybrid teas in very cold climates.

Are there many varieties of miniature roses? Yes, a great many, with more introduced each year. Several nurseries devote themselves exclusively to production and sale of miniatures.

What are some of the best miniature roses? 'Baby Darling', 'Beauty Secret', 'Cinderella', 'Mary Marshall', 'Judy Fischer', 'Pixie Rose', 'Red Imp', 'Starina', 'Yellow Doll', 'Simplex' (white single), 'Toy Clown' are a few, but there are many others.

I have heard about a miniature moss rose; is there such a thing? Yes. The tiny buds of mini moss roses are covered with a fragrant mossy growth. Some of the cultivars are 'Dresden Doll', 'Fairy Magic', 'Fairy Moss', 'Dara', 'Mary Kate', and 'Mood Music'.

How do you grow miniature roses indoors? Keep pots on damp pebbles in a cool, sunny window or 3 to 6 inches below fluorescent lights. Clay or plastic pots may be used. Fertilize lightly, but regularly.

Water carefully. Mini roses must never be allowed to dry out. Fungus diseases are not usually a problem indoors. Wash off foliage, including underneath surfaces, to control insects. The spray attachment on your kitchen sink is good for this.

Are there really climbing minis? It seems like a contradiction. Climbing minis make excellent hanging-pot plants, and also lend themselves to special landscape effects. Not all climbing minis bloom as profusely as their bush counterparts.

MOSS ROSES

What are moss roses? Most moss roses are sports of the centifolias. They have a mossy covering on sepals and stems composed of tiny, sticky glands, which are often pine scented. Common moss ('Muscosa') is probably the most desirable, in pink. There is also a white sport called 'White Bath', dark red 'William Lobb', and 'Striped Moss', small pink- and white-striped blooms with reddish moss and stems. 'Gloire des Mousseaux' is a large mauve-pink rose. 'Crested Moss' has a fringe just on the edges of its sepals, which makes it resemble a three-cornered hat, giving it its alternate name of 'Chapeau de Napoleon'. These, and other centifolia moss roses, bloom only once. There are just a few moss roses derived from the damask rose, which are more sparsely mossed, but do repeat later in the season after the bushes have become well established. 'Salet' and 'Alfred de Delmas' fit into this group.

POLYANTHA ROSES

What are polyantha roses? The term "polyantha" (meaning many flowers) well describes the class. The plants are usually dwarf and give a continuous profusion of small flowers in large clusters. They are especially hardy but less adapted for cutting than other types. For garden display, they are unequaled. They were formerly called "baby ramblers" because the flower clusters were similar to those produced on older varieties of ramblers.

What varieties of polyanthas are worthwhile? 'Cameo', 'Cecile Brunner', 'China Doll', all pink; 'Margo Koster', orange to salmon; 'Mother's Day', a red sport of 'Margo'; 'White Koster', pure white. Taller than these are 'Mrs. R. M. Ginch', light pink; 'Golden Salmon', an orange-red; and 'The Fairy', but the latter is best classed as a small shrub.

ROSE RATINGS

The pictures in the catalogs are all enticing. How can you tell if a variety is really good?   Two excellent ways. The American Rose Society rates rose varieties from reports sent in by gardeners all over the country. The results are published each year in the *Handbook for Selecting Roses*. However, it must be remembered that these ratings represent an average over the entire continent. A rose that does not rate highly in the *Handbook* may grow wonderfully well in your area.

The "Proof-of-the-Pudding," published each year in the *American Rose Annual,* gives much more information about newly introduced varieties. The *Annual* is sent to ARS members, but may also be purchased from the society. A Consulting Rosarian near you will be happy to make any information available to you, if you know which varieties you wish to inquire about.

All-American Rose Selections, Inc., rates roses by sending professionals to judge roses for two years as they are grown in test gardens throughout the country. Each year the coveted AARS Award is given to a very few varieties, seldom more than two or three, and roses thus designated are sold with an AARS tag. Very often these roses also rate high in the "Proof-of-the-Pudding" reports, and eventually they may be assigned high ratings in the *Handbook for Selecting Roses*. But unless you like to gamble, wait a year or two to see how they do in other gardens nearby before you buy them for your own garden.

RUGOSA ROSES

Will you tell me something about rugosa roses?   This hardy species and its many fine hybrids are among the toughest and most long-lived of all roses. They are suitable for planting at the seashore, where they make themselves thoroughly at home in sandy soil. They grow in the very cold sections of the West where few roses can survive, and they can be used as large shrubs or hedges wherever there is room for them. The species (*Rosa rugosa*) has deep rose or white flowers. Rugosa foliage is shining dark green and rugose (wrinkled). (For some of the best hybrids, see under Shrubs.)

SCOTCH

What are Scotch roses? A strain of old garden roses with fine foliage and spiny growth. Hardy and disease-resistant, they can be planted with shrubs or as specimens. 'Harison's Yellow', 6 to 8 feet, is semidouble; 'Stanwell Perpetual', double, pink, is a constant bloomer; 'Frühlingsgold', single, yellow; and 'Frühlingsmorgen', pink with maroon stamens, are modern hybrid spinosissimas properly classed as shrubs. Scotch roses are varieties or hybrids of *Rosa spinosissima*.

SHRUBS

What are shrub roses? Many of the more vigorous, hardy roses can be used in the garden in the same fashion as any flowering shrub. Some are officially classed as shrubs and some are listed as species or in the rugosa or other groups. 'Golden Wings', with very large, sulfur-yellow single flowers, was introduced as a hybrid tea, but when it proved to be exceptionally vigorous, too tall and broad ever to be planted with hybrid teas, it was reclassified as a shrub. 'The Fairy', with continuous clusters of small pink flowers, is still classed as a polyantha, but it is really a shrub, spreading to 4 to 5 feet and 3 to 4 feet high. 'Sparrieshoop', with light pink fragrant flowers, sometimes repeating, is halfway between a shrub and a climber and so is 'Pax', which repeats its creamy white, almost single blooms on willowy canes all summer.

Please list some good rugosa shrubs. 'Therese Bugnet', hardy in Alaska, has fragrant pink flowers. Other good rugosas include 'Agnes', yellow; 'Conrad F. Meyer', pink; 'Frau Dagmar Hartopp', pink, and a relatively low bush; 'Grootendorst Supreme', red; 'Pink Grootendorst', clear pink, fringed petals; *R. rugosa* 'Alba', white; 'Sarah Van Fleet', pink; 'Vanguard', large, double, salmon-pink, very fragrant flowers, not recurrent.

SPECIES

What are rose species? Please name some. These are the wild roses that have been found throughout the Northern Temperate Zone. Some of them are the ancestors of our modern roses. Among those that make beautiful and interesting garden plants are *Rosa eglanteria*, Shakespeare's Eglantine, the sweetbriar. It is a tall, upright bush which may also be trained to a trellis or pillar. The foliage is fragrant of apples, especially noticeable after a rain. The small pink flowers are delightful in June, and there are bright red hips in the fall. *R. hugonis,* Father Hugo's rose or the golden rose of China, is an early blooming bright yellow rose that makes a spreading mound and is best planted in poor soil. Others are *R. foetida* and its sport, *R. foetida* 'Bicolor' or Austrian copper; *R. paulii,* white; *R. rubrifolia,* pink with red stems and foliage beloved by flower arrangers; *R. rugosa,* mauve-pink, very fragrant, and its color sports *R. rugosa* 'Alba', white, and *R. rugosa* 'Rubra', deep pink or red; and *R. soulieana,* a rampant white climber.

What is a sport?   A sport is a spontaneous mutation in the plant cells. The cause is not understood, but the phenomenon is eagerly watched for by nurserymen, hybridizers, and rosarians. Roses have a proclivity for sporting that is matched by few other plants. Many of our most beautiful varieties have occurred by sporting. 'Chicago Peace' is a sport of 'Peace'. 'Flamingo Queen' is a sport by X-ray of 'Queen Elizabeth', but such experiments have not led to any outstanding varieties so far.

SUPPORTS

How can I support my climbing roses?   On a split-rail fence, over a trellis bought or made for the purpose, over an arch, or on cedar posts with crossbars added for extra support (the latter method is especially suited to pillar-type roses).

What is a pillar rose?   The term "pillar" refers more to a method of support than to an actual type of rose. Roses adapted to a post or pillar include some climbing varieties that do not have excessively long canes and some of the tall-growing hybrid perpetual varieties.

How can an overgrown rambler be attached to the side of a house?   The plant should be properly pruned by cutting off at ground level all but the new basal shoots. These can be trained as desired by tying them with soft twine to nails driven into the side of the house. However, the house wall is not an ideal form of support. The roses will interfere with painting and other aspects of maintenance. It is better to use some form of latticework, which should be held out from the wall itself at least 6 inches, or preferably a foot.

SWEETBRIAR HYBRIDS

What are hybrid sweetbriars? They are hybrids of *Rosa eglanteria,* having scented foliage, single or semidouble flowers on arching canes, and strong growth. The species, with small, pink single flowers, has been known since 1551 and is commonly found in pastures. The hybrid 'Lady Penzance' has single pink flowers with yellow centers. 'Lord Penzance' is fawn-colored, with fragrant flowers as well as foliage. 'Meg Merriles' is deep pink. Although the species is available in this country, the hybrid eglanterias are getting hard to find, and are currently available only by import.

TEA ROSES

Why are varieties of roses called "tea roses"? Because the scent of the flowers resembles fresh green tea leaves (not the beverage). Pink and yellow forms of *Rosa odorata,* the original "tea" rose, were brought to England from China in 1824 and thence to the United States. They are mostly grown in the South and on the Pacific coast, although a few may survive elsewhere. In mild, moist climates, they are very recurrent and grow without much care, being tolerant of black spot and intolerant of pruning. The fragrant flowers are of medium size, without bold colors, and are well formed.

What varieties of tea roses are available? 'Catherine Mermet', flesh-pink; 'Duchess de Brabant', rosy pink; 'Maman Cochet', cream to pink; 'Safrano', yellow; 'Sombreuil', white; and a few others.

What is the difference between a tea rose and a hybrid tea? The hybrid tea rose is descended from the tea, which is one of the parents of the hybrid tea. In appearance, the tea and the hybrid tea are alike, but the hybrid tea is more vigorous and hardy, has a wider adaptation and bolder colors.

TERRACES AND PATIOS

My property is limited and I don't have space for a real rose garden. Could I grow a few roses in large redwood tubs on my patio, which receives enough sun to keep geraniums and petunias flowering abundantly? Yes, select floribunda and grandiflora varieties, as they are more floriferous than hybrid teas. You can also grow miniature roses in planters or in clay pots sunk in window boxes filled with peat moss (do not allow to dry out!).

Why did the roses on my terrace, which did well during the summer, die during the winter, when rosebushes set in the open ground near the terrace wintered well? The roots of container-grown plants are much more subject to winter damage from low temperatures than are the roots of plants in the ground. Most plants grown in containers need special care to survive the winter. One suggestion is to group containers together in areas protected from winter sunshine and wind and then pack their sides and tops with marsh hay, straw, leaves, evergreen boughs, or whatever is at hand. It would be simpler to move containers to a garage or other enclosure for the winter; if heavy tubs are on casters, this might be possible. Of course, city gardeners don't have garage space and will have to take their chances with the winter elements. The few roses grown in containers can always be replaced in the spring if necessary.

Do roses grown in pots need any special care? They require the same attention as roses growing in gardens, plus the added care needed by a plant restricted to a pot. Each tub or container should have holes to drain off excess water; watering the soil thoroughly, before it becomes bone dry, is most important. A regular fertilizing schedule is essential since the roots of container-grown plants cannot forage for nutrients as can roots in a garden.

I need two tall accents in tubs on each side of the steps leading down from my terrace. Would tree roses be satisfactory? What would I do with them during the winter? Tubbed tree roses should make rather formal, yet most attractive, accents. In cold climates about the only way to carry the bushes safely through the winter would be to remove them carefully from the tubs in late fall and bury them horizontally in a trench covered with soil. After the ground freezes, they should be covered with evergreen boughs or rough compost. In the spring replant the bushes in tubs or open ground.

TREE ROSES

What is a tree (standard) rose? Instead of the bud being inserted close to the ground (as is done in propagating other types), tree roses are budded near the top of a tall understock cane. The plant that develops from the bud is therefore on a trunk, or standard. The trunk, usually of *Rosa rugosa* stock, is itself often on a different rootstalk, so 3 roses are involved in creating a tree rose.

Can tree roses be grown in cold climates?   They are difficult to grow in cold climates because they are hard to keep during the winter. In regions where the temperature does not drop below 10° F., they are usually satisfactory.

WALLS

I have a low rock retaining wall in front of my house that is 175 feet long. Should roses be planted on the inside, which is on a level with the yard, or on the outside, so they would have the wall for support?   Plant on the inside so the rose stems can overhang the wall.

What rose varieties would you suggest for a low rock retaining wall? (Kansas.)   'Max Graf', *Rosa* x *paulii*, *R. wichuraiana*, 'Sea Foam', if you cannot spray; climbing mini roses, if spraying is possible.

Organizations

What is the American Rose Center?   A dream come true, it is the home of the American Rose Society and a mecca for all gardeners. Administered by the tax-exempt American Rose Foundation, the Center is located in Shreveport, Louisiana, on a 118-acre tract donated to the foundation. There is a visitors' center and gift shop, and many rose gardens to stroll through. The address is P.O. Box 30,000, Shreveport, Louisiana 71130. The American Rose Society provides information for all rose lovers, mainly through its nationally appointed Consulting Rosarians. Write for a list of those in your area. They are eager to answer any questions about roses, and there is no fee or obligation for this service.

What is the Heritage Roses Group?   An international association of people who love the old garden roses of yesteryear, the Heritage Roses Group was formed for the purpose of sharing information, enthusiasm, and cuttings or budwood of roses that are no longer on the market. It is not connected with the American Rose Society, although many rosarians belong to both organizations. A quarterly newsletter is distributed to members. Information may be obtained from the American Rose Society.

7. Perennials

FEW GARDENERS TODAY have the space or will to make the 100-foot long, 8- to 10-foot-wide borders that used to be the fashion. But perennials can assume an important role in even the smallest garden, whether they be used as a few plants for accent or by the dozens. Besides near permanence, they offer a certain decorative quality that's hard to achieve with annuals, shrubs, or bulbs alone.

The perennial gardens of today and tomorrow will be much simplified so care will be minimal, their impact on the landscape maximal. For example, a classic combination of three favorites—peonies, bearded iris, and day-lilies—can border a driveway and provide color from spring until fall if the varieties have been carefully selected to spread the bloom sequence. The peonies and iris will flower first, then day-lilies will flower over most of the summer, according to variety. The area itself need be no more than 4 feet wide and 25 feet long and the gardener has only to master the simple needs of three rugged perennials that grow well under similar conditions. Such a narrow border eases maintenance considerably since all plants can be reached without actually stepping into the garden.

Another popular approach to a perennial garden is the irregularly shaped island garden, perhaps with a few large boulders or a small tree placed strategically for accent. Again, this garden is easy to work in, and different effects can be had from the various sides. In such a garden it's possible to accommodate both sun- and shade-lovers as well as rock-garden plants. Or annuals and perennials can be mixed. If only a few plants are desired, an attractive mulch or perennial ground cover can be used to fill the remaining spaces.

The single accent perennial is very effective, but it must be chosen with great care as it has to be decorative in bloom as well as out of bloom. Dramatic accents that come to mind are a clump of peonies or day-lilies by a garden gate, a grouping of Japanese iris by a small pool, or an ornamental grass against a fence.

Not to be overlooked is the use of perennials as ground covers to replace high-maintenance lawn areas. Such perennials as ajuga, lily-of-the-valley, sweet woodruff, and sedum offer a great deal more eye appeal than grass or gravel under certain circumstances.

For the advanced gardener who enjoys combining colors and textures to weave living tapestry, there is no better group of plants to work with than perennials. The challenge is there and the possibilities are limitless. The cost is reasonable, the results fairly soon achieved. The scene can be changed frequently—something not so easily done with more permanent shrub plantings.

What is a hardy herbaceous perennial? A plant which lives for several years, whose tops die in winter but are renewed from the same roots each spring.

What is the average age of perennial plants? About 1 to 3 years.

I am a rank beginner. Should I buy perennials from my local garden center or from mail-order catalogs? To start off, you might find it easier to buy a few perennials in containers from a garden center. The advantages are that the plants are usually in full growth, which gives you an idea of their size, and you can set them out any time during the growing season without disturbing their root systems. However, such potted perennials are much more expensive than mail-order plants. A mail-order nursery specializing in perennials usually offers more kinds of perennials and their varieties than a garden center can.

How do I arrange plants in a new perennial garden? Make lists of the plants you intend to use, dividing them according to height, color, and blooming season. Making a plan on paper is a help, but you can do quite well just working with the lists. Place the tall plants in the background, those of medium height in the midsection of the garden, and those of low height in the foreground. Since there will be some variation in heights and habits of growth among the three, the final effect of this arrangement will not be rigid. Even so, it is a good idea to drift some tall plants and some low plants toward the center of the garden. For maximum effect, group three to five plants of one kind together, except for such large, strong accent plants as peony, globe-thistle, and baby's-breath, which can stand alone.

What To Grow

Can you name a few good perennials for succession of bloom from spring to fall? Spring: bleedingheart, basket-of-gold alyssum, dwarf iris, and the blue *Phlox divaricata*. Summer: astilbe, various *Campanula* species such as *C. carpatica, C. glomerata* 'Joan Eliott', and *C. persicifolia,* day-lilies, summer phlox, globe-thistle, platycodon, delphinium. Late summer and fall: hardy asters, chrysanthemums, monkshood, helenium, and *Ceratostigma plumbaginoides.*

What would be an interesting layout for a perennial bed that is backed with shrubbery? First, set out groups of delphiniums—3 or 4 to a group—spaced at irregular intervals over the bed, 8 to 12 feet apart, depending upon the size of the bed. Set out hollyhocks in the same manner—2 to 3 plants in each group. Intersperse in the same way varieties of summer phlox, then various hardy asters. This will give distribution of bloom. If spaces are left, fill in with Oriental poppy, achillea, aconitum, *Anemone japonica, Campanula persicifolia,* cushion chrysanthemums, dianthus species and cultivars, gaillardia, gypsophila 'Bristol Fairy', helenium, heliopsis. These will lend support to the 4 main kinds at different parts of the season. The principle is to weave the pattern back and forth across the border.

What are good combinations of ordinary perennials in a border? The overall border plan should be based upon the distribution of bloom over the planting and over the season. Color combinations, although effective at the moment, leave gaps in the planting unless planned to be followed up with other plants. Some good color combinations are lupines, anthemis 'Moonlight', and *Oenothera missouriensis;* poppy 'Helen Elizabeth', Shasta daisy, and *Linum perenne;* purple iris and *Aquilegia chrysantha;* delphinium hybrids, *Thermopsis caroliniana,* and day-lilies and globe-thistle. These are only a few of the countless combinations possible. Be sure that all flowers selected for a combination bloom at the same time, as usually their season is short.

I have a collection of 24 varieties of day-lilies for continuous bloom during the season. They are all in shades of cream and yellow. Which hardy perennials do you suggest for harmonizing and contrasting bloom

from early spring to fall in such a border? Siberian iris, bearded iris, astilbe, cimicifuga, delphinium, globe-thistle, *Salvia azurea,* regal lily, veronica 'Blue Champion', goats-beard (*Aruncus sylvester*), platycodon, liatris, summer phlox, and helenium.

FOR SPECIAL PURPOSES

Which perennials can be planted around Oriental poppies to cover their unsightly fading foliage? *Anemone japonica,* baby's-breath (*Gypsophila paniculata*), *Thalictrum aquilegifolium,* hardy chrysanthemums, *Eupatorium coelestinum.* This latter perennial starts very late in the spring and fills out by midsummer.

My yard is made up of rock and ashes. Which perennials will grow well here? Everything seems to burn up from the heat of the sun. *Euphorbia myrsinites, Tunica saxifrago, Sedum acre, Silene maritima, Saponaria ocymoides, Nepeta* x *faassenii, Lathyrus latifolius, Echinops ritro.*

What plant or flower (perennial) do you suggest for cemeteries? For shade: *Ajuga reptans, Dicentra eximia,* vinca 'Bowles Variety'. For sun: *Dianthus plumarius, Sedum spectabile, Sedum acre, Aegopodium podograria.*

Which perennial can I grow in a small bed bordering my terrace? The terrace faces north and I want something at least 1 foot high. *Dicentra eximia, Phlox divaricata, Nepeta* x *faassenii.*

Which are the best perennials to grow in a border along an active red-cedar hedge? If there is at least a half day of sun: hardy asters, *Eupatorium coelestinum,* helenium, *Heliopsis scabra, Nepeta* x *faassenii, Oenothera missouriensis,* day-lilies, and summer phlox are some of the most satisfactory.

Which perennial flowers can be satisfactorily grown in a city garden where there is practically no sunlight? *Ajuga reptans* and *A. genevensis, Dicentra eximia, Mertensia virginica,* day-lily, *Pulmonaria saccharata* and *P. angustifolia,* and *Phlox divaricata.*

Is there a reliable perennial for shade? Many perennials classified as ground covers because of their spreading growth habits are reliable subjects for shade where they are often grown as grass substitutes. These include lily-of-the-valley (*Convallaria majalis*), which produces its very fragrant white flowers in late spring; bugle-weed (*Ajuga*), short spikes of blue flowers in midspring; sweet woodruff (*Asperula odorata*), white flowers in spring; epimedium, white, yellow, or rose flowers, according to species, in midspring; wild-sweet-William or blue phlox (*Phlox divaricata* and *P. stolonifera*), blue flowers in spring; and the fragrant plantain-lily (*Hosta plantaginea*). The last is a nonspreading perennial with clumps of bright green foliage and showy white flower spikes in summer. There are other fine hostas for shade, most of which are sought for their handsome, variegated, or huge bluish leaves rather than their flower displays. Hardy ferns are also reliable perennials for shaded areas but of course do not provide any flower color.

Can you suggest perennials for a small plot of ground facing the east? A house is in the background. Violets and lily-of-the-valley have not been successful. Aquilegia, anemone, *Phlox divaricata,* anchusa, epimedium, monarda, *Hosta* (syn. *Funkia*) *sieboldii* and *H. ventricosa.*

What are some easily grown blue-flowered perennials? *Veronica* 'Crater Lake Blue', *Veronica longifolia subsessilis,* globe-thistle, tradescantia 'J. C. Weguelin', *Platycodon grandiflorus, Campanula persicifolia, Ceratostigma plumbaginoides,* and amsonia.

What should one plant on north, east, and south fences to act as a screen, and also as a background for perennial borders? *Clematis montana rubens, Lathyrus latifolius, Polygonum aubertii,* bignonia 'Mme. Galen'. Or plant annuals such as sweet pea and morning-glory.

Will you name some very hardy perennials? Achillea, ajuga, aquilegia, artemisia, astilbe, coreopsis, dicentra (bleedingheart), eupatorium, day-lily, lythrum, mertensia, *Nepeta* x *faassenii,* peony, phlox, platycodon.

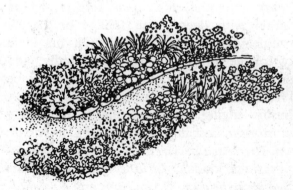

Facing flower borders follow the curves of a gracefully meandering path.

I want to plant a small perennial garden with plants that require no care and that are good for cutting. Can you give me a list? Most perennials require some care—removal of faded flowers, dividing of clumps every few years to keep them vigorous, and attention to weeding. The following are about as rugged as any: astilbe, bearded iris, hardy chrysanthemum, *Helenium autumnale*, peonies, hardy asters, *Lysimachia punctata* (this is an attractive cut flower and drifts are effective in early summer borders but eventually it becomes invasive), baby's-breath 'Bristol Fairy', platycodon, gaillardia, nepeta, day-lily. Delphinium plants can be spectacular, either for cutting or in the garden, but require regular spraying to control the cyclamen mite. The tall varieties also must be staked.

Are there any shade-tolerant perennials? Aconitum (monkshood), ajuga, anemone, aquilegia, astilbe, bleedingheart, bugbane (*Cimicifuga*), Carpathian bluebell, day-lily, doronicum, epimedium, ferns, eupatorium, lily-of-the-valley, *Lobelia cardinalis* and *L. siphilitica*, mertensia, *Monarda didyma*, *Phlox divaricata*, hosta, plumbago (*Ceratostigma*), primroses, thalictrum, vinca, and violets. (See also Wildflowers, Section 2.)

What are the best perennials for a sunny, dry place? Basket-of-gold, *Veronica incana*, *Cerastium tomentosum*, *Aethionema grandiflorum*, *Arenaria montana*, *Arabis alpina*, *Linum perenne*, dictamnus, heliopsis, iris (bearded), day-lily, *Oenothera fruitcosa* (sundrops), sedums.

Can you give me the names of some low-growing perennials that can be used for a border? Basket-of-gold alyssum, candytuft, *Ceratostigma plumbaginoides*, *Aster novi-belgi* dwarf varieties, primrose, *Sedum hybridum* and *S. sieboldii*, *Veronica incana*, *Geranium grandiflorum*.

What low-growing, neat, easy perennials with good foliage can be used for edging? Ajuga, either with deep green foliage or variety 'Bronze Beauty', with bronze leaves, is a good choice; it has blue flowers in the spring, husky foliage all season, spreads rapidly, and stands shade and city conditions. Several varieties of sedum may be used for edging, if controlled from spreading too much.

Will you name some bushy edging perennial plants for along walks? *Epimedium alpinum rubrum*, best in partial shade; *Campanula carpatica*, *Lamium maculatum*, *Iberis sempervirens*, *Aegopodium podagraria*, 'Variegatum', *Hosta* (various kinds), *Liriope muscari* and its striped variety, 'Variegata', *Sedum hybridum*, *S. spurium* and *S. sieboldii*, and *Nepeta*.

Can you give a list of low perennials to be grown in beds bordering a terrace? *Achillea tomentosa*, *Ajuga genevensis*, basket-of-gold alyssum, *Anemone japonica*, aster (cushion type), *Campanula carpatica*, cushion chrysanthemums, dianthus, various species and varieties, *Ne-*

peta x *faassenii, Phlox subulata* varieties, pyrethrum varieties, *Veronica incana, Geranium endressii* 'Johnson's Variety'.

Will you name some perennials for planting along the front of the border? *Aurinia saxatilis* 'Compacta', *Dianthus plumarius, Limonium latifolium, Ceratostigma plumbaginoides,* dwarf asters, *Veronica spicata nana, Arabis alpina, Silene maritima, Tunica saxifraga, Veronica incana, Nepeta* x *faassenii,* and santolina.

What are some medium-height perennials for the center of the border? Astilbe, *Campanula persicifolia* varieties, *Artemisia* 'Silver King', *Achillea ptarmica, Aquilegia coerulea, Paradisea liliastrum, Dicentra eximia, Eupatorium coelestinum, Veronica longifolia subsessilis, Gypsophila paniculata,* Siberian iris, gasplant.

Which are the best tall-growing perennials for a border? *Bocconia cordata, Thalictrum glaucum* and *aquilegifolium, Phlox paniculata* hybrids, *Helenium autumnale, Rudbeckia purpurea,* delphinium hybrids, asters (tall, named varieties), *Cimicifuga racemosa, Campanula pyramidalis, Echinops ritro,* most day-lilies.

Will you give a list of plants for a small perennial border with a succession of bloom as long as possible and no plants which are difficult to obtain? *Arabis alpina, Phlox divaricata,* bearded iris, astilbe, veronica 'Blue Champion', day-lily, heuchera, dianthus, phlox 'Miss Lingard', Shasta daisy, hardy asters, coreopsis, gaillardia, summer phlox, helenium varieties, cushion chrysanthemums, nepeta.

Can you give me a list of perennials to use in a border 2 to 3 feet wide and 50 feet long that would keep it looking well all season? *Brunnera macrophylla, Dicentra eximia,* delphinium 'Connecticut Yankee', gaillardia, geum, day-lilies, nepeta, pyrethrum, summer phlox, *Heliopsis scabra, Eupatorium coelestinum,* hardy asters, cushion chrysanthemums, and such gray-foliaged plants as santolina, nepeta, and *Ruta graveolens.* Constant color can be secured only by introducing annuals for later summer bloom.

Can you name about six perennial plants I can find in my local garden center to plant in front of shrubs? They must be easy to grow, last well, and require no care. No complicated botanical names please—I don't understand Latin. You don't say whether the situations are in sun or shade. The following do well in sun or light shade: day-lily, hosta, bugleweed (*Ajuga*), dead nettle (*Lamium*), astilbe, and catmint (*Nepeta* x *faassenii*). There is hardly a plant that requires no care, however, and the six named, though tough, will eventually need dividing. Weeds must be removed and bugleweed may need restraining. The common names of many plants are the same as the botanical names, examples being astilbe (*Astilbe*), delphinium (*Delphinium*), and phlox (*Phlox*). Sometimes the same common names are used for very different plants or are regional in origin and not known in other places. Also there are many different species of plants: the name catmint is used for many kinds of *Nepeta,* but *Nepeta* x *faassenii* is the best one to use in a flower garden.

Will you suggest varieties for a perennial bed 30 × 10 feet, so as to have continuous bloom from early spring to late fall?   Make a selection from the following: *March*—crocus, snowdrop, squill, winter-aconite (all bulbs and tubers). *April*—rock-cress, goldentuft, daffodils, moss phlox. *May*—perennial candytuft, columbine, globeflower, iris, Virginia cowslip, bleedingheart, polyanthus primrose. *June*—Japanese iris, astilbe, Shasta daisy, painted daisy, pinks, coral-bells, Oriental poppy, hybrid columbines, day-lilies, delphinium, hollyhock. *July*—baby's-breath, false dragonhead, summer phlox, loosestrife, Carpathian bluebell, perennial sunflower, balloonflower. *August*—plantain-lily, rose-mallow, sneezeweed, coneflower, cardinal-flower, hardy asters, sea-lavender. *September* and *October*—Japanese anemone, hardy asters, perennial sunflowers, goldenrod, showy stonecrop, hardy chrysanthemums, monkshood, hardy asters, leadwort (*Ceratostigma*), *Helianthus, Salvia azurea grandiflora.*

Is there a perennial that blooms nearly all summer?   No—despite claims in catalogs! *Heliopsis scabra, Gaillardia aristana, Nepeta* x *faassenii,* and *Dicentra eximia* all come very near it.

Which dwarf border plants bloom over the longest period of time?   *Silene vulgaris maritima, Dianthus deltoides flore-pleno, Nepeta* x *faassenii.*

General Culture

SOIL PREPARATION

How deep should soil be prepared for a new border?   For best results, the soil should be dug and prepared not less than 12 inches, but 18 to 24 inches deep will give superior results.

How shall I prepare new ground for perennials?   Dig the ground to a depth of 12 inches, 18 inches if you can, mixing in well-rotted or dehydrated cow manure, leafmold, peat moss, or compost, with 10 pounds superphosphate to 100 square feet. Spread the organic materials in a 3- to 4-inch layer. Small gardens can be spaded, but rent a rotary tiller for larger areas.

In preparing a border, should all stones be removed? Should the soil be screened? For perennials, annuals, and shrubs, stones the size of a lemon or smaller may be left in the soil. Do not screen the soil.

Is sand or clay better subsoil for a perennial border? If sand is too loose and porous, drainage will be excessive; if the clay is hard-packed, drainage will be stopped. Generally speaking, a sandy subsoil is preferable. Hard clay should be broken up and lightened with peat moss, cinders, gravel, or sand.

What element is lacking in the soil when perennials have good color and flower well but lack sufficient strength to stand upright and spread all over the beds? Possibly insufficient phosphorus and potash; but crowded planting, too much watering, and overfeeding with nitrogenous fertilizers will cause weak stems. However, many perennials need support by staking.

For 20 years we have had a perennial border. The last 5 years it has deteriorated; replacements, fertilizer, etc., have not solved the problem. Maple and elm trees grow nearby; there is sunshine for one hour a day. Can soil be improved to overcome a lack of sunshine? Nothing can be done to improve the soil so that it will overcome the lack of sunshine and greedy tree roots.

Why don't my plants near red-cedar trees thrive? Are there any perennials that will grow fairly well in the shade of trees? The soil may be "poisoned" by the accumulation of years of dead red-cedar foliage. Try removing this periodically. Give the surface a light application of ground limestone and a generous supply of rotted manure, compost, peat moss, or leafmold. Work until the ground is in good "tilth." Most shade plants, especially the "woodsy" ones, will grow well if the soil is friable and not super-acid. Some are ferns, dicentra, *Vinca minor,* hepatica, *Pachysandra terminalis,* primula, *Ceratostigma plumbaginoides, Phlox divaricata, P. carolina* and *P. ovata,* aquilegia.

FERTILIZERS

Which is the better time to put fertilizer around perennials—spring or fall? Chemical fertilizer is best spread when plants are actively growing. Superphosphate and animal manures can be worked into the soil when planting.

Will fresh sheep manure hurt perennials?   No, providing it is not put on too heavily and is not allowed to come in contact with the roots. Use 1 pound per 100 square feet and cultivate into the surface soil.

What is a good fertilizer for asters, phlox, peonies, and delphiniums?   Well-rotted or dehydrated animal manure, supplemented during the growing season by a balanced commercial fertilizer. A little lime may be needed if the soil is acid.

Is there anything to be gained by fertilizing perennials during the growing season?   In some cases, yes. Many kinds—phlox, delphinium, chrysanthemums, etc.—are helped by supplementary feedings of liquid manure or quick-acting commercial fertilizer applied when flowers are about to be formed. Whether or not this is necessary depends on the character of the soil, the initial preparation of the border, and annual routine practices to maintain its fertility.

How do you prepare and fertilize perennial beds in the spring so as not to disturb the plants?   By forking in the manure, compost, or fertilizer lightly. Or if plants are very close together, you may have to work carefully with a trowel.

Do all perennials need lime? My soil is cleared-off pine woodland.   Most garden flowers need a soil near the neutral point or slightly acid. Your county extension agent probably will be glad to advise you on how much lime to apply to your soil after you have it tested.

PLANTING AND TRANSPLANTING

What is the method of planting bare-root perennials?   Make a hole of sufficient size with a spade or trowel (depending on the size of the root system) to accommodate the roots without crowding. Put the plant in the hole, no deeper than it grew in the nursery. Work the soil between and over the roots and pack firmly. Soak with water.

Is it all right to plant perennials when the soil is sopping wet?   No. Soil structure can be harmed as a result. Wait until the soil is crumbly but still moist.

When is the best time to remake a perennial border?   Fall is best. Early spring is also good, but early-blooming plants should be replanted in the fall, except for those on the border line of hardiness in the region.

However, a certain amount of rearranging is possible throughout the growing season, especially if you buy plants in containers.

Is August a good month to revamp borders? Definitely not. It is the hottest and driest month as a rule, and newly transplanted stock (with the exceptions noted below) is likely to suffer.

Which perennials should be moved in midsummer or early fall? Bearded iris can be moved after flowering; bleedingheart, Christmas-rose, and peonies in late summer and early fall; Oriental poppies in late summer; madonna lilies, as soon as the tops wither.

Should all perennials be cut back, either after they are replanted or transplanted in the fall? Tall perennials are better if cut back before being moved. Whatever foliage remains down near the soil matters little in the fall.

What is the time for dividing and transplanting perennials in northern Maine—fall or spring? Fall, if it can be done at least 4 weeks before heavy freezing. It can be done in the spring, too—but as early as possible.

How do you suggest I rejuvenate my perennial garden? In early fall obtain a supply of wooden nursery flats or grocery cartons and fill them with the lifted perennials, taking care not to mix up varieties of the same plant. Then spread as much organic material, up to 2 to 4 inches deep, as you can afford. Use peat moss, your own garden compost if you have it, half-rotted leaves or leafmold, rotted animal manures, etc. Also spread superphosphate, about 3 pounds per 100 square feet, or steamed bone meal at the same rate. If you know that your soil is very acid (or a soil test shows this), also spread ground limestone over the area at the rate of 5 pounds per 100 square feet. Then use a rotary tiller to mix all these ingredients with the soil. (If you don't own a tiller, rent one from a garden center.) Then rake over the area and, as soon as the soil seems settled, replant. You will want to divide many of your plants at this time. (See Propagation, this section.)

Should flowers be planted in straight rows or staggered? The effect is better in a staggered planting. When they are grown for cut flowers only, it is more convenient to have them in rows.

When is the correct time to plant perennials in the spring? Will they bloom the same year? Plant as early as the soil can be worked or when received from the nursery. Plants, if large enough, will flower the same season.

My nurseryman sells perennials in pots and other containers from spring until fall. He says they can be planted anytime during the grow-

ing season. Is this true?   Yes. More and more plants, including trees, shrubs, and roses, are being handled in this way. Obviously the rules about only spring and fall planting don't apply because pot-grown plants suffer no disturbance when being transplanted.

CULTURE

What constitutes good year-round care of a perennial border?   In the spring (when frost has left the ground) remove the winter mulch. If rotted manure or partly rotted leaves were used, leave finer portions and lightly fork into the soil, along with a topdressing of complete fertilizer. Reset any plants heaved out of the ground by frost. More mulch can be applied to suppress weeds and prevent the formation of a surface crust. Support those plants that need it. Water thoroughly when necessary. Put on more mulch after the first severe frost.

What is the best way to keep down weeds in a border of perennials?   Use a narrow scuffle hoe frequently to chop off weeds before they attain much size. Run the hoe through the soil about an inch below the surface. Weeds among the flowers must be pulled out by hand. Certain mulching materials also help to keep down weeds.

How close and how deep shall I keep the soil worked around different plants?   The depth depends on the type of plants: shallow-rooted plants need shallow cultivation; deep-rooted plants will take deeper cultivation. All can be worked close, but with care not to cut the stems.

Will straw mulch help in weed control and to hold moisture? If not, what will help besides pulling and hoeing?   A straw mulch or any similar material helps in the summer to keep down weeds and hold moisture.

Which flowers should be pinched back to become bushy? Can Oriental poppies or lilies be treated like this?   Chrysanthemums, hardy asters, helenium, some tall-growing veronicas and penstemons. Most plants, such as summer phlox, that tend to send shoots from the axils of the leaves can be pinched. Poppies and lilies should not be pinched.

When is the best time to cut back perennials; and how far?   This can be done in the late autumn, when the herbaceous stems have died down. Cut down to within an inch of the soil for most plants. Some plants have a clump or rosette of green leaves which should not be cut off; just cut the old flower stems. Some gardeners prefer to wait until spring before cutting off the tops of the perennials. Their argument is that it helps to prevent winter injury because snow and tree leaves are held by the stems.

Why do some hardy perennials die off after one or two luxuriant seasons? Most perennials need to be divided and transplanted after 2 or 3 years. Many are short-lived. Some do not do very well during the winter; still others succumb to diseases or insects.

How often should perennials be watered? No definite time can be set; the kind of soil, the needs of the various plants, as well as other factors have an influence. See that at all times during the growing season the soil is kept moist. This is the safest rule in mixed plantings.

Can plants be watered too much to bloom? I have some shade from maple trees and my soil gets hard if I don't water often. I have very little bloom on my perennials and roses. Iris do quite well. Shade, rather than too much water, is responsible for the lack of bloom. Use shade-tolerant plants. Improve the soil by adding humus-forming materials. Or move your garden to a better location.

Is it true that water should not touch the leaves of perennials? There is scant danger of water on the leaves doing any harm.

Do you have to water perennial flowers in the winter or do you just cover them? No watering is then needed, since there is no growth. Cover them after the ground is frozen. With half-rotted leaves, compost if you have it, marsh hay, etc. (See section on Winter Protection that follows.)

WINTER PROTECTION

Why are plants covered for the winter? The theory varies with the kind of plant and climate. Plants that are not hardy are covered *before* hard freezing to protect them from low temperatures, which would destroy the cells and thus kill the plant. Truly hardy plants are covered *after* the ground freezes; not to protect them from cold, but to keep them cold. The theory here is to prevent fluctuation of ground temperature, resulting in alternate freezing and thawing, which cause the injury. A mild spell in late winter, followed by a sudden hard freeze, is dangerous. In some cases, shading plants from the winter sun is sufficient. Most winterkill occurs in late winter or early spring.

Shall we let mother nature blanket our border garden with maple and locust leaves and, if so, when shall we remove the leaves? This is not the best way of protecting most garden perennials. Maple leaves tend to make a sodden mass and smother to death any but the most robust plants. Light, litterlike material, such as marsh hay, through which air can circulate, is best. The covering should be removed gradually when signs of growth are observed underneath. Take off the final covering on a cloudy day.

Is it necessary to protect newly planted perennials for the winter? What is the best method? It is advisable in colder regions to protect plants for the first winter. Marsh hay, straw, evergreen branches, or cornstalks can be used. Lay loosely, so as not to smother plants; do not put on until after the first hard freeze.

I planted perennial seeds in my cold frame in July. They have made good growth. Can I leave them in the frame until the spring? Should I put a mulch in the frame after December? A mulch will help. You may want to cover them earlier than December, depending on when you get heavy freezing. Seedlings from seed sown in July ought to make strong plants by late fall, particularly if planted out in a bed. If they are hardy perennials and are well grown, they do not need cold-frame protection.

How much winter coverage is needed on established perennial beds of iris, phlox, tulips, and various small plants? How early should this be put on? What is the best type? (New York.) A covering of about 3 inches is sufficient for the average planting of perennials. Wait until the ground has frozen before putting it on. Use some litterlike material that will not pack down, such as marsh hay, pine needles, or evergreen branches.

Is peat moss a good winter covering for my garden of peonies, iris, hollyhocks, delphiniums, nicotiana, dicentra? Peonies and bearded iris should not be covered in the winter. This favors rot. Delphiniums are better if covered with several inches of coarse ashes, if you can get them. Nicotiana is not usually hardy in the North. Hollyhocks and dicentra are the only ones that might benefit from the peat moss. Peat moss is not a good mulch; it is better used as a soil conditioner at planting time.

In mulching plants, should you wait until the ground is frozen? As a rule, it is best to wait until the ground has frozen before putting on a protective mulch. Delay up to this point helps to harden the plants somewhat and also encourages rodents to find winter quarters elsewhere.

Should perennials be carefully covered in the fall in very changeable climates? The covering is not to keep out the cold but to protect against the bad effects of alternate spells of freezing and thawing. Delay it as long as possible in the fall—at least until the ground freezes. With the approach of spring, partially remove the covering; watch the plants and the weather; complete it on a cloudy day if possible.

Which perennials need a winter mulch and which prefer none? What kind of mulch?   Most perennials—except those with heavy green tops like tritoma—are the better for a winter mulch, particularly in regions of alternate freezing and thawing. Leafmold, marsh hay, and evergreen boughs are some of the better materials. Light covering should be strictly observed.

Propagation

SEED

When is the best time to sow perennials in a greenhouse?   In late February or early March, in a greenhouse of moderate temperature. With most kinds, seedlings will soon be large enough to be transplanted into flats, from which they can be set outside in a nursery bed in May. In this way only the usual summer cultivation is required and strong plants will be available for fall planting in the garden if need be.

Can perennials be raised successfully from fall-sown seed?   Where winter is severe and a cold frame is available, seeds of perennials can be sown in the fall, so as to remain dormant for an earlier start in spring than would be obtained from spring sowing under similar conditions. Losses would be great in trying to carry small seedlings through the winter.

Can you provide a specific list of the best planting dates for popular perennials from seed?   If greenhouse space is available, in March; if only a cold frame, in April; if no glass protection, outdoors in May. Some growers prefer to sow in August, thus securing the advantage of having fresh seed of the current season; but sowing in the first half of the year ensures huskier young plants, better able to face their first winter.

What is the latest date for planting perennial seeds for bloom the following spring?   Possibly in early August; but May sowing is better.

If you have no sunny window available, can you start perennial seedlings indoors?   Yes. Under fluorescent lights.

Is it advisable to sow seeds of perennials in the open ground?   Yes.

Make a special seed bed by mixing in fine leafmold or peat moss and sand in the top 3 or 4 inches of soil. Sow as early in May as possible and keep the soil moist. A good method would be to sow in seed pans or flats, bury these to the rims in sand, and cover with polyethylene until germination.

Can any perennials be grown from seed by simply scattering the seeds where they are to bloom?   There is no doubt that it could be done with certain kinds; but it is not the best, nor, in the long run, the easiest method. This method works better with annuals.

Should perennial seedlings be transplanted?   Yes. If the seeds were sown during the summer, transplant when they have developed their first true leaves. Water immediately and, if possible, provide light shade for a few days. Cultivate and water when necessary to promote growth.

Why do the seeds I save come up so well, while the seeds I buy, especially perennial, do so poorly?   Because, being home-grown, they are fresh; and they may be sown soon after ripening if need be. Buy only from a reliable dealer.

Which perennials are easiest to grow from seed?   Alyssum, aquilegia hybrids, *Campanula persicifolia* in variety, delphinium hybrids, *Coreopsis grandiflora,* erigeron, *Gaillardia grandiflora,* heliopsis, *Heuchera sanguinea, Lilium regale, Linum perenne, Lupinus polyphyllus* hybrids, primroses.

Can Thalictrum dipterocarpum seeds be planted in the late fall or the early winter? Will they bloom the following season?   Yes, in a cold frame; but they probably would not be strong enough to flower the following season.

What is the best method of raising thermopsis from seed?   Sow the seed when ripe in a flat of sandy soil and keep it in a cold frame during the winter. If seed is at hand in March, sow indoors and grow under fluorescent lights, first placing them in hot water to soak overnight.

How can I raise trollius from seed?   Sow the seed when ripe in a flat of rather porous soil. Keep it in a shaded cold frame and, as far as can be possible, maintain cool, moist conditions. It will probably not germinate until the second year.

CUTTINGS

How are perennials propagated by cuttings?   Cut off young shoots in the spring when they are about 3 inches long, making the cut below the ground if possible. Insert in sand or in perlite in a propagating case indoors. Also, by nonflowering shoots in the summer.

Will you tell me how to start cuttings in sand—such as chrysanthemum and carnation? Use a box about 10 inches deep; make drainage holes in the bottom; put in a 1-inch layer of coarse cinders or perlite and cover this with peat moss; add 3 inches of sand, tamped firmly. Cover the box with polyethylene and keep it where there is good light but out of the sun. Chrysanthemum cuttings are taken from the base of old plants in the spring; carnations can be rooted in August.

DIVISION

What is the best way to divide most perennials? Dig up the plants and pry the rootstock apart into pieces of suitable size with the help of 2 spading forks (or hand forks, if the plant is small).

When should perennials be divided? Early bloomers, in early fall; late bloomers, in the spring; bearded irises and Oriental poppies, in the summer.

HYBRIDIZING

How are flowers crossed by hand so that they produce seed? Remove the anthers from the flowers you want for the seed bearer before the pollen is ripe. Cover the flower with a transparent bag. When the

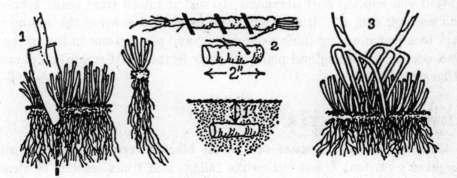

PROPAGATING PERENNIALS
Clumps or crowns can be cut apart with a knife or spade (1); or torn apart with two digging forks (3). Root cuttings (2) of some subjects (Oriental poppy, phlox, platycodon), buried about an inch deep, form new plants.

stigma is ripe (or sticky), put on the ripe pollen from the male parent, return the bag, and tie securely.

How does one go about producing a new color in a perennial? By taking the pollen from the flower of one species or variety and placing it upon the stigma of another. Both should belong to the same genus.

Specific Perennial Plants

ALYSSUM or BASKET-OF-GOLD (AURINIA)

What soil is needed to raise alyssum (Aurinia saxatilis)? It grows best in a light, porous soil with good drainage and sun.

My alyssum lives only one year. Why is this? It needs a well-drained soil and full sun in order to live from year to year. Remove the flower heads before they set seed.

Does alyssum need full sun? It does best in full sun; it will grow in partial shade but not flower as freely or live as long.

How do you make cuttings of alyssum that will root and grow? Take cuttings soon after the plants have flowered. Make them about 3 or more inches long, with about 1 inch of bare stem below the leaves; cut just below a leaf scar. Put in sand; water; keep shaded for a few days.

Will you explain how perennial alyssum is raised from seed? I have had no luck with it. It may be raised from seed sown in the summer, kept in a frame or bed during the winter, and planted out in the spring; also, sow in the spring and plant out early in the fall. Established plants often self-sow.

AMSONIA or BLUESTAR

Can you tell me the name of a lovely blue-flowered perennial in my neighbor's garden? It has willowlike foliage and bears clusters of clear blue, star-shaped flowers in midspring. Its height is about 3 feet. You are probably describing bluestar or willow amsonia (*Amsonia tabernaemontana*). It is native to much of the upper South and as far west as Texas, but it is quite hardy in northern gardens. Propagate by seeds or division in the fall.

ANCHUSA

Will you please give cultural care of Anchusa 'Dropmore'? Good garden loam, with fair moisture and full sun. Divide roots every 3 years.

Is Anchusa azurea 'Dropmore' a true perennial or should it be treated as an annual? Is it hardy in Massachusetts? It is a perennial and should be hardy in Massachusetts. However, it is not a long-lived perennial and often dies during cold winters.

ASTERS, HARDY

When should hardy aster seeds be planted? They can be sown in a greenhouse in March; in a cold frame in April; or outdoors in May.

When is the best time to plant hardy asters? In the spring, before they have more than an inch or two of growth.

How can I keep asters (Michaelmas daisies) from growing too high? Pinching them back in early summer should help them stay bushy.

Name some strong-growing hardy asters—preferably blue. 'Violetta' grows to 3 feet or more and has lavender-blue flowers. Also, 'Sailor Boy' and 'Eventide' are good, strong, blue varieties.

ASTILBE

Are the garden forms of astilbe that flower in the late spring related to the shrub spirea? No, but we can't blame you for wondering, as many nurseries and catalogs persist in labeling these herbaceous perennials—which are decidedly nonwoody—as "spirea." The flowers are fluffy, like some of those of spirea.

I would like to grow astilbe plants in my flower garden but I've been told that I can't as they require constantly wet soil. My garden's soil is average but phlox and day-lilies thrive in it. I always water the garden during drought. You should be able to grow astilbe under the conditions you describe. While the plants of astilbe revel in moist, rich soil, they also adapt to more average conditions. When planting, add rich compost, leafmold, or peat moss to the planting holes so that soil moisture will be retained.

BABY'S-BREATH (GYPSOPHILA)

What kind of soil is needed for growing perennial baby's-breath? It will grow in any reasonably good soil; it does not have to be rich, but it should be well drained and deep, and not more than slightly acid.

Can perennial gypsophila be successfully transplanted? Yes, if care is taken not to break the fleshy roots. It is best done in the spring.

What's wrong when gypsophila petals are so small that you can barely see them? Probably you have a poor seedling or another plant, *Galium aristatum,* which is sometimes sold as baby's-breath, which it resembles.

I have a 'Bristol Fairy' baby's-breath that grows beautifully but never blooms. Can anything be done to make it bloom? Some do not bloom when planted in too rich a soil. Try transplanting it (being careful not to break the long roots) and lime the soil.

How is gypsophila 'Bristol Fairy' propagated? Propagation is done by division, by cuttings, or by grafting on pieces of roots.

Does gypsophila 'Bristol Fairy' come true from seed? No.

BLEEDINGHEART (DICENTRA)

I had a large bleedingheart die last winter. Was this because I covered it with leaves? Probably you used too many leaves and smothered the plant; or perhaps you covered it too early. Wait until the soil is frozen, then cover lightly. Remove gradually in the spring. Mice will eat the roots.

My bleedingheart plants grew to become large, healthy bushes, but they would not bloom. Why? They were probably planted in too dense shade.

When is the best time to move bleedinghearts? In early autumn or very early spring.

When is the correct time to divide bleedingheart? September.

CACTI

What are the hardiest kinds of cacti? *Opuntia humifusa, O. fragilis, Echinocereus viridiflorus,* and *Pediocactus simpsonii.*

Are there any varieties of cactus, other than Opuntia, that can be left

outside all winter in southern Jersey? You might try *Echinocereus viridiflorus* and *Pediocactus simpsonii*.

Will cacti from the Arizona desert thrive in Oklahoma? Those native north of Phoenix will possibly grow if given a thoroughly well-drained and sheltered position.

Can spineless cacti be grown in a climate that is hot and dry in the summer and cold and wet in the winter? No. The spineless opuntias do not thrive where wet winters are experienced.

What are the names of some cacti that will live outdoors in south-central North Carolina? *Opuntia humifusa, O. fragilis, O. erinacea utahensis, O. polyacantha, O. imbricata, O. basilaris, Echinocereus viridiflorus, E. reichenbachii* and varieties, and *Pediocactus simpsonii*.

CANDYTUFT (IBERIS)

How can I propagate Iberis sempervirens (evergreen candytuft)? By seeds sown in the spring; by dividing the old plants in autumn or spring; or by cuttings made in the summer of the young growth inserted in a cold frame.

What is the best way to get a quantity of evergreen candytuft, for edging, from seed? Sow in an outdoor bed in May or June. Transplant seedlings to nursery beds, allowing 6 to 8 inches between plants. Set in their flowering quarters in the fall or the following spring.

Will you give me the proper culture directions for iberis? Mine are all dying. Iberis usually grows satisfactorily in any well-drained garden soil that is not too acid and needs no special care. There are perennial and annual iberis. The perennial kind sometimes does better when the plants are cut back to within a couple of inches of the crown after they have flowered.

CARNATIONS (DIANTHUS)

Is it possible to grow the English border carnation in the East? The heat of summers is not favorable to their culture, nor are they hardy during the winter in this region. Some success can be attained by sowing seeds in a greenhouse in February, potting the seedlings, and planting out in May in as cool a spot as possible; a little shade in July and August will help. Pinch them several times to make them branch; give some support to keep the plants from sprawling. Keep nearly all the buds removed until late summer and let them flower in the fall. Summer flowers are inferior.

What kind of fertilizer is best for carnations? The basic need is for some kind of humus; rotted or dehydrated manure is the best. Peat moss, compost, or leafmold can be substituted, but lime and fertilizer must be added to these. To a bushel of any of the above, add ½ pound of pulverized limestone and 1 pound of complete fertilizer. Mix thoroughly, spread this 3 inches deep, and mix with the soil. When plants begin to bloom, feed with dried blood, tankage, or dehydrated manure, ½ pound per square yard.

The soil here is sandy and the water supply very limited. Will carnations get along on natural rainfall? It will not be possible to get the best returns under these conditions. Set the plants out as early as possible, while the weather is cool. In July put on old leaves, grass clippings, or weeds as a mulch, and maintain it. This will assist in keeping the roots cool. Don't let the plants exhaust themselves by overflowering. Remove most of the buds until cool weather sets in.

Will you give the culture of hardy carnations? Sow seeds indoors in March in a soil mixture containing equal parts of loam, sand, and leafmold. Transplant the seedlings into flats, 2 inches apart, or into peat pots. Plant outside in May, about 12 inches apart. Prepare the bed by forking in leafmold or peat; add 10 pounds dried cow or sheep manure per 100 square feet. Water after planting; pinch out the tips to induce branching. Keep the soil stirred until the end of June, then mulch with old leaves or compost. Keep the plants watered; disbud for larger blooms.

What is the follow-up care of carnation seedlings? What is their winter care as far north as Pennsylvania? After hardening off the seedlings in a cold frame, set them out in the open in May in a well-prepared bed. (See the previous questions.)

How can I grow pinks and carnations in upright clumps instead of spreading all over the ground? Pinks and carnations have a tendency to spread, although some of the improved Marguerite strain are less inclined to spread than others. Insert small pieces of twiggy brush among the plants while they are still small. This will tend to hold them upright. A little tying here and there will keep them tidy.

I am able to raise most kinds of flowers except hardy carnations. Just what do they need to do well? They need a well-drained soil. The plants should be set out early to become well developed before hot weather. Give them plenty of moisture during hot weather. Some believe in keeping the buds removed until late summer because they flower best in cool weather.

Why do my carnations have thin stems? The flowers are large, but the stems are so small that they will not stand up. Try applying superphosphate to the soil, 4 ounces per square yard. Look at the variety; this sometimes is a vital fault that no amount of care will eliminate.

I have 2 choice carnation plants that are now 2 years old. One is full of buds and blooms; the other doesn't even have a bud. Why? The fault in the nonblooming plant is in the way it was propagated—hard growth from nonblooming stock. Discard it and propagate from the plant that blooms.

I read in a magazine that if you take cuttings from perennial pinks in October that they would grow indoors. I did this but they are not thriving. Why? What the article probably meant was to take the cuttings in October and winter the young plants over in the house and plant out in the spring. They are not house plants. They need full sun and bloom only in the summer. In any case, cuttings are better if they are taken in August.

Our pinks formed large plants their second year but did not blossom. In the same soil sweet Williams did very well. What do you suggest? The soil may be a little too rich, too wet, or lacking in lime. A well-drained soil, full sun, and the chance to ripen off in the fall are necessary. Do not feed or water after August.

Which dianthus species are dependably hardy? *Dianthus arenarius, arvernensis, plumarius* (cottage pink), *deltoides* (maiden pink), *petraeus, gratianopolitanus* (cheddar pink), *pavonius*.

Which kind of pinks are perennial? Is it better to sow new seed every spring? The most important perennial pink in the garden is *Dianthus plumarius*, of which several varieties (both single and double) are grown. *D. alpinus, D. gratianopolitanus, D. deltoides, D. knappii,* and *D. pavonius* can be grown in rock gardens or the foreground of a garden. It should not be necessary to sow seed every spring. Named varieties of *D. plumarius* are propagated from cuttings or divisions.

Will you name a dwarf compact dianthus that is not straggly? *Dianthus deltoides* 'Brilliant', *D. arvernensis, D. subaculis, D. gratianopolitanus* 'Tiny Rubies'.

CHRISTMAS-ROSE (HELLEBORE)

What is the botanical name of the Christmas-rose? *Helleborus niger*.

How should I establish Christmas-roses?   Select a position in partial shade where the soil is rich and moist; add well-rotted manure, peat moss, compost, or leafmold. Obtain young plants from dealers and set out in early spring.

I have a Christmas-rose that I have had for 3 or 4 years, and last February was the first time it bloomed. Now I would like to move it. Will that set it back again for 3 or 4 years?   The Christmas-rose does not like to be disturbed, and if you move it again this will probably set it back for a few years. Moving it carefully with a very large soil ball would help, but it would be best to leave it where it is.

To what location should I transplant my Christmas-rose? It doesn't bloom and it is on the south side of the house.   The southerly aspect is too warm. Put it in a cooler spot and let it get established. Never allow it to become dry. (See the preceding answer.)

Do Christmas-roses need much sun?   Christmas-roses do best in partial shade, where they are not subject to being dried out in the summer.

What makes my Christmas-rose die down, then get new leaves but no bloom? It has not bloomed this year.   The plant failed to set flower buds due to some factor like drying out in the summer or poor soil. It may have been disturbed during cultural operations.

Will you tell me how to divide a Christmas-rose? Mine is doing wonderfully well, but I would like to give some away.   It is best divided in late summer or autumn by taking a spading fork and lifting the side shoots without disturbing the main plant. It resents any disturbance and when well established it should be left alone.

I planted a Christmas-rose in the spring a year ago. It seems to be showing no signs of buds; in fact, no new shoots have come up this fall. It is in a well-drained spot, partially shaded, and covered with a box, one side of which is glass. What is the proper care? How early shall I cover it? What kind of fertilizer should I use?   Put fertilizer on in the spring. Do not cover the plant at all. A few leaves drifting in among the stems is enough covering. Let the plant become well established and avoid all disturbance. (See answers to the preceding questions.)

How can I start Christmas-roses from seed?   Sow as soon as ripe in a mixture of soil, leafmold, and sand in a cold frame and keep moist. They are slow to germinate and will probably take from 3 to 5 years to reach flowering size.

CHRYSANTHEMUM

The garden chrysanthemum, originally from the Orient, has been so changed through centuries of cultivation that it scarcely resembles the species from which it was derived. In the year 1750 it was introduced into English gardens but at that time created very little interest. About a century later it was brought to America, and for years was grown only as a greenhouse plant. Within the last half century it has become a prominent garden flower—a result of the successful development of hardier and earlier-flowering types and varieties.

Chrysanthemums in the garden give a profusion of bloom in bright autumn colors as a grand finale to the gardening season. Light frosts do little damage to either the flowers or the foliage. If planted in protected spots, they will often remain attractive until mid-November in the latitude of New York State. Farther south, and in other milder climates, they are even better adapted, and a much larger selection of varieties can be used.

While hardy chrysanthemums are comparatively easy to grow, they will not stand neglect. They need to be divided and reset every second or third year, and kept well fertilized and free of disease and insect pests. Considerable care should be given to the selection of varieties for outdoor planting. There are many kinds available but only relatively few of these bloom early enough in the fall or are sufficiently hardy where winters are severe to be dependable garden plants.

What type of soil is best for hardy chrysanthemums? Any friable, free-working soil is satisfactory. It should be well drained yet reasonably retentive of moisture and it should be deep.

How should a bed for chrysanthemums be prepared and fertilized? Spade it deeply (without bringing up large quantities of subsoil), incorporate a 3- or 4-inch layer of rotted manure, compost, or peat moss and a dressing of superphosphate. Lime, if necessary, to keep the soil approximately neutral.

How shall I prepare a bed for chrysanthemums? My ground is quite low and has a heavy clay subsoil. Spade or till in the fall, adding manure, compost, leafmold, or peat moss. In early spring apply a dressing of lime, and a week or so before plants are set out, fork in a light application of complete fertilizer. Chrysanthemums will not succeed in waterlogged soil.

Do hardy chrysanthemums like lime or limestone in the soil? They prefer pH 6 to 7. They have much the same requirements in this respect as most garden vegetables.

What and when should chrysanthemums, carried over in a cold frame for winter, be fed? Do not feed while they are in a cold frame. Add rotted manure and superphosphate, or a complete fertilizer, to outdoor beds prior to planting; possibly add a light side dressing of complete fertilizer when they are half grown. Liquid fertilizer applied in late summer and early fall works wonders.

How can rotted manure be used on cushion chrysanthemums? Around second-year plants, work a 2-inch covering well into the soil together with some superphosphate and a dusting of wood ashes. Prepare the soil for new plantings the same as for other hardy chrysanthemums.

Do cushion chrysanthemums need summer feeding? No. Not if the soil is fairly good.

When should one plant chrysanthemums? In the spring, but potted plants can be set out any time during the growing season.

Where should chrysanthemums be planted? Any location that receives sunshine at least two thirds of the day, providing soil and air circulation are good. Avoid overhanging eaves, walls, and stuffy corners. Don't crowd them among other plants.

What is the best way to plant bare-root chrysanthemums? In well-prepared soil, make a hole of ample size, with a trowel or spade, to accommodate roots. Set the plant in position; spread out its roots; work the soil in among them and press the soil firmly with your fingers. Do not plant when the soil is wet and sticky. Water after planting.

How often should chrysanthemums be replanted? Strong-growing kinds should be divided every year; moderate-growing, every second year.

Would it be advisable to divide and reset chrysanthemums in the fall after they have finished blooming? No. It is safer to do this in the spring. (See the following questions.)

When is the best time to divide hardy chrysanthemums? How? In the spring, as soon as the shoots are 3 to 4 inches high. Dig up the clump; discard old center portion; separate young offshoots; plant as single divisions, 10 or 12 inches part, in well-prepared soil.

Is spring or fall the best time to transplant chrysanthemums that are in a too-shady place? Spring is best, but if necessary, they can be moved any time during the growing season if thoroughly watered first and carefully lifted with a good ball of soil.

Can hardy chrysanthemums be moved when in bloom? Yes. Be sure the soil is moist; take up the clump of soil with a good root ball; replant immediately. Firm the soil around the roots; shade for 2 or 3 days; and don't neglect watering.

What is the best way to store early chrysanthemums during the winter in Washington? Cover lightly with evergreen branches, leaves, or similar protection.

What is the best way to care for chrysanthemums after they stop blooming in the fall? Cut the stems back close to the ground. If brown foliage appeared during the summer, burn the stems and all dropped leaves—they may harbor insects or diseases. Cover lightly with evergreen branches and dry leaves.

What is the winter care for chrysanthemums, without a cold frame, in southern Vermont? A blanket of evergreen branches intermingled with leaves would make the best covering. Apply when the soil is slightly frozen. Good soil drainage is an important factor.

Can well-rotted manure be placed around chrysanthemums as a winter mulch? Yes, but not close to the crowns. Pack dry leaves immediately around the plants themselves.

When should chrysanthemums be covered—before or after frost? After the first killing frost and when the soil is slightly frozen.

How can I keep a cushion chrysanthemum during the winter? (Minnesota.) Cushion chrysanthemums should winter over in Minnesota with a light blanket of evergreen branches and dry leaves applied when the ground is lightly frozen.

How may I protect large-flowering chrysanthemum blooms in the outdoor garden? A double-thick cheesecloth covering stretched over a framework affords considerable protection. Avoid growing varieties that are late in flowering. The 'Harvest Giants' are early.

Can you take a nonhardy chrysanthemum, cut it off a few inches from the ground, keep it inside until spring, and then set it out? Yes, if you pot the roots and carry the plant over in a cool, well-lighted cellar or room. The soil must be kept slightly moist. There are, of course, many reliable hardy chrysanthemums that do not require this attention.

Is December 1 too late to put a chrysanthemum plant outdoors that has been in bloom in the house for about 4 weeks? Too late for sure results in most northern areas. If planted in a sheltered corner or cold frame and covered lightly, it has a fifty-fifty chance.

Can semihardy chrysanthemums be kept in soil in a barn cellar dur-

ing the winter? Should the cellar be dark or light?   A well-lighted barn cellar that is cool should do. Be careful that soil does not dry out.

How do you care for cushion chrysanthemums? I know they are heavy feeders and I care for them very well, but why do they bloom one year and not the next?   Divide them every second year. Water copiously, but only when needed during dry periods. Reasonable feeding should be sufficient. Tarnished plant bug and other insect injury can prevent flowering.

How should chrysanthemums (cushion type) be cared for so that they bloom freely and look like the pictures in catalogs?   Choose a sunny location. Don't crowd together or among other plants. Add a complete general-purpose garden fertilizer plus compost or other form of humus to the soil under your plants. Cultivate frequently but lightly and water copiously when needed. Divide plants every other year.

Will you give me information on how to grow large chrysanthemums outdoors?   Grow 1 to 2 stems only to each plant; remove all side buds. Shading with black sateen cloth to hasten blooming, or other special protection may be necessary. Or grow early 'Harvest Giants'.

I've read that covering chrysanthemums with black cloth for a certain time during the day brings them into bloom earlier. Will you give me detailed instructions for its use?   There is a special black sateen cloth made for this purpose. Starting in mid-July, keep plants in complete dark from 5 P.M. until 7 A.M. Discontinue when the buds show color.

Can the blooms of large, exhibition chrysanthemums grown outside in the garden be hastened by enclosing them in darkened frames? If so, when should these frames be applied? I am an amateur but sell quite a few flowers to florists.   Yes. Build a framework of wood and cover with black cloth so it is as nearly lightproof as possible. (See reply to the previous question.)

What care should be given exhibition chrysanthemums?   They require careful attention to all details of cultivation, such as propagating, soil preparation, watering, staking, disbudding, etc. When buds appear, apply liquid fertilizer every week or 10 days until the flowers begin to open.

Will you please give culture instructions for pompon chrysanthemums?   Pompons are easily grown in the garden. Good rich soil, thorough watering when needed, and frequent cultivation are the essentials. Only the tallest varieties require pinching.

How should I care for chrysanthemums in the spring?   Divide and replant if they have been growing 2 years in the same place; if possible, give them a different location. Otherwise, fork some manure, compost, or fertilizer into the surface soil.

My chrysanthemums have been in 3 years and are large clumps. Should they be thinned out? Into what size clumps? Strong-growing chrysanthemums should be divided every year; moderate-growing kinds, every 2 years. Do this in the spring, leaving each division with 1 or 2 shoots.

How do florists manage to keep the foliage on chrysanthemums green down to the ground? By starting with young plants, taking care that they are never allowed to dry out but that they are not overwatered. Most florists spray the plants every 10 days so that insects cannot get a start.

How can I grow many-branched chrysanthemums? Keep plants young by frequent division and pinch them back 2 or 3 times during the growing season. Keep staked and watered during dry periods.

What is the correct way to disbud chrysanthemums? Many plants produce larger flowers if just 1 (the terminal) bud remains on each branch. Remove unwanted buds by picking them out with your thumb and index finger when the buds are about ⅛ inch in diameter.

When should chrysanthemums be pinched back? Tall-growing types, at intervals during spring and early summer. Pinch when they are 9 to 12 inches high; next, when they are about 15 inches high; and possibly a third time in late July. Cushion-type varieties require no pinching.

Should I pinch every shoot on a chrysanthemum or just the center one? All strong shoots are cut back early in the season to cause low, bushy growth.

Should cushion and pompon chrysanthemums be pinched back in the spring? All cushions and many pompons branch naturally and do not require pinching. A few of the taller pompon varieties should be pinched.

What is the best method of pruning and disbudding hardy chrysanthemums? "Pruning" consists of pinching out the tips of the shoots when the plants are 9 inches high, and the tips of all subsequent side branches when they are 6 inches long. This practice is discontinued in late July. Disbudding consists of removing many of the young flower buds so that the one or more allowed to remain on each stem will develop into especially fine blooms.

What is the proper way to stake chrysanthemums? Each year the weight of mine bends over the stems. Wooden or bamboo stakes can

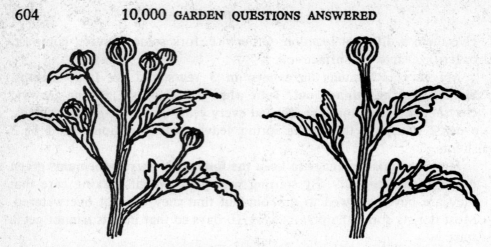

Disbudding a chrysanthemum. In order to secure a flower of large size, only the top terminal bud (of the several that form) is left.

be pushed into the ground near the plants and the stems neatly tied to these. Place the supports before the plants begin to flower, and try to preserve the natural habit of the plants. Avoid tying so that a plant is bunched together like a shock of corn. Brushwood staking, inserted so that shoots grow up through the sticks, is also very satisfactory.

Pruning or "pinching" a chrysanthemum. In order to throw the plant's strength to the terminal bud, or a crown bud, side shoots or laterals are removed.

I understand that there is a chemical for reducing the height of chrysanthemums. What is this and how is it applied?   There is a chemical called Phosfon sold for this purpose. It is widely used by commercial growers for controlling the height of potted chrysanthemums, less so by home gardeners, since it is not widely available and must be applied carefully. It should not be considered a substitute for proper culture.

Are hardy chrysanthemums reliably hardy throughout the United States? Not where extremely cold winters are experienced.

Is there anything one can do to make chrysanthemums bloom earlier in the fall? I had several new varieties this year and they budded so late that they didn't bloom at all. When selecting new varieties, choose early-flowering kinds.

Why didn't my chrysanthemums bloom this fall? They are the old-fashioned type and are planted on the south side of my house. Was it because they need dividing and transplanting or because of an early freeze? Old-fashioned chrysanthemums naturally bloom late and are sometimes caught by an early freeze. Why not try some of the many good kinds that flower in September and October?

My chrysanthemums grow very tall but have weak stems and few blooms. What shall I do? Divide them in the spring; pinch back (nip out tips of growing shoots with your thumbnail and index finger), starting when the plants are about 6 inches tall and continuing every 2 weeks until mid-July. This will make the plants bushy and more floriferous. Grow in full sunlight.

If seedling chrysanthemums bloom in October the first year and in August the second year (in the same place and about the same conditions), what is likely to be their regular season of blooming? From mid-September on, if your plants are divided and reset every second year, as they should be.

Two chrysanthemums, full of buds that seemed ready to burst several weeks prior to freezing weather, did not bloom. Can their blooming season be hastened in any way? Your varieties are too late for your particular locality. Try earlier kinds. The buds of some varieties are not frost-hardy, even though the flowers may be.

How can I keep chrysanthemums from growing out of bounds? Both hardy and exhibition types are 5 to 6 feet tall. Use phosphates rather than nitrates for fertilizing. Grow in full sun and do not crowd. Pinch back vigorous shoots during May, June, and July.

Our cushion chrysanthemums have very few blossoms. This is their second year. What is wrong? They should be at their best in their second year. Don't crowd. Prepare the soil deeply and water copiously whenever needed during the summer. They do best in full sun. Tarnished plant bug may prevent flowering. Do not overfeed with fertilizers.

I had a fine collection of chrysanthemums, but each blooming season I find that I have more bronze colors and fewer yellows and reds. Do

they revert?   Chrysanthemums do sometimes exhibit the phenomenon known as mutation; but more probably self-sown seeds have germinated and reverted to other colors. The bronze varieties are especially vigorous and would take the lead.

Do different chrysanthemums mix and change color if planted closely together? (Louisiana.)   No. But seedlings which differ in color can spring up among the parent plants. This would be very likely in your climate.

How can I best increase choice chrysanthemums?   If hotbed or greenhouse facilities are available, take cuttings (in February or March) from stock plants kept during the winter in a cold frame. Root in sand, transplant to pots or flats of soil, and set outdoors in the spring. Plants wintered outdoors can be taken up and divided in early spring.

What is the method of splitting or dividing a cushion chrysanthemum plant?   Same as any hardy chrysanthemum. (See the previous and following replies.)

Is it better to start new chrysanthemums from slips or to divide old plants?   Cuttings or small healthy divisions give equally good results. The former are better, however, if stock plants are infested with nematodes.

Will chrysanthemums grow from cuttings made from the tips of shoots that are removed when the plants are pinched back?   Yes.

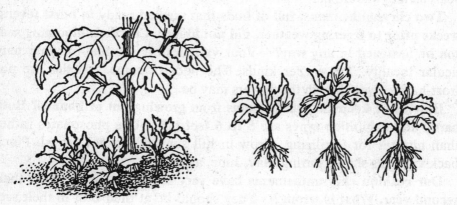

Old chrysanthemum plant in late spring. Remove young rooted divisions to provide vigorous new plants and discard the old plant.

When is the proper time to start to root chrysanthemum cuttings for best results?   For large plants, cuttings should be started indoors in late February and the cuttings taken in March. Cuttings taken in April and May are quite satisfactory, but the plants are smaller.

How can I graft several colors on a single chrysanthemum plant? Grow a strong, early-started, young plant to a single stem. At the desired height, say 2½ feet, pinch the tip out to promote side branches. On these, insert the grafts. A humid atmosphere should be maintained after grafting and the grafts should be kept sealed with polyethylene until they have formed a good union.

Can one buy seeds of the large-flowering-type chrysanthemums? They are listed by a few large seed houses. More readily available from seed are low-growing, small-flowered varieties, both single and double. This is an inexpensive way to acquire chrysanthemums. Seed germinates readily if sown early outdoors in a cold frame. Plants should flower by fall. In cold climates, select the earliest flowering chrysanthemums.

How can I grow chrysanthemums from seeds in order to get blooms the first year? Start seeds indoors during March. Transplant once to flats or a cold frame before planting in an outdoor garden.

What insects and diseases commonly attack hardy chrysanthemums? See Chrysanthemums, Section 13.

Why didn't my hardy chrysanthemums bloom this year? The leaves became gray. Evidently the plants were badly mildewed. Do not plant too closely together or in shade.

What spray do you recommend for black aphids on outdoor chrysanthemums? Spray with malathion.

How can I control chrysanthemum leafspot disease? First, be sure that the plants have this disease. The effects of leaf nematodes are often mistaken for it. Leafspot produces in the diseased areas masses of white spores which are easily seen with a magnifying glass. To control, pick off and burn infected leaves; spray with zineb or folpet; avoid wetting the leaves when watering.

What is the care of chrysanthemums? Mine die down every fall, lose their leaves (which turn black or brown), and flower very late. They are probably infested with leaf nematodes (eelworms). After the plants bloom, cut them back close to the ground. Remove and burn all stems and leaves, which harbor this pest during the winter. In the spring propagate from tip cuttings and set the plants in a new location in good soil, or in soil disinfected with dizomet or metam-sodium.

My chrysanthemum blooms turn brown before fully opening. Why? The foliage is in good condition. Send a few affected leaves to your

State Agricultural Experiment Station to be checked for leaf nematodes. (See the previous reply.)

In cold climates how can one be assured of buying plants that will bloom before the killing frost?   Buy from a specialist and be guided by the blooming dates given for each variety. If your area is different from that from which the catalog comes the dates can vary a week or two, since the dates are usually based on the blooming time in the nurseries' growing fields.

I have always admired the large chrysanthemums worn as corsages. Can these be grown in the garden and what should I ask for?   These are known as "football" chrysanthemums. They can be grown, but need a little more attention to disbudding and staking than regular varieties. In cold climates they need protection from frost as they are rather late to bloom, although the 'Harvest Giants' bloom earlier.

Is there a difference in the hardiness of chrysanthemum varieties?   Apparently there is. If you live in very cold regions, try to buy those developed in northerly regions. The University of Minnesota and the University of Nebraska have introduced quite a few varieties.

What is a cascade chrysanthemum?   These are plants grown so that they cascade down over a pot on a special frame. Sometimes they are trained up a frame. Special varieties are used for this purpose so it's best to consult the catalog of a chrysanthemum specialist.

What are spider chrysanthemums?   These have long narrow petals, curled at the tip. They are very exotic-looking and, because the flowers are somewhat delicate, they are generally grown in a greenhouse or with some form of protection against the elements.

COLUMBINE (AQUILEGIA)

My columbines never grow into healthy plants, as I have seen others do. They have full sun and the other plants around the columbines grow very well. Why?   They need a well-drained sandy loam, neutral or slightly acid. Prepare the ground at least a foot deep; incorporate a 2-inch layer of rotted manure, peat moss, or rich compost; space the plants at least 9 inches apart.

What is the best location for columbines? What fertilizer should I use?   Almost any location, except a hot, dry, windy one; light shade is beneficial. A topdressing of leafmold, with well-rotted manure or compost, is good in early spring.

What is the proper way to plant columbines? I planted them in a rich

soil in a woods where they got sun in the morning and shade later in the day. The spot was fairly well drained. The columbines never came up. The soil and position should be all right. You probably planted them too deeply and the crowns rotted. They are subject to a soft rot.

Can columbine seedlings, from seed planted in August, be transplanted next spring? Yes.

Is it possible to transplant old columbine plants? When? Yes. It is best done in early spring. Water until established. Don't plant too deeply.

How shall I divide columbines? Lift the clumps, shake off the soil, and gently pull the plant apart, taking care not to break the roots.

DAY-LILY (HEMEROCALLIS)

Today's day-lily is perhaps the perfect summer perennial. It is the answer for gardeners who demand an "easy" plant and it is difficult to think of another perennial that requires so little care. The ribbonlike foliage is superb, remaining in good condition throughout the growing season. Although each lily-shaped flower, often deliciously fragrant, lasts only a day (but often into evening), each stalk is so abundantly budded that the actual flower display goes on for weeks. The clumps are vigorous and can be divided every few years or, if they do not outgrow their space, can be left indefinitely without disturbance. Some of the delicate pastel varieties fade in full sunshine, but in general day-lilies seem to adapt to just about any garden situation except dense shade. They are especially useful in informal landscape schemes and look well in the foreground of shrub groupings or borders.

When is the best time to plant day-lilies? How? Spring or summer planting is all right. They can even be lifted in full bloom if a good clump of soil is taken and care is used not to damage the roots. Plants must be watered deeply and kept well watered for a week or two. Dig the soil deeply, adding well-rotted manure, leafmold, peat moss, or compost; dig the holes deep enough when planting so that the roots are not crowded and set the plants with their crowns just level with the soil.

Do day-lilies have to be planted in the shade? No. Day-lilies will grow in full sun if the soil is rich and moist, but the more pastel varieties do best in light or partial shade.

Can day-lilies be successfully grown planted among other perennials in a border? Yes, provided that you give them enough space to grow, at least 3 feet.

Perennial companions for midsummer: Yellow day-lilies and blue globe-thistle (Echinops).

What is the cause of day-lilies failing to blossom?   Failure to bloom is most commonly due to too-dense shade or the plants being over-crowded and the soil exhausted.

How can I get lemon-lilies (Hemerocallis flava) to bloom?   Divide and replant in full sun in soil that has been dug deeply (18 inches) and enriched with a 3-inch layer of rotted manure, leafmold, peat moss, or compost, plus bone meal or superphosphate at the rate of 6 ounces per square yard.

How shall I divide day-lilies?   These are sometimes hard to divide, especially old clumps. The best method is to first dig up clumps, then push two spading forks through the clump, back to back, and pry the clump apart. Do not make the divisions too small if you want flowers the next year.

Can you give me the name of an exquisite, dainty, lemon-yellow day-lily that blooms profusely in the early spring? The foliage is the same as the dark day-lily, only lighter and much daintier.   In all probability the lemon-lily, *Hemerocallis flava*. This species is fragrant.

What is the main blooming season for day-lilies? This is July and August. However, some bloom in June and others in September and October.

What is the orange day-lily that I see growing wild by the wayside? This is *Hemerocallis fulva*. It's a fairly rampant grower and is best used where it can multiply. There are better orange hybrids for garden use.

Are there any miniature day-lilies? Yes, they are becoming increasingly popular and a few more are listed each year. In general, the flowers are smaller than for the taller varieties, but they are showy nonetheless.

Will you name some good varieties of day-lilies that will give me a succession of bloom from early to late summer? Check a catalog of a day-lily or perennials specialist and choose two or three plants from each group—early, early midseason, midseason, and late. Here are a few suggestions: *Early:* 'Channel Islands', creamy yellow; 'Fire and Ice', velvety red. *Early midseason:* 'Aglow', melon blend with lavender ribs; 'July Gold', gold; 'Christmas Carol', velvety red; 'Mary Todd', gold. *Midseason:* 'Hyperion', yellow; 'Loyal Subject', gold and pink; 'Master Touch', pink. *Late:* 'Bright Banner', gold and bronze; 'Lacy Queen', salmon-pink; 'Carnival Flair', rose-red-edged yellow; 'Pink Taffy', pink.

Must I remove the spent day-lily flowers every day? I have so many plants. No, although the faded blooms snap off the stem quickly and make for a neater appearance. However, you should remove them before seeds form.

Is there such a thing as a double day-lily? I have one and thought maybe it was a freak. Yes. There are quite a few. Two doubles are 'Kwanso' and 'Double Gold'. There are also tetraploids, which have extra petals.

Can you tell me how to hybridize day-lilies? The flowers that are to be used as the seed bearer should be emasculated (remove anthers) and enclosed in a waxed or cellophane bag; when the stigma becomes sticky, the ripe pollen from another variety is transferred to it.

What is the best time of day to hybridize the day-lily? From about 12 noon until 2 P.M., as the pollen will be driest at that time.

DELPHINIUM

The modern delphinium is one of the most spectacular of our garden flowers. Most common garden hybrids are tall-growing and are best used toward the back of a mixed border where they create strong vertical lines and accent points. However, a few dwarf strains have been developed, so look for these in your catalog. (There are also the Chinese strains from *D. grandiflorum,* with loose flower sprays about 3 feet high.) While the clear blue colors are most highly prized, sparkling whites, rich violets, and soft, pleasing mauves are available. Some have yellow or red flowers, but they are not so easy to grow in the average garden; nor are the flower spikes as showy as those of the more common types.

The geographic distribution of delphinium species is more or less limited to the northern hemisphere, but they are used in gardens on every continent. While their culture varies in different regions, they are grown successfully throughout the United States and Canada.

There are four main types of delphiniums. The erect and tall-growing *elatum* or garden hybrids bear single or double flowers in dense spikes. The *Delphinium belladonna* types are low-growing, with more finely cut foliage and looser spikes of blue or white flowers. The Chinese delphinium (*D. grandiflorum*) is comparatively dwarf, seldom attaining a height of more than 3 feet. The foliage is finely cut and the clear blue or white flowers are borne in a loose, informal arrangement. They are the easiest to grow, and especially valuable for cutting to be used with other flowers in mixed bouquets or arrangements. The annual delphinium is the larkspur (*Consolida ambigua* syn. *Delphinium ajacis*).

What kind of soil is desirable for delphiniums?   A rich, friable loam containing a high percentage of organic matter.

How can one increase the amount of organic matter in the soil for delphiniums?   Mix thoroughly decomposed leafmold, compost, rotted manure, or peat moss in the soil.

Is peat moss good for delphiniums?   In some experiments carried out to determine the best type of organic matter, peat moss was found to be less desirable than leafmold. However, if leafmold or rich compost are lacking, use peat moss and add limestone, a slight handful to each hole when planting.

What soil mixture is best for starting delphinium seeds?   A mixture of 1 part good garden loam, 1 part sand, and 1 part leafmold is satisfactory. Sift through a sieve having ¼-inch mesh. A commercial mixture sold for seed starting is also suitable.

Can manure be used on delphiniums?   Manure, if well rotted, is excellent. It may be mixed with the soil at the time it is prepared or it may be used as a topdressing. Apply about 5 bushels per 100 square feet.

Do delphiniums need fertilizer? Yes. They require an abundance of nutrients. They have a higher nitrogen requirement than almost any other garden flower. Unless the soil is already very rich, they should be fertilized at least twice a year with a complete commercial fertilizer such as 5–10–5.

When should delphiniums be fertilized? Make the first application in the spring when the new shoots are about 4 inches tall. A second application can be made about 5 weeks later.

Do delphiniums require lime? They do best in a slightly acid soil (pH 6.8). If the organic matter content is very high, they will do well over a much wider range of pH values (pH 5.5 to 7.2). Lime is required only when a pH test shows that the reaction is pH 6.5 or below.

What type of lime should be used for delphiniums and how should it be applied? Ground limestone is best. Where the soil is very acid or very heavy, hydrated lime or wood ashes can be used. Spread it evenly over the soil surface and work it into the top 3 or 4 inches.

Should lime be applied to delphiniums every year? No, only when a soil test indicates that it is necessary.

How can one tell by observing the plants when the soil is too "sweet" for delphiniums? The leaves appear mottled with yellow or, in severe cases, with white. The veins usually retain their dark-green color. A pH test of the soil will confirm the plant symptoms.

In what situation should delphiniums be planted? In full sun or very light shade and, if possible, with some protection from strong winds.

How far apart should delphiniums be planted? In perennial borders, 2 to 3 feet apart; in cut-flower gardens, 3 to 4 feet between rows and 2 feet between the plants in rows.

When should delphiniums be transplanted? Very early spring is best; but they can be transplanted with success in the fall or immediately after their first period of bloom.

When should full-grown delphiniums be moved? In very early spring, if possible before growth starts. Move with a large ball of soil.

How can I keep my delphiniums healthy? Give them a rich, well-drained soil. Fertilize twice a year. Spray with a miticide.

How can delphiniums be made to bloom in the fall as well as during their regular season? By cutting the flowering stems off as soon as possible after they have finished blooming. New shoots will then come up and flower in the early fall.

How can delphiniums be staked?   Begin when the plant is about 3 feet high and place three 6-foot stakes in the form of a triangle around it. Tie a band of raffia or soft twine around the stakes about 1 foot above the ground. As the plant grows, tie additional bands around the stakes. If desired, individual stakes can be used for large-flowering spikes. This latter method is to be preferred in decorative plantings.

Should delphiniums be watered?   Delphiniums require large quantities of water, especially during, and just prior to, the flowering period. They will be improved by thorough watering when the weather is dry.

What winter care should be given delphinium seedlings started in a cold frame in August?   Cover with about 2 inches of medium-coarse clean sand. Later, mulch with straw or salt hay. Put a sash on the frame to keep out snow and rain.

Should young delphinium plants, set out in the fall, be mulched?   It is always a good idea to protect seedlings transplanted in the fall from heaving. Covering the plants with about 2 inches of sand, and later mulching lightly with marsh hay or straw, will give the necessary protection.

Should established delphiniums be covered during the winter?   In all but the coldest climates, this is unnecessary. Delphiniums are more likely to be killed by poor drainage, smothering, or diseases than by low temperatures.

Should a beginner buy delphinium plants or start them from seeds?   Either is satisfactory, but for quick results, buy plants.

Do seeds from hybrid delphiniums produce desirable plants?   If seeds are saved from superior plants, they should be satisfactory but they are seldom as good as the plants that seeds were collected from. However, for uniformity, it is usually best to buy seeds from reliable growers who have taken special pains in producing them. Try to buy fresh seed.

Why have my delphiniums failed even though I moved them to a better spot and replanted them 1 foot from a hedge where they get south sun?   Probably the moving is responsible. They may do better when they become reestablished. However, you have set them too near the hedge. They should be at least 2 or 3 feet away and kept well fertilized and watered.

How can I prevent my delphiniums from growing tall and having brittle stems even though I withhold nitrogen?   Vigorous delphiniums are likely to be brittle and to break off during wind- and rainstorms. Withholding nitrogen will not make the stems less brittle; in fact, it may make them more so. Nothing can be done except to stake the plants adequately. Or buy lower-growing kinds.

Can delphiniums have their tops pinched out like zinnias, in order to make them branch? No, the shoots that arise from the bases of the plants terminate in flower spikes. When the growing point is removed, the lateral buds do not develop as they do with zinnias.

Why do delphiniums freeze in the winter? Delphiniums are really very hardy plants. They are seldom killed by low temperatures. They are more likely to be smothered by snow, ice, or poor drainage. Diseases, especially crown-rot, can develop during the fall, winter, or early spring, and kill the plants. Heaving is another hazard. Some leading growers consider the English strains hardier than the American strains developed on the Pacific coast.

How long will delphiniums live? Where the crown-rot diseases are not serious, they live indefinitely. However, since these organisms are widespread over much of the United States, from 1 to 3 years is the expected life of the ordinary plant.

How can Delphinium cardinale be kept in cold climates during the winter? It can't. This species is tender and will not stand freezing. It can be kept during the winter only in a greenhouse, and even then it is not very successful.

How can delphiniums be grown in a warm climate, such as Florida? Grow them as annuals by sowing seeds early each spring. The plants are not usually successfully carried over a second year.

Is there a truly perennial delphinium? In their native habitats many species persist for years, but under garden conditions they are more subject to diseases and are less long-lived. They also live longer in regions where summers are fairly cool. Hot, muggy weather is not to their liking.

Why do some delphiniums live longer than others? Natural variation in vigor, disease resistance, as well as weather conditions, account for the difference in longevity.

What is the best temperature for germinating delphinium seeds? The optimum is 55° F.

What is the best way to raise delphiniums from seed? Many different methods are successful; it is difficult to state which is best. Where many plants are needed, sow in well-prepared soil in a cold frame in August. Leave the seedlings in the frame during the winter and transplant to the garden in the spring.

Does it speed germination to refrigerate seeds?   If seed is fresh (recently harvested), it does not need refrigeration before being sowed. When not fresh (as in spring), refrigeration in an airtight container in the refrigerator for several weeks will help. If seed is to be stored during the winter, keep it in the refrigerator in an airtight jar.

What conditions are necessary for growing delphinium seedlings? Good light, plenty of moisture (but the soil must not be kept soaked), and a temperature of 55° to 60° F.

Can delphinium seeds be sown in the open ground?   Yes. If you do so, prepare a bed with special care where the tiny seedlings can be protected. It is really better, however, to sow in a cold frame or in seed flats.

When should delphiniums be started indoors?   Seeds can be sown any time between February 1 and May 1. If started early, many of the plants will bloom the first year.

How thick should delphinium seeds be sown and how deep should they be covered?   Sow in rows spaced about 2 inches apart. The seeds in the rows should be about ¼ inch apart. Cover so that the seeds are barely out of sight.

Should delphinium seeds be disinfected? How is this done?   Disinfecting is desirable, especially where the soil is not sterilized. The use of a disinfectant, sold for the purpose, is satisfactory. Merely place a pinch of the powder in the seed package and shake until the seeds are evenly covered.

Is it necessary to sterilize the soil in which delphinium seeds are sown?   It is not necessary, but it is good insurance. Measure out 2½ tablespoonfuls of formaldehyde (40 per cent strength) for each bushel of prepared soil; dilute with 4 or 5 times its volume of water; add to the soil and mix very thoroughly. Place the soil in seed boxes, saving a little for covering the seed; stack the boxes one above the other to confine the fumes for a day or two, then uncover them. When the odor is no longer perceptible, it is safe to sow the seeds. However, all this bother can be avoided by sowing the seeds in a commercial soilless mix that is sterile.

Will delphinium seeds sown indoors in the spring produce flowers in the summer?   If sown indoors before April 1, most of the plants will bloom in late August or early September.

Should delphinium seedlings grown indoors be transplanted or may one wait until they can be planted outdoors?   Transplant to flats as soon as the plants are big enough to handle conveniently. Use a soil mixture of 1 part leafmold, 2 parts garden loam, and ½ part sand. Good drainage must be provided so that the soil never remains soggy. Seedlings can be put in individual peat pots and grown under fluorescent lights.

Is it wise to divide delphiniums that have grown to a large size? How often should this be done? Ordinarily it is better to start new plants from seeds, but old clumps can be divided if they have become too large; this will usually not be until they are at least 3 years old. An old but healthy clump is often best left alone.

How are delphiniums divided? How large should the divisions be? Lift the plants, shake off the soil, and cut the clumps apart with a strong knife. Replant immediately in well-prepared soil. Each division should contain 3 to 5 shoots.

My delphiniums suffer from "black"; they are deformed, stunted, and marked with black streaks and blotches. What is wrong? Your plants are infested by an exceedingly minute pest—the cyclamen mite. Cut off and destroy badly infested shoots. Spray every 10 days from early spring to flowering time with Kelthane. Avoid planting delphiniums near strawberries, which are also host to this mite.

What is a cure for crown-rot of delphiniums? Crown-rot is really a name for a group of diseases. All are very difficult to control. Sterilize the soil with Terrachlor and destroy infected plants. When possible, plant delphiniums on the ground where the plants have not been previously grown.

I planted some delphiniums but several were eaten off by slugs. How can I prevent a recurrence? Use metaldehyde, according to directions.

Is mildew on delphiniums caused by the soil? No. Mildew is a fungus disease that infects the leaves. It is controlled by spraying the plants with Benlate or Karathane. Avoid setting the plants too closely together.

How many colors occur in delphiniums? If all the species are considered, they cover an unusually wide range. The garden hybrids contain white and tones of blue, violet, and mauve. *Delphinium nudicaule* is orange and red; *D. cardinale* is clear red; *D. semibarbatum* is yellow.

Is there a true pink perennial delphinium? The variety 'Pink Sensation' comes nearest to this description, but apparently is no longer available.

How can I get the colors I want by growing my own delphiniums from seed? The 'Pacific Giant Hybrids' exist in blue and light blue, violet and dark blue, white, and in pastel and mixed shades. Consult seed catalogs for other strains.

I have heard of a delphinium called 'Connecticut Yankee'. I believe it was developed by a famous photographer. What is this?   This strain was developed by the noted photographer Edward Steichen. The bush-type plants are about 30 inches tall, which makes them excellent subjects for the average garden. The color range includes shades of blue and purple. The flowers are large and single. The foliage resembles that of delphinium species more than the regular hybrids. If seed is sown outdoors in early spring, the plants will usually bloom by August.

EREMURUS

When is the best time to plant eremurus (foxtail-lily)—in the spring or fall? Will 2- or 3-year-old plants bloom the first season after being planted or must they be older?   Plant in the fall, since top growth begins early in the spring. Usually plants younger than 4 years bloom little, if at all. For first season results, 4-year-old plants are set out. They will require a winter mulch (10 or 12 inches of coal ashes or coarse sand) to protect the roots from too-severe freezing in the North.

Does eremurus (foxtail-lily) require a special kind of culture?   It is best to give it a deep, well-prepared soil, but see that it is well drained. Work in some superphosphate each fall.

How do you plant foxtail-lily (eremurus)? Do you spread the roots out or do you plant with the roots down, like Oriental poppy?   They should be planted with their roots spread out flat. The roots will snap off if bent when planting.

How deep should 4-year-old eremurus roots be planted?   Plant so that the crown is about 2 inches below the soil surface. Too-deep planting is apt to cause the crown to rot, especially in a heavy soil.

I have some 3-year-old eremurus. What care do they require? Do they prefer light or heavy soil?   Plant in a sheltered position in rich, well-drained soil, in full sun, with the fleshy roots spread out and the bud 2 inches under the soil. Plant in late September and cover before winter with a loose mulch.

Can eremurus be divided, and when?   They can be divided only with difficulty, unless they make offsets freely. Early fall is the best time. Each division must have a bud, or eye.

Can eremurus be raised from seed? When and how long until they

bloom? It can be raised from seed sown in flats or pots in late autumn or spring. It will bloom from seed in about 4 to 6 years.

EUPATORIUM (HARDY-AGERATUM)

How deep should hardy-ageratum be planted? It is shallow rooting; plant it about 2 inches deep. The roots are stringy; spread them out and cover. This species is not related to the familiar ageratum grown as an annual, but is a relative of Joe-Pye-weed, a popular native plant.

When should hardy-ageratum be moved? It is best done in the spring before growth starts.

How often do you have to move hardy-ageratum? It is probably best lifted and transplanted every year or two, as it grows into quite a mat, which usually dies out in the center.

FUCHSIA, HARDY

Is hardy fuchsia (Fuchsia magellanica) a shrub or can it be included among herbaceous perennials? It is really a low-growing shrub, but in northern climates it is often killed down to the ground by the winter, making it in effect a herbaceous perennial.

In what kind of soil should a hardy fuchsia be planted? I had no luck with mine. A light, well-drained garden loam with some leafmold added. It is often planted in rock gardens. Keep it out of exposed situations and try a light winter cover.

GERBERA (TRANSVAAL DAISY)

What care does gerbera require, in regard to cultivation, pests, and diseases? (New York.) This South African perennial is not hardy, although it can be grown outside in sheltered situations if given winter protection, or lifted in the fall and wintered over in a cold frame. It is more commonly grown as a greenhouse plant or in a window garden. Grow in well-drained, fairly rich soil; keep crowns just above the soil level. Fertilize in the spring with liquid fertilizer. Propagate from seeds (slow to germinate) or (better yet) by cuttings of side shoots. Spray for leaf roller and aphids, two of its worst enemies.

What garden soil, exposure, moisture, and food is necessary for gerbera? They are hardy here. (Delaware.) Provide them with well-drained soil in full sun. Water only in dry weather. Apply weak liquid fertilizer in the spring and early summer.

I have some gerbera roots. I have them in a box 18 inches underground covered with leaves and soil. Will they smother or will I have to install an air-vent pipe? The covering is too deep. Tender plants cannot be wintered over by burying them. Without a cold frame or similar protection, it is difficult to keep gerberas during the winter. An air vent would be of little help. Plant them next to a building; erect a wooden frame around them. Cover with hay and give them air in mild weather.

How can I grow gerbera outside? They should be grown in full sun in well-drained soil. Plant only in the spring and give cold-frame protection for the winter. They are not hardy in northern gardens.

Do gerbera roots need dividing, and when? They do not require dividing very often; but when the clumps get large and begin to fail, divide in the spring.

HELIOPSIS (GOLDEN-SUNFLOWER)

Where and in what type of soil should heliopsis be planted? Place in full sun, in any garden soil. The plants will probably flower better in a fairly dry situation.

Is there a double-flowered heliopsis? Yes, the variety 'Golden Plume' is a fine golden-yellow double that blooms from July to October.

Does heliopsis require frequent division? The plants are very vigorous so they tend to become crowded after about 3 years. At that time, it is advisable to divide them in early spring.

HOLLYHOCKS (ALCEA syn. ALTHAEA)

Do hollyhocks take an excessive amount of moisture away from surrounding plants? Not enough to harm nearby plants. The ground around hollyhocks usually looks dry because their large leaves shed a lot of rain.

IRISES

Irises have always been favorites among garden flowers because of their sparkling hues and exquisite forms. The many species are distributed throughout the Temperate Zone and are therefore adapted to culture in most of the civilized world. Like roses, irises have been a part of our historical and legendary heritage. They were named in honor of the goddess of the rainbow, the messenger of Zeus and Hera. In medieval times the fleur-de-lis became the emblem of France and its abstract form has been widely used as a motif in many forms of art.

While some iris species have not responded to the efforts of plant breeders as readily as many other kinds of plants, considerable development has taken place, particularly in the tall-bearded iris group. Much of this work can be attributed to amateur gardeners. Size, substance, coloring, and garden value have been greatly improved. Many of the species used in American gardens need no improvement to make them worthwhile garden subjects.

Irises are adaptable to many diverse uses in the landscape. They are often used as one of the important features in a mixed perennial border, but they are just as stunning when used as single accents by a wall or rock outcropping, for example. With today's emphasis on minimum maintenance, the border limited to three perennials—peonies, bearded irises, and day-lilies—has gained deserved popularity for the extensive period (early summer to late summer) of bloom provided and—because all these plants grow under similar conditions—easy care.

Do irises grow better in low, moist ground or in dry soil; do they grow better in sun or in shade?   Bearded irises require sharp drainage. Beardless kinds (such as Japanese varieties) need plenty of moisture but not waterlogged soil. The yellow flag of Europe and our native *Iris versicolor* and Louisiana irises succeed even in swamp conditions. Most do best in full sun.

What is the correct soil for bearded irises?   Any good garden soil. Add bone meal or superphosphate and gypsum when remaking the beds. If heavy, lighten with sand or ashes. They require good drainage.

Do Japanese irises require acid soil?   Yes, or at least a soil that is not alkaline. Never apply lime, bone meal, or wood ashes.

For Japanese and Siberian irises, what soil preparation is required?   Spade deeply; incorporate plenty of humus—old rotted manure, leafmold, peat moss, or compost. Also, if the soil is poor, spread a thin layer of manure or general fertilizer. Never apply lime, bone meal, or wood ashes to Japanese iris. Siberian iris are tolerant of alkaline soil, but prefer soil that is somewhat acid.

What kind of soil is good for Dutch irises?   Any fertile, well-drained garden soil other than heavy clay. This is true for all bulbous irises.

Is manure good for irises?   Animal manure should not be used on bearded irises, but the beardless species (including the Japanese and Siberian irises) appreciate well-rotted manure.

Should beds of bearded irises be fertilized each spring?   Not if the ground was well prepared and fertilized at planting time.

What fertilizer do you recommend for ordinary bearded irises?   Superphosphate and unleached wood ashes together with a commercial fertilizer low in nitrogen. Mix with soil when the beds are prepared.

Do bearded irises require lime?   Only if the soil is decidedly acid.

Are wood ashes good fertilizer for bearded irises? When should they be applied?   Yes. They are generally best applied in the spring. If they are saved from a stove or fireplace, store dry until the time of application, since their value is quickly lost in the rain. They supply from 5 to 25 per cent of potash as well as 30 to 35 per cent of lime. Water in after applying at the rate of 4 to 5 ounces per square yard.

What is the best fertilizer to use on Japanese irises?   Rotted or dehydrated manure (or, if this is not available, leafmold or peat moss fortified with a light dressing of complete fertilizer). A fertilizer formulated for rhododendrons and azaleas (acid-loving plants) is good. Apply as a mulch in May or early June. In fall, mulch with manure, leaves, or peat moss.

Are irises more attractive planted together or scattered in clumps throughout the garden?   By themselves, they are not attractive during the greater part of the year. Clumps of one variety in front of evergreens are very effective. Many people interplant irises with day-lilies.

When, where, and how do you plant bearded irises?   The main planting time is in June or July after flowering, in a good garden soil. However, they can also be planted in the spring and fall. June planting allows maximum time for recuperation before blooming the next year. Plant rhizomes level with the surface in well-drained, sunny beds. In

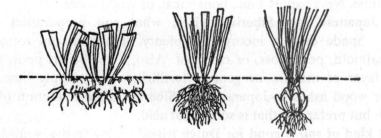

Planting depths for (left to right) bearded, beardless, and bulbous irises.

light, sandy soil, the rhizomes can be covered an inch or so; but in heavy soils they should be left with the tops exposed. Buy your stock from a reliable dealer so that you will receive good, healthy rhizomes.

What distances should be allowed between irises when planting? Tall-bearded, 9 to 18 inches; dwarf-bearded, 6 to 9 inches; Japanese and Siberian, 18 to 24 inches; bulbous, 4 to 5 inches with 12 inches between rows.

At what distance apart should purchased divisions of tall-bearded irises be set? For a substantial effect the first year after planting, 8 or 9 inches. A better spacing is 16 or 18 inches, but this takes 2 years to produce a good display.

Should iris rhizomes be dried out before being replanted? Not unless the rhizomes are rotted from disease, because if the feeding roots are dried, no new growth results until new ones develop. Irises can be divided and transplanted without much setback, provided their roots are kept out of the sun and they are soon replanted.

Will irises bloom if they are moved early in spring? The Japanese and Siberians usually bloom; the tall-bearded sometimes bloom (but with short bloom stalks). If possible, avoid moving bearded irises until after the blooming season.

When and how deep should Japanese irises be planted? Early spring, before growth starts, or late August. The crowns should be set 2 inches below the surface.

Can we grow irises successfully? We have a lot of shade. Ordinary garden irises will not thrive in the shade. Certain wild species, such as *Iris cristata, gracilipes, verna,* and *foetidissima,* are satisfactory in partial shade.

How often should I transplant irises? Whenever they become so crowded that the rhizomes are growing over one another, about every 3 years.

Can irises be replanted in the same bed? Yes, if redug and fertilized. If disease is present, the soil should first be sterilized.

Should irises be thinned out if they are not blooming freely? If lack of bloom is due to crowding, lift and replant. If there is some other cause, get a diagnosis and be guided accordingly.

What culture do Japanese irises require? The flower bed must be well drained (it is not a good idea to select a location where water stands during the winter). Enrich the soil with leafmold, well-decayed manure, or garden compost. Plant in August; replant every 3 years.

They like plenty of water before and during the blooming season. Never plant in alkaline soil or where lime has been used.

What are the conditions favorable to the growth of Siberian irises? Plenty of sunshine and well-drained, rich, slightly acid soil. They like plenty of rotted manure or rich compost, and plenty of moisture from spring until their blooming is over.

Do the Dutch, English, and Spanish irises all get the same culture? In general, yes. Plant bulbs 4 to 5 inches deep, October to November, in a sunny location and in good, well-drained loam. Let them remain for 2 years, then lift and replant in a new location. They are heavy feeders and deplete the soil very quickly. In severe climates a winter mulch is beneficial.

How are bulbous irises handled in the South? Dutch, English, and Spanish irises are dug after blooming and are stored in a cool shed until late fall, when they are replanted. This is because they make fall growth, and if left in the ground the flower stalks are usually killed by a freeze in late winter. When lifted and replanted in late fall, the stalks do not develop until the spring.

Do Dutch irises have to be dug up each year? Not unless they have suffered winter losses. In that case try planting as late in autumn as the weather permits. The following year dig the bulbs when the foliage dies down and store in a cool location until autumn. In extreme climates a winter mulch is beneficial.

When is the best time to move Dutch irises? As soon as the foliage has died down. In the South many people lift them at this time and store them in airy containers in a cool shed until late fall.

What is the correct culture for oncocyclus irises? These natives of the Near and Middle East require a dormant season without moisture. Grow them in pots or cold frames so that they are kept dry from mid-June to mid-December.

What culture do spuria iris require? These are best planted in early fall. They can take a year or more to bloom after being moved. Grow in sun or partial shade, in neutral to slightly acid soil. This iris is a heavy feeder, so fertilize each spring with a complete fertilizer (5–10–10) or use rotted or dehydrated manure.

When do you divide and replant Siberian irises? Late August or September.

I have a large garden of Japanese irises that were planted 4 years ago. When should I divide and reset them? They seem to be getting

crowded. Immediately after the blooming season, in September, or just before growth starts in the spring.

How much watering and cultivating do irises need? Bearded irises ordinarily need no watering. Japanese and other beardless types need plenty of moisture until their flowering is through. Cultivate shallowly and sufficiently often to keep the surface loose and free of weeds.

What care should be given bearded iris rhizomes after the blooming season? If overcrowded, divide them. Remove flower stalks immediately after flowering and be on the alert for signs of borers or rots. Keep all dead foliage cleaned off.

Does it injure iris plants to take green foliage off in the late fall? Leaves turning brown should always be removed promptly. Green foliage should not be removed or cut back in late fall because this may adversely affect next year's bloom.

When leaves are forbidden as winter protection for bearded irises, what can be used? No protection is necessary unless rhizomes have been planted in late fall. Evergreen boughs then make the best protection. Marsh hay or excelsior can also be used.

Should I cover iris roots? I have over 400 different kinds and it would be quite a task to cover them all. No. They need protection only if planted in late fall, and then only because their root growth will not be sufficient to keep them from heaving. A few irises of Californian origin need to be planted in sheltered spots.

How can I transport irises to shows? Obtain large florists' boxes. String tape across them in several places so that the stalks can be suspended without the blooms touching the bottoms or sides. Keep the boxes level; or if this is impossible, tie each stalk to the tapes.

How should I prepare irises for exhibition at my local garden-club shows? Bloom stalks should have at least 2 open flowers. Three would be better. These should be the first blooms. After cutting the stalks, stand them in water for 30 minutes or longer. The foliage should be displayed with the flower stalks. Dead or torn blooms count heavily against you. Varieties should be correctly labeled.

Why won't Japanese irises bloom for me? Too much shade? Alkaline soil? Dry soil? Water settling around the crowns during the winter? Any of the above may be responsible.

My bearded irises grow and look well, but rarely bloom. What is the reason? They have been established more than 2 years. They get full sun at least half the day. Most likely they are overcrowded and need to be divided. Some varieties of tall-bearded irises require dividing every year for good bloom. And the more sun, the better.

Are all bearded irises robust growers?   No. Certain varieties, especially dark-colored ones, are less vigorous than others. Some that have originated in Southern California are tender and do not do well in cold parts of the country.

Do irises change colors from year to year?   No. But in different gardens the same iris can vary somewhat in color intensity due to cultural and environmental conditions. Slight variations can occur in different locations in the same garden.

After a few years does a mixed planting of irises gradually lose color and turn white?   No. What sometimes happens is that the faster and more vigorous growers crowd out slower-growing varieties.

Why do irises stop blooming after being separated, even though carefully taken apart at the right season? They are free of pests and were planted at the right depth.   Perhaps the soil is deficient or exhausted. Try remaking the garden beds, adding superphosphate and perhaps lime. Sunshine is important.

I planted irises two years ago. Half of them grew to enormous size and bloomed, but the others remained small and spindly. How can I make these perk up and bloom?   Robust varieties produce a representative bloom stalk the first year after planting, others take 2 years to become established. Furthermore, varieties vary in height; it may be that you have some of the intermediate varieties growing together with tall-bearded sorts.

My irises (early dwarfs and Siberians) bloomed the first year but not the following 2 years. What is wrong?   Perhaps they do not get enough sunshine, or they may be too crowded and need to be divided. Siberians are heavy feeders; they require plenty of fertilizer.

My irises do not do well; they have decreased in size and stopped blooming. The soil is stiff clay. What would you advise?   Perhaps your soil is so heavy that just enough feeding roots develop to keep your plants alive, but not enough to build strong plants. Lift, divide, and replant in well-drained beds improved by the addition of coal cinders or sand, superphosphate, and a dressing of agricultural lime if the soil test shows the need for it. Incorporate organic matter.

What is the difference between the Dykes Medal and Dykes Memorial Medal?   There is no difference. The complete name is the Dykes Memorial Medal, but it is generally spoken of as the Dykes Medal. Most catalogs of iris generally indicate the winners of this medal.

How should I divide tall-bearded irises? After flowering, cut the leaves back halfway, lift the clumps, then with a sharp knife cut the rhizomes into pieces so that each has one (or, if preferred, 2 or 3) strong fan of leaves attached. Be sure that divisions are disease-free before being replanted. Divide every 3 or 4 years.

Newly set divisions of bearded iris.

How and when should Japanese irises be divided? It is quite a job if the clumps are large. A heavy-bladed knife or billhook is the best tool. Cut the leaves halfway back and then chop the rootstock into pieces, each having 3 or 4 growths. Discard old, lifeless material. Save only young, vigorous portions. Do this work in the autumn, in the shade, and keep the roots from drying out.

Should iris seeds picked in the fall be planted in the fall or spring? In the fall; if planted in the spring they will not germinate until the following year. Plant in open ground or in a cold frame—the

Typical divisions of tall bearded, dwarf bearded, and beardless irises, ready to be planted.

latter is preferred. In a cold frame the plants start coming up in late February and should be transplanted in late June to nursery beds.

How do you grow irises from seed?   After seed is harvested, plant immediately in a cold frame, or save until late fall and plant in open ground. If sown earlier outdoors, young seedlings come up and are heaved out during the winter. Be sure that the soil is well prepared and on the light side. Transplant the seedlings in late June to a nursery bed, spacing them at least a foot apart each way. Nearly all should bloom the following year.

My iris leaves are spotted. What shall I do?   This is leafspot disease. Cut back diseased foliage and burn it. If this is not done it will spread disease through the garden. Be sure and keep all dead leaves picked off and in two years you will have eliminated the disease. Leaves may also be dusted or sprayed with zineb. Avoid splashing water on leaves as this spreads the disease.

Are irises subject to virus disease?   Iris mosaic disease attacks both bearded and bulbous kinds, causing mottling or yellow striping of leaves and lack of vigor. Destroy all infected plants.

My iris roots have rotted and watery streaks appear on the leaves. What is the cause?   Bacterial soft rot. It often gains entrance through wounds made by the iris borer. Dig and destroy rotted plants; sterilize the soil by soaking it with ½ cup of a household bleach in ½ cup water. Also, pour it on the rhizomes and leave them exposed to the air until healing takes place. Avoid planting diseased rhizomes. Sterilize knives and tools with the solution, since, unsterilized, they can spread the disease. Clean off and burn dead leaves and rubbish in the fall.

How can I control thrips on Japanese irises?   By spraying or dusting with diazinon or Sevin.

Grayish plant lice have attacked my iris roots underground. What control measures shall I take?   Root aphids are destroyed by soaking the soil with nicotine sulfate, 2 teaspoonfuls to 1 gallon of water; or by the use of malathion or diazinon (follow directions on the package).

What controls are recommended for iris borers?   Clean up and burn all old leaves and debris in the fall. In severe infestations, spray with Thiodane, Sevin, malathion or methoxychlor in the spring.

How are irises classified?   They are broadly classified into bulbous and rhizomatous. In the bulbous group are included Dutch, Spanish, English, Reticulata, and Juno. In the rhizomatous group are found the bearded (Euopogon, Aril, Oncocyclus, Regelia, and Pseudoregelia) and beardless iris (including Siberian, spuria, Louisiana, and crested).

Which group of irises is most useful in the home garden? Undoubtedly, the tall-bearded (often miscalled German irises). The Japanese and Siberian groups are very popular.

In reading about the flowers of bearded irises, I often come across these terms that I don't fully understand—amoena, plicata, variegata, blend, bicolor, bitone, and self. Can you tell me what they mean? *Amoena:* tinted white standards and colored falls; *plicata:* stitched or stippled margin color on a white background; *variegata:* yellow or near yellow standards with deeper falls which may be either veined or solid tones of brown or purple; *blend:* a combination of two or more colors (one always being yellow); *bicolor:* light or medium standards in one color and deeper contrasting falls in another color; *bitone:* two tones of the same color; *self:* uniform color.

Do all bearded iris bloom at the same time? No, there is considerable variation. The catalogs of iris specialists are very helpful on this point. For each variety they indicate the relative blooming period as VE (very early), E (early), EM (early midseason), M (midseason), ML (midseason late), L (late), VL (very late).

What is meant by "dwarf," "lilliput," and "intermediate" when referring to bearded iris? Miniature dwarf iris are under 10 inches tall; lilliput or standard dwarf-bearded, 10 to 15 inches tall; and intermediate, 15 to 28 inches tall. Most tall-bearded iris are about 36 inches, but a few can reach 40 inches.

Can you tell me the relative blooming times of the various irises? This varies in different localities. However, in the New York City area it starts usually in March or April with *Iris reticulata* and is soon followed by the miniature dwarf-bearded (April–May); then the dwarf-bearded, aril, and intermediate bearded (May); then tall-bearded and Siberian (May–June); followed by Dutch, Louisiana, spuria, and Japanese (June–July). Last to bloom are the reblooming bearded (late July, August, September).

Is the bulbous iris Juno known by any other name? Can I obtain hybrids in the Juno group? No. It and other species of the Juno group are rare in American gardens. Only a few hybrids exist. They are suited only for skilled growers and comparatively mild climates.

LUPINE

What can I use to build up the soil for lupines? They need a well-drained medium soil. Use sand, leafmold or peat moss, and well-rotted manure. Lime should not be used on lupines, as they require an acid soil.

Is acid soil or lime soil better for perennial lupines? Most lupines seem to do better in an acid soil.

What should I use to fertilize lupines? Well-rotted compost, animal manure, or any general garden fertilizer, but don't overdo it!

Will you give soil and cultural directions for Russell lupines? Russell lupines thrive in any good garden soil in full sun. Seed can be planted indoors (see below) or outdoors, in the spring or summer, about ½ inch deep. The spikes do not generally grow as large here as in England, where they originated. Nevertheless, these are among our finest perennials. Lupines are short-lived in many gardens and may not persist after the first year. The soil must be well drained. Cut off fading flower spikes before seed forms.

What is the best way of raising the improved types of perennial lupine from seed indoors? I have had poor germination. Sow individual seeds in small peat pots filled with a sterile soilless mix or in the "one-step" Jiffy-7 peat pots in a sunny window or under fluorescent lights. Soak the hard-coated seeds overnight in water first. Sown in March, the seedlings will show in a week and be ready to plant outdoors in May, without the roots being disturbed. You can nick the seed; or place it in hot water for an overnight soak and sow thinly outdoors in April or later.

Will lupine seeds "stratified" come up the following year? They should. If kept during the winter in a seed container, germination is aided by making a nick in the seed coat with a sharp knife.

Can lupines be transplanted? Do they last many years? Old plants do not like to be disturbed and are very hard to transplant. Young plants can be transplanted in very early spring if care is used to protect the roots. Lupines are short-lived. For a constant supply, sow seed each year.

Is there a dwarf form of lupine? There are several fine dwarf forms that grow only 18 inches tall. Check seed catalogs.

I was told that lupine seed should be treated with an inoculant (Legume-Aid) the same as for pea seed. Is this true? Since lupines are legumes, it generally improves the germination to treat the seed. However, it's not absolutely necessary.

MONKSHOOD (ACONITUM)

How often should aconitum be divided? These plants flower very freely when they are in established clumps and can be left undisturbed for years.

How deep shall I plant aconitum and in what kind of soil? They are best planted with the crown about 1 inch down, in rich, moist soil, neutral or slightly acid.

Do aconitums need winter protection? They are hardy but should be protected for the first and second winter after being planted.

When should I sow the seed of monkshood? In late autumn, using fresh seed.

Will monkshood grow in the shade? They do best in partial shade.

Is it advisable to plant monkshood? I have heard that it is poisonous. Monkshood does contain poison. It is said to have been mistaken for horse-radish on occasions and eaten with fatal results. But it is widely grown in gardens, as are many other poisonous plants.

PENSTEMONS

I have several penstemon plants which stayed green long after a frost. Is it a hardy variety? You may have plants of the bedding penstemon, which is not hardy but which stays green until late autumn. The other kinds are hardy and, with the exception of the alpine sorts, are treated like ordinary perennials. Many of them remain green until long after frost appears.

How do you trim and care for large penstemons? They need no trimming. The wiry stems of the tall kinds need support, best supplied by using twiggy brush inserted among the plants when they are about a foot tall. Growing up through this, with loose stems tied up and the tops of the brush cut away when flower buds form, they will be held neatly and securely. Cut the stems after they bloom and topdress with bone meal.

What is the best way to divide penstemon plants? Lift the plants in early spring, pull them gently apart, and replant.

PEONIES

The modern peony is the achievement of years of steadfast devotion and effort on the part of plant breeders. For more than 2,000 years the peony has been cultivated in China, not alone for its highly prized flowers, but for its roots, which in early times were used for food and medicinal purposes. It was named in honor of Paeon, the physician of the gods, who—according to mythology—received the first peony on Mount Olympus from the hands of Leto.

Present-day gardeners are inclined to take the peony for granted because it has become so common. The very fact that it is common only serves to emphasize its many worthwhile qualities. Hardiness, permanence, ease of culture, and freedom from pests are but a few of its merits. Diversity in flower form, attractive colors, clean habit of growth, and deep-green foliage combine to produce a plant of exceptional value for mass plantings or for the mixed border. Peonies rank high as cut flowers because of their extraordinary keeping qualities. They are primarily plants for the North, for they require the low temperatures of winter to break the dormancy of the buds before spring growth will take place.

There are two main classes of peonies—herbaceous and tree. The herbaceous peonies die back to the ground each year while the tree peonies merely drop their leaves, and the somewhat woody stems persist year after year. Tree peonies are generally taller than the herbaceous, the flowers are somewhat larger, and in general they bloom a week or two earlier. Both are valuable garden subjects and although herbaceous peonies outsell tree peonies, the latter are fast gaining popularity as good varieties become more readily available.

Some horticulturists consider that the interest in peonies is on the wane; that their potentiality for further improvement is exhausted. This does not seem to be the case, however, for within the last few years several new varieties have been introduced that eclipse all previous originations in perfection of form and color. They have always been garden favorites and will continue to be so.

What type of soil is best for peonies?   They grow well in a wide range of soil types. Any rich, friable garden soil is satisfactory.

Is a very heavy soil satisfactory for peonies?   Yes, providing it is well-drained. Some form of organic material, such as well-rotted manure, peat moss, or leafmold, should be added to make it more friable.

Will peonies thrive in a sandy soil?   The soil must first be improved by adding organic matter. Well-rotted manure or rich compost and commercial fertilizer should be used.

What is the proper method of preparing the soil for peonies?   Spade it to a depth of 12 to 18 inches. Thoroughly work in some well-rotted manure or other form of organic material at the rate of 4 bushels per 100 square feet. Incorporate 3 pounds of superphosphate to each 100 square feet. If the soil is acid, apply lime (5 pounds per 100 square feet) several weeks before planting.

Do peonies need lime? Peonies grow best in a slightly acid soil (pH 5.5 to 6.5). If the soil is very acid (below pH 5), the addition of ground limestone is beneficial.

What kind and how much fertilizer should I use for peonies? A mixed commercial fertilizer of 4–12–4 or 5–10–5 analysis is satisfactory. Use 4 pounds per 100 square feet. Well-rotted manure is also satisfactory. Avoid the use of fresh manure.

When peonies are planted in the fall, should they be fertilized then or the following spring? Work the fertilizer thoroughly into the soil before planting. No additional fertilizer will be needed the following spring, but each succeeding spring, use a mixed commercial fertilizer.

Do peonies need fertilizer? When should it be applied? Yes. Apply commercial fertilizer in the spring. When growth is about 4 inches high, work it into the soil around the plants. Rotted manure makes a good fertilizer to put on in the fall.

Should peonies be planted in full sun? The best results are obtained when the plants are exposed to full sunlight. They should be protected from strong winds.

Can peonies be grown in partial shade? While they do best in full sun, they will grow satisfactorily in light shade. They require at least 6 hours a day of direct sunlight for good results.

Does the peony plant need to be kept away from other flowers in the beds? Providing they are properly spaced and cultural conditions are right, other plants exert no influence whatever on the blooming of peonies. They are often used in mixed perennial borders and are excellent for the purpose.

When should peonies be planted? In the fall or early spring.

How deep do herbaceous peonies need to be planted? The crown, from which the buds arise, should be only 1 to 2 inches below the soil level.

Does it matter whether the eye of a herbaceous peony is 1 inch or 2 inches below the surface? No. It is important, however, not to exceed 2 inches. If planted too shallowly, there is danger of the roots being heaved out during the winter before they become established.

I planted peonies the last of November; was it too late? Planting can be done any time until the ground freezes, but the ideal months are September and October. This gives them an opportunity to become partially established before winter.

I planted peonies in a temporary location in late November. When and how should I transplant them to their permanent place?   It would be desirable to leave them where they are until October, when moving would be much easier. However, you can move them in the spring as soon as the ground has thawed and replant them immediately.

If I move peony plants in the spring, will they bloom the same year?   Yes, if moved *very* early, before growth starts. The soil must be kept moist at all times.

Will peony roots that have been kept in the cellar all winter grow satisfactorily?   It is never advisable to treat them in this manner. However, if they have not dried out and appear to be in good condition, they will survive. It may take 3 or 4 years before they regain their full vigor.

Will peonies bloom the first summer after being transplanted?   Usually, if the plants are vigorous and were not divided into small pieces, and if the transplanting was done at the right time. The blooms may not be as large and perfect as those produced in succeeding years.

Why does it take peonies so long to bloom after being divided?   Dividing the clumps is a severe operation; it results in the loss of roots in which food is stored. Dividing at an improper time causes recovery to be especially slow. If the divisions are very small, it may take 2 to 3 years before the plants are sufficiently vigorous to bloom.

How do you recognize healthy peony roots suitable for planting?   They should be approximately 1 inch in diameter, smooth, free from bruises, and each containing at least 1 plump bud and several smaller ones. No decay should be evident near the cut surface.

How can you bring an old peony border back into bloom?   If the plants are very old, it is advisable to divide the clumps and replant them in well-prepared soil. Keeping the bed free of weeds by maintaining a mulch, and applying fertilizer in the spring, will increase the quality and quantity of the flowers.

Is it necessary to dig up peony roots every year and break them up to obtain more blossoms?   No. It is best not to divide and transplant peonies any more often than is necessary to maintain vigorous growth. Ordinarily, every 5 to 8 years is often enough. Better-quality blooms can be had by fertilizing and making certain that the plants do not lack moisture at the time they come into flower.

Why should peonies be disbudded?   The size and quality of flowers are improved by disbudding. The practice is advisable if blooms are to be used for cut flowers or for exhibition purposes. In the garden, where mass color effects are desirable, it is not as important.

When should peonies be disbudded? The earlier, the better. Ordinarily, it can be done when the plants are about 18 inches tall. Just as soon as the secondary buds become visible, they should be removed.

How are peonies disbudded? A peony stem usually has from 3 to 7 buds. The main, or terminal, bud produces the largest and most perfect flower. All of the buds except the terminal bud can be picked off, leaving only 1 on each stem.

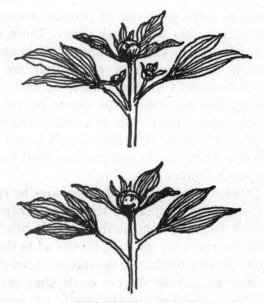

Disbudding peonies.

Should the flower buds of newly planted or transplanted peonies be removed the first year? Some growers do this to help the plants build strength, but it is not absolutely necessary. Most gardeners allow their plants to bloom even though the flowers are not as large and perfect as they will be later.

Do peonies need to be cultivated? Very little cultivation is necessary, except to remove weeds. The best time to destroy weeds is very early in the spring before the plants have made much growth or late in the fall after the tops have been cut off. A constant mulch will suppress most weeds.

Do peonies require much moisture? A moderately moist soil is suitable. In the spring when the flowers are developing, if the natural rainfall is not abundant, thorough watering increases the size and quality of the flowers.

Does irrigating peonies when in bud bring the flowers on sooner or does it hold them back?   It tends to hasten flowering. If the soil is very dry, irrigation also greatly improves the size and quality of the blooms.

How can I keep the stems of peonies from falling over?   Support with special, circular wire "peony stakes," or use individual stakes to each stem. Good growers shake the water out of the peony heads after each rain. Planting in a location sheltered from the wind helps to prevent damage.

Is there any way to make the stems of peonies stronger?   Some otherwise fine varieties naturally have weak stems. There is little that can be done except to give them artificial support. It is also well to plant them in full sunlight and, if possible, where they are protected from strong winds. Single-flowered varieties stand up better.

In picking peony flowers, should the stems be cut at the ground level?   Do not take more stem than is actually required for the arrangement. It is advisable to leave at least 2 or 3 leaves below the point where the stem is cut. These leaves will produce food for the production of the succeeding year's flowers.

Should the old flowers and seed pods of peonies be removed?   During the flowering season, old blossoms should be picked off before the petals fall since this helps to control the botrytis blight disease. Seed pods compete with the roots for the food produced in the leaves. Do not remove leaves when picking off the old flowers and seed pods.

Should the foliage on peonies be cut back after the blooming season?   No. The foliage should not be cut until it has been killed by hard frosts. The food manufactured in the foliage is stored in the roots and thus helps produce flowers the following year. If the foliage is cut back shortly after blooming, the plants are deprived of their next year's food supply.

Should the dried foliage of peonies be cut off to the ground in the fall or left on until spring?   In the fall. Its removal helps to prevent the spread of disease.

When is the proper time to cut down a peony?   After the foliage has been killed by frost. The autumn coloring of peony foliage is usually quite attractive.

Should peonies be protected in the winter?   Peonies should be mulched the first year after planting to prevent heaving. After they are well established, no protection is necessary.

Will peonies do well in warm climates such as Florida? No, they require low temperatures to complete their rest period.

Are peonies hardy in cold climates? They are among the hardiest of garden flowers.

Why do peonies that are several years old fail to bloom? The following conditions may prevent blooming: too deep planting; too shady a situation; poor drainage; plants need dividing; disease, especially of the roots; botrytis blight disease; roots infested with nematodes; lack of fertilizer; lack of moisture; lack of sunlight; injury to buds due to late frosts.

I have peonies about 12 years old that have only a blossom or two a year. The soil is black, sandy loam. They are not planted too deep. Are they too old or what can be the trouble? An application of complete fertilizer at the rate of 4 pounds per 100 square feet can correct the trouble. Nematodes also can cause failure to bloom. If infested with nematodes, the best thing to do is to discard the roots. To check on nematode presence ask your county extension agent where to send plant parts for testing.

Is there any way to tell the color of peonies from the roots or from the buds on the roots? No. Experienced growers can recognize certain varieties by root and bud coloring, but there is no general rule to follow.

What should I do with peonies that have been in the ground for many years and are not doing well? Dig and divide them during October. Replant them in well-prepared soil in a good sunny location.

I have some very old peonies. Last summer the flowers were almost single and many did not bloom well. Why? Old plants often fail to produce perfect flowers. They should be dug, divided, and replanted in well-prepared soil.

When should peony flowers be cut for use indoors? Preferably in the early morning. For cutting, select buds that have just started to open.

How are peonies scored or rated? On a scale of 10. A rating of 10 represents the highest possible excellence in both plant and bloom. Varieties rated at 9 or above are very high in quality. Between 8 and 9, they are considered good. Few varieties are grown that rate less than 7.5.

Can peony roots be divided in the spring with as much success as in the fall? No, early fall is the best time.

How are peony plants divided? Dig the clumps carefully so as not to injure or bruise the roots. Wash off all the soil. With a heavy, sharp knife, cut each clump through the crown into several pieces. Each division should have several plump buds, which in the fall are approximately ½ inch long. Roots without such buds rarely produce plants.

Would it be advisable to separate a peony root with a spade, leaving part in the ground and removing the other part? This method can be used and has the advantage of not interrupting the bloom of the portion that is left in place. However, it is usually better to dig the entire plant and divide it carefully. Before replanting, there is an opportunity to prepare the soil to improve growing conditions.

Can peonies be raised from seeds? Yes, but this method is used only for the production of new varieties; it is slow and tedious.

How should the seeds of peonies be sown? Collect when ripe. Keep in damp moss until November. Sow in a cold frame or protected bed. Cover the seeds to their own depth and mulch with peat moss the following spring. Keep the bed shaded and reasonably moist. They usually take 2 years to germinate.

How long does it take peonies to bloom from seeds? They ordinarily germinate 2 years after being sown. After 3 years' growth, a few flowers can be expected. This means 5 or more years from seed-sowing to bloom.

What can I do to control ants that are eating the flower buds of my peonies? Ants do not eat peony buds; they feed on the sweet, syrupy material secreted by the developing buds. They do no harm to the peonies except, possibly, to spread botrytis blight disease.

Why do peony buds dry up without developing into blossoms? The plant seems disease-free. The leaves do not dry and there is no sign of bud rot. Probably botrytis blight. This can be prevented by carefully cleaning the bed in the fall and by keeping it clean of dead leaves during all seasons. Spraying with zineb or captan every 10 days from the time the leaves show until the flowers open is a good control measure. Late frosts in the spring can also kill buds, but disease is the more likely culprit.

Is there something lacking in the soil when peony leaves turn brown at the edges early in July? Usually this is the result of drought or of infection with some root disease.

What are the names of the different types of peony flowers? The most distinct are single, Japanese, anemone, and double.

What is the difference between single peonies and the Japanese type? Singles have 5, or possibly a few more, true petals around a center of showy, fertile stamens. Japanese types have a single row of large petals, but the center consists of much enlarged stamens which bear very little, or no, pollen.

What is the anemone type of peony? It somewhat resembles the Japanese type, but the centers of the flowers are composed of much enlarged, petal-like stamens which bear no pollen whatever. These center petals are long and narrow, more or less incurved, and imbricated.

What varieties of anemone-flowered peonies are desirable? There are many fine varieties, but here are three: 'Nippon Beauty', red; 'Nippon Gold', pink and yellow; 'Prairie Afire', fiery pink.

What are a few good single peonies? 'Krinkled White', pure white; 'Sea Shell', pink; 'Red Warrior' and 'President Lincoln', red.

Which are some popular varieties of the Japanese type? 'Mikado', red; 'Nippon Brilliant', bright red; 'Amo-No-Sode', bright pink; 'Leto', white; 'Nippon Gold', dark pink, yellow center.

Which are a few of the best double peonies? 'Bowl of Cream', white; 'Elsa Fass', white; 'Festiva Maxima', white; 'Nick Shaylor', pink; 'Reine Hortense', rose; 'Sarah Bernhardt', deep rose; 'Pillow Talk', pale rose; and 'Pink Lemonade', pink.

Which peony flowers 2 weeks before the common herbaceous ones? The fern-leaf peony (*Paeonia tenuifolia*) is a very early-flowering species with delicate, finely cut leaves and single or double red flowers.

Is there a yellow herbaceous peony? Yes. There are several, one being 'Age of Gold', a double lemon yellow. Among the species, there is *P. mlokosewitschii*.

PEONIES, TREE

What is the difference between Japanese, European, and lutea hybrid tree peonies? The European and Japanese types are developed from the same *Paeonia suffruticosa*. The European tree peonies are usually fully double with thickly petaled flowers and the foliage is broad. The Japanese type have single or semidouble flowers, often with crinkled petals, and most have a lovely circle of yellow stamens; the leaves are finer than in the Japanese type. The lutea hybrids are crosses of *P. suffruticosa* with *P. lutea*. They are notable for their colors, ranging through many shades of yellow to orange, to orange tints and combinations of red and yellow.

What is the proper type of soil for tree peonies? A friable rich soil is necessary. Incorporate well-rotted manure, compost, peat moss, or leafmold. The optimum pH value is between 5.5 and 6.5.

How deep should tree peonies be planted?   The crowns or eyes should be set from 4 to 7 inches deep.

Are tree peonies completely hardy?   They have been known to survive 20° to 30° below zero.

How should the soil be prepared for tree peonies?   By spading as deeply as possible. Mix in some organic material, such as well-rotted manure, peat moss, or leafmold. The addition of a complete commercial fertilizer is also desirable. If a 5–10–5 or some similar grade is available, use it at the rate of 4 pounds per 100 square feet.

Can tree peonies be planted in the spring?   While October is the best season, success can be had from very early-spring planting.

How old do tree peonies need to be before they will flower?   Tree peonies are often slow to begin blooming. Normally, however, they produce a few blooms the second or third year after being planted.

How can I propagate tree peonies?   The usual method is by grafting in August or September. The scion should have at least 2 eyes. Its base is cut wedge-shaped and is inserted in a piece of root about ½ inch in diameter, 3 or 4 inches long, taken from a herbaceous peony plant. The scion is held in place with raffia or with a rubber band. The grafted roots are placed in good soil, in a cold frame, where they can be protected during the winter. If a cold greenhouse is available, the grafts can be placed in a deep pot and kept indoors during the winter. One of the eyes of the scion should be below the soil surface. Tree peonies can also be propagated by layering, division, and by seeds.

Which are some of the best tree-peony varieties?   'Hana Kisoi', flesh-pink; 'Banquet', strawberry red; 'Fuji No Akebono', bright scarlet; 'Reine Elizabeth', salmon and copper; 'Osirus', chestnut-brown; 'Akashi Gata', peach-pink; 'Kamata Fuji', purple; 'Souvenir de Maxine Cornu', yellow.

PERENNIAL PEA (LATHYRUS LATIFOLIUS)

How do you start what is called "wild sweet pea"? I have tried planting seeds and roots without success.   The perennial pea (*Lathyrus latifolius*) is best started from seeds sown in autumn, preferably where they are to grow permanently. The plant has long, fleshy roots and resents disturbance. Once established, it can be invasive.

What is the best way to plant and care for everlasting peas?   If by "everlasting" peas you mean the perennial kind, they rarely need special soil preparation or care. A sunny location and average garden soil are about all they require.

I have a well-established perennial sweet pea which failed to bloom last year. What can I do to it to produce bloom? The perennial pea usually flowers freely when established, even in poor soil. Try mixing superphosphate with the soil, 6 ounces per square yard.

Should hardy sweet peas be cut back in the fall? How far? They can be cut back to just above the ground level any time after the tops have dried up.

Is the perennial pea a good plant for a large lattice fence? Yes, if the slats are not too large for the tendrils to grasp. It will grow to a height of about 8 feet.

PHLOX (SUMMER OR GARDEN)

How is soil prepared for phlox (Phlox paniculata)? The soil should be dug to a depth of 1 foot to 18 inches and mixed with a 3-inch layer of rotted manure, leafmold, or mixture of peat moss and compost.

When is the best time to plant garden phlox? Either in early fall or early spring. Plants in containers can be planted even in midsummer. If fall planting is practiced, the plants should be mulched with a 3-inch layer of rough litter, hay, or straw, to prevent possible heaving as a result of freezing.

What is the best exposure for phlox? They thrive in full sun, but will grow in partial shade. A minimum of 3 to 4 hours of full sunshine is desirable.

What are some good varieties of garden phlox? *White*—'Mount Fujiyama', 'White Admiral', 'World Peace', 'Snowball'; *Lilac*—'Lilac Time'; *Red*—'Starfire'; *Orange-Red*—'Orange Perfection', 'Dramatic'; *Salmon Pink*—'Cecil Hanbury', 'Salmon Beauty', 'Sir John Falstaff'; *Dark Red*—'Leo Schlagater'; *Pink*—'Dodo Hanbury Forbes'; *Soft Pink*—'Dresden China'; *Purple*—'Royalty'.

Are there any dwarf varieties of garden phlox? Yes, there are several. 'Juliet', a pale heliotrope-pink, is only 2 feet tall, and 'Pinafore Pink' is 6 inches tall with large flower heads. 'Norah Leigh', pale lilac, is 15 inches tall with variegated foliage.

What is the earliest blooming garden-type phlox? The earliest are probably 'Miss Lingard' and *Phlox carolina,* pink.

How far apart should phlox be planted? Set them 15 inches apart and allow 3 or 4 shoots to grow from each plant.

Do phlox require much water? They need plenty of water during the growing season, but the soil must be well drained.

Do phlox require summer feeding? If the bed was well prepared by deep digging and the incorporation of organic matter, it may not be necessary; but they do respond to sidedressings or fertilizer or to applications of liquid fertilizers when flower buds are about to form.

How can I handle phlox to get more perfectly shaped heads of blossoms? They now grow ill-shaped. Probably your plants are old and need lifting, dividing, and replanting. Good trusses are obtained by thinning out the shoots that appear in the spring, leaving several inches between those that are left. Give liquid fertilizer weekly. Perhaps you have a poor variety or the plants could be infested with mites or nematodes.

I would appreciate some tips on raising phlox. Is it advisable to reset plants and how can I do this? Phlox grow best in a well-drained rich soil; they need a fair amount of water. Lift, divide, and replant about every 3 years, even more often for vigorous varieties. Cut off old flowers. They are subject to mildew; spray or dust regularly with an all-purpose insecticide-fungicide.

In transplanting phlox, how deep should they be set? Phlox should not be planted deeper than 1 to 2 inches.

Do you spread out the roots when planting phlox or leave them straight? Phlox roots should be planted straight down, so dig the holes deep and give them plenty of space.

My yard is on a slope. I have trouble with hardy phlox. They don't seem to bloom as they should. Is the soil the cause? Maybe. Phlox need a rich, moist, but well-drained soil. It might be the variety—some are poor bloomers. Disease or a pest like red spider may be responsible. It might be due to drying out of the roots, which are close to the surface.

Why don't my phlox thrive? The foliage is sometimes whitish-looking, turning to brown. The lower leaves drop off and the blooms are poor. (New York City.) Phlox are subject to red spider mite infestation, which causes a whitish appearance at first, then the leaves turn brown; they are also subject to mildew and a disease that causes the lower leaves to drop. Deep, rich, moist, but well-drained soil and periodic dusting with sulfur or spraying with Karathane will help. Phlox are extremely difficult to grow in the city.

Do phlox "run out"?   Yes. Phlox will deteriorate if not lifted, split up, and replanted in good soil every 3 or 4 years.

Should phlox be pinched back, thus preventing top-heavy plants while in bloom?   Pinching would induce branching, resulting in smaller heads of flowers and later blooming.

Could I plant hardy phlox at the base of poplar trees to follow tulips?   It depends on what kind of phlox. *Phlox divaricata* or a similar species, *P. stolonifera,* which would flower with the tulips, grow very well in partial shade. The regular summer phlox will have too much competition from the tree roots and probably too much shade.

What is the procedure in propagating perennial phlox by cutting up the roots into small sections? When is the best time to do this?   The plants are dug in September and the roots are cut into lengths of 1 to 2 inches. They are scattered in a cold frame and covered, ½ inch deep, with a half-and-half mixture of sand and soil. The young growths are kept in the frame until spring and are then planted out in nursery-bed rows.

How should I start the better varieties of phlox? Mine always die.   Phlox are propagated by being lifted and divided in the fall. Choose the new divisions from the outer edge of the clump and discard the old center, which is too woody for good growth.

Why did my phlox change color? Many plants which were white, salmon, or deep red are now a sickly magenta.   You probably allowed the seeds to ripen and self-sow. Unfortunately, self-seeded phlox tend to revert to their ancestral purplish color; and as they are usually exceptionally vigorous, they crowd out the desirable but less sturdy varieties. Weed out the seedlings and do not permit the plants to go to seed.

I have been told that unless phlox seed heads are kept cut off, they will revert to their original lavender. Is it possible for the roots of any plant to change like that?   The reason for the so-called reversion is self-seeding. The seedlings are always different in color, are very vigorous, and in time will displace the original variety. The original roots normally do not change. Cut off faded flowers to prevent reseeding.

Does dwarf phlox reseed itself? Please name a few kinds.   Yes, some of the dwarf phlox seed themselves but will probably not be the same color as the original plant. *Phlox subulata* with many varieties, *P. stolonifera, P. divaricata,* and *P. d. laphamii.*

PLATYCODON (BALLOON FLOWER)

Do platycodons need a rich soil?   No, any garden soil will suit them in the open. It must be well drained.

When should platycodon plants be set out?   In the spring.

How deep should platycodon be planted?   The crown should be barely covered with soil.

How do you keep platycodon in bloom?   Keeping the old flowers pinched off to prevent seed formation will help.

Should platycodon be pinched back?   It is not necessary, but permissible if a bushier plant is desired. It must be done when the plants are about 6 inches tall.

How tall does platycodon grow?   Most varieties grow about 2 feet tall, but there is a lower-growing variety that grows 10 to 12 inches tall —*Platycodon grandiflorus* variety *mariesii*.

Does platycodon come in any color other than blue?   Yes. There is a shell pink and a white.

Are platycodons difficult to transplant?   Yes. They do have long, fleshy roots, so you must take care when digging not to break them. Old plants' roots often go down 18 inches or more. Young plants are easier to move.

Do platycodons need winter protection?   They are perfectly hardy and need no protection, but mice may eat their roots.

How is platycodon propagated?   By careful division, in the spring; or by seed, sown in the fall or spring. Division is not as simple as for most fibrous-rooted perennials. Cut off the outer sections of the thickened crown so that both buds and roots are present on each division. Dust cuts with fungicide to prevent infection. Fortunately, platycodon needs infrequent division.

I have been told that platycodon is slow to appear in the spring. Is this so?   Yes, it is one of the last perennials to appear above the ground. Therefore, it's best to mark the location in the fall so as to avoid injuring the plants in the spring before they emerge.

PLUMBAGO (LEADWORT)

What perennial of easy culture has bright blue flowers late in the season?   *Ceratostigma plumbaginoides*. It is tolerant of city conditions, thrives in sun or partial shade, and blooms until frost arrives. It is often used as a ground cover.

POPPY, ORIENTAL (PAPAVER ORIENTALIS)

What fertilizer should I give perennial poppies? Any balanced one will give good results. Take your pick of the several special garden fertilizers such as 5–10–5 or a similar formula, but do not overfeed.

Will you give full planting instructions and the care of Oriental poppies? They should be planted out in August or September, making the hole big enough so that the fleshy roots are not broken or twisted upward; water well if the weather is dry. A few weeks after being planted, a crown of leaves will appear. In relatively mild climates, these can remain green for part of the winter. Protect in the winter with marsh hay or dry leaves to prevent crown rot.

How shall I care for Oriental poppies? (Maryland.) They don't need much attention. Cut off the flowers as they wither. In the spring work in sidedressings of balanced fertilizer.

After flowering, the leaves of my poppies start to turn yellow and then die. Is this normal? Yes, poppies will lose their leaves but they will reappear in the fall. If you find them unsightly, plant something like day-lilies nearby to hide them after they bloom.

My Oriental poppies come up and grow well, but never bloom. They get afternoon sun. Should they be in a different place? Transplant in April or August into a sunnier spot.

When is the best time to plant or transplant Oriental poppies? In August, after the leaves have withered, and early in the spring before growth commences. They dislike being transplanted, so injure the roots as little as possible; don't keep them out of the ground long, and water in thoroughly. If you grow them from seed, transfer the seedlings from flowerpots with the ball of soil intact.

When is the best time to thin out plants such as Oriental poppies? Thin out seedlings whenever the young plants tend to crowd. In growing practically all plants, thin out so carefully and continually that the seedlings do not touch each other. If you mean dividing the roots of large plants, August is the time.

Will Oriental poppies planted in the spring bloom the same year? Yes, but you should buy large established plants. Plant them in March or early April, give them good care, and you are quite likely to get some flowers.

Can I sow Oriental poppy seed in May, to bloom next year? Yes, if the plants are given good care. Transplant the seedlings into individual pots to avoid root disturbance when they are planted in their flowering positions.

How do you protect Oriental poppies in the winter? I have lost 3 different settings. They can be set out in very early spring, but the best time is in August when they are dormant. Is the soil well drained or waterlogged in winter? They resent the latter. Little protection is needed. A light covering of marsh hay or coarse ashes over the crown will suffice.

Is it necessary in this area to mulch fall-planted Oriental poppy before December? (South Dakota.) Tuck excelsior or dry leaves around the crown beneath the leaves; then mulch them with cut-up evergreen boughs after the soil freezes.

Is there any danger of Oriental poppy plants "mixing" if they are planted close together? Occasionally parent plants will mix. After a few seasons you can hardly help having in your group of plants some which are self-sown from seed dropped from the parents unless you are diligent about removing faded flowers before seed is formed. These will be mixed.

Do poppies come in any color besides orange? Yes. *White*—'Barr's White'; *Pink*—'Helen Elizabeth' and 'Salome'; *Flesh Pink*—'Lighthouse', 'Spring Morn'; *Salmon*—'Victoria Dreyfus'; *Salmon with Silver Edge*— 'Mahogany'.

Is there a double poppy? 'Crimson Pompon' is a fine blood-red double; 'Salmon Glow' is a salmon-orange double.

PRIMROSE (PRIMULA)

What kind of soil do primroses need? A fairly rich and moist soil; the addition of leafmold or peat moss mixed with rich compost is good. Primroses should be planted in partial shade. Some, such as *Primula japonica* and *P. rosea,* will grow in full sun where the soil is constantly wet.

Do primroses need fertilizer? Yes, they need a fairly rich soil. Use well-rotted or dehydrated animal manure or an organic fertilizer recommended for camellias and rhododendrons.

What summer care and winter protection do primroses need? (Virginia.) They should be given shade and not allowed to dry out in the summer. They are hardy and should not require any winter protection in Virginia.

What time of year is best for dividing primroses? After they have finished flowering in late spring.

Are primroses easily raised from seed? When is seed sown? Primroses come readily from seed. It's best to sow the seed as soon as it is ripe, which is in early summer. Spring-sown seed should be subjected to alternate freezing and thawing in the ice-cube tray of a refrigerator. Freeze and thaw several times for a week. Always refreeze immediately after thawing. Sow seed immediately after the final thawing. Seeds can also be sown early in the year in a greenhouse or under fluorescent lights. Some growers sow in late fall in a protected frame where seeds are subjected to natural freezing and thawing. They then germinate in the spring and sometimes through the summer. Protect the seedlings from hot summer sunshine.

PYRETHRUM (CHRYSANTHEMUM COCCINEUM)

How do you separate pyrethrums? They should be divided after they have finished flowering. The clumps are dug up and pulled apart, or pried apart with two spading forks.

ROSE-MALLOW (HIBISCUS MOSCHEUTOS)

How shall I treat hibiscus (mallow) before and after flowering? In the spring, dig in rotted leafmold and bone meal or superphosphate. Cut off faded flowers and prune back to the ground in the fall after frost.

Should rose-mallow be left in the ground all winter? Yes, the roots are perfectly hardy.

How can hibiscus (mallow) be grown successfully from seeds? How many years before the plant will be large enough to bloom? Hibiscus seeds are best sown, two in a pot, and then planted out from the pot in permanent position. They will take about 3 years to bloom. However, a fairly new hibiscus, an F_1 hybrid called 'Southern Belle', will bloom the first year if seed is started early indoors. Plants grow 4 feet tall and have blooms 10 inches across. Colors include rose, pink, and white with a red eye.

Rose-mallows are beautiful plants but they attract Japanese beetles in

droves. Are there any means of keeping the beetles off them? Use a spray such as Sevin.

SALVIA

What extra care would you advise for Salvia pitcheri? *Salvia pitcheri* has been reclassified as *S. azurea grandiflora*. It grows well in good garden soil with a reasonable amount of moisture and in full sun. Lift and divide the plants about every 3 or 4 years. The plants usually require staking.

Are there any perennial salvias? Yes, there are many. The ones usually found in gardens are *Salvia farinacea, S. officinalis, S. pitcheri, S. pratensis, S. jurisicii,* and *S. x superba. S. farinacea* is often treated as an annual in northern gardens. In addition, there are a few fine hybrids. For example, 'East Friesland' with intense violet-purple flowers on spikes 18 inches long, which appear in early summer.

SCABIOSA

When and how do I divide my scabiosa roots, grown from seed planted last spring? Your plants would hardly have grown enough from seed last spring to be divided now; plants 2 or 3 years old can be divided by cutting or pulling the plants apart in early spring and replanting them.

SHASTA DAISY (CHRYSANTHEMUM X SUPERBUM)

What is the best way to protect Shasta daisy plants in the winter? Cover with marsh hay after the ground is well frozen and gradually uncover in the spring.

How should Shasta daisies be divided? By digging up, in early spring, the outside rooted shoots either singly or in clumps. Shasta daisies are usually short-lived in the North and should be divided every year or two.

Can Shasta daisies be grown from seed? Yes, there are strains of both single and double forms that can readily be grown from seed. There is also an excellent dwarf—'Little Miss Muffet'—that is only 15 inches high.

SPURGE, FLOWERING (EUPHORBIA)

When should flowering spurge (Euphorbia corollata) be planted—spring or fall? Best in the spring.

What is the full name of the euphorbia that blooms at the same time as tulips? It is *Euphorbia epithymoides,* sometimes commonly called cushion euphorbia. It is showy because of its very bright yellow bracts just below the inconspicuous flowers. It is an excellent nonspreading subject (although it will self-sow to some extent) for the spring garden among other perennials. It is especially effective with tulips, as you mention, but the plants remain neat all summer.

TRADESCANTIA

What is the botanical name of "widows' tears"? *Tradescantia virginiana.* It is also known as common spiderwort and snake-grass.

Can you name some improved forms of tradescantia? Look for 'Iris Pritchard', white flushed with blue; 'Pauline', pale pink; 'Purple Dome', bright purple; 'J. C. Weguelin', pale blue; and 'Snow Cap', white.

What growing conditions does tradescantia require? It will grow well in any ordinary garden soil in sun or partial shade. The plants are very hardy. Although the flowers are pretty, the plants tend to be sprawly and invasive, and mice will eat the roots.

TRITOMA (KNIPHOFIA)

Can you grow tritomas from seed in the winter and transplant in the spring? Yes, grow the seedlings in 2½-inch pots, and transplant in early May.

Should tritoma be cut down to the ground after blooming? Just the flowering stems should be cut away after blooming. The foliage usually persists through the winter and affords some protection to the crown.

How do you prepare tritomas for the winter along the north Jersey coast? When is the best time to separate tritomas? Give winter protection with marsh hay or some other suitable material; do not cut off their leaves until spring. Separate tritomas in the spring only.

Is it possible to divide tritomas? How should it be done? Divide them in the spring only. It can be done by division of the roots, but it is much easier to dig up the offsets that come on the side of the main crown. See that these have roots.

VERONICA

The crowns of my veronica are rising above the surface. Can I remedy this?   Veronicas tend to raise their crowns if left in the same spot for some time. Lift and replant every 2 or 3 years.

Why does my veronica 'Blue Spires' sprawl instead of growing upright? I have plants from 3 different nurseries and all are the same.   It is characteristic of this variety to have weak stems. Little can be done to overcome this, other than to support the stems. This is best done by sticking twigs in the soil around the plants before the shoots begin to sprawl. Try variety 'Blue Champion' or the taller *Veronica longifolia subsessilis.*

VIOLA

Are violas just small versions of the familiar pansy?   For all practical purposes, yes. Both are botanically *Viola* and those commonly referred to as viola were developed largely by hybridizing *V. cornuta* with the pansy (*V. tricolor hortensis*). In general, violas have smaller flowers than pansies and bloom over a longer period. Many violas are hardy and live through the winter in cold climates for years; others behave like pansies and die the winter after the first year's bloom.

What is the proper time to plant viola seed for spring bloom?   In the latter part of the summer.

Will you discuss the culture of violas? I planted good plants last year but blossoms didn't form and there was frost.   Nearly all violas need cool conditions, moisture, and partial shade. Hot, exposed locations are not conducive to good results. Provide a moist soil containing plenty of leafmold or peat moss and the above conditions.

VIOLETS (VIOLA)

Are the so-called sweet, native or wild, and Russian violets related to violas and pansies?   Yes, they are all separate species and varieties of the genus *Viola,* to which both the pansy and viola belong.

Does Viola pedata, the birdfoot violet, prefer sun or shade?   It grows naturally in full sun and in an acid, sandy soil. It is difficult to retain under cultivation.

I am very much interested in growing sweet violets. I have a cold frame and yet don't seem to have any success. The plants have good

roots and healthy leaves; the few flowers are very small. Will you give me some information? Remove the sash and shade the frame with lath screens in the summer to keep the plants cool; cut off all runners as they appear; feed and water to build up vigorous plants for late fall. Ventilate freely in the fall, winter, and spring, whenever the temperature is above 35° to 40° F.

Should the runners be clipped off violet plants? Why do the plants grow up out of the soil instead of staying in it? How may large blooms and long stems be secured? In commercial culture, the runners are cut off as fast as they appear in order to build up the plants for flowering. The plants root at the surface, with the crown above; as they develop, the crown rises still higher above the soil. Young plants give the best bloom, hence a number of these must be kept coming along. Long stems and good flowers are produced on young, well-developed plants in a rich but well-drained soil. Thin out old plants in the spring.

My sweet violets produce seeds but I never see any blooms. Maybe they bloom without petals, for they never come out of the ground like a flower, but they develop into seed pods. Can you explain? Violets produce cleistogamous flowers, which are mostly on or under the ground. These are small, self-fertilizing flowers which never open.

My neighbor insists that African-violets grown as house plants are related to the hardy, woodland violets. Is she right? No, they are not related at all. The tropical African-violet is in the genus *Saintpaulia* and the true violets belong in *Viola*.

YUCCA (SPANISH BAYONET)

How old must a yucca plant (from seed) be to blossom? Will it bloom frequently? About 4 to 5 years old; then the clump should bloom every year or at least every second year after that.

Is it necessary to mulch a yucca plant? No, the common yucca is very hardy and prefers a dry, sandy soil.

What is the preferred time for moving yuccas? It is best done in early spring, when the plant is dormant.

I have several yucca plants that were on the property when we moved here 5 years ago. Why don't they bloom? They were probably planted in the shade, or in too heavy a soil. They prefer a light, sandy soil, good drainage, and full sun.

When can I separate yucca? Detach young suckers in early spring; or divide old clumps immediately after flowering or in the spring.

8. Annuals and Biennials

ANNUALS OFFER THE gardener the means—when it comes to beautifying his or her new home with flowers—of getting the fastest and the most for the least.

By no means, however, should annuals be considered merely as stopgap plants, to be used for temporary results until one can obtain something better. For many purposes, and for many special effects, there *is* nothing better. Many of the famous gardens of England make lavish use of annuals to obtain the breathtaking color displays for which they are noted.

While most annuals are so easily grown that they present no great challenge to the gardener's skill as a grower, they do test his skill—and offer him endless opportunities—in the employment of color and design in ways that will give his or her place individuality as well as beauty. And they do possess the great advantage of *flexibility*. Shrubs and perennials, once established, become more or less permanent fixtures. Annuals, used to supplement them, make it possible to shift the emphasis as one wishes, from year to year, or even during one season, and thus to obtain a series of interesting focal points not otherwise possible.

The flower arranger, too, will find that some annuals are almost indispensable to maintain a really constant supply of blooms for cutting and for supplementary foliage.

For pots, tubs, window boxes, and planters, annuals are the perfect answer. In fact a fabulous display can be assembled by using a multitude of pots and tubs of various sizes—some raised on props to give an allusion of height. Many city gardens are made up entirely with plants so displayed.

What is an annual? An annual is a plant that lives only one season, from seed sowing to flowering, setting of seed, and death.

What is meant by a hardy annual? A half-hardy annual? A tender annual? Hardy annuals are those whose seeds can be planted in the fall or in very early spring. Half-hardy annuals are cold-resistant and seeds of these can be planted early in the spring. Tender annuals are easily injured by frost and must be planted only after the ground has warmed up and all danger of frost is past. There are several plants treated as annuals that are really tender perennials. Examples are wax begonia and snapdragon.

What Annuals To Grow

Can you give me a list of a few annuals that will stand early planting in the spring? (Vermont.) Sweet-alyssum, scabiosa, candytuft, sweet peas, cosmos, cornflowers, larkspur, Shirley poppy, prickly-poppy (*Argemone*), California-poppy (*Eschscholtzia*).

Will you give me a list of annuals requiring the least care in home gardens? Marigold, verbena, gaillardia, cosmos, spider-flower (*Cleome*), calliopsis, petunia, zinnia, salvia, scabiosa, annual phlox, sweet-alyssum, impatiens.

What annual flower would you recommend for planting in a completely shaded area? There are no annual flowers that will grow well in *total* shade. A perennial ground cover such as *Pachysandra terminalis,* English ivy, *Ajuga reptans,* and periwinkle (*Vinca minor*) would be more suitable for such conditions. Your best choices, if you want to try annuals in partial shade, would be cleome, lobelia, nicotiana, wishbone-flower (*Torenia fournieri*), and impatiens.

Which annual flowers are best for flower beds—along sidewalks and on the side of a house? Ageratum (dwarf forms); *Begonia semperflorens* (wax begonia) varieties; dusty miller (*Centaurea cin-*

eraria); *Lobelia erinus;* marigolds (*Tagetes;* dwarf varieties); petunia (dwarf varieties); sweet-alyssum.

What annual would you suggest that I plant in the borders around my terrace? The area is partially shaded. Impatiens should do very well. There is a wide color range to choose from, heights from 6 inches to 1½ feet, and you can count on the plants remaining in good condition all summer. Wax begonia varieties should also do well.

How do I go about planting an annual garden from seed sown in place? The garden is about 4 feet wide and 15 feet long and receives sun all day. What annuals would be the most reliable to sow? After raking the soil as smooth as possible, use lime to outline the various sections or rectangles where the seeds are to be planted—as though you were making a giant plan on paper. For the easiest annuals to sow directly in place (you can broadcast the seeds), select sweet-alyssum as an edging, then nasturtium, and several varieties of marigolds and zinnias of medium height, and finally cleome and tall African marigolds and zinnias for background. Once the seeds germinate, you can transplant or thin; but in a display of this sort, a certain amount of crowding is permissible and even desirable. If one kind of seed doesn't germinate, spread out those from other sections to fill in its space.

Which are the easiest annuals to grow in a sunken garden? I prefer fragrant kinds. Ageratum, sweet-alyssum, calendula, centaurea, dianthus, four-o'clock, iberis, lobelia, dwarf marigold, nicotiana, petunia, phlox, portulaca, stock, torenia, nasturtium, viola, dwarf zinnias, if low-growing plants are desired, otherwise any variety.

Will you give me the names of a few unusual annuals, their heights and uses? Bells-of-Ireland (*Molucella laevis*), green, 24 inches; flower arrangements. Nemesia, various (except blues), 18 inches; edging, bedding. Nierembergia, lavender-blue, 12 inches; window boxes, edging. Nigella (love-in-a-mist), blue or white, 12 inches; bedding. Summer-poinsettia or Joseph's-coat (*Amaranthus*), colorful foliage, 2 to 4 feet; background.

What are the quickest-to-flower annuals that I can sow in patches (no transplanting) in my terrace garden? Sweet-alyssum; California-poppy; certain dwarf marigolds such as 'Lemondrop', 'Yellow Boy', 'Golden Boy'; annual phlox (*Phlox drummondii*); portulaca, annual baby's-breath. The phlox and baby's-breath may not last the summer; sweet-alyssum will need some shearing back to stimulate new flowering growth; and California-poppy seeds must be sown early for best germination.

Propagation

INDOOR

What are the basic requirements for starting seeds indoors? A sterile starting medium, adequate sunlight or fluorescent light, steady moisture, good air circulation, and suitable temperature.

What are the various methods of starting seeds indoors? Traditionally, seeds have always been started in flats or pots. However, today many other specially designed units are sold for the purpose to help simplify the process, especially for beginners. All are really just modifications of the traditional system. One such unit consists of a small plastic tray filled with a sterile planting medium (usually vermiculite and nutrients) plus seeds that adhere to the plastic cover. To activate the tray, all one does is to punch holes in special indentations in the cover to release the seeds and then add the specified quantity of water. Such a unit eliminates the handling of seeds, provides a sterile starting medium, spaces the seeds a reasonable distance apart, and helps to avoid the danger of over- or underwatering.

Other trays contain 6 or more compressed blocks of a special peat-based growing mixture in which one or two seeds per block are either presown or sown by the gardener. The unit is then watered.

Still another popular variant is the Jiffy-7, a flat peat-moss wafer when dry; but when moistened, it expands to form a small, filled pot in which a seed or seeds are sown. The wafers are usually placed side by side in a flat or other container. Large seeds can be sown one to a wafer and the plants that result are left to grow until ready to transplant outdoors. Small seeds are usually sown several to a pot or seed tray and transplanted once before being set outdoors.

Must I use a seed disinfectant? Yes, if you sow seeds indoors in untreated garden soil that may contain such fungus diseases as damping off.

What is a flat? A shallow, topless box (usually about 3 inches deep) with slits or holes in the bottom to allow for drainage of water from the soil. It is used for sowing seeds, inserting cuttings, etc. More shallow flats, usually of plastic, can be used without drainage holes if particular care is taken not to overwater. One disadvantage of a shallow flat is that it dries out quite quickly, but this size is better for window culture. Various discarded kitchen containers, such as aluminum foil pans, can also be used. Drainage holes can easily be punched in the bottom.

Is there any rule about the dimensions of flats? There is great variety in flat sizes. Usually they should be not less than 2½ inches or more than 4 inches deep. If more than 14 × 20 inches, they are likely to be too heavy to carry with comfort.

What soil mixture is preferable for seeds sown indoors? One part good garden loam, 1 part leafmold or peat moss, and 1 part sand, screened through a ¼-inch mesh screen; or half sand and half peat moss; or pure fine sand, vermiculite, or sphagnum moss watered with nutrient solution. The most convenient material is a prepared mix sold for this purpose and containing sufficient nutrients to carry sterile seedlings through until transplanting time.

What is the procedure in raising seedlings in sand with the aid of nutrient solutions? Take a flat 3 to 4 inches deep, with provision holes, and fill with clean sand. Soak it with water, then with the nutrient solution (liquid fertilizer) diluted 1 part to 5 parts water. Sow seeds thinly; cover with sand; firm well. Keep the sand moist with the dilute solution. When the seedlings have made true leaves, use equal parts of nutrient solution and water.

How do I go about sowing seeds of annuals indoors in a flat? Cover the drainage holes in containers with moss or pieces of broken flowerpot; follow with an inch of flaky leafmold, moss, or screenings; fill with screened (¼-inch mesh) soil mixture; press down level and sow the seeds. If you prefer, use a prepared mix sold for this purpose. Garden centers carry several kinds.

How deep should seeds be planted in flats and pots indoors? How deep in rows outdoors? Indoors, very small seeds are merely firmly pressed into the soil with a tamper, or covered with a dusting of fine soil, sand, or vermiculite; medium-sized seeds are covered ⅛ to ¼ inch; large seeds, about 3 times their diameter. Outdoors, seeds are customarily covered a little deeper.

What is a tamper? An oblong piece of board with a handle attached (similar to a mason's float) for tamping soil firmly in flats. For use in pots or bulb pans, the base of a tumbler or flowerpot can be used.

Is it better to scatter the seeds or to sow them in rows? When flats are used, it is preferable to sow in rows. You can judge germination better, cultivate lightly without danger of harming seedlings, and transplant with more ease. When pots are used, seeds are generally scattered evenly and thinly.

How can very small seeds be sown evenly? Mix thoroughly with sand before sowing. Hold the seed packet between your thumb and forefinger and tap gently with your forefinger to distribute the seed.

When starting seeds in the house in the winter, what do you put in the soil so that plants will be short and stocky, not tall and spindly? No treatment of the soil will prevent this. Good light, moderate temperature, and avoidance of overcrowding are the preventives. Turn the pots daily to keep the plants from "drawing" to the light. If your windows supply insufficient light, use fluorescent lights.

When should seeds for annuals be planted in seed flats in the spring? Mid-March usually is soon enough, in the North especially, if raised under space limitations. Allow from 6 to 8 weeks before it is safe to plant the seedlings outside.

What fluorescent unit is best for starting seeds under fluorescent lights? The most commonly sold unit consists of two 20-watt fluorescent tubes 2 feet long. This will usually grow most seedlings satisfactorily until they reach a sufficient size for planting outdoors. However, for superior results and for flowering of many annuals and house plants indoors, use a larger unit. The most popular setup is a unit consisting of four 40-watt fluorescent tubes 4 feet long. The light unit should be adjustable so that it can be raised or lowered according to the needs of the plants. When plants are small, the lights are set about 3 inches above them and then gradually raised as the plants grow. If the plants show signs of burning, the lights should be raised.

Are there any good books giving detailed information on raising both indoor and outdoor plants under lights? There are several helpful books. They are *The Indoor Light Gardening Book,* by George A. Elbert (Crown Publishers, Inc.); Gardening Under Lights (Time Life Books); and *Gardening Under Artificial Light* (Brooklyn Botanic Garden, 100 Washington Avenue, Brooklyn, New York 11225).

Are fluorescent lights left on constantly or should the plants have a dark period? For growing seedlings, the lights are generally left on from 14 to 16 hours. This should be during the day. A time clock is a great convenience in turning the lights on and off.

What are the advantages of growing seedlings under fluorescent light as compared to growing them in a sunny window? The lights give a steady supply of light at all seasons, whereas in a window there will be cloudy days and in winter the light intensity is low and the duration of the light period is short.

How should seed flats be watered after the seed is sown? Water thoroughly after seeding with a fine overhead spray from a watering can or a bulb-type or mist sprinkler until the soil is saturated. Subsequently, water when the surface soil shows signs of dryness. Do not overwater or permit the flat to dry out. (See the following question.)

Can seed flats be watered by standing them in a container of water? Yes, if more convenient. Do not leave in water any longer than necessary for moisture to show on the surface. Do not submerge the flat so water washes in and displaces the seeds; place in water about 1 inch deep. Many growers prefer this method to watering the surface, as there is less danger of washing out fine seeds.

I have tried starting annuals indoors but without much success. Is there some trick about watering, or soil, that I should know? I've always bought good seeds. The soil for seeds should be porous. A mixture of equal parts of loam, peat moss, and sand is good, but you might have better success with the prepared soilless mixes sold for this purpose. These are sterile and don't carry such soil-borne diseases as damping off, which can kill your seedlings. Keep the medium just moist, but not sodden. Sometimes poor germination comes from covering seeds too deeply. Sow them no deeper than twice their diameter.

Why do my seedlings, grown in the house, grow to about an inch, bend over, and die? Damping off, a fungus disease. Prevent it by disinfecting seeds with benomyl or Rootone, thin seeding, not overwatering, and giving seedlings fresh air without drafts. It can be virtually eliminated if you use the sterile soilless mixes.

The seedlings in my seed flat get very tall and leggy, and very light in color. Why? Seedlings in this condition are said to be "drawn." The causes are insufficient light and too-high temperature. Overcrowding may result in insufficient light. Grow them under fluorescent lights.

What is the best germinating temperature for annual nicotiana and annual gaillardias? I have planted both late in the spring with dubious results. Must they have a cooler temperature to start? Indoors in the spring, a night temperature between 50° and 55° F. is suitable. The fine seeds should be barely covered and in fact need light for adequate germination. Annual gaillardia germinates well outside in late May or early June. Self-sown nicotianas often germinate in early June, but are a bit late for best effect in most northern regions.

What is the proper time to plant indoors seeds of pansy, petunia, and

other annuals that should be started early but not too soon, as we often have frost here in May? (New Hampshire.) Pansies can be sown inside in January, but the best plants for spring display come from seed sown in July or August. The pansy can stand some frost; March is a good time to sow petunias for good plants that can be set out as soon as the weather is warm enough.

How can I start seedlings indoors so as to prevent too-rapid growth and decay? When shall I plant outdoors? Too-high temperatures and too early a start often account for the conditions described. Few plants need to be started indoors around New York before March, except for begonia, periwinkle, and a few others. Most of these are ready for planting outdoors in late April or early May.

How do you make new plants blossom early in the spring? There is not much that can be done to make them bloom early unless they are forced in a greenhouse. Most plants have to reach a certain age before they will flower.

Among annuals and plants treated as annuals, which ones take the longest time to come into flower in the North and therefore should be started indoors under fluorescent lights? Ageratum, wax begonia (*Begonia semperflorens*), snapdragon, petunia, lobelia, impatiens, nicotiana, salpiglossis, blue and red salvia, verbena, Madagascar periwinkle (*Catharanthus roseus,* formerly *Vinca rosea*), coleus, torenia, tithonia, nierembergera.

OUTDOOR PROPAGATION

What should the temperature be before planting annuals in the garden? (New York.) There can be no set temperature figure. Hardy annuals can be seeded as soon as the ground is ready to work; half-hardy annuals, about 4 weeks later; tender ones, when all danger of frost is past for the region. In and around New York, this is usually during the second week in May.

How early can annuals be planted in the Philadelphia, Pennsylvania, area? Hardy annuals, late March to April 1; half-hardy kinds, mid- to late April; tender kinds, from the first week in May to the end of the month.

I have purchased a self-ventilating cold frame. When can I sow annual seeds in it? These solar-powered frames usually open automatically when the temperature reaches around 70° F. and close when it drops to 68° F. In most northern areas, hardy annuals can be sown in

March, half-hardy annuals in April, and tender annuals a few weeks later.

What does this mean: "Sow seeds when the maple leaves are expanding"?   The unfolding of the maple leaves in the spring indicates that the season has sufficiently advanced for the gardener to sow certain hardier seeds outdoors.

How does one sow seeds of annuals in patches outdoors?   Fork over the soil, then rake the surface to break lumps and remove large stones. If the seeds are small (sweet-alyssum, petunia, portulaca), scatter evenly and pat down the soil. For medium-sized seeds, rake the soil again lightly *after* sowing and pat down. For seeds that have to be covered ¼ inch or more, scrape off the soil to the required depth, sow the seeds, and return the soil that was removed or cover the rows with fine vermiculite.

English sparrows take dust baths in my newly planted seed patches. How can I prevent this?   Lay pieces of burlap or of fine brush over the seeded areas. Remove when the seeds have germinated. Keep the seed bed constantly moist.

What is the best method of ensuring germination of small flower seeds in a heavy clay soil which consists mostly of subsoil due to excavation for a house? It grows plants very well once they get started.   Hoe out rows 2 inches wide and deep, fill with good screened compost, and sow the seeds in that. Before sowing, work in a generous amount of peat moss, sifted compost, or rotted manure, if possible, to improve the general texture of the soil.

Which annual seeds are suitable for autumn planting?   Larkspur, annual poppy, California-poppy, gilia, sweet pea, portulaca, nicotiana, salvia, celosia, cleome, sweet-alyssum, centaurea, petunia, coreopsis, kochia, euphorbia, balsam, cosmos, candytuft. They must be sown sufficiently late so that they will not germinate before freezing weather.

Can larkspur, centaurea, and other seeds that are recommended for planting in the fall be planted in February? (Maryland.)   Seeds of these plants can be sown outdoors just as soon as the soil is dry enough to work in the spring. For a broad naturalistic effect, the seed can be scattered in February even if the ground is not ready to be raked.

Is it advisable to sow seeds of cosmos, zinnias, and marigolds in late autumn, so that they can germinate the first warm days of spring?   They won't germinate until the soil is warm—considerably later than the "first warm days of spring," so you won't gain any time with these particular annuals.

How late is "late" when we are told to plant seed in late autumn? Usually about the average time of killing frost. Some seeds (sweet peas and other hardy annuals) can be sown after the frost, provided the ground is not frozen.

Is it necessary to prepare the soil for seed planted in the fall? For best results, yes. However, for an informal garden, seeds can be scattered on lightly raked-over soil.

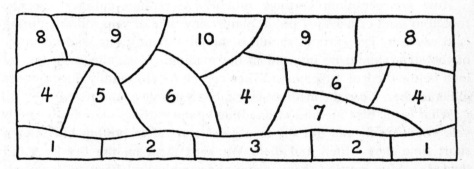

Plan for a rectangular garden of annuals. Such a garden can be adapted to any site and shape, but should receive full sun for best results. Plants can be purchased or seeds can be sown in place and transplanted or thinned as necessary. A third choice is to sow seeds in a special seed bed and then transplant the seedlings later. (1, 3) Dwarf or French marigolds; (2) sweet-alyssum; (4) petunias; (5, 7) 'Peter Pan' zinnias (different colors in each bed); (6) triploid marigolds; (8) 'Golden Triumph' plume celosia; (9) 'Primrose' or 'Yellow' Climax-type African marigold; (10) 'Sensation' cosmos.

Which flower seeds should be sown where they are to grow because of difficulty in transplanting? Poppy, annual larkspur, calendula, California-poppy, nasturtium, dwarf lupine, portulaca, mignonette, Virginia stocks.

If such plants as petunia, phlox, etc., are permitted to self-seed, is there a true-to-original-color reproduction? Not usually. Impatiens seeds self-sow and often produce very clear colors, many of which resemble their parent.

CUTTINGS

How are plants like snapdragon, petunia, verbena, and other annuals started as cuttings from the original plant? These may be rooted if short side shoots, 3 to 4 inches long, are placed in sand in a closed container in July and August. If the shoots have flower buds, these should be pinched off. Or the slips (or cuttings) can be taken in the fall and through the winter from plants potted up from the garden and brought indoors.

Why does coleus wilt so badly when I try to start new cuttings in soil?   The air around the cuttings is too dry. Cover them with a preserving jar or polyethylene bag until they have formed roots. Trim large leaves back one half.

How are geranium cuttings rooted?   Geranium cuttings may be rooted in sand or a Jiffy-7 pot at almost any time of year indoors during cold weather. The cuttings should be about 4 inches long, and about ⅓ of the stem should be inserted in the medium. Make the basal cut ¼ inch below the leaf attachment. They can be rooted readily out-of-doors in September. Keep the medium moist, but not soggy.

What is the best method of handling latana cuttings—our cuttings this year rooted well and got off to a good start after potting but after a short time they wilted and died. We kept them on the dry side and shaded.   After potting them, water thoroughly and keep in a closed, shaded propagating case for a week or two. Then gradually admit more air and remove the shade.

TRANSPLANTING

When should flat-raised seedlings be transplanted? How many times?   First, transplanting should be done when the seedlings have formed their first true leaves. Many plants, when they are 2 or 3 inches high, benefit from a second transplanting to individual pots before they are moved outdoors. However, seedlings grown in flats can be thinned and the remaining plants allowed to grow in the original tray or flat until they are ready to go outdoors. They may need a light feeding before being set in the garden.

What is the best mixture of soil for transplanting seedlings from flats to pots or to the cold frame?   Four parts garden soil (2 parts sand if the soil is excessively clayey), 2 parts peat moss, 1½ parts dried manure or compost, and ½ cup of 5–10–5 to each peck of the mixture. Mix all ingredients well. Or use one of the soilless mixes, which can be purchased at local garden centers, and follow fertilizer recommendations on the container.

What annuals do you recommend as foliage plants for use in arrangements?   Castor-bean; sideritis, gray; coleus, variegated; prickly-poppy, white-veined foliage; *Amaranthus tricolor,* variegated; snow-in-summer, white and green; dusty miller, gray.

What are the best tall annuals for background planting? Amaranthus, celosia, cleome, cosmos, datura, larkspur, marigolds (tall varieties), salvia, tithonia, snapdragons (tall varieties), zinnias (tall varieties).

I have difficulty in removing annuals from flats without ruining their root systems. Any pointers? Water thoroughly a few hours before transplanting. With an old knife or a small mason's trowel, cut the soil into squares, each with a plant in the center. The plants can easily be removed with their root systems almost intact. Annuals that have been grown individually in peat pots can be left in the pots when planting so that the pot and the plant are set out as one unit. However, it is advisable to break the pot in a few places to help the roots penetrate into the soil more readily. Be sure to set the top edge of the pot below the soil level or it will act as a sponge, drawing water, which will quickly evaporate, from the soil; the plant can suffer. Water thoroughly after planting and as necessary thereafter until the plant roots have penetrated through the pot into the soil.

What is the right technique in setting out annual plants? Remove the plants from the flats with as little root disturbance as possible. Stab the trowel in the soil, pull toward you, set the plant in the hole, remove the trowel, push the soil around the roots, press the soil firmly, and leave a slight depression around the stem to trap water.

How does one "thin out" seedlings? Choose cloudy weather when the soil is moist and spread the operation over 2 to 3 weeks or as necessary as the plants develop. Pull up the weakest seedlings before they crowd each other, leaving 2 to 6 inches between those remaining, according to their ultimate size. When those left begin to touch, again remove the weakest, leaving the remainder standing at the required distance apart.

How much space should be given annuals when thinning them or planting them out? The distance varies according to the variety and habit of growth. A rough rule is a distance equal to one half their mature height. Swan-river-daisy, Virginia stock, and similar weak growers, 4 inches; marigold, Shirley poppy, etc., 1 foot; strong growers, such as spider-flower and sunflower, 2 to 3 feet.

When can seedlings raised indoors be transplanted into the open? Hardy annuals, as soon as they are large enough. Tender annuals, when all danger of frost is past. First, harden them off by placing them in a cold frame or protected spot for several hours each day, increasing their time in the open until they are adjusted.

General Culture

Is it wrong to plant the same kind of annuals in the same space year after year?   As long as the soil is well dug each year and the humus content maintained, there is nothing wrong with the practice. However, China-asters, snapdragons, and marigolds may well be changed each year to avoid soil-borne problems.

What type of soil and what fertilizing programs are best for annuals?   Most annual flowers do best in a well-drained, rather light soil in full sun. Unless it is really run-down and deficient in plant nutrients, only a light annual application of rotted manure, peat moss, and/or compost, plus some standard commercial fertilizer, is advisable.

What is the best fertilizer for annual and perennial flower beds?   For most annuals and perennials, a 4–12–4 or 5–10–5 fertilizer is satisfactory.

How deep should the soil be prepared for annuals?   Nine inches for good results. Some growers go twice this depth to assure maximum growth.

Do popular annuals have decided preferences for acid or alkaline soil?   Most popular garden flowers tolerate either a slightly acid or alkaline condition and thrive in a neutral soil.

My 3-year-old garden is on a slight slope and has sun all day. The first year, cosmos and pinks did fine. Now everything dwindles and dies. Even petunias won't grow. What can I do?   Dig deeply and add a 3-inch layer of well-rotted manure, compost, or peat moss. Set the plants as early as you can, depending upon your conditions. A sloping site and a hot sun are not conducive to good growth because of the moisture conditions. Get moisture down around the roots of the plants; keep a heavy mulch of partly decayed leaves, grass clippings, or other material over the soil in the summer.

How shall I top annuals to make them bushy? What does one do— pinch them or cut them with a knife or scissors?   Pinch out no more than the growing point with your thumbnail and index finger, if possible, so as to avoid wasted energy on the part of the plant.

What is meant by "pinching back"?   Pinching back is the removal of the tip of a growing shoot to induce branching.

Which annuals and at what stage should they be pinched back for better growth and more flowers?   These annuals can be pinched to advantage when they are from 2 to 4 inches high: ageratum, snapdragon, carnation, cosmos, nemesia, petunia, phlox, salvia, schizanthus, marigold, and verbena. Straggly plants of sweet-alyssum can be sheared back in midsummer for better growth and to induce flowering later in the season.

Is it true that if flowers are picked they bloom better?   On plants that continue to make flowering growth, it is best to pick off flowers as soon as they fade to prevent the formation of seed, which is a drain on the plant's energy.

What would cause annuals to grow well but come into bud so late in the summer that they are of little use? The seed was planted late in April.   Most annuals are blooming at midsummer from April-sown seed. Lobelia, scarlet sage, torenia, and tithonia are examples that should be sown indoors in March for good results. The late, older varieties of cosmos usually do not have time to flower in the North, even if sown early indoors. Did you fertilize heavily? This could cause strong leaf growth at the expense of the flowers.

Why do I have to stake so many plants—zinnia, marigold, and other common plants? They grow fine and bloom generously, yet if not tied, they do not stay erect.   Insufficient phosphorus in the soil; or perhaps they are exposed to too much wind; or heavy rains could have beaten them down. Full sun all day helps produce sturdy plants.

Most of our annuals cease blooming about August, leaving few flowers for fall. Is there any way we can renew our plantings so that flowers are available until late in the season?   There are numerous annuals which, sown in the summer, will provide bloom right up until the frost. These are browallia, calendula, celosia, and the little fine-leaved marigold (*Tagetes signata pumila*), sweet-alyssum, *Torenia fournieri*, verbena, and all types of zinnias. The dates for sowing must be closely adhered to. These apply to the vicinity of New York City and so would suit a rather large region. The date of the first killing frost in fall must be allowed for in the more northerly section. With care, seeds can be sown outdoors and seedlings transplanted directly to their flowering quarters, or potted up and held over and used as needed. The latter plan is better for torenia and browallia. Sow these the first week in June; transplant to 3-inch pots. At the same time sow celosia, nicotiana, dwarf scabiosa, and tall marigolds. The third week in June sow California-poppy (sow where it is to bloom or in pots), globeflower, candytuft, *Phlox drummondii,* and marigold. None of the above will grow to the size of spring-sown plants. The last week in June to the first week in July sow calendulas, sweet-alyssum, and zinnias of all types. Sweet-alyssum, calendula, and verbena will survive light frosts.

How long is it from the planting of seed to the cutting of flowers on China-asters, stock, snapdragons? The length of time required will vary according to the type and variety, the time of year, and conditions under which grown. Early varieties of either might be ready in 14 to 16 weeks. Snapdragons will be bushier if pinched when they are about 3 inches high, but pinching delays flowering.

How can I save the seed from annual flowers? Select healthy plants of the best type and allow the seeds to mature on the plant; but gather them before they are shed, then dry in an airy, rainproof place that is safe from mice.

Will seed from hybrid annuals flower the following year; if so, will they come true? Seeds of annual hybrids saved one year should give flowers the next. Some may come close to true (resemble their parents), but wide variation will more likely result.

I have looked and looked for the answer to this question and haven't found it yet. When different shades of the same flower are planted together, which ones may I save seeds from and have them come true to their parent? Which ones not? You don't have much chance of getting seed which would come true from any of them.

Do the following come up without replanting: bergamot, ageratum, four-o'clocks, sweet-alyssum, morning-glories, moonflowers? Of this group, only bergamot is a perennial; this will come up each year. All the others are annuals. They come up from the seeds dropped from the plants the previous year. However, to be on the safe side, it is best to sow seeds each spring.

Specific Annual Plants

AGERATUM

How is ageratum started for outdoor planting? Sow seeds indoors in March or outdoors early in May when the danger of frost is past. The best method is to sow them in seed pans or small pots of fine-screened soil or a sterile soilless mix available at garden centers. Sow on a level surface and press the seeds in. Set the pan in water until moisture shows on the surface; cover with glass or polyethylene and shade; remove when germinated; transplant 2 inches apart when the first true leaves show, and grow under fluorescent lights or in a sunny window.

What is the proper care of ageratums during the winter? Young plants, started late in the season, may flower as house plants during late winter. Cuttings are taken from the young growth in September and rooted in sand.

ALYSSUM, SWEET-

Why does white sweet-alyssum come up year after year when purple varieties don't? The white alyssum reseeds itself prolifically, but the purple varieties are not as vigorous and are of more complex parentage.

ARCTOTIS (AFRICAN-DAISY)

I would appreciate instructions for success with African-daisies (arctotis). Mine achieve the bud state but never blossom, falling off at that point. Can it be too much water, or are they perhaps pot-bound? (Kentucky.) Dropping of buds can be caused by extremes. Too much moisture around the roots or their dying out; warm, humid conditions or a sudden chill. Use superphosphate for fertilizer; have the soil open and well drained. Don't plant in very large pots. Give them full sun.

ASTER, CHINA- (CALLISTEPHUS)

How can I grow annual asters? Select wilt-resistant seed. Plant indoors in flats or pots in late March or April; transplant into the open when the danger of frost is past. Or sow seed outdoors in May. Select "early," "midseason," and "late" varieties for continuous bloom. If in a region where aster "yellows" (a virus disease) is prevalent, grow under cheesecloth screens to prevent the leafhopper that spreads the virus from reaching the plants.

What culture do asters require? Prepare the seed bed by forking over the soil and working in peat moss or leafmold. Make drills 2 to 3 inches apart and ¼ inch deep; sow seeds, 6 or 8 per inch, about mid-May. Cover with a half-soil, half-sand mixture, and water with a fine spray. A light covering with hay or strips of burlap will help retain moisture until germination; then remove immediately. Keep the seedlings watered. Transplant when the seedlings have formed their first true leaves. Soak the soil a few hours before, lift the seedlings with all the roots, and keep them moist. If wanted for cut flowers, set in rows 18 inches apart, the plants 9 to 12 inches apart in the rows. Set the seedlings in the soil so that the bottom leaves are resting on the surface. Give a good watering; keep the soil cultivated until the plants get large or apply a mulch. Enrich the soil prior to planting by digging in 3 inches of rotted manure; or use compost or peat moss mixed with dried manure—6 pounds manure to 1 pound compost or peat moss. When flowers show, feed with liquid fertilizer weekly.

We have China-asters. Do they reseed themselves? (New York.) Yes, occasionally, especially the single-flowered kinds. However, it is better to raise new plants under controlled conditions annually.

Is it true that asters cannot be planted in the same space a second year? No—not literally. Asters can be grown in the same spot by using disease-resistant strains, by disinfecting the seeds, by mixing tobacco powder, diazinon, or malathion with the soil to discourage root aphids, and by screening with cheesecloth to keep out leafhoppers, which transmit the virus disease known as aster yellows.

What is the best procedure in disbudding asters? Should the tops be pinched out when they are young to make them branch? Asters usually are self-branching, producing a number of branches, and do not need pinching. Each branch will bear a terminal flower, together with numerous other buds on small side shoots. All these must be removed, retaining the main bud only.

Do annual asters come true from seed collected from a flower bed? Variation can be expected, especially if several varieties are growing together.

BALSAM (IMPATIENS BALSAMINA)

Is balsam worth growing? Yes, especially for positions in partial shade. Try the camellia-flowered double strains on bushy, branching plants.

BELLS-OF-IRELAND

How are the seeds of bells-of-Ireland germinated? Mine don't come up. Sow in a carefully prepared cold frame in May when the soil has warmed up. Keep constantly moist until germination. Transplant to garden beds in late June.

My bells-of-Ireland don't look like the ones in the flower-show arrangement. Why? Flowering stems are "groomed" by removing all the foliage, leaving only the bell-like bracts with the little flower "clappers" in the center of each.

BROWALLIA

When should browallia be sown for outdoor flowers? Which varieties should I use? For early flowering, sow in late March indoors, or in a cold frame after mid-April. Outdoor sowing can be done about mid-May. These dates apply in the vicinity of New York City; farther north it would be 7 to 12 days later and correspondingly earlier farther south. *Browallia americana* and *B. speciosa* are the best for summer.

What is the method of growing browallia for the house? What is the best variety to choose for this? Sow seeds in August; transplant into 2½-inch pots; as the plants grow, shift to 4-inch pots, then perhaps to 5-inch pots, but don't overpot; water sparingly after November. Sow again in January for early-spring bloom. Use *Browallia speciosa*.

CABBAGE, FLOWERING

On a visit to Mystic Seaport in Connecticut, I was impressed by a display of chrysanthemums and bright-colored foliage plants I was told were flowering cabbages. Can I grow them? Most seed catalogs offer the seed (there is also an ornamental kale), which can be sown in late spring or early summer so that the plants reach maturity in the fall when the foliage color is most brilliant. Their culture is the same as for regular cabbage. Both ornamental cabbage and kale are edible.

CALENDULA

Can you tell me why my calendula or pot-marigold plants are so feeble? I sow them outdoors at the same time I sow marigold and zinnia

seeds, which do very well for me. Try sowing the calendula seeds earlier so that their roots become established during cool weather. Also, select varieties bred for heat resistance, such as 'Juliette' and any of the 'Pacific Beauty' strain.

CAMPANULA

Are annual Canterbury bells easy to raise from seed? Yes, annual types bloom in less than six months from seed, but you must start them early to get a good display in the North.

CANDYTUFT (IBERIS)

My annual candytuft bloomed only a short time, then died. Why? Annual candytuft blooms very quickly from seed but only for a short time. Plant seeds at 2- or 3-week intervals for constant bloom during cool spring and fall weather. Annual candytuft does not do well in the heat of summer.

CASTOR-BEAN (RICINUS)

Can you tell me about cultivation, and if there is a market for the bean? (Ohio.) Castor-bean plants grow best in a rich, well-drained soil. Seeds can be planted in May where they are to grow, or started earlier indoors and then set out later. There is a market for the seeds, of course, but it is well supplied by commercial growers. The commercial crop is produced in the South, where a long season allows for maximum production.

Is it advisable to plant castor-oil-bean seeds around lawns in order to prevent molehills and mole runs? Castor-bean plants have very little, if any, effect on the mole population.

Is there anything poisonous about the castor-bean plant? The seeds contain a poisonous principle called ricin. They are best planted where children cannot be tempted to eat the beans. Fatalities have been reported from eating as few as three seeds.

CLEOME

I have seen lovely pink and white spider-plants. Are they something special? 'Pink Queen' is a fine variety which won a silver medal for excellence. 'Helen Campbell' is a pure white. If your plants self-seed, pull up all purplish-red self-sown seedlings, that is, if you don't like this color.

COLEUS

Is it possible to raise coleus from seeds? Coleus are easily started from seeds sown any time indoors. Germination is rapid (in about 1 week) and plants are ready for transplanting in another 2 weeks. For pot-plant use, look for one of the low-growing types such as 'Carefree'.

Can coleus be rooted from cuttings? I have a favorite pink-leaved variety that I would like to increase. Coleus roots very readily. Stem cuttings 2 or 3 inches long can be rooted in water, sand, vermiculite, or a regular rooting mixture.

CORNFLOWER (CENTAUREA)

Why do our bachelor-buttons or cornflowers show retarded growth and weak flower stalks? Sow the seeds in a finely prepared soil in the fall or as soon as you can work the soil in spring. Sow thinly; cover about ¼ inch. Thin out the seedlings to 9 inches apart when they are large enough. Yours probably were too crowded or were sown too late in the spring.

What treatment do you prescribe for bachelor-buttons for large blossoms and a long period of bloom? You should get good results by giving them a moderately rich, well-drained soil and extra watering during dry weather. Keep faded flowers picked off. (See the preceding answer.)

COSMOS

When should early (Klondyke) cosmos be started from seeds? Sow seeds indoors 5 to 6 weeks before the date of the last frosts in your region. Or use a cold frame.

I like to grow cosmos. A pink plant blossomed in early July which seems very unusual to me. Why should this happen? The rest of my plants blossomed in the fall as usual. There are several forms of early-flowering cosmos, including pink varieties. The 'Sensation' type blooms in 8 to 10 weeks after the seed is sown. 'Candystripe' blooms two weeks earlier than 'Sensation'.

DAHLIA

Is it true that some dahlias flower the first year from seed?   Yes, especially the dwarf bedding dahlias like 'Redskin', an All-America winner. Many others are listed in seed catalogs.

DIANTHUS

What are the best annual pinks?   Look for forms of *Dianthus chinensis* such as 'China Doll', an All-America winner with double flowers in mixed colors; 'Merry-Go-Round', a pure white single with a scarlet center; 'Bravo', a red single; 'Gaiety', fringed petals in mixed colors; and 'Baby Doll', a dwarf single in mixed colors.

Dianthus 'Zing', although a perennial, starts to bloom a few weeks after sowing. Its flowers are single in brilliant scarlet. It is a *Dianthus deltoides* hybrid.

DIMORPHOTHECA (CAPE-MARIGOLD)

How long can dimorphotheca be expected to stay in bloom? The plants I had last summer bloomed from about June 1 to July 15 and then died.   Six weeks of bloom is about all you can expect, although the time might be lengthened somewhat by snipping off all withered blossoms to prevent seed formation. It is a good plan to make a second sowing of seed 4 to 6 weeks after the first sowing, to provide blooming plants for the second half of the summer.

What are the requirements for dimorphotheca? It never comes up. Can it be planted early? I buy good seed. (Washington.)   Sow the seed outdoors in the spring when the ground has warmed up, or indoors 4 to 6 weeks earlier. Give the plants light and well-drained (not specially enriched) soil. Be sure they get plenty of sun.

EVERLASTINGS (ANNUALS FOR DRYING)

I want to grow some everlastings for winter bouquets. What shall I select?   Globe amaranth; helichrysum; helipterum; statice; honesty; xeranthemum.

When should everlastings be cut for drying?   Cut when the flowers have just started to open. Dry in a well-ventilated room and store away from any dampness.

FOUR-O'CLOCK (MIRABILIS)

I have been told that you get larger bushes and a greater amount of flowers from four-o'clock roots the second season. Should they be left in the ground or dug up and dried like certain bulbs? (Missouri.) They are mostly used as annuals; the roots would be very unlikely to live through the winter outdoors in your region. The large, tuberous roots can be lifted before a hard frost and stored indoors for the winter, like dahlias. They will flower earlier and produce better bloom. Try it, but sow some seeds outdoors in May to be sure of a crop of flowers.

GLORIOSA DAISY (RUDBECKIA HIRTA)

I thought gloriosa daisies were perennial. My plants never seem to live through the winter. Although perennial by classification, these plants tend to exhaust themselves by their prodigious blooming and seed production (unless fading flowers are removed before seeds form).

GODETIA (SATIN FLOWER)

I have no luck with satin flower. Can you help me? These lovely, bushy, 18-inch annuals with their masses of hollyhock-like salmon, orange, pink, red, and lavender flowers, prefer partial shade and a cool, moist location. They thrive in regions with cool nights in a well-watered garden and cannot stand areas where the nights are hot and humid.

GOURDS See Section 10, The Home Vegetable Garden.

IMPATIENS

How much shade will impatiens endure? Quite a bit and probably as much as any annual. Good light and a few hours of sun are needed for the best flowers, though.

KOCHIA

I have heard of an annual which can be used instead of a real hedge. What is it? Burning bush or kochia. The rounded plants, like sheared evergreens, grow 3 feet tall. During hot weather, the foliage is light green, but in autumn it turns a rich red.

LARKSPUR (ANNUAL DELPHINIUM)

How early should larkspur be planted? (Virginia.) As early in the spring as the ground becomes workable, or in late fall about November.

What month is the best to plant larkspur and ragged-robin? (Virginia.) Larkspur and ragged-robin (*Lychnis*) can be sown in November for spring bloom, or as early in spring as possible.

Will larkspur do well if they are transplanted? It transplants very poorly; sow the seeds where the plants will flower, and thin out the seedlings to 9 inches.

What is the secret for successful larkspur? Ours start well but fade away before flowering. The secret is an early start—about the time you sow peas. Sow seeds in well-drained, moderately fertile soil, in full sun or light shade. (See the preceding answers.)

LOBELIA

Will lobelia grow in partial shade? Yes, the low-growing varieties are ideal for window and porch boxes or hanging baskets, as well as for partly shaded edgings around terraces. Choose trailing varieties for boxes and dwarf varieties for edgings.

MARIGOLD (TAGETES)

What types of marigolds do you suggest for an all-marigold garden? African tall, double including carnation-flowered, chrysanthemum-flowered, dahlia-flowered, peony-flowered; French single; French double; dwarf 'Signet'.

What large-flowered, tall marigolds shall I grow for variety in color? 'Primrose Climax', pale yellow; 'Yellow Climax', bright yellow; 'Toreador', orange; 'Golden Climax', gold; 'Burpee's First Whites'.

Would you kindly tell me why my marigolds didn't blossom well last

summer? Could it be the fault of the ground? It may have been any one, or several, of a number of reasons: too late sowing; too much rain; too-heavy or too-rich soil; pest and disease attacks; insufficient sun; overfeeding or overwatering. Also, some dwarf varieties simply stop flowering in excessively hot weather.

Are seeds good which have not been picked until after a killing frost, such as marigolds? The first killing frost would not be severe enough to harm the seeds.

NASTURTIUMS (TROPAEOLUM)

What nasturtiums shall I grow to produce seeds for pickles and salads? What shall I do to keep them free of little black bugs? The old-fashioned singles, either dwarf or tall. The much more beautiful and attractive sweet-scented doubles produce few seeds. Keep young plants sprayed with malathion to kill aphids.

NICOTIANA (FLOWERING TOBACCO)

I have seen flowering tobacco in mixed colors. What variety is this? 'Sensation Mixed' is about 32 inches tall. 'Crimson Bedder' is deep red, 12 inches tall. There is also a lime-green variety, 'Lime Sherbet', that grows 16 inches tall. A dwarf red, 'Idol', only 8 to 10 inches tall, and 'Nicki Red', 16 inches tall, look well with 'White Bedder', 12 inches tall. All are delightfully fragrant and will grow in light shade.

NIEREMBERGIA

How shall I grow nierembergia from seed? Start indoors in February or early March for early bloom.

PERIWINKLE

How and where shall I plant the annual periwinkle? Periwinkle (*Catharanthus roseus,* formerly *Vinca rosea*) is a native of the tropics and practically everblooming. Sow seeds in January in a warm temperature in the North. The seeds are sometimes difficult to germinate, and at first the seedlings are slow-growing. Have the soil well drained and don't overwater. When these seedlings produce the first true leaves, transplant to 2¼-inch pots, later to 3-inch pots. From these, transplant to the open ground when all danger of cold weather is past. Provide a fairly rich soil. Once established, they need little care beyond watering occasionally.

PETUNIA

Can petunias be grown successfully with only 4 hours of afternoon sun?   Yes, provided other conditions are suitable.

How can I prepare a seed bed for petunias? When shall I plant in the St. Louis area?   Have the soil well drained, moderately rich, and very thoroughly cultivated so that its texture is fine and light. Sow thinly in the spring when the soil is in good workable condition. You will get flowers sooner if you start the seeds indoors under fluorescent lights.

When is the best time to plant petunias? In what soil? (New York.)   The new hybrid petunias are best started indoors in March in the vicinity of New York. (See Propagation Indoors, this section.)

When is the best time, and what is the best way, to plant petunia seed? (Alabama.)   In your region, outdoor sowing of petunia seed is likely to be the most satisfactory. It can be done as soon as the soil has warmed up in the spring. Have the soil finely prepared and it should barely cover the seed.

Can petunias be sown in the fall? (Ohio.)   Fall-planted petunia seeds sometimes live through the winter and germinate in the spring—this depends chiefly on climate, location, and the character of the winter. Spring sowing is preferable in the middle and northern sections of the country.

How long does it take petunia seeds to germinate, and when should one transplant them?   Good petunia seeds sown on prepared soil, only lightly covered and kept at 65° to 70° F., should germinate in 8 to 12 days. Transplant when the first *true* leaves appear. (The leaves that show at germination are only seed leaves.) This might be approximately 10 to 14 days after germination.

Should petunias always be transplanted or will they bloom well where they were originally planted?   If the soil and other conditions are favorable, they should do well where originally planted. But thin the seedlings to 6 inches or so apart if they come up thickly.

I set out petunias in my garden with partial shade when they had just begun to bloom; the plants withered and died until 90 per cent were

Good companions: Petunias and ageratum.

gone. **A soil analysis said that nothing was wrong. Gladiolus did well in the same bed. What was wrong?** Perhaps root injury when being transplanted, plus too much or too little water. Petunias will stand some shade but not too much.

I'd like a mass of petunias for borders but have no success growing from seed. How can this be done? (Connecticut.) Petunia seed for a mass planting is best sown as soon as the soil has warmed up. Have the soil very thoroughly pulverized and it should barely cover the seed. Keep watered and thin out the plants to 6 or 8 inches apart when they are a couple of inches tall. For earlier bloom, start the seed in flats indoors in March and transplant outdoors early in May. If you have no success sowing seeds, try one of the preplanted seed trays such as Punch 'N' Grow. Or buy seedling plants at your local garden center.

Is there any way to prevent petunias from growing lank during late summer? I keep seed pods picked off pretty well, but they look straggly by August. This tendency is hard to prevent in some varieties unless the flowers are cut quite often; prune back the longer stems to encourage stockiness. Use compact-growing kinds.

Why can't I raise petunias? They are the only plants with which I am not successful. I buy good seed but the plants that grow just get tall (leggy), with very small blooms. This is a hard question to answer without more information. The plants may be too crowded or the soil may be too heavy and shaded. Try careful thinning and pinching back young plants.

Why can't I raise any petunias? They come up but die. Perhaps the soil is too heavy and claylike, or it may be too wet. A light, well-drained soil in practically full sun is best, and it should be only moderately rich.

What makes petunia plants turn yellow, especially if grown 2 years in succession in the same soil?   Petunias are subject to several virus diseases that discolor the leaves. The condition may also be due to a highly alkaline soil. Dig in peat moss or leafmold, change the location, and prepare the soil deeply.

Why do petunia plants grow large but have no blooms?   The soil was probably too rich, thereby forcing excessive stem and leaf growth at the expense of blooms. Try them in another place where the soil is poorer. Don't overwater.

Can you explain how to snip off a petunia plant (brought in from outdoors) so that it will have many blooms instead of spindly stems?   Cut back about half of the stems to 4 or 5 inches. When these have developed new growth, cut back the remaining stems in the same way. Grow under fluorescent lights if you don't have a sunny window.

Can I grow petunias indoors as house plants?   Yes, if you can grow them under fluorescent lights about 16 hours a day. Poor flowering results when the plants are grown in windows, even south-facing ones, because there are so many cloudy days during the winter. Petunias need plenty of light and a cool temperature at night. You can sow seeds during the summer for indoor bloom or take cuttings. Or you might try digging up old plants in the fall, cutting them back, and planting in 4- to 5-inch pots.

Will petunias reseed successfully? (Indiana.)   Sometimes they will; it depends on the conditions. The more common kinds reseed freely, but the colors will be unsatisfactory. For good petunias, secure good seed each year.

How can I root cuttings from double petunias?   If the plants are growing indoors, take the cuttings in August or September. Select young growths about 2 inches in length that grow from the older stems. Trim off the bottom leaves and insert them ½ to 1 inch deep in pure, moist sand in a cold frame in a warm atmosphere. Shade and keep the sash on for about a week. Give light when they are rooting; this will be indicated by the foliage remaining erect. Keep the sand moist.

How can I root petunia cuttings in winter?   About February, take young side growths, trim off the lower leaves, and set them firmly in moist sand or vermiculite in a propagating box. (See the previous questions.)

Dwarf compact annuals, such as petunias, are useful for the foreground of mixed borders and for edgings along patios or walks.

Which kind of petunias shall I get to grow against a small white fence? I prefer something not tall, but rather bushy. Choose your favorite colors in the hybrid multiflora and grandiflora classes.

What type of petunia is best for all-summer beauty? Multiflora and grandiflora types are generally the most satisfactory.

POPPY

Do California-poppies (Eschscholtzia californica) and Shirley poppies (Papaver rhoeas) reseed themselves? Yes, usually, but much digging of the soil in the spot where reseeding took place will bury the seed so deeply that it may not germinate.

When is the best time to plant the Shirley poppy? Can it be successfully planted on top of the snow? (Kansas.) If in your region the

Garden centers and local nurseries offer well-developed, often flowering, annuals (usually called "bedding plants") in various kinds of containers—ready for quick planting. Be sure to water the plants thoroughly after setting out.

poppy usually reseeds itself and plants come voluntarily the following spring, you can very well sow on the snow. Otherwise, sow the seed just as early as you can get to the soil.

When is the correct time to plant poppy seed? How is it best sown? Just as early as you can work the ground in the spring. Rake the soil as fine as possible; make it level and firm it slightly; scatter the seeds thinly, press them firmly into the soil but don't cover. Thin out the seedlings when they are 2 inches high, spacing them 3 inches apart. Two weeks later, thin them again to 6 or 9 inches apart.

PORTULACA

How can I make portulaca germinate and grow? Portulaca is usually easy to grow from seed sown outdoors in either October or early spring. It should have a well-drained, light, but not rich soil, in full sun.

Does portulaca self-sow? Someone told me to let them go to seed and I'd have plenty of plants next year. They self-sow readily. Seedlings don't generally appear until fairly late in the spring after the soil has warmed. If they are crowded, they should be thinned or transplanted.

SALPIGLOSSIS

How can I grow large, healthy salpiglossis plants? (New Jersey.) Sow seeds in a well-prepared bed in May. Work peat moss or leafmold into the surface, sow the seeds thinly in rows 2 inches apart. Cover them not more than ⅛ inch deep. Transplant 12 inches apart in soil deeply dug and enriched with rotted manure or compost; or with peat moss mixed with dehydrated manure, 10 pounds to a bushel of peat, plus ½ pound of ground limestone. Spread an inch deep and dig in. Do not soak the soil until the plants are steadily growing and have some size. Cultivate frequently. When flower stalks form, feed with liquid fertilizer; or apply 5–10–5 or similar fertilizer. Hoe and water in; repeat every 2 weeks during bloom.

SALVIA

How do you start red salvia seeds? (South Dakota.) The seed should be sown indoors in a warm temperature, about the latter part of March, in small pots or seed pans. Cover the seeds ⅛ inch, and set the pot or pan in water until moisture shows on the surface. Cover with glass or polyethylene film and newspaper, but remove as soon as the seeds germinate.

Are there other colors of bedding salvia besides the red and blue? Yes. White, salmon-pink, purple, mahogany, and lilac. The blue salvia (*Salvia farinacea*) is a different species from the preceding and, though a perennial, it is better handled as an annual in cold climates. Sow seeds of blue salvia indoors in winter to get good-sized plants for the garden.

SCABIOSA

What is the best method of culture for scabiosa? (New Jersey.) Sow seeds outdoors about April 15 or indoors in March in the North. Give the plants a sunny position where the soil is rather light in texture, moderately rich, and in full sun. Do not cover the seeds deeply; not more than ⅛ inch. Transplant when the seedlings have made their first true leaves, setting them in the soil so that the lower leaves are resting on the surface. Set 9 inches apart each way.

SNAPDRAGON (ANTIRRHINUM)

Do snapdragons require a rich, shady place? (Idaho.) No shade. They should have full sun and a light, well-drained soil that is only moderately enriched. Early planting is desirable for best bloom.

What is the best fertilizer for snapdragons? Rotted or dehydrated manure or peat moss when preparing the soil, which should be neutral or slightly alkaline. Feed with liquid fertilizer when the plants come into flower, or give a dressing of complete chemical fertilizer such as 5–10–5.

Can snapdragon be sown in the fall? (Kentucky.) Yes, in your part of the country, but it must be done sufficiently early to provide young plants that will be large enough to withstand the winter with protection. Sow in August.

When shall I plant snapdragons? The best time to set young plants out is in the spring when the ground has begun to warm up. Seeds should be started indoors in March and grown under fluorescent tubes.

Are snapdragons strictly annuals? Mine bloomed after several frosts and continued in leaf. (Virginia.) No, in the South they are often treated as biennials or even perennials. Generally speaking, they are handled as hardy annuals (more cold-resistant than most). Botanically, they are perennials.

Must snapdragons be supported by stakes at planting time? Mine were all in curlicues and staking them after they were 8 or 10 inches tall didn't help at all. It is a good idea to put in the stakes at the time the young plants are set out, and start tying as soon as signs of flopping begin. Another method is to insert twigs 18 inches long among the plants. The growths will work up among the twigs. In an open situation, with proper care of the soil, they should not need much support. Some varieties are base-branching and require less staking.

Can you tell me how to grow snapdragons? I buy the plants and they bloom a little while, then die. (Mississippi.) Probably it is too warm or perhaps the soil is too rich, too heavy and claylike, or poorly drained. Or there may be too much shade. Snapdragons like an open situation, light soil, and not too much feeding. They dislike a hot situation and bloom best in cool weather.

How can I attain many-flowered snapdragons in my summer garden? I get good plants but there are many stems and few blooms to a stem. Thin out the weakest shoots, apply superphosphate and pulverized limestone to the soil at the rate of 8 ounces per square yard, and scratch into the surface. Full sunshine is necessary. Set out well-developed plants in early May.

Why can't I grow snapdragons from seed? They never come up. (Kentucky.) Sow in late April in a well-drained place where the soil is light and only moderately rich and has been raked into fine texture, free of stones and lumps. Cover the seed with sand not more than $1/8$ inch deep, and do not pack hard. Cover with burlap, which should be removed as soon as the seed germinates. Water regularly in dry weather. Disinfect the seed with Semesan before sowing. It's easier to sow such fine seeds indoors in pots or other containers and grow under fluorescent lights.

Can snapdragons be kept during the winter in a cold frame? (New York.) Yes, if they are less than 1 year old. Actually, these plants can be considered as biennials in the South, or in the North when cold-frame protection can be given during the winter.

How shall I protect snapdragons outdoors so that they survive sub-zero winters? (Kentucky.) Attempts to bring snapdragons through such winter weather outdoors often fail, whatever precautions you take. Try mulching with 3 or 4 inches of coarse straw or marsh or meadow hay after the ground freezes. A cold frame is about the only safe means of protection.

Are there such things as perennial snapdragons? No, from the practical gardening standpoint. Technically, they are all perennials, but in the North they are too tender to be treated as such.

What are the best snapdragons for the garden? I haven't had good luck with "snaps" recently. By all means get rust-resistant kinds. Select the colors you prefer from among the tall (3½ feet), medium (15 inches), and dwarf (7 inches) varieties listed in seed catalogs.

STOCKS

What causes stocks to mature without blooming? It may have been the common stock (*Matthiola incana*), which acts as a biennial and does not flower until the second year. 'Ten-weeks' and 'Trysomic Seven-weeks' stocks are annual and flower the first year if conditions are to their liking. They require cool growing weather and should be started in early spring.

Of 100 'Ten-weeks' stock plants in our garden, 20 of the smallest, most puny ones bloomed. The other 80 grew into beautifully thrifty plants from early summer until a hard freeze came, but did not bloom. Why? 'Ten-weeks' stocks usually fail to bloom if subjected to constantly high temperature—60° F. and over. Yours were grown under borderline conditions, enabling a few individuals to bloom. Next time, try the 'Trysomic Seven-week' stocks, which are more heat-tolerant.

How can I make stocks blooms? (New Jersey.) Buy 'Trysomic Seven-week' stock seed. Start indoors in March and set them outside late in April. This enables them to make their growth before hot weather comes.

Can stocks be wintered through? (Kansas.) Yes, if you have the biennial kind, *Matthiola incana,* and a mild, dryish winter climate. For the average gardener, this type is not worth trying or bothering with.

SWEET PEAS (LATHYRUS ODORATUS)

When is the best time to plant sweet peas? As early as the ground can be worked in the spring; or the seeds can be sown in a cold greenhouse or cold frame a month or more ahead of the time when frost can be expected to be out of the ground and then transplanted. Or sow one seed in an individual peat or Jiffy-7 pot and grow in a cool sunny window; or *after germination,* place under fluorescent tubes. Cool temperatures, about 50° F., are needed for germination and good growth.

When and how shall I plant sweet peas to ensure blooms? If you have a frost-free frame, you can sow the seed in September or October in a flat or in small pots, and in March transplant where the plants are to flower. Or if you have a cool porch or window (temperature not above 45° to 50° F.), you can sow in February, shift into pots, and, after hardening, plant out in late March. If there are no such facilities, sow where they are to flower as early in March as you can; prepare the ground the preceding fall. (See the preceding question.)

Can sweet pea seeds be sown in the fall for earlier and stronger plants in the spring? If so, at what time, and how deep? Sweet peas can be planted in the fall just before the ground freezes, putting them 4 inches deep and mulching lightly with straw or litter after hard freezing. It is doubtful, though, whether the plants would be appreciably earlier or finer than if they were spring-sown as soon as the ground could be worked.

Can sweet peas be planted in very early spring if the ground softens to a depth of 2 inches? No. Wait until all the frost is out; otherwise the soil will be too muddy to work.

What is the planting date for sweet peas in Oklahoma? Sow in November and give protection during the coldest part of winter; or sow in late winter, as soon as it is possible to work the soil.

How shall I prepare the ground for sweet peas for cut flowers? Dig a trench 1½ feet wide and deep. Mix with the soil a 3- to 4-inch layer of rotted manure or peat moss and compost, and bone meal or superphosphate at the rate of 1 pound to 10 to 15 linear feet. If possible, do this in the fall so the seeds can be planted without delay early in the spring.

I want sweet peas in clumps in a flower border. How do I go about it? Prepare the soil as described in the previous answer, except that instead of a long trench, you should make circular planting stations 2 to 3 feet in diameter. Support the peas on brushwood or a cylinder of chicken-wire netting held up by 4 or 5 stakes. Or you can use a dwarf variety such as 'Little Sweetheart'.

Will you let us know something about the cultivating of sweet peas? How far apart should the plants be? Should they have commercial fertilizer? See the preceding answers for soil preparation. The plants should not be closer together than 4 inches. Commercial fertilizers, used according to the manufacturer's directions, are good for application along the sides of the row after the plants are 4 inches high.

How deep should sweet pea seeds be planted? Usually about 2 inches. Some gardeners prefer to sow them in a trench 6 inches deep, covering them at first with 2 inches of soil. As the plants increase in stature, the trench is gradually filled in. This works well in sandy soils.

How early must I place the supports for sweet pea vines? When they are about 4 inches high. If left until they topple over, they never seem to grow as well as they do when staked early. Twiggy branches stuck in on both sides of the row, or in among the plants if they are grown in clumps, make good supports, but chicken-wire netting or strings supported by a frame will do.

Can you give me some general-care instructions for sweet peas? Full or nearly full sun is best; some shade is tolerated. The soil should be deep, well drained, rich, and well supplied with humus material. Be sure it is neutral or somewhat alkaline—never acid. Spray with malathion for plant lice. Keep weeded and cultivated; water regularly; feed weekly with liquid fertilizer when the buds begin to show.

I have never been successful with sweet peas, my favorite flower. I get about 3 bouquets and then they die. Can you help me? I have used a number of methods with no success. (Oklahoma.) Maybe the summer sun is too much for them; try shading with cheesecloth as soon as really hot, dry weather starts. Water thoroughly and regularly. Try preparing the soil and sowing in November or December, giving a little protection in cold weather. Select heat-resistant strains from catalogs.

I have very healthy-looking sweet pea vines but no blossoms. Why? The soil may be deficient in phosphorus; or the vines may have been planted too late for buds to open before the hot weather blasted them.

How can the blooming season of outdoor sweet peas be prolonged? By picking the flowers as fast as they mature and by shading from the hot sun with cheesecloth or similar material, plus abundant, regular watering. Usually hot weather limits the season.

Sweet peas that are planted in November usually make some winter growth or early-spring growth. Will it be advisable to shear this top growth and let the base of the plant start new and tender growth? (Virginia.) Yes, pinch the growth back to where the stem shows signs of sprouting at the base. This later growth produces better flowers.

Is there any way to keep birds from eating my sweet peas and ranunculus as they come up? Lay a few pieces of garden hose or rope alongside the rows; birds are afraid of snakes. Or cover with cheese-cloth. Strings with white rags hanging from them may also help.

How can I successfully grow sweet peas in a greenhouse in Texas? For your region, the seed should be sown in late August. These plants should give a crop the greater part of the winter. Try another sowing in late September. Prepare soil 18 inches deep, with dehydrated manure ¼ the soil volume. Add 1 pound ground limestone and ½ pound superphosphate per 20 square feet. Sow in rows 36 inches apart, 1 ounce to 35 linear feet. Thin to 4 plants per linear foot. Support the vines by stretching a wire at ground level along the row, another at 10 to 12 feet above. Stretch strands of string between the rows and train the vines up the string. Watering and feeding must be related to growth and flowering. In the winter, water only when moisture is low, as seen by examining the soil 1 to 2 inches below the surface. After flowering begins, feed every 2 weeks with liquid fertilizer. Use only the greenhouse sweet pea varieties.

Which varieties of sweet peas are the best for our hot, dry Kansas climate? What is the best method of planting? Sweet peas rarely succeed outdoors in a hot, dry climate unless sown very early. Your best chance is to plant in early spring, keep well watered, and shade with cheese-cloth from direct sun. There are, as far as is known, no varieties especially adapted to your conditions. The giant heat-resistant and spring-flowering types are quite heat-resistant but need abundant moisture.

TITHONIA

My tithonia plants never bloom. Can you tell me why? This Mexican sunflower with its handsome, single, brilliant orange blooms must be started early indoors to give generous bloom before frost arrives. The variety 'Torch' grows only 4 feet tall as against the original species, which reaches 6 feet. 'Torch' also blooms earlier. Use it at the back of the border or as a screen plant.

TORENIA (WISHBONE FLOWER)

What can I use instead of pansies in late summer? *Torenia fournieri,* an attractive little plant, very bushy with purple, lavender, and gold flowers like miniature snapdragons. Its foliage turns plum-colored in late autumn. Start the seeds in May in a seed bed, as they are very tender, or sow indoors in a warm temperature about March. Torenia grows well in sun or shade.

Bricks make an artistic edging to a flower border and also make it easier to mow the grass without cutting off plants. Flagstone can also be used as a "mowing strip," as such a barrier between lawn and garden is called.

VERBENA

How can I raise verbenas? I have not had much luck with them. (Kansas.)   Verbenas are not easy to raise unless you have adequate facilities. The seed is variable in its germination. Requiring a long season, seeds must be sown about March 1 in a temperature of 60° F. at night and 70° to 75° F. during the day. The seedlings are transplanted into flats, after the first true leaf appears, using equal parts of loam, sand, leafmold and rotted or dehydrated manure or compost. Keep in the same temperature until established (10 days), then harden off the plants in a cold frame before planting outside. Set out in the ground when the danger of frost is past.

When is the season to plant verbena?   The plants should be set out when warm weather is established. The seeds are best sown indoors 2 months prior to setting out the plants. (See the previous question.)

ZINNIA

What soil is best for zinnias?   Zinnias appreciate a fairly heavy, rich loam. Additions of rotted or dried manure, compost, or peat moss and commercial fertilizer will produce sturdy plants.

We have been unable to grow zinnias. Our soil is rich and well drained. We are able to grow asters but they attain no height or size. What could be the cause?   Maybe the soil is too acid. Have it tested, and if it is below pH 6, bring it up to neutral.

Is the middle of April too early to plant zinnia and marigold seed outdoors in central Pennsylvania?   A few weeks too early—May 1 to 15 would be better.

Should zinnias be transplanted?   Zinnias are very easily transplanted. They can, if desired, be sown where they are to grow, and then thinned out.

How should I gather zinnia seeds?   Select the healthiest plants with the best flowers. During late August or early September, allow the flowers to mature on the plant, and when the seeds are quite dry and dark, harvest them. Spread on paper in a dry, airy place. When thoroughly dry, discard the chaff and place the best seeds in sealed envelopes or jars. Label and store until planting time. (See also the following question.)

Why did seeds from a certain zinnia, when planted the next year, not come true to color?   Because it was a variety not capable of transmitting its characteristics by seed, such as the new hybrids; or the flowers were fertilized with pollen from other plants of a different color.

Biennials

Biennials are plants which start their life cycle one year, pass the winter in a state of dormancy or "suspended animation," and then grow on to complete their lives in the following year. Pansies, best known of the biennials, and one of the easiest of all flowers to be grown from seed, are usually bought in spring as plants in full bloom, instead of being raised from seed—at a fraction of the cost of plants—by the gardener himself.

Biennial seed should be sown in May or early June in the North—or for some of them, such as pansies, as late as August to take advantage of the new crop of seed that becomes available—and transplanted as soon as the true leaves develop. By mid-September or October the little pansy plants are ready to be transferred to their allocated positions in the garden or (in severe climates) carried over winter in a frame under a protective covering of straw, rough compost, or evergreen boughs, applied after the ground has frozen slightly. Covering with glass sash, except in *very* severe climates, is not necessary.

One of the great advantages of using some biennials in the garden scheme is that they provide very early color out-of-doors weeks before spring-sown annuals will be in flower. They are unsurpassed for "filling in" wherever color can be lacking in the spring garden.

When is it best to sow seeds of most biennials? May to July is considered the best time. This gives a fairly long season to produce good-sized plants for blooming the following year and most kinds grow better in the coolness of spring rather than in summer's heat. Hollyhocks, for extra-heavy plants, are best sown early; but pansies and forget-me-nots can be sown in August, as very large plants of these may die during the winter. Other biennials fare very well from May–June sowings.

How are biennials best used in the garden? They are valuable in a mixed border for early-summer bloom. Solid plantings can be made of such kinds as foxgloves, with early lilies and day-lilies. Combinations like Canterbury-bells in different colors, with sweet William, pansies, English daisies, and forget-me-nots, are used as a ground cover for a bulb garden. The biennials must be followed with annuals to fill the bare spots left when the biennials die. In a mixed border use in small groups near later-blooming perennials that will tend to cover the bare spots left. The later-blooming biennials (like hollyhock) can be given due prominence in a mixed planting of perennials and other annuals.

Will you give a list of biennials, with their time of bloom? This will include many that are perennial but which in garden practice are grown as biennials. Canterbury-bells (*Campanula medium*), cup-and-saucer (*C. medium* 'Calycanthema'), steeple-bellflower (*C. pyramidalis*), June and July; English daisy (*Bellis perennis*), April and May; foxglove, June–July; hollyhock (*Alcea rosea*), July; honesty (*Lunaria annua*), May; rose campion (*Lychnis coronaria*), May to June; pansy (*Viola tricolor*), April to June; English wallflower (*Cheiranthus cheiri*), May to June; sweet William (*Dianthus barbatus*), June to July; forget-me-not (*Myosotis sylvatica*), April to May.

Do any biennials self-sow?   Yes, quite a few, such as foxglove, for-get-me-not, rose campion, steeple-bellflower, pansy, and hollyhock. But if the soil is too assiduously cultivated, the seedlings may be killed.

Are biennials winter-hardy in northern gardens?   The hardiest are the campions, foxglove, hollyhock, steeple-bellflower, honesty, sweet William, wallflower. Most other biennials (see list) need considerable protection, preferably a cold frame.

At what time of year should biennials be transplanted?   Plants started the preceding year are set out in early spring for blooming the same year. Pansies begin to bloom with the spring bulbs.

Specific Biennial Plants

CANTERBURY-BELLS (CAMPANULA)

What is the best time of year to plant the seed of Canterbury-bells and foxglove?   May to June is a good time to sow seeds of these plants. If sown later, the plants may not be big enough to flower the next year.

Will Canterbury-bells grow well in upper New York State? When should the seed be sown?   Yes, they will do very well but must have adequate winter protection. Do not stimulate growth by watering or feeding after mid-August. After a hard freeze, cover with brush, over which spread a layer of marsh hay or similar covering. Sow seeds in May for bloom the following year.

How can I grow Canterbury-bells and cup-and-saucer?   The cup-and-saucer type ('Calycanthema') is a variety of the regular Canter-bury-bell (*Campanula medium*). The cup-and-saucer requires the same culture and conditions as the regular Canterbury-bells.

What is the best winter mulch for Canterbury-bells? (Wisconsin.)   Light, littery material that will not pack to a sodden mass over the leaves. Before covering, remove any bad basal leaves that might rot. Tuck the material in around the plants and stick a few twigs among them to keep the light covering from lying directly on the leaves.

Why is it that Campanula medium sometimes does not blossom? This spring I had two dozen nice-looking plants that were transplanted in the fall of last year, but none of them blossomed.   Plants of Canterbury-bells, unless they reach a good size, can fail to bloom the first summer.

Many, however, will persist through the second winter and bloom the second summer. It usually means the seed wasn't sown early enough.

FOXGLOVES (DIGITALIS)

What do you do with foxgloves that do not bloom the second year? Will they bloom the third year if kept on? Yes, they probably will; foxgloves frequently behave this way, especially when the seeds are not sown early enough.

Should we cover our foxglove plants heavily in the winter? (Vermont.) In your region they will need adequate protection. Mulch the soil with decayed leaves, lay cherry or birch branches over the crowns, and on top of this spread an inch or two of marsh hay or straw. If covering packs on top of the crowns, it will cause rot, hence the branches. Evergreen boughs—not heavy ones—are also valuable. These are used alone.

Will foxglove, if separated in winter, bloom the following year? If you refer to the common foxglove (*Digitalis purpurea*) from seed sown the previous summer—probably no. The perennial kinds can be separated in the spring.

What parts of foxglove are poisonous, if any? Probably all parts. The drug digitalis (poisonous in overdoses) is obtained from the second year's young leaves, so presumably the poisonous principle is most abundant in them.

What is the best method of gathering foxglove seed? Gather the lower seed capsules from the stem as soon as they show brown but before they open to shed the seed. Select from the best type.

PANSY (VIOLA)

What is the best location for pansies for good bloom? A cool, moist, well-drained soil, in a sunny location.

What is the best soil for pansies? Any soil that contains plenty of humus. Well-rotted manure, peat moss, or leafmold, mixed with the soil, will help. A neutral or slightly acid reaction is best.

When is pansy seed sown in Minnesota? In late July or August to produce plants large enough, before cold weather, so they can be wintered in a covered cold frame.

What is the best method of growing pansies? Plant seed in cold frames in July–August, transplanting 6 × 6 inches when the second set of leaves appear. When freezing weather arrives, cover the plants with straw and keep the frames closed. About March 1 remove the straw but keep the glass on and ventilate freely. Remove the glass about April 1 and set the plants in permanent position between April 1 and May 15. The best soil is a good loam with plenty of humus and moisture.

What conditions are necessary to get pansy seed to germinate? First, obtain *fresh,* plump seeds. For the seed bed, use a mixture of 1 part each of soil, sand, and leafmold or peat moss, put through a ¼-inch mesh screen. Select as cool a spot as you can—a cold frame that can be heavily shaded is ideal. Level and lightly firm the soil. Broadcast the seed on the surface (or sow in rows 4 or 5 inches apart) and cover with ⅛ inch of fine soil, press lightly, and shade, but leave space for ventilation. As soon as seeds have germinated remove the shading, except during the hottest part of the day. Give full sun when seedlings are well through.

Would pansy seed sown in the open in April come up and bloom by June 15? Pansy seed sown the first of April might possibly show a few flowers by June 15 if growing conditions are favorable. The finest spring display comes from fresh seed sown in midsummer.

Are pansy plants, from seeds sown outdoors in September, likely to survive the cold weather during the winter and to flower next summer in New York? No, the seed should be sown in late July or early in August. In the vicinity of New York City, young plants will live outdoors with light covering. Farther north they should be grown in cold frames during the winter.

Will you tell me when to transplant pansies? (Texas.) Presuming you mean pansy seedlings, you should plant them in their permanent locations (from seed beds, flats, or pots) in September or October for bloom during late winter into spring. Young plants, grown in cold frames or in open beds, may be transplanted in the early spring.

Is it better to purchase pansy plants for autumn planting or for very early-spring planting if one desires them for sale purposes around Mother's Day? Purchase seedling plants in September and grow these on to blooming size.

Why don't pansy plants bloom and grow all summer when planted in the spring in full bloom? Mine don't. They bloom best in the cool weather of spring and early summer. In an exposed place they deteriorate in the heat; also, the earlier heavy bloom exhausts the plants.

What would be the cause of pansy plants growing long stems and very small flowers? Too much shade or overcrowding. A good strain of seed, August sowing, winter protection, a good soil, and not too much shade are the prerequisites for success.

Why do blue pansies often have petals streaked blue and white? The seed strain is not good. Blue pansy seed that comes true to type is offered by reliable sources of seeds.

When wintering pansies in a cold frame, should one wait until the soil in the frame has frozen, then close the frame and keep it covered with a mat or leaves until spring? No. The best plan is to give plants light, ventilate whenever frost on the glass melts, and cover with mats only on the coldest nights. Do not remove snow from the frames.

What is considered a foolproof winter mulch for pansies? (Wyoming.) Branches of spruce, fir, or pine; straw or hay held down with chicken wire. If hungry mice or rabbits abound, spray the pansies first with aluminum sulfate or commercial rabbit repellent.

When is the best time to apply winter protection for pansies? (Wyoming.) As soon as the surface inch or two of the ground freezes.

When is it safe to remove the winter covering on pansies? (Wyoming.) When severe freezing is past. It is well to remove this (and all such mulches) on a cloudy or rainy day. Sudden exposure to sun and wind is unkind to leaves and buds.

Last year's pansies did such a wonderful job of self-seeding for this season that the resulting plants are lovelier and stronger than the new ones we grew from seed with great care. Any particular reason? It was probably due to some cross-pollenizing which developed strong, healthy plants. However, continuous intercrossing year after year will result in deterioration. To maintain the strain, weed out poor plants and poor colors as soon as flowers open.

ROSE CAMPION (LYCHNIS)

Will you please give the botanical name of mullein pink or rose campion? *Lychnis coronaria,* of easy culture and hardy.

SWEET WILLIAM (DIANTHUS BARBATUS)

When shall I plant sweet William? What kind of soil is required? In a sunny spot or in shade? Set plants out as early in the spring as the ground can be worked. They like a well-prepared soil with plenty of humus-forming material (like compost, leafmold, or peat moss) in addition to a good dressing of dried manure. They prefer a sunny location.

Can seeds of sweet William be planted in late fall or early winter? Will they bloom the following season?   This is a biennial normally sown in the summer for bloom the following year. There are annual varieties that blossom the same summer from spring-sown seeds.

Sweet William will not live through the summer for me. Why?   Sweet William is grown as a biennial. It usually dies after flowering.

Do foxglove and sweet William come up a second year?   The common foxglove (*Digitalis purpurea*) is a biennial. Sweet William is used as such. Rarely do they appear the second year except from self-sown seedlings. It is best to sow seeds of these kinds every year to ensure a supply of plants.

WALLFLOWER

What is the difference between wallflower and Siberian wallflower?   Wallflower (*Cheiranthus cheiri*) grows to a height of 2 feet and produces yellow, mahogany, and brownish flowers in spring and again in autumn. Siberian wallflower is a confused name that probably belongs to another genus, *Erysimum*. Most erysimums have fragrant yellow flowers in early spring.

Please tell me how to grow wallflowers.   Wallflowers require cool nights and moisture in the air during the growing season to thrive. They are supposedly lime-lovers but sometimes grow well in acid soil, such as near the seashore, when other conditions suit them. *Cheiranthus cheiri* is quite tender inland, but grows well near the coast in New England. Wallflowers need full sun and a sandy soil. They are usually grown as biennials but occasional plants will behave as true perennials, lasting for several years.

9. Lawns and Turf Areas

THE FIRST "LAWNS" were probably little more than open ground around dwelling areas, "mowed" by grazing livestock. Some grassy swards were of importance enough during the Middle Ages to have been kept within bounds by scything; even today much mowing, particularly in the Tropics, is by hand with sickle or bush knife.

The first mechanical lawn mower was not invented until 1830 in England. During the century that followed, mowing the lawn became increasingly customary, although little other attention was given. Well-kept lawns were far from universal and most only a hobby of the well-to-do; working and rural people gave little heed to their lawns until about the time of World War II. Then with intensified migration to the suburbs, lawn-tending was destined never again to be a casual thing. The customary close-clipping of whatever vegetation volunteered (or arose from seeding with farm grasses and legumes), with little recognition of grass habits or requirements, gradually gave way to the more involved maintenance procedures used today. Remember, only a few decades ago very few people even bothered to fertilize a lawn, and what weeding was done was by hand digging or pulling.

The Modern Lawn

A "good" lawn typically consists of an overcrowded population of dwarfed grass plants, all so very much alike as to create an unblemished carpet. This provides a superlative backdrop for home landscaping, whether the emphasis is flower gardens or the form and texture effects created by trees, shrubs, or varying grasses themselves. Because of the crowding, often a thousand or more shoots to the square foot, individual grass plants are apt to be weak compared to what they might be if uncrowded and unmowed. If all are hereditarily alike (i.e., a monoculture), they are fair game for plagues which spread from one plant to another, encountering no resistance. That is why lawn experts advise the planting of grass blends or mixtures, so that there is the likelihood that some resistant grass will confront whatever disease or other pest chances on the lawn.

This dense, perpetually defoliated carpet is expected to be constantly solid underfoot, to keep pets and people walking over it "out of the mud" at all seasons. It must not only look good, even if given inexpert attention, but it must refresh the air, cool the environs in summer, insulate the ground in winter, prevent soil wash, endure de-icing salts, be a playfield and a picnic ground, and whatever else is demanded. The grass family almost alone provides the rather few candidates able to meet these requirements. Such plants have their growing points close to the soil (only the elongating leaves are mowed); the foliage exhibits basal rather than tip growth; most spread by underground stems (rhizomes) or surface runners (stolons). This pattern of growth equips the plants to survive under constant low mowing.

Only about a dozen grass species find much service for lawns, a few each for the northern ("cool season") and southern ("warm season") regions (see map). The growth habits of these few grasses (and their multitudinous cultivars or varieties) must be understood for intelligent lawn maintenance. It is not only a case of doing the right thing, but of doing it at the right time as well.

The Basic Needs of Lawn Grass

Although growth influences vary due to environmental differences, these principles prevail in general:

Southern grasses, typically planted from Tennessee southward, grow best at relatively warm temperatures, above 80° F. They are exuberant in spring and summer, and should receive major attention then. Northern grasses, however, grow best when temperatures don't exceed 80° F. (at least at night); they conserve resources best in autumn, winter, and spring. By and large they benefit most from attention in autumn, and are weakest during the heat of summer. It is thus evident that July fertilization of Bermuda grass in the South may help it compete with weeds

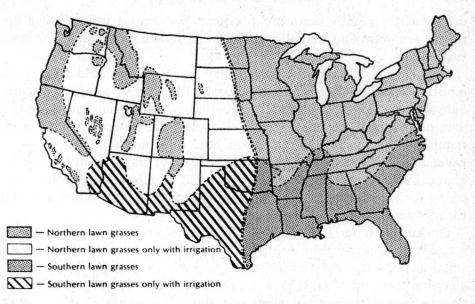

— Northern lawn grasses
— Northern lawn grasses only with irrigation
— Southern lawn grasses
— Southern lawn grasses only with irrigation

then, while in the North summer feeding could help weeds such as crabgrass more than the perennial bluegrass!

All lawns are mowed, and height of mowing can have considerable influence. Of course some grasses are better adapted to low-mowing than are others (bent grasses and Bermuda grasses, for example; newer low-growing cultivars of bluegrass as contrasted to the old-fashioned types). But in general, reasonably high mowing benefits the grass, probably because more green leaf is retained (the food-making resource for the plant). Disease is less severe and weeds are fewer in a tall-mowed turf than in a short-clipped one. Roots below ground correspond to top growth above ground, and are usually about 40 per cent dry weight of the tops. Taller-mowed grass thus roots more deeply, with the consequent benefits of reaching a greater soil mass for moisture and nutrients.

The water needs of a well-kept lawn do not vary greatly from grass species to species, although certain grasses are more able to endure prolonged drought than are others (for example, buffalo grass, though not making a good sod, does survive unirrigated in the arid High Plains). At peak season, any flourishing lawn will transpire about an inch of water per week, which must be provided from stored moisture in the soil, by irrigation, or by rainfall, if the lawn is to be kept attractive. Of course location has a tremendous influence on water need. Sunny, windy spots in the southwestern deserts will lose far more moisture than will a protected northern lawn, especially if it is in a cloudy upland location where nightly dews are prevalent. In regions where water demands are great and rainfall insufficient, irrigation is essential for lawn survival.

Soil is quite influential. A heavy (clay type) soil can hold 3 inches of moisture in its top foot, whereas a Coastal Plain sandy soil perhaps only half an inch. Obviously, watering must be more frequent on such sand than on clay. On the other hand, relatively brief watering is all that is required on a sand (because it will hold only the half inch or so of water anyway), and water will soak in readily; clay, however, may be almost impervious to water penetration, and usually requires a slow watering for a prolonged time until 2 or 3 inches of water have reached the root zone.

Obviously, natural fertility (have certain nutrients become unbalanced?), mowing history, acidity-alkalinity, organic content, and so on will influence not only maintenance procedures (liming, fertilization, etc.) but the kind of grass most suited to the situation. In general, clays poor in organic content are much more difficult to handle than are loams or even sands. They are cultivatable only a few times during the year, when moisture content is just right for tilling without clodding. Wet clays tend to compact from being walked upon or having equipment run over them. On the other hand, loam soils (rich in organic matter), and especially sandy soils, are little injured by tillage, traffic, or abuse at almost any season.

Homeowner preferences vary. Some people insist upon mowing the lawn very low, whether or not the kind of grass is adapted to such treatment. Others insist upon watering whether needed or not (thus bringing in water-loving weeds). Many will overfertilize ("if a little is good, a lot is better"), and some will apply "remedies" unrelated to the problem at hand.

Actually, no lawn-keeping program need be burdensome or unduly expensive if the homeowner takes time to learn about his grass-growth requirements. He can then work with the lawn's natural needs rather than against them. Because tastes vary, assess your preferences, willingness to provide care, and budget that will be available before choosing your grass (avoid high-maintenance cultivars such as are used for golf greens, unless you are willing to provide the intense care that they require). One pays a price in increased upkeep the greater one's demands are for special luxuriance.

The Lawn Grasses

The box on the following pages gives major fine turf species for lawns in the United States. The subsequent chart names some of the many cultivars that had reached commercial status during the 1970s.

To be effective, any lawn grass should be perennial, even though occasionally temporary cover may be had from annual species. Also, most lawn grasses spread well to make a thick sod and fill in gaps. All of the southern species listed spread by surface runners (stolons) with some rhizoming (underground spreading stems) as well in Bermuda grass and zoysia. Of the major northern lawn grasses listed, only bent grass spreads by stolons; bluegrasses and fescues produce rhizomes, and ryegrass is a bunch grass (not spreading). Trailing stoloniferous grasses do tend to build up a mat of vegetation above the soil surface, which, if slow to decompose, can add appreciably to spent tissues, thus making a layer of interfering thatch.

More new cultivars have been bred for the seeded northern grasses than for the vegetatively propagated southern ones. Apomictic Kentucky bluegrasses have been especially abundant, because a newly created genotype can be perpetuated more easily than a highly sexual grass species. Kentucky bluegrass in large measure produces seed on the mother plant without fusion of a male gamete (apomixis). Some sexuality occurs in bluegrass, but strains that are strongly apomictic can be maintained "pure" rather easily by roguing the few viable offtypes that occasionally occur. A high level of sexuality in southern species, such as Bermuda and zoysia, has mitigated against obtaining true-breeding cultivars from seed. As was noted, most southern grasses are vegetatively propagated, as are many golf-green creeping bent grasses and zoysias recommended in the North.

LAWN GRASSES

Southern

Bahia Grass (*Paspalum notatum*): Fairly open, coarse; seedheads unattractive and hard to mow. One of the easiest southern turf grasses to plant and to care for; sometimes used in mixtures.

Bermuda Grass (*Cynodon dactylon* and hybrids): Fast-growing, aggressive; attractive texture and deep color if well tended. Sun only; so vigorous as to require frequent care (a pest in borders); will form thatch; dormant near freezing; doubtfully hardy north of Tennessee.

Centipede Grass (*Eremochloa ophiuroides*): Medium texture, low-maintenance grass, resenting heavy fertility; turns chlorotic unless soils are acid (needs iron).

St. Augustine Grass (*Stenotaphrum secundatum*): Coarse but not unattractive; few seedheads; usually dark green. Tolerant of shade; subject to chinch bug and several diseases, hence not a carefree grass, but resistant cultivars are being bred; will form thatch.

Zoysia Grass (*Zoysia matrella*): Growth is slow; dense and among most attractive of southern grasses. Slowness is a disadvantage on planting, but reduces mowing demand later; does not require a great deal of attention, but is very fibrous and tough to mow (heavy-duty reel mower recommended); billbug becoming more serious; 'Meyer' cultivar hardy in North, but with short season.

Northern

Bent Grass (*Agrostis species*): Low, trailing or semitrailing; small leaf blades with excellent texture. "Show" grasses for well-tended turfs (fertilized, watered, frequently mowed); prone to diseases in muggy weather and to snow mold under cool, damp conditions.

Kentucky Bluegrass (*Poa pratensis*): Deep green, gracefully arching shoots, spreading by rhizomes. Among world's best sod formers; widely adaptable; one of best all-around grasses; rather easily cared for.

Fine Fescue (*Festuca rubra* in varieties): Slowly spreading, attractively fine-textured, beautifully dark green, rather stiff and "windswept" in appearance. One of the best shade grasses in the North, persisting on poorish soils in dry locations; at its best in cooler seasons (often becomes patchy under hot-humid conditions).

Perennial Ryegrass (*Lolium perenne*): New "turf types" bred for lawns are just as attractive as bluegrass; shiny green leaves; a nonspreading bunch grass. Quick to sprout and with rapid seedling growth; reasonably hardy although not so widely adapted to climatic extremes as Kentucky bluegrass.

IMPROVED LAWN GRASS VARIETIES

Kentucky Bluegrass: Sow Kentucky bluegrasses 1 to 2 pounds to 1,000 square feet (in mixtures a bit more heavily) for a fairly dense stand after several weeks of favorable weather. Fertilize, especially in autumn.
'Adelphi'—Rutgers hybrid, widely recommended; attractive appearance, habit, and winter color; tolerates diseases well and can endure low maintenance.
'Arboretum'—Ecotype from stressful Missouri habitat; tenacious under minimum care; natural habit, best mowed fairly tall.
'Baron'—Decumbent selection from Holland with all-around capabilities; much used for sod; seed blends are suggested for greater longevity.
'Birka'—Selection from Sweden, top-rating there; tolerant of low maintenance and light shade; winter color and drought resistance not outstanding, but adapts well generally.
'Bonnieblue'—Hybrid beauty from Rutgers, low, with excellent color and long season; good disease tolerance and ability to endure some acidity.
'Ennumdi'—Top-notch selection from Holland, notably resistant to fusarium; decumbent, dense, and tolerant of some acidity.
'Fylking'—Elegant Swedish selection, decumbent and well adapted to low mowing; disease usually not too serious; salinity tolerance noted in California; not aggressive, so especially suited to mixtures and blends.
'Glade'—Selection from New York, dwarfish, dark, fairly slow-growing; good in shade because of mildew resistance; endures moderate acidity.

'Majestic'—Handsome hybrid from Rutgers, rather diminutive and with excellent general qualities; noteworthy in hot weather in California.

'Merion'—The classic improved bluegrass, exceptionally dense and aggressive, wears well; suffers from certain diseases regionally and is not persistent under low maintenance (a "heavy feeder"); shows tolerance to drought and iron chlorosis but not salinity.

'Nugget'—Selection from Alaska best adapted northward, outstanding as a dense, dark-green carpet; great in summer but "greens-up" late; suffers somewhat from dollar spot and fusarium; good in shade because of mildew tolerance; withstands low maintenance.

'Plush'—Widely adapted selection from New Jersey with moderate disease resistance; can withstand low maintenance, drought, and acidity rather well.

'Ram I'—From a Maine golf course, adapted to low mowing and acid soil; spreads unobtrusively in blends and mixtures.

'Sydsport'—Vigorous, boldly textured Swedish introduction with excellent ratings, much recommended for sports turfs; only mildly susceptible to most diseases; resists iron chlorosis.

'Touchdown'—Popular selection from a Long Island fairway, dense, low, and "solid" even with only moderate fertilization; vigorous, so may thatch a bit; resists disease well.

Perennial Ryegrass: Ryegrasses sprout quickly but do not spread, so should be sown rather densely when planted alone (4 pounds or more per 1,000 square feet). Leading cultivars are polycrosses mostly developed from Rutgers germ plasma, and most of them are rather similar in appearance and performance. Compared to common ryegrass they are low and dense, rich green, winter hardy, and mow neatly.

'Blazer'—Dark green with good heat tolerance and appearance.

'Citation'—A cultivar resistant to heat and wear, companionable for mixtures.

'Derby'—Highly rated nationally; among the top three in California.

'Diplomat'—A cultivar of overall fine quality.

'Fiesta'—An excellent polycross that withstands stress and most diseases.

'Manhattan'—the definitive Rutgers University polycross, derived from a group of grasses growing in Central Park, New York City; excellent hardiness; among top three in California.

'NK-200'—A Minnesota selection, noted for winter hardiness (may be weaker in hot weather).

'Omega'—A cultivar that is attractive summer and winter; wears well.

'Pennfine'—A leading national cultivar developed at Penn State, competitive and especially strong in summer; among top three in California.

'Regal'—A newer release, attractive and strong under summer heat.

'Yorktown II'—Highly rated, elegant but durable.

Fine Fescue: Fescues are well adapted to dry soil, low fertility, and shade but often suffer stress from summer humidity (permanency is better in northern climates). Ordinarily best used with bluegrass in mixtures and handled like bluegrass.

'Banner'—Rutgers 45-clone Chewings polycross, doing especially well under coastal conditions.

'Ensylva'—A spreading polycross from Holland, well adapted to mixtures.

'Highlight'—Handsome Chewings release from Holland, strikingly brilliant.

'Koket'—A Chewings polycross from Holland, strong, generally undamaged by disease.

'Ruby'—A spreading fescue from Holland; used mostly in mixtures or for special purposes (e.g., coverings for bermlike constructions).

Colonial Bent Grass (*Agrostis tenuis*): 'Highland' is a natural ecotype that persists under minimum maintenance; mow frequently at ¾- to 1-inch height to avoid stubble.

Creeping Bent Grass (*Agrostis palustris*): This "golf green" species requires intensive care, especially frequent low mowing (say at ¼ to ½ inch).

'Emerald'—A pedigreed pure line, attractive and not too demanding.

'Prominent'—An 8-clone Scandinavian selection said to survive neglect and resist the weedy annual bluegrass (*Poa annua*).

Rough Bluegrass (*Poa trivialis*): 'Sabre', selected at Rutgers, is a real beauty, adapted to moist shade; however, the species is delicate and not very resistant to wear.

Soil Is All-Important

While most lawn grasses are widely adaptable—grow in soils having a range of nutrient qualities, pH differences (acidity-alkalinity), and so on—their culture is simpler and their performance generally better if the soil is good. Once a lawn is established, not much can be done for the root zone; fertilizers and other treatments can be applied only at the surface. So, before a lawn is planted, improve the soil in which the grass will grow as much as possible. Especially if the soil is low in phosphorus, mix a phosphatic fertilizer into the root zone before seeding or sodding. Phosphorus is fixed on soil particles, and moves downward only very slowly from the surface.

It has been customary for lawn experts to give elaborate instructions for preparing the soil prior to seeding. Deep cultivation; mixing in organic materials abundantly; fertilization with fertilizers compounded according to soil tests; indeed even a fallowing-cultivation sequence (to reduce weeds); or the growing of a green manure (plowing the residues into the soil) are the recommendations often made. All of them can be helpful, of course. But, in the real world, few are attempted and rarely well accomplished. The truth is that soil adequate for growing a good lawn can generally be had from nothing more than shallow cultivation (disking, rotary tilling) and mixing in fertilizer 2 or 3 inches deep. With infertile soils, use double the normal rate recommended on the bag of a phosphatic fertilizer. The level of soil fertility—and whether it is unduly acid or alkaline—can be determined by a soil test, but it is generally known to gardeners and agriculturists in the area (you can consult your county extension agent).

A caution against cultivating heavy soils when they are wet has been noted earlier. Each lawn soil will have some virtues and some liabilities. Since we cannot foresee particular happenstances, the best advice to be given is "to use common sense." Procedures will vary from soil to soil, from region to region. The objective is to loosen compact soil so air and fertility can reach the root zone, and accomplish this at times and in ways which will not be detrimental to soil structure. As a general rule, soil preparation is easier in late summer for an autumn planting than in spring, when weather and soil conditions are less favorable.

Common sense should also guide you in grading. Avoid depressions that will accumulate water, or mounds and ridges that will be scalped in mowing. Where low pockets are inevitable, perhaps a drainage system will be needed (tiles laid a foot or so deep are conventional, but slit-trench drains—narrow cuts into the soil filled with loose rock—are often an economical substitute). Any drainage system should be accurately laid to slope gently away from the moist pocket into a free-flowing channel.

During home construction, piles of soil often accumulate from foundation diggings. These should be spread in a gentle contour to slope away from the house. If possible, have the richer topsoil bulldozed aside before construction and replaced on the surface in the finished contour. However, lack of topsoil does not ordinarily necessitate its purchase; bought topsoil is often of poor quality and generally quite weedy. Good lawns can be grown even on subsoil if adequately fertilized and watered. In fact subsoils typically have one bonus—fewer weed seeds. As grass grows, their structure will improve due to roots adding organic material throughout the root zone.

Seeding and Sodding

The lawn area should be prepared just as thoroughly for sodding as for seeding. After final grading, any compacted spots or crusted soil should be broken up and raked level. With many soils it is well to await a rain or to irrigate the lawn before seeding or sodding to note any uneven settling. Rake level again, breaking up surface crust so that seeds may settle into chinks and roots penetrate easily. A "pebbled" surface, with soil chunks ranging from pea to grape size, makes a better seed bed than one pulverized to dust; seeds will sift into the crevices readily, and water will soak in for a longer time before "melting" the surface into relative imperviousness.

Most sod is professionally laid, but if you do buy your own at a garden center, use common sense, laying it in a tierlike pattern if it is in squares (similar to the way bricks are placed in making a wall or path). Roll new sod after placement, and if soil or compost is available, sift it into cracks between the fittings.

Seed is most accurately sown with one of the modern spreaders, although it is possible to cast it by hand if carefully done. It may be wise to extend small, expensive seeds with an equal quantity of a like-size material, say cornmeal, to provide more bulk for casting. With either hand or spreader sowing, it is wise to spread half the seed in one direction, the other half at right angles, thus better ensuring against voids. If the seed bed is friable, probably no rolling will be needed; watering will settle the soil comfortably about the seed for good sprouting. Some seed beds, however, may be fluffy, and will profit from light rolling (not sufficiently weighty to compact the soil, but enough to restore capillarity). Generally, a rolled surface accepts water less satisfactorily than one left loose.

Whether the new lawn is seeded or sodded, it should be kept moist continuously until the grass is well established. This may require light sprinkling—daily in hot or windy weather. Watering can become less frequent (but more prolonged) as the grass roots grow deeper. Let a new seeding dry out a bit before its first mowing, so that the mower will not rut the surface or tear the very lush growth. Mowing ordinarily begins when the new grass reaches half again to twice what its customary mowing height will be.

Maintaining the Lawn

Once the lawn is established it should receive continuing reasonable care. Mowing is inevitable, and since it will be the most time-consuming task encountered in lawn tending, top-quality equipment is worth its cost. Make mowing relaxing and pleasurable rather than dreaded! Mowing should be frequent enough so that no more than half of the green foliage is removed at any one cutting. Mow at a height suited to the particular grass and owner preference.

Equally important is sensible fertilization. As was noted earlier, northern grasses benefit especially from autumn feedings as cool weather approaches. But the newer, disease-resistant cultivars have been selected for response to reasonable feeding year-round. Suggested lawn fertilizer rates generally provide about 1 pound of elemental nitrogen to each 1,000 square feet (say 5 pounds of a 20–5–10—these figures indicating the respective percentages of nitrogen, phosphorus, and potassium). A real boon for the gardener has been the development of the controlled-release, nonburning lawn fertilizers.

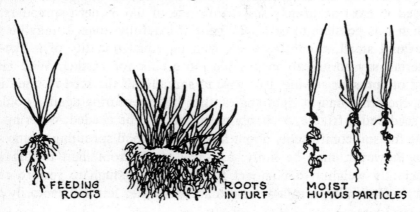

FEEDING ROOTS   ROOTS IN TURF   MOIST HUMUS PARTICLES

A square foot of turf contains many individual grass plants, each of which must be well fed. An abundance of humus in the surface soil is especially important in maintaining the moisture supply.

Less necessary generally, but often important locally, are irrigation, pest control, and bolster seeding. Earlier discussion pointed out that irrigation should match climatic needs, and supplement rainfall for a total of about an inch of water weekly. In most cases (depending upon soil) watering at infrequent intervals is best, so the soil dries out a bit and drains thoroughly between waterings. Home-lawn irrigation systems (some can be installed by homeowners) can be established underground with plastic pipe. Often they are set up to operate automatically. Even in regions of adequate average rainfall, there can be temporary droughts that cause lawns to go off-color unless they are watered.

Pest control has become quite complicated, not only because problems vary greatly from place to place, but because availability of pesticides has been restricted due to environmental concern. Some chemicals that were widely used are now prohibited, or their application is permitted only by licensed services.

The need for fungicides should diminish with the introduction of newer turf grass cultivars bred for disease resistance. When fungicidal protection is required, systemic fungicides (picked up by the grass sap stream) give long-lasting effectiveness with less bother. However, persistent use of any single pesticide can lead to buildup of resistance in the pest, so pathologists recommend alternating contact fungicides with systemic ones where disease prophylaxis is frequent. Fortunately, change of weather stalls most disease, and in most cases the homeowner can assist by being careful not to overwater or overfertilize.

When grubs, webworms, or chinch bugs attack, insecticidal sprayings thwart further devastation. "Hard" (long-lasting) insecticides have been mostly outlawed in favor of biodegradable types. And to complicate matters further, insect pests develop strains resistant to certain insecticides, so it may be necessary to alternate insecticides. Always follow product directions exactly, for insecticides are the most hazardous environmentally of any of the pesticides.

Weed control is a more general necessity, even though well-managed turf fights most of its own battles. Newly planted lawns generally have a fair abundance of weeds, but these tend to disappear because of mowing and crowding by the grass as the seedlings grow older and become more aggressive. Broad-leaf weeds, such as dandelions, plantains, and chickweed are no longer the problem they once were because of ready availability of phenoxy weedkillers. The herbicide, 2, 4-D, more broadly effective in combination with additives such as dicamba, applied at an appropriate season, takes care of most dicotyledonous (broad-leaf) pests. Crabgrass is controlled by several excellent pre-emergent chemicals, or after it has sprouted with arsonate sprays. No really good selective herbicides exist for taking perennial weed grasses out of perennial turf grass, but several chemicals are effective for killing all vegetation and then allowing reseeding or sodding with a wanted grass. Certain herbicides scorch all vegetation encountered, but are inactivated in the soil; these prove useful for edging plant beds, and for control of grass around base of trees to facilitate mowing.

Lawn renovation without the cumbersome plowing of the old sod has become feasible with the advent of specialized scarifying equipment ("power rakes," thinners, dethatchers, aerifiers). When used in combination with a knockdown herbicide, the seed bed can be made receptive to a bolstering with improved strains of grass. Even without chemical knockdown, occasional bolster seedings at an appropriate season may help thicken thin turf, and can perhaps upgrade quality by introducing preferred cultivars.

Grading

How should a lawn be graded? What operations are involved? Grading first depends upon the particular site and whether paths or driveways are to be laid out. Existing trees and areas for planting must also be considered. Outline the paths and drives with stakes. Remove the topsoil from these and spread it over the lawn area. Slope the grade as gradually as possible away from the dwelling. Unless wanted as an architectural feature, or if the situation demands it, do not construct terraces; terraces require extra maintenance effort and are not amenable to mechanized equipment.

How much pitch must be given a lawn, and how is the pitch determined? A pitch of 1 foot in 20 feet, or even 30 feet, is sufficient to give surface drainage. The grade can be established by using a line level, but in most cases the slope is sufficient so that simple sighting is adequate to provide drainage (watering, to note runoff and any areas of ponding, is the "acid test").

If there is much unevenness in the ground, should it be dug or plowed before grading? The soil, of course, will have to be loosened to move it. The practical thing to do is to remove all the topsoil, loosen the sub-soil, and do the grading; then finish the grade with the topsoil. This ensures an even depth of good soil over the entire area.

Our house sits quite a way back from the street and several feet above it. How should the front lawn be graded? A low, contoured slope is appropriate. Strategic placement of shrubs can help.

How is the soil leveled to make it even for seeding? In most cases, basic grade and leveling is completed with big equipment, such as a bulldozer or backhoe. If the soil becomes compacted, loosen by disking or rotary tilling. A tractor with a rake attachment or a chain-link mat drag can level off high spots and fill depressions quickly. More tedious is hand raking. Final touch-up and removal of debris (stones, small boards, etc.) must be done by hand with a rake or broom rake. If you are doubtful about the uniform firmness of the soil, soak the lawn (and after it dries sufficiently, rake again) or roll lightly and rerake to fill depressions.

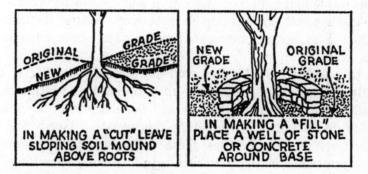

Grading around an established tree to obtain a properly sloped lawn surface.

We need to fill in to get a good slope for a lawn, but there are large trees in the way. Will the grading injure them? If the grade is to be carried much over the existing level, some protection must be given the trees. It may be necessary to build a dry well of stone around the trunks to allow air and moisture to reach the roots, although this is no guarantee of survival. One must weigh the value of the tree against the cost (and uncertainty) of preservation measures.

How high can the soil be raised around a tree without injuring it? This varies with the kind of tree, soil, and effectiveness of surface drainage. In general, where the soil is light and well drained, the grade may be raised around trees a foot or more without appreciable injury. If the soil is heavy and not well drained, raising the grade as little as 6 inches may cause waterlogging and an unhealthy anaerobic environment for the tree roots.

How large should a tree well be? As generous as possible, but at least four times the diameter of the tree. Deep wells should be provided with the drains running out laterally from the bottom.

Preparation for Sowing

When is the best time to prepare the soil for a lawn? For northern (bluegrass) lawns, late summer or early autumn. The soil is easier to cultivate then, having dried out through the summer (usually heavy soils are soggy in the spring). Preparing the soil for seeding is usually done a week or so before the desired seeding time. This allows for any settling to show, and debris or vegetation clumps can be noticed and removed. If chemical sterilization is practiced, follow instructions for the product used; many chemicals require days, some even weeks, to dissipate.

How thoroughly should the soil be cultivated? Work the soil sufficiently so that clods are broken up into chunks no larger than your thumbnail, but avoid pulverizing the soil (which breaks down its structure). (See discussion in Introduction, this section.) Needs will vary locally. Seed-bed cultivation has these objectives: destruction of unwanted vegetation; mixing fertilizer into the soil; loosening the soil enough so that air exchange occurs well beneath the surface (permitting deeper root growth); loosening the soil for easier leveling; and creating a pebbled surface that accepts seed well and allows for water penetration.

What about planting a lawn on sandy soil? Sandy soils have the advantage of not compacting easily and needing little cultivation. On the other hand, they do not hold moisture or fertilizer nutrients well. The latter deficiency can be helped by thoroughly mixing in about an inch of clay or, more practically, organic residues (such as peat moss, weed-free compost, etc.). Even without special modifications, a sandy soil can be made to support grass by practicing frequent, light fertilization and watering.

How about starting a lawn on heavy soil? The problems with a heavy soil are just the opposite from those with a sandy one. Clays become compacted easily, especially when wet, and can be cultivated well only when slightly damp. If compacted, they should be loosened at least 2 or 3 inches deep, care being taken to cultivate when the moisture content is such that the soil will crumble rather than form clods (which become like rocks when they dry). As with sandy soil, organic material is a good leavener, helping to loosen heavy soils; but adding sand is useless (for the sand will "set up" in the clay as it does in concrete). However, heavy soils do have the advantage of being relatively retentive of soil nutrients and moisture.

What about thin soils and stony ground? If there is sufficient soil to support grass roots and the drainage is adequate, a stony soil can be made into a good lawn, although any obtrusive stones that materially interfere with the level (and the use of equipment) should be removed. Rocky outcrops are very difficult, tending to hold moisture in rainy periods and to dry out quickly during dry weather; in such instances, there are two possibilities: to purchase enough good soil to provide at least 4 inches of rooting area over the indifferent base before sowing seed or to forget about a lawn here and instead treat the area as a semirock garden with appropriate plantings.

Must the soil for a lawn be fertilized? There are very few soils that will not benefit from fertilization. A soil test will provide a clue to the fertility level. Even with fertile soils, additional fertilization will cause no harm and should contribute to the nutrient "bank account." As noted in the Introduction, it is especially important to mix phosphorus-rich fertilizer into the soil before planting the lawn. With infertile soils needing rather heavy fertilization, it might be wise to choose gradual-release lawn foods.

Is the bringing in of topsoil advisable? This will depend on how adequate the residual soil is. If the soil is very thin, perhaps topsoil will be needed. But in most instances, the residual soil can be improved sufficiently to make a good seed bed much more economically than additional topsoil can be purchased. Moreover, topsoil is often of poor quality, not necessarily fertile, and almost invariably full of weed seeds (unless it has been expensively sterilized).

Should the seed bed be rolled? See the discussion under grading. Unless needed for pointing up irregularities, or for reestablishing capillarity on fluffy soils, rolling is probably not needed, and with heavy soils it can be more harmful than helpful.

Can steps be taken to prevent future problems? Yes, as, for example, through the buildup of nutrient reserves in the soil. Soils destined for "show-place" lawns can be sterilized to control residual weed seeds, disease-causing fungi, or even eelworms (nematodes), and sometimes pesticides can be introduced on a preventive basis. Most of these procedures are fairly complicated and expensive; unless you feel the problem is really serious, it may be more sensible to forgo elaborate treatments until you are sure you have a problem.

Can the seed bed be sterilized?   Yes, indeed it can, but completing the operation thoroughly, safely, and efficiently usually calls for professional help. Widely used is gaseous fumigation with methyl bromide—applied to a loosened seed bed under a tarpaulin, something few homeowners are equipped to handle. However, sterilant drenches such as DMTT, SMDC, or Vorlex usually can be applied by a homeowner with a sprinkling can; but the cost, hard work, and potential hazard to ornamental plantings (through their roots) must be weighed against the possible benefits. Sterilization is temporary; sooner or later pests reinvade, although by then the grass should be established and in position to check most weeds.

Will it be necessary to till the ground in order to sow grass seed?   Soil cultivation makes the best seed bed, but it is possible to renovate an old lawn or sow a new one if the grading is satisfactory. Powered scarifying machines can be purchased or rented which chop surface vegetation and scratch the soil, making a reasonably receptive seed bed. If old vegetation is first killed chemically (as with glyphosate) to forestall competition with the new seeding, surface scarification has an even better chance of being effective.

What about a temporary lawn?   If home construction is finished at a season inopportune for planting the permanent lawn, certain temporary plantings can keep you "out of the mud." It is best to sow cover that will not compete later with the permanent grass, or if it does persist, will not be an eyesore. Examples: Korean lespedeza, a hot-weather annual which gives way gracefully to bluegrass in northern lawns; fine-textured ryegrass, which in the South makes a pleasing autumn-winter cover before spring planting of lawns.

How quickly does newly sowed lawn seed sprout?   How fast seed will germinate depends both upon the kind of grass and the weather. Ryegrass is fastest; fescues, slightly slower; bluegrasses and bent grasses, still a bit slower. Under ideal conditions, ryegrass sprouts in just a few days, while bluegrass may take two weeks. Seed must be kept moist and warm for fast sprouting; germination is most rapid when daytime temperatures get into the seventies (F.). Also, seed that has been properly produced and handled will be more vigorous than that which has been mishandled. Seed can lie dormant in the soil during freezing weather, and will sprout only very slowly at temperatures below 50° F. Still, for spring sowings, it is best to seed the lawn as early as possible, letting the seed imbibe water and begin the sprouting process even though much "action" won't be seen until there are warmer temperatures later in the spring.

Lawn Grasses

What is the best lawn grass? "Best" will vary with the climate, local conditions, and your own preference. Bluegrass is the species most widely utilized in the northern two thirds of the country; Bermuda grass in the upper South; perhaps St. Augustine in the Deep South; but where conditions are suitable, bent grasses, fine fescues, and perennial rye-grasses can be equally appropriate in the North; zoysias in the South, and centipede or Bahia for the Deep South. Except for the special needs of the Deep South, almost all of the preferred lawn grasses are "fine-textured," i.e., have relatively narrow foliage that does not have a coarse appearance. They are also longlasting (perennial), and in most cases spread by runners or rhizomes.

What grass seed do you suggest to make a lawn under maple trees? Grass has a hard time under surface-rooting trees, having to compete for food and moisture as well as being shaded. High mowing, more frequent (but light) fertilization, thorough soaking if watering is practiced can help. So will trimming the trees for maximum light penetration. Sowing a fast, vigorous species like ryegrass in autumn usually results in a good stand during the tree's leafless season; though it may thin in summer, it usually lasts sufficiently to give some cover. Consider such bolstering as a regular autumn practice. Some bluegrass cultivars (e.g., 'Birka', 'Glade', 'Nugget') are more shade-tolerant because of their resistance to mildew, which is a frequent problem under trees.

There are so many new grass varieties (cultivars) now that I am confused. How can I choose intelligently? It is helpful to realize that all bluegrasses behave somewhat alike; all fine fescues like fescues, and so on. The difference between individual cultivars is mostly a matter of preferred color, texture, or growth habit, and not too much of a consideration as far as care is concerned. Seed firms provide helpful information concerning their proprietary cultivars, and responsible houses will utilize quality components in their seed mixtures which you can accept on faith. The new cultivars would not have been brought to market had they not exhibited at least some superior characteristics. They are chosen for reasonable resistance to the usual lawn diseases, for comparatively low rather than tall growth, and for attractive appearance. Examples of typical improved cultivars are given in the Introduction to this chapter.

How can I avoid confusing good lawn grasses with poor ones? Unfortunately, some uncertainty occurs with common names, and the botanical names seldom appear in component listings or are misunderstood by the uninitiated. "Bluegrass" generally refers to the valuable Kentucky bluegrass species (*Poa pratensis*), while "annual" bluegrass is a weed and other bluegrasses (such as "Canada" or "woods") are of lesser quality. But 'Kentucky-31' is the legal name for a coarse fescue, not to be confused with Kentucky bluegrass. Indeed, the unwanted coarse fescues (*Festuca elation,* in such cultivars as the 'Kentucky-31') should not be mistaken for the red fescue group (*Festuca rubra*), generally termed fine or lawn fescues, including the desirable 'Chewings' and creeping and spreading varieties. These are perhaps the major cases causing confusion, but one must become sufficiently acquainted with lawn grasses to recognize their names on the required component listings of the seed box to feel entirely confident.

Why are mixtures of several kinds of seed advocated? This was discussed at some length in the Introduction. In brief, it is an effort to introduce enough variability into the lawn so that not all grass will be susceptible to the same affliction; although a certain disease may attack one cultivar, another is likely to be resistant. Some grass suited to the many micro-habitats (shade-sun, south-north slope, poor-good soil pockets, high-low ground, etc.) is apt to be found in a mixture, whereas a single cultivar might not be adapted to all of these situations. Bluegrass-fescue combinations, with perhaps a touch of perennial ryegrass for quick cover, is a typical mixture; the bluegrasses are great for open areas, but fescues usually survive better in the shade and on dry-infertile soil under trees. Even where an all-bluegrass lawn is wanted, blends of cultivars are advocated to better "spread the risk."

What is meant by "nurse grass"? A nurse grass makes a stand quickly, until the permanent turf (generally slower in getting started) can take over. Unfortunately, the nurse grass competes for space and nutrients, slowing the permanent grass or even preventing its establishment. Ordinarily, a nurse grass should not constitute more than about 20 per cent of a mixture on a seed-count basis. A nurse grass is expected to protect the new seeding, then gradually give way to better grasses. The concept is rather outmoded these days, what with modern planting techniques and mulches, and reasonably fast-sprouting permanent cultivars. In a sense, fine fescue in a bluegrass blend serves as a nurse grass, and is useful if it persists. More often perennial ryegrass would be used. Annual ryegrass and redtop were formerly much used, but annual ryegrass is overly aggressive and redtop often carries a few unwanted species (such as timothy) with it.

Are timothy and other farm grass species suitable for lawns? Where the better lawn grasses can be grown, "hay grasses" are best left to the pasture; in the lawn they become coarse and clumpy. An exception would be for very difficult sites where survival of the finer grasses is questionable. Such sites are often seeded to tall fescue, the only turf possible without a great deal of maintenance.

What grasslike ground covers other than grass are used? A number of creeping broad-leaf species make excellent ground cover, but only dichondra (in the morning-glory family) is handled in the same fashion as are lawn grasses (seeding, mowing, etc.). Dichondra use is pretty well confined to Southern California. Creeping legumes, such as white clover, are acceptable for warm weather cover, but are generally not favored because of their contrasting appearance in turf.

What grasses are recommended for shade? Essentially the same species are planted for shade as for sun, although the proportion of shade-tolerant types may be increased. Grasses perform better in the shade if helped by tall mowing and more frequent fertilization and watering. Rough bluegrass (*Poa trivialis*), an attractive but shallow-rooting grass that does not wear well, adapts well to moist shade. Fine fescues are good for dry shade. All southern grasses except Bermuda stand shade reasonably well.

What are some good but economical grasses for large lawns that can't be pampered? Some of the "old-fashioned" self-reliant cultivars so well adapted to the casual care of yesteryear might fill the bill. Among the Kentucky bluegrasses are 'Arboretum' (Missouri) and 'Kenblue' (Kentucky) strains for the southern portions of the bluegrass belt, 'Park' (Minnesota) for northern and western zones. They are best mowed fairly tall (at least at a 2-inch clipping height). Some of the newer cultivars, such as 'Birka' and 'Plush', are similar; but as was noted, most improved cultivars not only rate highest in the well-tended lawn but under some neglect, too.

What are the advantages and disadvantages of white clover in the lawn?   White clover is an excellent companion to Kentucky bluegrass, having microbial nodules on its roots that trap nitrogen from the air; thus, clover enhances soil fertility. However, clover is patchy in the lawn and especially disruptive when white flower heads form. The flowers attract bees. Clover foliage is "soft" compared to grass, may be slippery underfoot, and is likely to stain clothing more readily than would grass. Clover leaves die down in winter and are not as good cover as cool-season grass foliage.

What grasses are best for winter color?   Southern lawn grasses turn dormant and brown near freezing. So do the native American prairie grasses. Lawns must depend almost entirely on introduced grasses from Europe, such as the bluegrasses, fescues, bent grasses, and ryegrasses, for persistent green in winter. Sow ryegrass or a mixture of these cool-season species for a green lawn in the South. In the North the same grasses remain green much of the winter and turn brown only when exposed to drying winds or bitter cold. Lawns adequately (but not excessively) fertilized show better late color. Green dyes are sold for spraying dormant southern grasses in the upper South. Dyeing is especially appropriate for zoysia, a grass typically too dense for good winter-grass overseeding, and, unlike Bermuda, with persistent enough foliage to stand winter wear.

What are the advantages and the disadvantages of establishing a zoysia lawn in the North?   The chief advantages to using zoysia are its competitiveness against weeds in hot weather and good density without a lot of mowing. Its chief disadvantage is an abbreviated growing season in the North; seldom is zoysia attractive before May and it turns off color again when frost arrives. Zoysia lawns in the North typically take several years to fill in from plugs or sprigs.

What selections of zoysia would you recommend for vegetative planting in the North? I have admired my neighbor's lawn which was planted from seed of Zoysia japonica, but he has advised me to seek one of the selected zoysia grasses, as he says they are less coarse.   The 'Meyer' strain of *Z. japonica* is most frequently offered for northern lawns, being quite hardy; the finer-textured *matrella* strains usually don't perform as well in cool climates as does the 'Meyer' strain. 'Meyer' zoysia is not as coarse as would be the variable population resulting from sowing *Z. japonica* seed (because of sexual crossing, zoysia seed does not come true-to-type).

How far north can Zoysia japonica and its selections be expected to grow without winter injury or kill? 'Meyer' zoysia should be hardy through the northeastern states, except perhaps at higher elevations and particularly exposed situations. Hardiness is perhaps less a concern than is its unattractive color where the summer is short and coolish.

I understand that there are green plant dyes used in the South on winter lawns. Would these dyes be practical in the North? Lawn colorants can be used on discolored grasses having dead foliage that is resistant to withering and wear, as with zoysia. The practice is most frequent in the upper South, and for commercial properties meant to attract visitors. Application of dye is difficult in winter weather, especially to northern grasses that are still succulent even though discolored. With northern grasses (which normally stay attractive at least until Christmas, and are then under snow during the winter), natural color is probably more pleasant than dyed turf.

Sowing Seed

Is it all right to sow lawn seed in winter? Seed will not sprout until the warm weather of spring, but where feasible it is good to get it in place as soon as you can (it may "work down" and become better imbedded in the soil from freezing-thawing cycles). Old almanac advice was to sow grass seed on the "last snow of the year." Seed will not be injured by winter weather, but where it might wash away it is better to wait until warmer weather.

Is spring or fall better for lawn seeding in Illinois? The best possible time for seeding northern lawns is in the autumn. Grass seed germinates well in this period with cold nights and sufficient moisture. Autumn-sown grass becomes firmly rooted. There is no weed competition, and the grass has an early start in spring. With spring sowings the danger is that the young grass will not have matured enough to withstand hot weather and compete well with weeds.

When is the best time to sow grass seed? In the section of the country extending from southern New York west to Omaha, the first half of September is the best. Farther southward, somewhat later; farther north, somewhat earlier.

How early in the spring can lawns on Long Island be seeded? As early as the soil can be worked; early March, if possible.

Is it best to wait until warm weather to sow grass seed? No, northern grasses thrive best during the cool, moist periods of spring and autumn.

What methods ensure sowing seed evenly? Use a mechanical seed spreader, sowing half in one direction, half at right angles. For hand sowing, see suggestions in the Introduction.

Why are there differences in seeding rates? Whether the grass plants are large or tiny, customarily crowded or spread out, will have some influence. But mainly, it is a question of seed size. Bent grass seed runs about 8,000,000 seeds to the pound; fescues, over 500,000; Kentucky bluegrass, 1,000,000 or more; and ryegrass, about 250,000. The more seeds per pound, the less poundage needed. Most mixtures are sowed two to three pounds to 1,000 square feet.

Is a spreader which casts or throws seed or one which drops it from the hopper preferable? Both the cyclone-type seeder (which throws seed from a whirling disc) or the kind that lets seed drop from regulated apertures at the bottom of a hopper will do an excellent sowing job if it is in good working condition. The casting spreaders complete seeding quickly, since they cover a band up to 10 feet wide in a single pass. They will not, however, define a course as accurately as will a drop spreader. When operating the drop spreader, more passes are needed, and one must be careful to overlap wheel tracks in order to avoid missing strips. With either type, more assured coverage can be obtained by sowing half the seed in one direction, the other half crossways.

Does a new grass seeding need protection? Protection is essential only in special cases, such as on strongly sloping ground or a poorly prepared seed bed that leaves the seed perched right at the surface. Most grass seed is too small to tempt birds, and it sifts into soil crevices where it is hidden. However, any seeding will benefit from a protective mulch, more to keep the seed bed moist than to "protect" the seed.

What is mulching? A surface blanket of any inert material that is open enough to let sprouts emerge (and rain soak into the seed bed) can serve as a mulch. Straw—a few straws deep—has been widely used, but it is difficult to procure in urban areas. Excelsior, chopped twigs, grass clippings, sphagnum peat moss, woven nettings, evergreen boughs, and similar materials can be used.

Why is a mulch helpful? A mulch helps prevent soil wash, serving as a barrier that breaks the force of rain. This is especially important on slopes. But perhaps even more important generally, a mulch acts as a partial barrier in retarding the drying out of the seed bed. Seed will sprout quickly only if kept continuously damp. A mulched seeding requires less frequent watering than one exposed directly to air and sunlight, and usually makes a stand more quickly.

What mulch is best? Mulches thick enough to retard evaporation but loose enough not to interfere with water penetration or seedling emergence work best. Mulches that will not blow easily in the wind and which decay naturally (not requiring later removal) have advantages. On the whole, nothing has proved much more satisfactory than straw, if material free from weeds can be procured. Most of the time, a straw mulch stays in place if walked upon to press it down; in especially windy spots it can be held down with string tied between stakes. Excelsior is another excellent mulch.

Is mulching a large area feasible? Machines have been developed for mulching large areas, such as newly seeded roadsides. Some blow straw along with an asphalt "tack" that binds the straw. Other hydraulic seeders pump a slurry, typically containing woodpulp fibers as the mulch. These machines can cover acres per hour. Many landscaping services have smaller versions which can be engaged for custom service.

What mulch is good for lawn repairs or important small seedings? Perhaps the most effective "mulch" for bringing a new seeding up rapidly is a clear polyethylene cover fastened at the margins by large nails or wire wickets pushed into the soil. This is not unlike a greenhouse. If the seeding is watered initially, the polyethylene not only prevents evaporation but condensation drips back and no additional watering is needed for days. In sunny weather, warmth is trapped; the soil temperature rises enough to speed sprouting early in the season. However, unless carefully watched, the temperature under the polyethylene can reach lethal levels quickly on a sunny day; sprouting seed and young seedlings will not survive temperatures much above 100° F.

How should a new seeding be watered? New seedings are best watered with a fine spray, frequently applied. Forceful watering, especially on an unmulched seed bed, disperses soil, preventing water penetration. Sprinkle lightly, frequently enough to keep the seed bed moist without surface runoff.

What about sprinkler systems for new lawn seedings? Most convenient would be underground piping activated by a time clock set for brief waterings at frequent intervals. Installations using plastic components

Underground sprinkler systems aid lawn maintenance.

(which do not require plumbing talent for installation) are now available. Or above-ground sprinklers can be set to cover sectors of a circle; these can be placed at the edge of the seeded area to prevent walking in the soft ground. Heavy or cumbersome above-ground sprinklers—apt to tear a seed bed—are to be avoided, as are ones that apply water more rapidly than the particular area can absorb it.

What assistance other than mulching and watering can be given a newly seeded lawn? Seedling grass derives its nourishment from stored reserves in the seed and will not need fertilization for some time. Seedlings are tender and susceptible to chemical injury. The grass must mature at least until it has been mowed a few times before applying any weedkiller. An exception is bromoxynil, which, at the recommended rate, can be safely applied to most seedling turf for elimination of broad-leaf weeds.

When should a new lawn be mowed first? Seedlings need a fair root system before being mowed in order not to be torn out of the ground. But don't let the grass grow so long that it flops over. It is generally wise to begin mowing before the grass has reached twice again what will be its customary mowing height. By then the grass should be rooted deeply enough so that the soil can be allowed to dry out sufficiently to prevent foot-printing and mower-rutting. Obviously, new grass should be dry for its first mowings.

Are there special precautions for seeding slopes with grass seed? Because of the obvious danger from erosion and the incon-

venience of operating on steep slopes, consider sodding rather than
seeding. Even a strip or two of sod across the slope helps control wash.
A seeded slope should receive all the protective measures that have
been discussed, possibly a nurse grass in the seed mixture and certainly
a good mulch. In the case of a really steep slope, grass may not be the
solution at all. Rather, consider the planting of ground covers, such as
creeping junipers, English ivy, or myrtle.

Planting Lawns Vegetatively

What is sod?   Sod consists of a community of mature grass plants
started elsewhere, delivered as flat squares or "rolls," like carpets, for
laying to make an "instant lawn." In effect, you pay a sod farm, the
"nursery," to oversee the seeding through the tedious seedling stages.
Only grasses having spreading stems make sod able to hold together
during lifting and replanting. Bluegrass is one of the best sod grasses.

Is sodding worthwhile?   Having your lawn sodded is certainly more
expensive than seeding it, but you gain cover instantly. Professionally
grown sod should provide just as good a grass in your lawn as if you
had planted it yourself.

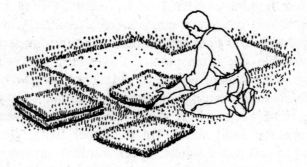

*Most garden centers sell grass sod in the
spring for new lawns or for patching up
established lawns.*

Does sodding make seed-bed preparation less necessary?   Sod
planted on poorly prepared soil will perform no better in the long haul
than would a seeding given inadequate seed-bed preparation. Before
laying sod, prepare the soil the same as for seeding, i.e., mix in fertil-

izer, add lime if needed, loosen the root-zone soil, remove debris, level, etc.

Are special pains needed with a newly sodded lawn?   It takes several weeks for sod to reroot, and during this interval it should be watered regularly. Firm newly laid sod into the soil by light rolling with a roller, and, if possible, topdress (with sterilized soil) where the sod blocks meet or where depressions are noted. Fertilize later as you would an established lawn.

Can I save costs by sodding my own lawn?   Yes, sod can be purchased from a garden center and laid at home. It is more difficult to do a smooth job from lifting your own sod from another part of the lawn; sod growers use machines that cut sod squares to an exact thickness, something not possible with ordinary garden tools. However, a certain amount of patchwork sodding can be successfully done by the homeowner.

Is there anything to be wary about in purchasing sod?   Buy sod from reputable sources which identify the grasses. Look for weeds or offtype grasses. Ask for assurance that there are no pests in the sod, such as crabgrass seed, harmful insects, etc. Sod that is cut thin roots most rapidly, but it also dries out more readily than does thicker sod; before accepting delivery, be certain that the sod is fresh and has not dried out (is not yellowing).

Are there less expensive alternatives to sodding?   Yes, small biscuits of sod (called plugs) or stem fragments (called sprigs) can be planted. Either will spread into a tight turf in time. Southern grasses—for which no seed is available—are often planted this way. Sprigs will give more coverage than an equivalent weight of plugs, but sprigs dry out readily and require immediate planting. Zoysia sprigs spread a bit more quickly than do plugs. Even so, zoysia is so slow-growing that a year or more is required to make a solid stand. On the other hand, Bermuda grass makes a stand in just a few weeks. Other southern grasses fall between these extremes.

Can grass fragments be used to start a lawn?   With certain grasses, yes, particularly creeping bent grasses and Bermuda grasses. Sod is shredded—or stem clippings cut—to make what are called "stolons," and these are scattered over a prepared seed bed just as is grass seed. Because these stolons dry out quickly, they should be topdressed immediately with about ¼ inch of soil (or at least be firmly pressed into the ground). The new stolons must be watered without fail until roots develop at the joints and new growth appears. This is more a practice for the professional than for the homeowner.

Are sodded lawns or lawns planted from sprigs or plugs preferable to seeding? The only advantages to sodding are quickness in providing mature turf or perpetuation of cultivars (in sprigging or sodding) that don't come true from seed. Sod may forestall weed appearance, but the potential for weeds is still in the soil if the sod fails. Such vegetative planting risks the introduction of pests and diseases more than does direct seeding, and some experts feel seeded grasses—rooting directly in "home soil"—do better than grass that is transplanted.

What grasses are most often used for vegetative plantings? While all lawn grasses can be transplanted vegetatively, the extra effort or expense (compared to seeding) makes quality sod or select cultivars the best investment. 'Floratine' St. Augustine grass is available in Florida and the Southeast; the 'Tift' series ('Tifgreen', 'Tifway', etc.) and 'Santa Ana' Bermuda grasses are available throughout the South and California. 'Emerald' and local zoysia cultivars are available in the South; 'Meyer' zoysia, in the North; the bluegrass and fescue cultivars cited at the beginning of this section, alone or in mixture, are used for northern sod.

Would you recommend vegetative strains of greens-type bent grass? Excellent creeping bent grasses from seed (such as 'Emerald', 'Penncross', 'Penneagle', and 'Prominent') are now available, and for lawns "like a golf green" this would be recommended. Seed of 'Kingstown' velvet bent grass, the ultimate in fine-textured turf, is also on the market. However, if you want a particular golf course clone (such as 'Cohansey', 'Evansville', 'Toronto', etc.), live starts must be procured from a nursery and be planted vegetatively, since these cultivars do not come true-to-type from seed and no seed supplies are available. However started, a lawn of creeping or velvet bent requires more attention than bluegrass-fescue, especially more frequent and precise mowing.

Must colonial bent grasses be started vegetatively? No, colonial bents such as 'Highland' are available as pure-line seed. Colonial bents do not require the intensive care that the lower-growing creeping bent grasses do. Colonial bents are best mowed at a ¾- to 1-inch clipping height.

Tending the Established Lawn

What are the main lawn-care needs? Mowing is inevitable, of course. With few exceptions, fertilization is needed (the exact program will vary with the kind of grass and climate). In many cases, watering will be required, and, alas, when things go wrong, such necessary procedures as weed, pest, and disease control must be resorted to.

Do maintenance programs differ for differing kinds of lawns? Yes, indeed. Obviously timing will differ for northern grasses compared to southern ones (see Introduction). Some grasses require more attention than do others, especially the "heavy feeders" such as Bermuda and bent. Fast-growing types, such as Bermuda, require more of just about everything (especially mowing and fertilization) than will a "poor man's grass" such as centipede (which actually suffers if fertilization is generous). Some grasses, such as fine fescues and zoysia, can get by with little attention, but look better when well cared for. Zoysia is slow-growing and stands infrequent mowing, but looks more attractive if clipped each week or so.

What attention can an "average" lawn be expected to need, say in bluegrass country? Weekly mowing (perhaps each five days at the height of spring growth, maybe each ten days during summer "slow-down"); a few fertilizations annually (particularly in autumn for bluegrass); probably a 2, 4-D treatment for broad-leaf weeds (the weeds are most noticed in spring–summer, but autumn weed control helps prevent spring occurrence); perhaps watering during dry periods and occasional chemical treatments to combat specific afflictions if they threaten.

What makes a lawn "look good"? Good looks are due mainly to density, uniformity, and rich color. Planting of improved cultivars helps greatly, but you still must mow regularly, eliminate discordant weeds, and fertilize (both for deep color and to keep the grass vigorously contesting weeds).

What are the main lawn problems to be expected? Probably most noticeable will be weeds, although after a while these should lessen, succumbing to vigorously growing grass and occasional chemical treatments. Selective herbicides exist for broad-leaf weeds, such as dandelions and plantains, and for annual grasses such as crabgrass, but not for perennial grass weeds. Disease can be troublesome seasonally, although this has become less of a problem with the newer disease-resistant cultivars.

Should clippings be collected? This is a matter of preference and to an extent depends upon the kind of grass. Bent and Bermuda cultivars probably should have the clippings collected, since their density prevents the clippings from sifting down near the soil where decay is rapid. Clippings of most grasses, if regularly mowed, are short enough to work into the sod and not be noticeable. Some pathologists feel that a mass of clippings constitutes a reservoir for diseases. The collection of clippings is a bother, and in general they are removed only on highly manicured turfs.

Are collected clippings of any value? Yes. They make an excellent mulch or a fine addition to a compost pile. Fresh clippings mold rather quickly unless spread out. Scattered about the garden they can be a valuable soil additive, both for nutrient value and for the humus they provide.

What is lawn thatch? Thatch is the accumulation of incompletely decayed tissues and other debris at the base of sod. It consists mainly of ligneous grass roots, stems, and lower leaf sheaths. Thatch is continuously decomposing at the bottom, while additions accrue above. Clippings, being succulent and easily decayed, contribute rather little to thatch buildup.

Is thatch harmful? If not excessive (up to ½ inch thick), it is normal and probably a useful recycling of vegetative remains, an aid to wear and to soil aggregation. Thatch may harbor certain pests, however. If excessive, it can insulate the soil so thoroughly that fertilizer or other surface applications will not penetrate evenly to the root zone, and the grass may root shallowly in the thatch instead of deeply in the soil. Zoysia thatch is so indestructible that some zoysia lawns shed water—as if shingled—rather than letting it soak through to the soil.

On a trip through northern New England in the spring, I saw farmers burning pastures and fields. (I used to see this as a child, but had thought it might now be outmoded.) Is this still a good practice? I know the new grass growth after the burning is very green, but aren't nutrients lost in the process? Would you recommend this as a practice in the spring on our very large zoysia lawn that is choked with thatch (although it performs quite well once it turns green)? We have plenty of hoses and good water pressure, so there would be no fire hazard. With restrictions on air pollution, burning, whether of field or lawn, is indeed "outmoded." Burning is an effective way to remove accumulated duff, especially pronounced with zoysia; burning dormant turf will not kill the grass and may have a rejuvenating effect. But a burned-over lawn is messy and an eyesore until new growth occurs. Nutrient loss is not consequential and can easily be compensated for through fertilization.

I plan to rent a dethatching machine. Should I use it in the spring or fall? Should I apply fertilizer after I use it? It is generally best to dethatch just prior to a season favorable for grass growth (which will vary with the kind of grass and climate); that way, fresh grass, rather than weeds, fills in the scars. Fertilize your lawn according to its needs (see discussion of fertilization), whether or not the lawn is dethatched. For efficiency's sake, it would be more sensible to apply fertilizer after, rather than before, thatch removal.

Why is thatch more of a problem now than formerly? Modern standards call for vigorous, dense cultivars, which are made to grow profusely by fertilization, watering, etc. Tissue decomposition cannot keep up with production, especially on stoloniferous turfs where the thatch hardly contacts soil—needed to speed decay. Pesticides can sometimes inhibit thatch decomposition, too. When earthworms are eliminated, as with soil pesticides, thatching generally increases.

How can thatch be controlled? Try to keep natural processes in balance so that decomposition is rapid. (Speedy decay requires moisture, moderate pH, some nitrogen, and reasonable aerification.) The most effective means for reducing thatch is to topdress lightly with weed-free soil, something more practical for a golf course than for a home lawn. Thatch can be reduced for a growing season by mechanical removal; powered equipment variously termed "vertical mower," "dethatcher," "thinner," "power rakes," etc., can be rented. These slice into the thatch and kick it to the surface for pickup. Aerification machines, which can also be rented, punch holes through the thatch into the soil and should help, especially if the soil cores are then scattered back over the thatch layer.

What is the nutrient value of grass clippings? Nutrients equivalent to one or two fertilizations at normal rates are contained in a year's clippings. Most of the nutrients are recycled as the clippings decay.

How can lawns be contained (that is, the grass restrained at borders)? This requires persistent attention. The problem is most pronounced with grasses having vigorous runners and rhizomes, such as Bermuda and zoysia. If only surface runners are involved, edging tools and powered edgers can trim the runners. If spread is by underground stems, metal or plastic barriers driven several inches into the soil may help. Sometimes it may be possible to toxify soil strips, although this is hazardous because the chemical may leach elsewhere. Chemical edging is also possible with a contact foliage spray of such substances as paraquat, cacodylic acid, glyphosate, or even petroleum derivatives. This is a useful approach for driveways and walks, and to create a grass-free mowing zone around trees.

What causes earth mounds on my lawn? Moles and gophers are usually responsible for tunnelings and soil piles at a burrow entrance. Other mammals may dig or scratch. Large earthworms ("night crawlers") leave castings that are noticeable on low-clipped turf such as bent grass. Mole cricket mounds are found on sandy soils of the Deep South, and those of crayfish on soils with a high water table.

How can damage from moles, gophers, or larger burrowing animals be checked? Poison baits and traps are helpful, although seldom completely successful. A more general approach is to remove the food that attracts these animals—in most cases, soil insects. A "grub-proofing" of the soil with an insecticide may be a solution.

What about earthworm castings? Insecticides make the soil unattractive to earthworms, which retreat to lower levels or move elsewhere (doubtless, the population is also reduced by the insecticide). However, before eliminating earthworms, remember that their burrows are beneficial where soil aerification is needed and the worms do consume thatch.

Should a lawn be rolled to make it level? Rolling can flatten mole runs or reset sod plugs and grass clumps heaved by winter's alternate freezing and thawing. It will squash, but not eliminate, soil mounds. Instead, scatter mounded soil by raking. It is usually preferable to level a lawn surface by filling in depressions with additional soil than to crush high spots. Rolling compacts the soil and undoes the benefit of cultivation (whether mechanical or due to freezing).

Is lawn liming necessary? As a regular procedure similar to fertilization, no. The chief value from liming is to make acid soils "sweeter" (more alkaline). If soil is near neutral, within a pH range of 6 to 8, lime is probably not needed. Very acid soils, some with a pH as low as 4, should benefit from liming, especially if planted with such grasses as bluegrass or Bermuda, which prefer a higher pH. The only sure indication of the need for lime is to have a pH soil test made.

What is the action of lime on a lawn? If the soil is heavy, lime will help to keep it aggregated, permitting air and moisture to penetrate. Lawns tend to become acid in rainy climates, and most fertilizers are mildly acidifying. Lime will counteract this tendency, helping to balance plant-food release for the grasses.

Both gypsum and ground limestone have been recommended to "break up" the very heavy clay on which our lawn grasses are struggling—without much success. Now I realize we should have applied the limestone or gypsum before sowing the seed, but since there is grass cover, though sparse, I'd like to save it. Which material now would work faster—the gypsum or limestone? The clay soil is acid, since it came from a potato field. Both materials are effective for aggregating soil where the calcium ion is needed (as in substituting for sodium in soils that slake readily). Gypsum is more soluble, and in that sense the more "immediately" effective. But other factors, such as acidity, may be a more important consideration. Gypsum would probably be preferable on alkaline soils in the West, while limestone would probably be preferable on acid soils in humid climates.

If lime is needed, what kind should I use? The best is crushed limestone, preferably the dolomitic type (containing magnesium). Spread 50 to 100 pounds per 1,000 square feet as you would fertilizer each few years, if need be, until the pH is at least 6. In northern climates, a good time to lime is in the winter or fall.

Is it necessary to acidify alkaline lawns? The need is less frequent than for liming, but may be required in arid regions. Ten to 50 pounds of sulfur per 1,000 square feet may be needed, depending upon the degree of alkalinity; however, the problem is often one of sodium excess rather than alkalinity alone, in which case gypsum (calcium sulfate) would prove a better corrective than sulfur.

What are the causes of lawn blemishes? This is sometimes hard to determine. Try a process of elimination: what about—soil adequacy (buried debris or spilled contaminants); pattern relating to dog urination; the possibility of spilled salt, fertilizer, etc.; insects associated with damage (such as grubs in the soil chewing off roots; webworms burrowing deep in the sod and chewing off foliage; tiny chinch bugs sucking juices from the foliage); possibility of physical damage, such as from scuffing or the repeated passage of equipment; past treatments, which with overusage may have accumulated to toxic levels (of arsenic or of crabgrass preventer). If none of these seems to fit, probably disease is the culprit, of which there are many kinds that are not easily identifiable. Your county agent may help and be aware of local problems causing the trouble.

How can I most easily repair a lawn blemish? Injury is generally quite localized and the spot can be reseeded, sodded, or planted to plugs and sprigs, just as with a new lawn. If soil is at fault, remove obstructions and replace toxic soil with fresh soil. An inexpensive hollow-tube plug lifter can cut plugs where the turf is thick for replacement in voids. As the plugs exit from the top of the tube, simply drop them in holes that the plugger makes in the repair area and firm them in place with your foot.

Is spiking a lawn helpful? Spiking may loosen thatch with attendant advantages, but it is generally not worth the trouble for improving the soil. Indentations forced into the soil are more likely to intensify compaction than to relieve it. Aerifying machines that remove cores of soil would be better.

Will tree leaves injure a lawn? Anything that obstructs light from reaching green leaves will reduce the grasses' food-making ability; but no toxicants occur in tree leaves that will appreciably inhibit the growth of familiar lawn grasses. Thus, the problem is mainly a mechanical one, not a chemical one. Tree roots, however, may reduce grass growth by competing strongly for fertilizer and moisture. Small leaves, or larger ones shredded by a mower, should cause no difficulty in the typical lawn (of bluegrass-fescue or other open-textured turf) if not more than an inch or two thick. The leaf fragments will settle into the grass foliage, which will soon overgrow them. Where fallen leaves are so abundant as to smother the grass, they should be gathered for the compost pile or mulching around shrubs.

Mowers and Mowing

Of what value to the lawn is mowing? Except that mowing is harder on most weed plants than on the grass, mowing does little to benefit the lawn other than to improve appearance. We all strive for a level grass carpet, and to achieve this, mowing becomes necessary. Foliage lost as clippings is a physiological drain on the grass, for each green leaf is productive food-making tissue. Mowing *does* stimulate side branching, causing the lawn to become denser, though the individual plants become stunted and more shallowly rooted. Lawns left unmowed form seed, become patchy, and gradually weeds and brush overwhelm the grass.

Does disease enter through the sheared tips of grass blades?   Some diseases are thought to, but in most instances, if conditions are right for a disease, it will find ways of infecting grass, mowed or not. But un-mowed (and tall-mowed) grass has some advantage in resisting disease, probably mostly due to the extra food-making power of additional green leaves.

How frequently should the lawn be mowed?   This, of course, will vary with the growth rate. Well-kept lawns, at peak seasons, may have to be mowed every few days. This is especially true with luxurious turfs, such as a golf green, which are usually mowed every other day. A good rule of thumb is to mow any time that the grass gains an additional 50–100 per cent of its customary mowing height.

What if I can't "keep up" with the mowing, due to rain or other cause?   If the grass gets excessively tall, cut it back a little at a time, gradually reducing the height. If a grass plant is suddenly bereft of most of its green leaf (is "scalped"), it will certainly be weakened; roots can fail to grow for many weeks. This is especially damaging in the spring when stored food has been used to make fresh leaves; eliminating this growth then may kill the plant.

Our house has a field of grass on which we look out. We enjoy the daisies and first stand of young grass. After that, when should it be cut, and how often per year, to keep it attractive? It is now full of red bunch grass.   Cut the first grass before the seed ripens in the heads. Two more (tall) cuttings at monthly intervals during the summer should keep it orderly.

What mowing equipment should I get?   This will depend upon the size of the lawn, the kind of grass and its ideal mowing height, and funds available. Since mowing represents most of the time people spend on their lawn, it should be made as pleasant an occupation as possi-ble; top-quality equipment, with the capacity to get the job done quickly and conveniently, is strongly recommended. It can range from simple hand-push unmotorized mowers that can easily handle postage-stamp size lawns in urban locations to tractors and riding mowers for estates almost as expensive as the family automobile.

What are the advantages of reel mowers?   Reel mowers cut with a scissors-like action of rotating a reel against a fixed bed knife. If in good repair, this is the most precise mowing instrument available. Reel mowers are especially recommended for low-mowed turfs that are well tended. Reel mowers are somewhat safer than other types.

What are the disadvantages of a reel mower? Reel mowers are rather hard to adjust and sharpen. They are also somewhat more expensive. Because their wheels protrude beyond the cutting edge, adjacent mowing passes must overlap and the machine cannot get very close to barriers. Riding on two wheels only, a reel mower maintains a constant cutting height above the soil and thus reflects any unevenness occurring in the lawn's surface.

What are the strong points of a rotary mower? Rotaries are less expensive and easier to maintain than reels. They are also more versatile, get close to obstructions, and are especially useful for mowing tall, floppy grass which is "sucked up" into the cutting chamber (a reel "blows down" lanky foliage ahead of the bed knife).

What are the disadvantages of rotary mowers? They can be hazardous, sometimes flinging with the speed of a bullet metal fragments or rocks that are struck. Cutting by the impact of a speeding blade, rotary mowers tend to bruise and fray leaf tips more than do reels, especially when dull. Rotary cutting is generally not as "neat" or precise as a reel cutting, but is far more popular.

Are there any "tips" to be aware of in selecting mowing equipment, things an inexperienced person might not think about? They are legion. Consider these: good dispersal of clippings, not wads or windrows; flotation tires that don't rut the lawn or "catch" in holes and crevices; sufficient power for the "worst" (i.e., fastest-growing grass) season; adequate range of height adjustment, easily made; not unwieldy, able to approach borders closely for "trimming"; noisiness; weight (ease of lifting); reliability of service and ease of servicing; with riding machines, maneuverable turning radius and compactness, reverse gear, mower speed independent of forward speed, simplicity of handling (including attachments), gas consumption, up-front or belly-mounted mower, and so on.

Are there other types of mowers for home use? None that are widely used. A hammer-knife design, in which loose-hanging blades are extended from a rotating reel by centrifugal force, has found some favor; it is safer than the typical rotary, but not so easily maintained. A few garden tractors still have sickle-bar attachments, the farmer's familiar hay-cutting tool; a sickle bar is not very suitable for low-cut home lawns and may be hazardous for inexperienced users.

String- or cord-powered trimmers have been widely introduced, patterned after the original Weed Eater. How useful are they? Those that are quite portable, powered by a lightweight (usually two-cycle) motor, are quite handy for controlling tall (but soft or fleshy) vegetation in out-of-the-way corners inaccessible to a conventional mower. Where an electric cord must be dragged for power, of course the versatility is limited. However, "mowing," if you can call it that, is even more brutal than with a rotary machine, accomplished by a rapidly rotating length of cord that whips and tears the vegetation. The machines throw out fragments of anything "cut," often unpleasant on the ankles and splattering clothing. The machines will not cut woody stems of any size, and can skin the bark off young trees or shrubs if brought too close to them; they are mainly of value for rough mowing of hard-to-reach places.

How soon after it rains can I mow?   Use common sense. Wet grass clippings tend to wad and disperse poorly, but sometimes wet weather is so persistent that getting the mowing job done outweighs performing it well.

What about electric mowers?   Now that battery-powered models are available, electric mowers may become more versatile. The inconvenience of dragging a cord makes mowing a large lawn (especially if there are trees) cumbersome with an electric mower using a power outlet. Electric power is superior for quietness, easy starting, and low maintenance. Corded electric mowers should not be used on wet turf.

Is occasional lawn scalping of benefit?   Removal of foliage scorched brown by winter weather may let sunlight reach the soil and grass crowns more abundantly and speed spring revival. There is little disadvantage to scalping the grass then, since this foliage no longer has much food-making capacity and will soon be replaced by new leaves. Such a scalping is permissible only in late winter before new foliage grows. Low mowing of a weedy lawn is sometimes practiced in the summer on the theory that seeds of crabgrass and similar weeds are thus removed; probably there will be plenty of weed seeds anyway, and the setback from low mowing to whatever good grass exists probably more than offsets any weed reduction benefits. A slight reduction in mowing height may stimulate new growth and help "tidy up" a lawn when done shortly before some special occasion.

What mowing pattern should I follow?   Efficient mowing varies with the contours of the land, but in general should minimize the need for turning and backing. Obstructions (such as flower and shrub areas) should be located so they don't make mowing any more complicated than necessary. Try to alternate or vary the direction of mowing—to avoid "grain" due to continuous sweep of the mower in one direction.

What is a suggested mowing height for northern grasses?   Velvet and creeping bent grasses are typically mowed quite low, no taller than ½ inch; colonial bent grasses are generally mowed ¾ to 1 inch. The newer low-growing bluegrass cultivars, such as 'Fylking' or 'Baron', do well at 1 inch, but most bluegrasses are better mowed at 1½ inches or taller. Rough bluegrass (*Poa trivialis*), such as 'Sabre', is mowed like topflight Kentucky bluegrass cultivars. Fescues and ryegrasses should be handled the same as bluegrass, although tall fescue is often mowed quite tall for bermlike, relatively untended turf.

What is the suggested mowing height for southern grasses?   Improved Bermuda grasses are generally mowed quite low, from ¼ inch with golf-green types such as 'Tifdwarf', to 1 inch or taller with common Bermuda. Zoysia and centipede are generally mowed at an intermediate height, between 1 and 2 inches. Bahia and St. Augustine are mowed fairly tall, typically 1½ to 2½ inches.

No matter how sharp I try to keep the blades of my rotary mower, they seem to "tear" rather than clean-cut my grass (Zoysia japonica). The result is that the tips look ragged and usually turn brown soon after mowing. A neighbor has suggested I use a reel-type mower. Do you think this would help?   Zoysia tissue is unusually fibrous. Heavy-duty mowers are recommended, and a well-adjusted reel mower should mow more neatly than a rotary. (See discussion of lawn mowing.)

How early in the spring should mowing start?   Mow just as soon as there is appreciable growth, weather permitting, or before the grass has doubled its usual mowing height.

How late should mowing continue in autumn?   As long as there is appreciable new growth. However, bluegrass lawns develop much shorter recumbent foliage in autumn than in spring, tending to thicken then rather than grow tall; mowing is not nearly as burdensome in autumn as in spring.

Should the lawn be clipped short for winter?   No. Continue at the customary mowing height through autumn so that the grass gains full advantage of ample green leaf.

Lawn Irrigation

Is watering the lawn essential?   Only in arid climates or during prolonged drought. The ability to resist drying varies with the kind of turf grass, but east of Kansas drought is seldom bad enough to kill the usual lawn grasses even though they may brown temporarily.

Would a covering of peat moss over the grass in summer help to hold the moisture and do away with watering?   No. Most water loss occurs from transpiration from the grass foliage, and would not be influenced by soil coverings. Moreover, normally accumulating thatch would be the equivalent of applied peat moss, free of charge! So save your peat for mixing into the soil.

What is the advantage of lawn irrigation in humid climates?   Mainly an assured supply of moisture whenever it is needed. This is especially important for newly seeded lawns and for keeping the lawn attractive when rainfall fails.

What is the best irrigation system?   See discussions in the Introduction and for new seedings. Any system that supplies an adequate amount of water uniformly, at a rate such that it soaks into the soil rather than runs off, should prove excellent.

Is it good to water the lawn frequently?   This will partly depend upon the kind of grass and its use (low-clipped, shallow-rooting turfs, such as bent grass, will benefit from more frequent watering than a bluegrass lawn would need). It is usually best to water the average home lawn only frequently enough to prevent drought discoloration, letting the soil surface dry between waterings. Intermittent drying-out above the root zone helps control disease and weeds.

Can lawn irrigation cause difficulties?   Watering is not a cure for any problem other than drought, and, indeed, it can intensify disease. Overwatering can result in more problems than no watering at all; it especially encourages unwanted wet-habitat vegetation (annual bluegrass, volunteer bent grass, nut sedge, *Poa trivialis,* etc.) at the expense of the lawn grass.

How heavily should I water?   Enough to soak the root zone, in most cases to percolate a foot deep or deeper. An application of less than an inch of water may suffice with a sandy soil, but a clay may need 3 inches for a good soaking. Apply water only as rapidly as it can soak into the soil. Sandy soils may accept an inch of water in a few minutes, but a clay soil may have to be watered at a light rate for hours to achieve a 3-inch penetration.

Are there ways to improve water penetration?   Growing grass itself helps, through organic additions that loosen tight soils. Wetting-agent sprays, such as Aqua-Gro, reduce surface tension, often enabling water to seep through thatch and into tight soils more readily. Aerification opens channels in compacted lawns. In preparing a new seed bed, amendments such as ground limestone and gypsum can be included to loosen tight or slaking soils.

Can the lawn be watered at any time of day?　Watering in the heat of the day can waste water through evaporation, but the cooling effect should benefit the grass. There is no truth to the idea that water droplets act as magnifying lenses, causing burn. Watering late in the day is efficient, but some custodians have an aversion to leaving a lawn "wet" through the night for fear of encouraging disease (much of the time, dew wets the grass anyway). This leaves early morning as perhaps very slightly favored for watering the lawn.

Is treated water all right for grass?　Any water suitable for general home use will not injure grass, even if heavily chlorinated. Muddy water from ponds, even treated sewage effluent, is satisfactory for irrigation. In arid regions, where the soil is already quite salty, highly saline water from wells could worsen the soil structure, especially if not applied heavily enough to leach completely through the root zone.

Lawn Fertilization

Why should lawns be fertilized?　Fertilizer is perhaps the most helpful tool for achieving the objective of a dense, attractive stand of grass. Lawn grass fertilized at the proper stages of the growing cycle is in a much better position to make a tight cover and to overpower weeds than is "weaker" unfertilized turf. Balanced fertilization also gives the grass a deeper color.

What is a complete fertilizer?　A complete fertilizer contains all three of the major nutrients: nitrogen, phosphorus, and potassium. They are listed by percentage in that order in the analysis (20–8–12 means 20 per cent nitrogen, 8 per cent phosphorus, and 12 per cent potassium).

Do I need to worry about secondary nutrients in my lawn fertilizer?　In most cases, no, unless soil tests or experience indicate that they are particularly deficient. Calcium and sulfur are typical secondary elements; much of the time they are included as unlisted ingredients in a complete fertilizer and often reach the lawn in small quantity in rainfall or dust. Acid soils especially benefit from calcium; alkaline ones, from sulfur (but sulfur has improved grass performance in western Washington and Florida, where alkalinity is not the problem).

What about minor nutrients? Minor or trace nutrients are required in only very small proportions. Their lack causes the so-called deficiency diseases, more often the result of the minor element being tied up by soil imbalance than because of complete absence. The only trace deficiency that occurs with any frequency in lawn grass is iron, often immobilized in alkaline soils of semiarid climates such as the High Plains. Centipede grass is very sensitive to iron deficiency and may turn chlorotic (blanched) with only a slight rise of pH or merely a fertility imbalance. Application of iron sulfate or iron chelates (a quick-acting form of iron sulfate available from garden centers—follow directions on container when applying) corrects iron chlorosis, but often a better solution is to acidify alkaline soils, making the iron tied up in the soil available. Copper, zinc, manganese, molybdenum, and a few other trace elements occasionally restrict crop growth but seem not to be a problem with lawns.

Don't lawns recycle their nutrients more than do agricultural crops? Yes, especially if clippings are left on the lawn. However, additional nitrogen will almost always be needed, since nitrogen compounds are readily volatilized and leached. Potassium may leach or be removed in clippings. Phosphorus, secondary, and trace nutrients are often supplied sufficiently by decaying vegetation and soil reserves.

What is the most important nutrient for lawn grass? Nitrogen. Its addition gives the greatest growth response. The value of a lawn fertilizer is viewed chiefly on the basis of nitrogen content, and application rates are usually set to provide about 1 pound of elemental nitrogen to each 1,000 square feet regardless of other nutrient percentages.

What are the chief sources of nitrogen in lawn fertilizer? There are three general classes of nitrogen-yielding components: 1) soluble or inorganic chemicals, such as nitrate or ammonium salts; 2) natural organic materials, such as sewage sludge, tankage, or processing residues; 3) tailor-made synthetic organics, such as ureaform and IBDU (see below).

What are the features of soluble fertilizer materials? Dissolving readily in water, they are immediately and abundantly available. This may be advantageous for quick spruce-up, especially in cold weather, but it can also cause overstimulation followed by debilitating letdown. Soluble fertilizer salts easily desiccate or "burn" foliage upon contact, and they may temporarily increase the salt concentration in the soil to deleterious levels. Soluble fertilizers are relatively inexpensive and can be effective when skillfully and carefully used.

What about organic fertilizers for the lawn? Organics are quite safe but also quite expensive in terms of nutrient value. Upon decay, organic substances release the whole gamut of nutrients found in tissue and should contribute a balance of minor nutrients as well as major ones. Manures were once widely available but are expensive and difficult to procure today. Their nutrient content varies with the kind of fertilizer and its handling, and they often contain weed seeds. Agricultural by-products, such as cottonseed or soybean meal, have become expensive for fertilizer. Tankage, leather scraps, seaweed materials, and other less valuable by-products vary in quality and usefulness. Processing sewage to acceptable form is expensive; in some instances sewage may carry unwanted heavy metal components from industrial wastes. Sewage sludge composted with wood chips has produced an effective lawn fertilizer, partly "subsidized" by urban communities anxious to dispose of sludge. Most of these materials are excellent sources of humus and when available locally can be mixed with the soil before the seed is sown. (See Introduction to Soils, Section 1.)

What about synthetic organic nitrogen sources? These are especially tailored for lawn usage, their composition regulated to provide limited immediate effect but long-lasting release as the more complex polymers are broken down by soil processes. Most often used are a copolymer of urea and formaldehyde called ureaform, or UF, and IBDU, synthetic isobutylene-diurea; both are frequently components of mixed lawn fertilizers. The synthetic organics are nonburning and long-lasting.

Do you suggest the use of horse manure for a grass lawn? Only in the preparation of a new lawn when it could be incorporated in the soil to supply organic matter. Moreover, its availability varies from region to region.

I live near a riding academy and can get all the horse manure I want. Should my lawn be covered with it in the fall? It is probably not as desirable as a bagged fertilizer. It would probably be hard to spread evenly, and might be unpleasant underfoot. However, it can be mixed with soil to make a new lawn or is valuable in flower, vegetable, and shrub gardens.

Would you advise using well-rotted cow or horse manure in preparing a lawn? How much on 1,500 square feet of area? Because of its beneficial action on the soil, rotted cow or horse manure would be an excellent material to use in preparing any soil for a lawn or garden. If the soil is poor, mix in 2 to 3 inches of the material if you can get this much.

Are there other controlled-release lawn fertilizers besides ureaform types? Yes, prills ("beads") of soluble fertilizer coated with resin or sulfur (SCU) to retard release of nutrients. Their effectiveness will depend on the uniformity and thickness of the coating, whether it has been cracked during handling, and how resistant it is to soil decomposition.

Should a complete fertilizer be used on the lawn, or nitrogen alone? Nitrogen alone is satisfactory if a soil test indicates ample other nutrients. It is often no more costly to utilize a mass-marketed complete fertilizer rich in nitrogen than nitrogen alone, thus assuring that other nutrients will not be in short supply. As a general rule, use a complete fertilizer at least once a year.

What is a good lawn fertilizer analysis? No single analysis fits all soils, depending upon which nutrients are abundant or lacking. It can be assumed that nitrogen will be needed by any lawn, and that this nutrient should predominate (be 2 or 3 times as abundant as other components). Lawns in humid climates generally need potassium more than do those in arid climates. A good lawn fertilizer analysis for lawns in the eastern United States might be 23–5–8, or something similar.

Is an analysis such as mentioned in the previous question equally suited to young and old turf? Yes, except that in mixing fertilizer into a seed bed, more phosphorus should be included (the phosphorus equaling or exceeding the other nutrients).

At what rate should I apply lawn fertilizer? Authorities suggest about 1 pound of elemental nitrogen to each 1,000 square feet (i.e., 5 pounds of a 20 per cent nitrogen fertilizer such as 20–6–6). Follow the recommendations on the bag. Lawn fertilizer directions usually indicate appropriate spreader settings.

How is lawn fertilizer best applied? If at all possible, use a spreader; it is very difficult to apply fertilizer uniformly by hand casting. (See discussions under Sowing Seed and use the same techniques.) Follow product directions.

Is there any advantage to one chemical form of nutrient compared to another? The grass doesn't care just as long as the nutrient becomes available to its root system. Ammonium nitrogen is held by soil particles better than nitrate (or urea) nitrogen, but soil microorganisms are continuously oxidizing ammonium so that it becomes about equally soluble in warm weather (and may volatilize more). UF nitrogen is very stable. The sulfate of potassium rather than the usual chloride may have some advantages, sulfur typically being useful and chloride unneeded; the sulfate has a slightly lower salt index, too.

When is the best time to fertilize lawns? Adjust to the seasonal needs of the grass (see introductory discussion). Some species are heavier feeders than others, such as creeping bent grasses and 'Merion' bluegrass in the North, Bermuda grasses and some St. Augustines in the South. Four or more pounds of elemental nitrogen may be required annually for intensively managed turfs, applied no more than 1 pound at a time (except when controlled-release fertilizer is used). Pace the fertilization through the growing season, keeping in mind that fertility is not lost from heavy soils when they are cold (below about 50° F. nitrogen mostly becomes fixed; you can advantageously feed northern lawns in cold weather).

Does fertilizer have to be "watered in" after its application? Not with most modern formulations; even soluble forms are generally prilled (not dusty) and roll off grass foliage to the soil, hardly risking burn. There is no risk with ureaform types of nitrogen, but other salts of a complete fertilizer may adhere to damp foliage; then a sprinkling will ensure against burn. Used on dry turf, few present-day lawn fertilizers need immediate watering in. Of course, when rain fails to appear, you will want to water your lawn to speed action by the fertilizer.

I bought some black material that I was told was a good lawn food, but it did no good. Was this a fertilizer? No, it probably was not fertilizer. A lot of dark materials are sold as "humus," and may be virtually worthless from the standpoint of nutrient content. Lawn foods are required to have percentage listing of major nutrients on the bag; check to compare nutrient content and unit costs.

Should shaded grass be fertilized differently from that in the sun? Conflicting forces are at play here. Many of the shade-tolerant species do not require high fertility, but on the other hand, tree roots will be grabbing a good bit of the sustenance. As a general rule it is probably helpful for grass in the shade of trees to be fertilized more frequently rather than more heavily, thus taking care of the needs of both tree and grass. Of course, controlled-release fertilizer can be applied more heavily without overstimulating the grass and intensifying disease (often the *coup de grâce* for turf in the shade).

What influence do the individual fertilizer nutrients have on grass? Nitrogen stimulates growth, especially of foliage, and a deep green color. Phosphorus is necessary for general balance and good root development and may reduce succulence that makes grass prone to disease. Potassium contributes to disease resistance, sturdier foliage, and winter hardiness. Insufficient minor nutrients generally cause chlorosis (blanched foliage).

Will lawn fertilization help the trees?   Yes, indeed. A tree on a fertilized lawn will probably grow twice as fast as its counterpart unfertilized. Some gardeners prefer to place fertilizer more deeply in holes in the soil around the periphery of a tree. Fertilizer compressed into spikes which can be driven into the soil with a hammer has become available, eliminating the need to bore holes.

Are hardwood ashes good or not good for lawns?   Hardwood ashes are rich in nonvolatile nutrients such as potassium, calcium, and phosphorus. Where these are needed, ashes make a good grass fertilizer. Unfortunately, wood ashes are hard to distribute, and may more easily be used in the garden than on the lawn.

When should lime and wood ashes be put on the lawn?   It would not be necessary to put both on at the same time. Wood ashes contain a high percentage of lime, as well as potash. Apply the lime—if needed—in the winter, and the wood ashes in April.

Is it possible to renew an old lawn by adding fertilizer and some seed?   Provided the turf has not deteriorated too seriously, a program of this sort coupled with weed eradication consistently kept up would go far to restore an old lawn. Annual overseedings to introduce new cultivars, accompanied by scarification to implant the seed, will be more effective than merely scattering seeds and leaving their progress to chance. (See discussion of renovation.)

Lawn Weed and Pest Control

What are the chief kinds of pests apt to bother a lawn?   Perhaps most obvious are weeds. Diseases are ubiquitous but more subtle, and insects are infrequently serious pests.

Are pests a major lawn-keeping concern?   Fortunately, most lawns, if at all healthy, endure pest attack without permanent damage and revive again seasonally. However, if your lawn is under fire, you will probably want to take corrective action in order to minimize damage.

Is it difficult to control pests?   Yes and no! Yes, in the sense that some type of pest is always around ready to attack any time lawn resistance weakens. No, because for most pests, effective controls are readily available these days and, too, nature provides predators for pests.

What kind of lawn pests are most apt to give a homeowner difficulty? Probably diseases, because inoculum is ever-present and because the causal fungi are obscure; disease is usually not evident until too late. Weeds and insects are more conspicuous and better controlled, when first noticed, by direct attack with herbicides and insecticides.

What pesticides should I stock for my lawn? This will vary with local conditions, but you should almost certainly include a phenoxy broad-leaf weedkiller (usually 2, 4-D in combination with an additive such as dicamba); an approved (biodegradable) insecticide such as malathion, carbaryl, chlorpyrifos, or diazinon for emergencies; possibly a fungicide, if your lawn is prone to a seasonal disease attack of serious proportions.

Can such pesticides be readily procured? The compounds mentioned above are available at retail stores, but new restrictions are constantly being reviewed, making uncertain what pesticides will be available on a continuing basis. Check local sources.

Why is it difficult to procure useful lawn pesticides? Environmental concern has given pesticides a "bad press"; harmless products are often considered environmental pollutants, along with harmful ones, even though only a few pesticides have been proved deleterious under normal usage.

How are lawn pesticides best applied? This varies with the pest and the product. Many pesticides are impregnated on granular materials and can be applied to the lawn with a seeder-spreader. Crabgrass preventers, weed-and-feed products, some broad-leaf herbicides, a few fungicides and insecticides are examples. As a rule, however, sprays will coat vegetation more fully and economically than will granulars. Most weedkillers (as contrasted with preventers operating in the soil) and the great majority of fungicides and insecticides are more efficient as sprays. A good pressure sprayer is about as essential around the home as is a seeder-spreader. Pesticide dusts are little used on the lawn because of their tendency to drift. Granular materials often depend upon volatilization to protect foliage not directly contacted; for more certain foliage coverage, spray materials (wettable powders and liquids) are usually preferred.

Will pesticides toxify the soil? Most pesticides are inactivated in soil or are broken down by soil microorganisms in short order. A few, especially if containing heavy metals, can build up to toxic levels with repeated use. Some organic types are fairly slow to break down or dissipate, perhaps requiring a year or more before their influence is no longer felt. Most soils are highly buffered and subject to great insult before their biological balance is upset. The majority of pesticides cause only temporary soil toxicity, or none at all. Always observe cautions on the label before using any pesticide.

LAWN WEEDS

What are the most frequent weed pests?   These will vary from region to region. They are apt to be more diverse in the South, more abundant (as a particular species) in the North. Several broad-leaf weeds (particularly dandelion, plantain, chickweed, knotweed, clover) are widespread in lawns, but are readily controlled with phenoxy chemicals. Annual grasses, such as crabgrass and foxtail, are abundant, too, but are controllable with preventers and post-emergent sprays. The perennial grasses, such as tall fescues and other forage species, are perhaps not as prevalent, but nonetheless are really the worst lawn weeds (because they are difficult to control selectively). Ordinarily a general herbicide that kills back all vegetation must be used to stop perennial grasses and should be followed by replanting.

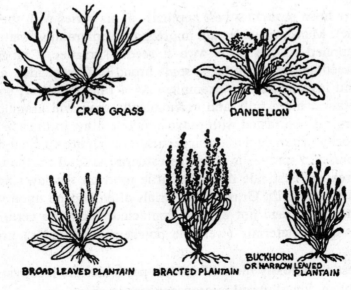

CRAB GRASS   DANDELION

BROAD LEAVED PLANTAIN   BRACTED PLANTAIN   BUCKHORN OR NARROW LEAVED PLANTAIN

SOME COMMON LAWN WEEDS

What is the herbicide for broad-leaf weeds? Phenoxy compounds, of which 2, 4-D is the most familiar and most economical; some broad-leaf (dicotyledonous) weeds are resistant to 2, 4-D, but succumb if a bit of mecoprop, dicamba, or something similar is combined with the 2, 4-D.

When are dandelions, plantains, and similar broad-leaf weeds best treated? Weeds are more susceptible to weedkillers when young or when vigorously growing; 2, 4-D (but not dicamba) is apt to be more efficient in reasonably warm weather. Thus, for summer weeds, treatment in spring might be most efficient, although hazards to budding ornamentals are greater then than later. Winter weeds, like cresses, are best treated in autumn. If weeding is needed at a less opportune season, increase the herbicide strength.

What about crabgrass prevention? A number of very effective crabgrass preventers are on the market, applied in spring before crabgrass seed sprouts (crabgrass germinates when soil temperature rises above 50° F.). The materials must be used exactly as directed, be spread uniformly to blanket the soil (since they affect only sprouting seed, not growing plants). Most preventers are 90 per cent effective or better; examples include bensulide, benefin, DCPA, oxadiazon, siduron, and others. Overapplication sometimes retards rooting of the permanent grass, so be judicious about repeated application. Siduron is fairly specific for crabgrass and will not harm new lawn seedings made at the same time as treatment.

Is there control for crabgrass after it has sprouted? Yes, 2 or 3 arsonate (AMA, DSMA, etc.) sprays made a week or 10 days apart should kill crabgrass and certain other annual grasses without injuring the permanent turf. Arsonates are also fairly effective against nut sedge.

Is there anything to control weedy perennial grasses like tall fescue and quackgrass? Nothing reliably selective. That is, there is no chemical that will kill the unwanted perennial grass without also damaging the turf grass. Amitrol, dalapon, and similar herbicides are effective against perennial grasses, but the chemical must be allowed to dissipate before reseeding or planting the lawn grass. Glyphosate may take a few days to show its effect, but it is immediately inactivated by the soil so that reseeding can proceed at once. Paraquat is also immediately inactivated, but is not labeled for homeowner usage (it is not systemic, as is glyphosate, so kills only the above-ground foliage sprayed).

Would you advise hand-digging weeds instead of using a herbicide? For a few weeds—yes. Also, hand-digging is obviously appropriate for weeds for which there is no selective herbicidal control, such as clumps of tall fescue, nimble Will, or small patches of any unwanted perennial.

Are herbicides hazardous to animal life? Scarcely, although of course they shouldn't be ingested or carelessly handled. Herbicides are probably the least likely of the pesticides to harm animals or to cause irreversible ecological change.

Is there a specific weedkiller for wild garlic (or wild onion—I don't know which) that comes up in clumps in my lawn? I've tried hand-digging but I can't keep up with it. Each spring there seem to be more clumps. Repeat treatments with 2, 4-D and/or dicamba will eliminate onion or garlic (both are *Allium*) if made in early spring (and perhaps again in autumn, if the weeds persist).

I am tired of my zoysia lawn and would like to start over with a 'Merion' bluegrass-fescue mixture. How can I get rid of the zoysia? It appears to be indestructible. One solution would be to have the sod removed, perhaps sold. The zoysia could be killed chemically (as with glyphosate), but dense sod left in place, even if dead, is difficult to seed into without cultivation.

Aren't there natural controls for weeds? Letting the lawn dry out occasionally (rather than keeping it continuously moist) helps restrain water-loving weeds; some years favor certain weeds over others (we experience good and bad nimble Will [*Muhlenbergia*] years, for example, and see appreciable tall fescue killed some winters). Many weeds in a new lawn will surely be squeezed out as the grass matures, a transition aided by proper fertilization. But nature dislikes monoculture and leans toward diversification, so some weeds are inevitable.

DISEASES

Are lawn diseases particularly a problem? They are ubiquitous, especially in lawns not planted with disease-resistant cultivars. Most of the time, however, diseases weaken turf rather than killing it outright and the grass snaps back as weather conditions change. Disease prevention is burdensome (usually repeated fungicide application is required to keep new foliage covered), costly, and difficult for an inexperienced person to time properly (by the time damage is obvious, the disease has probably run its course).

What brings on a disease attack? Several conditions favorable to the disease must coincide. The weather and season must be appropriate, the lawn must be physiologically susceptible, and the pathogen must be present and in an active phase. Most fungi are quite particular! Disease is generally favored by monoculture, generous fertilization, wet weather (some diseases like it hot, some cool), and, of course, by a handy source of inoculum.

How is lawn disease best checked? Fortunately, changes from moist to dry weather, or in temperature, or in seasonal rhythm of the pathogen do much to end the attack. The gardener, of course, can help check diseases. Apply a fungicide before the disease has made serious inroads (it is necessary to anticipate on the basis of weather and past experience when a disease is likely to attack). Also withhold water and reduce fertilization (especially soluble nitrogen).

What particular diseases should be looked out for? Hundreds of diseases can attack turf, and you should consult a book or pamphlet picturing different diseases and detailing measures for their control for specific information. Bluegrass lawns often suffer leafspot in the cool weather of spring (this may change to crown-rot in the summer), and depending upon the cultivar, lawns may suffer a serious attack of stripe smut or *Fusarium* patch in the summer. Bent grasses often come down with brownpatch in warm weather, snowmold in winter. Rust often attacks ryegrass and other species, especially in autumn; and mildew, almost any grass in the shade. Fine fescues often die in patches in hot weather (especially if the soil is wet) and this is often attributed to "disease." Diseases attacking southern grasses are even more profligate than in the North. Check with local authorities, such as a county agent.

Can I identify diseases in the lawn? Some symptoms, such as those of leafspot, are quite evident; consulting books in which diseases are pictured (Extension Publication No. 12, *Lawn Diseases in the Midwest*, University of Nebraska, or similar publications from other states and from commercial companies) should help. But even the experts are uncertain about many diseases, short of isolating the fungus in a laboratory and reinoculating with it.

What do I do if my lawn is diseased? General control measures have already been mentioned. If it is not too late, apply a fungicide, and in most cases reduce watering and fertilization (fertilization helps control dollar spot). If you know that disease is the problem, put the lawn on lean rather than generous fare, even though the latter is the normal reaction to a declining turf. If the disease is chronic, consider introducing new disease-resistant cultivars into the lawn.

Do some grass diseases evolve resistant strains? This is not as serious as with insects, which quickly build immunity, but some resistance to specific fungicides often builds up. Authorities advise alternating contact fungicides (those which kill spores or fungus tissue touched by the spray) with systemic ones (types like Benlate absorbed and carried through the plant in the sap stream).

INSECT PESTS

Do insects often damage the lawn?   Not often, but when attacking in force, they can devastate a turf almost overnight.

What are the most serious insect problems?   Although there are many pests of localized importance, soil grubs (the larvae of such species as June and Japanese beetles and chafers), sod webworms (the larval stage of the lawn moth), and chinch bugs (both juveniles and adults) are probably the three most serious lawn insects nationally.

What do I do about soil grubs?   Grubs eat grass roots and can often be identified by pulling up a section of sod (if it lifts easily like a carpet, most of its roots have been severed). An insecticide soaked into the soil is the obvious answer. Restrictions prevent the sale of long-lasting insecticides such as chlordane, so repeated flushings at intervals with biodegradable insecticides may be needed. A slow-acting but eventually effective remedy for grubs is milky spore disease, preparations of which are often useful where some grubs persist to carry and spread the disease.

How do we defend against sod webworms?   Webworms live in silk-lined burrows deep in the sod and are seldom seen because they feed at night (they chew off the grass near the soil level, leaving grass and chaff). An insecticide soaked deeply into the soil is usually the answer. However, some strains of webworm have developed resistance to insecticides used repeatedly. If so, alternate insecticides. Webworms are the larvae of lawn moths, which are frequently seen flitting over the lawn about twilight, laying eggs. The cycle from egg to moth is about one month in warm weather, so that drenching the lawn with insecticide about 10 days after lawn moths are abundant should catch most of the young webworms. Webworms are seldom prevalent enough in the first generation to be a bother, but become damaging as populations build up later in the summer.

How do I check chinch bugs?   Grass attacked by chinch bugs turns off-color and eventually browns in irregular patches; active insects are most abundant in adjacent green grass. They can be discovered by shaking grass over white paper and looking for white and black (some with red spots) insects not much bigger than a pinhead. Chinch bugs suck the sap from grass culms, debilitating and eventually killing the above-ground parts. Spray insecticide well into the undamaged turf.

Are there other kinds of lawn pests besides weeds, diseases, and insects? There is no end to pests, but fortunately few others are serious. Eelworms (nematodes) are widespread and often quite troublesome in Florida. Drenching the soil with a nematocide helps, at least for a while. Arthropods such as chiggers are often nuisances, as are slime molds, algae, and other lower organisms.

With all of the lawn pests, it would seem that prospects for having a good lawn are not cheery. Reciting the many troubles a lawn can have may overemphasize the negative. There are numerous things going for success, too! The favorite lawn grasses have proven themselves; they wouldn't be around if their progenitors hadn't had the stuff to fight most of their own battles. We may seduce them with soft living, but inherent toughness and the balance that nature imposes usually end blights and predations without disaster. Especially helpful are new lawn grass cultivars selected and bred for pest resistance (mainly disease, but increasingly for insect damage and weed invasion). Most lawns recover quickly from calamity, especially if aided by intelligent maintenance. It should prove possible for anyone to have an acceptable lawn in almost any location without lawn care becoming burdensome!

Moss Lawns

What is the name of the "moss" that is used for planting lawns? Will it grow anywhere? Its botanical name is *Sagina subulata,* commonly called pearlwort. It is used extensively in the Pacific coast states. It will grow almost anywhere in the United States, except the Rio Grande Valley and the region south of Fort Pierce, Florida. In extreme northern latitudes, it usually dies in the winter. It is not a true moss.

Does the "moss" used for lawns need a good soil? It thrives best on a fertile soil, but it has grown well on the adobe soils south of San Francisco. Having a shallow root system, it can be surface-fed like bent grass.

Is the "moss" that is used in lawns grown from seed? How is it planted? Pearlwort is planted from divisions. Two-inch squares are planted 6 inches apart. A quicker effect can be had by planting them 3 or 4 inches apart. When planting, see that the roots are well covered and firmed, and the crown (sprig) is kept above the surface. However, pearlwort is most commonly used between stepping-stones or on a terrace or walk.

How many years can I expect a "moss" lawn (pearlwort) to last? In a climate where no great winter cold occurs, it can last for several years.

Would the fact that "moss" has flowers add to its value in the lawn? True, it blooms very prolifically in early summer with tiny flowers on 1-inch stems and it is very pretty. The flowers, however, do not last long.

10. The Home Vegetable Garden

BY FAR THE most important reason for "growing your own vegetables" is that only by so doing can one be certain of getting vegetables of the finest quality. The local market gardener, who used to provide really fresh vegetables to neighborhood stores, is all but extinct. Vegetables that have to be shipped hundreds or thousands of miles before being graded and repacked for chain-store distribution lose much in quality and flavor. Many of the best quality varieties are never grown for market because they lack eye appeal, or do not mature uniformly so a crop can all be harvested at one time; or because they do not keep well when shipped. Lettuce is an example. The real quality varieties, such as 'Buttercrunch' and 'Oakleaf', are seldom if ever to be found in a market; the shopper must go without lettuce or be satisfied with the coarse and tasteless sorts which possess about as much flavor as a piece of aluminum foil. Such things as cantaloupes and tomatoes must be picked "firm" (a euphemism for "half-green") in order to be safely shipped to the wholesaler, and by him distributed to the retailer. They may "color up" by the time the consumer gets them, but they never gain their full flavor, or their full value as food. Sweet corn that is picked not more than an hour or two before it reaches the table is very different from the semiwithered article in the supermarket bins.

Even if one does not have space for a full-scale vegetable garden (say 50 × 30 feet), a supply from some of the most productive crops—such as tomatoes, pole beans, broccoli, bush squash, and lettuce—can be grown on a very small plot; or even in combination with garden flowers. In addition to getting better quality, the home gardener is likely to find —after deducting the cost of seed, fertilizer, spray materials—that he has made a dent in his food budget. Of course greater savings result from large gardens offering a surplus for freezing and canning.

Location

The location of the vegetable garden is important, but in the home garden plot there is not likely to be much choice as to where it can be placed or as to the type of soil to be selected. One thing, however, is absolutely essential—an abundance of sunshine.

The shade of a tall tree that casts a constantly shifting shadow upon the vegetable rows will not be too serious, but every square foot of the garden should get daily at least 5 or 6 hours of full sunshine, and preferably more. Asparagus and rhubarb, which make their most rapid growth in early spring, will stand considerable shade later in the season; lettuce in hot weather is rather benefited by slight midday shade, but as a general rule—the more sun the better.

Size of Plot

"How large a plot should I have to make it worthwhile to grow vegetables?"

That is a question often asked by the beginner, and it is a very sensible one. The answer, however, cannot be too definite. A well-worthwhile supply of quick-growing, closely planted crops—such as lettuce, onion sets for green onions, bush squash, carrots, radishes, mustard, cress, New Zealand spinach for a summer-long supply of "greens," and some tomatoes and beans (both bush and pole)—can be grown on an area as small as 10 × 10 feet or in a long border 5 × 20 feet.

A larger plot, however, is advisable, if it is at all possible to secure one. On many a small place a plot at least 10 × 25 feet can be provided for vegetables by the simple expedient of transplanting some of the existing shrubbery and possibly doing away with a shade-casting and root-hungry tree or two not really needed to maintain an attractive landscape planting around the house.

A plot 30 × 50 feet (or its equivalent) is recommended by government experts as desirable where the object of the gardener is to grow an important part of the family's food supply. Unfortunately the prevailing "lot" system used in subdividing suburban real estate makes it impossible, in many cases, to allocate even this moderate amount of space to home food production. But very often it is possible for the homeowner to obtain the use of additional land at a not-too-inconvenient distance.

Drainage

"Can vegetables be grown on wet ground?"

Drainage is another important factor in the growing of vegetables. Soil in which the average run of flowers and shrubs grow will prove suitable for the vegetable garden; but a boggy or a swampy location, in which the water has a tendency to remain after heavy rains, at less than 12 inches below the surface, should be drained before any attempt is made to employ it for vegetable gardening.

Low-lying ground that has a tendency to collect and hold surface water, but is not actually swampy, can often be made suitable for vegetable growing by the simple process of using raised beds in which to plant. Such beds—made up into shape and size convenient for planting— are formed by merely digging out paths 4 to 6 inches deep and distributing the removed soil over the surface of the beds. It is desirable, but not essential, to have the paths slope slightly to a low spot, so that surplus moisture draining from the beds into the paths will in turn be drained out of the paths.

Protection

Many a first-year gardener has seen much of his efforts go for naught because his plot was not adequately protected from mechanical injury— damage by dogs, rabbits, woodchucks, gophers, or children not trained to have a proper respect for plants. Without such protection the experienced gardener would not think of attempting to plant a garden where injuries from such sources are possible; but the average beginner will go gaily ahead and "take a chance"—only to regret it later.

Chicken wire with a 2-inch mesh, and at least 2 feet (and better 3 or 4) in height, supported by posts firmly set in the ground at intervals of 8 or 10 feet, will supply adequate protection. The lower edge of the wire should be buried 2 or 3 inches deep and firmly pegged down to prevent small animals from burrowing under it.

Such protection will of course make an additional item of expense the first year, but it is a worthwhile investment, and if kept in repair will last for many seasons. A 4-foot fence will also serve as a permanent and space-saving support for tomatoes, peas, cucumbers, or (with some additional support) for pole beans. It is quite worth its cost for this purpose alone. Only a 4-foot fence will offer much protection against pheasants, and a much higher one is necessary to discourage deer.

Equipment

The equipment required in caring for a moderate-sized vegetable garden need not be extensive or expensive, but it pays to have tools of the best quality.

For a small plot a spading fork, an iron bow rake, a hoe, a trowel, and a watering can are the essential implements. A hand duster or a small sprayer (preferably both) will be needed in the control of insects and diseases.

In addition to these tools for working the soil, an adequate supply of water, used intelligently, will increase the yields of many crops 50 to 100 per cent. Nobody wants to waste water, and methods for conserving it are emphasized in this section and in other sections as well.

What Vegetables to Grow

"What vegetables shall I grow in a small garden?"

In arriving at the answer to this question, several things must be considered.

How small is the garden?

What vegetables does the family like?

What crops will do well in your locality?

Is it planned to grow some crops for freezing and storing or only summer supplies?

Without knowing the answers to these questions, it is not possible to suggest a definite list of what vegetables to grow. It is possible, however, to give the beginner some guidance. Here are five lists that will help him.

I. Vegetables That Yield Most

(In proportion to space they occupy and the time required to grow them)

1. Tomatoes
2. Pole beans
3. Broccoli
4. Onions (from sets)
5. Beans, bush
6. Beets
7. Carrots
8. Chard
9. Chinese cabbage
10. Spinach, New Zealand
11. Mustard
12. Lettuce
13. Turnips
14. Cress
15. Cabbage
16. Radishes
17. Spinach
18. Bush (summer) squash

II. Requiring Least Space

1. Tomatoes
2. Pole beans
3. Beets
4. Carrots
5. Leeks
6. Turnips
7. Bush squash
8. Onions
9. Lettuce, leaf
10. Chard
11. Chinese cabbage
12. Beans, bush
13. Mustard
14. Radishes
15. Cress
16. Tampala

III. Requiring Considerable Space

(Look for varieties of some of these vegetables that have been bred for small-space gardens)

1. Broccoli
2. Cabbage
3. Cauliflower
4. Spinach, New Zealand
5. Corn
6. Eggplants
7. Peppers
8. Parsnips
9. Potatoes
10. Sweet potatoes
11. Peas
12. Cucumbers
13. Melons
14. Winter squash

IV. Short Season

(Can be followed by other crops)

1. Beans, bush
2. Beets
3. Early cabbage
4. Carrots
5. Cress
6. Lettuce
7. Mustard
8. Onions (from sets)
9. Peas
10. Radishes
11. Spinach
12. Turnips

V. Difficult to Grow in Many Regions

1. Cauliflower
2. Celery
3. Chinese cabbage
4. Cucumber
5. Muskmelons
6. Onions
7. Peas
8. Potatoes
9. Pumpkins
10. Spinach
11. Squash (winter varieties)
12. Watermelons

Plan Ahead

It will be seen from all this that the planting of a vegetable plot, if it is to yield maximum returns, is not merely a matter of walking into a garden center, picking out, more or less at random, a dozen or two packets of vegetable seeds, and then starting in at one end of the vegetable plot and sowing each as far as it will go.

A carefully thought-out plan for the vegetable garden should be made before any seed is bought—and this is even more important for a small plot than for a large one.

Making such a plan is not difficult, and it is a lot of fun—quite as interesting as solving a crossword puzzle. The first step is to make an outline plan, showing the shape and dimensions of the plot. It will help greatly if this is drawn to scale—say ½ inch equaling a foot for a small plot or ¼ inch or less a foot for a larger one. On the former basis, a garden plot 20 × 30 feet would be represented by a rectangle 10 × 15 inches. Each row of vegetables to be planted is then indicated. "Planting Tables" showing the proper distances between rows of the various

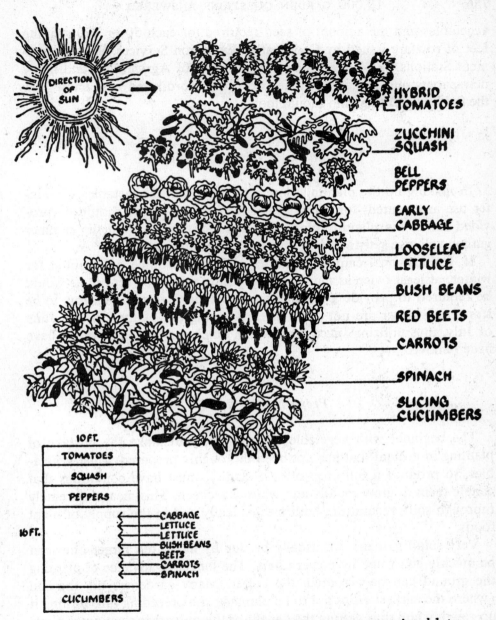

DIRECTION OF SUN

HYBRID TOMATOES

ZUCCHINI SQUASH

BELL PEPPERS

EARLY CABBAGE

LOOSELEAF LETTUCE

BUSH BEANS

RED BEETS

CARROTS

SPINACH

SLICING CUCUMBERS

10 FT.

| TOMATOES |
| SQUASH |
| PEPPERS |
| CABBAGE |
| LETTUCE |
| LETTUCE |
| BUSH BEANS |
| BEETS |
| CARROTS |
| SPINACH |
| CUCUMBERS |

16 FT.

Here is a vegetable garden that is ideal for a space-restricted lot and a small family. Ten feet wide by 16 feet long, it features easy-to-grow vegetables that will yield worthwhile produce. The early cabbage, lettuce, and spinach will not last all season, so their space can be filled by more bush beans, eggplant, or broccoli and lettuce (planted in early summer) for fall harvesting.

vegetables and the amount of seed required for each 50 or 100 running feet of row are issued by Cooperative Extension Services, State Experiment Stations, the United States Department of Agriculture, and many newspapers and magazines. The two plans reproduced here show how the finished planting plan should look.

Planning for Winter Supplies

In making up the planting plan, remember that if vegetables for winter use are wanted—for canning and for freezing—these should be provided for in the planting plan, although "surpluses" from the summer garden will give satisfactory results for small families.

If, for instance, canned tomatoes and tomato juice are wanted for winter, at least twice as many tomato plants should be set out as would be required to provide a summer supply alone. Beets and carrots to be stored for winter are not sown in early spring but planted in late June or July, thus utilizing space from which quick-growing early crops have been removed.

Preparing the Ground

The beginner with vegetables is very likely to make the mistake of planting in ground that has not been thoroughly prepared. Most vegetables, to produce a full crop of first quality, must have conditions that enable them to grow rapidly and without a check. This means extremely thorough soil preparation, both mechanically and in the supply of plant foods.

Very small gardens can usually be dug by hand, but larger ones can be quickly cultivated by power tillers. The longer in advance of planting the ground can be prepared, the better. Many gardeners dig the soil (where the earliest crops are to be planted) the preceding fall, turning it up roughly and thus getting the benefit of the pulverizing action of alternate freezing and thawing during the winter. A further advantage of digging in advance of planting is that many weed seeds have a chance to germinate. The tiny weed seedlings are destroyed when the soil is worked over before sowing or planting.

(*Details of soil preparation and fertilizers will be found in Section 1.*)

Row	Width
5/15 BUSH SQUASH (4 Hills acorn, 1 row zucchini)	24"
LEAF LETTUCE 4/10 ... LETTUCE 5/15	18"
TOMATOES (8 staked plants) 5/15	18"
KOHLRABI 4/10	18"
TOMATOES	18"
EARLY CABBAGE PLANTS 4/10	18"
PEPPERS (10 plants) 5/15 ... EGG PLANTS 5/15	18"
SPINACH 4/10	15"
LIMA BEANS 5/20	15"
SPINACH 4/10	15"
LIMA BEANS 5/20	15"
SNAP BEANS 5/15 ... LETTUCE 8/15	21"
SNAP BEANS 5/10 ... BEETS 7/20	12"
BEETS	6"
	6"
BROCCOLI 7/15 ... BEANS 7/10	12"
BROCCOLI 7/15	9"
SWISS CHARD 4/25	PARSNIPS 4/25	PARSLEY 4/25	18"
BEETS 4/25 ... ENDIVE 7/15	15"
BEETS 5/15	12"
CARROTS 4/25 ... CHINESE CABBAGE 8/1	12"
CARROTS 5/15	12"
RADISHES 4/10 ... CARROTS 7/1	12"
ONION SETS 4/10 ... CARROTS 7/1	12"

30 Feet · 20 Feet

PLAN FOR A 20 × 30-FOOT GARDEN

A typical northern garden with suggested planting dates for regions where the average date of the last freeze is May 10 or thereabouts. Both seeds and transplants (tomatoes, eggplants, peppers, broccoli, and cabbage) have been used. Full advantage has been taken of all space by interplanting (lettuce sown April 10 and May 15 between rows where bush squash and tomatoes are to be planted about May 15, for instance). Space is also conserved by succession crops—snap beans after broccoli, lima beans after spinach, etc.

Sowing and Planting

"When should the vegetable garden be planted?"

In the well-arranged vegetable garden, planting is a more or less continuous operation from the time the frost is out of the ground until 6 to 8 weeks before hard frost is to be expected. The 3 most active planting periods, however, are very early spring, when the hardy, frost-resistant vegetables are put in; 4 to 6 weeks later, when the tender ones are planted; and 4 to 8 weeks later than this, when many crops for late fall and winter use are sown. North of the Mason and Dixon line these dates are normally:

Mid-March to mid-April for early, hardy crops.

May 1 to June 1 for tender crops.

Mid-June to late July for "succession" crops for fall and winter use.

The *hardy* vegetables include beets, broad or fava beans, carrots, turnips, lettuce, onions (sets, plants, or seed), leeks, radishes, parsnips, salsify, witloof chicory; the cabbage group (cabbage, broccoli, cauliflower); mustard, spinach, and chard; parsley; early celery; peas; potatoes.

The *tender* sorts include most beans; corn, tomatoes, eggplants, and peppers; the vine crops (squash, cucumbers, melons, and pumpkins); okra; sweet potatoes.

The *late* sorts (some of which are hardy and some tender) for fall and winter use include bush beans; beets, carrots, turnips, rutabagas; lettuce, Chinese cabbage; cabbage, broccoli, Brussels sprouts, kale.

Information covering the details of seed sowing, transplanting, and cultivating is given in Section 3.

Planning the Garden

Is it necessary to make a ground plan of the vegetable garden before planting? It will save time, seed, and mistakes later on. However, seasonal developments may make minor changes necessary.

Should plant rows run east and west? The direction of the rows is of minor importance. Other factors being equal, there is a slight advantage if the rows run from north to south.

When the land slopes from north to south, should the rows be made across the slope or down it? When the land slopes perceptibly so that there is a tendency for heavy rain to run down the slope instead of soaking in, rows should always be run across the slope. If this makes the rows too long, a path can be run down the center of the plot, cutting the rows in half. On steep slopes it is desirable to make a series of terraces, held in place by stone or permanent sod, so that the ground under cultivation will be fairly level.

In what direction is it best to plant a vegetable garden—north and south or east and west? It makes very little difference. What is more important is the location of the tall-growing vegetables with reference to the low-growing kinds. Plant the low plants on the east or south sides. Keep tall ones in the back where they will not shade the others.

Should root vegetables and leafy sorts be planted in alternate rows? Since the fertilizer requirements differ—the leafy vegetables need considerable nitrogen and the root vegetables require a higher percentage of phosphorus and potash—it is usually more convenient to group the two types rather than to plant them in alternate rows.

Shall I plant rows of tall vegetables between those which are low-growing? As far as is practicable, tall growers should be together at the north end of the garden and low growers at the south or east. Often, however, rows of lettuce, radishes, or other low growers can be grown between tomatoes or other tall growers and can be harvested before the latter attain much height.

My garden is 22 × 30 feet. Should the tall vegetables, like corn and climbing beans, be on the south side of the garden in order to prevent shading smaller plants? Always plant tall-growing vegetables on the north or west side of the garden, if possible.

On what sides of the garden should trees or shrubs be planted as a protection against winds? Ordinarily, on the north and west sides, unless prevailing spring winds are from some other direction.

Which vegetables are easiest to grow in a beginner's garden? Explain how to arrange beds. For vegetables that are easiest to grow, see the introduction to this section. It is not necessary to make beds in a vegetable garden. Practically all types of vegetables do best planted on the level surface. Merely mark off rows for sowing the seed after the ground is well worked and prepared. A narrow path can be left through the center or along the sides of the garden.

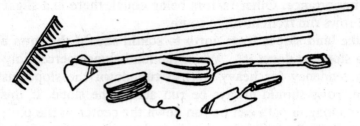

These tools—a rake, hoe, spading fork, trowel, and line for marking rows—are sufficient for most small vegetable gardens.

I have an area 50 × 15 feet. What is the best way to plant it? How can I obtain extra crops, earlier and later?   Plant the rows crosswise; 14 feet of carrots, beets, leaf lettuce, or other greens are enough for one planting. For beans and other vegetables of which larger amounts are wanted, plant two or three 14-foot rows. Keep tall-growing sorts, like tomatoes, corn, or pole beans, at one end, preferably north or west. Set out plants of as many vegetables as possible (such as cabbage, broccoli, lettuce, tomatoes, eggplant, beets) to get extra-early crops. Be ready to plant succession crops at once, when early crops are finished.

What are the so-called warm-weather plants?   Warm-weather plants will be killed by light frosts and cannot be placed in the garden until all danger of frost is past. The following may be grouped under this heading: beans (all types except broad beans), cucumbers, eggplant, muskmelon and cantaloupe, okra, peppers, pumpkins, squash, sweet corn, sweet potatoes, tomatoes, and New Zealand spinach. Seeds of tomatoes, however, can be sown as early as the soil is workable. They will germinate as soon as conditions are favorable. Transplants of tomatoes are tender. New Zealand spinach must be sown early, but it is often slow to germinate.

Where can I get a chart on how long it takes to grow various vegetables?   In pamphlets on vegetable growing issued by most State Experiment Stations or in vegetable gardening books. Most of this information is given in seed catalogs. The information is given with the description of each vegetable. (See individual vegetables, this section.)

What should I plant in a garden 90 × 90 feet?   For a garden of this size consult your State Agricultural Experiment Station or county agent of the Cooperative Extension Service. This size garden will permit growing unusual crops which would not be economical in smaller gardens.

What are the frost-hardy vegetables? The following vegetables survive light frosts: beets, broccoli, Brussels sprouts, cabbage, carrots, cauliflower, celery, chard, collards, dandelion, endive or escarole, kale, kohlrabi, leeks, lettuce, mustard greens, onions, parsley, peas, potatoes, radishes, roquette, spinach, and turnips; also broad or Windsor beans.

What crops can be grown on the edge of a city plot that gets hard in the hot summer and isn't very fertile? Can more than one crop be harvested during a year's time? Sweet potatoes, peanuts, bush beans for use dry, and soybeans. You would get only one crop of these. Any crop will take moisture. These will take the minimum amount of care.

What types of vegetables grow best in a sandy soil? While sandy soils are not recommended for commercial growing of some vegetables, satisfactory crops of most of them for home use can be obtained. The soil, however, must be kept well supplied with humus, and fertilizer in small amounts should be applied frequently. Water is usually the limiting factor on sandy soil.

What vegetables would grow best in ground that has never been cultivated before? This ground contains a lot of quackgrass. This would depend largely upon the character of the soil. Root crops—beets, carrots, parsnips—do not do as well on new ground as on land that has been worked for a few seasons. This is especially true of onions. Turnips, however, often do excellently on new soil. Corn and the various vine vegetables, if generously fertilized, should do well. Also, potatoes should do well if the ground is suitable for them. However, the quackgrass is likely to prove troublesome unless killed with dalapon two months before planting.

What is best to plant on newly cleared land? The soil is a little sandy. Would potatoes do well? (Rhode Island.) Potatoes need good soil. This is especially true of the 'Chippewa' variety. Snap beans, sweet corn, and sweet potatoes would probably be all right. Other vegetable crops are heavy feeders and would require very thorough soil preparation.

Which of the common vegetables can satisfactorily be grown in clay soil? Practically all of the usual home garden vegetables can be grown in a clay soil if it is properly handled. Root crops (carrots, parsnips) may be poor if grown in stiff clay loam.

What small vegetables can be successfully raised to mature before September 15 on the north shore of Cape Cod? (Northeast storms are

frequent and devastating.) Most of the frost-hardy plants, including cauliflower, broccoli, and turnips.

What could you recommend for a vegetable garden 50 × 100 feet in northern New England? This will make a very big garden which should produce a surplus for sale unless you decide to grow a large area —say one half—in potatoes. That leaves a lot of space for cabbage, broccoli, cauliflower, carrots, turnips, rutabagas, lettuce, Swiss chard, and sweet corn. If you grow tomatoes, you probably should have at least two dozen plants.

We own a vacant lot on a hillside—the soil is heavy yellow clay (brick clay). What sort of garden should we contemplate? Tomatoes do well enough. Since tomatoes do well on this soil, most other crops, except asparagus and melons, will do better. You will have to grow a short, stubby variety of carrot. You probably cannot grow parsnips. This soil needs considerable limestone, and the addition of plant refuse and coal cinders would tend to loosen it. Use limestone freely. Start out with a 25 × 25-foot garden and grow tomatoes, cabbage, broccoli, and Brussels sprouts as well as lettuce, carrots, and beets. Then add to it each year.

What vegetables would you recommend for the garden of a person who works all day and has a minimum of time to work in the garden? It isn't a question of which vegetable takes the least effort, but how big a garden you have. Radishes and turnips can be grown by sowing seed and forgetting them until it is time to pull them out of the weeds. Timely control of weeds when they are small will save much labor, regardless of the crop.

What kind of vegetables can be grown over a wire fence? Tomatoes, cucumbers, melons, squash, pole beans.

How can we garden at our summer home? We spend long weekends there in early spring, sometimes a week or more at Easter, and are "in residence" from mid-June, when school lets out, until Labor Day. Two or three weekends in the fall wind up the year. Your best solution is fall digging or tilling, after a light frost or two. Collect all the organic matter you can find—leaves, garbage, sawdust, etc., plus any plants left in the garden. If local farmers can spare manure, you are in luck. In the soil, work under all the organic matter you can. In the future, compost all table scraps and other available organic matter for use the following fall. Don't overlook the scraps from cleaning fish, hunting, etc., which add to the richness of a compost pile.

Let the tilled soil settle. Arrange to be there just before a hard freeze is expected. Rake the soil level and plant the seeds of any of the follow-ing crops your family will eat: beets, broccoli, Brussels sprouts, cab-bage, carrot, Chinese cabbage, cress, endive, escarole, kale, kohlrabi, lettuce, New Zealand spinach, onion sets or top onions, parsley, pars-nips, peas, radish, rutabaga, spinach, Swiss chard, and turnip. Seeds of tomato and 'Butternut' squash can be treated with captan or thiram to protect them from soil fungi and sown at the same time.

There is better than a 50 per cent chance that these seeds will survive the winter and begin growth before you can work the soil in the spring. If they fail, there is still time to seed all these crops before hot weather.

When the soil warms up and the danger of frost is past, plant seeds of warm-season crops such as snap beans, pole beans, sweet corn, cu-cumber, eggplant, okra, peppers, and melons.

Weeds will be a problem; ask at garden centers for information on the annual weed-control chemicals that can be used to spray the soil (after the first crop of seedlings in spring has been killed) and will keep the surface weed-free for up to two months.

Growing seedlings at home and carrying them to the garden on a spring visit (early for hardy vegetables; after the danger of frost for ten-der crops) is another way the problem of planting can be handled. They will transplant easily in peat-fiber pots (for most kinds) and in berry boxes filled with compost (for melons, squash, and cucumbers).

Rely heavily on mulches to conserve moisture and reduce weeds. In-crease the organic content of sandy soils all you can. Save wood ashes from the fireplace as a soil amendment and fertilizer.

In the North, how late can vegetables be planted? Except in cold spots such as near the Canadian border, the following dates will give edible produce in 9 years out of 10:

June 15: Brussels sprouts, cabbage, carrots, and beets for fall use. *July 1:* Chinese cabbage, broccoli, carrots and beets for storage, sweet corn, cucumber, zucchini, and snap beans. *July 15:* rutabaga. *August 1:* turnips, endive, escarole, garden cress, kohlrabi, lettuce, radish, peas (use 'Sugar Snap' for highest productivity and 'Wando' for heat resist-ance), spinach. Even if immature when frost comes, many vegetables then are gourmet treats, i.e., baby carrots, finger-length zucchini, tiny snap beans.

ROTATION

Is rotation of garden vegetables important? If space permits, it is a good idea occasionally to give the whole garden a rest for a year or two, but space in a garden is too limited for any real benefit from moving crops just a few feet.

What is the difference between planting crops in "rotation" and in "succession"? Rotation cropping is the practice of planting, in a given area, different crops each year. Succession planting means following one crop with another in the same season—for instance, the planting of snap beans in the row from which early carrots have been harvested.

How do I rotate plantings of vegetables to get the most out of them? Simply change the location of the different vegetables from year to year. However, in a small garden most vegetables can be grown in the same spot for several years in succession, if the ground is kept fertile. Rotation in the home garden is of little or no advantage.

Can you suggest a rotation of crops for the small garden? If you can use a big enough area, a garden planted every other year or every third year makes a good rotation. During the vacant years the garden may be seeded to green-manure crops, which are plowed under or put into a permanent sod. If weeds are permitted to grow and are mowed down when they begin to blossom, they will make a good green-manure crop. Rotating the vegetable crops in a small garden, except in a limited way, is not practical.

SUCCESSION PLANTING

What vegetables can be planted in the same area in a current season, one following the other? (New York.) In general, any vegetable that is removed from the ground sufficiently early in the season can be followed by any other which will have time to mature. Crops which are out of the way in time to be followed by others are early cabbage and cauliflower, lettuce, peas, beets, radishes, carrots, kohlrabi, turnips, and spinach; also, onions from sets that are used green. These can be followed by peas (in cool regions only), late celery, and late plantings of lettuce, beets, carrots, and turnips; cabbage and cauliflower, and early varieties of sweet corn. Chinese cabbage, mustard, kale, and collards for late autumn and winter use can also be grown after early crops.

Define "intercropping." Is it desirable? It may be defined as the planting of rows of quick-growing crops, such as lettuce, radishes, or spinach, between widely spaced, slower-growing items, such as celery, peas, and tomatoes. Intercropping is desirable because, if carefully planned, it results in producing more food from small gardens.

What are the combinations for intercropping vegetables? In general, intercropping vegetables in the small garden gives less yield per square foot of space than extra-close planting without intercropping. There are some exceptions. Early cabbage and lettuce transplants, for instance, can be set between the rows where tomatoes are to be set out later. Bush beans can be planted between the rows where peppers and eggplant are to be set later. With close planting (12 inches between rows for many crops), the ground will be so completely covered that there is not room for another crop in between. In general, two crops can be grown on the same ground only when one of them will be removed *before the other needs the entire space;* or when long-season crops are widely spaced to permit intercropping.

How can I get the largest number of vegetables from a small plot of ground? By intensive culture. This implies careful planning, thorough soil preparation, adequate fertilization and irrigation, succession and companion cropping, proper selection of varieties, constant control of pests and diseases, and keen attention to details at all times.

Two gourmet lettuce varieties: the heat-resistant 'Oakleaf' (left) and 'Buttercrunch', a 'Bibb'-type lettuce that is heat-resistant. 'Royal Oakleaf' is an improved version of 'Oakleaf'.

What is the trick to intensive gardening? I have about 4 × 15 feet to devote to vegetables. There is no trick or magic involved. Lay out 3 rows, 13 feet long. Plant 1 row of beets, 1 row of carrots, to be followed by 2 rows of snap beans planted after their roots are out. Plant ½ row of radishes or onion sets to be followed by Swiss chard, and ½ row leaf lettuce to be followed by late turnips or other root vegetables. Plant a staked tomato at each end of each row, allowing 1 foot from the stake to the planting of other vegetables. A fence on the north edge can be used to grow pole beans or cucumbers.

Is the custom of planting beans, corn, and pumpkins in the same space a good procedure? While this practice is often followed on farms, in the home garden it is better to keep them separate. In the small garden pumpkins have no place unless they can be planted near the edge of the plot and allowed to run out over the grass or climb along a fence.

USE OF SPACE

How many square feet will I need to supply each member of my family with vegetables for one year? Much depends upon soil fertility, crops grown, methods of cultivation, as well as varying needs of different families. From 300 to 500 square feet per person would perhaps be a fair answer. This would include crops for storing and canning for winter.

What is the size of the smallest plot one can use for a vegetable garden? You can use a patio planter to grow radishes and lettuce; you can grow tomatoes and peppers in pots or tubs. An area 4 × 20 feet is practical.

Would it be worthwhile for us to have a garden in a space 10 × 17 feet? There are just two of us. Yes. Highly perishable crops like lettuce and greens are always worth growing. You can grow a large part of your green vegetables as well as a few tomato plants in this area if you plan carefully.

Which are the five or six most practicable vegetables for an inexperienced person to try to raise in a home garden (20 × 25 feet) in New England? Tomatoes, snap beans, onion sets, radishes, Swiss chard, carrots, beets, and head or leaf lettuce. Follow one crop with another. Snap beans could follow radishes and lettuce.

What vegetables shall I plan to grow in a medium-sized garden? Anything you like with the exception of kinds which are known to be uncertain in your locality (consult local growers or your State Experiment Station) and such space consumers as corn, potatoes, squash, and pumpkins. (See the Introduction.)

How would you plan a vegetable plot 60 × 90 feet using principally the ordinary, easily grown items: corn, beans, peas, potatoes, tomatoes, radishes, etc.? Use 30 feet of the 90 for potatoes and divide the remainder among other crops, giving most space to those the family likes best.

What is the best way a plot 50 × 200 feet can be utilized so that it will include a home 20 × 32 feet, a little orchard of about 18 trees, a vegetable garden, and space for housing chickens? The chickens and the orchard can occupy the back 50 × 100 feet, with the poultry house in the center. The area between the house and the orchard could be the vegetable garden. If the house used up 75 feet, it would still give you a 25 × 50-foot vegetable garden.

How can I plan my garden, which is 90 × 100 feet? My husband died and I want to make a garden for myself and two children. This is almost a quarter of an acre, which would require a tremendous amount of work unless you possess a small power cultivator or rotary tiller. An area 25 × 50 or 75 feet will give you all the vegetables you need for your family. You might use that much for the garden and use the other land for some crop like tomatoes, potatoes, or sweet corn which you could sell to the neighbors.

What is the most profitable crop on an acre lot (part sandy and part loam and clay)? I have raspberries and strawberries, corn, and most garden vegetables. (Ohio.) Any crop is profitable if it will grow in your locality and you have a market for your produce. Strawberries, with irrigation and mulching, are usually profitable. If your vegetables are good and you live in an area where you can sell good produce, a general assortment can be profitable. First, you must learn to grow the crop well, and then sell it to good advantage.

Which vegetables would you recommend for planting in a small area (10 × 12 feet) that would produce the best yield? Onion sets, leaf lettuce, carrots, beets, 6 staked tomato plants, and 2 rows of snap beans. Make more plantings after the first crops are finished.

What vegetables could I plant in a sunny place where I have dug an extra foot of border on my flower bed; also, in an old rose garden about 9 feet square? Radishes, leaf lettuce, carrots, and beets in the narrow border; staked tomatoes and snap beans in the rose garden. Plant the beans between the tomato plants.

What is the usual size of a backyard garden? What vegetables could best be grown in that size? What could be used for second-crop or succession planting? An average-size backyard garden would be 20 × 25 feet. This will grow most vegetables for a family of four and you will still have some left over that you can freeze. Lettuce, beans, beets, carrots, cabbage, tomatoes, and onions (from sets) are good to start with.

You can make several plantings of all these vegetables, except tomatoes. Rutabagas, turnips, spinach, and lettuce are good for the fall.

Would you advise planting a few vegetables in border flower beds? We have very little rainfall and must irrigate most of the year. This is easily done. Plant tall vegetables north and west so they won't shade the low-growing plants. Keep the low-growing plants near the edges on the east or south side. Tomatoes can be set 2 feet apart and trained to stakes set alongside the plants. Low-growing plants can be set or planted in rows in the borders. Avoid crowding for vegetables which set pods or fruits. Parsley and chives make handsome edgings.

We are planning to convert some of our flower garden into a vegetable garden. Will you suggest suitable vegetables to plant against a brick wall 4 feet wide, facing south? Tomatoes, pole beans (especially limas), and cucumbers trained on a trellis would do well in such a situation.

What vegetables can be grown in flower beds in limited space? Half a dozen tomato plants scattered along the back of the flower beds, tied to stakes or grown in wire cages of wide mesh so they won't sprawl. Radishes and lettuce can be planted in the border toward the front. Asparagus can be planted so that the summer growth will serve as a background. Snap or pole beans can be planted between later-flowering plants. Rows of carrots and beets can be grown between rows of flowering plants, as they do not take much space. Onions can be grown from sets. There is always the possibility of growing a few cucumber vines in a tub or barrel in a vacant corner. Various herbs can be used as low edgings.

What steps must one take to start a home garden? (1) Decide on your crops and how much you want of each. (2) Select the ground and make your plan. (3) Sow seed for the plants 5 to 7 weeks before you plan to set them outside. (4) Get your ground ready with lime and fertilizer. (5) Plant frost-resistant crops about 3 weeks before the last spring frost (usually about mid-May). (6) Get warm-weather plants started, to have them ready by the middle of May.

LOCATION

What exposure should I choose for my vegetable garden? Providing the site is sunny, the precise exposure is less important than soil and other details. A southern or southeastern exposure will produce earlier crops. Even a northern exposure has advantages for cool-weather crops, such as late peas and summer lettuce.

What is the ideal location for a vegetable garden?   A well-drained, gentle slope facing the east or southeast, in full sunshine throughout the day and protected by shrubbery or a fence on the north and northwest.

Can I have a successful vegetable garden in a low, wet spot on my grounds? The soil is rich.   Vegetables must have good drainage. The only way you can successfully grow them in the location mentioned is to drain the area thoroughly by ditching or tilling, if necessary. (See Section 1 and the introduction to this section.)

What food plants can be planted in wet places such as undrained muck ponds, bayheads, etc.?   Except for watercress, which prefers running water, there are no vegetables which will grow in undrained soil. Stay away from salt water. Make beds 4 to 6 feet wide and at least a foot higher than the paths to get rid of the free water. Then you can grow lettuce, carrots, beets, collards, and similar types of vegetables. If the soil stays fairly dry, celery, tomatoes, and beans will grow well.

Can my vegetable garden be made on the west side of my house?   This is not a good spot for vegetables. Try to find a place that has full morning sunshine and as much sun in the afternoon as possible. The west side would do, however, if the garden is not too close to the house.

How much sunshine is necessary for vegetables?   Vegetables need all the sunshine they can get. A minimum of 5 to 6 hours of direct sunshine per day.

What is the best vegetable to plant in the shade?   There are none that will grow well without some sunshine. With partial shade, but sunshine in the morning, some of the leafy vegetables grow fairly well.

What vegetables are most suited to a shady garden? Will any of them yield successive crops, or is each good for only one crop?   Vegetables, to amount to anything, must have sunshine during the morning. The leafy vegetables are the only ones that will stand any shade. If they will grow, they may be planted in succession.

What vegetables will grow close (5 feet) to the north side of a house?   None.

I have a plot of 36 × 50 feet, one side of which lies in the shadow of my house. What vegetables (if any) can I plant in the shade?   If the garden is to the south of the house, you will have little difficulty. If it's on the west side, your only chance is some greens that may grow in the shade. On the north side, forget vegetables.

We have a large space of fertile ground underneath our fruit trees which gets sunshine only part of the day. I have not planted anything that has grown satisfactorily. Will you please inform me as to which vegetables will grow well in partial shade? Leafy vegetables are the only ones that will do well. Your difficulty may be that the tree roots rob the vegetables of water and fertilizer.

Would it be worthwhile to dig up a partially shaded area to plant vegetables such as beans and tomatoes? No, absolutely not. Some of the leafy vegetables might make a fair growth but not tomatoes and beans.

How can I raise a vegetable garden surrounded by oak trees that are at least 25 feet in height? It is hardly worth trying unless the trees are 20 feet or more from the vegetable plot. Plants must get morning sun, at least, and the roots of the trees would rob the vegetables of water and nutrients.

What vegetables will grow near maple trees in dry earth? None. Maple roots are too competitive.

Our new home was built on land that formerly was occupied by many tall trees, mostly oaks. We have some trees left which shade all parts of our grounds at some part of the day. The soil is acid and heavy. We have turned over half of the backyard and removed stones, roots, etc. Some land was left rough; another section was planted with rye and vetch, and we intended to turn it under in the spring. Can you suggest vegetables which we might grow under these conditions? To grow good vegetables, stay at least 10 feet from the outer edge of the branches, where the vegetables will receive at least the morning sun. The biggest problem is to keep the roots of the growing trees from robbing the water and fertility from the vegetable plants. Put on sufficient pulverized limestone to sweeten the soil. If this soil is very heavy, it should have considerable leafmold or manure, or even coal cinders, mixed with it.

What flowers and vegetables will grow close to the shady side of a privet hedge? Most vegetables, if the privet does not rob the vegetables of water and fertilizer. The shading effect is not serious unless it is on the south side of the vegetable plants, where it may produce too much shade. Five to six hours of direct sunshine are essential.

Are there any vegetables that will grow and produce in a plot 4 × 20 feet, which gets only morning sun and is within a few feet of pine and birch woods? The main problem here would be water and nutrients for the vegetables. The shading is not so serious unless the spot receives less than five hours of direct sunshine. Probably frequent watering would be required.

How do you develop a hillside garden? This requires the building of terraces, the width of which will be determined by the steepness of the slope. The rows must run crosswise of the slope.

What vegetables can be grown in sandy soil where wind and salt spray attack them? We have grown kale, broccoli, and lettuce fairly well. What others would you suggest? This can be answered only by your experience. Any smooth-leafed vegetable, including asparagus, should grow well. Plants with hairy or rough leaves probably would be injured by any appreciable amount of spray.

What vegetables grow and produce best in sandy and decomposed granite soil? This depends on how well the soil has been fertilized previously. If the soil has some lime in it, most vegetables can be grown provided that sufficient water and plant nutrients are added. Dissolving a cup of a mixed fertilizer in 3 gallons of water and watering the plants with this every 2 weeks will help. These usually are good soils.

COMMUNITY GARDENS

I would like to plant a vegetable garden, but don't have the land. How can I start a community garden? The most important requirement for a community garden is land. In city areas, tour your neighborhood and check out vacant lots, particularly city-owned vacant sites and park areas. In the country, talk with farmers, private landowners, and church groups—also corporations and local planning authorities. The next most important need is a "leader"—someone with enthusiasm, plus a gift for planning and organizing.

The best location is one with easy access to a water supply. Secure a location that is not temporary. There's nothing more discouraging than cultivating a plot of land only to realize that it won't be available the following year.

Divide the land into equal-size plots, and allocate one plot to each gardener or family group. Don't expect to garden the entire area like one big happy family. Each person with his or her own plot to look after is a better system. Don't make the plots too large if you are beginning gardeners. A well-cared-for small plot will yield far more than a large area that is neglected.

Try to have everyone start on the same day, having paid a farmer to plow the ground. This gets everyone off to an enthusiastic start, and the experience of planting the seeds becomes pure pleasure. Leave room for pathways between plots. Toilet facilities and a handy shed to lock up equipment should also be considered. In areas with potential vandalism, it may be necessary to erect a fence.

Soil Preparation

DIGGING OR TILLING

What's the case for fall digging versus spring digging? Dig in the fall, leaving the ground rough. Winter weather breaks up clods and aerates the soil through freezing and thawing. Many overwintering insect enemies are turned up, and there is less liability of leaving air pockets in the turned soil. Light, sandy soils, however, can suffer from washing by winter rains and usually are best left until spring for tilling or digging.

When digging a sodded plot of ground for the first time, to be used for a vegetable garden (in the spring), how should the ground be treated? Plow or till in the fall, leaving the clods on an angle instead of turning them over flat. This is done to avoid leaving a layer of sod between the subsoil and the surface soil. If lime is needed, also apply that in the fall, raking it in lightly so that rains will not wash it into hollows and low spots. If the sod is heavy, the plot should be tilled or dug in the spring at right angles (if reworking is necessary) to the direction in which it was first dug, so that the decomposing sod may be more thoroughly broken up and mixed through the soil.

When should spring digging or tilling be done? Digging should not be undertaken in the spring until the ground has begun to dry up after spring frosts are out. A simple test is to squeeze a handful of soil into a firm ball. If this ball under pressure from the fingers crumbles apart readily, the soil is ready to work. If it tends to remain in a sticky mess, digging should not be attempted until it has dried out further.

Should the vegetable garden be spaded up after the harvest in the fall and then again in the spring before the new planting? Or is spading in the spring sufficient? Spading or tilling in the fall is advantageous on most soils, except very light, sandy ones. Ground prepared in this way in the fall will need much less work done on it in the spring to get it ready for seed sowing and planting.

A power-driven rotary tiller can be a work-saver.
Use it to prepare the soil in the vegetable garden
and for mixing in fertilizers and organic matter.

When should a new vegetable garden be tilled or dug? Any time before seed-sowing time. Heavy or medium soils are better tilled or dug in the fall; very sandy soils, in the spring. However, if you have missed out on fall preparation, don't hesitate to begin a new garden in the spring.

When should the established vegetable garden be tilled or dug? If the soil is at all clayey, it should be turned over in the fall and left in a rough condition all winter. Very light, sandy soils should be tilled or dug in early spring.

How deeply do you think the ground should be dug for a vegetable garden? As deeply as possible providing that (1) not more than an inch or so of infertile subsoil is turned up; (2) labor is available. From 8 to 12 inches is a fair depth, but a somewhat greater depth is by no means excessive as the ultimate goal.

Does deep preparation of the soil help to make long, sturdy roots? Yes indeed. All crops benefit from deep soil preparations. Onion roots have been traced to a depth of 5 feet. Parsnips may be grown that are 3 feet long, with roots extending deeper.

Should ground be more deeply worked in dry areas? In general, yes. Some sandy soils are exceptions. Especially in dry locations it is necessary to encourage roots to strike deeply in search of moisture.

Do you advise turning over old sod ground, not used for 15 years, in late fall? By all means. Leave the ground in ridges rather than turning it over flat; this will permit alternate freezing and thawing during the winter to pulverize it more thoroughly. If the ground slopes, dig it

In digging soil with a shovel or spading fork, thrust the blade or tines straight down instead of at an oblique angle. Cultivating while weeds are very small saves backbreaking "chopping" later when weeds reach full size. But easier than cultivating weeds is the application of mulches or, in very small gardens, planting vegetables close together so most weeds are crowded out. Those that do manage to appear can be pulled out by hand.

across the slope of the land to check any tendency to erosion. A rototiller may usually be rented to turn over small pieces of ground. These small machines do an excellent job. If your grounds extend to even as much as an acre or two and the actual creation of your garden is still ahead of you, the purchase of a rototiller is often a wise move.

LIME

What is the best ground conditioner? For most soils, raw ground limestone is the best conditioner, as it both improves the mechanical condition of the soil and corrects acidity. For most vegetables, however, lime should not be applied to alkaline soil. Under such conditions, gypsum or land plaster is better, as it will not make the soil more alkaline—as will lime. Ashes and sifted cinders improve the physical condition of any heavy soil.

Should lime be spread over a vegetable garden early in the spring or in the fall? It is much better, if possible, to apply lime in the fall after the ground is dug. Then cultivate it in so that heavy rains will not wash it away.

What are the relative lime requirements of the common vegetables? With few exceptions, most vegetables do best in a soil which is slightly acid—that is, a soil showing a pH reaction of 6 or 6.5 to 7. (See

Acidity, this section.) The vegetables most tolerant of a somewhat acid soil are potatoes, sweet potatoes, watermelon (to a somewhat lesser degree), eggplants, peppers, and tomatoes. Those least tolerant of acidity (and therefore most in need of lime) are asparagus, cauliflower, celery, leeks, lettuce, onions, and spinach.

PROBLEMS WITH SOIL

What soil treatment do you recommend for a lawn dug up for a vegetable garden? If the sod is very heavy, it may be desirable to remove the turf, cutting it as shallowly as possible and making a compost heap of the sod thus obtained. However, if the sod can be dug under (mixing it thoroughly with the soil so that it does not remain in unbroken lumps), that is preferable. On soil prepared this way, an application of 5 to 10 pounds per 100 square feet of a complete fertilizer should give good results the first year.

Do you think removing all the stones from a vegetable garden is a good idea? Our garden was cleared of every stone for about 10 inches down; lots of manure was spread over the ground in the winter. My theory is that the fertilizer sank too far into the ground, as there was no foundation, and was lost to the crop. The year before we had a fine crop —it was only the second time for using this garden. Removing stones is not at all essential, except that their absence makes it easier to work the soil. However, taking them out would not injure the soil or make fertilizers leach away more quickly. Roots of most vegetables go down 2 feet or more.

How can I prepare a 10-acre plot to good advantage? First, supply sufficient liming material to bring the pH up near the neutral point, and plant some cover crop to plow under. Then fertilize for the vegetable crops. Consult your county agent.

What types of vegetables can be grown in clay-loam soil? How can that kind of soil be made to grow any kind of garden? This is a cold, late soil, best suited to frost-hardy plants like members of the cabbage family. Such soil should be well limed and have organic material mixed with it. After a year or two of use it should be suitable for most vegetables.

Our vegetable garden has a rather heavy clay soil. What treatment would you advise? Manure, compost, and humus supplied by growing green-manure crops will all help to lighten a clay soil. Applications of lime or of land plaster (gypsum) will also help greatly in improving the mechanical condition and make it less likely to form hard lumps. Clay soil should never be dug or cultivated while wet.

I have never done any vegetable gardening; I want to dig up part of my lawn to plant a vegetable garden. There is only about 2 inches of topsoil; the rest is sand. How should I go about it? Your problem is a difficult one, as very shallow soils are not the best for vegetable growing. Dig about 4 inches deep, breaking the sod up as thoroughly as possible and mixing it through the soil. If well-rotted manure can be obtained in the spring, apply a heavy coating—2 to 4 inches deep—and dig this under just sufficiently to cover it up so that the surface will be clear for planting. Lacking manure, apply a 2-inch layer of peat moss (available in 6-cubic-foot bales from garden centers). Your problem will be to keep the soil well supplied with humus to absorb and hold moisture; sandy soils dry out too rapidly. In using fertilizer, make frequent small applications while the plants are growing instead of putting it on in advance of planting, as is often done on heavier soils. Sandy soils require frequent watering.

How is newly spaded soil prepared for a vegetable garden? If the soil is acid, lime should be added and cultivated in. Unless the soil is already in very good condition from previous applications of fertilizer, 4 to 5 pounds of complete fertilizer per 100 square feet is broadcast and raked in before planting. Before seed sowing, the surface of the soil should be gone over with an iron-toothed rake, removing all small stones and trash and leaving it as smooth and level as possible.

What is the best time to prepare the ground for early planting of potatoes, corn, and various vegetables? As a general rule, it is best to prepare the ground for planting a month or more in advance. This is particularly true if sod or a green-manure crop is to be turned under. Advance preparation makes possible partial decay of the green vegetable matter before the vegetable crop is planted; otherwise, the decaying plant material will temporarily draw upon the nitrogen in the soil, thus robbing the planted crop, unless additional nitrogen is added when the crop is planted. Wherever very early planting is to be done, it is advantageous to till the ground the previous autumn if it is possible.

How do I prepare a former flower garden for a vegetable garden and what are the best vegetables for a beginner to grow? A flower garden that has been well fertilized should be in excellent shape to grow vegetables. Thorough and deep digging and the application of a complete fertilizer will put it into condition. The vegetables that it would be advisable to grow will depend on the size of the plot and the gardener's experience (see lists in the introduction to this section).

If clay soil is turned over in the fall, how early can the first vegetables be planted in the spring? (Ohio.) Clay soils dug in the fall can usually be planted much earlier than if the preparation of the ground is left until spring. The hardy crops (see Introduction) can be put in just as soon as the soil is sufficiently dry to be cultivated and raked without sticking to the tools and forming hard lumps. Ordinarily this would be in early April, but will vary with the season.

Is it necessary to have different types of soil for the common vegetables, such as carrots, lettuce, cabbage, etc.? No. In a well-prepared garden plot practically the complete list of vegetables can be grown satisfactorily. It is important, however, that the soil be slightly acid. If it is too acid or too alkaline, many vegetables will not do well. (See Acidity, this section.)

We live near salt water; our soil is not very good. The only flowers that we seem to grow successfully are marigolds and zinnias. If this soil agrees with them, what vegetables could we grow? If protected from high winds and salt spray, most vegetables can be grown. Add as much organic material to the soil as possible—peat moss and seaweed, for example.

In our vegetable garden we always have excellent results with green beans, tomatoes, butter beans, cucumbers, but poor results with peas, carrots, spinach, beets, and turnips. The soil is sandy, with pine trees in an adjoining pasture. Does this experience suggest that something is lacking? (Texas.) This indicates that the soil may be low in lime, boron, and potash. A complete soil test should be made, and if calcium is low, some pulverized limestone (preferably dolomitic) should be spread on the surface when the soil is prepared.

Why did my carrots, beets, and turnips grow only to about one fourth their normal size? My flowers mostly stayed very short with small blooms. The ground hadn't been turned over in 75 years. Does it require some special care? Few vegetables (particularly the root crops) do well on soil not previously cultivated. With good culture you will undoubtedly see an improvement each year for two or three seasons. Other than the usual cultivation, the incorporation of humus, and fertilizing, the soil probably does not require any special treatment. For root crops, use fertilizers that are high in potash and phosphorus, and irrigate during dry spells.

FERTILIZERS

What is the difference between "fertilizer," "manure," and "plant food"?   In a general sense, any material added to the soil which will aid plant growth is a fertilizer. As more commonly used, the term "fertilizer" refers to manufactured products in dry form sold in bags; "manure" refers to such animal products as cow, horse, or sheep manure. "Plant food," as usually employed, is an incorrect term; the only true plant foods are manufactured or developed *within the plant*. However, the term "plant food" is frequently employed as a polite word for fertilizer or manure.

What is the difference between organic and inorganic fertilizer?   The former is made from animal or vegetable sources, such as bone or blood or cottonseed meal; the latter is made from mineral or synthetic substances, such as phosphate rock, nitrate salts, or potash salts.

What is meant by the term "complete plant food"?   As used by manufacturers, a commercial fertilizer containing all three of the main elements which are required for plant growth, i.e., nitrogen, phosphorus, and potassium. "Complete fertilizer" is the correct term, rather than complete plant food.

What is the meaning of the three numbers which appear on every package of complete fertilizer, such as "5–10–5"?   The first number always stands for the percentage of nitrogen, the second for the percentage of phosphorus, and the third for the percentage of potassium.

What is meant by "trace elements"? Do any complete fertilizers contain these?   Trace elements are substances such as manganese, boron, sulfur, and iron, required for plant growth but in smaller quantities than the three main elements (nitrogen, phosphorus, and potassium) and usually present in most soils. Yes, most complete fertilizers do contain some of the trace elements, either in the raw materials from which the fertilizer mixture is made or they are added purposely to supply them. Since the law does not require manufacturers to declare the presence of trace elements on the bag, you must take this on faith.

What is the best all-round garden fertilizer—one which is of high, medium, or low percentage in plant nutrients?   A medium-percentage fertilizer such as 5–10–5 or 4–12–4 is usually recommended for general garden use.

What is a "starter" or "transplanting" solution?   This consists of a small amount of high-analysis chemical fertilizer dissolved in water. A cup is poured directly on the roots of plants when they are transplanted or a cup is poured directly on the seed for every 3 feet of row. An ounce of 13–26–13 fertilizer, or 3 ounces of a 5–10–5 fertilizer, in a gallon of water, makes a starter solution.

What is a "sidedressing" solution?   This is the same as a starter solution, but sometimes made stronger, used to pour around the plants after they are well established and growing. Two to three times as much fertilizer is dissolved in the water. It gives a quick response and there is somewhat less danger of burning the plants than when a dry fertilizer is used.

How should nitrogen be applied to the soil?   In a complete fertilizer, or in the form of ammonium sulfate, nitrate of soda, dried blood, or tankage, usually at the time of transplanting or in the early stages of plant growth, at the rate of 2 or 3 pounds per 100 square feet of row. Nitrogen helps in the development of leafy vegetables.

Sidedressings of fertilizer during growth are helpful to most vegetables. Fertilizer with high nitrogen is desirable for leaf crops, such as lettuce and Swiss chard. Seed- or fruit-producing crops, such as beans or tomatoes, require abundant potash.

When and how should phosphorus be applied to a vegetable garden?   Apply phosphorus in a complete fertilizer, or in superphosphate, at the time of soil preparation, at the rate of 3 to 5 pounds per 100 square feet. Phosphorus *must* be worked into the soil as it does not move down from the surface.

When should I apply potash and in what form?   In a complete fertilizer, 3 to 5 pounds, or in the form of muriate of potash 2 to 3 pounds, per 100 square feet. Or add this material to the manure or compost used in the garden. Potash is especially helpful in building up soils which do not grow good root crops or produce satisfactory stem plants, such as celery.

When should dried blood be used as a fertilizer? Dried blood is used when an organic source of nitrogen is wanted. It is usually applied at the rate of 4 pounds per 100 square feet.

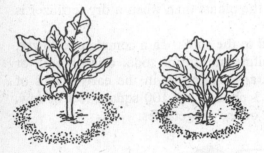

A sidedressing of fertilizer applied in a ring around the stem of young eggplant and cabbage.

What is "superphosphate," and what is its chief use in a vegetable garden? Superphosphate is ground and treated phosphate rock that carries (usually) about 20 per cent phosphorus. ("Treble" phosphate carries about 45 per cent.) It is used in almost all complete fertilizers. On most new soils it can be applied separately in addition to other fertilizers, being thoroughly mixed with the soil in advance of planting, 4 to 6 pounds per 100 square feet.

Can a successful garden be made using only complete fertilizers and peat moss or humus without manure? If manure is not obtainable, you can still have a successful garden by planting and turning under cover crops yearly, maintaining compost heaps to be used in the garden when rotted, and adding complete fertilizer when preparing the ground at planting time and as sidedressings during plant growth.

If manure and fertilizer are available, which do you recommend? Use both: manure, when preparing the ground and when planting many crops; complete fertilizers, just before planting and as a sidedressing during the growth of the plants.

Is there a good general fertilizer for the vegetable garden? Most fertilizer companies put out a "vegetable formula" fertilizer designed for use with most vegetable crops. This varies somewhat in different regions of the country. In general, a 5–10–5 mixture is a good all-purpose fertilizer for vegetables. For root crops, a 2–10–10 fertilizer, if available, is better; or supplement the 5–10–5 fertilizer with extra potash.

What are the food needs of different vegetables? While there are many special formulas made up for different vegetables that are grown on a commercial scale, in the home garden it is not practical to attempt to work out these differences. Homemade compost, plus a generous application of a high-quality complete fertilizer, will produce good crops. Where some special need exists, this can be provided for by an additional application of one of the several materials that carry nitrogen, phosphoric acid, or potash.

What is a good general fertilizer that can be used on potatoes, celery, tomatoes, and cabbage? A 5–10–5 or 5–10–10 fertilizer if your soil needs the extra potash. The first is better for cabbage and celery; the second is good for tomatoes and potatoes.

What fertilizer (grade of mixture) should be used on plants such as potatoes, tomatoes, corn (sweet), cabbage, and cauliflower? See the answer above. A general-purpose fertilizer can be supplemented by other materials for particular crops. For instance, lettuce, cabbage, and cauliflower during their early stages of growth are benefited by an abundance of nitrogen, and this can be supplied in the form of nitrate of soda or ammonium sulfate applied around the growing plants in addition to the general-purpose fertilizer which has been used.

What is the best way to fertilize new ground for vegetables? If the soil is acid, spread lime over the surface and apply at least 25 pounds of a 5–10–5 fertilizer on a 1,000-square-foot area before the ground is

There are different ways to apply fertilizer. The fertilizer can be broadcast over the ground and raked in (far left); dry fertilizer can be spread, about 4 inches from the root and stem area of plants, along rows; and liquid fertilizer, mixed according to directions on the container, can be applied to individual plants or groups of plants.

plowed or spaded. Then set all the plants and plant all the seed with starter solution.

How shall I fertilize a small space to produce the largest possible crops of different vegetables? (North Dakota.)   In areas where water is at a premium, it is difficult to use chemical fertilizer in the dry form. Keep the soil limed only if needed, and use animal manure if available. Then use a starter solution for setting the plants and when sowing. If more fertilizer is needed, use a sidedressing solution.

What can I do to enrich a vegetable garden plot 20 × 20 feet which has been planted regularly for 15 years and does not produce very good crops?   Very likely the soil is deficient in humus. If this is the case, commercial fertilizer alone will not produce good crops. Dig in a generous coating of compost or, if available, manure, applied 2 to 4 inches deep over the surface, or half that amount of compost.

Can you tell me the fertilizer necessary to make an active, producing vegetable garden soil out of former woodland?   This would depend upon the type of soil. It is best to make a test for acidity (see Section 1), then apply sufficient lime to bring the soil to a "slightly acid" condition—the best for most vegetables. Phosphoric acid is almost sure to be needed. Consult your local county Cooperative Extension agent or State Experiment Station for the general requirements of soil in your vicinity.

What should I use on a leaf soil in the woods to be able to grow a vegetable garden? I tried squash; the plants flowered but never produced any squashes; the blossoms all fell off. The same happened with cucumbers. Please tell me what kind of fertilizer to use.   The falling off of flowers without setting fruit usually indicates a deficiency in phosphoric acid and potash. Probably these should be used, in addition to a complete fertilizer, for two or three seasons, until the plant nutrients in your soil are more evenly balanced. Full sun is needed for all vegetables.

Does rotten manure have any effect on root crops, like scabbing or stunting?   Manure that is not thoroughly decomposed does sometimes make rough or scabby root crops. Other conditions, however, may be the cause. Potatoes grown in soil that is too heavily limed are almost certain to be scabby although no manure has been used on the ground for years.

Is there a connection between the type of fertilizer and the taste of vegetables or fruits?   Supposedly, no, but poor soil fertility will affect the flavor of fruiting vegetables such as melons.

I have room to place tomato plants between my rows of daffodils during the month of May. What would be the best fertilizer to use? Would

manure dug in be injurious to the bulbs? Manure can cause bulb diseases; use a complete fertilizer for the tomatoes. Superphosphate may be added, as this would not only help the tomato crop but would also be of decided benefit to the daffodils.

What causes tough-skinned and very small carrots and beets grown in the same ground that grows excellent tomatoes? Some deficiency in the soil, such as a lack of phosphorus, which builds strong roots. Apply superphosphate, 4 to 5 pounds per 100 square feet. If possible, have the soil tested by your county agent, who will give you advice on its improvement.

Our soil is sandy. What amount of fertilizer should we use? We have heard so much about the damage caused by too much fertilizer that we're confused. Sandy soil usually requires larger additions of humus and nutrients (in the form of compost—manure, if available—or fertilizer) than heavy soils. The method of application, moreover, is different. Sandy soils are likely to leach badly. Several light applications during the season give better results than one heavy application. Everything possible should be done to increase the humus content of sandy soil by using manure, humus in the form of compost, peat moss, or green crops for turning under.

What is the best time to fertilize a vegetable garden—fall or spring? Slow-acting materials such as lime and superphosphate may best be applied in the fall; or, if in the spring, as early and as far in advance of planting as possible. The more quick-acting materials (such as the ordinary "complete" fertilizer) and well-decomposed compost should be applied in the spring. The very quick-acting fertilizers, like nitrate of soda or sulfate of ammonia, and the somewhat slower dried blood or tankage is best used at the time of planting or applied around plants after some growth has been made.

Is it best to put stable manure on a vegetable garden in the fall or spring? This depends largely upon the condition of the manure. If thoroughly decayed, it is usually best to apply it in the spring. If in a fresh state, apply it in the fall or winter. If manure is applied long in advance of planting, there is a considerable loss of nitrogen, especially in light soils.

If a vegetable garden is covered with manure in the fall, is fall cultivation really necessary? Fall tilling is highly desirable unless there is danger of erosion. The manure will decay more thoroughly and evenly instead of merely drying out and it will also increase the bacterial action in the soil. Mixing the manure with the soil will also help retain nutrients. Earlier planting is made possible.

Is there anything I can do in the fall to improve a plot to be used for vegetables in the spring? A heavy application of compost or manure dug into the ground in the fall will put it into good condition for spring planting. Even if manure or compost is not available for tilling or digging, leaving the ground in ridges and furrows will help put it into better mechanical condition. If lime is needed, fall is the best time to apply it.

Is it a good idea to use wood ashes on a vegetable garden plot? When is the best time to apply them? Wood ashes contain potash and are also an excellent soil conditioner. Usually it is preferable to apply them in the fall, as they are not as quick-acting as most commercial fertilizers. However, if this cannot be done, they can safely be applied in the spring.

Do wood ashes on the ground make parsnips woody, and if not, what is the cause? Wood ashes, which add both lime and potash to the soil, are excellent for almost all vegetables. It is much more likely that woody or fibrous parsnips are the result of conditions causing slow growth. All root crops, to be brittle and tender, must develop quite rapidly and without a check. Lack of sufficient nitrogen, or a prolonged period of dry weather, would cause a woody condition.

Is soot from a furnace motor stoker beneficial for a vegetable garden? No.

Should coal ashes be used on a vegetable garden? If so, when? Sifted coal ashes are beneficial to the physical condition of most soils, especially to heavy ones. The winter's supply of ashes, screened and spread over the surface as they are produced in the winter, can be dug or tilled under in the spring.

In growing vegetables, is there much difference in the results of broadcasting commercial fertilizer before planting or spreading it in the rows when planting? Formerly, most fertilizers were applied by broadcasting before planting or in the row at the time of planting. The modern practice is to use ½ or ⅔ of the fertilizer in 1, 2, or 3 side-dressings along the sides of the rows during growth. This has been found to produce a bigger yield and to maintain growth at a more even rate of development—highly desirable for most crops.

How should fertilizing be done when transplanting vegetable plants from a cold frame to an open garden? Fertilizer is applied about a week in advance and thoroughly mixed in with the top 3 or 4 inches of soil. Or compost or a complete fertilizer is thoroughly mixed with the soil in the bottoms of holes in which plants are to be set.

Should vegetables be fertilized after being sown or transplanted into an open garden? If so, when and how? If the soil is rich and fertile, this may not be necessary. Otherwise many vegetables, when about half grown, benefit from the application of a sidedressing. Use 3 to 5 pounds of fertilizer to each 100 feet of row. Spread it thinly down each side of the row, 3 or 4 inches from the plants, and cultivate in.

ACIDITY

What is meant by an "acid" soil? One in which the chemical reaction is acid instead of alkaline, as measured by the pH scale. This scale corresponds, in a way, to the thermometer scale for measuring temperature.

What is the meaning of pH? See the introduction to Section 1. A pH reading of 7 indicates the neutral point. Figures below pH 7 (pH 5.5, for instance) indicate the degree of acidity; figures above pH 7, the degree of alkalinity.

Is it worthwhile to have my soil tested before I plant vegetables? It is well to have the soil of an untried piece of ground tested before starting to improve its condition, especially if you have reason to think it is worn out or unfertile. Consult your county Cooperative Extension agent or State Agricultural Experiment Station about testing your soil and how to improve it.

How can I tell if my soil is acid? There are available inexpensive testing kits which anyone can use.

Do vegetables prefer acid or alkaline soil? Most vegetables are grown most successfully in slightly acid soil, i.e., soil with a pH of 6 to 7. Soil with a pH 5 to 5.6 will grow potatoes, sweet potatoes, watermelons; pH 5.2 to 6—eggplants, peppers, tomatoes; pH 5.6 to 6.8—beans, carrots, corn, parsley, parsnips, pumpkins, salsify, Swiss chard, turnips; pH 6 to 7.2—beets, broccoli, cabbage, cucumbers, endive, leaf lettuce, muskmelons, peas, radishes, rhubarb; pH 6.4 to 7.6—asparagus, cauliflower, celery, leeks, head lettuce, onions, spinach.

What vegetables are good for a very acid soil? We cannot raise peas. Potatoes, sweet potatoes, and watermelons. Liming the soil (see Soil Preparation) would make it suitable for peas.

What treatment is necessary when beans, carrots, and beets are stunted, but 10 feet away they grow fine and strong? If poor drainage is not the cause, there may be an extremely acid spot in the soil. A soil test would prove this. If not, an additional application of a complete fertilizer should correct the trouble.

What steps can I take to correct the condition of my vegetable plot, which is very acid? See the introduction to Section 1, and Soil Preparation, this section.

GREEN MANURES (COVER CROPS)

When a garden writer advises the use of "green manure," what is meant? Any crop grown for the purpose of digging or tilling it under to decay in the soil—and thus add humus—is called a green manure. Long used in farm practice, green manuring in the home vegetable garden is rapidly gaining favor.

Is the practice of green manuring worthwhile for the home garden? Most decidedly, especially in sections where it is difficult to procure animal manures. This is a good inexpensive way to build up the humus content of the soil.

Do you advise the use of green manures for conditioning a vegetable plot? Yes, by all means. By putting in a cover crop in late summer or autumn as soon as vegetable crops are harvested, and digging it under in the spring when 6 to 10 inches high, the humus content in the soil will be maintained. (See Section 1.)

What is the best way to handle a green-manure crop (rye) that has grown too tall to be dug under conveniently? Mow the tops and add them to a compost heap, or use for mulching; dig under stubble and roots, which will add considerable humus.

What is the best way to maintain garden fertility? One of the most important factors in maintaining fertility is to keep up the humus content of the soil. This can be done by using manure or compost, and by growing green crops whenever possible to be turned under to decay. (See Section 1.) After the soil is producing well, the practice outlined above, plus moderate yearly applications of a complete fertilizer, should maintain the fertility indefinitely.

What should I sow after plowing my garden plot in the fall? Unless the ground is tilled or spaded by the first of September (in the latitude of New York) there is little use in sowing a green-manure or cover crop where early planting is to be done. Rye and rye grass are the two most satisfactory crops for fall and winter growth to turn under for green manure. In the latitude of Washington, D.C., and farther south, these crops will make considerable growth during the winter months and can be sown in late September or early October.

Which makes a better green-manure crop for a vegetable garden—rye or rye grass? Both winter rye and perennial rye grass make excellent green-manure crops. Both can be sown any time from midsummer until frost, and are perfectly hardy through the winter. Rye germinates somewhat faster and makes a more rapid early growth. It is coarser and more difficult to dig under in the spring if the job is not done early. Rye produces more bulk in a shorter time than rye grass, but both are satisfactory. Rye continues to grow whenever air temperatures are over 40° F. during the winter.

Sowing a cover crop in the fall and turning it under in the spring is one way to increase the humus content in the soil, as this forkful of winter rye shows.

What is the best time to plant sweet clover and soybeans, and when should these two cover crops be turned under? Sweet clover, a biennial, may be sown early in the spring but will make a suitable growth for green manuring even if sown as late as mid-June. Turn under when it is 8 to 12 inches high, or any time before its stalks become hard; sow in midsummer to turn under the following spring. Sow soybeans after the danger of frost has passed and turn under any time after sufficient growth has been made and before their main stems begin to get hard.

What are several good summer and winter cover crops? Summer: cowpeas, soybeans, oats, buckwheat, and Hubam or annual sweet clover. Winter: rye, perennial rye grass, or (if sown not later than mid-August) crimson clover or vetch.

Is there any evidence that growing vetch on land will inoculate peas? Yes. The bacteria left in the soil from the vetch roots will help the growth of peas.

My vegetable garden is covered with leaves; because of furrows, it is difficult to rake them off. Shall I burn them or turn them under in the spring? By all means, plow or dig under the leaves instead of burning them. Anything which will decay that can be turned into the soil will help add humus.

What vegetables or flowers will grow in 100 per cent humus? A shallow pond drained many years ago is dry black humus that I am told should be mixed with topsoil, now hard to get. Undoubtedly topsoil mixed with the humus would improve it. Many humus-rich soils, however, will grow good crops of most vegetables, provided a complete fertilizer is applied. Such soils are used by many truck gardeners. Celery is the most productive crop on high organic soils. Try it for one season before adding topsoil and then use it only for such vegetables that may not do well in the humus.

Seed Sowing

SEEDS

How can I be sure that I am buying good vegetable seed? By making your purchases only from reliable firms that specialize in seeds. The great skill and effort that go into producing high-quality seeds are not apparent in the seed packet—only in the crop that results.

For how many seasons are vegetable seeds good? There is considerable variation in the length of time that different vegetable seeds maintain their vitality. Onions, okra, and parsnips, for instance, can be counted on for only one year. Beans, beets, members of the cabbage family, and most vine crops are good for three or four years.

Will seeds that are purchased for one season, and not used, germinate the following spring? If they have been stored in a dry place, they probably will germinate well except for those mentioned above. There is no treatment that will improve their germination but the germination can be tested before planting. (See below for method.)

I have considerable green bean seed left. Can it be used for the next planting season? The seeds usually germinate well for several years. However, to make sure that germination will be satisfactory, sprout a few of them on moist blotting paper (in a saucer) before planting them. The percentage of germination can then be accurately determined.

What vegetable seeds can the home gardener harvest without risking deterioration or cross-pollination? What steps can a gardener take with the more difficult varieties? This is a big question to answer here. In a dry season, with good, clear weather, many kinds can be grown. Tomatoes, beans, peppers, eggplants, lettuce, endive, and onions are self-pollinated. Most of the others are cross-pollinated, and for good seed would have to be hand-pollinated under bags.

What is the proper method of saving and treating seeds from a vegetable garden so they will grow the following year? In general, vegetable seeds are gathered as they begin to reach maturity, indicated by the seed pods turning brown and hard. They can then be spread out on trays or in flats until they ripen further. During this period they must be protected from moisture. When completely ripened, they are stored in tight containers. Short-lived seeds can be stored at below freezing temperatures. In regular storage, temperature and humidity combined must not exceed 100° F., i.e., at 60° F., humidity should not exceed 40 per cent; at 50°, not above 50 per cent.

INDOOR SOWING

What vegetable seeds can be started in a house, greenhouse, hotbed, or cold frame in the spring? Tomatoes, peppers, eggplants, early lettuce, celery, celeriac, early cabbage, early cauliflower, and early broccoli; beets also transplant readily, if a few extra-early ones are wanted; also, sweet potato vines.

What is needed in the soil to start vegetable seedlings indoors? The soil for starting seedlings need not be rich. The mechanical condition is more important. A mixture of ⅓ garden soil, ⅓ sand, and ⅓ peat moss or compost, thoroughly mixed and passed through a sieve, gives good results, but may carry damping-off disease. Therefore, the sterile soilless mixes, such as Jiffy Mix, Readi-Earth, etc., are more convenient. They can be bought at garden centers.

Is it possible to have any amount of success in starting vegetable seeds indoors if there is no direct sunlight? Seeds will start but will not progress satisfactorily unless they have long hours of direct sunshine. Fluorescent tubes can be used successfully to supplement daylight by turning them on at 4 P.M., off at 9 P.M. Without daylight, keep the tubes on 14 hours.

When is the best time to seed vegetables in a flat before transplanting them in the spring? This depends on what vegetables you are growing, whether they are hardy or tender, and the length of time these take from seed to food crop. In general, seeds are planted in flats in late February and early March to be set out in April and May. Cabbage and broccoli started in February can be set out in early April. Tomatoes started at the same time are transplanted first into 2- and then into 3- or 4-inch pots before they can be set out in May. Peppers and eggplant seeds, which are very tender, can be sown in March as the plants cannot go into the open garden until all danger of frost is past and the ground has warmed up.

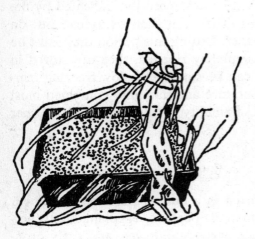

After sowing seeds, slip the flat into a plastic kitchen bag to retain moisture. Place the flat in a warm place out of direct sun. As soon as seedlings appear, remove the flat from its bag and place in sunshine or under fluorescent lights.

Should vegetable seedlings in flats, pans, or a seed bed be thinned before they are transplanted? If seeds are sown far enough apart, thinning will probably not be necessary. If the little plants are crowded, however, thinning is advisable, just as soon as they are well up.

What temperature should one have to start plants from seed indoors or in a greenhouse? Night temperature for hardy plants, 40° to 50° F.; for tender plants (tomatoes, peppers, eggplants), 50° to 60°. These are minimums; 5° to 10° F. higher will do no harm. To germinate the seeds, 60° for hardy plants (cabbage, etc.) and 70° for tender ones.

How can lettuce, tomatoes, peppers, cabbages, and other plants from seed be grown indoors? (New York.) To grow vegetable plants successfully indoors from seed you must have a very sunny window or a sun porch with a southern or southeastern exposure. Use fluorescent tubes to supplement sunshine during short days in late winter. Start hardy vegetable seeds (cabbage family, lettuce, etc.) February 15 to March 1 in flats of prepared soil. Start tender vegetables (peppers, eggplants, and tomatoes) about March 15, also in flats. Transplant to other flats when true leaves are formed and (for extra good plants) finally to small pots. Harden off the hardy vegetables outdoors in a cold frame from about April 1 to April 15 before setting in an open garden. Tender vegetables are hardened in a frame beginning about May 1. For other localities, seeds are started about 2 months before they can go out into a cold frame for hardening off.

Can vegetable seedlings be grown under artificial light? Fluorescent tubes can be used with the tubes about 4 inches above the upper leaves. If the seedlings are growing in a very cool basement, daylight white or warm white tubes can be used in combination with 4 20-watt incandescent bulbs spaced between the tubes. If the incandescent sockets are wired in series, instead of parallel, they will emit more red light (the color lacking in the fluorescent tubes).

Use an artificial soil medium such as vermiculite, calcined clay, perlite mixed with peat moss, or one of the packaged soilless mixes available from garden centers. Water whenever needed, but add a house-plant fertilizer (at about $\frac{1}{10}$ the strength recommended on the package) every time you water.

Before transplanting out-of-doors, harden the plants in a sunny window or cold frame for two or three days.

The seedlings growing in my south window grow spindly. What is wrong? Probably cloudy weather in March and April. Elevate the seed planter with a book. Or supplement daylight with a 60-watt incandescent light turned on all day during dark days and at 4 P.M. on clear days, off at 9 P.M. One bulb suspended 3 feet above flats will stimulate an area a yard square.

How should I label newly planted seeds? Each group of seeds planted should be labeled. Place a small wooden label with the name of

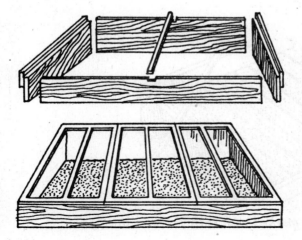

The use of a cold frame or a hotbed helps to get the vegetable garden off to an early start in the spring. (Above) Wooden sections for the frame before being assembled in the garden. (Bottom) Typical frame with a lightweight sash (cover), each 2 × 4 feet.

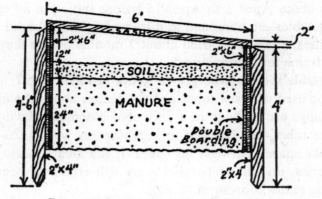

Cross section of a manure-heated hot-bed. Or use electric cables for the heat source.

the plant, variety, source, and planting date in a pan or at the end of a row in a flat or bed.

What is "bottom" heat? When is it used in growing vegetable seedlings? Warmth applied beneath the soil in which the seeds are grown, as by placing a flat of seeds on a heater or radiator. It is used to hasten the germination of tender or difficult seeds. *It should not be continued after seedlings are well up.* Soil readings above 90° are harmful. Insulate the top of a radiator if used: Direct heat could injure the seeds. A cardboard carton flattened out will do. Electric heating cables can be purchased at garden centers or from mail-order seed houses and can be regulated to exact temperatures.

End of cold frame marked with rows for seed sowing.

How long can newly sown seeds in pans, flats, or seed beds be kept covered from the light? Until germination takes place. They must then be uncovered *immediately*.

How can I water young seedlings to keep them from being beaten down by the spray of water? If grown in flats, pans, or pots, they should be watered *from the bottom*, by placing the container in a tray or pan partly filled with water. If grown in a seed bed or in an open garden, they should be watered with a very fine spray, but long enough to thoroughly soak the soil; water early in the morning, so they can dry off before night.

How can I heat a cold frame for early seed sowing? You can grow your own plants (to be set out in a garden) in a one-sash hotbed built against a cellar window, if you have some heat there. Otherwise, 4 100-watt light bulbs placed in the sash along the sides and lighted on cold nights would give sufficient heat to keep the plants growing. Or buy electric heating cables from a garden supply center. You can cover the sash in late afternoon to hold in as much heat as possible from the sun. Grow the frost-tolerant plants first and the warm-weather plants later.

A temporary cold frame can be made in a jiffy with scrap lumber. The sash or covering can be plastic sheeting stapled to a wood frame.

How can I prevent seedlings in flats from turning to the light so that their stems are crooked? Give them all the sunshine possible. If they still "draw" to the light, turn the flat or pan daily. (See the previous questions on supplementing daylight with artificial light.)

OUTDOOR SOWING

How should the ground be prepared for seed sowing of vegetables? Spade or till. Lime, if necessary. Fertilize. Rake or harrow to a fine, crumbly surface immediately before the seeds are sown. The surface should be even. If in doubt, consult local gardeners or your county

*For the lazy gardener: Preplanted
seed flats can be purchased that
require only water to initiate seed
germination. Other aids include
various kinds and sizes of peat
pots. The roots grow into and
through the peat so that the pot
and the plant are set out together
in open ground.*

agent through the Cooperative Extension Service in regard to your lime
and fertilizer needs.

**In planting seeds (in the open) for later transplanting to permanent
positions, shall I broadcast or plant in rows?**   Plant in rows so that you
will know where to look for seedlings and to facilitate weeding and
transplanting.

**Should vegetable seeds be treated with anything prior to being
planted?**   The only seed treatment home gardeners should be concerned with is a fungicide treatment. Peas, beans, corn, and similar
large seeds that are highly susceptible to rot diseases are best treated

with captan, a mild, protective, nonpoisonous fungicide. Some seed companies provide this service automatically for the seeds that need it; others will do it on request. Another harmful fungus disease is called "damping off," which attacks seedlings at the soil line, causing them to keel over and die. The disease is most troublesome indoors and is best prevented by using only clean, new containers and sterile soil mixes, or sterile planter pots such as Jiffy-7 peat pellets.

How can I hasten the germination of hard-shelled seeds like peas, New Zealand spinach, celery, and parsley? By soaking them in tepid water for 24 to 48 hours before they are sown. Then dry them off and sow at once. New Zealand spinach seed will not sprout in warm soil. Sow as early as the soil is workable.

What vegetable seeds are planted in the open garden in early spring? Peas, radishes, lettuce, cress, roquette, spinach, onions and leeks, parsnips, salsify, dandelions, early beets and carrots, kohlrabi, turnips, Swiss chard, fava or broad beans, and New Zealand spinach.

This well-developed eggplant seedling, with its roots growing through the peat pot, is ready to be planted—pot and all—in the open ground, if frost danger is past. Such tender vegetables as eggplant, pepper, and tomato are excellent subjects for peat pots.

Which tender vegetable seeds cannot be safely planted until the soil is thoroughly warm? Snap beans, lima beans, corn, cucumbers, squash, pumpkins, melons, and okra.

What is a trench, a furrow, a drill, and a hill? *Trench*—A ditchlike excavation 6 inches or more wide and a foot or more deep, made when spading soil. Or the term is also applied to deep drills in which celery or peas are planted. *Furrow*—The hollow between the ridges of soil thrown up in the process of tilling or of digging. Also, a very deep drill (such as a "furrow" for planting potatoes). *Drill*—A shallow mark in the soil in which seed is sown; usually less than an inch deep. *Hill*—A low, broad, flat mound in which seed is sown. Also, the spot where a few seeds are sown when the rows are not continuous but have spaces between a group of plants—as a "hill" of corn or of beans—even though the ground is perfectly level.

How can I get my seed rows straight? By stretching a stout cord taut between two stakes so that the cord lies along the ground where the row is to be made. In using the hoe to form the seed row, keep one side of the blade against the cord, which acts as a guide to the hoe. Or use a pointed stick, run along the cord for very shallow drills.

How should rows be fertilized before seeds are sown? In the intensively cultivated garden, it is better to broadcast the fertilizer over the surface and rake it thoroughly into the top 2 or 3 inches of soil a few days before seed is sown. Where rows are 2 feet or more apart, the fertilizer may be worked in only along the rows.

How deep should seeds be covered with soil? Not more than 2 to 4 times their own smallest diameter. For early sowings, and in clay soils, cover somewhat less than normal depth.

I planted lettuce and dandelion seed last spring and they did not grow. Why? Mustard seed did grow. The trouble may have been too deep planting. Lettuce seeds should be scarcely covered and sown in very well-prepared light soil. Lettuce seedlings cannot push up through a hard surface. Dandelion seeds also should be planted very shallowly. Often the germination is low. Mustard, which is an unusually strong grower, will generally sprout even under unfavorable conditions. Some lettuce seed, particularly 'Grand Rapids', will not sprout if covered. The seed must have light to germinate.

How thickly should vegetable seeds be sown? Small seeds, 4 or 5 times as thickly as the plants will finally stand. Thus, if turnips need 3 inches of space between the plants to develop, sow from 12 to 20 seeds per foot. This permits proper spacing after thinning out. Large seeds (such as pole beans or squash) may be sown 1½ to 2 times as thickly as plants are to stand after thinning.

Is it advisable to water vegetable seed rows after sowing? If the ground is at all dry, it is very much better to water the seed rows *before* sowing. After the drill is made, run a slow stream of water from a hose or watering can along the bottom. Let the water soak in, then sow the seed.

How early and how deep should vegetable seeds be planted? (Maryland.) In most parts of Maryland the planting of hardy vegetables (see the Introduction) can begin about the middle of March. This, however, will vary with the season. Practically all seed packets contain directions for when to sow and the depth of planting for the varieties enclosed. For more complete instructions, get the bulletin on this subject published by the State Agricultural Experiment Station at College Park.

What time should a garden be started in western Suffolk County on Long Island?   For hardy seeds such as lettuce, between April 1 to the middle of the month, but peas and broad beans can be planted in mid-March.

Is there anything gained by planting by signs—such as the phases of the moon?   Many gardeners believe so, but there is no scientific evidence to this effect. Planting by such a sign as "when white oak leaves are the size of squirrels' ears" (for corn) is quite different, as the size of leaves is determined by seasonal weather conditions.

Maintenance

THINNING

What is meant by "thinning" vegetables?   This is the term applied to the practice of pulling out surplus seedling plants so that those left can have room to develop properly. In order to be sure of having rows without skips, gardeners sow extra seeds in the row. If germination is good, a surplus of plants is the result.

How can one tell how many plants to remove when "thinning out"?   In directions for growing vegetables, the distance apart at which they should stand is given. Carrots, for instance, are usually thinned to about 2 inches apart; onions, 2 to 3 inches; beets, 3 inches; beans, 4 to 5 inches, etc.

Can any use be made of thinnings?   Thinnings of many vegetables can be used. Young beets, for instance, make excellent boiled greens; small onions may be used as "scallions," for eating green. Baby carrots may be canned. Or the thinnings of many kinds may be used for transplanting, if additional plants are wanted.

After being thinned, my plants wilted badly; can anything be done to prevent this?   Yes. First of all, begin thinning just as soon as seedlings are well up—the bigger they get, the more those left will be disturbed. Thin when the soil is moist, after a rain or a good watering. Cutting off surplus seedlings with a pair of sharp-pointed scissors avoids disturbing those left to grow and prevents wilting.

How soon should rows of small vegetable plants be thinned? Just as soon as the individual plants begin to crowd each other and before there is the slightest chance of their becoming "leggy" for lack of light and air.

Is more than one thinning advisable? With plants that grow closely in the row—such as onions from seed, carrots, and beets—two or three thinnings are often made as the plants grow; this leaves a margin of safety in case of injury or loss among the plants that are left.

TRANSPLANTING

How large should seedlings be before being transplanted? Seedlings should be transplanted as soon as they form their first true leaves (these are the third and fourth leaves to form) and before they become crowded in the flat, pan, or seed bed.

How often should vegetable seedlings grown indoors be transplanted before being set in the garden? Usually once—from the seed flat to a peat pot and then outdoors. However, there are seed-starting systems that avoid any indoor transplanting, such as Jiffy-7 peat pellets. These are pellets of compressed peat that expand to seven times their height when water is added to them. The peat is held in place by a netting. Two or three seeds are sown in a depression at the top, and on sprouting the weakest seedlings can be thinned out, leaving one strong seedling to grow into a healthy transplant. When transplanting time comes, you can plant pot and all into the garden, although gently removing the netting will ensure stronger root development.

What are the advantages of pot-grown plants over young plants cut out of the flat and planted in the garden? Pot-grown plants suffer little or no shock when they are set in the open garden, while plants removed from flats or seed beds have to recover from the disturbance to their root systems.

When are tender plants set out in the vegetable garden? When the ground warms up and the weather is settled. Tomatoes can be set out about May 15 to June 1 in the vicinity of New York; peppers and eggplants, a little later.

When can hardy vegetable plants be set in the open garden? Just about the time the last expected hard frost is past. Many beginners delay planting much longer than necessary.

How can I prevent newly set vegetable plants from wilting? Set after sunset or on a cloudy or rainy day. Water well after setting. If necessary, cover during the hours of high sun for a day or two, using newspapers or baskets. Uncover as soon as the sun is low.

Should newly transplanted vegetables be watered after the plants are set? Yes, they should be thoroughly watered. Leave a slight depression around the stem when planting and fill this with water.

When transplanting, does it help to trim back vegetable plants? Such plants as lettuce, cabbage and other members of the cabbage family, and beets may have their outside leaves trimmed back before setting. This practice is particularly helpful in setting plants which are apt to wilt.

What are Hotkaps? Are they useful in transplanting? Hotkaps are miniature paper tents to be set over seeds or young plants in the open garden to protect them from frost, wind, and insects during the early part of the season. They are of use in transplanting. They must be removed, however, before the plants are crowded; preferably, as soon as they are established and begin to grow after setting. Discarded plastic milk and other beverage containers can also be used (cut off the bottom of the container first; leave the top open for ventilation).

Hotkaps, available from garden centers, are miniature greenhouses for individual plants. With Hotkaps, tender seedlings grown indoors can be planted outdoors nearly 3 weeks earlier than normal. After a few weeks, tear a hole in the top of the tent to allow room for the growing plant.

If a late frost is forecast after setting young plants in the open garden, can anything be done to save the plants? Yes, they may be covered with Hotkaps, newspaper tents, or gallon-size plastic beverage containers (with their bottoms cut off) until the weather warms up.

CULTIVATION

Just what is meant by the term "cultivation" as used in garden articles and bulletins?   Cultivation is the breaking up and stirring about of the soil around and between growing plants.

How do "deep" and "shallow" cultivation differ?   Shallow cultivation means stirring the soil to a depth of 1 or 2 inches. Deep cultivation may penetrate the soil as much as 5 or 6 inches, but usually less.

Should plants be cultivated to the same depth throughout the season?   No. Usually deep cultivation is given just after transplanting or when plants from seed are still small. As they grow, and the roots spread out into the space between rows, the depth of cultivation is reduced.

What tool do you recommend for hand cultivation?   The scuffle hoe is the most useful tool for hand cultivation. Sometimes known as the Dutch hoe or the English scuffle hoe, this tool, with various minor modifications, is now manufactured in the United States.

How long should cultivating be kept up?   The longer, the better; and at least until crops have neared maturity and pretty well cover the ground. If a mulch is used, stop cultivating as soon as it is in place.

How can I prevent heavy crops of weeds from developing among my vegetables?   By using a mulch. The only other way is by clean cultivation, which takes far more time.

What is meant by "hilling"?   Drawing the soil up around growing plants with the hoe for the purpose of (a) covering small weeds; (b) supporting the plants; or (c) blanching the stems to make them more tender.

What vegetables require hilling?   In the home garden, very few (in farming, the practice is more general). Potatoes, corn, broccoli, and bush beans are often hilled for support; celery, leeks, and sometimes asparagus are hilled for blanching. As a rule—except in heavy soils—the less hilling, the better.

WEED CONTROL

Are weed killers available for vegetables?   Yes, but since they can be used only on certain crops, read the directions on those sold in your local garden center for specific information.

What general procedure would you suggest for keeping down weeds in a vegetable garden? Cultivate between the rows with a hoe or roto-tiller (the latter is practical only in a large garden) and remove weeds *by the roots* from the rows of seedling vegetables. Water thoroughly and then mulch with grass cuttings, hay, marsh hay, straw, or other available light material such as shredded sugarcane or ground corn cobs. Black plastic mulch is also highly effective and saves work. The prevention of weeds is much more practical than their removal after they are well established. Check your local garden center for chemical controls for annual weeds.

WATERING

Which vegetables need water in dry weather? In prolonged droughts, all vegetables benefit from irrigation. Those most susceptible to drought injury are peas, celery, spinach, and lettuce.

Does it harm plants to water in the heat of the day? Not if water is fed slowly and deeply into the soil from the end of a hose from which the nozzle has been removed. Lightly sprinkling the surface of the soil and the leaves in high sunlight in addition to deep watering reduces leaf

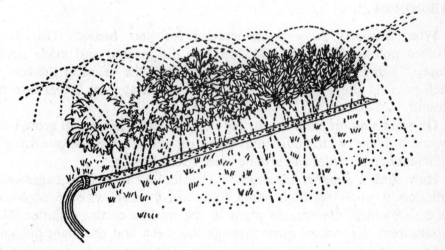

A sprinkler type of hose applies water through minute holes in a gentle spray that soaks the soil without packing its surface or spattering mud. Another type of perforated hose applies a trickle of water, without a spray, directly to the soil.

and soil temperature and may prevent the loss of seedlings. Growing crops are often watered with overhead irrigation in full sunshine, but early morning or evening is better, as less water is lost by evaporation.

Does irrigation tend to bring plant roots to the surface and thus weaken plants? Only if the watering is insufficient. If a "rain machine" or rotary sprinkler is used, it should be left on long enough in each area to really moisten the soil several inches deep, just as when watering slowly with a hose.

How often should an area be watered in dry weather? Often enough to keep the soil uniformly moist at all times to a depth of several inches. Fluctuating moisture is bad for tomatoes. It causes blossom-end rot.

How deep should the soil be moistened by watering? Water long enough to moisten the soil to a depth of at least 4 inches. One watering will then last a week to 10 days.

Some authorities contend that watering vegetable plants weakens their root systems and makes them "soft." Is this true? No. Lack of moisture is one of the biggest causes of poor results in a vegetable garden. If it is possible to get water to the vegetable garden, the crops harvested on watered areas will well repay the gardener for his effort and expense.

SUPPORTS

What supports do you recommend for pole beans? Use 8- to 10-foot poles driven 1 to 1½ feet into the ground and made into a "tepee," using 3 poles for each support. Plant the beans at the foot of each pole. If single poles are used, drive them at least 2 feet into the ground.

On what support shall I grow my lima beans? These will grow readily on a fence with additional wires or cords added above to give sufficient height. Poles can also be used. (See above.)

How shall I support tomatoes? Use tomato towers or cages—wire cylinders 5 to 6 feet high made from heavy mesh wire (6 × 6-inch mesh). Position the tomato plant in the middle of the cylinder. Side shoots from the tomato grow through the mesh and the plant becomes self-supporting, saving the gardener work. Other methods, such as staking (tying plants to 7-foot-long stakes) and using tripods, where tomato plants are tied to form a "tepee," are satisfactory, but more time-consuming. Staking tomatoes is not necessary, but it produces cleaner fruit, makes harvesting easier, and uses less space.

Do side shoots need to be pruned from staked tomatoes? When growing tomatoes up a single stake, pruning of suckers and side shoots is advisable, but the modern method is to use tomato towers (see previous answer), where all side shoots are allowed to grow. Providing that the soil is fertile and adequate irrigation maintains proper moisture in the soil, the growth of side shoots and suckers will not reduce crop yields.

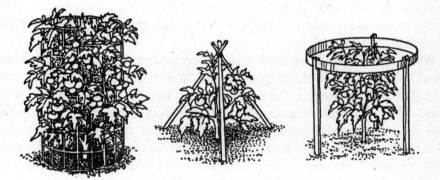

Three methods of supporting tomato plants. (Left) Within cylinders of heavy-mesh (about 6 × 6 inches) wire. The cylinders should be held upright by heavy stakes. (Center) "Tepee" and (right) hoop methods.

How shall I grow my tall peas to support them adequately? Peas can be planted along a 4- or 5-foot fence. Encourage vines to climb by setting cut brush as soon as vines begin to form. Set the brush *outside* the row of peas, on an angle to the fence. Netting for supporting peas is sold in garden centers for those who don't have access to a wood lot.

Should dwarf peas be supported? If dwarf peas are held up with a section of chicken wire or pea brush (cut about 3 feet long and driven firmly into the ground), they will bear more heavily and be easier to pick.

When brush is not available to support peas, what is the best substitute? A special coarse netting of cord, made for the purpose, is available. Sections of chicken wire will do, or buy special netting at garden centers.

Can vine crops be grown on supports and thus save ground space? Yes, cucumbers, melons, and even squash do well on trellises or fences.

MULCHING

What are the advantages of using black plastic as a mulch? Black plastic is highly desirable with warm-weather crops such as tomatoes, melons, cucumbers, and peppers. Black absorbs heat, so black plastic warms up the soil early and helps to maintain that warmth even during periods of temperature fluctuation (such as cool nights), allowing plants to make rapid growth and yield earlier. The plastic also helps conserve moisture and suffocate weeds. Most garden centers offer biodegradable plastic.

What can be used for mulch in a vegetable garden in place of peat moss? Peat moss is not a good mulch unless mixed with other materials. It is better used in the soil to supply humus. Moreover, there are many other materials that are less costly. Select a material locally available in your vicinity such as sawdust, ground corn cobs, buckwheat hulls, pine needles, salt marsh hay, bagasse (sugarcane waste), peanut hulls, seaweed, leaves, ground bark, or black plastic (see previous answer).

When should mulching be applied in the vegetable garden? As soon as the plants are well started, the ground can be cultivated, weeds removed, area thoroughly watered, and mulch applied.

Is a summer mulch advisable in the vegetable garden? It can be used successfully to keep weeds under control with crops that do not need frequent cultivation. It also serves to conserve soil moisture, to absorb rain where it falls, and to keep the soil beneath it loose and friable.

Can old newspapers be used as a mulch? Yes, especially to form walkways between rows of vegetables to create a clean, weed-free walk area. Consider using strips of black plastic for your rows of plants and layers of newspapers between the plastic strips. The heavy newspapers will also effectively anchor the plastic to prevent damage by wind.

HARVESTING

How can I tell when vegetables such as onions, potatoes, beans, and squash are ready to pick? This depends upon the purpose for which they are wanted—whether for immediate use, for storage, or for freezing. Onions can be pulled when small for green onions. For storage, they should be picked when the tops have fallen over. For pickling, you want them when they are an inch in diameter. For immediate use, potatoes can be used as soon as they are big enough to make it worthwhile to dig them. For storage, they should be dug when the vines are practically dead. For freezing, canning, or immediate use, snap beans should be picked before the pods show the location of the seeds. Cabbage and head lettuce should be picked when the heads are solid. Fruits should be picked green or ripe, depending on the use you wish to make of them. Green fruits, such as tomatoes, are best when they are full grown, just before they begin to turn color.

What vegetables can be gathered after frost? There are two types: those that will withstand a light frost without being injured and those that will survive after fairly hard freezing. Among the former are cauliflower, lettuce, chard, celery, and such root crops as beets and carrots. Celery well banked up will stand fairly hard frost. The real tough ones, which resist quite heavy freezing, are Brussels sprouts, cabbage, kale, broccoli, parsnips, salsify, rutabagas, turnips, leeks, spinach, Chinese cabbage, and escarole.

How can one tell when melons are ripe? As soon as they can be lifted easily from the stem.

When New Zealand spinach grows too fast and gets ahead of us, what can be done with it? Use the tips for pot greens. Cut back the old stems to within a few inches of the crown to stimulate bushy new growth. It can also be frozen for winter use.

Our okra grew well, but was woody and tough. What was wrong? You did not harvest it soon enough. Pods should be barely finger length.

When are edible soybeans ready to cook green? When are they harvested to be used dry? As soon as the pods have filled out. They remain edible as green shell beans for about 2 weeks. After the pods turn brown, they must be dried for use as dried beans. Harvest these before the pods burst open, as this will result in the beans shelling out on the ground. Pull up the plants and strip off the pods into a basket. Keep in a dry, warm place until they shell out.

When should summer squash be picked? When very young (about 5 to 6 inches long), less than half grown, and while the skin is very tender. Though edible when better developed, the flavor and texture are inferior.

When should sweet corn be picked? When in the full milk stage, i.e., while its kernels can still be readily punctured with a thumbnail, releasing the juice, or "milk"—and as short a time as possible before it is to be cooked.

When should sweet potatoes be harvested? After the first killing frost blackens the vines.

When are winter squash and pumpkins harvested? Before frost.

WINTER STORAGE

Is there any simple and inexpensive method for the small gardener to use in storing vegetables for winter? The simplest method for storing vegetables is in a bushel basket filled with dried leaves in a garage. Another method is pit storage. Dig a pit in a well-drained location. Place a layer of gravel or sand in the bottom. Line the pit with straw. Store your vegetables in the pit. Cover with straw and then at least 6 inches of soil, or deep enough to ensure safety from freezing in your climate. A 3- or 4-inch pipe sunk into the storage space and extending well above the ground gives ventilation.

How are root crops and cabbages stored outdoors in a barrel? An excavation is made in a well-drained spot and a tight barrel is buried in an upright or tilted position with its top 6 to 10 inches below the ground level. Vegetables are packed in the barrel. The opening is covered with a bag thickly packed with dry leaves, peat moss, or sand. The soil is then filled in to a depth to make the contents of the barrel frostproof. (See illustration.)

How should vegetables be stored for winter use in a root cellar? How should a root cellar be properly constructed? An ideal root cellar can be constructed by making a double wall, with an air space between, and an insulated roof. An 8-inch terra-cotta flue is placed in the bottom and run through a trench to a point well outside the root cellar, where it is brought up to the surface and hooded with a wind-operated ventilator several feet above the soil level. The roof also has a ventilator with a damper. The action of the wind forces air (which takes on the temperature of the soil) down through the terra-cotta duct to the storage. This maintains a constant temperature in the storage house and at the same time maintains good aeration. The root cellar must be well drained to prevent water from standing on the floor or from gathering in low spots.

What are the proper temperature and moisture conditions for fruit and vegetable storage? The best temperature for winter storage of root crops, cabbage, and most fruits is 35° to 40° F. The cellar, pit, or other storage space should be dark, with a dirt floor, but well drained. Though humidity is needed, no water should collect and stand on the floor or in the bottom of the pit or barrel.

How do you store carrots, beets, and turnips to keep them from shriveling? Store in a cool, dark place, 35° to 40° F., packed in sand or slightly moist peat moss, or in boxes covered with bags containing sand, leaves, or peat moss.

Can Chinese cabbage, leeks, kale, and celery be stored indoors? Yes, in a basement room or root cellar at a temperature of 35° to 40° F. They will need moderate air circulation and plenty of moisture. Leave some dirt about the roots and pack closely in boxes placed on the floor. Kale can be kept growing in a covered cold frame in the garden through most of the winter.

How can squashes, pumpkins, and onions be stored? These vegetables require dry storage. The vine crops should be "cured" for a week or two in a temperature of 80° to 85° F., then stored on a shelf in a dry cellar at 45° to 60° F. Onions should be kept in the dark, in a dry place, at 35° to 40° F. But cure them in trays or boxes, under cover, but with free circulation of air, for several weeks after harvesting.

How do I store sweet potatoes in order to keep them through the winter? Sweet potatoes are dug when their vines are killed by frost and are handled with care to avoid bruising. Perfect tubers are cured at a high temperature (80° to 85° F.) for 2 weeks. They are then stored in a dry place at 45° to 50° F.

We have strong, healthy roots of French endive. We do not wish to force them until spring. How shall we winter the roots? Leave them in the ground in the open garden. Dig when ready to force. Hard freezing does not injure French endive.

Where one does not have a place cold enough to keep potatoes from sprouting, is there any other method one can use to prevent them from sprouting while in storage during winter months? A frostproof pit is

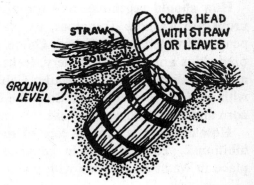

Traditional barrel type of outdoor storage pit. The cover must be tight to keep out moisture. Another method that works quite well is packing root crops (beets, etc.) among dry leaves in a bushel basket in the garage.

most satisfactory for storing potatoes. They need to be kept in the dark, just safely above freezing, in a humid but not too moist atmosphere. Otherwise, they will sprout; rubbing the sprouts off is of some benefit. Or they may be treated with a chemical "sprout inhibitor." Potatoes stored at temperatures *below* 42° F. will taste sweet. Bring out of storage into a warm room for a week before cooking.

What is the best way for a city gardener to store vegetables? Lacking better storage (see above questions), canning or freezing is the best answer, although drying has also become popular, and a number of food dryers are now commercially available.

My family dries beans for winter use. These dry beans are infested by worms which render them unfit for consumption. What can be done to remedy this condition? After drying the beans, place them on screened trays in a cold oven. Heat very gradually to 180° F. After 10 minutes at 180°, cool and store.

How are dried peas and beans stored for the winter? If possible, in airtight containers of tin or glass in a dry, cool room at a temperature from 45° to 60° F. Treat with heat before storing. (See above.)

Is sand the only suitable material in which to store cabbages and other crops in an outdoor pit? Vermiculite, peat moss, or buckwheat hulls can be used instead. These materials should be very slightly dampened.

Exhibiting

In what condition should vegetables be picked for exhibition purposes? In prime eating condition. The overgrown specimens often shown by beginners will not win prizes on size alone.

How should vegetables and fruits be prepared for exhibition? Root crops are washed. Tomatoes, eggplants, peppers, squash, apples, and pears are wiped and polished. Onion tops are cut off and outer, discolored skins are removed. Celery, leeks, and Chinese cabbage are washed and the roots are cut off neatly. Cabbage stems are removed, together with outer imperfect leaves. Strip the husk from a section of each ear of corn and cut it off near the base.

How can greens and the tops of root vegetables be kept fresh for exhibitions? Harvest well in advance and harden overnight in a cool place in water or sprinkle with water. If they are unwilted and of good color at the end of the hardening period, they will probably stand up through the show.

How are vegetables displayed in harvest shows? Try to have each exhibit made up of items of uniform size. The schedule usually calls for a specific number of potatoes, tomatoes, beans, etc. Select perfect specimens of uniform size and place each group neatly on a paper plate. Lay out pea or bean pods side by side where they can be counted and seen easily by the judges. Turn tomatoes stem end down; fruits, stem end up. Carrots, beets, and other roots may be displayed with their tops if they can be kept fresh, but they are usually shown with their tops removed.

Is it important to show only perfect vegetables in an exhibit? Yes, in order to win a prize each item shown must be of high quality, well grown, and well displayed. Uniformity of size is also important.

How shall I display a vegetable collection in a show? Make an arrangement of the vegetables, placing squash, melons, and other large items at the back center with corn, root vegetables, etc., radiating from the center. Smaller vegetables are placed in the foreground.

Equipment

What tools are needed for a vegetable garden? Only a few tools are needed for a small garden. The most important are a spade or a flat-tined spading fork, an iron rake, a hoe, and a hand weeder. It is highly desirable to have two hoes—one with a fairly large blade for "hilling" and heavy hoeing and one with a small, narrow blade for cutting out small weeds. In a vegetable garden of considerable size a rototiller is a great time-saver.

Is a spading fork essential equipment for a vegetable garden? Many people consider a spading fork indispensable. It is useful in breaking up the soil when digging and in lifting roots or other crops. If only a small number of tools are to be purchased, however, get a spade first and a spading fork later.

What sort of spade do you recommend for a vegetable garden? Most gardeners prefer a long-handled pointed spade with a diamond-pointed blade. The handle should reach to the top of your ear when held upright.

What sort of knife shall I use to cut asparagus? An asparagus knife with a fishtail blade is best for the purpose; it cuts stalks below the ground without injuring new stalks that are developing. However, it is not necessary to cut asparagus stalks. You can snap them off instead.

What type and make of power machinery do you suggest for tilling, cultivating, etc., to lighten hand labor and that is suitable to use in a garden 50 × 100 feet?   You might consider an electric-powered unit called a Soil Blender, which will churn up bare soil, but isn't effective on sod. Otherwise, there is no power machine particularly suitable for use in a plot as small as 50 × 100 feet, especially if the area is fenced in. Probably the nearest thing to it is a small-sized rototiller. It isn't worth owning for so small a garden. Rent it instead. This is for preparing the land, not for cultivating. It would be much more satisfactory to have the garden tilled or dug by hired labor and depend upon mulching to lessen the work of cultivating. However, the old-fashioned wheel hoe is still available from dealers in garden supplies.

What is a scuffle hoe?   A scuffle hoe is a tool used for cultivating the ground by using a backward and forward motion to destroy weeds and break up the surface soil. In purchasing a scuffle hoe, it is essential to select one with a sharp cutting blade.

Which is more useful in the vegetable garden—a wheelbarrow or a garden cart?   A garden cart with big wheels will carry many times the weight of a wheelbarrow but most carts are too large for average lots. If your space is limited, a small wheelbarrow will be more useful.

Are seed sowers worth buying?   Yes, they are very helpful to the vegetable gardener. There are a number of different sorts. A small hand sower helps to drop seeds evenly in flats, seed beds, and even in the garden.

What is the best piece of equipment for measuring the space between vegetable rows?   Secure a long, narrow strip of wood about 1 × 2 inches and 8 or 10 feet long. Mark it off at 3-, 6-, and 12-inch intervals with a heavy carpenter's pencil.

Are rotary sprinklers helpful in a vegetable garden?   As a rule, it is better to water slowly around plant roots with a hose, without a nozzle.

What is a "porous" hose, and how is it used?   This is a canvas hose to be attached to the end of the rubber hose. It can be obtained in 25- or 50-foot lengths. Water seeps through the canvas very slowly and is at once absorbed by the soil. It is especially good for watering vegetables in rows and in soaking the bottoms of drills before sowing seeds in very dry weather. A three-ply or two-ply plastic, perforated hose throws many fine jets of water along its length, watering a 25-foot or 50-foot row or length of border at one time.

Would creosote-treated fence posts affect vegetable plants very near them? No. The creosote will not spread through the soil.

Are Hotkaps worth using? Hotkaps, properly used, are of great assistance in getting an early start in the garden. Not only do they make possible earlier planting, they also furnish protection from insects and from wind and heavy rains while the plants are small and struggling to get a start. They are particularly useful in starting vine crops such as cucumbers and melons, and protecting tender plants such as tomatoes, eggplants, and peppers when they are first set out. Discarded gallon-size plastic jugs are especially useful for protecting tomato seedlings. For smaller seedlings, clear plastic jars used for food packing are convenient.

Miscellaneous

What edible foods can be raised in a basement or cellar and sold at a profit? As practically all vegetables require full sunshine for several hours a day, they cannot be successfully grown in a basement. Witloof chicory, a salad plant, can be grown in the dark from roots which have been produced by sowing the seed in early spring and gathering the roots in the autumn. A local market for this crop might be developed. Another possibility might be mushrooms, but this crop requires quantities of horse manure or a special mushroom compost handled in just the right way and would not prove feasible unless the manure were readily available.

How does one build and manage a cold frame? What vegetables can be kept in it for winter use? (Ohio.) See Cold Frames, Section 3. In a tight frame in a well-protected spot, lettuce can be grown until late December or January if the plants are started in August or September. Root crops, such as beets, carrots, and turnips, can be stored for the winter, but they should be covered with several inches of soil, leaves, or other mulching when the ground begins to freeze. Boards instead of glass are used to cover the frame when used for storing purposes. Celery taken from the garden on the approach of freezing weather, with the roots on and replanted in the frame close together, will blanch nicely and remain crisp for several weeks. Cabbage, Chinese cabbage, and cauliflower replanted in the frame may be held for several weeks longer than out-of-doors.

What vegetables would you suggest for raising in boxes, pots, and tubs on a city roof that is very high and exposed to the wind and sun?   Many roofs are too weak to support the load of enough soil for good growth, so use one of the soilless mixes that contains vermiculite, or use peat moss as a substitute. Parsley, onion sets, lettuce, herbs, peppers, eggplant, New Zealand spinach, cucumbers and bush squash, melons, and tomatoes would be some of the best vegetables to try.

What vegetables can be eaten from the garden in the winter? My basement is too warm for storage. (Michigan.)   About the only vegetables that can be used direct from the garden in cold weather in the North are parsley, Swiss chard, broccoli, kale, collards, and Brussels sprouts; these will stand quite hard freezing and can be picked through December and often into January. Also, parsnips, salsify, and leeks are hardy enough so that they are not injured by severe freezing. To use the latter during the winter, they should be heavily mulched to prevent the ground from becoming too hard to dig. The Jerusalem-artichoke is also perfectly hardy and the tubers can be dug and used any time they can be gotten out of the ground.

I have learned by experience that there are two kinds of fruits and vegetables. (1) Those that can stand shipping. (2) More delicious and delicate ones for home gardens. How can I select the latter?   A recent increase in the interest in home vegetable growing has focused attention on this point. Many of the leading catalogs now take these differences into account in their descriptions. Such phrases as long bearing season, for local market, high quality, etc., mean noncommercial varieties.

Is there any danger of germ contamination in having a vegetable garden over a septic-tank drainage system?   There is some question as to whether contamination may occur in soil over a septic-tank overflow field. In theory, it cannot. The natural drainage of the soil is, however, an important factor. If another location for the vegetable plot could be found, it would be better.

What is organic gardening?   Organic gardening or farming is the growing of vegetables without the use of chemical fertilizers or sprays. It is accomplished by keeping the soil limed to a near neutral pH and following a rotation of crops where a good leguminous crop like clover or a sod crop occupies the land 2 out of 3 or 4 years. Animal manures are used to maintain the fertility of the ground. Also, plant refuse is composted and applied to the soil. Organic fertilizers are also used. Although perfectly feasible in home gardens, the big question is whether organic gardening on a commercial scale could feed America's large population.

What kind of soil will produce the best vegetables containing the most vitamins and minerals; is commercial fertilizer necessary to obtain such vegetables? Any garden soil in good tilth. While commercial fertilizer is usually used, it is not essential; minerals exist in the soil.

Can we have a garden on a sandy soil that is full of ants? Most sandy soils, if improved with humus and fertilizer, will grow excellent vegetables. If ants have made nests or hills, they can readily be eliminated by treating the soil with diazinon according to directions.

Pests and Diseases

(See individual plants, and also Section 13.)

Specific Vegetables

ARTICHOKE, GLOBE (CYNARA SCOLYMUS)

In what section of the country can globe artichoke be grown successfully? As a winter crop, in California, between San Francisco and Los Angeles; on the Gulf Coast, and in the South Atlantic states. In the eastern states (as far north as Massachusetts) as a summer crop, the roots being mulched during the winter. Globe artichoke is a difficult crop for the home gardener, usually requiring two seasons to grow if started from seed.

How does one grow large globe artichokes? (Pennsylvania.) They cannot be grown satisfactorily in Pennsylvania, unless you can protect them against winter freezing or buy started plants in the spring. They require a fertile, well-limed soil; the plants are grown from offshoots from old plants. They are vigorous growers. The part used is the bud of the flower, which should be picked before it is open.

ARTICHOKE, JERUSALEM- (HELIANTHUS TUBEROSUS)

Can you tell me something about Jerusalem-artichokes grown as a garden root vegetable? The tubers are started like potatoes, from cut tubers set 18 inches apart. It is really an American sunflower and ought to be known by its Indian name of sun-root; it grows 5 to 6 feet tall. No attention is required until the roots are dug in late fall or early spring, when they must be thoroughly removed from the soil or the plants will spread and are likely to become a pest. Jerusalem-artichokes are best planted by themselves, outside the garden.

Are Jerusalem-artichokes desirable as a garden vegetable? They are easy to grow and produce a heavy crop of nonstarchy tubers. However, they spread rapidly and can become a weed. The plants are subject to black aphids and mildew, and so should be kept at a distance from choice flowering or vegetable plants.

What time of the year should Jerusalem-artichokes be dug? Does freezing improve them? Freezing does improve their flavor and therefore they should be dug as late as possible in the fall, during a winter thaw, or early the following spring before they have a chance to sprout.

How are Jerusalem-artichokes prepared for the table? They are boiled and served with cream or Hollandaise sauce or diced raw, chilled, and added to mixed salads. And in numerous other ways such as glazed, au gratin, etc.

ASPARAGUS

Where can I purchase roots or plants of asparagus? Most seed suppliers and garden centers offer asparagus roots in the spring. In many cases they are rather small. It is advisable to order about twice as many as needed and plant only the best.

How should a new asparagus bed be fertilized? See that there is plenty of humus in the soil, preferably by turning under a cover crop, compost, or manure during the fall before planting. When preparing trenches for planting, enrich thoroughly with compost or manure and superphosphate. Be sure that the pH is not below 6.5. If it is, add lime.

What is the proper procedure for starting an asparagus bed from plants? Since asparagus is to occupy the ground for a long time, it is well to have the land in good fertility and tilth and free of weeds. Asparagus does well in a fairly wide variety of soils, from sandy to moderately heavy; good drainage is important. In early spring, make trenches 4 or 5 feet apart and about 8 inches deep in well-prepared soil. The very deep planting that was formerly recommended is not now considered necessary; if the soil is heavy, planting shallower than 8 inches may be better.

Is it advisable to attempt to plant a bed of asparagus roots in the fall of the year? Early spring is better.

How many asparagus roots should be planted per person? Under favorable conditions, 10 plants or 15 feet of row may be expected to furnish asparagus for one person through the season. One-year-old plants are best to purchase.

If young asparagus is covered too much, would that stop its growing? Yes, especially if the soil is heavy and planting is deep. Eight inches is deep enough for asparagus roots, and the first covering should be only 2 inches, gradually working soil in as the plants grow.

If I transplant asparagus that has been cut before, can it be cut the first year after it is transplanted? It is not ordinarily best to move old asparagus roots, but if this is done, it would probably be best not to cut the first year. Good top growth is necessary to reestablish the crowns. After that, judgment can be based on the vigor of shoots as they come up.

Is it possible to purchase asparagus roots to plant in the spring and have the shoots to eat the following spring? If asparagus plants are set out in the spring, the shoots should not be harvested until the second spring following. Then they may be cut for a period of about 4 weeks and for a full crop the next year.

How late in the season can asparagus be cut? For an established bed, 8 weeks is about the usual cutting period. If the shoots become spindly, quit cutting so that good growth can be made for the following year. The tops have the job of storing food for next year's crop in the enormous root system underground.

I started an asparagus bed this year. Next year, when it's time to use the spears, how are they cut? Asparagus is best cut with a special asparagus knife just below the surface of the soil. Care must be exercised not to jam the knife into the crown or to injure the buds of shoots that may be coming up. The knife should be slipped down fairly close to the shoot that is being cut, and then tilted to avoid injury to other shoots. Some prefer simply to snap off the spears at ground level.

Is it necessary to bank or ridge asparagus each year?   Most people prefer green asparagus to white or blanched; hence, banking is not necessary. Slight ridging may be effective in smothering young weeds just when they appear in the row.

Should asparagus be deeply cultivated?   Asparagus should not be deeply cultivated as this practice damages the roots and crowns and so hinders growth.

How do I care for and harvest asparagus plants (roots) set out last spring?   During the summer, pull the weeds and give shallow cultivation; mulch with manure or rich compost in autumn and work it lightly into the surface soil in early spring, keeping a little away from plants and remembering that their roots are shallow and spread horizontally. In the fall, when the old plants have lost their green color, cut the tops a few inches above the ground and destroy them.

Why do some authorities advise cutting asparagus stalks in the fall, while others prefer leaving them until spring to help hold the snow and form a winter mulch?   Cutting the stalks in the fall before the seeds mature and sow themselves prevents an infestation of seedling plants in the bed. These may become troublesome weeds. If cut 6 or 8 inches high, the stems will help hold mulch or snow.

When should asparagus be fertilized and what fertilizer should be used?   Once a year is often enough to fertilize the asparagus bed. It doesn't make a great deal of difference whether it is done in early spring or at the end of the cutting season, when plants are allowed to grow up. Fertilizing before cutting is generally preferred. In sandy soils, use a 5–10–10 fertilizer at the rate of 35 pounds per 1,000 square feet. In heavier soils, a 5–10–5 would probably do as well. Compost and manure are also first-rate for asparagus.

How does one apply salt to asparagus?   Don't. In the old days farmers found that while asparagus could tolerate salt, weeds could not, and so it became known as an effective form of weed control. However, excessive salt buildup in your vegetable garden soil can be harmful. Instead, use a weed-smothering mulch to achieve weed control, such as layers of shredded leaves or other organic material.

How do you protect asparagus during the winter?   It is root-hardy and needs no extra protection.

How often should asparagus beds be reset?   Never. If an old bed runs out, start a new one, using young plants.

Do asparagus crowns gradually come to the surface of the soil?   This is true, not because the crowns actually move, but because the new growth of the root stocks which make up the crowns is nearer to the soil surface than the old growth. This, however, is of little harm since most people prefer green asparagus. When they come within 2 or 3 inches of the surface, cultivation over the row before and after cutting is likely to injure the buds.

What is the best method to revive an old asparagus bed? The yield is light now and stalks are small.   If an asparagus bed is in good shape except for lack of fertilization, it can be revived by starting a good program of fertility maintenance. If the crowns have become spent or the stand is poor, it is better to start a new bed.

Is it practical to interplant between asparagus rows?   No. Roots of asparagus are not deep and spread horizontally. Interplanting would injure these spreading rootlets.

How are asparagus plants grown from seed?   For growing asparagus roots, select a fertile soil in good tilth. Mark out rows 18 inches apart. Sow seeds 2 inches apart in the row and cover ½ to 1 inch deep. Soaking the seed in water at room temperature for 3 to 5 days will hasten germination. Then plant at once, in late April or early May.

Does asparagus do well in the Deep South?   Asparagus is successfully grown commercially in South Carolina, but in such states as Florida and Louisiana it does not do well.

What causes asparagus to be tough and pithy?   Insufficient fertilizer; poor soil preparation; a pH below 6.5; allowing it to get too old before being cut.

How can I avoid asparagus rust?   Purchase seeds or roots of a rust-resistant variety such as 'Mary Washington'.

What is the control for asparagus beetle?   Dust with rotenone or methoxychlor.

What asparagus varieties are suitable for the Washington, D.C., metropolitan area?   'Mary Washington', which is partially resistant to asparagus rust, is the leading variety everywhere.

What is your opinion of 'Paradise' asparagus compared with 'Mary Washington'?   Indications are that 'Paradise' is very similar to a good strain of 'Mary Washington'. It cannot be expected to give a full crop a year ahead of other varieties, as is sometimes claimed.

BEAN, BUSH AND POLE (PHASEOLUS VULGARIS)

What is the difference between string beans, stringless beans, and snap beans?   All older varieties of beans had strong, fibrous, stringy growths running the length of the pods. The removal of these strings was a tedious job. Many years ago, plant breeders began producing varieties in which these "strings" were eliminated. These were called stringless beans. Stringless beans are easy to break or "snap" into pieces; hence they are now called snap beans.

How should the ground be prepared and fertilized for planting snap beans and shell beans?   Beans need a well-prepared, thoroughly drained soil. Use a 5–10–10 complete fertilizer, 2½ pounds per 100 square feet of row. Apply as a sidedressing, 3 inches from the row or hill. Beans do well on soil too poor for most other vegetables. Fertilizers high in nitrogen are to be avoided.

How are snap beans best grown in the home garden?   Bush snap beans are planted after the danger of frost is fairly well past, 2 or 3 weeks after the last killing frost, or a week before tomatoes are set out. They will not withstand frost after they are above ground. They thrive in a wide variety of soil types. Leaf diseases are controlled by getting seed that is disease-free. Dusting is necessary in areas where Mexican bean beetles prevail.

How many plantings of snap beans shall I make each year?   That depends on the length of your growing season. Beans require about 60 days to mature. The last planting should not be made later than 70 days before the first killing frost. Therefore, you can plant every 2 weeks until that date. If you make a planting May 1, you can plant 5 or 6 times.

Is there really a bean, either snap or lima, that can be planted early and will stand cool weather?   Broad or Windsor (*Vicia faba*) beans resist frosts and are usually planted about the same time as peas. (See below.)

What varieties of yellow wax beans will ripen in rotation?   All the bush beans ripen about the same time. They can be planted, however, for succession crops, at intervals of 2 to 4 weeks. You can grow the pole varieties and have beans over a longer period.

Do varieties of beans mix when planted in a garden near each other?   Some degree of crossing in the field occurs among beans, differing with varieties and conditions. However, this would not affect the immediate crop. It might result in hybridization if seed were to be saved for the next year.

Can beans be grown in the same place two successive years? Yes.

How and when should I plant 'Kentucky Wonder' or other pole beans? Plant when the danger of frost is past. Where seasons are very long, a late planting can be made for fall. Sow seed along a fence or trellis, 3 or 4 seeds per foot and an inch or two deep. If a hill system is preferred, plant 6 to 8 seeds per hill; set poles at least 3 feet apart.

Can pole beans be grown successfully along a fence about 4 feet high? Yes, on a wire fence. A higher fence is better. A little trellis can be set above the fence to allow for greater height of the plants. If the fence is of stone or boards, it will be desirable to use strings or chicken wire from the ground to the top of the fence.

When do you harvest kidney and other shell beans for use in the dry state? Should they be shelled right away? Dry beans are harvested when the pods have matured and begun to dry up, but before they open and begin to drop the beans. One has to strike a happy medium for minimum loss from immaturity on the one hand and shattering on the other. Leaves ordinarily turn brown to a considerable degree. Vines can be harvested entirely and allowed to dry on a shed or garage floor, and then the beans can be flailed out. Of course, in small quantities they can be picked by hand. They will shell out easier after the pods have become dry.

How should I care for snap, lima, and soybeans in the fall so as to get seed for planting or winter eating? Conditions in the Northeast are not very favorable for saving the seed of beans. Commercial production has moved to the West to irrigated areas where there is bright, dry weather at curing time. On a small scale, one can pick the pods, dry them, shell them, and put the seeds away. On a larger scale, the whole plant can be pulled when leaves begin to drop and taken in to a barn floor, garage, or other suitable place. Then they can be flailed out, cleaned, and put away. Plants from which seed is saved should be free of anthracnose and bacterial blight. Storing seed in a refrigerator will stop bean weevil and protect germination.

When bean vines turn yellow, is it an indication of too much water, cold weather, or lack of fertilizer? This could be an indication of either lack of fertilizer or cold weather.

What beans for use green or dry are not bothered by the bean beetle? There seems to be little difference in susceptibility of bean varieties to Mexican bean beetle. People are sometimes confused because there are early and late broods of the beetle with a period of relative immunity between. The beetle is not particularly difficult to control with methoxychlor or Sevin.

What is the best control for Mexican bean beetle?   Methoxychlor or Sevin dusted on the underside of the leaves when the grubs hatch from the orange-colored eggs. Don't dust until you see the grubs or beetles, as the dust does not last long. (See Section 13.)

What are the names of stringless bush beans, both green and wax?   'Green Pod', 'Tendergreen', 'Tenderpod', and 'Wade' for green; 'Pencilpod', 'Brittlewax', and 'Goldcrop' for the yellow.

What is the best green bean to plant for canning?   'Bountiful' is a heavy bearer. 'Tendergreen' is of better flavor and retains its tenderness even when quite fully grown.

What variety of green stringless beans would you recommend for freezing?   'Tendergreen', 'Topcrop', or 'Tenderpod'.

What beans are resistant to the blight?   Most modern varieties are bred for disease resistance.

In a small vegetable garden, would you recommend pole beans instead of bush beans?   The question of bush versus pole beans is largely one of choice. Bush beans are less trouble to take care of, bear considerably earlier, and succession plantings can be made to give a supply throughout the season. On the other hand, pole beans bear over a longer period of time, and a good many like the pole varieties such as 'Blue Lake', 'Romano', and the old 'Kentucky Wonder'. 'Burpee's Golden' is a distinct type, with yellow pods of fine flavor.

BEAN, LIMA (PHASEOLUS LIMENSIS)

Do large lima beans need to be planted right side up to grow?   Lima beans do not need to be planted right side up (or, more correctly, with the eye down). Experiment has shown small difference in results when planting in this way. But in heavy soil in the home garden, it is probably worth the extra trouble.

How can I grow lima beans successfully?   Lima beans (bush type) can be grown on well-maintained garden soil, being planted after the danger of frost is past. Seed at the rate of 3 or 4 per foot, 1 to 2 inches deep, with rows 2 to 3 feet apart. Dusting for Mexican bean beetle may be necessary.

How long will pole lima beans grow and produce?   Pole limas will yield edible beans over a longer period of time than bush beans—4 to 5 weeks, or even more, depending on climatic conditions.

When are lima beans ready to eat? When they are about full grown but still green. If they stay on the vines long enough to begin to turn white, they are usually too hard.

Do large limas require acclimating? No. Acclimating a stock of seed generally means breeding for adaptation to a specific soil and climate. Lima beans seem to be about as widely adapted as most of our vegetables.

How and when do you harvest lima beans? If left till dry, they mold; if green, they shrink. I have too many to go over them every day or so. Most gardeners prefer to harvest lima beans when tender—and then freeze or can them at this stage. Most of the dry lima beans are grown in western areas where conditions are particularly favorable for their production and curing. If left to mature in the garden, they can be harvested when the pods have dried, but if the climate or weather at this time is humid, there is likely to be trouble in drying and curing.

What can I do to pole limas to make them mature? Lima beans, especially the pole varieties, require a fairly long season for maturity of the crop—90 to 120 days. Thus, in northern climates it is important that they be planted as soon as possible after the danger of frost is past. They can be started earlier if Hotkaps are used. Or for bush limas, erect a plastic tunnel over the row.

Will pole lima beans mature in Massachusetts? The growing season in Massachusetts varies from 150 to 200 days. Pole limas require 90 to 120 days for maturing, so it is possible to grow them. The length of the season is measured between the average date of the last killing frost in the spring and the average date of the first killing frost in the fall.

I have been trying to raise pole lima beans for 3 years and have had no success. The vines grow 10 to 12 feet long with lots of bloom, but the beans fall off when they are about a half inch long. A few will get full-size pods but no beans. My garden is sandy loam and I use the best seed I can obtain; I also use a 5–10–10 fertilizer at the rate of about 1,000 pounds per acre, applied in the hill. What is wrong? Lima beans do not set well when there is a period of hot, dry, sunshiny weather with low humidity during the blossom period. Night temperatures below 50° F. cause blossoms to drop. One study showed that under certain conditions, where there is boron deficiency in the soil, applications of 15 pounds per acre of borax made increases up to 40 per cent in yield of limas. Whether this is directly associated with the set of the pods or with other factors is not clear. Use of a hormone spray, such as Blossom Set, is recommended. Factors such as insect injury and unbalanced nutrition are probably involved. Inoculating the seed with Legume-Aid before sowing is recommended.

How can I raise lima beans without blight? The best insurance against blight (including both anthracnose and bacterial) is the use of clean seed that has been grown in territory free from the disease. Some progress has been made in developing resistant strains. Cultivating beans when wet will spread anthracnose if it is present. Bean refuse in the garden is likely to harbor and carry over the disease.

Do Mexican bean beetles attack lima beans? Yes, very much so. Control by dusting with rotenone dust or methoxychlor.

BEAN, SOY- (GLYCINE MAX)

What type of soil is needed to grow soybeans? Soybeans are among the thriftiest of plants and will make the most of any soil in which they find themselves. But better soil means more and better beans.

Where can I obtain United States bulletins on the culture of soybeans? Publications of the United States Department of Agriculture can be obtained from the Superintendent of Documents, U. S. Government Printing Office, Washington, D.C. 20402.

Do soybeans require any special care? Soybeans should not be planted too deeply, about 1 inch. Rows should be 2 to 3 feet apart, 5 to 8 seeds per foot. Protect soybeans from rabbits and Japanese beetles.

Should soybeans be inoculated? When growing soybeans for the first time, it is wise to get inoculating material with the seed or from a seed store. They can be grown on the same soil for a year or so, and from that point on inoculation should not be necessary. Even though not inoculated, they will usually make a fair crop.

Are edible soybeans satisfactory in the home garden? Yes, if you have use for them and you like them. They are used as green shell beans or dry, but require 3 to 4 months to mature and more space than snap beans.

Is it feasible to grow edible soybeans as a green-manure or cover crop, to be plowed under after harvesting the beans? They will do, but snap beans grow faster as a cover crop for plowing under.

We had a lot of soybeans. It was a big job to pick them but far worse to shell them. Is there an easier way? Soybeans should be blanched in boiling water, 3 to 5 minutes, before shelling them out. This makes the process much less difficult. Or try the Japanese method: Drop the green pods into boiling water and boil them for about 15 to 20 minutes. Drain the water and sprinkle the pods with salt. Then take each pod separately and squeeze the beans into your mouth. (See also next question.)

How do you cook soybeans?   Green soybeans may be scalded in the pods to make shelling easier. Shell, boil until tender (like limas), and serve buttered. *Baked:* Soak dried soybeans overnight; bring to a boil in fresh water and boil ½ hour; then use them as pea beans for baked beans. *Soy Loaf:* To one pint of cold, boiled (dried) soybeans, add a beaten egg, a cup of bread crumbs, 1 tablespoon chopped onion, 2 tablespoons tomato catsup, and salt and pepper to taste. Form into a loaf and bake for 1 hour. Serve with tomato sauce. *Salted:* Soak dried beans overnight; boil for 1 hour in fresh, salted water; spread in a shallow pan (after removing excess moisture) and roast in an oven at 350° F. until light brown; butter and sprinkle with salt. Or French fry dried, boiled beans in deep fat and sprinkle with salt.

BEAN, BROAD (VICIA FABA)

What soil is preferred by broad or Windsor beans?   A heavy, well-drained soil, limed and manured or enriched with compost.

When should Windsor (or broad) beans be planted to bear before hot weather?   Broad, Windsor, or fava beans thrive under cool conditions. They can be planted as soon as soil is dry enough to work, usually about the time that peas are planted. They mature in early summer, or in about 80 to 90 days.

How can black aphids be avoided on broad beans?   Plant early, as soon as the danger of hard frost is past. Spray with malathion according to the directions on the package when first aphids appear; repeat as frequently as needed. Pinching off the growing tips of the plants where the aphids cluster is a control method that should appeal to organic gardeners.

BEAN, MUNG (PHASEOLUS AUREUS)

What is the botanical family and species of the small mung beans used by the Chinese for sprouts, and how do they compare with soybeans in protein and vitamin value? (California.)   The small-seeded or green mung bean used for bean sprouts by the Chinese is *Phaseolus aureus*. Like other beans, the family name is *Leguminoseae*. The mung bean, although belonging to the same genus as our common field beans, is of a different species. The protein content of the mung bean is about the same, or slightly higher, than that of our common beans. The comparative figures on percentage composition are 23.3 and 22.7 per cent respectively. For soybeans, the protein value is about 50 per cent higher.

How do you grow bean sprouts used to make chop suey? Bean sprouts are usually produced by placing a layer of the dry seed on a rack in the bottom of a moist chamber, preferably in a large earthen jar. (The beans should not lie directly in water, hence the advice to place them on a screen or rack above the water.) The vessel should be covered to exclude light and maintain a moist atmosphere. A minimum of 5 to 7 days is the period usually required to produce sprouts 2 to 4 inches long. The room temperature will promote rapid sprouting. In the winter, water should be added twice daily; in the summer, preferably three times a day. Before placing the beans in the jar for sprouting, the seed should be thoroughly washed and the jar made sterile to prevent molding.

BEET (BETA VULGARIS)

How shall I sow beets and when? Sow as soon as the ground can be worked, in rows 12 to 15 inches apart, a dozen seeds to the foot, ½ inch deep. For late beets, sow deeper, up to 1 inch. If the soil is dry, water well before sowing.

What fertilizer should be used for beets? Beets require very fertile, well-limed soil, not deficient in potash and in good tilth. Apply compost or a complete fertilizer (preferably 5–10–10) at the rate of 3 pounds per 100 square feet of row.

Why are there spaces in the beet row where seed did not come up? Possibly the seed did not germinate because it was too old. Or damping-off organisms may have been at work. Use a seed disinfectant (captan or thiram) before planting to prevent damping off.

Is it profitable to transplant beets? I have never had them grow as well as the ones left in the row. However, I don't seem to be able to prevent the seed from coming up too thickly. Each beet seed (so-called) contains several true seeds, hence the thick growth of seedlings. Those thinned out may have been damaged at the roots, or when transplanted the taproot may not have been set vertically. When carefully transplanted, plants grow well.

Why do beets that are apparently healthy fail to produce large

roots? Possibly because the plants are getting too much nitrogen and too little potash. Have your soil tested.

I have heard that beets need boron. Could I put some borax in a watering pot and add it to the soil that way? My beets were a failure. The carrots growing beside them were fine. This may have been because of a lack of boron. One ounce of borax in 16 quarts of water will prevent it. The trouble may have been due to a lack of potash. Use wood ashes where you grow beets.

What variety of beets do you recommend for winter storage? 'Detroit Dark Red' is a standard variety for late keeping. 'Winter Keeper' or 'Lutz Green Leaf' are others. 'Winter Keeper' has the best flavor after long storage.

BROCCOLI (BRASSICA OLERACEA)

How is broccoli grown? In exactly the same manner as cabbage. The spring crop is started in the house under fluorescent lights, or in a greenhouse or hotbed in early March, taken to the garden in mid-April, and harvested in June. The fall crop may be directly seeded in the garden about July 1 to 10, thinned out about August 1, and harvested in September or October.

How do you fertilize broccoli? Broccoli requires a lot of nitrogen. If it is kept fertilized well, it will grow until freezing weather. Sidedress the plants every month or so.

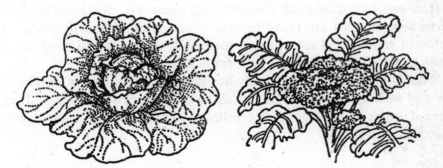

Cabbage and broccoli, two important vegetables for the home garden, can be set out in seedling form as soon as frost is out of the ground. Sow seeds in early summer for a fall harvest or in mild climates in the fall for winter and early spring harvests.

What is the secret of obtaining early broccoli in the North? Grow your plants from seed sown indoors about March 1. Or buy young plants from a local grower and set them out as soon as the ground can be worked and danger of hard frost is over.

When should broccoli be planted? It can be started with plants set in the garden as early as the ground can be prepared. These plants will produce good broccoli all season in most regions. If a second crop for fall is wanted, sow seeds outside in May–June.

Is there any way to hurry along broccoli? I planted some late in April. September arrived and there still were no blooms. Up until severe freezing it was still growing, but there were no heads. Sow seed May 15 to June 1 and set out plants in July; or sow indoors in February or March for an early crop. Early strains are now available. 'Green Goliath' and 'Green Comet' are 15 to 20 days earlier than older varieties.

What treatment of broccoli plants will cause them to produce thick clusters of buds rather than sparse clusters? Plant in rich, deep, friable soil. Cultivate constantly. Water during dry periods and sidedress with nitrogen or liquid manure when plants are established. The side sprouts never produce heads as large as those that first form at the top of the main stalk, but they still taste good.

When and how should broccoli be cut? When flower heads have formed, but while florets are in tight bud. Cut with a sharp knife a few inches below the head. New heads will form from side shoots, and cutting can continue as heads form. Keep heads cut regularly.

How can I keep broccoli producing all summer? Keep the heads cut off as soon as they are ready to use. When cutting broccoli, cut 2 to 4 inches of stem. If cut too close to the heads, the plant will send out too many small side shoots rather than fairly large ones.

What is the cause of apparently healthy broccoli suddenly turning yellow and wilting? It could be caused by any one of a number of things: lack of water or food, cabbage yellows (a disease), or root maggots. (See Section 13.)

BROCCOLI RAAB (BRASSICA OLERACEA RUVO)

The fresh-produce department of our supermarket has recently been selling a vegetable called "broccoli raab" in the winter and spring. Can I grow this in my summer vegetable garden? Yes. Broccoli raab (also known as "sparachetti," "broccoli-headed turnip," or "Italian turnip") is an annual, a member of the cabbage family, and tastes more like mustard or turnip than broccoli. It is a cool-season crop as are most in the family. For late spring or early summer harvest, seeds must be planted in early spring, just as soon as the ground is workable. The plants grow about 18 inches high and must be harvested just as soon as the flower buds form, otherwise they quickly become tough and go to seed. Flower buds, foliage, and upper stems are all eaten after being boiled for a short time. Don't overcook. Serve with butter or oil and garlic.

BRUSSELS SPROUTS (BRASSICA OLERACEA GEMMIFERA)

When should you plant Brussels sprouts seed?   Sow seeds May 15 to June 15. Set plants out about August 1.

What cultivation and type of soil are needed for Brussels sprouts?   Set plants out in rich, friable soil; cultivate constantly; water in dry weather and sidedress with nitrogen or liquid manure during its early stages of growth.

How can I raise Brussels sprouts? They grow up, and I break off outer leaves, except a few on top. The little balls start, and there they sit!   Try an application of liquid manure or water-soluble fertilizer when sprouts begin forming (see preceding answer). Pinching out the growing tip will often force heads to form.

Can Brussels sprouts be grown in the climate we have in St. Louis?   Not too well. Seed should be sown in your area June 1, plants should be set out July 20 in cool soil, and watering should be frequent.

Should we cut the leaves off Brussels sprouts when heads start to form?   Remove lower leaves only, to facilitate cutting of the sprouts.

My Brussels sprouts are beautiful plants, but the sprouts are loose and leafy. How can I get firm sprouts? (South Carolina.)   Heat may be the cause of this trouble. Try an application of water-soluble fertilizer when sprouts begin forming.

When and how are Brussels sprouts harvested?   Brussels sprouts are harvested by cutting the "sprouts" (like tiny heads of cabbage) off the stems with a sharp knife after the leaves have been broken off. The leaves will usually snap off easily as far up the stem as the "sprouts" are ready to cut.

CABBAGE (BRASSICA OLERACEA CAPITATA)

What kind of soil is suitable for cabbage?   In the home garden, cabbage can be grown successfully in a wide variety of soils. For commercial culture, a rather heavy loam is usually preferred, although early varieties are frequently grown on fairly light soil. All of the cabbage group are heavy feeders and do best when two or three applications of fertilizer are given during the growing season.

What kind of soil and fertilizer are required for growing cabbage successfully? (California.)   Any soil that will not bake too hard is suitable for cabbage. Frequent cultivation is essential. Fertilizers high in nitrogen are preferable when setting plants out, plus a sidedressing of nitrogen or liquid manure when they are half grown.

How can I make cabbage head early? (New Jersey.)   Set out in early April, choosing early varieties, as soon as the ground can be worked. Apply good fertilizer immediately. Sidedress with fertilizer high in nitrogen or liquid manure one month later. Water frequently in dry weather.

I cannot raise cabbage or cauliflower in my garden. Why?   If the soil is not poor, it may be infested with club root, which attacks cabbage and cauliflower. Try new soil in a different part of the vegetable garden. Dig to a depth of 12 inches; use plenty of compost or rotted manure. Cultivate frequently; water during dry spells; sidedress with nitrate of soda or liquid manure when the plants are established. Cabbage yellows, a disease, is another problem. Plant only yellows-resistant varieties.

Why do our cabbage and broccoli plants, carefully tended in newly turned soil that is rich and black, form foliage instead of heads? (Illinois.)   Probably a lack of lime, phosphorus, or potash. Boron deficiency can cause the heart to die out. You can see this by examining the leaves in the center of the plant.

I have been planting cabbages for four years, but they do not do well; they make long stems but few heads. What is the trouble?   The seed purchased may be of doubtful quality. The plants may be held out of the ground too long before being planted. The soil may be deficient in phosphorus and potash or may not be sufficiently cultivated. The weather may be too warm.

We have a small plot of Savoy cabbages. Some of them are large and some are very small. Why?   Evidently your seed was of uneven quality;

soil fertility may be spotty. Buy the best seed and distribute your fertilizer evenly.

Why do cabbage heads crack? How can I prevent this? This is usually due to rapid growth during warm weather on early cabbage, causing premature formation of a seed stalk when the head is maturing. Heads should be cut as soon as they are full grown. With the fall crop, there is less difficulty. Loosening the roots by pulling or bending over the head to break the fibers on one side of the stem delays cracking.

When should cabbage seed be started? (Missouri.) For a spring crop, 60 to 90 days before the danger of the last hard frost. For a fall crop, May 15 to June 20.

When is the best time to plant cabbage for early setting? (New Jersey.) Sown indoors, 60 to 90 days before the danger of the last hard frost, usually late March to mid-April.

How is fall cabbage grown? When is it planted? (Missouri.) Sow seed May 15 to June 20. Set out your plants August 1. Harvest before hard freezing.

How do you control worms on cabbage and other crucifers? Dust the foliage with rotenone dust, methoxychlor, or Sevin when the worms make their appearance. In the home garden, catching the yellow or white butterflies (which lay the cabbage worm eggs) with a net is helpful—and good exercise!

Cardboard or foil discs placed around the stems of cabbage plants prevent injury from root maggots.

What insects and diseases attack crucifers? Root rots are the most serious diseases. Cabbage yellows is serious in some parts of the country but there are resistant varieties to overcome this disease. The main insect trouble is the cabbage worm, which eats the leaves, the harlequin plant bug, and aphids (plant lice), which suck the juices. On early cabbage the root maggot does much damage unless controlled by using cardboard discs around the stems when setting out your plants.

How can cabbage be stored for winter?   A few heads of cabbage can be stored by pulling the plants out by the roots and covering the head with a paper sack, tying the sack shut around the stem, and then hanging the head up by the roots. A cool cellar is best. For large quantities, cabbage should be stored in pits out-of-doors and covered with layers of straw and soil so it won't freeze.

What are good early and late varieties of cabbage?   *Early:* 'Jersey Wakefield', 'Golden Acre', 'Stonehead' hybrid. *Late:* 'Danish Ballhead'. *Red:* 'Red Danish'.

CARROT (DAUCUS CAROTA SATIVUS)

What soil is best for carrots?   Well-limed and aerated sandy loam soil. Incorporate plenty of humus. Unless loose and friable, roots will be tough and crooked.

Do carrots need plenty of water to grow large, or is fertilizer more important?   Carrots need a well-limed soil and average moisture conditions. Use a 5–10–10 fertilizer if the soil is poor.

Does the flavor of carrots vary with the condition of the soil? The carrots that I raised last year had a flat, unsavory flavor. They were grown in ground uncultivated for 10 years.   A well-grown carrot is sweeter than a stunted carrot. You may need more lime, humus, and potash in the soil. Too much nitrogen as well as continued hot weather will cause poor flavor.

How does the market gardener plant carrot seed and cultivate to keep down the weeds? What are the newest methods of carrot growing?   The market gardener's soil is freer of weeds because the ground is cultivated so much. The rows are thinned while the plants are still very small, and chemicals are used to control annual weeds, not later than 50 days before the carrots are harvested.

I can never get a good stand of carrots. Why?   Probably the ground bakes too hard. Try sprinkling some pulverized magnesium limestone over the seed before you cover them. Don't plant the seed too deep; barely covering from sight is sufficient.

How should carrots be planted for succession crops?   Make 3 plantings: early spring, early summer, and midsummer—mid-July to August.

Why doesn't carrot seed germinate?   It may be too old. Or it may be due to a lack of lime in the soil. Use pulverized magnesium limestone and sprinkle it over the seed in the row before covering with soil.

When is it best to thin out carrots? When the seedlings are about 2 inches tall. Thin them when the soil is moist—soon after a rain or a good watering.

How are carrots transplanted? This cannot be done satisfactorily. Anything that breaks off the main taproot causes them to produce branched or forked carrots.

Why do my carrots so often lack color? The soil may be too dense, contain too much nitrogen, or lack lime. On black soil, 20 to 50 pounds per acre (1 to 2 ounces per 100 feet of row) of copper dust will improve their color. Plant newer coreless varieties, which are solid orange in color.

What would make carrots (good seed) which grew rapidly very tough, even the baby ones? Probably a deficiency of potassium, or insufficient lime in the soil. Hard clay soil forces the roots to twist or "corkscrew." Fiber forms with each twist.

What makes forked carrots? Failure to pulverize thoroughly the soil in which they are to grow; the use of manure which is not well rotted; or perhaps allowing seedlings to grow too big before thinning, which is apt to make their roots twist around one another.

I have read about treating soil with borax for carrots. When advisable, how is it done? Is regular kitchen borax used? One ounce of ordinary borax to 16 quarts of water, poured along the row, is enough for 50 to 75 feet.

My carrots sometimes have many roots instead of one straight one; or sometimes they are full of little nodules like root bumps. How can this be prevented? This sounds like nematode injury. Try to grow them where carrots have not been grown before. Fall tilling will tend to minimize the trouble. A lack of lime sometimes causes forked carrots.

Carrots grown during the past season have sprouted many smaller roots from around the main root. The main roots are healthy, about 7 or 8 inches long, with as many as 6 or 8 smaller carrots all around the main stem. Only some of these in the same row showed this peculiarity, while others were normal. Soil tests were: slightly alkaline, good nitrogen content, deficiency in potash. A good dose of 20 per cent superphosphate was given the soil three weeks before planting in a sandy loam soil in southern Connecticut. What is the matter? Try some magnesium limestone as well as more potash. It is doubtful whether the high pH is due to lime in the soil.

Do carrots poison the ground? No, but they do use up nutrients which cause deficiencies for other crops. This is not poisoning, but it does affect later crops.

My carrots come up and grow very well until the first week in July, then their tops die down rather suddenly. About the middle or last of August, new shoots appear. The carrots get no bigger than my middle finger, although the tops look healthy. This has occurred every year for five years. Other things grow on. What is it? This sounds like leaf blight. Many commercial growers spray with Bordeaux mixture to control this disease.

What is the proper time to plant carrots for winter storage? (Iowa.) Plant seed June 1 to 20, for usual table size. If deluxe "baby" carrots (about half grown) are wanted, two or three weeks later.

We replanted the carrots in a box of soil in the cellar this fall. Now they are developing new tops and rootlets. Will the rootlets spoil the carrots for use as a raw vegetable? Not unless they make considerable growth, in which case they will be bitter. The soil should be air dried when used for storing roots. Very slightly dampened peat moss, sand, or vermiculite is better than soil for packing around roots in winter. Root crops will not start to grow if the temperature is kept below 40° F.

When shall I dig carrots for winter storage? Just before a hard freeze; early frosts do not injure them. Storing them too early can cause them to sprout.

At what stage of development should carrots be pulled for canning? In the "baby" stage—finger size—for best table quality.

What is the best carrot to plant on a rather heavy soil? 'Oxheart', 'Chantenay', 'Danvers', or 'Nantes Half Long'. Use plenty of magnesium limestone.

Can you name a good sweet variety of carrot for the home garden? There are many, such as 'Coreless Nantes', 'Sweetheart', and 'Short 'n Sweet'.

CAULIFLOWER (BRASSICA OLERACEA BOTRYTIS)

What is the best method for growing cauliflower? Get high-quality seed. For a spring crop in northern areas with cool, moist weather, sow indoors in February or early March. Set out your plants as soon as the danger of frost is over. The soil must be deep and very rich. Cultivate constantly and sidedress with a high nitrogen fertilizer. Fall crop: Sow seed June 1 to 15; set out plants in August.

Why didn't some of my cauliflower form heads, while Brussels sprouts and other cauliflower did? Both crops dislike high summer temperatures, which cause irregular growth.

What causes cauliflower heads to turn yellow or purple? The heads turn yellow or purplish if not protected from the sun. Pull leaves together over the top of the head as soon as it begins to form and tie them together at the tips to hold them in place. This will keep the heads perfectly white. 'Early Purple Head' and 'Royal Purple' do not require tying.

How do you bleach cauliflower? When I tie the heads together, they turn black and rot. I have been told to use lime, but I hesitated to do so. Do not tie the heads until they are about 2½ inches in diameter. Never tie too tightly or too closely over the head. Be sure the "curd" is dry when tied.

I planted cauliflower and grew nice, snowy-white heads, the first one in 62 days. When they were cooked, they turned a light brown color. What was wrong? Evidently your water contains a considerable amount of iron. Cauliflower should be steamed rather than boiled.

CELERIAC (APIUM GRAVEOLENS RAPACEUM)

How do I grow celeriac; what are its soil and light needs? Does it have to be blanched? How long can it be left in the ground? Is it subject to celery blight? Celeriac (also known as root celery or knob celery) is grown by the same methods as other celery, with about the same type of soil and light requirements. It doesn't need to be blanched and seems to be more resistant to disease than ordinary celeries, but it may require Bordeaux dusting. It can be left in the soil until the danger of freezing weather has passed. The roots will not freeze quite as quickly as the leaf stalks of ordinary celery. It does require good soil and ample irrigation to develop large, smooth roots of fine quality. These, with their tops removed, can be stored in sand or soil for the winter.

CELERY (APIUM GRAVEOLENS DULCE)

Can celery be grown in the home garden? If so, what variety is recommended? It *can* be grown, but requires so much care, patience, and space that most home gardeners prefer to buy it. 'Golden Self-

Blanching' is one of the best for the home garden, though—despite its name—it requires blanching. 'Fordhook' is another.

How should early celery plants be started?   Sow seed in flats of a soilless mix. Mark out rows ¼ inch deep and 2 inches apart or scatter the seeds over the surface. Sow seed 10 to 15 per inch; cover very lightly by sifting on not more than ⅛ inch of soil. Cover the flats with newspaper or plastic and water moderately. As soon as seedlings break ground, remove their covering. When seedlings are 1½ or 2 inches high, transplant them to other flats, spacing them about 2 inches apart. Firm well, with the crowns just about even with the soil but not above. Watering should be managed to give steady but not too rapid growth; a temperature between 55° to 65° F. is about right. Plants should be hardened by watering sparingly.

A flat of celery plants ready for transplanting into a garden.

What is the best time to start celery seed for early planting?   Celery seedlings start slowly and seed should be sown indoors 8 to 10 or even 12 weeks before setting outdoors. Celery will withstand moderate frost, and it may be put out about the average date of the last hard, killing frost, or 2 to 3 weeks before tomato-setting time. Celery plants for a fall crop may be started in a well-prepared outdoor seed bed about 8 weeks before field setting. Celery will withstand light frost but not hard freezing in the fall, and 100 to 125 days should be allowed from the time of setting out plants until harvest or storage.

How should celery be spaced and transplanted in the garden?   Celery plants should be dug with minimum breaking of the fine root system. In transplanting, avoid doubling up or bunching of roots; pack the soil firmly and set the plants at about the depth they were growing in the plant box or seed bed. If set too shallowly, roots are exposed; if too deeply, soil is likely to get into the crowns. Rows may be 2 to 3 feet apart and plants spaced 6 inches apart in the rows. For partial blanching, celery may be planted in rows 18 inches or 2 feet apart. For blanching with earth, 3 to 4 feet between rows should be provided.

What is the best kind of soil for celery? Should celery be planted in sun or shade? The soil best for celery should be fertile and well filled with organic matter. The soil range is from moderately sandy to sandy loam to moderately heavy soil, provided the other requirements are met. Muck or peat soils are especially suitable. Rich, well-maintained garden soil containing compost and/or rotted manure will give good results. It responds well to liberal applications of commercial fertilizer— up to 1 pound per 20 square feet. A 5–10–5 fertilizer will not be far wrong on most soils. On peat soils, a high potash fertilizer may be desirable. Celery does not do well under shady conditions.

How much water does celery require? A great deal. The root system of the celery plant is not spread far or deep and a liberal water supply is needed, more so than for most vegetables. The soil should be kept moist throughout the growing season.

Can an outdoor seed bed be used for late celery plants? Yes, but it should be well-prepared, rich, friable soil. If seed is sown thinly, transplanting may be omitted, but this uses up garden space. Watering is likely to be necessary, but it should not be overdone, so that the plants will not be soft and spindly. Good plants for setting out are about 6 inches high and should be managed so that leaf pruning will not be necessary. It takes about 8 weeks to grow the plants.

How do I grow and care for celery in Southern California? Celery is not likely to do well in the hotter, dryer parts of California, but a good deal is grown near the coast. Cultural methods are not greatly different from other places. Ample irrigation is likely to be necessary.

We grew our first celery this year. It seemed to thrive, became a good size, blanched well, but is hollow and tough. What does it need to grow large and tender? In the fall, the stalks were soft and stringy. The quality of celery is very much dependent upon favorable growing conditions, especially fertility and moisture. It is not likely to be good if the weather is hot and dry. Pithiness or hollow stalk is generally traceable to poorly bred seed. Stringiness varies widely with varieties, being more prominent in the 'Golden Self-Blanching' group than in the late green celeries. It is much more prominent where celery has been grown under unfavorable conditions of fertility, moisture, or heat.

How does one grow the celery that develops large hearts that will be used for braising or eating raw? The proportion of "heart" in celery depends a good deal upon variety. The 'Golden Self-Blanching' strains are good in this respect, the old 'Giant Pascal' are not as good, but a number of green celeries of high quality (such as 'Fordhook' and

'Utah') have been developed. The heart comes up and becomes more prominent late in the growth of the plant or even in the storage space (see below).

How should celery be blanched? Commercial growers use boards or stout paper along the rows; home gardeners may slip a tube over each plant or tie paper around it. The old method of pulling up earth around the plants involves much washing in the kitchen. Only the stalks, not the foliage, are to be blanched.

I would like to know what causes celery blight. What can I do to check it? Celery "blight" (there are three different leaf diseases) is controlled by faithful dusting or spraying with Bordeaux, taking special pains to cover the lower leaves, especially the undersides. The soil should be free from celery refuse, and it is best if the soil has not grown celery for a period of three years. Spraying or dusting may well begin in the plant bed, especially if disease has been troublesome in the past. Treatment every week or ten days is necessary, unless the season is very dry and disease is not developing.

What will prevent celery from rotting in the ground after it has been hilled up? Celery for storing and hilling ought to be practically free from disease. Hilling should not be done until really cool weather, and the plants should be dry.

Cross section of celery stored in a trench for fall use, or later in mild climates.

How can celery be stored, and for how long? The plants are lifted complete with roots (which are light and should be disturbed as little as possible) and replanted in a shallow trench, in boxes in a storage house or cool cellar, or in a cold frame. The roots should be kept moist but the stalks should be dry. The plants can be kept for many weeks. The temperature should be just above freezing.

CHAYOTE (SECHIUM EDULE)

What is chayote? A perennial tropical vine native to America. It is grown as an annual in cooler climates, where 220 days may be counted on between killing frosts. Fruits, which are melonlike, are edible baked or steamed. The tuberous roots are also edible in climates where the vine is perennial and able to produce small tubers. Young shoots are also edible.

What is the culture for chayote? Plant the entire fruit on its side with the point slightly exposed where the vine is to grow; or plant shoots from the base of an established plant. A rich, well-fertilized soil is needed and a support on which the vine can climb. Fruit may be expected in late fall from spring planting in climates with at least a 220-day growing season.

Can chayote be grown in Maine? Not very well. Chayote is a tropical perennial vine. It may be grown in greenhouses, or as an annual for its fruit, in sheltered places where the growing season is at least 220 days between killing frosts.

CHICORY, WITLOOF, FRENCH ENDIVE (CICHORIUM INTYBUS)

Why does my chicory seed, planted in the spring, fail to come up? Much of the seed used in this country is often several years old. French seed should come up readily no matter how early it is planted. Buy seed from a reliable source.

How is chicory grown in the garden for winter forcing? Plant out-

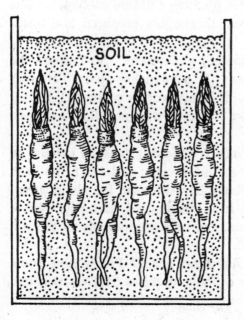

Cross section showing roots of Witloof chicory packed in a deep box of moist soil or peat moss and sand for forcing for winter salads.

of-doors in early spring in rows 18 inches apart; thin out to 4 inches apart; grow on through the entire summer. Summer foliage is not used but permitted to grow and feed roots. Dig the roots just before a hard freeze for forcing indoors.

How do I force chicory? What should be done with the roots saved for successive forcing? Dig the roots just before a hard frost and trim to a uniform length of 6 to 8 inches; cut the tops off just above the roots. Pack in a box, 12 to 16 inches deep, in peat moss and sand (or peat moss and loam), close together, and cover with 6 inches or more of soil. Place in a cool, dark cellar, water well, and cover with a board. When shoots appear at the surface, reach down through the soil and cut just above the roots with a sharp knife. Save the roots wanted for a second crop by planting—as above—in dry soil; do not water until ready to force the crop.

Growing chicory in the cellar, how do we take off the leaves—cut or tear them off? The chicory seems to be having good growth and the leaves are very good to eat. If the chicory is forced properly, you shouldn't have to remove any leaves. The "heads" are cut. If the outer leaves are loose, it is an indication that the soil above the crowns is too loose. This should be compact and firm. (See the previous question.)

CHINESE CABBAGE (BRASSICA OLERACEA PEKINENSIS)

How should the soil be prepared for planting Chinese cabbage? The soil should be well drained but moist, thoroughly prepared and fertilized, especially with nitrogen.

How is Chinese cabbage seed planted, and when? Sow where the plants are to grow, very thinly, in rows 18 to 24 inches apart. Thin to 3 inches apart, then to 6 or 8 inches. The fall crop is planted 2½ to 3 months before frost. Chinese cabbage is a cool-weather plant and must be grown quickly.

How can one keep Chinese cabbage from going to seed instead of heading? Plant in late midsummer for a fall crop; it doesn't like heat. Plant as late as possible to mature. Keep the soil moist, the plants growing without check—80 to 90 days from seeding to maturity. Newer varieties from Japan, i.e., 'Springtime', can be sown as early as the soil can be worked and will not go to seed.

Why does my Chinese cabbage not form heads? Please give some pointers on its cultivation. Chinese cabbage requires cool weather and short fall days to make heads. It should be grown on very fertile soil with lime and plenty of moisture. Thin to 8 inches.

What is the trouble with our Chinese cabbage? It grows well until ready to head, then begins to wilt; then the leaves begin to rot. This is probably due to a crown or heart rot. A specimen should be sent for diagnosis to your county agent at the Cooperative Extension Service, usually listed in phone books under the county government.

Why is our Chinese cabbage so buggy? Plant lice or aphids can be a nuisance on Chinese cabbage. Spray or dust the plants with methoxychlor or rotenone just as soon as lice appear. Repeat as frequently as needed.

CHIVES (ALLIUM SCHOENOPRASUM)

What are the soil and light needs of chives? They are easy to grow, but in view of the fact that the seed may not be too good, it is best to start with plants, dividing them into sections. They need a well-limed, loamy soil and full sunlight or light shade. Divide and replant old clumps every two or three years to prevent overcrowding.

Is it necessary to cut blossoms from chives in order to keep the tops (foliage) good for use? Removal of the flowers makes new growth easier to cut because old flower stems are tough. This also encourages the growth of new foliage instead of letting its strength go into seeds.

How are chives used in cookery? Young foliage and bulbs are used for flavoring in soups, salads, in cream cheese, in sour cream, on vegetables—wherever a very delicate onion flavor is desired.

CORN, SWEET (ZEA MAYS)

How is the ground prepared for corn planting? It should be thoroughly dug or tilled. Soil along the rows or in hills should be well pulverized when fertilizer is being added prior to planting.

How should corn be fertilized? Corn needs a 5–10–5 complete fertilizer and/or compost to make the soil fertile. Rotted manure is also good. Fertilize when preparing the ground a week or more before planting. In garden soil in good tilth, pour a cupful of starter solution over the seeds in a hill before covering with earth and omit other fertilizer.

Does sweet corn need lime? Corn likes a pH of 6.0 to 6.8; that is, slightly acid.

How should corn be planted? Either in rows 30 inches apart, 3 or 4 kernels to the foot, 1 to 2 inches deep, 3 or 4 rows being planted at once to ensure cross-pollination; or in hills or groups 3 feet apart each way, 5 or 6 seeds to the hill, planting always 2 or more rows of hills for cross-pollination.

When should sweet corn be planted? Plant sweet corn a week before the probable date of the last killing frost in the spring, if for an early crop; 10 days or so later for a main crop. A late planting (of early varieties) can be made 80 to 90 days before the probable date of the first fall frost.

Can corn be successfully started in pots indoors for transplanting? Yes, providing they are not kept too warm and set in the ground too early. This method has limitations but will give you earlier corn. Peat-and-fiber pots, 3 or 4 inches square, are better for this purpose than clay pots.

In order to have a supply of young corn fairly late into the fall, what is the latest date it should be planted? (New York.) July 4 to 15, depending on the length of the growing season (between last spring and first fall frosts) in the locality. This calls for using seed of an early variety.

Is there any advantage in planting sweet corn in blocks instead of single rows? When planting three varieties of sweet corn at one time for succession, it is better to plant a third of each of three rows in a little block than to have single rows of each variety. This makes for better pollination, since each row helps pollinate the others and so ears are better filled.

How should corn be cultivated? Cultivation should be frequent to control weeds, but should be shallow. Hill up as plants grow.

How many stalks of sweet corn are left to a hill? Usually only 3.

My sweet corn was a complete failure this season. It grew heavy, tall stalks but no ears. I planted 6 rows at a time, about 6 inches apart in a row. Rainfall was exceptionally heavy, which was the only unusual thing. What was wrong? (Soil analysis shows a deficiency of potash.) I used commercial fertilizer with a heavy percentage of potash and a small amount of nitrogen. The stalks were too close together. They should be a foot apart.

I have never succeeded in growing good corn. The stalks grow well but the ears are few and small. I buy seed from a good house and plant in accordance with instructions. I have planted the seeds in three widely separate locations; in fact, one garden is 7 miles away from the others. This sounds like too close planting or too much nitrogen and too little lime, phosphorus, or potash. The soil may be too dense below the tilled layer.

Last spring I planted corn (two kinds) and it tasseled when it was about 2 or 3 feet high. That was all we saw of the corn. Why? This sounds like an acid soil, dry weather, dark days, or a lack of fertilizer was the cause—possibly all four.

What is the cause of incomplete development of kernels on an ear of corn? All around the ear the kernels may be plump, sweet, and full of juice, but 2 rows or more may be dry and flat. Plant in blocks rather than single rows, in order to assure cross-pollination and development of every kernel. It may also be the result of the corn borer working in the stalk just below the ear.

Can the fact that my corn failed to produce one single ear, when planted in two 250-foot rows, as per directions, be due to the fact that the 3–8–7 fertilizer used was too poor in phosphate? The fertilizer should be O.K. Perhaps the stalks were too close together. Ten 50-foot rows would ensure better pollination than two 250-foot rows. Sometimes hybrid varieties set their pollen in one short period. If this period coincides with windless days, no pollen will fly.

Should suckers be removed from corn? If so, when? Nobody has been able to prove that there is any advantage in removing the suckers from sweet corn. From a physiological point of view, to do any good the suckers should be removed when they are not over 3 inches tall. Most people sucker corn when it is a foot high. This is too late and injures the parent plant when the suckers are removed.

How can I keep crows from stripping sweet corn after it is in ear? Hang up tin cans or other noisemakers. Scarecrows may help.

What can I do to control the corn borer? Dust the plants every 5 days with Sevin. They should be dusted from the top so that the dust gets into the axils of the leaves. Rotenone dust once a week is another control. All infested stalks should be burned in the fall as the pest winters over in the plant refuse.

How can I prevent the corn-ear worm from ruining the ears? You can put 10 to 20 drops of mineral oil containing rotenone on the silk about 3 days after the silk comes out of the ear. Or you can cut off the silk close to the ear every 5 days. Or grow varieties developed with close-tipped husks to prevent entry of the worm.

Is there any method of controlling corn smut during the growing period? There is no complete control except to remove and burn as soon as discovered and before powdery spores are released into the air to spread disease. Smut is a fungus growth that comes through the stem into the ear or tassel.

Are any varieties of sweet corn absolutely smut proof? No. You might try spraying the plants with Bordeaux mixture when the ears are beginning to form. Be sure to destroy smutty ears before the powdery spores are released into the air.

What is hybrid sweet corn? A hybrid is the first-generation progeny resulting from the crossing of two inbred lines. The breeder first works several years purifying and fixing the character of his inbred lines. He then crosses two of these, hoping to secure a combination of several desired characters and more vigorous growth.

What kind of sweet corn is the sweetest? The sweetest sweet corn varieties are hybrids, known as "supersweets," but there are two types of "supersweets"—those that need isolating in order to retain their supersweet qualities, such as 'Early Xtra Sweet', and those that don't, called 'EV' (short for a gene known as Everlasting Heritage). The isolated sweet corns came first, and the 'EV' sweet corns are an improvement. 'EV' sweet corns, such as 'Kandy Korn EV' and 'Earliglo EV', not only require no isolation to retain their supersweetness, but they also stay sweet for up to 10 days after picking. Among white sweet corn, a variety called 'Silver Queen' has developed a reputation for being the sweetest, milkiest, tenderest sweet corn, and it requires no isolation. Even though it is not a "supersweet," it matches supersweets for flavor.

How can I get succession crops of sweet corn? Take any one variety and make plantings every 2 weeks. If you make only small plantings (a dozen hills or so), make plantings every week. Or you can pick a group of varieties that will mature at different dates.

Where can I get seed for varicolored corn? (Michigan.) Most seed houses carry various kinds, such as 'Rainbow'.

CRESS (CURLY CRESS, UPLAND CRESS)

I have tried in vain to establish watercress in our wet meadow, which often becomes dry in the summer. Are there substitute greens we can grow? Watercress needs constant running water to grow properly, although it can be grown in rich, damp soil. As an acceptable substitute, obtain seed of curly cress, which has a peppery tang, or upland cress, which is more similar in flavor to watercress. The plants do best in the cool weather of spring and fall and mature fast, so seeds should be sown every few weeks to maintain a supply. In hot-summer regions, postpone sowings until late summer for fall use. Curly cress grows well indoors in a cool sunny window or under fluorescent tubes.

CUCUMBER (CUCUMIS SATIVUS)

How is cucumber seed planted?   In the open ground after the danger of frost is past. Rows can be 4 to 5 feet apart, with a plant every 2 to 4 feet in the row. Many gardeners plant seeds too thick and fail to thin out. For an earlier harvest, sow seeds indoors in peat pots or outdoors under Hotkaps.

How are cucumbers fertilized?   With plenty of well-rotted manure or compost placed under the soil in which the seed are planted, either in hills or rows.

How are cucumbers cultivated?   Cultivate carefully for weeds until the vines spread, when hand weeding is necessary. Mulching between rows or hills can be used to keep weeds down.

How often should cucumbers be picked?   To ensure production through their full bearing period, pick regularly (which may be daily, certainly every few days); the younger the better. If fruits are allowed to mature, the vines soon stop bearing.

Can cucumber plants be transplanted?   Cucumbers can be started inside, 3 weeks ahead of garden setting, using any good greenhouse or plant-growing soil in peat pots. Sow 3 to 4 seeds per pot and thin out to 1 or 2; keep at a temperatue of about 65° F.; water moderately so plants grow vigorously but will not have started to vine before field setting. Care must be taken in setting them out not to disturb the root system, as they do not stand transplanting as well as cabbage or tomatoes.

Should cucumbers be trained upwards? If so, how?   They can be trained on a fence or over a wall to save space, but are usually allowed to run over the ground. In small gardens, plant bush varieties.

Can cucumbers be planted near melons?   Cucumbers can be planted close to melons without fear of "crossing." What causes melons to "taste like cucumbers" is exposure to cool or cold weather sometime during growth rather than cross-pollination.

Do cucumbers and muskmelons cross?   No. However, the belief that they cross is widespread, and many experiences are related that seem to confirm it. The most carefully conducted and scientifically correct experiments have been made in vain attempts to cross them.

Should cucumbers be picked when their foliage is wet? What makes

cucumber vines turn yellow before all fruit is mature?   Cucumbers are subject to several leaf and vine diseases which would probably be spread somewhat more freely when the plants are wet. These diseases are best controlled by rotation of land and by seed treatment as mentioned in the following question.

Why do cucumber vines die so soon?   Because the fruits are not picked or because of diseases, such as bacterial wilt, scab, anthracnose, and angular leaf spot. Most reputable seed catalogs list the tolerance of varieties to these diseases. As cucumbers come up, they should be dusted with rotenone, pyrethrum, Sevin, or methoxychlor for striped beetles, which are carriers of bacterial wilt. Use of Hotkaps will protect small plants from the cucumber beetle, which spreads the wilt.

Where do cucumber beetles come from?   Cucumber beetles pass the winter as adults. Some are in the garden under old cucumber or melon vines and unharvested fruits and some are in fence rows, ditch banks, wood lots, and rubbish piles near the garden. They come out of hibernation about May 1 and feed on weeds for a few days while waiting for the cucumbers and melons to come up.

My problem is growing cucumbers and squash. I can grow the plants but they get many empty blossoms; when the fruit comes on the plants and I get a few small ones, the plants start to die. I use plenty of well-rotted manure and give them lots of water when needed. What is the trouble?   Probably wilt spread by striped cucumber beetles. (See the previous questions.) "Empty" blossoms may be male.

Are there wilt-resistant cucumbers?   Some results have been achieved in breeding mosaic- and mildew-resistant strains, but so far none have been developed that are resistant to bacterial wilt. 'Burpee Hybrid' is resistant to both mosaic and downy mildew; 'Marketmore 70', to scab and mosaic. 'Gemini', an all-female variety, is resistant to five or more diseases. Of the pickling sorts, 'Pioneer', 'Mariner', and 'Wisconsin SMR18' carry multiple resistance.

Are there any advantages to growing all-female cucumbers? If so, how do the female flowers get pollinated?   The advantage of an all-female cucumber is that most of the flowers are capable of producing fruit. Older varieties of cucumbers are generally "male dominant," meaning that they produce more males than females, and the males have a tendency to appear first. However, there are three kinds of so-called all-female cucumbers: The first kind is truly all-female and a normal cucumber vine with male blossoms must be planted nearby to ensure pollination. When seed suppliers sell this kind, they include seeds of a pollinator, stained a distinct color so you can recognize them. Another kind of all-female produces a small percentage of male flowers—sufficient to ensure pollination—and a third kind (which must be isolated) produces all-female flowers requiring no pollination whatsoever from a male flower, since it is self-fruitful. This third kind is mostly for greenhouse growing. In order to determine which is which when buying seed, check the catalog description or packet instructions carefully.

DANDELION (TARAXACUM OFFICINALE)

How do I grow dandelions? You can buy dandelion seed and sow it in rows in late summer and harvest them the following spring. They require a fertile soil that is well limed.

Would dried dandelion leaves make good winter eating? What about other edible weeds? Most of the common nonpoisonous weeds, if harvested when young, are quite nutritious from the standpoint of vitamins. They can be dried and used later. The main question is their palatability. Lawn grass and young alfalfa are very nutritious if you like them.

DASHEEN (COLOCASIA ESCULENTA)

I have heard about the "dasheen," the rival of the potato, and I wish to try it. Can you tell me of its cultural necessities and if it is possible to grow it at an altitude of nearly 5,000 feet with a relatively short season? No, it is a tropical plant.

EGGPLANT (SOLANUM MELONGENA ESCULENTUM)

How is the soil prepared for eggplant? The soil should be well drained and rather sandy, well worked with compost or rotted manure.

What is the secret of growing eggplants successfully? Don't grow the young plants too fast until the fruit is set. The use of Blossom Set will help. Grow them on well-aerated soil that is amply supplied with lime. Use plenty of compost in holes when setting out and keep well watered. If subjected to temperatures below 50° F., flowers will drop off and no fruit will set; the same result will occur at temperatures above 90° F.

What is the best way to grow eggplants? Buy young, healthy plants or raise from seed indoors in peat pots in a warm place under fluorescent lights. (See Seed Sowing.) Set out when the ground is thoroughly warmed up or earlier under the protection of Hotkaps. Set 2 feet apart in rows 2½ to 3 feet apart. Work in 5–10–10 complete fertilizer around each plant as it begins to grow. Cultivate often or mulch.

Why do the blossoms of eggplants continue to drop off? Care is taken that they do not get frostbitten; manure has been applied and the ground is kept cultivated, but the blossoms still will not hang on. You probably grow the plants too soft with fertilizer, or at too high or too low a temperature. Grow them slower, with less nitrogen.

What makes eggplants develop a rot all over them in spots while only half grown, resulting in practically no crop? This is a bacterial or fungus spot and is caused under conditions where the fruit tends to stay moist on the surface. This often happens on poorly prepared soil. Check soil acidity. It may need more lime.

Eggplant in this area was destroyed by a "wilt." Dust and sprays failed completely. Can any helpful information be given? (Kansas.) There is no control for eggplant wilt after it has once gotten into the plants. The prevention is to grow seedlings in soil which has not grown them before and set the plants in fields which have not grown eggplants for at least 10 years. Some varieties, such as 'Black Beauty', are more resistant than others.

How do you keep bugs off eggplants? Dust the plants with Sevin or methoxychlor if the bugs eat the foliage; or spray with malathion if plant lice are present.

Which are the best varieties of eggplant? 'Black Beauty' is the old standby but there are several hybrids with smaller fruits, such as 'Dusky', that bear earlier and more bountifully. 'Florida High Bush' is especially suited to the South.

ENDIVE AND ESCAROLE (CICHORIUM ENDIVIA)

How is endive grown? In the North, sow seeds about July 15 for fall use. When endive reaches maturity, it is usually blanched by tying the outside leaves around the heart, as with cauliflower. After being tied, the head can be covered with waterproof paper to prevent rotting. Endive is frost-resistant and provides salad greens late in the fall. It can be stored in a cool cellar like celery, where it blanches in the dark. Endive that is tied up will rot in wet weather, particularly if the soil is not well limed.

FENNEL (FOENICULUM VULGARE DULCE)

What is Florence fennel, and how is it grown? Florence fennel (or finocchio) is a celery-like vegetable with an anise flavor. It matures quickly (in 90 days) and is sown in garden rows, thinned to 6 inches, and grown without special attention until approaching maturity. Then it is hilled up by having the soil drawn high on either side of the row to blanch the stalks. The blanching process takes about 3 weeks.

GARLIC (ALLIUM SATIVUM)

How does one grow garlic? Garlic can be grown just like onions, either from the "cloves" (divisions of the bulb) or from seed.

How do you divide garlic to plant? I want to grow large bulbs. You divide the garlic bulb into cloves and plant the individual sections. The size of the bulb is determined by soil and weather conditions. A fertile soil in good physical condition with ample rainfall will produce large bulbs.

When is it best to plant garlic—spring or fall? It can be planted either time. Spring planting is best where the soil freezes.

How deep should one plant garlic? Cloves are planted with their tops ½ inch below the surface. Seed should be planted not over ¼ inch deep. Plant in moist but not wet soil so the ground over the seed does not bake.

Can I grow the garlic chives used in oriental cuisine? Yes. Garlic chives (*Allium tuberosum*) are very hardy and bear attractive fragrant white flowers in late summer so they can be grown in herb or flower gardens. Their bright green leaves are used to flavor many Chinese dishes. The plants do self-sow and may become weedy.

GOURD

Is there an edible gourd? A variety called "vegetable gourd" is described as ornamental (it is creamy white, mottled, striped with dark green) and of good eating quality.

Which kinds of gourds are suitable for bird houses? The ordinary dipper gourds as well as others of the *Lagenaria* genus.

How can I produce dipper-type gourds? I have heard that it is necessary to tape the neck of the gourd. Dipper-gourds culture is the same as for other gourds. The shaping of necks is not ordinarily necessary for dipper gourds, but if you want to modify their shape this could be done with string or wire.

Is there any fertilizer that will cause gourd plants to grow more rapidly? The same provisions that are made for cucumbers and melons will work well with gourds. Use a 5–10–5 fertilizer or a combination of dried manure and a smaller amount of fertilizer, or compost and superphosphate.

How do you raise gourds? Gourds are not particularly difficult to grow. They can be allowed to run on the ground but are better planted along a wire fence or provided with a trellis. Their general requirements are about the same as for cucumbers and melons—a moderately rich, well-fertilized soil with reasonable moisture supply. They thrive under a wide range of conditions, and most varieties of small gourds will mature in the northern part of the country. Seed is sown about 1 inch deep and plants are thinned to 2 or 3 feet apart, according to varieties. Dusting may be necessary to control the striped cucumber beetle. In northern climates, plants can be started indoors in peat-fiber pots under fluorescent lights. Shallow cultivation should be practiced to control weeds.

What is the earliest date gourds can be planted? Gourds are planted at about the same time as cucumbers, 2 or 3 weeks after the average date of the last killing frost in the spring, or at about the time tomatoes are set out. Gourds will not stand frost.

How do you start gourds from seed? Ornamental gourds are usually raised in peat-fiber pots from seed sown in April or May and transplanted in June. When the peat pots are set out in the ground, they quickly disintegrate but save the roots from being disturbed in the transplanting operation. Seed can also be sown outdoors when the danger of frost is past.

How can one take care of gourds after they are picked so that they will not decay? Gourds should be thoroughly matured on the vines before they are picked. They will not stand freezing if they are still succulent. If by necessity they are taken at the immature state, they should be handled with the utmost care and allowed to dry and cure indoors, but mold is likely to attack them. Some recommend washing gourds, but wiping with a soft cloth is probably better. Disinfectant solutions may be of some service, but not too much. To keep gourds in their natural state, waxing is one of the best methods, using ordinary floor wax and polishing lightly. Some use shellac, but this changes the color and appearance. Some also like to decorate and paint them in simple or fanciful fashion. Stems should be left on the gourds, removing them from vines by cutting. Maturity may be judged by feeling them, but it is not wise to test with the fingernail. They should be dry and the stem should be withered.

What is a good spray to combat the stem borer of gourds? It is best to grow the gourds on ground where cucurbits (members of the squash family) have not been grown the previous year or where their refuse remains. Early summer squash may be used as a trap crop. When the borer is already at work in the vines, surgery is resorted to, cutting lengthwise of the vine with a thin knife to destroy the larvae. Then the cut portion is covered with earth and little harm is done to the plant. Methoxychlor spray or dust applied 3 or 4 times beginning in early summer may be effective in destroying the borers just after they are hatched.

HORSE-RADISH (ARMORACIA RUSTICANA)

How do you raise horse-radish? What kind of soil do you use? Horse-radish must be grown on a well-limed, sandy loam soil that has a subsoil which is well aerated to permit deep penetration of the taproot. The crop is grown from root cuttings which are set (large end up) 10 to 12 inches apart in rows 2 to 3 feet apart. The roots can be set in deep trenches and covered 2 inches over their tops. Set horse-radish roots in the spring for that season's crop.

I am interested in growing horse-radish. My plants that are 1 year old show no signs of root deterioration. However, plants that are 2 to 3 years and older show excessive dry rotting of the roots. To your knowledge, can this be remedied? This is a natural sloughing off of tissue which cannot be prevented. The best horse-radish comes from 1-year roots from small root cuttings that are planted every year.

When do you harvest horse-radish? Should it be dried before being grated? Horse-radish is harvested in the fall and the grating is done while the roots are in their natural fresh state.

KALE (BRASSICA OLERACEA ACEPHALA)

When and how is kale planted? Kale is improved by cold weather and should therefore be sown in the open, about 2 months before freezing is expected. Seed should be thinly sown, as the plants will eventually stand 18 to 24 inches apart. While kale will grow almost anywhere, it will be of better quality on good soil.

How late in the season can kale be cut for table use? Until heavy frost kills it, although in much of the North it survives the winter. Cut the bottom leaves first, before they get tough. Neglect of this point has given kale a worse name than this vitamin-richest of the potherbs deserves.

I have planted kale two different years. In all, about 3 plants have appeared. How do you make it come up? Buy high-grade seed. Seed should be covered ⅜ to ½ inch, and the seed bed should never be allowed to dry out.

How can I keep kale in the garden from freezing? (Ohio.) Kale is considered hardy in your area of the country and nothing but extremely low temperatures should cause damage. The leaves are improved by hard frost.

Can kale be kept green for table use during cold weather? By taking up plants and growing them in a covered cold frame it is possible to have kale through most of the winter.

How should kale be cooked? Kale can be chopped, boiled as a green, and served buttered. It can be cooked with ham hocks or ham, which flavors the kale. *Scalloped kale:* Boil chopped kale until tender. Drain. Mix with chopped hard-boiled egg. Place in a baking dish. Moisten with soup stock or bouillon. Cover the surface with slices of cheese and sprinkle with seasoned bread crumbs. Bake in an oven about 15 minutes, until heated through and the crumbs and cheese are browned.

KOHLRABI (BRASSICA CAULORAPA)

How should one plant and care for kohlrabi to get best results? Plant early on a well-limed, fertile soil. Kohlrabi is easy to grow and should give no trouble on a good soil. On poor soil, some fertilizer and a complete fertilizer applied as a sidedressing should be used. Thin out to about 3 inches. Harvest when not over 2 inches in diameter.

How should kohlrabi be harvested? Many gardeners plant kohlrabi but few eat it. Kohlrabi should be harvested while the bulb is still growing and tender. When growth stops, the bulb quickly becomes hard and woody in texture, bitter in flavor, and entirely inedible.

LEEK (ALLIUM AMPELOPRASUM PORRUM)

What is the culture of leeks? Leeks are grown from seed in well-limed, very fertile soil with ample water. They must be grown in full sunlight. Shade will not produce good growth.

A dibble (planting gadget you can buy or make) is handy for setting out many seedlings, such as those of leeks and onions.

What is the proper way to transplant leeks? Make a trench 5 to 6 inches deep; enrich the bottom with old manure or compost and fertilizer. Set young plants (trimmed back, both tops and roots) in the bottom, 5 to 6 inches apart. As they grow, fill the trench and draw earth up to blanch them.

Part of my crop of leeks is still in the ground. I have been told they could be left there and used next spring. Is this information correct? (West Virginia.) Yes, this is true for the home garden where the appearance of the leaves is not so important. For market, the leaves will be ragged, which will hurt their sale.

LETTUCE (LACTUCA SATIVA)

How should the soil be fertilized for head lettuce? Lettuce has a scanty root system; therefore, it must have good soil with enough humus to hold the moisture so necessary for such a crop and to provide equally necessary nitrogen. Compost or rotted manure is needed and as much lime as is needed to counteract any acidity.

When can lettuce seed be planted outdoors? Loose-leaf lettuce should be one of the earliest crops sown and is preferred, for several reasons, by the average home gardener. Head lettuce should be started indoors and transplanted (after hardening off), so that the heads may be well grown before hot weather comes. The variety 'Buttercrunch' can be sown out-of-doors both early and late and will form loose heads.

Use a cold frame for early harvests of lettuce.

How soon should lettuce be thinned? How far apart should the heads be? Leaf lettuce, sown in the open, can be thinned a couple of times while still very small, until the final plants stand 8 to 10 inches apart. The larger head-lettuce varieties should stand 10 to 12 inches. Small varieties, such as 'Bibb' and 'Tom Thumb', which are among the best, need only about 6 inches.

How can I be sure to get good head lettuce? By growing it in ideal conditions; namely, a fertile soil, well drained but not dry, in a climate where the nights are cool and the days warm. Raise seedlings indoors or in a cold frame; harden off by gradual exposure to the outdoors; transplant them on a cloudy day and protect them from strong sunlight until well established in the garden.

How can I raise large heads of delicious, crisp, tender, loose-leaf lettuce? (Vermont.) You should have no trouble in your climate. Prepare soil with plenty of lime and well-rotted manure if available, and sow the seed as soon as the ground can be prepared in the spring; thin so that the plants stand 8 inches apart; or start seed indoors, sidedress with liquid fertilizer if needed. 'Salad Bowl', 'Green Ice', and 'Oakleaf' are good varieties of the type you describe.

How can I, with Missouri soil conditions and without replanting, raise

head lettuce rather than leaf lettuce? Head lettuce requires a good, well-limed soil with ample moisture and cool nights. You can't grow head lettuce if the weather gets hot. Sow the seed as early as possible and thin the seedlings to stand 8 to 12 inches apart. See that the ground has plenty of humus—in the form of well-rotted manure, if available, and compost.

How can I get lettuce to grow faster? Lettuce requires a limed soil with a good balance of nutrients, especially nitrogen in early spring. The soil must have a clean odor and drain easily. You probably need lime and humus.

How can head lettuce be grown for a small family to have plenty all summer? You may not be able to grow head lettuce during the summer months because of hot days and nights. During the season of cool nights, you should have good heads by making plantings at 2-week intervals. 'Matchless' is a heat-resistant variety of head lettuce. Leaf lettuce is more nutritious and is usually grown during the summer months. 'Buttercrunch', a loose-head variety, does well in heat, as does 'Ruby'.

Why doesn't lettuce grow in our soil? (Pennsylvania.) Perhaps you have insufficient lime in the soil or too little phosphorus. Have your soil tested and if necessary add lime to bring it up to pH 6 or 7. Use well-rotted manure or compost.

What makes lettuce heads rot in the center, and why does the first early crop seed before heading? This may be due to a lack of available calcium or to one of the lettuce diseases that cause the heart to decay. Head lettuce goes to seed because of hot weather or other conditions that check normal growth. It needs cool nights to head well.

What causes "tip burn" in head lettuce? Tip burn is usually caused by uneven growth where the leaves get too soft. It may be due to too little calcium in the soil or too free use of a fast-acting fertilizer such as nitrate of soda as a sidedressing, especially if hot sunshine follows a cloudy, moist spell.

Can lettuce seed be planted in the house? Not unless you have good light and cool temperatures. The temperature should not be above 55° F. It can be grown in a cold room in a south window or under fluorescent lights.

I would appreciate suggestions for vegetable window boxes. Can lettuce be grown in pots or boxes? Yes, if you have sunshine and the night temperature is not too high. Head lettuce requires cool nights to make it head. Leaf lettuce will grow in any window box. Keep the plants 6 to 8 inches apart. Use a soil with plenty of lime and humus in it. Fluorescent lights will help in the winter.

Where can I obtain lettuce seed which produces a plant for all winter? (Pennsylvania.)   No varieties are hardy in the northern states unless grown in a greenhouse. 'Salad Bowl', 'Boston', 'Buttercrunch', and 'Oakleaf' are good varieties for a late fall crop. Endive, similar to lettuce and used for salads, is considerably hardier and should survive through fall and early winter in a cold frame.

Please recommend some lettuce varieties for the home garden, including some that are heat-resistant.   'Salad Bowl' and 'Green Ice' are the best of the loose-leaf type, which is easier to grow and gives a plentiful yield of leaves that are higher in vitamin content. 'Buttercrunch' has high quality, heads well, and resists heat. 'Royal Oakleaf' and 'Ruby' are especially heat-resistant.

What members of the lettuce family (or other salad greens) can be planted throughout the summer months?   Use head lettuce in the early spring and late fall. 'Bibb' is a good very early variety. 'Oakleaf' is another. In summer, grow mustard greens and such heat-resistant lettuces as 'Ruby' and 'Salad Bowl'; in autumn, 'Salad Bowl', 'Oakleaf', and 'Buttercrunch' head lettuce and endive, which is frost-resistant. Witloof chicory can be forced indoors for winter salad. Other greens to add to the salad bowl in spring and summer along with lettuce are curly cress, roquette, and spinach.

What is 'Bibb' lettuce?   'Bibb' lettuce is a loose-heading or bunch-heading variety having very thick, smooth, dark green leaves quite different from any other type. It is especially adapted to growing in cold frames in the southern states during the winter months and makes a good spring lettuce in the open garden in the North. 'Burpee Bibb', 'Buttercrunch', and 'Tom Thumb' are very similar.

MUSHROOM

I would like to know about growing mushrooms in the cellar. How do you start a bed? Is there a special temperature you have to keep? Can you be sure of having nonpoisonous kinds?   Use composted manure; pack in beds 6 inches deep; inoculate with pure-culture spawn; cover with an inch of soil; grow at 55° to 60° F. It sounds simple but is really very difficult. Write to your Agricultural Experiment Station for detailed information or purchase prepared flats or pots with the spawn already planted. Water and care for according to directions. Purchased spawn will not contain poisonous mushrooms.

How can a home mushroom bed be made under a front porch? You would have to close the area so that you could maintain conditions described in the answer to the previous question.

How can mushrooms be grown outside? You will have difficulty in doing this. Wild mushrooms grow only when weather conditions are favorable. You would have to provide those favorable conditions; therefore, mushroom growing in the open is not practicable.

How can I safely tell edible wild mushrooms? There are several regional as well as general books on the subject. One of the best is *The Mushroom Hunter's Field Guide,* by Alexander H. Smith, published by the University of Michigan Press, Ann Arbor.

MUSKMELON AND CANTALOUPE (CUCUMIS MELO)

Please give information on raising muskmelons. Muskmelons do well in lighter soils and need a warm, sunshiny season for maturing quality fruits. Seed can be sown out-of-doors, but in northern sections it is better to start seed indoors, using Jiffy-7 peat pellets to grow healthy transplants for setting outside after all danger of frost has passed. Start seeds 4 to 5 weeks before outdoor planting time. Set 3 to 4 feet apart, in rows 4 to 5 feet apart. Cultivate frequently; some pulling of weeds will be necessary after the vines spread. Black plastic mulch works well with muskmelons. Where the season is short, early varieties such as 'Harper Hybrid', 'Champlain', and 'Delicious 51' may be grown. Temperatures below 50° F. during growth reduce the sugar content of melons and decrease flavor.

How are muskmelons fertilized? They need a well-manured soil, light and thoroughly prepared, and a complete fertilizer. Two to 4 shovelfuls of well-rotted manure or rich compost are usually worked into the soil under each "hill" when planting.

When can I plant muskmelons? After the danger of frost has passed, about tomato-setting time. About the middle to the last of May in most of the northern states, or a few weeks earlier under Hotkaps or similar protection.

How can an early crop of muskmelons be achieved without starting it indoors? Use plant protectors such as Hotkaps. In this way, seed or plants can be put out 2 or 3 weeks earlier than would otherwise be advisable. As plants begin to make growth, the protector should be torn open at the top to provide ventilation.

Cucumber, melon, and squash seeds can be sown while frosts are still possible if the seeds are sown under Hotkaps or similar protection. The Hotkaps will warm the soil, which is necessary for germination.

Can muskmelons be started indoors? Yes, clay pots, paper pots, peat-fiber or Jiffy-7 pots, or the like can be used with a good plant-growing soil. Sow seed 3 to 4 weeks before setting out-of-doors. Grow at a temperature of 65° to 70° F., watering to provide vigorous growth; but plants should not start to run before they go to the garden. When setting in the garden, do not disturb the roots.

How can I tell when muskmelons are ready to pick? Most varieties of muskmelon develop a yellowish color as they mature. Watch the place where the stem joins the fruit. When this begins to crack and the stem comes off cleanly and freely, the melons are ready to harvest. Some varieties are not quite ready for the table at this stage but should be kept a few days in a sunny windowsill until they become a little soft at the blossom end. Varieties differ considerably in the application of these tests. When ripe, the fruits must be refrigerated, as they can spoil very fast.

Can you please tell me how to grow good quality muskmelons? I planted some last summer on a pile of old sod. I had melons, but they were quite tasteless and flat. Lack of sweetness and flavor in muskmelons may be due to cool, moist weather during the maturing period and to loss of leaves by disease. Active foliage is required to make sugar. Varieties also differ in quality.

Our muskmelons grow only as large as an egg. Why? There are many possible reasons for this. This may be due to a lack of phosphorus and lime in the soil. It may be due to a lack of water or the presence of insects. On sandy soils, it may be a lack of fertility. If the vines are vigorous, it may be due to a lack of potash.

Can I raise muskmelons in the clayey but well-drained soil of this region? (New Jersey.) Yes. Add humus; do not plant until the soil is warm. Try the variety 'Hearts of Gold'.

How can I fight muskmelon diseases? Plant disease-resistant varieties. Treat seed with captan or thiram. When plants come up, they should be faithfully dusted for striped cucumber beetle. Keep free from weeds; some of them carry mosaic, which injures the crop.

How can I keep cantaloupe vines from wilting about the time the fruit starts to grow? This is due to the work of the cucumber beetle when the plants are young. As they feed on the foliage, they inoculate the plants with the wilt organism. A cold frame with mosquito netting over it placed over the plants until they are well started will keep the beetles off and thus prevent the wilt. Methoxychlor will control beetles.

I live on the north shore of Long Island; I should like to grow some melons. What kind is best? Growers on Long Island and in Connecticut have had good success with 'Delicious 51'. Other good varieties are 'Burpee Hybrid', 'Saticoy', 'Iroquois', 'Harper Hybrid', and 'Supermarket'.

What are the best varieties of muskmelons? Muskmelon varieties vary widely in their adaptation to regions. In the southern half of the country the 'Hale Best' group does very well, but it does not thrive under the cooler, more humid, conditions of the North. 'Mainerock' is both early and adapted to cool weather. 'Delicious 51' is a good early. 'Harper Hybrid', 'Burpee Hybrid', 'Iroquois', and 'Gold Star' all do well in various sections of the North.

OKRA (ABELMOSCHUS ESCULENTUS)

How much seed is necessary to plant 30 feet of okra? One half ounce of okra seed will plant 100 feet of row, usually enough seed in a packet for 25 or 30 feet. The plants should stand at least 12 or 15 inches apart.

How and when should okra be planted? I have been unsuccessful in trying to raise them. When the soil is well warmed—that is, about the same time as beans. The soil should not be acid, and better plants and pods will result if it is fertile. Okra needs, in addition, lots of sun and a location where there is little risk of cold winds.

What caused most of my okra to grow to immense size but to set only a few pods? In all probability, some fertilizer too rich in nitrogen has been used. Unfavorable weather conditions, however, may have been the cause. Long periods of rain often result in poor pollination.

In a fairly good soil where other vegetables grow well, for 4 years in succession, okra has done poorly. The leaves turn yellow, wither, and die. This sounds like either a disease working in the stems or root lice or other insects working on the fine roots. The soil should be well limed. Dig up a plant next time and see whether root lice are causing the trouble. They infest okra at times. Aphids are carried by ants. Treat the soil with diazinon before planting to get rid of ants.

At what size should okra pods be picked? When they are young and tender—finger length, and not too thick through. Large pods are too pithy and tough to be palatable.

ONION (ALLIUM CEPA)

What is the correct way to raise onions? Grow onions from sets for summer, or from seed or plants for winter storage. The soil should be well limed, fertile, and abundantly supplied with nitrogen; work in 5 pounds of a complete fertilizer to 100 square feet. Harvest when the tops begin to break over and die. Use small sets to prevent large neck and seed stalks.

What is the best way to grow onions in the small garden? From onion sets—very small onions which made their limited growth the previous season. These will furnish the early onions. They are available in early spring from garden centers and mail-order houses. Those for later use and winter storage can be grown from seed. The soil must not be acid and should be extra-well-fertilized.

For fall and winter use, is it best to plant seed, plants, or sets of onions? Sets for early onions, and plants for late onions for storage. Growing from seed is more difficult and uncertain.

When should onion sets be planted? How deep? As soon as the soil can be made ready in the spring. Push into prepared soil, leaving ½ inch above the top of the sets. If large onions are wanted, the sets should be 3 to 4 inches apart; for scallions or bunch onions, about 1 inch apart. Do not plan to thin out and use alternate onions for scallions, as this disturbs the roots of those left to form large bulbs.

What are onion sets? Onion sets are grown by sowing seed thickly, 50 to 60 pounds per acre, in drills or rows 2 or 3 inches wide. The seedlings should be grown on fairly clean soil. The tops will begin to turn yellow in July. When mature, they are pulled and the tops cut off.

They are piled in the field in shallow piles for a week if the weather is dry. Then they are stored under cover in shallow trays with good ventilation. Only varieties that store well as mature bulbs will keep as sets. Spanish types are worthless.

Please give the easiest way for the home gardener to raise onion sets for the following year. Or is it better to raise onions from seed in one season? For home use it is better to buy sets or plants in the spring and raise a crop of bulbs from these.

What is the proper way to grow onions from seed? Plant the seed in rows early in the spring as soon as the ground can be worked. Make rows 12 to 15 inches apart; sow 8 to 10 seeds per inch; cover ¼ inch deep; thin to stand 2 to 3 inches apart in the row. Use fertile, well-drained soil, liberally limed, then cultivate to keep out weeds. Watch for thrips on the young seedlings. Harvest when the tops begin to die after they break over. Cure thoroughly, under cover, before storing for winter.

What kinds of onion seed do I need for my market garden to supply good green onions all summer? What kind of fertilizer do they require? (Michigan.) 'White Portugal' and 'Evergreen Long White Bunching' are grown for this purpose, but any variety recommended for the northern states is good for growing green onions. In order to have them all summer it is necessary to make successive plantings of seed at 2- to 3-week intervals. An 8–6–6 fertilizer at the rate of 400 pounds to the acre, broadcast over the surface when the ground is prepared, should be ample for green onions.

Can I raise 'Bermuda' onions from seed? (Ohio.) Yes, but unless the seed is sown early (in a greenhouse) and transplanted, the onions will be much smaller than those sold in stores. The 'Sweet Spanish' types have all but replaced 'Bermuda'.

How and when should 'Bermuda' onions be planted to grow large? Get plants from a southern plant grower or from a seed supply firm. Set the plants, as soon as the ground can be prepared, in rich soil, and make provision for watering during dry weather.

How should 'Bermuda' onions be stored for best results? They store poorly. Use storage types instead.

What fertilizer is best to use in a sandy soil to grow big onions from sets? A 7–7–7 or an 8–6–6. Compost or well-rotted manure, plus a complete fertilizer (such as 5–10–5), usually give a satisfactory crop. Wood ashes are excellent for onions.

Do onions need lime? Onions should be grown on soil with a good lime content—not because the onion actually needs so much calcium but because the presence of lime helps to aerate the soil, enabling the plants to grow better.

What is the botanical name of the onion that bears little bulblets at the top?   This is the perennial tree (or Egyptian tree) onion, *Allium cepa proliferum*. It is winter-hardy.

What are "multiplier" onions good for?   The multiplier onion is probably a sport of the regular onion and is used for flavoring, just as regular onions are used. It is often confused with the species mentioned above.

What is the botanical name for shallots and how are they grown?   The shallot is *Allium cepa aggregatum*. It is propagated by planting the sections or cloves of which the large bulb consists.

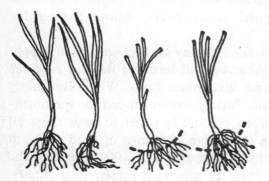

Onion seedlings ready for transplanting. Tops and roots (right) are trimmed back as indicated.

I had very bad luck with onions. They were no bigger than seed onions at the end of the season and the green onions were very thin. What was wrong?   If they did not stay green, it may have been due to thrips on the leaves, lice or maggots on the roots, poor soil, a lack of lime in the soil, or too much nitrogen.

Could onion seeds be sown in the fall, or in February? I'm especially interested in 'Sweet Spanish' types. (Missouri.)   Both seed and sets can be planted in the fall and winter months if the soil can be prepared properly. The large Spanish onions are usually sown in seed beds and then transplanted in the spring only.

Should blossoms of onions be cut?   If the flower stalk is cut, water might rot the bulb. If the flower stalks are forming, they can be recognized when the neck of the onion is small. They should be broken over (not cut) to prevent the neck of the onion from getting too large. A big-necked onion does not keep well in storage.

How do I grow large onions? When should they be taken up?   Their size depends on the weather, how well the soil has been prepared, adequate thinning (2 to 3 inches apart while plants are small), and keeping the crop absolutely free from weeds. Only large-type onions, such as the 'Sweet Spanish' varieties, produce big bulbs. Dig bulbs when they are large or when tops fall over.

What causes onion tops to fall over and turn brown? This is normally the sign that the bulbs have attained maturity. The tops, then of no further service to the plant in manufacturing its food, naturally shrivel and collapse. If the onions are not matured, drought may be the cause, or thrips.

Does planting onions near gladioli increase the possibility of the latter being attacked by thrips? It would not make much difference; if thrips are bad, it is because of weather conditions being favorable for their multiplication. Any crop that harbors thrips will increase their population for crops that follow. Control thrips with Sevin or diazinon according to the directions on the container.

How can I prevent onions from becoming sunburned? White varieties sometimes sunscald or turn green. Gather as soon as their tops begin to die; spread out thinly, under cover, but with good ventilation until their tops dry up, then remove the tops.

How do I keep dry onions from sprouting in the winter months? If onions are kept too warm in a room where the air is moist or where light enters, they will sprout. Some onions will sprout more than others because the bulbs have not been properly cured. Some varieties keep better than others. The best winter keeper of all is 'Spartan Sleeper', which can be stored at room temperature for 6 months or more before spoiling.

Please name some good varieties of onions for the home garden. *Early:* 'Crystal White Wax', 'Silver Skin' ('White Portugal'). *Midseason:* 'Yellow Globe', mild. *Late:* 'Southport White Globe', 'Sweet Spanish' types, 'Gigantic Gibraltar', all mild; 'Ebenezer', 'Yellow Globe', medium mild. Best storage onion is 'Spartan Sleeper'.

PARSLEY (PETROSELINUM CRISPUM)

How should parsley be grown? Does it tolerate shade? Parsley does not do well in a shady place. As a matter of fact, there are very few vegetables that do, not even the ones that do not tolerate too much heat and drought. Parsley can be sown in good, friable, well-enriched garden soil as soon in the spring as the ground can be prepared. Make rows shallow and cover lightly with fine soil. Sow seed about 10 or 20 to the foot, or thicker if you want to use the thinnings. If sizable plants are wanted, they should be thinned to from 5 to 8 inches apart. Adequate water supply is important.

Should the parsley bed be covered during the winter? If so, what material should be used?   Excelsior or dry leaves or some other material that will not become wet and form a mat will keep the plants green well into the winter. Still better, transfer some of the plants to a tight frame; if the latter is reasonably frostproof, they should last through the winter.

My parsley plant stops growing when taken indoors, ball, root, and all, even though it stands with other plants that thrive. Why does it do this?   This sounds like the turnip-rooted parsley, which will become dormant. It is better to use the regular parsley, which is fibrous-rooted.

How can I successfully transplant parsley from outside beds for winter window gardening?   Soak the ground around the plants the day before you wish to move them. Dig the plants by leaving a small ball of soil around the roots and set in a window box in soil that has not been treated with chemical fertilizer. Trim off at least half of the outside leaves.

Why does my parsley, brought in from out-of-doors and potted, turn dark at the edge of its leaves and look as if it was dying?   Parsley brought in from out-of-doors should be cut back to the crown so it can make new growth. Old leaves will wither. Water sparingly at first, increasing as growth starts. Parsley requires several hours of sunshine a day to do well indoors. Young plants started in August are much better for winter use than old roots. All herbs grown indoors do better if fluorescent tubes supplement daylight.

Are the bottoms of parsley plants good to eat? If so, how would you use them?   The roots of turnip-rooted (or parsnip-rooted) parsley are edible. Use in soups.

How can I make my parsley seed germinate more quickly?   The natural germination period is long. Soak the seeds for 24 hours in tepid water before planting to soften the hard shells. After soaking, run tepid water through the seed to remove a natural chemical that slows germination.

PARSNIP (PASTINACA SATIVA)

How can I have long, fleshy, well-developed parsnips?   Soil for parsnips should be very well and deeply worked to a depth of 12 to 18 inches. If perfect roots are desired, all stone and hard clods must be removed from the soil, which should be enriched with compost. Plant seeds early in the spring in rows 18 to 20 inches apart, covering ¼ to ½ inch deep. Thin to 4 inches apart. Grow on through the entire season, cultivating the ground as needed. The crop will be ready in autumn and can be stored, or some can be left in the ground (as they are perfectly hardy) for digging in winter and spring.

How are exhibition parsnips grown? Deep holes, 4, 5, or 6 inches apart, are made with a crowbar, in well-prepared, pulverized soil. These are filled with sifted soil and compost and 3 or 4 seeds are planted on top of this. When seedlings develop, all but one are removed. Such roots are often 3 to 4 feet long when dug at the end of the season.

What variety of parsnip is best to grow? Though 'Hollow Crown' is the standard, 'All-American' is newer and preferable because the roots are thick but chunky, and so can be well grown without such deep preparation.

PEANUT (ARACHIS HYPOGAEA)

What is the proper time for planting and care, cultivation, and harvesting of peanuts? The nuts (removed from the shells) are planted an inch deep and about a foot apart in well-prepared, light soil. Manure and nitrogenous fertilizers are avoided. Rows should be 3 feet apart. Give clean cultivation until after the blossoms at the base of the plant (which are not readily found) are produced. Mulching around the base of the plant at this time is beneficial and helps keep down weeds for the balance of the season. Plant about the same time as the first sowing of sweet corn. At least 4 months are required to produce the crop.

What should one do to make peanuts give a better yield in sandy Michigan ground? This may be a water and a fertility problem. Perhaps the season is too cool for peanuts to grow satisfactorily. They require warm nights for a considerable period.

Do you think it is possible to grow peanuts successfully as far north as I live, in Spokane, Washington? The season in your part of the country should be amply long even if the seed is sown outdoors in the usual way, but night temperatures are unfavorable. While peanuts do not transplant readily, they can be started in small peat or Jiffy-7 pots and the young plants set out after the danger of frost has passed. The time gained results in a larger crop and is best in a region like yours with cool nights.

PEA (PISUM SATIVUM)

Are green peas very hard to raise?   In areas where hot weather, and especially hot nights, is likely to come suddenly, they are difficult. Peas are easy to grow if the soil is in good condition and the seed is planted very early in the season. Only one variety, 'Wando', will set pods in hot weather.

What sort of weather and climate do peas prefer?   Cool nights with bright, cool days.

What kind of soil, weather conditions, etc., are necessary for growing green peas in a home garden? What variety is best?   A good soil that is well limed and does not contain an excess of nitrogen. The subsoil should be open so the roots can penetrate it. Peas should be planted as early as possible to get them to set pods before hot weather. 'Little Marvel', 'Novella', and 'Green Arrow' are good dwarf varieties. 'Freezonian', 'Midfreezer', 'Mammoth Podded Extra Early', and 'Lincoln' are good 2½ footers. 'Alderman' and 'Sugar Snap' (edible-podded) are excellent tall ones. Only the variety 'Wando' will set pods in hot weather.

Do garden peas require a new soil to do their best?   Not unless the soil is infected with root diseases. Lime will work wonders for peas. Don't overfertilize them. Use a starter solution. Water in dry weather.

What fertilizer is necessary to produce a good growth of peas?   If the soil is properly limed and generally fertile, you do not need any fertilizer. In a garden, a starter solution poured on the seed when it is planted should be enough.

What particular soil feeding do peas need? I have good loam soil that produces excellent beans, tomatoes, etc., but peas do not do well. The plot is well manured each year although I haven't used any commercial fertilizer.   You may need some lime. Also the soil may have too much nitrogen. Peas must be planted as early as the ground can be prepared.

Is hen manure good fertilizer for growing peas? What causes pods to dry up instead of maturing properly?   No. Peas do not need the nitrogen that is present in the chicken manure. If peas grow too rapidly because of too much nitrogen and water, the pods may start to grow without being fertilized and will dry up, as there is no seed in them. Hot weather also causes them to shrivel.

When should peas be planted, both smooth and wrinkled sorts?   Either type may be sown just as early in the spring as a good, mellow seed bed can be prepared. The sole advantage of the smooth-seeded sorts is that they are a trifle hardier and can be planted a few days earlier; usually this is scarcely sufficient compensation for their lower quality.

When is the proper time to plant peas on the eastern shore of Maryland? Late fall or very early spring.

When is the right time to plant garden peas, also sweet peas, in this locality? (Missouri.) In the fall or as early as the ground can be prepared in the spring.

Is it possible to raise peas in the fairly well-drained, rather clayey soil of this region? (New Jersey.) Yes, if the soil is properly limed. Don't use too much nitrogen. Plant the peas before the first of April, if possible. Try 'Little Marvel' for early peas and 'Laxton's Progress' for a little later.

Can you tell me if it is possible to raise peas on light soil? Yes. Be sure that the soil has sufficient lime and humus, then use a starter solution on the seed when it is planted.

Is it possible to grow peas near salt water? (Massachusetts.) Yes, if the spray does not hit them and the ground does not contain salt.

How early can garden peas be started in my locality? Also, will peas grow in practically full shade or do they require some sunlight? (New Jersey.) Plant as early as possible. This may be April 1 or even earlier. Peas will not grow in the shade; they require full sunshine, especially in the morning.

Why are peas a poor crop in northern Virginia? This may be due to a lack of lime in the soil or to hot dry weather when the pods are ready to set. Peas must be planted in the fall or very early spring.

Is there any type of garden peas that can be planted in the fall or winter for an extra-early crop? (New Jersey.) Any variety of garden peas can be planted in the fall if they are planted late enough so that they won't germinate until spring. Drainage must be perfect; how they will come through depends largely on the winter weather.

Do dwarf peas need support? If so, what kind? While they do not need support, it is well to use it if possible in the home garden; the rows can be planted closer (24 inches or so) and the crop is more easily tended and picked than when the vines are allowed to sprawl.

What is the best support for peas and sweet peas? Cut brush, if it can be obtained; if not, use wire or string. Most seed firms sell a reusable trellis netting that pea vines can cling to. The support should be 15 to 18 inches for dwarf peas, 5 to 6 feet for tall peas and sweet peas.

What makes pea vines wither and turn brown before they mature? Hot weather; aphids; diseases; soil in poor physical condition or with poor aeration.

What insects are most common on peas? Plant lice or aphids. (See Section 13.)

What do I do for garden pea weevil? Place seed in an airtight container, drop a few drops of carbon disulfide in the can, and cover tightly.

What fungus diseases attack garden peas? How can they be identified? How can they be prevented or controlled? Powdery mildew on the leaves can be controlled with dusting sulfur. Root rots causing brown roots, caused by poor aeration of the soil, can be corrected by deeper tilling and more lime in the soil. When possible, rotate plantings each year.

What is the most effective way of protecting young peas and other succulent seedlings from slugs during wet weather in the spring? Sprinkle some hydrated lime on the ground under the vines and even on the lower leaves on the vines. Or use slug baits sold in garden centers.

What treatment do you recommend for mildew on peas? Dust with flowers of sulfur or a sulfur-lime dust.

How can sparrows be kept from eating the peas and beans as they come through the earth? Some short pieces of rope should be placed where the birds will see them. (Birds fear snakes.) Or cover the row with a strip of close-mesh wire.

What is the difference between smooth-seeded and wrinkled peas? Smooth-seeded are hardier for very early sowing, but the crop is inferior in quality. Smooth-seeded peas take two months to mature. Wrinkled-seeded are a little less hardy, the seeds being more apt to rot in cold, wet ground, but the quality and yield are superior. Treat seed with captan to prevent rot. (For varieties, see the following questions.)

What are the best edible-podded pea varieties? The variety called 'Sugar Snap' belonging to a new class of edible-podded pea called snap peas, growing fat, edible pods and sweet, succulent peas is outstanding. (Unlike old-fashioned garden peas that need shelling, edible-podded peas can be eaten pod-and-all.) All that's needed with 'Sugar Snap' is the removal of a string along the top of the pod. This comes away automatically when the stem part of the pea is pulled off. Some of the older edible-podded pea varieties, so much used in oriental cuisine, are also easily grown in the home garden. The advantages of these varieties, such as 'Snowbird' and 'Dwarf Gray Sugar', are that they come into bearing before 'Sugar Snap', which requires about 70 days to reach harvest, and they do not grow taller than 2 to 3 feet. 'Sugar Snap' grows 6 feet tall and needs sturdy support for the heavy vines. Other snap pea varieties ('SugarBon', 'SugarMel', and 'SugarRae') grow only about 30 inches high.

What varieties of peas are best for freezing?   Edible-podded or snow peas are excellent for freezing. Among standard peas 'Freezonian' is the outstanding variety for freezing. 'Little Marvel', which is one of the best home-garden varieties, is also a very good freezing variety, as are 'Lincoln' and 'Wando'.

PEPPER (CAPSICUM ANNUUM)

How can I have early sweet peppers?   Buy plants from a local grower or start seeds indoors in March under lights. Set out when all danger of frost is past—just a little later than you set out tomatoes in your locality.

How do you make pepper plants bear? Mine grow beautifully but bear late and little.   Grow them with little or no nitrogen. Use only lime and a 0–12–12 fertilizer.

Why do I have no success with sweet peppers? The plants have many flowers and tiny peppers but very few that can be used, yet the plants are nice and big.   The plants are too vigorous. Try growing them on less fertile soil and do not put any nitrogen or manure on until the peppers are set and partially grown. Try using a liquid fertilizer side-dressing. Temperatures below 50° F. or above 90° F. cause flowers and small fruits to drop off.

What makes fruit drop off pepper plants in the summer?   Too much nitrogen, a boron deficiency, or high or very low temperatures when the flowers are setting fruits. Grow them slower until the fruit is set.

Should green pepper plants be pinched back?   Pinch out the growing tip of the plants at 6 inches. Later pinching will slow their harvest.

If sweet pepper plants are brought indoors in the fall, will they continue to bear during the winter?   Yes, if moved carefully and with sufficient soil, but it would be difficult. Peppers need high temperatures, humidity, and sunshine.

What peppers shall I grow?   *Sweet:* 'Early Pimiento', 'Better Bell', 'Big Bertha', 'Gypsy', 'Fordhook', 'Ace', and 'Sweet Banana'. *Hot:* 'Long Red Cayenne' or 'Hungarian Wax' (yellow).

POTATO (SOLANUM TUBEROSUM)

Are there any tricks about raising enough potatoes for our own use next winter? How many potatoes should we plant to get about seven bushels?   Potatoes are somewhat more difficult to grow for home use than most other vegetables. A few fundamentals must be observed. These include choosing a loamy soil, using healthy stock, and practicing a thorough program of weed control and of spraying for insects and blight. To raise about seven bushels of potatoes, plant about 30 to 50 pounds of seed stock. The former figure assumes a fifteenfold increase, which is somewhat above the average. If soil temperatures go above 85° F., tubers stop growing. A heavy mulch keeps soil cool.

Is it profitable to grow potatoes in the home garden?   It depends on whether potatoes grow well in your locality, on the size of the garden, and similar considerations. In the suburban garden of a family with a normal liking for potatoes and located near a store, the answer is probably "No." Potatoes are a big commercial crop that does not suffer too much in quality by being stored and shipped. For another opinion, see below.

Are home-grown potatoes of superior eating quality?   Definitely yes! Fresh-dug potatoes are tender, mealy, and delicious, with an especially fine flavor.

What soil do you suggest for potatoes?   Potatoes are not adapted to heavy and poorly drained soils. Farmers who do not have good potato soil grow other crops. A good potato soil is one which is loamy or friable to a depth of at least 12 inches. In choosing a soil for potatoes, it is fortunate if one can be found which is naturally quite acid in reaction. Otherwise, there will be trouble with potato scab. It is fairly easy to change, by liming, a soil which is too acid, but it is difficult to acidify a soil which is naturally within the range favorable to scab, i.e., anything above pH 5.6.

What are the best commercial fertilizers on a sandy loam for a potato crop? For clay soil?   Sandy soils are particularly deficient in soil nutrients, especially in potash. For this reason, potato growers on the sandier soils usually use large applications of such fertilizers as 5–10–10 and 4–8–12. For heavier soils, use a fertilizer relatively high in phosphoric acid, such as 4–12–4 and 5–10–5. Soil with a high clay content tends to tie up or make unavailable the phosphorous element, thereby increasing the danger of deficiency unless supplied in excess.

What is needed in fertilizer for potatoes in home gardens? My soil has a good deal of oak-leaf humus.   Since such soil is well supplied with humus, the principal need for nutrients would be phosphoric acid and potash. It may be desirable to add some form of commercial nitrogen to hasten the decomposition of the humus—such as sulfate of ammonia. Whether or not this garden soil needs lime depends on its present reaction. Lime can cause trouble. A pH reading of 5.6 or lower will prevent scab. Use calcium sulfate (gypsum) if a soil test shows calcium is needed. There is probably enough acid, but you should have the soil tested.

What are certified seed potatoes?   Certified seed potatoes are potatoes stored, treated, planted, and harvested under definite rules of sanitation. They are inspected for symptoms of any virus disease. There is a final bin inspection before the potatoes are bagged for shipment. If the potatoes pass inspection, they are certified by the state as being free from virus diseases.

How should seed potatoes be prepared for planting?   Cut the seed potatoes into several pieces, each of which should have one strong eye, or two, and a good piece of the tuber. The "eye" is a dormant bud from which a new plant will grow, and its first food will be derived from the piece of tuber. Plant only certified, disease-free seed potatoes. Small seed potatoes need not be cut.

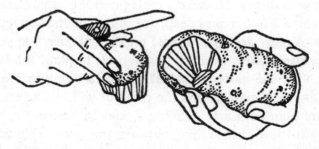

Large potatoes can be cut up into seed pieces. These should have at least two good, strong eyes.

Are seed potatoes planted immediately after cutting?   They may be, but it is better practice to lay the cut pieces out in flats or shallow trays, skin side up, and leave them in a sunny but airy place for from 1 to 4 weeks until the "eyes" sprout. Or the whole potatoes may thus be sprouted before cutting. Unlike sprouts produced in the root cellar on stored potatoes, these sprouts will be dark green and closely clustered in the eyes close to the tuber. They are then planted, eyes up.

Should I use large or small seed potatoes?   Small tubers of certified seed potatoes are best.

How many pounds of seed potatoes are needed for planting a half acre? (Illinois.)   Most experiments show that 9 to 10 bushels of seed would be the approximate amount needed to plant a half acre of potatoes on upland soil.

How many potatoes should be planted in a hill?   Place one piece of tuber every 12 inches and cover with 3 inches of soil.

When is the best time to plant early potatoes?   About a month before the last spring frost is expected. By the time the young plants have come up through 3 inches of soil, any frost likely to hurt them should then be past.

When should late potatoes be planted?   The word "late" as applied by gardeners means late in reaching maturity, not late in time of planting. Your seed catalog will show approximately the number of days for the variety you select; count back this number from the expected date of first frosts in the fall.

How deep should early and late potatoes be planted?   Early varieties of potatoes (planted early) should be planted shallower than late potatoes. Shallower planting results in earlier emergence, which in turn tends to hasten maturity. However, most potatoes, regardless of variety, should be planted 3 to 5 inches deep, depending on the soil type.

Since July–August droughts almost regularly injure late potato plantings in the central states, would it not be well to plant the late potatoes early, along with the early potatoes?   The late potatoes are varieties which take longer to mature, and the drought will affect them no matter when they are planted. Early planting would be better. Try spreading a mulch of straw 4 to 6 inches thick between the rows. This will conserve moisture and keep down weeds.

Is it practical to mulch potatoes in this area? (Southeast Kansas.) How do I do it?   Yes, entirely practical. Before dry weather, spread straw to a depth of 4 to 6 inches between the rows and close up to the plants.

Should potatoes be grown under straw?   The effect of a straw mulch is to maintain a lower soil temperature, to conserve moisture, and to control weeds. The straw should be applied about the time the potato plants are emerging. If applied too early, growth is retarded; if too late, the plants already started will be injured by the straw. Often as much as 12 inches of straw is used when the entire growing area is covered.

Is it possible to plant potatoes in January, February, and March? There are frosty nights but sunshine in the daytime; there is no snow. (California.) Plant the seed potatoes four or five weeks before the frosty nights are expected to end.

What is lacking in the earth that our potatoes don't grow to a normal size? They are perfect and of good flavor but remain very small. They seem to grow well and have plenty of top. There are two probable reasons. Your soil may be deficient in nitrogen, phosphoric acid, or potash. Too little fertilizer or too little organic matter in the soil may be responsible. High soil temperature (above 85° F.) stops suberization (tuber growth). If in your judgment none of these factors is involved, the most likely explanation is that the seed you have planted is infected with virus disease. The principal virus diseases are mosaic and leaf roll. Purchase certified or disease-free seed.

I grow wonderful potato vines in my garden, but the tubers are seldom larger than marbles. What can I do about it? Large potato vines and poor yields may indicate an excess of nitrogen or a deficiency of potash and phosphorus. This can be corrected by an increased application of phosphoric acid and potash. If the garden has had an abundance of organic matter, the difficulty might be corrected merely by using superphosphate, broadcasting it and working it in when preparing the plot. Another possibility is that the garden does not get enough sun. Too much shade causes an excessive ratio of top to the tuber in potatoes.

In potato growing, when should I harvest them? When the vines have completely died down. The tubers make no growth after that.

Is light harmful to potatoes after they are dug? Yes, they acquire an unpleasant flavor and should be exposed to the sun only long enough so that the adhering soil may be easily removed. (Greened potatoes are poisonous.) Then they should be taken to the cellar or some other dark storage area.

How should potatoes be stored? In a very cool cellar, and so piled or arranged that a little air can circulate around them; otherwise they are likely to sweat. Loosely woven potato sacks are satisfactory, or slat crates—much better than solid boxes or bins.

How can flea beetle and potato beetle be controlled on home-grown potato plants? When insect pests appear, use an all-purpose potato dust or spray that controls both pests and diseases. A bacterial culture containing *Bacillus thuringiensis* and sold under various trade names kills beetles as they feed. Also, look at the underside of leaves for their little clusters of orange-colored eggs and destroy these.

What causes scab on potatoes? A fungus, *Actinomyces scabies,* which thrives best in light, alkaline soils. It can be brought into the garden by infected seed potatoes; if it is already in the soil, be very wary of using lime on the potato patch. This organism does not endure acid conditions.

How often and with what should potatoes be sprayed to control late blight? The best safeguard against this disease is maneb or chlorothalonil applied as a spray. As plants increase in size, more spray is needed for thorough coverage. The spray should be applied often enough to keep all of the new growth completely covered throughout the season. Under conditions favoring rapid growth, this means an application at least every 7 to 10 days after the plants are 6 inches high.

What are early, medium, and late varieties of potatoes? First, the type of soil, climate, and other local conditions should be considered. In general, 'Irish Cobbler' is the favorite early, though many prefer 'Chippewa' or 'Early Ohio'. For midseason, 'Katahdin' and 'Kennebec'. 'Green Mountain' does well on heavier soils. For the late crop, 'Jersey Red' and 'Sebago' are among the best.

What are the best-tasting potatoes to raise? Plant 'Early Ohio' for the first crop, 'Katahdin' for the second, and if your soil, culture, and climate are good, the potatoes will be of fine flavor.

Does the 'Katahdin' potato do well in the corn belt? (Illinois.) When grown as a late potato, the 'Katahdin' does as well or better than the members of the Rural group in the northern part of the corn belt. Trials in the southern part of the corn belt have been inconclusive.

What experiments have been made with 'Sebago' potatoes and with what result? 'Sebago' has proved widely adaptable and very satisfactory as a late variety in the New England states and in New York. 'Sebago' is definitely later in maturity, white-skinned, lower in starch content, and much more resistant to scab, blight, and mosaic than is 'Green Mountain'. Experience to date would indicate that it is also more widely adapted to adverse potato soil and climate than 'Green Mountain'. Seed-spacing tests both in Maine and New York indicate larger seed pieces and more seed to the acre are desirable with 'Sebago' than with 'Green Mountain'.

Has there been any real improvement over the 'Early Rose' and 'Green Mountain' potato? No variety exists today that has a higher starch content than 'Green Mountain'. Such varieties as 'Chippewa', 'Katahdin', 'Sebago', and 'Sequoia' are lower in starch content but much more resistant to disease and more productive. However, some varieties, such as 'Houma' and 'Mohawk', have as much starch content and are as mealy as 'Green Mountain' and 'Early Rose'.

PUMPKIN (CUCURBITA PEPO)

What is the best way to grow good pumpkins? Soil for pumpkins should be well enriched. If good garden ground is used, it is not necessary to make up special hills, but if the soil is a bit poor, work a forkful or two of compost into each hill. Plantings should be made after frost danger is past, with rows 8 feet apart and hills 4 to 8 feet apart in the row. Cover the seed about an inch deep. Dusting for striped beetle will be necessary during early growth.

Are pumpkins planted in sun or shade? Pumpkins should have little or no shade.

What method does one follow to force or produce supersized pumpkins or squash? Does it help to cut off branch tips and keep them in a dish of milk? The plants should be grown under favorable conditions of soil and climate. The soil should be fertile and moisture-holding. If rainfall is short, water frequently. Plants are spaced widely, about 8 to 12 feet. Allow the whole plant to grow, but remove extra fruits, leaving only 1 or 2 per plant. Sidedress the plants with a little complete fertilizer as the season goes along. Nothing is gained by cutting off the tip of the branch and keeping it in a dish of milk.

What are some good pumpkin varieties? 'Big Max' is a variety of large pumpkin, but 'Small Sugar' is considered better for cooking and pies. The 'Cushaws' (including the 'Green Striped', 'Tennessee Sweet Potato', 'Golden Cushaw', and 'Large Cheese') are favored in the South. 'Cinderella' is a bush variety for smaller gardens (6 square feet to a single plant).

RADISH (RAPHANUS SATIVUS)

What soil and plant food are necessary to produce good radishes? Any soil that does not bake too hard will produce good radishes. Use fertilizers low in nitrogen. All organic materials such as leafmold, compost, and humus are beneficial. Sprinkle land plaster (gypsum), 3 or 4 pounds to 50 feet, along the rows and work into the soil before planting.

Why can't we raise radishes of any kind?   This is hard to understand. Radishes are very easy to grow. Plant seed from April 1 to May 15, using early varieties. Thin seedlings to stand 1½ inches apart when the first set of true leaves appear. They are a cool-weather crop. Perhaps you plant them too late in the spring.

What should be done when my radishes all grow into tops instead of radishes?   Probably the weather is too warm. (See the above question.)

What happened to my second crop of radishes and lettuce planted in July? They came up 2 inches and would go no farther. The first crop was fine. I have sandy soil. (Indiana.)   July is a poor month to sow radishes and lettuce. Midsummer temperatures are not conducive to the production of these crops in your area. The variety 'Icicle' does better in hot weather but still must be sown earlier than July in most northern regions.

I have a small greenhouse and the radishes I planted have long, thin red stalks between the green leaves and the radish itself. What is the remedy for this?   Evidently the soil is too rich in nitrogen, the night temperatures are too high, and they are not being thinned out sufficiently.

What are the names of some improved radish varieties?   'Cherry Belle', 'Champion', 'Comet', 'Sparkler' (red with a white tip); 'Giant Butter' (very large, and remains a long time in good condition); 'Long Scarlet' and 'White Icicle', both long and narrow, the latter less peppery than the former. Winter radishes: 'White' and 'Scarlet Chinese' and 'Long Black Spanish'.

RHUBARB (RHEUM RHABARBARUM)

How do you prepare the bed for rhubarb roots?   Make sure that the soil is rich and well drained. If you have rotted manure or compost, it should be liberally spread and dug in. Set the roots in holes 6 inches deep and 18 to 24 inches apart, with crowns just below the surface. Firm the soil about them with your feet, applying full weight.

What yearly care is needed for established rhubarb roots?   In autumn, mulch the entire surface of the bed with compost or rotted manure. In the spring, dig this into the bed lightly, being careful not to cut the roots. An application of high-nitrogen fertilizer will hasten spring growth and produce tender, juicy stalks.

How is rhubarb propagated? Rhubarb is usually propagated by dividing the older roots. This is best done in the early spring just as the first buds appear. Use a sharp spade to cut the old root into pieces, having at least 1 and preferably 2 or 3 buds at the top. Set the cut pieces in the new location immediately, with the buds just at the surface of the soil; water in well.

Do rhubarb roots ever need to be divided? Yes, about every second or third year for the best quality stalks.

When is the best time to reset pie-plant (rhubarb)—fall or early spring? Reset rhubarb in the early spring, as the first buds appear.

When is the best time to take up and move rhubarb? How many roots are placed in a hill and how do you fertilize them? I have plenty of barnyard manure. (See the above question.) Barnyard manure on a well-limed soil will grow good rhubarb. Divide old roots (free from any rot) into 2, 3, or more sections and place 1 section in a hill.

How do you cut rhubarb? Rhubarb is not cut, but *pulled,* as the whole leafstalk is usable. When young, vigorous leaves come up during the summer, rhubarb makes just as good sauce as in the spring. Pull only a few stalks for the first season, however, to give the plants a chance to get well established.

When should you divide rhubarb in California? Soon after it has stopped growing and has become dormant. If under irrigation, it should be made dormant by withholding water. After the leaves have dried, the plants can be divided and moved.

In forcing rhubarb, does it kill or injure plants for outdoor garden use? Forcing is very debilitating. Most forced plants are discarded. However, if you have space and patience, some clumps, replanted, may recover.

I have tried to grow rhubarb several times and in several locations. It always starts out well and grows part of a season, then the stalks seem to begin to rot, fall over, and the plant dies. Can you tell me what is wrong? This is due to a crown rot. If it gets into the plants and the soil, there is not much you can do except to get clean plants and set them where rhubarb has not grown before. The soil should not be acid. Rhubarb does better in the cooler parts of the country.

What is the best variety of rhubarb? 'MacDonald', 'Valentine', and 'Victoria' are considered tops.

ROQUETTE OR ROCKET SALAD (ERUCA VESICARIA SATIVA)

What is the lettucelike greens with a distinctive pungent flavor often served in salads in Italian restaurants? You probably mean roquette or rocket salad (*arugula* in Italian), a cool-season annual member of the mustard family. It is easy to grow from seed sown early in the spring at the same time you plant radishes and lettuce. The leaves can be cut, as needed, 3 to 4 weeks after sowing. Keep flowers and seedheads cut off. In warm weather, the leaves become tough and "hot," but sometimes the plants can be cut back nearly to the ground, and the resulting leaves can still be mixed with lettuce in a salad. Generally, though, it is best to make another sowing in late summer for fall use.

SALSIFY, OYSTER-PLANT (TRAGOPOGON PORRIFOLIUS)

What information can you give on the growing of vegetable-oyster or oyster-plant? Oyster-plant (salsify) requires 120 days of growing weather and a fertile, sandy loam soil. Sow seed early, in rows 18 to 20 inches apart, and thin plants to 4 inches. It requires a well-aerated subsoil to get long, fleshy roots. The flavor of the root is improved by freezing. It is better taken directly from the soil than if dug and placed in storage.

How hardy is salsify? Perfectly hardy. The roots can be left in the ground during the winter and dug during a thaw or in early spring.

I planted salsify last spring but it did not come up. Why? Salsify seed has a low germination at best and if it is several years old it will not germinate. It should be grown in well-limed soil. Obtain seed from a reliable source; sow thickly enough for the seeds to touch; if thinning is needed, do it early.

What caused my salsify to go to seed? It also rotted. Anything that causes a dormant period or a stoppage of growth processes due to dry weather can cause it to go to seed. The decay may be due to a boron deficiency in the soil or a lack of sufficient calcium. Usually a small percentage of roots will throw seed stalks; these should be pulled out.

Why does salsify grow 3 or 4 sprawly roots instead of one good root? This is the nature of the plant. The roots can be made to grow deeper and longer by extra-thorough and deep preparation and by loosening the subsoil. Make sure that the calcium supply is adequate.

SHALLOT   (See Onion.)

SORREL (RUMEX SCUTATUS)

Recently in a restaurant I was served a soup made from sorrel which was very refreshing on a hot summer day and which had a "sour" flavor. Can I grow this plant in my vegetable garden? How else is it used in cooking?   Yes, you can grow French sorrel. It is a perennial which will last for several years if the seedheads are removed. Most seed houses offer seed. Sow early in the spring. Consult French cookbooks for recipes. Sorrel is often used with fish.

SPINACH (SPINACIA OLERACEA)

What are the soil requirements for spinach?   Any fine, friable soil that can be worked into a mellow seed bed, and which is well supplied with organic matter and nitrogen, will grow spinach. The optimum pH level is 6.0 to 6.7, mildly acid.

When should spinach be planted?   *Very* early in spring, making 2 or 3 sowings, timed so that the last will mature before hot weather comes. Sow again in late summer, 50 to 60 days before frost for the fall crop. Seed should be treated with captan or thiram to prevent damping off.

What variety of spinach is satisfactory for the home garden?   'Bloomsdale Long-standing' does not throw up seed stalks quite as readily as some others. 'Melody' is disease-resistant.

Can you expect more than one cutting from spinach? Ours usually turns yellow after one cutting.   No. The whole spinach plant is cut at the soil surface—not picked off a leaf at a time.

Can spinach be grown in midsummer? If not, please suggest substitute greens.   Spinach bolts to seed in hot weather. The best substitute—and a very good one, too—is the so-called New Zealand spinach, which resembles spinach only when cooked. It loves heat and is very easy to grow, but makes a slow start. Soak seed 2 or 3 days before planting; sow 8 to 10 seeds to the foot in rows at least 24 inches apart; thin to about 8 inches. Although it grows best in hot weather, seed of New Zealand spinach will sprout only in cool soil. Seed early.

What is summer-spinach?   New Zealand spinach (*Tetragonia tetragonioides*), which is not spinach at all but is used as such and is often called summer-spinach. Seeds planted about April 1 will yield a harvest from about July 1 until frost. The plant is a tremendous yielder and only a few feet of rows are necessary for the average family. Like beets, there are a number of seeds in each seed pod. Seedlings can be readily transplanted to fill out a row, especially as the seed pods are apt to produce quite a large group of seedlings growing close together. (See the preceding question.)

SQUASH (CUCURBITA)

How should summer squash be planted to produce abundantly? Summer squash is not difficult to raise. Start with good seed. Seed can be sown when the danger of frost is past, with rows 4 to 5 feet apart and plants thinned to about 3 feet apart in the row. The soil should be well fertilized. Plant protectors, such as Hotkaps, will permit planting 2 or 3 weeks earlier, or plants can be started indoors in peat pots and grown under fluorescent lights. Faithful dusting for a few weeks with Sevin or methoxychlor will be necessary to control the striped cucumber beetle.

Are squash grown more successfully in hills or rows? In gardens where fertility is well maintained, the practice of making hills with compost or manure has been largely abandoned. This practice may be good where soil is not rich, stirring a couple of forkfuls of well-rotted compost into the soil under each hill.

When should summer squash be picked for best table quality? When the skin of the fruit is soft. On vigorous vines, the fruit will be about 6 inches long. They should be a lemon-yellow color. When orange-yellow, they are too old and the flesh gets coarse and tasteless. Zucchini types should be picked when they are 6 inches long or smaller.

What kind of soil should I use to grow winter squash? When and how should the seed be planted? Winter squash thrives in a rather wide variety of soils. Moderately heavy soils retain moisture better, are likely to be somewhat more fertile, and give good results. Seed should be planted about the time that tomatoes are set, when the danger of frost is past. In northern climates, practically the full season is required to mature them, for they need 100 to 130 days. They must be harvested before frost in the fall. Hills should be at least 6 feet each way; or thin to single plants 4 feet apart in rows.

How are winter squash harvested and stored? Winter squash should be harvested as late as possible before a fall frost. Cut with an inch or so of vine on either side of the stem. They must have a hard rind to keep well. You should not be able to dent them with your thumbnail. If well matured, they should be kept near the furnace for several weeks to cure them. After that they can be placed on shelves in a single layer in a dry place at 45° to 60° F. Don't pile them up. *Handle like eggs!*

How can striped cucumber beetle be controlled? By dusting the plants with methoxychlor or Sevin.

What can I use on the "stink bugs" that infest the squashes? The squash bug (commonly, and not without reason, called the "stink bug") can be trapped by laying a shingle or little board on the ground near the plants. This shelters the bugs at night and they can be destroyed in the morning. Removing and destroying egg masses and young are also helpful. Dust must be applied to the underside of the leaves as well as the surface. If you have only a few hills, make cases 2 × 2 × 1 foot, covered with mosquito netting, and keep these over the hills until the vines crowd the cases. This will give the vines a good start before being subjected to insect injury.

How can I protect my vine crops from stalk borers? By mulching with aluminum foil; squash borer moths are confused so they cannot locate the base of the stalk to lay their eggs. The variety 'Butternut' is immune to borers. Vines should be examined occasionally for borers. If found, they must be removed by carefully slitting the vines and removing. Also, keep the points of vines covered with soil to encourage them to root, thus by-passing the borers. Or spray or dust the plant stems with malathion or methoxychlor weekly.

What can be done about root maggots in vine crops? Root maggots are probably the larvae of the cucumber beetle. Keep the vines covered with Sevin or methoxychlor while they are young and the beetles won't come near them.

Can acorn squash be grown in southwest Ohio? 'Table King' acorn squash grows under a wide range of conditions, matures in 60 to 75 days from seed, is prolific, and is not difficult to grow. Grow in the same way as other squash but with a somewhat closer spacing of the plants.

Can acorn squash be stored through the winter months? Acorn squash can be stored successfully for several months, using the same method as with Hubbard or other winter squash. It probably will not keep in good shape as long as 'Blue Hubbard'.

Will 'Buttercup' squash produce satisfactorily if staked up in a garden to save or conserve space? The added exposure to heat, sun, and wind might be damaging. Saving space would be offset, at least partially, by shading other crops. However, they are sometimes grown this way.

What is the best small early winter squash to grow in northern Michigan? 'Kindred', a semibush squash, is early and prolific. It matures in about 60 days from seed; an early start may be gained by starting plants indoors as with muskmelon or by using plant protectors, such as Hotkaps, in the garden. For winter use, such small varieties as 'Table King', 'Butterbush', and 'Delicata' require only 60 to 75 days to mature from seed.

What are some satisfactory summer squash? 'Seneca Butterbar' and 'Gold Rush' for yellows; 'Aristocrat', 'Elite', 'Chefini', and 'Diplomat' for green.

What is the best variety of zucchini squash? 'Aristocrat' is very dark green, a heavy bearer, and edible until quite large. Many people consider it the best of the summer squashes in flavor and quality, although some of the new yellow zucchinis such as 'Gold Rush' are becoming extremely popular.

What are the best winter squashes to grow? 'Delicious', 'Buttercup', and 'Butternut' are good for fall and early winter; 'Golden' and 'Blue Hubbard' are good for winter.

SWEET POTATO (IPOMOEA BATATUS)

Can I grow sweet potatoes? If so, how? Yes, if you have lots of room and a long, hot summer. Buy cuttings (young, rooted plants) from a reliable source to avoid transmission of diseases and set them out 18 inches apart, with 4 feet between the rows. They prefer a rather light soil.

How should soil for sweet potatoes be prepared? No other preparation than for the usual vegetable crops is required. A sandy soil is best, and it should not have a hard subsoil, which would prevent the roots from reaching down to moisture.

Should sweet potato vines be trimmed? No, injury to the vines would cause loss of nourishment to the potatoes. If the vines grow too large, it is better to loosen them from the soil, where they root at the joints.

Will sweet potatoes grow in the North, just for an experiment? (Illinois.) This is by nature a tropical plant, but it can be successfully grown where the summer is warm and free of frost for 5 months. As the vines spread extensively, their culture is more for the field than the garden.

How do you grow sweet potato plants? Growing the cuttings, or plants, to set out for sweet potatoes is rather tedious, and the home gar-

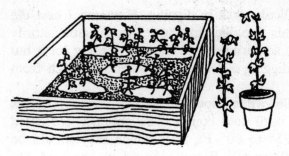

Sweet potatoes are started in a covered box or frame to supply "sets" for the garden.

dener would be better advised to buy them. They are started in hotbeds or cold frames, the sprouts or cuttings being removed with adhering roots from the old potatoes.

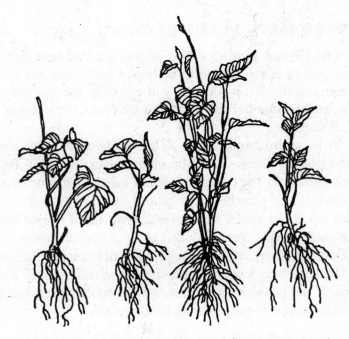

Sweet potato "sets"—young rooted sprouts started in a frame and then transplanted to the open. The "sets" or cuttings can also be bought from mail-order nurseries.

When should I start sweet potatoes in the house for sprouts? When should I plant the sprouts outside in the garden? Start 6 weeks before the date when frost is sure to be over for the season. Set out the plants only when the soil has become well warmed.

During the past season I have raised delicious, large sweet potatoes in

my garden, but my great difficulty was in digging. How can I best dig without breaking them? This problem has never been satisfactorily solved because the tubers are so very tender. There is nothing for it but to exercise great care—start digging a little way off and approach from the side instead of the top.

Do sweet potato tops die when ripe? How are sweet potatoes "cured"? The tops survive until cold comes. The potatoes are cured by storing 2 to 3 weeks at 75° to 80° F., after which they should be stored at a temperature of 50° to 60° F. until the tubers are used. Do not handle them while in storage. At all times, handle with the greatest care to avoid bruising them. Broken or injured ones should be used first.

SWISS CHARD (BETA VULGARIS CICLA)

How is Swiss chard grown? This is really a leaf beet and is grown in the same way as beets, but only the leaves and stalks are used. It is a "cut-and-come-again" crop—that is, you cut only the amount you wish at one time, rather than harvesting the entire plant. New leaves continue to appear all summer.

How is Swiss chard harvested? A leaf or two at a time may be cut from several plants. These should be outer leaves; they will be replaced as the plant grows. Or the center top is cut off, 2 inches or so above the crown, so that all new growth will be tender.

Last year my Swiss chard was covered with small brown spots. How can this be controlled? Probably this is a potash deficiency if the spots occurred along the margins; or a magnesium deficiency if in the body of the older leaves. Magnesium, lime, or wood ashes will correct the deficiencies. If the problem is serious, send a specimen to the Cooperative Extension Service in your county for diagnosis.

Swiss chard is a nourishing vegetable for summer-long harvest. Pick individual leaves with their white stalks. More will form on the plants.

What are good varieties of Swiss chard? 'Rhubarb' chard, with crimson stalks; 'Fordhook Giant', dark green leaves with white stalks; and 'Lucullus'.

TOMATO (LYCOPERSICON LYCOPERSICUM)

What is the surest way to get a crop of tomatoes? High points in tomato culture are: using the seed of a good disease-resistant variety; planting on fertile, moisture-holding soil; buying or starting strong plants; and keeping the weeds under control. Tomatoes thrive under a very wide variety of soil and climatic conditions, but will not fruit if night temperatures fall to 50° F. or lower.

Do tomatoes thrive best on alkaline or acid soils? Tomatoes seem to thrive under a fairly wide range of soil reaction. Experiments have not shown much benefit from liming when the crop is grown in acid soil. It also seems fairly tolerant up to a pH of 7.5 or so (7.0 is neutral).

Do tomatoes require much fertilizer? Tomatoes need to be well supplied with nutrients, whether this is achieved by the use of compost or phosphorus, complete fertilizer, or a combination. Phosphorus is particularly important for tomatoes, contributing to good yields and to earliness. An oversupply of nitrogen under some conditions, and with some varieties, may result in an overgrowth of vine and a poor set of fruits.

How many tomato plants will I need per person? Just for the table, 3 plants are plenty. For canning and freezing, 6 average plants are needed.

I notice some tomato varieties are described in catalogs as being "determinate." What does this mean? Determinate varieties are those with a bushy rather than a vining habit and generally require no supports. These varieties are most suitable for pot growing and for any small-space garden. Some determinate varieties are 'Patio Prize', 'Dwarf Champion', 'Stakeless', 'Patio Hybrid', and 'Pixie'. The majority of tomatoes are indeterminate and continue to grow at their stem tips, thus making support almost a necessity in a small garden.

How far apart should tomatoes be planted? The spacing of tomatoes depends on the variety as well as the size of the garden and whether the plants are to be staked or supported in wire cages or towers. Where space is ample and no support is planned, the sprawling, vining (indeterminate) plants should be set about 4 × 4 or even 4 × 6 feet apart. Most staked and caged plants can be set from 1½ to 2 feet apart in the row. Small, determinate varieties can be set even closer.

When is it safe to set out tomato plants?   They are set out when the danger of killing frost is past. This is usually 2 to 4 weeks after the average date of the last killing frost in the spring. Local experience is valuable; talk to other gardeners.

Is it best to buy tomato plants or plant seed yourself?   Growing plants require a suitable place and a little equipment, such as fluorescent lights, and the gardener must look after the plants regularly. With care, better plants can be grown at home; *and they are on hand when planting conditions are right!* It is easier to buy plants—if good ones are available at a reasonable cost—but many poor plants are offered for sale, and if more than a few plants are needed, the cost becomes significant. Growing your own seedlings usually allows wider varietal choice.

Is February too soon to start tomato seeds in the house?   In most climates, tomatoes are set out in the garden about 3 weeks after the average date of the last killing frost. For much of the Northeast, this means setting them out the last week of May. Seed may be started about 8 weeks ahead of this to get good-sized plants, although 10 weeks is preferable. Too early sowing results in ungainly plants that often outgrow their space.

How should one manage the starting of tomato plants?   Use a little box or flat, 2 to 3 inches deep, filled with good potting soil or one of the prepared mixes, such as Jiffy Mix, well firmed around the sides and corners. Sow seed in rows 2 inches apart, 8 to 12 seeds per inch. Seeds may be treated with captan or thiram. Keep the box in the window, under fluorescent lights, or in a greenhouse or hotbed at a temperature of about 70° F. Water so that the soil is moist, but not so heavily as to

Young tomato seedlings—about 4 weeks old—at the right stage for transplanting.

result in tender, spindly growth. As soon as the seedlings come up, give them full sunshine or place under fluorescent tubes. Transplant into peat-fiber pots when the seedlings are about 2 inches high. Or sow a couple of seeds in Jiffy-7 peat pellets, pinching off the weaker seedling, in which case no further transplanting indoors should be necessary.

When should tomato seedlings be transplanted in the greenhouse? When seedlings are about 2 inches high and showing the first true or rough leaves, transplant with spacings of 2 × 2 up to 4 × 4 inches. Set the plant almost down to the seed leaves and firm the soil securely around the roots. If only a few plants are involved, they can be kept in a sunny window or under fluorescent lights in the house, or they may continue their growth in a greenhouse, hotbed, or cold frame. The temperature should be 65° to 70° F. and the plants should have the benefit of full sunshine. Water just enough to ensure steady, vigorous growth without plants becoming soft. If this is well managed, little hardening is necessary before being set out in the garden.

My staked tomatoes were high in quality but quit fruiting by late July. What did I do wrong? The mistake was in planting a determinate variety, one that sends up a single growing stem, then quits growing vegetatively and produces fruits. While determinate varieties are early and heavy fruiting, their period of production is usually short. Instead, for staked or cage-supported tomatoes, use indeterminate varieties that keep growing and throwing out new branches. They will produce until killed by frost. Staking is not essential to fruit production—both types will bear if allowed to sprawl on the ground, but few gardens can spare the space for this method.

Do you advise staking tomatoes? Does this cause sun blister? Use of wire cages (18-inch wire cylinders with 6 × 6-inch mesh) is better than staking and reduces the risk of sunscald, which can be caused when fruit are totally exposed to the sun's rays with insufficient leaf covering. With wire cages, the plant's side branches grow through the wire mesh and become self-supporting, whereas staking requires tying and pruning of side shoots. It is always better to support tomato plants than to let them sprawl on the ground, since vines on the ground take up more space and the fruit is subject to rotting and greater insect damage.

Should tomatoes be pruned? At one time pruning was recommended for tomatoes that are staked, because this made them easier to tie up, and it was thought that more fruit would result from all the plant's energy being directed into one main stem. However, this no longer is advised. As long as the soil is fertile and the plant's moisture needs are met, there is no need to prune side shoots. The side shoots also help to provide protection for the fruit against sunscald.

Can tomato plants be pruned at the top to keep them low and bushy? No. Varieties listed as determinate are usually lower than others without any pruning. Pruning tomato plants is no longer recommended.

Can new growth taken from tomato plants be rooted to make new plants? Yes, if the growth isn't too watery. Cuttings should be firm, but not too old. Cuttings made in early July often escape blight and continue to bear until frost.

My tomato plants went all to foliage. Why? This may be due to too much shade (perhaps from planting too closely) or to too much nitrogen in the soil. Use a fertilizer high in phosphorus, especially at the time of flowering, and this will encourage heavier fruit yields and early ripening.

How far away from the growing plants should tomatoes be cultivated? My tomatoes were a failure this year. Mulch rather than cultivate. This is less work and there is less chance of injuring the plants' roots.

Should you hill up the soil around tomato plants? It is now generally agreed that there is little to be gained by hilling up the soil around most vegetables. It results in damage to the roots, which spread wider than the tops.

Is mulching of tomatoes a good idea? Yes. A 2- or 3-inch layer of hay, straw, old leaves, lawn rakings, or anything of the sort serves to retain moisture in the soil, smother weeds, keep fruit clean, and the material is a good addition of organic matter for the next year. A little extra nitrogen on the soil may be necessary to balance the demand of organisms which decompose the mulch material.

Our tomatoes are finished by early fall. How can we have good ones later on in the fall? It is a good practice to set some tomato plants a bit late for fall maturity. Seed for these ('Burpee's Long-Keeper' is a good late variety) can be sown in the open May 1 to 15 in most northern climates. This also furnishes good mature green tomatoes to put away for fall use. Cuttings made from shoots on old plants are good to use in setting plants for late crops.

Our tomatoes had an acid taste. Testing indicated that the ground had too much potash. Could this account for it? It does not seem very likely that the nutrients in the soil would have very much to do with the acidity of the tomatoes. Varieties differ a good deal in this respect. Varieties of the 'Ponderosa' group and also the yellow tomatoes are milder in flavor and acidity than most varieties.

Will tomatoes do well if planted in the same location several consecutive years? Tomatoes do not seem particularly sensitive on this point, unless disease accumulates in the soil. The fusarium wilt or "yellows" is a soil disease, and long rotation helps in its control if you have the space available. It is best to use fusarium-resistant varieties, of which there are now many.

We have grown tomatoes in the same plot for several years; we find that we get a tremendous growth of vine but not very large or many tomatoes. Would you advise what to add to the soil? Probably there is too much nitrogen. Use superphosphate and wood ashes as fertilizers.

How can tomatoes be ripened in very high altitudes or in the extremely cold northern section of the Midwest where the growing season is very short? Varieties 'Starfire', 'New Yorker', 'Presto', 'Valiant', 'Coldset', and 'Springtime' have been especially developed for growing under these conditions. Get the plants to the flowering stage in 4-inch pots by the time the ground is ready to receive them. Sow seeds in flats or Jiffy-7 pellets first. Have the soil in good condition. Use a mulch. If fertilizer is needed, use it in liquid form.

What shall I use to control flea beetles on tomatoes early in the season? Dust rotenone on the plants or use Sevin or methoxychlor.

What causes tomato leaves to curl? The leaves curl for a number of reasons. Most common is a virus disease called "shoestring top." It is carried by aphids, which winter over in weeds. Spray transplants with malathion as soon as they are set out and again 10 days later. Direct-seeded plants usually escape. Spraying near tomatoes with weedkillers such as 2, 4-D can cause them to drift onto plants and curl the tips or the entire plant. Drying out of the soil (loss of spring moisture) in late June often results in curled leaves.

Should tomatoes be sprayed or dusted? If leaf diseases are prevalent on tomatoes, use an all-purpose dust specifically recommended for tomatoes.

Why do tomatoes get black spots at the blossom end? This trouble is ordinarily called blossom-end rot. It is not caused by a definite disease organism, but seems to be physiological in its nature—a failure of moisture to reach the tender tissues at the blossom end. The trouble may be due to a lack of rainfall, droughty soil, or alternating dry and wet spells. The trouble is often followed by secondary mold or fungus infection. It sometimes occurs when the soil is not particularly dry, either because the root system is defective or because there is not enough oxygen in the soil for proper moisture intake. Control is by any measure that ensures adequate water supply, such as irrigation, maintaining organic matter in soil; in some cases, improved drainage.

Can tomatoes be saved after frost?   Healthy, mature green tomatoes (that is, tomatoes that have attained full size but have not begun to show color) can be kept for 4 or 5 weeks in the fall. They will keep longer at a temperature of 45° F., but will ripen more quickly at temperatures up to 70° F. Precaution should be taken against evaporation and shriveling; that is, the storage place should be fairly humid. Tomatoes at the half-ripe and turning stage will also ripen up well in a few days. The flavor, however, will be inferior to vine-ripened fruit. Keep them away from direct sunlight. Temperature, not light, is more important for ripening tomatoes.

Are vine-ripened tomatoes more nutritive than those picked when only partially ripe?   Vine-ripened tomatoes are of better quality and flavor, and are much better for canning. It is probable that they are more nutritious, although some authorities dispute this.

Why do tomatoes grown in the northern United States lack the flavor and brightness of color of those grown 500 miles farther south? (Wisconsin.)   Tomatoes like warm weather, but with careful cultivation you can grow northern tomatoes of equal merit. Planting varieties which were specifically bred for cool climates will mean better flavor. 'Fireball', 'Springset', 'Coldset', 'Starfire', 'Valiant', and the 'Sub-Arctics' are recommended.

Is the acid and food content much different in various varieties of tomatoes, such as white, yellow, and red kinds?   Most yellow types of tomatoes are less acid than the red, while white tomatoes are almost free from acid. Food content is about the same in all types.

For late tomatoes, should one plant late varieties, or is it as well to plant early varieties at a later date?   It is better to plant late varieties for late tomatoes.

What is the earliest tomato for home or market?   'Pixie', 'Early Salad', 'Springset', 'Starfire', 'Presto', and 'Early Girl' are some good ones.

Which main-crop tomatoes are considered best for the home garden?   'Big Boy', 'Better Boy', 'Supersteak', 'Supersonic', 'Fantastic', and 'Burpee VF Hybrid' are main-crop varieties of merit. 'Sunray' is the best yellow. There are many others.

What kind of tomato plants would you recommend for a very small place, where I have room for only 4 or 5? What can be done to make the tomatoes less spindly, outside of pruning, which did not seem to make much difference? Look for determinate varieties and those suggested for pots on patios. Your spindly plants are evidently caused by lack of sun or poor soil. Add humus to the soil, if possible.

What is the best tomato variety for low, sturdy plants and early fruit? 'Pixie', 'Starfire', 'Fireball', 'Early Bird', 'Floramerica'. These should be grown on rich soil that retains moisture well. Since the vines are short, the plants may be set 30 inches apart with rows 3 feet apart. They produce a large number of fruit close to the center of the plant.

What is meant by "resistant" varieties of tomatoes? These varieties have been bred to resist the attack of the common fusarium wilt. They are attacked by the disease but do not succumb to it. There are no immune varieties. Among the resistant varieties are varieties that are identified by the initials VFN and VF. All are highly resistant. Those with an N are resistant to nematodes.

What are the best varieties of low-acid wilt-resistant tomatoes in a small garden? Most low-acid tomatoes are the yellow or orange type. Good varieties of these are 'Sunray', 'Ponderosa', 'Jubilee', and 'Golden Boy'.

In this locality, probably due to late spring and much rain, tomatoes do not mature. What would you suggest to overcome this difficulty? (Minnesota.) Grow an early variety in pots to the flower stage or early fruit stage, and set them in the ground as soon as it is ready. Put up some protection on the north and west sides of the plants. Try 'Sub-Arctic Maxi', 'Rocket', 'Scotia', and others recommended for cold climates.

What large-fruited tomato would you recommend? We have tried 'Beefsteak' but the fruits were rather late and misshapen. (New York.) Most large-fruited varieties of tomatoes are late and have a tendency to produce fruit with deep ribs. A variety called 'Supersteak VFN' is not only earlier than other 'Beefsteak'-type tomatoes, but it also produces smoother-skinned fruit and has excellent flavor.

What is the best all-around tomato for this climate? How should the seed be planted? (Missouri.) 'Supersonic' or the VF hybrids are excellent selections for all-around use. Start seeds in flats indoors under fluorescent tubes and transplant when a few inches high into peat pots. (See directions for starting tomato seeds in this section.)

Where can I get the cherry tomato varieties—those tomatoes that

grow only as large as a cherry?   Most commercial growers or seed houses have a good selection of cherry-type tomatoes.

Are so-called climbing tomatoes a success?   'Trip-L-Crop' and 'Early Cascade' are the climbing varieties of good flavor.

What is the best canning tomato?   Any solid-meated variety.

What type of tomato is best for juice?   Any of the more common types can be used. 'Big Boy', 'Moreton Hybrid', and 'Supersonic' are excellent. 'Sunray' (yellow) makes mild juice of a distinct flavor.

TURNIP (BRASSICA RAPA RAPIFERA)

How do you grow large, yet tender, rutabagas, turnips, etc.?   Plant the seed in late July in a well-limed soil that is thoroughly aerated. Don't use too much nitrogen, but plenty of potash.

When should turnips (yellow) be planted for a fall crop? (New Jersey.)   About August 1.

I was perfectly successful in raising large crops of lettuce, carrots, beans, beets, tomatoes, and mint, but my white turnips, seeded in two different places, refused to ball up and grew long like carrots. Why?   Probably due to a lack of potash. Put on some wood ashes or muriate of potash at the rate of 2 pounds per 100 square feet. Be sure that the lime content is satisfactory.

When do you dig turnips?   Turnips can be dug at any time when they are ready and one feels like eating them. For winter storage, they can be left until the first light frosts have come, then they should be lifted, topped, and stored in the root cellar.

What makes small marks on the outside of turnips?   It may be due to growth cracks or wireworms that rasp the young roots, leaving scars. Also, insufficient lime may cause this condition.

What makes turnips grow corky?   Too much nitrogen or hot weather. If they grow too fast, they get pithy. Plant late enough so that they develop during cool nights.

Our turnips, which grew fine, are hard and bitter when cooked. What is the cause?   This is probably due to hot weather when they matured or they were allowed to remain in the ground too long.

What is the best variety of turnips to grow for winter storage?   The Swede turnip, also known as rutabaga. If you prefer yellow, use 'American Purple-top', but if you think, as some do, that the white sort is milder and better flavored, try 'Purple-top White Globe'.

VEGETABLE SPAGHETTI (CUCURBITA)

How do you grow vegetable spaghetti and how do you cook it? Vegetable spaghetti is a type of vining squash that is as easy to grow as a cucumber vine. You can let it sprawl on the ground, but it is better grown up a trellis or chicken-wire fence. The fruits are ripe when they turn yellow, and they can be stored for several months without spoiling since they have a hard shell. The best method of cooking is to bake the

The vegetable spaghetti is a squash that can be boiled or baked. After it's cooked, cut it in half and remove the pasta-like pulp. The fruits can be used in the "green" stage in late summer or stored in a cool but frost-free place for use in fall or early winter.

whole fruit in an oven at 350° for 45 minutes. Then remove, slice lengthways across the middle, separate the two halves, and discard the seeds by scooping them out with a spoon. Then take a fork and scrape out the spaghetti-like strands all the way to the shell. Add butter and seasoning or a spaghetti sauce. You can also boil the fruit for about 25 minutes.

WATERCRESS (NASTURTIUM OFFICINALE)

How should watercress be started? Seeds can be germinated in a flowerpot set in a pan of water. Thin out to avoid crowding and, when large enough, transplant to a shallow stream. Or root cuttings in water; take from bunches of watercress purchased at a produce market. Plants can also be grown in moist soil if watered frequently enough to prevent the surface from becoming dry.

WATERMELON (CITRULLUS LANATUS)

How would one manage a watermelon planting in the garden? Watermelons need well-drained sandy or light soil. Use compost or rotted manure or commercial fertilizer, or a combination of all three—liberally. Seed is planted outdoors after the danger of killing frosts has passed; or plants can be started indoors in peat-fiber pots or Jiffy-7 pellets, as with muskmelons. Rows should be about 8 feet apart and plants should be thinned (or hills made) 4 to 6 feet apart, according to the variety and how well they grow under local conditions. Careful dusting to control striped cucumber beetle is usually required. Shallow cultivation is practiced as long as possible to control weeds; some pulling of weeds after that may be necessary. Mulching with black plastic will suppress weeds and warm the soil.

How do you tell when watermelons are ripe? If the sound, by snapping with your fingertip (or knocking with your knuckle), is sharp and high, the melon is immature. If there is a dull, hollow sound, it is more likely to be ripe. When the tendril or curlicue by the melon is alive and green, it is almost certainly immature. If the curlicue is dead, the melon is at least approaching maturity. Another test is to watch the change in color—a yellowing of the spot where the melon rests on the ground. A ripe melon, when pressed with a bit of weight, will usually "crackle," but this is not good for ones that are to be kept. There is a variety called 'Golden Midget' that turns yellow when ripe.

How would you raise watermelons in the North? What varieties are best here? (New Jersey.) Watermelons are very much at home in southern New Jersey, less so in northern New Jersey. However, they can be grown successfully much farther north than is ordinarily supposed. To grow watermelons successfully in northern regions, use an early variety. One of the finest is 'Sugar Baby'. This variety will mature as early as most muskmelons (in about 80 days from seeding) and thrives under northern conditions. Other early varieties are: 'New Hampshire Midget', 'Fordhook Hybrid', 'Crimson Sweet', and 'You Sweet Thing'. However, yellow-fleshed varieties such as 'Yellow Baby' and 'Honey Island' are the most cold-tolerant and earliest of all watermelons. Watermelons can be started indoors in peat-fiber pots under fluorescent lights.

Can watermelons be raised in this climate? (Massachusetts.) Yes, in the warmer parts of the state, particularly in the eastern and Cape Cod sections. The sandy soils are best suited to them. Some of the small-fruited varieties should be tried where the growing season is less than 120 days.

Please name some good new midget melons. 'Sugar Baby', 'You Sweet Thing', 'Yellow Baby', and 'Honey Island'.

Is it true that there are now seedless watermelons? Yes, but the seedless varieties need a normal watermelon to act as a pollinator since the former is not self-fertile. Several seed suppliers now list seedless varieties with precise instructions on how to grow them. Seedless watermelons are worth the trouble, since they are sweeter than the regular kinds.

II. *Home-grown Fruits*

NUTRITIONISTS ENCOURAGE the inclusion of fruits in the human diet. Yellow peaches, apricots, and strawberries are especially valued for their vitamin content. All fruits supply sugars of several types in easily digestible form. Minerals are found abundantly in many. Above all, the flavors and aromas that abound, while they may not add anything essential to the diet, certainly contribute something that makes eating fruits a delightful experience. Every home gardener can expect to be amply rewarded when he grows some of his own fruits.

Growing fruits in the home orchard is somewhat more difficult than growing common vegetables, but even with proper care, apples, pears, strawberries, raspberries, and others are easy to grow.

Pears produce a high proportion of usable fruits without any sprays. However, apples generally require sprays if a good portion of the fruits are to be edible when harvested. One of the most difficult problems in many regions is to control mice, which chew the trunk bark at the ground level. Also, the control of insects and diseases by sprays requires considerable vigilance and careful timing. Despite these challenging problems, mouth-watering, luscious fruits can be grown right in your own backyard if you are willing to put a little effort into it.

Before deciding what to plant, look around your state or county and see what kinds of fruits grow well in your area. Apples, for example, do not grow well in Florida or Southern California because there is insufficient winter chilling to cause the trees to break dormancy in the spring. Also, in northern districts, do not attempt to grow peaches where temperatures drop below minus 20° F. or apples where they drop below minus 40° F.

Why Grow Your Own?

Home-grown fruits, if properly cultivated and handled, are, as a rule, much superior to market fruits. Fruits for shipment must be picked in a slightly immature condition, so that they can stand packing and handling. They must often be harvested before the sugars and flavors are developed up to the point where the ripening process will continue after the fruit is removed from the tree. This is especially true of the more perishable fruits, such as the berries. One has not really had peach ice cream until he has picked from the tree a suitable variety, so fully ripe that it would squash in the hand, and used this for the making of a most delectable dessert, quite different from the supermarket product. Or, with blackberries, there is absolutely no comparison between the fruits as purchased in the market—even if you can find them—and those ripened on the canes to the point where a touch will make them fall off.

High-quality fruit varieties, not available in the markets, can be grown in the home fruit garden. Tasting these tree-ripened varieties can be a gourmet treat and a revelation to those who have only experienced the market product. Most fruits can be frozen, canned, or made into juice, jellies, and preserves. Fruit trees are attractive in bloom and contribute beauty to the landscape. Blueberry bushes, for example, would be attractive ornamentals if they never bore fruits. Children should have the opportunity of observing the marvels of fruit development—virtually impossible today unless the home garden gives them access to ripening fruit throughout the summer months.

Of course location with respect to production has a bearing. If you live in a region where fruits are harvested and delivered to a local market, the quality will more nearly approach that of home-grown fruits; but even for such local handling many sorts must be picked before fully mature.

Dwarf Fruit Trees

As home grounds become smaller, so does the available space for gardens—and standard fruit trees, such as apples and cherries. But dwarf fruit trees, which require far less space than their standard counterparts, can give home gardeners on small properties the happy experience of growing and picking their own apples, peaches, apricots, plums, and pears. (A regular-size apple tree will eventually occupy an area 20 × 20 feet or more, but nearly ten dwarf fruit trees can be planted in the same space and could include peach, plum, pear, and apricot as well as apple. However, even dwarf trees will eventually become crowded in such close spacing, so some thinning in this miniature orchard will be necessary; but before that time arrives, the harvest will have been varied and bountiful.)

Dwarfing in fruit trees is caused by the rootstock. A one-year-old fruit tree from the nursery ready for orchard planting is really made up of two different kinds of tree: the top, which will bear the fruit, and a completely different kind of tree, the rootstock. In the nursery, the rootstock of one kind was first grown, then the top fruiting variety, called the scion variety (such as 'McIntosh'), is budded onto the rootstock. There are specific varieties of rootstocks which cause the dwarfing growth of the apple tree. A 'McIntosh' apple tree can be either dwarfed or nondwarfed, depending on what rootstock is under it.

Apple varieties budded onto seedling roots grow into full-sized trees, perhaps 25 feet tall at 15 years of age. Nurserymen can grow seedling rootstocks by planting the seeds of any apple variety. However, these trees on seedling roots have no size-controlling effect on the new orchard tree. Generally, the home gardener should not purchase apple trees with seedling roots and should insist on trees having size-controlling roots.

Dwarfing rootstocks are propagated vegetatively and are removed from mother plants in the form of rooted cuttings. These are planted into the nursery and the scion variety, such as 'McIntosh', is then budded on them and allowed to grow for a year before the tree is ready for orchard planting. Dwarfing rootstocks have specific varietal designations, such as 'Malling 9', abbreviated as 'M9'.

Truly dwarfed apple trees grow to a height of about 8 feet at 15 years of age, depending on pruning practices, scion variety, and soil fertility. Trees having the dwarfing 'M9' rootstocks do not have good anchorage and tend to fall over a year or two after planting if not supported. It is necessary to drive a post or construct a trellis beside the tree and tie the tree to it.

Apple trees on 'M26' roots or interstem trees develop into semidwarf trees, about half the tree volume of large trees. By double budding in the nursery, interstem trees, such as 'McIntosh/M9/MM106', have a 6-inch interstem trunk section of 'M9' which causes the size control. Trees on 'Malling-Merton 106' and 'M7' roots grow to about three-fourths full size. There are many other varieties of vegetatively propagated size-controlling rootstocks, but most are not widely grown. Most of the widely used rootstocks are available as virus-free material.

Fruits borne on dwarf trees are just as large and are otherwise identical with fruits of the same variety borne on full-sized trees.

Pear trees are dwarfed by budding them onto quince rootstocks.

Sweet cherry trees have no satisfactory dwarfing rootstock. Peach trees are small enough that they do not require a dwarfing rootstock.

In addition to their space requirements, dwarf fruit trees offer other advantages for today's home gardeners. They come into bearing early, often after the second year of planting. Spraying the trees is easily accomplished with average equipment rather than high-reaching power sprayers, and, of course, harvesting the fruits from such low-growing trees is also easily accomplished. Because of their slow rate of growth, dwarf fruit trees require less pruning than standard trees. (See also Rootstocks for Fruit Trees in this introduction.)

Small Fruits

Especially suitable for home gardens of limited space are those fruits that are usually referred to as small, although there is nothing "small" about their yield. They include raspberries, blackberries, strawberries, currants, gooseberries, and blueberries. They can provide a continual supply of fruit from the first strawberry in early summer to the last autumn-fruiting raspberry. They are second only to dwarf fruit trees in their space requirements. Moreover, spraying is simpler than for all tree-borne fruits and often unnecessary.

A small strawberry bed should produce about one quart of strawberries for each foot of row. To achieve the best strawberries, space the plants adequately to prevent overcrowding, control weeds by mulches, provide water as needed, and protect the plants with additional mulching for winter before temperatures drop below 20° F. The everbearing varieties will produce lightly during late summer and fall.

Red raspberries are also excellent for the garden and are one fruit almost impossible to buy fresh because they do not keep long or withstand shipping well. Raspberries are easy to freeze—an additional attraction they offer homeowners who possess their own freezers or freezing compartments in their refrigerators. The raspberry cultivar 'Heritage' bears a summer crop and then a fall crop on the tips of the new canes, beginning in late August in central New York State (earlier southward) until a killing frost in October. While red raspberries and blackberries should be grown in rows, ideally about 7 feet apart—a luxury in space that not all home gardeners can afford—a single row of plants 20 feet long can yield enough fruit for immediate eating and freezing. Even a small "patch" of raspberries—an area about 5 × 3 feet convenient to the kitchen door and perhaps used as a screen for trash cans—will provide a sufficient harvest for a small family.

Currants and gooseberries are another example of small fruits that bear heavy crops annually. They form neat, low-growing shrubs, and only a half dozen or so plants of each are necessary to provide the makings for currant jelly and gooseberry jam.

Blueberries are attractive shrubs at all seasons, but especially so when laden with the blue fruits or when their foliage is bright red and orange in the autumn. They make a handsome boundary hedge for suburban properties and in larger gardens can border one or more sides of a vegetable garden. Or blueberry plants can be grouped among other shrubs (at least 2 varieties are needed for the most efficient cross-pollination). The major requirement of blueberries is an acid soil; if you can grow rhododendrons and azaleas successfully, your soil should also be suitable for blueberries. Otherwise you can test the soil and if necessary adjust the pH by adding sulfur. (See Section 1.)

Soil and Site

The home gardener has little choice of a site, but a consideration of its characteristics will indicate whether fruit plants can be set out with some hope of success. Soils that have been messed up in grading operations are sometimes poor places to grow plants, but they can be improved by the addition of organic matter (peat moss, compost, etc.), sand if the soil is heavy, or hauled-in topsoil (see Section 1).

The ideal soil is a deep, fertile, sandy loam at least 4 feet deep and well drained. Lighter soils can be improved by growing and then plowing under green cover crops, adding stable manure or peat moss, using more fertilizer, and watering the plants in dry weather. Heavier soils can be improved the same way, but may be in need of supplementary drainage.

Fruit soils must be well drained. In soggy situations, if tile drainage is not feasible, then the soil may be raised in wide ridges 6 inches or more in height. This will increase the chances of success in growing plants if good natural drainage is not present. Provision should be made to drain the surface water away from the planting. Peach and cherry trees are less tolerant of poorly drained soils than apples, blueberries, pears, or grapes. However, no fruit plant will grow in soil that is always wet.

A slightly acid soil is best for most fruits. Blueberries require an acid soil, preferably with a pH below 5.0. The regular use of sulfate of ammonia fertilizer on blueberry soils will tend to increase the acidity.

The best sites for orchards or home fruit gardens are on slopes so that on still, frosty nights the cold air will drain away. Frost pockets, or low spots surrounded by higher land, are less suitable for fruit plants, as frosts during bloom will injure the flowers. At the other end of the growing season, early frosts shorten the growing season.

Check with your county extension agent to find out if peach and sweet cherries bear regularly in your area. If so, the site is probably satisfactory for most Temperate Zone fruits. Also if 'Concord' grapes ripen well each year, the growing season is long enough for most fruits. All fruit plants must have full exposure to the sun for most of the day. Fruit trees will grow in partial shade, but the harvest will be very light.

On small lots the proximity of large trees should be avoided as their roots offer too much competition and their tops cast too much shade.

Planting

Fruit trees can be planted either in late fall or in early spring as soon as the soil can be worked without packing. In the northern tier of states, spring planting is usually considered to be safer. Raspberry plants set in the fall should have the soil mounded up around them or a mulch of leaves or sawdust to prevent the plants from being heaved out of the soil by frost during the winter. Strawberry plants are best set out in the spring.

One- or 2-year-old fruit trees are the preferred size for planting. Older or so-called bearing-age trees are slow to become established, if they survive the moving, and will not yield worthwhile crops as quickly as young trees properly planted and then well cared for. Dwarf apple trees and other dwarf fruit trees bear early anyway.

On arrival from the nursery, plants should be unpacked promptly and "heeled in" (roots well covered with soil) in a shady spot if they can't be promptly planted. If the bark is shriveled and the cambium is not bright green, the plants may not grow. The nursery should be notified promptly.

The plants should be set at the level or slightly deeper than they grew in the nursery in a hole large enough to hold the roots without crowding.

Dwarf apple trees on 'M9' rootstock should have the bud union about 2 inches above the soil level to prevent the scion from rooting and thus spoiling the dwarf habit of the tree. If the scion (top) is covered at the base with soil, it will develop roots and become a full-size tree.

It is helpful in getting the young tree off to a good start if the soil to be put around the roots is mixed with a pailful of wet peat moss. The soil should be packed firmly around the roots by stepping heavily on it as the hole is filled.

If the season is dry after planting, the young tree should be watered weekly until rainfall is adequate. A 3-foot-square black polyethylene mulch around the base of the young tree is helpful in getting it off to a good start. No fertilizer should be used in the planting soil during the first year. Adequate water and weed control are most important for the first 2 or 3 years.

Insects and Diseases

It is usually not possible to produce unblemished fruit without controlling the insects and diseases to which most of the fruits are susceptible. Usually, unsprayed tree fruits will not be usable because of insect or disease injuries. Some fruits and some varieties are more susceptible to injury than others, and injury varies from year to year according to weather. Plants on sites where air circulation is poor experience more injury from fungus diseases than where air circulation is good. Any insect or disease which reduces the vigor and efficiency of the leaves, even though it does not destroy them, tends to make the plant less winterhardy and reduces the crop the following year. Pear trees produce cleaner fruit when they are neglected as to spraying than do other tree fruits.

Codling moth is the most serious insect pest of apples everywhere. Apple maggot and aphids are other apple pests. Several others can occasionally be troublesome. Scab is serious with most apple varieties, but scab-resistant varieties are being developed by breeding.

The stone fruits—peaches, plums, apricots, and cherries—are seriously damaged by brown rot, which attacks the fruit in humid weather and can destroy the entire crop if the weather is not suitable. Wormy peaches are caused by the larva of the Oriental fruit moth and the plum curculio. The latter causes wormy plums. Cherry fruit flies are the cause of wormy cherries. Aphids are also pests of these fruits.

Virus diseases, which are systemic and live in all parts of the plant, decrease plant vigor and productiveness. Some can even kill the plant.

Several viruses of different fruits are known and more than one virus in a plant can ruin it.

Techniques have been developed to eliminate viruses from plants by heat treatment and meristem culture. The resulting virus-free plants are maintained under virus-free conditions and used as sources of propagating material for nurseries. Many kinds and varieties of fruit plants are now available as virus-free plants. When ordering plants, virus-free plants should be specified, as the older virus-infected plants are still around. When possible, virus-free plants should be isolated from older plants of unknown virus content.

Spray programs for controlling insects and diseases of fruit plants are available from your State Agricultural Experiment Station or Cooperative Extension Service. The programs are revised each year as new pesticides are developed and the older materials are superseded or eliminated because of hazards to the environment.

The programs for the commercial orchardist are complicated, but simpler schedules are available for the home orchard. They will give fair control of insects and diseases and their recommended chemicals are safer for the user. These chemicals are available as mixtures or can be made up by the user. Directions for the use of pesticides should be followed exactly as to amounts and timing.

Selection of Varieties

Fruit plants should be purchased from nurseries specializing in them. Nurseries that feature ornamentals with a few fruits listed in the back of the catalog, sometimes not even by variety names, are not as good sources as the specialists.

The order should be placed early in the winter before stocks of some varieties are sold out. Varieties should be chosen carefully and ordered by name. Picking up a few fruit trees of whatever is available at the garden center at the last minute is not the best way to start a fruit garden!

Your Cooperative Extension Service (under county government in the telephone book) or State Agricultural Experiment Station issues lists of recommended fruit varieties, revised occasionally, to help you make an intelligent selection. These lists should be consulted as space does not permit a listing of varieties for all the climatic regions of the country. Some varieties are widely grown, others only in limited areas.

Older varieties that may have been superseded by newer sorts are usually just as good as when they were introduced and are often just about as satisfactory for home use as the newer varieties.

The varieties below are listed in order of ripening:

Apple: 'Julyred', 'Jerseymac', 'Viking', 'Tydeman Early', 'Burgundy', 'Jonamac', 'McIntosh', 'Macoun', 'Cortland', 'Empire', 'Jonagold', 'Golden Delicious', 'Idared', 'Melrose', 'Mutsu'.

Disease-resistant apple: 'Prima', 'Sir Prize', 'Nova Easygro', 'Macfree', 'Liberty', 'Priscilla'.

Old apple: 'Gravenstein', 'Snow' ('Fameuse'), 'Twenty Ounce', 'Cox Orange', 'Pound Sweet', 'Tolman Sweet', 'Baldwin', 'Northern Spy', 'Granny Smith'.

Crab apple: 'Hyslop', 'Dolgo', 'Young America'.

Pear: 'Clapp Favorite', 'Bartlett', 'Aurora', 'Anjou', 'Flemish Beauty' (hardiest), 'Gorham', 'Seckel', 'Bosc', 'Highland'.

Peach: 'Brighton', 'Garnet Beauty', 'Reliance' (hardiest), 'Redhaven', 'Raritan Rose', 'Harken', 'Triogem', 'Glohaven', 'Madison', 'Cresthaven', 'Redskin'.

Nectarine: 'Pocahontas', 'Morton', 'Nectared No. 4', 'Nectared No. 6', 'Nectacrest'.

Apricot: 'Alfred', 'Goldcot' (very hardy), 'Veecot', 'Hargem'.

European plum: 'Oullins', 'DeMontfort', 'Mount Royal' (very hardy), 'Mohawk', 'Seneca', 'Green Gage', 'Richards Early Italian', 'Iroquois', 'Stanley', 'Golden Transparent Gage', 'Italian Prune', 'Oneida'.

Japanese plum: 'Shiro', 'Formosa', 'Santa Rosa', 'Abundance', 'Burbank'.

Damson plum: 'French'.

Tart cherry: 'Montmorency', 'Meteor', 'North Star'.

Sweet cherry: 'Venus', 'Emperor Francis', 'Stella' (self-fruitful), 'Compact Stella' (compact tree, self-fruitful), 'Vogue', 'Ulster', 'Hedelfingen', 'Van', 'Windsor'.

Quince: 'Orange', 'Smyrna'.

Grape: 'Van Buren', 'Ontario', 'Seneca', 'McCampbell' (large-clustered sport of 'Fredonia'), 'Alwood', 'Buffalo', 'New York Muscat', 'Lakemont', 'Concord Seedless' (for grape pie), 'Glenora'.

Wine grapes: Several American grapes make good wine. These French-American and *Vitis vinifera* hybrids are excellent: 'Aurore', 'Marechel Foch', 'Seyval', 'Cayuga White', 'Baco Noir', 'DeChaunac', 'Chardonnay', 'White Riesling'. A specialist should be consulted about other French-American and *V. vinifera* hybrids.

Red raspberry: 'Jewel', 'Allen', 'Bristol', 'Huron'.

Purple raspberry: 'Brandywine' (large fruits, productive).

Blackberry: 'Darrow'. Thornless varieties for areas south of Washington, D.C.: 'Smoothstem', 'Thornfree'.

Currant: 'Red Lake', 'Wilder', 'White Grape'.

Gooseberry: 'Poorman', 'Downing'.

Strawberry: 'Sunrise', 'Holiday', 'Canoga', 'Catskill', 'Fairfax', 'Redchief', 'Midway', 'Raritan', 'Garnet', 'Fletcher', 'Sparkle', 'Geneva' (everbearing). The best-flavored strawberries are 'Suwanee', 'Fletcher', 'Fairfax', 'Holiday', 'Geneva'.

Blueberry: 'Earliblue', 'Collins', 'Blueray', 'Bluecrop', 'Berkeley', 'Herbert', 'Coville'. In the South, rabbit-eye varieties: 'Premier', 'Woodard', 'Tifblue', 'Powderblue', 'Homebell', 'Garden Blue', 'Aliceblue', 'Beckyblue', 'Centurion'.

Mulberry: 'Wellington'.

Pollination Requirements

Many fruit trees do not set fruit if the flowers are self-pollinated. Hence, at least two varieties blooming at approximately the same time should be planted to ensure cross-pollination.

All apples and pears require cross-pollination. In some areas with ideal weather during bloom, single-variety apple orchards of 'Golden Delicious', 'Rome Beauty', 'Baldwin', and others have been known to produce good crops by self-pollination without the presence of other varieties as cross-pollinators. However, in the northeastern United States, with cool, damp weather during bloom, all apple varieties should be considered self-unfruitful; that is, two different varieties having similar blooming dates must be planted within 100 feet of each other so that cross-pollination can occur between them in order for the blossoms to set fruits. Perhaps a close neighbor has a tree of a different variety that will effectively serve as a pollen source. Pollen of triploid apples is infertile, so two other varieties are needed if a triploid variety is planted.

Sweet cherries require cross-pollination, but an exception, 'Stella', is self-fruitful. The Japanese plums require cross-pollination, but some of the European types are self-fruitful and some are not. European and Japanese varieties do not pollinate each other. All the peaches, nectarines, grapes, and small fruits, except blueberries, are self-fruitful. Although blueberries are partially self-fruitful, blueberry flowers, if cross-pollinated, set much better and produce much larger berries than when self-pollinated.

Rootstocks for Fruit Trees

Clonal rootstocks are now being used generally for apple trees. The ultimate size of the tree, age of coming into bearing, and productiveness are influenced greatly by the rootstocks. The rootstocks are designated with M (for Malling) numbers. 'M9' produces the smallest tree and is most suitable for backyard trees. The trees on 'M9' grow 6 to 8 feet tall and in an orchard arrangement should be planted 6 to 8 feet apart in rows 10 to 12 feet apart. 'M7' produces trees somewhat larger than 'M9'. Trees on 'M26' are intermediate in size between 'M9' and 'M7'.

Dwarf apple trees on 'M9' and 'M26' should be staked at planting time, as the shallow root system can cause them to tip over with a load of fruit or from a high wind. Stakes are desirable for 'M7' trees during the first 5 years.

Pears are dwarfed by budding on quince roots but the trees may be short-lived. *Pyrus communis* (pear) seedlings are better rootstocks for dwarf pears. Oriental pear rootstocks should not be used, as the resulting trees are more susceptible to pear decline, a mycoplasma disease, than on *P. communis* roots.

Dwarfing stocks for peaches and plums are Nanking cherry, sand cherry, and 'St. Julien A' plum. However, trees on seedling roots are small enough for most sites and can be kept dwarf by pruning.

There are as yet no suitable dwarfing stocks for sweet cherries. The sour varieties 'Meteor' and 'North Star' are much smaller trees than 'Montmorency' and make attractive ornamentals as well as fruit producers.

Some American grape varieties are susceptible to injury by phylloxera, an insect which feeds on the roots of susceptible varieties. The rootstock 'Couderc 3309' is resistant to phylloxera and susceptible varieties or varieties that are to be planted where grapes have recently been grown will perform much better on 'Couderc 3309' rootstock.

Herbicides and Mulching

Herbicides are much used in commercial orchards, where they eliminate labor and prevent injury to the roots of the plants that result from power cultivating. They can be used in home fruit gardens, but instructions must be followed exactly to avoid plant injury. The margin of safety is narrow and unless one is exact the damage to the plants can be substantial.

Herbicides are numerous and new ones are appearing frequently, so information should be obtained each year from your county agent.

If sufficient mulching material is available, it is an excellent way to control weeds and conserve moisture and of course it is free from the hazards inherent in herbicides. A hay mulch provides nutrients as it rots. Black polyethylene is also very good for small operations. Straw should not be used where there is a fire hazard.

Why Fruit Trees Fail to Bear

The trees may not be old enough. Some apples and pears require several years to reach bearing age if on seedling roots. Dwarf apple trees (on 'M9' rootstock) fruit at 2 or 3 years. Peaches bear at 3 years as do sour cherry trees. Sweet cherries begin at 5 to 7 years and plums a year or two earlier.

Low winter temperatures, or spring frosts, when the trees are in bloom, may kill the flowers. Apricots, peaches, and sweet cherries, which are early blooming, may fail to fruit because of a frost at that time. Prolonged cold wet weather during fruit bloom prevents the bees from flying, and cross-pollination, which is essential for the flowers to set fruit, may not take place.

Some fruits are self-unfruitful. (See Pollination Requirements, this section.) If only one tree is planted and other varieties of the same species are not nearby to provide pollen, then the flowers fail to set.

Excessively vigorous trees are slower to come into bearing than trees of normal vigor. Trees low in vigor because of poor drainage, lack of nitrogen, and injury to the leaves from insects or disease can be slow to begin fruiting. Trees in shady situations will fail to fruit or bear only lightly.

The Orchard

SOIL

How can soil for orchard fruits be built up? Building up the soil is accomplished by increasing its content of organic matter to improve the physical condition. This can be done by adding large amounts, 20 tons or more per acre, of manure or peat moss; or more cheaply by seeding the land to a green-manure crop, such as grass or a legume, and fertilizing it heavily. Mow it several times a summer, leaving the clippings to rot. Turn it under after 2 or 3 years.

Does sandy soil retard the growth of apple and peach trees? Mine are 4 years old and only about 5 feet tall. Will other soil put around the trees help? Apple and peach trees will grow well in sandy soil if it is properly fertilized and provided it contains ample moisture. Adding heavy soil might help, but it would require a great deal. It would be more feasible to improve the soil by adding a 5–10–5 commercial fertilizer at the rate of about 800 pounds per acre. If the soil is dry, either irrigate with a sprinkler system or mulch with some strawlike material to conserve moisture. Heavy mulching will gradually increase the humus content of the soil. Compost, leaves, lawn clippings, or any organic materials are good mulches.

Will fruit trees grow in a scrub oak section on Long Island, New York? The soil in question is probably low in fertility and very acid, but with good care might produce enough fruit for home use. Liberal applications of stable manure or other humus-forming materials such as peat moss, annual fertilizing, and mulching to conserve moisture should make it possible to produce fruit on this soil.

Our soil is mostly sand. Would it be suitable for the raising of strawberries, red raspberries, and fruit trees? A sandy loam soil, or even a loamy sand, is suitable for these fruits if it has a reasonable supply of moisture. If it is very dry, sandy soil, you will probably have poor results unless you irrigate. Coarse sands will probably need heavy and frequent fertilization with complete fertilizers. Peaches will thrive in sandier soil than is needed for apples. Black-plastic mulches are excellent if appearance is not important.

Will fruit trees grow in muck ground? Yes, provided the muck is well drained, not too acid, and contains the necessary nutrient elements in sufficient quantities. Muck land is usually low; hence, cold air may "drain" into such an area and result in frost damage. Frost damage to the flowers may be so frequent on muck that crops will be few and far between. Winter injury may be much more serious than on upland soils. Fruit trees should have good "air drainage," so are usually set on relatively high land.

Is there any reason why fruit trees will not grow on soil adjacent to black walnut trees? Black walnut roots are known to excrete a substance that is toxic to the roots of some plants, including apples, tomatoes, and alfalfa. Grass will grow under black walnut trees, but to be on the safe side, other plants should be kept well away from the roots of the walnut.

FERTILIZER

Must fruit trees (such as apple and peach) be heavily fertilized? Fruit trees should have sufficient complete fertilizer to supply any nutrient elements which may be deficient in the soil in which they are growing. However, it is easy to overfertilize these fruits. They do not require as heavy fertilization, for instance, as is needed by most vegetable crops.

Should manure be placed on a new garden plot on which fruit trees and berries are to be planted? A good coat of manure would be about the best treatment you could give. If manure is not available, turn under a ground cover such as grass or legume sod that has been previously planted.

How is nitrate of soda applied when used for fruit trees? Nitrate of soda is usually used for fruit trees at the rate of ¼ pound for 1- to 2-year-old trees, to 5 to 10 pounds for trees 20 to 30 years old. Ammonium nitrate, which contains twice as much nitrogen, is used at one half this rate. On fertile soils, if leaves are large and dark green, omit these fertilizers.

Can you give some data on fertilizer to help fruit trees produce well and at a younger age? (Illinois.) Good production will be secured only if the trees have the proper supply of nutrients, and that in turn will depend a great deal on the natural fertility of the soil. Check with your Cooperative Extension Service for specific recommendations for your soil. No particular type of fertilizer will cause the trees to bear at a younger age. The age of bearing is influenced chiefly by the variety, the pruning, and by some rootstocks. The age of bearing can be delayed, however, by applying too much nitrogen or by heavy pruning. For the quickest-bearing fruit trees, plant only dwarf trees.

What type of fertilizer should be used for fruit trees in acid soil? Most fruit trees in the East are grown in acid soil; that is, soil which is below the neutral point of pH 7.0. If soil is very acid (below pH 5.5), lime should be added to bring the reaction to around pH 6.0, then use ordinary commercial fertilizer as required.

I have heard that fruit trees do not require lime. Is that correct? Fruit trees require lime as much as any other plants. Whether it should be used or not depends on the acidity and calcium content of the soil. The pH should be between 5.5 and 6.0. However, generally it is not necessary to add lime to garden soils for fruit plants.

PLANTING

What is the best age at which to buy apple, peach, cherry, plum, and pear trees for setting in the home garden? Apple, 1 or 2 years; peach, 1 year; cherry, 1 or 2 years; plum, 2 years; pear, 2 years. Larger trees are not recommended, and nothing is gained by planting so-called bearing-age trees.

How many fruit trees will be necessary to supply a family of 4 with an adequate amount for the year? This will vary greatly according to personal preferences. Six apple, 2 pear, 6 peach, 1 sour cherry, and 2 plum trees would provide about as much as the ordinary family would want, if varieties with a succession of ripening dates are chosen, and if the trees are on suitable soil and well cared for. Additional varieties can be grafted onto these trees to extend the season.

How early in the spring should fruit trees and berries be planted? Plant just as early as the soil can be worked. There is no danger of planting too early, provided the soil has dried out enough to be worked into good tilth.

How far apart should fruit trees be planted? I plan to plant about 10 acres. Planting distances of fruit trees depend on the kinds of fruits, their rootstocks, and, to some extent, on soil and climate. The following are average distances between trunks and rows: apple, 20 to 40 feet; pear, 24 to 30 feet; peach, 20 to 25 feet; plum, 22 to 24 feet; cherry (sour), 22 to 24 feet; cherry (sweet), 24 to 30 feet; apricot, 22 to 24 feet; quince, 18 to 20 feet.

How far apart should the trunks of dwarf fruit trees set in rows be planted and how far apart should the rows be? Dwarf apples, on 'M9' rootstock: 10 × 12 feet; on 'M7' rootstock: 6 × 12 feet; dwarf plums: 8 × 8 feet; dwarf peaches: 10 × 10 feet. Home gardeners who plant only a few trees can cheat a bit on spacing.

How should I go about planting a fruit tree? How big a hole should I dig for an apple tree? A hole 12 to 15 inches deep and 15 inches across should be large enough for the average nursery tree. If the roots are too long to fit in a hole this size, cut them back. As the soil is filled in, jiggle the tree up and down a little so that all the roots will make contact with the soil. When the hole is half full, and again when it is full, step on the soil around the trunk of the tree in order to compact it.

Finish filling the hole. If the soil is at all dry, pour in a pail of water before the hole is quite full.

How deep should fruit trees be planted? If the nursery tree has been budded onto size-controlling rootstocks, such as apple on dwarfing 'Malling 9' or pear on quince roots, it is essential, at planting time, to identify the height of the rootstock-scion bud union. Generally, there is a slight crook in the tree trunk at the bud union. The tree must be planted as deep as it was growing in the nursery or at a depth so that this bud union will be about 2 inches above the soil level. If the bud union is planted below the soil level, the base of the top scion variety will be in the soil and it will send out roots. This is known as scion rooting. Roots produced by the scion portion of the tree have no dwarfing effect; they will cause the tree to grow to full size. The dwarfing benefits of the 'Malling 9' will be completely lost. If the tree has been budded onto seedling rootstocks which have no dwarfing effect, the depth of planting is much less important, but having the bud union at ground level is still a good depth.

How should nursery-grown trees be treated upon receipt? Remove from packing at once and plant immediately or heel in. Examine carefully. If the plants are dried out, soak in water, completely immersed, if possible, for 24 hours. If they do not plump up, return them. The bark when cut into should be bright green.

I received nursery fruit trees in the fall. What is the best way to hold them until spring? If they cannot be planted at once, heel them in, in a shaded place. Dig a trench wide enough and deep enough so that the root systems will almost go in them. Place the plants in the trench, packed close together, at any angle of about 45°. Place loose soil around the roots, work down and pack tight, then mound. No grass or weeds should be against the roots. The object is to keep the roots moist during the winter.

How large does a body of water have to be to cause conditions to be favorable for fruit growing? The moderating effect of the body of water is caused by the changes in temperature occurring in air masses as they move across the water toward the fruit-growing section. If prevailing winds do not blow across unfrozen water long enough to have their temperature raised, then there will be no effect on temperatures in the orchard. This means a body of water will have to be several miles wide and remain unfrozen in order to have very much effect.

Is locality taken into consideration in regard to the types of trees that should be planted? Yes. Fruits that thrive in Louisiana would not survive the winters in New England, and New England varieties would not do well in Louisiana. Cultural methods also vary greatly in different localities. The length of the growing season and summer heat are also important factors.

SPRAYING

We have a new orchard of fruit trees. What should they be sprayed with, and when? The damage likely to be caused by certain pests varies a great deal in different localities; hence, spraying recommendations vary from one producing region to another. Unless the trees are sprayed regularly and intelligently, the fruit will be worthless and the trees severely injured by diseases and insects. Each Agricultural Experiment Station has developed spraying directions to fit conditions within the state. These directions may change from year to year as chemicals are changed. Get directions each year from your Cooperative Extension Service or your state university.

How and how often should orchard trees be sprayed? The number of sprayings varies according to the locality, the insects and diseases, and whether one wants perfect fruit or will be satisfied with fair control. They should have a minimum of 4 sprayings, with a good pressure sprayer. One dormant spray should be given, and at least 3 before and while fruit is forming. Commercial growers use as many as 11 sprayings in one season.

Does the Japanese beetle do much harm to fruit trees? What spray can be used against it? Carbaryl (Sevin) is quite effective. Check the label for precautions to observe on ripening fruits.

MULCHES AND COVER CROPS

How does a mulch of straw provide more water to young trees? No more water is provided, but what is already there is conserved. The mulch prevents wind and sun from striking the ground and evaporating moisture from the surface. It also prevents the growth of weeds and grass which would compete for water with the trees. During a very hard rain, the mulch prevents or lessens surface runoff.

How should fruit trees be mulched? They were 3-year-old trees when planted, and have been growing in a yard for 3 years. By mulching is meant the placing of enough strawlike material around the tree to keep down weeds and grass and thus conserve moisture. The mulch is usually applied from the trunk to a point under the tips of the branches; hence, the area mulched increases as the tree increases in size. Straw, spoiled hay, lawn clippings, or leaves can be used. Black plastic is good, but must be anchored and covered with additional mulch for the sake of appearance if trees are included in the landscape scheme. If leaves are used, place some hay or brush over them to prevent their blowing away. Mice often injure mulched trees, so it is best to rake the mulch away from the trunk in the fall (a distance of 3 or 4 feet) and spread it again in the spring.

Is the growing of fruit trees in grass sod satisfactory in a small orchard? Peach trees are better with cultivation or a mulch, but the other fruit trees may be grown in sod if it is mowed as frequently as a lawn so that the competition for moisture is reduced. Thick vigorous sods may need occasional partial breaking up with a disk-harrow or a rototiller to reduce competition. Herbicides are very useful if properly applied.

What is the best ground cover for a young orchard of 2-year-old trees? Cultivate near young trees. Maintain closely clipped sod elsewhere.

What are the advantages of mulching trees? Moisture is conserved, weeds are controlled, plant food is added by the decaying mulch, and drop fruits do not bruise much when they fall on the mulch. Root injury from tillage is eliminated.

What are the disadvantages of a mulch? It creates a fire hazard and should not be used if there is danger of fire. Mice are much worse under a mulch and they should be poisoned and the tree trunks protected by a wire collar or a mound of gravel around the trunk.

If I grow my trees in sod, how should I manage it? Mow it frequently, several times a summer, to reduce competition with the trees. Leave the mown grass to rot under the trees.

PRUNING AND TRAINING

How and how often should fruit trees be pruned? Trees are pruned during the dormant season, preferably toward spring in severe climates. The object of pruning is to produce a structurally sound tree that will not experience limb breakage from a heavy crop or ice storm. The scaffold branches should be about 6 to 12 inches apart and pointing in different directions. Crotches with each member of equal size should have one member cut back a little each year until it becomes a branch of the other. Interfering and broken branches should be removed as well as those with disease. Pruning should be a little each year rather than a lot at longer intervals. It is better to err on the side of too little rather than too much pruning.

When and how much should I cut back fruit trees planted this fall? The tops should be reduced about one half, leaving 4 or 5 branches 6 to 12 inches apart and pointing in different directions. It is better to wait until spring to cut back the newly planted trees, especially in the northern states.

Is it advisable to cut the heart or center limb out of a fruit tree to prevent its growing too tall? Peach trees are usually trained to an open center, so the central leader is cut out. Apple trees are well adapted to the modified leader system, in which the leader is allowed to grow to a height of 8 to 10 feet before it is cut out.

How should fruit trees be pruned so that branches will not bend down or break off when fruit gets large? We would like to make the branches stronger and not lose more fruit than necessary. The branches are bound to bend down if a crop is being produced. However, heading back the long, leggy branches will reduce their length in relation to their diameter. Such branches will not bend or break so badly because the leverage exerted by the load of fruit is not so great. Breakage can also be prevented by propping with poles and by thinning off excess fruit.

Is root pruning the proper way to reduce wood and leaf growth on a fruit tree? Root pruning is seldom justified unless the tree is growing in a greenhouse or is used as an ornamental where its size must be strictly limited. If a tree is making too much wood growth, it can usually be checked satisfactorily by withholding nitrogen from the fertilizer application or by growing it in a grass sod.

What is meant by the "ringing" of fruit trees? Taking out a ring of bark around the trunk or one or more main limbs of a tree—usually an apple tree. This causes carbohydrates synthesized in the leaves to stay in the top of the tree, above the ring. The result usually is a heavy set of fruit buds followed by a large crop, but the roots are starved for carbohydrates, so the tree is weakened. It will die if the ring is too wide to heal over in one season; therefore, scoring by cutting through the bark in one or more places, all around the trunk, but without actually removing any bark, is a safer method. Ringing or scoring is usually used only on filler trees which are to be removed in 2 or 3 years anyway. Dwarf apple trees (on 'M9' and 'M7' rootstock) bear much earlier than do regular-size trees.

PROTECTION

Is whitewash beneficial to fruit trees? How should it be applied? Whitewash was once considered of some benefit in preventing sunscald of fruit trees, but it is rarely used by fruit growers now and is probably of doubtful value.

Would it be advisable to use a good white-lead and oil paint on fruit trees? No paint should be used on fruit trees except possibly on pruning wounds. Most commercial growers do not paint wounds unless they are much larger than that. The paint does not cause the wound to heal faster but may help to keep the exposed wood from decaying before the new bark grows over the wound and seals out decay organisms. Small wounds, 2 inches in diameter or less, do not need painting. Larger wounds may be painted with an asphalt emulsion in water.

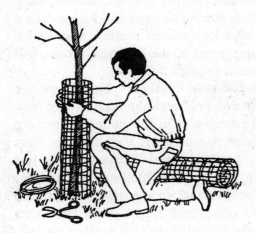

Cylinders of hardware cloth protect young fruit trees from winter injury by rabbits and rodents.

How are young fruit trees best protected from mice in the winter? Remove the mulch and loosen the plant material from around the trunk for a foot or more. Use strychnine-poisoned oats in the runways under matted grass. The county Cooperative Extension Service can advise as to the best poison baits and where they may be obtained. Cylinders of hardware cloth placed around the trunks with their bases embedded in the soil are good protection.

What is the best protection against rabbits, for young fruit trees, other than using wire netting? Guards of wire-mesh cylinders are the best protection. County agents can supply information about chemical repellents, but these may be short-lived and must be replaced frequently.

POLLINATION AND FRUITING

What is cross-pollination?   Cross-pollination is the transfer of the pollen of one variety to the pistil in the blossom of another variety.

What is meant when you say that a plant is self-sterile or self-unfruitful?   The two terms are commonly used synonymously, but there is a slight difference. Self-sterile means that a variety will not form seeds with its own pollen. Self-unfruitful means that it will not form fruits with its own pollen.

Is there any explanation as to why a variety may be self-unfruitful?   It is based on genetic factors. Sometimes the pollen may be sterile, i.e., not capable of germinating. In other cases, it will be able to germinate but will fail to function on its own pistil, functioning on the pistils of other varieties.

Which fruit trees are not self-fruitful?   Fruits that are not self-fruitful are most apples; all varieties of the European pear and its hybrids; a few varieties of peaches; all sweet cherries (except 'Stella') and 'Duke' cherries; many of the European plums, most of the Japanese plums, and many of the hybrids arising from American plum species.

Will any variety of apple cross-pollinate another?   No. There are certain varieties that definitely will not pollinate themselves, nor will they act as pollinators, because of a weakness in the pollen. These are called triploids because of the chromosome number. Varieties that bear a close relationship, as 'Delicious', 'Starking', and 'Richard' (the last two being bud sports of 'Delicious'), will not cross-pollinate each other.

Do crab apples require cross-pollination?   Like the large-fruited apple varieties, crab apples are also self-unfruitful, i.e., they fail to set fruits by their own pollen. They must be pollinated by another variety. Large-fruited apple varieties, such as 'Liberty', will effectively pollinate crab apples, and vice versa, crab apples will pollinate large-fruited apples. However, they must bloom at approximately the same date. Like large-fruited apple varieties, some crab apple varieties bloom very early, some midseason, and some late.

Are there some varieties of apples and cherries that will act as pollinators for one variety and not for another?   'Delicious' forms good pollen but will not cross-pollinate its bud sports, 'Starking', 'Richard', and several others. Among sweet cherries, there are a number of varieties that are cross-unfruitful.

Why do seedlings of fruit trees differ so much from the parents in fruit quality?   Nearly all of our fruits are of complicated parentage, so that when seeds are sown all sorts of variations may be expected to occur. Often the weakest qualities of the genus show up, or susceptibility to disease. Some do come relatively alike; 'Elberta' peach seedlings, for instance, may all resemble 'Elberta' in shape and color, but many will be clingstones and many will be of poor quality. Very few seedlings are superior to their parents.

For how many years can the following fruit trees be expected to bear heavily: apple, pear, peach, sour cherry, sweet cherry, plum, quince? It will depend somewhat upon variety, and definitely upon climate, site, soil, culture, and control of insects and diseases. Apple, 50 to 75 years; pear, 35 to 50 years; quince, 25 to 30 years; peach, 15 years; plum, 30 years; sour cherry, 30 to 40 years; sweet cherry, 50 to 60 years. Profitable commercial production may be less. Virus diseases often shorten the productive lives of stone-fruit trees.

Can I have young transplanted fruit trees bearing in a year or two? The age at which a young tree begins to bear fruit depends on the kind and variety (some are early bearing, some may take a number of years), the rootstock and the care, especially pruning. Many fruit trees should begin bearing at 4 to 6 years of age. Peach trees bear at 3 to 4 years. Dwarf apple trees may bear at 2 or 3 years of age. Frosts and disease or insect troubles may cause delays.

My fruit trees were set out 2 years ago but seem to show small progress. What should I do to get more rapid growth? (Tennessee.) Give them good growing conditions by cultivating and applying fertilizer. It may be necessary to spray to control pests. Dry weather may have been a factor; if so, mulching will help. As they become well established and older, they will grow faster.

How can I develop fruit trees quickly? I set out 15 trees 2 years ago and have had poor results. Fruit trees normally develop rather slowly —apple trees, for instance, take 4 to 12 years, depending on the variety, to come into bearing. Give them good growing conditions, full sun, sufficient moisture, weed control, and the fertilizer needed by your particular soil.

I have a few fruit trees: peach, pear, and plum. None bear any fruit. Why? There might be several reasons: too young; weak, because of faulty nutrition; overvegetative, because of too heavy pruning or too much nitrogen in the fertilizer; injury to buds or blossoms by low temperatures; injury by pests; and possibly, if they blossom, because cross-pollination is not provided.

I have a home fruit orchard: apples, peaches, pears, plums, and cherries. The fruit seems small. How can the size be increased? The size will depend on the variety, planting distance, natural fertility of the soil, fertilizer treatment, moisture supply, and the amount of pruning and thinning. Overbearing is a common cause of small size. Severe thinning of plums, peaches, and apples is necessary for good fruit size. Try to determine which factors were responsible, then improve conditions with respect to those factors. The system under which they are grown is a factor, whether on sod, cultivated, or mulched. Build up the humus content of the soil by the use of cover crops if the trees are on cultivated soil. If the soil is light and tends to dry out, use the mulch system and apply fertilizer early in the spring. Trees in their first years should be well grown to eventually make vigorous trees.

Can I get quick returns from berries and grapes? This is the second season for berries, the third season for grapes. Strawberries fruit the second year and raspberries a little the second year and nearly a full crop the third year. Everbearing strawberries will fruit the first fall. Autumn-fruiting raspberries fruit the first fall if well grown. Grapes bear some the third year and nearly a full crop the fourth year.

Does covering berry bushes with cheesecloth to keep birds away retard growth and ripening of fruit? Cheesecloth to keep birds away from berry bushes should be put on just as the fruit starts to ripen, and at this stage it will not appreciably retard the growth or date of ripening. However, the special netting, usually of plastic, sold by seed and nursery firms, is easier to use than cheesecloth.

How can heavily laden branches of fruit trees be prevented from breaking? Proper thinning of the fruits should be done after the so-called June drop; if still heavy, prop with stout, crotched stakes.

HARVESTING AND STORING

What is the right time to pick apples, cherries, and pears? For home use, summer and fall apples may be left on the tree until ripe enough to use or until they start to drop. Summer apples keep only a few days unless stored cold. Winter apples are picked before eating-ripe and stored until they are ready in late fall or early winter. Most varieties of pears should be picked when fully grown but still relatively hard—when the first few specimens begin to acquire a yellowish tinge and start to drop. Cherries should be picked when fully ripe.

How should fruit be harvested that is to be stored for the winter? Each apple or pear should be picked from the tree, by hand or with a picker, before it is dead ripe. Avoid bruises, scratches, and cuts. Store only perfect fruits.

Where apples are stored in a fruit cellar and the temperature is controlled only by opening windows to outside air, but where humidity can be controlled, what degree of humidity should be maintained? Give as much ventilation as possible, and a relative humidity of 85 per cent. To prevent shriveling, store in polyethylene bags.

Should the door of a fruit house (built into a bank, with stone sides, wooden roof, ventilating opening in roof, concrete floor) be kept closed in early fall for apple storage? Close on warm days and open at night on cold days to bring the temperature down close to 32° F.

Should apples in storage be kept dry or moist? The air should circulate and the room should be ventilated. The air should, if possible, have a relative humidity of around 85 per cent.

Should apples in storage be sprayed with water? The floor of the storage area, rather than the apples, should be sprayed to maintain the humidity.

Will apples keep longer if waxed? Commercial-wax emulsions will reduce shriveling in storage but may increase "scald" if not properly used. Moistureproof polyethylene wraps will also reduce shriveling. The best assurance of good keeping is to store a long-keeping variety where the air is moist and as near 32° F. as possible.

Should apples be wrapped when stored? Wrapping will help to prevent shriveling and will keep decay from spreading if a few bad apples are mixed with the good ones. Special oil-treated wraps will prevent scald. Most apples stored commercially for any length of time are wrapped in oiled paper or have oil-impregnated paper strips scattered through the package.

Some apples placed in a cold storage room looked fine when they came out, but 2 days later they looked as if they had been dipped in hot water. Why? This is a storage trouble known as apple scald. It is worse if the fruit is picked before it is fully matured and colored. Some varieties are much more susceptible than others. Good ventilation in the storage area will help to some extent. Wrapping the apples in thin paper impregnated with oil will prevent scald almost entirely. The immediate cause seems to be certain gases given off by the apples themselves, and the oil in the wraps will absorb these gases.

I have had some very fine apples but no place to store them; my cellar is too warm; the attic and garage are too cold. How can they be stored inexpensively somewhere outdoors? You could build an insulated storage room in the cellar near a window. Or they can be stored in a barrel pit. (See Storage.)

Can I successfully store fruit in a cellar with a central heating sys-

tem?   The cellar is much too warm. You should construct an insulated room which can be ventilated through an outside window. Try to keep this room as close to 32° F. as possible. A bulletin from the United States Department of Agriculture describes several simple types of home fruit and vegetable storage.

EXHIBITING

How are tree fruits selected for shows?   They are usually shown as plates of 5. Select fruits that are typical in form, size, coloring for the variety and vicinity; that are uniform in form, size, and color; and free from insect and disease injury. Do not wash or polish: soil may be wiped off, but even this may mar the natural appearance.

PROPAGATION

What are Malling rootstocks?   Apple rootstocks were formerly mixed in the trade so that variety names were meaningless. The East Malling Research Station in England collected all the types and classified them according to their effect on tree growth. They are now being used by many nurseries for propagating apple trees. Some produce dwarf or semidwarf trees; others produce large trees. 'Malling 9' produces the smallest tree, 6 to 8 feet tall and generally considered best for home garden use. 'Malling 7' produces semidwarf trees 8 to 10 feet tall.

Can grapes, peaches, cherries, and apples be grown from seeds obtained when you get them from the fruit you buy?   All fruits are originally grown from seeds. They seldom resemble their parents and more often than not are decidedly inferior. This is why superior types are propagated vegetatively.

Would it be practical for me to attempt budding or grafting named varieties of apples on some young wild apple trees growing on my property?   Yes; neither process is very difficult, although in this, as in most things, "practice makes perfect."

How and when should seeds of cherry, peach, plum, apple, and pear be planted?   Mix with sand in the fall and place outdoors, where they will be kept moist. Freezing is not essential; however, the temperature should not rise above 51° F. The optimum temperature is about 36° to 40° F.

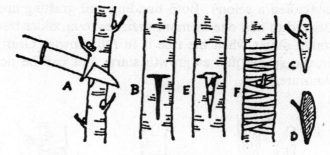

BUDDING

Budding is the simplest method of propagating a desired variety upon another of the same (or a closely related) species. (A) Bud stick; (C and D) different views of bud, after being cut from bud stick; (B) T-shaped cut in bark on stock (stem or branch that is to be budded); (E) bud inserted; (F) bud bound in tight with raffia or rubber band.

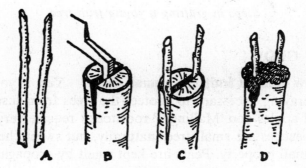

BARK (CLEFT) GRAFTING

A simple method of grafting. (A) Scions, or sections of small branches of the variety it is desired to obtain. (B) Heel of grafting tool holding open the split or cleft in the end of the branch on which the graft is to be grown. (C) Scions cut to wedge shape and inserted so that the bark layers of the branch and scions come into direct contact. (D) Grafting wax applied to protect wound and prevent drying out.

What is the difference between "budding" an apple tree and "grafting" one? Both budding and grafting are used by nurseries in growing young fruit trees. In the former case, a bud (with a sliver of bark attached) is used; in grafting, a small section of a branch or shoot, with

several eyes (called a scion). Both budding and grafting are also used
when it is desired to add one or more varieties to an older tree. Budding
is done in midsummer when the tree is in full growth. Grafting is usually done in the spring just as growth starts, but can be done later if
dormant scions are used.

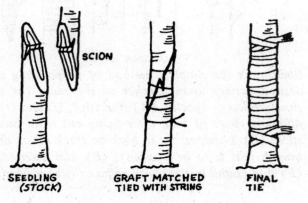

Steps in grafting a young fruit tree.

WHAT TO GROW

Can I grow orchard fruits on a small place?   Yes, if you are willing
to do the spraying necessary to protect the trees from insects and diseases. Dwarf apples (on 'Malling 9' rootstock) require very little space.
Plums and peaches are small trees naturally, but sweet cherries are too
large for a small property. Pears are kept small by propagating them on
quince stocks.

**Which are the best kinds of tree fruits for home gardens in northern
New Jersey?**   This will depend somewhat on the personal preferences
of the gardener. If there is room for only 1 or 2 trees, the apple would
probably be most generally satisfactory: it makes a fair shade tree and
can stand neglect better than the peach. Most pear varieties blight
badly, except 'Seckel', 'Kieffer', 'Magness', and 'Moonglow'. The sour
cherry 'Montmorency' is fairly easy to grow, but birds are likely to get a
good share of the fruit.

**What kinds of fruit trees shall I plant in a space 75 × 150 feet to give
our family of 5 the best selection of fruit and assure fertilization of the
blossoms? (New York.)**   The varieties, and to some extent the kinds
of fruit to plant, will depend on how cold it gets during the winter. If
you are in a part of the state where peaches can be grown, try the following plan: Row 1 (4 feet from the fence), strawberries. Row 2 (8

feet from the first row), raspberries, currants, or other bush fruits. Row 3 (10 feet from the second row), grapes. Row 4 (20 feet), 4 peach, 2 sour cherry, 2 pear. Row 5 (23 feet), 6 dwarf apple trees. This will make the apple row 10 feet from the edge of the plot, which may be too close or not, depending on who owns the adjoining land and the purpose for which it is used. There will be no pollination problem with the small fruits or sour cherries. With peaches and pears, planting of more than one variety will practically ensure a satisfactory supply of pollen. 'McIntosh', 'Delicious', 'Cortland', 'Grimes', and many others are good pollinizers for other varieties of apples.

We plan to put in a few fruit trees. Our soil is fairly good but somewhat shady. Choose dwarf fruit trees if your space is limited. However, they require open sunny situations.

In planting a new orchard (of as few as 6 trees) on a property having no fruit at present, what would you advise? Your choice of fruits should be governed by your soil and climatic conditions. Plant what is already growing well in your community or consult your Cooperative Extension Service. Unless you plan to spray, stick to the small fruits, such as blueberries and raspberries.

What fruits can be grown in a cold region with a short growing season? Elevation, 5,700 feet. (Montana.) Only the hardiest varieties, such as some of the new fruits produced by breeding at the Minnesota and South Dakota Experiment Stations. Write to your own Experiment Station for a list of recommended varieties.

What fruits are best for the home garden? The small fruits require less space, bear early, have less trouble from insects and diseases than tree fruits, and need less equipment for their care. Strawberries are the first choice, with red raspberries, currants, gooseberries, blackberries, and blueberries nearly as good.

Specific Tree Fruits

APPLE (MALUS)

What are spur-type apple trees? For several apple varieties, genetic mutations have occurred in nature or by artificial irradiation resulting in new sports that have smaller tree size. For example, 'Oregon Spur Delicious', 'Starkcrimson Delicious', 'Redchief Delicious', and a score of others are spur mutations from the original, larger tree, 'Red Delicious'.

Similarly, 'McIntosh', 'Golden Delicious', and other apple varieties have spur types, but no spur types have yet been discovered for many varieties. 'Compact Stella' is a spur type of the 'Stella' sweet cherry. Because spur types grow into trees that are about two thirds normal size, they are preferred for planting in the home garden as well as in commercial orchards. They bear more fruit per unit volume of tree.

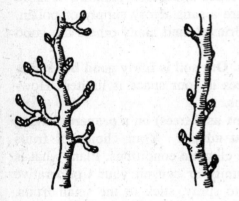

FRUIT TREE SPURS
(Left) Spur-type branch showing how productive spur varieties can be. (Right) Spurs of regular fruit tree branch.

Are genetic dwarf fruit trees the same as spur-type dwarfs? Do they tend to be more dwarf? I have a nursery catalog that lists several genetic dwarfs among cherries (including a self-fruitful 'Garden Bing'), apricots, almonds, apples that are on standard-size rootstocks rather than the usual dwarfing stocks. The degree of dwarfing among different varieties of the various fruits is a relative thing. Some varieties are much more dwarfing than others. In today's commercial apple orchards, a large portion of the new plantings of 'Red Delicious' are spur types. Spur-type apple varieties could be referred to as mild genetic dwarfing.

The term "genetic dwarf" is usually reserved for varieties that are truly dwarfed, perhaps only one fourth as large as most standard varieties. The 'Bonanza' peach is a genetic dwarf. Genetic dwarfs are usually characterized by short internodes (lengths of twig between leaves). Thus, the several genetic dwarfs you asked about are true dwarfs. These genetic dwarfs grow small even when they are propagated onto vigorous standard-size rootstocks.

A word of caution, however: Dwarf nectarine trees of such commonly grown varieties as 'Pocahontas', 'Cherokee', 'Nectared No. 4', or 'Nectared No. 5' are dwarfed, not because they are genetic dwarfs, but because they have been budded onto seedlings of dwarfing rootstocks, *Prunus tomentosa* or *P. besseyi*. Nectarine or peach varieties budded onto seedlings of these two *Prunus* species will produce trees that are dwarfed, but the rate of mortality at 3 or 4 years or younger is generally excessive. This is not a good type of tree to buy if longevity is your aim.

When is the proper time to plant apple trees? Some say fall; others say spring. Either spring or fall. If you can get the plants and you live in a region where the autumn is long, fall will perhaps be better, as the soil can be handled and the trees planted when there is not much pressing work.

Can an apple tree be transplanted without injury to it if it has borne its first crop of fruit? Transplanting any tree is a shock, and if a tree has been bearing, transplanting (unless the entire root system is taken with it) may result in rapid vegetative growth that will retard fruiting. If the tree is 4 or 5 years old, it will be better to set a new young tree.

How should a 13-year-old apple tree be fertilized? Apple trees require a complete fertilizer treatment containing the important nutrient elements. The amount of each element needed is determined by the natural fertility of the soil and its past treatment. Therefore, the requirements of a 13-year-old tree might vary from nothing in a very fertile soil to 20 pounds of a 5–10–10 formula on light sand. (See Fertilizer.) Most soils will need nitrogen in the form of ammonium nitrate or nitrate of soda. A few soils are deficient in potash.

What is the best time to plant apple and pear trees in the state of Connecticut? What is the best time of year to prune such trees? Prune and plant in very early spring before the buds begin to swell.

Should an apple tree be fertilized at planting time? No, it is too easy to burn the limited root system with chemical fertilizers. During the first growing season, water is most important.

How can I improve a heavy soil at planting time? Mix the soil removed when digging the hole with a pail of wet peat moss and work this mixture around the roots as the hole is filled. Firm the soil by stepping on it as the hole is filled.

When is the best time to prune apple trees? Any time during the dormant season is satisfactory. Actually the best pruning weather is likely to be in late fall, just after the leaves have dropped and before the weather becomes too cold. In regions where unusually severe cold (25° to 30° F. below zero or lower) may occur, pruning should be delayed until the severe cold of winter is past, as winter-injured trees may experience much more damage if pruned than if not pruned.

What are the main points to keep in mind when pruning a bearing apple tree? Do not remove a branch unless there is a good reason why it should come off. Some varieties will require very little pruning. Take out limbs that are dead, broken, or badly diseased, too low or too high; remove water sprouts (sucker growth, usually whiplike and nonfruiting) from the trunk and main limbs; thin out a little in the top, if necessary, to admit light to the lower limbs; remove slender, obviously weak twigs.

How can I prune so there will not be a lot of water sprouts?   If large branches are to be removed, take them out gradually, over 2 or 3 years. This will result in fewer water sprouts, and these can be detected and rubbed off before they become large.

Is it true that fall pruning of fruit trees cuts down sucker growth?   Fruit trees react the same to dormant pruning regardless of whether it is done soon after the leaves fall in the autumn or just before growth starts in the spring.

What happens when apple spurs are pruned off?   Most of the fruit in certain varieties is borne on short, crooked growths known as spurs. These spurs start to form on 2-year-old wood and grow very slowly. If spurs are pruned off a particular section of a limb, they will not be replaced and that part of the tree cannot produce any fruit.

Is summer pruning of trees advisable to make them bear fruit earlier?   Most experiments have indicated that dormant pruning is preferable. The reduction in leaf area from summer pruning may be a disadvantage to the tree by preventing normal ripening of the fruit. Certainly summer pruning is not of any practical value as a means of hastening fruit production by young trees. Some summer pruning, really pinching back of succulent growth, is recommended for dwarf fruit trees to keep them compact and to improve their shape.

How often should apple trees, just planted, be pruned?   Prune at planting time and early each spring thereafter.

Should bearing-age apple trees, which were pruned when shipped from the nursery, be further pruned when planted?   It may be necessary if the trees are shipped bare-root. If there appears to be any drying out, more pruning may be necessary—back to live wood. The top should be reduced proportionately to the size of the root system. Heavily pruned large trees are really no better than young trees.

How should I prune apple trees that are in their second or third season?   Apple trees of this age should receive only corrective pruning. In other words, do not remove any branches except those that especially need to come off. This would include branches that are broken, too low on the trunk, crowding other branches, or that make a narrow angle with the trunk. Crotches with narrow angles (less than 45°) are more likely to split apart than are wide-angled crotches. If two members of a crotch are of equal size, cut one back each year until it is a branch from a larger limb or remove it entirely. Keep the central leader dominant at this stage by shortening branches that may be competing with it

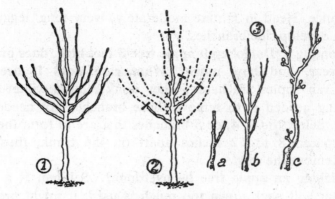

APPLE TREE PRUNING

(1) A 2-year-old nursery-grown tree, as received and planted. (2) The same tree after being pruned. The "X" signs indicate branches removed entirely. (3) Effects of cutting back compared with thinning. (a) Twig severely cut back. (b) Growth from cut-back twig is all vegetative (no flowers). (c) Growth from tree with thinning pruning only; good balance of twig growth and flowering spurs is clearly evident.

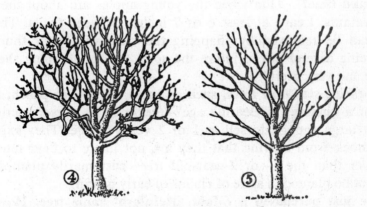

(4) Neglect of early training results in poor framework. A 'Stayman' apple about 6 years old with three leaders (very undesirable), polelike growths, and bad crotch. To correct these faults now means a high head. (5) Early training results in good form. 'Stayman' apple about 6 years old; good spacing of scaffold branches. Central leader still present. Note development of secondary branches.

for dominance. Head in (prune moderately) very long, leggy limbs to make them develop side branches.

After planting a 'Dolgo' crab apple tree 3 feet high, does one prune it the first year, and how much? What care does it need in the winter?   Crab apples are hardy. They don't require winter care. The only pruning needed is to remove those branches not needed for the framework. Select the 3, 4, or 5 branches that are to form the frame so they are spaced 8 to 12 inches apart on the trunk, thus avoiding crotches. Remove the rest.

Can mulching an apple tree be overdone?   Seldom. If a mulching material that will pack down too much is used, it might prevent root aeration. Loose material to a depth of 4 to 12 inches is good. Heavy mulching for several years with a hay mulch relatively high in nitrogen, or a legume mulch, may make the tree overvegetative. The apples may color poorly, drop prematurely, and lack keeping quality. Susceptibility to injury from low winter temperatures is another possibility.

What special care do apple trees need in the spring?   Proper pruning and spraying, and then attention to the fertilization of the soil. (See Fertilizer.)

How should the fruit of an apple tree be thinned? What is the best method and time?   Thin when the young apples are about the size of hulled walnuts. Leave at least 6 or 7 inches between fruits. The small apples can be removed by snapping the stem with your thumb and finger, being careful not to injure the spur. Special thinning shears are available and very useful.

Can bearing-size fruit trees, such as apple, cherry, or peach, be purchased at a nursery?   "Bearing age" trees may be nursery scrubs that were not large enough to sell at 1 or 2 years of age. They experience such a shock from moving that they are not likely to bear much fruit any earlier than the 1- or 2-year-old trees customarily planted. They should not be planted in spite of claims of early bearing.

I have just purchased a 6-foot 'McIntosh' apple tree. How many years, approximately, until it bears fruit?   With good care it should bear in the sixth year.

How much should a 'Red Delicious' apple tree grow a year if planted at 2 years of age?   The first year it should increase its height about 2½ feet; the next year, 2 feet. Ordinarily, 3 to 6 shoots, 30 to 48 inches long, may be produced in the first year.

My apple tree bears fruit by halves—that is, first one side bears apples and the next year the other side. How do you explain this? (New York.)   Some varieties bear a full crop in alternate years. In the case of your tree, something happened to upset the periodicity on one side. This is a desirable condition.

We have an 'Astrachan' apple tree that bore no fruit last year. It is about 12 years old and bore abundantly the previous year. Would you have any explanation? 'Red Astrachan' is generally an alternate-year bearer.

I have two early apple trees bearing only every other year, but together. Can I change the bearing years of one of them? Thinning sprays applied during the bloom of early apples will make alternate bearers into annual bearers.

What can be done to an apple tree (about 5 years old) to get it to blossom and bear fruit? It is now about 10 to 11 feet high. Any variety of apple must reach a particular state of internal development before it will set fruits. Do only corrective or formative pruning, and do not fertilize too heavily with nitrogen. When the proper balance is reached, the tree will fruit; to use means to hasten this might prove dangerous. Some varieties bear in 3 or 4 years; some take 10 to 12 years.

What causes a young medium-size apple tree to have only one large flawless apple? Probably it is a self-unfruitful variety and needs to be pollinated by a compatible variety.

We have a 'Wealthy' apple tree about 8 years old that seems to produce a lot of foliage but few apples. What is the reason? 'Wealthy' is one of the earliest varieties to bear. Your tree probably had too much nitrogen or too heavy pruning. Inexperienced persons have been known to prune off the fruiting spurs. Lack of cross-pollination, if the tree blossoms, could be the answer if there are no other apple varieties nearby.

I have a 'Grimes Golden' apple tree in my yard that is 8 years old. It has been pruned by people from an experienced nursery for 2 successive years, yet it will not bloom; hence, no fruit. Why? 'Grimes Golden' should bear in about 5 or 6 years in the orchard. Probably the pruning was too heavy and encouraged vegetative growth.

I have a 'Golden Delicious' apple tree, 10 years old, that has had only 5 apples on it. The tree looks fine and is 12 feet high. Why are there no apples? Although 'Golden Delicious' is capable of some self-pollination, much better results can be expected with another compatible variety nearby.

I have a small orchard of 10 apple trees, 16 years old, which do not bear any fruit. Can anything be done to make them bear? (Wisconsin.) This may be due to winter injury; if so, there is little chance of correcting the condition. If a tree is making very vigorous growth and does not form fruit buds, the lack may be caused by pruning too heavily, or by using too much nitrogenous fertilizer, in which case the remedy is evident. If the trees are all of one variety and do blossom, then lack of cross-pollination is a possible reason. Severe injury to the foliage from disease (apple scab) or insects is another possibility.

How can immature apples be prevented from dropping? Nearly all species of fruiting trees lose some fruits by dropping them when the fruits are small; this is called the June drop. The reason is that more fruits are formed than the tree can support, but sometimes the drop is because of imperfect fertilization by pollen. And sometimes it is caused by codling moth or curculio, which can be prevented by spraying.

What spray is used to prevent premature dropping of apples? Various commercial brands of hormone sprays or preharvest sprays can be obtained. These are for prevention of premature dropping of nearly mature fruits.

My 2 apple trees have full bloom, but when the apples form they fall off. Spraying helps very little. Can you offer a solution? If the fruits attain a size of ½ to ¾ inch, the spraying may be with the wrong material, or applied at the wrong time, or otherwise inadequate. If they drop at a smaller size, it may be a question of incompatible pollination or too rapid growth.

How old must a 'Northern Spy' apple tree be to produce fruit? What is the matter if an apparently healthy tree does not yield? A 'Northern Spy' apple requires the longest period of any variety to reach the stage of fruitfulness. This can be as much as 15 or 20 years in some instances. Try to reduce its vigor by growing it in sod. Do not prune the tree. They will fruit much earlier on 'M9' rootstock, which then makes them a dwarf fruit tree.

What is the best method to make apple and pear trees 50 to 60 years old profitable? Pruning, spraying, soil enrichment, etc. If they have been long neglected, it might be better to start anew. They may be too tall for profitable handling, and then many new and better varieties have come along since these were planted. If in fair condition, a renovation pruning, together with fertilizer and spraying, may bring them back.

How about apple trees that have been neglected for several years and no longer bear fruit fit to eat? Can these trees be brought back to a normal condition? If so, how? Renovation pruning, fertilization, and proper spraying are indicated. These measures will gradually restore the trees to vigor, provided, of course, that they are not too old.

How can I preserve an old apple tree that is beginning to de-

cay? Remove all dead wood. If space is available, plant replacements, since old, declining trees are not good producers, although they can be picturesque in the landscape.

How can I tell flower buds from leaf buds on apple trees in late summer? Apples form most of their flower buds at the ends of short spurs. Some varieties may form them laterally, on longer twigs of the current season's growth. Flower buds are plump and more rounded than the narrow-pointed leaf buds.

Old, neglected fruit trees can be cut back severely to form new, lower heads to make them easier to care for and eventually productive.

Is there any way to keep apple trees from blooming too early? Frost always gets our blossoms. There is no practical way to delay the blooming date. Certain varieties, such as 'Rome Beauty', 'Northern Spy', and 'Macoun' bloom later than most. Consult your State Experiment Station as to hardy varieties for your locality. Trees in a frost pocket experience much more injury to flowers from spring frosts than trees well up on a slope. You may be in a place where the climate does not permit apples to be grown successfully.

Is it possible to determine the variety of apples by the appearance of the leaf on a "5-in-1" apple tree? Probably only a few people in the country are qualified to determine, negatively or positively, some varieties of apples by their foliage. It would require an unusual knowledge in this field.

What varieties should I look for on a "5-in-1" apple tree? Whatever the nursery chooses to put on. (Usually the varieties are stated.) However, as far as possible, they should be uniform in growth, because there is great variation in the growth of various varieties. There must be at least one good pollinator in the lot.

What special care do dwarf apple trees require?   Apple trees on 'Malling 9', the most dwarfing rootstock, should be planted with the bud union (indicated by a swelling) about 2 inches above the ground. The soil must not be allowed to get above this point or the top may develop roots and soon become a full-sized tree. Dwarf trees should be tied to a stout stake since the roots are brittle and the tree may topple over with a heavy crop. (See also Dwarf and Espalier Fruit Trees.)

Is an apple tree that bears several kinds of apples good to grow?   If there is space for only one apple tree, one with several varieties may be used, provided the varieties are carefully selected. Several dwarf trees (on 'Malling 9' rootstock) will occupy no more space than one large tree and because of their lower height, 6 to 8 feet, they are easier to manage.

About how much room is needed for a "5-in-1" apple tree?   If these are grafted on standard roots, they will require a space about 35 × 45 feet. For ease in management, get one on a dwarfing rootstock, such as 'M9' or 'M7'. 'M9' needs 6 × 12 feet; 'M7', 12 × 20 feet.

How soon can I expect fruit from a "5-in-1" apple tree?   It depends upon the varieties used. Some varieties will produce fruits in 3 to 5 years after being planted; others require 5 to 8 years, and sometimes more. Growth conditions, as governed by site, soil, fertilization, and disease and insect control, will also have an effect. A dwarf tree will bear sooner.

Will a "5-in-1" apple tree continue to bear heavily over a long period of years?   If properly cared for, it should bear as long as if the same varieties were planted individually.

What precautions should be taken in pruning a nonbearing "5-in-1" apple tree?   Try to secure as uniform a development of each variety as possible. If one is weaker than the others, prune it more lightly than the more vigorous kinds. Prune only in the winter, but pinch back rapid growths in the summer to act as a stopper.

My "5-in-1" apple tree is lopsided. Why?   The varieties are such that they do not grow at a uniform rate, or the union on one may not be as good as with the others. The exposure as related to shading may affect one more than another. (See also Section 13 for more on plant problems.)

My apple tree is turning green around the trunk. What is the cause? What is the remedy?   The green color is probably caused by moss or lichens growing on the dead outer bark. It will do no harm, but could indicate poor circulation of air or too much shade. Possibly pruning has been neglected. This condition usually does not occur on sprayed trees.

What causes hard brown spots in apples? The trees appear healthy, but the apples are not fit to use. Probably "bitter pit," usually associated with excessive tree growth late in the season. Some varieties are especially susceptible, such as 'Baldwin' or 'Northern Spy'. In some localities, lack of boron in the soil can cause brown spots in the flesh of the apple.

Is it the same kind of aphids that we have on other plants that curl up apple leaves? These are "green" and "rosy" apple aphids. A summer infestation can be controlled with malathion.

Are there borers that attack apple trees? There are 3: round-headed apple tree borer, flat-headed apple tree borer, and leopard moth borer. The round-headed usually attacks young trees, and the laying of eggs may be prevented by means of repellent paint or by covering the trunks with fine-meshed wire or with paper. The flat-headed borer usually works in old, neglected trees. The leopard moth attacks young trees or branches. Examine the trees frequently, and if sawdust is seen near the trunk, look for the hole. Sometimes the larvae can be killed in the hole with a fairly stiff wire. There are commercial preparations such as Borerkil. If you have many trees, consult your Cooperative Extension Service.

My apples all have worms in them. What shall I do? The worms are codling moth, the most serious insect pest of apples. Consult your Cooperative Extension Service, since the spray program is rather complicated and new insecticides vary from year to year.

What causes young apples to fall off? They have crescent-shaped marks on them. This is the egg-laying mark of curculio. Methoxychlor is effective in controlling the curculio. Pink-bud and petal-fall sprays are important, but others may be necessary in different localities. Consult your county extension agent for a spray schedule.

In July, when I approach my apple trees, myriads of little flies come out. What are they? They may be leafhoppers. Keep watch just after the trees bloom. The nymphs cannot fly then, but are very shy and sidle away. This is the time to kill them with malathion. They are not as easy to kill as adults.

What is San Jose scale? A sucking insect which forms a hard circular covering that attacks orchard fruits and related plants, especially apple, peach, and pear. It may kill young trees in 2 or 3 years. It is indicated by a scurfy appearance when the scales are thickly clustered on young twigs. There may be a reddish discoloration along the veins of the leaves or small circular red spots on the fruits. Control is miscible oil as a dormant spray.

How can I get rid of tent caterpillars?   Apple tree tent caterpillars east of the Rockies, and a similar species west, infest wild cherries, apples, etc. In regularly sprayed orchards they are usually no problem, but in home fruit gardens they may be. Do not burn them, as this will injure the tree. Spray with malathion when the nests are about the size of a silver dollar. Better still, follow the regular spray schedule for your state, which will control them.

What are the brown and somewhat star-shaped spots on my apples?   This is apple blotch, prevalent in the South and Southeast. Consult the spray schedule from your county extension agent.

Why should red-cedar trees be cut down near apple orchards?   The red-cedar and the apple are alternate hosts for the so-called cedar rust, which is indicated by light-yellow spots changing to orange on apple leaves and fruits in the spring and summer; cedar rust galls on cedar in winter, developing to release spores in early spring. If there are only a few red-cedar trees, destroy all within half a mile to protect the apples. If too numerous to destroy, ferbam sprays on the apple will give good control.

What makes the leaves on some of the twigs of my apple trees turn black and dry up, just as if they had been burned?   This is fire blight, a bacterial disease. Cut these off well back from the dead part. Use a solution of zinc chloride to sterilize tools after each cut. Look for cankers on the trunk or limbs and clean these out. Regulate the growth of the trees so that it is not too vigorous. Spraying with Bordeaux mixture while the trees are in full bloom will often prevent infection through this means. Antibiotic sprays have also proved effective in controlling fire blight in some areas.

What is apple scab?   Apple scab is the most serious fungus disease of apples in the North. It partially, or sometimes nearly completely, defoliates apple trees, thereby greatly reducing them in vigor and productiveness as well as making them susceptible to winter injury. The scab lesions, if numerous, also disfigure and spoil the fruit. Ferbam, captan, and other materials are used in controlling scab. Because of the importance of this disease, the county Cooperative Extension Service issues special bulletins on the latest control measures. These should be followed for best results, since careful timing is important in securing good control.

What is the best and quickest-growing apple tree?   If you want apples in a hurry, plant dwarf trees that are propagated on the 'Malling 9' rootstock. Most varieties will start bearing on this root in 2 or 3 years. 'Golden Delicious', 'Jonathan', 'Tydeman Early', and 'Jerseymac' are good varieties.

Which varieties of apples have proved suitable in New York? 'Jerseymac' ripens in August, 'Tydeman Early' in September, 'McIntosh', 'Cortland', and 'Macoun' in early winter. 'Mutsu' is a good winter variety.

For a family that likes crisp, hard, slightly tart, and very juicy, old-fashioned apples, and which has room for only 2 or 3 trees, which varieties would you recommend for central New Jersey? You might try 'Tydeman Early' for medium early, 'Jonathan' for early winter, and 'Stayman' or 'Mutsu' for a late variety.

What is the best all-round or all-purpose apple tree to plant in New England? 'Mutsu'.

APRICOT (PRUNUS ARMENIACA)

Can apricots be grown in central Massachusetts? Yes. If peach trees are hardy, 'Alfred' and 'Farmingdale' are good. 'Sungold' is one of the hardiest varieties.

We have 2 apricot trees, 8 to 10 years old. What can I do to prevent fruit rotting just before it becomes ripe? (California.) Get the current spray schedule from Agricultural Experiment Station, Davis, California.

CHERRY (PRUNUS)

Under what conditions of soil and climate can sweet cherries be grown successfully? They need a sandy loam, deep and well drained. Climate is even more important. The shores of the Great Lakes, the Hudson Valley of New York, and the Pacific coast are the areas where sweet cherries are grown commercially. They are susceptible to winter injury and late frosts and do not like extremely hot summers.

Are sour cherries fussy as to soil and climate? These can be grown over most of the Atlantic coast and in the Mississippi Valley. Commercially, they are grown in New York, Wisconsin, and Michigan. They are hardier than the sweet varieties. They can be grown on sandy or heavy soils, if well drained, and can stand drought better than sweet cherries.

When should young cherry trees be fertilized to bring them most quickly into bearing? If young cherry trees need fertilizing, do it in early spring. As a general rule, they would start bearing at an earlier age if they were grown a bit slowly. It is desirable to grow good-sized trees as quickly as possible, in order to get a large crop; hence, the trees are usually forced while young, thus sacrificing very early bearing for the larger size of the tree.

What is a good fertilizer for cherries and how should it be applied?   On young trees, apply 10–10–10 at a rate of ½ to 3 pounds per tree. On older trees, use ammonium nitrate at a rate of 1 to 3 pounds per tree, depending on its vigor. Broadcast complete fertilizer in early spring and the ammonium nitrate later as needed.

What is the best age to buy cherry trees and when should the trees be planted?   One- or 2-year-old trees. Plant in early spring in the North; farther south, in late autumn.

What rootstock is best for cherries?   Cherries are propagated on two rootstocks, mahaleb and mazzard. Sweet cherry trees on the mazzard root are longer lived than trees on the mahaleb root and generally more satisfactory, especially on heavy soils. Mahaleb roots are used generally for sour cherries. To get cherries on mazzard roots, you must specify them and pay more as they are more expensive to produce.

Are there dwarfing rootstocks for cherries similar to apples?   No suitable dwarfing stock for cherries has been found. Tart cherry varieties, such as 'Montmorency', are generally budded onto mahaleb cherry rootstocks, and sweet cherry varieties, such as 'Stella', onto mazzard (wild sweet cherry) rootstocks. 'Colt', introduced in 1974 in England as a dwarfing cherry rootstock, has proven not to have any significant dwarfing effect.

Should cherry trees be pruned and at what age?   Cherry trees should be pruned lightly each year, but removal of a few undesirable twigs may be all the pruning needed. They require less pruning than the apple or peach.

When is the best time to prune cherry trees?   The best time is in early spring—during the latter part of March. They may, however, be pruned at any time during the dormant season. Do not prune after unusually cold winters.

How should cherry trees be pruned?   With sweet cherries, little need be done except to remove dead or injured branches and twigs that are growing in an undesirable position and that are too high or tending to make a weak crotch. Sour cherries should be started as delayed open-center trees with a short trunk about 6 feet high and several well-spaced scaffold limbs. Besides the "corrective" pruning, as recommended for sweet cherries, some thinning of tops will be needed to keep the trees from becoming too dense and so shading out fruit-bearing wood in the lower part. If trees are pruned every year, not a great deal of cutting will be needed at any other time.

I have been told a 'Bing' sweet cherry will not produce fruit when planted by itself. What variety will? I don't want more than one tree. 'Compact Stella', a spur-type sweet cherry, will produce fruit on its own pollen. Nearly all sweet varieties will pollinate others. In your case, you might top-work (graft) 'Windsor' or 'Black Tartarian' on a branch of the 'Bing'. This will provide enough pollination for one tree. 'Bing', 'Lambert', and 'Napoleon' are cross-incompatible and do not pollinate each other successfully.

I have a 'Black Tartarian' cherry tree surrounded with plums, peaches, Rocky Mountain cherry, and apples. Does it need any other cherry for fertilization? None of these is an effective pollinator. You could use 'Bing', 'Windsor', 'Napoleon', and other good varieties.

What do you recommend doing for a white cherry tree when very small green cherries fall off before maturing? Plant another variety to act as a pollinator.

What causes the small green cherries (sour cherry) to drop off the tree? It may be due to a lack of pollination, attacks by curculio, or frost injury during bloom or shortly after.

I planted 3 cherry trees and 2 days later we had frost. How should I protect these trees from frost? If the trees were dormant, as they should have been for transplanting, frost a few days after planting would not hurt them.

I have a 15-year-old sweet cherry tree. Why does it bear only a few large fruits? This tree is located in a strip 4 feet wide separating two cement driveways. This is a very poor location for a tree. And probably there is no other sweet cherry variety in the near neighborhood to act as a pollinator.

How long does it take for a cherry tree to blossom? A sour cherry should produce its first blossoms 3 or 4 years after being planted. A sweet cherry tree may take 1 to 3 years longer.

How can I retard the blooming of cherry, peach, plum, and apricot trees? There is no practical method of retarding blooming dates of fruit trees in order to avoid frost injury. Some varieties naturally bloom a little later than others.

We raised a cherry tree from a pit; it is 3 years old. Will it bear fruit? It will bear eventually but is not likely to resemble the parent.

A sour cherry tree bore fruit one year and none the next. Why? The blossoms or buds were probably injured by cold weather.

I have 4 cherry trees which bloom but have only a dozen or so cherries. Why? Probably because of imperfect pollination. If your trees are all of one variety, plant some other. There are 7 distinct groups which will not pollinate each other, so the variety must be selected with care and also as to the possibility of frost injury.

I accidentally broke a branch in the lower part of a cherry tree that left a groove in the bark; the sap keeps running out at the foot of the tree. What must I do to correct this? Sap will run from any kind of an injury on a cherry tree. There is no practical method of repairing an injury such as the one described. If the tree is growing vigorously, the wound may heal over eventually.

How can I keep my cherries free of insects and diseases? Plum curculio, cherry maggot, and brown rot are the worst enemies of cherry trees. Cherry leaf spot appears first as yellow spots in the leaves. These turn brown and fall out. They look like shot holes. The leaves themselves turn yellow and then fall. Sometimes the tree is completely defoliated. Follow the spray schedule obtainable from the Cooperative Extension Service in your county or from the state university.

How can I keep birds from eating my cherries and other fruits? This is a hard question to answer. The enclosure of the tree or its branches is the only sure method. Covering the branches with large cheesecloth bags will save a few of the fruits for you and rarely can the birds eat the entire crop!

I have heard of virus diseases of cherries. What can I do to avoid them? As the result of an extensive search for virus-free trees of the important cherry varieties, nurseries are now propagating virus-free trees. These should be specified when ordering trees. They are superior to stock of uncertain virus status.

PEACH (PRUNUS PERSICA)

What kind of soil is needed for peach trees? Any good soil that is well drained. They prefer sandy loam, however.

Should I mix fertilizer with the soil when I plant a peach tree? Do not mix fertilizer with soil used to fill in around the roots, as it might cause some injury. Dig it under before the tree is planted or work into the soil around the newly planted tree but outside the limits of the hole in which it was planted.

Should I plant a peach orchard in the spring or fall? In general, except where winters are quite mild, spring planting is best.

Is it wise to plant new peach trees in the same places from which the old ones have just been removed? It is not. Peaches so planted often fail. The trouble is not well understood, but it may be nematodes, root aphids, or possibly something else from the roots of the old trees.

I have a bearing peach tree. When can I move it? Moving a bearing-age peach tree is hazardous. It must be pruned heavily and might be as long coming into bearing again as a new tree. It can be moved in the fall, but very early spring would be better.

How does one care for a peach tree in a suburban backyard? The ideal treatment would include preventing weed or other growth around the tree; use of a complete fertilizer; adequate pruning; some spraying and thinning of fruit whenever a heavy crop is set. Control of the peach borer, which works in the trunk just above the level of the soil, is very important.

My peach tree has 3 main trunks at the ground level, forming a sort of cup which is filled with gum. How shall I treat it? This is probably the result of killing the leading shoot when the tree was a year or two old. Cut away 2 of the trunks as close as possible and arrange drainage so the water will not stand in a "cup," if one is left. Paint the wounds.

I have a 'Halehaven' peach tree which has had only a half-dozen peaches. Could you explain why and what to do to improve the fruit? The tree may be too young to bear a full crop. It should have a full crop by the fourth year if it is making good growth and has not been injured by cold weather. Low winter temperatures or spring frosts at blooming can prevent fruit from forming.

Do peach varieties have spur types like apples? 'Compact Redhaven' is identical with 'Redhaven', except that it develops into a smaller, more compact tree. Unlike the enhanced productivity of spur types in apples, this compact peach variety is less fruitful than the normal, non-compact 'Redhaven'. 'Bonanza' is another very dwarfed, dark-green peach tree with very dense leaves; but again, it is not sufficiently fruitful to be recommended except as a novelty. It can be grown in a tub.

Why do some peach trees fail to bear? (California.) This might be due to any one or more of these factors: lack of enough winter cold to complete the rest period; frost injury to buds or flowers; lack of pollination (if a self-sterile variety); or faulty nutrition.

I have a 3-year-old peach tree about 8 feet high which has not blossomed. It grew from a 'Halehaven' pit. When will it bear fruit, or must I graft it? Peaches usually bear at 3 or 4 years of age. Whether a seedling will bear good fruit is a matter of chance. Some seedling peaches are good enough for home use.

What is the approximate life of a peach tree? With good care, peaches can be made to produce for about 20 to 25 years. However, severe winter temperatures or borers can shorten the life of peach trees.

I have a young peach tree about 12 feet away from a large oak tree.

Will it grow and produce fruit there as well as it would in the open or should it be moved? You have two handicaps: competition of roots, and shade. Better move it. Peaches need full sun.

Will a peach tree that came up from seed ever bear good peaches? It may or may not. If it is a seedling of 'Elberta', it will resemble that variety. Keep it until it fruits and decide then whether you want to keep it.

My peach tree is simply loaded with fruit but it never gets large enough to amount to anything. The fruit should be thinned when it is a little larger than a robin's egg. Take off all small or stunted peaches, leaving at least 6 inches between the fruits that remain on the tree. Thinning will result in larger size, better color, and less breakage of limbs.

What is the best method of "domesticating" wild-grown or neglected 2- to 3-year-old peach trees? It is probably better to start anew if they were badly neglected. If not too bad, plow, fertilize soil, prune, and give good spraying. Take out very bad trees and replace.

How can a peach tree, 4 years old, be changed to another variety? Peaches can be top-worked (see Grafting), but cleft grafting used for apples or pears is not successful with peaches. The way to proceed is to cut off branches 2 or 3 inches in diameter in late winter. During the summer, shoots will appear, and these can be budded in July, August, or early September, just as seedling peaches are budded.

Will peach tree roots block up a drain or sewer? Peach roots will not seek out a drain or sewer; but roots of any tree planted above or very close to a loose-joint sewer will enter it.

When and how should I prune newly planted peach trees? Prune just before the trees are planted or just after. Small nursery trees, 3 to 4 feet high, should be pruned to a "whip" (a single stem) and cut back to a height of 24 to 30 inches. Larger trees, 5 to 6 feet, should be cut back to about 30 to 36 inches, but instead of cutting off all side branches, leave 3, suitably spaced to be used as scaffold limbs, and cut them to stubs 4 to 6 inches long.

What is the proper way to prune a young peach tree? Develop an open center, bowl-shaped type of tree with its lowest scaffold limb at least a foot from the ground. Remove limbs that are too low, that head in and tend to fill up the center, or that crowd other limbs and make any part of the tree too dense. The tallest limbs should be headed to side branches pointing outward in order to get maximum spread and keep the center open.

What time and method should be used in pruning old peach

trees? Pruning is best done in late winter or early spring after the time when dangerously low temperatures may occur. Pruning should be more severe than for younger trees. Cut out weak twigs and limbs, thin out year-old shoots by taking out weaker ones. Cut back shoots that are longer than 12 inches. As the tree gets older, severe pruning needed to maintain vigor may cause it to be smaller than it was as a younger tree.

When is the best time to remove a limb from a peach tree? Any time it seems necessary, although it is usually done during the dormant season.

What is the best way to fix a peach tree limb that was broken because of the heavy crop? If the branch can be spared, cut it off. If it is split in the middle, prop it up and put in a few small bolts with washers. Early thinning prevents limb breakage from overbearing of fruits.

Should one cut all dead limbs from peach trees? All dead limbs should be removed from all trees, as they present a disease and insect hazard. You should have no dead limbs if you prune peach trees properly.

How do you prune a nectarine tree? The fruit of a nectarine is essentially a peach without fuzz, and so the tree is pruned in the same way as a peach.

Must peach trees be cross-pollinated? Only varieties that have poor pollen need other varieties near to provide good pollen. 'J. H. Hale', an old variety, has poor pollen, but all satisfactory recent varieties have good pollen.

When I cut open peaches that appear to be sound, why are there little pink worms in them? These are the larvae of the Oriental fruit moth. Spray trees according to the Cooperative Extension Service directions obtainable from your county agent.

Do peach trees need a mulch for winter? Mulching the soil around peach trees will have no appreciable effect on their susceptibility to injury by cold weather.

What is the best method to protect young peach trees from freezing in the winter and from rabbits? There isn't much that can be done in a practical way to protect peach trees from freezing. If they are of a hardy variety and in good growth condition, they will be as resistant to cold as it is possible to make them. Rabbits usually are not as likely to bother peach trees as apple trees. Mechanical protection, by use of wire cloth, building paper, or even newspapers wrapped around the trunk, is probably the most satisfactory method.

What is the best method of propagation for peaches? Peaches are usually budded on seedlings grown from wild peach seeds. (See Budding.)

What are the main insects and diseases that trouble peaches? See Section 13, and consult bulletins from your state Cooperative Extension Service.

What are the best varieties of peach trees to plant? See the introduction to this chapter.

PEAR (PYRUS)

When does one fertilize young pear trees to bring them into early bearing? The trees will bear earlier if making a moderate growth than if growing too vigorously. Overfertilization is also conducive to fire blight. If the soil is poor, make a light application of a complete fertilizer in early spring. Otherwise, if the tree is making good growth, do not use fertilizers.

What soil is best for pear trees? Heavy sandy loam or clay loam with plenty of humus, which will hold moisture, yet assure good drainage.

When is the best time to plant pears? Plant trees as early in the spring as the soil can be prepared. Planting should be completed by the time fruit-tree buds begin to expand.

How do I plant, care for, and prune 'Bartlett' pear trees? I am setting out 100 trees this spring. A hundred trees of 'Bartlett' pears will involve considerable care and expense. It would be advisable, therefore, to get rather complete information from your Cooperative Extension Service as to fertilizing, spraying, etc., under your particular local conditions. When making planting plans, some provision should be made for cross-pollination by planting at least 5 or 6 trees of another variety which should be something other than 'Seckel', as 'Bartlett' and 'Seckel' do not pollinate each other.

Our 5-year-old 'Bartlett' pear has twice borne fruit sparingly. It is of good size and its leaves look healthy, but they are very small and few. This tree is doing well to have borne fruit twice the first 5 years. 'Bartlett' leaves are normally rather small, so perhaps the tree has nothing wrong with it. If you stimulate its growth too much, you may have trouble with the disease known as fire blight.

Are there dwarf pear trees? Are they worth planting? Pear trees are dwarfed by propagating them on quince roots. They are suitable for the home garden.

Will one pear tree alone in a garden bear fruit? Most varieties of pears will bear a much better crop if cross-pollinized, so in making a new planting it would be highly desirable to include at least 2 varieties unless there are other varieties growing in the immediate neighborhood. However, single trees sometimes prove to be fairly reliable croppers.

Is the 'Bartlett' pear self-fertile? If not, what variety should I plant near it? 'Bartlett' will set a much better crop if cross-pollinated. Any of the common varieties, such as 'Sheldon', 'Bosc', or 'Anjou', would be satisfactory pollinizers.

Does a 'Duchess' pear need cross-pollination? Experiments in New York and in California indicate that this variety can bear a fair crop if self-pollinated but a better crop if cross-pollinated.

How should mature pear trees be pruned? Mature pear trees of most varieties require very little pruning and are likely to be injured by fire blight if pruned too heavily. Simply remove dead and broken branches. If the trees become too high, leaders can be cut back a little to a side branch.

How do you prune pear trees at planting time? One-year trees will be unbranched whips. Head a 5-foot tree back to 3½ or 4 feet. Two-year nursery trees will have 2 to 6 side branches; remove all side branches below 30 inches, except 2 to 4 of the stronger ones well distributed around the trunk and spaced at least 4 inches apart. Remove the rest; head the leader back by about one third.

Our pear and plum trees have not had very much fruit for several years. They have never been pruned. How and when should this be done? The lack of fruit is probably due to other factors than lack of pruning, such as frost injury, insects, or diseases. Pruning would probably result in larger fruit. Remove dead, very weak, or broken branches, limbs that are too low or that rub and crowd other branches. If the trees are getting too high, the tallest limbs should be cut back to side branches. Avoid overpruning. The pear can be injured by fire blight if cut too hard. If there is a great deal of cutting needed, spread it over 2 or 3 years. If the soil is fairly fertile, withhold fertilizers during the years when heavy pruning is done.

How should I prune a young 'Seckel' pear tree? The 'Seckel' pear makes a rather dwarfish, compact tree which requires very little pruning. Remove only dead or broken twigs and those branches which are definitely out of place.

When pruning pear trees, is it harmful to remove some of the branches which had borne fruit during the past summer? It is claimed that this helps the growth of trees. No effort should be made to re-

move those branches which have borne fruit, as they should continue to
bear for many years.

**The trunk of our 20-year-old pear tree has produced 3 offshoots this
year. If I cut them off and set them in a container of mud and water,
will roots develop?**   No.

Is there anything to be done for fire blight on pears?   Not much.
Prune off the afflicted limbs. 'Bartlett' is reputed to be less subject to
blight when not overstimulated by fertilizers or pruning. The varieties
'Moonglow', 'Maxine', and 'Magness' are considered to be blight-resistant.

Is it necessary to spray pears to secure good fruits?   Pears are attacked by San Jose scale, codling moth, and fire blight. (See Apple.)
Fire blight is serious. Pear psylla is sometimes called a jumping plant
louse. A black fungus grows in the excreta on the leaves. Pear trees produce better fruit without spraying than other fruit trees. Consult your
Cooperative Extension Service for instructions.

What pear varieties are suitable for home-garden planting?   See the
list in the introduction to this chapter.

Can you give some information on the 'Comice' pear?   The 'Comice'
pear has excellent fruit but the tree is a poor grower, subject to blight,
and not very hardy. It is a valuable commercial variety on the Pacific
coast but likely to prove disappointing elsewhere.

**What is the best pear for the Lake George region? (New
York.)**   'Flemish Beauty' and 'Clapp Favorite', both of which are
more winter-hardy than most other varieties, are suggested for the Lake
George region. Two varieties are necessary to provide cross-pollination.

PLUM (PRUNUS)

Do plums require a special type of soil?   Heavy soils are preferred
for the European types and lighter soils for the Japanese varieties; but
they will all do well enough for home use on a fairly wide range of well-
drained soils if the site is otherwise suitable.

**How should young plum trees be fertilized to bring them into early
bearing?**   Young fruit trees usually make a rather vigorous growth if
the soil is reasonably fertile. The addition of fertilizer, if not carefully
regulated, may make growth too vigorous and delay bearing instead of
hastening it. Fertilize only enough to maintain good growth and trees
will bear early. On sandy soils, of course, fertilizer will be needed every
year if good growth is to be secured. The fertilizer program must be
adapted to local soil conditions.

What is the proper way to plant plum trees? Order 1- or 2-year-old trees and plant in early spring 20 feet apart (or a little less for Damsons). Dwarf plum trees can be planted 8 feet apart.

Can a single plum tree bear fruit? A few varieties such as 'Stanley', 'Italian Prune', 'Reine Claude', and the Damsons will set fruit if self-pollinated. Most varieties of plums, however, will set a very poor crop, or none at all, unless their blossoms are fertilized by pollen from another variety of the same species of plum. All Japanese plums are self-unfruitful. Bees will carry the pollen for some distance, but it is better to have trees close together to ensure cross-pollination.

I have a young plum tree which bloomed last spring but no fruit followed. Can you tell me the reason? There are various possible reasons for the failure to produce fruit. The variety may be self-unfruitful and require another variety to pollinize it. Frost may have injured its blossoms and prevented them from setting fruit. A young tree may sometimes be overvegetative and fail to set on that account. Pruning would make the tree more vegetative and would not induce fruiting.

We have a plum tree that blooms but never sets fruit. What causes this and what can be done to set fruit on this tree? It is probably a self-unfruitful variety requiring pollen from a tree of another variety. If this is a Japanese plum, plant another Japanese variety nearby and let the bees do the rest. If it is a European variety, plant another European, as the European and Japanese plums are not satisfactory pollinizers for each other.

Does the purple-leaf plum bear fruit? Yes, if pollinized by another variety of the same species.

I have a plum tree and think it needs pruning. Should I cut the branches short or just thin them out? Some cutting back may be needed to prevent the tree from getting too tall and "leggy." Most of the pruning should be a thinning out to remove undesirable branches and keep the top from becoming too dense.

How should a Japanese plum tree be pruned? This type of plum grows and bears much like the peach and should be pruned a good deal like it. Train the young tree to an open center and practice fairly heavy annual pruning to keep the top from becoming too dense. This will help maintain the vigor of the tree and the size of the fruit.

I have several year-old plum trees grown from pits. Can I expect these to bear eventually, or should I have planted only grafted trees? As the seedlings may not bear fruits worth having, it is much better to plant trees of a known variety. However, you might get a tree or two worth keeping.

When and how should sand (or cherry) plum seed be planted? If you want named varieties of plum, they must be budded onto seedlings, as seedlings do not "come true." To produce seedlings for budding purposes, plant seed in the fall in furrows about 2 inches deep. If only a few seeds are to be handled, it will be better to stratify (that is, mix the seed with sand and bury in a well-drained place). It can be protected against rodents by hardware cloth. Take up the seed in early spring and plant in shallow furrows.

What causes my plums to rot and fall off? This is the brown rot of stone fruits. It is more difficult to control on plums than on peaches because of their smooth skins. Follow the spray schedules obtainable from your Cooperative Extension Service.

Why are my plums wormy? The plum curculio is probably responsible. Follow spray schedules obtainable from your Cooperative Extension Service.

What caused all my plums to drop off? The tree is 6 years old. The trouble may be frost injury to the young fruits, and plum curculio if they are wormy. A virus disease may also be responsible. If the trouble continues, the tree should be replaced with one that is free from virus troubles.

Dwarf and Espalier Fruit Trees

How many dwarf fruit trees can I plant in my backyard? There are no trees of any kind there now. Probably several, but this of course depends on the size of your property, the dimensions of which you didn't give. Dwarf fruit trees (apples on 'M9' rootstock) can be planted as close as 6 × 6 feet (between trunks), but 8 × 8 feet, or 10 × 10 feet, or 10 × 12 feet in the case of an orchard (when the trees are set in rows), is better. The so-called dwarf cherry trees, varieties such as 'North Star' and 'Meteor', soon reach the proportions of a small tree, such as a flowering dogwood, and require more space than other dwarf trees. Write to your State Agricultural Experiment Station or Cooperative Extension Service for bulletins on dwarf fruit trees.

Do dwarf fruit trees require any special care? Yes. They must be looked after in the same way as are standard fruit trees: spraying to control pests and diseases, fertilizing, and some pruning. In addition, they may require staking when their fruit load is heavy. Plant with the bud union at least 2 to 4 inches above the ground.

When should I prune my dwarf fruit trees? Late winter through early spring are the best times.

Do dwarf fruit trees require as much pruning as standard fruit trees? No, because they are grafted on stocks that limit their growth to maintain a dwarf habit. The major pruning of dwarf trees is for special training, such as when the plants are grown against a fence or wall (see espaliers below) or when they are planted too close to one another. Some initial pruning may be necessary to prevent bad crotches and to help make the tree structurally strong.

Are dwarf fruit trees generally as long-lived as standard trees? Probably not, because of problems that can arise between the understock and scion.

I have had 2 dwarf apple trees for several years. In the past year or so, one plant has grown very fast, the new shoot growth considerably exceeding its former growth rate and making it much taller and wider than the other tree. What should I do? It would appear that you have become the victim of a fairly common occurrence among home gardeners who grow dwarf fruit trees! What may have happened is that your tree has lost its "dwarfness" because the scion—the variety grafted onto the dwarf understock—has formed roots and is outgrowing the dwarf understock. If you want to retain a dwarf fruit tree, the only course you can follow now is to cut down the tree and buy another dwarf plant. When planting, be sure that the graft is 2 to 4 inches above the soil level to avoid scion rooting.

What are some good apple varieties available as dwarf trees? Most nurseries specializing in dwarf fruit trees offer the following: 'McIntosh', 'Beacon', 'Lodi', 'Red Delicious', 'Golden Delicious', 'Spartan', 'Cortland', among many others.

Is it true that dwarf apple trees start to bear fruit sooner than standard apple trees? Yes, much sooner. For example, a 'Red Delicious' dwarf apple tree, planted on 'M26' rootstock, at 4 years of age, can produce between 40 and 50 fruits. The tree could be barely 4 feet tall. It will eventually reach a height of about 8 feet, about 2 feet more than the ultimate height of a tree dwarfed by 'M9' rootstock.

What is an espalier fruit tree? It is a tree trained in formal shape to a given number of branches, usually in a vertical plane. The tree is planted against a wall, building, or trellis where it takes up little space and provides decoration as well as fruit. It can be trained to a single shoot or to 2 shoots opposite each other, or in a fan or other shape. The training is begun when the tree is very young. Espalier fruit trees have always been popular in Europe, where the protection afforded by wall training makes it possible to grow orchard fruits in climates less favorable than those in this country.

Are espalier trees practical for the average home garden? If you want fruit trees on a small property, they may do, but since most of them are on dwarfing rootstocks anyway, you might find it easier to grow dwarf fruit trees and give them only moderate training rather than trying to follow the intricate practices and patterns of formal espaliers. The yields, while often of high quality, are never plentiful on true espaliers.

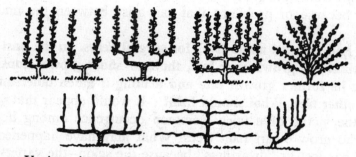

Various forms of espalier (or trained) fruit trees.
They are usually grown against walls or fences, or
secured to very strong wires or trellises.

What is the place of espalier fruit trees in the garden picture? Where there is limited space or if novelty design is wanted or in climates where severe weather changes prevail, this type of tree has its place. Training espalier fruits in traditional shapes is a garden art and can be time-consuming.

What part of the season is fertilizer applied to dwarf fruit trees? Two to 4 weeks before the trees come into bloom, when ½ pound of ammonium nitrate can be applied.

What fertilizer materials are used to feed dwarf fruit trees? Nitrogen has been found to be the main element in the growing of tree fruits but a complete fertilizer such as a 5–10–5 is usually satisfactory. (See also the above question.)

How is fertilizer applied to dwarf fruit trees under the mulch system? Broadcast the material on top of the mulch. Water in if dry weather is encountered.

How should espalier trees be pruned? The object is to maintain the skeleton form into which the tree has been trained. This means frequent pruning at an early stage to prevent undesired branches and suckers from getting a start.

Will dwarf fruit trees continue to bear as many years as standard-size fruit trees? With proper attention to pruning, training, fertilization, and spraying, they might. However, the general expectation is that they will not.

In training one's own trees, which are the most suitable varieties of apple, pear, peach, and apricot to use? Any varieties can be used. The fruits mentioned should be on dwarfing roots. The standard tree grows too vigorously to permit the intensive pruning an espalier is subject to.

Where may dwarf fruit trees be obtained? Any first-class mail-order nursery should be able to supply them.

Can fruits be grown in pots as indoor plants? Fruit trees in pots are very practical for persons who have very small garden areas or for those who wish to see fruit blossoms in the very early spring while the snow is still blowing. Peach, cherry, and apple trees have been grown continuously in pots for 20 years, with good results. Potted crab apple trees make beautiful displays of bloom.

In early March, purchase 1-year-old, not 2-year-old, dormant nursery trees of your preferred variety. The trees must be budded on dwarfing rootstocks: apples on 'M9' or 'M26'; pear on quince; cherry on mahaleb; peach on peach. Plant into 9- to 14-inch pots. Hold in a cool cellar for 2 weeks after potting, then move to a cool, sunlit area of the living room. Trees may not bloom the first year after potting, but in the second or third year, blossoms should open 2 or 3 weeks after the trees are brought into the warmth. If fruits are to be set, hand-pollination, using pollen of another variety, must be done as blossoms open.

In May, when the fruits are one third grown, they should be thinned if there are too many. Early shoot pruning should also begin in May by pinching back the tips of shoots. Keep strong upright growth in check. Shape the trees into pyramids.

In June, move the potted trees out-of-doors; keep watered. Most fruit plants require winter chilling of three months below 45° F. before they are ready to break leaf again in the spring. Potted fruit trees must be kept outside or in a cold cellar for 3 months, during which time the pots must be insulated by deep mulching to prevent root freezing and pot breakage. Protect from rodents.

Every other year, just before the trees are brought into a warm atmosphere in March, they should be removed from the pots, one third of the roots pruned off, and the trees repotted. Root pruning reduces excess shoot growth and promotes fruit bud formation.

I plan to grow a few dwarf fruit trees in containers on my terrace as ornamentals and (I hope) for some fruit. Will these survive the winter

in their tubs? Is any special winter attention needed?   The roots of fruit trees are much less tolerant of severe winter temperatures than are the tops. In midwinter in the orchard, apple tree tops may withstand a temperature as low as 40° F., but roots are killed at plus 10° F. Roots of peach and cherry trees are even less hardy than those of apple. Thus, fruit trees grown in tubs require special care to protect the roots. During the winter, the tubs must be kept in a cool cellar or a hole can be dug in the garden and the pot put into it and covered with heavy insulating material such as a thick layer of leaves or several layers of a heavy fabric.

Small Fruits

BLUEBERRY (VACCINIUM)

What is an ideal blueberry soil?   A well-aerated mixture of sand and peat moss, with the water table 14 to 22 inches below the surface. In such a soil, there is excellent drainage near the surface, but water is always available within the reach of roots. A plentiful supply of peat moss means plenty of organic matter and usually the required acid reaction of pH 4.5 to 5.5. Such soil conditions are seldom available in the home garden, so they have to be approximated by spading in peat moss or leafmold, by mulching, or irrigation, or all three.

How can I make my soil sufficiently acid for successful blueberry culture?   The soil should be moist, full of peat or other organic material, and with a reaction of about pH 5.0. The soil may be made acid through the use of acid peat moss, oak leafmold, and sulfur. The quantities of sulfur necessary have to be calculated in relation to the composition of the soil and its pH reaction. Have your soil tested and get recommendations from your Cooperative Extension Service.

How can hybrid blueberries be grown on neutral soil?   Limestone soils vary. Sometimes, if the underlying rock is limestone, the topsoil can be acid. If the soil is deep and of limestone origin, the conditions are different. Investigate. Why try something that may be troublesome in later years? For instance, you might make the soil acid enough originally, but if it is necessary to irrigate, and the water is hard, trouble will develop. However, if you must have blueberries, try this: Excavate a bed 4 feet wide and 2 feet deep, and put in a layer of 6 or 8 inches of peat moss or acid leafmold. Fill with soil that has been acidified chemically or by being composted with acid peat or leafmold. Use water that does not contain lime. Line the hole with a polyethylene sheet with drainage holes in the bottom.

How is ordinary soil prepared for growing blueberries? Is there any way to test it? Most State Agricultural Experiment Stations or Cooperative Extension Services will test the soil for residents of the state. Methods of acidifying the soil are discussed elsewhere. In many cases, it will not be necessary to acidify artificially, and then the main requirement is assurance of a uniformly plentiful supply of moisture. If the soil is dry, it may be necessary to irrigate. If it is fairly moist, a permanent mulch of straw, rotted sawdust, or peat moss will give the best results by conserving what moisture there is.

Our soil is too rich for blueberries. What can we do about it? It probably isn't too "rich," as blueberries will grow in very fertile soil provided other conditions are right. Your soil may be alkaline, deficient in one or more elements, or too wet or too dry.

Would you recommend blueberries for an acid garden? Blueberries will do excellently in an acid garden and will usually be an asset to it. They require the same cultural conditions as azaleas and rhododendrons. Full sun most of the day is essential, although some berries are produced in partial shade.

Is the soil in Cleveland satisfactory for blueberries? The ground is quite clayey. (Ohio.) Blueberries probably will not grow successfully in unmodified Ohio clays. They are lowland plants that like acid soils stuffed with humus and with a strong acid reaction.

We are much interested in trying to raise blueberries in an ashy soil in a dry climate; we have plenty of water to irrigate, but the atmosphere is very dry. Can it be done? (Idaho.) Your main difficulty would be in getting your soil acid enough. It would be best to start in a small way first. See the suggestions above.

How should blueberries, already planted, be fed and cared for? Assuming that the soil is acid, apply a mulch to a depth of 2 to 4 inches, and renew as needed to control weeds. Rotted sawdust, peat moss mixed with rich compost, pine needles, strawy manure, etc., are suitable mulches. Fertilize with sulfate of ammonia at the rate of 1 ounce for each year of age of the plants up to 8 years. During the first years of the mulch, double this amount may be necessary.

What is the best fertilizer for blueberries? I have a field of very fine native lowbush berries in Maine, which I wish to improve for marketing. Experiments at the Maine Agricultural Experiment Station have indicated the value of a complete fertilizer for lowbush blueberries provided that weeds are kept under control. Since this is to be a commercial venture, write for the latest recommendations from the Maine Station at Orono, Maine 04473.

How and when should blueberry shrubs 3 years of age be pruned? Prune during late fall, winter, or early spring. Three-year-old bushes will need comparatively little pruning. Remove small, rather weak lateral twigs to prevent their fruiting. Long shoots, well covered with fruit buds, may need to be cut back to leave only 2 or 3 fruit buds. Remember that 1 fruit bud will produce a cluster of flowers and of fruit. If the fruit buds are not thinned by pruning, too many berries will be set, the fruit will be small and late in maturing, and the bush will be weakened.

When is the best time to make blueberry cuttings, and how are they cared for? Make hardwood cuttings in late winter or early spring and place them in peat moss, or ½ sand and ½ peat moss, in ground beds under a lath house, or in a special raised propagating frame. Cuttings should be about 6 inches long, of good 1-year-old twigs, preferably without fruit buds. Place them at an angle in the moss, with at least ⅔ of the cutting covered. Great care must be taken in watering and ventilating, especially in raised frames which are covered with a hotbed sash and kept closed in the early stages of rooting.

Are 2 blueberry bushes sufficient to assure fruit, or is it necessary to have more than that number? If so, how many? Two bushes are enough if they are different varieties that bloom at the same time. If only 1 variety is planted, a fair set might be obtained, but the berries would probably be a little smaller than if they had been cross-pollinated.

Is any progress being made in adapting blueberries to dry land? The only way this can be accomplished is by crossing those which require moist soil with one of the dry-land types. The cultivated blueberry has been crossed with the lowbush blueberry of Maine, a dry-land type, and also with 2 or 3 dry-land species of the South. Suitable varieties have been developed for the South. Mulching and irrigation are helpful if the soil is dry.

What are the requirements of hybrid blueberries? The so-called hybrid blueberries are essentially like other plants with respect to most of their requirements, the two principal exceptions being that they require a rather acid soil and an ample and uniform moisture supply.

Where should blueberries be planted in the home garden? Blueberries require acid soil, good drainage, full sun, and aeration. They need a space of 6 to 8 feet between bushes.

Can blueberries be cultivated in a limited space under favorable conditions? Yes. Favorable conditions, however, include full exposure to sunlight, which is not always possible in a very limited area.

How can I promote faster growth of blueberry bushes? Be sure that growing conditions are favorable with respect to weed control, soil fertility, and moisture supply. Some varieties grow more rapidly than others, but all are rather slow-growing compared, for instance, with a peach tree.

Will blueberries grow under tall, large oaks in semishade? They may survive in this environment, but the yield of fruit will not be equal to that of plants grown in the open.

How are weeds controlled in the blueberry regions of Maine where cultivation isn't practical? By burning over the blueberry fields every other year or every third year. Straw is spread thinly over the area and burned when conditions are right for a quick fire that will not injure the blueberry roots.

I have 2 acres of well-drained swampland; how and when should I plant highbush blueberries? Be sure that the swampland is well drained but not too dry; blueberries are very sensitive to moisture conditions. Plant as early in the spring as the soil can be put into condition. Set the plants carefully, slightly deeper than they were in the nursery row, about 5 feet apart in rows 10 feet apart.

We have very large blueberries in a pasture. Can they be moved to a garden with good results? Very large bushes would be difficult to move, but you could move smaller ones. Some would need to be split up to make several plants. The size, color, and quality of the fruit are not likely to be as satisfactory as that from the named varieties, plants of which you can buy. Be sure your soil is properly prepared with humus-rich materials before digging the wild bushes.

My cultivated blueberry plants have been neglected for approximately 3 years. Will transplanting and proper care revive these plants? Prune them to thin out the probably too dense bush, control weeds with shallow cultivation or a mulch, and fertilize with sulfate of ammonia.

How often should a planting of blueberries be renewed? Blueberries, with good care, should be as permanent as tree fruits, that is, 15 to 25 years or more.

Under ideal conditions, are the leaves of blueberries light or dark green? Could a yellowish-green color be due to any factor other than incorrect soil reaction? The leaves of blueberries that are doing well are large and dark green, although the intensity of the green may vary somewhat in the different varieties. The yellowish-green color might be due to nitrogen deficiency; a too wet, poorly aerated soil; a too alkaline soil with which might be associated iron deficiency; or a virus disease known as stunt.

I have blueberries which are not doing well. What can be done? Check the following, which may be responsible: soil that is not acid enough; soil lacking in fertility, especially nitrogen; too dry; too wet; injury by low temperatures or by some pest.

How can I grow blueberries successfully in Ohio? For soil requirements, see the previous questions. Plant 5 feet apart in a row, using balled and burlapped stock, either in the fall or spring. Always plant 2 or more varieties to ensure good pollination. Water once a week if rain does not fall for the first season. Cultivate shallowly or mulch the plants with rotted sawdust, compost, or oak leaves. In the spring, apply 1 ounce of sulfate of ammonia for each year of the age of the plants. After the plants are in full bearing, remove old, unfruitful branches during the winter.

Will the large blueberries grown in south Jersey do as well in northern New Jersey? Yes, if proper growing conditions are provided. However, there is not nearly as much good blueberry soil in the northern part of the state as in the southern part.

Does the blueberry make a good ornamental shrub? Yes, it is attractive in bloom when the fruit is ripe and when the leaves turn red in the fall. The twigs in winter are also striking. Results will be disappointing, however, if the growing conditions are not right. If they are favorable, it may be possible to raise an adequate crop of fruit in a border of ornamental shrubs. The fruits are attractive to birds, so unless you want to share the harvest, cover the bushes.

What are the advantages of mulching blueberries? Blueberries are shallow-rooted, so that the advantages of mulching are very substantial and greater than with many other plants. The mulch conserves moisture, eliminates most of the weeds, keeps soil temperatures lower, and prevents injury to the roots from too deep cultivation.

How hardy are highbush blueberries? They will stand temperatures down to 20° to 25° F. below zero and sometimes even lower. When in bloom, they will stand more frost than other fruit blossoms. Injury may be expected in bloom when temperatures drop below 22° F.

How are blueberries protected from birds? The plants should be covered with plastic netting sold for this purpose or a cage made of poultry netting small enough to keep out birds or to keep the birds from strangling themselves. Scaring devices (except the family cat) are of little value as the birds soon become used to them. Birds rarely can clean up all the fruits on established bushes.

What is meant by hybrid blueberries? The term is commonly used to designate the named varieties of the type known as the highbush, swamp, or cultivated blueberry. The first varieties to be cultivated were merely wild highbush blueberries that were somewhat superior to the general run of wild blueberries. All of the good cultivated varieties now are several generations of breeding removed from their wild ancestors.

What is the difference between blueberries and huckleberries? The term huckleberry is often erroneously applied to blueberries outside of New England. Blueberries (*Vaccinium*) have many small seeds, 60 or 70, that are not noticeable, while huckleberries (*Gaylussacia*) have 10 comparatively large seeds that are very noticeable and crackle between the teeth. Huckleberries have small yellowish dots on the underside of the leaves; blueberries have none.

What are the best blueberry varieties for the home garden? Ripening from early to late, the best varieties are 'Earliblue', 'Bluetta', 'Collins', 'Blueray', 'Bluecrop', 'Berkeley', 'Herbert', 'Darrow', 'Coville', 'Late Blue'. 'Jersey' is still a good variety and one of the hardiest.

I have seen blueberries growing in western Florida. What kind are they? These are a different species than grows in the North. It is known as *Vaccinium ashei,* the rabbit-eye blueberry. It is suited to the Deep South and makes a much larger bush than the northern types. Improved varieties now being grown are, in order of ripening: 'Woodard', 'Coastal', 'Garden Blue', 'Callaway', 'Tifblue', 'Homebell', 'Menditoo'.

What is the difference between the cultivated blueberries and the ones that grow in Maine? The species usually meant when the term "cultivated blueberries" is used is *Vaccinium corymbosum,* otherwise known as the highbush or swamp blueberry. The ones commonly seen in Maine belong to the species *V. angustifolium,* the lowbush type, which grows in dry upland in both sun and shade.

What are the important blueberry-producing states? New Jersey, North Carolina, and Michigan produce the most cultivated blueberries. There are some commercial plantings in Massachusetts, New York, and Maryland. Maine is in the lead in the production from wild lowbush blueberries. Nurseries in New Jersey, Michigan, Massachusetts, Maryland, and North Carolina are propagating blueberry varieties.

CRANBERRY (VACCINIUM MACROCARPUM)

Is the highbush-cranberry worth planting for jelly? The highbush-cranberry, *Viburnum trilobum,* is not a true cranberry, but is a red-fruited viburnum with fruit of about the same size and color as the true cranberry. It makes a fair jelly, but is not equal to jellies made from currants, grapes, quince, and several other fruits. It is most useful in regions too cold for these other fruits.

Where is the creeping cranberry native? *Vaccinium macrocarpum* is native to Newfoundland, south to North Carolina, Michigan, and Minnesota.

What are the soil requirements of the cranberry? Cranberries are grown in acid peat bogs that can be flooded. A level peat bog with a clay subbase is selected. The growth of weeds is killed by flooding for a year. Clear sand is added to a depth of 2 or 3 inches, and cuttings are thrust through this into the peaty soil beneath, 12 to 18 inches apart. They fruit in about 3 years. Bogs are flooded from December to April or May, and at other times to control insects, to prevent frost, and to harvest loose berries. Bogs are fertilized every year or two and are sanded at intervals to prevent too rapid, tangled growth.

Can cranberries be grown from seeds? Cranberries can be grown from seeds stratified in the fall, but the plants grow well only in very acid wet soil, as described above.

Is it safe to collect and eat wild cranberries that grow in a swamp near our summer place? (Long Island, New York.) Yes, quite safe! You will want to wear boots, as the bogs are usually full of water in late fall when the berries are ripe.

CURRANT AND GOOSEBERRY (RIBES)

Are currants and gooseberries particular as to soil? They can be grown successfully on an average garden soil that will grow vegetables and flowers.

How should currants and gooseberries be fertilized? Ammonium nitrate at the rate of about 4 ounces per plant, or nitrate of soda at the rate of 8 ounces per plant is most likely to be profitable. On light soils, sulfate of potash, at about 3 to 4 ounces per plant, may be useful, but it will not be needed every year. A hay or straw mulch is also useful.

Where should bush fruits such as currants and gooseberries be planted? They are somewhat tolerant of shade and may be planted on the north side of buildings or fences and between young fruit trees and grapevines if space is limited. In such a case, beware of spray residues on the currant and gooseberry fruits from sprays used on the trees.

When should currant and gooseberry bushes be planted? These plants start growth very early in the spring, so they should be set either in the fall or by the latter part of March.

How far apart are currants and gooseberries planted? In the garden,

3 to 4 feet in the row and ideally 5 to 6 feet between rows, but less if space is limited.

Can gooseberries and currants be planted near pine trees? In regions where white-pine blister rust is serious, and white pines are important, the planting of gooseberries and currants may be forbidden. Consult your county agent.

How many currant and gooseberry bushes should be planted per person in the home garden? Currants—2 plants. Gooseberries—2 plants.

What care do currants need? Annual pruning, fertilization, and cultivation or mulching to control weeds. A dormant spray to destroy aphid eggs and summer sprays for anthracnose may be necessary.

Do red currants need to be cultivated? Currant bushes sometimes struggle along in sod and produce some fruit, but they will do much better if weeds and grass are suppressed by shallow cultivation or mulching.

Should I purchase bearing-size currant bushes? Good 1- or 2-year plants are much superior to bearing-age transplants. They are cheaper and more likely to survive.

How often should currants and gooseberries be picked? For jelly, currants are all picked at once, as soon as ripe, but for dessert, they can be picked as needed for 3 or 4 weeks, since they remain in good condition for some time. Gooseberries may be picked when they are half grown to make green gooseberry pie or sauce, delicious desserts known to very few these days. This early picking of part of the crop amounts to a thinning which makes the late berries much larger. Gooseberries are sometimes scalded by unusually hot weather (90° F. and above) so they should be harvested promptly.

Can gooseberries be successfully grown in the small home garden? Gooseberries are easy to grow and have few pests. The plants are very compact, so that the few needed by an average family will not require much room.

Why are gooseberry bushes not grown more in Massachusetts? Currants and gooseberries are alternate hosts for white-pine blister rust, a serious disease in New England as well as other parts of the country. Various state and federal laws provide for eradication of these plants in certain areas, and in Massachusetts, state authorities have the right to remove them when deemed necessary, thus aiding in the control of this disease.

At what time of the year should currant bushes be pruned? Late fall, winter, or very early spring. Since so many things have to be done in the spring, autumn is the most practical time.

What is the best method of pruning red currant bushes? Remove canes 4 years old or older; low-growing canes that droop to the ground when heavy with fruit; broken or diseased canes; the weaker 1-year shoots. After pruning, an ideal bush might consist of about five 1-year shoots, four 2-year canes, three 3-year canes, and possibly two or three 4-year canes, if they are vigorous.

Do red currant bushes that have borne heavily for 3 years have to be trimmed? They don't seem to have any dead wood. When the canes get to be about 4 years old, they usually weaken and become unproductive. Such canes should be taken out, down to the ground, before they actually die.

Do gooseberry bushes need pruning? They may continue to produce for a long time without being pruned, but the bushes will be more vigorous and the fruit larger if they are pruned.

When should gooseberries be pruned? At any time during the dormant season; that is, after the leaves fall and before growth starts in the spring.

How does one prune gooseberry bushes? Remove any dead or broken canes, then those branches that are borne around the lower part of the bush, low enough to touch the ground when loaded with fruit. Canes more than 4 years old usually are too weak to be productive, so they should be cut out. This will usually be all the pruning needed, although it may be desirable to remove a few twigs here and there to shape up the bush or open up a crowded part of it.

Are currants raised from cuttings? That is the usual method—hardwood cuttings taken in late winter. Cuttings are made of 1-year canes and are usually 6 to 8 inches long. Currants can also be propagated by layers; that is, low-growing branches covered with soil except for the tips. After roots have formed, cut the branches from the plant and set where desired.

Will gooseberry bushes root from cuttings? Hardwood cuttings are usually used, but they will also root from half-ripe cuttings in the summer. They are easily layered—often branches resting on the ground will root.

What causes currants to have distorted, crinkly leaves? Aphids feeding on the leaves cause them to become distorted. These are best controlled by spraying the bushes with malathion at the first sign of leaf distortion. Use at the rate of 8 tablespoonfuls in 5 gallons of water, being sure to hit the underside of the leaves.

We have found our currant bushes stripped entirely bare of leaves. What causes this? This is undoubtedly the work of the imported currant worm, which usually works in large numbers and can strip a bush in a very few days. Watch your bushes carefully in early summer. When the greenish worms appear, spray with malathion, 6 tablespoonfuls to 5 gallons of water. Or dust with rotenone or pyrethrum. Bordeaux sprays used for disease control may kill many of the worms.

Do early browning and dropping of leaves from currant bushes mean that the bushes have died? Or will they come out again next spring? The leaf-spot disease and injury by the currant aphids may make leaves turn brown and drop prematurely. If the twigs are still plump and the bark, when scraped, is bright green, you can expect the leaves to come out again next spring. However, premature defoliation weakens the plants so that they are less productive the next year.

We have been told that currant and gooseberry bushes and pines do not mix. Must one or the other necessarily be the host of the attacking disease? Currants and gooseberries are the winter host for the white-pine blister rust, which attacks only those species of pines that have 5 needles in a bundle. The disease is limited in areas, and where not present, the fruits may be grown. Black currant is the worst, gooseberry next, and the red currant is permitted except in seriously infested areas. Your county extension agent should be consulted if you have doubts.

What varieties of currants are recommended for the home garden? Try 'Red Lake', one of the newer varieties.

What is a good gooseberry variety? (Pennsylvania.) 'Poorman' is a good red-fruited variety. 'Chautauqua' is very large-fruited and yellowish green when ripe.

ELDERBERRY (SAMBUCUS)

Is the elderberry worth planting for fruit for pies and canning? Yes, if you have the space. Elderberries are ornamental, and many people like the blossoms for wine and the fruits for pies and jelly. They are of easy culture, growing almost anywhere. Elders need cross-pollination, so more than one variety should be planted. Good varieties are 'York' and 'Nova'.

Does the 'Adams' elderberry spread and become a nuisance? All elderberries spread by means of suckers from the roots. With watchful care, these can be eliminated.

FIG (FICUS CARICA)

What is the best fertilizer for a fig tree in acid soil? A good garden fertilizer, such as 5–10–5, used at the rate of 1 pound per 50 square feet, will probably supply sufficient nutrients.

What is the best time to prune a fig tree growing in a tub? If it's in a greenhouse, at any season when it is not maturing fruits. If out-of-doors, prune in early spring.

How are fig trees pruned? (Maryland.) Figs require very little pruning. Most of this is done in training the tree while it is young. It is especially desirable in regions where winter injury is probable and the trees must be protected. If trained to 3 or 4 branches, it is easy to lay these down and cover them with soil, mounding up over the center point, for protection from the cold.

How can one keep a fig tree from freezing in the winter? (New York.) Many methods are used, depending upon the protection afforded by buildings. One way is to tie up the branches and wrap them with several layers of burlap. Or heavy waterproof paper may be used. The surest way is to train the plant so that it branches close to the ground. These branches may then be pressed to the ground, fastened, and covered with a foot or more of soil, with the soil mounded over the central point.

Should a fig tree on Long Island, New York, on the side of a house, be covered for winter? Fig trees will need good winter protection on Long Island. (See previous questions.)

What is the method of propagating a fig tree by layering? (Pennsylvania.) Bend a branch over in the early spring until a portion that is 2 years old may be fastened down and covered with soil. A notch in the underside of the covered portion, held open by a sliver of stone, may help. Keep this covering of soil moist. Roots should form by the middle of summer, when the new plant may be detached and planted.

In what parts of the country will figs bear successfully for the home garden? In the southeastern Atlantic and Gulf states, in parts of California, much of Arizona, and New Mexico. In northern states, figs need winter protection and usually bear little fruit.

What is the treatment for fig trees in a greenhouse? The soil should be rich in humus, and it is advisable to keep the trees mulched with well-rotted manure or compost. Winter temperature, 50° F. night, 65° F. day. In spring, increase to 65° F. night and 70° F. day. Figs must have plenty of air and moisture until the fruit is set.

I have a fig tree that is covered every winter, but only a few of the figs ripen before frost. Is there any way of forcing them to ripen earlier? (Ohio.) The variety factor enters here. Some varieties, such as 'Brown Turkey', mature fruits earlier than others.

How can I learn the variety of fig trees I have? (California.) Your county agent might be able to identify the variety.

GRAPE (VITIS)

What soil is most suitable for the cultivation of grapes? A good loam or sandy loam is probably ideal, but grapes will grow satisfactorily on a wide range of soil types, provided the moisture supply is adequate. Extremely dry or extremely wet soils should be avoided.

Do grapes like alkaline or acid soil? Grapes thrive on soils showing rather wide ranges of soil reaction. On the whole, acid soils seem preferable to alkaline soils.

Will grapes grow on muck soil? Grapes are never grown commercially on muck soil. Grapevines are usually planted on slopes because they will not tolerate poor drainage, and most muck soils offer drainage problems at some seasons of the year. Also, grapes should have good air drainage, and the level surfaces of muck soils do not favor air drainage. Frosts are worse on muck soil sites than on elevated land.

What is a good fertilizer for grapes? Grapes on the average soil are most apt to respond profitably to nitrogen at the rate of 60 or more pounds to the acre. Apply 200 pounds of ammonium nitrate or 400 pounds of nitrate of soda. Per vine, this would be ¼ pound of ammonium nitrate or ½ pound of nitrate of soda. On light soils, a need for potassium may be indicated by a marginal browning of the leaves. Here, sulfate of potash may be used. A hay or straw mulch will supply potassium, too.

What is the best way to apply fertilizer to grapes? Broadcast the fertilizer, covering an area a foot from the trunk out to 4 or 5 feet away from the trunk.

My 'Caco' grapevine is 5 years old, has made wonderful growth, but it bears no grapes. What fertilizer should I use on it? The fact that your grapevine is making wonderful growth indicates that it does not need more fertilizer, but, on the contrary, needs to have all such materials withheld from it. It is possible that you have been pruning it too closely. Leave at least 40 buds on it the next time you prune it. If it is still too vigorous and nonfruitful, leave 60 buds a year later.

What location is best suited for grapes? Do they grow well near trees? The ideal location for a vineyard is gently sloping land. Air and water drainage must be good to avoid the danger of late spring frosts and "wet feet." Steep slopes should be avoided because they favor erosion unless rows are planted on the contour. Southern exposures favor earlier starting of growth in the spring and earlier ripening of fruit, but are more susceptible to late-spring frost injury and to summer drought. Northern slopes are less susceptible to injury from late-spring frosts and summer droughts, but ripen their crops later than southern slopes. Deep, sandy soils that contain a good amount of organic matter will give best results for grapes. Soils too poor for other crops are not good grape soils. Planting grapes close to trees is usually not a good practice because the trees compete with the vines for water and soil nutrients as well as furnish cover for insects which may attack grapes. Shade from trees may favor diseases, delay ripening of the fruit, and reduce productiveness of the vine.

Where should grapes be planted?   On fences, trellises that mark boundaries, or on arbors especially constructed for the purpose.

Do grapevines need much sun?   Grapes are sun-loving plants, as is shown by their tendency to climb over the tops of tall trees. The outstanding grape regions of the world are in areas that have much clear, sunny weather and few fogs. Lack of sunlight favors the spread of mildew and black rot and retards the ripening of fruit. However, grapevines will do fairly well if they receive direct sunlight at least half of the day. Though grapevines will grow fairly well in partial shade, they will not produce well under such conditions.

How far apart should grapes be planted?   A suitable spacing for most varieties is 8 feet between rows and 8 feet between vines in the row.

How should grapevines be planted?   After the ground has been prepared and the rows have been marked, dig holes of sufficient size to accommodate the roots of the vines after they have been cut back to within 8 inches of the trunk. The top should be cut back to a single strong cane of 2 buds' length. The vine is then placed in the hole and the roots spread out evenly. A few shovels of soil are then thrown in on roots while the stem is shaken gently to sift fine soil in around the fine roots. More topsoil is then thrown into the hole and thoroughly tamped into place with the feet. Holes should then be well filled.

My 'Concord' grapevines, now 5 years old, should be moved to a better location. When is the best time? Will it destroy them if their root systems are cut?   Any time in the fall after the vines are fully dormant. A good-sized ball of earth should be moved with the vine, so that as many roots are kept intact as possible. The tops should be cut back severely so that the top growth is kept in balance with the greatly reduced root system. Vines should not be allowed to bear fruit the first year after being moved, and only a light crop the following year. It is really much better to set a new vine than to move a 5-year-old vine.

How many grapevines will a family of 4 need? This will depend on how you use the fruit. For table use, include 2 plants of very early varieties, 2 early, 6 to 10 midseason for jelly and juice, and 2 to 4 late to very late.

Is it necessary to dig around grapevines? Cultivation is only to control weeds and should be shallow. Mulching is a good substitute for cultivation.

What treatment should I give my grapes? They are fruiting poorly on clay soil. The fact that grapes are not fruiting well on clay soil indicates that the vines are probably not making enough growth to permit heavy fruiting. As a rule, grapes prefer lighter and sandier soils, but many good vineyards are found on clay soils. Fertilize vines with ⅓ pound of nitrate of soda or sulfate of ammonia per vine. Apply when the shoots are starting their growth in the spring. Frequent cultivation to keep down weeds and close pruning will encourage more vine growth and eventually result in heavier fruiting. Be sure that insects and diseases are not responsible for the poor cropping.

What can I do to make my grapevines bear heavily? An application of proper fertilizers, plus cover cropping and cultivation, should result in vigorous vines capable of bearing good crops of fruit. Pruning vines properly to not more than 40 buds per vine should enable them to set good crops. Spraying to control mildews, black rot, and leafhoppers favors ripening of such heavy crops. If vines overbear, the grapes do not ripen well and vines may winter-kill.

How soon and how much will grapes bear? Grapevines should not be allowed to bear any fruit until their third season, and then only a small crop. The fourth season may be expected to give a good crop of fruit, and by the fifth season, if vines are well grown, they may be expected to have reached full production. This may be from 10 to 20 pounds per vine, and vigorous vines, properly pruned, should produce twice that amount. An average of 10 pounds per vine would give about 3 tons per acre for vines spaced 8 to 10 feet apart.

Why do my grapes grow all to vines and bear no fruit? How often and at what season should they be trimmed? The vines have probably been thrown into an overvegetative stage by being grown on too rich a soil, by overfertilization, or by being pruned too closely. Very vigorous vines should have from 40 to 60 or more buds left to fruit. Grapevines require pruning only once each year, when the vines are fully dormant.

Dense shading encourages excessive vine growth and tends to discourage fruiting.

My 'Concord' grapevines, 15 years old, in recent years have ripened fruit very unevenly, with green and ripe berries of uneven sizes on each bunch. What is the cause and remedy? The primary cause of uneven ripening is high night temperatures, as in coastal plain areas south of Washington, D.C., or in portions of Oklahoma and similar climatic areas.

What is necessary to have grapes grow in nice bunches and have all the grapes ripen at about the same time? Uniform ripening of fruit is more likely to occur when the vine does not bear too heavy a crop. This

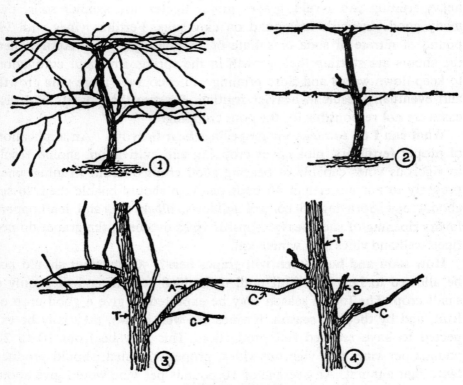

GRAPE PRUNING

(1) 'Concord' grapevine (several years old) before pruning.
(2) Same vine, pruned back during winter (Kniffin system).
(3) Detail, before pruning. T—main stem or trunk; A—arm, or lateral, 2-year-old wood; C—cane, 1-year-old wood. (4) Detail, after pruning. T—trunk; C—renewal cane, 1-year-old wood, tied to wire; S—spur, 1-year-old wood, cut back to 2 buds.

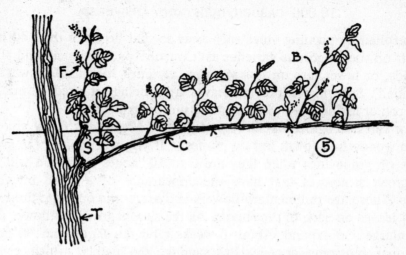

(5) Vine is early summer growth, showing fruiting habit. T—trunk; C—renewal cane; B—shoot, current year's growth; F—flower cluster; S—spur, producing new shoot, which may be used as a renewal arm the following year.

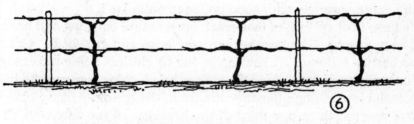

(6) Trellis for Kniffin system; wires 3 feet and 6 feet above ground; posts are placed 15 to 20 feet apart.

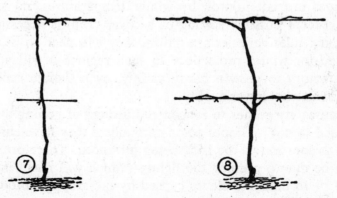

(7) One-year-old grapevine after being pruned, tied in 3 places to top wire. (8) Two-year-old vine after being pruned; 5 buds left on each lateral cane on top wire; 4 buds on each at bottom wire.

is controlled by pruning vines each year so that no more than 40 buds are left on such vigorous varieties as 'Concord' or 'Fredonia', and about 30 buds, or fewer, are on less vigorous varieties such as 'Delaware' or 'Diamond'. Spraying to prevent leaves from being attacked by mildew, black rot, or leafhoppers will also favor uniform ripening.

How can I recognize the flowers of grapes? My 3-year 'Caco' vine has shown wonderful growth but no grapes. If you will look at the young shoots on grapevines when they are 6 to 10 inches long, you will find tiny green structures that have the appearance of a small bunch of grapes. These are rudimentary flowers and are borne opposite the lower 3 or 4 leaves on each of the shoots. As the shoots grow, the flower clusters enlarge and expand. About 6 weeks after the shoots start to grow, individual blossoms appear. In opening, the petals, which remain greenish in color, are shed, leaving only pistil and anthers. The reason for nonfruiting may be overfertilization or underpruning, which produces lush, soft growth at the expense of fruit. Perhaps your vine is not 'Caco' but is another variety that may produce poor pollen and hence require another variety with good pollen to pollinate it.

We have 'Tokay' grapes that crack open before ripening and are sour; also, some dry up. The bunches are very large and crowded. Cracking of the berries followed by souring is due to clusters being too compact. The only remedy is to reduce the cluster by pinching some of the berries from each cluster soon after they are set in the spring. A good plan is to remove one fourth to one third of the branches of the cluster. This will reduce the size and should loosen it enough to prevent cracking.

What prewinter care should be given to grapevines? In regions where grapes are not injured by winter temperatures, no special fall treatment, except possibly sowing of a cover crop, is necessary. In the far North, if tender varieties are grown, they will need to be laid down and covered for winter protection. In such regions it will probably be more satisfactory to grow a hardy variety, even though such varieties may be of somewhat lower quality.

What causes my grapes to remain red instead of getting blue as they are supposed to do? Grapes color normally if they have sufficient leaf surface in proportion to the fruit being produced. Therefore, failure to ripen may be due to pruning too lightly (which will result in an excessive crop) or to injury to leaves caused by the grape leafhopper, Japanese beetle, or mildew.

Can good fruit be grown on an arbor or must there be more sun available? It is the sunlight on the leaves, not on the fruit, that determines whether grapes can be grown. The shade of nearby trees and buildings should be avoided. An arbor can produce heavy crops of fruit if the vines are sprayed and pruned regularly.

When is the best time of the year to prune grapevines? Grapevines should be pruned when the vines are fully dormant, in late fall, winter, or early spring. Pruning in late winter means the canes that have suffered from winter injury can easily be detected and cut out, thus leaving only sound canes on the vine. Spring pruning is not recommended because as buds begin to swell they become brittle and break off easily, thus reducing the size of the crop.

What is the difference between grape training and pruning? Training is the arrangement of the trunk and canes to facilitate care of the vines. Pruning is the removal of excess wood growth to adjust the number of buds to produce a crop that the vine is capable of maturing.

How are grapevines trained? The single stem 4-cane Kniffin system is a good method. A vine trained this way consists of a trunk 6 feet tall with two arms 3 feet from the ground and two at the top of the vine. A two-wire trellis with the lower wire 3 feet from the ground and the top wire 6 feet from the ground is used.

How are young vines pruned after the first year? The second year, the best cane is cut off at 6 feet and tied to the top of the trellis. All blossom clusters are removed to prevent fruiting. The third year, a vigorous vine should have two 10-bud canes left at the top wire and 2 spurs at the lower wire. A light crop is allowed to be produced. If the vine is weak, prune it the same way but remove all blossom clusters.

What is the umbrella Kniffin? A single stem reaches to the top wire and all canes arise near the top of the trunk and are twisted slightly over the top wire with their ends tied to the lower wire. This is a good system.

How are grapevines pruned the year that they are planted? The vine is cut back to 2 buds. Several shoots will grow. The strongest is saved and tied to a stake so that it will make a straight trunk. The others are removed. Vines over 3 years old are pruned as bearing vines.

How should bearing grapevines be pruned? Pruning is the removal of excess wood growth to adjust the crop to the vigor of the vine. To take this operation out of the realm of guesswork, a method has been devised. The pruner first selects 6- to 10-bud canes to fruit and cuts off all the rest of last year's growth. This is weighed. If the prunings weigh 1 pound, reduce the number of buds to 30 by leaving three 10-bud canes. For each additional pound of wood, leave another 10 buds. Thus, 2 pounds of wood would require that 40 buds be left. This is for the 'Concord' variety. For 'Fredonia', leave 40 for the first pound and for

'Catawba' leave 25 for the first pound. Two budspurs should be left near the trunk for canes for the following year.

I have been told to prune my grapes in the summer to let the light in to the fruit. Is that necessary?   It is not only unnecessary but undesirable. The fruit will color normally even if no light at all gets to it—quite different from the apple in this respect. Furthermore, removal of leaf surface at this time of year will delay or prevent normal ripening; hence, it will defeat the very purpose for which it is done.

Would you recommend thinning foliage on grapevines in the fall to hasten the ripening of fruit before frost?   Thinning the foliage would not hasten the ripening of the fruit but would delay ripening, inasmuch as leaves are the food-manufacturing organs of the plant. Nothing can be done at this stage of the season to hasten the ripening of fruit. Thinning the crop shortly after blossoming might have speeded up the ripening of the remaining fruit if the vine had set too heavy a crop.

How do you trim grapevines that have been neglected for years?   Neglected grapevines should be renewed by cutting the old trunk back to the ground. New shoots will start from the roots. Only 3 of these should be allowed to grow, and at the end of the first season the strongest one should be selected for a new trunk and the others should be removed. The new trunk should be cut back to the desired length and 4 side branches, of about 10 buds' length each, are then selected.

How can I best revitalize an old, neglected grapevine?   Cut back the old vine severely. If the old trunk is in bad shape, cut it back to the ground and start a new trunk from one of the new shoots. If you do not care to cut it back that severely, and if the trunk and old arms are still in fair condition, cut the vine back to the point from which most vigorous shoots, closest to the trunk, are arising. Leave a few, preferably 4, spurs of 2 buds each when the vine is cut back to provide new growth. It will be necessary to sacrifice a year's crop in order to get the vine back to a desirable form and fruiting condition.

Can I cut an old grapevine stem that has grown too long?   Renew the trunk of the old vine (see above) by cutting it back to the ground. Many new shoots will start, but only about 3 should be allowed to grow the first season. The next winter, remove 2 of these.

Will you please advise me as when and how to trim 'Scuppernong' grapevines?   'Scuppernong' grapevines are usually trained on overhead trellises or arbors in home plantings. This system calls for a single trunk running to an overhead trellis. At that height, 8 arms, radiating from the trunk like the spokes of a wheel from a hub, are selected and trained to grow out over the trellis. After the arms have been established, they are pruned by cutting back all side branches on them to short spurs 2 or 3 buds long. As the arms become older, it may be desirable to renew some of them by cutting them back to a strong lateral cane near the trunk. It is a good plan to renew 1 arm each year in this way. The best time to prune is in late winter, after the danger of severe freezing has passed. At that time, one can easily tell which wood is alive. Avoid leaving injured wood. Pruning after the buds begin to swell is not desirable because the buds break off easily.

How do you construct the standard grape trellis? The standard grape trellis in the East is the Kniffin trellis. This is simply 2 wires, one 3 feet from the ground and the other 3 feet above the first, supported by posts every 18 to 20 feet. No. 9 wire is the best size for this purpose.

Do grapes cross-pollinate? If so, how close can different varieties be planted? Yes, grapes frequently cross-pollinate when several vines are planted near each other. This is true in spite of the fact that most commercially important varieties are self-fruitful. Grape pollen is very light and fluffy, is easily scattered about by winds, and is carried about by many small insects. However, you need not fear that the pollen of one variety will in any way influence the fruit of another variety. It has been shown many times that there is no immediate effect produced by pollen of one variety being placed on pistils of another variety. Only the seedlings produced from such cross-pollination will show any effect.

Should all grapevines be grafted? In some areas of the country, grapes should be grafted on rootstocks that are resistant to the grape phylloxera or root louse. Where this insect is not prevalent, vines can be grown from cuttings. Grafted vines of some varieties often perform much better than own-root vines. Consult your State Experiment Station concerning your own locality.

How can I get another vine started from the one I have? The easiest way is to lay a cane on the ground, peg it down if necessary, and cover a portion of it with soil. Roots will form at the joints that are covered, and the cane can be cut loose from the old vine and used as a new plant. Most vines are propagated commercially by means of cuttings.

What is the best way to get grape cuttings started and set out so that they will grow? Should grafting wax be used? Select straight, vigorous, well-matured 1-year-old wood of pencil size. Cut into sections 3 buds long, making a lower cut through the node opposite the lowest bud and an upper cut about an inch above the third bud. Tie the cuttings in bundles of 50 and bury them in a trench, butt ends up, and cover with 6 inches of soil during the winter. After the ground has warmed in the spring, set the cuttings in well-prepared soil so that they are about 3 inches apart and with only the upper buds above the soil. Hoe, cultivate, and water them during the summer as needed. On good soil they should make enough growth in one season to permit transplanting them to the vineyard the next spring. No grafting wax or other materials need be used on cuttings handled in the manner described.

My grapes have begun to look like raisins on the vine but don't taste like them.   Your grapes have been affected by black rot disease, which is caused by a fungus. It can be controlled by spraying with Bordeaux mixture. The most important times to spray are when new shoots are about 1 inch long, when they are 12 inches long, right after blooming, and again 10 days later. (See Grapes, Section 13.)

How can I protect my grapes from birds?   Cover the clusters with 2-pound white paper bags such as are used in bakery stores. Do not use the brown bags as they give the grapes an unpleasant flavor. The bags are put on as the grapes begin to color and are folded around the cluster stem and fastened with a stout pin.

How can I keep bees and wasps from destroying my grapes?   The bees and wasps are secondary; the birds puncture the skins and the insects move in. Sprays that will poison them will poison the grapes and spoil them for food. Bag the clusters as described above.

Is there a seedless 'Concord' grape on the market?   There is a variety of grape available to growers which is known as 'Concord Seedless'. It is thought that it originated as a sport or mutation of 'Concord' grape. The berries are much smaller than those of 'Concord' and have only very rudimentary seeds which are hardly noticeable.

How does 'Sheridan' grape compare with 'Concord' grape?   Where it can be grown properly the 'Sheridan' grape is an improvement over 'Concord'. It has a larger berry and cluster, a more compact bunch, is more attractive, has a finer flavor, tougher skin, and will keep in fine condition in storage until January. It requires a long season to mature, however, ripening about 2 weeks after 'Concord' in central New York.

Are there any varieties of grapes which will keep better than 'Concord', either on the vine or after picking?   Long-keeping grapes are 'Seneca', 'Buffalo', 'Yates', 'Sheridan', and 'Steuben'.

What grape variety is usually made into grape juice?   The most common sweet grape-juice variety throughout the East is the 'Concord'.

What varieties of grapes should I plant for a long season of harvesting?   In order of ripening, from earliest to latest, the following are good varieties: 'Van Buren', 'Fredonia', 'Seneca', 'Buffalo', 'Delaware', 'Concord', 'Yates', 'Steuben', 'Sheridan', 'Golden Muscat', and 'Catawba'. Unless you have a long season, you may not be able to grow those ripening after 'Concord'.

What are some good varieties of hardy seedless grapes? The new seedless grapes—'Canadice', 'Glenora', 'Himrod', 'Lakemont'—originated at Geneva, New York, will endure winter temperatures down to about −15° F. These four varieties are much like the 'Thompson Seedless' of California. 'Concord Seedless' is like 'Concord' in flavor, but the berries are much smaller. The vine is as hardy as 'Concord'.

I would like to grow some of the California varieties of grapes in New Jersey. Do they require special culture? Yes. If disease control is very good and overbearing is prevented by proper pruning, some of the earlier ripening north European varieties are worth trying on an experimental basis where winter temperatures are not lower than −5° to −10° F.

Will 'Scuppernong' grapes grow in Pennsylvania? You are too far north for this type, which is widely grown in the South. The northern limit of the 'Scuppernong' or 'Muscadine' type is southern Virginia.

Do ordinary table grapes make good wine? Some varieties that are good table grapes—'Delaware', 'Iona', and 'Catawba'—make excellent wine. Generally speaking, the best wines are made from grapes suitable only for wines. Recently, French hybrids have been planted considerably in New York for wine and several have considerable promise.

Can the California grapes like 'Tokay', 'Malaga', etc., be grown in the eastern United States? Some California grapes may be grown in the East where winter temperatures are not lower than −5° to −10° F. and disease and insect control is excellent. They should be grafted on phylloxera-resistant roots. 'Seneca' and the seedless varieties listed above are much like California varieties.

Are there any grape varieties hardy enough to be grown in northern Minnesota? 'Beta' is one of the hardiest of all grapes. The Minnesota Agricultural Experiment Station at University Farm, St. Paul, Minn. 55101, can supply information as to the best grapes for northern Minnesota.

JUJUBE, CHINESE (OR DATE)

What is the Chinese-date fruit like? How old are the trees before they fruit? (Kentucky.) Fruit of the Chinese-date, more commonly called the Chinese jujube, is a drupe (stone fruit), oblong, up to 2 inches long, brown, with a sweet, whitish flesh of applelike flavor. The trees bear when young, usually in their second or third year where growing conditions are favorable. Several jujube seedling trees have survived at Geneva, New York, for many years, but produce very few fruits because of high humidity.

JUNEBERRY (AMELANCHIER)

Is the Juneberry worth planting? The dwarf Juneberry or serviceberry bears heavy crops of bluish-black fruits about the size of wild blueberries. The flavor is insipid, but if they are cooked with lemon juice they make fair pies. The bushes grow 3 to 4 feet in height, are covered with white flowers in early spring, and are very hardy, which makes them useful in the cold Great Plains region. Birds are very fond of the berries and, in most cases, this is a major reason for growing them. There are several species with similar characteristics.

MULBERRY (MORUS)

What are the chief uses of the mulberry? The fruit is good to eat and quite sweet. The trees grow fast and bear large quantities of fruit ripening over several weeks, which makes it a fine tree to attract birds. Since the fruit is messy, the mulberry should not be planted near the house or a sidewalk.

Are mulberries easy trees to grow? Yes, they like almost any soil and thrive under varying conditions.

Did the so-called Russian mulberry actually come from Russia or is it just a name? Yes, it really came from Russia. It was brought to the western states by Russian Mennonites in 1875 to 1877.

Is it true that there are male and female mulberry trees? Must you have both to have berries? Also, is there a difference in the foliage? Yes, the sexes are separate, but usually both are present on one tree. There is little difference in the foliage. Both should be present to ensure fruiting.

We have 2 mulberry trees planted about 30 feet apart. They are over 15 years old. Why are they full of blossoms every spring but never set fruit? Mulberries are often dioecious, that is, staminate (male) and pistillate (female) flowers on separate trees, although generally both sexes are borne on the same tree. The failure to set fruit is undoubtedly due to lack of pollination. Both your trees may either have all flowers of one sex or the male and female flowers do not mature at the same time. If you cannot judge, cut a small branch of each tree just before the flowers open and submit them to a botanist for examination.

How can a mulberry tree that has sprouted from the bottom (top dead) be cultivated to grow right? It is about 2 years old. Cut off all but the strongest sprout. If the stub of the original stem remains, cut this (with a sloping cut) close to the shoot that was selected to carry on.

What are the best varieties of mulberry for fruit production? Mulberry varieties true to name are hard to get. 'Wellington', an old unknown variety renamed, is good.

PERSIMMON (DIOSPYROS)

Are persimmons reliably hardy in the North? The native American persimmon, *Diospyros virginiana,* is native from Connecticut to the Gulf of Mexico. Selected varieties are hardy at Geneva, New York, and some mature early enough to ripen fruits nearly every year. The Oriental persimmon (*D. kaki*) is grown in the South and on the West Coast.

Is the native persimmon worth growing for its fruit? Most of the wild trees produce fruits that are small and very astringent. However, there are a number of selected varieties that produce large, sweet persimmons that are well worth growing.

Do persimmons need frost to make the fruit edible? Frost does not hasten the ripening of the persimmon or make it edible. On the contrary, a hard frost before the persimmons are ripe will spoil them. After they are ripe, the frost will not spoil the fruit. Probably many persimmons ripen about the time of the first frost, hence the idea that frost is needed to ripen them.

Is the persimmon tree fussy about soil? No, they often grow on very poor soils. In the South, on abandoned eroded farmland, the persimmon is one of the first plants to come in. They respond to good soils and care, however.

How should a persimmon tree be transplanted? With a burlapped ball of earth, even if the tree is of small size, in early spring.

How should persimmons be cared for in order to ensure fruits? Very little care is needed. Reduce competition from competing trees, shrubs, grass, and weeds. Be sure that a male tree is nearby to pollinate the flowers or there may be no fruit.

Do persimmon trees have staminate and pistillate varieties? Persimmons are usually dioecious; that is, staminate and pistillate flowers are on different trees. Some pistillate trees produce parthenocarpic (seedless) fruits without having been pollinated.

I have some persimmon seeds. How should I start them? Plant the seeds about 1 inch deep as soon as they are ripe.

QUINCE (CYDONIA OBLONGA)

Does the quince make a good home-garden fruit? If it is sprayed thoroughly to control the Oriental fruit moth, to which it is very susceptible, and if it is not allowed to grow vigorously, thereby making it subject to fire blight, it is a good garden fruit. It can be used to make very fine jelly, quince honey, etc.

What soil does the quince require? How are the trees planted? Quince needs somewhat heavy, moist soil. Set 1- or 2-year specimens, in early spring, 8 to 10 feet apart.

Are the quinces of an ornamental flowering quince bush edible? Are they useful for jelly or quince honey? They can be used in any way the ordinary quince is used, but their jelly is not equal to other jellies in flavor. In addition, they can be dried and used among linen for their aroma.

How and when are quince trees pruned? Pruning should be very light to avoid stimulating vigorous growth that may be attacked by fire blight. Remove dead twigs and those which are growing "out of bounds"—too low, too high, etc. The bush form is probably preferable to the tree form. Prune in early spring.

I wish to cut back a tall quince tree. How many branches should I leave? It is difficult to spray as is. Remove a few of the tallest branches one year and a few more the next in order to reduce the height gradually. Too severe pruning all at once will probably result in an outbreak of fire blight.

It seems to me that the books I have consulted give contradictory advice regarding pruning a quince. My tree is suffering from fire blight. The instructions are to cut back the diseased wood, but won't this compound the problem since heavy pruning helps induce fire blight? Fire blight on quince, pear, or apple does, indeed, present a paradoxical situation. It is important to prune off infected shoots during the summer, making the cuts 4 to 5 inches below the last visible signs of dying. This heavy pruning causes more vigorous growth on the other shoots, and it is the most vigorously growing shoots that are most susceptible to new infections by fire blight.

However, do not feel that the situation is hopeless. A general recommendation is to convert the tree into a lower state of vigor. This may mean withholding fertilizer applications completely for 3 or 4 years. Eventually, the tree may lose all of its blight infection and grow normally.

How do you graft a quince bush? It is not necessary to graft quinces, as they can be propagated by cuttings—a much easier method of getting new plants.

STRAWBERRY (FRAGARIA X ANANASSA)

In what sort of soil should strawberries be planted? What advance fertilization is necessary? A sandy loam soil is good, but any well-drained soil that is fairly retentive of moisture can be made to produce good strawberries. Turn under manure or compost combined with commercial fertilizer (see below) before the plants are set.

Do strawberries require an acid soil? I have a patch that does not do very well. My soil has a tendency to be alkaline. The alkalinity of the soil probably has very little to do with the failure of your strawberry bed to do well. (See below.) Various diseases and insects are more likely to be causing the trouble.

Is lime needed for strawberries? There is a popular belief that lime may be injurious to strawberries, but actually they will respond to lime about as well as other crops. If the soil is alkaline or only mildly acid (pH 5.6 or above), then lime won't be needed and might even be harmful. But if the pH is down around 4.0 to 5.6, then by all means use lime.

Should you use fertilizer on strawberry plants? What is the best kind to use? A complete fertilizer, such as 5–10–5, at the rate of 2 to 4 pounds per 100 square feet should be broadcast and worked into the soil before planting.

Is animal manure too alkaline for applying to strawberries for the winter? A straw mulch applied before temperatures drop below 20° F. is better for the winter. Manure is best used in adding humus to the soil before planting the strawberries.

How can a strawberry planting be tied in with a vegetable garden? A good plan is to have it adjacent to the vegetable garden. When an old row of strawberries is removed, vegetables can take their place, as it is not desirable to keep strawberries in one place too long. If space permits, strawberries should not be grown on land that has grown tomatoes, peppers, eggplants, and potatoes during the previous 2 or 3 years. A few feet between them is enough.

How much space should be planted in strawberries for each person in the family? Twenty-five feet of row per person in fruit, and another 25 feet of young plants coming along for the following year.

I have a slope in the back of my yard that I wish to have covered with strawberries. If I plant them at the bottom, will they climb? Do the leaves stay green in the winter? Better to plant in rows 2 feet apart across the slope. As runners form, you can place them where needed to cover the soil. The leaves remain more or less green during the winter, depending upon the site. In cold regions, where winter temperatures drop below 20° F., they will need to be covered.

I plan to start a strawberry patch for a family of 2. I want some for freezing. How many plants do I need? One hundred feet of row would take 40 plants, set 30 inches apart, and would yield 30 to 40 quarts if all goes well. Decide how many quarts you want and compute the number of plants needed.

How far apart are strawberry plants set? Varieties that do not make runners freely (especially the everbearers), about 18 inches apart; a fair plant takes 24 inches; a good plant takes 30 inches. The rows should be 36 to 48 inches apart.

When should strawberry plants be set? Strawberry plants are usually set in the spring as soon as the ground can be worked. If dormant plants from cold storage are used, then later planting is all right. Late October and early November is also a good time to plant. Fall-set

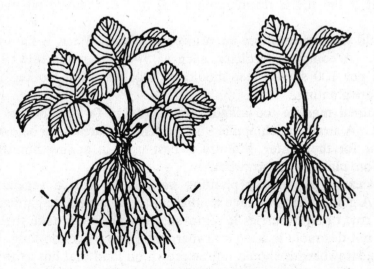

SETTING OUT STRAWBERRY PLANTS
Old leaves removed and roots trimmed back.

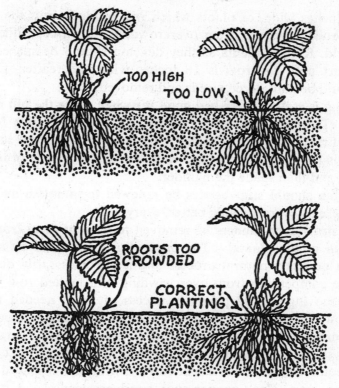

SETTING OUT STRAWBERRY PLANTS

plants should be mulched the first winter, the mulch removed in the spring, and the blossoms removed to prevent fruiting the first summer. Care is then the same as for a spring-set bed. Midsummer is not a good time to plant strawberries.

How should strawberries be planted? Have the soil in good tilth. Scoop out a hole with a garden trowel to a depth of 4 or 5 inches; plant firmly, being sure that the roots are well spread and extend down into the hole and are well covered. The plants should be set as deeply as possible without covering the crown. If set too deeply, the plants will be smothered; if not deeply enough, part of their roots will be exposed and will dry out.

What is the hill method of strawberry growing? The plants are set a foot apart and all runners removed as they appear. Single rows are often used, but much higher yields will be obtained if 2 to 4 rows are set a foot apart with an alley between each set of rows.

What is the matted-row method of strawberry growing? The plants are set 18 to 30 inches apart, in rows 30 to 48 inches apart. The runners are allowed to develop and take root, forming a "matted row,"

18 to 30 inches wide, of plants which will produce fruit the following season. Matted rows are often overcrowded, with a consequent reduction in yield. Runner plants as they develop should be spaced about 6 inches apart until the row is 18 inches wide. Thereafter, the runner plants should be considered weeds and removed.

How long is a strawberry bed good for when using the hill method of planting? If properly cared for, a bed will be productive for 3 or 4 years; the first crop will be the best, and later crops will be successively poorer. It is best to set new plants each spring, let them fruit the following spring, and then spade them under.

How often should strawberries be renewed to maintain an abundant yield? At least every 2 years; better, every year.

Should strawberry runners be removed to prevent them from sapping the strength of the plants? The production of runners by strawberry plants is a perfectly natural process and is not necessarily devitalizing. The severe competition from overcrowding in a matted row is the reason for removing runner plants in excess of those needed to form a fruiting row. In the hill system of growing, all runners should be removed in order to keep the plants properly spaced. In the common matted-row system, the only runners removed are those in excess of the number required to produce a matted row, with plants spaced at least 7 to 8 inches apart. Each runner soon produces leaves and roots of its own and becomes a "self-supporting," individual plant.

How many runners should be allowed to develop from each mother plant in the matted-row system? Allow at least 7 or 8 inches (in all directions) between runner plants. If the plants are 30 inches apart in rows, allow 12 to 14 runner plants to develop from each mother plant. The excess runners should be cut off, preferably before they take root.

What shall I do when my strawberries grow too thick? Keep the runners spaced and thinned so the plants will stand at least 7 or 8 inches apart in the matted row. Usually the beds are replanted every year or two, setting runner plants in a new location.

We have been advised to cut strawberry leaves off in the fall. Is this correct? The leaves definitely should not be cut off in the fall. They are the organs in which those foods which feed the plant are manufactured. Cutting off the leaves "starves" the rest of the plant.

Can strawberries be weeded in the spring? Most strawberry beds need weeding in the spring unless the ground is unusually free from weed seeds. Some weed seeds come in the mulch. Many of the weeds should be pulled by hand to prevent damaging the strawberry plants. Herbicides, properly used, can reduce the amount of weeding needed.

Why did my strawberry plants bloom so profusely but set no berries? The blossoms may have been injured by frost, which, without injuring the petals, often kills the part which will develop into fruit.

My strawberry plants blossom and set berries, but they do not develop after being half grown. Why? Misshapen and knotty berries are often caused by the feeding of the tarnished plant bug, an insect which feeds on the blossoms. It is easily controlled by spraying the plants, following current instructions from the Cooperative Extension Service.

I seem to have no luck with strawberries. They do not bear very heavily. First, be sure that you have a productive variety and one suited to your soil and climate; set a new bed frequently and keep the soil well, but not too heavily, fertilized. Do not let the plants crowd in the matted row. Do not fertilize in the spring of the bearing year.

How are strawberries propagated? In the summer strawberry plants produce long, stringlike growths called "runners," at the tips of which grow new plants. These send roots into the soil. They are allowed to develop until the following spring, when they are dug up and set out in new beds. Some varieties make many runners; others make only a few.

How should strawberry runners be cared for before they are set out in a new bed? If using runners from your own beds, dig only when ready to plant. Remove old ragged or dead leaves, leaving the small leaves at the tip of the crown. If you purchase plants, try to plant them as soon as you receive them. If this cannot be done, "heel in" in a shallow trench in a cool place and keep them well watered until planting time.

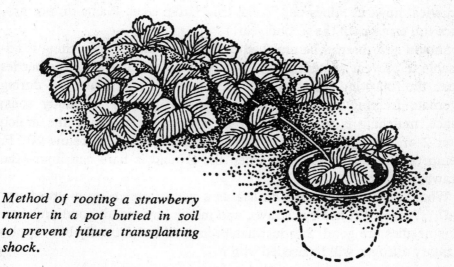

Method of rooting a strawberry runner in a pot buried in soil to prevent future transplanting shock.

How can runners be rooted in pots?   Fill 2½- or 3-inch pots with a good humus-rich soil and sink them in the ground around the mother plants. Place a runner tip over each pot and hold in place by putting a stone or clod on the runner near the tip, or bend or twist wires into hairpin shape and peg the runners down, or use clothespins. When the new plant is well developed, the runner can be severed from the old plant.

Are potted strawberry plants any better than those runner plants which have been allowed to become well established in the garden before transplanting?   For starting a new bed in late summer or early fall, only potted plants will stand transplanting satisfactorily. However, spring planting of ordinary runner plants is preferred.

Pot-grown strawberry plants for late-summer planting.

Can strawberry seeds or plants be started in the spring and produce worthwhile results the same year?   There are certain small-fruited European varieties which "come true" from seed and will fruit the same year the seed is planted. The common garden strawberry of North America, however, does not "come true" from seed. Plants do not produce full crops until the second year.

Should strawberries be mulched during the winter?   Mulching is advisable to prevent winter injury, conserve moisture, and keep the berries clean the following spring. Plants are more likely to heave out during alternate freezing and thawing on heavy soils than on sandy soils; hence, mulching is more essential on heavier soils. Apply the mulch after 2 or 3 sharp freezes, but before temperatures drop below 20° F. Temperatures lower than this when the ground is bare can injure the strawberry plants.

What is the best material to use as a winter mulch on a strawberry bed?   Wheat, oat and rye straws, and marsh hay are all good mulches. Pine needles are good. Sawdust has been used satisfactorily but supplementary nitrogen will be needed with it.

How is mulching material applied to a strawberry bed? The straw is scattered over the bed with a fork to a depth of 3 or 4 inches. In windy situations, weight it down with brush.

What are the advantages of mulching strawberries with marsh hay, and when should it be applied? This hay is freer from weed seeds than wheat, oat, and rye straws, and is easy to get in coastal areas.

Is it all right to mulch strawberry plants with tree leaves? Tree leaves are a fair mulch, but if too thick they can mat down and make it difficult for the strawberry plants to push through in the spring.

How soon is the mulch removed from the strawberry bed? The mulch is removed in early April when inspection of the plants shows that the new leaves are beginning to grow from the crown. Part of the mulch is pulled off the plants into the space between the rows and part is left over the plants. The leaves and flower clusters push through the mulch and the berries rest on the straw, which keeps them clean.

What are "everbearing" strawberries? These are varieties that form a crop of fruit in the spring and another in late summer. The total yield is smaller than that of one-season berries.

Are everbearing strawberries successful? They do not live up to the descriptions in some of the catalogs, but if you like strawberries well enough to put up with the faults of everbearing varieties, then they can be termed "successful." One of the faults is that the crop is produced over such a long period that only a very small picking can be made on any one day.

Are everbearing strawberries as prolific as the ordinary kind? If the plants are grown in hills and mulched with sawdust and the blossoms removed until the middle of July, most varieties will produce a fairly large crop per plant. The soil should be fertile and watering is essential in dry weather. An inch of water per week from rain or a hose is desirable. The fruit will then ripen over a period of 2 to 3 months, but the picking on any one day will be rather small. If the blossoms are not removed, the plants will exhaust themselves by producing heavily during the hot midsummer months. The fruit produced in cooler fall weather will be of better quality than that produced in midsummer.

Should the runners be removed from everbearing strawberry plants? A maximum fall crop will be produced if the plants are set close together, about 12 to 15 inches apart, in rows 2 feet apart, and all runners removed as they form. This is known as the hill system.

How and when are everbearing strawberries thinned? Most varieties will need no thinning unless grown in hills, in which case all the runners should be kept off. Set a new bed each spring rather than try to rejuvenate the old one.

Should the first blossoms be removed from everbearing strawberry plants? When should they be allowed to bear?   Best results will be secured if all blossoms are removed up to the latter part of June. The first fruit would then ripen about the middle of August.

If I transplant everbearing strawberry plants in the spring, will they bear the same season?   Yes, they should bear their maximum crop in the fall of the year in which they are planted.

My everbearing strawberries do not have the flavor of standard strawberries. Are there any that compare with usual spring berries?   'Geneva' is of highest quality. 'Ozark Beauty' is another popular variety.

What care should be given to everbearing strawberries to keep them bearing from year to year?   It can't be done. You could get some fruit for 2 or even 3 years, but many plants would die and the others would get progressively weaker. Don't count on one planting to produce more than one fall crop, followed by a spring crop.

What care should be given everbearing strawberries through the winter? Do they thrive better in moist ground or dry?   They should be winter-mulched like any other strawberries. Everbearers are getting ready during the hot, dry weather of midsummer to produce a fall crop; hence, they must have ample moisture or the results will be disappointing.

I have a 50-gallon oak barrel in which I want to grow strawberries. How should I prepare the soil and set the plants? How far apart should the holes be?   Beginning 1 foot from the bottom, bore holes at irregular intervals, 9 inches apart and large enough to hold a plant without cramping. Bore a number of smaller holes in the bottom for drainage and set the barrel on flat bricks. Put in 6 inches of drainage material—coarse gravel or cinders, topped with finer material. Mix good garden soil with ⅓ its bulk of rotted manure or rich compost and ⅓ screened cinders. To every bushel, add 1 pound of a complete fertilizer. It is not necessary to fill the whole interior with this soil. Maintain a 6-inch thickness around the inside and fill the center with any gravelly material available. Planting and filling are done at the same time. Begin by covering the drainage with soil to the level of the first holes. Push the plants through from the inside, spread their roots, and cover with soil. Repeat to within 12 inches of the top; fill this with good soil and plant the entire top. See that the moisture conditions are uniform.

What variety of plant should be used in a strawberry barrel? How should the plants be wintered over?   Select a variety of high quality adapted to your climatic conditions. It is desirable to use potted plants if you can get them. Mulch with straw over the top; protect the side plants, if possible, with straw or burlap after the first heavy freeze. Unless well protected in cold regions, the plants will be injured or killed by winter cold. Check moisture conditions occasionally to prevent drying out.

What is the proper way to handle strawberry plants in a strawberry jar (barrel) after they are through bearing? Remove the old plants and replace a little later with newly formed runner plants that have been rooted in small pots.

Do strawberries need to be sprayed? Probably not—only if certain pests (such as leaf roller, tarnished plant bug, or weevil) are bad. Most strawberries in the home garden do quite well without being sprayed.

What causes the purplish spots on the leaves of my strawberry plants? One of two diseases—either leaf spot or leaf scorch. During most seasons, the modern varieties will not be injured enough to make it worthwhile to spray.

What causes the buds to drop from my strawberry plants before they bloom? The strawberry weevil, a tiny insect, lays an egg in the bud and then cuts the stem just in back of the bud. Follow the current spray program from your Cooperative Extension Service.

Are any strawberry varieties resistant to the red stele root rot? 'Sparkle', 'Redglow', 'Surecrop', 'Midway', 'Redchief', 'Sunrise', and 'Guardian' are resistant.

What are "virus-free" strawberries? They are plants which tests have shown are free of virus diseases. They are much superior to the old stock, most of which was infected with a virus disease that reduced the vigor and productiveness of the plants. Most good strawberry plant nurseries are selling them. Plants that are obtained from sources that are not attempting to produce virus-free plants should be avoided.

What are the best strawberries for freezing? 'Sparkle' and 'Midland' are two good ones.

What are "runnerless" strawberries? These are a strain of the alpine or European strawberry, *Fragaria vesca,* that produces no runners so they must be raised from seeds. The berries are small, pointed, and have a distinctive flavor. The plants fruit throughout the summer.

Can wild strawberries be transplanted in a regular bed? If so, do they give a good crop? Wild strawberries in cultivation (that is, fertilized and weeded) will give better yields than in the wild, but it requires a good many to fill a quart basket. Berry size is improved very little under cultivation. But they *are* flavorful!

Cane Fruits

What is meant by the term "bramble or cane fruits"?   This group includes the fruits belonging to the genus *Rubus:* the red, black, and purple raspberries, the dewberry, and the bush and trailing blackberries. The loganberry, boysenberry, etc., can be classified as dewberries.

Have the "brambles" any preference as to soil?   Raspberries and bush blackberries do best in heavier soils; dewberries like sandy soils and will not thrive on heavy soils. If the soil is well drained and in good physical condition, the brambles will grow satisfactorily on a fairly wide range of soil types.

Can cane fruits be grown successfully in a sandy soil?   A sandy loam soil is satisfactory, but coarse sands are too subject to drought and are low in fertility. Irrigation and mulching are helpful here as well as the incorporation of peat moss, compost, and/or rotted manure at planting time.

What fertilizer should be used for brambles?   Use a nitrogenous material such as ammonium nitrate or nitrate of soda. If marginal burning of the foliage is present, sulfate of potash should be used.

Where should cane fruits be planted?   They should be planted on fertile well-drained soils that are well supplied with organic matter. The black and purple raspberries should not be planted on land that has grown tomatoes, peppers, eggplants, and potatoes within the past 3 years or near wild raspberries or runout cultivated raspberries, which often harbor diseases and insects that can ruin the new planting.

Can you plant berry bushes during the winter when the ground is soft?   It could be done, but if the soil has much clay in it, it will be too sticky to do a good job. If there is much freezing and thawing afterward, the plants might heave out of the ground unless mulched and mounded up with soil. Fall or early-spring planting would be preferable.

How much space should be planted with cane fruits for a family of 4?   Personal tastes must be considered, of course, but here is one suggested assortment: plants 3 feet apart in a row, in rows 6 to 8 feet apart. Red raspberries, 50 feet of row; black raspberries, 24 feet of row; blackberries, 50 feet of row.

Can raspberries be planted near pine trees?   If there is distance enough between them so that there is no root competition or shade.

What berry bushes thrive in the shade? No plants that bear fruit will thrive in much shade. The more sun they receive, the better the crops.

When do you plant everbearing raspberries? Everbearing raspberries can be set either in the fall or spring and should have the same care that the ordinary one-crop varieties receive.

Can bramble or cane fruits be grown in a very small city garden? They may be grown if sunlight is adequate (most of the day). Keep them in bounds by hoeing off unwanted suckers.

Do cane fruits need support? Cane fruits do not require support, but most growers use some means of training to keep them from growing too "ragged" and occupying too much space in the garden.

How would you construct a trellis for dewberry vines? A 5-foot stake driven 1 foot into the ground beside each plant will be quite satisfactory. Cut out old, dead canes and tie up new, vigorous canes in early spring, cutting them off at the top of the stake.

How should I care for the 'Heritage' raspberries that I set out last spring? How should they be pruned and sprayed? (Vermont.) In the same manner as the one-crop varieties. (See the question on pruning raspberries below.) Spraying is not necessary.

What is the correct yearly cultural care of established cane fruits? Constant shallow cultivation to control weeds is important. Mulching is a good plan, using well-rotted manure or rich compost. Prune living canes only where necessary for the training of plants. Prune out all dead canes after the fruiting season. Apply nitrate of soda (or a similar high-nitrogen fertilizer) in the spring, 1 to 2 pounds per 100 feet of row.

How often should berries be picked? Pick red raspberries every day; blackcaps and blackberries, every third day.

How can I increase my stock of raspberries? Black and purple raspberries are propagated by tip-layering. The tips of the new canes are inserted vertically in the soil in late August to a depth of 4 inches. Roots form on the tip in late fall, and in the spring the tip is dug, severed from the mother plant, and planted where desired. Red raspberries send up many sucker plants, which can be dug in late fall and early spring for planting elsewhere.

How often should the brambles be planted? Usually in 5 to 10 years, but if weeds are not bad and diseases are kept under control, the plantings last longer.

What kind of fruit bushes can I grow on a strip 3 × 40 feet? (New York.) If the area is exposed to full sunlight, you could grow any of the small fruits, such as grapes, strawberries, raspberries, currants, or gooseberries, or combinations of the ones you like best. For instance, 3 currant bushes would take up about 10 feet, leaving 30 feet for strawberries if you particularly like these two fruits; or all the area may be planted with raspberries or blackberries.

Our garden is in Maine, rather far east on the coast. Can you give some information on varieties of small fruits we can plant? 'Sparkle', 'Catskill', and 'Fairfax' are good home-garden strawberries; others are 'Fletcher' and 'Raritan'. 'Latham', 'Newburgh', 'Heritage' (fall-bearing), and 'Taylor' are good red raspberries. 'Bristol' and 'Dundee' are the best black raspberries. 'Brandywine' is the best purple variety.

What would be a profitable fruit planting, producing in about 3 or 4 years, that could be tended on weekends and will produce for at least 10 years without being replanted? There are 2 acres, a half mile from the ocean, and full sun. Red raspberries are rarely grown commercially now so there is no competition for a crop that can be very profitable. Or you might make a miscellaneous fruit planting for your own use and sell the surplus. In that case, choose the fruits you like and take a part of your "profit" in personal satisfaction. If profit is the main objective, secure enough land to make an economic farm unit. Be sure that the land is a good farm soil. Consult your Cooperative Extension Service.

What different kinds of berries should be planted in order to have a continuous supply from late spring until frost? Start off with strawberries, then raspberries, currants, gooseberries, and blueberries. These will cover the season until late August. Everbearing strawberries and raspberries will fill out the rest of the season.

What kind of everbearing raspberries are suggested for south of Boston? The best variety is 'Heritage'. This is really fall-bearing. The fall crop is produced at the tips of the new canes and next summer the same canes bear another crop.

Can we grow the 'Oregon Evergreen' blackberry in this state? (Massachusetts.) Grow the 'Darrow' variety instead.

What is the best variety of blackberry for Maine? 'Darrow'.

BLACKBERRY (RUBUS)

Will blackberries grow on any soil? They do best on good sandy loam soil containing plenty of humus but well drained.

Can manure be used on blackberries? Yes, manure or complete fertilizer can be used to improve poor soils on which blackberries are grown. A yearly cover crop, turned under in the spring, or the turning under of summer mulch, adds needed humus to the soil.

When is the best time to transplant blackberry or raspberry bushes? Early spring, although fall planting can be successful if the plants are set rather deeply and mounded somewhat to prevent heaving during the winter. This applies to red raspberries; black raspberries should be set in the spring.

How far apart should raspberries and bush blackberries be planted? Three feet apart in the row and rows 7 to 8 feet apart are standard distances, but when space is limited in the home garden, you can plant them much closer.

How far apart should blackberries of the trailing type be planted? Trailing blackberries such as 'Black Diamond' (called 'Oregon Evergreen' in the West) need plenty of room. Set the plants at least 6 feet apart in rows 6 to 8 feet apart.

When and how should blackberries be pruned? In June the tips of new shoots are pinched off at a height of 3 feet to make them branch. The following spring the branches are cut back to a length of about 15 inches. After the crop is harvested, canes that have borne fruit are removed.

Why do some blackberries blossom and not have any berries? There are two possible causes. A sterile blackberry has been widely distributed by nurseries. It produces no fruit although it blooms. Another cause is the feeding of the tarnished plant bug on the flowers, causing them to develop into sterile or partially sterile fruits. The plant bug is easily controlled by spraying the plants with malathion at the rate of 6 tablespoonfuls of the 25 per cent Wettable Powder in 5 gallons of water. This is applied just before the plants bloom. Make a second application immediately after the petals fall.

Are the trailing blackberries (that is, dewberry, boysenberry) propagated the same way as regular blackberries? These are usually propagated by tip-layering.

Can the suckers that come up from the roots of blackberries be used to make plants of the same variety? Yes. Usually nurseries use root cuttings 3 to 4 inches long and the thickness of a lead pencil.

Why do blackberry leaves get a bright orange color and then seem to die? The orange color is made up of spores of a disease known as orange rust. Infected plants will die. The only control is to dig out diseased plants before spores have been discharged to infect other plants. Be sure to dig out the roots, since shoots coming up from these would be diseased.

Is it satisfactory to transplant wild blackberry bushes for home use?   This is all right if you can find really superior wild bushes; otherwise, you will have much better results by planting named varieties. Wild blackberries sometimes do not do as well under cultivation as they do in the wild. Try the 'Darrow' variety.

Is the thornless 'Thornfree' blackberry as good as the thorny type?   Yes. Thornlessness is a very valuable asset, as can be attested by anyone who has picked from or pruned the thorny type.

Would raspberry and blackberry plants make a good ground cover for a steep embankment?   Raspberries and blackberries will grow satisfactorily on a steep bank if the soil is fertile and the ground is mulched to prevent its being washed away. Steep banks, however, can be badly eroded, in which case the soil is not suitable for the brambles. Also, caring for the plants and harvesting under such conditions would be a chore.

BOYSENBERRY (RUBUS)

Are boysenberries worth growing in the East?   Boysenberries are not winter-hardy north of Washington, D.C., and even though protected, the crops are very light. The other small fruits will produce much more fruit with less effort. Boysenberries are an excellent fruit in California and Oregon.

How should boysenberries be fed?   Boysenberries can be fertilized with nitrate of soda or sulfate of ammonia at the rate of 1 pound per 100 square feet.

I have some boysenberries that I set out last spring which I would like to move. When can this be done? (Washington.)   Boysenberries can be moved in late fall or early spring before their growth starts. In mild sections of your state, they can be moved any time during the winter.

How are boysenberries pruned and trained?   Boysenberries are a trailing vine. The canes grow one year, bear fruit the second, and then die, other canes taking their place. To facilitate the harvesting of fruit and tillage operations, fruiting canes are tied up to a trellis at the beginning of the second season. A suitable trellis consists of a wire 3 or 4 feet above the ground. Canes are gathered together and tied at the top of this wire. The ends are cut off or tied along the wire. Canes can also be tied up to 5-foot posts, their ends cut off at the top of the post. After the crop is harvested, the fruiting canes are removed and new canes, which will fruit the following year, are tied in.

I have 6-year-old boysenberry bushes that were planted close to young shade trees and now are shaded too much. Can I transplant them this coming spring? The plants are very large and strong. Can I divide them and make more plants? (Oregon.) Old berry plants are not transplanted and reestablished readily. Either buy new plants or cover the tips of new canes with soil in late summer. Roots will form at the tips. New plants may be severed from the parent plant the following spring and moved to their permanent location. Dividing old plants is hardly practical.

RASPBERRY (RUBUS)

When is the best time to plant red raspberry bushes? Red raspberries can be set in late fall if the soil is mounded around the plants to a height of several inches to prevent heaving from frost. In the spring the soil is worked down level. Raspberries can also be set in early spring.

Is it wise to plant virus-free raspberry plants back onto ground formerly occupied by virus-infected plants? No. Many viruses of fruit plants are carried in the soil by certain species of nematodes, which are very small eelworms about $\frac{1}{16}$ inch long. As long as weeds or other plants are growing in the soil, nematodes can feed on the roots and remain alive in the soil year after year. If a virus-infected raspberry planting is removed in the fall with the intent of replanting with new, virus-free plants the next spring, these new plants will soon become virus-infected if planted on the same ground. They will become infected by virus-carrying nematodes, which will chew on the roots.

Commercial raspberry growers fumigate the soil with a poisonous gas in the fall. This kills the nematodes and virus-free raspberry plants can then be safely planted. Fumigating the soil is probably impractical for most home gardeners. Viruses, of course, are not always the cause of poor growth and low yields. The home gardener should not allow these potential virus problems to deter his enthusiasm. In most cases you will be delighted with the delicious raspberries you are able to produce.

When is the best time to transplant black raspberries? Tip plants are set in the spring, but "transplants" can be set either in the spring or in the late fall.

How far apart should raspberries be planted? Plant suckering varieties 3 feet apart, in rows 5 or 6 feet apart; blackcaps, 4 or 5 feet apart, in rows 6 or 7 feet apart.

Can raspberry bushes which were not planted in the fall be held over until spring without heeling them in? They must be heeled in (that is, their roots covered with soil) or packed in moist material such as sphagnum moss and stored in a cellar where the temperature stays 32° F. The roots must not be allowed to dry out and the temperature must be low enough to prevent the canes from sprouting. Surely you have space to heel them in during the winter.

Is it possible to plant between the rows of raspberries? It seems as if there is space going to waste. Small vegetables, but not tomatoes, pepper, eggplants, or potatoes, may be planted between the rows the first season, but not close enough to the raspberries to compete with them. After the first year, the raspberries will need all the ground.

Should raspberries and blackberries be pruned in the summer? Red raspberries should not be summer pruned except for old canes of ever-bearers which can be cut out at the base after harvesting ends in early summer. Blackcaps and bush blackberries should have their canes pinched back when they reach the height at which branching is desired. This would usually be at 24 to 30 inches for black raspberries and 30 to 36 inches for bush blackberries. If pinching is done at the proper time, it will consist of merely nipping out the growing tip of the cane with your fingers.

How should red raspberries be pruned and trained? Red raspberries are commonly tied to stakes or a wire trellis in the garden, but support is not necessary. Plants should be grown in hedgerows not over 1 foot in width. In early spring, canes that grew during the previous season are cut back about one fourth of their height. Weaker canes should be removed so that the remaining canes are spaced about 6 inches apart in rows 1 foot in width. Canes that fruited the previous summer should be removed if this was not done after the crop was harvested. Red raspberry plants send up a multitude of suckers between the rows and unless these are subdued by vigorous use of a hoe, a veritable thicket will result.

How should black raspberries be pruned? Remove canes that are dead, broken, obviously diseased, or that grow at such an angle that they will bend to the ground when in fruit. Cut back good canes to about 24 to 30 inches and then shorten the lateral branches to about 6 inches.

Do red raspberries need a trellis? Not necessarily. If they are pruned rather short (cut back about one half, if 5 to 6 feet tall), they will hold themselves up. However, a trellis of one wire on each side of the row, supported by posts and crosspieces, will hold the canes up during storms, prevent breakage, and keep the berries from getting into the mud. Mulching protects lower berries from being splashed with mud.

Last summer I planted some 'Sodus' purple raspberries. They have grown to a length of 9 to 12 feet. How far and when should they be cut back? In early spring, the canes should be cut back to a length of 4 or 5 feet and tied up to a stake or wire trellis. To eliminate the need for support, pinch off the tips of new shoots when they reach a height of 30 inches. This makes the canes branch and they are sturdier and self-supporting. The following spring, cut the branches back to a length of 10 or 12 inches and no support will be needed.

What, if any, winter protection should be given 1-year-old black raspberry bushes? (New York.) Black raspberries are hardy without winter protection except in the coldest parts of the country like northern New York.

How can I protect raspberries during the winter? (Massachusetts.) Hardy raspberry varieties should not need protection in Massachusetts. If protection is desired, bend the canes down and cover the tips with soil. In this position, snow will provide protection. Where snow blows off, straw or earth can be used to cover the canes.

What materials are suitable as a mulch for raspberry bushes? Compost, rotted manure, straw, old hay, and decayed leaves are good mulching materials for raspberries.

Do everbearing raspberries bear continuously? Two crops are borne, the first in June or July on canes which grew during the previous season, and the second or fall crop in September and October on the tips of the new or current season's canes.

My red raspberry patch has grown so profusely. Would it be wise to take out every other row and start a new patch? It is rather difficult to subdue and restore order in a raspberry patch that has run wild. It will be easier and more satisfactory to take up healthy sucker plants and set a new patch, resolving to take care of it and keep suckers in bounds. Have the rows in the new patch 6 or 7 feet apart and keep the rows of plants about 1 foot in width.

Can shoots of red raspberry be cut away from their parent plant and transplanted in the spring? If so, how and when? New shoots of red raspberries can be taken up in June after they have reached a height of 6 or 8 inches. Care should be taken to get part of the old root. Cloudy, moist weather is essential and the plants should be watered in. This method of starting raspberries is not successful in hot, dry weather.

When is the best time to propagate "wild" red raspberries? Red raspberry sucker plants can be taken up and set either in late fall or early spring. They are usually not worth growing as the berries are too small and the crops are too light, unless they happen to be a good variety that has escaped cultivation.

How can I get new plants to renew my raspberry planting? Red raspberries are propagated from suckers from the roots of old plants. These are dug up, the large root severed, and new plants set in place. Black and purple cane raspberries are propagated by tip layers.

Will red and black raspberries mix if planted close to each other? No. Not at all.

How can I keep birds from devouring my red raspberries? Cover the plants with netting or cheesecloth. Usually the birds can't catch all the crop on established plantings.

How can I keep rabbits from gnawing raspberry bushes during the winter? Fence them out with poultry netting, 30 inches high.

What causes the mosaic disease of raspberries? This is a virus disease spread from one plant to another by aphids. The only remedy is to keep digging out and destroying diseased plants. Be sure to take out the roots, as all the shoots coming up from the roots of a diseased plant will also be diseased. Nurseries now sell virus-free plants, but if exposed to diseased plants they will soon become infected.

What are the symptoms of viruses in raspberries? Unlike the mosaic virus, which is visible, several viruses which infect raspberries are referred to as being latent. This means that they do not exhibit distinctly visible external symptoms on the raspberry plant; the infection will, nevertheless, cause reduced plant vigor and yield. Several cultural factors, such as wet soil or too much shade, can also reduce plant vigor and yield. Therefore, it may not be possible for a home gardener to know whether virus is present. Scientists can detect the presence of latent viruses in raspberry plants by transferring leaf sap to virus-sensitive indicator plants such as the lamb's-quarters weed, which does show distinct symptoms.

Some of the latent viruses in raspberries are tomato ring spot virus (crumbly berry), mosaic virus, tobacco streak, black raspberry latent and raspberry bush dwarf virus. Latent viruses are widely distributed in raspberries. In some varieties, all plants are infected. Extensive testing of plants from many sources has located some that are free of all known viruses. Heat treatments of many varieties can remove viruses. The most that the home gardener can do is to buy virus-tested raspberry plants from a reliable nursery so that he or she can start out with healthy material.

What causes a hard, woody knot to grow at the ground level on my raspberry bushes? This is caused by the disease known as crown gall.

There is no cure for a diseased plant, and the disease will live in the soil for some time. Set clean, inspected plants in soil that has not recently grown any of the bramble fruits.

What causes the tips of my 'Latham' raspberry plants to wilt over? The raspberry cane borer, a beetle, lays an egg near the tip of the cane, then cuts a girdle just above and below the egg, which usually causes the tip to wilt and die. The most practical control consists of breaking off the wilted tips and burning them. Break or cut a couple of inches below the girdle in order to get the larva, which will start to bore down through the pith of the cane as soon as it hatches.

My black raspberries have gray spots on the canes and on the fruit. What can I do? This is the disease known as anthracnose. A delayed dormant spray of 1 part lime sulfur to 20 parts water, when the buds are out about ½ inch in the spring, will usually give control. In seasons favorable for anthracnose (prolonged wet spells), ferbam at the rate of 12½ tablespoonfuls to 5 gallons of water should be applied when the new shoots are 12 to 15 inches high and again just before they bloom.

Why aren't red and black raspberries supposed to be grown together? Because of certain diseases, mosaic in particular, which are carried by the reds and readily transmitted to the blacks. Mosaic infection may not injure a red variety very rapidly but will kill a blackcap in a much shorter time (that is, the reds act as carriers of the disease). The blacks would be much safer a couple of hundred yards away, far enough so that aphids will not get from one to the other.

Why aren't purple raspberries more widely grown? They are susceptible to the mosaic disease. They are not very attractive in the box and do not sell well. But those who know them frequently prefer them to the reds and blacks. The plants are very productive and the tart berries are useful in the kitchen.

Are everbearing raspberries more desirable than standard sorts? For the home gardener, everbearing sorts are desirable to extend the season. 'Heritage' is the best everbearing variety. It bears two good crops in one season.

What black raspberries are the best producers for home use? 'Bristol' and 'Dundee' are both productive, high-quality varieties.

What red raspberry do you consider best for home garden and market garden? (Wisconsin.) For Wisconsin, 'Latham' is a standard variety. 'Taylor', 'Newburgh', and 'Heritage' should also be tried.

What are good early and late red raspberries? 'Newburgh' for early and 'Latham' for late would make a good combination.

Nut Trees

GENERAL

What is the best soil for nut trees? I have an open field.   Any well-drained soil that will produce good farm crops is suitable for nut trees. The native walnut especially prefers fertile bottom-land soil, while the Persian (English walnut) is thought to need limestone soils. Poor, eroded soils are not suitable for nut trees.

What is the general care for nut trees?   The principal care required is to eliminate weed competition by cultivation or mulching. If the soil is not fertile, an annual application of nitrate of soda or sulfate of ammonia, at the rate of ¼ pound (or ½ that rate of ammonium nitrate) for each inch of trunk diameter, should keep the trees growing.

Will the planting of nut trees in a fruit orchard react against either the fruit or nut trees in the presence of each other?   Nut trees are too vigorous and grow too large to be grown in the same orchard with fruit trees.

Can nut trees be grown as far north as Brunswick, Maine?   Those best suited are the native hazelnuts, the shagbark hickory, and butternuts. The growing season in Maine is too short and too cool for many nut trees. Also, the winters are too cold.

How can nut trees be grafted?   Several methods of grafting are used in nut-tree propagation. Splice grafting or whip grafting is used when propagating young Persian walnuts in nurseries in the West and for young pecans in the South. Scions are grafted onto a 1-year-old seedling understock. In the Persian walnut, the union is waxed but not tied; in the pecan, the union is tied with raffia. Soil that was removed from around the seedlings before grafting is pushed back and the scions completely covered to a depth of 2 inches. When trees are being top-worked to another variety, the cleft graft method is used. This method, however, has been largely supplanted by that known as bark grafting. (See Grafting.)

Is there a miniature nut tree?   No dwarfing stock for nut trees has as yet been introduced.

What kind of nut trees will grow in the East? (New Jersey.)   Black walnuts, butternuts, and Chinese chestnuts are probably the most satisfactory. Hickories are slow-growing and the trees take up a lot of space.

What kinds of nuts can be successfully grown in the southern Pennsylvania climate? How do I start such an orchard? Is it necessary to purchase trees from nurseries or can they be grown successfully from nuts? Southern Pennsylvania has suitable soils and climate for all of the nut trees of the eastern states such as black and Persian walnuts, shagbark hickories, Chinese chestnuts, and filberts. Heartnuts and Japanese walnuts grow well, but the nuts are not of high quality. The practicability of commercial nut culture in this region has not been demonstrated, and plantings should be experimental or for pleasure. The named varieties available from nurseries as grafted trees are much superior to seedlings. Seedlings should be used only for reforestation or as food for game.

What are several quick-producing nut trees that can stand cold and strong wind? (New York.) Filberts will bear nuts in 4 or 5 years and are about as hardy as peaches. Grafted black walnuts also bear young, but will not produce many nuts until the trees develop sufficient bearing surface, which takes 8 or 10 years. Some Chinese chestnuts, most of which are seedlings, also bear fairly early.

ALMOND (PRUNUS DULCIS VAR. DULCIS)

Can almond trees be grown in this country? Commercially, only in California. They are almost as hardy as the peach, but because they bloom earlier, they are especially susceptible to damage by late spring frost. Their care and culture are the same as for peach trees.

Will almonds come true from seeds? (Oregon.) No. Named varieties are increased by budding them onto seedling almonds or seedling peaches.

BUTTERNUT (JUGLANS CINEREA)

Would you advise the home gardener to plant butternut trees? Butternut belongs to the walnut family but is hardier than our native black walnut, growing from New Brunswick to Arkansas. It is a good choice for an extensive property in the North, but grows too large for small gardens. The oblong nuts have a rich but delicate flavor, preferred by many to the stronger-flavored black walnut. Butternut trees reach 50 to 75 feet in height.

CHESTNUT (CASTANEA)

What kind of soil do chestnuts need? Well-drained, acid soil, preferably sandy. They will also grow fairly well in neutral soils.

Are the blight-resistant Chinese chestnuts hardy? Less so than our native chestnut. They may suffer injury in severe winters in the northern United States. Nuts of the Chinese chestnuts are usually larger than those of the American chestnut and of equally good flavor. The trees branch like apple trees.

Have the Chinese chestnuts which I see advertised been definitely proven to be blight-resistant? Chinese chestnuts are generally sufficiently resistant to blight to permit their culture in regions where the blight has destroyed the native American chestnut. Many of the Chinese chestnuts in the trade are seedlings instead of grafted trees and exhibit considerable variation in blight resistance. Several named varieties are available from nut-tree nurseries, among which are 'Abundance', 'Nanking', 'Kuling', and 'Meiling'. Because of the incompatibility between the scion and rootstock, the grafted trees often die young. Seedlings, in spite of their variability, are preferable. Chestnut flowers require cross-pollination to produce nuts; hence, two or more seedlings should be planted.

Where can I get Chinese chestnuts and the thin-shelled black walnuts and pecans? A list of nurseries specializing in those named varieties of nut trees may be had from the New York Experiment Station, Geneva, N.Y. 14456.

Will any chestnut stand the climate of Montreal, Canada? It is doubtful if any chestnut trees are hardy enough for Montreal.

I have in my garden a chestnut tree severely afflicted with blight. Is there any effective treatment which might be applied to save this tree? If this is an American chestnut, it is hopeless to attempt to save it.

We have an American chestnut tree which bears many false (empty) burs. If a Chinese chestnut was planted, would it fertilize the American? This tree has died down several times, but sent up a few shoots which would live about 3 years and then die. No treatments will save the American chestnut. It will send up shoots for many years, but these will die as they become infected with blight. Planting another tree alongside this one would have no effect whatever on it.

FILBERT, HAZELNUT (CORYLUS)

Will filberts grow in this country? What are the best varieties? The European filbert (*C. avellana*) is grown commercially in Oregon and Washington. In the northeastern states near the Great Lakes where peaches are hardy, filberts may be expected to grow well. They will grow as far south as southern Pennsylvania at least. Hybrids between the native American hazels (*C. americana* and *C. cornuta*) and the European filbert grow well in the North.

Where should filberts be planted? Any good well-drained soil is suitable. A north slope or the north side of buildings and a site protected from cold winds are desirable.

Should filbert (hazelnut) trees be trimmed to the tree shape or allowed to grow as bushes? They may be grown either as trees or bushes; but as suckers are freely produced by many varieties, a bush is much easier to grow than a tree with a single stem.

How should filberts be pruned? Prune them like peaches, only not as severely. Severe pruning may result in winter injury. A moderate thinning is sufficient.

HICKORY (CARYA)

Are hickories worth growing? The shagbark hickory (*C. ovata*) nut is of very fine flavor, excelled only by the best pecans. 'Wilcox', 'Fox', and a few others propagated by nut nurseries are worth growing and they are much superior to seedling hickories. Hickory trees are difficult to transplant and establish because of the long taproot. They are suitable only for extensive rural properties.

Where should one report good nut trees, when found, so that they may be preserved (for instance, hickory and black walnut)? The New York Experiment Station, Geneva, N.Y. 14456.

MACADAMIA (MACADAMIA INTEGRIFOLIA)

What is the macadamia nut? This is an edible nut of a species of Australian tree. It is commonly called the Queensland nut.

Is the macadamia nut tree grown in this country? Yes, these nut trees are cultivated in California and in parts of Florida. They are a commercial crop in Hawaii. They thrive in rich, loamy soil with plenty of moisture, although they have been reported growing in dry sections. The tree is an evergreen and is ornamental as well.

PECAN (CARYA ILLINOINENSIS)

Are pecans successfully grown in the North?   Pecan trees are hardy in the North, but the growing season is too short and too cool to mature the nuts. Several northern pecans, as they are called, will mature nuts as far north as Washington, D.C., and the Ohio River Valley. The nuts are not as large as the southern varieties.

Of several small pecan trees I planted, all have died but one. Is there some special way to dig holes or set them out to make them live and grow well? (Georgia.)   Vigorous pecan trees that have been carefully dug and not allowed to dry out should not be difficult to establish. Set the trees in the fall; firm the soil tightly against the roots; keep down weeds; and water and mulch the trees when drought threatens during the first year or two.

What should be done for pecan trees when the nuts do not fill properly? They hull themselves as they should, but do not fill out. (Virginia.)   Control diseases and insects that attack the foliage. Varieties suitable in the Deep South may not fill well in Virginia. Grow northern varieties there.

How old does a soft-shell pecan tree have to be before bearing nuts?   The age of bearing depends on the variety of the tree, but not many nuts will be had until the trees are 6 to 8 years of age.

How should pecans be grafted? (Alabama.)   Varieties of pecan are propagated almost entirely upon seedling stocks of pecan species. Stocks of certain varieties are said to have some influence upon the growth of the grafted tree. Various pecan stocks are used in Texas. In Louisiana some use is made of the water hickory as a stock. Study local conditions as to the stock used.

PISTACHIO (PISTACIA VERA)

In what part of the country can the pistachio nut tree be grown?   Only in California and Mexico. It needs a climate like that required by olive trees.

WALNUT, BLACK (JUGLANS NIGRA)

Is the black walnut a good tree for the home garden?   If you live where winter temperatures do not drop too low and want a handsome specimen tree which will produce nuts, the black walnut is a good choice. The tree requires lots of room and is hardly suitable for most suburban properties. Some plants will not grow within the reach of its roots as these produce a substance toxic to these plants. Grass will grow all right under a black walnut. Although individual specimens live for years in New York State and similar sections, black walnuts are not considered reliably hardy where winter temperatures drop below −20° F. Butternut is hardier.

What special requirements has the black walnut? Wild specimens are often found growing in dry, rocky upland pastures as well as in woodlands. To produce nuts, this tree needs good, well-drained soil with regular supplies of moisture. A wild tree in a dry, unfertile location, if subjected for a few years to fertilization and sufficient moisture, will increase its yield tremendously. If caterpillars, such as canker or inch worms or gypsy moth caterpillars, defoliate the tree, they should be destroyed. They gather in clusters on the trunk at night, at which time they can be destroyed by rubbing out the colony with a broom. If the leaves are destroyed prematurely by caterpillars, anthracnose, or early fall frost, the nuts may not fill properly. Spraying the foliage with malathion or any stomach poison is also effective.

What are the dirty-white worms all through the outer husks of my black walnuts? What can I do to get rid of them? (New York.) These are the maggots of the walnut-husk fly, distributed throughout the East to the Kansas–Nebraska line on black walnuts and butternuts. A closely related species attacks the central and western black and English walnuts. Flies, a little smaller than house flies, with transparent, black-banded wings, lay their eggs in the husks in August. The maggots tunnel through the husks for several weeks, drop to the ground before or with the nuts, and pupate several inches down in the soil. They emerge as flies the next summer, or wait until the second or third summer. They do little injury to kernels, but they stain the surface of the nut. This insect is difficult to control, and hardly worth the trouble for most home gardens.

How can I grow native walnut seedlings from walnuts? So far I have had no luck. (Missouri.) Plant the seeds in the fall about 2 inches deep. If squirrels are troublesome, store the nuts in a box of moist sand outdoors and cover with wire netting to keep out rodents. Plant the nuts in the spring.

WALNUT, JAPANESE (JUGLANS AILANTHIFOLIA)

Can you give some information about a Japanese walnut?   The Japanese walnut is a rapid-growing, very handsome tree. The nut is elongated, smooth, cracks poorly, and is inferior in quality to other walnuts. The heartnut, a supposed sport of the Japanese walnut, is much superior in cracking quality.

WALNUT, PERSIAN (ENGLISH) (JUGLANS REGIA)

Is the Persian walnut hardy in the East?   Many seedling trees have been grown for years in the fruit-growing regions of the Great Lakes and on the eastern end of Long Island, New York, but occasionally a severe winter that injures peach trees may kill or seriously injure many of these trees. Several superior varieties, supposedly of greater than average hardiness, are now being propagated by nut-tree nurseries. Among them are 'Metcalfe', 'McKinster', 'Broadview', 'Littlepage', and 'Hansen'.

What are the soil and cultural requirements of the Persian walnut?   Good, deep loam, well drained but with plenty of moisture to produce large crops of nuts. Where peaches are hardy in the North, the walnuts are worth trying. Farther south, many of them start their growth too early and are injured by frost.

Are Persian walnut trees harmful near shrubs?   The Persian walnut is not considered to be harmful to shrubs, but of course it will compete with them for plant food and moisture.

I have a Persian walnut tree that is 14 years old. It never bore until the last 2 years. All its nuts fell off both years when they were quite small, but nuts inside were formed. Why does this happen?   The nuts may not have been pollinated. If no other Persian walnut is near this tree, another should be planted to provide pollination.

What can I do to have more walnut nuts mature? The tree sets plenty of fruit, but nearly all drop off when they reach the size of large cherries.   Lack of cross-pollination may be the cause of the trouble. Another variety of the same species should be set nearby. The tree may need fertilizing to increase its vigor. Nitrate of soda or sulfate of ammonia at the rate of ¼ pound for each inch of trunk diameter may be tried.

Is the Persian walnut self-pollinating?   Persian (English) walnut varieties usually require cross-pollination by another variety, since its own pollen often is not shed at the time when the pistils are receptive.

How are Persian walnuts washed and dried to be stored for the winter? Remove the husks promptly and wash the nuts immediately. Lay the nuts out one layer deep in an airy room until they are thoroughly dried. Keep them in a cool, dry place.

We have a Persian walnut tree. Is there some way to treat the nuts to prevent mold while drying and to keep nut meats white? The nuts should not mold if they are husked promptly, washed, and thoroughly dried in an airy place.

Do you know a good soft-shelled walnut—better than 'Manchurian'—that will stand 10° or 20° F. below zero if need be? Our average winter temperature is 10° F. (Washington State.) The 'Hansen' variety of the Persian walnut and the Carpathian strain of the same species are thought to be somewhat hardier than the usual varieties and may be worth trying.

12. House Plants

HOUSE PLANTS HAVE two delightful functions—they make charming decorations for our rooms and they are fun to care for. The degree of satisfaction they give depends first on the conditions you can offer in which they can thrive. If your house is flooded with winter sunlight, you can grow almost any plant you wish; if it is well lighted, you also have a wide selection; but if it is quite dim, the light cut off by nearby walls or heavy evergreens, your selection must be very limited unless you install fluorescent lights. With these, a great variety of plants will flourish in previously dark corners or even in basements.

Although plants suitable for indoor culture have to a degree different individual requirements, there are certain basic needs of light, heat and humidity, moisture, food, and rest common to all. Keep them in mind as you become familiar with the individual nature of each indoor plant. Thus, African-violets, begonias, and ferns are kept barely moist all the time, but the sansevieria and aspidistra are allowed to dry out a little in between waterings.

Today in modern houses and office buildings floor-to-ceiling windows offer a handsome setting for tree-form lantanas or geraniums if there is sun, and for great foliage specimens in fully lighted locations—bamboos, ferns, philodendrons, Norfolk-Island-pines, aralias, and the schefflera. Attractive containers of brass, china, earthenware, or basketry add to the charm of house plants individually or in groups; for vining plants, there are, besides ceramic and brass baskets on chains, wicker cages, brackets that are copies of kerosene lamps, and wrought-iron pedestals to set off graceful cascades.

The great thing is to have only healthy plants. Sickly specimens are better discarded than pampered, and if you have had less success than you wish, try the easy ones—spider-plant, grape-ivy, Swedish-ivy, tradescantia, philodendron, asparagus-fern, pick-a-back plant, and ever-blooming wax begonia, all nearly foolproof but offering possibilities for attractive displays.

Light, Natural and Fluorescent

Most plants require a fully lighted location. Fresh-from-the-greenhouse specimens hung on a bracket in a dark hall or set at the mantel ends of a dim living room are destined, no matter what their original condition, for a short life—and not a very merry one. Light permits the plant organism to turn certain substances into usable foods. There are, of course, a number of excellent foliage plants which need no direct sun. The wax begonia and the patience-plant will bloom to some extent in a fully lighted location, without direct sunshine, but for most flowering plants sunshine is required—not an occasional hour or so, but every bit a southern or eastern window (from 4 to 6 hours) can offer. Without a maximum of sunshine, the geranium will fail to bud, and the jasmines and wax plants will remain an enduring green.

Fluorescent lights make it possible to grow plants in otherwise dark areas. Tubes can be fastened under kitchen cabinets and bookcase shelves and above counters. Table fixtures with hoods can be purchased and set over pebble-filled plastic trays. Carts fitted with fluorescent tubes are available by mail order, as are various special growth lamps. However, it has been found that standard tubes, available locally, are perfectly satisfactory, especially in a combination of one warm white and one cool white tube.

It is important to allow 15 to 20 watts of fluorescent light per square foot of growing area: for instance, two 48-inch 40-watt tubes for a 1×4-foot plant shelf. The center of the tubes gives the strongest light. Most plants thrive with tops 8 to 10 inches from the lights, which are kept on 12 to 14 hours a day. African-violets, other gesneriads, small begonias, and many miniature plants are a delight under fluorescents.

Temperature

Grown at 60° to 65° F., almost every house plant is better off than at 70° or 75° F. (indoor temperatures once normal in most northern winter interiors but virtually obsolete because of higher heating costs), while a night drop to 55° F., similar to nature's outdoor falling of temperature after sunset, is a further cultural benefit. Many of the most decorative plants can be grown in a really cool house window where the average is 50° to 60° F. For this reason a plant room, today's version of yesterday's sun porch, makes an ideal location for indoor gardening, since temperatures are usually lower there than in the house itself.

On record, for example, is one where night temperatures dropped to 35° and 40° F., and where only a small amount of electric radiation supplemented the effects of the sun during the day. Here begonias and geraniums bloomed incessantly. The cyclamen, with never a yellow leaf, opened bud after bud for a full 3 months. Primroses and paper-white narcissus kept fresh for extra weeks, while ivies, wax plants, *Asparagus* 'Sprengeri', many ferns (even maidenhairs), and strawberry-begonias maintained marvelous health. Of course these plants were all set back somewhat from the glass and, if outdoor temperatures threatened to go below 20° F., they were covered at night with newspapers.

When plants develop weak, soft, spindly growth, foliage color is light, and buds blast or fall prematurely, it is very often because they are suffering from too warm an atmosphere.

Air conditioning is not generally harmful. In areas of high humidity in summer, it is beneficial, a safeguard against leaf rot. However, air conditioning can have a drying effect, decreasing the atmospheric humidity so that plants require extra water.

Humidity

The greatest foe to successful indoor gardening, however, is lack of humidity. Outdoors the air is moist. Inside it is usually much too dry. This results in parched foliage, especially on English ivy, even when the owner has never neglected moistening the soil.

Now how can humidity be increased? A humidifying device can be added to the furnace or a room humidifier, cool-vapor not hot-steam type, placed in the room where plants are growing. Supplying the window garden with metal or plastic trays filled with 2 to 3 inches of pebbles is probably the easiest means of increasing humidity. Excess water from the pots runs through to the trays, and more water is added as needed to keep the level just below the surface pebbles. (Plants must never stand in water.) Water beneath the pebbles serves as a source of evaporation for constantly moistening the air circulating about the plants.

An occasional cleansing of the foliage with water from a sprayer during the day keeps house plants in good condition and free from insect pests.

Extra-large, pebble-filled saucers with water can be set under each plant or, better yet, large trays that will hold several plants can be used. Furthermore, humidity as well as cleanliness is increased if plants are frequently sprayed from a bulb syringe or set under a shower or faucet. Usually this can be managed only monthly or weekly, while a light syringing may be a daily matter. But again there must be interpretation according to individuals. The hairy-leaved African-violet, gloxinia, and rex begonia, and the tightly crowned cyclamen or pandanus, may be harmed by heavy showering, but light misting also benefits these. Always use room-temperature water.

Watering

The question most often asked by house-plant growers is, "How often should I water my house plants?" or, "Is there a rule, so much water for so much soil?"

Only in a very general way can a rule be offered. *When the topsoil feels dry to the touch, then it is time to water.* Then water so thoroughly that the entire root system is saturated and in a little while excess seeps out into the pot saucer. Empty this excess from the saucer; roots rot if pots stand in water.

The most important "Beware" in connection with watering applies to the little-and-often method. Pouring water on plants just for the fun of it does them no good. Often it results in a too-wet upper half of soil and a too-dry lower. Especially is this true of thick-rooted plants such as palms or very large specimens of almost any plant, particularly those of the shrubby type—gardenia, azalea, and the like. All such are wisely set,

Use a mister with a fine spray to increase the humidity temporarily. Several mistings a day can be very beneficial.

about once a week, in a pail filled with water to within an inch of the pot rim. Here they remain until enough moisture has been drawn up to make the surface feel moist. Then they are removed in a thoroughly refreshed condition, especially if tops are syringed at the time.

Most plants are safely moistened by applying water at the edge of the pot rim. Some with thick crowns, like the cyclamen or bird's-nest fern, are better moistened from below by pouring water into the saucer and letting the plant draw it up according to its need. Saved rainwater is better than faucet water, especially in places where the local supply has been treated with chemicals, the residue from which often collects on the soil and discolors the containers. Room-temperature water also is better than cold, which may have a retarding effect on growth. Most plants, however, are fairly tolerant and given regular care will not be too fussy about the type of water supplied, only the amount. Actually, most beginners tend to overwater rather than to neglect. Experience reveals which plants, like the African-violet, begonia, cyclamen, and ferns, want a "just-moist" soil at all times; while others, notably the jade plant, many of the cacti, and the sansevieria, thrive only when allowed to become quite dry between drinks.

In addition to the drinking habits of the plant itself, other factors influencing the amount of water required are: the size of pot (little ones dry out faster); the type of pot (plastic ones permit less evaporation); the stage of plant growth, whether active or resting; and the temperature of the room. The weather is also a factor: on sunny days more water is required than during dull ones. All these conditions are to be taken into consideration. Complicated as all this may sound, however, it soon becomes second nature to water the poinsettia twice a day and the big jade plant only once in 10 days, when the feel of the soil is made the actual guide.

Ventilation

A close atmosphere is very hard on house plants. Even when the weather is definitely cold, they require a fresh atmosphere. The best plan then is to admit fresh air indirectly through a window or door in an adjoining room, or through a window ventilator in the same room, but not directly beside the plants. It is most important to provide an abundance of fresh air for several weeks after plants are brought in in autumn; and again in spring, as the midday hours become increasingly warm.

Where manufactured gas is used for heating and cooking, plenty of fresh air is especially necessary; but even this will not counteract the effects of escaping gas, the fumes of which spell ultimate death to most plants. Some of them are extremely allergic to gas. The Jerusalem-cherry, for instance, is one of these. First it drops all the fruit, then the leaves shrivel, and finally the plant dies. Natural gas, however, is not harmful to plants.

Air is essential to the roots as well as to the tops of plants. A constant loose condition of the surface soil, and hence aeration of the roots, is readily obtained by an occasional stirring with a fork.

Pruning and Training

Plants are kept shapely by being turned frequently so that all sides receive an equal amount of light, and by the cutting back of overlong growth, which tends to make ungainly specimens. Sometimes, too, a drastic pruning back is necessary to promote health. Thus in autumn the summer geraniums are cut back to stubs 3 to 6 inches long, while the dormant poinsettia in summer is started all over again by hard pruning.

Fertilizing

Extra fertilizer is not nearly so important as good texture and structure of soil and proper potting. Sickly plants especially are more likely to be suffering from too much heat and water, or from some insect pest, than from starvation. Usually a plant from the grower requires no extra nutrients for a month or more. If a plant is at a standstill when, by all the rules of its own nature and the time of year, it should be growing, or when its buds are not maturing, or its foliage color is poor—although a proper system of culture is maintained—then extra feeding definitely is to be considered. Generally speaking, flowering plants require more nutrients than foliage ones, at least up to the time the buds show color. Plants growing under fluorescent lights require more food than those at windows. For slow-growing plants, occasional light top dustings of complete fertilizer are good. Any one of the "complete" fertilizers especially prepared for house plants is excellent, provided directions are followed and it is not assumed that because a little is good for a plant a lot will be better. Nor should a resting plant be "pushed" with a quick-acting fertilizer when the need is for quiet and not for action. Thus the summer-weary geranium or wax plant in fall requires not fertilizer but coolness and time to resuscitate itself.

Certain items are *not* suitable fertilizers—notably tea, coffee, cigar ashes, castor oil, and leftover alcoholic beverages!

Repotting

When a plant has actually outgrown its living quarters (when, after the pot is removed, a fine web of roots is seen on the outside of the earth ball), that plant needs another container, but probably one only a size larger. Usually established plants need shifting only once a year; some only once in 2 years. Often, worn-out soil can be carefully washed from the roots of a large plant and the plant then repotted in the same size pot.

Repotting is not a panacea. A too-large pot with unneeded amounts of soil and moisture more often kills an ailing plant than cures it. The best general policy is to keep plants in as small pots as possible. Overlarge antique specimens of plants, dear as they may be sentimentally, are rarely, when dispassionately viewed, very attractive in themselves or as part of the general window-garden arrangement. Institutional-size plants do not belong in people's houses, nor do sickly plants which, outside a greenhouse, will be unlikely to regain health under the trying conditions of most houses in winter.

The best time for repotting is in spring; then the resulting shock is offset by months of ideal outdoor life. In the spring, when the weather is settled, a practical plan is to take all the plants outdoors, discard some, divide others (repotting the divisions into smaller pots), and then shift the remainder into larger pots.

Arranged in a row, small to large, with a few pots on hand larger than any already in use, plants are easily repotted—the largest plants going into the new pots, which if of clay have first been soaked in a pail of water for 24 hours, and the others, successively, to the outgrown pots, which are thoroughly scrubbed out before receiving new occupants.

Plants are readily depotted for examination or repotting if they are first watered and then inverted on the gardener's left hand, with the main stem placed between the index and middle fingers. The pot rim is then knocked sharply against a table or step. So loosened, the pot is lifted off by the right hand and the root condition examined.

When needed, a larger pot is fitted with an arching piece of broken flowerpot above the drainage hole and, if it is above a 3-inch size, a few more pieces of broken crock are fitted over this. In large pots a handful of gravel or pebbles is placed above the "crocking" and a drainage layer of coarse compost or sphagnum moss (saved from mail-order packing) is spread over this. (When pots have no hole, the drainage layer of this coarse material is especially necessary; also a bit of charcoal mixed in the soil to ensure "sweetness.")

When the drainage layer is in place, a sifting of soil is added. Then the plant is centered in the pot and extra soil firmly pressed around it with a potting stick—a piece of lath or an old ruler. The soil is kept ½ inch or so below the rim of the pot, this space being needed to receive water.

Potting Soils

Although there are almost as many soil formulas as there are types of house plants, it is a matter of experience that plants try to accustom themselves to any soil that is of proper texture or friability and well drained. A generally good formula (which may be altered in its proportions according to the type of plant to be grown) consists of 1 part loam from vegetable or flower garden, 1 part compost or other humus such as leafmold, commercial humus, or peat moss, and 1 part sand (builder's, not seashore) or perlite. For enrichment, a 4-inch pot of a complete fertilizer is added to a wheelbarrowload, or its close equivalent, of soil or 1 teaspoonful to an 8-inch pot of soil.

The loam contains nutrients, sand facilitates drainage and aeration of roots, while humus materials increase the water-holding capacity and thus prevent too-rapid evaporation of moisture and caking of soil. Humus also helps to produce a light, mellow mixture which roots can easily penetrate. To these essentials may be added, when convenient, a little charcoal to "sweeten" the soil (especially in pots lacking a drainage hole).

Apartment gardeners as well as others who value convenience can procure ready-made soil mixtures from florists or hardware stores or artificial soil mixes compiled according to the famous Cornell and other universities' formulas. Versions of these are available under such trade names as Jiffy Mix, Readi-Earth, etc. These mixes usually include vermiculite, sphagnum peat, superphosphate, limestone, and a complete fertilizer. Using prepackaged potting mixes is an easy way to avoid soil pests and disease organisms frequently found in garden soils.

If the plants have heavy roots—such as those of pandanus, sansevieria, or palm—less sand and more loam is used, because such roots have force enough to penetrate a firm mixture, and the plants prefer it. The fibrous-rooted ferns, begonias, and fuchsias thrive in a lighter medium—about ½ leafmold or peat moss, ½ loam, and plenty of sand.

Summer Quarters

Summer is the ideal time for all plants with future possibilities to be resuscitated after the trying months indoors. Summer quarters can be established outdoors on porches, terraces, breezeways, or in garden beds. (Even a cool, light window indoors will do, if plenty of fresh air is available.) Wherever placed, the plants should be out of the way of strong winds and grouped to facilitate watering and syringing. Pots are not removed because house plants, freed of their containers, develop in an open garden bed such extensive root systems that autumn repotting becomes almost impossible.

It is a healthful procedure to place your plants in a garden bed that offers suitable gradations of light for the varying needs of sun-loving geraniums and shade-requiring ferns. A location under some open-leaved tree, like an apple or a honey locust or an oak, with branches not too low, is ideal. Nearest to the trunk, where the shade is deepest, go the ferns; below the open branches in light shade are set resting geraniums and heliotrope, vines, foliage plants, and most of the flowering subjects: gardenias, azaleas, fuchsias, and shade-loving begonias; near the edge, but not under the overhang, where sun daily penetrates, are placed the young geraniums, wax begonias, and poinsettias.

A bed is dug deep enough to contain the largest pot, plus a 3-inch layer of stones or other worm-deterring drainage material. Here the plants are arranged according to their light requirements, and around them is packed light soil containing plenty of water-holding humus, preferably peat moss. When placing is completed, pot rims remain slightly above the soil surface. About once a week each plant is turned. This prevents anchoring roots from taking hold through the drainage hole, and also facilitates the development of shapely tops.

The watering of house plants should not be forgotten in summer. Even when placed outside, they require, because of their restricted root systems and location under tree branches, more frequent watering than average summer rainfall supplies.

The best procedure is to let a hose with its nozzle removed trickle slowly into the bed for a period long enough to moisten it completely to a depth of 6 inches. This will suffice for a week or 10 days even in hot weather. During long, hot, dry spells, an oscillating sprinkler played on the bed through the late afternoon hours will give the plants a lift. The cool night hours to follow should revive them completely.

An ordinary rotary sprinkler should not be used unless it produces a fine spray, for heavy drops falling successively in the same spot or on the same leaf or flower over a long period may do more harm than good.

Some pruning may be required to promote shapely growth, and insect pests must always be watched for. Usually frequent hose syringing deters them, but sometimes, as in winter, aphids or mealybugs must be sprayed with an insecticide.

Plants in Autumn

Plants are prepared for winter well before frost. It is a good precaution to remove the pot from each specimen and, if necessary, to renew the drainage arrangements. At this season, however, roots should be disturbed as little as possible.

Plants should be brought inside before the first touch of frost, for many are from the tropics, and hence are easily harmed by cool fall weather. Pots should be scrubbed and tops sprayed with an insecticide. Then set plants on a sheltered porch or terrace for a week or so, when another spraying is given. During the first weeks indoors much attention to ventilation and syringing is necessary. Now more than at other times plants are particularly inclined to resent the dry, close air of the house. Falling leaves and blossoms are signs of unfavorable reaction. A thorough drenching under a faucet will often immediately check leaf dropping. This is also the time for insect pests to attack. A sharp eye should be kept out for these and an all-purpose house-plant aerosol bomb used if any pests are discovered.

If a systemic is mixed in the potting soil, many pests are unlikely to appear. The material, drawn up through all parts of the plant, is lethal to insects that suck and particularly efficacious against whitefly. The systemic must be used exactly according to the manufacturer's directions.

Rest Period

All plants have growth cycles that include periods of rest. As trees lose their leaves in fall and enter into a dormant period, so do house plants at some time rest in greater or lesser degree. In winter, ferns and palms are less active and produce fewer new leaves than in spring. In early fall many of the cacti remain utterly quiet. After flowering, some plants, such as cyclamens, appear on the point of death, when really they are only going to sleep.

All plants that are resting require less water and warmth than when they are in a period of active growth. None should be fed at this time. The resting condition of plants is not always an easy one to identify, but constant observation of each kind eventually reveals it, and the indoor gardener is accordingly guided in the treatment given them.

General Culture

SOIL

Are all house plants potted in the same soil mixture?   No, there are variations in soil mixtures for different types of plants, although most house plants do very well in general-purpose mixtures. (See the following questions.)

What is a good standard or general-purpose potting mixture for house plants?   Two parts garden loam, 1 part leafmold or peat moss, 1 part sharp sand. For general use, add 1 pint of a complete fertilizer and 2 quarts of a commercial cow manure, or well-rotted cow manure if available, to each bushel of mixture.

An alternate (although more expensive) approach is to purchase ready-to-use commercially packaged potting mixtures, which are free from weed seeds and pests. Common garden soil often contains organisms that are harmful to house plants. Some of these mixtures contain soil and some, such as Jiffy Mix and Readi-Earth, are soilless. They can save time and trouble and can be modified to fit specific plant requirements. For example, sand and fine gravel can be added for desert cactus or fine fir-bark chips for jungle cactus and columneas, extra-coarse peat moss for azaleas and gardenias.

What are the proportions of a typical soilless growing medium? I would like to mix my own to save money. One bushel of vermiculite; 1 bushel of peat moss; 1¼ cup of ground limestone (preferably dolomitic); ½ cup of 20 per cent superphosphate; 1 cup of 5–10–5 fertilizer. Mix thoroughly before using.

What mixture of soil is best for azaleas and other acid-loving plants? Add to a standard potting mixture (see the previous question) 25 per cent in bulk acid (hardwood) leafmold or peat moss, and to each bushel, add 2 quarts of a commercial (dehydrated) cow manure and 1 pint of a complete fertilizer.

What mixture of soil do I need for ferns grown indoors? A fibrous mixture. Add to the standard potting mixture 25 per cent in bulk leaf-mold, compost, or peat moss, 2 quarts of a commercial manure, and 1 pint of a complete fertilizer.

How shall I prepare the potting mixture for house plants which need an alkaline soil—some herbs, for instance? To each bushel of standard mixture, add 1 quart raw ground limestone, 1 pint bone meal, and 2 quarts well-rotted or commercial cow manure. Some potted herbs, such as rosemary or lavender, benefit from an occasional dusting of wood ashes from the fireplace, which should immediately be watered into the soil.

What potting soil shall I use for desert cacti and other succulents? A sandy mixture. Add 25 per cent in bulk sharp sand or crushed soft stone (or crushed flowerpots) to a standard potting mixture (see the previous question). Add to each bushel 1 quart raw ground limestone and 1 pint complete fertilizer or bone meal. Make up the mixture 2 weeks or more before its use. (See Cacti.)

Do tender bulbs, such as amaryllis, tuberous-rooted begonias, etc., need a special potting soil? Yes. Place 1 to 2 inches of manure or rich compost in the bottom of the pot, and for potting soil use well-rotted compost. If compost and cow manure are not available, use 1 part garden loam, 1 part peat moss or leafmold, and add to each bushel 3 quarts of a commercial (dehydrated) cow manure and 1 part complete fertilizer.

Which house plants prefer peat moss in the soil? Please add information concerning its use. Most house plants can tolerate peat moss in the potting soil, as it is a source of humus. Azaleas and gardenias thrive with up to 50 per cent coarse peat in a potting mix.

What do you think of the prepared potting soils sold by garden cen-

ters and stores? Most of these are well-balanced mixtures suitable for African-violets, begonias, ferns, etc. Although they do differ in quality and usefulness, there is little way of judging them until you try them and see the plant's performance. More reliable are the soilless mixes, which consist of formulas devised by Cornell University and the University of California.

How should the soil surrounding house plants be prevented from getting solid? Is there any danger of cutting rootlets if the soil is dug in to loosen it? Stir the shallow, surface soil frequently. Use the soil mixtures recommended in the previous questions. Then spread a little fresh soil on top if the soil appears "watered down."

POTTING AND REPOTTING

Which are better: clay or plastic pots? Most plants grow well in both, as long as cultural care is satisfactory. As a rule, those in plastic pots need less water than those in clay. Plastic is easy to keep clean. Some modern plastic pots look like wood or ceramic, come with snap-on saucers, and are available in different colors. But top-heavy plants in small plastic pots often tip over, especially when the lightweight soilless mixes are used.

What size pots are best for winter-blooming plants? It depends on the plant and its stage of growth; 3½-, 4-, and 4½-inch pots suit most of them. As a rule, flowering plants give more bloom if grown in pots just big enough to hold the roots.

Should the soil on a potted plant be changed? If so, how often? See the introduction to this section.

When should house plants be repotted? This varies with the kind of plant. A good general rule is to repot each year in the spring when plants are taken outdoors. Some, such as agapanthus, need attention only every few years. It is best to examine the roots in the spring when the plants are first taken out.

How can I tell when my plants need repotting? When the plants are knocked gently from their pots (see the introduction to this section) the root system shows whether repotting is necessary. If roots have formed a thick, dry web on the outside of the root ball, repot. If visible roots are few and appear succulent and healthy, return to the same pot; if a rotted condition is seen, knock off as much soil as possible, cut back any soft roots, and plant in a smaller pot with fresh soil.

When repotting house plants, how much larger should the new pot be? Usually one size larger is adequate. Overpotting does not produce healthy plants. (See the introduction.) For most plants, use one size larger in the spring for plants that are to be sunk in garden beds in their pots. For fast-growing wax begonias and impatiens, use two sizes larger. Even so, these may need fall repotting in spite of this precaution.

How should tender bulbs be potted for indoor bloom? Most of these bulbs, such as amaryllis, calla-lily, and tuberous-rooted begonia, are planted with the top third of the bulb exposed.

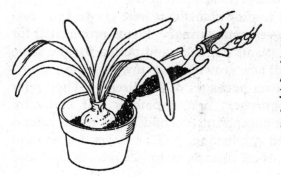

With some bulbs (such as amaryllis) and other plants in large pots, the soil is renewed (usually yearly), without repotting, by removing as much as possible of the old soil and then refilling with new soil.

How can I provide good drainage in the pots of my house plants? Place a bit of broken flowerpot, curved side up, over the drainage hole of small pots before adding soil. For 4-inch or larger pots, use several pieces of this "crocking"; for large bulb pans and large pots, cover the entire bottom with broken bits of pot, always being sure that the piece which covers the drainage hole is placed so as to allow the free outflow of water. Then spread a thin layer of roughage, such as gravel, small driveway stones, unmilled sphagnum moss, or very coarse compost.

FEEDING

When shall I feed my house plants? See the introduction to this section.

What fertilizers are best for house plants? In the questions on Soil in this section and in the introduction, recommendations are made for fertilizing the soil mixtures. In addition to this, complete fertilizers may be given in liquid or tablet form according to package directions. Instant liquid cow manure is easily prepared from a commercial mix. An organic fish-emulsion fertilizer is useful for many plants and available from garden centers and house-plant specialists. Special foods are sold for some plants, such as African-violets. (See Culture of Specific Plants.)

Do you think liquid manure is a good fertilizer for house plants? Yes. It gives excellent results. You can use it sparingly about once a week on plants in active growth that prefer a pot-bound condition (amaryllis, pandanus, palms, nerines, etc.) and on plants that bloom steadily with every watering if you apply a very weak mixture.

Several of my house plants look very sick indeed. Shall I give them fertilizer? It is wise to discard such plants, for they rarely can be brought back to health under average home conditions.

What is the proper means of feeding plants that were grown from cuttings as house plants to carry over until spring? Plants propagated for carrying over to spring, or old plants cut back and potted for the same purpose, don't need feeding until new growth shows toward spring.

What do the numbers mean on packages of fertilizers? They refer to the three basic elements—nitrogen, first, promotes leaf and stem strength and stimulates growth; phosphorus, second, is for roots, gives a steady push to flower and seed production, and improves foliage and flower color; potash, third, wards off disease, stabilizes growth, and also intensifies color. (See Section 1.)

Is black tea of any value to ferns? No.

WATERING

What is a good general rule for watering house plants? Water only when the plants *need* water, not whenever it seems that they may stand watering. Whenever water is supplied, give enough to saturate thoroughly the whole ball of soil. Never merely sprinkle the surface.

How often should one water house plants—namely, ferns, wax begonias, and geraniums? Watering is governed by the temperature and humidity of a room. Keep geraniums barely on the dry side if they are not actively growing; begonias and ferns in a room of 60° to 70° F. will need water almost every day. The feel of the soil is the best guide.

Can you tell me why growing house plants rot or decay from the roots up? This sounds like overwatering. Do not permit the plants to stand with their roots soaking in water. Surplus water should be poured from the saucer after each watering, and water should be given only when the surface of the soil feels dry—or almost dry.

What can be done to counteract the effect of watering house plants with the hard water we have in this locality? If the hardness of the water is merely due to lime, use an acid fertilizer such as sulfate of ammonia.

Do plants kept in the cellar in winter need much water? If the cellar is poorly lighted and not warm, the plants should be kept fairly dry. Most modern basements are too hot.

How can I give enough water to azaleas, hydrangeas, and other house plants which seem to dry out completely? Once a week, when the topsoil is a little dry, set the potted plant in a pail or dishpan of water so that the water is absorbed from the opening in the bottom of the pot and the soil is thoroughly soaked.

How can I keep my house plants from having "wet feet"? Pot them properly and place a handful of large pebbles or gravel in the saucer under each pot or in the tray or on the shelf on which the pots are set. If there is surplus water, the pebbles will provide good drainage.

Must all flower pots have drainage? Plants can be grown in pots without drainage and no outlet for surplus water, but care must be taken not to overwater. During the winter and spring, narcissus and some other bulbs can be grown in pebbles in pots without a hole at the bottom.

How often should house plants in glazed pots be watered? More sparingly than those in clay pots since evaporation does not occur through the walls as with clay pots. A quart of charcoal bits added to each bushel of potting soil helps keep the mixture "sweet."

How often should plants in plastic pots be watered? Usually less often than those in clay pots because of slower evaporation, but let the feel of the soil guide you. As a rule, a plant in a clay pot may need water every day; one in plastic, only every second or third day.

TEMPERATURE

What temperature is best for most house plants? Many flowering house plants are happiest at 55° F. or lower. Cineraria and calceolaria prefer 45° F. That's why so many people fail with house plants in hot rooms. It also explains why cyclamen, Jerusalem-cherry, ornamental pepper, etc., last such a short time after coming from the florist. If your home is kept at 70° F. or above, day and night, grow semitropical foliage plants, cacti and succulents, African-violets, some orchids, and poinsettias. If a low night temperature can be maintained, many plants preferring a cool temperature will do quite well.

Why do my house plants die within a short time—all except a Chinese-evergreen and some ivy, both in water? I tried different soil and fertilizers. I put them in the sun and in the shade with no result. They grow nicely outside in the summer but die in the house even in the sum-

mertime. Probably too high temperature, too low humidity, poor drainage, or too much water or a combination of these factors.

I am determined to keep my house temperature at 65° F. during the day and 60° F. at night to cut down on my oil bill. How will this affect my vast and varied house-plant collection that has formerly done quite well at winter temperatures about 70° F.? Your house plants should do very well. The majority of house plants prefer cooler temperatures. African-violets and some of the other strictly tropical plants prefer warmer temperatures, but they should adjust and continue to bloom well, especially if you grow them under fluorescent lights where the temperature will be a few degrees higher.

What plants can be grown in an unheated but enclosed breezeway? I am trying geraniums, sweet marjoram, parsley, sage, winter savory, and ivies. Your suggestions will be appreciated. (New Jersey.) Such a room in winter is difficult, since in severe weather everything will freeze. However, if you can protect the plants when the temperature dips below freezing and remains there, you may have success. Other plants to try are azaleas, chrysanthemums, camellias, Norfolk-Island-pine, and French lavender.

Will house plants survive in a home that has a temperature of 75° F.? They may survive or even do well if the temperature drops to 60° F. at night. When high temperatures are the rule, house plants are apt to develop many difficulties such as falling leaves and buds, pests and diseases, and general unthriftiness. Tropicals such as African-violets, poinsettias, semitropical foliage plants, etc., are exceptions to the rule when humidity can be kept above 40 per cent.

Why do house plants do well in country farmhouses? Because the temperature is low, especially at night, and the humidity high, due to a lack of central heating. The steaming kettle on the farm kitchen range is a first-class humidifier. Although most farmhouses today have central heating, their rooms are generally cooler and better lighted than those of most city apartments and suburban houses.

Is a very cool sun porch suitable for house plants in the winter? If the night temperature is safely above freezing, house plants such as camellia, azalea, gardenia, and cymbidium orchids, which prefer coolness (see individual plants), will be far happier there than in the warmer living room.

VENTILATION

Do my house plants need fresh air in the winter? Yes, decidedly.

See that fresh air is admitted daily to the room where they are kept, but avoid direct drafts. A window or door opened for half an hour each day in an adjoining room will provide the needed ventilation. (See the introduction to this section.)

SUMMER CARE

What shall I do with my house plants in the summer? See the introduction to this section.

How can I arrange my house plants outdoors in a garden bed so that they will receive the right amount of sunshine and shade? Choose a location near a water supply where part of the bed receives morning sun and partial shade. Place geraniums and other flowering, sun-loving plants in the sunniest location. Ferns, foliage plants, and other shade lovers go in the shade.

What house plants suffer from being sunk in a garden bed in the summer? African-violets and other gesneriads, calla-lily, most begonias, and other delicate-leaved plants cannot endure beating rains and winds. Place these on a sheltered terrace or at an open window.

Will house plants take care of themselves if sunk in garden beds in the summer? Rarely, and only if there is adequate rainfall. In a drought, they must be watered slowly and deeply by letting the hose run into the ground around them with the nozzle removed. Keep weeds down and cultivate the soil occasionally.

AUTUMN CARE

When should house plants be brought indoors in autumn? At least 2 to 3 weeks before you plan to turn on the heat, and of course before frost. This permits plants to acclimate gradually to the more difficult winter environment of the house. A few kinds of cold-hardy plants should not be rushed indoors. They include Thanksgiving and Christmas cacti, citrus plants, and azaleas.

How shall I prepare my house plants for the autumn move to the house? Two weeks before they come in, loosen the pots in the ground. Prune back long, unsightly branches. If the plants tend to wither, prune more severely. At the end of a week, lift the pots and place the plants on a sheltered patio or against a retaining wall where they will have outdoor light and air. At the end of a 2-week period from first loosening the pots in the ground, scrub the pots, spray for pests, and remove them to the house.

Do house plants need special care when they first come indoors in autumn?   Yes, the leaves of glossy-foliaged plants should be frequently syringed. Water moderately. Ventilation should be good. Pests are apt to appear now. Keep a close watch and have an aerosol spray handy.

Is it possible to leave coleus, geraniums, and begonias in the ground during the winter (covering them for protection) or should they be taken into the house? (New Jersey.)   They positively will die however well you protect them. Take cuttings of those you want. There is only one begonia that is hardy with protection, the tuberous *Begonia grandis*.

What shall I do with fuchsias, lantanas, and other summer bloomers when they come indoors in the fall?   Place in a cool cellar window or a cold (but never freezing) sun or plant room. Water very sparingly until new growth appears in late winter. Then cut them back and give them light and more water.

What shall I do for house plants that turn brown when brought in the house during the winter? I am losing all of my plants.   Grow them cooler. Do not overwater. See that they get fresh air. Cut back withered portions. Check your humidity.

VACATION CARE

How can I safely leave my plants when I go away in the winter for two to three weeks?   One way is to get a "plant sitter" who knows plants and will follow your written instructions for their care. Or leave them untended and turn down the thermostat to 60° F. Water the plants (to the moist, not soggy, stage), remove buds, open flowers, and any old leaves. Place each plant in a light, not sunny, place. Cover with a plastic bag held by a long enough stake to keep the plastic from

There are various means available to ensure house-plant survival while the gardener is on vacation. One of the most simple, good for 2 to 3 weeks, is encasing the plant's pot in a plastic bag that is closed around the stem. Some gardeners prefer to enclose the pot and the entire plant in a plastic bag.

touching the foliage. Cut a small hole in each bag to allow for more ventilation.

When I go away in the summer, how can I leave my plants untended? I have a great many. Two New Jersey indoor gardeners give these directions for a two-week summer absence. One gardener says, "Take one, or more, large cartons. Put on cellar floor. Fill with sphagnum moss. Wet down until thoroughly soaked. Allow plants to go without watering until leaves are limp enough to pack pots closely. Remove blossoms, water well from the top, and pack. Be sure to leave a window slightly open. The plants will do all right without much light in the cellar for a couple of weeks, but they *must* have fresh air." The other gardener tells how she sets her plants on a well-soaked 2-inch layer of builder's sand in a big washtub in which she rigs up a wick system. A canvas ironing board cover serves as a wick. One end is pushed well down in the sand under the plants; the other rests in a big pail of water placed beside the tub. This system works for a week or more, depending on the rate of evaporation.

EXPOSURE

What flowers and vines are suitable for a mostly sunny (full west exposure) window? Most flowering plants including amaryllis, geranium, abutilon, shrimp-plant, miniature roses, kalanchoe, oxalis, cacti and other succulents, forced spring bulbs, chrysanthemums, veltheimia, citrus plants, herbs, azaleas, most begonias, and many orchids, such as miniature cymbidiums. *Vines:* tradescantia, Kenilworth-ivy, *Campanula isophylla,* nasturtium, and morning glories.

Which house plants will grow in a window in the winter? It has all of the morning sun. Flowering plants that will keep blooming if the temperature is not high (55° F. at night) are primroses, bouvardia, begonia, impatiens, and all kinds of bulbs which potted in the fall will keep up a succession, including paper-white and other narcissus (daffodils), amaryllis, veltheimia, and the other plants listed above.

What house plants will blossom with only 2 or 3 hours of sunshine during the winter months? The small-flowered begonias are dependable; also, various bulbs potted in the fall will help out. African-violets and bromeliads will sometimes bloom without direct sunshine. Four to six hours of sun will give more and better-colored flowers.

What house plants would you suggest for east windows partially shaded most of the time, and in a steam-heated room which is consistently overheated? Why expect the impossible? Plants will not tolerate extreme heat unless they are tropical subjects that require high humidity, which almost never prevails in overheated rooms. About the only things we can suggest are sansevieria (snake plant) and the kangaroovine (*Cissus antarctica*). Both can stand dryness and warmth to an unusual degree.

What house plants are suitable for rooms having little sunshine? Much depends upon the temperature maintained. Dry, hot rooms will kill anything, but if the temperature is moderate and you maintain a fair amount of humidity, you can grow small palms, ferns, ivies, philodendrons, many large-leaved begonias, bromeliads, and tropical-foliage plants.

What plants can be grown in a sun porch without southern exposure? Almost anything you fancy if there is sufficient heat during winter to keep the night temperature around 45° F. Both blooming and foliage plants from the florists will get along in such a porch.

What flowers and vines are suitable for a shaded window? Begonias, lobelia, English ivy, German-ivy, variegated panicum, strawberry-geranium, trailing fuchsia, creeping fig, grape-ivy, Kenilworth-ivy, ceropegia, chlorophytum, palms, Chinese-evergreen, dracaena, dieffenbachia, nephthytis, rubber plants, and ferns. Keep the night temperature down to 55° F. if possible.

What flowering house plants can be grown successfully without a great amount of sunshine? Other than wax begonias and bromeliads, you won't find many that will bloom in poor light. The room temperature counts for a lot, and if about 65° F. in the day and about 50° F. at night, you can expect all kinds of ferns, palms, and ivies to get along well. Better install fluorescent tubes if your plants receive less than 4 hours of sunshine daily.

Can I keep house plants in a west window? Yes, plants that do not need full sunlight, such as African-violets, large-leaved begonias, foliage plants, ivies, etc.

What plants other than Chinese-evergreen and nephthytis will grow in water in a northern exposure? Philodendron, tradescantia, English ivy, grape-ivy, redwood burls, and umbrella-plant (*Cyperus alternifolius*).

What can I grow in a north window? All kinds of ferns, ivies, philodendron, and other foliage plants; African-violets; large-leaved begonias; pick-a-back plant; bromeliads; strawberry-begonia.

ENVIRONMENT

What are the conditions under which my house plants will flourish in the winter? See the introduction to this section.

The atmosphere in my house in the winter is very dry and I have difficulty getting house plants to live. Place humidifiers on your radiators or stand your house plants on pebbles in water-filled trays to increase humidity. See that they get fresh air daily, without direct drafts.

Does coal gas injure house plants? Yes, it is deadly, even in very small amounts.

Does cooking gas affect house plants? Manufactured gas is harmful only if there is a leak. Natural gas does no harm.

How does a plant room differ from a greenhouse? A plant room, usually opening off a living room, dining room, or hall, makes it possible to enjoy and care for plants easily, as part of the room is used for everyday living. If there is sun, and humidity is maintained with pebble-filled trays of water, most plants do almost as well as in a greenhouse; tending them is a more incidental and personal procedure. Also, the plant room can be a very decorative addition to your house. Usually light comes only from windows and doors, not through the roof. A greenhouse of glass or plastic offers a more businesslike, less decorative way of raising plants with greater control of heat and humidity.

What is a lath house? This is a structure made of laths or slats that admits a good circulation of air but only about half the usual amount of light. Slats are usually set about an inch apart.

Is it possible in Connecticut to grow plants in a lath house like those you see in California? It can serve in the summer as protection for tender foliage from strong sun but it is not for year-round use in cold areas, as it is for tropical and subtropical regions. There, the lath house is much used for growing orchids and ferns.

Is the cold from windows injurious to plants? Definitely so, if the plants are tender kinds; take them out of the window at night or place thick paper between the glass and plants. Cold drafts are very bad. Various kinds of plastic sheeting are useful to put between the plants and the glass in freezing weather.

What house plants can be easily kept in a hot, dry room with only a small amount of diffused sunlight? No plant can thrive in a hot, dry room, but some of the cacti and other succulents can put up with a lot if kept mostly dry during the winter.

Do plants grow under incandescent light? Yes, incandescent light can be used as a substitute for sunlight, although plants do better under natural conditions or under fluorescent light. Incandescent light is very hot and can harm plants too close to it.

How do you grow house plants under artificial light? Install fluorescent light fixtures over the bench or table on which the plants are to be grown. The tubes should be 8 to 10 inches above the tops of growing

Many house plants thrive under fluorescent lights, such as this tabletop model, which contains 2 tubes.

plants and long enough to illuminate the entire growing area. Leave the lights on 12 to 14 hours a day for optimum results. Use daylight or white fluorescent tubes, or a combination of the two. Plants require more water and food than under natural conditions. Keep cacti and other succulents very close to the tubes. Orchids will do best with fixtures that hold at least 4 lamps, but they will also thrive with a mixture of sun and fluorescent light. Using lamps over a greenhouse bench and under the bench is an excellent way to supplement sunlight for a too shady greenhouse. You may want to experiment with the special lamps developed for plant growth.

What house plants grow best under artificial light?   African-violets and all their relatives seem particularly happy under these conditions, also many other flowering plants. Among orchids, *Paphiopedilum* and *Miltonia* are some of the orchids that thrive under fluorescents. Planters and carts are available commercially with built-in light fixtures above them, but more reasonable are the general-purpose "shop" lights. For more information, write the Indoor Light Gardening Society of America, 128 West 58th Street, New York, N.Y. 10019.

Why do my house plants have luxuriant foliage but the buds dry up and fall off before opening?   This may be due to high temperatures and low humidity and irregular or too heavy watering. (See Watering, Temperature, and Sanitation.)

What causes the lower leaves on a small palm plant to turn brown and then die? What is the remedy?   Unsuitable soil. Dryness at the root. Dry atmosphere.

How can I prevent plants, grown indoors from seeds or cuttings, from growing spindly?   This is caused by too much warmth and not enough light and humidity. Direct sunshine is needed by most seedlings. Pinch out the tops to make the plants branch. Or grow them under fluorescent lights, about 4 inches from the tubes.

INSECTS AND DISEASES

How can I prevent pests from getting a start on my house plants? Spray all house plants before bringing them inside in the fall. If any specimens from the garden or purchased from a florist are infested with pests of any sort, segregate them and get them entirely clean before letting them join your healthy plants. Make it a habit to look all plants over weekly for possible pests. Sponging with soap and water at intervals checks such pests as scale, mealybugs, and red spider. Keep all dead leaves picked off. Use a pressure-bottle all-purpose house-plant spray as soon as pests are discovered and keep infested plants segregated until clean. Frequent "fogging" or spraying is a good preventative.

What shall I use to get rid of aphids on house plants? Give a strong water spray at the sink for a mild infestation; for a heavy attack, spray with a weak malathion solution or dip the top of the inverted plant in it. A granular insecticide, such as 2 per cent Di-Syston Dexol Systemic House Plant Insecticide, added to the soil according to directions, will control aphids without your having to spray.

What is the best method to clean mealybugs off plants? Place the plants in a bathtub and wash off the bugs by directing a spray of water at them forcibly. Go over hairy-leaved subjects like African-violets with an alcohol-dipped swab.

Kill mealybugs by dabbing them with a cotton swab dipped in alcohol.

How can I get rid of red spider mites on my house plants? Forcibly syringe with clear, cold water, particularly the underside of the foliage.

For heavy infestation, spray with a miticide such as Kelthane or discard the plant.

An occasional cleansing of the foliage with a stream from the hose on plants summering outdoors is recommended. This is especially important just before the plants are brought indoors for the winter.

What is the scalelike pest which adheres closely to the leaves and stems of ivy, and which seems to attract ants? What will kill this pest?   It is probably brown scale. Hand-pick a light infestation; for a heavy attack, spray with a weak malathion solution or dip inverted tops of the plant in a basin filled with the solution.

What can be done about white jumping insects in the soil of house plants?   These are probably springtails, which usually breed in the organic matter in the soil. Try standing the pots in a vessel of water kept at 110° F. for a few minutes. This temperature is fatal to many insects, and most plants are unaffected by it even when completely immersed. The springtails, however, are harmless.

How can one kill whiteflies? Do these flies hatch in the earth or on the leaves of plants?   They are difficult to control on house plants. Repeated sprayings with resmethrin, found in formulas such as Dexol Whitefly Spray and Pratt's Whitefly Spray, have proved to be very efficient. The eggs are small translucent bodies laid on the undersides of the leaves.

SANITATION

How often should house plants be syringed or washed under a spigot?   Glossy-leaved plants profit from a monthly syringing or sponging. Fuzzy-leaved plants should be dusted with a camel's-hair brush or very lightly with warm water.

In washing the leaves of house plants, should soap be added to the water?   Many green-fingered gardeners do use soapy water in sponging off the foliage of glossy-leaved foliage plants. Plain water is just as good if all dust is removed, unless the plant is infested with red spider, scale, or other pests, when soapy water helps to destroy them.

What causes the white and brownish moldlike substance on the out-side of clay flower pots? The white film is the lime or alkali in the clay. Wipe the pots occasionally; scrub with a wire brush dipped in hot soapy water.

Why does the soil of house plants get moldy? It is not mold, but algae, the spores of which are in the air and perhaps in the water. Loosen the surface of the soil occasionally with a fork. Wipe off the pots occasionally.

Why does the soil in my house-plant pots smell sour and musty, and sometimes have a green, mosslike coating on the top? See the intro-duction to this section on Potting Soils. Bits of charcoal mixed through the soil will help keep it "sweet." Do not overwater; try to admit fresh air daily, without direct drafts. Check the drainage in the pot.

PROPAGATION

How should I take cuttings from house plants and make them grow? Take shoots or tops of the plants, 4 to 6 inches long with firm, but not hard, stem growth. Fill a pot with sandy soil, vermiculite, or other rooting medium, dip the lower ends in a hormone rooting powder, and insert the cuttings around the edge. Make the holes with a stick and press the soil around the cutting firmly. Sink about 1 inch. Shade from the sun and keep only just moist. When growth starts, pot singly. (See also Section 3, Propagation.)

Is there any way of dividing very large house plants so they will not take up so much room in the house? It is usually better to root cut-tings, discarding the unwieldy parent plants. Geraniums and many others can be pruned back very severely. Large tropical foliage plants such as dieffenbachia, monstera, and rubber plant can be air-layered.

What can I feed house plants that will encourage blooms? I have a fairly cool room and southern exposure. My geraniums and fuchsias re-fuse to bloom during the dreary winter months. I have taken my rose-mary indoors, but it will not grow in spite of all my efforts. If your ge-raniums and fuchsias have been in bloom outdoors in summer, they are now resting. Start cuttings in the summer for late-winter bloom. Rose-mary can also be readily rooted by cuttings and the young plants will grow more thriftily than the old, sometimes even coming into bloom. Use low-nitrogen fertilizer to encourage bloom. Are they receiving sufficient light?

Which blooming house plants can be started in March? If you have ample light, a temperature not above 68° F., and understand the rudiments of plant raising, you can have success with begonias, African-violets, gloxinias, and other gesneriads. For lower temperatures, cinerarias, primroses, and calceolarias can be grown for temporary color effects.

What is the procedure for starting house plants from seeds, rather than from the usual cuttings? Use milled sphagnum moss. Sow each kind thinly in a pot, making moss fairly firm and level beforehand. Use hot water to moisten the moss. After sowing, cover with glass held several inches above the seed or put the pot inside a clear plastic bag. Give shade and a temperature of 60° to 70° F. Always water from the bottom. Transplant into other pots or window boxes when true leaves show. (Seeds can also be sown in prepackaged soilless mixes and the seedlings can be transplanted into the same mixes. Using these mixes, which are sterile, eliminates disease problems.) The best time for sowing such seeds is between January and March; but some, like primroses, can be sown in June, and cinerarias and calceolarias can be sown in August or September. Miniature plastic greenhouses and casserole dishes with covers that can be lifted for ventilating can be used instead of pots. Seedlings will thrive under fluorescent lights.

What is "damping off" and how can it be prevented? This is a fungus disease prevented by using soilless mixes or by sterilizing the soil or treating the seed with a disinfectant such as benomyl.

How can one start bougainvillea cuttings in the house? Take short side growths or tips 6 inches long. Insert in sandy soil in a small pot or insert several around the edge of the pot. After watering, stand them in a big pot and cover with a plastic bag, giving them a warm place. Don't overwater but never allow to dry.

How can one take cuttings from a rubber tree? *Ficus elastica* can best be propagated by air layering. Make a slanting cut halfway through the stem with a sharp knife, insert a toothpick to keep it open, bind around with a ball of damp sphagnum moss, then wrap tightly with a sheet of plastic film, fastening near each end with wire fasteners. While rooting, stake the branch to avoid breakage. When the moss is filled with roots (3 months or more), cut it from the parent plant and pot the cutting in soil.

Can I start seeds under fluorescent lights? Yes, lights make it possible to get good plants in short order for outdoor planting. Sow seeds on milled sphagnum moss or packaged seed-sowing mixes mentioned above, all of which are available at garden centers or from mail-order seed houses. Set the trays close to the lights, about 3 to 4 inches. If you can't regulate distances by moving the light canopy up and down, then set the tray on inverted flowerpots, big ones at first, then smaller ones as the seedlings grow and have to be placed farther from the lights, about 6 to 8 inches. Give no fertilizer until the seedlings are well advanced, then quarter-strength fertilizer once a week will be about right.

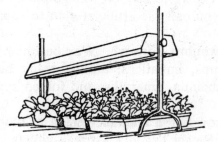

Wax begonias, impatiens, African-violets, and other gesneriads can be started from seed under fluorescent lights.

How can I propagate pick-a-back plant? The small plants on the leaves will quickly root if the leaf is taken off the plant and pegged on the surface of the soil in a pot. This is about the easiest of plants to propagate.

Decorating with House Plants

How can I make a window garden? Have a 12- to 15-inch shelf built to fit a sunny bay, deep-silled window, or in front of one or more windows. Support the shelf with brackets. Buy plastic plant trays in sizes to fit your shelf, available by mail order or from local hardware or garden centers. Trays are green or gray, in 4 × 8-inch to 11 × 22-inch sizes. Fill the trays with pebbles and set the plants on them. Keep the trays filled with water to humidify the atmosphere around the plants, but don't push the pots down into the pebbles where the roots would be kept constantly wet.

What sort of indoor window box do you recommend? A box with a waterproof metal lining will work, but plastic window boxes are less expensive. Some plastic window boxes are made very narrow to fit on small windowsills and other models have clip-on drainage trays. You can plant directly in drained window boxes. Undrained boxes can be used to hold individually potted plants. The pots can be hidden under sheet moss or set on wet gravel or coarse perlite inside the window box. Or the box can be filled with peat moss, into which the pots can be sunk.

Which flowers can be grown in the house throughout the year? I have a planter about 8 × 4 feet; the earth is about 3 feet deep with drainage. A box of this size needs to be in a glassed porch or greenhouse. If your room isn't especially well provided with windows, don't expect all plants to be a success, unless you expect to rely on foliage plants that get along on less light. Of course, you can use artificial light to supplement natural light.

What are sure-to-bloom winter window flowers? Wax begonia, jasmine, many orchids, crown-of-thorns, impatiens, azalea, many bulbs such as paper-white narcissus, veltheimia, amaryllis, and forced spring bulbs.

What are ten good plants for providing a long succession of blooms during the winter? Wax begonia, Rieger begonia, African-violets, and shrimp-plant give constant bloom; paper-white narcissus and hyacinths can be started for succession and are very fragrant; scented geraniums, veltheimia, amaryllis, and jasmines strengthen the picture. Also, you can pick up azaleas and chrysanthemums in flower at your local florist's. Laelia, miniature cymbidiums, and slipper (*Paphiopedilum*) orchids have very long-lasting flowers.

What blooming flowers may I put in my fernery to keep in the house during the winter? I have it in front of south windows, but I have venetian blinds which I keep tilted just a trifle—the sun is not there all day because of the next house. Better give up the idea of much flowering in a fernery that gets no sun, but you might try the African-violet, impatiens, or some of the winter-blooming begonias.

What flowers and other plants can be grown in a window box in the heart of the city? Begonias, geraniums, lobelias, chlorophytum, English ivy, sansevieria, German-ivy, and Kenilworth-ivy. Some dwarf orchids, such as *Epidendrum* and *Oncidium,* will thrive if the light is bright.

What house plants will survive in a city apartment with little or no sunshine? Snake-plant, aspidistra, Chinese-evergreen, English ivy, pothos, tradescantia, bromeliads, palms, fatsia, dieffenbachia, grape-ivy, dracaena, rubber plant (*Ficus elastica* and *F. lyrata*), pandanus, monstera, and peperomia.

What house plants require a great deal of moisture? Calla-lily, Chinese-evergreen, ferns, hydrangea, primula, cineraria, cyclamen, Jerusalem-cherry, baby's-tears.

Which house plants do well if kept on the dry side at the roots? Aloe, bromeliads, agave, crassula, sedum, sansevieria, and other succulents including most cacti (except the orchid cactus).

Modern interiors require the presence of large foliage plants, such as this Dracaena marginata, *which is treelike in its growth habit.*

How can I supply needed humidity in the room where I keep my house plants? By fitting humidifiers to the radiators or to the heater; by placing shallow trays or wide saucers filled with pebbles or sand (which must be kept moist) beneath the pots; by spraying the plants more than once a day with a fine atomizer.

Is there any way of safely leaving house plants during a vacation of a week to 10 days without care? Would it be harmful to leave them standing in saucers of water so that they do not dry out? Standing house plants in water is rarely a good idea. An alternative is to water the plants well and then stand the pots in a box packed around with wet paper or peat moss. Set in a cool, not sunny, place and cover with plastic supported by stakes to hold it above the foliage. (See Vacation Care.)

What are the names of some house plants that are easy to raise? Wax and other begonias, most ferns, English ivy, grape-ivy, Swedish-ivy, philodendrons, jasmines, carissa (Natal-plum), sweet-olive, and spider-plant respond well to regular care.

Which low-growing plants would be suitable for house use in small containers without drainage holes? (Michigan.) Containers without drainage or a vent at the bottom will soon sour the soil. If not carefully watered, air is driven from the soil and no plants can stand that. With care you may, for a time, keep ivies, African-violet, cacti, and succulent plants in variety in good shape. Succulents and most cacti need very little water until spring. Mix finely broken bits of charcoal in your potting soil and place a layer of pebbles in the bottom of each container.

What dwarf plants are best suited for growing in small containers to keep on glass window shelves? (Maine.) Small-leaved ivies, Kenilworth-ivy, wax begonias, various ferns, small crotons and other tropical foliage plants, cacti, and succulents in variety; African-violet, Hoya lacunosa, miniature orchids, and many others according to fancy, room conditions, light, etc.

How shall I place house plants in a window garden with a southern exposure? Put the flowering plants that need full sun close to the glass. On the edge of the shelf, facing the room, use small-leaved ivies or ferns that do not need sun. Against the walls on each side can go foliage plants with colored leaves to give a variety of color. When the forced bulbs are ready for bloom, these can be placed just behind the ivy, away from the full heat of the sun. Such flowers as amaryllis, primula, and fuchsia can also occupy this less sunny space when they are in bloom.

The only place I have for a window garden gets little sun. Is there any special way to arrange the plants? If plants are used that do not need sun, like the ferns (but which nevertheless require light to perform well), these can be placed next to the glass to give the best effect. Use foliage plants with variegated and colored leaves, like the spider-plant, purple velvet-plant, coleus, and fittonia.

Miniature Gardens

TERRARIUMS

What type of soil should I use in planting a terrarium? Use a packaged terrarium mix or make your own with a third good garden soil, a third humus, and a third sand or perlite with bits of charcoal added to keep the soil "sweet."

How can one make a terrarium? Use any large glass container, like an aquarium; cover the top with a sheet of glass. (A glass or hardware store will cut it for you.) Other possibilities are candy and pickle jars, clear glass wine jugs, covered glass casseroles, Victorian domes, and bubble bowls. Spread a layer of coarse gravel or small stones over the bottom. Add ½ inch of granulated charcoal, then the soil mixture above or whatever mixture is appropriate for the kind of plants you plan to grow.

How should the interior of a terrarium be arranged? After the drainage layer and soil have been placed in the bowl, a grade may be

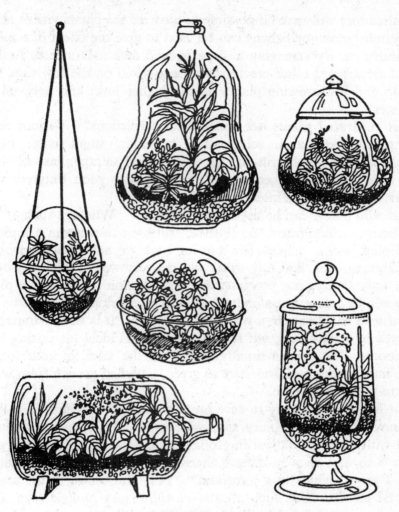

BOTTLE GARDENS AND TERRARIUMS

*To the traditional fish bowls and discarded aquariums, long
used for terrariums, can be added new or used bottles, ginger jars, and the imaginative hanging "egg" container shown
above. Terrariums can be satisfying and successful if a few
rules are followed: Don't overwater—once watered, it is unlikely that additional moisture will be required for months
unless the container is kept open. Don't keep the container
in direct sunshine for more than a few hours. Don't use containers of colored glass or plastic that will shut out light.
Choose the correct plants that will thrive in a humid atmosphere. Good ones are small terrestrial orchids, ferns, fittonia,
baby's-tears, and Sinningia pusilla and varieties.*

established that will make it possible to have all the plants visible at one time. Stones, moss, or lichens can be used to give the effect of a miniature landscape. By arranging a slope instead of a flat surface, seedling trees of shrubs and other erect growers can go in on the low side, with creeping and low-growing plants on the higher level and between the taller ones.

What cultivated plants are suitable for terrariums? Various ferns, small palms, pellionias, selaginellas, begonias, small ivies, pileas, fittonia, maranta, small crotons, peperomia, and saintpaulias—whatever plants appreciate humid conditions. Some plants soon outgrow their quarters, so replanting at intervals is necessary.

What wild plants can be used in a terrarium? Wildings such as partridge-berry, wintergreen, pipsissewa, rattlesnake-plantain, hepatica, ground-pine, moss, lichens (on bits of bark or half-decayed wood), seedling evergreens, and tiny wild ferns do very well in a glass garden. Collect only species not protected by conservation laws or save plants endangered by construction on land soon to be developed.

What seed can I sow in a woodsy terrarium? It is not customary to sow seeds in a terrarium, but such a container is ideal for raising ferns from spores. The spores usually found on the back of fern fronds, shaken into a terrarium, will start as green, flattened growth from which tiny ferns will duly emerge.

What is the proper way to care for a terrarium? Keep it in a light, not sunny place. Water very sparingly, especially if the container is topped with glass. Don't wet the foliage when watering. Wipe the glass top dry each day, also the sides if there is a great deal of condensation.

Can I grow orchids in a terrarium? Yes. Those best suited are the terrestrial jewel orchids such as *Anoectochilus* and *Ludisia* (syn. *Haemaria*). Some dwarf lady's-slipper (*Paphiopedilum*) species and their primary hybrids thrive in large terrariums under fluorescent lights. Miniature epiphytic orchids such as *Ornithocephalus* and *Pleurothallis* will also do well in larger terrariums under fluorescent lights.

What flowering plants thrive in a terrarium? Miniature African-violets grow well, also related gesneriads such as the tiny gloxinia species *Sinningia pusilla* and the almost white *S.* 'Wood Nymph' and lavender *S.* 'Bright Eyes'. 'Cupid's Doll', 'Dollbaby', and 'Cindy' are a pretty trio of small gloxinias, all treated about the same as African-violets, with the terrarium top left open a little all the time and completely removed for an hour or so each day to ensure adequate circulation of air.

TRAY AND DISH GARDENS

What plants are suitable for dish or tray gardens? Cacti and other succulents such as small specimens of crassulas, gasterias, echeverias, kalanchoes, and sedums. *Saxifraga stolonifera,* cryptanthus, ferns, myrtle, seedling evergreens, pileas, small *Begonia semperflorens,* peperomias. Go to a garden center and select any very small potted plants that will fit in your dish or tray. Or try small plants from your own garden or window garden.

How is a dish or tray garden arranged? A shallow dish or tray is lined with coarse gravel or small pebbles, over which is placed a thin layer of light garden loam, sandy for cacti and other succulents, mixed with peat moss or leafmold for woodland plants. The plants are set in to simulate a miniature landscape and earth is packed firmly about their roots. Moss can be used to cover the bare soil of the surface.

How should a tray or dish garden be watered? When the garden is made, enough water should be given to moisten thoroughly the roots of the newly set plants, but not enough to leave them soggy and waterlogged. After first watering, give water sparingly when the soil feels dry to the touch. Pour water directly to the roots with a small pitcher or long-spouted watering can.

How can I keep the soil "sweet" in my dish garden? Mix small pieces of charcoal through the soil mixture that you are using.

How long will plants survive in a dish garden? That depends on the plants used and the care given. Cacti or other succulents often live for months or even for years if planted in sandy loam and watered sparingly. Foliage plants do not last quite as long, but if given proper care they will remain fresh and green for weeks or longer.

What is bonsai? This is the Japanese art of dwarfing plants by restricting roots and pruning tops so that even a century-old plant may thrive in a pot or on a tray.

Is a miniature garden the same as a dish garden? Not exactly. The dish garden, more often than not, is a collection of small plants in a "dish" that have not been given any studied arrangement or consideration as to their appropriateness with each other. A miniature garden is more likely to be what its name implies—with the creator of the garden trying to reproduce a landscape in miniature—whether house plant or hardy plant material is used.

What is saikei? Saikei is another garden art from Japan, the creation of miniature landscapes in shallow ceramic pots or clay trays. It is akin to bonsai but the emphasis is on reproducing a part of a landscape —trees, mountains, or islands (suggested by rock), sand and moss (to serve as water and grass), etc. Usually hardy dwarf evergreens or trees are used, but variations of saikei can be made by the house-plant enthusiast with tender material. (See *Saikei: Living Landscapes in Miniature*, by Toshio Kawamoto, and other books on Japanese tray gardening.)

I have been given a potted juniper which has been trained as bonsai. What should I do with the plant in the winter? Do you have a plant room, enclosed breezeway, sun porch, or the like that remains protected and above freezing but very cool in the winter? If so, this would be a good place to keep your bonsai, which should receive some sun and ample light during the day and water as it dries out. A second choice would be a cool window ledge where the temperature remains several degrees cooler than in the rest of the house. A third choice is to winter the plant outdoors, in a cold frame, or in the open ground where the container must be protected by soil and a mulch. Or the plant can be carefully removed from the pot and planted. It can be repotted in the spring. Hardy plants grown in bonsai style just do not thrive indoors in the winter in warm dry rooms.

What plants make good bonsai subjects? A great many, especially dwarf evergreens and shrubs. Fake bonsai subjects can be achieved by selecting certain house plants that resemble trees and potting them in special bonsai containers. A common house plant used this way is the jade plant (crassula), but many others are suitable. They, of course, are much easier to take care of in heated rooms than hardy trees and shrubs that need to rest during the winter. There are many books on bonsai that explain the technique and also suggest ways to adapt it to house plants and indoor gardening.

THE KITCHEN-WINDOW HERB GARDEN

What herbs can I grow in my sunny kitchen window? *Annuals:* parsley, sweet marjoram, basil, anise, coriander. *Perennials:* mint, chives, thyme, sage, lemon balm, tarragon. *Tender perennial shrubs:* scented geraniums, lemon-verbena, rosemary, French lavender.

What kitchen-window herbs can be grown from seed? Sweet marjoram, parsley, basil, anise, coriander. Sow seeds in late summer or fall for winter use.

What kitchen-window herbs do better if purchased as plants? Rosemary, lemon-verbena (tender shrubs), tarragon, mint, chives, thyme, sage, and lemon balm are perennials and give quicker results when purchased as plants.

Where can I purchase herb plants and seed for growing indoors in the winter?   Most leading seed houses now carry lists of herbs. Some firms offer herb-growing kits with seed, soil, pots, and instruction book.

What kind of soil is necessary for herbs grown indoors?   Three parts of good garden soil and two parts of sand or perlite make a good mixture with a teaspoon of lime added to a 5-inch potful. Or use one of the soilless mixes.

Can chives be grown indoors in the winter? If so, how?   Yes, chives do well for a while in a kitchen herb garden. Bring in a clump of bulbs from the garden, setting it in a bulb pan of light, "sweet" soil. Cut back the foliage and let new growth start. Grow in a sunny window or under lights at a low temperature, preferably 55° F. Keep on the dry side.

Can I grow scented geraniums in a kitchen herb garden?   Yes. (See Geranium.)

Do you think one should bring in lemon-verbena during the winter? I did, potted it, and kept it in my basement near a window and watered it once a week. Am I doing the correct thing? (Michigan.)   Being a native of Argentina and Chile, the lemon-verbena would not winter over out-of-doors in Michigan. You are doing the right thing with it, if it stays alive all winter in the basement. It can be cut back when brought in from the garden and grown through the cold weather in a sunny window. It can stand a higher temperature than that preferred by most herbs.

Can I leave my rosemary plant outdoors the year round? I have seen plants as big as shrubs in gardens on Cape Cod but my friends tell me to bring it indoors here in the vicinity of New York City.   Rosemary is unreliably hardy in the North but where humidity is high and temperatures not too frigid, as along the seacoast, it survives outdoors surprisingly far north. However, you were well advised to take it in. When pruning it back in the fall, preparatory to bringing it indoors, root some of the cuttings in moist sand or vermiculite. They are easy to propagate.

How can parsley plants be grown in a house during the cold months?   Cut back, lift, and pot strong plants in the fall and give them a well-lighted window with a temperature never above 55° F. Don't overwater and don't fertilize.

Why does house-grown parsley become very pale, with long, weak stems? I give fertilizer every 2 or 3 weeks.   It probably lacks sun and is grown too warm. Parsley grown indoors is almost always weaker and less thrifty than that grown in the garden. It wants plenty of sun, a temperature of not more than 55° F., and enough but not too much water (keep it rather on the dry side). Try growing it under fluorescents.

Should parsley and chives be kept very moist when growing in a kitchen window? No. Be careful with watering; with a little practice, you can tell by the weight of the container or the feel of the soil if it needs water or not.

Does it injure tarragon, rosemary, and marjoram to pot them every winter for use indoors? It does not injure them if they get the proper care and the plants are not too large. They should be set into the garden again in the spring to recuperate. Eventually they will get too big to pot up. Cuttings should be propagated to produce young plants, leaving the parents in the herb garden out-of-doors. If the young plants are left in their pots and placed in the garden through the summer, they will sustain less shock when brought indoors in autumn.

What is the truth about growing herbs indoors? The truth is that few herbs do well indoors unless they have the conditions which they prefer; namely, no soaring day heat—70° F. is acceptable but 60° is better. They need a night temperature of about 55° F.; plenty of light and sunshine (grow under fluorescent tubes if natural light is inadequate); sufficient humidity, as from pebble trays; good air circulation; and regular care with adequate water (no drying out of the soil but no sogginess, either). These conditions are hard to provide in the average heated home. A plant room, cool window, or lean-to greenhouse offer good possibilities.

Specific Flowering House Plants

ABUTILON (FLOWERING-MAPLE)

Does abutilon make a good house plant? Abutilon used to be a favorite house plant and was also a good garden subject, growing tall and bushy and blooming freely in sunny, open beds. It deserves a comeback. It will thrive in a cool window but needs several hours of sun to flower abundantly. The foliage and bell-shaped flowers are most attractive. Cuttings root readily. If an old plant is brought indoors in fall, cut it back severely to prevent wilting and to encourage new growth. It rapidly becomes pot-bound and therefore needs a lot of water. It is subject to whitefly. Repot in a standard potting mixture. (See Soil, this section.)

I have a small plant with leaves almost exactly like a maple. After I set it outdoors in July, it thrived, producing orange-colored flowers like "Japanese lanterns" on long, fine, drooping stems. What is it? What winter protection does it need? (Pennsylvania.) The plant is abutilon or flowering-maple. It is not hardy and must be grown as a pot plant indoors in your part of the country. If possible, grow cool, at 50° to 60° F., and it will flower freely in the winter. Root cuttings to make new plants. It grows quite large.

How can abutilon or flowering-maple be raised from seed as a house plant? Sow the seed in a pot in February or March in sandy soil, barely covering the seed. Place a sheet of glass on the pot and keep in a warm room. Give some light when germination starts, but use care in watering, as the seedlings are tiny. Transplant into another pot, 1 inch apart when in rough leaf, and grow on like any other tender plant. Variegated *A. pictum* 'Thompsonii' is propagated by cuttings.

AFRICAN-VIOLET (SAINTPAULIA)

Please suggest the best soil mixture in which to grow African-violets. A light mixture easily penetrated by the fine roots is best, such as 1 part peat moss, 1 part perlite, and 1 part vermiculite. Add fertilizer according to the directions on the container. If there are no nematodes in the soil in your area and you have well-decayed compost, which is all humus, sift this through a half-inch screen and add sand or perlite until the texture feels light and open.

Packaged soil from hardware stores, garden centers, or by mail order are available. Some are fine right from the bag; other mixes may need lightening with sand or perlite (or added fertilizer). Here is one well-tried formula that contains fertilizer:

Mix 2 parts (by bulk) good garden loam, sterilized (see below)
    1 part vermiculite or sterilized sand
    1 part peat moss
Add 1 quart broken bits charcoal per bushel
    2 quarts commercial cow manure or rich compost per bushel
    1 quart fine bone meal or superphosphate per bushel

Is it necessary to pasteurize African-violet soil? If so, describe the method. Yes, it is usually advisable, since African-violets are susceptible to a number of soil-borne pests and diseases. Only loam, sand, and pots need be sterilized, as vermiculite and packaged peat moss are free from harmful organisms. In a roaster that has a cover, moisten the soil, etc., with hot water and bake at 180 degrees for 1 hour. (The odor produced is offensive to some people.) Let stand uncovered in a cool place for about 2 weeks. Stir occasionally.

What is the best temperature for African-violets?   The minimum night temperature in the winter should be 60° to 65° F. At 50° to 55° F., saintpaulias only struggle along. The day temperature can reach 75° F. or a little above, but 70° F. is preferred. Plants seem to adjust to cooler daytime temperatures as low as 65° F.

Will an African-violet thrive without sunshine?   Frequently these plants bloom even at north windows, but better results are obtained in the winter with plants grown in a sunny (4 or more hours of sun) exposure, with pots set back a little from the glass. Under fluorescent lights, African-violets bloom prolifically. (See the discussion of fluorescent lights under Light, Natural and Fluorescent, in the introduction.)

How should African-violets be watered?   Because of its thick crown and velvety leaves, moisture is avoided around the heart of the plant, and water is supplied from the saucer or around the edge of the pot. Pour excess water from the saucer after about half an hour, when the plant will have drawn up all it needs. Let the soil approach dryness but not really dry out between waterings: the soil should never be sopping wet or be dry for long.

Is cold water bad for African-violets?   Yes. Lukewarm water is essential.

My African-violet has white rings and spots on the leaves. Is this a disease or fertilizer deficiency?   Neither. It is the result of applying cold water to the soil or letting it fall on the leaves. Warm water sprayed on the leaves is not harmful.

Please tell me how to get African-violets to bloom. My plants remain green and healthy, but shortly after they leave the florist's they cease flowering. Shall I repot them?   The difference in humidity between a greenhouse and an ordinary living room is probably the reason for their not blooming. For best flowering, plants should be kept standing on moist pebbles, which afford a constant "aura" of humidity. Faded flowers must also be promptly snipped to prevent seed formation, which is always a deterrent to further bud development. Plenty of fresh air indirectly admitted in cold weather is likewise important. Repotting may be necessary but usually is not in the case of a newly purchased plant, so other factors in culture are first considered. Perhaps your plants are not receiving enough light! An African-violet plant food or one of the several reliable house-plant foods may be applied according to the directions on the package when buds begin to appear. *Do not* feed during the short periods when plants are resting and producing no new growth, usually during the summer in the North.

How often should I feed my African-violets? You can feed them very lightly at every watering except in prolonged periods of overcast weather or when the plants are taking a brief rest after heavy bloom.

Should African-violets be grown in small pots? Yes, the root system is small and plants do not thrive if overpotted and then overwatered. "Squatty" 2¼-inch plastic pots will do for quite large plants, and 3-inch pots are as large as you should get.

Does keeping an African-violet plant in a glazed flower pot prevent it from blooming? In such a pot, even if it has a drainage hole, the plant will not dry out as readily; but it does not do as well in glazed pots as in porous clay pots because air circulation in the soil is poorer. Wick-fed plastic pots are satisfactory.

What is the best location for African-violets in the summer? They are either set in a light north window in a well-ventilated room or else on a sheltered porch or patio except when heat and humidity are high; then they are better indoors, and air conditioning is not harmful. They should never be grown in a garden because hard rains and wind can injure the brittle leaves.

How are plants kept free of dust, if spraying is harmful to the hairy leaves? Dust is removed with a soft brush. A flat camel's-hair paintbrush is ideal. Leaves may be sprayed occasionally with a fine mist of room-temperature water. Until completely dry, plants must remain in complete shade, away from drafts, and out of direct sun. .

What makes the blossoms of an African-violet fall off while they are still fresh? It is natural for them to do so. They fertilize or pollinate readily, and after that happens they slide off.

Why do African-violets drop their blooms before they open? Probably the temperature or the humidity is too low. They prefer 70° F. by day, not less than 60° at night, and humidity around 60 per cent.

Will gas heat cause the buds to fall from African-violets? Leaking manufactured (not natural) gas, however slight, will make any plant drop its leaves or buds.

How can one keep the leaves of African-violets from drooping onto the edge of the pot and thereby rotting away where contact is made? This condition, due to deposits of fertilizer salts, occurs more often on clay than plastic pots, especially if the plants are overwatered or grown too cold. Cut the center from a small paper plate, slit one side, and fit like a collar under the foliage. This prevents contact and encourages the plant to grow up, not down. Because of this problem, most growers prefer plastic pots for African-violets.

What can I do to prevent my African-violets from developing long bare "necks"? Probably you can't prevent this. As the plant grows, old leaves are discarded. But you can conceal the stem by repotting the plant, cutting off or spreading out the lowest roots, and setting the plant low enough, often in the same pot, to cover the bare stem. If you can't fit it again in the pot, use a deeper one.

How can I keep my African-violets from growing lopsided? These plants grow so readily toward the light that giving a quarter turn once a week is necessary to keep the plants shapely. Plants grown under fluorescent lamps are the most uniform.

What causes a gnarly condition on African-violets? New leaves and blossoms have no stems; they just grow out from the base of the plant. Need of division might be the explanation, but more likely the invisible cyclamen mite is at work. Use an aerosol spray recommended for mites or apply a miticide like Kelthane. Discard badly infested plants.

How can I clean up mildew on the leaves and mold on the stems of African-violets? What causes these? These thick-leaved velvety plants are often a prey to mildew and mold without any apparent cause, although poor ventilation and insufficient sunlight seem to be contributing factors. Badly affected sections are sharply cut away and the leaves, both upper- and undersides, dusted with fine sulfur, or one of the dusts with sulfur as an active ingredient. The "mold" on stems may be mealybug.

How can mealybugs be cleaned up on African-violets? The end of a skewer or matchstick is wrapped with cotton and dipped in wood alcohol (or in a little cologne). This is applied to all affected sections of the plant. Repeat as needed.

I have 7 African-violets which had blossoms steadily for 3 years, but now are infested with a webby substance on the underside of the foliage. The leaves are spotted yellow. What causes this? This sounds like red spider, a minute insect forming colonies of red dots on the underside of the foliage where webs are formed for protection. Increase the humidity in the room. Forceful syringing with clear, lukewarm water to break the web and wash away the insects is somewhat effective, but you will probably also have to spray regularly with a miticide like Kelthane.

My African-violets have developed pale, limp leaves and the flowers collapse before they fully develop. What causes this? Probably nematodes. Remove the plant from the pot and examine its roots. If swellings are present and decayed areas visible, destroy the plant and pour boiling water through the potting soil before discarding it. Next time, pasteurize the soil.

Can African-violets be successfully divided? Readily. Indeed, as soon as the crown gets overthick, flowering usually wanes. Carefully pull apart and reset; each fair-sized repotted section usually begins to flower soon afterward. It is also easy to maintain your stock by rooting leaf cuttings. But you usually get more shapely plants if you prevent thick multiple crowns by removing with tweezers the little side growths that push out from the main stem, and grow only single-crown specimens.

Which is the better time to divide African-violets—in the spring or the fall? The spring is better. The divisions then grow on into good plants by the following winter.

What is the best method of propagating a large number of African-violets? The leaves may be sharply cut with 1½-inch stems from the base of the plant at any time (although commercial growers prefer October and November). These are inserted in small separate pots, which are placed in a large bulb pan of light soil or in a plastic bread or shoe box with a lid. Half sand and half peat moss or vermiculite seems to give the quickest results. Leaves are inserted the length of the stem. The soil is kept warm, in a light place, and moist while roots are forming. Keeping the pots or flats in a propagating case helps to maintain ideal, quick, humid rooting conditions; or the pots may all be set in a box containing a layer of sand always kept moist and covered with plastic. When roots are formed, new leaves will begin to appear at the base of the old ones. The cover is then removed and new "plants" are separated from the parent leaves and potted up separately in an African-violet

PROPAGATION OF AFRICAN-VIOLET (*Top*) *Leaf cutting inserted in pot of sandy compost.* (*Below*) *Potted young plant, with saucer for watering from beneath. Plant* (*right*), *repotted, has reached flowering size.*

potting mixture in 2-inch pots. Generally speaking, it takes 4½ to 5 months for young plants to be ready for separate potting. The first blossom by this method will show at 6 to 12 months.

How can African-violets be rooted in water? Mature leaves cut with plenty of petiole or leaf stem will root if placed in a glass with just enough water to cover the end of the stem but not up to the leaf. As soon as roots develop, the "plant" is moved to a small pot of sandy soil. It helps if foil is crimped over the glass and the leaves inserted through holes punched in the foil. This method is slower than inserting leaves in a rooting medium such as vermiculite or sand.

Where did the African-violet originate? *Saintpaulia ionantha* was first discovered in East Africa in 1893 by Baron Walter von Saint Paul. Forms of it introduced at that time were *purpurea,* dark purple; *grandiflora violacea,* large flowered; and *albescens,* white tinted pink. These forms seemingly were all lost, as up to the time 'Blue Boy' was originated in California the only saintpaulias available were forms of the species *S. ionantha,* usually grown from seed on a limited scale.

ANTHURIUM

What are the requirements of an anthurium plant to make it bloom? Anthuriums are tropical and demand high humidity and heat while in active growth but accept cooler conditions while in flower. The pot must be well drained and a mixture of sphagnum, peat moss, fibrous loam, and sand should be used. The crown must be above the soil, and as the base rises, it should be wrapped with moss. Most adaptable are selections of *A. scherzerianum,* such as brilliant red 'Flamenco'.

AZALEA   (See Gift Plants.)

BEGONIA

What is the best soil mixture for begonias? A loose, humus-rich mixture suits most begonias best. One part good loam, 2 parts leafmold, 1 part sand, ¼ part small lump charcoal, ¼ part dehydrated cow manure, plus bone meal at the rate of 1 pint to the bushel is satisfactory. Packaged potting soils like Jiffy Mix and Readi-Earth are also satisfactory, with a third part of sand or perlite added for drainage.

What type of soil and amount of moisture do fibrous-rooted begonias need; what room temperature and humidity? Should they be kept in a

sunny window or shaded? They need a light, humus-rich, well-drained soil. Never permit the soil to become really dry, but avoid a saturated condition and grow them at 55° to 70° F. Provide them with sun or fluorescent lights in the winter, partial shade in the summer. Increase humidity by using pebble-filled saucers or trays under the plants.

How should I feed begonias growing in pots? They respond best to organic fertilizers, one of the best of which is diluted fish emulsion, but any complete house-plant fertilizer that will dissolve in water may be used. Never feed plants that have not filled their pots with healthy roots, unless they are in soil-free mixes.

What are the best winter-blooming begonias? Nothing equals the wax begonia (*Begonia semperflorens*). Even plants lifted from the summer garden bud again quite quickly and never completely stop through the winter and then continue through the summer, too. Wax begonias are one of the most dependable of all house plants and are available in many floriferous hybrids. The trick in their culture is not to overwater.

What are some good smaller-growing begonias? I have very little space for the plants. Six-inch miniatures that bloom during the winter and spring include 'Baby Perfectifolia', 'Bow Joe', 'China Doll', and 'Robert Shatzer'. 'Dew Drop', 'Robin', and 'Wood Nymph' are rex types. Dwarfs up to 10 inches include 'Black Falcon', 'Silver Jewel', and 'It', a silver-spotted rex type. Some small begonias perform best in terrariums and include *Begonia prismatocarpa* and *B. quadrilata*. Consult specialists for additional kinds, as there are many.

What are the rules for repotting a healthy, fibrous-rooted begonia that has filled its pot with roots? (1) Water thoroughly a few hours before repotting; (2) the new pot should be only an inch or two wider than the old pot; (3) put crocks (drainage material) in the new pot; (4) avoid damaging roots; (5) moderately firm the soil around the root ball; (6) water thoroughly. Shade from bright sun for a few days. Do not overwater!

What is the proper care for begonias? They grow well but hardly ever blossom. About once a year they bud and then the buds drop off. Bud dropping suggests lack of light or too low humidity (45 to 70 per cent is desirable). Try fluorescent lights.

Can begonias in the house be pinched back severely to prevent them from growing leggy, or does this condition indicate some cultural defect? Pruning back can be done. Some varieties (the *coccineas*, for example) send up long, canelike growths. Lack of light and too high temperatures may also be responsible for legginess.

Where in the house do begonias do best? A sunny window during the winter where the night temperature is not below 50° F. and the day temperature is not above 65° F.

How should fibrous-rooted begonias be watered? The soil should be kept moist but not waterlogged. When water is given, thoroughly saturate the whole ball of soil (preferably by immersing a big pot in a pail), then give no more water until the soil begins to show signs of dryness. Use water at room temperature.

How do you take care of begonias? My plants are withering. Begonias that have tuberous roots die down and rest for a period each year. Most others thrive in 55° to 70° F., provided the atmosphere is not too dry and the light is reasonably good. The soil should be light, humus-rich, and moderately moist. Begonias with thick rhizomes should be allowed to dry out slightly between waterings.

Should begonias have a rest; if so, when, and what care should follow? It is impossible to generalize. The tuberous kinds need a complete rest through the winter. *Begonia socotrana* and some South African kinds rest during the summer. Many benefit from a partial rest (but are not dried off), while others continue their growth year-round.

What is your method for growing a calla-lily begonia? One person's directions contradict another's. (New Jersey.) Place the plant in the window of a country home and see how it grows! This prima donna seems to do best under cool and well-lighted conditions. Professional gardeners often fail. A west window in a room with a night temperature of about 60° F., reasonable humidity and fresh air, with moderate watering from below (or without wetting the heart of the plant), may keep it alive. It should be grown quite dry during the winter, with just enough water to keep its leaves from drooping, and not overwatered in summer, which is their time of active growth.

Why is it so difficult to grow the calla begonia south of New England? This seems to be due to the extremes of summer weather. Like sweet peas, delphiniums, and some other garden plants, this house plant abhors spells of weather when both days and nights are hot and humid.

How can I keep a Christmas begonia over summer so it will bloom next winter? Rest it for a few weeks after it blooms; cut back and repot in light soil in the spring; grow in a humid atmosphere (minimum temperature, 60° F.). Shade from bright sunshine; repot as necessary during the summer. Control pests. You can scarcely expect success without a warm greenhouse.

How do you care for 'Gloire de Lorraine' (Christmas) begonias after they are through blooming? They are usually discarded because young plants develop into better specimens for the following year. If you wish to continue growing old plants, rest awhile by reducing the water supply somewhat. In the spring, cut partly back, repot, and start into growth again.

How can I make my angel-wing begonia bloom?   Provided that the plant is growing well, it should bloom after it attains a reasonable size if it is kept in a fully lighted or sunny place and fertilized regularly.

Why do my angel-wing begonias, after a few days' growth, dry up and lose the leaves? I keep them well watered and cool.   The common causes of leaf dropping are too much or too little water, low temperatures, exposure to drafts, too dry an atmosphere, and careless repotting. The minimum temperature should be 55° F.

What disease causes begonia leaves to turn yellow?   This is usually not due to any organic disease but to the plants receiving a check to their growth due to dryness, too strong sunshine, an arid atmosphere, or too low temperature.

Why do begonias bloom in greenhouses and not after I get them home? I have one now, it grows just fine, but has no flowers.   Possibly there is too little light. Begonias need light shade from intense summer sun, but sunlight is necessary for flower production, especially during the winter. Also, humidity of 45 to 70 per cent is needed.

Most begonias grown for their foliage effect rather than flower display require a fairly moist atmosphere and do not thrive in hot, dry rooms.

The begonias kept on my terrace during the summer, and brought into the house in the fall, dropped all their leaves. What can be the cause or causes? We use bottled gas in the house.   Leaking gas may be the cause, but much more probably the dry air inside (especially after heat is turned on) is responsible. Install humidifiers. Stand the plants on trays in moist gravel.

My potted, wax begonia blooms on one side branch only. What can I do with it? It is about 9 inches tall and has 4 stalks full of foliage so it should be bushy.   The plant needs good light to bloom well. It will stand more sunlight than most other begonias.

When a rex begonia droops, is it going into a rest period? It has just finished blossoming. Should I water it less often? When grown in the house, this often happens at the approach of winter. Reduce the water supply (but keep the soil somewhat moist). Repot and water more when signs of new growth show in the spring.

My rex begonia never seems to increase in size. As soon as a new leaf appears, another leaf turns yellow and dies. What is wrong? The wrong soil, too low temperature, or too dry an atmosphere. The soil should be humus-rich but porous; the temperature should not be below 55° F. A humid atmosphere suits these plants best.

Why do my begonia cuttings rot instead of root when I try to start them in water? While some people report success with *some* varieties of begonias in water, a generally preferable method is to use moist sand (not sea sand) or vermiculite as a rooting medium. If water is used, add a few lumps of charcoal.

Can calla begonias be made to grow from cuttings, and how? (New York.) Yes. You must be careful to select the greenest shoots for cuttings. The white ones are devoid of chlorophyll and will not grow. The green ones produce white tips later. Root in a covered plastic dish.

When is the best time to take cuttings of double-flowered begonias? At the same time that cuttings of single-flowered varieties, belonging to the same section, would be taken; thus, of most fibrous-rooted and tuberous-rooted kinds, in the spring; of most winter-flowering hybrids, in early winter.

How can rex begonias be propagated? They can be increased by seed, division, or from leaf cuttings. Cuttings are best made from mature leaves in the spring. Insert them in sand, or sand and peat moss. Keep moist and shaded from direct sunlight. Young plants should develop in a few weeks.

How do you start the new plants of a Christmas begonia? Most commonly from single leaves treated as cuttings and inserted in a bed of moist sand in December. They need 70° F. temperature and moist atmospheric conditions to succeed. They can also be grown from ordinary stem cuttings inserted in the spring.

My Begonia sutherlandii has developed swellings or lumps on its stems. Can these be used to start new plants? Yes. If planted in the spring, these bulbous growths will develop into new plants.

Which is the best way to propagate the hardy Begonia grandis? Collect the small bulblets that form so freely on the stems in late summer. Store them in a cool place for the winter and plant them in boxes of light soil in the spring. Also by division of old plants.

What precaution should be observed in sowing begonia seed? Use soilless mixes or milled sphagnum moss (sold in bags in garden centers or by mail-order seed firms). Water well *before* sowing. Scatter the dustlike seed evenly and press in lightly. Do not cover with soil. Cover the pot with glass or clear plastic and set in a dim place—temperature, 60° to 70° F.—until seed germinates. Then place under fluorescent lights, 3 to 4 inches beneath tubes. Never allow the soil to become dry. Water by standing the pot in a dish so that moisture seeps up from below.

How can begonias be grown from seed? I have difficulties; they always damp off. Damping off is caused by a fungus that thrives when conditions for the seedlings are unfavorable. Avoid overwatering, too heavy shade, extreme fluctuation of temperature. Sow seed on milled sphagnum moss, not on soil or on soilless mixes. Be sure that the mix is well drained. Water only on sunny days.

How should seedling begonias be transplanted? They are such tiny things. Prepare shallow boxes or pans by placing drainage material in the bottom and filling with a mixture of pasteurized house-plant mixture or any soilless mix, much preferred over garden soils. Top the mix with ½ inch of moist milled sphagnum moss. Loosen the seedlings and lift them with their roots intact (use a wooden label with a V notch) and plant with leaves on the surface, roots covered. Water with a fine spray or from below. Keep warm and shaded. Grow under lights.

What causes the younger leaves on begonias to crinkle and get a crumbly, webbed, grayish look? Mites (microscopic insects), which suck the juices from the plant. Spray forcibly at the sink to break webs and spray with Kelthane.

My begonias fail to grow. I have been told that they have root knot. What shall I use? Root-knot nematode causes swellings on roots and, finally, decay. The only control is to repropagate from tip cuttings, throw out old plants, and keep new ones growing in sterilized soil.

Little green plant lice are on my begonia plants. What shall I do? Use malathion as a spray or dip. When using as a dip, cover the soil with foil, invert the plant, and dip the foliage and stems so that they are thoroughly wetted.

What kinds of begonias are best in the house? A good selection of easy-growing kinds includes: *B.* x *feastii* (beefsteak), *B. semperflorens* (wax), *B.* x *argenteo-guttata* (trout), *B. coccinea* (angel-wing), *B. heracleifolia* (star), *B. scharffii*, 'President Carnot', and *B. foliosa miniata*. *B.* 'Tom Ment' is a graceful, arching angel-wing with dwarf habit, pink flowers, and spotted foliage.

What are 'Lorraine' begonias?   Commonly known as Christmas begonias, they are the result of hybridizing *B. socotrana* and *B. dregei*.
The first hybrid produced was named 'Gloire de Lorraine'. More adaptable are recent *B.* x *hiemalis* hybrids such as 'Aphrodite Red' or
'Aphrodite Pink'.

**What is the name of the begonia with green and white, and some all-
white, leaves and small red and deep pink flowers?**   It is often called
calla begonia or calla-lily begonia. These are varieties of *Begonia
semperflorens*.

Can you tell me the name of a hardy begonia?   *Begonia grandis,* a
native of China, is the hardiest species. In a sheltered position, it will
live outdoors in New York. It comes in both pink- and white-flowered
varieties.

BROMELIADS

What is the correct care for bromeliads?   Bromeliads, of which there
are many species, are relatives of the pineapple. A few, such as *Dyckia,*
are considered succulents. They like a winter temperature of 55° to
60° F. Most popular are nonsucculent epiphytic sorts. The common
name is air-plant because they derive most of their nourishment from air
and water, being tree perchers in their native habitats. A number make
fine house plants and include *Billbergia, Vriesia,* and *Aechmea.* The
leaves of many species are vaselike, rising from a tight base, and the
exotic, colorful, long-lasting flowers on stiff stems are borne in winter.
Vaselike bromeliads should be watered in the "vase," which holds
moisture well. They are excellent for city conditions.

What are the best bromeliads for beginners to grow?   You could
hardly go wrong with varieties and species of *Aechmea* and *Billbergia.*
Vriesia and *Tillandsia* are a little more temperamental and need more
care.

Can you give me some information about watering bromeliads?   The
majority of bromeliads—*Aechmea, Billbergia, Guzmania*—need their
growing medium just slightly moist, but they absolutely require that the
"vases" be filled with water all through the growing season. Those without water reservoirs—*Cryptanthus,* silvery *Tillandsia* species—need an
evenly moist growing medium through spring, summer, and fall, with a
slight drying out in winter. Small, silvery *Tillandsia ionantha* and similar species thrive when mounted on chunks of tree fern or cork bark.
Mist them with room-temperature water on bright mornings.

What is the best potting medium for bromeliads?   A half-and-half mixture of shredded osmunda or tree-fern fiber with soil. Also, a handful of pebbles suits most bromeliads. Exceptions would be the terrestrial species—*Cryptanthus,* for example—which can be grown in a standard house-plant soil.

Do bromeliads need sunlight to bloom indoors? Any flowering plant, bromeliads included, will do better with some sunlight, not only to encourage bloom, but also for good leaf color. This is especially true for bromeliads. Much of their beauty is in their colorful foliage.

Is it true that putting an apple in the "vase" of a bromeliad will make it bloom? Yes, the gas given off by the apple apparently stimulates flowering. Cover the plant and apple securely with plastic.

CALCEOLARIA

How can I grow calceolarias from seed? If you propose to do this in an ordinary window, you have chosen a tough subject. Like cineraria, the spotted and other hybrid calceolaria varieties need coolness. Sow the fine seeds on the surface of a level soilless mix in a pot in July or August; provide full shade and never leave dry; transplant the tiny seedlings to a flat and keep in a shaded cold frame. Pot later and keep in the frame until late fall, then move to a light place with a temperature around 40° to 45° F. at night. If the temperature runs above 50° any time during the winter, failure is almost certain. Beware of aphids and whiteflies.

CAMPANULA ISOPHYLLA (LIGURIAN HAREBELL)

There is a plant common in Cape Cod homes which is generally called star-of-Bethlehem. This is not the same as the hardy plant that grows in our garden from a bulb. It is a larger plant with beautiful blue or white flowers. Can you give me some idea of the right name? This is *Campanula isophylla,* a native of Italy. It is a trailing plant with beautiful gray-green foliage, a summer to late-winter bloomer. It can be purchased by mail order from house-plant specialists.

How can star-of-Bethlehem, or Ligurian harebell, be grown in the house? Grow in sandy soil that has humus added. Provide a sunny window in the winter, light shade in the summer. Supplement short winter days with fluorescent light for maximum bloom or grow the plants under lights for 16 hours in the winter if a sunny window is not available. Keep moderately moist in the winter; water freely in the summer. Feed with diluted fertilizer when in growth. Propagate by cuttings in the spring.

CINERARIA (SENECIO X HYBRIDUS)

Can cinerarias be grown in a south window? Can they be carried through the summer for flowering again the next season? Cinerarias are short-lived plants in a warm room. They are grown at 40° to 45° F. and never above 50° F. When they are through blooming, discard them, as they don't like summer weather.

How can I raise cinerarias from seeds? I used moist sand and covered them with a glass, but one by one they died. As cinerarias have to be sown in July or August to get sizable plants for winter or early spring, damping off in hot weather is always a menace. Use soilless mix and don't cover. Stand the pan where it is shaded, and keep as cool as possible. Sow late in August or early September to escape the hot days and nights. Cinerarias must at all times be grown cool, 40° to 45° F.

What causes cineraria leaves to curl and dry at their edges? Probably too hot and dry an atmosphere; possibly the plants are dry at the roots. Cinerarias don't last long in a hot, dry temperature; 45° F. at night is plenty. Aphids are prone to attack them. They are greenhouse subjects that rarely last more than 2 to 3 weeks in the average house. It is best to discard them when their bloom is finished.

FUCHSIA

How are fuchsias handled as house plants? Cuttings are rooted in the spring, taken from old plants that have been started after a winter rest. If you keep them growing all year in a warm room, without a rest and subsequent new growth, you won't get flowers. Most are spring and summer bloomers. They like full light but not full sun, and rich soil, plenty of water and humidity when in growth. Feed liberally when in growth with one of the "complete" house-plant fertilizers.

What fuchsias will bloom indoors in the winter? *F. magellanica macrostema* is a winter bloomer. It will look well in a hanging basket, as it is a drooping, almost vinelike variety. The small flowers are ruby red. Variety 'Variegata' has white markings on the leaves. The winter-blooming hybrids of *F. triphylla,* including 'Gartenmeister Bohnstedt' with pink and orange-toned flowers, are adaptable to intermediate temperatures, even to growing under fluorescent lights. Most fuchsias are summer bloomers. By taking slips from larger plants in the summer and having them well rooted by early winter, you may get bloom in late winter or very early spring. Or buy young, blooming plants from a grower who has forced them.

I have a fuchsia that blossomed in May and June. What should I do so it will bloom during the winter months? Fuchsias are not naturally winter bloomers. The winter is their resting season.

Should fuchsias be given a rest period or can they be kept in bloom all through the year? Fuchsias are not everblooming, and in the winter old plants are best kept dry and cool until early spring. They should be potted and rested in a cool cellar or room and watered very little. Cut back in February or March and give warmer quarters, watering more when new shoots begin to appear. If you can't accommodate growing plants so early, keep practically dry and cool until April, then place them outdoors on warm days, indoors at night. Don't plant outside until all danger of frost is past.

What is the cause of buds and blossoms falling off a fuchsia plant on a window shelf indoors? Too hot and/or dry an atmosphere, resulting in red spider or whitefly attack. Possibly they are either too wet or too dry at the root. Root injury always causes leaf drop. Spring and summer are the blooming seasons. Don't expect flowers in the winter. The plants should be resting unless they are young plants. Daily misting of growing plants is a good deterrent to pests.

Can fuchsias be kept during the winter in a cold frame? If the frame is absolutely frostproof and the fuchsias are kept dry and dark until March, they might survive. The so-called hardy variety *Fuchsia magellanica* is the only sort that will stand real frost.

GERANIUM (PELARGONIUM)

Which kind of soil should be used for geraniums to get good flowers? A half-and-half mixture of good garden loam and sand or perlite will grow good flowering plants. Apply a liquid fertilizer when the plants are growing, not when they are resting. The old idea of poor soil kept dry is no longer acceptable.

What is the best fertilizer for geraniums? A low-nitrogen fertilizer is best. Nitrogen is the first number in the fertilizer formulas. It encourages growth rather than bloom.

What do you suggest feeding geraniums for Christmas blooming? Provided you have a good winter-blooming variety, and have grown it especially for winter bloom, any good complete fertilizer that is moderately quick-acting may be used after the final pots are well filled with roots.

What must I do to start geraniums left to hang in a cellar (root upward) when spring arrives?   Take them down, prune them back somewhat (cut back roots as well), and pot in a sandy soil in pots just large enough to hold the roots. Give one good soaking and put in a light, cool place. Unless you have a cellar that is really cool and not a warm basement, hanging plants through the winter is rarely satisfactory. Avoid watering frequently until new growth is well started.

When is it safe to plant geraniums from a window into an open garden?   After all danger of frost has passed and the ground has warmed up (about the time beans are planted). Harden the plants gradually before planting by standing them for a few days in a cold frame, on a porch, or in a sheltered place outdoors.

Should I break the soil and spread out the roots of potted geraniums when I plant them in a garden?   No, leave the root ball intact. Thoroughly soak it an hour before planting it. Make a hole big enough, press soil firmly around the root ball; water well. The top of the root ball should be a half inch below the surface.

What window is best for geraniums?   The sunniest one. They like it cool, somewhat below 68° F. and about 10 degrees less at night.

Should geraniums always be kept toward windows, one side always facing the window, or can they be moved? (Maryland.)   They can be moved if desired, but it is advisable to turn them frequently only at the same window so that all parts get the light and the growth is shapely.

How should one care for geraniums in the house? What about using milk on them? What size pots should be used?   Do *not* use milk. Pots must be adjusted to the size of the plants. Avoid pots that are too large. When the pot is well filled with healthy roots, transfer the plant to a pot a size or two larger, using the soil mixture suggested in the first question on geraniums. A 4-inch pot is a good average size.

How shall I water my potted geraniums?   Watering must be adjusted to the individual plant and environment. Your aim is to keep the soil moist (but not wet and boglike) throughout. When water is given, saturate the whole ball of soil. Let the soil approach dryness between waterings. Sunshine, high temperature, breezy weather, and vigorous growth all make more frequent watering necessary.

I have potted my garden geraniums. What procedure do I follow to keep them blooming in the house? Please give directions for watering, sunlight, clipping tops, and temperature.   See other questions. Cut tops about halfway back at potting time. Give all available sunlight, and fresh air, without drafts. Plants potted from the garden are unlikely to bloom again until late February or March.

Can anything be done to correct the growth habit of a pink-colored geranium which is growing too tall and not sending out any side shoots below a distance of about 10 inches from the flowerpot? Yes. You may "stop" the plant by pinching out the tips of the growing shoots, or, if necessary, you may prune the stems back to force new growth nearer the pot.

Is it true that if geraniums bloom continuously outdoors during the summer they seldom bloom freely in the winter? Garden geraniums are unlikely to be good winter-blooming types. Furthermore, potting them from garden beds causes considerable root disturbance and adjustment must be made before the plants set buds again.

How can I make my geraniums bloom through the winter? To get good winter bloom, take cuttings from May to June. Repot until roots fill 4-inch pots. Young plants should be blooming size by October. August-to-September cuttings probably won't bloom before February. Mail-order specialists can supply geraniums of many types (not just the familiar zonals) that will give you a variety of winter bloomers.

Should geraniums be repotted and how often? Mine are scrawny and do not blossom since being brought in from outdoors. Plants that have given a good display all summer can scarcely be expected to continue throughout the winter. Prune back severely when you bring them indoors. Rest them somewhat by keeping them drier, but not completely dry, until new growth begins in late winter.

How do you treat and store geranium plants through the winter? The best procedure is to cut the plants back partway and pot them a couple of weeks before a killing frost may occur. Winter in a cool plant room or window where the temperature does not drop below 55° F. Water sparingly during the winter.

I have geraniums in flower boxes in my basement. Last summer they developed rather long stems and I want to cut them back this year. How shall I do it? I had these boxes in an unheated porch, but when the weather got too cold I put them in the basement for protection against frost. They lost all their leaves while in the porch (which I wanted to happen, to give them a rest during the winter), but now in the basement they are producing small buds all over and it will not be long until they have new leaves. What shall I do? Prune away ½ to ⅔ the length of each shoot. Repot into new soil, put in a light place, and they will develop nicely by summer.

Can geraniums planted outside be successfully wintered by storing

plants in peat moss or similar material, or must they be potted? They probably could be planted in peat moss and sand, but potting would undoubtedly be surer and better.

Will geraniums keep all winter if pulled up by the root and kept in a cool fruit cellar? I have some beauties I would like to keep. Yes, under the conditions you mention. Hang them up by the roots from the ceiling and pick off all leaves that decay.

What is the best care for ivy-leaved geranium? Mine becomes straggly and root-bound in spite of being cut back and continuously changed to larger pots. Perhaps your plant is so old that it would be wisest to start afresh from a cutting. When plants are well rooted, feed with liquid fertilizer at weekly or biweekly intervals. Pinch the tips out of growing shoots occasionally to induce branching.

What is the proper treatment of ivy geranium—soil, exposure, watering, etc.? Pot in a rich, mellow soil that is well drained. Grow in full winter sun; light shade is desirable during the hottest part of the day in the summer. Water to keep the soil always evenly moist, but not wet and stagnant. Good ventilation and plenty of room are essential.

Why do ivy geraniums always have some dead leaves during their blossoming season? This seems a common complaint except with plants grown in a comparatively humid (and perhaps lightly shaded) greenhouse.

What are conditions favorable to growth of the Lady Washington geranium? Soil and moisture required? Cool, airy, sunny conditions (minimum night temperature 45° F.). Porous, fertile soil with some lime added. Plenty of moisture when growing rapidly; little or none when resting.

How do I care for my Lady Washington geranium that bloomed this summer? These are difficult to care for in a house; it is better to treat them as disposable pot plants after their 4- to 6-week spring display is over. Obtain new plants each year from a mail-order house in a 2½-inch size.

Why do the leaves on my normally blooming geraniums turn brown and drop off? There are many possible causes: too dry an atmosphere; lack of water; too much water; damage to roots when repotting; or too strong fertilizer or spray.

What causes brown edges on geranium leaves? Probably too low humidity. Try standing the plants on pebble-filled trays of water and syringing their tops about once a week.

What causes my geranium leaves to turn pale green and not thrive? They have been recently repotted, but long enough ago to be growing

and thriving. Probably you are growing them with too little light. Low temperature could also be a factor. Try full sunshine and a minimum temperature of 55° F.

Will geraniums thrive inside in a window box when the house is heated by gas? Unless artificial gas is escaping into the room atmosphere, the method of heating will make no difference. Good light, reasonable temperatures, proper soil, and good care are the factors that count.

What makes our geranium house plants thin and spindly instead of short, stocky plants as they are outside? Too high temperature coupled with too little light. Pinching tips out of plants occasionally will help. (Read other questions and answers on this subject.)

My geraniums won't blossom. They are in a southeast window, and the room temperature is between 75° to 80° F. most of the time. What is wrong? The temperature is much too high for them, and most other plants. The ideal temperature for geraniums is 50° to 60° F.

What causes the buds of a geranium to turn brown and dry up? Low humidity is the most likely cause of trouble.

What causes a geranium to have flowers of different colors—first red, then pink? Plants sometimes "sport" or mutate. A red-flower geranium may produce a branch that bears pink flowers, and vice versa. Temperature and fertilizer also influence flower color.

When I cut off pieces of my rose geranium and put them in a bunch of flowers, they start wilting almost at once. What can be done to prevent this? Very little. It will help to cut the geranium ahead of time and put it in cold water in a dark cool place for a few hours.

What is a good method for propagating geraniums? By cuttings (terminal pieces of stem 4 or 5 inches long with lower leaves removed and bases cut cleanly across just beneath a joint). Plant firmly in clean sand; keep shaded from direct sunshine and in a fairly moist atmosphere at about 60° F.

What is the best way to start geraniums from cuttings? What kind of soil should be used, and how much water? Start with good, clean cuttings made of shoots that are neither hard and woody nor yet very vigorous and watery. Plant in sand. Keep just moist (not sopping wet). When roots have formed, pot singly in small pots, using for this first potting a very sandy soil.

What is the recommended time for taking cuttings of rose geraniums? Cuttings will root any time, but the most favorable months are May, August, and September.

When is the right time to take cuttings of geraniums so they will

flower for Memorial Day? August or September. Many of the hybrids flower in 4 months from seed.

When should geraniums be started for planting in outdoor planters? From August to February, depending on the size of the plants needed. Early cuttings will finish in 5-inch pots; late cuttings, in 3½- or 4-inch pots.

Why don't my geraniums bloom in the house before February? I usually start them from cuttings in August. They are very beautiful otherwise, with very large, thick, glossy leaves. The flowers are large and beautiful when they do bloom. For early bloom, propagate in May.

Is it better to root geraniums in water or in sand? What is the best time to root them for early blossoming? Moist sand is best. Take cuttings early in September for late spring blooming; in May, for winter blooming.

Before frost in October, I take geranium cuttings and plant them in sand in a pot indoors for rooting. About 90 per cent eventually rot at the soil line. What is wrong? You will stand a greater chance of success if you take your cuttings in late August or early September. Let the cut ends form a dry callus for a day, then dust the cut end with a hormone powder, available in garden centers. Set the cuttings no more than 1 inch below the sand. Shallow placement encourages sturdy new roots and discourages rot. Keep the sand moist but not wet. You are probably keeping the rooting medium too wet. (See also diseases of Geranium.)

My geranium cuttings looked very healthy at first, but now the leaves are turning yellow and dying. The plants are in a south window. What is the trouble? The cuttings are losing water faster than they can take it up. Reduce the transpiration by shading from bright sun, syringe plants lightly every day, and increase ventilation.

When and how do I pot geranium cuttings rooted in sand? As soon as the roots are ½ to 1 inch long, plant singly in small pots, using very sandy soil without fertilizer added. Do not press soil too firmly. Water well immediately; syringe for a few days.

I have a rose-scented geranium and can never start a new cutting. When and how should I try? In May or August. Make the cutting 4 or 5 joints long; cut with a sharp knife below the joint; remove lower leaves; plant firmly in moist sand; keep moist, shaded from strong sun, in a moist atmosphere at 60° F. or more.

How does one take cuttings from Lady Washington geraniums? Very much as any other geranium. The shoots that root with greatest ease are young ones produced after plants have been started into growth in late summer, but tips of older shoots can also be used.

How can geraniums be grown from seeds? Sow seeds in the spring in pots of soilless mix. Cover very lightly, keep moist (and shaded until seedlings appear) in a temperature of 60° F. If the seed is good, it will soon germinate, and under favorable conditions the transplanted seedlings will make rapid growth. 'Carefree' geraniums grow easily from seed and make fine pot plants.

Why don't my seedling geraniums bloom? Possibly they are growing too vigorously because of the too-rich soil. Too much shade also reduces blooming. Try keeping some plants in pots.

How long after geranium seed is planted may blooms be expected? From 4 to 6 months for standard types, slightly faster for 'Carefree' and 'Firecracker'.

How can a large geranium plant be divided into smaller plants? What fertilizer is recommended? Geranium (*Pelargonium zonale*) plants do not lend themselves to this method of propagation. Increase stock by means of cuttings. Any commercial fertilizer can be used advantageously.

Can geraniums be grown under fluorescent lights? Yes, the miniatures and dwarfs. Taller types require too much space and equipment. Place plants with their tops about 3 inches below the lights; raise tiny growers on inverted flowerpots. Pinch tops to make the plants bushy and give 14 to 18 hours of light. More water and fertilizer will be needed than for window plants.

I have an ivy geranium that is almost 3 feet tall. It was a cutting last spring; now the leaves are starting to curl down. What is the cause of this? It may be due to a severe attack of aphids. Examine young shoots and the undersides of leaves; if plant lice are found, spray with any good contact insecticide.

I have a pelargonium, 6 years old; it bloomed once with gorgeous red and brown blooms. It has never blossomed since. I've changed soil and pots, and started new cuttings, but none will bloom. Whiteflies bother it all the time. What shall I do for it? This is a Lady Washington (*Pelargonium* x *domesticum*) variety. To control whiteflies, spray at weekly intervals (until the trouble is cleared up) with malathion used according to the manufacturer's directions, or with an aerosol resmethrin spray recommended for the purpose. For cultural details, read answers to other questions. Lady Washington geraniums are difficult as house plants.

Why do geranium cuttings rot while in the sand and turn black and die without rooting? The fungus disease known as black leg causes these symptoms. The rot begins at the base and works upward to the leaves. It is wise to discard rotted cuttings and start over. Use clean flats and sand that has been thoroughly baked or use sterile vermiculite. Propagate from healthy plants only.

There is a small-leaved geranium similar to rose geranium, with a most unusual and delightful scent from the leaves. What is its name? Perhaps you mean *Pelargonium crispum* (lemon-scented), *P. denticulatum* (pine-scented), *P.* x *fragrans* (nutmeg), *P. odoratissimum* (apple- or nutmeg-scented), or one of the numerous other scented-leaved geraniums with small leaves.

I have seen a geranium on the market in both red and light pink. The green leaves have a white border. What is the name of this geranium? There are many geraniums that can fit this description: 'Mme. Salleroi', 'Hills of Snow', 'Madame Languth' (pink).

What are some good small geraniums that are easy to grow? The tiny miniatures are difficult, but the larger dwarfs, smaller than the standard zonals, will give you continuous color and are of easy culture. These include: 'Bumblebee', 'Dancer', 'Dopey', 'Emma Hossler', 'Gypsy Gem', 'More Mischief', 'Mr. Everaarts', 'Pride', 'Prince Valiant', 'Robin Hood', and 'Sparkle'.

GERBERA

Does gerbera, or African-daisy, when brought indoors from the garden, get a rest period; or should the plants continue to show leaves? Gerberas do best when kept growing during the winter at 55° F., as that is their real flowering season. They are not likely to prove good window plants at ordinary room temperatures.

GESNERIADS

I hear that there are plants similar to the African-violet that require the same culture but will give variety to my window garden. What are they? These are the fibrous-rooted gesneriads; among them, *Aeschynanthus* (the lipstick-plant), *Columnea* (the goldfish-plant), *Episcia* (peacock-plant), *Nematanthus,* and *Streptocarpus* are all excellent flowering subjects.

Are there any trailing gesneriads I could arrange with my African-violets? Episcias make delightful trailing plants, as do *Aeschynanthus,* especially 'Black Pagoda', and the various kinds of *Nematanthus.* However, you will not find them as free-flowering as their African-violet relatives.

What is the best temperature for gesneriads, and how should I water and fertilize them? Like the African-violet, the other gesneriads thrive in a daytime temperature of 65° to 72° F. with a drop of some 10 degrees at night. Keep the soil just evenly moist while plants are in active growth and feed them at every watering with a diluted solution of a water-soluble house-plant fertilizer according to the directions on the container.

Do other gesneriads require as much humidity as African-violets? About the same and not less than 50 per cent. Mist the tops frequently with warm water. This misting, plus the regular fertilizing, promotes bloom.

What is a good soil mix for gesneriads? An open porous soil that drains perfectly, about the same as for your African-violets—good garden loam (pasteurized) plus sand or perlite, or use one of the soilless mixes available at garden centers.

HELIOTROPE (HELIOTROPIUM)

Is heliotrope a satisfactory house plant for winter bloom? Heliotrope can be made to bloom in the winter only by purchasing plants forced by the grower (its normal flowering time is summer) or by starting cuttings in the summer that are ready to bloom by late winter. To force winter bloom on mature plants, they must be kept pinched back and disbudded through the summer. Heliotrope must have a very sunny position in a cool window garden. Water moderately. Cut back long, sprawling branches occasionally. Watch for whitefly.

Can a heliotrope potted from the garden be kept during the winter and set out again in the summer? Yes. Cut back a bit and keep cool—not above 55° F. Cuttings can be rooted in February to make more plants to set out in late May.

Can heliotrope and lavender be treated in the same manner? It depends on which lavender you mean. The French (*Lavandula dentata*) and Spanish (*L. stoechas*) lavenders are not hardy and can be treated as heliotrope is (see above).

IMPATIENS (PATIENCE-PLANT)

How do I care for impatiens indoors? Impatiens plants make excellent everblooming house plants provided they can be grown fairly cool, not above 65° F., and with the humidity above 40 per cent. Setting pots on pebble-filled saucers of water and syringing the tops once or twice a day promote humidity. If long bare stems develop, cut these all the way back. Patience-plants established in clay pots need a lot of water and will drop or show yellow leaves if allowed to dry out for even a few hours. They require a position in good light and do well under fluorescent tubes.

Do patience-plants come in other colors than pink?   Yes, hybridizers have extended the color range and you can grow from seed or find in the spring at your garden center dwarf or standard-size plants in shades of coral, red, orange, scarlet, lavender, and purple as well as white (also some that are variegated red and white, such as 'Go-Go'). Hybrids bred from New Guinea species have both colorful flowers and variegated foliage. Garden centers and several mail-order sources offer New Guinea hybrids suitable for indoor growing in bright light.

Can I dig up impatiens plants from my garden and expect them to bloom indoors in the winter?   Yes, pot them carefully early in September; set in a somewhat shaded, sheltered place outdoors for a couple of weeks; spray to clean up any pests; then bring indoors and provide good air circulation and bright light, including at least 4 hours of sunshine. Given proper care (as above), they will produce a wealth of bloom. Don't overlook seedlings in the garden. In small pots, they will also begin to bloom soon. You can also take cuttings of especially good seedlings.

MARGUERITE DAISY or BOSTON DAISY (CHRYSANTHEMUM FRUTESCENS)

Are marguerites satisfactory as house plants?   Yes. Purchase blooming plants from a florist. They will do well in a sunny window. Sink pots in a garden bed in the summer where they will do almost equally well. For winter bloom, keep plants disbudded through the summer. New plants root readily from cuttings. Marguerites need ample water. Watch for aphids. Use a standard potting mixture. (See Soil, this section.)

NEOMARICA

Is the neomarica sometimes called "twelve apostles"? Does it make a good house plant?   Yes, the neomaricas are sometimes given this nickname because of the number of their irislike leaves, which sometimes reaches twelve. *Neomarica gracilis* is the smaller-leaved of the two generally grown and has white and violet, irislike fleeting blossoms which appear at the tips of leaflike peduncles in late winter. *N. northiana* has larger leaves and blooms about the same time, having larger violet and white fragrant blossoms. It blooms less freely than *N. gracilis*. New plants can be started from the peduncles, which produce young plants after bloom. These plants need sunshine and warmth for early bloom. Sponge the glossy leaves to keep them free from dust. Use a standard potting mixture. (See Soil, this section.)

I have a Neomarica gracilis which grew lustily and increased greatly in size. Why didn't it bloom? Perhaps you kept it too cool. At 50° to 60° F., bloom is considerably delayed. The flowers should appear in late winter if the plants are kept at a day temperature of about 70° F. Pot-bound specimens seldom bloom well. Yours may need division; or discard the old plant and start new stock.

Is it safe to divide old plants of neomarica? Yes, they can be easily divided. Or start new plants from those which develop on blooming stalks.

How old does the "twelve apostles" have to be before it blooms? This plant (*Neomarica,* formally classified as *Marica*), if grown from a small offshoot, can take 2 to 3 years to reach blooming size. Put the plant outdoors in partial shade during the summer. Bring in before frost.

Does the "twelve apostles" require much sun and water? It can take its full share of sun and light in a window, but do not overwater; placing it outside in partial shade during the summer is desirable. It blooms in late winter or early spring, depending on the species.

What makes the tips of my neomarica leaves turn brown? Probably they were watered too much. This plant is related to the iris, and, while evergreen, it has its resting season. When the leaves go bad, repot it in fresh soil (after cutting away dead roots) and give only enough water to prevent wilting until it becomes active again. Too low humidity also causes leaf-tip browning.

ORCHID

I would like to try growing a few orchids but I am confused by the many kinds available. How do I begin? First of all, see the questions and answers that follow. Obtain a good book on orchids, such as the books listed in Section 16. Then survey your growing conditions. Orchids are divided into warm (day temperatures of 70° to 80° F.; nights, 65° to 70° F.), intermediate (days, 65° to 70° F.; nights, 60° to 65° F.), and cool (days, 60° to 65° F.; nights, 55° to 60° F.) groups. There is obviously some overlapping between the last two groups. Orchids also require several hours of sun (or fluorescent lights) and humidity—the same requirements of most flowering house plants.

Is it true that orchids can be grown successfully indoors at a window instead of in a greenhouse? If so, which ones?   In recent years much has been learned about orchids as house plants. Excellent results have been obtained at windows with varieties of *Cattleya* (corsage), *Paphiopedilum* (lady-slipper type), *Epidendrum, Oncidium* (butterfly type), and *Phalaenopsis* (moth orchids) as well as many others. These are mostly intermediate to warm growers that bloom from winter to late spring. The monthly bulletins of the American Orchid Society (84 Sherman Street, Cambridge, Mass. 02140) usually contain one or more articles on orchids as house plants.

What is the culture for orchids at windows?   This is a complex business (see the above question). The epiphytes (tree-grown), which represent the majority, thrive in coconut fiber, a fir-bark mixture, or chopped tree fern. Those with moisture-holding pseudobulbs (cattleyas are an example) are allowed to dry between waterings; those without pseudobulbs (paphiopedilums, phalaenopsis) are kept evenly moist, not soaked; orchids potted in a humus-rich soil, such as paphiopedilums, are watered like other house plants. Frequent fogging benefits all of them and they do very well under fluorescent lights. Advances in meristem propagation (cloning by tissue culture) have made prices of superior clones more reasonable (although orchids are still more expensive than most house plants). See color catalogs for mericlone orchid selections, especially dwarf clones well suited for window ledges or gardens under fluorescent lights.

I have an east-facing large window that is too cool in the winter for most house plants (as low as 50° F. on some winter nights). I was surprised when a neighbor (who has a greenhouse) suggested cymbidiums, as I thought orchids liked warmth.   Not all orchids require warm temperatures and cymbidiums are a prize example of this exception. They should do very well in your window but you will want to grow miniature hybrids only, as the standard kinds grow much too large. Even the miniatures in some varieties can reach 18 to 24 inches or more *above* their 6- to 8-inch pots. Most of the hybrids are terrestrial and thrive in a peat moss-bark mixture or something similar that is humus-rich but drains well. The plants can be summered outdoors in partial shade and toward the end of summer moved into a sunnier spot and watered less. The cool autumn nights will force flower spike initiation for many varieties. (Others should form buds during winter and spring.) Bring the plants indoors before heavy frosts begin. To maintain humidity indoors, place the pots on pebbles in water-filled trays in an east, south, or west window.

PRIMROSE (PRIMULA)

What primroses can I grow indoors in winter? *Primula sinensis* (Chinese primrose), single or double, bears pink, magenta, or white blooms. It has a long blooming period. *P. malacoides,* fairy primrose, has small, frothy violet blossoms throughout the winter. *P. obconica* (poison primrose), with vigorous hairy leaves, has larger flowers. Water daily, in the saucer. Keep in a cool east window, standing the pots on pebbles in water-filled trays.

What can I do to make a primrose bloom? It is about 3 years old. Not knowing the kind of primrose, we can't advise. There are several types grown in pots for winter and spring flowers in greenhouses, and dozens of hardy kinds that bloom outdoors in the spring and early summer if conditions are right. The greenhouse kinds are usually discarded after one season.

What conditions are best for primroses as house plants? How much water? How much light and sun? How much heat and how cool at night? For *Primula malacoides* and *P. sinensis,* not above 50° F. at night; even less is better. *P. obconica,* 50° to 55° F. at night. All like partial shade, ample water, but plenty of drainage in the pots.

What care does the Christmas-blooming primrose require? If you mean *Primula obconica,* this is raised from seed sown in February or March, grown in pots in moderate shade through the summer, and from fall on kept at 55° F. or so. Don't give it too much water, yet never allow it to wilt for lack of moisture at the roots. Discard the plant after it blooms. This is the species that can cause a painful dermatitis on allergic people who handle the plants.

How can I propagate a Chinese primrose? The Chinese primrose (*Primula sinensis*) is raised from seed each year. Choice double sorts that do not form seed usually produce side growths that can be cut off with a knife and rooted.

SHRIMP-PLANT (JUSTICIA BRANDEGEANA)

What exposure does a shrimp-plant like? Shrimp-plants like plenty of sun and plenty of water. This is a fine house plant, untroubled by any insect pests.

What will I do with my shrimp-plant when it gets tall and leggy? Cut the plants back each spring and root cuttings for new plants to bring indoors in the fall. Cuttings will root easily, either in pots of sand or in a cold frame. Of course, you can keep the big plant, simply cutting it back enough to promote bushy growth rather than letting it achieve a 3- to 4-foot height.

Can a shrimp-plant be wintered in a cold frame? No, it is too soft and will die, even with protection. Even at a temperature of 45°, the shrimp-plant is unhappy. It grows best at 55° to 60° F.

Can you tell me the native habitat of the shrimp-plant and any legend or general information about the plant and its care? It comes from tropical America. There are no legends, as it was practically unknown except to botanists up to 1905.

SPATHIPHYLLUM

What is the correct growing medium for Spathiphyllum? Pot in terrestrial orchid mix or 50 per cent coconut fiber with 50 per cent houseplant soil, all over good drainage of gravel and a few chunks of hardwood charcoal.

Which spathe flower varieties are best as house plants? Choose the compact, adaptable sorts such as hybrid 'Mauna Loa' and the dwarf species *S. quindiuense*. Both of these have shiny strap-shaped leaves and long-lasting white spathes. Spathiphyllums thrive in intermediate to warm temperatures (65° to 70° F. nights), 50 to 60 per cent relative humidity, and diffuse light. *S. quindiuense* is mature at 6 to 8 inches, so it is suitable for many fluorescent light gardens.

STRELITZIA

How is bird-of-paradise (Strelitzia) handled in the winter? Should I take it out of its pots and plant it in the ground in the summer? The strelitzia is a big subject for a house plant, needing a tub—since it won't bloom until of some size. In the winter, give it only a moderate amount of water; good rich soil with plenty of drainage; full light but no feeding while semidormant. Don't take it out of its pot or tub in the summer; sink it in the ground to the rim and feed it regularly. Strelitzia generally blooms in late summer and fall. In the winter it should have a temperature of 45° to 50° F.

Whenever my bird-of-paradise makes a new leaf, an old leaf dies. Why doesn't it bloom? You won't get blooms until the plant has 10 or more healthy leaves. The dying leaves indicate something wrong at the roots. The cause may be either insufficient size pot, poor drainage, not enough water while in active growth during the summer, or too much water in the winter when it should be semidormant.

SWEET-OLIVE (OSMANTHUS FRAGRANS)

How shall I care for a sweet-olive as a house plant? Sweet-olive does well in an east or west window if you can give it a day temperature of 60° to 65° F. It needs plenty of water and a humid atmosphere. Syringe the leaves daily and feed occasionally with a "complete" plant food after the pot is filled with roots.

Annuals and Biennials as House Plants

Is it possible to raise annuals indoors in the winter without the plants becoming stalky? Yes, if you choose varieties that are dwarf and use fluorescent lights (a combination of cool-white and warm-white tubes will be satisfactory unless you want to experiment with the special plant tubes, which will be more expensive), either solely or as a supplement to sunshine on cloudy days. The lights should be on from 14 to 16 hours.

ALYSSUM, SWEET- (LOBULARIA MARITIMA)

Can I make sweet-alyssum bloom indoors? Yes, if you have enough sun or fluorescent lights and a really cool window or plant room. Sow the seed in late summer and fall for winter bloom, in early winter for spring bloom.

BROWALLIA

Is the browallia an annual? I potted mine in the fall and about January the leaves withered and it died. *Browallia americana* is an annual for outdoor use. *B. speciosa* is a biennial or perennial, but not hardy. It is sown in the fall, carried along in a greenhouse through the winter, and planted out in the spring; or sown in the spring to flower indoors in the winter.

Are browallias suited to a window garden?   Yes, *Browallia speciosa* makes a most satisfactory house plant. The tubular flowers, rather like small petunias, are blue, violet, or white, and literally cover the plants through a long blooming season. They are easily grown biennials that form shrubby, compact plants. Purchase them in bloom from a grower or grow them yourself from early spring-sown seed.

FORGET-ME-NOT (MYOSOTIS SYLVATICA)

Can forget-me-not be made to bloom indoors?   Yes. It needs a cool but humid atmosphere and, unlike most other annuals and biennials, can stand some shade, though not much indoors. Plant the seed in the spring for the following winter's bloom. This is really a greenhouse subject for winter bloom, but with the right conditions, such as fluorescent lights, you may have flowers.

LOBELIA

Is lobelia a plant which can be made to bloom indoors in the winter?   Yes, you can grow lobelia from seeds or cuttings to produce winter bloom. It does not need as much sun as many other flowering plants but will require artificial light for best results. You will have a good chance of success if the window or location under lights is cool.

MORNING-GLORY (IPOMOEA)

Can I grow morning-glory in my window garden?   Yes, if you have a cool, sunny window. Plant seeds in individual pots in August. Transplant to larger pots as needed. Have strings ready near the glass to encourage the vines to climb.

NASTURTIUM (TROPAEOLUM)

How can nasturtiums be grown indoors in the winter?   They must have a cool, sunny window or plant room. Plant seeds in late summer in pots of soil without too much fertilizer. Or take cuttings of some of the summer bloomers in the garden, keeping them cut back to prevent bloom until winter. Of course, black aphids will attack them indoors as well as out. Use some of the double fragrant varieties. Long, budded sprays cut early in the fall and placed in a vase of water will bloom for weeks indoors.

PETUNIA

How can I grow petunias in the house during the winter? I took a few in this fall and they wouldn't grow. Petunias make fine blooming house plants, especially under fluorescent lights. Lift in September, cut back tops, and set in quite small pots, for the root systems are not large. Give a clean-up spray, and after a week or so in a sheltered place outdoors, take to a sunny window. New shoots will appear and buds will develop about January. Syringe frequently at the sink to ward off aphids. Take cuttings from established plants to maintain a succession of bloom.

My petunia plants potted from the garden are growing well but the foliage feels sticky and there are a number of yellow leaves. Although petunia foliage is naturally a little sticky, this sounds like an attack of aphids. Examine the underside of the leaves; if you see tiny white dots and if water spraying (see above) doesn't clean up the infestation, try a house-plant bomb, or for a bad attack, a *weak* malathion spray.

SNAPDRAGON (ANTIRRHINUM)

Are snapdragons practical house plants? If you have a very cool sun porch or bay window (40° to 50° F. night temperature), you may be able to have blooming snapdragons (*Antirrhinum*) through the winter. Though these are perennial in the South, they are grown as annuals in the North. Buy budded plants or grow your own from seed planted the previous spring. Select dwarf, rust-resistant varieties. Or you can start plants in the summer for winter bloom by propagating by cuttings those growing in the summer garden. Whether plants are started from seeds or cuttings, they should be kept pinched back to encourage winter bloom.

Foliage Plants

GENERAL

What temperature is best for foliage plants indoors? No one temperature is best for all. The majority grow well in a night temperature of 55° to 60° F. with a rise of 10° in the daytime permitted. For cooler rooms, try English ivy, leopard-plant, Australian silk-oak, aspidistra, baby's-tears, pick-a-back plant, strawberry-geranium, spider-plant, and Norfolk-Island-pine.

Does it help to spray water on the leaves of foliage plants grown in the home?   Daily sprinklings with mist benefit all plants having leathery leaves, such as rubber plants, palms, and pandanus. On the mornings of bright, sunny days, syringe plants with thin or hairy leaves, such as coleus or pilea.

Some people tell me to wash my foliage plants with milk; others say to wipe the leaves with olive oil. Which is better?   Both are harmful. They merely result in an artificial gloss due to the oil or to the fat of the milk. When you sponge leaves, use lukewarm, soapy water.

My foliage plants indoors do well in the summer, but in the fall their leaves turn yellow and drop off. What is the cause?   When artificial heating is used the air becomes too dry for the plants. Lack of atmospheric moisture is one cause of failure with house plants. Install humidifiers. Stand the plants on shallow trays of sand or gravel, kept moist.

Can you give a list of foliage house plants that can easily be raised from seed?   *Eucalyptus globulus* (blue gum), *Eucalyptus citriodora* (lemon-scented eucalyptus), *Grevillea robusta* (Australian silk-oak), coleus, *Asparagus densiflorus* 'Sprengeri' and *Asparagus setaceus* (syn. *plumosus*) (asparagus-ferns), and *Cordyline indivisa* (*Dracaena indivisa*).

ARALIA   (See *Fatsia japonica*.)

ASPARAGUS

What kind of soil does Asparagus setaceus like—acid or alkaline?   More on the acid than the alkaline side. It likes a garden soil that has both peat moss and sand in it (2 parts soil, 1 part peat moss, 1 part sand); this should be enriched by ⅛ part (in bulk) of dried cow manure mixed with a sprinkling of superphosphate.

What are asparagus "ferns"?   Three are commonly grown: *Asparagus setaceus*, with flat sprays of fine foliage; *A. densiflorus* 'Sprengeri', with coarser and less regular leaves; and *A. densiflorus* 'Myers', with tightly clustered foliage. These foliage plants are not true ferns and are in the same genus as the vegetable. They are subject to red spider, so spray once a week with cool water. Transplant once a year, or whenever the pots become filled with roots. They like plenty of light and air. Water regularly and feed once a month. (See the next question.)

What are the water requirements of Asparagus 'Sprengeri'? Is it the moisture or temperature conditions that turn the foliage yellow? *Asparagus densiflorus* 'Sprengeri' likes adequate and regular watering. Once or twice a month, give liquid plant food. Leaves turn yellow from a lack of food, if the plant is pot-bound, or if the temperature is above or below 55° to 65° F.

How do I raise asparagus "ferns" from seed? Very easily. Soak the seed in tepid water for 24 hours before sowing, then plant 1 inch apart and cover to a depth of ¼ inch in light, sandy soil in a pot or pan. Keep moist, dark, and in a temperature of 65° to 70° F.

ASPIDISTRA ELATIOR (CAST-IRON PLANT)

Why do the leaves of my aspidistra turn yellow? Yellowing leaves mean either red spider mites are sucking the life out of them, that you have watered too much, or have exposed the plant to extreme drought. If red spider is the trouble, spray or sponge the leaves with any good contact insecticide.

Does the aspidistra plant ever bloom? Old, well-established plants sometimes do. The flowers are relatively inconspicuous, are reddish-brown, and are borne at soil level.

Can aspidistra be increased in any other way than by division? No. In nature it may propagate by seed, but seeds do not seem to form in cultivation. Divide in the spring and keep newly potted divisions in a warm room and a moist atmosphere until new roots become established.

AUSTRALIAN SILK-OAK (GREVILLEA ROBUSTA)

What kind of soil does Australian silk-oak (Grevillea robusta) like? A sandy and rather peaty mixture that does not tend to become waterlogged. Very heavy soil is unsuited to this plant, particularly in its young stages.

AVOCADO (PERSEA AMERICANA)

How can I raise an avocado plant from a seed? Select a seed from a ripe fruit. The seed should show signs of cracking and not appear hard

An avocado pit (seed) will develop into an attractive foliage plant. Insert toothpicks into the sides of the pit so it can be suspended in water. After it has sprouted and roots have formed, it can be potted.

and dry. Insert 3 toothpicks into the sides just deep enough to support the seed on the edge of a tumbler of water. Keep the water level just up to and touching the bottom of the seed; don't float or submerge the entire seed in water. In a few weeks, roots and shoot growth appear, and then the rooted seed can be placed in a 4-inch pot. Several pinchings of top growth will be necessary if you wish a bushy plant. When potting the seed, put about three fourths of it in the pot; the remainder can protrude above the surface.

BABY'S-TEARS (SOLEIROLIA SOLEIROLII)

What is the plant called baby's-tears and how can I grow it in the house? Baby's-tears, or creeping-nettle, formerly known as *Helxine soleirolii*, is a native of Corsica and Sardinia. It looks like a fine green moss and grows well in sandy soil, kept moist, in morning sun or very light shade, but it resents a hot, dry room. It is excellent for a terrarium. Baby's-tears is easily propagated by pulling it apart and setting the pieces in soil.

BAMBOO

Can bamboo be grown indoors as a house plant? Yes, some genera make handsome specimens in tubs in fully lighted, cool interiors. Keep the plants in relatively small containers and do not repot unless really pot-bound. They will need plenty of water and benefit from summering outdoors in light shade. The Chinese goddess (*Bambusa glaucescens riviereorum*) is often used indoors but may reach 6 feet in height. Other cultivars of *B. glaucescens* are worth considering and searching out, as some do not grow as tall.

BAY TREE (LAURUS NOBILIS)

Are there several varieties of bay trees, and how should they be treated? Mine were given me as a gift. I am at a loss as to how to keep them growing. You must be talking about sweet bay or laurel (*Laurus nobilis*), whose leaves are used as a flavoring. It is not hardy in cold climates. It eventually grows to large size. Tubbed specimens are best wintered in a cool, light situation with reduced watering.

BEAUCARNEA (BOTTLE-PALM)

What is the odd but intriguing plant with the swollen base and stem topped by a cascade of ribbon foliage? The elephant-foot plant or bottle ponytail or bottle-palm (*Beaucarnea recurvata*), an oddity that becomes handsome as it ages. It is a long-lived plant that enlarges slowly, tolerating a wide range of indoor temperatures and low humidity. The swollen part of the stem holds moisture. Allow soil to dry out between waterings and water sparingly during the winter.

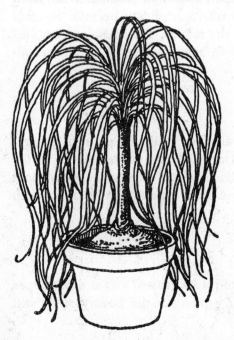

Ponytail or bottle-palm are two names for Beaucarnea recurvata. *This foliage plant has a gray trunk swollen at its base. The plant grows slowly and, though tolerant of neglect, speeds up its growth and improves in appearance when given daily sun and water as the soil dries.*

CHINESE-EVERGREEN (AGLAONEMA MODESTUM)

What are the requirements of Chinese-evergreen, so often grown indoors in water? *Aglaonema modestum* is a very satisfactory house plant for rooms with little sun. Grown in water to which a few small pieces of charcoal have been added to keep the water "sweet," it behaves well in average living-room conditions. A ¼-strength solution of water-soluble house-plant fertilizer can be used instead of water, once the stems have roots.

COLEUS

Can I dig up coleus plants from the garden and put them into pots for winter decoration indoors? If plants are cut back at the time of potting, they may grow into decorative specimens by late winter; but a much better plan is to take cuttings from outdoor plants in August, root them in sand, and pot them up to provide young new plants for your indoor garden.

How can coleus be raised as house plants? Mine always become sickly. Coleus are raised from seed or cuttings. They like full light, temperatures not above 65° F. in the winter, and protection from mealybugs.

Mealybugs on my coleus are a constant source of trouble. What shall I do? Mealybugs on coleus are difficult to eradicate because forceful syringing with water is apt to damage the leaves. Try brushing them off with a soft camel's-hair brush dipped in soapy water or denatured alcohol.

CROTON (CODIAEUM)

I have a croton, potted in fibrous loam, but while the plant in general does well, sometimes leaves wilt and drop. What causes this? If the plant is growing outdoors, cool spells may be the cause. This plant loves lots of heat. It is not a good house plant unless high humidity with heat is provided.

CRYPTANTHUS (EARTH STAR)

What is a cryptanthus and how should it be grown? It is a miniature bromeliad (pineapple relative) that is grown for the beauty of its stiff little leaves. For best foliage color, give some exposure to the sun or grow under lights. It grows best in a terrarium or in a warm room where the air is not too dry. Pot in a sandy, humus-rich soil with charcoal added, or in a mixture of bark and leafmold.

DIZYGOTHECA (FALSE-ARALIA)

How can I grow dizygotheca? This treelike false-aralia is not demanding and thrives at 55° to 75° F. Give it good light and keep the soil evenly moist. A 5-inch pot is usually about right.

DUMB-CANE (DIEFFENBACHIA)

I have a dumb-cane (dieffenbachia) in the house and the lower leaves turn yellow. What shall I do? Too low a temperature or lack of moisture in the air are the most common causes of yellowing. Excessive dryness at the roots may be a contributing cause. This plant likes warmth, a moist atmosphere, shade from strong sunshine, and a fair amount of soil moisture.

Why is dieffenbachia called dumb-cane? Is it poisonous? It is not poisonous, but, like its relative the Jack-in-the-pulpit, it contains sharp crystals of oxalate of lime. If the stem is chewed, these pierce the tongue, causing it to swell with intense pain. Speech may be impossible for several days—hence the common name.

Can a "leggy" dieffenbachia be successfully air-layered? The plant is 30 inches high. Cut halfway through, diagonally and upward. Insert a toothpick and bind with a large ball of sphagnum moss. Then wrap tightly in plastic, binding at each end with wire fasteners. A thick stem may take a year before it is rooted enough for you to cut below the moss and place it in a pot. Set leftover cane section on moist unmilled sphagnum moss if you want sprouts from the dormant buds.

FALSE-ARALIA   (See Dizygotheca.)

FATSIA JAPONICA

Is Fatsia japonica a house plant? It is an easy subject to grow in a light window where the temperature ranges between 55° and 65° F. Shade from bright summer sunshine is desirable. Water to keep the soil always evenly moist but not waterlogged.

How can Fatsia japonica be raised from seed?   Sow seed in pots of light, sandy soil in the spring; cover seeds with sifted soil. Keep moist and at a temperature of 65° F. When an inch or two high, transplant to small pots of sandy soil. Grow in a light window.

FERNS   (See under separate headings, this section.)

FIG, WEEPING (FICUS BENJAMINA)

Can I propagate the weeping fig from cuttings?   Yes. Use tip cuttings and insert them in a soilless mix. Enclose the pot or flat in polyethylene.

HOLLY (ILEX)

I have a dwarf holly plant in a pot. Can it be made to fruit indoors?   Holly is not a house plant, but some species are not hardy except in the South and can be grown for a time indoors in a cool location. Most hollies are unisexual and fruit is not possible unless both types (a male plant and a female plant) are grown near each other.

LEOPARD-PLANT (LIGULARIA)

Is the leopard-plant classed as a foliage or a flowering plant?   Like most "foliage plants," *Ligularia kaempferi* 'Aureo-maculata' blooms (and the yellow flowers are quite attractive) but it is grown primarily for the beauty of its large, rounded leaves, which are conspicuously spotted with yellow markings.

Under what conditions does the leopard-plant grow best? How is it propagated?   It likes a rather cool room with full sun or partial shade. Provide a freely drained soil, but enough water to keep it always moist. In the summer, plunge the pot to its rim outdoors in a partially shaded position in the garden. Propagate by dividing the old plant in the spring.

MANGO (MANGIFERA INDICA)

I am raising a mango tree from seed. Do you think it will bear?   Not indoors. The mango is a large tropical tree that sometimes attains a height of nearly 100 feet. It is hardy only in the most tropical parts of the United States. Fruits of seedling mangoes are very inferior to named varieties but they make very attractive foliage plants for a well-lighted, rather cool situation indoors.

MARANTA (PRAYER-PLANT)

How should Maranta leuconeura and its variety kerchoviana be cared for? Marantas, grown chiefly for their unusual foliage, are tropical plants which flourish in the winter at a north window with evenly moist soil and 40 to 50 per cent humidity. They rest in late fall. When some leaves turn brown, especially around the edges, cut them off. Then keep the plant quite dry until about February. Then water freely again and fertilize regularly. It is often called prayer-plant because it folds its leaves at night.

MONSTERA (SWISS-CHEESE PLANT)

What is the foliage plant, of climbing habit, with large, heart-shaped cut leaves? You are probably referring to *Monstera deliciosa,* a very showy foliage plant which looks well in modern rooms and which can be grown in good light without direct sun. Though a climber, it grows rather slowly and is usually treated as a foliage plant, trained on cork bark. It has many other common names, including Mexican breadfruit.

NEPHTHYTIS (SYNGONIUM PODOPHYLLUM)

What are the requirements of nephthytis? Nephthytis is a tropical vinelike foliage plant which usually comes from the grower trained on cork bark. It does not need full sunlight and stands ordinary living-room conditions well. Trailing portions cut from the main plant do well grown in water.

NORFOLK-ISLAND-PINE (ARAUCARIA HETEROPHYLLA)

How do we take care of Norfolk-Island-pine during the summer? This evergreen tree makes a good but slow-growing pot plant. During the summer, sink the pot outside in soil up to the pot's rim in light shade and syringe and water regularly. In the winter, it prefers a temperature of 55° to 60° F., and even light to keep it shapely. Spray regularly to prevent red spider mite and mealybug attacks.

I have had an araucaria for the past 4 years. It is now 40 inches high. The branches are starting to droop. Can you suggest the reason? It is natural for lower branches eventually to droop. If the plant is really wilting, you have either overwatered or given too much fertilizer with perhaps not enough light and too much heat. Stimulants are not called for when plants droop. Keep cool and water less in the winter.

The Norfolk-Island-pine is a beautiful evergreen that can eventually reach 5 to 6 feet. It grows best in cool indoor temperatures, 50° to 55° F. at night and 60° to 65° F. during the day.

PALM

How shall I take care of a date palm?   (1) Temperature from 55° to 65° F.; (2) soil—loam, peat moss, and sand, proportions 5–3–1; also, a 5-inch pot for a 6-foot specimen; (3) watering—never completely dry but not too wet; deep occasional soaking in a pail or tub; (4) exposure —bright light.

Is there any special fertilizer or treatment to give palm trees and how often must they be watered?   Palms need full shade and must never be dry, yet not constantly soaking wet. No feeding is needed until the pots are full of root.

What possibility is there of growing palms?   Many palms are good house plants if given full light but not direct sun and are not subjected to dry, hot rooms in winter. The dwarf *Chamaedorea elegans* adapts well to indoor pot culture.

PANDANUS (SCREW-PINE)

How should I care for a pandanus plant?   Keep out of bright sunshine and use care in watering. It is easy to kill this plant with overwatering.

My pandanus leaves are turning yellow, especially at the tips. What is the cause? This is a sure sign of root trouble; you probably have overwatered. Keep it on the dry side and don't use too large a pot. Don't expose it to bright sunshine.

How and when should shoots from pandanus be rooted? Cut off the suckers at the base and insert them in sandy soil. If you can place the pot in a box and cover it with a sheet of glass or plastic, all the better. Do this in the spring, when growth is active.

PEPEROMIA

How can I grow the striped peperomia (P. argyreia) successfully? Peperomias require fairly warm, humid conditions and protection from direct sunshine. A humus-rich soil (well-drained), kept uniformly moist, is desirable.

Rooted leaf cutting of peperomia.

What causes small brown spots on the underside of peperomia leaves? Spots on the underside suggest injury from thrips or other insects. Poor foliage generally is due either to sunburn, lack of moisture in the atmosphere, or too much water on the leaves.

My peperomia gets large, irregular brown spots on the back of the leaves. Can you tell me why and what to do? Such spots or patches are usually an indication of disease brought about by atmospheric conditions. Try to increase the humidity.

PICK-A-BACK (TOLMIEA)

What is the pick-a-back plant? *Tolmiea menziesii,* a native of our Pacific Northwest. It has the curious habit of producing young plantlets on its leaves from which new plants can be grown. It is an interesting, worthwhile house plant.

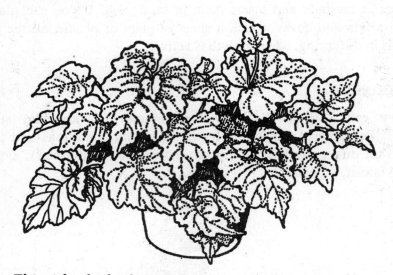

The pick-a-back plant (Tolmiea menziesii) *is an oddity among foliage plants. It forms plantlets on its growing leaves.*

How shall I care for the pick-a-back plant? Grow in pots of light, rich soil. Keep quite moist at all times. It thrives in full sun or partial shade. Although a hardy plant, it seems not to object to ordinary room temperatures as long as its potting soil does not dry out. Propagate by planting well-developed plantlets that are borne on mature leaves.

PINEAPPLE (ANANAS)

How can I start a pineapple plant? Cut off most of the leafy top, leaving a little attached to a small section of the fruit. Scoop out the pulp and let the cut surface dry for a few days. Then plant the top in a pot of sandy soil. (Do not keep sopping wet or rot will occur—and no roots.) New shoots will soon push out from the old top.

What can I do with a pineapple plant that is nearly 2 years old and does not seem to grow any more? It stands nearly 8 inches high now.

Doesn't it flower? If a true pineapple (*Ananas comosus*), grown from the tuft of the fruit, it needs full sun to bloom. Perhaps you have a different species. Flowers are not showy but dwarf *Ananas nanus* is interesting for the miniature pineapple fruit it eventually bears. Variegated-leaf pineapples (*A. comosus 'Variegatus'*) are also attractive in a sunny window. To encourage bloom and fruiting on a mature pineapple, place the plant in a warm room in a clear plastic bag with a ripe apple for a week. The ethylene gas from the apple forces flowering. Although the pineapple is an interesting plant, there are other members of the bromeliad family that make better house plants, take less space, and have more attractive foliage. For example, *Aechmea fasciata*, *Billbergia zebrina*, and the various dwarf terrestrial *Cryptanthus* cultivars.

The pineapple is a bromeliad. It can become a house plant by rooting the top saved from a fruit.

What care is needed for the pineapple plant? The true pineapple needs plenty of warmth, light, and sun, and very careful watering, as it quickly resents very wet conditions at the root. Frequent feedings (2 a week) with a balanced fertilizer are of great help to a healthy plant.

POMEGRANATE (PUNICA GRANATUM)

Can pomegranates be grown from seed? Yes, they can, and if wanted merely as house plants they are quite satisfactory. For fruit production (when they can be grown outdoors), named varieties are used, and these will not come true from seed.

How are pomegranates propagated? By hardwood cuttings planted in open nursery beds in February; by taking rooted shoots directly from the base of the plant; by layering; by green cuttings taken in the summer.

REDWOOD BURL (SEQUOIA SEMPERVIRENS)

How long will a redwood burl last? Also, can a sprout of it be rooted and grown as a pot plant? A burl kept with its base in a shallow container of water lived and thrived for many years at the New York Botanical Garden. Sprouts sometimes form roots when the atmosphere is humid. If you wish to encourage rooting, put damp sphagnum moss around the base of active green sprouts and keep the plant in a bright location at a moderate temperature, 50° to 60° F., at night.

RUBBER PLANT (FICUS)

What care is needed in watering and feeding rubber trees grown as house plants? *Ficus elastica,* the recognized rubber plant of early days, and *F. lyrata* like good light and lots of room, as they eventually become very tall, rarely branching. Give plenty of water except in winter when growth is less active. Occasionally wipe its leaves with a damp cloth. A more compact selection which often has small yellow "figlets" is *F. deltoidea,* the mistletoe fig. It makes a good indoor bonsai subject.

How does one encourage the rubber plant to branch out rather than grow as a single upright stem? *Ficus elastica* is not very responsive to being cut back, but if done after the plant has 6 or 8 leaves, removal of the point will induce 2 or 3 breaks. The natural habit is to grow single stemmed for many years before branching.

Can I cut back a large rubber plant when the trunk is thick? *Ficus elastica,* if cut back, may die from the shock if it is treelike and has no lower leaves. The regular method of propagation is to slit the stem partly through, wrap with moss, and keep constantly moist. If your plant has a branch with a ½-inch stem, you can so treat the branch, but if there are no branches and the trunk is really heavy, 1 inch or more, it's too large for this air-layering method.

What is the name of the rubber plant with leaves that widen out toward the tips? What culture does it need? This is the fiddle-leaved fig (or rubber plant), *Ficus lyrata.* It requires the same general care as the common rubber plant, *F. elastica.*

SAGO-PALM (CYCAS REVOLUTA)

I have a sago-palm in a pot. It is about 20 years old, but I've had it only 5 months. It hasn't done well since I brought it inside. Can you

give its proper care? *Cycas revoluta* likes bright light and a sandy soil. Avoid overwatering, especially in the winter when the plants are inactive, but never allow them to dry out completely. In the fall, don't be alarmed if the lower leaves turn brown and drop. It's natural for them to drop as new ones are produced.

SCHEFFLERA (BRASSAIA ACTINOPHYLLA)

Is the schefflera a good house plant? Yes, if you have plenty of room for a tub specimen. It is easy to grow, producing decorative leaves and sometimes red flowers (but only on aged plants), even under less than ideal conditions of 55° to 75° F. It requires full light, not sun, and water only when somewhat dry, about once or twice a week. It is decorative in front of a long window of a modern house, or for a well-lighted public room.

SENSITIVE-PLANT (MIMOSA PUDICA)

How can I grow a sensitive-plant in my sunny window? Sow seeds of *Mimosa pudica* in a pot of light soil in March. Transplant seedlings into a 2½-inch pot when the second set of leaves is well grown. Later, pot into a 4-inch pot. Use special care to keep as many roots as possible since *M. pudica* resents being transplanted. Grow in well-drained soil with a minimum temperature of 60° F. Never permit it to suffer from dryness.

SNAKE-PLANT (SANSEVIERIA)

Under what conditions will sansevieria do best? In dry, moderately warm rooms with full light. Water carefully once a week. This is enough under ordinary conditions, as it is easily killed by overwatering.

I can never get sansevieria to grow and do well. Why? Too much water and not enough light. This plant, when well rooted, does not require frequent watering. Shade is also detrimental.

My sansevieria plant had flowers on it this summer. Is this unusual? Not as unusual as is sometimes thought. Old, well-established specimens are apt to bloom, and once they begin, they repeat the performance year after year. The flowers are light greenish, on feathery spikes, and are very fragrant.

How does one increase sansevierias? These are grown from divisions of roots or rhizomes. Pieces of leaf planted in moist sand will root and make plants, but if you so treat the variegated sort, the young plants will be green-leaved rather than variegated.

SPIDER-PLANT (CHLOROPHYTUM COMOSUM)

Please describe the spider-plant.   The form 'Variegatum' has green-and white-striped leaves and sends out long, slender stems which bear young plants at their extremities. It is very easy to grow and also most decorative. Grow in a light place and take care not to overwater. Cut off the plantlets and pot them if you want more plants, but it does not harm the parent plant to let offsets stay. They are an added interest. Another name is airplane plant.

STRAWBERRY-GERANIUM (SAXIFRAGA STOLONIFERA)

What will encourage the growth of strawberry-geranium? Should it be kept on the dry side? In the sun or shade?   *Saxifraga stolonifera,* also known as mother of thousands, is usually winter hardy in the North if protected by a cover of leaves. Don't try to grow it in a hot, dry room, or it will become infested with red spider. Sun or bright light is good. Provide moderate supplies of water. If you want runners bearing young plants to develop, grow it in a hanging basket.

UMBRELLA-PLANT (CYPERUS ALTERNIFOLIUS)

What conditions does the feathery green plant called umbrella-plant require?   This is really a bog plant and needs a moist or wet soil. It is one of the few house plants that does well if the pot is kept standing in a saucer of water; it prefers plenty of sunshine.

How are young plants of the umbrella-plant raised?   *Cyperus alternifolius* is easily raised from seeds sown in soil kept constantly moist. Another method of increase is to cut off the leafy top with about an inch of stem attached and submerge the stem in a pot of sandy soil.

VARIEGATED PLANTS

What plants with colorful leaves can be grown among green plants at well-lighted windows?   These make pleasing accents with green plants: purple-tinted velvet-plant; prayer-plant (*Maranta*) with maroon or silver markings; also aucuba, aphelandra, columnea, sansevieria, episcia, fittonia, various kinds of dracena, *Cissus discolor,* and many kinds of begonia. In the summer, a few pots of caladiums will enliven collections of house plants sojourning on the terrace, as will New Guinea impatiens, which have brightly variegated foliage, too.

VELVET-PLANT (GYNURA AURANTIACA)

I have a foliage plant with velvety purple leaves. What is it and how shall I care for it? This is *Gynura aurantiaca* or velvet-plant. Place it in an east window and water freely. It is of easy culture.

Gift Plants

AZALEA (RHODODENDRON)

What is the proper soil for azaleas and other ericaceous plants? Acid, well-drained, and humus-rich soil. The addition of liberal amounts of oak leafmold or peat moss to the mixture is recommended. (See Soil, Acid Potting Mixture, this section.)

How shall I care for a tender azalea after it blooms? Keep it well watered, in full light, in a room at 50° F. If it is overlarge for the pot, shift to a pot 1 inch larger, soaking the soil well after repotting. Use an acid potting mixture. Pot firmly but do not ram the earth down hard.

Should I cut back my indoor azaleas, and when? No, merely pinch back any extra-long shoots, but don't prune in the usual way for shrubs or the plants may die. Azaleas make only short growths each year.

What care is needed for an azalea plant grown indoors? Pot azaleas should be indoors only during the winter and while in bloom. From mid-May on the pot should be sunk in the ground, with light shade, regular watering and spraying, and pinching back of overlong growths. Use a general or liquid fish fertilizer occasionally. Bring indoors to a cool room before severe frost.

How should I treat my tender azalea plants after bringing them indoors in autumn? Keep just moist, in a light, cool room at 40° F. until 4 weeks before you want full bloom, then bring into a warmer, sunny room, water plentifully, and mist foliage daily. Give a complete fertilizer until color shows on the buds.

Should an azalea plant have a rest period during the winter? Yes. After being brought indoors before severe frost, a potted azalea must be kept cool (40° to 60° F.) and just moist until after Christmas. In January or February, bring to a sunny but cool window, fertilize as new growth develops, and syringe the tops frequently to ward off red spider.

How can I tell whether my tender azalea is going to bloom? The buds should be well set when brought indoors in the fall.

An Easter azalea plant was put aside and forgotten after blooming until it was discovered in November in a dry, warm cellar. Is this plant dormant or really dead? An azalea so treated is dead—or it ought to be! Don't waste time on it. Azaleas after flowering need a cool place, moderate water, and good light before being sunk outdoors. The plants that flower in pots are practically evergreen and should never be bare of all leaves.

How are evergreen azaleas propagated? These are easily rooted from cuttings, using the short shoots that come after blooming. Root in sand and peat moss in a propagating box or in a pot enclosed in a plastic bag.

I was presented with a fine azalea plant. Why has it shed all its leaves? You either let it get dry at the roots or the foliage became infested with red spider. Both will cause defoliation, and, if complete, the plant cannot be revived.

I have an azalea which I purchased 2 years ago. Last year it bloomed beautifully. Now it is dying. Can you give me any help in the care of the plant? Your rooms are probably too hot and dry. Keep the plant in as cool a place as possible. Once a week, submerge the pot up to the rim and let it stay until the topsoil feels moist.

Should I plant outdoors a pink-flowered azalea purchased in a florist's shop? (Vermont.) If your azalea is small-flowered, it is a Kurume, and there's little chance of its surviving a winter outdoors in your state. If large-flowered, it positively will winter-kill. If you want garden azaleas, plant sorts listed as such. (For correct care of your azalea, see previous questions.)

I have a small-flowered and a large-flowered house azalea. Can you tell me what they are? There are many named varieties of azaleas grown as potted plants.

CHRYSANTHEMUM

How long can chrysanthemums be kept flowering indoors? Two weeks is average. Spraying daily with cool water will help to keep foliage fresh-looking and prevent its turning brown and dry before the flowers fade. Keep in a cool location.

Are any of the potted chrysanthemums used for gift plants hardy

enough to be transferred to a garden? Yes, but the kind of chrysanthemum as well as your climate must be considered. And, of course, the time of year you receive the plant determines when it can be planted in the garden.

Is there any way to save chrysanthemum plants sent in the fall from the florist? They don't winter over outside. After they bloom, cut their stems down, store the pot in a cool, light cellar or shed, and water occasionally. Sink in the garden in April. Lift in September and bring into a very cool plant room, water and fertilize, and hope for bloom.

How can one best grow chrysanthemums to bloom during the months of November, December, and January? We have the severe cold of Lake Erie and a long winter. Could they be brought into the house when winter comes and so bloom during these months? Pinch plants well early in the season. Pot from the garden in early October. Use late varieties. Give a sunny location in a cool room.

CYCLAMEN (CYCLAMEN PERSICUM)

Why does cyclamen always die a few days after it comes from the florist? The commercial grower grew the plant in a moist atmosphere and a temperature of 40° to 50° F. Living-room conditions are too warm and dry; however, you should be able to keep the plant for a few weeks if you can find a window where its ideal requirements are more nearly met.

The leaves on the cyclamen I received for Christmas are turning yellow. What caused this? The sudden change from a greenhouse to the dry, hot atmosphere of a house is responsible. Cyclamen should be kept cool, well watered, and away from too much sunlight. An east or west window is best. Syringe their tops daily, water more than once a day from the edge of the pot, and move to cold, not freezing, quarters at night—perhaps the garage floor.

How cold is it safe to have cyclamen when flowering, and when not flowering? At 40° to 45° F. a plant in flower will be far happier and last much longer than in a room of 60° to 70° F. After it blooms, gradually dry the plant off and rest it in the cellar or in a cold frame outdoors. Repot in July, and with luck you may get the corm to start again. Or try a newer system. Set on the porch or terrace in the summer and don't dry off the plant at all, just water less after bloom is over and until new growth appears.

How shall I water cyclamen plants during their flowering period? If cyclamens are kept cool enough—40° to 50° F.—they will not dry out quickly. If kept in a hot room, watering freely and frequently may prolong their lives for a week or two, although it will not take the place of a low temperature. Water from below or at the top around the edge of the pot, keeping the soil moist but not soggy.

How long must you let a pot of cyclamen soak in a pan of water to wet it thoroughly?   If the water in the pan is halfway up the pot and the soil is moderately dry, allow to soak 10 to 15 minutes, then stand in the sink to drain off the surplus. You can tell from the feel of the topsoil whether the whole soil mass has been moistened.

Are cyclamens difficult as window-garden plants?   Cyclamens are among the most difficult of all plants for the overheated living room. Old corms that have blossomed can be dried off and kept dormant in a cool place until July, but it's a 50–50 chance to get them to start up strongly again.

How long should a cyclamen bloom?   Cyclamen should flower either in a greenhouse or under favorable home conditions from Christmastime until April, depending on the number of buds. Remove faded blooms.

Should faded blooms be removed from cyclamen with a knife or scissors?   Neither. Get a firm grip on the stem of a dead flower or yellowed leaf and give a sharp pull. It comes out cleanly.

Can one grow cyclamens from seed? What soil should I use and how long is it before blooming?   Seedlings are easy to start if seed is sown thinly in a soilless mix in July or August; but after that, troubles begin. If you can simulate greenhouse conditions for 18 months and can keep the plants free of mites and other pests, you might succeed. Plants like a compost of good loam, sand, rotted manure or rich compost, and peat moss; shade during the summer, yet full light; careful watering; high humidity and frequent spraying; and in the fall and winter, a temperature not above 55° F. More adaptable and long-blooming are recently developed dwarf strains that can be grown from seed.

GENISTA (CYTISUS CANARIENSIS)

Can anything be done with a genista after it has stopped blooming? (New York.)   Genistas (the greenhouse kinds) are strictly gift plants, not even good house plants for any length of time. They are not hardy outdoors in the vicinity of New York. Keep in a sunny window, water well, and see that there is circulation of air around them. Don't crowd genistas in with a lot of other plants.

HYDRANGEA (HYDRANGEA MACROPHYLLA)

Why did my hydrangea die the day after I received it as a gift? The hydrangea does not die that quickly. If the leaves and flowers wilt, it is suffering from a lack of water. Immerse the whole pot in a pail of water for 20 minutes. It will revive immediately.

How long should a hydrangea flower in the house? It should flower not less than 3 weeks. Keep it away from a hot, sunny window and heat outlets. Water thoroughly twice a day.

What care and treatment should be given pot hydrangeas? Florists' hydrangeas are propagated from cuttings in early spring, grown in 4-inch pots that are sunk in the open ground during the summer, and well fed. Put into larger pots in September and place in a cold frame with a sash, but keep well ventilated. Bring inside before hard freezing and keep in a cool cellar at 40° F. until late December or January. Give just enough water to prevent drying, although leaves will fall off. Start in full light at 50° F.—never above 60° F. Give plenty of water at all times and lots of light. After blooming, cut back well and carry outside during the summer if a large specimen is wanted the next season.

What must I do to make a pot hydrangea bloom in March or April? If you have only living-room facilities, don't expect to do what commercial growers can't always manage. A hydrangea has to rest in a cold place until late December. Start into growth at 50° F. and never above 60° F. Grow it cool, or you'll have a flowerless plant.

Can my hydrangea be planted in the garden after it has stopped flowering? Yes. After it has finished blooming, cut back its stems about half their length, remove the plant from the pot, and plant in a garden where it will have plenty of room. It will grow into a big, shrubby plant. Water well.

I would like to know something about hydrangeas. Are they hardy? The florists' hydrangeas are hardy, but in areas where hard freezing occurs, the wood is killed to the ground. If you have a variety that will bloom on the new wood, well and good. If not, and the wood is killed back, you'll never see any flowers. Such kinds have to be kept in pots and brought indoors and rested during the winter.

Twice I have purchased plants of hydrangea 'Bluebird', and after potting, new shoots appeared, but in a week or two the plants died. The potting mixture had a pH of about 4.5. Temperature, watering, and light conditions apparently perfect. What was wrong? If you bought actively growing young plants, why not in pots? Why did you use such extremely acid soil? Unless your soil is naturally alkaline, forget the pH and use a good rich compost with waterings as suggested below.

What element is it that makes the hydrangea flowers blue or pink? Acidity of the soil causes blue flowers, but some varieties become blue more readily than others. Repeated watering with alum solution or aluminum sulfate (1 level teaspoon to 1 gallon of water) will cause blueness. Add 1 tablespoon of alum to the potting mixture to get pink flowers.

JERUSALEM-CHERRY (SOLANUM PSEUDOCAPSICUM)

Why do leaves and berries fall off a Jerusalem-cherry soon after I receive it? If your house is hot, Jerusalem-cherry will not survive. It likes a cool room (about 50° F.), plenty of water, and a location away from chills or drafts. Spraying the leaves daily may help. It is a poor house plant.

Are the fruits of Jerusalem-cherry edible? No. They are poisonous.

How shall I treat a Jerusalem-cherry after it has fruited? Unless you want to grow a big specimen, throw the plant away. Old plants can be cut back a little, kept on the dry side until spring, then shifted into a larger pot and put outdoors with slight shade during the summer. Give plenty of water and feed; bring indoors in September.

When should the seed of Jerusalem-cherries be sown for Christmas fruiting? Sow the seed in January or February. Grow in pots and plant outdoors in late May. Lift carefully with the root ball in September, pot, and shade until established, then place in a bright window or greenhouse. Selected types can be raised from cuttings taken early in the year.

KALANCHOE

What care does this holiday plant require? Cut off the faded flower stems above the foliage; more will push up and probably continue to appear until May. This succulent will thrive in a 72° F. living room and does not require high humidity. Take care not to overwater—every third day is usually enough. Be on the watch for mealybugs among the tight leaves.

How should I handle my kalanchoe to make it bloom again next Christmas? In the spring, repot it in a gritty soil—half humus and half perlite—and place in semishade for the summer. Bring indoors before frost. Since this is a "short day" plant, requiring 12 to 14 hours of darkness for 3 weeks before Christmas to produce buds, move it to a dark closet about 6 P.M. every night and let it stay until 8 A.M. from Thanksgiving on. Bring it to full sunshine during the day.

Are there kalanchoes in other colors besides red, which doesn't look nice with the color scheme of my living room? Yes, there are yellow, cream, coral, and pink varieties you can grow from seed or buy as plants from florists and garden centers.

ORNAMENTAL PEPPER (CAPSICUM ANNUUM)

How can ornamental peppers be kept small and full of bloom as you see them in the markets? Try the compact 'Holiday Time' and 'Holiday Cheer' and other varieties you will find in seed catalogs. Raise from seed annually in the spring and grow in full light. You can't expect the plants grown in a window to equal those grown in a greenhouse, but growing under fluorescent lights will result in well-shaped, bushy plants. Or plant outside for the summer and pot up in August indoors in 5-inch pots at temperatures of 50° to 60° F.

Are the fruits of the Christmas pepper poisonous? No, but they are hot and should be used as a condiment with discretion. You can dry the fruits as you would hot peppers grown in the vegetable garden. The fruits of Jerusalem-cherry, a pot plant also available around the holidays, are poisonous.

POINSETTIA (EUPHORBIA PULCHERRIMA)

Are the pink and white poinsettias harder to grow than the red ones? The Mikkelsen, Ecke, and other pink hybrids do beautifully, often holding their color until June, as do the newer red varieties. The greenish whites may not hold longer than two months and are difficult to make bloom a second year.

Will my poinsettia bloom again? How should it be treated? Care for it as you do your house plants, keeping it growing as long as possible. Flowers, really bracts, often last until June; if they drop sooner, set the plants in a 50° to 60° F. place and water just enough to prevent complete dryness. After frost danger is over, take your plant outside, cut its stems back to 2 to 3 inches, repot in fresh soil mixture, keep in a light open place, and water and feed weekly with a liquid fertilizer. As new leaves form, pinch back to keep growth low. Bring in about mid-September and make certain the plant gets complete darkness, as in a closet or cardboard carton, for at least 12 hours for 70 days. Water as necessary.

I carried over a poinsettia last year and it made good growth but never bloomed. What was wrong?   One cause is keeping it near a light at night. The poinsettia is a "short-day" plant, and if placed in a room where the lights are on several hours every evening, it won't bloom.

I raised a poinsettia this summer in a pot in the yard and brought it in the house in October. Just as the buds for the blooms started, they dried up and fell off. I saw some fine web. Has some minute insect done the damage?   Bring indoors earlier if in your part of the country it gets cool at night after August. The web suggests red spider. Regular spraying is needed to prevent this and mealybug attack.

After bringing in poinsettias from a summer in the garden (in September), how can one "hold them back" from blooming until about Christmastime?   Yours is an exceptional case. The trouble with most people is to get them to flower. Temperature should not be above 60° F. at night. Too high a temperature will cause premature, poorly developed blooms.

I brought some dormant poinsettias from California in May, planted them, and they grew; when cold weather came, I carefully potted them. Why did they wither and die?   Poinsettias in growth won't tolerate root disturbance.

If you cut poinsettias close to the soil, will they sprout again?   Poinsettias may be cut back two thirds while quite dormant, but when actively growing, no cutting back should be practiced unless the young shoots are to be rooted as cuttings.

When and how does one make cuttings from poinsettias and grow them into blooming plants?   The cuttings are taken off when they are 4 to 6 inches long and rooted in sand between June and August—the latter date for small plants. They need a greenhouse to grow successfully.

Should poinsettia cuttings be started in part sand? What temperature is needed?   Short 4- to 6-inch cuttings will root either in plain sand or a sandy soil. Successful growers use a bottom heat at 70° F. with high humidity. They can be rooted outdoors in June or July in a shady place.

Is it safe to remove the ferns that are sometimes planted around the base of a gift poinsettia?   Yes. These are probably *Pteris tremula* and make excellent house plants. When you take your poinsettia outdoors in June and repot it, remove the ferns and pot them separately.

ROSE (ROSA)

Are roses good house plants?   As a general rule, no. However, miniature roses thrive in a bright window or under fluorescent lights. Several nurseries specialize in these small roses. The large-flowered gift plants received at Eastertime will flower for about 2 weeks and then should go into the garden. While indoors, spray the foliage daily with tepid water and give the soil plenty of moisture. Placing the plant on a pebble-filled saucer of water increases humidity.

Can miniature or baby roses in small pots be grown indoors and if so how?   Miniature roses do well in the window garden or under lights if properly cared for. Give them a sunny spot in a cool room or window (not above 60° to 65° F. daytime temperature and 10° lower at night). Water daily or whenever the soil is dry, but do not let the water stand in the saucers. Frequent syringing of foliage is helpful. Turn the pots frequently to receive maximum sunshine. After their bloom is over, prune as you would garden roses and decrease watering to encourage a resting period of 2 to 3 months. In the spring, when outdoor roses are starting, repot and sink them in their pots in a sunny place. Or, if you prefer to grow them as outdoor plants, remove them from their pots and plant in a well-enriched bed. They are perfectly hardy.

Shrubs

AZALEA   (See Gift Plants.)

CAMELLIA

How should a camellia plant be grown?   Place a pot or tub in light shade outdoors in the summer. Bring inside in September. Its night temperature should be 50° F. It requires sun. Keep the soil always moist, but not waterlogged. In the spring, after the plant blooms, repot it or topdress as necessary. Feed once a week when good growth is being made.

When should I pot my camellia and in what soil mixture?   Never repot unless the soil is obviously unsuitable or unless the pots are crowded with roots. Do this as soon as flower buds have set. The soil should be acid and consist of good loam, leafmold and/or peat moss, sharp sand, with some superphosphate and dried cow manure added. After potting, spray frequently with clear water. Avoid overwatering.

What about pruning camellias? Prune only sufficiently to keep the plant shapely. Thin crowded plants by removing weak growths. Cut back any long, straggly shoots. Do this immediately after they flower. Remember, flowering shoots for the following year arise from the base of the flower; cutting back flowering shoots destroys the following year's bloom.

How can buds be kept from falling off a camellia plant? It was just loaded with buds when I took it in this fall and all but 3 fell off. Indoor camellias ordinarily lose buds: (1) because the indoor temperature is too high and the atmosphere too dry; (2) lack of sufficient moisture; (3) lack of light.

Can a camellia be grown in the house? How old must it be to bloom? Camellias are not satisfactory house plants unless, perhaps, you can keep them in a cool window or plant room. In the wintertime, they are harmed by temperatures higher than 50° to 60° F. Plants often bloom when quite young—3 or 4 years old.

The indoor camellia plant has conditions in my home similar to gardenias. Is this right? Is it a sun-loving plant? (New York.) Camellias need cooler growing conditions than the florists' gardenia. They enjoy sunshine and a free circulation of air. It is important that the soil be kept reasonably moist.

Can one start camellias from a bud in the winter? Not from a flower bud. Camellias are propagated by cuttings, grafting, and layering. July is a good time to take cuttings.

What shall I do to prevent scale on my camellia plants indoors? Frequent syringing of the leaves with cool water is helpful. You can pick off a few or rub them off with a soapy sponge. If the attack is severe, use an aerosol spray containing malathion.

CITRUS FRUITS

What sort of potting soil shall I use for citrus fruit trees grown as house plants? A general-purpose potting mixture.

I have a grapefruit tree grown from seed, now 10 years old, 8 to 10 feet tall, in good condition. I plant it out-of-doors during the summer and in a wooden tub in the winter. Why has it never bloomed? You should not be shifting your grapefruit plant from open ground and back into a tub. Keep it in the tub. But seedling grapefruits are capricious as to time of blooming, particularly when grown as house plants. In the winter, they should be grown in cool temperatures, 40° to 50° F., and light, airy conditions.

Can you give me information about the indoor culture of dwarf ponderosa lemon trees—type of soil, exposure, room temperature? The soil should be rich, rather coarse, and well drained. Expose to maximum sunshine. Night temperatures should be 45° to 50° F. with a 5° to 15° rise permitted in the daytime. Place the plant (pot and all) in an outdoor garden bed in the summer.

Will a lemon tree planted from seed ever bloom without being grafted? It is about 5 feet tall; its trunk diameter is 1½ inches. It may bloom with age. Seedlings often take many years from the time of seed sowing until they bear flowers.

What fertilizer could I use to feed a lemon tree? Any complete commercial fertilizer will be satisfactory. It is not necessary to select one having a particular analysis.

What is the correct care for orange trees—temperature and fertilizer? Can they be grown as other house plants with success? Essentially the same as for grapefruits and lemons. (See replies to inquiries on these subjects.) The plants grow well as house plants, but often they fail to bloom or develop fruits.

How can I treat an orange tree, as a house plant, to always have oranges on it? Don't expect the impossible. Oranges of all kinds, including the dwarf Otaheite (*Citrus* x *limonia*), need lots of light and to be kept free of insect pests such as scales, mealybugs, and spider mites. Plant the pot outdoors in the summer, as this may induce flowers to set fruit.

Why do the blossoms on dwarf orange and lemon trees drop and bear no fruit? Lack of light or improper water relations within the plant (due to unsatisfactory environment) are probably responsible. Or indoors, lack of pollination may be at fault. Pollinate the flowers by hand. Rub powdery pollen on the sticky stigma with a paintbrush. Take care that the plant is not kept too dry when flowers and fruits are developing.

What varieties of citrus fruits can be grown as pot plants? Plant the dwarfs such as 'Ponderosa' lemon, Otaheite orange, 'Meyer' lemon, Satsuma orange, and calamondin orange (x *Citrofortunella mitis*).

CRAPE-MYRTLE (LAGERSTROEMIA INDICA)

Could a crape-myrtle be grown in a tub like an oleander—outdoors in summer, indoors during the cold months? Yes, very easily. Store it in the wintertime in a frostproof place and at that season keep the soil very nearly dry.

GARDENIA

Can gardenias be grown as house plants?   Yes, if you can supply sufficient atmospheric humidity.

What type of soil do gardenias thrive best in—acid or alkaline?   Acid. A pH of 5 to 5.5 is generally considered best. Chlorosis (yellowing of the foliage) results from alkaline soil conditions.

Can you recommend a good soil mixture for gardenias?   Two parts mellow loam, 1 part coarse sphagnum peat moss, ½ dried cow manure, ½ sharp sand. To this, add a 4-inch pot of superphosphate and a heaping tablespoonful of iron sulfate (copperas) to each bushel, the last to prevent chlorosis (yellowing of the foliage). Or use Sequestrene, according to directions on the container.

What kind of food should be given to gardenias?   A 4–12–4 fertilizer is recommended. Particularly suitable are fertilizers that provide nitrogen in the form of ammonia, such as sulfate of ammonia.

The gardenia that I received for Christmas has developed yellow leaves at the tips of the shoots. What is the trouble?   This may be a deficiency of iron. To prevent as well as cure, apply ½ teaspoon of iron sulfate to the soil and water thoroughly. To keep the plant growing, apply ½ teaspoon of 4–12–4 or 5–10–5 every 6 weeks. Never apply lime. Acidity is promoted by watering with a vinegar solution—½ teaspoon to 1 quart of water. If high heat and low humidity are causing difficulty, try a cooler location and promote humidity by covering the plant for a time with a plastic bag.

When is the best time to repot my gardenia house plant? It appears pot-bound to me.   Any time from April to August that the plants show evident need of this attention. The final pots should be filled with roots before winter begins.

When and how should gardenias be pruned?   Pruning consists of "stopping" (pinching out the tips) growing shoots each time they attain a length of 6 inches or so from spring to mid-August. You can also shorten branches by picking flowers with long twigs rather than cutting only the bloom.

What causes gardenias to dry up? The leaves become brittle and drop off and the plant seems to be dead. I've had 3 plants do the same.   Gardenias need high atmospheric humidity. This is difficult to provide in the house and is one of the major causes of failure. Try covering with a plastic bag such as those used by cleaners to protect clothing.

What is the correct application of water to the gardenia? Because of varying environmental factors, no exact answer is possible to your question. In general, keep the soil evenly moist and once a week let it dry out just a little. Then set the pot in a pail filled with water up to the rim. Let it stay until the topsoil feels moist.

How would I treat a gardenia plant that was hit by frost or cold air in the house? If severely damaged, it probably won't recover. If the damage consists only of moderate injury to leaves, keep in a warm place. Water with great care, so that the soil is not kept in a saturated condition, and lightly mist the branches 2 or 3 times daily.

My year-old gardenia plant has never bloomed. Would sinking the pot in the ground outdoors in the summer help? Placing it outdoors in partial shade and in a deep peat moss mulch should help.

How do you make gardenias bloom? No simple method can be given. You must provide conditions that are to the plant's liking, so it grows vigorously. Flower buds appear on new growth at temperatures of 60° to 65° F. at night and 70° to 75° in the day.

Can limbs be cut off a gardenia plant and rooted, and, if so, when is the best time? Large branches that have become woody are not suitable material for propagation. Cuttings of the young terminal shoots that are firm, but not hard and woody, are started in the winter and spring.

What is the most successful way to root gardenia cuttings? Cuttings 3 or 4 nodes long are dusted with a rooting hormone powder, then inserted in sand or sand and peat moss from December to March and enclosed under polyethylene. The sand is maintained at a temperature of 75° to 80° F. and the surrounding atmosphere is 70°. A humid atmosphere is necessary and is easily maintained in an enclosed plastic container.

What are the white, woolly insects that cluster on my gardenia? How can I kill them? They are mealybugs, one of the worst pests of this plant. Wash them off with a forceful stream of water or spray with malathion and repeat in 10 days. You can clean up a few by touching with a Q-tip dipped in rubbing alcohol.

HIBISCUS (HIBISCUS ROSA-SINENSIS)

How shall I care for hibiscus as a house plant? Presumably you have the Chinese hibiscus. If so, prune the plant back hard in the spring and repot in any good, well-drained soil. Spray lightly with water each sunny day. Keep the soil moist but not waterlogged. Give full sunshine. In the winter, keep the soil just moist in a temperature about 50° F.

I have a Chinese hibiscus growing in a pot, as the cold here would kill it if I planted it outside. What is the best plan for keeping it safe all winter? Keep it in a light cellar or plant room where the temperature is not less than 40° F. or more than 50° F. Give only sufficient water to prevent the soil from drying out completely.

HYDRANGEA   (See Gift Plants.)

LANTANA (LANTANA CAMARA)

How are lantanas handled to bloom in the winter? Buy small plants in the summer and sink the pots in soil out-of-doors until autumn. Bring in before frost. Do not repot at this time. Keep in a cool, sunny window or plant room at not more than 60° F. Give water sparingly at first, then more water and liquid plant food. They should start into fresh bloom in December or January. In the spring, repot in a standard potting mixture (see Soil, this section) and sink outdoors in a garden bed. If winter bloom is desired a second year, keep the summer bloom pinched back. It would be better, however, to buy new small plants for winter bloom.

I have a weeping lantana. When does it bloom? Lantanas are naturally summer-to-fall bloomers. They must be brought indoors after September. Keep them moderately dry and cool throughout the winter. Cut back and give more water and warmth from March on; plant out in late May.

LEMON-VERBENA   (See Kitchen Herb Garden, this section.)

OLEANDER (NERIUM OLEANDER)

How can oleanders be grown successfully in tubs? Prune back old growths, topdress in the spring, and increase the temperature and water supply. Feed occasionally during the growing season. Give full sun. After midsummer, keep somewhat drier. Store in the winter in a light, cool, frostproof place and keep nearly dry. Spray to keep clean of scale and mealybugs.

My oleanders look perfectly healthy, but never bloom. I keep them on a glass-enclosed porch in the winter and around an outdoor birdbath

in the summer. What else do they need? This is often due to insufficient ripening of the wood. To induce ripening, make sure that the plant has ample light and air and rather dry conditions at the root after the season's growth is completed.

ROSEMARY (See Kitchen Herb Garden, this section.)

SWEET-OLIVE (See Flowering Plants, this section.)

Ferns

CULTURE

What soil is recommended for indoor ferns? Mix together 2 parts good loam, 2 parts leafmold, 1 part sand, ¼ part dried cow manure or rich compost, ¼ part broken charcoal, and add ¾ of a pint of superphosphate to each bushel. Or take it easy and mix pasteurized garden soil with plenty of humus from the compost pile and some perlite or sand. The aim is a soil that feels light and porous.

What is the best fertilizer for ferns? There are many good commercial preparations. Plant tablets, dry commercial fertilizers, or liquid fertilizers are all satisfactory if used according to the manufacturer's directions. Fish emulsion is excellent, but don't feed ferns unless they are in active growth. Many are in a somewhat resting state from November to February.

Should house ferns have large, roomy pots or do they prefer to be pot-bound? How deep should the plant be set in the soil? Most plants thrive in pots just large enough. Too-big containers allow an overabundance of food and water, resulting in plant "indigestion." Let the crown of the plant be level or just a little above the soil level. Allow a 1-inch space above the soil in order to receive water.

Is good soil enough or is it necessary to provide additional drainage for ferns? Although moist soil conditions are appreciated, drainage must be perfect for ferns. The soil should be porous, there should be an inch or more of small stones or coarse sphagnum over the broken crock in the bottom of the pot, and ferns should not stand in a saucer or jardiniere in which water has been allowed to collect. Some epiphytic ferns such as *Polypodium aureum,* platyceriums, and davallias thrive in tree-fern pots or grow well in coconut-husk fiber.

How often should ferns be repotted?   Usually not more than once a year. Divide, if necessary, and always give them fresh soil. Young ferns that have filled their pots with roots by July may need a second potting but should not be divided. With a large specimen, knock it out of its pot in the spring and crumble off as much old soil, top and bottom, as possible, replacing it with a fresh mixture.

When is the best time to divide and replant an old Boston fern?   In the spring, just as new growth is beginning. Select younger and stronger crowns from outside the plant for replanting rather than old woody interior parts, which can be discarded.

Are there any tricks to watering ferns?   The soil should never be allowed to "bake out" or be kept constantly soggy. Keep it medium-moist, and when water is given, soak the ball of roots and soil thoroughly. Never apply water in a stream heavy enough to settle in the heart of the plant. The best way is to immerse the pot in a pail or tub of water, then allow it to drain before replacing it in a saucer.

Do ferns like plenty of sunlight?   Ferns prefer light but not direct sunlight. In fact, too much sun may be the cause of a sickly, light-green appearance, but winter sunshine or fluorescent lights are rarely too strong.

What window is best for ferns?   An east, west, or north window, or any place within a room where they receive plenty of light.

Is there a general routine for keeping ferns looking bright and crisp? Dry leaves form on my ferns right away.   Probably a lack of moisture, either in the soil or air. Water regularly and keep away from a radiator or heat source; keep in a temperature above 55° F. When buying a new fern, look for a young one that has not been growing in a greenhouse too long.

How should ferns be cared for in a city apartment?   Use the same procedure as for the care of ferns in a house. They do not like direct sun and want plenty of light, moisture in the air and soil, warmth, and to be kept away from drafts. Choose only the thriftiest ferns for apartment conditions, such as rabbit's-foot, holly, and bird's-nest. Set plants on large saucers or in a plant tray filled with pebbles and water.

Will it help my fern if I cut off fronds that have turned brown at the tip or have been broken off?   Cut off brown or damaged fronds. Ferns must have plenty of room, for fronds are easily damaged either from close contact with other plants or people brushing past them.

Should one cut the runners on ferns grown in a house? A friend told

me to cut them off my fern, and it doesn't seem to be growing as well since I did it. By all means, cut the runners off house ferns. They never develop into fronds and only take the strength from the rest of the plant. Perhaps your fern needs repotting in fresh soil.

What special care should be given a house fern to produce luxuriant foliage? Mine has a tendency to turn yellow frequently. Is it possible the pot is too small? Yes, it is possible that the pot is too small, but even more likely, the humidity is too low.

Will ferns do well in a Wardian case or terrarium? Yes, many of them do better there than in the average living room. Pteris ferns are especially good for terrariums, as are the small rock ferns or polypodiums, small holly ferns, and possibly the maidenhair.

Should ferns (house plants) be put outside during the summer? Many ferns benefit from being plunged (planted nearly to the rims of the pots) in an outdoor bed of peat moss or humus-rich soil that retains moisture around the pots in a shady spot during the hottest months. They will also thrive in the summer on a sheltered porch or terrace.

What causes the fronds of ferns to turn brown and fall off? This may be due to people passing by and injuring their tips. It may also be due to growing conditions: too small a pot, too low temperature, too hot or too dry atmosphere, lack of water in the soil, poor drainage. Check up on conditions. However, it is normal for some of the oldest fronds to die after a season of growth.

How can I save my fern, just an ordinary house fern, after an overdose of fertilizer? Obviously, the roots were burned from the overdose of fertilizer. Better start over with a new fern.

I left a fern in an unheated room and it froze. What can I do for it? If only the tops and not the roots were frozen, the tops should be cut off and the roots repotted in fresh soil to encourage new top growth. If the roots as well as the tops were frozen, the plant is a total loss.

What is the proper care for a Boston fern? Provide well-drained soil, plenty of water, air, light (but not direct sunlight), and humidity in the atmosphere (most rooms are likely to be too dry). They should never be where the temperature drops below 55° F.

My Boston fern does not send out sprouts, only long stems, and very few leaves. Should it get fertilizer in the form of cow manure? Cut off long stems, or runners, which do not turn into fronds and only take strength away from the plant. If the plants are otherwise healthy, liquid fertilizer, such as fish emulsion, can be given when the plants are in active growth. (For other cultural directions, see previous questions.)

How should lace ferns be grown? Probably you mean one of the sports of the Boston fern. It needs essentially the same care as the common Boston fern, but special care must be taken to keep any dead leaflets off and to prevent water lodging in the centers of the plants.

Mold is beginning to show around the topsoil of my indoor planter in which are several plants of the common Boston fern. What does the soil need? Mold seems to indicate that the drainage is poor or that you are not providing sufficient ventilation. Are there drainage holes in the bottom and an inch of broken crock or small stones under the soil? Better change the soil and pay attention to drainage when repotting.

Why does an unusual type (ostrich-Boston) fern revert back to the Boston type? Your fern is a somewhat unstable sport from the Boston fern. Such mutants often tend to revert to type. Unless the typical Boston fern fronds are cut out, they will eventually displace the weaker-growing type.

Is there such a plant as a holly fern? The holly fern is a cyrtomium. Its fronds are divided into small leaflets, each one resembling a holly leaf in outline. It is one of the best ferns for the house and grows steadily. In the summer, put it outdoors in a shady spot.

What are the best growing conditions in the house for the maidenhair fern? Maidenhair fern is one of the most difficult to grow in the house. It likes a porous soil that contains plenty of humus and more moisture in the air than is usually found in any house. The Australian maidenhair fern (*Adiantum hispidulum*) is one of the most adaptable in the genus. A temperature of about 65° F. and shade from direct sunlight are necessary. A large terrarium is most likely to provide the requisite conditions.

What is the best time to pot and what is the best fertilizer for pteris? Several species and forms are available, all generally known as "table ferns." They grow rapidly under favorable conditions and should be repotted into the next size pot whenever their containers become filled with roots. Liquid plant food such as fish emulsion, applied once a month to well-rooted specimens, is sufficient.

How should rabbit's-foot fern be cared for? Rabbit's-foot fern (*Davallia*) can stand higher temperatures and drier air than any of the other house ferns. It should do well in the average living room. Keep it out of direct sunlight but see that it has plenty of light. Davallias will grow in well-drained porous soil, but they look best when grown in a tree-fern basket or tree-fern planter so the attractive fuzzy rhizomes can creep about in the open. Maintain a minimum relative humidity of 40 per cent. Let the roots dry slightly between waterings to prevent rhizome rot, but the fronds can be misted with room-temperature water any morning.

How are ferns propagated from the spores on the back of the leaves? The average person may find it difficult to do. Take a piece of soft brick and a clay saucer. Sterilize these by baking. Stand the brick in a saucer and wet thoroughly. Scatter the spores over the surface of the brick. Keep a little water in the saucer and cover with glass, leaving a slight opening at the bottom for ventilation. Keep in diffused light at a temperature of 60° to 70° F. The first growth of the fern looks like green scales.

Is it safe to divide fern plants? Yes, but not more than once a year. New crowns or heads which have sprung up around the original crown can be pulled or cut off gently and each piece potted in a pot of suitable size. Probably the original plant can go back into the same pot with fresh soil.

When ferns have black specks on the underside, is that fungi? If these black or brown specks appear in even lines or a regular pattern on the undersides of the leaves, they are sori, which contain the spores by which ferns reproduce themselves. They are not harmful to the plant.

My sword fern has little black spots on its stems. Is it a disease? If these black spots are on the stems, not on the back of the leaves, they are a scale insect. If there are only a few scales, hand-pick them with a toothpick or try to wash them off with a soapy sponge. For a bad attack, try a *very weak* malathion solution or discard the plant.

What are the best ferns for indoor culture? Boston fern (and its several variations), holly fern, bird's-nest fern, pteris (table) ferns, and rabbit's-foot. All of these will thrive in the average home if given reasonable attention.

Is ostrich-plume fern all right for the house? The native woods ostrich fern is hardy and not suitable for indoor culture. If by ostrich-plume fern you mean one of the feathery Boston fern types, it is a suitable house plant.

Vines for Indoors

WHAT TO GROW

Will most vines do better in a greenhouse than in the house? Yes, if ideal conditions and care are given; yet remarkably good results are obtainable in the house with vines that are adapted to such conditions. This group is by no means a small one.

What kind of house plants grow long and trailing, in addition to ivy and philodendron? *Cissus antarctica* (kangaroo vine) is one of the best and longest growing; grape-ivy, pothos, tradescantia, zebrina, *Setcreasea purpurea, Jasminium rex,* lipstick vine, waxplant (*Hoya*), and sweet potato.

What vines grow best in a light window? Can they be grown in water? Ivy, philodendron, and tradescantia are stand-bys to grow in water. They do not need sun. Pothos and nephthytis will grow in either water or soil. Grape-ivy, Kenilworth-ivy, German-ivy, passion vine, creeping fig, and kangaroo vine do well in soil.

What are the names of vines that will grow in water in the house? In a light place: English ivy, philodendron, tradescantia, pothos, nephthytis, passion vine, sweet potato. In sun: trailing coleus and *Zebrina pendula,* whose leaves are purple on the underside and silver-striped on the upper.

What vines are best for a city apartment? The thriftiest vines are philodendron, pothos, kangaroo vine, with grape-ivy a close runner-up.

What about growing vines indoors in water? Should the water be plain or are there solutions that should be added? Many vines grow satisfactorily in water—plain water plus a small piece of charcoal to keep the water "sweet." Don't disturb the roots by changing the water; simply add more as needed. Water-soluble fertilizers can be used at one fourth strength for sturdy plants.

Is it safe to use foliage vines to frame the sides of a sunny south window used for other house plants? Yes, if the foliage vines are not kept in the direct sunlight of the window but are fastened or trained to the window frame facing in toward the room.

How should the leaves of vines be kept clean? Spray vigorously once a week with cool water on both the upper- and the undersides of the leaves. This not only prevents insects but keeps the foliage fresh-looking. Or sponge leaves with soapy water occasionally.

Can any vines be grown from seed for use indoors? Morning-glory, especially the Japanese ones and 'Heavenly Blue'; black-eyed-Susan vine (*Thunbergia alata*), cup-and-saucer vine (*Cobaea scandens*), canary-bird vine (*Tropaeolum peregrinum*).

What are the names of some perennial flowering vines to grow in a light window? The passion-flower, *Hoya,* and also such gesneriads as the lipstick vine *Aeschynanthus* 'Black Pagoda'; the goldfish-plant *Columnea* 'Yellow Dragon'; the peacock-plant *Episcia* 'Yellow Topaz';

and hybrid *Nematanthus* with pouch-shaped flowers in red or orange tones and waxy green foliage. *N. wettsteinii* is an adaptable trailer with small green leaves, orange and yellow flowers, and restrained growth. Specialists also offer trailing African-violet hybrids, which are graceful and long-blooming when conditions are to their liking.

How should Boston-ivy be cared for in the house? True Boston-ivy is *Parthenocissus tricuspidata*. This is a large-leaved vine that drops its leaves every autumn. It is an outdoor, not an indoor, vine. Perhaps you are thinking of grape-ivy or kangaroo vine in the genus *Cissus*.

CREEPING FIG (FICUS PUMILA)

Can you suggest a creeping vine that will cling to a masonry wall behind a small pool in a plant room? The creeping fig will suit your purpose. It is small-leaved, intensely green, and makes a flat mat against the wall up which it creeps. A variegated variety is also available.

ENGLISH IVY (HEDERA HELIX)

How can hardy ivy be grown in the house? Keep in a cool, light place, away from radiators and direct sunlight. Spray foliage once a week with cold water to keep clean and free from dust and red spider. Keep its soil moist; feed monthly with a pinch of complete fertilizer. It also grows well in water and even better in ¼-strength water-soluble house-plant fertilizer.

Does ivy require sunshine when grown indoors? No. Ivy should not be in direct sun. It does need good light—a north window is preferable.

We have been unsuccessful in keeping ivy cuttings alive during the winter in the house in water. What is the proper method? A glass container is best; be sure to have a piece of charcoal in the water so that it will stay "sweet" and not have to be changed; add water as needed. A light but not sunny place is preferred.

My ivy, grown in water in the light, dries up and dies. How can this be remedied? The location is either too sunny and hot and/or the plant has red spider. Spray both sides of the leaves vigorously with cool water once a week. Keep in a light but not sunny place.

What is the best method of starting indoor ivy? By cuttings rooted in water. Take the tip ends of ivy, having at least 4 mature leaves. Remove 2 lower leaves and stand in water. Longer stems may be used but leaves must be removed from as much stem as is under water.

Why do the leaves of ivy turn yellow?   Too much sunshine perhaps, a too-hot and dry atmosphere, or a soil too dry.

My ivy (indoor) has a brown scale on its leaves. What causes this?   Brown scale is an insect. The most effective control is to dip the plants in water and malathion, mixed according to directions. If necessary, use a soft toothbrush to remove scale from the stems.

How can variegated ivy be grown successfully?   Variegated ivies should be grown in north windows only, or in eastern exposures if shaded by larger plants. Good soil, moderate watering, and spraying of the foliage once a week to keep it clean are of basic importance.

I have a green and white variegated ivy. As the new leaves come out, the old ones turn brown and die, beginning on one side of the leaf. Why?   Probably due to too much sun. Keep in a north window. Check other general factors—soil, watering, and cleanliness of foliage—for additional causes.

What are the best kinds of English ivy for indoor culture?   The standard English ivy (*Hedera helix*) and the 'Pittsburgh' cultivar are the two thriftiest kinds. Many variations have been developed and can be obtained by mail order from house-plant nurseries or at local garden centers.

GERMAN-IVY (SENECIO MIKANIOIDES)

I have seen German-ivy grown indoors in ferneries. Is this a difficult house plant?   No, *Senecio mikanioides* does well in window boxes or fern stands in full diffused light and without direct sun. Plant in a standard potting mixture to which charcoal has been added to keep the soil "sweet." When German-ivy is growing well, water it weekly with liquid fertilizer. Cuttings root easily in moist sand.

GRAPE-IVY (CISSUS)

I have a trailing house plant that looks like poison-ivy. What is its name and of what country is it a native?   *Cissus rhombifolia*. Its common name is grape-ivy and it is a native of northern South America.

Is the grape-ivy a satisfactory house plant?   Yes, it is splendid and will thrive with any reasonable care in a warm room. It appreciates sunshine except for shade from intense summer sunshine, a good rich soil, free drainage, adequate supplies of water, and feeding when pot-bound.

Is grape-ivy a form of English ivy?   No. Grape-ivy is *Cissus rhombifolia,* which is quite different in appearance from English ivy (*Hedera* *helix*). Its leaves are made of three leaflets while those of the English ivy are merely lobed. It is less subject to insect pests than English ivy and usually looks well longer.

HOYA   (See Waxplant.)

KANGAROO VINE (CISSUS ANTARCTICA)

Does kangaroo vine make a good house plant?   Yes, this is one of the toughest and least temperamental of house vines. It does not object to living-room temperatures. New plants can be propagated from cuttings.

KENILWORTH-IVY (CYMBALARIA MURALIS)

Can I grow Kenilworth-ivy as an indoor vine?   Yes, this dainty little vine, with its violet flowers and leaves tinted with red beneath, grows well in a sunny window if the atmosphere is not too dry. It requires a standard potting soil and about a 4-inch pot. Often it will seed itself in the soil around the base of other pot plants. In the summer, it grows riotously in a wall or rock garden out-of-doors and seeds itself freely (in the vicinity of New York City). The main indoor pest, especially under dry conditions, is red spider mite. Wash gently with lukewarm water every few weeks to discourage mites.

MYRTLE (VINCA MAJOR)

Will myrtle grow indoors?   Yes, it will, but it must be sprayed, without fail, once a week with cool water to ward off red spider, its greatest handicap to growing well indoors. It does not like too warm a location. Myrtle will root and grow in water or larger plants can be potted in soil.

PASSION-FLOWER (PASSIFLORA CAERULEA)

Would passion-flower grow in the house during the winter months? Should it be cut back before being brought in?   Passion-flower makes an excellent winter house plant. It grows luxuriantly outdoors during the summer and it may have to be cut back before being brought indoors. Train to a bamboo stake and put strings against the window up which it can climb. To encourage the growth of the vine, it *must* be provided with something on which to climb. Its growth depends on the height of the trellis or string provided.

My passion-vine, kept in a south window, grows well during the winter but does not flower. Will anything encourage blossoms? Early winter should be a season of comparative rest (temperature 55° F.; soil on the dry side). In late winter, increase the temperature 15° to 20°; give more water. Repot if necessary, or, if not, feed every 2 or 3 weeks. A rest season is important.

How can you propagate the passion-flower? By tip cuttings rooted in sand kept constantly moist or in water in a glass container. Keep in a light but not sunny window. When well rooted, pot up in a humus-rich soil.

PHILODENDRON

What are the cultural directions for philodendron? The philodendrons used as house plants are tolerant of warm rooms and some shade, although they appreciate atmospheric moisture and sunlight. Give well-drained, humus-rich soil, and avoid potting too frequently.

What is the proper method for growing philodendron—in water or soil? Philodendron grows well in either. If in water, keep a piece of charcoal in the container to keep the water "sweet." Do not change the water but add to it as needed. If soil is more convenient, any good garden soil that is porous is all right. See that it is watered regularly.

How does one obtain a cutting of philodendron? By cutting off the tip ends or any side shoot. The piece cut off should have at least 4 leaves. Remove the 2 bottom leaves so that the nodes from which the leaves grew can go under water. New roots will appear from these nodes. Sometimes cuttings can be selected with aerial roots already formed at the nodes.

What can be done to make a philodendron branch and to prevent it from becoming stringy? As soon as the distances between leaves start to get longer than normal, pinch off the ends of the vine. The plant will branch out and the several pieces, if long enough, may be rooted in water to make new plants.

What should be done with philodendron when the leaves become too small? It is probably growing in too dark or too cool a place. It does not need sun, but plenty of light and a temperature of 60° to 70° F. If the roots are healthy, give it a plant tablet or feed with liquid manure or a good complete fertilizer once a month. Overwatering also results in small leaves.

How should philodendron vine be taken care of? The leaves seem to die off. Do I water too much? Dying leaves are evidence of root injury or too dry atmospheric conditions. Never water a plant if the soil is really moist. Shake out your plant, and if the roots are decayed, cut back soft growth, repot, and water carefully. Don't use much fertilizer. Perhaps you have been overfeeding.

POTHOS (SCINDAPSUS PICTUS)

What kind of exposure does pothos like? Pothos is very adaptable. It will grow in either sunlight or good diffused light. It is good for a south window as well as for an east or west one.

SWEET POTATO (IPOMOEA BATATAS)

How do I start a sweet-potato vine in water? Select a good-sized sweet potato and a glass container about 8 inches deep and suitably wide. Wash, but don't scrub, the tuber to remove any chemical applied to retard sprouting. Thrust a toothpick in the middle of either side of the potato and let the toothpicks rest on the rim of the container. Keep water at a level so that the lower end of the potato is always covered. Remember to add water as evaporation occurs. Dryness would be fatal.

How long does it take a sweet-potato tuber to grow into a plant? After about 10 days in a cool dark place, a sweet potato, properly planted with the *root end* down in the water, will begin to develop roots. Move then to a light or sunny window and sprouts will show in 3 to 4 weeks after you put it in water. As growth develops, pinch out all but two or three strands and train these on a cord where you wish them to grow.

WANDERING JEW

What is the botanical name of the trailing indoor plant called wandering Jew? Two plants of very similar appearance go by this name. One, *Tradescantia fluminensis,* produces white flowers; its leaves are often variegated. The other, *Zebrina pendula,* flowers pink or red-purple; its foliage is striped above, purple beneath. Both are of the very simplest culture and will grow under similar conditions.

What is the best time to root cuttings of wandering Jew? They root readily at any time if planted about 2 inches apart in pots of sandy soil. Stand the pots in a box with 1 inch of sand or cinders in the bottom.

Water well, cover with a sheet of glass, and shade lightly from bright sunshine. Cuttings also root well when cut ends are ½ inch under water.

WAXPLANT (HOYA)

Please tell me about the house plant known as "parlor plant". It has thick waxy leaves and clusters of small, star-shaped waxy flowers. From your description, this must be *Hoya carnosa,* or waxplant. It is a native of southern China and Australia and is an old-time favorite. Botanically it is related to the milkweeds (*Asclepias*).

What kind of soil should be used for waxplant? A soil rich in humus. One part good garden soil, 1 part coarse sand, 2 parts leafmold or peat moss, with the addition of ⅛ part of bulk of dry cow manure or rich compost and a pint of superphosphate to each bushel.

Should waxplant have sunshine or shade, plenty of moisture, or kept on the dry side? It appreciates sunshine, good drainage, and plenty of moisture in the spring, summer, and fall, but should be kept drier and cooler (50° F. night, 60° to 65° F. day) in the winter.

Why doesn't my waxplant (5 feet long and 5 years old) bloom? Although slow to flower, your plant is large enough to do so. Does it get plenty of sun and has it filled its pot with roots? Plant must be pot-bound to bloom well; hence, avoid overpotting. A partial rest in wintertime is very beneficial.

Are there other waxplants suitable for growing indoors? Yes, several attractive varieties are available from mail-order firms. Some of the most beautiful are cultivars of *Hoya carnosa* but have red and cream markings on the foliage. Other species with larger leaves than *H. carnosa* are *H. kerrii,* with very thick, heart-shaped leaves, and *H. purpurea-fusca* 'Silver Pink', with long silver-spotted waxy leaves and red and white flowers in big clusters. Miniature types include *H. bella* and *H. lacunosa,* which has fine twining stems, small glossy dark-green leaves, and clusters of fuzzy fragrant flowers.

Cacti

SOIL AND FERTILIZER

Are cacti in the house grown in all sand? Cactus plants can be kept alive and will grow in sand for long periods but thrive better and are more permanent if planted in a loose, porous soil mixture.

What is the proportion of sand to soil for cacti grown in the house? From ¼ to ½, depending upon how sandy the soil is.

What soil do cacti require? Cacti form a large group and there are some differences in the soil requirements of individual kinds. In general, a loose, porous soil, fertile but not overrich in nitrogen, is desirable. Many species benefit from the addition of lime. (See Sandy Potting Mixture.)

When should we start feeding cacti, and what month? Never feed cacti unless they are strong, vigorous plants that have filled their pots with healthy roots. Feed only during their growing season (usually spring and summer), and then sparingly.

CULTURE

When should cacti be repotted? The repotting of healthy cacti that have filled their containers with roots should be done at the beginning of their growing season (in most cases, from spring to early summer). A plant that is planted in unsuitable soil and is consequently unhealthy may be carefully repotted at any time.

How can a cactus be made to bloom? The cactus group is a large one. Some kinds flower regularly and with ease while others are much more capricious. Study the individual plant, provide it with the best possible environment, and see that it has a period of rest immediately before its season of active growth in spring.

What temperature must be held to keep cactus plants healthy? A minimum of 50° F. for plants grown indoors. A few kinds are hardy outdoors even in the North.

What is the best method of watering cactus plants? Submerge pots nearly to their rims and leave in that position until water entering drainage holes in the bottom of the pots seeps through and wets the surface of the soil.

Can you tell me something of the care of cacti so they will blossom? I have one that blossoms about July; last year the buds formed and then dried up. You probably kept the plant too dry. Pot-grown cacti require moderate amounts of water over the greater part of the year. Supply quite a generous quantity when growth or flowers are developing.

How often should cactus plants in small flowerpots be watered? This depends largely upon the prevailing weather and other environmental factors. In general, water often enough to prevent the plants from shriveling. The soil should be allowed to become nearly dry before each watering.

How often should cacti in small pots be watered when they are in the house during the winter?   In the winter, most cacti are resting and the soil should be permitted to dry out completely before water is applied. The frequency with which this occurs varies with the individual plant and its environment.

How can succulents and cacti be kept thriving in an apartment with not much sun?   Grow them in a window where they will receive the maximum amount of light possible (even though this is not direct sunlight) or under fluorescent lights. Attend carefully to watering, potting, cleaning, and other details.

Will cacti grow and bloom better if set outside in the summer? Should they be left in pots or set directly in the ground?   If their indoor position is a sunny one and otherwise satisfactory, it makes little difference whether they are left indoors or are set outside. If set outside, they should remain in their pots.

How can cacti be carried successfully through the summer out-of-doors? We have a lath house. Would that be better than the rock garden?   A lath house is probably too shady for most kinds of cacti. It is better to bury the pots to their rims in a sunny open position.

Why do my miniature cacti fail to grow?   Because the soil or other environmental factors are not to their liking. Read with care the answers given to other inquiries and be guided accordingly.

I have 2 cacti, 6 feet tall, that have never bloomed. Why?   Some cacti do not bloom until they are several years old. Resting plants by keeping them decidedly on the dry side and cool (50° to 60° F. at night) during the winter often helps blooming, as does exposure to sunshine or fluorescent lights.

Will the peanut cactus plant blossom?   The peanut cactus (*Chamaecereus silvestri*) normally blooms from May to July. Its flowers are tubular, nearly 3 inches long, and orange-scarlet.

How should cactus cuttings be made?   Most cacti root readily from cuttings. Make cuttings in the spring or early summer. Leave them lying in the sun for a few days to dry the cut surface, then insert them in a sand bed. Keep the sand just moist and the atmosphere *not* close and humid as recommended for cuttings of most plants.

How should seedling cacti be grafted on larger or stronger stock? I have raised many from seeds.   Seedling cacti are not usually grafted. Grafting is reserved for varieties that do not do well on their own roots.

While a simple process, this can scarcely be adequately described in a brief reply. (See Grafting, Section 3.)

How can I start cactus seed? Plant the seeds in pots filled ⅓ with crocks and ⅔ with very sandy soil that has had no fertilizer added to it and that has been passed through a ¼-inch screen. Sow in the spring. Cover the seed to their own depth. Keep the soil moderately moist at all times. The temperature should be 60° to 70° F.

How long does it take cactus seeds to come up? From 1 to 2 weeks under favorable conditions.

How can I remove mealybugs and scale insects from my cactus plant? Mealybugs are easily washed off with a forceful stream of water. Scale can be removed by scrubbing gently with a soft toothbrush dipped in soapsuds or in a pyrethrum, rotenone, or malathion insecticide.

ORCHID AND NIGHT-BLOOMING (JUNGLE) CACTI

What kind of soil is needed for night-blooming cactus? The soil must be very porous, so that water drains through quickly, even when packed together. Mix good garden soil, sand, and broken brick until you get this result, then add $\frac{1}{10}$ part in bulk dried cow manure and a pint of superphosphate to each bushel. Or use a packaged mix that is porous; or try 4 parts leafmold, 1 part sand, 1 part perlite (or vermiculite), and 1 part charcoal.

What will make a night-blooming cereus-type cactus bloom and not lose its buds? Good light, suitable soil; proper temperature; plenty of water and feeding when growing (during spring and summer); little water during resting period (winter); freedom from scale and mealybugs.

How should a large night-blooming cactus be cared for during the winter? Would it do all right in a dark cellar? It should be kept in a light place at all times. Providing the soil is kept nearly dry during the winter, it may be kept in a temperature of 40° to 45° F. At warmer temperatures, more water is needed.

Could a jungle cactus be cut back? I had one given to me and it had been broken in many places, but this past summer it put out new growth. When is its blooming time? Yes, it can be cut back. Dust the cuts with finely powdered sulfur. Summer is its blooming time.

A night-blooming cactus started from a cutting bloomed once when it was 2 years old but hasn't had a flower since. It seems healthy enough and is growing well. What is wrong? Young plants bloom either irregularly or not at all, especially when growing vigorously. Your plant will probably bloom when it is older. Avoid overfeeding or overpotting.

How long does it take for a night-blooming cereus-type cactus rooted from a cutting to bloom? This cannot be stated with any degree of precision. Usually several years or when the plant becomes pot-bound.

When should a large night-blooming cactus be transplanted? In April or May.

I have two cactus plants that are night-blooming, with a cream-yellow waxlike flower about 5 inches in diameter. Can you tell me the correct way of increasing these to make more plants? Cuttings of the stems, each a foot or so long, taken in the summer and set in clean sand that is kept moist will soon form new roots.

What is a good potting mixture for an orchid cactus or epiphyllum? This needs a moister and richer soil than desert types of cacti. Two parts loam, 2 parts leafmold, 1 part sharp sand, plus a pint of bone meal to each bushel should be about right.

What is the best fertilizer for epiphyllums? Liquid fertilizer low in nitrogen.

What time of year do the orchid cacti bloom? Will they freeze in the winter? The epiphyllums and other orchid cacti bloom from April to July ordinarily. They are natives of the warmer parts of North, Central, and South America and are not adapted for outdoor culture where freezing weather is experienced.

What is the trouble when a night-blooming orchid cactus sets many buds which turn brown and wither when they are no larger than peas? The plant is well watered and sprayed with water after the buds appear. Lack of potash in the soil is said to cause buds to drop. Overwatering will also bring this about. Probably too low humidity is a factor.

What is the reason my epiphyllums grow but seldom bloom? To bloom satisfactorily they must be given a rest each year. This is done by keeping them as dry as possible (without permitting the leaflike stems to shrivel) for a period of 8 to 10 weeks during the winter.

CHRISTMAS, THANKSGIVING, AND EASTER CACTI

Are the Christmas and Thanksgiving cacti the same? No. The Thanksgiving cactus, also known as the crab-claw or claw cactus, is *Schlumbergera truncata* and usually blooms in late November. Its flat joints are decidedly "clawlike" and its flowers less symmetrical than those of the Christmas cactus, *Schlumbergera* x *buckleyi,* which is supposed to bloom around Christmas but is often late. Both kinds are often called Christmas cactus. Their generic name was formerly *Zygocactus.*

THREE KINDS OF HOLIDAY CACTI

Christmas cactus (left) blooms around Christmas or later and has leaf margins that are less indented than those of the Thanksgiving cactus (center). The Thanksgiving cactus blooms close to that holiday and is also called the crab-claw cactus because of its pronounced leaf indentations. The Easter cactus (right) blooms in the spring and has pretty star-shaped flowers.

I have a beautiful white-flowered Christmas cactus that always blooms around Thanksgiving. Why doesn't it bloom at Christmas? You probably have 'White Christmas', a hybrid probably more closely related to the Thanksgiving cactus (*Schlumbergera truncata*) than the Christmas cactus (*S.* x *buckleyi*).

I have been given a plant called an Easter cactus but to me it looks just like my Christmas cactus. Does it really bloom at Easter? The Easter cactus out of flower does resemble the Christmas cactus (*Schlumbergera* x *buckleyi*), but its flowers are definitely star-shaped and rose-red. They appear in late March or early April and usually coincide to some degree with the Easter season. Its botanical name is *Rhipsalidopsis gaertneri*.

What kind of soil is best suited to Christmas and Thanksgiving cacti? Equal parts of loam, leafmold or compost, and coarse sand (not seashore sand) together with a pint of superphosphate and a quart of wood ashes to each bushel is a good mixture. Or packaged mixtures, including soilless mixes, can be used.

How often should a Christmas cactus be repotted? Ordinarily every 2 or 3 years, or whenever the pot is filled with roots and the soil appears to be worn out. However, plants can exist many years without being repotted.

When should a Christmas cactus be transplanted? In the spring, if the plant is healthy. A plant that is unhealthy because of poor root condition may be carefully repotted at any time and is usually transferred to a smaller pot.

Must the Christmas and Thanksgiving cacti have sunshine to bloom? Both need exposure to sunshine, except from May to September; during this period, shade from the full intensity of strong sunlight.

How do I care for my holiday cactus after it blooms?   Rest the plant by keeping it nearly dry for 6 to 8 weeks. When new growth appears, repot or topdress with fresh soil and water so that the soil is kept fairly moist.

Why do Christmas cactus leaves turn yellow and fall off indoors each winter and come out again on the porch in the summer?   Because the indoor atmosphere is too arid for these epiphytic plants. Use humidifiers. Stand your pots on trays of moist gravel or sand.

What makes Christmas cactus leaves turn yellow and grow very small? They do not grow as broad as they should. They are planted in sandy soil.   The soil is probably too poor. Try repotting into a richer (but still porous) mixture.

What care must I give to my Thanksgiving cactus so that the buds will not drop off? Out of 25 buds appearing on the plant, about 7 or 8 develop into full-blooming flowers.   Common causes of bud dropping are overwatering, exposure to cold drafts, a position too close to a heat source, and low humidity. Syringe foliage frequently in autumn. Water the plant sparingly. Feed a little liquid fertilizer weekly after buds appear. Some bud drop is normal when a great many buds form.

I have a Christmas cactus plant several years old, and it hasn't bloomed. Someone told me it must be a male plant. Are there male and female plants? How can you tell?   No, there are not separate male and female plants. Both the Thanksgiving and Christmas cacti bear male and female parts in the same flower, not on separate plants.

What can I do to have my Christmas cactus bloom at Christmastime instead of in March?   Leave the plant outdoors as late as possible in the fall and not near artificial light. It can be kept outside until frost danger approaches and temperatures fall below 40° F. Buds will have formed when the plant is brought indoors.

Why does Christmas cactus send out tiny hair roots at each leaf joint?   This is quite a natural phenomenon and occurs particularly if the plants are grown in a moist atmosphere. This phenomenon is especially typical of the Easter cactus (*Rhipsalidopsis gaertneri*).

How can a claw cactus be started from an old plant?   By stem cuttings planted firmly in moist sand in the spring. By grafting onto pereskia, cereus, or other suitable stock in early summer. (See Grafting, Section 3.)

Succulents

GENERAL

What is the difference between cacti and succulents? A cactus is any plant of a fleshy character adapted to conserve water and store it in its tissues. Nearly all cacti are succulents, but not all succulents are cacti. Century-plant, aloe, air-plant, stapelia, and many others are succulents that belong to families other than Cactaceae.

Do succulents need the same kind of soil as cacti? Generally, yes, but succulents that are not cacti form a much more diverse group than those that are, and, in consequence, their specific needs tend to vary more. However, they also need good, sharp, soil drainage.

In what kind of soil should succulents be planted? This varies to some extent with the individual needs of the large number of species that comprise this group. It *must* be porous but should not, as beginners often think, be nearly all sand. Many species appreciate lime.

Do succulents need a resting season? Yes, all do. As they come from many different parts of the world, their seasons of rest vary. Thus, most South African succulents grow in our winter and should be rested in the summer, while species that are native to lands north of the equator commonly rest in our winter. When resting, keep cooler and drier than when growing.

What are some of the most interesting succulents, other than cacti, for the window garden? The list is vast. You might try euphorbia, echeveria, stapelia, haworthia, gasteria, senecio, cotyledon, crassula, kalanchoe, and some of the South African rock plants (lithops).

CRASSULA (JADE PLANT)

What could cause a crassula (jade plant) to drop most of its leaves? Too much water or possibly very extreme drought. This succulent plant should be treated like a cactus—plenty of drainage in the pot but water enough to prevent shriveling. The exact frequency of watering depends upon the size and condition of the plant as well as upon the weather and its position in the house.

What can be done to encourage a jade plant to bloom? It has been kept in good health for 10 or 15 years. The jade plant does not normally bloom until it is many years old. Younger specimens sometimes bloom if pot-bound.

I have a so-called rubber plant about 10 years old; it bloomed 2 years in succession, the last time 3 years ago, and not since. Why? Your plant is probably the so-called Japanese rubber, *Crassula argentea;* its failure to flower regularly is probably due to giving it too much water, so that it never rests. This plant is a succulent and needs to be kept on the dry side in late summer and early fall.

How can I propagate my jade plant? It is now so large I can no longer handle it. You can scarcely help doing so! Branches and leaves of *Crassula argentea* or jade plant, which makes a showy, treelike house plant, root so easily that if a piece is accidentally broken off and falls in the pot, roots soon form in the surface of the potting soil. The thick, glossy, rounded leaves will also produce roots if the bases are inserted in damp, sandy soil.

CROWN-OF-THORNS (EUPHORBIA)

How can I keep my crown-of-thorns (Euphorbia milii var. splendens) green? The leaves come on and drop off. It just refuses to bloom in the house. Probably you are keeping the plant too dry. It cannot produce leaves and flowers without a constant supply of moisture during its growing season.

Does crown-of-thorns require a dry soil? The soil should be exceedingly porous and well drained but should be kept moist whenever leaves are present on the stems. When the leaves fall off, keep the soil nearly dry until new growth begins.

Which plant food is best for crown-of-thorns? Avoid the excessive use of fertilizer. A vigorous plant with a strong, healthy root system will respond to small amounts of any complete fertilizer applied during its active growing season.

What window should a crown-of-thorns stand in? Why do the buds blast? The sunniest possible window. Bud blasting (failure to develop properly) may be due to extreme dryness, gross overwatering, or low temperature. Ordinarily temperature should not go below 45° F. Increase humidity by placing the plant on a saucer of wet pebbles or gravel.

Is the crown-of-thorns a constant bloomer? Yes, if kept in good growing condition, it will bloom much of the year. (See previous questions for culture.) *Euphorbia fulgens* (sometimes listed as *E.* x *keysii*) has pink flowers throughout the year when given good light. Other interesting selections have yellow flowers.

ECHEVERIA

I have a tender succulent which resembles the common hardy hen-and-chicks. What is it? Probably an echeveria. The handsome rosettes of these succulents are often silver-gray, gray-green, or almost white, touched with pink. Plant them in the rock garden in the summer and bring them indoors in the winter, before the first frost.

KALANCHOE

What is the proper soil and care for successful blooming of the Kalanchoe blossfeldiana? The soil should be moderately rich and quite porous. Grow in full sun. Propagate by cuttings in the spring. Repot the plants as roots fill the pots. Water fairly freely when in active growth and feed gently when the final pots are root-filled. (See also under Gift Plants.)

How can I make an air-plant (Kalanchoe pinnata) bloom? Give good culture that has as its object the rapid production of a large, vigorous plant. It needs a rather warm temperature (60° to 70° F.), plenty of sun, rich but quite porous soil, rather ample supplies of water, and feeding when it has filled a 6-inch pot full of roots. Low temperatures, too dry soil, and lack of light prevent blooming.

What is the name of the house plant that produces many little plants along the edges of its fleshy leaves? Several species of kalanchoe possess this habit. They are easily propagated from the plantlets.

LIVING STONES (LITHOPS)

How should living stones be treated? Plant closely together in shallow pans filled with exceedingly porous soil. The tops of the plants should be well above the soil level. Cover the surface of the pans with gravel or small stones. Water freely from October to May but let the soil dry out between waterings. Keep nearly dry at other times. Shade lightly from bright summer sun. Grow in a temperature of 50° to 60° F.

SEDUM

How can healthy, small, potted sedums be kept growing? Grow them in the sunniest window in a room where the temperature is not excessive. Pot them in a porous, well-drained soil and keep moderately moist at all times. Sedums are easy to grow.

STAPELIA

I can never get stapelia to grow and do well. Why? They are sometimes rather tricky. They need an open, porous soil and regular watering in spring and summer. Give light shade during the summer when they should bloom. They should be kept nearly dormant in the winter by giving less water. (See below.)

Concerning stapelias: mine are rested, kept fairly dry in the summer, and form buds in late August or early September. The buds wilt, however, without maturing. How should they be treated? Perhaps you keep them too dry in the summer. A usual practice is to rest them by keeping them nearly dry in the winter and to water them moderately and encourage growth in the summer.

Hardy Bulbs for Forcing

IRIS

Can 'Wedgwood' iris be grown successfully in the house in the winter? If you have a cool room (50° to 55° F.), plant the largest size bulbs in 6- or 8-inch pots; give full light and sun; keep free of aphids and don't disturb the roots. This iris may flower, but it really needs greenhouse or outdoor culture. Don't use small bulbs for indoors, as they won't bloom.

LILY (LILIUM)

Will regular garden lilies bloom indoors? The regal lily is a good pot plant but rather tall. Potted in late fall and given a temperature of 55° to 60° F., with full light, it will flower in April or early May. Other hardy lilies recommended for forcing include the Mid-Century Hybrids, such as 'Enchantment'. For others, see catalogs of bulb specialists.

How can Easter lilies be made to bloom in time for Easter? The starting temperature should be 50° to 60° F. After rooting, provide a minimum night temperature of 65° to 70° F.; day temperature, 75° F.

When the plants are 3 to 4 inches high, move them to a lower temperature (60°) for 14 days, then to high temperatures. Water frequently.

What lilies will succeed in a bright window or greenhouse? The new dwarf lilies such as fragrant 'Little Rascal' and 'Connecticut Lemonglow' will succeed in pots with temperatures of 55° F. at night, 65° to 70° F. during the day in bright light. Plant the bulbs in containers with 2 to 3 inches of soil over the top of each bulb.

LILY-OF-THE-VALLEY (CONVALLARIA MAJALIS)

Can I make lily-of-the-valley bloom indoors? Yes. Order large, cold-storage pips sold for forcing. Plant in moist fiber or mix, leaving the tops exposed. Place at once in a sunny window and give plenty of water. These are especially treated—your own roots won't work.

Hardy Spring Bulbs for Indoors
(See also Section 5.)

What spring-flowering bulbs can be forced in pots of soil for winter bloom? Follow recommendations for best forcing varieties in bulb mail-order catalogs. These include hyacinths, daffodils, tulips, and crocus.

How are hardy (spring-flowering) bulbs forced for winter bloom? In late October, pot the bulbs in a standard potting mixture or any garden soil that drains well. Allow 6 to 7 crocus bulbs, 3 to 5 daffodil bulbs, 5 to 9 tulip bulbs, and 3 to 6 hyacinth bulbs to each pot (bulbs are set much closer for forcing than they are in the open ground). The tips of the bulbs should be level with the surface of the soil in the pot. The bulbs require a cold period of 8 to 14 weeks to form roots, best accomplished by burying the pots in a trench so the tops of the pots are about 4 inches below the ground surface.

After watering the pots well, pack peat moss and/or leaves or straw around and on top of the pots about 4 inches deep. You can also place inverted flowerpots on the top of each pot before applying the mulch, which will keep out rodents. Or use a sheet of hardware cloth.

An alternative to the trench method, which makes it difficult to lift the pots when the ground freezes solid, even with the 4-inch mulch, is to put the pots in a cold frame—if you have one and there is space for the pots. Another alternative is to keep the pots in a cellar or basement

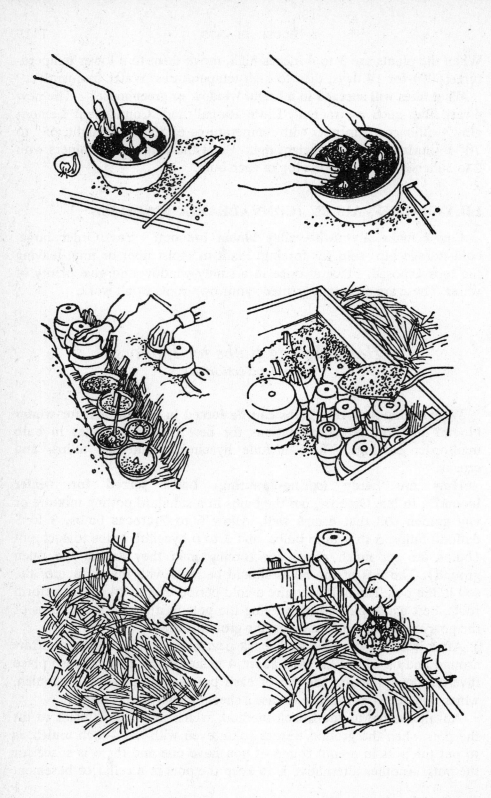

where the temperature does not go above 40° to 50° F. Do not let the soil dry out during this cold-storage period indoors.

As the pots develop shoots about 2 inches long, bring indoors to a cool, partially light place for about 10 days, then to a sunny window. Water as necessary. When blooms open, remove from full sun (but keep cool) to prolong the display.

Do you water daffodils or tulips that are potted and kept in a cold cellar for later forcing?   After the bulbs are potted, they should be thoroughly soaked. If conditions are right (i.e., if there is proper humidity in the cellar), they will not require additional watering. However, if pots dry out, they must be watered.

In how many days will tulips bloom after they are taken out of the cold-storage pit?   They will bloom in 4 to 8 weeks, depending on the earliness of the variety, the temperature, and how close the blooming period is to spring.

Can we plant tulip bulbs in indoor pots to bloom at Easter?   Yes. Bring pots into 60° F. about 3 to 4 weeks before Easter.

What care is given to spring-flowering bulbs forced for winter bloom after they have bloomed?   Foliage is ripened as in a garden, being kept green as long as possible. When leaves turn yellow and dry off, plant outdoors for garden bloom. Forced bulbs are unlikely to bloom again indoors and can take several seasons before recovering sufficiently to bloom again in the garden.

FORCING SPRING BULBS FOR INDOOR BLOOM

(Top row) Bulbs are planted close together, but not touching, in a pot or special bulb pan (a squat pot) so that the tips of the bulbs are at or just below the surface. (Second row) After covering the bulbs with soil, water thoroughly, then place the pots in a trench or cold frame. Inverted flowerpots protect the bulbs from rodents (or use a length of hardware cloth). Pots are covered with soil. Straw or leaves can be added to prevent the soil from freezing solid. (Bottom row) After several weeks, pots with sprouted bulbs can be brought indoors, but avoid very hot, dry rooms. Put the pots in your coolest rooms, especially when they are first brought indoors.

Tender Bulbs for Indoors

In what sort of soil should tender bulbs be grown?   Light, well-drained, and fertile soil. Avoid the use of *fresh* manure.

ACHIMENES   (See Section 5—Bulbs, Tubers and Corms.)

AGAPANTHUS

What is the proper care for an agapanthus in both the winter and summer?   In the winter, rest it. Keep nearly dry in a temperature of 45° F. In the spring, increase its water supply and temperature. In the summer, stand it outside in a sunny position; water and feed it freely. Repot in the spring only when growths become crowded. Expect bloom in April and May, water freely, and feed then. If you have space, dwarf varieties in small tubs will be most attractive.

How deep should lily-of-the-Nile (agapanthus) be planted in pots to take into a basement for the winter?   The tuberous roots should be planted just beneath the soil surface, so that the crown of the plant is practically at the surface.

AMARYLLIS (HIPPEASTRUM)

Are amaryllis bulbs planted inside or out? If outside, should they be lifted for the winter? When do they bloom? (Ohio.)   Plant in pots indoors, leaving the upper half of the bulb sticking out of the soil. They bloom from January to April, but the same bulb does not produce bloom over this entire period.

What soil should be used for amaryllis?   Garden soil enriched with superphosphate (1 pint per bushel) and commercial cow manure or compost (2 quarts per bushel).

How shall I plant an amaryllis bulb?   Select a pot just large enough to hold the bulb, comfortably surrounded by soil. Pot in the potting mixture described in the previous question, with the top half of the bulb exposed. Water well from below after potting.

When should I plant an amaryllis bulb? I planted one last year and there are no blooms.   Plant new bulbs from December to March.

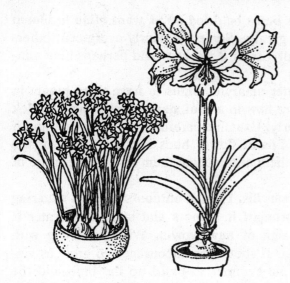

Two satisfactory house plants to grow from bulbs: the quick-growing, fragrant paper-white narcissus (left) and the flamboyant amaryllis (right).

Should amaryllis bulbs be kept in the dark until rooted? This is not necessary. A temperature of 60° to 70° F. and just sufficient moisture to keep the soil damp (all the way through) is all that is needed.

How can amaryllis bulbs be kept from year to year? Keep the plant growing by watering and feeding it during the season when leaves are developing or present—usually in the spring and summer. When the leaves die down, keep the plant dry. Repot every third or fourth year; topdress at the beginning of the growing period during other years. (See answers to other inquiries.)

How shall I topdress a potted amaryllis? By scraping off the top inch of soil in the pot without disturbing the bulb and substituting good garden loam containing a complete fertilizer.

Is there some fertilizer that I can feed an amaryllis to produce better and more blooms? When the plant is growing, and provided that the pot is well filled with roots, use any complete house-plant or garden fertilizer.

What is the trick of raising amaryllis indoors? Make sure that it is rested in the fall and early winter. Water freely, feed and otherwise encourage growth when the leaves are growing. Plunge (bury pot to its rim in soil) outdoors in a partially shaded spot during the summer. When potting, do not bury the bulb more than halfway in the soil.

How long do you leave an amaryllis bulb in dry soil before applying water? From the time the leaves are yellow and die away in late summer to fall, until the first signs of new growth can be seen sprouting out of the top of the bulb.

How long should amaryllis bulbs be dried off? I want mine to bloom in March.   Individuals vary greatly. Some are nearly evergreen; others die down quite early in the fall. Six or 8 weeks would perhaps be a minimum.

When should I start to water amaryllis bulbs to have them bloom in January or February? They are now in a cool, dark room in pots.   Pick out bulbs that went to rest early. Examine carefully in December, and if you can find any that show tips of flower buds out of the top of the bulb, start these by watering them and placing them in a temperature of 70° to 75° F.

Last Easter I bought an amaryllis. I left it outdoors without watering it until September, when I brought it indoors and started to water it again. To date there is no sign of any growth. What is wrong with it?   You dried it off too soon. It should be encouraged to grow as vigorously as possible through the summer to build up the bulb and the following year's bloom.

In what window should amaryllis be kept—south or east?   Either exposure should be satisfactory. They need as much sunlight as possible during the winter and spring, and light shade during the summer.

I have some fine hybrid amaryllis bulbs which bloomed the first year; now—in spite of following directions for resting, feeding, etc.—I get no more blooms, though the bulbs are growing well with big leaves. I have had bulbs 2 years. What is the trouble?   Amaryllis bought and flowered the first year often fail to bloom the second year. Their energy is used to establish a new root system. As good foliage has developed, your plants should bloom from the third year on. Usually 2 to 3 leaves guarantee that the bulb will form buds.

Why don't hybrid amaryllis bulbs brought home from Florida bloom? I have about 3 dozen bulbs and all bloomed before we got them.   It may be that they have not established themselves yet. This may take a year. (Read other replies on this subject.)

What is the best way to grow amaryllis bulbs to a really large size? Mine seldom reach 3 inches in diameter.   Good cultivation over a period of years is the answer. This implies potting, watering, feeding, resting when required, suitable soil, temperature, and light conditions, as well as maintaining the plants free from pests. (See previous questions.)

Is bulb fiber as good as soil for growing an amaryllis bulb?   No. To grow these successfully so that they will last from year to year, nourishment is needed, and this is not contained in most kinds of bulb fiber.

Is it unusual for an amaryllis to bloom in December?   No, it is not particularly unusual, although most bulbs produce their flowers later in the winter.

Do amaryllis often bloom more than once a year? Mine bloomed 3 times this year. The amaryllis (*Hippeastrum*) does not bloom more than once a season. Strong bulbs will sometimes produce more than one flower scape, however. If your plant blooms every 3 or 4 months, it is something other than *Hippeastrum*. There are many bulbs of the amaryllis family (*Amaryllidaceae*) with varying characteristics.

How can a fine hybrid amaryllis (Hippeastrum) be propagated vegetatively to make a rapid increase in the stock of bulbs? By cutting the bulb into segments, each containing a small part of the basal ring. These pieces are planted in sand and peat moss and placed where a bottom heat of 70° F. is available. Keep just moist and shaded and new bulblets should arise in a few weeks.

I have amaryllis hybrids, from seed, already as big as marbles, but they have stopped growing. Should the bulb be nearly out of the soil? What fertilizer should be used and how often? What soil is needed? Bulbs of young amaryllis naturally grow out of the soil. They will cease growing for a period in late summer. Use superphosphate in the soil, which should be a medium porous loam. Feed when in active growth with liquid fertilizer.

AMAZON-LILY (EUCHARIS GRANDIFLORA)

Can I grow the beautiful Amazon-lily outside a greenhouse? Yes, this very fragrant member of the amaryllis family will thrive in a light, rather than a sunny, location.

How should I plant bulbs of Eucharis-lily? This makes a big plant with 18-inch stems and glossy evergreen leaves. Allow a 5-inch pot for each bulb and provide a fairly warm place, 70° to 75° F., until buds appear. Then cooler growing, about 65° F., is better. Water well after potting and fertilize until the bloom is developed; then stop feeding until a new set of buds appears. After each period of bloom, induce a 4- to 5-week rest with the soil somewhat dry, but not to the point that the plants' leaves wilt.

AMORPHOPHALLUS   (See Hydrosme.)

ARUM PALAESTINUM (BLACK-CALLA)

What is the history of the black-lily-of-the-Nile? *Arum palaestinum*, also called the black-calla, is a native of Palestine, a relative of our common skunk-cabbage, of the tropical anthurium, and of the white calla-lily. It was first discovered by the Genevan botanist M. Boissier near Jerusalem.

What can I do to make a black-calla come into bloom? I have tried but to no avail. Perhaps your tuber is too small and will bloom when older. Grow it in rich soil, keeping it moist and in a light place during the summer. Dry it off completely during the winter.

BOWIEA VOLUBILIS (CLIMBING-ONION)

How can bowiea be grown? The climbing-onion is a South African plant with large onionlike bulbs from which are formed tall, delicate, green vinelike growths. Pot in a porous soil with only the base of the bulb buried. Give it a sunny window. Keep the soil moist when green growth is in evidence, dry at other times. It goes many years without needing to be repotted.

CALADIUM

What is the proper culture for caladium tubers? Set each tuber in a 5-inch pot of humus-rich soil. Their growing time is April until October so they are more useful as terrace rather than house plants. At the start, give shade and heat, 70° to 80° F., and keep well watered. Gradually dry off toward fall. *Caladium humboldtii* is a dainty miniature useful in large terrariums and gardens under fluorescent lights.

After getting caladium bulbs to start, I find that the leaves are small, but the stems of the leaves are abnormally long. What causes this? The bulbs are growing in a window which gets some sun during the day. This is usually true of the first few leaves. If the condition persists, it is probably because of a lack of light or humidity, which should be 60 per cent or higher.

How should a caladium that has finished blooming in the house be treated? As soon as the plant begins to lose foliage in the fall, gradually reduce watering. When all leaves have gone, withhold water completely and store the pots containing the bulbs in a dry place, at 60° F., or remove the tubers, dry them off, and store each one in a heavy paper bag for 2 to 3 months of rest.

CALLA-LILY (ZANTEDESCHIA)

When should calla-lilies be planted for Christmas bloom? Pot tubers in August, each in a 4- or 5-inch pot of humus-rich soil; water and set in a dim place at 55° to 60° F. until growth is well started; then move to light and warmth, but below 70°, and fertilize. As flower stalk develops, move to a sunny place. Water moderately at first but keep almost wet as the plant develops.

How should calla-lily tubers be cared for after blooming? Keep feeding the plants (good organic fertilizer) and encourage strong growth until June, then gradually dry them off, turn the pots on their sides, and rest until September. Repot and start into growth at this time.

I have a white calla-lily 5 years old which never has blossomed. What is the reason? This plant needs rich soil, ample moisture during the growing season, at a temperature of 50° to 60° F., feeding when in active growth, and a definite rest period during late summer.

CLIVIA

Can clivias be grown as window plants? Yes. Stand potted plants outdoors in the summer; feed and water them regularly. Bring indoors before frost and give them a light window. Water enough to prevent shriveling, as the plant is evergreen. When buds push up, give the plants more water.

I have had a clivia 6 years which bloomed only when I bought it. Are there any secrets of how to make it bloom? Clivias need cool growing conditions and full sunlight, except during summer months, when light shade is appreciated. They resent disturbance at their roots. The soil should always be moist but not waterlogged. During the summer, feed at weekly intervals with liquid plant food.

CRINUM

Can you give me information on crinum-lilies? When grown in large pots or tubs, they need good drainage and rich soil. Plant them half out of the soil. Store them in the winter in a light place, at a temperature of 50° F., and water only a little. In the spring, increase the temperature and water more freely. In the summer, water freely; feed generously; place outdoors in a sunny location. These are summer-blooming.

What is the proper culture for crinum (milk-and-wine-lily)? Mine does not bloom but develops many bulblets. Plant in a very rich but well-drained soil in large pots or tubs. Set the bulbs with their top half protruding above the soil. Water and feed established plants generously in the summer and grow in a sunny position (outside in hot weather). Keep in a cool, frostproof place and nearly dry in the winter. Repot only every 3 to 4 years.

EUCHARIS   (See Amazon-lily, this section.)

FREESIA

When is the best time to start freesias in the house and how should they be taken care of? Plant bulbs in September in fertile, porous soil. Space them 1½ inches apart. Put in a cool place. Give only a little water at first, more as growth develops. Place in a cool, sunny window, 50° to 60° F., when the tops are 1 to 2 inches high. Avoid overwatering. Feed lightly when flower buds appear.

How can I have a succession of freesia blooms in my window garden? Plant bulbs at 2-week intervals from September to November; 3 months are needed from planting to flowering.

My freesias planted in pots grew well but did not bloom. Why? After being planted, freesias need a period in a cool, frostproof, light place to develop root growth. When growth starts, the temperature should be 40° to 50° F. at night, with a 5° or 10° rise in the daytime.

My freesias last year were more beautiful than all expectations, exceeding those at the Philadelphia Flower Show. This year I took care of them but they are spindly and small-leaved; I used fertilizer this year but not last. This has happened before. Why? I bought giant-sized bulbs. It is advisable to buy new bulbs each year. The quality of bloom depends largely upon the cultivation the bulbs received the *previous* year. In a house or small greenhouse, it is difficult to provide ideal conditions for bulb development.

Why are my freesia leaves turning yellow? They are 8 to 9 inches high. Overwatering will quickly cause freesia leaves to turn yellow. Lack of sufficient light, low humidity, or extreme dryness of the soil will cause a similar condition.

My freesias are growing spindly without blossoming and are drying

up. Why? The temperature may be too high, the atmosphere too dry, and possibly there is a lack of sufficient sunlight.

How should freesias that bloom in the house be cared for to have bulbs for another year? Mine will bloom about Christmastime. If brought into bloom as early as Christmas, it may be difficult to provide conditions that will ensure good bulbs for the following year. Water, feed, and keep them growing in a sunny, cool position until the foliage fades, then gradually dry them off. It is more satisfactory to start with new bulbs each year.

I've grown freesias from bulbs and have lots of little bulblets. Will they bloom? They are planted now. They will not bloom while very small, but if grown under good conditions they should soon make blooming-size stock.

GLORY-LILY (GLORIOSA)

What is the proper culture for this climbing lily? This is *Gloriosa superba* or *G. rothschildiana,* two excellent plants for a warm, sunny window. Plant in February in a 6-inch pot half full of house-plant soil. Lay the flat tuber on this and cover with more soil to within an inch of the top. (Insert three equidistant 2-foot stakes unless you plan to train the plant on strings around a window.) Growth will start in about 2 weeks. Apply liquid plant food every other week from then on. Buds will appear in about 12 weeks, the yellow or yellow-marked scarlet blooms continuing through spring and summer.

Does the glory-lily require a rest period? Yes, gradually reduce watering and withhold by October. Leave the tuber in the pot. If possible, do not repot when growth is started again in February; try to scrape away the topsoil and add a fresh mixture.

My gloriosa tuber looks healthy but it will not sprout. What could be wrong? Most gloriosa tubers have only one live bud or "eye." If something happens to this primary growing point, the tuber may remain sound (like a potato) for several years without sprouting. If your tuber does not have a plump live bud, it would be better to start with a new tuber. When selecting tubers at garden centers, be sure to pick sound tubers with an obvious bud.

GLOXINIA (SINNINGIA)

What soil mixture should gloxinia tubers have for best growth? Should gloxinias be watered from the top or bottom? A loose, humus-rich soil. Adding flaky leafmold, compost, sharp sand, and broken charcoal to the mixture is helpful. They can be watered from top to bottom, provided that the soil is thoroughly wetted and no water is splashed on the leaves.

What are the cultural requirements for the gloxinia (Sinningia speciosa), from tuber planting to maturity and back to rest again?   Put tubers in pots just large enough to hold them, in light, humus-rich soil, February or March. Keep just moist in a temperature of 70° F., increasing the water supply as growth develops. Pot into 5- or 6-inch pots when the first pots are filled with roots. Feed a complete fertilizer biweekly when in full growth. Shade from the sun. Dry off gradually after flowering.

Will you please tell me if gloxinias grow best in a shady or sunny place?   Shade from anything but weak early-morning and late-afternoon sunlight is necessary. They thrive under fluorescent tubes.

What is the correct temperature for gloxinias? How should watering be done?   During the growing season, a minimum temperature of 60° F. (rising to 70° in the daytime) is satisfactory. Watering should be done with caution until a good growth of leaves has developed, then it may be given more freely.

Why do my gloxinia buds turn brown and die?   This may be due to an infestation of mites, but more probably the air is too dry. A moist, but not stagnant, atmosphere and freedom from draft provide congenial conditions.

Why do my gloxinias grow tall and lanky? Those I have seen at florist shops are bushy.   This can be due to too little light. They need shade from bright sun, but good light otherwise. Grow your gloxinias 6 to 8 inches below three or four 40-watt broad-spectrum fluorescent lamps.

Why do gloxinia leaves curl and look limp? I drop no water on the leaves.   You probably are keeping the soil too dry or you have watered it so much that the roots have rotted off. Gloxinia leaves normally die down after flowering.

What is the proper care for gloxinias after they bloom?   Shortly after their blooming is over, begin to reduce the moisture supply by increasing the intervals between applications. As the leaves die down, intensify this drying-off process; finally store the plants (leaving the tubers in the soil) in a dry place at a temperature of 45° to 50° F.

When can I take my gloxinia out of storage and start it growing?   From mid-February to the end of March. If it shows signs of activity (new leaves appearing), it should be potted and started without delay.

What is the proper blooming season for gloxinias? Under greenhouse conditions, with skilled cultivation, they may be brought to bloom at almost any time. However, they are naturally summer and early-fall bloomers, and it is easiest to have them in flower at those seasons.

Are there any compact or dwarf gloxinias suitable for small gardens under fluorescent lights? Yes, hybridizers have developed dwarf gloxinias with 4- to 8-inch mature height although the flowers are large and showy. The red and white 'Tom Thumb' is a popular dwarf gloxinia. Then there are the miniature sinningias, which vary in spread and height from a few inches to about 6 inches. They have small tubers and tend to be nearly everblooming, especially in the humid atmosphere of a terrarium or brandy snifter. *Sinningia pusilla,* one of several small species, has tiny lilac flowers; 'Dollbaby' has larger lavender-blue flowers.

Which gives the better result in starting a new gloxinia: to plant a leaf after it has rooted in water or to plant the unrooted leaf in soil immediately? The best plan is to root the leaf cuttings in moist sand or sand mixed with leafmold or peat moss.

How and when does one start new gloxinia plants from their leaves? Leaf cuttings consist of partly matured, medium-sized leaves with some of the apex portion cut away. They are taken in early summer and planted in sand and leafmold, or sand and peat moss, in a warm propagating bed. Keep only just moist until new tubers form.

In starting gloxinias from leaf cuttings, what is done after a tuber and roots have formed? Mine don't seem to start. If cuttings are started late in the season, the young tubers are rested through the winter and started up in the spring. Even with early summer-rooted cuttings, a period often elapses between the formation of the roots and tuber and development of leaves.

What is the best method of starting gloxinia from seed? Sow in January or February on milled sphagnum moss. The seeds are exceedingly small and should not be covered with soil but firmly pressed into the surface. Sow sparsely or you will be inundated! Keep evenly moist at all times in a temperature of 70° F. Shade seedlings; feed with ¼-strength water-soluble fertilizer when fully germinated. Transplant as soon as they are large enough to handle.

HAEMANTHUS (BLOOD-LILY)

Can the blood-lily, a native of South Africa, be started in the house in the winter and set out in the spring, then taken in the house again and

the same culture repeated? Haemanthuses should not be taken out of their pots and set in the garden. If desired, pots could be plunged to their rims in soil outdoors (in light shade) during the hottest months.

HYACINTH (HYACINTHUS)

I have seen hyacinths forced in the winter in dishes of fiber or pebbles. What kind are they, and how should they be handled? These are the delicate, fragrant Roman hyacinths. For Christmas bloom, plant in mid-October and grow cold for 5 to 6 weeks while roots form. Then bring first to a cool, light window, then to a sunny place as buds form.

(*Left*) *Bulb pan removed from prerooting storage, ready to be brought indoors.* (*Right*) *Paper cone with a small opening at the top is used during early growth of hyacinth* (*center*) *to draw flower stem from foliage.*

HYDROSME

What is the sacred lily-of-India? This plant has been known as *Hydrosme* but is now called *Amorphophallus rivieri*—a relative of the calla-lily and a native of China. In the spring, large tubers produce a tall, dark-colored, fetid, callalike bloom; in the summer, a single, stout leaf of umbrella shape finely divided into many leaflets.

I have been given a sacred lily-of-India which is supposed to bloom black. It looks like a large potato. How do I care for it? Grow it in a pot of loose, humus-rich soil or plant it out in a garden in the summer. A leaf is produced in the summer, a flower in the spring. In the fall, dig up (if in the garden) and keep dry until the following spring. The flower is exceedingly interesting, but it has an offensive odor. However, the flower doesn't last long and the leaf that follows is very ornamental.

IXIA

How can ixias be grown? I cannot make them live. Bulbs start, then die off. Treat exactly like freesias. Pot in early fall, spacing the bulbs about 2 inches apart. Water carefully at first, more freely afterward. Grow in a cool, well-lighted position (night temperature, 45° F.). Dry off gradually after flowering. Avoid overwatering and high temperatures.

NARCISSUS (DAFFODIL)

Which tender narcissus bulbs are grown as house plants in water and pebbles for winter bloom? Is the culture the same for all? Paperwhites, pure white, fragrant; 'Soleil d'Or', golden yellow, fragrant; Chinese sacred-lily, two shades of yellow, fragrant. Yes, all are forced in the same way.

How can I grow tender narcissus as house plants? Buy bulbs from a reliable source so that you will know that they have been well grown. Plant in a soilless mix or soil, or put in dishes of water and pebbles to which bits of charcoal have been added. Place for 2 weeks in a cool dark closet or cellar until growth starts. As roots develop, bring to more light. Keep cool. When foliage growth begins to develop, place in a cool, sunny window.

I started some paper-white narcissus the first of November; now they are about 3 inches high. How long before I should bring them into the light and a warmer temperature? They should be brought into the growing temperature immediately.

When narcissus bulbs are planted in the house, is there any way to keep them from getting so tall? My present ones are now 30 inches high. These are undoubtedly being grown at too high a temperature. The best daytime temperature is 65° to 70° F. The lower the temperature, the shorter and more satisfactory the plants will be. Moving plantings to a cool garage at night helps to keep growth lower and to prolong bloom after the flowers open.

Why do my narcissus bulbs have only leaves and not flowers (bulbs grown indoors in water)? If the bulbs are of good quality, failure is most often caused by excessively high temperatures.

My paper-white narcissus, growing in pebbles in a cool cellar, grow tall and fall over before blooming. Why? They must have been planted too early and kept in a dark place too long. They must have full light to mature. If planted about September 5 to 10, they should bloom by Thanksgiving, a matter of 10 weeks. Later plantings take less time; plant in mid-November for Christmas.

What procedure should be used in keeping paper-white narcissus bulbs for next season? It is impractical to keep paper-white narcissus over from year to year. Discard after flowering unless you live in a mild climate. Then the bulbs can be planted in the open ground.

ORNITHOGALUM (STAR-OF-BETHLEHEM)

What is the proper culture for Ornithogalum arabicum? Is it a good house plant? Excellent. You can plant 6 or 7 bulbs, 1 inch deep, in a low flowerpot (bulb pan) in a mixture of half-and-half leafmold and sand. Plant from September to February. Grow cool, about 60° F., in a light place, particularly until the foliage is well advanced. Then move to a sunny place and keep the soil just moist. Let the foliage go on growing until it begins to die down naturally. Store the pots in a cool, dark place until fall. Then repot in a fresh soil mixture.

I have carefully followed the directions for Ornithogalum miniatum, with poor results. Only 1 bulb out of 4 in the same pot has started and that has blossomed low. What is the trouble? This species needs considerably more warmth and more moist conditions than most ornithogalums. A temperature of 60° F. at night and 65° to 70° F. in the daytime is not too much.

OXALIS

How should I care for oxalis? I have several different kinds. Tender oxalis are potted in September, 3 or 4 bulbs in a 4-inch pot or bulb pan in porous, fertile soil. Water carefully at first; more freely as growth develops. Repot into a 5-inch pot when the 4-inch pot is filled with roots. When blooming is over, gradually reduce water and keep quite dry through the summer. Grow in a temperature of 60° F.

Why can't I grow oxalis successfully in the house? Because the environment is likely not suitable. They need plenty of sunlight, ample water during their growing season, none during the dormant period, a loose, porous soil, and a temperature of 55° to 65° F.

How do you store, and where is the best place to plant, oxalis bulbs? During their dormant season, leave the bulbs in soil in the pots, keep dry, and store in a cellar or shed. They may be grown in pots or in hanging baskets in a greenhouse, sun-room, or sunny window.

Why do my oxalis bloom for only a short time in my window garden? Oxalis have a definite season of bloom. Unlike some geraniums, begonias, and fuchsias, they do not produce flowers over a period of months.

Why don't my oxalis bloom? I have one in an east window and one in a west window. Possibly lack of sufficient light. These plants need full exposure to sunshine for good results. Overcrowding or an unsuitable soil may be contributory causes, or too low humidity.

RANUNCULUS

My ranunculus is dying leaf by leaf; it's in a north window. What is the cause? Probably it is too warm and dry. This bulbous plant must be grown indoors in cool (night temperature, 45° F.) moist conditions for best results. A cool sun or plant room would afford the right conditions.

VALLOTA SPECIOSA

What can you tell me about Vallota speciosa? The Scarborough-lily is a tender evergreen bulb. It needs rich, porous soil. Repotting is resented and should be resorted to only when absolutely necessary. Never let its soil become dry. Grow in full sun and feed the plants vigorously.

VELTHEIMIA VIRIDIFOLIA

How shall I plant and care for my veltheimia bulb? Pot in a standard soil mixture in a 6- or 8-inch pot with the upper half of the bulb exposed. Give regular water and sunshine through autumn. The bloom should begin to develop around Thanksgiving and be open for Christmas or soon after. It lasts several weeks. After flowers fade, cut off the blooming stem but continue to give water and light while the handsome foliage remains green. As it dies back, toward spring, gradually reduce its water. Store in its pot turned on its side on the damp floor of a potting shed or outdoors during the summer. When new growth starts in the fall, increase its water, feed it with a complete plant food, and give it full sunlight in a cool window.

Veltheimia is a winter-flowering bulb native to South Africa. In a cool, well-lighted window garden the bloom remains in good condition for 5 to 6 weeks.

What shall I do with the small bulb which has appeared on the side of my veltheimia? When its leaves die back, gently remove the offset from the parent bulb and pot it separately.

13. Plant Troubles and Their Control

PLANT PESTS ARE probably as old as the plants themselves. We know that insects antedated man by millions of years and we know that plant diseases plagued the ancient Romans. Some diseases, like the potato blight that caused the Irish famine of 1846, have changed the course of history. The application of pesticides is likewise not new, sulfur being recommended as early as 1000 B.C., but our modern concept of protecting plants with chemicals starts with the discovery of Bordeaux mixture in 1882.

For many years gardeners took care of their problems with a limited number of pesticides. The plant medicine chest usually included nicotine sulfate and soap for sucking insects, lead arsenate for chewers, or sometimes pyrethrum and rotenone, lime-sulfur or oil for dormant spraying, and sulfur or copper for plant diseases.

The development of DDT during World War II brought spectacular success in control of plant as well as human pests and encouraged a flood of synthetic organic chemicals. In 1947, the Federal Insecticide, Fungicide and Rodenticide Act (known as FIFRA) provided for the registration of all pesticides with the U. S. Department of Agriculture. A further requirement of this act was that complete information concerning the chemical be carried on the label of the container. Soon, more than 60,000 formulations were registered under trade names and it became difficult to select the right product for a particular problem.

In 1961, it was one woman, Rachel Carson, and the publication of her *Silent Spring* that focused attention on the effect of all these pesticides on the environment. Since then the flood of new chemicals has been reduced markedly and registration has been shifted from the U. S. Department of Agriculture to the Environmental Protection Agency, formed in 1970.

In 1972, the Federal Environmental Pest Control Act, which drastically amended the Federal Insecticide, Fungicide and Rodenticide Act, was signed into law to become fully effective by 1976. This legislation regulated, for the first time, actual uses of each pesticide by making it illegal to apply a chemical inconsistent with the directions on the label. Thus, an insecticide or fungicide could be used legally only for those pests and plants specifically named on the label. In 1978, amendments were passed to permit the use of a pesticide for a pest or pests not on the label, *if* the chemical is labeled for use against another pest on the same plant and if the label does not say for use *only* against those pests listed. Also allowed under the amendments are application methods other than those outlined on the label unless expressly prohibited, and dilution rates *less* than specified.

The amended FIFRA also provides for the classification of pesticides into two categories—*general use,* for home gardeners, and *restricted use,* for certified applicators, either private or commercial.

A process has been devised to evaluate the registration of pesticide uses by the EPA, including the reregistration of uses on existing labels. It is based on the known and probable disadvantages and advantages or risks and benefits of pesticide usage. The EPA is responsible for determining the risks of pesticide use and the USDA, the benefits. The process is referred to by the acronym RPAR (Rebuttable Presumption Against Registration). In applying this process, when a potential risk is identified by the EPA it becomes the basis for a presumption against registering specific, or, in some cases, all, uses or restricting certain uses. That presumption can be rebutted, followed by a benefit-risk evaluation, and a decision by EPA to register, not to register, to restrict, or to ban existing or newly developed pesticides. This is and will be a continuing effort for the foreseeable future, making it essential that you keep in close contact with your local and state Cooperative Extension Service for current, legal recommendations.

The quality of the environment is the main concern, and under the amended FIFRA legislation, penalties may be incurred by anyone who uses a pesticide in a manner inconsistent with instructions on the label. States can legislate further restrictions, and many have already done so. At the present time, a number of pesticides are either under or being considered for RPAR review, including carbaryl (Sevin), lindane, benomyl (Benlate), and others.

The pesticides that the home gardener can now purchase without restrictions are relatively safe for plants, the environment, and the user but they should still be applied with caution. Carbaryl, for instance, is widely recommended for performance and for safety, but it does kill bees and some other beneficial insects. Rotenone, long used on vegetables, kills fish. Pesticides should be applied only as necessary, at the proper dilution rate and at the *right time,* after proper diagnosis of the problem. In some cases, protection of the environment may mean less-than-perfect control of a pest.

Importance of Diagnosis

In plant medicine, as in human medicine, accurate diagnosis is nine tenths of the cure. You must know what is wrong with your plant before you can select the right control measure. The wrong medicine, or even unnecessary medicine, can do more harm than good.

Some diseases and pests are readily recognized by home gardeners; others are extraordinarily difficult even for a specialist to identify. If you are in doubt, do nothing until you get advice from some competent person. (Your neighbor is usually not qualified, even though his advice is profuse and free!) The most reliable source of advice is your county agent or your State Extension Service. It is helpful to send a specimen and a description. Send a whole plant if feasible, for the trouble you think is in the leaf may originate in the stem or roots. Diseased material travels best flattened out between layers of newspaper. Don't send live insects about the country, for they can escape and establish themselves in some hitherto-uninfested area. Insects may be quickly killed by dropping them into a small jar or vial of 70 per cent rubbing alcohol.

In making your own diagnosis, check the obvious things first. *The name of the plant is of primary importance.* Some insects and diseases are promiscuous, attacking a wide variety of plants; but others are highly selective, attacking only the members of a certain family, or even genus, so that the name of the host plant can mean almost immediate identification.

Consider also the time of year. A webby mass in a tree in the spring probably means tent caterpillars; in late summer it indicates fall webworms. An elm leaf perforated in May is probably chewed by a cankerworm; in June, by the elm-leaf beetle; in July, by the Japanese beetle. These dates are for New Jersey. If you live in Florida, or California, or Maine, your dates, as well as your pests, may be quite different. That is one reason for you to keep in close touch with the information put out by your own local Cooperative Extension Service.

Diagnosis is a process of elimination. After knowing the plant that is being attacked and the time of year, look at the foliage. Holes in leaves are probably the work of some chewing insect, although there are one or two diseases that cause shotlike holes.

Disease is the term applied to the abnormal condition that comes from the work of bacteria, fungi, nematodes, viruses, one or two higher forms of plants, or unfavorable environmental conditions.

Injury is the term applied to havoc caused by insects. The different chewing insects make their own patterns in the leaves. When all the leaves of a single twig or branch are chewed off down to the midrib, or, as in the case of pine, the needles are chewed down to the fascicles, then sawfly larvae may be responsible. Flea beetles make tiny round perforations, so familiar in newly set tomato plants unless they have been coated with a protective dust; weevils produce rather typical angular openings; beetle larvae (grubs) and certain caterpillars often "skeletonize" leaves, chewing everything but the epidermis and veins.

If the leaf is yellowish, or stippled white, or gray, the loss of color may be due to sucking insects. You may see them or their cast-off skins, eggs, or excrement on the underside of the foliage. Yellowed or finely stippled leaves that are cobwebby underneath indicate red spider mites, while whitish streaks mean thrips. If there is no sign of insects, the yellowed leaf may be a symptom of malnutrition, perhaps lack of nitrogen or unavailable iron. Leaves curled up or cupped down may harbor aphids; deformed leaves may be due to the cyclamen mite or to sucking insects on buds or developing new growth; blotches or tunnels, to leafminers; round or conical protrusions, to mites, aphids, midges, or gall wasps.

Leaf spots with definite outlines and filled with numerous minute dark pimples are of fungus origin; smooth spots are usually symptoms of a bacterial disease. Fungi may produce irregular blotches on a leaf, but if the black specks or pimples are missing, the blotches may be sunscald or windburn—the result of cells collapsing when water could not get up from the roots fast enough to replace that evaporated from the leaves. Spray injury also produces leaf spots. When phlox leaves die progressively up the stem, it very likely is due to some unbalanced water relation; but if chrysanthemum leaves die in the same fashion, it may be due to drought, leafspot fungus, a wilt fungus in the soil, or to leaf nematodes, the latter being more probable with Korean varieties. Reddish pustules on a leaf indicate rust, very common on hollyhocks; a white felty growth, mildew; and dark soot, a mold living on aphis honeydew.

A dark lesion, or canker, on a stem indicates a fungus disease; a sawdustlike protrusion is the sign of a borer; but a gummy substance exuding on a peach tree may be caused either by the peach-tree borer or the brown-rot fungus.

Wilt—the partial collapse and dying back of a plant—can result from any one of many causes: high temperature, lack of moisture, root injury from too-close cultivation, too-strong fertilizer, a soil fungus that invades the vascular system, or one that causes a crown or stem rot, large grubs, or microscopic nematodes working on the roots. Rots may follow physiological disturbances, and then millipedes and other small animals feast on the disintegrating tissues. *Determine, if you can, the primary cause, and don't worry about the secondary effects.*

It all sounds enormously complicated, but with a little practice you learn to recognize at a glance the signs and symptoms of common pests and diseases, just as you recognize your acquaintances when you pass them on the street. You don't stop to analyze why that is Mrs. Smith; you just know that it is. With a little more training you'll be noticing signs in spite of yourself and walking along the street muttering, "The lacebugs have certainly made Mrs. Smith's azalea look sick; I wonder why Mrs. Jones never sprays her junipers for scale; Mr. Brown's corn smut is a public menace. If the Board of Health makes me cut down my ragweed they ought to make him clean up his smut boils."

Types of Control

Having, as far as possible, diagnosed your plant trouble, how are you going to control it? There are four main avenues of approach: immunization, exclusion, suppression, and protection—and sometimes it takes all four.

1—Immunization means the development, by hybridization or selection, of varieties which are resistant to certain pests. One hundred per cent resistance, or total immunity, is impossible, but if you can buy varieties reasonably resistant to the pests most prevalent in your locality, that is the first, and easiest, control method to attempt. Most seed catalogs list resistant varieties, and your Cooperative Extension Service will help you out with suggestions.

There is a theory, widely held by gardeners, that vigorous plants are more resistant to diseases and pests. This is more often due to coincidence rather than to any true relationship between lack of vigor and susceptibility. The same cultural practices which produce a vigorous plant often check the spread of pests. Spider mites flourish and plants languish in close quarters where there is little air circulation. Proper pruning and feeding of elm trees check the spread of Dutch elm disease only indirectly by reducing weak or dead wood in which the bark beetle, disseminator of the fungus, lays its eggs. Some fungi, weak parasites, can enter plants only through wounds, and thrive on decaying tissue; but other parasites, such as rusts, smuts, and mildews, can operate only on a vigorous plant. In corn-breeding experiments it has. been found that hybrids of high vigor are more susceptible to smut than those of low vigor; but since vigor is more important than smut resistance, we must continue to control this fungus by eradication methods. Vigorous plants can better withstand many pests, which may make them appear to be more resistant.

Japanese beetles definitely prefer young, succulent leaves to old and wilting ones, and you never find Mexican bean beetles waiting until plants are weakened before they move in!

There are some rather hazy theories about plant nutrition as a factor in disease resistance, but we have not yet gone very far along this line. No matter how well plants are cultivated and fed, one still cannot ignore their insects and diseases. The sooner this fact is recognized, the sooner the gardener will get over having nightmares about pests and learn to take them in his stride. He cannot have a garden without planting seeds; he cannot continue to have a healthy garden, year after year, unless pest control becomes a routine operation.

2—*Exclusion* is practiced by counties, states, and countries by means of quarantine laws and regulations, backed up by careful inspections. You can apply the same principle to your garden by looking at every plant, whether acquired by gift or purchase, with a suspicious eye before allowing entry. If you insist on acquiring a diseased plant, either disinfect it or put it in isolation, far removed from your healthy plants.

Buy certified seed when you can. That means that government inspectors looked at the seed plants in the field and certified them as being free from specific diseases. Treating seed with hot water or a disinfectant is another exclusion measure. Farmers, through their cooperatives, have been able to obtain treated seed more readily than the home gardener, but many seed dealers do disinfect seeds sold in small packets.

3—*Suppression,* of course, means the destruction of a pest after it gets established in an area. It includes soil sterilization to kill soil fungi or nematodes, or treating the soil with an insecticide to kill grubs—or eliminating an ant nest, or breaking off a tent caterpillar egg mass or hand-picking bagworms. It means picking Japanese beetles and dropping them into a can of kerosene, or putting milky-disease bacteria into the soil where their grubs develop. It may mean taking up an entire plant and its surrounding soil (as in crown rot), or cutting off a branch of apple or pear that has fire blight. It means removing rose leaves infected with black spot; cleaning up peach or plum "mummies" (wizened, dried-up fruits) or maggot-riddled apples; or spading under all vegetable refuse after harvest. Burning is now restricted in an effort to decrease local air pollution.

Suppression may mean crop rotation to starve out the insect or disease, or cleaning up additional weed hosts, or eliminating some plant that is an "alternate host" and so a necessary factor in the life cycle of a certain disease. Pest-control measures were applied long before people understood the nature of the plant disease. The first barberry eradication law was passed in France in 1660, when it was noticed that wheat rust flourished when barberries grew nearby. Nowadays we sometimes try to isolate red-cedars to prevent the apple rust fungus from completing its cycle, and take out black currants to save nearby pines from blister rust.

To sum it up, suppression is really garden sanitation, the removal of all factors injurious to plant health. *It is probably the most important control method available to the home gardener.*

4—Protection involves the spraying and dusting of plants to prevent or to keep away insects or diseases. (Some dormant spraying, however, is more properly a suppression measure.) When chemicals are applied in a wet mist, we call it "spraying"; and when they are applied as a dry powder, the operation is known as "dusting." There are many arguments as to the relative advantages of dusting and spraying; but each has its place, even in the small garden. The lazy gardener will use an aerosol can or his small dust gun more often than his sprayer, which should be—though it seldom is—thoroughly cleaned after each use.

A spray or dust used against insects is called an "insecticide," and one against bacteria and fungi a "fungicide." In addition there are "fumigants" and "disinfectants," "attractants" and "repellents," as well as materials called adjuvants to make the sprays spread and stick.

Sometimes one chemical serves two purposes. A dormant lime sulfur is used both as a fungicide and a dormant spray for scale insects and aphid eggs. Sulfur dust is effective against mildew and red spider mites. Bordeaux mixture—a copper fungicide—sometimes serves as a repellent for insects.

Insecticides can control insects by being swallowed; by hitting their bodies or touching their feet; when their vapors enter the insects' breathing organs; and when they repel them because of odor or taste.

Just how any given insecticide affects insects may depend on its characteristics, when it is applied, how it is applied, and the nature of the pests involved. Most of our newer insecticides will destroy insects in more than one of the above ways.

Insecticides and fungicides are sold under hundreds of different brand names, all variations in one way or another, based on a relatively small number of chemicals. The brand name is unimportant except as it indicates a reliable manufacturer; *it is important to read the label on each package and know you are using the right chemical at the right dilution for your particular purpose.* Most pesticides have both a trade name, such as Sevin, with its first letter capitalized, and an accepted common name, carbaryl, with a small letter. Both names, unlike the brand name, do indicate the pesticidal ingredients. Other examples are: benomyl (Benlate), folpet (Phaltan), maneb (Manzate D, Dithane M-22), mancozeb (Manzate 200, Dithane, Fore), malathion (Cythion), diazinon (Spectracide, Gardentox), dicofol (Kelthane), chlorpyrifos (Dursbar), and dimethoate (Cygon, DeFend).

The possibility of spray injury is ever present. Some plants are at all times sensitive to certain chemicals; others can stand them if it is not too warm or too cold. There is grave danger of injury when two incompatible chemicals are mixed together.

It is not possible to cure all garden troubles with one general spray any more than one kind of pill will cure all human ills, from a sprained ankle to cancer. Sometimes, however, sprays or dusts can be combined to take care of both insects and diseases of certain kinds. Such combination sprays or dusts can be purchased under brand names or, occasionally, mixed at home.

The timeliness of the application is most important. Fungicides should be applied *before* rains, so that a protective coating will be present when the fungus spore or the bacterium starts to grow in the presence of moisture. For fungus diseases, spraying should start *well before the disease is expected,* and should be continued, at whatever intervals are needed, to keep it in check. For rose black spot, in New Jersey, that means weekly treatments from early May until the end of October; but July 1 to September 1 usually covers the spraying period for late blight of potatoes. The adult Japanese beetle is with us from mid-June to mid-September, but for the pine needle scale there is only a two-week period in May, during which the crawlers are active, when spraying will have any effect.

Know your insects and know your diseases, and don't waste your money and your patience by spraying too early or too late, or with any material but the right one.

Biological Control

Biological control is defined as the suppression of the reproductive potential of organisms through the action of other organisms. Natural enemies include lady beetles, lacewings, syrphid fly larvae, praying mantises and other predators, and various parasitic wasps. Lady beetles can be purchased by the gallon but they frequently fly away to other gardens when released. It may be just as helpful to encourage the lady beetles already present in a garden by leaving some plants unsprayed to harbor their food, mostly aphids. Praying mantises will eat some beneficial insects as well as plant pests.

There are some fungus and viral diseases that attack injurious insects. A very useful microbial insecticide, prepared from the bacterium *Bacillus thuringiensis,* has been widely used as a spray against gypsy moth caterpillars and cankerworms. Spores of the bacterium *B. popillia,* causing milky disease, are applied to sod for the control of Japanese beetle grubs.

A relatively recent development in biological control is the release of male insects, sterilized by irradiation, to mate with normal females and so render the eggs infertile. Chemical sterilants have been developed but these have proved to be quite toxic. Sex attractants have been made synthetically to be used as bait in traps. As gardeners, we can only practice an integrated program, using chemicals with discretion and in ways that will least affect our insect friends.

Insects, Diseases, and Their Controls

ACEPHATE   (See Orthene.)

AEROSOLS

Please explain how an aerosol insecticide works.   Aerosols are pesticides dispersed in the form of a fog or mist by means of a liquefied gas or superheated stream ejected through an open valve; or in the form of a smoke by igniting a combustible material in which they are dispersed. Practically all pesticides (insecticides, fungicides, weedkillers) that can be dissolved in sufficient concentration in organic solvents can be applied in aerosol form. Generally, insecticides are much more quickly applied and more potent when used in this form, but how aerosols act on insects is determined by the nature of the insecticide and the amount deposited on the plants.

How do I go about selecting a suitable aerosol? It all depends on the pests involved and the area to be covered. Sprays in aerosol form are now available as combinations of insecticides, and insecticides and fungicides. They are purchased in small to large hand-borne metal containers (aerosol bombs) with a valve release for home, garden, or greenhouse use; in cans for combustion in the greenhouse. The small pressurized cans sold for house and garden use are very useful for spot treatment of aphids and some other pests. Remember to hold the can 18 inches away from the plant to avoid injury.

ANTS

What can be done about ants in the garden? Ants are undesirable in the garden not so much because of their feeding but because they loosen the soil around the roots, causing the plants to wilt and die, and they cart around and nurse aphids and mealybugs for their honeydew. They may be fought either by applying carbaryl, diazinon, or malathion to the nests.

How can you exterminate the large red ant leaf eater which strips the bushes clean? (Texas.) The leaf-cutting ant does not eat the leaves but carries them to its nest where it chops them up in pieces as a medium on which to grow fungi it uses for food. Spraying the foliage with carbaryl might have some deterrent effect. Ordinarily the injury by this ant is more interesting than serious.

How can I get rid of half-inch-long black ants that live inside the trunk of my English walnut tree? The entrance is a narrow fissure 18 inches long. I have tried filling it with cement but they burrow around it. This is the black carpenter ant, which does not chew through healthy bark or wood but enters through wounds to construct a nest inside the tree. Ants do not eat wood as do termites, but chew large excavations in dead and decaying heartwood to make room for a nest. Piles of "jawdust" often can be seen expelled from areas where carpenter ants are constructing a nest. If the nest site can be located, soak the entrance and the bark of the tree where the ants crawl with a residual aerosol or garden sprayer from an approved insecticide for ants.

APHIDS (PLANT LICE)

What year-round program would you suggest for aphids? Aphids are soft-bodied sucking insects controlled by contact or systemic insecticides; in general, spray for them when you see the first few individuals. They are more numerous at certain seasons of the year, the time varying with the host plant, so that spraying is generally spasmodic rather than regular. Often an aphicide may be included in a spray put on for other purposes. Or spot treat with an aerosol.

What should I use to destroy plant lice? Nicotine sulfate, 1 to 1½ teaspoons, and 1 cubic inch of laundry soap, not detergent, or 2 level tablespoons of flakes to 1 gallon of water is an old and successful spray for aphids, but now seldom available.

Malathion or diazinon is at present the most effective spray material for use on aphids, but pyrethrum, rotenone, dimethoate, or Meta-Systox-R can also be used. Acephate (Orthene) is excellent on ornamentals, but should not be used on food plants.

Can anything be done to destroy the white aphids which feed on the roots of plants? Malathion, when used at 1 tablespoon a gallon and poured into a depression around the plant stem, is helpful. Root aphids are usually tended by ants, so that ant-control operations should also be started.

How do I control aphids on trees? A dormant oil spray applied to fruit trees kills aphid eggs. The same spray will also kill aphid eggs on shade trees but should not be used unless needed for scale insects. The spray is not safe on all evergreens. The fluffy white bark aphids on pine and the spruce gall aphid are best controlled with malathion applied on a warm day in the late winter or early spring.

ARMADILLOS

How do I get rid of the armadillos that root up my garden at night? (Florida.) Armadillos are as difficult as rabbits to control. The best method is a fence of 2-foot chicken wire around the garden, otherwise shooting, if permitted, or trapping in rabbit traps put across their paths. They cannot be easily poisoned.

ARMILLARIA ROOT ROT

What is the fungus disease, especially prevalent in California, which

kills trees, shrubs, and other woody plants, being most destructive on lands recently cleared of oak? It may be recognized by the white mycelial threads or fans, black shoestring strands extending through the soil, and honey-colored toadstools that grow near the base of the trunk. Remove dead trees and shrubs, taking out all roots. Rhododendrons and azaleas may sometimes be saved by exposing crowns and main roots for a season. Avoid planting in areas of high-moisture content. The soil where diseased plants have been taken out can be disinfected with methyl bromide. However, its use is restricted to a commercial applicator.

ARMYWORMS

What is the dark-green, white-striped worm, similar to a cutworm, which attacks grasses, corn, and grain crops, feeding at night and hiding under clods, stones, or leaves during the day? Armyworm. Controlled by scattering poison bait in late afternoon or by spraying with malathion or methoxychlor. (See Cutworms.)

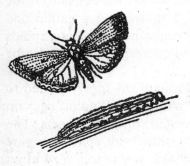

Armyworm with female moth. The worm is dark green with white stripes or is light tan and resembles a cutworm. It feeds at night on corn, grain, and grass.

ASIATIC BEETLES

How do you identify the Asiatic beetle? (New York.) There are two: the Asiatic or Oriental beetle (*Anomala orientalis*) and the Asiatic garden beetle (*Maladera castanea*). As grubs, they both are the size and shape of Japanese beetles and feed on grass roots. The adult Oriental beetle varies in color from light brown to black, with or without mottled marking. It is sometimes found feeding on roses and other flowers but does not do much damage there. The Asiatic garden beetle is a smooth copper brown, and has been described as an animated coffee bean. It stays in the ground during the day and feeds on foliage, bangs against windows, and flies into cars at night. The larvae injure grass roots and some vegetables. The adults injure leaves of asters, zinnias, and other low ornamentals and carrots, parsnips, turnips, beets, and pepper tops.

How do you combat the Oriental beetle? (New Jersey.) Treat lawns with diazinon or Dursban and spray foliage of ornamentals with carbaryl (Sevin). Rotenone may act as a deterrent on food plants. (See Japanese Beetles.)

Are castor bean plants a protection from Oriental beetles? (Connecticut.) Their efficacy has been greatly overrated. Entomologists claim that tests in cages show that the foliage is practically nontoxic and they cannot be used as trap plants in the field because beetles do not go to the castor bean before their favorite food plants have been exhausted.

Last summer I found hundreds of young Oriental beetles in a semi-dormant state around my garden plants. How do they hibernate? Will my garden be eaten up next summer? (Massachusetts.) They will hibernate as grubs in the soil under grass roots, and the beetles may fly to feed on your plants late next summer. However, treating your lawn with diazinon or Dursban in early September should reduce the infestation. Adults can be killed with Sevin.

Is it possible that Oriental beetles came from the roses and destroyed the bent grass in large spots? (Iowa.) The Oriental beetle is not prevalent in Iowa. The lawn may have been injured by white grubs or chinch bugs or the fungus disease called brown patch, and your rose pest is probably the rose chafer. (See Rose.)

What should I do to prevent the Oriental beetle? (California.) Nothing. According to statistics, the Oriental beetle is not a problem in California.

BACILLUS THURINGIENSIS

What are biological insecticides? They are naturally occurring diseases of insects that can be produced commercially and formulated for application as sprays or dusts as are chemical insecticides. They include two spore-forming bacteria, *Bacillus popillia* (milky disease), for Japanese beetle, and *Bacillus thuringiensis* (Dipel, Thuricide, Baktur), effective against various caterpillars, such as cabbage loopers, gypsy moth, bagworm, and others. The specificity of toxic action to the limited insect hosts make them safe to use around food, water, and animals. When susceptible insects feed on the host plant, spores are consumed that cause fatal disease in the pests.

BAGWORMS

How do you destroy bagworms? (Georgia.) This pest, generally distributed in the East, is more severe in the South. Hibernation is in the egg state in the female bags, made from interwoven twigs and leaves. The young hatch late in the spring, spin their own bags, and immediately start feeding on evergreen and deciduous trees. Control by picking off bags by late winter and by spraying with Sevin or Kelthane, malathion, dimethoate, acephate (Orthene), *B. thuringiensis,* or diazinon when feeding starts in late May to mid-June.

BEETLES

What are real "beetles"? Members of the insect order Coleoptera, with chewing mouth parts and hardened front wings forming convex shields. Except for a few beneficial types, such as ground and lady beetles, they are injurious both in their grub or larval stage and as adults. They are controlled by stomach or contact poisons used in the ground or on the foliage.

Do beetles ever come through closed windows into the house in the winter? No. In the fall, lady beetles and elm leaf beetles (and box-elder bugs, too) get in through very small cracks and crevices around windows, eaves, and siding to spend the winter. They may become active during warm spells in the winter and crawl on windows as they go toward the light. In the spring, they are more active and conspicuous as they try to get back out of the house.

BENEFICIAL INSECTS

What bugs are harmful and which are harmless in the garden? (Ohio.) The harmful bugs are discussed under the different host plants. Of the harmless or helpful ones, lady beetles, ground beetles, and praying mantises are most often seen in the home garden, although sometimes, if you look closely at a group of aphids, you will see a sluglike creature, larva of the syrphid fly, preying among them.

BENLATE

What is Benlate? Benomyl, sold as Benlate, is a systemic fungicide. It is excellent for control of powdery mildew on roses and other plants,

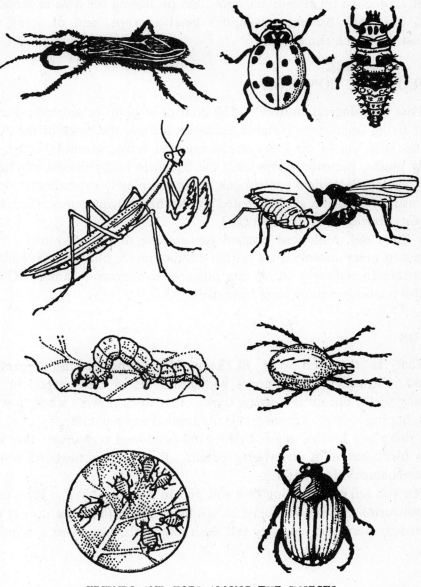

FRIENDS AND FOES AMONG THE INSECTS
(Top row, left to right) The friends: assassin bug; lady beetle, adult and larva. (Second row, left to right) Praying mantis; tiny wasp depositing egg in an aphid. (Third row, left to right) Some foes: cabbage looper; a spider mite, much enlarged. (Bottom row, left to right) Aphids on underside of leaf; Japanese beetle.

usually effective for rose black spot, and promising for a wide range of fruit, nut, turf, ornamentals and vegetable crops, and of some use against the Dutch elm disease.

BIOLOGICAL CONTROL

What is biological control? The control of plant or animal pests by other living organisms. Notable examples include the work of the Australian lady beetle on the cottony cushion scale, ground beetles on gypsy moths, parasitic wasps, and the bacterial milky disease on Japanese beetles. Biological control can never completely exterminate a pest and usually must be supplemented by mechanical measures. (See also *Bacillus thuringiensis,* this section.)

Is there any biological control for codling moth? (Illinois.) Yes, birds and many insects work on the codling moth, but they have never been able to reduce it below the point of commercial damage. Other control methods usually must be used.

BIRDS

What is the best way to keep birds from eating vegetable seeds? Farmers' supply stores sometimes sell a crow repellent for treating seeds, but some say that crows often work down a whole row of corn, hoping to find a kernel that is not treated and palatable.

Is there any known object besides old-fashioned scarecrows that will keep birds out of a strawberry patch? Cover the strawberries with coarse cheesecloth or netting.

Can you tell me anything that will poison sparrows? The baits used for cutworms and slugs sometimes kill birds by mistake, but do not put it out for sparrows; you may kill desirable birds, also. Use a sparrow trap.

BLISTER BEETLES

What are those long bugs that attack potatoes and other plants? (North Dakota.) Blister beetles. They are common in most states, feeding on vegetables and many ornamentals, especially China-asters and Japanese anemones. They are as much as ¾ inch long, plain black, or black with gray margins, or yellow or gray stripes, or brown or gray. When crushed on the skin, they can cause blisters.

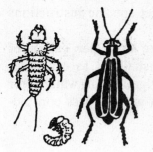

Adult blister beetle (right) feeds on asters, anemones, potatoes, and many other plants. Yet in its triungulin form (left) it eats eggs of certain grasshoppers.

What is the best insecticide for blister beetles?   They are hard to kill. Sevin should do a good job. Knocking the beetles off into a jar of kerosene or chlorine bleach is a helpful measure.

BORDEAUX MIXTURE

What is Bordeaux mixture?   An old fungicide still of some value in the control of plant diseases. The regulation formula is 4–4–50, meaning 4 pounds of copper sulfate and 4 pounds of hydrated lime to 50 gallons of water, but for many ornamental plants a weaker solution is used. Bordeaux mixture may be purchased in dry powder form to be mixed with water at the time of spraying or it may be made at home by preparing 2 stock solutions, 1 made by dissolving 1 pound fine copper sulfate crystals in 1 gallon of water and the other by dissolving 1 pound of lime in 1 gallon of water. Dilute only at the time of use, the amount of water determining the strength of Bordeaux; never put 2 stock solutions together, but add the water to the lime solution and then stir in the copper sulfate solution. For a 4–4–50 mixture, use 1 part of each stock solution to 10½ parts water; 3–3–50, 1 part to 14⅔ parts water; 2–2–50, 1 part to 23 parts water.

Please define 3–5–50 Bordeaux mixture or any such combination of figures. What do they stand for?   They are a kind of shorthand to describe the strength of the spray. The first figure is for the copper, the second for the lime, and the last for water; in this case it means 3 pounds of copper sulfate and 5 pounds of lime to 50 gallons of water. Ordinarily lime and copper are used in equal amounts, as 4–4–50 or 3–3–50, but sometimes lime is increased to avoid injury to specific crops.

What can you substitute for Bordeaux mixture when you do not have an agitating sprayer? Will tribasic copper act the same? (Oregon.)   There are several metallic copper sprays that may be used to replace Bordeaux mixture and they are safer when lime is undesirable.

Tribasic copper is one of these, but you should get specific instructions from your county extension agent.

What amount of Bordeaux mixture should be used per gallon of water? The directions come on the package, usually 8 to 12 table-spoons of prepared dry Bordeaux powder to 1 gallon of water. For most ornamental spraying, about half this amount is safer, less conspicuous, and equally effective.

BORERS

How can borers be prevented from doing their deadly work? Borers are caterpillars or grubs, larvae of moths or beetles, that work in woody or herbaceous stems. Some, like the European corn borer or common stalk borer, are best prevented by cutting down weed hosts and burning old stalks at the end of the season. Twigs infested with borers should be cut out and destroyed. Once the borer is in a woody trunk, such as rhododendron or lilac, little can be done to control it. Newly set trees should be protected from borers by wrapping trunks with Kraft crepe paper wound spirally from the crown to the first branch. Three or four applications at 3- to 4-week intervals of lindane or methoxychlor to the trunks and branches of trees and shrubs beginning in mid-May will help to protect them from borers.

BOX-ELDER BUGS

What will destroy the bugs that infest my trees and eat the fruits and flowers? The young are red and the adults are dark gray, with a red border. (Arizona.) These are box-elder bugs. Spray with carbaryl to prevent their swarming into the house. Avoid planting the pistillate tree nearby, for the eggs are laid on the fruits.

BUGS

What is a bug, horticulturally speaking? A term used by the layman to denote any insect, but by the scientist to mean a sucking insect of the order Hemiptera, which means half-winged. The basal half of the fore wing is thickened and the other half is membranous. They often have an offensive odor. True bugs include stink bugs, lacebugs, plant bugs, and chinch bugs.

What can I do to kill sucking bugs? Use a contact or systemic insecticide. (See also Insects.)

CANKERWORMS

What should be done about inchworms?   There are two species of these inchworms or measuring worms. Both have green- and brown-striped caterpillars and wingless female moths. The fall cankerworm female crawls up trees to lay her eggs in autumn; the spring cankerworm deposits her eggs in the spring. A sticky band of Tanglefoot (available from garden centers or garden-supply firms) has sometimes been suggested to prevent egg laying but spraying is far more effective. In seasons when a heavy infestation is forecast, have your trees sprayed with carbaryl (Sevin), methoxychlor, or the bacterium *Bacillus thuringiensis*. Oaks and elms are most seriously affected. These pests are cyclical and most years they are not a serious problem in the home garden.

CAPTAN

Is captan really as wonderful as some writers would indicate?   It is an excellent general fungicide sold as a 50 per cent Wettable Powder or a 7 to 8 per cent dust for foliage and fruit diseases but it is not a "cure-all." Many general-purpose spray mixtures contain captan. It will not control powdery mildew or rust diseases. Captan is widely used as a seed protectant; in drenches, it controls damping off of seedlings and cuttings; and in dips for corms and tubers, it prevents storage rots. Its toxicity to warm-blooded animals is quite low. Dogwoods, apples, and crab apples have had their foliage injured by early season captan sprays.

CARBARYL

Is Sevin safe to use?   Carbaryl, sold under the brand name of Sevin, is a very useful broad-spectrum insecticide comparatively safe for plants and the user. It does kill bees and some other beneficial insects and can increase the spider-mite problem. Sprays should usually include a miticide. However, carbaryl will suppress or control some rust and gall mites.

CATS

How can cats be kept out of the garden? (Massachusetts.)   They can't very well. Aside from a small city garden, where numerous cats may congregate, they do little damage to the garden itself, but of course they are destructive to birds. Automobiles kill more birds than cats do and cats can be a great help to the gardener in the control of rabbits, mice, and moles.

CENTIPEDES

When digging, I see quite a few slender, orange and brown insects, about 2 inches long, that run fast, seek the dark, and look like thousand-legged brown or tan miniature snakes. Are they injurious to plants? (Kentucky.) These are probably centipedes, meaning hundred-legged, although literally they have about 15 pairs of legs. They are usually beneficial in the garden, preying on other insects, but the larger ones may inflict painful bites on people.

What is the color of a centipede in infancy? (New York.) The true centipede is yellow to brown, like the adult. The garden centipede, so-called, but really a symphyllid, is small and white. This creature injures plants and has become an important pest in greenhouses and truck-garden fields in some states. Lindane is effective but may be restricted in some states. Try malathion.

CHINCH BUGS

How do you guard against chinch bugs? (Ohio.) Chinch bugs are very small, black and white sucking insects, red when young, which injure corn and small grains of the farmer and lawns of the homeowner. In hot, dry seasons, large brown patches in lawns are very commonly chinch-bug injury. Treat lawns with granular Sevin or with diazinon. Growing soybeans between the corn rows will shade the base so that the chinch bugs will avoid the corn (they do not touch soybeans or any plant outside the grass family).

The chinch bug is a very small black and white sucking insect that is destructive to lawns.

CHIPMUNKS (See Squirrels.)

CHLOROTHALONIL

What is a good fungicide to use for leaf spots and blight on vegetables? Chlorothalonil is marketed by the trade name Bravo, Exotherm, or Daconil 2787. It is a broad-spectrum fungicide recommended for leaf spots, leaf blights, anthracnose, powdery mildew, and several other leaf diseases of tomato, potato, celery, cucurbits, onions, watermelons, and some ornamentals.

COMPOST

Is there a way of combating insects and diseases by treating the compost heap and using it where plants are to be grown? The compost itself may be treated to ensure against its being pest-ridden, but it will confer no immunity to the plants in the garden bed.

What is the danger of carrying over fungi and insect pests in compost? There is some danger, and that is why we recommend disposing of plant material known to be diseased or likely to harbor insects.

CONTACT INSECTICIDES

What is meant by a contact insecticide? A chemical that kills insects by direct contact in contrast to some older materials such as lead arsenate, a stomach poison, or *Bacillus,* effective only if eaten. Most modern contact insecticides act as stomach poisons also, when ingested with plant material. Contact action occurs when insects are hit directly by sprays or dusts, when they simply walk on insecticide deposits, eat the foliage, or chew through the bark. There is considerable variation in the toxicity of different insecticides to different pests; some insects may be killed by one insecticide but not another. Those that are effective against many kinds of pests are called broad-spectrum insecticides. Generally, most insecticides do not control mites, and miticides do not control insects.

CRAWFISH

I am having considerable trouble with crawfish digging up my lawn. How do you exterminate them? (North Carolina.)   Mix 8 tablespoons of Sevin in 1 gallon of water. Pour 1 ounce into each hole. Or dig them for food. They are a delicacy, like lobster.

CROWN GALL

I noticed swellings on the roots of my roses when transplanting them. What shall I do about this condition?   This is crown gall, a bacterial disease that is soil-borne as well as plant-borne and gradually weakens and kills the plants. Take up the plants and burn them, if possible, or place them in plastic bags in a trash disposal. Then plant in a new area or in sterilized soil. Refuse new plants with galls.

CROWN ROT

What will prevent crown rot?   Crown rot is a disease causing sudden wilting of plants from a rotting at the crown or soil line. *Sclerotium rolfsii* is the causative fungus. The best prevention is to put healthy plants in a new location. The fungus may live for several years in the soil in the form of reddish-tan sclerotia, which resemble mustard seeds. Therefore, it is important to take out all surrounding soil when the diseased plant is removed. Unless the soil can be dug out for 1 foot deep and 2 feet or more in the area and replaced with fresh soil, Terrachlor (PCNB) should be poured over the earth and the crowns of nearby plants.

CUTWORMS

How can I prevent cutworms from nipping off new seedlings or transplants?   One way for newly set bedding or vegetable transplants is a heavy paper on a thin cardboard collar around each stem, 1 inch into the ground and 2 inches above the ground. Another way is to apply diazinon granules to the soil prior to planting or using diazinon spray or dust applied to the plants and soil immediately after planting. It is best to treat in the late afternoon or evening.

Do cutworms stay in the soil in some form during the winter?   Usually cutworms overwinter as larvae in cells in the soil, or under trash, mulch, or in clumps of grass. Sometimes they overwinter as pupae or adults. The larvae are active in the spring, cutting off seedlings at the soil level or nipping off young tender leaves at the petiole. They pupate to adult moths that give rise to one new generation in the North and several in the South. Both adults and larvae are nocturnal and hide during the day.

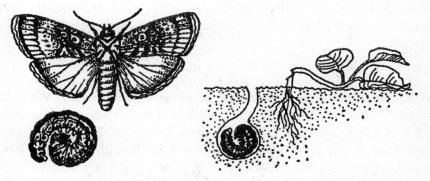

Cutworms attack young cabbage and tomato plants and other seedling vegetables and flowers. (Left) Greasy cutworm; (right) dark-sided cutworm.

In midsummer, many annuals had their foliage devastated, but no insects could be found. What caused this? (Virginia.)   If there were no slime trails to indicate slugs, it most likely was climbing cutworms, such as the variegated cutworm. The larvae hide in the soil or under debris during the day and feed voraciously on the foliage at night. In small patio gardens, hand-picking at night while searching with a flashlight will reduce populations. Spraying the plants and soaking the soil with diazinon is effective.

DAMPING OFF

What would cause seedlings in flats to rot at the stems just at the top of the soil?   This is known as damping off, a disease caused by any one of several soil fungi. There are two types: pre-emergence damping off, when the sprouted seeds rot in the soil; and post-emergence damping off, when the young seedlings wilt and fall over. For growing in flats, either soil or seeds may be treated, but seed treatment is more practical for sowing directly in the garden. That is why most seed is now treated prior to sale. It pays to buy treated seeds.

What is the safest preparation for soil treatment to prevent damping off in seed flats? Formaldehyde, perhaps. Dilute 2½ tablespoons of commercial formaldehyde with 6 times as much water and sprinkle over a bushel of soil, mixing thoroughly. Place in flats. Wait 24 hours before planting, and water well immediately after planting.

When starting seeds in the house in boxes, what is the safest thing to use to prevent damping off? See the above question. However, the various soilless mixes (Jiffy Mix, Readi-Earth, etc.) are virtually sterile since they contain no soil. They can be bought at garden centers.

DDT

DDT was once acclaimed as a miracle insecticide. Why is it banned? DDT was the original chlorinated hydrocarbon whose amazing insect-killing powers led to the development of many other potent insecticides. Used as a public-health aid in World War II, DDT is credited with saving 5 million lives and preventing 100 million illnesses. It is, however, persistent in the environment and builds up in the food chain, an example being birds killed by eating earthworms that had ingested DDT. It may be related to the thin eggshells that may have caused the decline of bald eagles and some other endangered species. Some insects became resistant to DDT and it increased the mite problem by killing certain beneficial insects. DDT was probably safer for man than some of the highly toxic phosphates that are replacing it on some commercial crops and we do not yet have an adequate substitute for the control of some pests.

DERRIS

What is derris? One of the plants used as a source of rotenone. It is imported from the Far East.

DIABROTICA BEETLES

What do you do about the 12-spotted beetles? They ruin all the late blooms—roses, gerbera, carnation, chrysanthemum. (California.) These are the 12-spotted cucumber beetles, Diabroticas, very common in your state. They are hard to kill, but dusting or spraying with methoxychlor or carbaryl would be helpful.

DICOFOL

I often see the name dicofol suggested for mites. What is it? Dicofol is the accepted common name for Kelthane, a very effective and widely available miticide for spider mites on ornamentals.

DIMETHOATE

Is dimethoate a systemic insecticide? Yes. Sold as Cygon or De-Fend, this reasonably safe phosphate is used as a foliage spray and sometimes for soil treatment to control insects and mites. It is injurious to some plants; apply only to those listed on the label.

DOGS

What are your views and advice on the dog-nuisance question? Owners should be willing to keep their dogs restrained and, when walking them on a leash, should keep them curbed rather than allowing them to ruin lawns and shrubs near the sidewalk. Moth balls around shrubs and various chemicals sold as dog repellents in garden centers or through mail-order houses may help. Also, a barberry hedge and a few chopped twigs of barberry scattered about is one idea that might work. Wire shrub guards are usually quite successful.

DORMANT SPRAYING

What is a dormant spray? A spray applied while plants are dormant, which means sleeping; that is, while deciduous trees are bare and before evergreens have started into new life. At this time, the plant can stand a stronger spray than during the growing season, and a strong spray is needed to get hard-shelled insects like scales.

When and how should the dormant spray be applied to trees and bushes? (Illinois.) The safest time is toward the end of their dormant season, just before new growth starts. In Illinois, that might mean the end of March for lilacs and early April for evergreens. For dormant spraying, the home gardener usually has a choice of lime-sulfur or an oil spray, or a commercial mixture of both. The liquid lime-sulfur should be diluted with 7 to 9 parts of water. It is safe, but unpleasant to use, impossible near painted surfaces because of the indelible stain, and leaves an objectionable residue on evergreens. Miscible oils—colorless oils which mix readily with water to form a white liquid—are sold under many trade names. Most manufacturers suggest a 2 to 3 per cent dilution for deciduous trees and 1 to 2 per cent for evergreens. Oil sprays may be injurious unless they are used on a bright, clear day with the temperature well above 45° F. Do not use on beech, black walnut, butternut, Japanese or sugar maple, or magnolia. Do not use on such evergreens as false-cypress, cryptomeria, Douglas-fir, true firs, hemlock, Japanese umbrella, pine, or yew. Oil sprays will remove the "bloom" from evergreens, especially blue spruces.

DURSBAN

What is Dursban and what is it for?   Dursban is an insecticide, also called chlorpyrifos, that is recommended for some ornamental pests and chinch bugs, cutworms, and sod webworms in lawns. It has a warning label and most of its uses are restricted to commercial applicators. For many of those uses it is sold under the trade name Lorsban.

DUSTER, GARDEN

What is a garden duster?   A machine for applying insecticides or fungicides in dry dust form. For the small garden, choose a hand rotary duster, or a dust gun, ranging in size from 1-pint to 2-quart capacity. Choose one with an extension rod and a flange, which will allow you to stand up while using the duster and yet drive the dust from the bottom of the plant up through it. For the larger garden, a knapsack bellows or a rotary duster will save much energy in operation.

DUSTING

How do you know how much garden dust to use? I tried a dust gun which didn't cover the leaves sufficiently without extreme labor and the dust when tossed out by hand seemed too much. Many plants wilted. I used sulfur and rotenone. (Virginia.)   Apply only as much dust as will cover the plants with a thin, even coating. This can be done only with some sort of duster. If yours was too hard to work, it either was the wrong type for the number of plants or else needed adjusting. Coverage of the underside of the leaves is most important and can be done only with the right apparatus, never by throwing it on. Your method of application together with the sulfur in your dust would account for the plants wilting. Sulfur may be injurious to any plant in hot weather, but vegetables are particularly sensitive. Beans occasionally require sulfur, but cucurbits should never have it.

Do you dust plants when they are wet with dew or when they are dry? There is always an argument on this question, but if ornamental plants are dusted when they are wet, they are left with a too conspicuous residue.

EARTHWORMS

Do earthworms or angleworms feed on and destroy peony, iris, and other tubers? I have dug them up and found worms imbedded in them and nothing left but the outer shell. Your peony probably succumbed to botrytis blight and the iris to borer and rot. Earthworms do not feed on living plant tissue.

When garden worms are found in flowerpots, do they feed on the roots of the plant? No. Worms in pots are chiefly a nuisance because they clog up the drainage holes. Watering with lime water will get rid of them.

EARWIGS

Is there anything possible on this earth to exterminate earwigs? Earwigs resemble beetles and have two claspers on the hind end that look like large "jaws." They hide under debris, crawl into picnic baskets and other household belongings used out in the yard during the summer. There is little that can be done to exterminate them, since they may be scattered all around the yard. Spraying with diazinon, carbaryl, chlorpyrifos, or malathion will kill those that come in contact with the spray.

Earwigs

FALL WEBWORMS

What is the difference, if any, between the fall webworm and the fall cankerworm? The fall webworm makes increasingly large silk webs or tents from June to September on the outer ends of branches of many trees, unlike the eastern tent caterpillar that constructs its nest in branch crotches only on wild cherry and flowering fruits. The caterpillars are hairy, white to orange, about 1 inch long, and gregarious, feeding in broods on foliage within the webs. Fall cankerworms, prevalent only in the spring (usually May) on many tree hosts, are light green or dark gray, hairless, and "inch" along, resulting in such names as inchworms, loopers, or measuring worms. (See Cankerworms.) All of these defoliators can be controlled with carbaryl or methoxychlor.

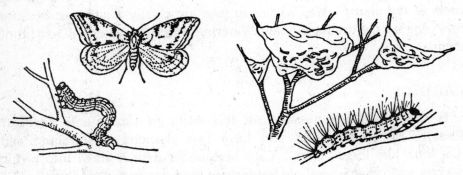

Fall cankerworm (left) and fall webworm (right).

FERBAM

Can you give me some trade names under which ferbam is sold? Trade products containing ferbam are Fermate, Carbamate, and Karbam Black. It is a good general fungicide, especially for rust diseases of plants. The usual dosage is 2 tablespoonfuls per gallon of water.

FLEA BEETLES

What about flea beetles? (Florida.) Flea beetles, which get their name from their habit of quickly springing several inches when disturbed, are small, black, oval beetles that chew tiny shot holes in the foliage of most garden crops. Two species in Florida are most troublesome on beets, cabbage, and tomatoes. In the North, potatoes and seedling tomatoes, peppers, eggplants, and crucifers are almost sure to be riddled by flea beetles early in the season. Dusting or spraying with carbaryl, diazinon, or methoxychlor will control flea beetles.

FOLPET

What is folpet? An excellent fungicide, sold as Phaltan, used on fruits, vegetables, and ornamentals and very safe for the operator. It is recommended for apple scab, cherry leafspot, rose black spot, and many other diseases.

FORMALDEHYDE (FORMALIN)

What is formaldehyde? A useful soil disinfectant. (See also Soil Sterilization.)

Is it safe to use a weak solution of formaldehyde (1 to 50) on a seed bed that has been planted, but seed not germinated, to curb damping-off fungus? (West Virginia.) This is not a weak solution of formaldehyde; it is the standard strength for drenching *fallow* soil, which will probably have to air out at least a week before planting. It would not be safe to use after the seed is planted. (See Damping Off for the formaldehyde method of treating soil for flats, and see Seed Treatment for ways to prevent damping off in garden soil.)

What concentration of formaldehyde will kill insects and larvae without destroying the foliage on seedlings? None. Formaldehyde is never to be used around living plants. If you must disinfect the soil, the plants will have to be moved out for a couple of weeks, and since you do not want to set infested or infected plants back in treated soil, you have to start a new batch of seedlings. So try some other method of controlling your insects.

FUNGI

What are fungi? Members of the Thallophytes or lowest plant group. Lacking the power of manufacturing their own plant food, they live as saprophytes on decaying plant tissue or as parasites on living higher plants. They are characterized by a vegetative stage, consisting of fungus threads or mycelium and fruiting bodies which contain the reproductive organs. Some fungi are readily recognized at a glance: mildew with its white weft of mycelium growing over a leaf; rust, which produces reddish dusty spore pustules; and smut, with its masses of black spores. Some can be differentiated only by microscopic examination.

What do you do for white fungus? (California.) Such a question is too indefinite. A white fungus may be the coating of mildew on a leaf; it may be the white weft of mycelium at the base of plants in crown rot or southern blight; or it may be the fans of white mycelium peculiar to the armillaria root rot, prevalent on woody shrubs in California. Then there is downy mildew and many other possibilities.

What do you recommend as treatment for mustard-seed fungus? (Missouri.) This question is almost as brief as the one above, but it can be answered definitely because there is only one fungus, *Sclerotium rolfsii,* that would be present in Missouri, known as the mustard-seed fungus. It causes the disease known as southern rot or blight or crown rot and gets its name from the reddish sclerotia which look like mustard seed. It is fairly common as crown rot of delphinium. (For control, see Crown Rot.)

FUNGICIDE

What is a fungicide? A material used to eradicate bacteria and fungi in the soil or on seeds. It is more commonly used as a protectant to cover susceptible plant parts before the disease organisms arrive. Most of the older fungicides are compounds of either copper or sulfur. The most common newer ones are dithio-carbamic acid derivatives (ferbam, zineb, mancozeb, maneb, etc.) and captan, folpet, and benomyl.

GOPHERS

What is the best way to poison California pocket gophers? There are many species of pocket gophers (ground rats) found in California, Oregon, and Washington. There are special gopher traps on the market. Consult your county extension agent for regional restrictions and recommendations for available baits.

GROUND BEETLES

I have found several June bugs in the ground this fall. Are they harmful? (New York.) You would not be apt to find June beetles in the ground. You probably found ground beetles, black or brown or iridescent large beetles with very prominent jaws that live in the ground or under stones. These are beneficial insects, feeding on cankerworms and other pests, and should not be disturbed.

GRUBWORMS   (See White Grubs.)

GYPSY MOTHS

What is the history of gypsy moths?   The gypsy moth, *Lymantria dispar,* is an example of an introduced pest that has wreaked havoc in a new country. In 1868 a few moths were brought to Massachusetts from France by a professor who thought he could make a hybrid to produce silk. Their cage was broken open by a windstorm and the caterpillars, brown, hairy, with red and blue tubercles, escaped, prospered, and now feed on many deciduous and evergreen trees, with a particular preference for oaks. They are so voracious that a single caterpillar can eat a square foot of leaf surface in 24 hours. Evergreens, eaten only after deciduous foliage is gone, may be killed by a single season's defoliation; other trees may die after 3 or more successive defoliations. Massachusetts has spent millions of dollars trying to cope with this pest and for many years a barrier zone confined it east of the Hudson River. Now, however, the gypsy moth is a menace in New England, New Jersey, New York, Pennsylvania, and Maryland, and has been spotted in Virginia, Michigan, and other states.

In 1957 a large-scale aerial spray program, using DDT, was launched

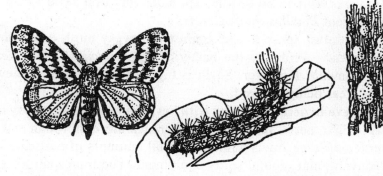

Gypsy moth caterpillars attack tree foliage and, occasionally, vegetables and other plants. Caterpillars are 2 inches long with conspicuous blue and red markings. (Right) Egg cases on tree trunk.

but had to be given up because of public outcry against the environmental effects. To prevent further spread, it is vitally important that individuals cooperate in observing quarantine regulations. The tan egg clusters, with a feltlike texture, about an inch long, may be attached to almost any object, but are especially conspicuous on tree trunks and limbs. Don't try to bring Christmas trees or other plants out of the regulated area without inspection. Check your automobile or trailer if you have vacationed in gypsy moth country and your home is in an uninfested area. If you expect a heavy infestation in your area, trees can be sprayed with carbaryl (Sevin) or *Bacillus thuringiensis*. The U. S. Department of Agriculture is releasing parasites for control of gypsy moths, experimenting with sex attractants in traps, and utilizing insect growth regulators as sprays.

Most of our property (about 2 acres) is a woodland, mostly of oak trees. Last summer, for the first time in this area, we had a severe infestation of gypsy moth caterpillars and most of the tree foliage suffered accordingly, although I can't report that there was total defoliation in all cases. My neighbors predict that a second and third year of devastation by these caterpillars will result in the death of the trees. Is this true? Predicting when a tree will die, short of chopping it down, is not easily done, as many factors must be considered. Certainly successive defoliations weaken trees, especially old ones and those that are sick or diseased, but usually it is a combination of factors rather than a single cause, such as the gypsy moth, that finally kills the tree. Oaks are most susceptible to gypsy moth infestation and repeated defoliation may contribute to the death of some. In your case, it is doubtful that all or even any of your trees will die, and the caterpillars will probably move on after a few years. But to be on the safe side, why don't you spray with the bacterial agent *Bacillus thuringiensis*?

What is the safest spray to use against the gypsy moth caterpillar in the home garden? Probably the bacterial agent *Bacillus thuringiensis*, or carbaryl (Sevin). However, Sevin is highly toxic to bees if they are active in the areas being sprayed.

Do you believe in aerial spraying with Sevin to control the gypsy moth caterpillar? First, aerial spraying permits much more thorough and uniform coverage of large tracts with very small amounts of pesticide compared to conventional ground spray equipment. The time span for effective spraying in good weather conditions is very limited and large areas can be treated quickly and economically. Second, Sevin is highly efficacious against gypsy moth, does not persist in the environment, and is very low in toxicity to warm-blooded animals. However, it kills shellfish and fish, as well as bees, and should not be used over bodies of water or in coastal areas.

Sevin may destroy many parasites and predators of the gypsy moth, so it should not be used where those natural enemies have developed moderate to high population densities. Where Sevin cannot or should not be used, Bt (*Bacillus thuringiensis*) can be applied to reduce gypsy moth infestations without harming bees, fish, or natural enemies. Where trees or woodlands are of low value in generally infested areas, it is best not to use insecticides and let natural enemies function. Control strategies depend on whether the location in question is within the generally infested gypsy moth range, within the fringe or leading edge of its spread west and south, or in a previously uninfested area.

What are methods the home gardener can use to control a gypsy moth infestation? You can have your trees and shrubs sprayed with Sevin or *Bacillus thuringiensis* in midspring just after the eggs hatch. (If the spray chemical is mixed with molasses, usually only one treatment is necessary.) Consult your State Extension Service for other recommended methods. In the fall and winter, when the tan egg clusters are most conspicuous, you can coat them with creosote. A sponge or rag fastened to a long pole will reach some of the higher-up clusters. Or you can scrape the clusters into a can and then burn them in the fireplace, where they will pop like little firecrackers. In early summer, when the large caterpillars are crawling down tree trunks, they can be trapped by wide bands of overlapping burlap wrapped around the trunks. The caterpillars, which are most active at night, hide in the burlap during the day when it is quite easy to collect and drop them into containers of liquid bleach.

Most home gardeners prefer the first method—spraying, which is not a serious environmental hazard when done by competent, careful professionals. For tall shrubs and trees, power sprayers are essential. The majority of home gardens are artificial situations composed of ornamental plantings designed to give enjoyment and comfort to the owners, quite different from the complex environmental factors referred to in the preceding question on aerial spraying.

HARLEQUIN BUGS

How do you get rid of harlequin bugs? (Kansas.) These brilliantly colored red or yellow and black or blue bugs cause the leaves of horseradish, mustard, cabbage, and related crops to curl and turn brown. They lay clusters of black-banded eggs that look like barrels. Hand-picking before egg laying and removal of eggs are the best control. Destroy all old plant parts and dust with rotenone.

HYDROXYQUINOLINE SULFATE

How is hydroxyquinoline sulfate used for the prevention of soil rots? For cuttings of succulent plants, use a 25 per cent material at the rate of 1 teaspoon per gallon of water, and soak cuttings for 5 minutes. Use the same strength for a seed-bed drench and apply at the rate of 1 gallon to 10 square feet. This compound acts as a chemotherapeutic or systemic fungicide. It is now sold as Chinosol.

INFORMATION

What we need is plenty of information on pests. We find some that are different from those of eastern states. Are they harmful or beneficial? (California.) Your own State Extension Service is set up to give you exactly that knowledge. Not many gardeners realize what a wealth of information, applicable directly to their own state, may be obtained by a phone call or visit to your local county agent. In your particular case, you can write to the College of Agriculture, Berkeley, Calif. 94720, and ask for a list of publications. Practically every state's land-grant university has concise information ready for the home gardener as well as the farmer. Ask for it.

INSECTICIDES

What is an insecticide? Chemical compounds that are used in the control of insects are generally called insecticides. Any given insecticide may act on insects in one or more ways. However, it is generally grouped according to its main mode of action: a *stomach poison* attacks the internal organs after being swallowed; a *systemic insecticide* is a stomach poison absorbed and translocated in the sap of plants, destroying sap-sucking pests mainly; a *contact insecticide* kills upon contact with some external portion of the insect's body; a *residual contact insecticide* kills insects by foot contact for long periods after application; a *fumigant* is a chemical that produces a killing vapor in the air; and a *repellent* is a substance that is distasteful or malodorous enough to keep insects away. Of the older insecticides, the arsenicals are stomach poisons; nicotine sulfate, pyrethrum, and dormant oils are contact poisons; rotenone kills in both ways; and chloropicrin and methyl bromide are typical fumigants. The newer organic insecticides are generally effective for a variety of pests regardless of the way they feed. Many chewing and sucking insects are readily destroyed by either malathion or carbaryl.

INSECTS

Just what are insects?   Members of the animal group Arthropoda, meaning jointed legs. True insects, of the class Hexapoda, meaning 6-legged, are characterized by always having 3 pairs of legs and 2 pairs of wings in the adult form, except for flies, which have only 1 pair. The body is composed of a head, thorax, and abdomen. Along the abdomen are small holes, spiracles, which form the breathing apparatus. Contact poisons work through their action on the spiracles or directly through the chitin. Chewing insects have jaws and bite holes in plant tissue; hence, they can be controlled by spreading a stomach poison in advance of the insect. Sucking insects cannot bite but obtain their food through a beak that pierces the plant epidermis to get at the sap. Since they cannot be injured by stomach poisons unless they are systemics, contact sprays are necessary.

JAPANESE BEETLES

What are effective ways to suppress Japanese beetles? (New York.)   Chemical treatment of soil in lawn areas; biological control by distribution of a natural parasite, the milky-spore disease dust; spraying foliage during the flying season; hand-picking; trapping in special beetle traps.

How and when do you fight the Japanese beetle? (Pennsylvania.)   Lawn treatment is done either in late August or early September. Summer spraying for adults normally starts at the very end of June and may have to be continued until the end of September on plants like roses, although beetles often stop feeding on vines in late August. If shade trees are sprayed with carbaryl at the end of June, one or two sprayings will normally give protection for the season. With shrubs, vines, and flowering plants, the number of applications depends on the rapidity with which new growth is formed. Roses and ampelopsis require a spray weekly to keep the new growth covered.

Is there any control, other than chemical, for Japanese beetle grubs in lawns?   Yes. The spore dust of milky disease—a natural enemy of the beetles—is another means of controlling and eliminating this pest, and it is available commercially as Doom. Directions for use are printed on the packages. Do not apply to areas treated with insecticide.

Is there anything I can do to the soil in flower beds? The beetles destroy hollyhocks, cannas, petunias, roses, and geraniums.   Soil treatment for flowers is ineffective. Beetles lay their eggs primarily in turf grass. For flowers, the most effective control is picking off the beetles; for roses, cutting the buds when they show color and enjoying them in the house. Aerosol bombs for use on flowers will paralyze or kill beetles without disfiguring blooms, but in general you have to rely on carbaryl (Sevin) or methoxychlor in a spray or dust to take care of the foliage and hand-picking the beetles into a jar or can of kerosene.

Can you tell me something to get rid of Japanese beetles? I have tried traps and they seem to attract them.   That is exactly the purpose of a trap: it is painted bright yellow and baited with geraniol just to attract the beetles. Unfortunately, the trap attracts more beetles than get caught in it, so that the nearby plants serve as beetle food and suffer proportionately.

What is the best method of exterminating Japanese beetles before they are hatched?   Spraying for the adults before they can lay their eggs in the grass. Otherwise, eggs will hatch into grubs. If the soil has been treated, the poison in the soil will kill the grubs as they feed on grass roots.

Is it possible to recognize the Japanese beetle in the daytime? How can you fight the Japanese beetle on rose bushes? (Louisiana.)   In Louisiana, you probably will not have to fight Japanese beetles on rose bushes. If and when you do, carbaryl or methoxychlor or a combination spray will keep the foliage reasonably whole; but to save the flowers, you should cut the buds and let them open indoors. The beetle is readily recognized. It works in the daytime and prefers hot sunshine. It is about ½ inch long, shiny metallic green, with bronze wing covers and tufts of white hairs protruding from under the wing covers. It is a very handsome beetle, one of the scarab beetles.

What do you do about Japanese beetles? (California.)   Nothing in California. It's not your problem yet. (But see preceding questions.)

What is the most effective repellent of the Japanese beetle? (Connecticut.)   Hydrated lime will serve as a repellent on grapes. Grape foliage is a favorite target of the beetles.

Can I check Japanese beetles with castor-oil beans?   Probably not. (See Asiatic Beetles.)

Does fall spading help exterminate the Japanese beetle?   No. But it helps for other white grubs in the garden, if you take the trouble to destroy or throw out to the birds the grubs you turn up. Birds, by the way, are great allies. The holes you see in the lawn in late summer are where the robins, starlings, and other birds have gone in after the grubs. The starlings are given the most credit for eating the hard beetles, but some other birds work at them. Brown thrashers will pick a beetle off a rose bush and then whack it down onto a cement path to soften it up for eating. Skunks will mutilate turf with a lot of grubs.

Is the Japanese beetle nuisance likely to abate soon? Does severe cold tend to kill them? (Connecticut.) The menace has abated, due to natural enemies and man-made control methods. Any newly introduced insect does more damage initially than after it is a long-established pest. Beetles, as with tent caterpillars and cankerworms, are nuisances to be expected each season but not to be unduly excited about.

Do Japanese beetles bother geraniums? They are attracted to them; indeed it is a derivative of geranium that is used as bait in traps, but there is some evidence that beetles are killed by eating certain varieties of geraniums.

Which plant is easy to cultivate, a free bloomer until frost, and free as possible from Japanese beetles? (Connecticut.) Phlox and the 'Heavenly Blue' morning-glory answer your requirements. Roses, marigolds, and zinnias are favored food plants; delphiniums are not much bothered by beetles, but they are not easy to grow. Blue eupatorium will contrast with your phlox and give you color until frost. It has few insect enemies. To replace marigolds, try 'Goldcrest' cosmos. It has almost no pests or diseases and grows with no effort at all. Scatter the seeds in any odd corner; rake them in lightly. With no more attention, they bloom from early July to November.

Japanese beetles devouring a ripening apple. The beetles attack many ornamental plants as well as fruits and vegetables.

Which vegetables would be least affected by Japanese beetles?   Most vegetables are little affected by Japanese beetles. However, they are extremely fond of soybeans, pole beans, and sometimes appear on snap and lima beans; they injure the silk of corn; they are numerous on, but seldom injurious to, asparagus foliage; and they often play havoc with rhubarb leaves.

I have a pet cat. What spray is safe on garden flowers and vines? I have Japanese beetles.   Sevin will not harm the cat. It is one of the treatments applied for fleas. Dogs and cats like to follow around when you are spraying and kittens want to play with the nozzle, but if you shut them in the house during the actual mixing and application of the spray, there is no problem with the residue on the plants. Of course, you do not want to leave the pail of any pesticide standing where a dog or cat might try to take a drink. Mix up your spray and dispose safely of what is left in your spray tank and you will have no trouble.

JUNE BEETLES

What is a June beetle?   It is the adult of any of a number of scarab beetles in the genus *Phyllophaga*.

KARATHANE

How often is it necessary to apply Karathane to plants to control powdery mildew?   Karathane should be applied about 3 times at weekly or 10-day intervals to stop the progress of this disease. The normal dosage is 2 level teaspoons in 3 gallons of water plus a spreader. It may also be obtained as a ½ to 1 per cent dust. Mixtures with the common summer insecticides and fungicides are safe on foliage.

LACEBUGS

How do you kill lacebugs? (Iowa.)   Lacebugs, small bugs with lace-like wings that work on the underside of leaves, sucking out the sap so that the upper surface becomes a stippled white, gray, or yellow, are killed by any contact or systemic insecticide applied with a good spreader and sufficient pressure. Malathion, Orthene, or carbaryl is effective.

LEAD ARSENATE

What is lead arsenate? A formerly widely used stomach poison, valuable for spraying ornamentals and for some food plants like apples. Because of the residue problem, lead arsenate being the most poisonous of the arsenicals, and because it burns some tender foliage, it was of little value in the control of vegetable pests. Arsenicals are now restricted or banned.

LEMON OIL

Is it harmful to put lemon oil on plants? If you mean the furniture polish that goes by that name, yes; but there is a tried-and-true insecticide called lemon oil sold for years for use on house plants and perfectly safe when used according to directions.

LIME-SULFUR

What is lime-sulfur? A fungicide, often acting as an insecticide also. Formerly valuable in dormant spraying for the control of fungus diseases and scale insects, but also useful as a summer spray to control apple scab and other diseases, boxwood canker, red mites on fruit trees, spider mites on evergreens. Liquid lime-sulfur is used at a 1 to 7 or 1 to 9 dilution as a dormant spray and 1 to 40 or 1 to 50 as a summer spray. It stains paint and leaves an objectionable residue, but is relatively safe. Do not use it within one month of using oil. It is not as available in stores as it once was.

LINDANE

Is lindane safe to use on my vegetables? Lindane is no longer recommended for home use on vegetables. It had been used widely for many types of insects both because of its residual effectiveness and vaporizing activity. It is now used primarily for borers, bark beetles, white pine weevil, and leafminers on deciduous trees. It is an excellent aphicide, but may not presently be registered for that use.

MAGGOTS

What causes ground maggots and how can you get rid of them?

(Maryland.)　Maggots are legless white larvae of flies that lay their eggs in plants near where the stem meets the ground or in crevices in the soil. The cabbage maggot is the one most bothersome to the home gardener. (For control, see Cabbage.) Maggots are also pests of radishes, turnips, onions, beans, and corn. Diazinon is effective for control.

MALATHION

I have a cat and dog which roam around in my gardens. Will malathion sprays applied to the plants harm them?　Very unlikely. Malathion is one of the least toxic insecticides to warm-blooded animals and in addition loses its toxic properties rapidly on exposure to air moisture, so that in two days no toxic residue is left. The only precaution I would suggest is to keep pets and children away from freshly sprayed plants.

MANCOZEB

Is mancozeb another name for maneb?　No, it is a coordination product of zinc iron and maneb plus zinc sulfate. Maneb is sold under trade names Manzate 200 and Dithane M-22. It is effective against rusts, potato seed-piece decay, scab on cucurbits, and blights and leaf spots on many ornamentals.

MANEB

What is maneb?　It is the "coined" name for the manganese salt of dithiocarbamic acid. This is another valuable general fungicide safe to use in combinations for fruits, vegetables, and ornamentals, but like captan it will not control powdery mildews or rusts. Delay applying to cucurbits until they are beginning to branch out. Trade names are Manzate and Dithane M-22.

MEALYBUGS

What are the fuzzy white bugs on my house plants?　Mealybugs, sucking insects closely related to scales; flattened, oval, with short, white, waxy projections from the body, and often looking like bits of cotton fluff because of the eggs carried by the females in a cottony sac. Mealybugs are serious pests of house and greenhouse plants, and in the South on such outdoor plants as gardenia, azalea, and citrus fruits. In the

North, yew is often heavily infested, and the Comstock mealybug is an apple pest.

What is the life history of the mealybug? How does it travel? The female mealybug deposits her eggs in a cottony waxy sac attached to the rear end of her body. When she has laid 400 to 600 eggs, the sac is left at the axils of branching stems or leaves and the female dies. The eggs hatch in about 10 days, and the flattened, oval, yellow young crawl over the plants, sucking the sap, and soon a waxy covering is exuded from their bodies. They are sluggish and do not move much. The males transform into small, active 2-winged flies to mate with the females and then die. Mealybugs are disseminated by ants, and by moving about infested plants.

Mealybugs are small, soft bugs covered with a cottonlike fluff. They attack many house plants.

How can I rid a small greenhouse of mealybugs? Plants can be sprayed with or dipped into a solution of 1 pound of soap to 3 gallons of water, but this must be washed off within 2 hours to prevent burning. Spraying with malathion or Orthene is probably the easiest solution, provided that the manufacturer's directions are rigidly followed.

What is the best method of getting rid of mealybugs and how long does it take? (California.) First, wash off your plants with a strong spray from the hose, then use malathion or Orthene. It may be necessary to spray malathion 2 or 3 times at weekly intervals to clean up an infestation. For a few small plants, an aerosol plant bomb is very effective.

What will destroy mealybugs in the soil? (Ohio.) Remove the soil from around the roots and pour in some of the spray described above as in a light watering.

Can window boxes once infested with mealybugs be used again? (Connecticut.) There is no reason why not, if the soil is cleaned out and the box thoroughly washed with strong soap and water.

We are plagued with mealybugs on our flower and vegetable plants. Can you recommend a safe spray so as not to harm the plant or poison the vegetables? (Pennsylvania.) I cannot believe that mealybugs in an outdoor garden would be that much of a pest in Pennsylvania, although I have occasionally seen coral-bells and yew with bad cases of mealybugs in this region. Perhaps you have root aphids. (See Aphids.)

METHOXYCHLOR

What advantages has methoxychlor? It is very safe to use around warm-blooded animals; its residual toxicity lasts only about a week; it does not injure cucurbits; and it controls the plum curculio and the Mexican bean beetle. It does not adversely accumulate in the environment.

MICE AND RATS

How can you keep rats from eating plants in a city garden where, because of lack of cooperation from neighbors, it is impossible to get rid of all of them? (Maryland.) Poison put out for the rats would probably harm a pet cat or dog, and even traps would have to be used cautiously to avoid maiming a pet. When the house plants on my window were mysteriously chewed, I could not believe it was a rat until I caught it in the act one night. It was killed in a trap baited with sunflower seed. A pival-cornmeal or warfarin-cornmeal poison bait placed in a protected feeding station so that larger animals cannot get to it is a most effective and relatively safe way of killing rats and mice by internal hemorrhage. Rats and mice must be allowed to feed on this bait daily for at least a week for it to take effect. Constant rat and mouse protection will be obtained by leaving the bait and replenishing it when necessary.

Is there any practical way to get rid of mice in the garden? Not really, and what little can be done is only moderately helpful at best. The experts on rodents tell me that persistently using snap traps is the best, and certainly the safest method. Having cats around that are good mousers will help, although winter snows as well as mulches provide mice with protection. Wire screen around the base of trees, as for rabbits, helps. The poisons available in years gone by are not available generally and were extremely toxic to use around yards and pets. Chlorphacinone (Rozol) and diphacinone (Ramik-brown) are used commercially but may not be available to the home gardener in most states. They are also very poisonous to cats and dogs, if not used properly. You should consult your local extension agent for recommendations and currently available products.

MILDEW

What makes mildew on plants? (Texas.) A fungus, of the type they call an obligate parasite, because it must get its food from living plants. When the wind carries a spore (little seed) to a leaf and the moisture conditions are right, the spore sends out a germ tube that grows into white threads, mycelium, which branch over the leaf in a soft, white, felty coating. This fungus does not grow inside the plant but sends little suckers, haustoria, into the sap. In a few days, chains or spores are built up from the mycelium which gives the powdery effect. Later, black fruiting bodies with the sexual or overwintering spores are formed. Because it is on the surface, mildew is more readily controlled than many other fungi and may even be eradicated after the first signs of it appear.

How can one control mildew? (Minnesota.)   Sulfur is a specific for mildew and the easiest way to apply it is in dust form, but sulfur or copper sprays may be used. Karathane and Actidione PM are used specifically for mildew control. Benlate is also very effective.

MILLIPEDES

What is the best way to rid a garden of the dark-brown, hard-shelled, spiral variety of worm which eats root vegetables? (Massachusetts.)   This is a millipede. The name literally means thousand-legged, but the number falls far short of that, although this animal comes in many segments and there are 2 pairs of legs on each segment (the centipede has only 1 pair to each segment). Ordinarily, millipedes in the garden act more as scavengers than as a direct cause of injury, but they do some feeding on potatoes and other root vegetables. For control, use malathion, carbaryl, or diazinon. (See Wireworms; Sowbugs.)

MITES

What can be done to avoid or control mites?   There are 3 kinds of mites apt to be troublesome in the home yard: spider mites, gall and rust mites, and cyclamen mites. Mites are relatives of spiders since they have 8 legs rather than 6, like insects. They are microscopic in size, so a hand magnifier is necessary to identify mites as the problem. Spider mites have silk glands and make webbing on the undersides of leaves or between needles. Their sucking of plant sap stipples foliage and needles, resulting in yellow foliage or rusty brown needles. Spruce mite and southern red mite should be controlled in the spring (May) or fall (September); honey locust mite in mid-June to early July; and two-spotted mites throughout the growing season whenever they occur. Spider mites are encouraged by the use of carbaryl (Sevin), but can be controlled with Kelthane, tetradifon, chlorobenzilate, or Omite. Gall mites are common on trees but seldom injurious. Rust mites can bronze or yellow the foliage of hemlock, privet, elm, and honey locust. Sevin suppresses these mites (*Eriophyidae*), but use Kelthane to control them. The cyclamen mite is most common on African violets and cyclamens as house plants, but stunts and deforms some outdoor flowers, especially delphiniums, causing blackened buds that never develop. Destroy severely infested plants and spray others every week or two with Kelthane.

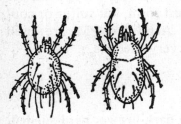

Red spiders are very tiny. They make fine webbing on the undersides of foliage.

What is the best material to use for spider mites on my garden and greenhouse plants?   There are several specific miticides on the market. (See the above question.) Spider mites can be partially checked by washing the foliage with strong jets of water.

MOLE CRICKETS

How do you get rid of mole crickets? (Florida.)   Mole crickets are dark-brown burrowing insects, about 1¼ inch long, with their front legs enlarged for tunneling. They come out at night to feed and are destructive because they eat the vegetative parts of seedlings as well as disturb the roots. Diazinon or Dursban will control mole crickets.

MOLES

How do I get rid of moles?   This is a very common problem. It was sent in by 91 gardeners in 32 different states. It is unfortunate that moles, which really do a lot of good in the world by eating white grubs and other insects, should also have the bad habit of making unsightly ridges and mounds in lawns and of disturbing the roots of flowers and vegetables by their tunnels. Actual feeding on plants is done by mice that use the mole runs. (See the following questions.)

Do moles eat bulbs?   No. They are carnivorous. Mice eat bulbs.

How do you get rid of moles without traps or poison? (Pennsylvania.)   There is not much left except patrolling the ridges and watching for movements indicating that the mole is at work and then killing it with a spade or a fork. A dog after a mole is disastrous, but cats may catch moles without any extra damage to the garden. One cat of an acquaintance had an unbroken record of a mole a day. Flooding the mole runs with water in the spring will drown young moles and mice in some soils.

What is the best method of controlling moles? (Oregon.)   Trapping. The Fish and Wildlife Service in Oregon and Washington report negative results with poison baits and cyanide dust but success with traps correctly set. Traps should not be set in the shallow runways but in the deeper main highways. Two types of traps may be used: the scissors and the diamond-jaw. Both depend on a trigger, sprung when the mole follows its natural instinct of burrowing through an obstruction of loose earth placed in the runway. Use a strong trowel to set the trap in the runway, aligning it so that the jaws of the scissors trap straddle the course or so that the choker trap encircles it. Pack the earth firmly under the trigger so the mole cannot work through without springing it. In gravelly soil, the choker works best.

What will eradicate Townsend moles? (California.)   These are Oregon moles. (See the previous question.)

Can one ever get rid of moles? (Iowa.)   Maybe, with persistence, but you don't want to get rid of those that are not actually injuring your garden. Think of your white-grub problem in Iowa. The loop or choker trap has been found to be very effective in Iowa soil.

How do you combat moles? (New York.)   New York State has 3 different moles. The naked-tail mole does much of the damage to lawns and golf courses on Long Island and in the lower Hudson Valley. In central and western New York, the star-nosed and the hairy-tail moles are present. The star-nosed mole throws up earth in a mound similar to a gopher mound, but the other two make the familiar ridges. Use mole traps for these, but snap-back mousetraps for the star-nosed variety. Treating the lawn for white grubs is often helpful in discouraging moles.

MOTHS

What is the difference between moths and butterflies?   Both are adults of caterpillars, often called worms. Moths are night fliers and their antennae are never clubbed.

I have small golden moths infesting my shrubs and grass and when I use the hose they fly up in great numbers. No one seems to know what they are or have not noticed them. They last from June or July to September. What are they? (New York.) They are probably the crambid moth, adults of sod webworms. Webworms are not a major lawn pest in New York, as they are in California and some other states, but sometimes the larva, a fat caterpillar which lives in a silklined nest, injures the grass roots. Spray your lawn with chlordane, carbaryl, or diazinon. In your particular case, the larvae of your moths may not be doing enough damage to bother about.

NEMATODES

What are nematodes and in what manner does soil become infested? (Georgia.) Nematodes are roundworms or eelworms, too small to see with the naked eye, that live in moist soil, in decaying organic matter, or as parasites in living plant tissues. They can travel only a short distance in the soil by themselves but are spread by surface water, by moving infested soil from place to place, and, very commonly, by local transfer and shipment of infested plants. Nematodes are more serious in sandy soils in southern states and in California. In the North, they may live during the winter in perennials and can also survive free in the soil.

How do you recognize the presence of nematodes? (Texas.) Injury to plants is slow to show up and not at all dramatic. Usually conspicuous above-ground symptoms do not appear until a heavy population of nematodes has built up. Nematodes should be suspected when plants show a slow decline in vigor and growth, when they become stunted and unthrifty, when water does not help them much in drought, or when the foliage becomes discolored yellow or bronze, as from a nutritional deficiency. You may or may not find swellings on the roots. The feeder roots may be lacking and the root system stunted and sparse or matted and shallow. Washed roots may disclose abundant small reddish-brown lesions in the epidermis. A hairy root condition occurs in some plants. Often roots are partially to wholly decayed because of secondary fungus or bacterial infections starting in lesions made by the nematodes. Foliar nematodes, common in chrysanthemums, produce angular brown lesions in the leaves; and bulb and stem nematodes produce discolored streaks or rings in narcissus bulbs, thickened stems, and crinkled leaves. The root-knot nematode, most common in southern areas, infests more than 1,700 species of plants. The nodules formed by beneficial nitrogen-fixing bacteria on legumes should not be confused with the root galls produced by this nematode.

How can root-knot nematodes be destroyed without killing shrubbery and perennials in infested beds? (California.) Nematocides are now available that destroy nematodes without killing plants; however, not all plants are tolerant to them, so read directions carefully and use on the specified plants only. You may use either V–C 13, a complex phosphorous compound, or Nemagon, 1, 2–dibromo 3–chloropropone. Both may be watered directly into the lawn or under plants with a watering can or hose proportioner. Granulated formulations can be applied by hand or with a fertilizer spreader and then watered in.

What is the latest information on combating nematodes in the southern garden? (Texas.) Either of the above nematocides may be used some 2 weeks previous to planting on prepared soil for susceptible plants or after planting on tolerant plants. An excellent preplanting treatment that may be used in any garden area after the soil has been prepared, but some 2 weeks before planting, consists of applying sodium methyl dithiocarbamate (Vapam or VPM). Just apply it with a watering can or with your hose and hose spray proportioner. This treatment destroys disease-producing fungi and most weed seeds, as well as nematodes.

Is there a quick, economical method of ridding garden soil of root-knot nematode? (Georgia.) The chemical methods discussed above are quick but not economical for large areas. Both ethylene dibromide and methyl bromide are more economical but not as easily applied. Ethylene dibromide may be applied as an undiluted liquid with special equipment on a field basis or in furrows 6 inches deep and 10 inches apart by pouring a stream along the trenches at the rate of ½ cup for every 75 feet. A quart container with 2 nail holes in opposite sides of the lid will facilitate application. As the application is made, another person should follow, filling the trench with soil and tamping it down. Wait two weeks before planting. Methyl bromide (Dowfume MC–2, Bromo-Gas) is a volatile liquid that must be kept under pressure at ordinary temperatures. Small amounts of soil for use in flowerpots, flats, and greenhouse benches can be treated in a large garbage can with a tight cover. Use ½ ounce per cubic foot of soil for 24 hours and allow 3 days for aeration before using. This treatment destroys soil fungi, weed seeds, and insects, as well as nematodes. For larger prepared-soil areas such as cold frames, gardens, and seed beds, a plastic tarpaulin is essential to confine the fumes for 24 to 48 hours. The rate is 1 pound per 100 square feet, and allow at least 2 days for aeration. The soil temperature should be above 60° F. to make treatments effective. Avoid treating the soil under trees and shrubs, and the soil to be used for carnation growing. This is highly toxic; get a professional applicator.

Two other soil fumigants, D-D and chloropicrin (Larvacide), are used chiefly in commercial enterprises: the first, for nematodes and insects; the second, for all soil organisms including weed seeds. They are applied with special hand applicators or tractor-borne applicators attached to plows or cultivatorlike devices. A water seal is necessary, along with a 2- to 3-week wait before planting.

I have heard that growing marigolds in gardens with other plants controls nematodes. Is this true? Marigolds grown with or in advance of other plants produce a toxin that will reduce the number of root-lesion (meadow) nematodes, but *not* root-knot and other types. Best results come from growing a crop of marigolds one season, spading it under, and putting in susceptible plants the next.

NICOTINE SULFATE

What is nicotine sulfate? Formerly widely available as Black Leaf 40, it is now hard to obtain. It is a useful contact insecticide. It is poisonous, but not as hazardous in diluted form, to people. It is readily washed off, and so can be safely used on vegetables and fruits to within a short time of harvest. It is used ordinarily in a soapy solution but it can be added to fungicides and some other insecticides. The dosage varies according to the insect to be controlled. A normal solution (1 to 800 dilution) is made with 1 teaspoon of nicotine sulfate and 1 ounce of soap (1 cubic inch of laundry soap) per gallon of water. For more resistant insects, the dosage is increased to 1½ to 2 teaspoons per gallon. Ordinarily, nicotine sulfate can be used without injury to plants, but caution is needed on a very hot day in the garden or in an enclosed greenhouse that is too warm.

OIL SPRAYS

Where and when can oils be used on plants? Normally called "dormant oils" (see Dormant Spraying), petroleum oil is an effective insecticide against mites, aphid eggs, and scale insects, while being nontoxic to animals. At recommended dosage rates, it is not injurious to most plants, even when used as a summer oil spray. The spray oils of recent years are more highly refined and thus more insecticidal and safer to use on plants than those of 20 to 30 years ago. Be sure to follow label uses and directions carefully.

ORTHENE

My extension agent suggested that I use Orthene for aphids in my garden and for mealybugs on some house plants. Is it the same as acephate? Acephate is the accepted common name for Orthene (trade name). It is used against a wide range of insect pests and has systemic properties. It is very effective for aphids, leafminers, mealybugs, scales, some caterpillars, and other common pests. It is registered for use on ornamentals in the garden and many house plants, but not the vegetable garden or fruit trees. Some plants are sensitive to it, so be sure to read the label for precautions.

PESTICIDES AND PUBLIC HEALTH

Federal, state, and even local laws regulate the sale and use of pesticides and at the same time help to protect the public from dangerous residues and the environment from deleterious hazards. All pesticides must be label-approved by the Environmental Protection Agency for specific crops and pests. Any use inconsistent with label directions is illegal under federal and state laws. Residue tolerances on food crops and quarantine periods to control reuse of treated areas have been established by law. Pesticides have been and are still in the process of being designated for general use, or for restricted use only by certified private and commercial applicators. For large-scale or area-wide spray programs, environmental impact statements by the applicators are required and must be approved by local, state, or federal agencies before control operations begin. The home gardener often has misused pesticides by using more than the recommended rate given on the label (it does *not* improve results!), treating too often, treating when or where pests are not a problem, or by dumping excess spray material into sewage systems, storm drains, or sites where runoff ends up in streams or other bodies of water. It is very important to read and follow *all* of the label directions and precautions carefully with regard to uses for specific pests and crops or plants, safe intervals between last spray and harvest, and precautions for the applicator, pets, children, and wildlife.

PRAYING MANTIS

Can you tell me about the praying mantis? I am planning to purchase an egg case next spring. (Illinois.)   If the praying mantis is not naturally present in your neighborhood, it might not pay to purchase egg cases, for these ferocious-looking beneficial insects are not commonly found much north of 40° latitude. The mantis belongs to the grasshopper family. It is very long and thin, with prominent eyes and enormous front legs used for catching other insects (aphids, mites, caterpillars) but often held up in a praying attitude. The baby mantis looks just like the adult, except for lack of wings. Their cannibalistic instincts are so well developed that they often eat one another. Do not let the egg masses hatch in the house, for heat brings them out in the winter and there is no way to feed the young mantises until they can survive out-of-doors. The praying mantis is generally a good predator, but will not control all garden pests.

I have hundreds of praying mantises in my garden. What do the egg cases look like? I find so many tentlike formations. (Kansas.)   The egg cases are a sort of dingy cream or yellow, shaped something like an oblong hatbox, but not especially regular, about 1 inch across, and made of a frothy gummy substance which hardens in that same frothy texture. They are usually attached to twigs of trees or shrubs. Egg masses are produced in late summer and hatch the following spring.

PYRETHRUM

What is pyrethrum?   A contact insecticide obtained from the pyrethrum plant, mostly grown in Africa. It is especially effective against aphids and soft-bodied insects, but it will kill whatever chewing insects it hits. It is useful for spraying flowers where a stain would be objectionable. For use on the Mexican bean beetle, impregnated pyrethrum dusts are more efficient.

RABBITS

Other than by fencing, how can rabbits be kept out of the garden? (Pennsylvania.)   Some sort of fence is still the best solution. If you cannot get the poultry wire ordinarily recommended, a picket fence can be substituted, or a low concrete wall built. The expense of either of these would be justified if the vegetable garden is to be permanent, and would look better than a wire fence (although green wire fencing is inconspicuous). There are reports that a row of child's windmills, or glass bottles stuck in the ground (neck down) will act as a fence in scaring rabbits away. A few cats will greatly diminish the rabbit population.

Will dried blood sprinkled around the roots of beans or other vegetables prevent rabbits from eating them? (New Jersey.)   Dried blood has long been listed as an effective rabbit repellent, as well as being good for the garden. Some gardeners report that it is not always effective.

What is a good rabbit repellent? (Illinois.)   The New Jersey Fish and Game Commission has listed 9 repellents for harassed gardeners: (1) dust plants, when damp, with powdered lime; (2) dust liberally with dusting sulfur (some vegetables do not take kindly to sulfur); (3) sprinkle plants with red pepper; (4) spray with a solution of 3 ounces of Epsom salts in 1 gallon of water; (5) spray with 1 teaspoon of Lysol in 1 gallon of water; (6) spray with 2 teaspoons of Black Leaf 40 in 1 gallon of soapy water; (7) spray with a solution of common brown laundry soap; (8) spray with 1 ounce of tartar emetic and 3 ounces of sugar in 1 gallon of water; (9) sprinkle naphthalene flakes between the rows of plants. One of the easiest methods is the family's pet cat! (The more cats, the fewer rabbits.)

How can you keep rabbits from eating young soybeans?   Soybeans are often used to keep rabbits away from other plants. They worked that way in my garden, and I still get a lusty crop of soybeans. Formerly I credited moth balls with repelling the rabbits just enough to give the soybeans a fighting chance, but I visited a garden one summer where the rabbits had not allowed one soybean plant out of hundreds to get above 6 inches high and moth balls were so thick that the garden looked white. Now I have come to the conclusion that it is my neighbor's cats, hunting young rabbits, that keep the population down to reasonable proportions.

Rabbits have chewed the bark completely from the trunk of a young flowering crab planted this spring. Can anything be done to save the tree? (New Jersey.)   You might try bridge grafting, which has worked successfully for apple trees girdled by rabbits and mice. Unless you are acquainted with this art, it would be better to have the work done by a tree expert, and that might cost as much as a new tree. Next time, protect your tree with a cylinder of close-mesh woven wire, 24 inches wide, sunk into the ground a few inches, and held away from the trunk with stakes. Sometimes prunings left on the ground around the trees and bushes will feed the rabbits enough to keep them from injuring the trunks. (See the answer to the previous question.)

RACCOONS   (See Squirrels.)

RED SPIDER MITES   (See Mites.)

RESMETHRIN

I have read that resmethrin is good for whiteflies. What is it?   It is the common name for one of several man-made chemicals similar to natural pyrethrins that are derived from the chrysanthemum. These synthetic pyrethroids have become available in the 1970s, primarily for greenhouse and house-plant use, but not as yet for food crops or vegetable gardens, although they appear to be effective against many kinds of insects. For the first time, they provide for the kill of whitefly nymphs as well as adults. Other pyrethroids include permethrin (Ambush, Pounce) and tetramethrin. The aerosols available to the home gardener may have only the long chemical name on the label, but will also prominently display the designation "Whitefly Spray."

ROTENONE

What is rotenone?   The principal insecticidal constituent in roots of plants such as *Derris* or *Lonchocarpus*. It acts as a stomach and contact poison for insects, kills fish and other cold-blooded animals, but is not injurious to man except as a throat irritant. It leaves no poisonous residue on the plant. Rotenone formerly was obtained from the Far East and is now coming from South America. *Lonchocarpus* has been established there to provide a new source of rotenone. Rotenone dust is available in a 1 per cent dilution. *Derris,* with an analysis of 4 to 5 per cent rotenone, is used for spraying.

RUST

What is a good spray for rust on plants? (California.)   That depends on whether or not you have true rust, a fungus that manifests itself in erumpent reddish-brown or reddish-orange pustules of spores, or, in the case of red-cedar and apple rust, in long, gelatinous spore horns, for which there is no chemical control. Zineb, mancozeb, or sulfur and ferbam are the best fungicides for the control of rust. For ornamental plants, they can be applied as a dust. Very often gardeners speak of "rust" when they merely mean a reddish discoloration of the tissue, which might be due to a variety of causes but never to the true rust fungus.

SCALE INSECTS

What is the life history of scale? What plants are attacked? What are the treatments? Do you mean indoors or out? There are many different scale insects, but 2 general types. Those found in gardens in New York would be mostly of the armored-scale type, that is, after they finish the young, crawling stage, a hard, separable shell is formed on their bodies and they stop moving around. In this group is the oyster-shell scale on lilacs, scurfy scale on apples, rose scale on roses, euonymus scale on euonymus and bittersweet, juniper scale, pine-needle scale, and many others. This group is controlled by oil spray before growth starts in the spring (see Dormant Spraying) and malathion for the young scales or "crawlers" in midsummer. The second group includes the soft or tortoise scales, represented in a northern garden by maple, tulip tree, lecanium, and magnolia scales. More often seen on house plants are soft brown scales that have to be scrubbed off or sprayed with an aerosol plant bomb, Orthene or malathion. (See House Plants.)

How do you get rid of cottony cushion scale on trees? (Texas.) Ask your State Extension Service where you can get a colony of Australian lady beetles. A malathion spray can also be helpful.

SEED TREATMENT

Should seeds be treated before being planted? Yes, the application of a chemical protectant is insurance against damping off, either in the seed flat or the garden row, and in addition can prevent some diseases due to organisms carried on the outside of the seed. Nowadays, most seeds available to the gardener have been treated. It pays to buy seeds already treated. Also helpful is sowing the seeds in soilless mixes, such as Jiffy Mix, which are sterile.

What about the organisms carried inside the seeds? They cannot be killed with external dusts. The seeds must be soaked in hot water—a treatment usually not given unless the disease organism is presumably present. Tie seeds loosely in cheesecloth bags and keep the temperature of the water constant: 122° F., 25 minutes for cabbage, 15 minutes for other crucifers; tomato seed, 25 minutes; 118° F., 30 minutes for celery.

SLUGS AND SNAILS

Is there any way to rid my garden of slugs? (California.)   No, but they can be suppressed or minimized by a combination of good sanitation practices and proper use of slug baits. Slugs and snails live where it is very moist and hide in the dark in daytime beneath stones, boards, and trash on the ground and in the soil. By keeping the garden well tilled, free of weeds, and uncluttered by stones, stakes, and plant refuse, slugs will have few places to thrive. Two slug baits that may be sold under various trade names are metaldehyde and mesurol. Mesurol is not labeled for use around food plants, but metaldehyde is. Be sure to follow label directions carefully when treating the soil. Do not treat the plants directly. Supplementary measures for small gardens include trapping. Boards placed in the garden in the evening provide ready places for them to hide when daylight comes. Slugs can then be killed. Beer will attract slugs if placed in shallow dishes with the rim at soil level. Slugs crawl into the dish and drown. Salt or lime will kill slugs when sprinkled on them.

What is the best method for combating slugs? We use lime but it whitens our shrubs. The slugs attack cherry trees, purple-leaf plum, and flowering quince. (Utah.)   Put your lime on the ground in a circle, enclosing the tree trunk. Try spraying the slugs at night with a spray of ¼ to ½ pound of alum per gallon of water. Try metaldehyde baits or beer in deep saucers. If "slugs" are seen on the leaves during the day, they may be sawfly larvae. (See Rose.)

Will a boardwalk in a garden be the cause of an exceptionally large number of slugs?   It would provide the protected hiding place favored by slugs, but it should also prove a help in getting rid of them, for poison baits put under the boardwalk would not endanger children, pets, or birds.

What is the best way to destroy slugs and snails without the risk of poisoning birds or pets? (Ohio.)   If poison baits are put out under little jar covers or pieces of board, there is little danger to pets, but to play it absolutely safe, resort to lime on the ground, cleaning up plant debris, hand-picking, and probably spraying or dusting plants with an insecticide. There is practically no danger to pets when a poison is used on plants.

Are hard-shell snails or big, fat, soft ones harmful or beneficial in the garden? I have roses, iris, lilies, etc. (Pennsylvania.)   They are not exactly beneficial. Roses will be little bothered by true slugs in Pennsylvania, but they have their special brand of false slugs or sawfly larvae. (See Rose.) Any plant with leaves close to the ground like iris or lily will be apt to be eaten by slugs.

SOIL STERILIZATION

Isn't there some way to get the soil in such a healthy condition that insects and diseases will not bother a plant? Disease organisms in the soil can be killed by soil sterilization, but there is no known way to render plants immune to attacks by fungi or insects. There are a few instances where fertilizing is somewhat linked up with resistance, but there is little exact knowledge along this line.

How do you sterilize soil? The usual aim is not a complete destruction of all living organisms but a partial sterilization which will control harmful organisms. Heat is one of the best means, but there are difficulties. Steam is excellent but practical only for the commercial greenhouse operator; hot water can be used, but it is apt to puddle the soil; baking is used for small quantities, but toxic materials can be liberated; this can be true also when electricity is used. Formaldehyde is most useful for treating small lots of soil to prevent damping off of seedlings. Formaldehyde dust is used, but the liquid sprinkle method seems more generally satisfactory. For each 20 × 14 × 2 and ¾-inch flat of soil, use 1 tablespoon of Formalin diluted with 6 tablespoons water. Sprinkle it over the soil and mix thoroughly. Let stand 12 to 24 hours; after the seeds are sown, water immediately.

How do you treat the soil in a garden? It is rather an expensive procedure recommended only for the control of specific organisms when crop rotation is not feasible. Formaldehyde is usually used for root-rot fungi. Dilute 1 part commercial Formalin with 50 parts water and apply ½ gallon to each square foot of soil. Cover for 1 to 2 days with burlap, paper, or boards. Spade to air out the gas and wait about 2 weeks before planting. Vapam is registered and available for treating home gardens as a preplant treatment. It is effective against nematodes and other soil-borne plant pathogens. Soil preparation and temperature are very important. After applying either 1 pint per 50 square feet with a sprinkling can or 1 quart to 3 quarts of water per 100 square feet with a hose proportioner, immediately cover the area with a plastic film. Post-treatment cultivation during a waiting period is essential. Be sure to follow all directions carefully from Cooperative Extension recommendations and on the label.

SOOTY MOLD

I have had trouble in my greenhouse with a black sooty substance forming on the leaves. It is hard to wash off. What is it and how do I prevent it from forming? (Wisconsin.) This is a black fungus growth called sooty mold, but the fungus is not parasitic on the plant; it is merely growing in insect honeydew that drops on the leaves—in your case, very likely from aphids, scales, or mostly whiteflies, but on outdoor shrubs mostly from aphids or scale insects. There is not much hope of washing it off. You can prevent it by spraying to control your insect population.

SOWBUGS

How do you destroy sowbugs? The bug is flat and fairly round, and has hard legs along the side. (Virginia.) Sowbugs, probably named for female hogs because of their shape, are sometimes called pill bugs because of their tendency to roll up into little balls. Sowbugs are not true insects but crustacea, related to crayfish. They are grayish, segmented, with 7 pairs of legs about ½ inch long. They hide at the base of plants under clods of earth or manure. Dust the soil with malathion, carbaryl, or diazinon to control them.

Do sowbugs eat seed in flats? I am not certain about the seed itself, but they injure the seedlings by feeding on the stems and tender growth at the soil line.

SPITTLEBUGS

What causes the white frothy substance that looks like white foam to come on plants? This is the spittlebug, so named because the young nymphs have the habit of secreting a quantity of frothy material between molts. The adults leave the "spit" protection and look something like leafhoppers, but because of their bulging eyes, they are often called froghoppers. In Michigan, the pine spittlebug can be injurious to pines and other conifers by sucking the sap. Occasionally young trees are killed. Spray with methoxychlor or malathion, and apply the spray with great pressure.

What can I do to rid my plants of an insect in a sort of "bubble"? I have heard it called spitbug. Various species of spittlebugs occasionally injure garden plants. In New Jersey a while back, a devastating attack on strawberries was repulsed with *Derris* dust. Any fairly potent contact insecticide applied with enough pressure to penetrate the protective froth should be satisfactory. Spittlebugs do get around. They have been several times reported from penthouse gardens high over New York City.

SPRAY MATERIALS

Spraying charts are usually given for the large farmer, not the backyard gardener. Will you furnish a simplified spraying chart where a gardener needs to mix only a pint or a quart at the most? Label directions are usually given for 1 gallon. One pint, or even a quart, will not go very far, even in a backyard garden. Moreover, anyone capable of filling out income-tax blanks should be able to do a little arithmetic on garden sprays. Remember that there are 3 teaspoons in 1 tablespoon, 16 tablespoons in 1 cup, or 8 liquid ounces, 4 cups in a quart, and 4 quarts in a gallon. Buy a set of kitchen measuring spoons and a glass cup marked off in ounces. When the directions call for 1 teaspoon per gallon and you need only a quart, use the tiny ¼ teaspoon measure. When 1 tablespoon per gallon is needed, mix ¾ teaspoon in 1 quart.

What can I use on vegetables that is harmless to people or dogs and will kill the chewing bugs? Rotenone. Methoxychlor is also relatively safe and may be used within a week of harvest.

What are the main spray materials to have on hand? I understand some of these sprays are the same, only they are under different names. You understand correctly. Insecticides and fungicides are sold under hundreds of different trade names, but basically they now depend on malathion, carbaryl, methoxychlor, diazinon, acephate, *Bacillus thuringiensis,* pyrethrum, rotenone, and oils for action against insects; and copper, sulfur, and the new organic fungicides captan, ferbam, benomyl, folpet, maneb, zineb, mancozeb, and chlorothalonil for diseases. Miticides include Kelthane, Tedion, Omite, and chlorobenzilate. Always read the label on your proprietary mixture and know what you are buying. Only the plants you grow and the diseases and pests you have can determine how many different materials are required in your garden. Theoretically, 1 fungicide, 1 stomach poison, 1 contact insecticide, and a miticide would see you through, but not all fungi react to copper or to sulfur, and not all insects can be controlled by rule.

Isn't there some one spray I could use for all the garden ills to which the Deep South is heir? (Louisiana.) Unfortunately, no, but a general-purpose garden spray comes close to taking care of some of the most important southern pests. Write the Department of Entomology, State Agricultural Experiment Station, Baton Rouge, La. 70803 for help.

Would you suggest how to plan a spray schedule for a perennial border? It depends on the plants you have. Check through the alphabetical list of ornamentals in this section and see which problems apply to your garden. Consult the books listed in Section 16 under Pests and Diseases for further information.

What ingredients would you advise in a general-purpose spray mixture for use on fruits, vegetables, and ornamentals? A good general-purpose spray or dust may have malathion for sucking pests and mites; methoxychlor or carbaryl for chewing insects; captan, folpet, or zineb for diseases; and Kelthane as a miticide. Karathane or benomyl may be needed for powdery mildew control. General-purpose sprays applied periodically eliminate the necessity for knowing what foliage or fruit insects or diseases to worry about on your plants.

SPRAYERS

What are garden sprayers? Equipment to apply liquid insecticides or fungicides to plants in a fine mist. Sprayers vary from aerosol bombs and pint- or quart-size atomizers useful for house plants to huge power apparatus that will spray tall trees with 500 pounds of pressure. For the average garden, a cylindrical compressed-air sprayer or a knapsack sprayer of 1½- to 3-gallon capacity, which fits on the back, will be sufficient. For small trees and shrubs, a bucket or barrel sprayer mounted on wheels to move around the garden will be most convenient. Small motor-driven sprayers are also available. If a copper or stainless steel sprayer rather than a galvanized one can be procured, it will be worth the extra price in longer life. No sprayer is better than the care given it. Rinse thoroughly immediately after use and occasionally take it apart for cleaning. Strain all spray mixtures into the tank through cheesecloth to prevent clogging. Extra parts can often be obtained from manufacturers or distributors to keep old sprayers in operation.

Is any single sprayer, such as the hose proportioner type, sufficient for all average conditions? Hose sprayers of the proportioner type are very convenient and easy to use and are suitable for shrubs and small trees as well as flowers and vegetables. They handle solutions and emulsions readily, but you may run into trouble with suspensions because of clogging. Not all types give a suitable dispersion of the active chemical in the spray. Those with a shut-off near the nozzle are much preferable to those that have no shut-off and require you to place your finger over a hole to start the chemical mixing with the water spray. The 1- to 3-gallon compressed-air sprayers will handle all chemicals and will do a good job in most gardens. In addition, gardeners should have a few aerosol plant bombs on hand for spot treatments of pests.

SQUIRRELS, RACCOONS, AND CHIPMUNKS

How do I get rid of chipmunks? (Massachusetts.) It has been said, although I cannot prove it personally, that chipmunks are unsuspicious creatures readily caught in live-animal or snap-back traps baited with a nut, pumpkin seed, or peanut butter, and placed near their burrows. These ground squirrels eat some slugs and insects and should not be destroyed without reason. Bulbs can be planted in wire baskets to protect them. Cats will also discourage chipmunks.

Our corn patch was neatly devastated, a dozen ears per night, by some animal that shucked as it ate. Is it likely to have been squirrels? How can we combat such an unseen adversary? (Connecticut.) It may have been woodchucks or squirrels, but more likely raccoons if the ears were husked. There is not much solution except to trap or shoot them or to plant enough for you and the animals, too. In my garden, they are satisfied with the outside row. Creatures have their rights, too, and their place in the environment. (See Corn.)

How do you get rid of gray squirrels? (Virginia.) Get permission to trap them or to shoot them, which is easier said than done in many communities.

How do you prevent squirrels from monopolizing feeding stations? (New York.) If the feeding station is hung from a horizontal wire, metal guards can be placed on either side; or if the feeding station is on top of a post, a guard can be placed underneath; but if the station is anywhere within leaping distance of a tree, the guard is useless. Put out enough food for the squirrels—and the birds.

STREPTOMYCIN

Do any of the antibiotic drugs for people work on plant diseases? Yes, streptomycin has been used to control a number of bacterial plant diseases such as fire blight of apples and pears, bacterial spot of tomato and pepper, and bacterial wilt of chrysanthemum. The formulations are sold under the names Agrimycin, Agri-Strep, and Phytomycin. Effective dilutions range from 50 to 100 parts per million.

SULFUR

How is sulfur used in the garden? Sulfur is a valuable fungicide with many uses, but especially in the control of rust and mildew, and also of some value as a miticide in the control of spider and other mites. In the home garden, sulfur is usually used in dust form, and it can be safely combined with insecticides. Wettable sulfurs are available to use as liquid sprays. In very hot weather, sulfur should be used cautiously, for it is apt to burn the plants. It is incompatible with oil and should not be used within 30 days of an oil spray. It will injure viburnums.

SYSTEMIC OR CHEMOTHERAPEUTIC AGENTS

I have heard that some pesticides can be absorbed by plants to kill the pests and fungi that attack them. Which chemicals are they and how do they work? There are a number of systemic insecticides and at least one fungicide. Since this type of chemical tends to be relatively more toxic to animals also, most are restricted to use by professional applicators. Those that are available to the home gardener include the insecticides acephate (Orthene), dimethoate (DeFend and Cygon), and oxydemeton methyl (Meta-Systox-R or MSR), and the fungicide benomyl (Benlate). Whereas warm-blooded animals must be injected or eat chemicals (drugs) for medication, plants can take up chemicals through the roots, through the foliage, or be injected. Injection techniques are registered for use by professional applicators. Although it might seem that a toxicant within the plant would protect against any insect or disease, that is not the case. Systemic insecticides are effective primarily for sucking insects and mites that feed on the foliage, some caterpillars that feed on foliage and new growth, but seldom those feeding on or in the bark or wood. Extreme caution should be used when systemics are used, since the dosage rate that renders plants toxic to insects approaches the dilution rate that may be injurious to the plants. Granular formulations of disulfoton (Di-Syston) are available for mites and sucking insects on roses and some floral crops and leafminers on birch and holly trees.

TENT CATERPILLAR

How can I control the tent caterpillar, which attacks wild cherry and apple trees in the spring? As soon as the webs form, while worms are still very small, wipe them out of the crotches of branches with a pointed stick or a swab dipped in kerosene or spray them with carbaryl. If webs must be destroyed after the caterpillars are well developed, do so in the early morning or after sunset when the caterpillars have returned to the web for warmth. A preventive control is to cut off and burn the twigs bearing egg masses, which can be seen after the leaves have dropped in autumn or winter.

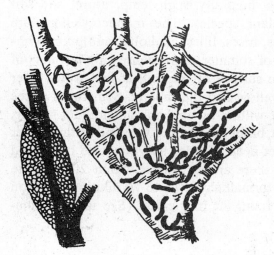

Tent caterpillars form large gray-white webs in the crotches of branches. (Left) Egg mass on a winter twig.

TERMITES

Where termites are in cordwood, 50 feet from a brick house, is there danger that they will get started in the house itself? (Maryland.) Not unless there is any woodwork on the building in direct contact with the ground. If there is, a metal shield can be inserted. It is wise to get rid of the termites in the woodpile by burning the wood and treating the termite nest with chlordane.

TERRACHLOR

My dealer does not have Terrachlor—where can he get it? Terrachlor, or PCNB, is manufactured by the Olin Chemical Corporation, Little Rock, Arkansas, as a 75 per cent Wettable Powder or a 20 per cent dust. It is very promising for some soil-borne diseases such as club root of crucifers and crown rot of iris and many other plants. Use Wettable Powder at the rate of 1½ pounds per 12 gallons of water per 1,000 square feet, or the dust at the rate of 5 pounds per 1,000 square feet. Work the dust into the upper soil before planting.

TEXAS ROOT ROT

Has there been anything found to control root rot? (Texas.)   Texas root rot, also called cotton or Phymatotrichum root rot, is probably the chief problem in gardening in certain parts of Texas, Arizona, and New Mexico. The fungus *Phymatotrichum omnivorum* is a native soil inhabitant in semiarid regions of low humidity, high temperature, and soil alkalinity. It attacks 1,700 plant species. The monocotyledons are immune, so you can grow palms, irises, lilies, gladiolus, and bulbs without trouble. During the period of summer rains, dense circular mats of fungus mycelium appear on the surface of the soil, at first white, later tan and powdery. Plants turn yellow and die rapidly. Sometimes a tree can be saved at the first sign of wilting by applying ammonium sulfate, 1 pound to 10 square feet, in a basin around the tree and letting water run in until the soil is wet 4 feet deep. Garden soil may also be treated with ammonium sulfate, but if there are no shrubs within 20 feet, the fallow soil may be treated with formaldehyde (1 to 70 dilution, 1 gallon applied per foot) or with soil fumigant fungicides. (See under Nematodes.)

THRIPS   (See Gladiolus.)

WHITE GRUBS

This spring I plowed and planted land that had not been farmed for 25 years; grubworms killed the potatoes, cabbage, etc. What was the reason? (Illinois.)   Grubworms are white grubs in your area, soft-bodied white worms with brown heads and curved bodies ½ to 1 inch long. They look like Japanese beetle grubs but are a little larger. They

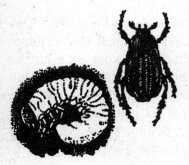

White grub, a large, soft, white grub with a brown head, is the larva of the June beetle (right) and eats roots of grass and other plants.

damage lawns in the same way and are much more injurious to root vegetables than are the grubs in the East. As you continue to garden your land, the injury should get less. It is most serious in areas neglected for a long time. White grubs are larvae of June beetles. There is a 3-year cycle, the grubs staying in the ground 2 years and the large brown beetles flying the third year and eating tree foliage. Injury from the worms is greatest the year after beetle flight.

How shall I rid my soil of grubworms? (Texas.) Prevent trouble, if possible, by not planting garden crops on sod land or land covered with weeds and grass the preceding year. If such land must be used, till or spade in the fall. Legume crops will suffer less than corn or potatoes.

WHITEFLIES

Is there a really good control for those clouds of little white flies among my house plants? Yes. Use an aerosol, according to container directions, that contains resmethrin. (See Resmethrin.)

WIREWORMS

I have a pest in the soil about the thickness of a darning needle, light brown, very tough. I have to cut off the head to kill it; it is ¾ to 1½ inches long and seems to live in the roots. Is it harmful to plants? (Indiana.) You have described a wireworm, a chewing insect that feeds underground on germinating seeds and underground roots, stems, and tubers. Potatoes, beets, beans, cabbage, carrots, corn, lettuce, onions, turnips, and other vegetables may be injured. Damage is worse on poorly drained soil or on land that has been in grass sod. The adult stage of the wireworm is a gray, brown, or black click beetle, an amusing creature that clicks itself right-side-up when it falls on its back.

What is the best method for exterminating wireworms? (New Jersey.) If newly broken sod must be used, till it thoroughly and then apply diazinon as a broadcast treatment prior to planting and thoroughly mix the top 4 to 8 inches of soil.

WITCHES'-BROOMS

What are witches'-brooms and their cause? (Massachusetts.) They are broomlike excessive development of twigs in response to an irritation caused by insects, fungi, or some virus. Hackberry is a notable example, with often hundreds of brooms, each a mass of stubby twigs, arising from a swelling at the base of a branch, on a single tree. A gall mite and a powdery mildew fungus seem to be jointly responsible for this deformation. There is no control in this case, but cutting out the brooms improves appearance.

WOODCHUCKS

How do you get rid of woodchucks?   The United States Fish and Wildlife Service has developed a special woodchuck cartridge, which can be obtained through county agents or at farm-supply stores. When lighted according to directions and placed in a den mouth, this will diffuse a lethal gas through the den.

How can I prevent woodchucks from eating strawberries?   A fence is the only sure protection, except a dog.

What can I do about woodchucks that eat my garden plants?   Watch for them in early morning and late afternoon and shoot them, if it is allowed in your area. Consult your county extension agent for local recommendations and restrictions.

Ornamentals and Their Pests

ACONITUM

Why do monkshood leaves and stems die? What is the cure? The roots look healthy. (Connecticut.)   If the vessels are black when you cut across the stem, dying leaves are probably due to verticillium wilt, the result of a soil fungus affecting the vascular system. There is no cure. Plant healthy roots in new or sterilized soil.

Can one prevent yellowing of leaves or complete defoliation of aconitum before blooming? (Ohio.)   Since this is presumably the same verticillium wilt, nothing will prevent the disease except starting over with new roots in fresh soil.

Is there any other cause of blight of aconitum except verticillium? (New Jersey.)   Yes, sometimes the crown-rot fungus so destructive to delphinium attacks aconitum. In this case, you usually see white threads or seedlike bodies on the soil, and the plant may topple over at the crown. Remove the plant and the surrounding soil. Disinfect the area with bichloride of mercury or Terrachlor.

Why do the flower buds of my aconitum turn black and not open?

(New Jersey.) The cyclamen mite affects aconitum as it does delphinium. Remove infested portions and spray weekly with Kelthane throughout the growing season.

AFRICAN-VIOLET (SAINTPAULIA)

My African-violets are stunted—they have twisted stems, misshapen foliage, and few and imperfect flowers. What is the trouble? The trouble is a cyclamen mite and bad news. It is too small to see with the naked eye and can spread from pot to pot of African-violets. Keep new plants isolated until you are sure they are healthy. Badly infested (deformed) plants are best destroyed. Kelthane is recommended as a dip (1 teaspoon to a gallon of water) and a spray (follow directions on the label).

How can I get rid of the mealybugs on my African-violet? It is difficult because spraying injures the foliage. Watch for the first signs of these white, woolly sucking insects and remove them with a small brush dipped in alcohol. Touch only the bug, not the leaf. Avoid a too hot, dry atmosphere. A house-plant aerosol bomb is also effective. Try Orthene; it is excellent for aphids.

How do I rid my African-violet of a small insect that leaves white cotton all over it? It is probably a mealybug, and if the infestation is that bad, you'd better destroy the plant and start with a healthy one.

Is there a remedy for lice on African-violet plants? You probably refer to mealybugs, for ordinary aphids are not as common on this plant. Constant vigilance is the remedy; pick off the first bit of cotton fluff you see, or touch each insect with a small swab of cotton on a matchstick (or a very small paintbrush) dipped in alcohol. A malathion or Orthene spray will also control mealybugs.

What causes a moldlike covering over the topsoil of houseplants, particularly African-violets? Insufficient aeration. Cultivate the soil occasionally with the tines of an old fork. Too much water compacts the soil and encourages the moldy surface growth. You may need to repot with a fresh mixture.

AGERATUM

What do you do for whiteflies on ageratum? The whiteflies, which usually come along when you get your plants from the greenhouse in the spring, cause minute white spotting on the foliage all summer, getting worse toward fall. Use a whitefly spray (resmethrin) or aerosol.

How can I keep "mooly" aphids or milk cows from my blue ageratum? I lose the plants each year. (Missouri.) "Mooly" is evidently mistyped for woolly, but the pun is too good to lose. Ants keep root aphids herded together so they can feed on the honeydew (milk) excreted. Make a shallow depression around each plant and pour in malathion solution. (See also Ants, for their control.)

ALYSSUM (AURINIA SAXATILIS)

Why does basket of gold alyssum die? Possibly because of wet feet. Good soil drainage is necessary; the foliage should be kept dry. This plant thrives on walls and other dry locations. The plants are not long-lived where summers are hot and humid, as they are alpines. Keep a fresh supply of seedlings to take the place of older plants.

AMARCRINUM

How do I get rid of thrips on x Amarcrinum memoria-corsii and Urginea maritima (sea-onion)? Spray or dust weekly with malathion.

AMARYLLIS (HIPPEASTRUM)

Can mealybugs be removed from the scales of an amaryllis bulb? I have tried alcohol sprays but there are still mealybugs. Be wary of alcohol sprays. You can remove bugs with a tiny cotton swab on a toothpick dipped in alcohol. Or try dipping in a malathion solution.

What is the grub that gets into amaryllis bulbs? Probably the larval form of greater or lesser narcissus bulb flies. Grub of the greater fly may be up to ¾ inch long; the lesser, up to ½ inch. Commercial growers often treat bulbs with hot water, but there is nothing for the home grower to do after the injury is noted.

Why do amaryllis leaves turn yellow and die? They do not dry up but have something like wet rot. If the rot is wet, it may be bacterial soft rot following the work of bulb-fly larvae. If the bulb is not sound, do not save it for another year. Destroy it.

ANEMONE

How can one protect Japanese anemones (windflowers) from the blister beetle? Only by constant vigilance when the beetles appear in midsummer. Dust or spray with carbaryl or methoxychlor. Pyrethrum-rotenone sprays are also helpful, as is hand-picking of the beetles. (See Blister Beetles.)

ARBORVITAE (THUJA)

What is the best chemical to use on arborvitae when the branches become a rusty color? (Illinois.) The rusty color is often due to spruce mite. The most potent spray is a miscible oil, applied before new growth starts in the spring. (See Dormant Spraying.) During the growing season, spraying with Kelthane, Tedion, or chlorobenzilate is effective in early May and late September. Treat when seen at other times in the season.

What might be the cause of arborvitae turning brown and dying? (Mississippi.) If the whole tree dies, it may be from prolonged injury from spruce mites, but the browning and dying of inner leaves are a natural shedding. Dying of the tips of the branches, twig blight, is a fungus disease, calling for cutting off the infected portions. Tiny tan patches in the foliage may be from arborvitae leafminer. (See the questions below.)

How do you destroy little red bugs that suck the sap from arborvitae? (Arkansas.) You may mean the arborvitae aphid, a very small, hairy, amber-brown plant louse. Apply a good contact spray, such as malathion, with as much pressure as possible, since these aphids are covered with a powdery film, which makes them hard to kill.

Why do the tips of arborvitae twigs turn white? (Connecticut.) This is the work of a leafminer, which winters in the leaves and emerges as a moth to lay eggs in June. Spraying with diazinon or dimethoate in late June and early July helps to kill larvae as they enter the base of the leaves.

ASPIDISTRA (CAST-IRON PLANT)

What causes the white-looking fungus or scale or whatever it can be called on aspidistra leaves? How can it be cured? (Louisiana.) There is a fungus disease, anthracnose, characterized by white spots with brown margins. Spraying is seldom necessary or profitable. Fern scale is also found on aspidistra. Perhaps you refer to mealybugs. (See House and Greenhouse Plants in this section, for control.)

ASTER, CHINA- (CALLISTEPHUS)

Will paper collars adequately protect transplanted seedlings, China-aster particularly, from grubworms? (Oregon.) Collars will protect against cutworms (fat caterpillars that cut off plant stems near the surface). Collars offer no protection against the white grubs, larvae of June beetles, which stay in the soil and feed on roots of garden plants.

After reaching full growth and flowering size, my China-asters dried up and died. What was the cause? (New York.) Aster wilt, a disease caused by a soil fungus, a species of fusarium, which grows into the roots and affects the vascular or water-conducting system of the plant. Young plants may be infected and not show symptoms until flowering, as in this case.

Why do some China-asters thrive until they are 7 to 8 inches tall, then turn brown, rusty, and die? I can't find anything at the roots or on the tops. (Idaho.) This is an earlier manifestation of the same aster wilt. Infection often takes place at transplanting time, with the leaves drying and dying somewhat later. Plant wilt-resistant seed, many varieties of which are now on the market.

When China-asters have blighted, how long a time must elapse before they can be safely grown in the same ground? (Illinois.) No one knows exactly how long the fusarium wilt fungus lives in the soil, but it is several years.

What can I do to prevent root rot in my China-aster bed? I plant wilt-resistant seed, disinfected with Semesan, without the desired results. (Illinois.) Certain soils are so infected with the wilt fungus that a certain percentage of "wilt-resistant" plants will succumb, the situation being worse in wet seasons. Try sterilizing the soil in the seed bed and transplanting seedlings to a fresh location. (See Soil Sterilization.)

Is there anything to sterilize the ground for infected China-aster plants? It is a large space. (Wisconsin.) It will scarcely pay to treat a large space. For a small area, try a formaldehyde drench, spading the soil, and then saturating with a solution of 1 gallon of commercial Formalin diluted with 50 gallons of water. Apply ½ to 1 gallon per square foot of soil, cover with paper or canvas for 24 hours, and then air out for 2 weeks before planting. (For other methods, see Soil Sterilization.)

What causes some China-aster flowers to open greenish-white instead of coloring? (California.) Aster yellows, a virus disease transmitted from diseased to healthy plants by leafhoppers. The leaves lose their chlorophyll and turn yellow, while the blossoms turn green. Plants are usually stunted. This is the most serious aster disease and occurs throughout the United States.

How can I prevent China-aster yellows?   Only by preventing insect transmission. Remove diseased plants immediately, so there will be no source of infection. Spray frequently with contact insecticides to kill leafhoppers. Commercial growers protect China-asters by growing them in cloth houses made of cheesecloth or tobacco cloth with 22 meshes to the inch.

How can I get rid of the small root lice that suck life out of China-asters and other annuals? (Illinois.)   Make a shallow depression around each plant and pour in the same malathion solution used for spraying above-ground aphids.

What treatment will reduce damage to China-asters by the tarnished plant bug? (Kansas.)   This small, light and dark brown sucking insect is hard to control. It is very active, occurs on many kinds of plants, stinging the flower buds and spotting the leaves, and has several generations a season. Spray with carbaryl or malathion. Rotenone dust is also effective. Cleaning up all trash and weeds will make hibernation difficult for the bug.

What is the control of the common black beetle on China-asters? (Michigan.)   You probably mean the long, slim blister beetle, which is very destructive to these asters. Dust or spray with carbaryl or methoxychlor. (See Blister Beetles.)

AZALEA (RHODODENDRON)

What is azalea flower-spot disease? (Louisiana.)   A fungus disease that has spread from South Carolina through the Gulf states since 1931 and has been reported from California and as far north as Connecticut, New Jersey, and Pennsylvania. Pinhead spots on the flowers enlarge to brownish blotches and the flowers collapse in about 3 days. Black resting bodies form in the petals and winter in the fallen leaves. The indica varieties are especially susceptible.

How do you control azalea flower-spot?   Spray with zineb 2 or 3 times a week starting when midseason varieties come into flower. Treating the soil with Terrachlor and a barrier mulch has been recommended but has little effect because spores are readily spread from untreated azaleas. Never purchase azalea plants in flower from an infected area.

What are the cause and treatment of moldlike white threads, resulting in a general decline of azalea plants? (California.)   Azaleas in California are subject to attack by the oak-root rot fungus (*Armillaria mellea*). Besides the white threads (mycelium), the fungus has shoestringlike black strands which go through the soil and produce honey-colored toadstools. Increase the vigor of plants by feeding; remove some of the soil from the crowns and roots; avoid a too high soil moisture content. Soil known to be infected should be sterilized. (See also under Nematodes.)

My azalea buds blight before they open. Why? (Ohio.)   There is a fungus that blasts terminal flower buds in the summer so they do not bloom the following year and sometimes kills leaf buds and twigs. Prune out and destroy all diseased material. Spray with Bordeaux mixture after blossoming.

What bores holes in my mollis azalea? It goes in near the ground and comes out at the top of the branches.   Probably the azalea stem borer, but this starts at the top and works down. The beetle lays its eggs near the tip and the young larvae enter near the leaf node and bore down through the twig into the crown. Cut off dead and dying tips; inject borer paste into holes showing sawdust.

My azalea plants (outdoors) have been attacked by lacebugs. How can I get rid of them? (New Jersey.)   Spray with malathion, Orthene, or carbaryl when the young nymphs hatch, usually in early June. There are 2 or 3 broods of the azalea lacebug, and it may be necessary to spray at 3-week intervals. Cover the undersurface of the leaves very thoroughly. The sucking of lacebugs turns the leaves of evergreen azaleas coffee-colored and those of deciduous varieties whitish.

What kills black aphids on azaleas? (New Jersey.)   Aphids are not ordinarily as common on azaleas as on other hosts, but they may be killed with the usual malathion spray or any other contact insecticide.

When and with what do I spray azaleas for spider mite and other pests? (West Virginia.)   Spray with Kelthane for spider mites. (See above for other pests.)

What causes the leaves to drop on a webby string from an azalea house plant? Is dry sulfur good for this?   This is probably the work of spider mites. Water is more important than sulfur. If the plants are bathed frequently, or treated with a fine mist spray from an atomizer, and kept under sufficiently humid and cool conditions, mites will never have a chance to cause this much damage. After the plant has been thoroughly washed and dried, spray with Kelthane.

In late August or early September, I found large caterpillars that seemed to defoliate my azaleas overnight. What were they and how can I prevent it next time? (Virginia.)   Caterpillars about 1½ inches long that feed voraciously like that must be azalea caterpillars. The apparent onslaught is because they are nearly full grown and consume large quantities of food. As young larvae, the caterpillars are inconspicuous and consume less foliage over a period of time. Sevin will control them most effectively when small. Careful surveillance during early and mid-August is necessary to detect this pest early. It is not possible to predict if and on which plants it might occur next year.

BEGONIA

What makes the leaves of begonia turn brown on the edge and get lifeless? Perhaps unfavorable environment and perhaps injury from leaf nematodes, which cause irregular brown blotches, enlarging until the leaf curls up and drops. Prune off and burn infested portions; do not let the leaves of two plants touch; water from below instead of wetting the foliage. The nematodes will be killed if potted plants are submerged in hot water held at 115° to 118° F. for 3 minutes, but this may cause injury and is more for the commercial grower than the home grower.

Dry spots form on the leaves of my begonias until they are almost eaten up. What is the cause and the treatment? Possibly sunscald, possibly the leaf nematode just discussed, and possibly lack of humidity.

I have a calla begonia, healthy a month ago, now with leaves withering and tops of new branches falling off. Why? (Wisconsin.) This is probably due to unfavorable environmental conditions rather than any specific organism. The calla-lily begonia is conceded to be difficult. Cool, moist air, fairly dry soil, and watering only from the saucer are recommended. Allow the soil to dry out between waterings.

When my tuberous begonia was budded to bloom, the leaves, then the stalk, turned brown and dropped. What was the trouble? (Nebraska.) It is hard to be sure without personal inspection, but there is a soil fungus, pythium, which causes a stem rot and may produce a soft rot and collapse of the crown and stalk. Avoid crowding the plants. Do not replant in infected soil without sterilizing.

A tuberous begonia rotted after a promising start. It wasn't overwatered. What could we have done wrong? (Ohio.) Tuberous begonias are sometimes attacked by larvae of the black vine weevil, which destroy the roots, so that the plants wilt and die. If the white grubs are found in the soil and if a good root system exists, knock the soil off the roots and repot. No insecticide is labeled for this pest.

What blight or insect attacks tuberous begonias to keep them from developing properly? (New York.) Insufficient light may be responsible, even though these are shade-tolerant plants. The cyclamen mite or possibly thrips may cause deformation. Frequent spraying with Kelthane before blooming may be of some benefit.

What spray shall I use for plant lice on a Lorraine begonia?   Malathion before flowering; pyrethrum while in bloom.

What is the tiny white or transparent worm that gets in the stalks and roots of begonias?   It is probably only a scavenger worm feeding on tissues rotting from some other cause, possibly a fungus stem rot. If the plant is this far decayed, you should start over with a healthy plant in fresh soil.

What causes a sticky sediment on my begonia?   It is honeydew, secreted by sucking insects, aphids, mealybugs, or whiteflies.

BIRCH (BETULA)

How can white birches be protected against a small worm that gets between the layers of the leaves? (New York.)   This is the birch leafminer, which causes a brown blotch on the outer half of the leaf. The worm is the larval stage of a black sawfly. Spray with carbaryl, Orthene, or malathion as soon as leaves are fully out. Or apply a systemic chemical to the soil, following the directions on the container.

How can I stop insects from eating the leaves of a cut-leaf birch? (New York.)   The birch aphid sucks the sap from the leaves of a cutleaved birch and may be controlled with malathion or Orthene spray. Cankerworms chew holes in birch leaves in May. Spray with carbaryl or methoxychlor.

How can I eliminate bronze birch borer from a weeping birch? (New York.)   The flat-headed, light-colored grubs, ½ to 1 inch long, make winding galleries underneath the bark; the adult beetles feed on the foliage. Trees growing under adverse conditions may die. Treat the bark of larger upper branches with lindane. See that trees are well fed and watered.

BITTERSWEET (CELASTRUS)

What is the treatment for scale on Oriental bittersweet?   The euonymus scale often covers bittersweet vines with a heavy infestation of slim white male scales and darker, rounder females. Spray before growth starts with a dormant oil, at a 1 to 25 dilution. Spray again in the summer, when your scales hatch, with malathion.

BOXWOOD (BUXUS)

What is good for boxwood with white scale? The leaves are dying on most of the bush and spreading to others. (D.C.) Oystershell scale may infest boxwood, but it is dark brown or gray in color. You may refer to nectria canker, a serious fungus disease that kills the leaves and twigs and produces pinkish-white spore pustules on the backs of the leaves and on the stems. Your area has been invaded by wax scale. It is white, ¼ inch across, and round. Spray with Sevin the second week in June.

How do you control boxwood canker? (New Jersey.) Chiefly by sanitary measures: cleaning out old leaves and dead twigs twice a year and getting rid of all material that can hold moisture. Never water boxwood so that the foliage is wet for long periods. Try a spray of Bordeaux mixture in the spring or summer. Direct the spray into the interior of the bush.

What should I do for my young boxwood, which is dying by degrees? (North Carolina.) Probably the canker disease just discussed is responsible, or possibly nematodes. This is somewhat more prevalent farther north, but it is sometimes serious in your state. Clean it out; avoid prolonged wetting of the foliage. Spray with Bordeaux 3 to 4 times during the spring and summer.

What treatment will keep boxwood leaves from turning brown? (Delaware.) Winter injury, nectria canker, serious infestations of scale, nematodes, or leafminers will all cause brown, unhealthy foliage. Winter protection and sanitary measures are most important.

What about the orange flies that come on boxwood in May? (Connecticut.) These are the adults of the boxwood leafminer. Spray with diazinon when the flies first begin to emerge or with dimethoate or diazinon in mid-June after the eggs have hatched.

What shall I do for red spider on boxwood bushes? (Tennessee.) Spider mites turn the leaves a light, unhealthy color. Spraying with a miticide, as recommended under azaleas, should be effective.

BROWALLIA

How do you treat the black spotty disease that infects the foliage of browallia? (Mississippi.) Smut has been reported on this host and would make black sooty masses over the leaves. The best thing to do would be to remove the smutted leaves. However, you may merely be having sooty mold growing in insect honeydew, in which case you use contact sprays for the insects.

BULBS

What formulas have been used with known success in combating fungus diseases of newly planted bulbs?   The most successful formula is to plant clean, healthy bulbs. Look them over carefully and discard any that show signs of black sclerotia, small, flat, hard bodies under the outer scales. Discard diseased bulbs. Plant in a new location or in treated soil if you have been previously troubled with much disease.

How can ants be destroyed that occur in clumps of bulbs? (Alabama.)   Soak a malathion, diazinon, or Dursban solution around the bulbs. (See also Ants.)

What are the minute white worms found in and around rotting bulbs? Do they cause the decay or are they scavengers that are cleaning up? (Minnesota.)   They are scavengers, doing their appointed job. Don't worry about them, but do hunt for the primary cause of the rotting.

CACTI

What shall I do for white furry web spots on small spiny cactus?   The spots are probably mealybugs, which can be removed with a toothpick or small brush; by washing off with water applied as a fine spray; by spraying with an aerosol bomb, Orthene, or with malathion, using caution. (See House Plants.)

How do you control mealybugs on cacti too spiny to use a brush on?   Use an aerosol bomb or spray as recommended above.

How do you cure cactus scab?   Maybe you refer to a corky spot due to unfavorable conditions, often prevented by increasing light and decreasing humidity, but perhaps you are describing scale. Remove scale with a brush dipped in a malathion solution or scrape off with a small piece of wood.

What causes prickly-pear cactus to get a white fungus or mold on it, and what can be done to prevent it? (Texas.)   A white mold is rather improbable on cactus. You may be describing mealybugs; or possibly one of the scale insects common on prickly-pear cactus. (See previous questions for control.)

My Christmas cactus is covered with a web and large pieces drop off. How can I prevent this?   The web is probably produced by red spider mites, which flourish in a dry atmosphere. The Christmas cactus does not need to be kept as dry as other cacti and should be frequently syringed with water to keep spider mites in check. Try also spraying with an aerosol plant bomb containing a miticide.

How can I use sulfur on cactus with mildew?   True mildew, a white powdery coating, would not be common on cactus. Perhaps you have a rot encouraged by overwatering. Cut out the diseased portions and dust the cut surfaces with captan. Reduce watering.

What is the cause of cactus plants dying off at the base?   Probably too much water. Cacti are very subject to rot caused by fungi that flourish in the presence of moisture. Infection often starts through wounds, which should be avoided as much as possible. Water the plants sparingly.

How do you overcome silver and brown rust on cactus?   This "rust" is more likely due to unfavorable light conditions than to a fungus. Increasing the light and decreasing the humidity may help.

CALADIUM

Worms have appeared in my caladium plant and all the brightly colored leaves have withered and died. What can be done?   Probably nothing at this stage. Worms in the soil can be flushed out with lime water, but they do no damage except to clog the drainage holes. It sounds as if the plants had either been drowned, with the roots in too soggy soil, or else had dried out.

CALENDULA

Is there something that will kill black bugs on calendula? (Minnesota.)   Malathion, Orthene, or diazinon spray applied thoroughly and often should clear up the black aphids, which are practically inevitable on calendula.

CALLA (ZANTEDESCHIA)

Why didn't the bud on my calla-lily open?   There are only two diseases of calla-lilies: a root rot that may prevent flowering and a slimy, soft rot that starts in the rhizome and spreads up into the flower stalk. Your plant may have been infected with the root-rot fungus or some physiological condition may have prevented blooming. In either case, it would pay to start over with a fresh rhizome.

CAMELLIA

What do you do when camellias have root lice? (North Carolina.)   If you are sure the trouble is root aphids and not the root-knot nematode, a weevil grub, or other pest, scoop the soil away from the trunk somewhat and pour in a solution of malathion. There are also root mealybugs. If they or root lice get too serious, you have to take up the plant, wash off the roots carefully, and replant in fresh soil.

I have a camellia that has small spots on its leaves, pinhead size. The leaves are light green and sick-looking. It is growing in a tub in a greenhouse. What can I do for it? (Texas.)   The soil may be wrong or the plant may be in too strong sun or improperly watered, but the light spots indicate that the tea scale is working on the underside of the leaves. This is the most serious pest of camellias. Spray with malathion or dimethoate. Two treatments may be necessary to clean up a heavily infested plant.

CANDYTUFT (IBERIS)

What is the cause of candytuft turning white? It looks like mildew and is dying. (North Carolina.)   A white rust is common on candytuft and other members of the crucifer family. White pustules appear on the underside of the leaves, which turn pale. Destroy diseased plants or plant parts and clean up cruciferous weeds, such as wild mustard. Spraying with Bordeaux mixture may help.

CANTERBURY-BELLS (CAMPANULA MEDIUM)

What can be done to prevent canterbury-bells from rotting just before blooming? (Ohio.)   Possibly growing plants in a new location or disinfecting the soil with formaldehyde, perhaps merely by improving the soil texture. It might be due to winter injury.

Why don't I have success with Campanula medium? They rot away. They have a dry soil. (Delaware.)   There are two soil fungi which may cause crown or stem rot under moist conditions, but your trouble may be physiological and due to insufficient water. Try another location and improve the soil with organic matter such as leafmold or peat moss.

CARNATION (DIANTHUS CARYOPHYLLUS)

What causes me to lose my clove pink? Foliage turns brown in the center of the clump and spreads until the entire bed is dead. (Tennessee.) It may be a fungus stem rot, partially controlled by spraying with captan. Try healthy cuttings or plant in a new location. They need a very well-drained soil.

Is there any pest that will cut carnations off at the joints? (Montana.) Cutworms, possibly. Try diazinon dust around the plants. A fungus, called branch rot, may girdle the nodes or joints and cause death of the branch. Remove infected parts.

What do you recommend for baby snails that feed on carnation buds? (California.) Hand-picking or a poison bait. Consult your Cooperative Extension agent for local recommendations. (See Slugs and Snails.)

My greenhouse carnations wilt and dry up. What shall I do to produce strong, healthy plants? (Rhode Island.) Several soil fungi cause wilts or stem rot, being more prevalent at high temperatures and in wet soils. Steam sterilize your greenhouse soil and bring in only healthy plants. (See also Soil Sterilization.)

What is wrong with my hardy carnations? I get them started and they bloom until August, then droop and die. (Iowa.) Are there rusty pustules on the underside of the leaves and do the leaves turn pale? If so, try zineb spray or dust to control rust. More likely, soil fungi are to blame. Try a new location. Perhaps your carnations merely dry out and require more organic matter in the soil. Or the weather may be too hot and humid.

CEDAR, RED-   (See Juniper.)

CHINESE-LANTERN (PHYSALIS ALKEKENGI)

What type of insecticide will kill the striped beetles that ruin our Chinese-lanterns? They resemble cucumber bugs but are much hardier. (Minnesota.) They probably are striped cucumber beetles, which are certainly hardy but should be killed by spraying the plants with methoxychlor or carbaryl. If you want to grow cucumbers, you'd better get rid of the Chinese-lanterns entirely, because the beetles carry a virus disease, mosaic, from one host to the other.

A yellow and black bug lays eggs, hatching a slimy, sucking bug.

What will destroy these? (Michigan.)   If your "bug" is spotted, it is the tortoise beetle; if striped, it is the cucumber beetle. (See above.) The "slimy" bugs are the larvae, or immature beetles. Those of the tortoise beetle carry their excreta in a pack upon their backs. Spray with methoxychlor or carbaryl.

CHRYSANTHEMUM

What causes the leaves of an outdoor chrysanthemum to curl up and turn brown?   This question, in one form or another, was asked most frequently of all the pest questions. Verticillium, or fusarium wilts, septoria leafspot, or improper watering will all turn foliage brown, but in 9 cases out of 10, leaf nematodes are to blame.

What are leaf nematodes and how do they work?   They are eelworms—microscopic animals that live in the soil and in wet weather swim up the stems of chrysanthemums and enter the leaves through the stomata—small mouthlike openings in the leaves. Infection begins with a yellowish-brown discoloration bounded by the larger veins, so that the discolored area is usually pie-shaped. Later the entire leaf turns brown and brittle, and may fall.

How can leaf nematodes be controlled?   First, by removing seriously infested plants; next, by cutting off all chrysanthemum tops after blooming. Make cuttings or divisions only from healthy plants or clumps, and either plant in a new location or sterilize the soil with a nematocide. (See Nematodes.) Propagate only by tip cuttings if plants are possibly infested.

How do nematodes spread from one plant to another?   If the leaves touch, they can swim across in wet weather. They can also be carried by the gardener on hands, tools, or clothing. Do not cultivate or handle the plants when they are wet with rain or dew.

Early in the summer my chrysanthemum plants start turning yellow on their lower leaves. The leaves turn brown and crisp. This moves up the stem until the entire plant is dead. The roots show no growth since planting. What should I do? (Utah.)   This may be nematode injury, but in your state it is likely to be verticillium wilt. Start fresh with healthy plants in a new location or in sterilized soil.

How do you prevent the lower leaves on tender chrysanthemums from spotting and shriveling? (Ohio.)   If your trouble starts as definite black spots, rather than brown wedges, you probably are dealing with a fungus disease, septoria leafspot, which is controlled by spraying with folpet and picking off infected leaves. If the spotting is white and powdery, it is due to the mildew fungus, and you should dust with sulfur or spray with Karathane or Benlate.

What causes my chrysanthemum plants to get black and wilted at the lower part of the plants? (New Jersey.) If you are sure it is a black wilting, it may be due to a leafspot fungus or a soil fungus. If the color is brown, it is probably the work of leaf nematodes. (See answers to the above questions.)

Will the fungus Sclerotium delphinii, which caused crown rot among hybrid delphiniums, be likely to affect chrysanthemums planted in that bed next spring? Infection is possible, since this fungus is known to occur on almost every garden plant, but the disease is far more prevalent on delphiniums. Play it safe and treat the soil with Terrachlor or Vapam this fall or very early next spring. (See Soil Sterilization.)

What do you advocate for exterminating dodder on chrysanthemum plants? (Pennsylvania.) This charming parasite seems to be increasing as a garden pest. Once a plant is entwined with the orange tendrils, there is no remedy except breaking off the parasitized plant parts before the white dodder flowers set and drop their seed for another year.

What insect causes chrysanthemums to open only partially? (Illinois.) If the foliage is not brown and crisp, suggesting leaf nematode injury, it may be the gall midge, which lives in little conical projections of the leaves and flowers. Pick off and destroy infested plant parts. A fungus disease, ray blight, also deforms flowers.

What shall I spray with to kill those little black bugs that get on chrysanthemums? (Missouri.) These are aphids, almost inevitable on chrysanthemum tips in late summer, and sometimes all summer. They are readily killed with any contact insecticide, such as diazinon, Orthene, or malathion. Spray often enough to protect the new growth.

I have a chrysanthemum plant with black insects creeping on it. If I cut the branches down, will it be all right to put it out in the garden in the spring? (D.C.) Yes, you may safely move your infested plant to the garden. Aphids are readily killed with any contact insecticide. (See the previous question.)

Each year my indoor chrysanthemum gets covered with little green bugs. How can I get rid of these pests? The green bugs are undoubtedly aphids, or plant lice. Spray with diazinon, Orthene, or malathion if they get numerous, but pure water will help in prevention. Wash the foliage frequently or apply a fine mist from an atomizer.

What can I do to prevent root aphids? (New Jersey.) Scoop out the soil from a shallow depression around each stem and pour in about a cupful of malathion, 1 tablespoon per gallon of water. Control ants.

What poison can be used in a cold frame for a small green caterpillar that eats young leaves? (New Jersey.)   Spray with carbaryl or methoxychlor; keep the glass sash off until the spray has thoroughly dried.

What is the little bug like a ladybug that eats the flowers of chrysanthemums every fall? (Texas.)   If the "bug" is green with black spots, it is the spotted cucumber beetle, known in your section as the diabolical diabrotica because it is so fond of so many garden flowers.

How do you eliminate diabrotica beetles?   Control is difficult because sprays discolor the flowers. Pyrethrum or rotenone would be best. As a last resort, spray or dust with carbaryl or methoxychlor.

What treatment shall I use for insects that eat the centers of chrysanthemums? (Missouri.)   Probably these are the 12-spotted cucumber (diabrotica) beetles discussed above.

What are the flying, hard-shelled, rather beetlelike bugs that attack some chrysanthemums during the blooming season? (Indiana.)   Black-spotted green beetles are diabroticas; long, black beetles are blister beetles. For the latter, try spraying or dusting with Sevin. (See Blister Beetles.)

What do you do for a small beetle, yellow with black spots, that eats beans and chrysanthemum flowers? (New York.)   The Mexican bean beetle is not ordinarily a chrysanthemum pest, but when it has devoured all the bean foliage in sight, it may seek other fields. Try spraying or dusting the chrysanthemums with rotenone or methoxychlor.

What can one use to keep grasshoppers from eating buds? (Kentucky.)   Spray the chrysanthemums with diazinon or malathion after the buds form but before they flower.

What is the treatment for gall on garden chrysanthemums and the disposition of infected plants? (New York.)   Assuming this is the bacterial crown gall that appears at the base of the plant, and not the gall midge, there is nothing to do for infected plants except to remove them.

Is the soil liable to harbor crown gall infection the succeeding year?   Yes, the bacteria may live for some time in the soil. Plant in a new location or sterilize the soil.

What is the gall midge?   A fly that lays its eggs on foliage and buds, where the larvae stimulate the formation of small conical galls. This is primarily a greenhouse pest (controlled with restricted pesticides by commercial growers only) that sometimes attacks outdoor plants. It is usually easier to remove infested chrysanthemums.

About July something attacked my chrysanthemums; they broke off about 3 inches from the ground, leaving piles of what looked like white ant eggs. What caused this? (Ohio.)   The stalk borer was probably responsible, the "ant eggs" being frass excreted by the caterpillar inside the stem. When you see borer injury, it is usually too late to help the plant. Cleaning up weeds, especially in the fall, is the best prevention.

What is the round black worm around the roots of Shasta daisies? (New Jersey.)   Likely a millipede feeding on roots rotting from some other cause, perhaps a fungus stem rot. Remove the diseased plant if the roots are destroyed.

How shall I exterminate termites in beds? (Texas.)   Water with a chlordane solution into the soil around the plants.

CITRUS

How shall I control scale on dwarf citrus fruits in the house?   Spray with malathion, Orthene, or a house-plant aerosol bomb. (See House Plants and Greenhouse Plants for special precautions.)

My grapefruit tree has become infested since being taken in from the garden. Same pest is on cacti. What is it?   The infestation is probably mealybugs, which flourish on cacti. Use the same treatment as for scale.

What is the cause and cure of syrup substance on the leaves of dwarf lemon and orange?   The sticky material is a honeydew secreted by sucking insects, probably mealybugs in this case, although possibly scale insects, whiteflies, or aphids. (For control, see the previous two questions; see also House Plants and Greenhouse Plants.)

CLEMATIS

In late fall, what attacks Clematis paniculata, which has flourished like a green bay tree? Hordes of beetles practically denude the vines overnight. (Georgia.)   These are probably blister beetles. Spray with Sevin or malathion. (See also Blister Beetles.)

How can I kill blister bugs that eat my vines in the summer? (Louisiana.)   Blister beetles are more prevalent on clematis in the South than in the North. They are hard to kill, but spraying or dusting with malathion or carbaryl may be effective. Knock off the beetles into a can of bleach.

My Clematis x jackmanii climbers, after getting several feet high, wilt unexpectedly. If dry stem rot causes this, what can be done? (Wisconsin.)   It sounds like stem rot. After the fungus has girdled the stem so that the vine wilts suddenly, nothing can be done. Spraying or dusting with sulfur through the season may aid in prevention. Start cuttings from healthy plants.

COLEUS

Are mealybugs on coleus caused by too much or too little watering?   Mealybugs, like most sucking insects, thrive in a dry atmosphere, but too little water cannot "cause" them. Also, if the plants are unhealthy from a waterlogged soil, they may succumb more readily to mealybug injury. Spray at the first sign of bugs with malathion, diazinon, or Orthene.

What is one to do to get rid of the soft white fungus scale on coleus? I scrape it off, but this is not drastic enough.   It is neither a fungus nor a scale that you describe, but mealybugs. (See above.) Spray house plants with a house-plant aerosol bomb.

What causes blistered or puckered leaves?   It sounds like the work of the cyclamen mite, which attacks so many indoor plants. (See Cyclamen.)

What can I do to stop a white moldy rot on coleus, kept as a house plant?   There is no white mold on coleus, but you may have a combination of white woolly mealybugs, very common on this plant, and a black rot called "black leg" because it rots the stalks at the base. For the mealybugs, spray with Orthene or malathion; for the rot, destroy infected plants and pot new ones with fresh soil.

What causes white fungus growth? I changed the plants from glazed to clay pots, but the white growth persists.   Changing the pot won't affect mealybugs on the foliage. Spray and spray again until you clean them up. (See answers to the previous questions.)

COLUMBINE (AQUILEGIA)

How can one keep the roots of aquilegia from becoming infested with worms? (Minnesota.)   The worms are probably millipedes, and usually they swarm around when a plant is weakened or dead from other causes, either disease or unfavorable cultural conditions. They cause little injury, but can be controlled with a diazinon drench.

What makes hybrid columbines pass out in a perennial bed where everything else is happy? (Pennsylvania.)   Hybrid columbines, like hybrid delphiniums, are usually short-lived, but sudden passing out may be due to crown rot, a fungus disease, or to the columbine borer.

What remedy will prevent crown rot? (Alabama.)   Crown rot in Alabama is caused by *Sclerotium rolfsii*, a fungus that is generally prevalent in the soil and kept viable because it can attack so many different plants. Soil sterilization is difficult and not too satisfactory. Remove infected plants as soon as noticed and pour a Terrachlor solution over the area.

What about the columbine borer?   This is a salmon-colored caterpillar that works in the crown of the plant. All you can do is pull up the victim and in the fall destroy all weeds and other debris that might harbor borer eggs during the winter. Protect other columbines with carbaryl or methoxychlor.

The leaves of our columbine have little silvery-white lines all over them. Could you tell me the cause? (Rhode Island.)   These are the serpentine tunnels of the columbine leafminer. The larvae work inside the leaf and a small fly emerges to lay eggs for the next generation.

What is the cure for white line discolorations in leaves? (Illinois.)   There is no cure, but picking off and burning all infested leaves as soon as they are noticed and cultivating the ground around the plants in the fall and early spring will help prevent further infestations. Spraying with Orthene or malathion may help.

What shall I do for plants turning brown because of a certain type of spider that gets on them? (Florida.)   If this is spider mite (the tiny mite that makes webs on the underside of the leaves), try sulfur dust, but not when the temperature is so high (above 90° F.) that the sulfur will burn the foliage. Kelthane or another miticide is more effective.

COSMOS

What is the cause of cosmos turning brown and dying? (Nebraska.)   It may be a bacterial wilt, but more likely a fungus stem blight. A grayish lesion girdles the stem and all parts above die. Spraying is of little value. Remove infected plants when they are noticed and pull up and destroy all tops after blooming.

CRAB APPLE (MALUS)

Why do the leaves of a Bechtel's crab curl up and drop in the summer?   Bechtel's crab is peculiarly susceptible to red-cedar and apple rust, a disease prevalent over much of the country. Spores are carried from the red-cedar galls in the spring and the resulting infection of orange spots on the crab apple leaves shows up in midsummer. Defoliation follows heavy infection.

How do you prevent rust?   Never plant red-cedars (*Juniperus virginiana*) and crab apples together. It is preferable not to have them on the same property, but at least get a windbreaker such as a house or trees between the two as a barrier to windborne spores. Remove red-cedar galls in the winter and early spring. Spray crab apples with sulfur and ferbam, zineb, or maneb when the leaves come out and every 10 days until July.

I have sprayed my Malus floribunda but it is always full of aphids. What can I do? (Michigan.) Try spraying with a dormant oil spray just before the buds break. (See Dormant Spraying.) If aphids appear during the growing season, spray with malathion.

What treatment shall I give a small flowering crab? There is no new growth, the leaves shrivel, and there is a fuzzy white substance that appears at crotches and twig intersections. (Rhode Island.) The fuzzy white substances are woolly aphids, controlled by spraying thoroughly with malathion. The tree is apparently dying from other causes—improper planting or some soil trouble.

What solution should be painted on the trunks of young flowering crab trees in March to prevent green worms from climbing up and depositing their eggs? (Illinois.) None. No chemical should be applied directly to the trunk. If you have time and money to burn, apply a band of balsam wood and cover with Tanglefoot. This will prevent canker-worm moths from climbing the crab apples but will not stop young worms from dropping onto crab apples from nearby shade trees. Spray with carbaryl (Sevin) or methoxychlor in May in any case, for the trunk treatment reduces infection not more than 10 per cent.

CRAPE-MYRTLE (LAGERSTROEMIA INDICA)

How is mildew on crape-myrtle controlled? (Alabama.) Either by a dormant spray of 1 to 8 lime-sulfur when the buds start swelling or by spraying with wettable sulfur, Karathane, or Benlate after growth starts. It is important to spray early; otherwise the white fungus will stunt the buds.

What spray formula will destroy the whiteflies covering my crape-myrtles, causing smut? (Louisiana.) The smut is a fungus, sooty mold growing in the honeydew secreted by aphids. Spray after blooming with Orthene or diazinon. If whiteflies are there, use Orthene.

Every year, without fail, my crape-myrtle are beset by plant lice. Isn't there a simple cure? Crape-myrtle has very few insect pests. However, wherever they grow, aphids are a common problem. Since aphids are winged and active, they may infest new succulent growth as it develops.

Apply aphid controls at 1- to 2-week intervals while the plants are actively growing. (See Aphids.)

CROCUS

Is there any method of preventing squirrels from eating crocus bulbs? (Massachusetts.) Plant the bulbs in wire baskets, which can be made at home from ½-inch wire mesh. A few naphthalene flakes may act as a repellent, but too many will injure the bulbs with their fumes. Plant a lot of crocus bulbs each fall; the squirrels won't destroy all of them.

CYCLAMEN (C. PERSICUM)

What causes a cyclamen to become soft and die? I watered mine carefully through the bottom of the pot, but it died within 2 weeks. It sounds like bacterial soft rot, usually serious only when plants are too wet, or shaded, or not well ventilated. Your plant may have been infected when it came from the greenhouse.

What would cause a cyclamen to wilt suddenly and the bulb to rot? Probably the bacterial soft rot suggested in the previous question. Possibly a fungus disease called stunt, although here the dying is usually gradual.

What is cyclamen mite, and how does it affect the plants? This mite is a microscopic relative of the spider mite, white to pale brown in color, that infests many varieties of ornamental plants, causing puckering, curling, or other deformation of the leaves; flower buds become blackened and distorted. If plants are kept close together, the mites can crawl from one to another. They can also be spread by hands, tools, clothing. Spraying with Kelthane will help.

DAFFODILS (See Narcissus.)

DAHLIA

What causes dahlia roots to rot? (Florida.) Any one of several fungus or bacterial diseases. With verticillium wilt, the lower leaves gradually lose their color, the roots are decayed, and the stem shows black streaks when cut across. With stem rot and soft bacterial rot, wilting is rather sudden.

How are the wilt diseases of dahlias cured? There is no cure. All you can do is remove infected plants immediately and plant healthy tubers in a new location, or sterilize the soil with chloropicrin or methyl bromide.

When the tubers rot, is the soil too damp? (New York.)   A heavy, wet soil encourages stem rot and bacterial wilt, but the organisms have to be present. Improving drainage and lightening the soil with sand or coal ashes will help.

There is a little brown worm about ½ inch long that eats my dahlia roots. How should I treat the ground before I plant? (Ohio.)   It is probably a millipede feasting on tissues rotting from one of the wilt diseases just discussed. (See the previous questions.)

When I dig my dahlias in the fall, the tubers are almost always rotted away. Why are gray-blackish insects present? (New York.)   They are probably millipedes. They look brown to some, grayish to others. They are hard, with many legs, usually coiled into a circle, and almost always scavengers feeding on rotting tissue.

My dahlia tubers are drying up and some show rot all through. How do you prevent this? (New York.)   Botrytis, fusarium, and other fungi and bacteria may cause storage rots. Use care in digging to avoid wounds, store only well-matured tubers, avoid any frost damage, and keep at 40° F. in sand that is only very slightly moist. Too much moisture will increase rotting. Dusting tubers with captan before storage may help.

Some dahlia leaves have bright yellow mottling; is that mosaic, and what can be done? (Montana.)   The mottling is a typical symptom of mosaic, a virus disease carried from one plant to another by aphids. There is usually dwarfing or stunting. Control aphids with contact sprays, and remove and burn infected plants.

What are the chief causes for dahlia "stunt"? (Illinois.)   Either mosaic or the feeding of sucking insects, often leafhoppers, but sometimes thrips or plant bugs. Stunted dahlias are short and bushy with an excessive number of side branches. Leafhoppers cause the margins of the leaves to turn yellow, then brown and brittle—a condition known as hopper burn.

How do you control stunt caused by insects?   Spray once a week with malathion, beginning early in the season and covering the underside of leaves thoroughly.

After plants are stunted, are the tubers good the following year? (New Jersey.)   Yes, if the stunting was due to leafhoppers and the tubers appear sound. But if the stunting was due to mosaic, a virus disease, the tubers should be destroyed.

My miniature dahlia is full of buds, but they rot. What is the matter? (Ohio.) It may be gray mold, the same type of botrytis blight that affects peony buds. Remove all diseased buds and spray with captan. Burn all plant tops in the fall.

How can I prevent mildew? (Pennsylvania.) Dust foliage with sulfur or spray with Karathane or Benlate, especially in late summer.

If dahlias mildew badly at the end of the season, will the tubers be injured? (California.) Probably not, but mildew is a serious disease on the West Coast, and dahlias should be sprayed or dusted with one of the above fungicides.

Is the borer which attacks dahlia stalks the corn borer? (New Jersey.) Yes, if the borers are flesh-colored when young, later turning smoky or reddish. If the caterpillar is brown, striped with white, it is the common stalk borer, also a pest of corn.

What can I do to prevent borers? (Illinois.) Clean up stalks of all herbaceous plants in the fall. Include the weeds, for many of these harbor borers during the winter. Spray or dust stalks with malathion plus methoxychlor.

How do you prevent the little black flies from biting or stinging buds so that they only partially open? (Vermont.) The tarnished plant bug is brownish rather than black, but it stings and blackens the buds. Control is difficult. Keep down weeds and spray frequently with carbaryl or malathion.

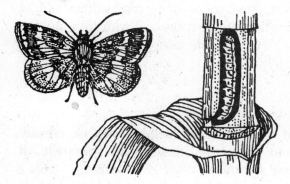

The pink larva of the European corn borer frequently attacks dahlias. The adult moth is yellowish brown.

Last summer I found a lot of black bugs and some ladybugs on my blooms. The petals had holes in them. Were the little black bugs to blame? (Texas.) The black bugs were probably aphids or plant lice, controllable by spraying with malathion. If the "ladybugs" were green instead of red, they were diabrotica or cucumber beetles and responsible for the holes. (See Chrysanthemum.)

What can I do about aphids on roots? I have tried ground tobacco. (Wisconsin.) Tobacco dust in the ground should help, but pouring a solution of malathion in a shallow depression made around each dahlia stem will be a more potent remedy.

This year grasshoppers ate our dahlia blooms. Is there any way to prevent this? (Mississippi.) Spray or dust the flowers with diazinon. Keep down weeds. (See also Grasshoppers.)

How do you rid dahlias of snails? (Michigan.) Try one of the metaldehyde or mesurol slug baits, obtainable under a commercial trade name such as Bug-geta or Slug-geta. (See also Slugs.)

Do spider mites attack dahlia plants? Yes. Spray with a miticide, such as Kelthane, being sure to cover the undersides of the leaves.

Do thrips ever attack dahlias? How may they be controlled? (Iowa.) They may infest the flowers, turning the petals whitish. Regular spraying with malathion for the control of leafhoppers may discourage infestation by thrips. (See Gladiolus.)

How do I prevent earwigs from destroying my dahlia flowers? Dust or spray your plants and the surrounding soil with diazinon, carbaryl, or malathion.

DAPHNE

The leaves of my daphne are turning yellow. Why? (California.) This may be chlorosis, due to an alkaline soil, which makes iron unavailable. Spray the leaves with 2 teaspoons of ferrous sulfate and ¼ teaspoon of glue in a quart of water. Or treat the soil with iron chelates available under trade names. Your *Daphne odora* may also be dying from armillaria root rot.

DELPHINIUM

Last summer I lost a great number of my delphiniums. A creamy, seedy substance formed around the plants, making the roots rot off. Later it spread to the phlox and buddleia. What is it? (Ohio.) This is a good description of crown rot, caused by the fungus *Sclerotium rolfsii*. White fungus threads, mycelia, form at the base of the stalk and spread over the ground. Seedlike bodies are attacked so that the plant is readily pulled up. This fungus attacks more than 100 species of ornamentals and readily spreads to the other plants in wet weather. A common name for this rot is the mustard-seed fungus.

How shall I grow delphiniums when the plants rot off at the ground

and the earth turns white and rust color? (Kansas.) This is another phase of crown rot. The sclerotia, which are at first cream-colored, turn reddish or rusty as they mature, and there may be so many crowded together at the base of the plant that it seems as if the earth itself has changed color.

How shall I keep delphiniums from getting crown rot? How can I stop its spread to other plants? (Illinois.) Stopping the spread immediately is very important. Dig up an infected plant as soon as noticed, using a shovel so as to get all the surrounding soil harboring the sclerotia. If you pull up the plant and leave the sclerotia behind, they may live for months or years, ready to infect other plants. Wrap the diseased specimen and soil in several thicknesses of newspaper and hurry it to the garbage pail. Treat the diseased area with Terrachlor, but don't plant delphiniums in the same area again.

Is there any other chemical to prevent crown rot? I have tried naphthalene flakes. (Iowa.) Naphthalene is somewhat effective in stopping the spread of the white mycelia, but it cannot be relied on to kill the sclerotia. Sulfur dust will likewise check the mycelial growth, and Terrachlor as a crown drench may be effective. The permanent remedy is to sterilize the soil, when all plants have been removed, with formaldehyde. (See Soil Sterilization.)

Can delphiniums be replanted after sterilizing the soil in a bed where others died of sclerotium rot? (New Jersey.) Yes, if you use soil sterilizers according to directions and wait until all the odor has disappeared from the soil before replanting—usually about 2 weeks. Naturally, put back only healthy plants. The treatment is not guaranteed; a new location is preferable.

What makes delphiniums get a mildewed appearance and what can be done to prevent it? (New York.) This is powdery mildew, a fungus appearing as a white coating on the leaves. In the East, it is seldom serious before late summer. Dust with sulfur, or spray with Benlate or Karathane.

Is it possible to prevent mildew? (Illinois, Minnesota, Colorado.) The mildew problem seems to increase in importance as one goes west, until a climax is reached in California. However, many of the new hybrid strains are fairly resistant to mildew, and spraying gives reasonable control. (See the above question.) There is no "prevention" except cleaning up all old plant material.

Why do delphiniums mildew so badly? (California.) It's the famous California climate, which seems to encourage mildew on delphiniums, roses, and other plants. Try to get California strains of delphinium more or less resistant to mildew and treat as above.

How do I prevent rust and white mold? (Wisconsin.) The white mold is mildew. (See the answers to previous questions.) True rust is not very common on delphinium. Discolored patches on the leaves can be due to the broad mite or the leafminer.

How do you control black spot? This bacterial disease appears as tarlike black spots on the leaves. It is not serious except in wet seasons, when it may be controlled by spraying with Bordeaux mixture or possibly streptomycin. In a normal season, picking off infected leaves and cleaning up old stalks in autumn are sufficient.

How should dry Bordeaux mixture be diluted for spraying delphiniums when they come up in the spring? (Pennsylvania.) Use about half the strength recommended on the package, which usually gives directions for a potato spray. If your brand calls for 8 to 12 tablespoons per gallon, use 4 to 6, adding 2 tablespoons of flour to the dry powder before stirring the water in very slowly. Strain through cheesecloth into the sprayer and use *immediately*.

Is there a remedy when leaves curl and the plants fail to bloom? Those that do bloom have green blossoms. (Utah.) This is a virus disease, probably aster yellows. There is no cure except taking out infected plants as soon as noticed and spraying with contact insecticides to control the leafhoppers, the insect carriers of the virus. Such diseases are common in the Northwest.

Why do my delphiniums grow large and thrifty, have one blooming period, and then get a black rot? (Ohio.) There are various delphinium rots besides sclerotium crown rot, caused by at least 2 bacteria and several fungi. Rotting is usually worse in wet weather and with succulent tissue. Some growers feel that the act of cutting down the old stalks after blooming spreads the rot organisms.

What causes the yellowing of leaves on hybrids? When the plants were treated with nitrate of soda every 10 days, they took on a healthy green again. (Illinois.) You answered your own question: evidently your plants lacked nitrogen. But be careful about applying too much. Getting too succulent a growth will mean more rot diseases.

Why do my delphiniums turn yellow? (Indiana.) Possibly due to fusarium wilt, this fungus being common in soils in the Middle West. There is usually a progressive yellowing of leaves from the base upward. But the yellowing may also be due to crown rot, lack of nitrogen, lack of water, or intense heat. Try a new location.

What causes delphinium buds to become black and wadded up? (In-

diana.)   The cyclamen mite, a light-colored relative of the spider mite too small to see with the naked eye, and a very serious pest on delphiniums. It deforms the leaves, blackens the flower buds, usually preventing bloom, and stunts the plant.

What can be done to overcome cyclamen mite on delphiniums? (Wisconsin.)   Spray weekly with Kelthane. Start spraying very early in the spring. Pick off deformed parts; discard severely infested plants.

What should be done for brown spots on the underside of leaves of delphiniums? (Illinois.)   If these spots are rather glassy in appearance, they are due to the broad mite, which is not as harmful as the cyclamen mite and more readily controlled with sulfur dust.

What causes blighted areas in the leaves?   The larvae of leafminers feed inside the leaves, which collapse and turn brown over rather large areas, usually near the points. Remove infested leaves. Spraying with malathion may help.

Why are there red lice during blooming time? (Michigan.)   Why any calamity? These are the same aphids so prevalent on annual larkspur. Spray thoroughly and frequently with malathion.

I have tried sulfur dust for the little red lice. How can I prevent them? (Michigan.)   Sulfur dust will be of little benefit. You need a malathion spray.

My delphiniums always get orange lice on the underside of the leaves. When shall I start watching for them and what shall I do? (Michigan.)   These aphids usually get serious toward midsummer, but sometimes appear in the spring. When the leaves start cupping downward, looking like umbrellas, you always know red aphids are underneath. Use a spray rod with an angle nozzle so you can cover the underside of the leaves.

My delphinium leaves get infested with tiny red insects. Are they red spiders? (New York.)   Probably they are red aphids. Red spiders are almost too small to see with the naked eye and form a mealy cobweb on the underside of the leaves. Use malathion for aphids, Kelthane for mites.

DOGWOOD (CORNUS FLORIDA)

What can be done for bark borers on flowering dogwood trees? (New Jersey.)   Twig borers can be taken care of by cutting below the infested portion, but bark borers are best prevented by wrapping newly transplanted trees in Kraft crepe paper, extending from the crown up to the first branches. Leave on for 2 years. After infestation, borers can be surgically removed, but it is not always possible to save the tree. Lindane sprayed on trunks twice in the spring and early summer will also help prevent borers, but lindane is a restricted chemical which in many states can be applied only by a professional.

I planted 2 flowering dogwoods. One died; its bark blistered, chipping off easily. Can the other tree be saved? (Ohio.)   A crown canker disease might have that effect but I do not know of it occurring in Ohio. It may have been bark borers. (See the previous question.) If you cut out all borers in the remaining tree, wrap the trunk and feed and water it, it may live.

Dogwood, pussy willow, other shrubs, and roses have some disease; they are covered with scales of a shell-like nature. The trees finally die. What is the remedy? (Maryland.)   All these and other plants are subject to attack by scale insects. There are many different types with various host preferences. Dogwood can have round scurfy scale, lecanium scale, or cottony maple scale. Oystershell scale occurs on willow and also on dogwood, as well as other shrubs and trees. Rose scale can be destructive to roses. Dormant oil sprays are effective for most scale insects, followed by a contact spray during the growing season when crawlers are active. Each species of scale insect has its own crawler period. Get a positive identification and information on crawler periods from your local Cooperative Extension Service.

ELM (ULMUS)

What is best to use for yellow striped bugs on Chinese elms in July? (Ohio.)   This is the elm leaf beetle, a chewing insect little affected by a contact insecticide. Have your trees sprayed with methoxychlor or carbaryl early in June.

What spring care can be given to an elm that gets covered with small worms, causing the leaves to turn brown and fall in midsummer? (New Jersey.)   Cankerworms chew foliage in May, but in June the dark, dragon-shaped larvae of the elm leaf beetle skeletonize the leaves, causing the browning and defoliation. Two carbaryl sprays are best: the first for cankerworms after the leaves come out in May; the second for elm leaf beetle in early June. Power spraying by a tree expert is required.

What is a practical insecticide for Siberian elms? The affliction is a black caterpillar worm that attacks the foliage. (New Jersey.)   This is the larval stage of the mourning-cloak butterfly, but it can be controlled by power spraying with carbaryl.

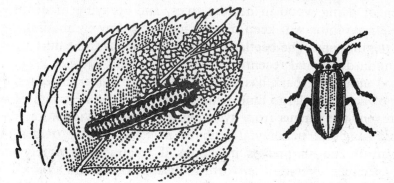

Black larva of the elm leaf beetle. The beetle has distinct yellow stripes.

What is the scale infecting the bark of my Siberian elms? (New York.) Elm scurfy scale and 2 or 3 other scale insects may appear on elm bark, causing the death of branches and occasionally of young trees. Use a dormant oil spray before growth starts. (See also Dormant Spraying.)

Why did my elm tree give off a black secretion so that the lily bed under it looks like a city garden? (New Hampshire.) The secretion was colorless honeydew from aphids on the elm, but when it dropped onto the lily leaves, a black fungus grew in it. (See Sooty Mold.) There is no control except spraying the elm for aphids, and the expense may not be warranted.

The leaves of our 5-year-old elm turn yellow and fall off in August. (Ohio.) The elm leaf beetle may be the cause, or the Dutch elm disease, or cephalosporium wilt, or a virus disease common in Ohio called phloem necrosis. Call in a tree expert for diagnosis, or send specimens of twigs to your county agent at your Cooperative Extension Service or to the Agricultural Experiment Station at Wooster.

What is the Dutch elm disease? A wilt disease, first reported in Ohio in 1930 and in New Jersey in 1933. It is transmitted by bark beetles, which came in from Europe on elm burls imported for furniture veneer, wood for dish crates, etc. Wilting is followed by yellowing, curling, and dropping of leaves. When the twigs are cut across, the vessels are black, but this is also true of cephalosporium and verticillium wilts, so that laboratory cultures are needed for a true diagnosis.

Area-wide integrated control programs are most effective in keeping Dutch elm disease at a low level. Demand for and support of sound municipal control programs are essential to reduce the probability of infection for privately owned trees. The prompt removal of infected trees, pruning of dying wood in healthy trees, and spraying of healthy trees with methoxychlor will keep disease incidence low by minimizing bark beetle populations. The beetles transmit the fungus to healthy trees after breeding in dying and recently cut or killed wood. Do not keep elm for firewood unless the bark has been removed. In numerous cases, the removal of an entire large limb within a week of the first sign of wilting will prevent the fungus from systemically infecting the entire tree. The systemic fungicide benomyl (Benlate) in some cases provides preventive control and suppresses infections if treatment is timely enough. Large specimen elms can be worth thousands of dollars and well worth a professional arborist's services. Keeping trees healthy and vigorous by feeding, watering, pruning, and spraying is essential.

What causes Siberian elm trees to bleed so long after pruning? Mine have been discharging for two years. (Illinois.) Elms are subject to a condition known as slime flux, which means a continuous exudation from wounds due to positive pressure in the sap. Often this bleeding flux has an alcoholic odor and attracts insects.

What will dry up sap flowing from a borer hole wound? (Oklahoma.) It is slime flux. Sometimes it helps to drill a hole below the bleeding wound into the heartwood and insert a drainpipe. This carries the flux out beyond the tree trunk and gives the wound a chance to heal.

EUONYMUS

Why do the stems of my Euonymus fortunei radicans variety, 15 years old, growing against a cement garage, become white? (Massachusetts.) Your vine is completely covered with the euonymus scale. Look closely and you will see thin white male scales, mostly on the leaves, and brownish or gray oval females on the stems. When the young scales hatch, they are yellowish and crawl slowly about, but the adults are motionless. Scale is always worse on a vine attached to a wall.

How shall I check or prevent euonymus scale? Use a dormant oil spray in the spring before growth starts; in the summer, when young scales hatch, spray with dimethoate or carbaryl. The temperature must be above 45° F. for spring spraying. If your plant is against a wall, try to get the spray in back of the vine, close to the wall.

What is a satisfactory treatment for blight of the evergreen shrub euonymus? (Virginia.) You probably have euonymus scale, treatment for which is given in the previous question. Sometimes, in the South and West, euonymus foliage is covered with the white coating of

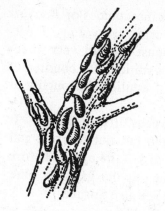

Oystershell scale, one of the most common pests on fruit trees, is controlled by spraying with a miscible oil spray (a spray that will readily mix with water).

the mildew fungus. A sulfur spray or dust will control this, but it must not be used within 30 days of an oil spray.

EVERGREEN

Is there any spray with an odor that will keep the dogs off my evergreens? (Tennessee.) There are on the market many dog repellents that may give some measure of protection.

Is there anything I can do to keep dogs off evergreens? The repellent sprays have only a fleeting effect. (Wisconsin.) Lasting and inconspicuous are the wire shrubbery guards, placed 3 or 4 around each shrub. If they are unavailable and you can spare some wire coat hangers, borrow some wire cutters and make your own guards. File one end to a point, make a right-angle bend so that the point sticks out from the tree, and put the other end in the ground.

Is it advisable to use a dormant oil spray for pines and junipers? Yes, if you have a serious infestation of scale insects. Spray only on a bright day, before new growth starts, with the temperature above 45° F., and follow manufacturer's directions for the dilution for evergreens. Oil sprays should not be used every year, but only when definitely needed. A dormant lime-sulfur spray is safer for evergreens but can be messy.

Should evergreens have a dormant spray in early spring for spider mites? (New York.) It is better to rely on Kelthane and syringing with a hose during the growing season. If you use a dormant oil spray, wait 30 days before applying any form of sulfur.

What is the most effective control measure for bagworms on evergreens? (Illinois.) If an infestation is small on one or a few shrubs, pick off and destroy the bags between fall and early spring. The easiest way is to spray plants with one of many effective insecticides or *Bacillus thuringiensis* in early to mid-June, when the worms are young. Treatments when bags become large in July and August are not very effective. (See Bagworms.) If carbaryl is used, add a miticide to counteract any mite buildup. Control is easy and effective if applied thoroughly at the proper time.

What is the best treatment for gall on evergreens? (New York.)   It depends on the evergreen. If it is red-cedar, then cut out the rust gall before the spore horns develop; if spruce, spray to kill the aphids before new growth starts, using a malathion spray. Cut out the galls on blue spruce before they turn brown in early summer. (See also Spruce.)

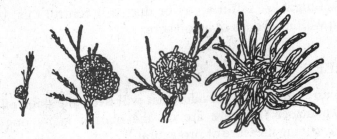

Stages in the development of rust galls on red-cedar (Juniperus virginiana) *in the spring.*

What can I use to prevent grasshoppers? They are destroying the evergreens around my new home. (Ohio.)   Grasshoppers occasionally are destructive to evergreens. Try a methoxychlor or diazinon spray.

The inside of my evergreens are brown, with their needles fallen off, but the outside looks all right. Could this be caused by grasshoppers in them all the time? (Maryland.)   Possibly this is due to spider mite injury. If the browning occurs in late summer and fall, it is merely the natural maturing of the needles. The individual leaves of evergreens do not stay on forever, but ripen and drop off as they do on any other tree. The new outer leaves stay green while the older inside foliage is lost each year.

What feeding procedure should be followed to revive dying evergreens? (Illinois.)   Feeding may kill them off more quickly, just like giving a large meal to a person with high fever. Have the cause of the dying evergreen diagnosed by an expert before you try to revive it by feeding.

FERN

What is wrong with a fern when it gets minute white specks all over it, and brown ones which are slightly larger? The white ones can be moved, but the brown ones are tight. This is a perfect description of the fern scale. The white bodies are male scales; the brown pear-shaped objects are female scales, which stay put. A severe infestation ruins the fern. Try spraying with malathion using ⅓ the usual dosage; repeat 3 times at 10-day intervals and wash off with a pure water spray several hours later, as malathion injures ferns. Remove badly infested fronds.

My fern is covered with brown spots and a sticky substance on the backs of leaves. A friend insists that these are not spores but living creatures. However, the spots don't move. What are they? Probably the brown soft scale or the brown hemispherical scale common on ferns. The sticky substance is honeydew. If you can't get rid of them with a brush dipped in soapsuds, try a house-plant aerosol bomb. Malathion, often used to control scales, may injure delicate ferns such as maidenhair and even Boston types. An alternative is to drench the soil with Cygon. Or spray weekly with rotenone or pyrethrum.

What is the most effective treatment for white lice on ferns? Do you mean whiteflies, those tiny mothlike creatures? See scale control in the above question.

My maidenhair fern gets brown areas on the leaves; what are the cause and cure? Nematode injury is a possibility; this may cause brownish areas in leaves, although more often they are black bands. Remove infested leaves.

I have a staghorn fern that is attacked by worms each year; they eat foliage at night and hide in the ground during the day. What will kill the worm and not affect the fern? (Florida.) This is the Florida fern caterpillar, pale green changing to black, which feeds at night, and may strip a fern in a day or two. Dusting with methoxychlor will probably be effective.

What "laces" fern leaves? We can find no insect that causes it. (Kansas.) Possibly the Florida fern caterpillar, with its nocturnal habits, has come to Kansas. (See the previous question.)

Will Bordeaux hurt Boston ferns? A weak solution of Bordeaux mixture should be fairly safe. It is sometimes recommended to control the rhizoctonia damping-off disease, which may rot the lower fronds of Boston ferns.

What causes rust on sword fern? (Washington.) Rust is a fungus disease somewhat common on outdoor ferns. In the Northwest, there are 8 fern rusts that have fir as an alternate host, causing white blisters on the fir needles. Ferns and firs should not be grown close together.

FIR (ABIES)

The lower branches of several fir trees are dying. Is this usual in this type of evergreen? (New Jersey.) There is usually a definite reason when branches die, even though it may be unfavorable location, crowding, or injury from spider mites. Lower branches of firs are occasionally infected with a fungus needle-and-twig blight. Prune out and burn infected parts.

Four beautiful Douglas-firs (Pseudotsuga menziesii) have died on our property this past year. Is it caused by an insect between the bark and wood and will it spread to more trees? (Washington.) Firs in the Northwest may succumb to various rust diseases and to the dwarf mistletoe. Bark beetles are also a possibility. The latter will spread to other trees if infested dead wood is left untreated. Call in a tree expert for exact diagnosis.

FUCHSIA

How can small whiteflies infesting fuchsias be controlled? (California.) Whiteflies seem to be inevitable on fuchsia, whether it be a greenhouse plant or grown outdoors. Spray with resmethrin or an aerosol whitefly bomb.

Black spots appear on the underside of fuchsia leaves, which turn yellow. What are the cause and remedy? There is a rust that comes in brown spots on the underside of leaves, but yellowing of leaves is probably due to sucking by whiteflies, and the black spots may be parasitized whitefly nymphs or whitefly pupae. (For control, see the previous question.)

What causes root rot in fuchsia? (Kansas.) Probably a waterlogged soil, although a verticillium wilt has been reported from fuchsias growing outdoors in California.

GAILLARDIA

How can I keep grubs out of the stems of gaillardias? Your grubs may be larvae of the common stalk borer, with the best control depending on cleaning up all weeds and woody stems in autumn. Frequent spraying with methoxychlor plus malathion may partly repel borers. (See also Dahlia.)

GARDENIA

What is the best insecticide for mealybugs on gardenias?   Probably Orthene, but malathion and diazinon are effective. (See Mealybugs.)

My gardenia has a little white speck that looks like mold, but when you mash it, it is alive. What is it?   The specks are mealybugs. Clean up the first you see, before the infestation gets serious.

How do you get rid of lice on gardenias?   You probably mean mealybugs. If you refer to aphids, the same sprays will do.

My cape-jasmine, which grows outdoors, had some sort of insect eat a fringe around the leaves, but I never can find the insect. What can I spray with? (North Carolina.)   It may have been some sort of weevil with nocturnal habits. Spray the foliage with methoxychlor.

How should I rid my gardenia plant of beetles? (New Jersey.)   It depends on the kind of beetles. Fuller's rose beetle, a gray-brown snout beetle, is sometimes reported on gardenias. It feeds at night. Spray with methoxychlor.

GERANIUM (PELARGONIUM)

Is there any way to prevent geranium stalk rot? Some of mine rot each winter, but I do not think they are too wet.   Stem rot is usually associated with poor drainage or excessive watering. Start with cuttings from healthy plants placed in fresh or sterilized sand or a growing medium.

About a third of my geranium cuttings have shriveled at the ground, turned black, and died. What is the cause?   Either a fungus or a bacterial stem rot. Take cuttings from healthy plants and place them in clean new sand. Keep them on the dry side.

What spray should be used to kill the tiny white insects on the under part of the leaves of a rose geranium?   These are whiteflies. Spray with resmethrin whitefly spray or Orthene.

My choicest pelargoniums have green bugs. How can I get rid of these pests?   Spray with malathion, diazinon, or Orthene for aphids.

After pruning geraniums and using a 45 per cent angle, the stems turn black and rot back for 4 or 5 inches. What can be done? (California.)   Try frequent pinching back instead of occasional heavy pruning. When you prune, do it close to a node and disinfect your knife between cuts in 5 per cent Formalin or denatured alcohol.

GLADIOLUS

How do I recognize thrips on my gladioli? (Wisconsin.)   The gladiolus thrips is a small slender insect, $\frac{1}{16}$ inch long and only as wide as a small needle. When young, it is yellow, but changes to black as an adult. It feeds by rasping petals and the leaf surface. It is hard to find because it hides under the leaf sheaths and inside the flowers.

What causes gladioli to fleck or get speckled and the foliage to turn whitish? (Wisconsin.)   These are typical results of thrips injury. Infested spikes may fail to bloom, or the flowers may be spotted, or they may dry and shrivel.

Does the planting of onions near the gladioli increase the possibility of thrips on the gladioli? (Illinois.)   No, the onion thrips is a different species.

What is the best spray for gladioli to avoid the difficulty caused by thrips? (New York.)   Spray or dust plants every 10 days with methoxychlor, malathion, or Orthene.

How high should gladiolus plants be before you start spraying and how often after the first time? (Wisconsin.)   Start when the plants are not more than 6 inches high and repeat weekly for about 6 weeks, or until flowering.

Why do my gladioli bloom only partially? Only 2 or 3 of the lower flowers open. Should the corms be left in the ground all winter? (Oklahoma.)   Thrips are probably to blame. Take up the corms and treat them with malathion dust. Make sure that all old tops and debris are cleaned up in the fall, since thrips may live through an Oklahoma winter. Plant in a new location if possible.

Is it harmful to next year's plants to leave thrips-infested gladiolus corms in the ground during the winter? (New York.)   In New York thrips would presumably be killed over the winter, but the corms might harbor various fungus diseases. Why not clean up?

Will it be safe to plant new gladiolus corms in the same ground affected by thrips this past summer? (Minnesota.)   I think you can rely on a Minnesota winter being cold enough to kill the thrips.

If in storing my gladiolus corms I keep the temperature near 40° F. from December 1 to March 1, will I be free of thrips?   No, you will need to treat the bulbs in storage, or else dip them before planting, or both.

I am using naphthalene flakes on my gladiolus corms this winter to check thrips. Will you tell me when, how long, and how much to use? Use malathion dust on the corms for greater safety, or soak in Lysol (1½ teaspoons to 1 gallon) for 3 hours before planting.

I lost almost 1,000 gladioli this last season. My husband refuses to use naphthalene flakes, as he says they injure the corms. How about this? They may. See the above question.

I have to store my gladioli, tigridia, and zephyranthes, side by side. Should they all be treated? (Michigan.) The gladiolus thrips does infest tigridia, its near relative. As far as I know, the gladiolus thrips has not been reported on zephyranthes.

Is Semesan good for treating gladiolus corms in the spring before planting? It has been used to control scab, a bacterial disease, but is restricted. Dust with thiram.

I have heard that soaking corms for thrips will delay blooming for 2 weeks. Is it true? (Wisconsin.) Disinfectants frequently have a slight retarding effect on growth and bloom; the length of delay varies with circumstances.

Are there any cultural practices which aid in the control of thrips? Digging early in the fall, before the corms are quite mature, and cutting off and burning the tops before the thrips can work down into the corms will help.

When bulbs are taken from the ground, a brown scale or spot appears. Is this a disease, and what steps may be taken? (Virginia.) This is probably scab, a bacterial disease that shows as circular black depressions with a raised margin. Clean off husks before planting in the spring. Discard corms where the scab has gone through to the corm itself and dust the rest with thiram.

The tips of the leaves start turning brown, and this continues down the stem until the plant dies and the corms rot. What will correct this? (Indiana.) This may be scab, although usually there are definite spots on the leaves. It may also be dry rot, a fungus disease that turns the leaves yellow and produces dark sunken lesions on the corms and root decay. Discard all spotted corms, treat before planting, and, if possible, practice a 4-year rotation—that is, do not replant gladioli in infected soil before 4 years.

How do you treat gladiolus corms for fusarium yellows? (Indiana.) You can't entirely prevent yellows by corm treatment. The fungus lives in the soil and is widely distributed throughout the Middle West. Some varieties are more resistant than others. Wait at least 4 years before replanting gladioli on diseased soil. Use only corms that bear cormels; treat as for scab.

If space is limited and you must replant gladiolus corms in the same place, is there any way of inoculating the soil against disease and thrips? (Mississippi.) You can't inoculate it, but you can disinfect a small area with soil sterilizers. (See Soil Sterilization.)

GLOXINIA (SINNINGIA SPECIOSA)

What causes gloxinia buds to blast when nicely started? Sometimes a gray mold fungus, botrytis, of the same genus that causes peony buds to blast. Usually poor ventilation and excessive humidity are contributing causes. Remove all diseased parts as soon as noticed.

GOLDEN GLOW (RUDBECKIA)

My golden glow was eaten this year by beetles, light green with black spots. What were they? (Kansas.) These were diabrotica, or spotted cucumber beetles. Dust with methoxychlor or spray with carbaryl.

GOURDS

How can I keep insects from ruining fancy gourds? (Georgia.) Gourds are afflicted by the same pests and diseases as cucumbers. A combination spray of methoxychlor, malathion, and captan should take care of wilt, borers, cucumber beetles, aphids, and whiteflies more or less successfully. Start spraying when the plants are small and repeat at 10-day to 2-week intervals. For chewing insects alone, methoxychlor may be used as a spray or dust. Wipe the gourds with a disinfectant to prevent spotting after harvest.

HACKBERRY (CELTIS)

How can leaf galls in hackberry trees be eradicated? (Colorado.) These galls are caused by plant lice. Spray with malathion or Orthene when the leaves are half out.

HAWTHORN (CRATAEGUS)

With what should red hawthorns be sprayed when red-cedars surround them? (New York.) Spray several times during May with wet-table sulfur and ferbam.

What should I do about a sort of mildew that turns the leaves on my English hawthorn yellow and causes them to fall in midsummer? (Iowa.) The orange rust will cause defoliation, and so will a fungus leafspot, to be controlled by spraying with zineb in May. If you have true mildew, a white coating on the leaves and buds, spray with Kara-thane or Benlate before the buds open and after the petals have fallen.

What is the remedy for the lesser borer in the trunk of Paul's scarlet hawthorn? I am not sure which borer you mean. If it is one that brings sawdust to the mouth of holes, you can gas it with a few drops of Borerkil, sealing up the hole with putty or gum. If it is the flatheaded borer, keep your tree growing vigorously, paint pruning scars and other wounds, and treat with lindane to prevent future attacks.

HELENIUM

What shall I do for white grubs in the roots of helenium? (Michigan.) There is not much you can do for plants where the roots are already eaten off. White grubs are usually worse in land recently taken over from sod. Perhaps you can transplant your heleniums to a bed that has been in cultivation for a long time. Spading a bed and leaving it rough during the winter will kill grubs. You can dust or spray diazinon or Dursban on the soil as a preventive measure.

What about the black "bugs" on helenium? (New Jersey.) The chief offenders are small black snout beetles, which start chewing the young shoots in early spring and often keep working until flowering. Frequent spraying with methoxychlor keeps them fairly well in check. Later in the summer, black aphids may appear. You can add malathion to the spray or use a separate application of malathion.

HEMLOCK (TSUGA)

The hemlock branches turned brown and died until 4 or 5 had to be cut off. What can be the cause? (Tennessee.) It might be spruce mite injury, or a fungus blight. You can dust with sulfur or spray with Kelthane for the former; for the latter, you can only cut out and burn the infected limbs.

HIBISCUS

What makes the leaves on Chinese hibiscus dry up and fall off?   It is hard to say. There is a fungus blight, a stem rot, and a leafspot which might have such symptoms, but your trouble is more likely one of water relations—either too dry soil or one waterlogged from overwatering.

The buds on my hibiscus formed but before blossoming turned brown and dropped off. Why? (Maine.)   If you had a spell of rainy weather, it might have been botrytis blight, gray mold, which possibly might have been prevented by spraying with captan.

HICKORY (CARYA OVATA)

What spray will kill the grubs that get in hickory nuts? (Ohio.) These are the larvae of the hickory-nut weevil in all probability. Spraying has not been recommended for the control of this pest. The larvae leave the nuts in the late fall and pass the winter in the soil, and it has been suggested that harvesting early may prevent them from producing weevils for another year.

HOLLYHOCK (ALCEA ROSEA)

What is the cause of the rusting, yellowing, and dropping of foliage of hollyhocks? (Maine.)   Rust is due to the rust fungus, which produces its spores in little reddish pustules on the underside of the leaves. Yellow areas appear on the upper surface, and with a bad case of rust, the leaves turn yellow, wither, and may fall off. There are usually rust lesions on the stem as well as on the leaves.

Is there any way to prevent rust on hollyhocks? (Connecticut.)   Remove infected leaves as soon as noticed, and clean up all old stalks and leaves in the fall. Dust with sulfur and ferbam or spray with zineb starting in early spring, being careful to cover the undersurface of the leaves.

I used dusting sulfur early on my hollyhocks but was unable to get more. What else could be used in place of it? (Maine.)   Zineb.

My hollyhocks rot. Why? I've put cinders, lime, and peat moss in the soil, as the area is damp. (New Jersey.)   Haven't you any well-drained place that has ordinary good garden soil? Any self-respecting plant might rot in such a mixture. Sand is the only thing you haven't tried, and that might work. Don't forget that hollyhocks are biennials. They usually die naturally after blooming.

HONEY LOCUST (GLEDITSIA TRIACANTHOS)

During July the leaves of my thornless honey locust gradually turn brown followed by severe leaf drop. What's the problem? This problem is widespread in the more temperate parts of the United States. It is caused by the honey locust mite, which quickly develops destructive populations beginning in mid-June. By spraying with Kelthane in late June or early July, leaf browning and defoliation can be prevented.

There has been some twig dieback on my two specimen honey locusts. I noticed that for 2 or 3 years the foliage had become increasingly webbed and brown as summer progressed each year. Is there any connection and what webs the leaves? (Virginia.) The mimosa webworm likes honey locust as well if not better than mimosa, which is on the decline due to mimosa blight. It is a moth in the adult stage, but the damage is caused by a small, green, half-inch-long, wriggly caterpillar. It can be controlled readily with carbaryl, diazinon, or Orthene in late June. Two or three generations occur, so a second spray would be advisable in late July or early August.

There are little nutlike growths on my honey locust where leaves should be. What is it? (New York.) Honey locust pod gall midge incites this growth. Though not severely destructive, it can be controlled with 2 or 3 biweekly sprays of diazinon beginning in early May.

HONEYSUCKLE (LONICERA)

How can I exterminate aphids on honeysuckle? (Kentucky.) It is rather difficult, for the aphids congregate on the young shoots in great numbers and dwarf the leaves. Even the flower buds may be injured. Spray frequently with malathion; start when you see the first few aphids and not the first few hundred.

HOSTA

My hosta last fall looked lacelike, the leaves were so badly eaten. What is the cause and what shall I do? (Ohio.) Slugs will have this effect on hosta leaves. A metaldehyde or mesurol bait is recommended, or beer in saucers. (See Slugs.)

HOUSE AND GREENHOUSE PLANTS

What are the white plant lice that look like cotton that appear on house plants?   These are mealybugs, sucking insects like aphids. They are prevalent in greenhouses and on many house plants—coleus, croton, cactus, crassula, gardenia, poinsettia, rubber plant, and many others. A severe infestation is evidence of neglect.

What can be done to rid house plants of woolly aphids?   These are mealybugs. It is easier to prevent them than get rid of them. Keep your plants frequently syringed or washed in a not too hot or dry atmosphere. Remove the first bit of white fluff you see with a tiny cotton swab wrapped around a toothpick and dipped in alcohol (omit the alcohol for cactus). Try a house-plant aerosol bomb.

How do you rid house plants of the white mealybug that leaves a sticky substance on the leaves?   The sticky substance is honeydew, secreted by various sucking insects. If mealybugs get started despite your picking them off, spray with Orthene or malathion. Have the plants somewhat shaded from the sun and rinse with pure water several hours later. Malathion may injure crassula and some ferns; try a rotenone-pyrethrum aerosol bomb.

Should house plants with mealybugs be repotted after control?   It is not necessary if you got control; if you did not, repotting would do no good. Of course, repot your plants if their growth requires it.

Do you know a home remedy good for plant lice?   Just ordinary soap and water will do, but spraying is preferable. Aphids are not hard to kill if they are sprayed frequently. Or use a house-plant aerosol bomb.

My house plants show a brown scale and a sticky substance. Can the scale be avoided by treating the sticky substance?   It's the other way around. You treat the scale and then it can no longer secrete the honeydew. Wash scales off in a strong soap solution, scrubbing them off with a brush, and then spray with malathion or Orthene spray, as used for aphids.

We are bothered with very small white bugs that suck the underside of leaves; when the plant is shaken, they fly off and settle back again. What are they?   These are whiteflies. Spray the plants in the morning, before the flies get active, with resmethrin or Orthene, hitting the underside of the leaves.

What can you use to get rid of little white maggots in the soil?   These are fly maggots, often present in soil with much humus or plants fed with organic fertilizers. Water the plants with a solution of malathion. Or the soil may be baked before using for potting.

What causes the small black flies on house plants, similar to fruit flies? These breed from the maggots or eggs that came in with the potting soil. Some recommend watering the soil with lime water as for earthworms, or working in tobacco dust, or watering in any contact insecticide.

Is there any way to keep red spider off my indoor plants, other than constantly washing them off under running water? A frequent bath is the best way to keep spider mites in check. A Kelthane spray, or houseplant aerosol bomb containing a miticide, will help fight spider mites, as will avoiding too dry an atmosphere.

How do you get rid of red spider in a greenhouse? Frequent syringing with pure water is helpful and this may be followed with a sulfur dust. However, too much syringing in a greenhouse is often accompanied by increased plant disease, in which case spraying with a miticide or using an aerosol or smoke bomb would be more satisfactory.

A small insect inhabiting my greenhouse looks like a crab, and spins a web from leaf to leaf. I have tried dusting and the force of plain water. What shall I use? If very small and if the leaves are turning yellowish, they may be spider mites. Otherwise they are probably some species of spider, harmless to plants.

Can insects, scale, etc., be controlled in a small greenhouse by fumigating only? You will probably have to supplement with some spraying or aerosol smoke bombs. Nicotine fumigation is effective against aphids and does fairly well for thrips, but is not so good for whitefly and scale.

Is there a way to destroy angleworms in a potted plant? Dust the surface of the soil with hydrated lime and water it in, or else water the plants with lime water. Earthworms do no damage in themselves, but they can clog up the drainage hole.

I am having trouble with soil nematodes in my house-plant soil. Can you recommend a procedure to be used on a small scale? Dispose of infested soil and use sterilized soil or soilless mixes available in garden stores. Small batches of garden soil or used soil from pots can be baked in a preheated oven for 1 hour at 200° F. (See Soil Sterilization.)

What is the yellowish-brown scale that forms on the top of soil in pots? An indication that your soil needs cultivating and a little oxygen allowed to get into it. Scratch it up with the tines of an old fork.

My jade plant, peperomia, and some others have a rust on the underside of the leaves. What is it? Probably not an organic disease as much as a reaction to the environment, possibly too much water and not enough oxygen in the soil.

What causes powdery mildew to appear on house plants? This is a fungus growth that usually comes only when plants are kept in a too moist atmosphere—something that seldom happens with house plants. Dusting sulfur or a house-plant aerosol containing a fungicide for mildew will control it.

What will destroy or prevent wiggle-tails, or mosquitoes, in a water garden or pots in the greenhouse without injuring the plants? Try spraying with pyrethrum or rotenone. Do not let water stand in cans, pots, or other containers around the yard.

HYDRANGEA

What shall I use on my hydrangeas to prevent brown spots on the leaves? (Texas.) To control leafspot, spray with captan or zineb. Remove infected leaves.

What solution should be used for mildew on hydrangeas, or should the soil be treated? (Texas.) Treating the soil won't do any good for mildew. Dust with fine dusting sulfur or spray with Karathane or Benlate. Spraying with potassium sulfide has sometimes been recommended for the Southwest.

IMPATIENS

Why do my impatiens plants get a sticky substance on them? They have something like grains of sugar all over them. These grains of sugar may be honeydew secreted either by scale insects or aphids, but are more likely drops of exudate unrelated to insects. (See House Plants.)

IRIS

Some of my iris rhizomes are rotting. Although the shell seems dry, the inside, if opened before destruction is complete, is wet and slimy. What is this? (New York.) This is a perfect description of bacterial soft rot. You put your thumb on a supposedly firm shell only to have it sink into slimy, vile-smelling goo. The rot may start in the leaves, following punctures by young borers, and there is often a water-soaked appearance to the leaves.

What can I do to overcome soft rot in iris? (New York.) In the first place, take control measures against the borer (see below). Next, remove and destroy immediately any rotting rhizomes. Dig them out with surrounding soil and disinfect your trowel.

Will applying hydrated lime to our soil prevent the dying out and disappearance of bearded iris? (Georgia.) No. Iris is said to like lime, but so do the bacteria that cause soft rot. If the soil is slightly acid, it will deter the bacteria responsible for the disappearance of your iris.

How do you destroy the borer that attacks iris, cosmos, calendula, etc.? (Illinois.) It is not the same borer. The iris borer, a fat, flesh-colored caterpillar with a dark head, specializes in iris. In cosmos, it is probably the stalk borer. Sanitary measures are most important in getting rid of iris borers. If you are dividing the iris, do it early while the borer is still in the stalk and before it has eaten out the rhizome; in any case, before it has left the rhizome and pupated in the soil. The moth lays its eggs on old leaves and debris during the fall. Sometime in October or November, after a killing frost, clean up and burn all this old material, leaving only a clean fan of new leaves. In the spring, start spraying new growth with lindane once when first signs of feeding show on the leaves, or with dimethoate weekly for 3 to 4 applications.

Is there an effective means of controlling the iris borer? You have to start early in the spring to get the borers before they actually enter the leaves. Use dimethoate or lindane. Kill young borers already in the leaves by squeezing leaf sheaths between your thumb and finger.

What ate long holes or skeletonized my vesper iris seedlings during the summer? (New York.) My guess is that slugs were at work, but a zebra caterpillar also chews iris leaves. Spray or dust with methoxychlor for the caterpillar; use bait for slugs.

Do you know anything about the little round iris-wrecking beetle? I have fought it for years but never found it mentioned. (Connecticut.) A small, round, flat, dark weevil is said to eat iris pods and sometimes the petals. Try spraying with methoxychlor.

How can you lick thrips in iris? Does dark, rainy weather foster their growth? (Minnesota.) Thrips are especially disastrous to Japanese iris, but bearded iris may also be infested. You can try malathion or Orthene. Thrips are usually more numerous in hot, dry weather.

What is the meaning of brown spots on iris leaves? (Texas.) This is a fungus leafspot disease, usually fairly well controlled by cleaning up all old leaves in the fall, but occasionally requiring 2 or 3 applications of captan or Bordeaux mixture during the summer.

Why do iris leaves turn brown and dry during July and August? (Wyoming.) Crown or rhizome rot fungi may be the cause, or perhaps merely overcrowding and lack of water. If there are any signs of gray mold or white fungus threads with seedlike bodies, remove and destroy infected rhizomes. Sterilize the area with Vapam.

Why do my iris blooms last only 1 or 2 days and die? (Oregon.) The life span of a single iris flower is only a day or two; that's the way it is made. But if you mean that after 1 or 2 flowers come out your whole stalk withers and dies, that may be some fungus disease working at the crown, or possibly a very serious infestation of thrips.

My beautiful iris garden is being ruined by root-knot nematodes. What can I do? (Arkansas.) The root-knot nematode is one of the worst southern problems since it cannot be killed by winter cold or readily starved because it attacks so many kinds of garden plants. If you have any land that has not been growing nematode-susceptible plants, you can start a new iris garden there. You'll have to start with new rhizomes also. If you must use the same location, you can take out the iris and disinfect the soil with Vapam, methyl bromide, or ethylene dibromide. Or try Nemagon around living plants. (See Nematodes; Soil Sterilization.)

IVY, ENGLISH; GERMAN-IVY; AND GRAPE-IVY

What can be done to keep red spider from killing English ivy (Hedera helix)? Give it a weekly bath. Water is the very best deterrent for spider mites, and if the foliage is washed frequently, the creatures will never get started. If, however, the leaves are yellow and cobwebby, dip the vines in a Kelthane or other miticide solution.

My ivy gets a brown (looks like a flaxseed) sucking insect on it. I have tried repeatedly to eliminate it. What is it? If it is brown and thin, it is evidently the soft brown scale, and not the white oleander scale, which is equally common on ivy. Frequent spraying with malathion or Orthene when the young are hatching and the scales are vulnerable is supposed to keep them under control.

How do I get rid of the tiny brown slugs on the leaves of an ivy plant? These are probably scale. (See the previous question.) The best way to keep the plant free from them is to note the first one that appears and wipe it off with a soapy rag.

My English ivy was infested with scale in September; I picked off most of it and then noticed a sticky clear fluid oozing from the leaves. Is it from the scale? Yes, honeydew secreted by the insect. You will have to spray to clean it up.

My German-ivy (Senecio mikanioides) is defoliated by a minute black insect. What is it and how can I make it feel very unwelcome? It is a black aphid, very common on ivy. Spraying with, or dipping in, a solution of malathion will make this plant louse unwelcome. So will the weekly bath that keeps red spider in check.

What makes ivy plants wilt and the leaves turn yellow? Spider mites, usually encouraged by too dry an atmosphere, will cause leaves to turn yellow, but a bacterial disease, encouraged by too high humidity and too high temperatures, will also cause yellowing of leaves and sometimes their wilting if there are bacterial lesions on the petioles. This disease would be far more common in a greenhouse than in the dry air of the average home.

What causes new leaves on grape-ivy (Cissus) to dry and drop? Grape-ivy is susceptible to a fungus leafspot and dieback, which may kill the young leaves. Spraying with captan will control it. More probably your grape-ivy does not like its soil conditions. The new leaves will dry if the soil is either too wet or too dry.

JAPANESE CHERRY (PRUNUS SERRULATA)

Why did my two Japanese cherries die after the fourth blooming year? (Illinois.) It sounds as if they might have had a harmful spray. An oil spray too strong, or applied when it is too cold, can kill ornamental trees.

JUNIPER (JUNIPERUS)

What spray shall I use for juniper scale? (Pennsylvania.) If your bushes are not too close to any painted surface, spray with a 1 to 9 dilution of lime-sulfur before the new growth starts, about the first week in April in Pennsylvania. If your junipers are close to the house, this spray will discolor the paint and you should use a dormant oil or malathion during the summer. (See Dormant Spraying; also Evergreens.)

How can I keep bagworms off junipers? Does spraying do any good? (New York.) Yes. Spray with a contact insecticide or *Bacillus thuringiensis* after the young worms begin moving around with their bags and chewing, usually by mid-June. Pick off the bags during the fall and winter. (See Bagworms.)

How can I get rid of all the red spiders in my juniper? (Idaho.) Thorough spraying with Kelthane. Or dust with fine dusting sulfur. Dormant oil will work, but oil sprays sometimes injure junipers. (See Arborvitae.)

What causes my pyramid juniper to be slowly dying? The needles turn yellow-brown and drop off. Another juniper on the other side of my doorstep is just fine. (Wisconsin.) It may be spider mites, and a juniper near a wall, in a very warm place with little circulation of air, is far more susceptible to injury. The upright junipers very often get brown and unsightly in a few years, no matter what control measures are used.

Do windbreaks of Maryland pines or red-cedar trees (Juniperus virginiana) harbor diseases that may be transmitted to fruit trees nearby? (D.C.) Pines are not dangerous to orchard trees, although I am not sure what you mean by Maryland pine. Red-cedar harbors the cedar-apple rust fungus. Brown galls put out orange spore horns in the spring and infective material is carried to apples as much as a mile or more away, although the amount of infection is roughly proportionate to distance. In some apple regions, red-cedars are prohibited by law.

Some of the red-cedars in my hedge are developing brown patches; I suspect red spider. Can you prescribe a remedy? (Georgia.) It is very likely spruce mite. Try forceful spraying with Kelthane or Tedion, or occasional drenching with a strong stream of water from the hose.

LARKSPUR (CONSOLIDA)

What will kill little yellow lice on larkspur? (Arkansas.) Spray frequently with malathion.

Why does my larkspur turn yellow, soft at the base, and rot? (South Carolina.) This is probably crown rot or southern rot (due to *Sclerotium rolfsii*). Remove infected plants and soil. (See Delphinium.)

Why do my annual larkspur plants turn yellow and die just before or after the first blooms appear? (Massachusetts.) This may also be crown rot. The fungus starts working in warm, humid weather, which may coincide with the blooming time of the larkspurs. (See Delphinium for control.)

LAWN

How can I prevent neighbors' dogs from tearing up the grounds to get at moles, aside from getting rid of the moles? Why not attempt getting rid of the moles that attract the dogs? A fence around your property and a gate tightly latched may be the best solution to keep the dogs off your grass. Even if dogs are kept on leash, sometimes their owners walk them on the lawn side of the sidewalk rather than curb them.

How can I get rid of moles in the lawn? We have tried traps, the pitchfork, castor beans, cyanide gas, Mol-o-gen, and we still have the moles. (Ohio.) Traps have to be set with great care. Treat the lawn with diazinon or chlorpyrifos to eliminate grubs that attract moles. (See Moles.)

Can chinch bugs be controlled by applying tobacco dust around the edges of the lawn? (Massachusetts.) No. You have to cover the entire area very thoroughly. Use Aspon, Dursban, diazinon, or carbaryl. Make one application in June, and one in August for the second brood.

What caused white, slimy mildew spots on my lawn under red oak trees? (New Jersey.) There are several fungus diseases of turf, most common being large brown patch, dollar spot, or small brown patch, and spot blight of pythium disease. The latter may be your particular trouble. It occurs in warm, humid weather and where the air is stagnant, as it might be under an oak tree, but thiram or captan will probably check its spread. Avoid overwatering. Avoid also, in humid weather, letting the clippings remain on the grass.

What causes the half-circle formation of toadstools, killing the grass, and what can we do to correct it? (Washington.) This is a fairy ring of mushrooms rather common in lawns. The fungus mycelium starts in one spot and spreads in a circle, sending up the fruiting bodies at intervals. Fungicides are ineffective. Various chemicals have been suggested: 4 ounces of iron sulfate to 1 gallon of water; 1 ounce of potassium permanganate to 4 gallons of water; cut the grass close for several feet around the rings and wet the ground thoroughly.

LILAC (SYRINGA)

I have a gray scale on the twigs and branches of my lilacs with some branches already dead. What can I do to get rid of this pest? (Massachusetts.) If the scale is round, it could be scurfy scale, but more likely it is elongate and is oystershell scale. A dormant oil spray before buds break in the spring will help, but not eliminate it. Follow up with 1 or 2 contact sprays when the overwintering eggs hatch, usually in the end of May. This scale insect has many host plants, so have a careful look at other trees and shrubs in your yard to see if it has a start elsewhere. Remember, even when you do achieve control the dead scales will adhere to the bark for several months.

The bark on my lilacs is flaking off in large chunks, especially near

the larger crotches and on the trunk, with holes underneath the rough places. What causes this and what can I do? (New York.)   Lilac borer adults (a clear-wing moth) lay their eggs on roughened bark, especially where there are wounds, branches broken off, or lawn-mower "burn." Tiny young caterpillars tunnel through the bark and bore into wood. It is important to prevent borers from getting in or reentering plants previously attacked. Three monthly sprays of lindane, beginning in mid-May, will help prevent lilac borer infestations.

How can I prevent lilac leaves from becoming mildewed during the summer? (Indiana.)   The mildew, or white powdery coating over the leaves, comes from a fungus that grows over the outside of the leaves and so can be killed by dusting with fine sulfur or spraying with Benlate. Mildew usually appears in late summer. It is unsightly but has little permanent deleterious effect.

What shall I do for an insect that rolls up lilac leaves, leaving eggs and a web? Eventually the leaf is eaten through in this spot and the leaves are scalloped, but I think this is done by another insect. (Washington.)   Probably 2 phases of the same insect, the lilac leaf roller, which is reported in the Puget Sound region. Spray with malathion, diazinon, or methoxychlor to kill the young larvae before the leaves are rolled.

What causes the foliage to turn brown and die shortly after blooming?   Any one of several blight or leafspot fungi, a bacterial blight, a wilt from verticillium fungus in the soil, a graft blight due to grafting on privet stock, too much fertilizer, or not enough water.

Why did large lilac bushes develop black and brown spots on the leaves and fall off?   Possibly a fungus disease, possibly weather, or a soil condition or graft incompatibility.

LILY (LILIUM)

What causes lily buds to have brown spots on them? (Illinois.)   Presumably botrytis blight, a fungus disease, which produces oval, orange, or reddish-brown spots on the foliage, a bud blight, and sometimes stem lesions. The disease is more prevalent in rainy weather.

Can you spray the growing lilies with something to bring them through the blossoming period? (New York.)   Spraying with benomyl (Benlate), or with Bordeaux mixture every 2 weeks, starting in early spring, should control botrytis blight sufficiently to obtain normal flowering. Pick off and burn each spotted leaf.

Just how does the lily-disease mosaic look on the foliage? (New

York.)   The leaves of infected plants are patterned with light- and dark-green mottled areas, varying with the species. Mottling is accompanied by stunting, and leaves may die, from the base upward, prematurely.

How do you tell the difference between mosaic and chlorosis in lilies? (California.)   Mosaic, the virus disease, shows up as a mottled green and yellow effect, while chlorosis, a physiological disease, often appearing in lilies grown with too much lime in heavy soil, is a yellowing of the entire leaf, except near the veins. Spraying with 0.5 per cent solution of ferrous sulfate, or applying iron chelates to the soil, will often bring back the green color.

My lilies were a complete failure last year. Leaves on gold-banded and pink-spotted varieties became yellow and twisted and the bud died. Can you advise procedures for next year?   This may have been basal rot, due to a fungus, fusarium, which came to you in diseased bulbs. The lower leaves turn yellow and the plants seldom come to flowering. In buying new bulbs, make sure they are healthy. It is said that some control is obtained by immersing diseased bulbs in Formalin diluted 1 to 50.

Why do lily bulbs turn yellow and die after growing a few inches? Some never come through the ground. (Iowa.)   This may be bulb rot from diseased bulbs, or stump rot, caused by phytopthora living in the soil and attacking the new growth as it emerges from the soil. Spraying with captan will help in the latter case.

What would you suggest is wrong with our regal lilies, which grow well, with firm stalks and buds, and then suddenly topple over with the stem withering halfway? (Minnesota.)   There is a disease called limber neck, which seems to be due to unfavorable physiological conditions, but no one knows very much about it or how to prevent it.

Why have my Madonna lilies grown smaller and poorer in quality? They have small white insects on the bulbs when dug up.   If these insects are very, very small, they are bulb mites, and doubtless responsible for your lilies getting poorer. Destroy infested bulbs; plant new ones in another place in a well-drained soil. If your insects are larger, they may be root aphids, and you may be able to kill them with a solution of malathion.

What can I use to keep bugs off lily blossoms? (Illinois.)   There are several species of aphids that infest lilies, one of which, the cotton aphid, carries the mosaic virus. In addition to aphids on the buds, the leaves, especially in late summer, are very often completely covered with these plant lice. Spray with malathion, repeating as needed.

How can one protect Madonna lilies from a worm that hollows out the stem? (Indiana.) This is the common stem or stalk borer that attacks many garden plants. Clean up the weeds around and burn in the fall any plant tops suspected of harboring borers. It may be possible to save a lily in bloom by slitting the stem and killing the borer with a knife or injecting some borer paste.

How can I keep moles away from lilies? Plant bulbs in wire baskets, but moles don't eat lily bulbs, as they are carnivorous. Mice eat bulbs and are especially fond of lilies.

LOCUST (ROBINIA)

I have noticed large bulges in the bark of our flowering locust. Is this a disease? What do you suggest as a remedy? (Connecticut.) The swellings are caused by the locust borer, a devastating pest not readily controlled. The larvae live in the wood, and the adult, black, yellow-marked beetles come out in September to feed on goldenrod and lay their eggs in crevices in the locust bark. If the trunk is painted or sprayed with a lindane solution, it will kill all the young larvae that come in contact with it. This practice may be restricted to professionals in some states.

I travel the Northeast extensively and have noticed that all the black locusts along the interstate highways are brown in midsummer from New York down through western Virginia. Is this from the herbicides used along highways? (Pennsylvania.) Weed spraying is not responsible. The locust leafminer is the culprit. The larvae of that leaf beetle brown the leaves during June and July. Apparently the trees survive attack year after year, though weakened.

LUPINE (LUPINUS)

What causes a large, healthy Russell lupine plant to die late in August? (Washington.) It may have been a fungus stem, crown, or root rot, but it may also have been unfavorable soil conditions. Russell lupines have often been short-lived in this country. Some think a rather peaty soil, well supplied with organic matter and phosphorus, and testing pH 5.5 to 6.0, works best for lupines.

Can anything be done to Russell lupines to prevent aphids? I have sprayed with everything. (Massachusetts.) You can't exactly prevent aphids, but you should be able to kill the first few before they multiply with a contact insecticide such as malathion.

MAGNOLIA

My beautiful small magnolia seems to have scale. Is this usual? I sprayed with lime-sulfur last spring. Was I correct? Large blackish magnolia scales are not unusual. A dormant lime-sulfur spray at 1 to 8 dilution should have gotten the scales, but it is an unpleasant spray to use. Try a dormant oil. (See Dormant Spraying.) Crawlers of magnolia and tulip tree scales are both active on magnolia in late August and September. Spray them with malathion.

MAPLE (ACER)

Last spring, after leafing out, my Norway maple began to die out in the small branches, finally getting so thin you could see through it. What caused this? (Virginia.) Verticillium wilt, a serious fungus disease of maples, works that way, with the sudden dying of a branch. There will be green streaks, later turning black, in the sapwood. Maples sometimes recover from mild cases of wilt if the infected branches are promptly pruned out. Often, however, the tree must be removed and destroyed as quickly as possible, getting out the roots also. Plant another kind of tree in that location.

My silver maple tree is all eaten up by worms. What can be done? (New York.) If it is the green-striped maple worm, a caterpillar 1½ inches long with dark and yellow-green stripes alternating down the back, spray with carbaryl or methoxychlor when the caterpillars are young, probably in June. The forest tent caterpillar, blue-black with white diamonds, chews in May, and hence requires an earlier spraying.

What insect works on the leaves of hard maple trees? (Illinois.) The green-striped maple worm and caterpillars of the tussock moth are reported to feed on the foliage of hard maples in the Midwest.

Can you tell me how best to control maple aphids? (Massachusetts.) The Norway maple aphid, a large, greenish plant louse, not only wrinkles the leaves but drops its sticky honeydew on cars parked underneath. If you can afford it, have the tree sprayed with malathion. A tree expert with a power sprayer will be needed for large trees.

Our Japanese maple drops its leaves about the end of July; they seem to dry up. We give it plenty of water. What is the trouble? (Ohio.) It is possible to give it too much water. Aphids sometimes get so numerous that the leaves curl and dry. This maple must be sprayed cautiously, for it is susceptible to spray injury, which may cause the leaves to burn or fall. Malathion may be used on a not too hot day.

Why do the leaves of my Japanese maple get rust spots on them and roll up and fall off? (New York.)   This may be sunscald or perhaps spray injury. (See the answer to the previous question.)

Is the spray used for leaf curl on peach trees injurious to dwarf red maples? (Oregon.)   It depends on what was in the peach spray. Ferbam should not be injurious.

I have a bug that splits my maple tree limbs. (Ohio.)   There are several maple borers, the work of any one of which would so weaken the tree that branches might be split off. The callus borer is marked by swellings and abnormal growths.

What do you do for borers? (New York.)   If they are in the branches of small limbs, cut out the infested parts and burn. If the sugar maple borer is the problem, spraying with lindane may help prevent damage.

Last season we had trouble with worms under the bark of young maples, causing excessive bleeding. Is there anything we can do to prevent their appearance this season? (Ohio.)   In Ohio, newly set maples are prey to the flatheaded borer. Trunks should be wrapped from the ground to the first branches with Kraft crepe paper or any good grade of wrapping paper. It may not be too late to wrap for another year.

Do maple trees normally require a yearly spraying? (New Hampshire.)   One treatment with carbaryl or methoxychlor after the leaves are well out will give protection against chewing insects, such as the forest tent caterpillar or green-striped maple worm, but in some seasons of light infestation you may not need it. A yearly dormant spray is not necessary on maples, and oil sprays may even be injurious.

MARIGOLD (TAGETES)

What insect, triangular in form, spotted brown or gray, stings the tops of marigolds before buds appear so they are flat and empty? (New York.)   The tarnished plant bug works on marigolds. It is oval, mottled brown, and stings the buds of many flowers. It is a sucking insect, subdued by malathion or carbaryl. Remove all nearby weeds.

Why do my dwarf marigolds turn brown and dry up after blossoming well for a month? It is not lack of water. (New York.)   Perhaps you cultivate too close to them, perhaps it is a fungus stem or collar rot or wilt. If the latter, you must remove diseased plants and either sterilize the soil or use another location for your next planting.

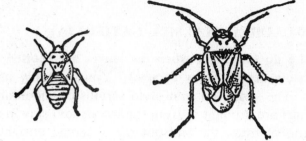

The tarnished plant bug attacks marigolds and many other garden flowers. It is triangular with brown or gray spots.

MATRIMONY-VINE (LYCIUM HALIMIFOLIUM)

What causes greenish warts on the leaves of matrimony-vines? I cannot see the insects. (Illinois.)   This is a leaf gall caused by an insect you can't see because it is inside the gall. It is a mite anyway, and almost too small to see. Try spraying with Kelthane when the leaves are half out.

MONKEY-PUZZLE TREE (ARAUCARIA ARAUCANA)

What can I do for a monkey tree whose branches are turning and dropping? (Virginia.)   The lower branches of the monkey-puzzle tree may be attacked by a fungus blight. All you can do is to remove dying wood.

MOUNTAIN-ASH (SORBUS)

How can I combat worms on my mountain-ash trees? They completely strip the foliage. (New York.)   This is the work of the wormlike larvae of the mountain-ash sawfly, which feeds a couple of weeks ahead of the Japanese beetle. Spray with carbaryl in late May and get ahead of the worms.

What causes the leaves of my mountain-ash tree to look grayish or bronzed in June? (Virginia.)   The European red mite is rather common on mountain-ash as well as fruit trees in the mid-Atlantic states and in the Northeast. A spray with Kelthane or Tedion should prevent this. Overwintering eggs on the twigs can be controlled with a dormant oil before they build up during the growing season.

MOUNTAIN-LAUREL (KALMIA LATIFOLIA)

What shall I do for blight when the leaves are spotted and burned, followed by slow death? (New Jersey.) You probably have two distinct troubles. The spotting is not often serious on mountain-laurel, but when the shrubs are brought in from the woods and stay in shady places under the drop of trees, the leafspot may become unsightly, in which case it may be controlled by spraying with zineb or ferbam. The burning is probably winter burn and sunscald, due to the drying effect of winter wind and sun. Death may be due to neither the leafspot nor the sunscald but to some unfavorable soil condition.

MYOSOTIS (FORGET-ME-NOT)

The stems of Myosotis scorpioides turned black from the soil toward their tips. What caused this? (New York.) A wilt due to a fungus, probably sclerotinia, in the soil. All you can do is remove the infected plants, digging out all surrounding soil and filling the hole with fresh soil from another location.

NARCISSUS (DAFFODIL)

What can I do to save my daffodils from destruction by a large, short grub, which eats the centers of the bulbs? (Idaho.) This is the larva, yellow-white and about ¾ inch long, of the narcissus bulb fly, which resembles a bumblebee and lays her eggs at the base of the leaves or in the neck of the bulbs. When the bulbs are taken up, infested ones will be of lighter weight and softer. Destroy those seriously infested.

Is there any specific spray for the control of the narcissus fly? Naphthalene flakes are not satisfactory. (Washington.) No, there is no spray or any satisfactory treatment for the bulbs. It is easier to burn all infested bulbs and purchase more.

My daffodil bulbs, which have been in the ground for several years, are now being destroyed by maggots. Someone gave us a lot of tankage. Would that be the cause? (New York.) The maggots are probably the larvae of the lesser bulb fly—yellowish-gray, wrinkled, about ½ inch long. There are usually several to a bulb, as opposed to the narcissus bulb fly, where there is usually one. The life history and control are about the same. The tankage did not bring your maggots but might provide a favorable medium for them, since they are not confined to living tissue. (See the previous section.)

If 'Von Sion' flowers come up green and yellow, instead of their original beautiful yellow, is the soil or the fertilizer to blame? (Georgia.) This particular narcissus often loses its original character after growing in gardens a year or two, but if the leaves were streaked with yellow along with the streaking of the flowers, you probably have mosaic, a virus disease, and the diseased individuals should be destroyed.

Why do my double white daffodils, just before opening, turn brown and black? I have tried lime, shallow and deep planting, and moist places. (New York.) These late-flowering double daffodils frequently blast before flowering. Lack of continuous moisture and hot weather have been blamed. Be careful of too much lime.

NASTURTIUM (TROPAEOLUM)

How do you control black aphids on nasturtiums? (New York.) By using malathion or other contact spray frequently, faithfully, and usually frantically. These aphids are very hard to kill. Use an angle nozzle to reach the underside of the leaves; start spraying early and continue through the season. Sometimes it seems simpler either to ignore the aphids and yellowing leaves or to omit nasturtiums.

What can I do to keep the plant lice formed by black ants off nasturtiums? (Michigan.) These black aphids (technically they are bean aphids) are not "formed" by ants and they may appear quite independently of them, but often they are protected from their natural enemies by ants, who feed on the honeydew secreted by the aphids. (For control, see the answer to the previous question.)

What do you use for cutworms among nasturtiums? (Michigan.) Not much, since paper collars are rather impractical for nasturtiums. Dursban or diazinon should be effective. (See also Cutworms; Slugs and Snails.)

OAK (QUERCUS)

My large oak is infested with borers. All summer small branches were falling off the tree and each branch had a large brownish worm. What can I do? (Connecticut.) This worm, the grub stage of a beetle, is known as the oak twig pruner because it cuts off the branches. Since the larvae winter in the fallen branches, your job is to clean up all these.

What can I do to put new life in an oak tree that was struck by light-

ning? (Maryland.)   If possible, have a tree expert go over it to note the extent of the damage, remove shattered limbs, and apply a wound dressing. Feed with a rapidly available fertilizer. Valuable trees should be equipped with lightning protectors—a very good form of insurance.

This fall there were loads of little white bugs clinging to the bark of our oak tree. Later they seemed to have disappeared. We are worried about the tree, which has not responded to treatment. (Kansas.) These could have been the young stage of scale insects, several of which infest oak; or, if they were fluffy white bits, some sort of woolly aphid, or else, if on twigs, mealy flata (planthoppers), rather common on many trees in late summer and causing no particular damage. The poor health of your tree may be due to borers or to scale. Have it examined by a reputable tree expert.

OLEANDER (NERIUM)

How can I keep my oleanders free from insects?   Malathion will control the young, motile stages of the oleander, cottony cushion, hemispherical scales, and mealybugs. (See House Plants.)

What is destroying the leaves of my oleander shrubs in the yard? I saw some large reddish caterpillars. (Florida.)   The oleander caterpillar is often a problem and can be controlled easily with carbaryl if you find them when they are still young and small.

PALM

The soil of my potted palm seems to contain many small insects like soil lice. Do they hurt the roots and how can I destroy them?   Your description is too vague, but they sound like root aphids. Root aphids can be killed by making a depression around the plants and pouring in malathion, diluted as for spraying.

Little white spots form on the leaves of my palm. They can be washed off but reappear. What shall I do to prevent this?   The spots are probably mealybugs, or possibly one of the many species of scale. Keep the leaves syringed frequently and control ants, for they often carry around young insects. Try malathion or Orthene applications. (See House Plants.)

PANSY (VIOLA)

What can be used to prevent rabbits from eating pansies?

(Ohio.) Probably a wire fence around the pansy bed is the best method. If that is impossible, try moth balls or some other of the many repellents suggested under Rabbits.

What is the white moth, similar to the cabbage moth, that lays its eggs on pansies? These hatch into small black hairless caterpillars that eat foliage and stems; during the day they lie on the ground, climbing up the plants at night. (Washington.) You have described the sluglike larva of the violet sawfly, the adult of which is a four-winged black fly, so the moth you mention must be something else. Spray with methoxychlor or carbaryl for false slugs or sawfly larvae.

What is it that eats leaves and flowers of pansies? I have found one mahogany-colored worm with short hairs. (North Carolina.) The woolly bear caterpillar comes close to your description. It has a brown body, black at each end, and clipped hairs. It eats all kinds of garden plants. Spray or dust with methoxychlor if large numbers occur; woolly bears are seldom numerous enough to warrant spraying.

How do you prevent pansy plants raised indoors from getting infested with lice? Keep them syringed frequently. Treat with an aerosol plant bomb.

PECAN (CARYA ILLINOINENSIS)

What should I spray pecan trees with, and when? (Texas.) A suggested spray schedule lists a dormant oil spray for scale, and 4 applications of captan for scab, starting when the nuts set and repeating at 3-week intervals. Add malathion for aphids and methoxychlor or carbaryl for caterpillars and leaf-case bearers. Clean up and burn old hulls and infested nuts to control shuckworm and nut weevils. Consult your State Experiment Station or county agent through the Cooperative Extension Service.

What caused my trees to shed the pecans before they matured? (Louisiana.) Pecan scab, a fungus disease, causes the nuts to dry up and fall. Control by spraying with captan. In buying new trees, choose resistant varieties.

PENSTEMON

Why didn't my 'Garnet' penstemon bloom? The tips of the branches blighted and turned black instead of forming buds. (Texas.) Crown rot, caused in Texas by *Sclerotium rolfsii*, is common on penstemon and would blight the buds; but generally the whole plant would wilt and die. (See Crown Rot.) Penstemon likes a well-drained but not dry soil, and dies out in a year or two if not kept in full sun.

The tips of penstemon buds are webbed together and a small worm bores down the center of the stalks. What shall I do to prevent this? (Indiana.) The tobacco bud worm reported on some garden plants is probably the pest you have. Spray thoroughly with carbaryl as the buds form. With the hydrangea leaf tier, also a bud worm, the leaves may be opened and the worm killed before it injures the flower buds.

PEONY (PAEONIA)

What causes peony buds to blight? (Michigan.) A disease called botrytis blight, caused by *Botrytis paeoniae* and *B. cinerea,* and widely distributed across the United States. Young buds turn brown or black and fail to develop; irregular brown to black areas show on the leaves, and black pimples (sclerotia) form at the base of the stalks.

Why do stalks wilt and fall over? (Wisconsin.) This is another symptom of botrytis blight. If the old stalks are left in the ground, the sclerotia will produce spores in the spring that infect the young shoots coming up. In wet weather, the shoots turn black and rot at the base, often being covered with a gray mold. If the weather is dry early in the season, the disease may not show up until the bud stage.

Why do peonies have brown spots on the petals? (Virginia.) Usually because of botrytis blight. The rain splashes spores from infected buds to opening blossoms, and everywhere a spore starts to germinate there is a brown spot on the petals. However, browning may also be due to thrips injury. (See Gladiolus.)

Is bud rot curable? (Wisconsin.) Not curable, but often preventable. In the fall, cut down and destroy all peony tops, so the sclerotia cannot overwinter. With a sharp knife, cut each stalk just below the soil level. Never use the tops for mulching. Spray several times in the spring with benomyl, mancozeb, or zineb, starting when the reddish new shoots are 3 to 6 inches high, and again when 10 to 18 inches.

Why does the foliage turn black after the blooming period? (Tennessee.) It may, in a wet season, be due to botrytis blight. Every infected bud or leaf should be cut off and every infected shoot carefully pulled up to prevent the spread of the fungus. Blackening may also be due to stem rot, a fungus disease characterized by blighted foliage, white film areas (mycelia) on the stem, and large black sclerotia in the pith.

What can be done for stem rot? Remove the infected shoots very carefully so as not to drop out any of the sclerotia, which are formed loosely in the pith and fall out of the stalks. Destroy.

What would cause roots to rot? (Montana.) Possibly botrytis blight or stem rot; or sometimes a downy mildew which causes a wet rot of the crown. It may help to sprinkle a solution of PCNB (Terrachlor) over the soil. Peonies should not be planted in a too wet soil; if it is heavy clay, lighten it with coal ashes. Never leave manure on as a mulch so the shoots have to push up through it.

What insects or worms eat out the insides of roots? (New York.) Worms are probably millipedes feasting on tissue dying from some rot disease. They are not apt to be injurious to healthy roots. Eelworms, or root nematodes, may infest peonies and cause galls on the roots, but these worms are too small to be seen with the naked eye.

Is it natural for peonies to die during August? Should they be cut back at this time? (Wisconsin.) No, they should retain foliage all summer and not be cut back until late September or early October—just before frost. Your peonies may be afflicted with one of the diseases discussed above.

The foliage on my peonies turns a light color and looks blistered. What is wrong? What is the remedy? (Colorado.) Apparently a physiological disease called measles or edema and associated in some way with too much soil moisture or atmospheric humidity. There is no practical remedy known.

How can I control rose chafers on peonies? (Massachusetts.) There is no very satisfactory answer to this universal question. Pick off as many as you can and spray with carbaryl or methoxychlor. If it is any comfort to you, when the Japanese beetles get worse in Massachusetts, the rose chafers diminish.

Should one discourage the big black ants that come on buds? (Pennsylvania.) They do no damage themselves, but merely feed on the sweet substance exuded from the peony buds. Some authorities think they carry botrytis spores around with them.

PETUNIA

We are bothered with slugs and sowbugs eating petunia stems. We used bran bait, which killed birds but didn't kill the pests. Is there something safer to use? (Michigan.) Use mesurol bait, put it out in the evening, and place it under boards or in special traps (see Slugs and Snails) designed for the purpose so that birds cannot get at it.

The petunias in my flower boxes dry up and don't bloom well near

the end of the season. What is the trouble? (Ohio.)   It may be purely
cultural difficulties—not enough water or poor soil conditions in the
crowded box, but it may also be due to one or two fungi causing basal
or root rots. Next time, be sure to use fresh soil.

By the end of June, insects start to eat petunia leaves in my window boxes. What kind of spray should I use, and how often? (Illinois.)   Spray with methoxychlor or carbaryl often enough to keep the
new growth covered. Look for hairless caterpillars feeding after dark. It
may be climbing cutworms, which can be controlled with diazinon.

PHLOX

What is the cause of phlox foliage drying up from the roots to the
bloom? (Colorado, Kansas, Illinois, Michigan, Minnesota, Missouri,
Ohio, Pennsylvania, Washington, Wisconsin.)   This question is almost
as universal as the one about chrysanthemum foliage turning brown,
and there is no real answer. It is evidently a physiological disease and
not one caused by any specific organism. It may be due to a checking of
the food and water movement at the point of union between current and
old growth. In the fall or early spring, cut old stalks back to ground
level.

Is there any remedy for phlox blight?   A liberal supply of water and
cutting diseased stems back to sound wood may help. (See the above
question.) Fungus leafspots may accompany the blight; these can be
checked by spraying with captan, ferbam, zineb, or Bordeaux mixture.

What is the best remedy for rust? (Maryland.)   There is no rust
common on phlox, gardeners all over the country notwithstanding. The
reddish discoloration of the leaves termed "rust" is merely one phase of
leaf blight. (For a definition of the fungus disease, see Rust.)

When our perennial phlox is in full bloom, a stalk or two in a clump
suddenly shows green wilted leaves, and in a day or two the entire plant
may be dead. What is the cause? (West Virginia.)   This may be the
leaf blight discussed above, or death may be due to the fungus crown
rot or southern blight. (See Crown Rot.)

How is mildew prevented? (New York, Texas.)   Dust or spray the
foliage with Benlate or Karathane, being careful to cover the undersurface. Except for the phlox variety 'Miss Lingard', mildew on phlox in
New York does not start much before July, so that treatment may be
delayed until then. In Texas, start when the foliage is well out. Phlox
that is crowded or shaded is more subject to mildew.

What can be done to prevent phlox from turning yellow before blooming? (Virginia.)   If the foliage is really yellow (and not brown, as in leaf blight), spider mites are probably to blame. These can be seen in silken webs on the underside of the leaves. Spray with Kelthane. Frequent syringing with water or spraying with other miticides will also give control. (See Mites.)

A small, soft-bodied insect, orange with black stripes, attacks my phlox. Nothing seems to control it, and I have never been able to find out what it is. What is it? (Indiana.)   Probably the phlox bug, a sucking insect with reddish or orange margins on the wings and a black stripe on the back. Kill the nymphs by spraying with malathion or carbaryl.

What shall I do for a striped flying beetle? (Virginia.)   Striped cucumber beetles attack flowers. Spray or dust with carbaryl or methoxychlor.

PHOTINIA

Please tell me what causes scale on photinia, and what to do for it? (Texas.)   Scale is a sucking insect. Usually, when adult, it is covered with a shell and attached to the plant, although the young scales may move around. In Texas, you can control scale by spraying with malathion when the young scales are crawling. Lacebugs are more common on photinia than scale, and can be controlled with the same spray. (See Scale Insects; Lacebugs.)

PIERIS (ANDROMEDA)

What can be done for lacebugs? (New Jersey.)   Yellowed or speckled white leaves, with brownish bits of excreta on the underside, are sure signs of lacebug injury. Spray with malathion or carbaryl (Sevin) or another contact insecticide when the young bugs hatch (usually late May or early June) and repeat in 2 weeks. Pieris is most susceptible to lacebugs when in the sun. Moving the plants to partial or light shade (not *deep* shade) often helps. (See Lacebugs.)

PINE (PINUS)

There is white scale on my mugo pine. What is the proper treatment? (Iowa.)   Lime-sulfur can be applied in the spring before new growth starts. If the pine is near a house, substitute dormant oil. Or spray with malathion when the young scales are in the crawling stage at the end of May and the end of July. (See Dormant Spraying.)

How can I save Scots pines that have an insect or worm in the buds? (Michigan.) The worm is the grub of the European pine-shoot moth; it emerges as a reddish, white-marked adult sometime in June. The easiest method of control on small trees is to break off and destroy the infested buds (readily told by light color, or crook, or mass of resin) before the moth comes out to lay her eggs. If the trees are too large, spray, about the middle of June and in early July, with methoxychlor and malathion or dimethoate.

Is there any control for the worm that starts boring through the new growth of pines, killing the very tops of the trees, if not found in time? (New York.) This may be the pine-shoot moth, but more likely is the white-pine weevil, the grub of which mines into and kills the leader of the tree. Cut out the infested shoot below the grubs between early June and mid-July. Remove some of the laterals and tie up one to replace the leader. Spray with lindane or Meta-Systox-R in early April.

Why are the needles chewed off my pine twigs, leaving only a brush of new growth at the tip? (New Jersey.) This is the work of a sawfly, which has become a very serious pest of pines in New Jersey. The larvae hatch from scalelike eggs on the needles in late April or the beginning of May. They work in groups and clean up one branch before moving to the next; but they feed only on the old growth, not the young needles. Spray with carbaryl at the first sign of feeding. There are many sawfly species working on pines in the spring and summer. One type webs the needles together. Spray at the first sign of feeding.

What insect works on white pine, boring small holes in the trunk? What is the treatment to save the tree? (Minnesota.) There are several bark beetles that make such holes. Treatment is difficult, and a badly infested tree should be cut and burned to prevent beetles migrating to other pines. Newly transplanted trees should have the trunks wrapped. Keep the trees fed and watered properly. (See Borers.)

What can I do to save my trees from the pine beetle? (Louisiana.) The southern pine beetle is distinguished by making pitch tubes midway up the trunk. The black turpentine beetle is at the base of the tree. Keep the trees well fed and watered, for these bark beetles work in weakened hosts.

How can pines be cleared of bagworms? (West Virginia.) Cut off all the bags you can reach. Spray with a contact insecticide or *Bacillus* when the young worms start feeding. (See Bagworms.)

What is the best insecticide for red spider? (Ohio.) Kelthane gives control of spruce mite, the common "red spider" on needled evergreens. (See Mites.)

What is the best way to get rid of white-pine rust? (Michigan.) Destroy all currants and gooseberries within 900 feet of the pines, as they serve as alternate hosts for the white-pine blister rust, probably the most important disease of this tree.

PLUM, ORNAMENTAL (PRUNUS)

I have a Prunus (pissardii) cerasifera 'Atropurpurea' which loses its leaves every summer. What causes this? How can it be corrected? (Pennsylvania.) Perhaps it was sprayed for the Japanese beetle, so prevalent on this host. This plum objects strenuously to many spray materials, dropping its leaves at the first treatment. Rotenone dust or methoxychlor will control the beetles without injuring the foliage. This tree often drops its leaves in unfavorable weather even when no spray has been used.

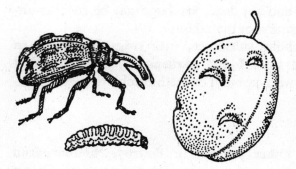

Plum curculio: a small, gray, humpbacked snout beetle.

POINSETTIA (EUPHORBIA PULCHERRIMA)

What can be done for mealybugs on poinsettias? Remove them singly with a toothpick. Spray with malathion, Orthene, or a house-plant aerosol bomb if the pest still persists. (See House Plants; Mealybugs.)

POPLAR (POPULUS NIGRA 'ITALICA')

What control is possible for a bug or beetle that works on the leaves of our Lombardy poplars? (Indiana.) If it is a yellowish beetle with black stripes or spots, and the grubs skeletonize the leaves, it is the cottonwood or poplar-leaf beetle at work. Control by spraying with methoxychlor or carbaryl in May.

A scale is forming on the trunk of our Lombardy poplar. Is there any cure? (Indiana.)   The oystershell scale is common on poplar. Spray with a dormant oil, or with malathion for crawlers. (See Dormant Spraying.)

PRIVET (LIGUSTRUM)

What is the best spray for a brown scale our privet hedge gets every summer? (California.)   Spray with malathion when the young are crawling. You may need to repeat the spray once or twice during the summer. A summer oil spray might help.

PYRACANTHA (FIRETHORN)

What causes the leaves of pyracantha to turn rusty brown and the berries to fall? (Texas.)   Pyracantha is subject to fire blight, a bacterial disease that will suddenly kill branches. Cut diseased branches out and spray with streptomycin when in bloom. (See Fire Blight.) If the leaves are merely discolored and not dead, lacebugs may be sucking underneath. If so, spray with carbaryl or malathion.

My pyracantha has a weblike substance, with twigs and leaves in meshes on the limbs. What shall I do? (Arkansas.)   It is probably pyracantha webworm. Spray with carbaryl or methoxychlor.

RHODODENDRON

How can I detect, and either prevent or destroy, rhododendron borers? (Pennsylvania.)   You can detect them by the sawdust (insect frass) protruding from holes in the trunk or branches. They can be prevented by spraying the stems and trunks with lindane in early May and again in early June. (See Borers.)

How can we get rid of red aphids on rhododendrons? (New York.) Are you sure you have aphids? They are most unusual on rhododendrons. The best rule for aphids on any shrub is to spray with malathion.

What is the cause of a black film on rhododendron leaves? (New Jersey.)   It is a fungus, sooty mold growing in the honeydew dropped by scale insects or aphids working on some tree overhead or nearby. There is little you can do for the rhododendrons, except scrubbing the film off. Having the trees sprayed for aphids or scales is usually expensive. Tuliptrees are the worst offenders.

How do I get rid of the pest that eats the margins of the rhododendron leaves? (Oregon.)   Any of several night feeders may do this, but the most important is the black vine weevil. Spraying plants and soil under the plants with chlordane in late June and 2 weeks later was the only control until it was canceled by the EPA. No insecticide is now registered, but keep in touch with your county agent for new developments.

My rhododendrons have a dry curling blight on the leaves. They eventually drop off. I have sprayed with rotenone, without results. What shall I use? (Massachusetts.)   This may be a fungus blight or canker, but it is more likely the effect of winter wind and sun. Spraying will not help in either case. Watering the rhododendrons thoroughly in the fall and providing some sort of windbreak over the winter will be most helpful.

Rhododendron leaves have dried up and turned brown. What can I do? (California.)   This can't be winter injury, as in Massachusetts, but it could be summer burning; or injury at the roots from the black vine weevil; or borer injury; or an attack of armillaria root rot; or injury from prolonged droughts. You'll have to call in some local expert for a real diagnosis, although it seems a little late to save your shrub.

What is the cause of large black spots on rhododendron leaves? The adjacent plant that gets more sun is healthy. (California.)   Sooty mold on the surface or fungus leafspots, which would be more likely to occur on a plant in the shade. It is probably not serious.

ROSE (ROSA)

The leaves of my roses have black spots. What is the cause? (New Jersey.)   The causative agent is a fungus. *Diplocarpon rosae,* which grows into the leaf and forms the black spots by its dark mycelial threads just under the cuticle. In a few days, little black pimples show up in the spots. These are the fungus fruiting bodies ready to discharge their spores, which are carried by rain or wind, by gardeners on hands, tools, or clothing, or even by beetles, to a healthy leaf. There they start another cycle if given 6 hours of continuous moisture for germination.

The leaves of roses turn yellow and all drop off before the summer is over. Why?   That's the way black spot works: first spotted leaves, then loss of color, and finally defoliation. There may also be lesions on the stems. Roses often put out a second set of leaves and lose these, too, thus weakening the plant so that it may not live through a hard winter.

What is an easy way to control black spot? (Nebraska.)   There is none. A control program means applying a summer spray or dust *weekly,* from the time the leaves come out until late frosts in the fall. It also means picking off infected leaves as soon as the spots appear.

What is an effective early spring treatment to kill the spots that may still be present on the canes? (New York.)   A dormant spray of lime-sulfur, 1 to 9 dilution, just as soon as the roses are uncovered and pruned in the spring, is often recommended, but summer spraying is more helpful.

Does sulfur really control black spot? If so, how should it be applied —on the foliage or on the ground around the bushes? (Michigan.)   It works very well, if used faithfully. It will do no good on the ground. Get a good dust gun and cover the plant with a fine film of dust, working from underneath and making sure that the lowest leaves are coated.

Is there a modern remedy for the prevention and cure of black spot? (Kansas.)   Yes. Spray with folpet (Phaltan), Benlate, Daconil, mancozeb, or maneb. Despite the best of care, black spot is apt to show up by the end of the season. For encouragement, compare your roses with those of your neighbor who has done no dusting or spraying.

Is it harmful to pick off all leaves when all are infected?   Yes, it probably is. Theoretically, you pick off every infected leaf, but this means starting early in the season and taking only an occasional one. If you wait until there is 100 per cent infection, the shock to the plant of sudden and total defoliation would be great. Pick off the worst leaves, remove all those fallen to the ground, and resolve to do better next year.

To control black spot, would it be wise to destroy all plants now in the garden and plant new stock? (West Virginia.)   No, you are more than likely to get black spot with your new plants from a nursery. Buy whatever new plants you like, but do not destroy the old plants for this reason. Start your spraying program with the dormant spray.

To destroy black spot, would it help to remove 2 or 3 inches of top-soil, then sprinkle sulfur and put on new topsoil?   No. This would remove some inoculum, old leaves rotting into the soil, but it might also injure some of the rose roots. Sulfur in the soil would not help much and might make the soil too acid.

Is there any way to sterilize the ground in a rose bed to prevent a recurrence of black spot? (Ohio.)   No, and even if you could, the next new plant you bought could bring it back to your garden.

If rose leaves turn yellow and fall off with no sign of spot, is this black spot? (Pennsylvania.)   Usually it is not. Leaves may turn yellow from too much moisture in the soil in early spring, or from drought in summer, or from nutrient deficiency.

Can cow manure cause black spot? (Virginia.) No.

Where no winter protection is required, what can be done through the winter to guard against black spot? (Maryland.) You might put on the 1 to 9 lime-sulfur spray in December, after the plants are dormant, and repeat in early March before growth starts, but this may be wasted effort. Spray regularly in summer.

Black spot has been unusually bad this year in spite of constant dusting with sulfur. Why? (Michigan.) The way the material is applied and the timing of the treatment before rains are important in control, but some seasons black spot flourishes in late summer despite the most careful control measures.

Does cold weather freeze black spot? (Indiana.) It kills the summer spores, but not the mycelia living in leaves fallen to the ground, or the special winter spores. In some states, probably including Indiana, the mycelia in lesions on the canes live through the winter and produce summer spores again the next season.

What causes mildew? (Utah.) The mildew fungus, which sends its white, felty, mycelial threads branching over the leaf or flower buds, gets its food by little rootlike suckers extending into the plant sap. The powdery effect comes from chains of summer spores growing upright from the mycelium. These spores are readily detached and carried by wind or rain to healthy leaves.

What was wrong with my polyantha roses this summer? The calyx was swollen and white, leaves wrinkled, stems white, bloom scanty. Is there danger of this spreading to a bed of hybrid teas? (Ohio.) Mildew will deform the buds, curl the leaves, and cover everything with a white coating. Ordinarily mildew is severe on certain ramblers and polyanthas in May and June, and may affect hybrid teas in late summer. If your hybrid teas are regularly sprayed with a fungicide throughout the summer, you need not unduly fear infection from the polyanthas.

Why does one of my climbing roses always have mildew, even the shoots as they come through the ground? (Missouri.) Some varieties are more susceptible than others. Either change your roses for others more resistant to mildew in your locality or make up your mind to keep them faithfully sprayed or dusted.

Can you tell me how to prevent blue mold from forming on my 'Dorothy Perkins' roses? I have cut back, every spring and fall, and sprayed, but it persists. (North Carolina.) Mildew is most persistent on 'Dorothy Perkins'. Cutting back shoots will do no good. The spores will come on the wind from somewhere. Start treating as soon as the leaves appear, and keep it up at least once a week through flowering, and occasionally thereafter. If it is a large arbor, you can probably get better coverage with a liquid spray than with a dust from a small dust gun.

What is the best treatment for white mold on rose climbers? (Massachusetts.)   Benlate is very effective; Karathane and Actidione PM are specific mildewcides.

What kind of spray is effective against mold on rose buds? (California.)   In California, you have a very special problem with mildew, and although sulfur dust is often recommended, spraying with Benlate or Karathane is sometimes more effective. Use a spreader and avoid spraying when temperatures are above 85° F.

How does one treat roses that build up big rust spots, like dust, on the stems of bush and buds, which finally kill the plant? (Michigan.)   These dusty pustules are made up of spores of the rust fungus; they are orange early in the season, later turning dark brown. Clean up all fallen leaves; treat with dormant lime-sulfur in the spring; and spray weekly with zineb or mancozeb through the growing season.

What can be used to rid bushes of yellow fungus growth? (Wisconsin.)   This is rust, which attacks the canes as well as the foliage. Prune out infected canes and follow the directions given above. Rust is prevalent in the Midwest, but is seldom seen on the East Coast, except sometimes north of Albany and Boston.

The foliage of my rambler rose is spoiled during the summer by brown spot on leaves. Spray controls this on later leaves, but the early leaves are infected while the plant is blooming and spraying then spoils the appearance of the plants. What is the trouble? (Illinois.)   There are several fungus leafspots, in addition to black spot, which may occur on roses, but control would be the same. Many sprays are inconspicuous on roses and may be used during blooming.

What is the best treatment for brown canker on roses? (Ohio.)   The very best treatment is to refuse to plant in your garden any rose that comes to you with its canes covered with little white spots with reddish margins. Next best is to remove all cankered canes at spring pruning, following this with the dormant lime-sulfur spray. Any treatment for black spot will reduce canker infection during the summer.

Some of my bush roses and climbers have long canes that turn brown at the ends, and eventually the entire cane dies. Why? (Illinois.)   Probably due to a canker that has girdled the base of the cane and cut off the water and food supply. Or it may be winter injury. Clean out infected canes at pruning. Use the dormant lime-sulfur spray.

What causes roses, when cut back, to start getting brown on the stems, and this brown to travel down until the whole stem is dead? (Florida.) Canker fungi often follow pruning cuts, unless these cuts are clean and sharp and made close to an eye, and on a slant, so that water will not stand on the tissue. If you have much trouble, disinfect your pruning shears between cuts.

What is an effective control for peduncle necrosis, a disease quite prevalent here, chiefly in red roses? (Illinois.) Peduncle necrosis, a drooping of the flower pedicle and a reddish lesion on the upper part, seems to be some physiological disease for which no control is known. Possibly a feeding program can be developed to get these roses to hold their heads up.

What causes rose leaves to turn a pale yellowish-green, and what will prevent this? (Florida.) Spider mites will do this, but in Florida the trouble is probably too alkaline a soil, making iron unavailable. The soil can be treated with ferrous sulfate or iron chelates but it will be better to acidify the soil by adding sulfur. Send a soil sample to your State Experiment Station and ask for directions.

Why do my climbing roses turn black toward the stalk during the fall? (New York.) If roses are fed in late summer with an excess of nitrogen, so there is much succulent growth, this will turn black and soft at the first touch of frost.

Will lime-sulfur spray help roses? (New Jersey.) Sometimes, when used as a 1 to 9 dormant spray, just after pruning in the spring. It controls scale and may "burn out" overwintered cane lesions of black spot. It is not ordinarily used for a summer spray on roses.

What will kill scale on the wood of climbing roses? (Pennsylvania.) If the bushes are not against the side of a garage or a house with light paint, give the dormant 1 to 9 lime-sulfur spray. If staining painted woodwork must be avoided, substitute a dormant oil. (See Dormant Spraying.) But, in my experience, this is a poor substitute for lime-sulfur on roses.

How do you kill the green licelike "beasties"? (Pennsylvania.) The "beasties" are plant lice, or aphids, sucking insects readily killed by thorough application of most contact insecticides; malathion or Orthene is very effective, or use Meta-Systox-R.

How early should one start spraying to get rid of aphids on roses? (Michigan.) Fairly early in the spring. Since a contact insecticide is required, wait until the first few start working. Ordinarily, cool, rainy weather in the spring and the cooler weather toward fall encourage aphids, and they are not as numerous in midsummer. One cannot predict insect invasions accurately, but must be prepared to cope with them immediately.

How can roses (indoors) be freed of a small black insect pest? Malathion should take care of aphids. Try washing them off and then spraying the entire plant. (See House Plants.)

My rose garden is located near 2 old apple trees. Spraying with a rose spray twice weekly proved ineffective against a plague of whiteflies in September and October. What should I use? (Connecticut.) These whiteflies are apple leafhoppers, whose late-summer brood is often difficult to control. Try malathion, carbaryl, dimethoate, or Meta-Systox-R, directing your spray underneath the leaves. The stippled white leaves are unsightly, but there is no lasting injury from this late brood of leafhoppers. The early brood comes in May and is more readily controlled.

What is the best control of spider mites on rose leaves? (California.) No one is best. Kelthane, Tedion, Omite, or chlorobenzilate are all good, plus an occasional washing with the hose. They are most serious in enclosed gardens or on roses under overhangs where there is little air circulation.

How can I get rid of big insects on 'Paul's Scarlet'? They eat up every plant. These bugs work in pairs by the hundred. They fly. (New York.) You describe the rose chafer, sometimes called rose bug, which is a long-bodied, long-legged tan or grayish, rather soft beetle. They are often found in pairs, mating. They feed on the flowers and are a destructive pest for about 6 weeks in late May and June. Their numbers diminish with the advent of Japanese beetles.

How can one eliminate the rose chafer? (Rhode Island.) It is not easy; hand-picking is really the best control. Or spray with carbaryl (Sevin).

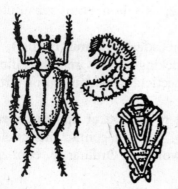

Rose chafer or rose bug is a tan beetle that attacks many garden flowers.

What is the best way to save roses from the Japanese beetle? How much insecticide is needed and when should I use it? (New York.) Carbaryl or methoxychlor in any combination spray or dust will keep rose foliage reasonably free from chewing by beetles. Pick them off the flowers. Beetles become numerous by the end of June and continue into September. To protect the new leaves, which the beetles prefer, a weekly treatment is required.

Japanese beetles destroy the buds of my roses. Should the buds be cut off shortly after they are formed, or would it be more beneficial to the stalk to leave the buds on? (Pennsylvania.) The plant does not care whether or not the buds remain; all it wants is plenty of green leaves to make more food. Leave the buds on until they show color, then cut them and enjoy them in the house. Cut in the morning or the beetle will get them before you do. Cut off fading, full-blown flowers, which attract beetles. When cutting, make a clean slanting cut just above an eye—as if you were spring pruning; it saves lots of canker trouble.

What is the Oriental beetle? What color is it; how can it be recognized and found? (Illinois.) It resembles the Japanese beetle in size and shape, but is duller in color, which varies—either light-brown, purplish-black, or mottled. The Asiatic garden beetle (another species) is copper-brown and feeds only at night. Both beetles are most dangerous in the grub stage, feeding on grass roots, and both are chiefly pests of the Atlantic seaboard.

Is the Oriental beetle the same as Fuller's rose beetle? (Oregon.) No, Fuller's rose beetle is a small gray snout beetle with grayish patches. It is also a pest of citrus trees on the West Coast. Spray with methoxychlor or malathion, and pick off by hand.

When rose buds open, you can see numerous very minute white insects running along at the bottom of the petals. What kind of disease is this? (New Jersey.) It is not a disease. The insects are thrips, usually the flower thrips, but sometimes onion or greenhouse thrips. They are rasping-sucking insects and injure the flowers rather than the foliage.

What makes my roses turn brown? Just before they open, the outside leaf is brown and dry, but if I take off the leaf, the bud will open. (Wisconsin.) Thrips very often cause roses to "ball" in this way. Sometimes the bud will open normally, and sometimes all the petals turn brown.

How are thrips on roses controlled? (New York.) Frequent spraying with malathion, dimethoate, or diazinon may help. They are hard to control. Thrips injury is usually worse in a dry season. After a wet spring, there is seldom a serious infestation of thrips in June.

I dug up some rose bushes this fall that had not thrived and found small white particles on the roots. What caused this? (New York.) If the particles were alive, you could have soaked the roots in a malathion solution, then poured the solution into the soil and replanted, for they may have been root aphids. If the particles were a fungus growth, it would have been too late to save the plants.

What is the trouble when new rose shoots die on the end and the buds dry and fall off when they are the size of small peas? (Pennsylvania.) The rose midge is to blame. The adult is a yellow-brown minute fly that lays her eggs in the leaf and flower buds; these hatch and the maggots burrow into the new growth, causing the result you describe. When each maggot reaches maturity (indicated by the orange color), it drops to the ground, where it pupates just beneath the surface and produces another midge. In warm weather, the whole life cycle takes only 10 to 12 days, so there are many generations in a season.

What is the control for rose midge? (Indiana.) DDT sprays once controlled them. Now Orthene is registered for this use. Remove infested shoots.

What can I do about the Asiatic beetle, which chews up my roses? (Michigan.) Are you sure you have the Oriental beetle? This one and its cousin, the Asiatic garden beetle, are chiefly distributed along the Atlantic seaboard and are not primarily pests of roses. Perhaps you have rose chafers or the rose curculio.

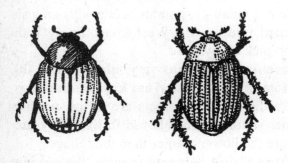

A Japanese beetle (left) and an Asiatic beetle (right).

How do I get rid of green beetles with black spots on them? They get inside my roses and ruin all the blooms. (Texas.) These are the diabrotica or 12-spotted cucumber beetles. They are controlled by the carbaryl or methoxychlor in your regular schedule.

Last year a little green worm (coiled) ate all the leaves off my roses. (Minnesota.) This is the coiled rose worm, a rose slug, controlled by spraying with carbaryl or methoxychlor and by cleaning up all decayed

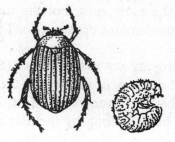

The Asiatic beetle feeds at night and attacks China-asters, zinnias, carrots, beets, peppers, and other plants. The grubs injure grass and vegetable roots.

wood and pithy stems in which the insect can hibernate during the winter.

Why do the leaves on my roses turn brown early in the summer? I find green worms on the underside; spraying does not seem to help. (Michigan.)   These are rose slugs, not true slugs, but sawfly larvae, which skeletonize the leaves, eating out everything but the veins and so cause the browning. Slugs work in the early spring, starting almost as soon as the leaves come out, occasionally in midsummer, and they often have a late summer brood. Spraying will control them but good coverage is needed on the undersides of the foliage.

What kind of a pest eats holes in rose leaves and buds? (Missouri.)   Perhaps the rose curculio, a red beetle with a black snout. Eggs are laid and larvae develop in the buds and young fruits, so pick off all dried buds. Spray with methoxychlor or carbaryl.

I have observed wasps chewing the edges of my rose leaves. Should I try to poison them? (Wisconsin.)   This is the leaf-cutter bee taking circles from the leaf to roll into a cylinder for a nest and then coming back to cut a larger circle that fits exactly and forms the top of the nest. I am always so intrigued by the seeming intelligence of this insect—which really does little harm—I never want to poison it. It is also a good pollinator.

In pruning my roses, I found the branches dry and dead inside, and a small black beetle. What will exterminate this insect? (Oklahoma.)   This is the rose cane borer or stem girdler. All that can be done is remove and burn infested shoots, cutting below the borer. Fall pruning sometimes encourages the insect. If you leave long canes in the fall and the borer works near the top, you can cut out the injured wood in the spring without any real damage to the bush.

What will kill ants around bushes and not kill the rose plants? (Missouri.)   Try to find their nests and apply an insecticide. (See Ants for more suggestions.)

How can I keep moles from eating our rose bushes? (Mon-

tana.)   The eating is done by mice in the mole runs, but the tunnels can dry up the roots. Step on the mole runs around bushes. (See Moles; Mice.)

How can I prevent rabbits from destroying my rose bushes? (Penn-sylvania.)   If you don't like the looks of a fence, or cannot get the materials, there are various chemicals that have an evanescent effect. Moth balls work for me, but I think they are helped along by the neighbors' cats. (See Rabbits.)

What is the best all-purpose spray for hybrid tea roses? I am not adept at diagnosing pests and diseases. How frequently should it be used? (New York.)   No one is best. I use Isotox Insect Spray (Sevin, Kelthane, Meta-Systox-R) plus Phaltan.

RUBBER PLANT (FICUS ELASTICA)

What is the cause of rust ruining the leaves of rubber plants?   There is a fungus disease, anthracnose, which appears as a scorching and tip burn of the leaves and has little rose-colored spore pustules; there is a true scorching from dry air in a too hot hothouse; and there is a red scale. Pick off spotted leaves; do not let drops of water stand on the leaves; keep the house cool and the atmosphere humid. Spray for scale with a contact insecticide.

SEDUM

What makes sedum rot off the top of the ground? (New York.)   Sedum is subject to both crown rot and stem rot, two fungus diseases. Remove the diseased plant and the surrounding soil and fill in the hole with fresh gritty soil before replanting; give perfect drainage.

SNAPDRAGON (ANTIRRHINUM)

Small brown dots appear on the underside of the leaves of my snap-dragons. Is this rust? (Louisiana.)   Yes, the rust pustules are chocolate brown and show on the underside of the leaves.

How can I control and kill snapdragon rust? (West Virgina.)   It can't be killed, but spraying with zineb biweekly until the plants are 15 inches tall will help prevent new infections. By far the easiest way to control this disease is to grow rust-resistant varieties.

What causes snapdragon to wilt and die? (Texas.)   In Texas, southern blight, cotton root rot, verticillium wilt, stem rot, and some other diseases. Remove diseased plants and try to replant them in a new location.

SPRUCE (PICEA)

What is an effective remedy against spruce gall? (New York.) Spruce galls are caused by adelgid aphids. The one that causes the elongation and swelling of the tips of blue spruce has Douglas-fir as an alternate host. When new growth starts, the aphids work at the base of the leaves, causing each cell to become enlarged and the whole gall to look something like a small pineapple. The best control is to remove the galls in midsummer before they open and free the new aphids.

What kind of spray shall I use for spruce gall, and when is the proper time to spray? (New York.) For Norway spruce, where the galls are located at the base of the twigs, rather than at the tips where they are easily cut out, spray with malathion in the summer after the galls open to expose the aphids; spray in the spring, just before new growth starts, with a carbaryl or malathion solution. With the blue spruce, if it was impossible to cut off all the galls while they were closed, spray in early April with malathion or Meta-Systox-R.

Why do the needles of a Black Hills spruce turn brown and fall off? (Illinois.) All spruces are subject to infestation by spider mites, which suck the sap from the needles, turning them grayish, and later brown, and often causing defoliation. A dormant oil spray or a spring or fall spray of Kelthane has been recommended. (See Mites.)

What causes the needles of our Norway spruces to turn brown and fall next to the trunk? I have found a small moth hidden in the branches. (Illinois.) There are several small moths the larvae of which mine in the needles of spruces, feeding on them and webbing them together. Ordinarily they are not serious and the browning of the inner needles may be natural ripening. Spray with carbaryl or malathion if necessary to control the larvae.

What diseases get on Koster's blue spruce? Should they be sprayed? The most serious disease is a canker or dieback of the lower limbs, which is not amenable to sprays. Cut out the diseased branches. Rust may sometimes attack spruce but is not serious in ornamental plantings. In general, you do not need to spray spruce for disease control, but occasionally for gall aphids and spider mites. (See the above questions.)

A blue spruce suddenly drops all its needles with no apparent cause.

Would you suggest a spray? (New York.)   No, never spray unless you have "apparent cause." A tree in that condition might be made sicker with a spray. It sounds like a drought reaction, but it could be too heavy, wet soil, or escaping gas, or too strong a spray or some other environmental cause.

Borers in my spruce trees cause white encrustations on the trunks. What spray should I use, and when? (Illinois.)   If these are bark beetles, there is no spray that will help, and seriously infested trees should be cut and burned before the beetles escape to other spruces. Ask a tree expert to diagnose the trouble.

STOCK (MATTHIOLA INCANA)

Why can't I raise good-looking stocks? Mine are always spindly and buggy. Even when I spray them, they are small and sickly. (California.)   Stocks in California suffer from several diseases. Young seedlings get a bacterial wilt, prevented by immersing seed in hot water held at 127° F. for 10 minutes and planting in a new location. A fungus crown rot appears on overwatered, poorly drained soil; mosaic stunts the plants. Remove the infected plants and spray to control aphids with malathion.

What can be done to control stem rot on stock? (Arizona.)   Stem and root rot are caused by a soil fungus which yellows the lower leaves, girdles the stem, causing wilting, and rots the roots. Since the fungus spreads for several feet through the soil away from the plant, it is not removed by taking up diseased plants and surrounding soil. Sterilize the soil (see Soil Sterilization) or plant in a new location.

SWEET PEA (LATHYRUS ODORATUS)

How do you control mildew on sweet pea? (Washington.)   Dust frequently with fine dusting sulfur, starting before mildew usually appears or spray with Karathane or Benlate. They can be combined with malathion to control aphids.

Will treating the soil prevent green lice on sweet peas? (Wisconsin.)   Di-Syston granules or dimethoate on the soil may help. Usually you spray for aphids during the growing season, using malathion up to blooming time.

Will treating the soil prevent the blighting of sweet peas? (Wisconsin.)   Soaking the soil with a benomyl solution before planting will help in the control of various root rot diseases that cause wilting or blighting of the plants. (See Soil Sterilization.)

What causes sweet peas to wilt just below the flower buds, then the whole plant turns greenish white and dies? (Connecticut.) A fungus disease called anthracnose, common on outdoor sweet peas, has this effect. The fungus also causes a disease of apples and lives during the winter in cankered limbs and mummied apples as well as on sweet pea pods and seed and soil debris. Spray with benomyl biweekly during the growing season. Clean up all plant refuse in the fall. Plant only those seeds that appear sound and plump.

Why do my sweet peas develop a curled and puckered appearance? I plant on new ground each year, treat seed with Nitragin, and give plenty of moisture. (Idaho.) This is probably mosaic, carried from plant to plant by aphids. Virus diseases are common in the Northwest and there is nothing you can do except try to control aphids by sprays and remove infected plants promptly.

SWEET WILLIAM (DIANTHUS BARBATUS)

What causes sweet Williams to rot and turn yellow? I do not over-water them. (California.) A stem rot caused by a soil fungus, usually most destructive during warm, rainy periods, which you don't often have in California. Change the location if you can or sterilize the soil; use a light soil; avoid wounding the stems in cultivating.

SYCAMORE (PLATANUS)

What causes sycamore leaves to turn yellow and drop all summer long? (Missouri.) The most common cause is the fungus disease known as anthracnose, scorch, or leaf-and-twig blight, but this usually appears as brown areas on the leaves and is serious, chiefly following a wet spring. It is controlled by spraying 2 or 3 times with zineb or benomyl in the spring and by cleaning up all infected leaves in the summer. Yellowing and leaf fall may be due to hot, dry weather rather than disease.

TIGRIDIA

What treatment should be given tigridia bulbs which, when lifted from the border, are found to be covered with aphids? (New Jersey.) This is probably the tulip-bulb aphid, which commonly infests

gladiolus, a relative of tigridia. For gladiolus, a 2-hour soaking in malathion solution can be used. You will have to experiment to see if this
treatment injures tigridia.

TRUMPET VINE (CAMPSIS)

**What do you use for green lice on a trumpet plant? (Pennsyl-
vania.)**   Spray with malathion, starting early, before the leaves curl.

**What can be done about leaves curling up on the trumpet vine,
caused, I think, by red spider? (Pennsylvania.)**   If the leaves are
curled, it is more likely that aphids are at work. Spider mites are more
apt to turn the leaves yellow and mealy. Spray with malathion or any
other contact insecticide for aphids, with Kelthane for mites.

TULIP (TULIPA)

What causes tulip blossoms to blister? Is it a disease?   Botrytis
blight causes brown or water-soaked spots on the petals, which might
be called blisters. This is a fungus disease, very contagious, often known
as gray mold or tulip fire. The spores are carried by the wind and rain
from infected leaves or blossoms to healthy ones. Small black sclerotia
are formed on leaves and petals rotting into the soil, and on the bulbs,
and serve to carry the fungus over the winter. Spray with zineb, benomyl, or mancozeb from early spring weekly until bloom is finished.

**Can the bulbs of diseased tulips be dug up and treated and used
again? (Maine.)**   If the blighted blossoms are picked off immediately,
and if all blossoms are cut off as they start to fade; if diseased leaves are
removed when seen, and all leaves are cut off at ground level as soon as
they ripen, the fungus may never get down to the bulb, and it is safe to
leave it in the ground. If the bulbs are dug, it is better to discard any
showing sclerotia than to treat them. If healthy new bulbs are to be
planted in old infected soil, then the soil should be treated. (See Soil
Sterilization.) If tulips are seriously diseased early in the season, the
bulb is also infected, and should be taken up and destroyed immediately
without waiting for the normal digging time.

**Why did my last year's tulips grow headless stalks? (New
York.)**   Botrytis blight often causes blind buds. These usually come
when the bulb itself was diseased in the ground, and not as the result of
secondary infection from plants nearby.

**Last spring most of my bulbs failed to grow; those that did were
sickly-looking. Was this due to not mulching the bulbs or a disease? I**

planted large, healthy bulbs. (Minnesota.)   It probably was disease. If you planted deep enough, there was no need to mulch. You either had botrytis blight from sclerotia in the soil or on the bulbs under the husk, so you did not see them, or else they had gray bulb rot. The latter also is a sclerotial disease; it is more often characterized by large numbers of tulips failing to come up than is the botrytis disease, which is characterized by a weak growth above the ground. Plant new bulbs in another location, and make sure there are no black bodies either on the surface of the bulb or under its outer covering.

Why do white or yellow tulip varieties seem not to be affected by the virus disease that causes "breaking" of the colors? (New York.)   The breaking is a depigmentation, and if there is no color pigment in the flower, or very little, it cannot "break." However, there is now known to be another virus that adds color to light-colored varieties.

How can I prevent my tulip bulbs from being eaten by very small insects? (Missouri.)   These are probably bulb mites, very small, yellowish-white spiders. A heavy infestation will pulverize the inside of a bulb. Discard all such bulbs; dip the rest in malathion, 1 tablespoon per gallon of water, for 10 minutes and replant in another location or in sterilized soil.

What are the thin white worms, ½ inch long, that eat bulbs in the ground? (Illinois.)   These are probably scavenger worms, feeding on bulbs rotting from some other cause. Seek for the original culprit.

What treatment do you recommend for the soil of tulip beds where ground aphids are present? (New Jersey.)   Soak it with a malathion solution according to the directions on the container.

Do moles eat tulip bulbs? (Washington.)   Moles are carnivorous, living on grubs and other animal life. Usually the mole makes the run to the tulip bed and mice follow along to do the actual eating. (See Moles; Mice.)

TULIP-TREE (LIRIODENDRON TULIPIFERA)

How can I save a tulip-tree that shows signs of fungus growth on the south side? (New Jersey.)   Consult a tree expert. If fungi are growing out from the trunk, it is a sign of internal decay.

Can anything be done for a tulip-tree, about 10 years old, that is badly infested with oystershell scale? (New Jersey.)   This may not be oystershell scale. The tulip-tree scale—oval, brown, ⅓ inch across—is far more common and injurious on this tree. A dormant oil, applied in early spring, should control it. (See Dormant Spraying.) The eggs of this scale hatch in late summer, so sprays for crawlers should be applied in late August or early September.

VIBURNUM

What treatment should be used on common viburnum to discourage pests that cause the leaves to curl? (Illinois.) This is the snowball aphid, and it starts curling the leaves almost as soon as they unfold. Spraying with Orthene or malathion when the buds first break will help to control this pest. Usually after you fight the aphid for a few years, you either ignore it or plant another variety of viburnum.

When a snowball tree or any other shrub is diseased, can one get it back to a normal, healthy condition or must it be replaced? (Minnesota.) That all depends on the disease, or the pest. The common snowball will curl up with aphids every season. You would have to select a different variety.

A bush of Viburnum carlesii has a deposit of rough white along the stems. Is it mealybug? What can I do to save the bush? (New Hampshire.) Probably not. Many woody shrubs in late summer are attacked by planthoppers, whose young leave flocculent white masses over the twigs. There seems to be no permanent injury. Spray with malathion and don't worry.

Each summer black spot comes on the leaves of my Viburnum carlesii and they drop off. What is the preventive? (Kentucky.) There is a bacterial leafspot listed for viburnum, but this may not be your trouble in Kentucky. Spraying with streptomycin may work. Try picking off infected leaves and cleaning up fallen leaves. Sulfur sprays may injure this species.

VIOLET (VIOLA)

What can be done to protect violets against caterpillars? (Louisiana.) Pick the caterpillars off by hand as far as possible. Dust with methoxychlor or carbaryl.

WALNUT (JUGLANS REGIA)

I have an English walnut that makes a new growth every spring and then the leaves drop off, and it is bare the rest of the summer. What causes this? (Pennsylvania.) It may be a leafspot disease, but more likely uncongenial surroundings. The English walnut is exceedingly particular as to soil requirements, being intolerant of wet soils but requiring very deep, fertile soil with no excess of alkali.

WILLOW (SALIX)

The beautiful willow on my lawn, which has reached gigantic proportions, keeps losing its leaves as a result of bugs. It seems a shame to cut down the tree. Is there something I could spray on the bark and branches within my reach? (Long Island, N.Y.) These are probably willow beetles. Have your tree sprayed once a year, in late May or early June, with malathion and carbaryl.

What can I do about the millions of dark red lice that get on our large weeping willow from midsummer to the time of frost? It is impossible to use the yard for my laundry. (Ohio.) Have your tree sprayed with malathion or another contact insecticide by a tree expert with power apparatus.

Will whitewashing a willow keep tree borers from attacking it? (Illinois.) It probably would have little effect. Wrapping the trunk with wrapping paper or Kraft crepe paper will keep borers out, but this is usually done only the first 2 years after transplanting. (See Borers.) Better get the advice of a reliable tree expert in your vicinity.

Is there any relation between scale insects and borers on pussy willow? What is the prevention? (Pennsylvania.) No relation. Spray for scale with a dormant oil. (See Dormant Spraying.) Cut down seriously infested trees and start over. Pussy willows grow fast.

YEW (TAXUS)

Are all insects injurious to yews controlled by applying chemicals to the surrounding ground? (Pennsylvania.) No. Chlordane was used to kill the grubs and adults of the black vine weevil, which is probably its most injurious insect pest. Now there is no registered control for this pest, but Orthene may be in the future. Yew is also subject to attacks by scale insects and mealybugs, which are controlled by spraying foliage with malathion.

YUCCA

What are the soft-bodied insects that infest yucca? What spray is there for control? (North Carolina.) Aphids are soft-bodied insects infesting yucca, but mealybugs—soft white creatures—are more likely to be the trouble. Spray forcefully with malathion. Repeat as necessary.

ZINNIA

What is the cause of the white, powderlike discoloration on zinnias? (New Jersey.)   This is powdery mildew, a fungus disease, which usually appears toward the end of the season and is chiefly of importance because of the unsightly foliage. Dust with fine dusting sulfur or spray with Benlate or Karathane.

What makes the leaves of zinnias curl up from the sides? (Vermont.)   Mildew sometimes has this effect. Or it may be a physiological condition.

My zinnias have been troubled by rust. What will stop it? Could it start from a narrow strip of brush and small trees adjoining my garden? (Massachusetts.)   There is no rust common on zinnias, but there is a bacterial, and also a fungus, leafspot that can cause reddish discoloration of the leaves in late summer. It is not usually serious, and it might be prevented by spraying with captan. You need not fear the strip of brush as far as "rust" is concerned, but if the weeds flourish, too, it would be a source of insect pests.

The roots of zinnias planted in open ground are covered with aphids; the plants withered after they had grown a few inches. How can we get rid of them? (Rhode Island.)   You can try making a shallow depression around each plant and pouring in a solution of malathion according to directions on the container; but if your soil is so badly infested, it would be better to plant more zinnias in another location. (See also Soil Sterilization.)

What should be used to get rid of tarnished plant bugs on zinnias and other plants? I have tried many sprays without success. (New York.)   Frequent applications of carbaryl or malathion spray might help. The first and most important step is getting rid of the weeds that harbor this plant bug.

This year my zinnias have been badly infested with stem borers, but there were no marks or sawdust visible on the outside. I cannot find material telling their life cycle or control. Can you supply me with information? (California.)   These probably are the common stalk borers, although they are listed as general only east of the Rockies. They winter as eggs on weeds and old stalks, so that the chief control measure is getting rid of these. (See also Borers.)

Vegetables

ASPARAGUS

Will rust-resistant asparagus always escape the disease? Not entirely. The 'Mary' and 'Martha Washington' varieties are reasonably rust resistant, but in some seasons in certain areas the red and black pustules show up on the leaves and stems, with yellowing of the tops. In that case, spray with maneb 3 times at 2-week intervals after the cutting season. Destroy old tops.

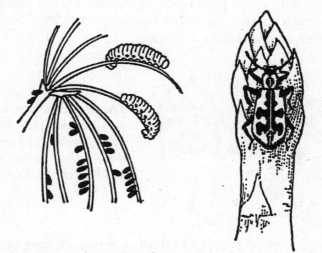

Asparagus beetles (right) eat tender shoots in the spring. Later the grubs feed on foliage (left) as they emerge from eggs.

Is there a spray or remedy of any kind for asparagus beetle? (Oregon.) This red, blue, and yellow beetle is chiefly controlled by clean cutting during the harvest season, although an occasional dusting with rotenone may be needed. After the cutting season, dust with carbaryl or methoxychlor.

Is it true that calendula plants interplanted with asparagus repel the asparagus beetle? No scientific evidence on record. Why don't you try it and judge the results yourself?

What about the Japanese beetle on asparagus? (New Jersey.) The

Japanese beetle may appear in swarms on asparagus foliage in mid-summer, but the injury is rarely sufficient to call for treatment.

BEAN (PHASEOLUS)

What is the chewing insect, colored yellow with black spots, shaped a little like the ladybug but longer? (Texas.) Either the Mexican bean beetle or the bean leaf beetle. The former looks more like a ladybug with its 16 small black spots, but it is larger, more convex, and coppery-yellow. Its spiny yellow larvae are also found on the leaves. The bean leaf beetle is prevalent in southern states. It is about the size of a ladybug, red to yellow, with 6 black spots and a black band around the wing covers. Its larva is a white grub which feeds on the stem and roots below the soil line. Both beetles are controlled by the same treatment. The yellow-green spotted cucumber beetle also feeds on bean foliage in Texas, and this, too, looks like a ladybug.

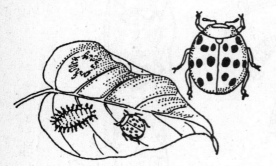

The Mexican bean beetle is coppery-yellow and has 16 black spots. Both adults and the spiny, dirty-yellow larvae feed on the undersides of foliage.

All known insecticides failed to destroy a ½-inch-long yellow creeper on my beans. It looks like a caterpillar. What is it? (Massachusetts.) Probably larvae of Mexican bean beetles, which are fat, soft, covered with black-tipped spines, and something under ½ inch long. They succumb to rotenone dust in this stage, or spray with diazinon or carbaryl. The larvae are easier to kill than the adult beetles.

Are little pests that look like a yellow bur on green beans the bean beetle? (Ohio.) Yes. That is a very good description of the larvae of Mexican bean beetle.

What are the time cycles of the Mexican bean beetle? With a succession of snap beans, I notice some plantings suffer more than others. (New York.) You are right. Beans planted in June in New York will mature in July between the two broods of beetles. The first beetles appear in May, when the early beans come up, feed for a week, and lay their eggs in orange-yellow clusters on the underside of the leaves. The larvae hatch in another week, feed for 2 to 5 weeks, pupate on the leaves, and in 1 more week produce the adults, which feed and lay eggs for the second generation. This is usually much more destructive than the first, untreated bean foliage being completely riddled during August and September.

How long a season has the bean beetle? (Virginia.) About as long as the beans are growing. In Virginia, the Mexican bean beetle will probably have 3 broods a season.

What is the cheapest and most effective way to destroy bean beetles without harming the plants? (New York.) Apply rotenone, preferably in dust form for ease of application and coverage, or carbaryl, diazinon, or methoxychlor as a spray.

Is daily picking of the bean beetles and eggs the easiest way to control them? (Virginia.) An occasional dusting will be a lot easier than daily picking off, unless there are very, very few beans. Combine the two methods, picking off as many as you can whenever you have time. Each female removed before egg laying, or each cluster of eggs burned up, means fewer beetles for the next brood.

Is there anything other than spraying, dusting, and hand-picking to control the Mexican bean beetle? (New York.) Yes, sanitary measures at the end of the season are very important. Clean up all plant debris, or else spade or plow it under deeply, and clean up all weeds and trash around the garden so there will be no hiding place for the overwintering females.

Is there anything to be done about such pests as bean beetles and cutworms during the winter? (Indiana.) Fall plowing or spading and keeping the garden clean during the winter will certainly help to discourage both of these pests.

What can I do for the little bugs that appear on lima beans? (Maryland.) The Mexican bean beetle is as destructive to lima beans as it is to string beans. Use the same control measures.

What will destroy the Japanese beetle on snap beans? (Massachusetts.) Rotenone dust or spray, or carbaryl, as recommended for Mexican bean beetle, will also take care of Japanese beetles.

How can I kill or prevent small green bugs with black dots on its back that eat bean foliage? I was afraid to spray on account of poisoning the vegetable. (California.) These are diabrotica, or 12-spotted cucumber beetles. You can safely spray with either rotenone or carbaryl.

My snap beans had little greenish bugs all over the plants all season.

What are these? How can I get rid of them? (New York.) The regular bean aphid is black; the pea aphid is green and sometimes attacks other legumes. A greenish leafhopper sometimes infests beans. Malathion or diazinon spray should keep any of these under control and may be applied almost up to picking time. Or rely on the rotenone used for beetle control.

What shall I use, and when, for very tiny whiteflies that rise in a cloud from snap beans? (California.) It is doubtful that whiteflies on beans are injurious enough to warrant control measures. They may be sprayed with diazinon or malathion up to within 5 days of picking to kill adults. Sprays must be repeated every 3 to 4 days until the adults are gone.

How does the bug called a weevil get into beans? (Massachusetts.) Eggs are laid on the pods while the beans are in the garden; these hatch into grubs, which burrow through the pod into the bean. There they change into the small, dull-gray adult weevils with reddish legs. Several broods may be produced in storage, ruining the beans for either seed or food.

The beans I raised last summer have little holes from which have come little beetles. What treatment should the vines have to prevent them? (Maine.) These are the bean weevils (weevil being merely the name given to a beetle with a little snout). There is no treatment for the vines except to clean them up. The beans have to be treated after harvest. (See the next question.)

How can I protect the beans from weevils during storage? There are several methods: (1) Spread out in pans and heat dry in the oven at 130° to 140° F. for 1 hour (some say 30 minutes). (2) Suspend seeds in a cloth bag in a kettle of cold water and heat to 140° F. Dry quickly. (3) Shake the beans thoroughly in a container, with 1 pint of lime to each quart of beans.

Does treatment injure the beans for food or seed? It should not, if directions are followed. The excess lime can be shaken off in a strainer and then the beans should be washed.

Last year my pole beans did poorly and when I pulled them up there were a lot of very small bugs on the roots. What were they? (Massachusetts.) Root aphids, in all probability. Push the soil away slightly from around each stem and pour in a cupful of malathion solution, 1 tablespoon to 1 gallon of water.

I had some fine 'Kentucky Wonder' beans, but after a while the leaves turned brown and the beans stopped growing. What caused this? (Massachusetts.) This might have been the root aphids just mentioned; or perhaps dry root rot, caused by a fungus that lives several years in the soil, necessitating a long rotation; or rust. (See below.) It could have been heavy, wet soil without the fungus. In our town, in an "experience meeting" at the end of a past season, we learned that pole beans did extremely well in the plots that were almost pure ashes, and hence well drained, and very poorly at the other end of town, where the soil was heavy clay.

Last summer I was bothered with "rust spots" on my green beans, varying from skin deep to the center of the pod. What was the trouble? (North Carolina.)   Not true rust but a fungus disease called anthracnose or pod spot, which shows up as round sunken spots with dark borders and pinkish spore pustules in the center. Anthracnose cannot be "cured" but it can be prevented by planting seed from healthy pods or else seed grown in the West where the disease is not a problem. Avoid working with beans when they are wet, as this spreads the spores from diseased to healthy plants. Resistant varieties are chiefly of the shell-bean type. Maneb or zineb sprays will prevent its spread.

What causes blight on the leaf of green beans? (Ohio.)   If there are small angular lesions and black veins, this blight is anthracnose. Look in catalogs for resistant varieties. If the blight shows up as irregular blotches on pods, it is bacterial blight.

How is bacterial blight controlled? (Ohio.)   Use disease-free seed, either from healthy pods or western-grown. Do not work with wet plants. Spray with Fixed Copper. Some varieties are more or less resistant.

What is the treatment for rust that comes about midseason on pole beans? (Massachusetts.)   True rust is a fungus disease that shows as reddish powdery pustules on the leaves. In Massachusetts it is generally serious only on pole beans, where it causes early death of the vines. The rust winters over on dead plants and on stakes. Destroy vines after harvest, and next year use new poles or soak the old ones in formaldehyde (1 to 100 dilution), and keep them wet overnight by covering. Spray with sulfur, zineb, chlorothalonil, or maneb.

What is the treatment for mosaic on green snap beans? (Washington.)   There is no treatment. The virus usually comes in with the seed. Destroy plants with mottled light- and dark-green leaves. Choose resistant varieties like 'Topcrop', 'Tendercrop', or 'Greencrop'. In Washington, curly-top, another virus disease, may affect beans. Destroy dwarfed plants with puckered leaves.

Why do my snap beans mildew? (California.)   Powdery mildew is a fungus disease very prevalent in California. It usually attacks beans in cloudy weather or toward autumn. Dust with sulfur; choose mildew-resistant varieties such as 'Greencrop'.

Does mildew appear on snap beans because of soil or atmospheric conditions? (California.) This is not a soil fungus; the spores are carried by the wind. For some reason, the California atmosphere is peculiarly conducive to mildew, not only on beans but many other vegetables and ornamentals.

BEET (BETA VULGARIS)

How are leafminers kept out of beet tops? (New York.) There is no spray that will surely prevent maggots from working inside the beet leaves, turning the tissues brown, but malathion may help. Pick off infested leaves and destroy the wild host, lamb's-quarters. Incidentally, lamb's-quarters when young is a perfectly delicious vegetable, preferred by many to spinach, so a good way to destroy it is to cook it for dinner.

What about beet webworms? There are several species of caterpillars which eat the leaves and web them together. Dust with 5 per cent methoxychlor dust or spray with malathion and remove weeds like lamb's-quarters.

Should beet seed be treated before planting to prevent damping off? Definitely. The rough beet seed may carry spores of several disease organisms. Thiram (Arasan) or captan is very effective for beets. (See Seed Treatment.)

What causes spots that resemble warts on beets? The same organism that produces potato scab. Do not grow beets on land that has grown scabby potatoes. If the soil is alkaline, make it slightly acid with sulfur, and avoid any alkaline agents such as lime and manure. Use a cover crop of rye in place of the manure.

How can I keep beets and spinach from blighting? Our soil is slightly alkaline. (Washington.) In Washington, blight probably means curly-top, a virus disease that used to be called western yellow blight, characterized by yellowing, stunting, and death. The virus is transmitted by the beet leafhopper, so that insect control with contact insecticides is important. There is little else you can do except destroy diseased plants immediately and keep down weed hosts. Soil acidity is not a factor, as it is in scab.

Is leafspot on beets prevented by spraying? Spraying with zineb can prevent the round, red-bordered spots from getting numerous, but in the small garden, picking off spotted leaves is ordinarily sufficient control.

BROCCOLI

How can I keep aphids off broccoli? (Oregon.)   Spray or dust with malathion until the heads form, then treat with pyrethrum if necessary. Often the aphids cluster on a single head or leaf, which can be removed and burned. If aphids are numerous on a head, cut for eating, separate into flowerettes, and soak in strong salt water. The aphids will float out and can be poured off. Then rinse the broccoli well in pure water before cooking.

How are root maggots and worms controlled?   See Cabbage. Broccoli is a member of the cabbage family, and while it is free from many cabbage diseases, it has its share of aphids, root maggots, and green worms eating the foliage and flower heads.

BRUSSELS SPROUTS (BRASSICA OLERACEA GEMMIFERA)

What is the best control for worms and aphids on Brussels sprouts?   Rotenone dust or carbaryl is allowed for worms on Brussels sprouts and will keep the aphids down to some extent. *Bacillus thuringiensis* is excellent for cabbage worms. Or they can be sprayed or dusted with malathion. (See also Cabbage.)

CABBAGE (BRASSICA OLERACEA CAPITATA)

Is there any way to prevent white maggots from attacking the roots of cabbage plants? (Wisconsin.)   When a young cabbage wilts and, upon being pulled up, discloses white maggots working on the underground stem and roots, it is too late for control. There are several ways of preventing maggot injury. Apply diazinon dust or spray to plant bases when the plants are set out.

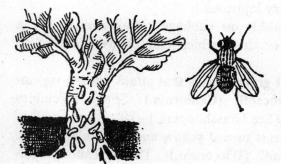

The cabbage root maggot's eggs are laid on stems, near ground level, in early spring.

The cabbage worm is green. The adult is a white or yellow butterfly, a familiar visitor to the summer vegetable garden.

How are tar-paper disks, for control of root maggots, applied? Cut a 4-inch square or circle; make a hole in the center with a spike, and make a cut from the outer edge to the hole, so you can get the paper around the stem. Work gently, so as not to bruise the young seedling. The disk should stay flat on the ground and fit snugly around the stem.

What is the calomel treatment for seedlings? This treatment has been replaced by the more effective diazinon dust or spray treatment to plant bases.

What is the best way to control the black flea beetle on small cabbage plants? (Virginia.) These small but very active beetles do considerable damage to young plants, often riddling the leaves with tiny shot holes. Spray with carbaryl.

Is there more than one type of cabbage worm? There are 3. The true cabbage worm, a green caterpillar of the common white or yellow butterfly; the cabbage looper, a striped pale-green worm that moves like an inchworm and changes into a brownish-gray moth; and a small, greenish caterpillar that is the larva of the diamondback moth. All these are controlled in the same way. Spray with rotenone, carbaryl, or *Bacillus thuringiensis*.

Is lump lime good to destroy cabbage worms and those little dark worms that hold themselves in ring shape? (Maine.) Lime has been used to control cabbage clubroot, if your soil is acid, but would have no effect on cabbage worms. For clubroot, use Terrachlor, 6 tablespoons per gallon of water, 1 cupful in a hole when planting. The little dark worms are millipedes and not very injurious.

How can I control blue aphids on cabbage? (California.) By a malathion or diazinon spray, or dust, which can be used almost to harvest time.

What treatment is best to kill grasshoppers that attack garden vegetables such as cabbage and broccoli? (California.) Spray vegetables with carbaryl or methoxychlor. (See Grasshoppers.)

The leaves of my cabbage plants turned yellow and the cabbage died. Is anything wrong with the soil? (Wisconsin.) This is cabbage yellows, caused by a soil fungus—a species of fusarium—very common in your state. Either plant in a new location or grow varieties marked "yellows-resistant" in your seed catalog.

In order to grow cabbage, do I have to buy yellows-resistant seed? (New York.) Advisable, but it may not be necessary in New York. The disease is not so prevalent as in the Midwest, and if you have no previous record of cabbages dying or yellows on your soil, you need not worry much.

For years I have had trouble with cabbage plants. Just before they are ready to head up, the leaves turn yellow and drop off. The plant dies. There is no evidence of insect pests. (Delaware.) Your soil is apparently well inoculated with the "yellows" or fusarium wilt fungus. Plant resistant varieties.

What causes cabbages to rot off the stalk? (Iowa.) Black rot or blight, a bacterial disease, is one cause. The plants are stunted; leaves turn yellow to brown, shrivel and drop off; or the head may decay and fall off in a slimy mass. The vascular ring in the stem and the leaf veins are black. Use clean seed or disinfect with hot water (see Seed Treatment); plant in disease-free soil; remove diseased plants; clean up all cabbage refuse.

What causes the tops of the cabbage leaves to turn black, sometimes running through the entire head? (Wisconsin.) Either the black rot just discussed or a fungus disease called blackleg. There are dark areas with black dots on stems and leaves. If the stem is girdled near the ground line, the plants wilt and die. Use cabbage seed grown near Puget Sound, where the disease is rare, or treat with hot water. Practice sanitary measures given above and a 4-year rotation.

What is the best remedy for preventing clubroot in cabbage and cauliflower? (Michigan.) Clubroot is the name of a disease that causes grossly enlarged and malformed roots and stunted, sickly plants. If the disease has been present previously, treat the soil with fresh hydrated lime, 10 pounds to 100 square feet, and rake it in shortly before planting; or try a soil treatment with PCNB (Terrachlor) when planting. Use 6 tablespoons per gallon of water and put in 1 cupful per hole when transplanting.

What is the cure for cabbage wilt—curled tips of leaves, whitish color? (California.) This may be powdery mildew, with the fungus growing over the leaves and causing the white color. If so, you can dust with sulfur. If it is a chlorosis (an actual loss of color in the leaf tissue), then perhaps some chemical is lacking for good nutrition or your soil is too alkaline.

CARROT (DAUCUS CAROTA SATIVUS)

We have trouble with maggots in the carrots. Can you give any help in controlling this pest? (Washington.) In western Washington plant early carrots so that they can be harvested by July 15, and in small blocks so they can be screened and the rust fly prevented from laying her eggs. Do not plant late carrots before June 1. Use diazinon in the seed furrow.

Please advise me about the small worms that make burrows in carrots. Are they wireworms? (Oregon.) Probably these are the maggots of the carrot rust fly discussed in the previous question. Control measures for Washington should also apply for Oregon.

What grub or bug eats tunnels through the sides of carrots? (Iowa.) In Iowa, the carrot grub, which looks like the common white grub and eats pieces out of the carrots, and the rust-fly maggots, which make rust-colored tunnels, are the chief insect pests. Control both pests by dusting the ground along the row, as soon as the seed is planted, with diazinon. Rotating is helpful.

Can carrot worms be avoided by harvesting early or by adding lime to the soil? (Michigan.) By planting in June, the first brood of the rust fly can be avoided, and harvesting can be done before the second brood. Lime is sometimes recommended to drive away the carrot beetle but should not be used unless your soil requires it.

What are the insects that look like blue lice and infest my carrot roots? How can I get rid of them? (New York.) These are root aphids (plant lice); they look bluish because of a powdery coating. If the infestation is bad enough to require control, pour malathion, 1 tablespoon per gallon of water, around the stems after loosening the soil.

How do I keep ants from putting plant lice on carrot roots? (New York.) Find the nest if you can and treat with an insecticide. (See Ants.)

How can I keep my carrot crop from rotting in the garden? (Arizona.) Your carrots either have southern blight (see Crown Rot) or else bacterial soft rot, a bacterial disease that more often appears in storage, but occasionally in the garden. The fungi and bacteria are in the soil, so you must plant in a new location or treat the soil. (See Soil Sterilization.)

Is there a foliage disease of carrots? (New Jersey.) There is a leaf blight that produces spots on the leaves, after which they turn brown and die, but it is not ordinarily serious enough in the home garden to require more than cleaning up old tops. If necessary, spray with captan.

CAULIFLOWER (BRASSICA OLERACEA BOTRYTIS)

How are cauliflower troubles controlled?   Treat the seed and practice the same sanitary measures as recommended for cabbage. Occasionally there is a bacterial or fungus spot on the heads; for this there is no practical control.

CELERY (APIUM GRAVEOLENS DULCE)

Is blight on celery in the seed or the soil? (Indiana.)   Both. There are 3 blights: early and late blight caused by fungi, and a bacterial blight. The organisms are carried over in celery refuse in the garden and on the seed. Practice a 3-year rotation and either use seed that is 2 years old or treat it with hot water at 118° F. for 30 minutes. Then dry and dust with thiram.

How can celery blight be prevented? (Pennsylvania.)   Spray with maneb, benomyl, or chlorothalonil at weekly intervals in the seed bed; and at 7- to 10-day intervals after setting out in the garden. Blight is worse in a wet season and is spread by working with plants when they are wet.

Our celery is injured by slugs; is there any remedy? (Pennsylvania.)   Clean up hiding places such as loose boards and old plant debris; sprinkle lime on the ground. (See Slugs and Snails.) Slug bait is not registered for use on celery.

How can I get rid of beetlelike bugs in celery plants? (Pennsylvania.)   These are tarnished plant bugs and very difficult to get rid of. Clean up weeds and try pyrethrum or malathion dusts or sprays.

COLLARDS (BRASSICA OLERACEA)

How can one overcome insects on collards? (Alabama.)   See Cabbage.

CORN (ZEA MAYS)

How can one tell when corn has been stung by the corn borer moth? (New York.)   The yellow-brown moth of the European corn borer lays its eggs in groups of 20 or more on the underside of the leaves, and the larvae, tiny, flesh-colored borers, tunnel their way into the stalk, leaf stems, and ears. Their presence is shown by tassels bending over or broken, fine sawdustlike castings on the leaves, and small holes in the stalks, often with protruding borings.

When should corn be planted to avoid the borer? (Michigan.) There are 2 broods of the European corn borer. Extra-early corn will be injured by the first, and very late corn will be attacked by the second brood. Corn planted between the middle of May and the first of June will mature chiefly between the broods and thus escape much injury.

What is the latest on the control of corn borer? (Vermont.) That the treatments for the borer must be related to growth stages of the corn. Give the first dusting when tassels can be seen on half the plants by looking down into the tops. Dust into the tassel whorl and give two more treatments at 5-day intervals, using carbaryl or diazinon. Ryania dust is also used, but it is more expensive.

How else can one fight the borer? The corn borer feeds on more than 200 kinds of plants and winters, in the larval stage, in old herbaceous stems. It is extremely important to clean up in the fall, not only old cornstalks and stubble, but dahlia and gladiolus tops, and to clean up weeds, especially pigweed and smartweed.

Is the common stalk borer injurious to corn? Yes, especially at the edge of the corn patch near weeds or where wasteland has been recently turned into a garden. The young caterpillars are brown, white-striped, turning grayish as they increase in size. The moths lay their eggs in September on giant ragweed and many other weeds. Cleaning up is the best control measure.

Can worms in sweet corn be avoided? (Washington.) The corn-ear worm is more widely distributed than the corn borer, and the caterpillars are large, brown to green, and striped. The moths lay their eggs

The corn-ear worm is a large, brown-to-green worm with distinct stripes.

chiefly on the corn silk, and the young larvae feed on that and the tip of the ear. Treat as for the corn borer. Repeat 3 to 4 times at 2-day intervals.

Can anything be done about Japanese beetles on sweet corn? (New Jersey.) They congregate on the silk, so the ear-worm applications will also control them.

How can squirrels be kept from eating corn? (Indiana.) Squirrels, and occasionally raccoons, are very destructive pests of corn, and there is little to be done except shoot them, which is not permitted in most localities. In my garden, the corn was planted in a square block. The squirrels started to eat on the outside row, and when this was left to them they ignored the rest of the corn patch.

How can I eliminate smut from sweet corn? (New York.) The only control measure is to cut off the large smut boil—from ear, tassel, or stalk—before it opens to discharge the black spores that will infect other corn. Avoid the use of manure likely to be infected, and burn up stalks after harvest. Spraying is not helpful and there are no resistant varieties.

Is there any other important corn disease? (New Jersey.) Bacterial, or Stewart's, wilt may be serious after a mild winter. There are discolored streaks in the leaves, and young plants wilt and die. The bacteria are spread by corn flea beetles. Many of the new hybrid varieties are resistant to this disease.

CUCUMBER (CUCUMIS SATIVUS)

What measures can be taken against striped cucumber beetles? They seem almost impossible to destroy. (Illinois.) They are hard to control, but there are many ways to fight these green, black-striped beetles: (1) Remove weed hosts, especially Chinese-lantern plants. (2) Protect young seedlings with Hotkaps or cheesecloth tents. (3) Plant extra seeds in the hills and discard the most injured seedlings. (4) As soon as the ground cracks over the seedlings, start dusting with rotenone, carbaryl, or methoxychlor. Repeat treatments as often as needed to keep plants covered with dust.

What causes bugs in the roots of cucumber plants? (Pennsylvania.) The larva of the spotted cucumber beetle works on the roots of many plants and is known as the southern corn rootworm. The beetle, green with 12 black spots, is controlled like the striped cucumber beetle. The spotted beetle also attacks many ornamental plants, where it is known as diabrotica beetle. "Bugs" may also be root aphids (see under Aphids).

A worm eats our pickle cucumbers. Is there a remedy? (Illinois.) The white or green pickle worm is especially destructive in southern states but is occasionally found as far north as Illinois. It bores into the ripening fruits. The dusts listed for the striped cucumber beetle should be helpful. Carbaryl will control but may injure cucumbers. Destroy all old vines.

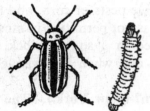

Striped cucumber beetle attacks cucumbers, melons, and squash. It is green with black stripes. The larvae attack roots.

What is the control for the large, flat, gray beetle that attacks cucumber, pumpkin, squash, and melon vines? I have used moth balls in the hills with the seed and it seemed to work. Was it by accident? (Arkansas.) Probably, although the moth balls might have some repellent effect on the squash bug. (See Squash for more details.)

How can I rid cucumber vines of lice? (Texas.) The melon aphid is very destructive to all cucurbits, causing leaves to curl, wilt, and brown; it attacks many other plants, including lilies, to which it carries mosaic. Spray or dust with malathion, being careful to get underneath the leaves.

How are whiteflies on cucumbers killed? (New York.) The treatments for aphids (see the previous question) should subdue them. They are often abundant on cucurbits, but of minor importance.

What pest or disease causes cucumber to wither, runner by runner, until the plant dies and semimature fruit shrivels up? (New York.) It is either the squash vine borer (see Squash) or wilt. The latter is a bacterial disease, very prevalent, disseminated by spotted and striped cucumber beetles, which carry the bacteria in their digestive tracts during the winter and deposit them in droppings on the leaves as they feed. The young vines can be sprayed or dusted to control the cucumber beetles. Malathion or methoxychlor will control the squash vine borer.

My pickles show mosaic. What can I do about that? (Michigan.) Control the weeds, such as burweed, milkweed, catnip, pokeberry, and groundcherry, which harbor the virus; control the melon aphids and cucumber beetles, which carry the virus from the weeds to the cucumbers. Try resistant varieties. Purchase treated seed.

My cucumber leaves look rusty and yellow. What causes this? (Mas-

sachusetts.)   Bacteria produce angular leaf spots and fungi, brownish circles. Spray foliage with captan or maneb, especially in the latter part of the season. Clean up and burn all old vines.

EGGPLANT (SOLANUM MELONGENA ESCULENTUM)

How can one get an eggplant that does not die of wilt? (Alabama.)   You have to set healthy plants grown from clean seed in soil that has not grown eggplant for 4 years. Eggplant wilt—also called foot rot, blight, leafspot, and wilt from its various symptoms—is so severe in the South that clean seed is rarely found. Soak in hot water, 122° F. for 5 minutes; then rinse in running water and dry thoroughly. Tie the seed in a cheesecloth bag before immersion. After drying, treat the seed with Arasan or captan. (See Seed Treatment.) To prevent fruit rot, use mancozeb or zineb every 7 to 10 days as the fruit ripens.

What makes eggplants wilt? (New Jersey.)   In New Jersey, it is probably verticillium, which stunts the plants and turns the leaves yellow. The plant wilts in the heat of the day and the vessels are dark if the stem is cut. Use a long rotation that does not include tomatoes, potatoes, or raspberries. The fungus can live in the soil a long time. Or try soil sterilization with Vapam.

LETTUCE (LACTUCA SATIVA)

Why did my head lettuce rot after it was transplanted from the greenhouse? It was covered with a grayish fuzz. (New York.)   This was botrytis blight, or gray mold disease, which infects seedlings if they are kept too wet in the greenhouse and shows up as bottom rot. Remove the plants carefully with the surrounding soil and soak the soil with a captan solution mixed according to container recommendations. Sterilize the soil used for flats in a greenhouse or cold frame. Plants can be sprayed with Botran. A similar rot, but starting from the top down, is called "drop," and is controlled in the same way.

MELON (CUCUMIS MELO)

How do you exterminate the small yellow chewing insect with black stripes known as the cantaloupe bug? (Texas.)   The striped cucumber beetle frequently congregates on melon fruit. (See Cucumber for control.)

What insect kills my cantaloupes almost overnight? It is the same

color as the leaves, small and egg-shaped, and the leaves scald and brown. (Missouri.) The melon aphid almost fits your description. (See Cucumber for control.)

Can root rot on melon vines be prevented? (Vermont.) Fusarium wilt, a soil fungus, causes the plants to become stunted and yellowed. Long rotations reduce the amount of wilt. No fungicide is registered.

My muskmelons did well up to ripening, then wilted and died. Why? (Michigan.) Perhaps the fusarium wilt just discussed; or cucumber wilt (see Cucumber); or the squash vine borer (see Squash).

ONION (ALLIUM CEPA)

Is there a practical method (for a small garden) to keep onions raised from seed free from the onion maggot? (New York.) Treat the soil at planting with diazinon or malathion. Use shallow planting.

What causes onions to rot? Seemingly a worm or bug bores through the stalk. (Wisconsin.) This is the onion maggot discussed above. When damaged onions are put in storage, they decay and cause the surrounding bulbs to rot.

I pulled and stored my onions and found that the majority are going bad. Why? (Pennsylvania.) Fungi following after maggot injury are responsible. Onions should be stored only where there is free air circulation, either in a string bag or else with the tops left on and braided into chains to hang up on the wall. The latter method is easy and very successful, and you can always cut off just the size onion you want without rummaging through a bag.

What is the best means of control for onion thrips? (Connecticut.) It is very difficult to control this small sucking insect, which rasps the leaves and turns them whitish. Early planting is said to be helpful, for most thrips are present after July 1. Spray weekly with diazinon or malathion.

Can cutworms be prevented from injuring young growing onions? (New York.) Paper collars are impractical, so use diazinon if the cutworms are too numerous to destroy by hand-picking. (See Cutworms.) The maggot treatment will also take care of cutworms.

What is the black powdery mass on leaves and bulbs? Onion smut, a fungus disease. The easiest way to avoid it is to grow onions from sets, because they can be infected only in the young, seedling stage. In growing from seed, start in a clean, new seed bed and transplant, or else treat seed with Arasan or captan before planting.

PEA (PISUM SATIVUM)

How are damping off and root rots on peas prevented? (Connecticut.) Early planting helps get peas started before the root-rot fungi can get in their work, but treating with captan helps prevent root rot as well as damping off. Avoid heavy, low, and poorly drained soils. Use a 3- to 5-year rotation if possible.

How can I control the pale-green plant lice that suck the sap from the vines? The pea aphid is very difficult to control, but malathion or diazinon spray or dust is helpful.

How can moles be prevented from destroying green peas? I have read that moles eat only worms. If so, what becomes of the pea seed? (Washington.) Perhaps the seeds are consumed by mice that use the mole tunnels.

PEPPER (CAPSICUM ANNUUM)

What should be used to kill lice on pepper plants? (Nebraska.) Malathion or diazinon should be safe if the fruits are carefully washed; but pyrethrum or rotenone can be substituted as nonpoisonous materials. In general, peppers have the same pests as potatoes, and control measures are the same.

Why do my peppers turn brown and fall off as soon as they are formed? (Connecticut.) This is probably due to unfavorable weather, which sometimes causes not only blossom and fruit drop of many plants, but a blossom-end rot of the fruits after they were formed. (See Squash; Tomato.)

POTATO (SOLANUM TUBEROSUM)

How do I prevent potato leaves from curling and turning brown, and the vine from dying before the tubers are full grown? (New York.) This is late blight, the most destructive disease of potatoes. Plant only "certified" tubers, of a blight-resistant variety, and start spraying with maneb or chlorothalonil when the plants are 6 inches high; repeat every 10 to 14 days until the plants stop growing.

How can the home gardener, with no power-spray equipment, prevent late potato blight? (Massachusetts.) Spraying is preferable, and can be done with a 3-gallon compressed-air sprayer, but dusting can be substituted, using chlorothalonil or maneb dust.

When should blighted potatoes be dug? (Massachusetts.) If the vines are severely infected, dig as early as possible before the fungus gets down to rot the tubers.

Is there any treatment of the soil to prevent potato rot? (Connecticut.) No, it would not pay or help much to chemically treat soil for potatoes, and the best seed treatment is to make sure they are sound when cut for planting. The practice of hilling potatoes is in a sense a helpful treatment because it interposes more of a barrier between the fungus spores developing on the leaves and the tubers below.

What is the cause of scab on potatoes? (Vermont.) A common soil organism closely related to bacteria, *Actinomyces scabies*. It is unable to grow in an acid soil, but as the soil becomes increasingly alkaline, scab injury increases, varying from slight russeting to greatly roughened scabby areas on the tubers.

What can be done for potatoes that get rough, scabby hides? We put plenty of cow manure on. Do we use it too green, or too much, or too often, or is it the weather? We used to have lovely potatoes. (Kansas.) You use it too much and too often for soil infected with scab organism. Manure has an alkaline effect, like lime and wood ashes, and the more alkaline the soil, the better *Actinomyces* likes it. Resistant varieties are available.

What can be done with soil that produces scabby potatoes? (New York.) Get your pH (soil acidity) down to around 5.4. Adding sulfur will increase acidity. The amount needed varies with the original pH, but might run around 10 pounds per 1,000 square feet or 300 to 400 pounds per acre.

The government puts out some kind of solution for potato seed. What is it? (New York.) State Experiment Stations or county agents may arrange cooperative seed treatments for farmers but it is doubtful if the government gives out any such material. To control scab and rhizoctonia, uncut potatoes may be dipped in nabam solution (1 pint in 30 gallons of water) just before planting. The backyard gardener would do better to make sure he is using clean, sound potatoes for seed and omit the treatment.

How are potato bugs controlled? (New York.) Spray or dust foliage with methoxychlor or carbaryl to take care of these large orange-yellow, black-striped beetles and their enormous humpbacked, reddish larvae. This is the famous Colorado potato beetle, one of the pests to become resistant to DDT in the heyday of that insecticide.

How do you control the old-fashioned black potato bug?

The potato bug is a double menace as both black-striped adults and fat, copper larvae feed on leaves.

(Ohio.) Blister beetles are hard to kill. Hand-picking is excellent. The potato beetle treatments should also work.

How shall I exterminate long-bodied gray or brown beetles that clean out a potato patch in one night? (Nebraska.) These, too, are blister beetles. They may be plain black, or striped, or margined, or brown or gray, but, in any color, they have voracious appetites. (See the previous question; also, Blister Beetles.)

We were warned that if we planted potatoes in soil where nothing had recently been grown they would be wormy. Why? (Ohio.) White grubs and wireworms are usually prevalent in sod land, and when this land is prepared for a garden, the worms remain until their life cycle is completed. Potatoes planted in newly broken sod land are very apt to have brown tunnels going through the tubers. If new land must be used, treat soil with diazinon. (See Wireworms.)

Last year my potatoes were scabby from wireworms. How can I raise clean potatoes in the same ground another season? (Ohio.) After one year of cultivation you may have fewer wireworms, but it would be safer to treat the soil before planting potatoes again.

Why do the edges of potato leaves get brown before the late blight season? (New Jersey.) This is a condition called hopperburn, due to the sucking of many leafhoppers. Carbaryl will control them.

What about virus diseases of potato? (New Jersey.) There are a great many, and the names describe the symptoms. Some of these are "yellow dwarf," "leaf roll," "mosaic," and "spindle tuber." Plant certified seed, or resistant varieties, and destroy any plant that seems to be infected. Control the aphids to prevent the spread of the disease.

Some of our potatoes had a layerlike black moss inside them. What caused it? (Virginia.) There are many causes of tuber discoloration: late blight and other fungus diseases, some bacterial and virus diseases, and a physiological disease called black heart. Your trouble may be the latter, and it comes from too great heat and lack of oxygen. If the potatoes stay out in bright sun after being dug, or if the storage place gets too hot, black heart may develop.

PUMPKIN (CUCURBITA PEPO)

How can cucumber beetles on pumpkins be controlled successfully? (Illinois.) Any of the treatments discussed under cucumber should be satisfactory on pumpkin.

How can the pumpkin vine borer be kept from entering vines as they are beginning to set fruit? (West Virginia.) For the control of the squash vine borer, and also squash bugs on pumpkin, see Squash.

RADISH (RAPHANUS SATIVUS)

What control is there for the light-green worm, like a caterpillar, that eats the leaves of radishes? (New Jersey.) This is probably the larva of the diamondback moth. (See Cabbage for control.)

Is it safe to eat radishes grown in soil treated with diazinon to eliminate wormy root crops? (Pennsylvania.) There should be no danger if the label directions for treatment were followed.

Why are my radishes small with a black spot up the middle? There is a disease called black rot of radish, caused by a fungus, but there is not much known in the line of control. Try a different location and the 'Red Globe' type of radish variety.

RHUBARB (RHEUM RHABARBARUM)

Why does rhubarb rot? (Virginia.) Phytopthora foot, or crown rot, causes sunken spots at the base of the leafstalks and a rot and wilting that progress from stalk to stalk until the whole plant dies. Dig out and burn diseased plants, being careful not to scatter infected soil. Disinfect the location with 1 to 50 formaldehyde. Plant only healthy roots.

What are the insects that bore holes in rhubarb stalks? (Pennsylvania.) Rhubarb curculios. Pick them off, because sprays do not seem to control them. They are yellow-snout beetles, which puncture stems and cause black spots. Destroy dockweed near the rhubarb.

SQUASH (CUCURBITA)

Is there any treatment for 'Hubbard' squash and the worms that burrow inside the stem? The squash vine borer is a white grub or caterpillar that works inside the vine, causing wilting beyond the point of attack, which is indicated by yellow excrement outside. The adult is a clear-wing moth. Spray or dust plant bases and stems with methoxychlor or malathion in late June and weekly in July.

Is there any way of exterminating the rather hard-shelled sucking insect, with a repugnant odor, which attacks squash plants first, then others? (Texas.) This is the squash bug, sometimes called stink bug, which is distributed all over the United States. The adults are brownish black, ⅔ inch long; they hide under the leaves and suck the sap, causing the vines to wilt. They attack all vine crops, but prefer squash. They can be killed with malathion, methoxychlor, or carbaryl sprays or dusts. Hand-pick the adults or trap them under boards. Destroy all old vines in the fall.

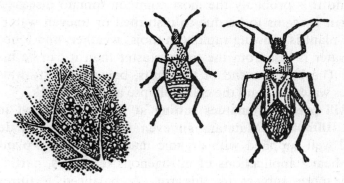

The squash bug is a large, lively rusty-black beetle, destructive at all stages, hatching from orange eggs on the undersides of leaves. It attacks squash and pumpkins.

What causes summer squash buds to drop off? (Connecticut.) Chiefly unfavorable weather conditions. However, the male and female flowers are separate on squash plants, and the male flowers, of course, drop off without setting fruit.

Why can't I raise crookneck squash? Something attacks the roots and prevents the fruits from maturing. (Michigan.) It may be a water relation rather than an organism at the roots. Blossom-end rot is common in squash, causing the small squash to wither at the blossom end, which is followed by secondary rot fungi. This disease is thought to be due to an insufficient or uneven water supply.

What caused about 8 out of 10 straight-necked squash to rot shortly after setting? (Connecticut.) The weather, and resultant dry soil, caused this blossom-end rot. (See the previous question.)

SWISS CHARD (BETA VULGARIS CICLA)

How can I control leafminers on Swiss chard and beet foliage? Spray with malathion every 7 days but wait 7 days before harvesting.

TOMATO (LYCOPERSICON LYCOPERSICUM)

What is the cause of blossom-end rot, which looks more like a fungus disease than a rot? It covers from ¼ to ½ of the fruit and is gray-black and quite firm. (Oregon.) Blossom-end rot does look like a fungus disease, and it is probably the most common tomato disease across the country, but it seems to be due to disturbed or uneven water relations. When the plant is growing rapidly in moist weather, and a hot dry spell follows, water is lost from the tissues faster than it can be taken up by the roots. The blossom end of the fruits, being farthest away from the roots, loses water first and the cells collapse and turn black.

What will prevent tomatoes rotting at the blossom end just before ripening? (Illinois.) Maintain an even water supply. A deeply prepared soil well supplied with organic matter helps; but plants that receive too heavy applications of nitrogenous fertilizers, particularly manure, are more subject to this rot. A balanced fertilizer high in superphosphate and available calcium decreases susceptibility. Calcium nitrate is good to use as the source of nitrogen. Although blossom-end rot usually shows up in periods of drought, it may appear when the soil has received so much rainfall that the small roots are killed for lack of aeration. Spraying with calcium chloride (1 tablespoon in a gallon of water) will help prevent blossom-end rot.

What causes rot inside perfectly good-looking tomatoes? (Connecticut.) Probably the same type of weather and soil conditions that cause the blossom-end rot discussed above.

Is tomato wilt carried on the seed or does it remain in the soil? (Mississippi.) Both. Primarily a soil organism, the wilt fungus may be carried on the seed.

What is the cause of blight on tomatoes that begins at the bottom of the plant and works up? The leaves curl; the fruit develops but does not come to completion; and the plant dies slowly. (Pennsylvania.) This is probably fusarium wilt, caused by a fungus that lives in the soil. At first, the leaves roll up and wilt in the middle of the day; later there is a permanent wilting, yellow leaves, and death.

If my tomato plants all succumbed to the wilt in a damp season last year, will they do so again this year when planted on the same ground? (Connecticut.) If you plant susceptible varieties, they are very likely to, for the fungus lives several years in the soil. Rotation or soil sterilization is necessary; also, cleaning up all tomato refuse.

My tomatoes wither and stop bearing about the first of August. What are wilt-resistant varieties? (Tennessee.) 'Better Boy', 'Heinz 1350', 'Campbell 1329', 'Supersonic', 'Roma', 'Louisiana Gulf State', 'Minalucie', 'Jet Star', and 'Springset' are reasonably resistant to fusarium wilt. Consult seed catalogs for others.

What are the causes and cure for the mosaic disease of tomatoes? (Pennsylvania.) The cause of mottled dark- and light-green misshapen leaves is a virus. The only cure is prevention: destroying diseased plants as soon as noticed, and also weed hosts, and controlling insect carriers.

What are the weed hosts of mosaic? Ground-cherry, horsenettle, jimsonweed, and nightshade are the most important. Tomatoes should also be grown as far away as possible from tobacco, petunias, and potatoes, for the same virus may be present in these plants.

Can tobacco dust or nicotine spray be used safely on tomato plants? I think I read somewhere that a virus disease results. (New Jersey.) The tomato mosaic virus is carried in ground tobacco, so that one should not smoke while working with tomatoes or use tobacco dust. However, nicotine sulfate used as a spray apparently does not carry the infective principle, and nicotine dust made from nicotine sulfate mixed with lime would also be safe. The gardener can carry the virus from plant to plant on his hands, which should be washed frequently with soapy water while working with tomatoes.

What can we do to overcome brown specks on our tomatoes? Will lime overcome this? (New Hampshire.) Brown spots on the leaves and sunken black spots on the stems and fruit may be due to early blight caused by a fungus (Alternaria). Look for resistant varieties in catalogs. It is better to use sprays without lime, because this causes blossoms to drop off (lime in the soil is a perfectly good recommendation). Spray weekly or biweekly with maneb, captan, zineb, or chlorothalonil. Use clean seed and practice crop rotation. Do not apply maneb or zineb later than 5 days before harvest.

What causes anthracnose on tomatoes? What is the remedy? (Indiana.) Anthracnose is a fruit spot rather common in the central states. The spots are dark, sunken, with concentric markings, and there are pinkish spore pustules in the center. The fungus lives in the soil, so that a 4-year rotation should be practiced. Avoid poorly drained soil and fertilize properly. Pick all ripe fruit as soon as possible. Spraying with maneb, zineb, captan, benomyl, or chlorothalonil is effective.

My tomatoes had an earthy flavor and were mushy. Was it the variety or the soil conditions? August was a wet month. (New York.) The rainy weather may have caused growth cracks in which one of the mold fungi grew to produce the mushiness and the flavor, which should not be charged against the variety. Staked tomatoes suffer less in a wet season. Pick tomatoes frequently, and remove and destroy all soft and rotting fruit.

What is the best formula to prevent rust on tomatoes in southern Florida? The "rust" is probably sunscald; there is no true rust common on tomatoes. Keep as much foliage as possible on the plants, so that the fruits are not exposed to the sun in hot, dry weather. Verticillium and other wilts that cause loss of lower foliage increase sunscald. A very light covering of straw over fruit clusters may reduce this disease.

Are there many diseases that attack tomatoes? There are many leaf and fruit spots, wilts, and blights; southern states have to contend with nematode root knot and southern blight, while virus diseases, curly-top, and spotted wilt are prevalent in the Northwest. Consult your Cooperative Extension Service if you need help. Despite diseases, tomatoes are an easy and prolific crop for the home gardener.

What is the easiest way to circumvent cutworms on tomatoes? A paper collar put around each seedling after it is transplanted. (See Cutworms.) Pouring ½ cup of diazinon spray mixture around each plant when transplanting is very effective.

What causes little holes in the leaves of tomato seedlings? (New Jersey.) Flea beetles. They may riddle the foliage if not controlled and seriously injure the young plants. Dust with rotenone dust or spray or dust with carbaryl. (See Flea Beetles.)

How can I get rid of the huge green caterpillars on tomatoes? (New York.) The large tomato hornworm is best controlled by picking off by hand. Or dust or spray with *Bacillus* or carbaryl. If the caterpillar is in the fruits, it is the corn-ear worm, also called tomato fruitworm. Destroy infested fruits as soon as discovered. The same treatment as for the hornworm will do, or use methoxychlor.

What is the pest on tomato leaves in August that looks like salt on the leaves and later turns into tiny flies? (Wyoming.) Your grains of salt are the nymphs of whiteflies, common on tomatoes in late summer,

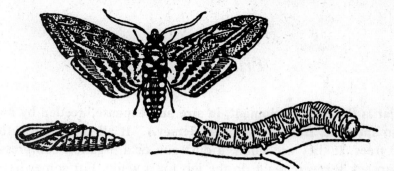

The tomato hornworm is a rather fierce-looking, large, and nervous green worm. It attacks tomato foliage and sometimes eggplants, peppers, and potatoes.

but not particularly injurious. Malathion or diazinon sprays or pyrethrum or rotenone dusts may control them. (See Whiteflies.) These insecticides kill only adults, so treat at 4-day intervals until eliminated.

How can I get rid of the yellow bug on tomato plants that looks like a ladybug? (New York.) The Mexican bean beetle occasionally wanders over to tomato plants but ordinarily does not require treatment there. (See Beans.)

A green bug, with shield-shape marking, stings and ruins our tomatoes. Is there a remedy? (Texas.) This is the green stink bug, a close relative to the squash bug. The nymphs are greenish with black markings and the adults are green or brown; they suck the sap of tomatoes, peas, beans, and other plants. Dust or spray with malathion or carbaryl when the young bugs first appear and repeat as needed. Also hand-pick.

Is there a way to get rid of the worm that enters the stalks of tomatoes in bloom so that the plant dies or falls over? (Missouri.) Getting rid of the weeds in the vicinity is the best and practically only way of getting rid of the common stalk borer. (See Borers.)

TURNIP (BRASSICA RAPA RAPIFERA)

What can be done about maggots in turnips? See Cabbage.

Why do yellow turnips rot in the ground? (New York.) Sometimes bacterial soft rot follows along with the maggots, especially in a wet season and if the plants are crowded together in the row. Thin your turnips early and space widely. See that the rows are far enough apart. Remove all diseased turnips immediately. Practice crop rotation.

Fruits—General

What is the least equipment, in size and expense, needed by an amateur to spray 12 fruit trees? (New Jersey.)   It all depends on the size of the trees. If they are small, a dust gun or a 3-gallon compressed-air or knapsack sprayer might do the job for a while. For somewhat larger trees, you might manage with a slide (trombone) sprayer or a hose-end gun or a bucket or barrel pump on wheels. For 12 mature trees, you would need some sort of power sprayer.

For backyard fruit trees, what sprayings are really necessary? (Mississippi.)   That depends on the backyard, but ordinarily several sprays including a calyx spray, when most of the petals have fallen, and a foliage spray 10 days to 2 weeks later are most indispensable. (See also discussions under the different fruit hosts.)

When should fruit trees be sprayed, just before or after the bloom opens? (Mississippi.)   It depends on the fruit and the pests you want to control. In general, sprays are not applied when fruits are in full bloom for fear of preventing pollination. The farmer usually applies

The 3-gallon compressed-air sprayer, knapsack type, is convenient for spraying small fruit trees.

what is called a "pink" spray on apples just before blooms open; but the amateur can often wait until it's time for the calyx spray, when most of the petals have fallen.

What is the best simple spray for fruit trees? (Michigan.) There is no one best spray for all fruit trees but various commercial fruit spray mixtures are available, to be used according to instructions on the label. If you want to make your own, one multipurpose spray consists of 2 tablespoons of captan, 50 per cent W.P. (Wettable Powder); 2 tbsp. malathion, 25 per cent W.P.; and 3 tbsp. methoxychlor, 50 per cent W.P., to 1 gallon of water. Kelthane is added to this mixture as necessary for mite control. In addition, peaches might have a dormant spray of ferbam or Bordeaux mixture and other fruits might have a delayed dormant (green tip) of oil. Ask your own county extension agent or State Experiment Station for a spray schedule suitable for home gardeners in your area.

What is advisable to use as a general spray for apple, cherry, and plum trees, and grapes? (Illinois.) The mixture given above would be a general spray for your fruit trees. For grapes, spray just before and just after bloom, repeat 10 days later, and again after 14 days. Your county extension agent or Agricultural Experiment Station can send you a circular on spraying fruits in Illinois.

When is the best time for dormant spray of fruit trees? What spray can be used? Can this spray be the same for apples, peaches, plums, and cherries? (New York.) The dormant spray is best applied after the buds have begun to swell but before they show green at the tip. Probably you could safely use a 1 to 9 dilution of lime-sulfur on all these fruits, or even an oil spray, but you will get much better results if the spray is directed at specific pests for each kind of fruit and timed for these. (See also the discussion below under different hosts.)

How and when should fruit trees too small to have fruit or blossoms be sprayed? Bulletins tell about pre-blossom sprays, etc., but with no older trees around, how are you to know when to spray? (New York.) Having no fruit, you do not have to use all the different sprays, for they are chiefly intended to provide sound fruit. If scale is present, put on a dormant spray; later you can spray the foliage to control cankerworms, Japanese beetles, aphids, etc., if these insects appear and are injurious.

Do you know what will kill rose chafers without killing fruit trees and bushes, which they attack so furiously in June that we get no fruit? (Michigan.) Your county Cooperative Extension Service or State Agricultural Experiment Station says that rose chafers attack in the vicinity of sandy quackgrass sod. You must be on the alert to spray as soon as they appear. Carbaryl sprays will help keep them in check.

What is the best method to deal with Japanese beetles in a young orchard? (D.C.)   Spray with carbaryl.

How can I get rid of lice on my fruit trees? (Minnesota.)   Add 2 tablespoons of malathion to a gallon of spray mixed up for other purposes. Malathion should be especially added to a delayed dormant spray to control aphids.

Mice or rabbits gnaw the bark of my young fruit trees. What shall I do? (New York.)   Mechanical protectors such as wood veneer, tar paper, cloth, or ¼-inch galvanized wire are most satisfactory in protecting young trees from injury. The wire is best. Keep it away from the trunk except at the top of the wrap. Protectors must be 20 inches higher than the winter snow line. For repellents, see Rabbits.

Young apple trees can be protected against injury from rabbits by tar-paper or hardware-cloth cylinders fastened around their trunks.

Is there any repellent I can put around young fruit trees to keep the deer and rabbits from eating the new leaves next spring?   Various repellents have been tried with success in some cases and no success in others. Contact your county extension agent or State Agricultural Experiment Station for regional help.

Specific Fruits and Their Pests

APPLE (MALUS)

How can I get 1 or 2 large apple trees effectively sprayed without spending more money than the fruit is worth? (Massachusetts.)   You cannot expect to get 1 or 2 fruit trees sprayed without its costing you much more than the fruit itself is worth. You have to balance the account by considering apples also as ornamentals and think of the fun you have picking your own fruit. The charge for several sprays must cover the time of 2 men, cost of materials, transportation of a special trip for only 1 or 2 trees, and the seasonal nature of the work. To save money, you must do the spraying yourself, which would not have much effect on a large tree, or else resign yourself to wormy apples. A surprising amount of pies and applesauce come from unsprayed apples. One unsprayed tree may provide 7 families one summer with all the applesauce they can set aside for winter. If trees are not sprayed, it is very important to clean up all dropped apples every week.

How many sprayings of apple trees are indispensable for reasonably satisfactory fruit in the home garden? When we have our trees sprayed 5 times, it is much cheaper to buy apples. (Ohio.) Five sprays are supposed to be the minimum for sound fruit: dormant, cluster bud, calyx, and first and second codling-moth sprays, but often the dormant spray may be omitted if there are no scale insects, and possibly one or two other sprays. The calyx spray, when 90 per cent of the petals have fallen, and the first codling-moth spray, 17 days after calyx, are probably most useful in providing reasonably clean fruits. Use a general-purpose spray.

About how many gallons of spray should be used to cover a 5-year-old apple tree and a 10-year-old tree—for dormant and full-leaf sprays? (New York.) A foliage spray for a 5-year-old apple requires 1 to 2 gallons; 10-year-old, 4 to 5 gallons; 25-year-old, 12 to 15 gallons. A dormant spray might take about half as much.

Can old apple trees that bear many infected apples ever grow sound fruit? (New York.) Yes, with a definite spraying program combined with rigid sanitary measures.

What is the easiest and best way to spray a few apple trees infested with codling moth? (Massachusetts.) There is no easy way, but in Massachusetts the calyx and second cover sprays are most important.

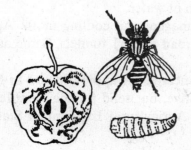

Apple maggot is a common pest. A small black and white fly is its parent.

What is a practical control of curculio on apples in the small garden? (Massachusetts.) Calyx and first cover sprays are most important in controlling curculio. (See the schedule below.) Gather and destroy dropped fruit every week.

My 'McIntosh' apples this year were covered with black spots, ⅛ to ¼ inch in diameter. The trees were sprayed. Can you identify it and suggest a remedy? It seems to be a local infection. (Massachusetts.) 'McIntosh' apples are very susceptible to scab, a fungus disease more prevalent following a wet spring. It is controlled by maneb, mancozeb, ferbam, captan, or wettable sulfur sprays, which must be carefully timed. (See the spray schedule below.)

A spray schedule for Massachusetts is as follows:

Delayed Dormant—Desirable spray if red mite or San Jose scale is present. Use dormant oil according to manufacturer's recommendations.

Pre-Pink—Desirable on 'McIntosh' and other susceptible varieties to control scab. Five level tablespoons of wettable sulfur or 2 tablespoons of captan and 3 tablespoons of methoxychlor to 1 gallon of water.

Pink Spray—Important for scab-susceptible varieties. Same mixture as pre-pink but add 1 tablespoon of malathion for aphids.

Calyx Spray—Important to control scab, codling moth, and curculio. When 90 per cent of the petals have fallen, apply 5 tablespoons of wettable sulfur or 2 tablespoons of captan and 3 tablespoons of methoxychlor to 1 gallon of water.

First Cover Spray after Calyx—Important to control curculio, leafhoppers, and scab. Apply when the temperature reaches 75° F., 5 or more days after calyx spray, using 5 tablespoons of wettable sulfur, 3 tablespoons of methoxychlor, with 1 tablespoon of malathion per gallon of water.

Second Cover Spray—Important to control codling moth, scab, and sometimes curculio. Apply 7 to 10 days after first cover spray, using same materials as first cover.

Third Cover—Important for apple maggot and scab. About July 10, when maggot flies appear, apply 5 tablespoons of wettable sulfur and 3 tablespoons of methoxychlor to 1 gallon of water.

Fourth Cover—Important for apple maggot and codling moth. Apply about July 25 to prevent maggot (railroad worm) tunnels. Same as for third cover.

What sprays should be used on an uncared-for apple orchard in New Jersey? About the same sprays as above, but send for the New Jersey Apple Spray Schedule from the State Agricultural Experiment Station, New Brunswick, N.J. 08903.

What causes brown spots through the interior of apples and what will prevent this? (New Jersey.) Probably the apple maggot, a slender white worm that feeds within the pulp and carries with it germs of a soft rot. The adult is a small black and white fly. The maggot winters in the soil as a small seedlike pupa; the flies come out in the summer, usually in July. The 2 sprays listed as third and fourth cover in the Massachusetts spray schedule above should work in New Jersey but check with the Experiment Station in New Brunswick or your county extension agent concerning the proper time to apply them. Cleaning up every rotten, dropped apple is very important in preventing more maggot trouble for another year.

How can I reclaim apple trees whose fruit is always badly infested with railroad worms or, I suppose, codling moth? (Vermont.) Railroad worms are apple maggots (see the preceding question) and quite different from codling moth larvae, which are larger, ¾ inch long, pinkish white with brown heads. The larvae winter in cocoons in the crotches and under the bark of trees. The moths emerge to lay their eggs in warm, dry weather about a week after the petals have fallen. The newly hatched caterpillars enter through the calyx cup of the fruit unless a poison spray is in place. Later-hatched caterpillars enter the fruit through the side. After 3 to 4 weeks inside the apple, the larva burrows through a mass of excrement to the surface and crawls down the branches for a suitable place for a cocoon. In addition to spraying, scraping the bark on the trunk up to 10 feet during the winter will be very helpful in reducing codling moth infestation. Chemically treated bands on scraped trees will collect larvae and prevent damage.

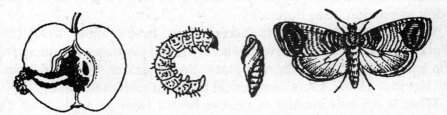

The codling moth is the parent of the worst apple pest. The larvae are pinkish-white caterpillars, ¾ inch long, and tunnel through apples and other fruits.

I spray my one apple tree 4 times as prescribed in all manuals, but recently the apples have brown spots throughout and are sort of knotty and misshapen. Why? (New York.) This is probably the result of apple maggot. You need a summer spray in addition, about June 25 to

July 1, which is a combined codling-moth cover spray and first apple-maggot spray. A second spray for maggots should go on about July 10 to 15. The misshapen, knotty apples are also occasionally the result of redbug punctures. Add malathion to the calyx spray if redbugs appear.

How do you prevent the apples from falling off the tree and getting wormy? (Illinois.) The 3 codling-moth sprays listed as minimum for Illinois are calyx, 17 days after calyx for the first brood, and 9 weeks after calyx for the second brood. Amounts of methoxychlor to use are given in the spray schedule for Massachusetts.

When and how often should I spray an old 'Baldwin' apple tree that bore very wormy apples this year? (New Hampshire.) For codling moth and railroad worms, the calyx, first cover, and third cover (about July 7) are most important. (See the Massachusetts schedule above for formulas.) Pick up all dropped apples and destroy them.

My apple trees are young but will soon need a spray. What can I use that will not be injurious to the bees? (Iowa.) Any insecticide may be injurious to bees; that is why spraying schedules call for treatment before the blossoms open or after almost all the petals have fallen.

I've had scale on an apple tree for more than a year. Will a dormant spray used next spring be effective to save this tree? (Illinois.) It should be. Unless there is an extreme infestation, scale insects will not kill a tree very quickly. Use a 3 per cent oil spray.

How can I raise apple trees without having them destroyed by borers? (New York.) Wrap the young trees when they are set out in Kraft crepe paper, starting several inches below the ground and going up to the lowest branch. Remove in August and rewrap in a few weeks for a second year. Wire wraps later will keep out rabbits and mice and check borer infestation. (See Borers.)

What should be done to borers deep in an apple tree? (New York.) Poke in a flexible wire where you see sawdust protruding from the bark and try to kill them in place. Borers nearer the outside can be cut out with a knife. Use a commercial fumigant such as Borerkil.

What is the best method to remove fungus from an apple tree? This runs from the ground to about 4 feet up. (New York.) If you mean a greenish moss on the trunk, that is of no consequence, but if you mean a collection of shelf fungi, they are indications of a heart rot inside the tree, which may or may not be worth saving by cavity treatment.

Why do red-cedar (Juniperus virginiana) evergreens harm apple trees? (Minnesota.) Because they form the alternate host for the cedar-apple rust. Spores are carried from the cedar galls in the spring to infect young apples and foliage, which will show rusty spots in midsummer. Maneb or ferbam sprays for apple scab will control rust. (See also Juniper.)

What is the cause and cure of blight on apple trees? (Illinois.) You doubtless refer to the bacterial disease known as fire blight, which kills back branches and blights blossoms so that they appear burned by fire, and produces cankers on twigs or the main trunk. Cutting out infected portions well below the visibly blighted area is most important, and so is breaking out blighted fruit spurs. If the disease is serious, apply a special full-bloom spray of streptomycin or a spray of Bordeaux (mixed according to instructions on container) to control the blight of blossoms.

What causes apples to rot on the tree and dry up? Is it a fungus disease or insects? What kind of spray should I use? (Illinois.) It sounds like black rot, a fungus disease characterized by mummied fruits and by frog-eye spots on leaves as well as a bark canker. Either ferbam, captan, zineb, or wettable sulfur in the regular pre-blossom sprays for apple scab should take care of black rot, provided that all mummied and rotting fruits are cleaned up. In southern Illinois, another fruit rot, called bitter rot, may be prevalent. The normal spray schedule will take care of this.

How can I get rid of powdery mildew on an apple tree? (Washington.) Cut out mildewed twigs at the time of pruning. Spray with 1 to 100 lime-sulfur or wettable sulfur in the cluster-bud and calyx stage and again 2 weeks after petal-fall stages. If a regular schedule for scab is being carried on, powdery mildew will be taken care of.

Is there anything that can be sprayed into the ground while the tree is in blossom to prevent 'Winesap' apples from ripening with specks and rottenness at the core? (Maryland.) Elgetol in earlier times was used to spray on the ground to eradicate the apple-scab fungus, but this would not be the cause of rottenness at the core. Rot and specks may be due to apple maggots, controllable by summer fruit spraying. Corky brown specks through the fruit sometimes come from lack of boron in the soil. In that case, you can apply powdered borax, ¼ to 1 pound, depending on the age of the tree. The larger amount is not safe on a tree under 25 years old. Apply it like fertilizer. One dose will last 3 years.

What is the cause and remedy of brown bitter spots on apples? (Wisconsin.) Either the bitter rot or boron deficiency previously discussed or a disease called bitter pit, due to some disturbed water relation with no very definite remedy.

What causes peculiar greenish sections in the flesh of some apples? (Connecticut.) Climate, variety, and water relations seem to have something to do with this physiological condition called water core. Maintain an even supply of water; maintain the proper balance between the root and the top by pruning; and pick the fruit at proper maturity.

My apples no sooner form in the spring than they become wormy and practically all drop off. (Long Island, New York.) This sounds like the European apple sawfly, a relatively new pest present in southeastern New York and Connecticut. This damage can be prevented by using a combination of malathion and methoxychlor in the calyx or petal-fall spray and in the first cover spray.

APRICOT (PRUNUS ARMENIACA)

What can be done against wormy apricots? A tiny worm starts eating around the stone and destroys the fruit. (Michigan.) This is the plum curculio, common also on apple, peach, and cherry trees. It is controlled by methoxychlor and malathion sprays and a stringent cleaning-up campaign. (See Plum.)

My apricot trees turn yellow and the fruit loses all its flavor. Is this a condition of the soil? (Utah.) In Utah it is probably a chlorosis due to a too alkaline soil, corrected by applying a fertilizer and equal parts of iron and aluminum sulfate, using 1 pound of mixture to each inch of diameter of the trunk. Apply beneath the branch spread, either in water solution or in holes 12 to 18 inches deep. Yellowing may also be symptoms of a virus disease. Consult your State Experiment Station.

BLACKBERRY (RUBUS)

How do you get rid of red rust in 'Alfred' blackberry? It acts like fungi but does not yield to sulfur; it is very contagious. (Missouri.) It is a fungus, officially named orange rust of blackberry. It lives all through the interior of the plant and cannot be controlled by fungicides as are other rusts. Remove diseased plants, getting out all roots, before the contagion spreads farther.

BLUEBERRY (VACCINIUM)

Why do my blueberry bushes have little pieces of wood, which look like worms, on the ground near the roots? (Massachusetts.) It sounds like frass (excrement) from a borer working in the stem. If you can find the hole, inject some borer fumigant, such as Borerkil.

CHERRY (PRUNUS)

When is the proper time to spray cherry trees to get better fruit and prevent insects? (New Jersey.) Write to the New Jersey Agricultural Experiment Station, New Brunswick, N.J. 08903 and request their extension bulletin on home-fruit-pest control.

After my cherry tree blossoms, the leaves curl up with aphids. When and with what will I spray? (New York.) A dormant oil spray helps to control cherry aphids. When the aphids first appear and before the young leaves curl, spray thoroughly with malathion, repeating as necessary.

How can I prevent the rot of cherries on trees? (Illinois.) Captan or benomyl will hold brown rot in check. Use captan in a multipurpose spray mixture at pink, petal-fall, and later stages, and also at full-bloom stage by itself. Insecticides must not be included during bloom; they kill the pollinators.

What causes cherry leaves to turn yellow in midsummer and drop off? What spray do you recommend? (Wisconsin.) This is a fungus leaf-spot, controlled by captan as in the preceding spray schedule.

What will kill worms that feed on the roots of cherry trees until the trees are killed? Will it be safe to plant another tree in this ground the following spring? (Michigan.) It is not clear whether you mean the peach tree borer, which works on the trunk under the soil surface, or the larvae of white grubs. Keeping the ground plowed and cultivated before replanting or treating for grubs will help get rid of the latter. The peach tree borer stays under the bark rather than in the soil; replanting in the same spot would probably be fairly safe. (See Peach.)

CURRANT AND GOOSEBERRY (RIBES)

Is gooseberry or any other berry harmful to pine trees? (New Jersey.) Gooseberries and currants are alternate hosts for the white pine blister rust. Where this disease is prevalent, they should be removed whenever they are found within 900 feet of white pines. Black currants are particularly susceptible to blister rust and should not be grown at all in rust areas.

Is there a disease-resistant currant? (Connecticut.) Variety 'Viking' is said to be resistant to white pine blister rust.

What causes red blotches on 'Red Lake' currant? (North Dakota.) Large reddish blotches on leaves of currants frequently indicate aphids working on the underside. If there are rusty patches on the underside of leaves, it may be white pine blister rust.

How can I rid currant bushes of aphids? (Illinois.) Add 1 tablespoon of malathion per gallon of water to any spray applied as soon as the foliage is developed, or put on a separate spray of malathion. Direct the spray toward the underside of the leaves.

What is the best insecticide for worms in gooseberries and currants? (Washington.) The currant fruit fly is a serious pest of currants and gooseberries in western Washington. White maggots feed inside the berry, causing the fruit to turn red and drop. Spray with malathion or contact your State Extension Service for the latest information on its control.

What is best to use on gooseberry bushes affected with leaf-chewing worms? (Indiana.) A combination spray of malathion and captan applied as soon as the foliage is well developed will take care of the currant worm (your "leaf-chewing" worm) as well as aphids and leafspot.

What causes leaves to turn brown in the early part of summer? (New York.) If there are dark spots on leaves and later defoliation, it is a fungus leafspot controlled by spraying with captan. If the whole shoot blights, it is caused by an internal fungus. There is nothing to do but cut infected canes at ground level.

GRAPE (VITIS)

What is the proper spray to use for black rot on grapes? (Ohio.) Black rot causes more loss than any other grape disease. The berries turn purple prematurely and change to hard, black, shriveled "mummies." Spray with captan, benomyl, or ferbam when new shoots are ½ inch long and again when they are 8 to 12 inches long; spray after blossoms fall with captan or folpet and repeat at 2-week intervals if the disease has been serious in other years.

What causes grapes to drop before they are ripe? (Pennsylvania.) Frequently the grape berry moth, which can destroy 60 to 90 per cent of the fruit on an unsprayed vine. Add 2 tablespoons of carbaryl to the ferbam spray applied just after petal fall, and again 10 to 14 days later. An additional spray might be necessary in late July or early August.

What do you do to keep Japanese beetles off grapevines? (Michigan.) Apply carbaryl when the beetles appear in numbers; repeat as needed.

How do you control rose bugs on grapes? (Massachusetts.) Cultivate the soil around the vines thoroughly in May and early June. Spray with 2 tablespoons of carbaryl to 1 gallon of water as soon as the beetles appear; repeat if necessary.

My grapevine is troubled with a small insect or fly early in the season, and a small bug or hopper in midseason. What spray should I use? (Wisconsin.) The early "fly" is probably a flea beetle, which will be controlled by the spray used for berry moths. Leafhoppers are sucking insects very injurious to grapes during the summer. Apply carbaryl in late June and early July.

How do you control mildew on grapes? (Michigan.) Spray with folpet, captan, benomyl, or zineb for downy mildew.

PEACH (PRUNUS PERSICA)

What is the white worm I find in the bark of my young fruit trees at the earth line? It buries itself in a jellylike mass. (New Jersey.) This is the peach tree borer, responsible for the death of many peach trees. The white, brown-headed worms, larvae of black and yellow wasplike moths, live in the bark from 8 to 10 inches above the soil to 3 to 4 inches below the surface. Control depends on chemical trunk treatments. Apply lindane as a drenching spray to the trunk from the first branch to the ground. Do not spray the fruit or foliage.

Is there anything we can do for the peach tree borer besides spraying? (Ohio.) You can fumigate in early fall after the young worms have hatched and are under the bark. The standard material is paradichlorbenzene. The crystals are placed carefully in a ring around the trunk, not closer than 1 inch or farther than 2 inches from the crown. The dosage must be very exact: 1 ounce for trees 6 or more years old, ¾ ounce for 5-year-old trees, and ½ ounce for 4-year-old trees. No treatment should be given to peaches set out for less than 3 years. Before placing the crystals, remove all grass, seeds, and debris from around the tree, and immediately afterward mound up with additional soil, being careful not to disturb the crystals. The time of treatment varies according to the state, usually September for New York and up to November 1 for the South. The soil temperature should not be much lower than 60° F. for effective results. After several weeks, the mound of soil should be leveled off. For more information, see Home and Garden Bulletin No. 211, *Control of Insects on Fruits and Nut Trees in the Home Orchard Without Insecticides* (USDA).

How do you get rid of the worms that make gum at the roots of peach trees? (Indiana.) If the trees are less than 3 years old, or there

A peach borer, a fat white grub, shown burrowing into a peach tree trunk. The adult moth, blue-black with an orange band, lays eggs at the base of tree trunks from early summer to fall.

are only 1 or 2, you can go after the worms with a knife or a wire, a process known as worming. See the previous questions and ask your own county Cooperative Extension Service for advice.

What, other than a borer, will cause peach trees to lose sap at the trunk and the tips of the branches to be coated with a gummy substance? (Pennsylvania.)   The gum is one manifestation of brown rot, controlled with sulfur, captan, or benomyl sprays or dusts and also by cutting out diseased twigs and branches and destroying all infected fruit or old "mummies."

Shortly before the time for peaches to ripen, they rot on the tree and dry up. Is there danger of next season's crop being affected? If so, what is the treatment? (Pennsylvania.)   There is very much danger of brown-rot infection from these mummied fruits on the tree or others that have fallen to the ground. Pick all the fruits and destroy them. Follow a spray schedule. (See Plum.)

What is the spraying program for peach trees? (Massachusetts.)   Write to the Experiment Station, Amherst, Mass. 01002, or your local Cooperative Extension Service, and request their latest spray program for peach trees.

Red blotches on peach leaves are causing them to curl up. Why? (Massachusetts.)   This is peach-leaf curl, a fungus disease. Its principal symptoms are much thickened distortions of the leaves, often followed by defoliation.

What is the best way to control peach-leaf curl? (Washington.)   Spray before buds start to swell during the dormant season with ferbam or Bordeaux mixture according to the directions on the container.

Some insect I have never seen cuts a thin slice in the skin of each peach, from which oozes a colorless syrup. What is it? (Massachusetts.) The cuts are made by the plum curculio, a snout beetle. (See Plum.)

The Oriental peach moth is attacking our 2-year-old peach trees, 3 different varieties. What remedy should be used? (Ohio.) This small gray moth with chocolate markings is the Oriental fruit moth and lays her eggs in the leaves; the young worms bore in the twigs and later generations attack the fruit. Spray with malathion or methoxychlor with 3 applications—early July, mid-July, and early August.

The green tips of my peach trees died back all last summer; little white worms were inside the shoots. I was told that it was caused by the tarnished plant bug. Is there any control? (Indiana.) Tarnished plant bugs do sting peach twigs and turn them black. There is little control except to destroy the weeds and sometimes to spray with carbaryl. However, since there were worms in the twigs, it was probably the Oriental fruit moth; this kills back the twigs also. (See the previous question.)

What should I do for yellows in young peach trees? (Alabama.) Yellows may be due to a virus or to an alkaline soil. Ask your county extension agent for a diagnosis and help.

Why do our peach seeds split, causing the peach to rot? What is the remedy? (Washington.) There is a physiological disease called split pit that results in rotting embryos and the gummosis of the fruit. The cause and remedy are not exactly clear, but the symptoms are more pronounced on a few varieties and in the years of a light crop. It is suggested that thinning be delayed 5 weeks after the pits start to harden.

What spray is used to prevent the dropping of premature fruits such as peaches? (Ohio.) Hormone sprays are used to prevent the premature dropping of some fruits, usually apples. It is doubtful if they will work on peaches.

PEAR (PYRUS)

What is the cause of fire blight in pear and apple trees? (Iowa.) Bacteria cause the disease but there are contributing factors. The more vigorous a tree, the more susceptible it is to fire blight because the bacteria prefer succulent tissue. Do not overfertilize (fall feeding is safer than spring), do not prune heavily, and do not cultivate around the trees. Some varieties, like 'Kieffer', are more or less immune.

Will spraying a pear tree while it is dormant check fire blight? There is no way to have all the diseased parts pruned out without ruining the tree. (New Mexico.)   You will lose the tree anyway if you do not have the diseased parts cut out, perhaps even if you do. The fire-blight bacteria are not on the outside, to be killed there by a spray, but are working down inside the twigs in the vascular system. Cut out *below* the infected portion of twigs and scrape away all dead wood from cankers on the main trunks and large limbs. Paint these wounds with Bordeaux paint, made by stirring raw linseed oil into dry powder. In the spring, the bacteria ooze out from the dead twigs and cankers in little droplets, which attract the bees. The bees, flying from blossom to blossom, carry around the bacteria and cause new infection. From blighted blossom clusters, the bacteria work down inside the twigs into the main branches. Spraying with streptomycin or Bordeaux mixture according to the instructions on the container when the blooms are open helps prevent this new infection. Break out all blighted blossom clusters.

Why did a few branches on my young pear tree die after the fruit was hanging on? (Pennsylvania.)   Probably fire blight. It may have been secondary infection from twigs or fruit blighted in primary early-spring infection.

Is there any practical remedy for curing fire blight on pear foliage? (Connecticut.)   No. If you see blighted foliage, you must cut the whole branch out 6 inches or more below the part that looks burned or blighted.

Is there anything that will cure pear blight? I had 4 dwarf trees. When the first one had it, I cut it down; the others all have it now. (Illinois.)   You cannot "cure" fire blight by any method. All you can do is to clean up infected parts and spray to prevent reinfection through the blossoms. Were you very careful to disinfect your tools after cutting down the diseased tree before working on the others?

I planted some pear trees in a 20-foot square space of apple trees. I am told that they will give the blight. Would you leave them, take them out, or use some spray to prevent it? (Indiana.)   Pears are much more susceptible to fire blight than apples, and if blight is in your neighborhood, which is more than likely, they will probably acquire the disease first, after which bees may carry it to your apple trees; your pruning shears will carry it unless you disinfect them between cuts. Formalin, at a 1 to 20 dilution, makes a good disinfectant. If you leave your pears where they are, plan on a blossom spray as described above.

What may I spray on a pear tree to kill a snail-like insect that kills the foliage? (Ohio.)   This is the pear slug, whose slimy dark-green to orange larvae skeletonize the leaves before they turn into sawfly adults.

If the pears are getting the regular apple-spray schedule, slugs will be controlled, or a separate spray of methoxychlor (3 tablespoons to 1 gallon of water) may be applied as soon as young slugs are noticed.

How can I get rid of the pear and plum leaf slugs? (California.) The pear slug attacks pear, plum, and cherry trees. It can be killed by any kind of finely ground dust, but a 5 per cent malathion dust is preferable. It can also be killed by regular malathion, carbaryl, or methoxychlor sprays.

How can I get rid of bugs on a pear tree? Little worms are eating the leaves. (New York.) See the two previous questions for the treatment of pear slug.

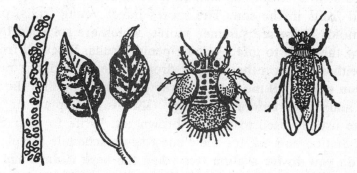

Pear psylla. The adult (right) is a reddish-brown fly with transparent wings.

Will you please give me information about pear psylla? (Massachusetts.) The pear psylla is the most serious pest of pears, especially in the Northeast. The adult psyllids are only $\frac{1}{10}$ inch long, reddish-brown, with rooflike transparent wings. They live during the winter under the bark and in orchard debris, emerging in early spring to lay eggs in cracks in the bark and on the buds; the eggs hatch into yellow nymphs, which suck sap from the leaf and fruit stems and leaves. To control, spray with dormant oil at the green-tip stages. Use a multipurpose spray at pink, petal-fall, and then as needed.

About the first of August, the leaves of my young dwarf pear turned black and fell off. What caused this? (Maryland.) The pear psylla, whose sucking causes defoliation. The black discoloration was due to a sooty mold, growing in honeydew surrounding the psylla nymphs. A summer spray of malathion is helpful if the psylla were not cleaned up by a dormant spray.

Is it proper to spray a pear tree in the winter that was covered with a

sort of mildew during the summer, or wait until spring? (Maryland.)   If you mean a true mildew, i.e., a white coating on the leaves, summer sulfur sprays or dust will control it, but more likely you refer to the blighted effect produced by pear psylla. (See the above question.)

PLUM (PRUNUS)

A fungus gathers on our plums each year and the fruit rots on the tree as soon as it starts to ripen. Why? (Michigan.)   This is brown rot of stone fruits, a fungus disease very common on peaches, plums, and cherries and sometimes injurious to apples as well. In early spring, spores are sent up from cup-shaped fruiting bodies growing out of old mummied fruits in the soil. The spores infect young fruits, producing grayish mold. These are summer spores, which are splashed by rain or carried by the wind to infect other ripening fruits. Diseased fruits wrinkle and either hang on the trees or drop to the ground as "mummies."

Will you please tell me how to spray plum trees so that the fruit will not rot and drop before ripening? (Illinois.)   Captan or benomyl sprays are usually used to control brown rot. Write to your State Experiment Station and ask for their latest spray schedule for plums.

What do you do for a plum tree when the bark is dark and splitting and in a few places gum or a jelly is running out? (Virginia.)   Gummosis is one of the symptoms of brown rot. (See the above question for advice.) Sanitation is even more important than spraying. Every mummied fruit fallen to the ground or left on the tree should be removed and burned.

How early do you spray plum trees? (Michigan.)   If there is scale, especially San Jose scale, use a dormant oil spray, although this is needed only in occasional years. You can put on a pre-blossom or cluster-bud spray of captan, methoxychlor, and malathion, but for the home garden, the shuck or husk-split stage may be early enough to start spraying.

What is the chemical that is put around plum trees to prevent curculio? (Florida.)   The curculio, a small, gray, hump-backed snout beetle, is the cause of wormy plums. There is no chemical for the soil, but keeping it well cultivated to destroy pupae and larvae in their earth cells and picking up and burning all dropped fruits are very important in controlling this serious pest. The methoxychlor recommended above is for the curculio.

What is the best spray for plums that will not be injurious to a small apiary in an orchard? (Iowa.) The spray schedule is so adjusted that there will be no poison on the open flowers when the bees go after nectar.

QUINCE (CYDONIA OBLONGA)

When and with what material should quince trees be sprayed? (New York.) A spray schedule for New York State calls for a dormant oil spray if lecanium scale is present, and a pink spray and a calyx spray of captan, methoxychlor, and malathion to control leaf blight, leafspot, codling moth, and Oriental fruit moth. Repeat the spray at 3-week intervals until 3 weeks from harvest.

RASPBERRY AND BOYSENBERRY (RUBUS)

What are the various diseases that attack black raspberries? How can they be controlled? (Ohio.) Virus diseases are green mosaic, yellow mosaic, leaf curl, and streak. Fungus diseases are verticillium wilt, orange rust, anthracnose, cane blight, spur blight, powdery mildew, leafspot, and bacterial crown gall. Most of these are controlled by sanitary measures—removing infected plants or plant parts. Many raspberry diseases are distributed in planting stock; order virus-free plants. A dormant spray of lime-sulfur, and pre-blossom and after-blossom sprays of ferbam or captan, will help control anthracnose and cane blight.

During the bearing season, we noticed overnight a bush or two stricken as if with heavy frost or a blowtorch, then turning black and drying up. We could find no insects. What caused this? (Michigan.) This is cane blight, caused by a fungus that frequently enters through insect wounds. Remove the blighted parts immediately, destroy fruiting canes after harvest; avoid sites with poor air and soil drainage; control weeds; spray with lime-sulfur when the buds show silver, for a dormant spray, and with ferbam or captan 1 week before, again immediately after blossoming, and again after harvest.

How do I control orange rust on boysenberries? (New York.) Orange rust is a systemic disease; that is, the rust fungus is found throughout the whole plant and not just on the leaves. Infected plants never recover; there is no control by spraying. Pull out diseased plants by the roots and destroy them before the rusty spores are shed to infect nearby brambles.

How can I rid my boysenberry vines of mildew? I used dry sulfur for 3 months but some of the runners died and the vines are all white.

(**Washington.**) Try spraying with Karathane or with wettable sulfur with a sticker. Consult your county extension agent for the best spray for your locality.

How can I get rid of crown gall without having to throw away all of my berry bushes? (Illinois.) You can't get rid of it. Even if you pull up these bushes, the bacteria will live in the soil for some years. Get healthy bushes and plant in a new location or sterilize the soil. Never bring in diseased stock from a nursery; refuse plants showing any signs of enlargements or galls.

What about insects on raspberries? (Wyoming.) Raspberry pests in Wyoming include aphids, false chinch bugs, fruitworms, grasshoppers, leafhoppers, leaf slugs, legume bugs, mites, scales, strawberry leaf rollers, and root weevils. Your county extension agent will help you work out a schedule for control of pests most destructive in your garden.

Some insect cuts rings about ¼ inch apart on my red raspberry canes and deposits its eggs between. What is the insect and what is its control? (Ohio.) This is the raspberry cane borer. The adult is a black and yellow beetle who deposits her eggs in new growth after first encircling the stem with 2 rows of punctures. The girdled tips wilt, and unless they are cut out, the young borers work down the canes. Remove all infested portions; cut out old canes after harvest.

Can red raspberries have little worms in the caps? (Ohio.) Yes, these are the grubs of the raspberry fruitworm. The adult is a light-brown beetle that feeds and lays eggs on blossoms. Dust or spray with malathion or methoxychlor as the blossom clusters are forming; repeat in 10 days.

Is there anything that can be grown to attract Japanese beetles away from raspberry bushes? (New Jersey.) They exert such a potent attraction that even soybeans may not entice them away. Pick your raspberries early in the morning, before the beetles are active, and keep the bushes dusted with rotenone.

STRAWBERRY (FRAGARIA)

How can you keep birds out of strawberry beds? (Illinois.) Cover the beds with a fine-enough mesh netting so that the birds won't get caught and strangle themselves. Most garden centers and nursery catalogs sell a light net made for this purpose.

What is the strawberry weevil? (New York.) The strawberry weevil, or blossom clipper, is a dark, reddish-brown to black, small snout beetle. It hibernates in rubbish in hedgerows and perhaps under the mulch in strawberry beds. It lays an egg in an unopened bud and causes it to fall by cutting the pedicel. The grub feeds on pollen and pupates inside the bud, going into hibernation in midsummer. Spray with carbaryl, malathion, or methoxychlor when the blossom buds appear and again before bloom. Dust with pyrethrum or rotenone after fruits start to form.

What causes strawberries to wilt and die just when they are in fruit? The roots turn yellow, brittle, and rot. (Wisconsin.) White grubs working on the roots will cause strawberries to wilt. These are most serious in land turned over from sod but may linger in soil in cultivation. They can be kept from injuring strawberries by treating the soil with Dursban or diazinon. Avoid planting strawberries immediately following sod. If no grubs are present, it can be a fungus root rot, in which case new plants should be set in fresh or sterilized soil.

What is the small black beetle that attacks our strawberries? (Illinois.) There are several beetle possibilities on strawberries. This one may be the adult of one of the strawberry root weevils. The grubs feed on the roots; later the weevils feed on the plants at night. Try a methoxychlor or carbaryl spray on the plants.

How do you deal with strawberry leaf roller? (Iowa.) This is a small greenish caterpillar that draws the leaflet together with a silken thread, feeds inside, and causes it to turn brown and die. Spray with diazinon or carbaryl in early spring just before the first blossoms open. Rotenone dust can be used after fruits form. Clean up the leaves after the crop is harvested.

Why do my strawberries turn white and the plants die? (Wyoming.) Chlorosis either from a virus disease or too alkaline soil. Send a specimen and a soil sample to your State Experiment Station, Laramie, Wyo. 82070.

14. Weeds

HOME GARDENERS, in common with farmers, nursery owners, golf greenskeepers, and others engaged in horticultural pursuits, are faced throughout the growing season with the problem of weed control. Keeping weeds out of garden areas where they compete with cultivated plants for nutrients and water is surely one of the most trying and time-consuming tasks of garden maintenance for the home gardener. While there has been much progress in the development of chemical weed-killers, the majority of them are for agricultural and professional uses and are often hazardous and may be of limited value to the home gardener and small property owner (see the second question below). The exception, of course, is in weed control in lawns, and here the home gardener is as much the beneficiary of modern technology as the nursery owner or greenskeeper.

The home gardener today, even though essentially still dependent on his own energy in controlling weeds among flowers, shrubs, and vegetables, can lessen his burden considerably by the use of mulches. Mulches look attractive, conserve soil moisture, improve plant growth, and contribute humus to the soil as they slowly decompose. In some home-garden situations, mostly in vegetable gardens, black plastic sheeting, available in rolls from garden centers or mail-order sources, is practical as a means of controlling weeds.

General

How can you keep weeds down? By constantly attacking them while they are still young, and above all by preventing them from seeding. In borders and shrub plantings, use mulches; on cultivated ground, use a tiller and hoe, plus hand-weeding; on lawns, weedkillers and good culture will encourage desirable grasses; on drives and paths, use weed-killers.

I keep hearing about miracle chemicals that will take all the labor of weeding out of garden maintenance. And yet when I read the labels and instructions on containers of weedkillers in my garden center, I find the chemicals are for very special and restricted uses and situations—none of which seem to apply to my home garden. Is there one weedkiller I can use among my flowers, shrubs, and vegetables to kill weeds? Selective herbicides are chemicals developed to control some plants but not be harmful to desirable ones. It is not likely that you would find one that will rid you of all your weeds and be safe on all desirable plants. It is much easier for the large-scale farmer or nursery owner who grows many of a specific crop to solve a weed problem than the home gardener with a limited growing area and a wide variety of plants in a vegetable garden or in ornamental plantings. The home gardener may best rely on hand-weeding, hoeing, and the use of mulches. The hobbyist who specializes in one crop may well find herbicides to solve his problem. The major exception is weed control in lawns. You have to admit that the elimination of crabgrass seed germination by the use of pre-emergent chemicals is quite a miracle.

I have 6 acres, not worked for about 20 years, that are full of weeds. What is the best way to get rid of them? Is it best to till in the fall or spring? Consult your Cooperative Extension county agent for specific controls for specific weeds.

We intend to fence our lot in the spring. Adjoining are open fields. How can I keep down weeds at the base of the fence on the outside? If you are not planting too close to the inside of the fence and there are no roots of desirable trees under the fence, use one of the nonselective long-lasting weedkillers such as Princep, Pramitol, Hyvar X, Spike, or Aatrex.

Is there any method to kill weed seeds in a seed bed? The best method for most home gardeners is to keep the bed moist to encourage germination and then to cultivate 2 or 3 times (allowing 10 days between each cultivation) to destroy seedlings. Sterilization with Vapam is also effective, but it must be carefully applied according to instructions.

How can I get rid of weeds before and during the growth of parsley, besides weeding? Hand-weeding in the rows and frequent hoeing between the rows are the best methods for annual weeds. Stoddard Solvent Oil has been recommended. Consult your county extension agent for advice.

Is it possible to spray carrots to control the weeds? Yes. Stoddard

Solvent Oil can be used. For latest information in your area, consult your Cooperative Extension Service.

In August I put Turf-Builder around a privet hedge. Six weeks later a broadleaf weed came in thick around the hedges. Could it be the Turf-Builder?   Turf-Builder is a proprietary plant food that certainly does not contain weed seeds. It probably stimulated the growth of weeds present in the soil, thus proving its efficiency as a fertilizer.

Is there anything that will kill weeds, yet not destroy flowers or vegetables?   Cultivation sometimes followed by mulching is the safest approach. There is no herbicide safe on all flowers and vegetables. Dacthal and Vegedax are labeled for use on many established flower and vegetable plants to prevent weed seed germination—consult the label for specific crops and weeds. Adequate mulch may reduce weed seed germination sufficiently.

What can be done to keep a gravel drive free from weeds?   This depends upon the weed problem, if there are tree roots under the drive, and where the surface water from the driveway drains. If the water from the drive does not flow onto desirable plants, including grass, some of the nonselective herbicides such as Pramitol, Hyvar X, Spike, or Aatrex can be used. Princep can be used over tree roots if they are not close to the surface. Use according to directions.

What is the name of a compound to put in paths between flower beds to eliminate weeds?   There are two choices, the best of which is to use a herbicide that is safe in the flower bed at a slightly higher strength. The other alternative is to use a short residual herbicide such as Paraquat on growing weeds, making sure to keep it away from desirable foliage.

What is best to use in killing weeds in a brick drain?   Providing the drain does not carry water into garden areas or into a pond or stream used by fish or animals, any commercial weedkiller should prove effective.

Is 2, 4-D dangerous to use?   All herbicides can be dangerous unless used with extreme caution. It is best to use 2, 4-D and similar herbicides in a sprayer used only for lawn spraying because it takes special procedures to adequately remove them from a sprayer. Apply 2, 4-D as a coarse spray with low pressure on a day that the wind will not blow the droplets onto desirable plants. There are special applicators for lawn treating that are much safer than hand-spraying. Use low-volatile esters or amines to prevent fumes from causing damage to desirable plants.

How can I tell different kinds of weeds? See *Common Weeds of the United States* (Dover Publications).

I am planting a garden over an old asparagus bed and have tried many ways to kill the asparagus, even to digging up the crowns, but the asparagus persists. How may I rid myself of this nuisance? Keep digging. Every time an asparagus stem appears, dig out the root from which it arises.

Specific Weeds

How can one get rid of bindweed on a lawn without killing roses, trees, and shrubs? If the bindweed is actually growing in the lawn, spray with 2, 4-D. Digging out would be the only solution in the shrubbery.

How can I exterminate an extremely hardy vine resembling a morning-glory, having white flowers and seemingly endless roots? Doubtless hedge bindweed, a pernicious weed with deep thick underground stems and roots, every fragment of which can grow. Where it exists, either don't plant anything and constantly hoe, so that no leaves can build up a food store in the roots, or plant only low-growing crops that can be hoed frequently so that no vines can get started. Also it has been determined that repeated applications of 2, 4-D while the weed is actively growing can kill it nearly 100 per cent. Avoid spray or drift of 2, 4-D to desirable plants except grass.

How can I get rid of Bermuda grass? The U. S. Department of Agriculture recommends 8 tablespoons (¼ pound) of dalapon in each gallon of water. Apply 1 gallon of the mixture to each 1,000 square feet of lawn to be treated. Make one application in late June and another within 3 to 4 weeks to kill any remaining plants. Reseed 4 weeks after the second application if temperatures have been high and the area has been kept moist. Otherwise, wait 6 weeks before reseeding.

What can I do for Bermuda grass in flower borders? (Tennessee.) In borders it must be kept down by frequent hoeing and treating the invading Bermuda grass on the edges with dalapon.

How can I clear land of blackberry vines? Spray the vines during the growing season with a combination of 2, 4-D plus Banvel D (dicamba). If the vines show signs of recovery, repeat the treatment. The solution reaches the roots through the vines and kills them.

Can you name a formula to kill buckthorn or plantain? At what time of year should it be used? The plantains are easily controlled in a lawn by spraying with 2, 4-D in the spring or fall. Cultivation is very effective in the garden.

Narrow-leaf plantain (left), a deep-rooted weed in lawns. Dig up seedling plants. The broad-leaved plantain (right).

What is dicamba? Dicamba is 3, 6 dichlora—0 anisic acid, a growth regulator different in composition but similar in action to 2, 4-D, although affecting different weeds. It is used in combination with 2, 4-D for lawn weed and brush control.

What is more effective in controlling weeds, 2, 4-D or Banvel D (dicamba)? Both are effective, but 2, 4-D is best against dandelion and poor against chickweeds and clover, while Banvel D is more effective on chickweeds and clover but ineffective against dandelion.

We have some patches of Canada thistle in our garden. Is digging them up the best remedy? Yes, if the work is well done. Any pieces of root left in the soil will grow, however, and digging should be followed by repeated hoeings. You might also use a 2, 4-D formulation as a spray or aerosol to treat only the foliage of the Canada thistle.

We have a large hay field next to us with a few bad patches of Canada thistle. The seeds blow over into our garden. Can these patches be eliminated by spraying? Yes. Use 2, 4-D as a summer spray and again in early September when regrowth has occurred.

What is the best way to clean cattails and rushes from a lake's edge? The best practicable method is to dig them out completely. If the surface of the lake could be lowered for a considerable period, they might die out from lack of moisture. Also try spraying with Dowpon, for it has given good results, but first check with local authorities for safety to water.

What is the best method of fighting crabgrass after it has germinated? Pull every seedling as soon as it is big enough to recognize, thus preventing seeding (crabgrass is an annual). Postemergence sprays that have given good results are DSMA, MSMA, and AMA. Make 3 applications at 7- to 10-day intervals, the first soon after the crabgrass emerges.

Crabgrass is the bane of lawn-makers. (For control, see Lawns.)

How can creeping Jenny or moneywort be eradicated? This is the yellow-flowered *Lysimachia nummularia*, sometimes used as a ground cover. The herbicide 2, 4-D gives excellent control.

What is the best method for controlling dandelions? They can be pulled if the soil is soft from rain, but all the root must be removed as any piece can make a new plant. It is easier and more effective to spray with 2, 4-D or apply 2, 4-D with a rag or a cane with a herbicide applicator on the bottom.

Dandelion: To control occasional plants, cut the taproot well below the ground with a knife and prevent plants from forming seeds. Spray colonies of the plants with 2, 4-D.

How can one effectively destroy dock weeds? Specimens of small size can be pulled out when the soil is very wet. With larger plants, use the spot treatment with 2, 4-D recommended for dandelions.

What can be done to get rid of dodder? Dodder, also called love-vine, goldthread, strangleweed, desire's-hair, and hellbind, is a parasitic annual. Cut down and burn all infected plants before the dodder has a chance to seed, or treat the soil with Dacthal spray or in granular form before the seeds germinate.

What method of controlling chickweed do you recommend to the home gardener? There are several kinds of chickweed. The most frequently occurring ones are common chickweed, which is a winter annual, and mouse-eared chickweed, which is a perennial. Both are best controlled in the garden by frequent cultivation and in the lawn by spraying with mecoprop, MCPP, or Banvel D in early spring or fall. Do not use over the recommended amount of Banvel D once a year near trees.

Chickweed is one of the worst garden weeds. Control its spreading roots by cultivation or 2, 4-D.

Will you suggest a remedy for a much-branched, green, leafy weed with tiny daisy flowers, each having 5 white petals? I think it is called galinsoga. This is an introduction from tropical America. It is very sensitive to frost, but is an annual and so overwinters as seed. Hand-pulling large plants before seeds form and cultivation to kill young ones are the most practical remedies.

Is it possible to remove Johnson grass or quackgrass from a vegetable garden so that it will not be back the next season? These are two distinct species. Both may be eliminated by forking out as much as possible by hand, taking pains to get every root, and then by repeatedly cultivating the surface throughout the summer. Johnson grass is particularly resistant, and vigorous methods must be used. Attempts might be made to cover the Johnson grass or quackgrass with black polyethylene plastic. If properly done, this can kill it after two full growing seasons. As far as using chemicals on these two vicious spreaders in the vegetable garden, better write your State Experiment Station or call your county extension agent to see if there is anything new to be recommended. State regulations regarding herbicides differ.

The weed lamb's-quarters is common in my garden. How do you keep it down? This weed usually favors rich soils. It is controlled by cultivating and is easily hand-pulled. When the plants are young, lamb's-quarters makes excellent salad greens.

We have a shrub called Japanese-bamboo that is becoming a nuisance. How can it be eradicated? This is *Polygonum cuspidatum,* with the more accepted common name of Japanese knotweed. It is very difficult to control by digging because of its massive underground root system. If there are no trees nearby, repeated applications of dicamba will work. Otherwise it may be advisable to have a professional apply glyphosate (Roundup) to the foliage in late summer or early fall.

What will kill moon-vine or wild morning-glory? Dig out as much as possible, then keep the ground surface cultivated at frequent intervals so that no new shoot ever attains a height of more than 2 inches before being cut off. Spraying with 2, 4-D or 2, 4-D plus Banvel D also gives good control.

How can a fairly large patch of nettles in a field be eliminated? By repeatedly mowing so that the plants are never permitted to get more than a few inches high. Also, by spraying the plants when young with a commercial weedkiller.

Nut-grass is a troublesome weed in my garden. Can you suggest a means of eliminating it? This could be yellow or purple nutsedge, either of which are extremely difficult to control and practically impossible to eliminate because of the dormant tubers that can remain in the soil for many years before growing. In lawn areas, use AMA, DSMA, MAMA, MSMA, or basagran as a spray on growing plants. In garden areas, use the same treatment or incorporate Eptam in the soil to retard tuber sprouting.

What can be done to destroy petunia seedlings? I would like to plant something else in a former petunia garden, but the petunias come up by the hundreds each year. Hand-weeding or hoeing after the seedlings are up is the only practical treatment.

Can you suggest any means of getting rid of plantain (both narrow- and broad-leaved) in quantity? Very effective is 2, 4-D spray on turf.

How can I get rid of a patch of poison-ivy? On areas where no food crops will be grown, spray or use a brush to dab the foliage with amitrole. In areas with fruit trees or where vegetables will be planted, use Ammate. Do not handle or burn live or dead poison-ivy leaves, vines, or roots. Use gloves when treating poison-ivy.

How may I get rid of poison-ivy growing in a planting of lily-of-the-valley? Get someone immune to poison-ivy to carefully dig up the bed. Transplant lily-of-the-valley to another location for 2 or 3 years. Meantime, eliminate any poison-ivy that appears on the old site with commercial sprays such as Ammate or amitrole.

What is the poison-oak plant and how can it be destroyed? Poison-oak (*Rhus toxicodendron*) is similar to poison-ivy (*R. radicans*), but has more oaklike leaves. Spray with amitrole in nonfood-crop areas or

Ammate in food-crop areas. Keep off the foliage of desirable plants.

Every summer my garden is invaded by purslane. What can I do?   This is an annual that develops rapidly in warm weather and rich soil. Attack vigorously with a hoe and cultivator while the weeds are still tiny. If the plants get large, rake them up and compost, otherwise they will root and grow again. Purslane, steamed in a little water, is an excellent potherb.

Which is the most effective way of ridding the ground of quackgrass? It grows in the soil around my shrubbery and cannot be exposed to anything that would harm these plants.   Incorporate Eptam into the soil by cultivation immediately after applying the granules—see the container for rates. In the spring, work the whole area over with a spading fork and carefully remove all underground stems of the grass. Follow this throughout the summer by forking out every piece of the grass that appears before the leaves are an inch high. Or cover all the ground about the shrubs with black polyethylene film.

How can I eradicate redroot (pigweed)?   This weed can be eradicated only by soil fumigation with Vapam, but usually adequate control can be secured by hoeing and hand-pulling.

How do you get rid of sandburs?   Practice clean cultivation. The plant is an annual and can be controlled by clean cultivation or using the herbicide Dacthal before the seeds germinate.

How can I destroy sheep sorrel and at the same time use the ground for vegetables and flowers?   Sheep sorrel is a sure sign of poor, infertile, and, usually, acid soil. Apply fertilizer generously and test for lime needs. Nitrogenous fertilizers are especially helpful.

Is there any method of destroying sumac other than digging it out?   Spraying young foliage with a mixture of 2, 4-D and Banvel D (dicamba) when it is half mature in the spring, and a second time when regrowth is at about the same stage, has given good control.

I have an old trumpet-vine root in the ground and want to plant a fruit tree instead. How can I kill the heavy root so it won't take the strength from the fruit tree?   Dig out the trumpet-vine root and turn over and fertilize the soil before planting the fruit tree. Or you can spray with a mixture of 2, 4-D and Banvel D (dicamba).

How can I get rid of white clover in my garden?   White clover is best controlled in lawns by spraying with MCPP or Banvel D in the spring or fall. In garden areas, it is easily controlled by cultivation and hand-weeding.

What is the best method of getting rid of white snakeroot?   Grub out the roots.

What is the best way to get rid of wild carrot?   The plant is biennial and does not reproduce itself if it is cut down before it reaches the seedling stage. Also, 2, 4-D will control it.

Wild garlic is becoming troublesome. How shall I eliminate it? This is a most pernicious weed, once established. If the area is not too large, hand-digging, followed by destruction of every bulb, is best. Cultivate the surface frequently. Repeat spraying for several years with 2, 4-D in the spring when the garlic is tall, before the grass is cut. Dormant bulbs come up for a period of years, making repeated treatments necessary.

How can wild grapevines and poison-ivy be killed? These seem to cover every rock and bit of space on our farm. Goldenrod and milkweed mingle with these weeds. If the farm grows good crops, the poison-ivy can be controlled with Ammate. If there is poor control of the goldenrod and milkweed, use 2, 4-D on young foliage, repeated until control is adequate.

Poison-ivy (left); Virginia-creeper (right),
often mistaken for it, has five leaflets.

Can wild morning-glory be exterminated around the trunk of fruit trees without killing or damaging the trees? Maintain a circle of bare ground around the tree and keep this clean of all growth by scuffle hoeing every few days throughout two successive growing seasons. As an alternative, cover the infested area with black polyethylene plastic film for two seasons.

How can I get rid of wire grass? This name is applied to several distinct species of grasses, and also to a kind of rush. Several of these indicate soils low in fertility. Some are annuals; some are perennials. Frequent cultivation and prevention of seeding are recommended treatments. Dalapon spray is effective on many perennial grasses, sedges, and rushes.

I have a poplar tree, recently cut down, but the roots keep sending up suckers. How can I kill this 2½-foot stump once and for all without having to dig it out? Make a groove or hollow in the stump and place a half cupful of crystals of sodium sulfamate there. This will gradually dissolve in rainwater and be absorbed by the wood.

Can I spray brush while it is dormant in the winter and still expect a good kill?   Yes, using a mixture of 2, 4-D and Banvel D (dicamba) in kerosene and directed to the base of the plants so that the stems are thoroughly wet on all sides.

In reading a trade magazine I saw an advertisement of a power company spraying brush along the power lines to kill the growth. Can I use this same material on my property?   Certainly, it is usually a mixture of 2, 4-D and Banvel D (dicamba) mixed with water for use when plants are in leaf, and mixed with kerosene when plants are dormant. It is easily applied and very effective on many plants. It is easily obtained under the general name of brush killer. Keep off foliage of desirable plants.

We have an old pasture covered in spots with hawthorns as much as 6 inches in diameter. How can I best eliminate these plants without having to pull each one out with a tractor?   Try spraying the lower base of the trees with a concentrated solution of 2, 4-D and Banvel D (dicamba) in oil in the winter while the trees are dormant.

We have a large flagstone terrace at the back of our house. Various low-growing plants—thyme, dianthus, etc.—grow between the stones, but are being crowded out by crabgrass. Is there a weedkiller to use that would not kill the desirable plants but eliminate the crabgrass?   Spreading siduron or any other preemergent crabgrass herbicide in the spring over the terrace should nearly solve the problem. Use your lawn spreader to distribute the chemical, then use a broom to sweep the chemical particles from the flagstones into the soil spaces between the stones. While most crabgrass will be eliminated, a few plants can be expected.

We have many plants of poke-weed at our summer place. I have been told the plants are edible but others say they are poisonous. What is the truth?   The truth is that the black berries, tap roots, and mature foliage (especially in late summer when it turns reddish) of the pokeberry (*Phytolacca americana*) are poisonous; but the emerging shoots in the spring are *not* poisonous and are delicious cooked in the same manner as asparagus.

Please give me a list of edible weeds.   Pokeberry (see above); purslane; milkweed (*Asclepias syriaca*); dandelion; watercress; upland cress. For others see *Billy Joe Tatum's Wild Foods Cookbook and Field Guide* (Workman Publishing Company, New York, 1976).

How can I get rid of wild veronica in my lawn?   There are many kinds of veronica (speedwell). You must have the veronica identified to determine which control measure to use. Consult your local county extension agent. Creeping veronica (*Veronica filiformis*) is best controlled at time of flowering by spraying with Dacthal.

How can I smother the unwanted growth of such woody brush as honeysuckle, Virginia-creeper, poison-ivy, and huckleberries that form patches in my woodland garden? I am afraid to use chemical brush killers as I have many groupings of wild flowers and shrubs, such as rhododendrons, yet the honeysuckle, etc., is too extensive for just hand-grubbing. This situation is not easily resolved. If you can use a rotary mower in such confined space, cut the brush as close to the ground as possible. Then pile on layer upon layer of newspapers. To hold the newspapers in place as well as conceal their presence, cover with half-rotted leaves, marsh hay, straw, grass clippings, or compost. Pull or cut any unwanted growth as it breaks through the papers and mulch. Eventually you will have a rich mixture in which to plant additional wild flowers, but in the situation as you describe it, there will always be a need for some hand-grubbing of alien growth For one thing, birds, which are attracted to woodland gardens because of the shelter and food they offer, are bound to scatter seeds of the plants you wish to eliminate. Very cautious spraying of a herbicide such as amitrole on a day when there is no wind might be safe on the larger weed patches.

Describe the plant marihuana. Marihuana (*Cannabis sativa*), also known as hashish or Indian hemp, is a tall, rather weedy annual with narcotic properties. It is often found in waste areas or in fields. (It was once grown as an ornamental foliage plant in the British Isles.) It is native to Asia. It has alternate, compound foliage in a digitate arrangement of 3–7 leaflets which may be 9 inches long. The inconspicuous green flowers appear late in the summer, with male and female flowers being carried on separate plants as with holly. The tough fibers of the stems were once used to make rope.

Marihuana (Cannabis sativa) *is also known as hashish or Indian hemp.*

15. Regional Garden Problems

(Arranged by States)

CLIMATIC AND SOIL conditions, of course, do not follow state lines. Even within state boundaries such conditions may vary to a very great degree. Altitude, the direction of prevailing winds, the proximity of large bodies of water—all these and many other factors enter into the picture.

However, a certain amount of generalization based on the broad factors of latitude, topography, and the prevailing movements of large bodies of air can properly be applied to the climate of any given state. The relation of this fact to the growing of plants in any particular section of the country is obvious.

The residents of different states will find in these pages much information that will be of use to them. Also, much regional information for New England and Mid-Atlantic States has been given in other sections. But let us emphasize again, wherever some particular local problem is involved, the importance of consultation with some local authority, such as one's county extension agent or State Agricultural Experiment Station. The locations of the latter are given on page 1444. (The addresses and telephone numbers of county extension agents are found in the telephone directory, listed under your county and under the designation "Cooperative Extension Service.")

$Q\mathcal{E}A$ *Alabama*

What do you consider good group plantings of perennials and annuals, separately and mixed? Day-lilies and angelonia; physostegia and Shasta daisies; violets and zephyranthes; verbena and bouncing bet. For color combinations of annuals blended to taste, try pink cosmos behind deep-blue petunias; lupines edged with pansies. The possibilities are limitless.

What flowers can we grow to send to shut-ins during the winter months? Pansies in little grape or strawberry boxes, as well as in many leftover kitchen containers. Freesias, paper-white narcissus bulbs in small bowls of pebbles, wandering Jew in attractive little pots, and many different kinds of easy-to-grow but much-appreciated succulents.

What apple can be raised in Alabama as a successful commercial venture? In extreme northern Alabama, 'Delicious', 'Black Twig', 'Jonathan', 'McIntosh', and several other varieties of apples should grow successfully. Varieties developed largely in Israel are worth trying farther south. Consult local nurseries.

When is the best time to set out azaleas and in what type of soil, for best results in this state? It is the custom, but not essential, to move azaleas when they are in full bloom. Balled plants should be moved carefully into beds that have been prepared with rotted hardwood leaves, peat moss, and aluminum sulfate if the soil is not acid. The beds should be entirely free from lime. Be sure to set the plants at exactly the same level they grew in the nursery and water well.

I am told that my azaleas and camellias will do better if I mulch with oak leaves around them. Is this true? Yes. These plants succeed much better under a mulch than they do with clean cultivation. Oak leaves are excellent when applied about 4 inches thick. As the leaves decompose and the mulch becomes more shallow, pile on more leaves to keep the blanket up to the original thickness. A mulch retains moisture, prevents extremes of temperature, and discourages weeds.

What are some of the best bulbs for fall planting on the Gulf Coast? Calla-lily, hybrid amaryllis, iris species (native), leucojum, lily, butterfly-iris (*Moraea*), narcissus, and zephyranthes.

Will the cushion-type chrysanthemums succeed in the Birmingham area?   Yes, these popular garden perennials do well in this locality.

What can I do for the powdery mildew on my crape-myrtle?   At first signs, spray with Benlate or Karathane fungicides. Use 1 ounce to 25 gallons of water. Do not apply when the temperature is above 85° F. Dusting sulfur will do as well, but it must be carefully applied after each rain until the mildew is under control.

Are any day-lilies evergreen in southern Alabama?   Yes, many of the choice hybrids are evergreen and are, therefore, of much value in the winter garden.

What sprays are recommended for various scales and insects common to fruit trees, and when should they be applied in Alabama?   Combination or all-purpose sprays are available for use on fruit trees in the home garden. It is necessary, however, to spray a number of times each season to get satisfactory results. Spray as follows:

1. When leaves begin to bud out: apple, peach, plum, apricot.
2. When bloom shows color: apple, peach, plum, apricot, pear, quince, cherry.
3. When all petals have fallen: apple, peach, plum, apricot, pear, quince, cherry.
4. When shucks fall: cherry, peach, plum, apricot.
5. Every 2 weeks from petal fall to shuck fall: apple, pear, quince, cherry, peach, plum, apricot.
6. Two weeks before harvest: peach, plum, apricot.
7. After harvest: cherry.

Can fuchsia plants be left in the ground outdoors during the winter in the South?   In certain areas and in certain well-protected places, fuchsias may be grown as garden perennials. If they are growing in the ground, they will be much hardier, of course, than if they are plunged in their pots. As potted plants they are quite likely to freeze. The plastic cones used for winter protection of roses can also be used on fuchsias.

When should gladioli be planted in Montgomery, Alabama?   February or March, so that newly emerging flower scapes will miss the late frosts.

When should Bermuda grass seed be planted?   Sow in early spring if it can be watered; during the summer rains; or in early autumn if winter ryegrass is not going to be used. When the grass shows definitely green, make a light application of a nitrogenous fertilizer and water in well. These feedings may be repeated at 4- or 5-week intervals during growing weather.

If grass (Bermuda or centipede) grows around the base of camellias

or azaleas, does it hurt them? It is better to maintain circles free of grass around the bushes. A mulch of compost, bagasse, or leafmold placed on the ground surface is very beneficial.

How can I eradicate nut-grass? Nut-grass is very difficult to eradicate in the lower South. It would be best to consult your regional county agent for recommendations based on your particular property.

What herbs are most suitable for southern Alabama? *For fall:* anise, chives, winter savory, sage, and dill. *For spring:* sweet basil, summer savory, sweet fennel, coriander, thyme, and sweet marjoram.

What are the cultural requirements for Japanese iris in this state? Japanese iris prefer a moisture-retentive soil of slightly acid reaction. The roots may be planted or transplanted after flowering or during the autumn and winter. Applications of a plant food in March, May, and July should take care of nutritional needs; a mulch is highly desirable.

What is the best fertilizer for nandina? I have strong, healthy plants, but the berries dry up and fall off before they turn red. Any good commercial fertilizer mixture should suit nandina. An application in January, spread around the shrubs and lightly scratched into the soil, and another in June to mature the new growth, should be adequate under normal garden conditions. Keep the soil moist to avoid the drying of berries. Nandina berries will color best in full sun; they may be destroyed by very low temperatures.

Can oranges be grown along the Gulf in Alabama and Mississippi? Yes. Satsuma oranges are dwarf citrus trees that belong to the kid-glove group. These are quite hardy, and when budded on hardy trifoliate stock, they will produce excellent early oranges along the upper Gulf Coast.

What is the proper method for growing pansies from seed in the South? Pansies are cool-weather annuals and the seeds will not germinate well in the warm weather of early autumn. Seeds sown after the weather turns cool in October or early November germinate well and give flowering plants in April and May. Sometimes germination in warm weather can be hastened by placing a small seed flat, properly prepared, in the refrigerator for a week or so.

Will peonies grow well in Alabama? I was told that they grow best near salt water. We are quite inland. Peonies are temperate-zone plants and in many parts of the lower South they will not succeed. It is not the proximity of salt water that assures success with peonies, but a combination of soil and a long, cold winter without warm breaks that will guarantee a complete dormancy in the peony crown.

Why are rhododendrons practically failures in the lower South, where soil conditions appear to be ideal, as both evergreen and deciduous azaleas and the white dogwood grow and bloom luxuriously?   In the South there is not a sufficiently long or sufficiently severe winter season for most rhododendrons. Soil conditions may be ideal but climatic conditions are definitely not right for most rhododendrons. However, you can probably grow *Rhododendron chapmanii, R. ovatum,* possibly *R. fortunei,* and there may be possibilities for warm climate gardens in the rhododendrons from Malaysia.

What rock-garden plants will grow in partial shade in central Alabama?   Most rock gardens are exposed to full sun, and the usual list of plants for rock gardens include few shade-loving species. There are many, however, that do excellently in partial shade. You could make a fine collection from the wildflowers of your locality. Deep pockets of earth may be prepared for hardy ferns, to be used as a dominant green note. Besides wildflowers, you could add sweet violets, viola, florists' anemones and ranunculus, alliums, zephyranthes, periwinkle, lily-of-the-valley, lady's-slipper orchids, and other native orchids of the Southeast.

What roses would you suggest for Alabama?   In addition to the hybrid teas, you can grow such tea roses as 'Duchesse de Brabant', 'Sombreuil', and 'Maman Cochet', which are too tender for northern gardens.

What about planting roses deeper than usual in the South?   In this locality tests have shown that it is much better to set roses at exactly the same depth that they grew in the nursery.

When should bush roses be pruned in central Alabama?   In February or in March, just before growth commences. Head the canes back to 4 or 5 good strong eyes if you wish to prune low to produce a few perfect flowers. If you prefer tall, luxuriant bushes covered with masses of smaller blooms, prune as high as you wish, but remove all half-dead or diseased wood and cut each healthy cane back somewhat. Pruning cuts should be made about ¼ inch above a strong eye that points away from the center of the plant.

I have been told that I cannot grow tulips on account of the winter temperatures here. Is this true?   Only partly true. Tulips cannot be successfully grown in the Deep South without special prior treatment. They require several months of cold weather and a cool spring to develop normally. Ask your supplier about specially treated bulbs. Do not, however, try to keep tulip bulbs in a refrigerator. Temperatures below

40° F. will start both root and top growth, spoiling the bulbs unless planted at once.

Alaska

We must move to Anchorage. Will it be possible for me to have a garden there? Yes, but because of the short summers (less than 100 days of growing weather), your choice of plants will be restricted. Most annuals do well—especially when started indoors under fluorescent lights. The University of Alaska (mailing address: Cooperative Extension Service, Fairbanks, Alas. 99701) maintains a display of ornamental plants suitable for home gardens in the region; you could write them for literature to study before your move. You will be able to obtain help and ideas from Anchorage's Parks and Recreation Department, which maintains a greenhouse and extensive public plantings.

What house plants can I grow in Alaska? Almost all the plants you can grow indoors in more benign climates. Your major concern must be with light and coping with the short days of winter. However, this is easy to remedy with the installation of fluorescent light fixtures, under which you can grow African-violets, succulents and cacti, orchids, coleus, geraniums, wax begonias, azaleas, asparagus-fern, chrysanthemums, etc. Greenhouses are very popular and, even though the amount of light is increased, many owners add fluorescent light units to improve plant growth and to make use of every bit of growing space. Many greenhouse owners also grow certain vegetables, such as tomatoes and cucumbers, which cannot produce fruits outdoors because of the short summers.

Where should I go in Alaska to see wildflowers? Mt. McKinley National Park, accessible from Anchorage and Fairbanks, is one of the best places. The park is open from June 1 to mid-September.

Arizona

What are the characteristics of the soils of Arizona, Colorado, and New Mexico? The whole Southwest region has, except for the mountain areas, few forests or other vegetation to provide humus. Hence, in general, the soil, whether sand, silt, clay, or caliche, requires the addition of much humus. The compost pile is very necessary here. Peat moss, rotted strawy manure, any decayed vegetation is useful. One successful gardener in central New Mexico began with a half acre of caliche—shale clay. She first put on a heavy layer of dairy manure and had a team plow and harrow this. Next came 20 bales of peat moss. A surface mulch of peat moss and manure each fall with constant additions from the compost pile kept her garden growing and blooming with a lushness unbelievable when one saw the surrounding soil and vegetation. The lack of humidity in the air, as well as low rainfall, makes much watering necessary. Incorporation into the soil of generous amounts of humus helps it to retain moisture and so reduces the labor of watering.

What are the best flowering plants to stand Arizona desert heat? Perennials that flower early, followed by annuals that can stand heat and dry air. Native plants should be most satisfactory. Such early perennials as dwarf phlox, dianthus, iris, euphorbia, oenothera. Annuals: verbena, zinnia, marigold, mesembryanthemum, mirabilis, petunia, portulaca, salvia, *Xanthisma texana* (star of Texas), California-poppy, venidium, xeranthemum, and Texas bluebonnet.

What kind of flowers can be planted in the fall in a high altitude (7,000 feet) where it is very cold? Fall planting of perennials is more successful in this climate if done early—even before the first killing frost. Plant shrubs and roses in either fall or early spring. For fall planting: lilies, narcissus, peonies, pyrethrum, iris, campanulas, tulips, phlox, dianthus, dictamnus, heliopsis. Hybrid tea roses can be planted, if covered during the winter. Polyantha and floribunda roses should be quite satisfactory, and will give a long season's bloom and require little or no winter protection. Among the sturdiest are 'Else Poulsen' and 'Spartan'. Climbing roses are more difficult, since in your climate they require protection from the winter sun. Some of the hardiest are 'Paul's Scarlet', 'White Dawn', 'New Dawn', 'Blaze'. Shrub roses include rugosa and rugosa hybrids, *R. hugonis;* and the best of the hybrid perpetuals. (See also Section 6, Roses.)

Can you advise me as to a good climber, either annual or perennial? I live in a hot, dry climate, and the season is long. Annual: madeira-vine, coral-vine, *Cobaea scandens,* gourds, thunbergia, cardinal-vine, morning-glory, moonflower. Perennial: passion-flower, trumpet vine, *Clematis texensis, Lonicera heckrottii,* silver fleece-vine.

When is the best time to plant chrysanthemums in Arizona? Spring. Even late-spring transplanting brings earlier and more profuse bloom than if the plants are left undisturbed. Divide old clumps in the spring.

Can wild Indian paintbrush be transplanted and if so, how and when? Indian paintbrush (*Castilleja chromosa*) is partially a parasite. To transplant successfully, its host must be transplanted with it. *Chrysothamnus* (rabbitbrush) is one host of *Castilleja chromosa*. Transplant any time when the ground is sufficiently moist to make a ball. They move easily in full bloom if kept well watered. Dig a trench around the plant, then lift it with a ball or clump not less than 1 foot in diameter, taking with it any other plants contained in the ball.

Can I grow Lilium bakeranum in Arizona? *Lilium bakeranum* is listed among the difficult ones. Since it is a stem-rooting species, bulbs should be planted about 3 times their own depth. To prevent drying, as well as alternate freezing and thawing, a mulch is necessary. In its western China home, it grows on steep, loamy slopes among shrubs and grasses.

When is the proper time to plant lily bulbs in our southern country? The time to plant lily bulbs is determined by the time of dormancy of the bulbs rather than by the climate of their new home. *Lilium candidum* is planted in August and September. Top growth begins immediately. Plant lilies whose bulbs mature later (the majority of species and hybrids), in September to November.

What climbing rose will do the best here? All the climbing forms of hybrid perpetuals and hybrid teas should do well. Some that are grown successfully in the Southwest are 'Blaze', 'New Dawn', 'Climbing Crimson Glory', and 'Climbing Talisman'. Protection from winter sun may be necessary on a southern exposure. Spruce branches or cornstalks may be woven into a rose trellis, or roses, support and all, may be laid on the ground and covered.

Arkansas

Will delphinium and Oriental poppies grow in this part of the country? Yes. *Delphinium* x *belladonna* is more likely to prosper than some of the fancy hybrids. Pacific Hybrid delphiniums can be grown in your area only as biennials.

What flowers can I plant in a coco-grass-infested area? Few plants have the persistence of these stoloniferous grasses. Some that may fight their way are goutweed (*Aegopodium* 'Variegatum'), Kenilworth-ivy, buttercup, strawberry, and moneywort (*Lysimachia nummularia*). Consult your county extension agent for a chemical control for hard-to-kill grasses.

Can I put poinsettia plants outdoors in the summer?   They can be put out during warm weather, in a spot with sunshine, but sheltered from strong winds. Be sure to bring them inside in the fall before night temperatures drop below 55° to 60° F. (See Section 12.)

California

What can I mix with adobe soil to make a garden?   Two very good materials to mix with adobe soil are decomposed granite and bean straw. A 3-inch layer of granite, dug in deeply, followed by a deeper layer of bean straw, also dug in deeply, will help greatly. Where available from electric utilities, steam cinders that have weathered over the winter make excellent soil conditioners. Decomposition of the straw should be permitted to advance well before planting is done. This treatment will not improve drainage, for adobe is generally too deep.

What kind of fertilizer is best for adobe soil?   Have your soil tested. Follow the recommendations made according to the results of the test.

What is the treatment for hard, black soil near Los Angeles?   (See Section 1.) The most important consideration of all is in respect to water. First, don't ever work adobe soil when it is wet, for it will cake and harden and be put out of condition for a long time. Second, do not overirrigate, for it drains poorly. Tile drainage, if not too costly, can be used to improve heavy soil. Check the soil to see how deeply it has dried, and aim to irrigate just enough to moisten the soil to that depth. Cultivate as soon as the soil surface is dry.

How can adobe soil be made to produce?   See the previous questions. Alkalinity must also be considered. If the plants look yellow and stunted, there may be an alkaline condition. Soil sulfur or ferrous sulfate, at the rate of 2 pounds per 100 square feet, will reduce the alkalinity. More or less may be used yearly, after the first application is made as a test. Normally, adobe soil produces heavily.

It is cold and often foggy here, and this seems to slow plant growth down. Would an extra amount of fertilizer give plants beneficial warmth?   No. Commercial fertilizers will not supply any warmth to the soil. However, nitrogen fertilizer will stimulate growth if the soil is not too cold, and phosphorus and potash may be used to hasten maturity.

We had to import soil for our garden, but now it is worn out. Can it be improved? The lack of humus in most California soils is the cause. The imported soil may have had some, but the thin layer was stripped very soon. Soils wear out from lack of humus. Addition of bean straw, manures, or peat moss would have helped maintain the purchased soil. Follow a yearly program of planting the garden area to a cover crop of cow peas or other legumes, to be tilled under when 6 inches tall. This will provide a constantly increasing supply of humus. Add compost, and if available, animal manures mixed with peat moss. During the growing season, feed little and often with a complete plant food or with liquid fertilizer.

What can be done with soil spoiled by the oil from the pods, leaves, and bark of eucalyptus trees? First, clean off all debris; then turn the soil as deeply as possible. Permit rains and heavy waterings to leach out the toxic oils. After lying fallow during the winter, the soil should be in fair condition. Constant raking must be practiced to keep off the debris.

My soil is light, has no clay subsoil, and requires too much water. How can I use less? The problem is not one of using less as much as of *losing* less. Add as much humus as possible, preferably with peat moss. Cultivate as soon as the surface is dry. In irrigating, do not wet the soil too deeply for annuals, vegetables, or shallow-rooted plants, for the water will drain away. Trees and shrubs should be irrigated deeply and seldom, to encourage deep rooting. One solution is to dig out light soil to a depth of 12 inches and lay down plastic. Replace the soil with added compost.

What is a good book on soils and fertilizers for California? Some of the very best information on the subject is to be found in bulletins of the State Agricultural College in Berkeley, Calif. 94720. Also consult your county Cooperative Extension Service.

Can one make an attractive garden with perennials alone? It often seems like less work to grow perennials, but if results are desired, they involve about as much work as annuals. One should start off with a good shrub background, not too tall, to add to the appearance and break the wind. Then select perennials that are proven in your region. Select them for durability, successive blooming dates, and reasonably clean habit. Interplant with bulbs and corms like lilies, muscari (grape-hyacinths), watsonia, calla, and others that grow in your area for several years without lifting. Although perennials do create spectacular effects, annuals will usually produce more bloom all summer long with far less time and effort.

What are the best flowers for winter, spring, summer, and fall? This could make a long list, but here are some good ones: *Spring:* freesia, calla, ixia, sparaxis, narcissus, minor bulbs, sweet peas, snapdragon, columbine, mesembryanthemum. *Summer:* geranium, heliotrope, lantana, fuchsia, dahlia, gladiolus, montbretia, tigridia, haemanthus, gaillardia, marigold, zinnia. *Fall:* hardy asters and chrysanthemums. *Winter:* sweet pea, calendula, snapdragon, stock, various kinds of dianthus, and wallflower.

What are some good border flowers or plants, not over 12 inches high? Annuals that might answer the purpose are lobelia, portulaca, ageratum, low-growing marigolds, sweet-alyssum, and *Phlox drummondii.* Perennials could be *Chrysanthemum mawii, Nierembergia hippomanica,* day-lily, coral-bells, *Aster* x *frikartii,* and gazania.

What flowers will grow in pots in the sun all day? The reason most plants fail under these conditions is the rapid drying of the soil. The soilless mixes tend to dry out more slowly although pots (in contrast to larger planters) usually need plenty of water under most circumstances.

What plants will hold adobe soil on hillsides? Nothing surpasses the common ice plant (mesembryanthemum) for this purpose; but other good ones would be honeysuckle, creeping lantana, geranium, and St. Augustine grass.

What are good plants for adobe soil, especially in the sun? As a general rule, the same plants will grow in adobe as in any other soil, but the difficulty caused by poor drainage eliminates some. The doubtful type of plant would include choisya, cistus, caesalpinia, helianthemum, leptospermum, and others known for their tolerance of dry conditions.

What flowers or shrubs would do well on the west side of a house where the temperature sometimes reaches 140° F.? In such hot, dry spots, one must have heat-loving plants. Leptospermum, oleander, lantana, bougainvillea, cistus, plumbago, *Cotoneaster lacteus,* diosma, felicia, helianthemum, leucophyllum, *Pittosporum tobira, Viburnum suspensum,* and *V. tinus* all should do well. For annuals, marigolds, petunias, portulacas, and tithonias will give summer color.

What low perennial may be planted in the shady strip between a drive and house? *Fragaria chiloensis* would be a happy choice. It is a creeper with bright-green foliage and bright-red fruits. *Campanula mayii* or *Bergenia crassifolia* would give some color, but would grow 12 inches to 15 inches tall. *Ajuga reptans* would also do very well.

What can be grown under eucalyptus trees? The heavy demand for food and water by the eucalyptus and the toxic effect of its leaves and bark make trouble for most plants. Grass, heavily fed and watered, is satisfactory, since debris can be easily raked off. English ivy is often used as a ground cover, but hand-picking of debris is necessary.

My house faces southwest, and the northeast corner gets little sun. What plants would do well there? This is an ideal spot for some of the shrubs that do not like full sun, especially camellia, azalea, gardenia, star jasmine, fuchsia, *Daphne odora,* hydrangea, eranthemum, ginger-lily, English holly, and nandina.

What flowers or vines will grow on the north side of our house, where it is shady all the time? There are many plants that grow well in the shade, the degree of shade being a limiting factor. Camellia, fuchsia, begonia, violet, fern, *Bergenia crassifolia* all do well in some shade. If very dense, use ferns, aucuba, sarcococca, and aspidistra.

We live under oaks, and find violets, iris, ferns, coleus, and begonias growing fine. What would do well in sunny spots in such soil? In sunny spots near oaks, most plants should thrive. If coleus and begonias overwinter, it would indicate a frost-free area, so try primroses, cineraria, calceolaria, and cyclamen for winter. In the shade azalea and camellia should do well. In the summer avoid rank-growing annuals, but try the rest.

What climber would grow on the wall of a summerhouse facing the ocean near Los Angeles? Few climbers compare with the blood trumpet vine (*Distictis buccinatoria*) under such circumstances. It has beautiful foliage, and for most of the year it produces huge red trumpets of bloom. It does not object to the salt breezes. It will need a trellis until it has something to hold on to.

What vine similar to trumpet vine can I put on the north side of my house? The trumpet vine itself, *Distictis buccinatoria,* does very well on the north, as will also *Bignonia violacea, Thunbergia grandiflora,* and *Distictis lactiflora,* all of lavender and blue shades. The Cape-honeysuckle, *Tecomaria capensis,* even more vivid than the trumpet vine, does well too. None of these like heavy shade, but normal conditions on the north are satisfactory. All are equally hardy.

How can I grow a beautiful dichondra lawn? The soil should be well enriched and perfectly graded. The plants are purchased in flats. They are divided with a knife into 2-inch or 3-inch squares. Planted about a foot apart, and well watered, these will soon spread. Frequent feedings with a balanced complete fertilizer and plenty of water are needed to keep the "lawn" green. It should be cut 3 or 4 times a year. A serious fault of dichondra is that chemical weedkillers will also kill the dichondra.

What time of year is the best for starting a lawn in Southern Califor-

nia?   A lawn may be started at any time, but the best time is fall—September or October. This will establish the plants well before heavy rains and give a good turf before the summer's heat.

How do you renovate an old lawn infested with "devil grass"?   It can hardly be eliminated, for a tiny piece of root starts a new plant. The customary procedure is to run a renovator over the lawn several times and rake out the roots as well as possible. This gives the new sowing a chance to fight the "devil grass" (Bermuda grass), though it will succumb again sooner or later. (Contact your local garden center.) Dalapon, a selective weedkiller, is the best chemical control to date.

How is a lawn of sagina moss made?   *Sagina subulata* is not a moss but a flowering plant. It is used as a shade-tolerant ground cover. It must have light soil and good drainage. It may be planted at any time of the year, but preferably in the spring. Flats may be purchased at some nurseries, and the plants are divided and planted quite closely. It has a serious failing in that it turns yellow in spots and must be replanted, but it is fairly permanent. (See also Moss Lawns, Section 9.)

What shrubs would make a good flowering hedge?   The list would be almost limitless in Southern California, but some of the best would be abelia, white and red, *Cassia splendida, Plumbago capensis, Murraya exotica, Choisya ternata,* cotoneaster, *Grewia caffra, Feijoa,* pyracantha, *Solanum rantonnetii, Viburnum suspensum* and *V. tinus,* and lantana. Properly cared for, a hedge of varicolored hibiscus can be beautiful. Oleander, with pruning, works out well.

How is a flowering hedge best planted?   Except for hibiscus, the plants mentioned above could be planted from containers at any time. (Hibiscus should be well established before winter.) Allow plenty of room for each plant to develop into a good specimen. Drop a line, and stake out the center of each hole along it. Dig generous holes and add plenty of manure or humus. In the rear, leave a good irrigation ditch. By all means, carry on a program of pruning, so that the hedge does not become an eyesore.

What are good plants for green hedges?   This would depend on the size required. For a very low hedge, nothing surpasses *Buxus microphylla* var. *japonica. Myrtus* 'Compacta' and *Ligustrum henryi* also make good low hedges. For a moderate-sized hedge (up to 5 feet), the wax-leaf privet (*Ligustrum lucidum*) is excellent. Boxwood is fine anywhere up to this height. For the tall hedge, *Pittosporum undulatum* outdoes any other. In hot, dry areas, *Ligustrum japonicum* is a tough, tall hedge.

Our dwarf eucalyptus windbreak blew over in a storm. What could

we use that would be sturdier? *Eucalyptus globulus* 'Compacta' is so shallow-rooted that it blows over easily. One good substitute is *E. cornuta*. Another would be *E. sideroxylon*, if it were topped out at about 20 feet. *Pittosporum undulatum* also makes a good windbreak if it need not be high.

What shrubs can be planted in Southern California in January and February? Since most shrubs are grown in containers, they can be planted at any time. Very tender plants, such as bougainvillea and hibiscus, are best planted later.

What are some shrubs that would make good foundation plants? Such a list should be made up of plants that will not cover the windows in a few years. Some good ones for sun are *Convolvulus cneorum, Correa reflexa, Juniperus* 'Tamariscifolia', *Turraea obtusifolia* —all of which grow very low. *Choisya ternata, Murraya paniculata, Viburnum suspensum, Myrtus* 'Compacta', *Ligustrum indicum, Abelia floribunda, Diosma ericoides, Gardenia, Pittosporum tobira*—all of which grow to moderate size, and can be kept low easily by pruning.

Will you name some shrubs that are quick to grow and easy to care for around a new home? This is really the worst thing to do in California, as quick-growing shrubs around the house in 3 or 4 years make a jungle and a mess. Be patient, and a permanent effect can be obtained by using slower-growing, more durable material.

My shrubs and trees grow too fast. How can this be prevented? Overwatering and overfeeding cause too rank a growth. Do not use fertilizer for several years, and water just enough to keep plants from wilting.

What are some good evergreen trees for a small home in the Los Angeles area? The evergreen elm, *Ulmus parvifolia* 'Pendens' (*sempervirens*), *Pittosporum undulatum,* and *P. rhombifolium* give beautiful fruits, as well as being good foliage trees. *Jacaranda acutifolia,* nearly evergreen, has a mass of blue flowers in the spring. *Calodendrum capense,* a mass of pink flowers in summer, is a good tree. *Magnolia grandiflora* is everyone's favorite. For certain types of homes, olive trees have a fine character.

What kind of tree do you suggest putting in a front yard only 40 feet wide? One of the finest trees is the evergreen elm, *Ulmus parvifolia* 'Pendens' (*sempervirens*). Care must be used in its purchase, for seedling forms vary too much. The best nurseries grow only from cuttings taken from fine trees.

What fruits are most likely to do well on the Pacific Coast? There is no fruit that does not do well somewhere on the Coast, except very tropical types. In the North, all the deciduous fruits, like apple, cherry, and plum, do very well. Farther south, the evergreen fruit area begins, and citrus, avocado, and other subtropicals do well.

How do you cure curly leaf on trees?   First, investigate for the presence of aphids. Most so-called curly leaf is the result of these plant lice. They are easily controlled by malathion, 2 teaspoonfuls of 50 per cent emulsion per gallon of water. If this is not the cause, it may be the curly-leaf virus. Consult your county extension agent.

Where can one obtain information on tropical ornamentals?   Not many truly tropical plants thrive in Southern California, where subtropicals are the rule. Tropicals generally demand a moist climate, with never any frost. They like light, moisture-retentive soils. They desire at least partial shade. Obviously, lath houses and conservatories are the answers. If attempts are to be made to grow them, contact one of the large nurseries in Southern California that specialize in exotic material, and the State Agricultural Experiment Station.

Would you please make suggestions for growing plants in a lath house?   On the whole, the plants that like shade prefer a light soil containing leafmold, which provides good drainage. This is often given by building raised beds and filling with prepared soil. Careful attention must be given to watering, but the results are worthwhile. Feeding should be done with cottonseed meal or an acid fertilizer. Do not grow heavy vines on the lath.

What plants are grown in lath houses?   Camellia, fuchsia, and begonia plants are raised by every lath-house owner. Other desirable subjects are gloxinia, streptocarpus, achimenes, caladium, anthurium, cyclamen, stephanotis, *Hoya carnosa,* and sarcococca. Many orchids also do very well.

What evergreen vine can I use over my lath house that will not freeze easily?   *Gelsemium sempervirens* is a good vine if the temperature does not drop below 15° F. It has a light growth that will not be too dense for the plants beneath, and in late winter is a mass of yellow bloom. It is very clean, and has refreshingly green foliage all year.

Why doesn't my almond tree bear?   A single tree never bears; 2 varieties must be planted together to get pollinization. Good combinations are 'Nonpareil' and 'Ne Plus Ultra', or 'Ne Plus Ultra' and 'I. X. L.'

I have an Arbutus unedo that blooms but does not set fruit. Why?   Some arbutus do not bear well. It would be well to investigate its environment before deciding that it is a poor type. The trees like good drainage. They do not like to be exposed to hot, dry winds; nor do they like an alkaline soil. If conditions are favorable and the tree is healthy, then the seedling is evidently a poor type.

I have an avocado tree 8 years old. Why do the blooms fall?   There may be many factors. The tree may be still immature. Drainage may be poor. Overwatering or feeding before the fruits set may have forced off the bloom. Oil sprays are sometimes given at the wrong time, before the fruit is set.

My seedling avocado has fruit. Will it be good?   There is a chance that it will be good. All the good varieties were once seedlings. For new plantings, seedlings are not worth the gamble, when there are such fine named varieties.

Should I destroy a seedling avocado with black fruit, growing 8 feet from another avocado?   One tree or the other would be best removed, for the tops spread wide, and you would end up with 2 poor trees. The black fruit is typical of many fine kinds of avocados.

What time of the year should avocados be picked?   Avocados are picked at any time of the year, depending on the varieties planted. For home use, they are best allowed to ripen on the trees. An avocado becomes somewhat soft when ripe.

Can azaleas be grown in Southern California?   Evergreen azaleas do beautifully with proper care. They should never be planted in full sun. A large amount of peat moss should be mixed in the soil. Drainage must be perfect, and in heavy soils this means raising the plant above the surrounding soil. During the summer, water heavily and feed generously with cottonseed meal or other acid fertilizer.

How can I encourage bananas to ripen in the Los Angeles area?   First, types that fruit in this area should be purchased. Plant in a rich, well-drained spot that is protected from hot, dry winds. Keep the plant growing in healthy condition and fruit should ripen.

Is there any special care for bird-of-paradise? Should it be pruned or divided?   If you have it outdoors in your California garden, let it grow as it pleases. Remove only dead foliage and don't divide before the foliage dies. Feed and water plentifully during the summer.

How are blackberries grown in California?   Blackberries grow fairly well here in heavy loam. Young plants are set out in early spring, about 3 feet apart. The first growth is pinched when a few feet tall to encourage branches that bear the fruit the next year. Each year canes that have fruited are cut out after harvesting. A mulch of manure or compost in the spring and copious watering in the growing season are desirable. In warm climates, blackberries are short-lived. Start new plants from root sprouts of existing plantings for replacement every 3 years.

Can blueberries be grown in California?   There are some places where they should grow well, but they seldom do. If you have a moist climate and cool winters, write to an eastern nursery specializing in fruits, and try its recommendations.

What is the best care of boxwood?   Boxwood is a very easily grown plant. It likes a fertile soil, with plenty of organic fertilizer. It must never be allowed to become dry or it will start to shed foliage. Frequent prunings or shearings will keep it dense. Be on the lookout for red spider, which mottles the foliage, and for scale. There are many sprays for red spider on the market, and scale is controlled by a 1½ per cent or 2 per cent oil spray or by malathion in June or July.

How are boysenberries grown?   Plant in early spring, at least 5 feet apart. Allow the vines to grow on the ground. Be generous with water and fertilizer. Early the next spring, tie the vines on trellises. As the berries start ripening, cut out new growth. After harvesting, cut off the vines that bore the fruit and allow new growths to grow on the ground. These should be tied up early the following spring. Plenty of fertilizer in the spring and plenty of water in the summer will produce tremendous crops.

In the West, should ranunculus bulbs be lifted after flowering?   Yes; when they are dormant, they resent the water given other plants. When the foliage is yellowed and dry, they are ready for digging. Seedling-grown ranunculus give far superior bloom but are troublesome to start.

What is the proper care for calla-lily in California?   Calla-lilies are almost weeds here, except in bad frost areas. They enjoy partial shade but it is not necessary. They like a very rich soil and plenty of water and rich compost. They do not need a rest period. They can be divided at any time, but early fall is best.

Could you suggest a tree similar to the Deodar cedar?   There are a number of fine coniferous trees for Southern California. The atlas cedar and its blue variety, the canary pine, the Aleppo pine, the stone pine, the Monterey pine, the coast redwood, and the California incense-cedar all do well in most areas.

When should chrysanthemums be planted, and how?   New plants can be set out in the spring and planted about 12 inches apart to the same depth they were growing. They enjoy a rich soil and reasonably generous watering. Pinch several times in the summer to encourage branching and strong stems. Divide yearly, after blooming. Container plants are available nearly year-round.

We water our citrus trees by trenches and daily sprinkling. Is this too much?   Citrus trees do not need much water when once established.

Overwatering forces growth at the expense of fruit and may kill the tree. A well-established tree need not be watered more than once a month. This will encourage deep rooting.

How old must a seedling citrus tree be before it bears fruit?   This would be extremely variable, but a guess would be between 4 and 8 years. Seedlings are seldom worth growing.

Why does a young lemon tree produce hard lemons?   The first fruit of citrus trees often has a very thick rind. If the tree is a seedling, there is a good chance that it is a hard type. Citrus is one fruit that responds to good care. Instructions can be obtained from your local county extension agent.

I have a lemon that is losing its leaves. Why?   A very heavy crop of fruit often will strip a lemon of most of its foliage. Overwatering in poorly drained soil may cause the condition, but the poor health of the tree will be obvious. Less water and a feeding of commercial citrus food in the spring should bring it back. Lemon trees require very little water.

When should lemons be planted?   Lemons and other citrus and evergreen fruits are best planted in a well-worked soil in the spring when cold weather is over and before summer's heat. A stake should be provided immediately, and some kind of shade on the south side to prevent sunburn on the trunk. Watering should be liberal the first year.

How are 'Meyer' lemons and dwarf limes grown?   There are no true dwarf limes, though the 'Rangpur' (*Citrus* x *limonia*) is somewhat small. Lemons are quite hardy; limes (*Citrus aurantifolia*), definitely not. Where each can be grown, requirements are the same. Good drainage is essential. They want plenty of water when young, much less as they mature. Light feeding in the spring is beneficial. Most 'Meyer' lemon trees tend to overbear. Thin out fruits in clusters to a single lemon.

How can one tell the difference between young oranges and lemons?   The best way is to note the foliage. The lemon has much paler foliage than the orange, if the orange has been growing well. It sometimes is very difficult, except for an expert, to tell.

How does one apply lime around orange trees?   Lime is sprinkled on the soil rather heavily, as far out as the branches spread. It is cultivated in a few inches. Irrigation then carries it evenly through the soil. Ground limestone is the best form to use.

What do you spray oranges with?   Under normal conditions, oranges are sprayed in the summer with a dormant oil, usually a 2 per cent solution of light medium. This will kill red spider, scale, aphids, etc. It should never be applied when the temperature is above 90° F. in the shade. A perfect coverage is essential.

How do you prune cotoneasters to get good berries? Cotoneasters fruit on 1-year-old wood. After the berries fall, the wood on which they were borne should be cut back about 6 inches from the ground. New growths for the following year's berries will spring freely from the stubs. Never be afraid to cut the sprays for decoration, for this can become a part of the pruning if the stems are cut back to about 6 inches.

My cotoneasters, though faithfully watered and fertilized for over a year, have had no berries. Could they be "duds"? Cotoneasters have perfect flowers and do not require pollination to set berries. Dead wood, caused by dieback from fire blight, usually strikes the stems bearing flower buds, causing sterility. Probably too much shade, too much water, too immature, or pruning off the flowering wood would be the difficulty. Since they are almost foolproof, patience will probably reward you with their showy berries. (See the previous question.)

My cypress tree yellows, then browns. It seems to be dying. Why? This is a disease called coryneum canker and has no permanent cure. Cutting out the first cankers to appear will retard the disease, as will a spray of Bordeaux mixed according to the instructions on the container. Monterey cypress is the most frequent victim. Forbes' cypress seems resistant.

What special culture is needed for tree ferns? The tree fern, *Alsophila australis,* is not a temperamental plant, but it must be treated as a fern. It likes shade, leafmold, perfect drainage, and must never be allowed to dry out, even for an hour. During the spring and summer, it likes feedings of dried blood or liquid fertilizer high in nitrogen.

How often should figs and peaches be watered? The texture of the soil decides this. Sandy soils need more water; heavy soil, less. During the growing season, deciduous fruits require a moist soil. Watering every 2 weeks in sandy soil might not be too much. On the other hand, 2 or 3 good soakings during the season might suffice in adobe soil.

What kind of soil and care do fuchsias require? They like protection from hot sun; the north and east sides of the house are good. If possible, provide a light, well-drained soil high in humus. They must never suffer from a lack of moisture. Regular monthly feedings of acid fertilizers are appreciated, the best being cottonseed meal. This feeding should be started in March and continued until September.

How should fuchsias be pruned when in the ground? In February or March, cut back hard, leaving only a little of the previous season's growth. The best plants are obtained if the new growth is pinched when about 6 or 8 inches long, thus making the plant bushy.

How are potted fuchsias cared for? Fuchsias are generally grown in 6-inch pots as rapidly as growth permits, and then shifted into 8-inch pots. If feeding is carried out, every 2 years should be often enough to shift plants to larger pots. During the growing season, they should be watered heavily and food applied monthly. Each February or March, they should be pruned hard to force new flowering growth.

How often should gerbera plants be divided? Do they require fertilizer? Gerbera plants really demand rich, well-drained soil. They particularly like organic fertilizer. Divide every 3 or 4 years in the early fall. They are subject to aphids, so spray with malathion.

In California, should gladiolus bulbs be lifted? Yes. They multiply fast and need separation; they should be kept dry when dormant. They can best be treated for thrips when out of the ground. After digging, keep them in a sack for about 2 weeks with naphthalene flakes to kill thrips, then remove them and screen or shake the naphthalene off. Store in a cool, dry place.

When should we prune grapes set out last spring? 'Tokay', 'Muscat', 'Ribier', and 'Zinfandel' all require hard pruning. Pruning the first winter is to restrict the plant to one stem to form the trunk. It should be the most vigorous branch and should be cut back to 2 eyes. (See Grape.)

What is the difference between strawberry guava and pineapple-guava? Although both belong to the myrtle family, they are different genera. The strawberry guava is *Psidium littorale;* this and its variety *littorale* make 2 fine fruits and very attractive plants with light-green, glossy foliage. The pineapple-guava (*Feijoa sellowiana*) has very pleasant fruit that is excellent for jam, and is a beautiful large shrub with silvery foliage and bright-red flowers. Both are well worth growing for fruit and ornament.

I am interested in a small herb garden. Can you suggest some herbs for it? Herbs do well in Southern California, especially in light soils. They like poor soil and little water. Except for mint, they will not survive in the shade. Plant in early spring. The plants should be renewed every 3 or 4 years. A good list would include sweet basil, thyme, sweet marjoram, savory (both winter and summer types), tarragon, sage, rosemary, lavender, chives, mint, and lemon balm. (See Herbs.)

Why is it that some people have such bad luck with English holly in California? English holly is grown to perfection in California, but it will not thrive in the full blazing sun in the summer. A slight shade must be provided.

What planting and care is necessary for iris in adobe soil? Irises are exceedingly easy to grow. The only precaution to take in adobe soil is not to plant too deeply. Barely cover the rhizomes and do not water heavily. Every third year, clumps should be dug, saving only the new, strong rhizomes. Except in interior hot areas, this is best done as soon as flowers fade in the spring. In the hot areas, September is better. Feeding in spring and fairly generous watering until they flower will ensure good bloom.

How should jasmines be pruned? True jasmines grow so abundantly that they should be severely pruned in the winter. Old stems should be cut out at the ground each year, as the bloom is much finer on young growth. The bad reputation of the yellow jasmine is due to its excessive growth, but it can be kept in bounds and attractive by regular pruning.

What lilacs would bloom here in Los Angeles County? Eastern lilacs are unsatisfactory, suffering either from excessive heat or mildew. The lilac that does very well is the Persian lilac, *Syringa persica*. It has lavender flowers in the spring that are fine for cutting, and the plant is of graceful habit. Easterners who remember lilacs with nostalgia should plant the lovely species of *Ceanothus,* often called California-lilac.

When should lilies be planted in California? Lilies should be planted as soon as they are available in the fall. They like full sun and rich soil, but resent poor drainage or fertilizer touching the bulbs.

Does lily-of-the-valley do well in the California coastal region? There are a number of successful plantings here. They need shade and a light soil.

Can mangoes be grown in Southern California? They can and are grown in frost-free areas. They need plenty of water and the soil should be constantly mulched.

What would be a good covering under oak trees? Three very good ground covers would be the evergreen ornamental strawberry (*Fragaria chiloensis*), bugle-weed (*Ajuga reptens*), and English ivy (*Hedera helix*).

How are oleanders pruned to keep them vigorous and flowering freely? After the plant is several years old, old stems, as soon as they have finished flowering, are cut off almost to the ground. No plant suckers more freely, so do not be afraid of harsh cutting.

Can papaya be grown in California? Only in a few areas that never have frost. The trees are difficult to pollinate, and several trees must be planted. Though they are delicious and have been fruited, they are a gamble.

How are flowering peaches pruned? These plants have an unhappy life in the Southern California area because most people fail to cut them hard enough. They need the stimulus of hard pruning. They should be cut back each year after flowering, leaving only about 6 inches of growth of the previous year. If pruned right after blooming, there will be plenty of time for the plant to send out and mature strong growth for next year's bloom.

Is the peony plant a shrub? Will it grow in Southern California? Though there is a shrubby type, most peonies are herbaceous, dying to the ground in the winter. In Southern California, they grow well in only a few favored locations. The long, hot summer is too much for them. They are not a good choice. North of San Jose, tree peonies are reliable and beautiful.

What should I do to have success with perennial phlox? Hardy phlox grows well in Southern California, but it takes clean, healthy stock, planted in rich soil, with some little protection from the afternoon sun. They should be divided, in the fall, every few years. Flower heads should be removed immediately after fading.

What is the culture for Norfolk-Island-pine in order to get rapid development? This plant is not a rapid grower even in California. If your area is not subject to hard frost, treat like any other tree. It will not make more than 1 or 2 tiers a year.

How is the dwarf pomegranate grown? Dwarf pomegranates are grown chiefly for their decorative bloom. They require little care. Like most deciduous plants, they enjoy plenty of food and water during the growing season. Thinning out occasionally in the winter encourages better bloom. Do not allow fruit to mature on the plant. There are some new types that are really showy.

How should a 'Santa Rosa' plum be pruned? Pruning fruit trees is a long subject, well covered by bulletins obtainable from your county agent. Training should be started the first year and practiced every winter. (See Plums.)

How should pyracantha shrubs be pruned? Pyracanthas (firethorns) and cotoneasters have the same habits, and should be pruned much alike. After a plant is several years old, each berry-producing branch should be cut back to within about 6 inches of the trunk; each year thereafter the producing branches should be cut to within 6 inches of their bases. They should never be sheared, for it will result in a top-heavy plant. The time for pruning is when the berries fall or dry. Some species will grow into small trees if left unpruned.

When should roses be planted?   When available in your region, probably about December 15 to May 1. Or buy container-grown plants, which can be planted anytime.

How should roses be planted?   Holes generous enough to receive the roots without cramping should be dug. Mix a shovelful of rich compost or manure in the bottom, then hold the plant at the required depth (the bud union—the swelling between roots and branches—should be even with or an inch above the soil surface), pull in a little soil, and work it around the roots with the fingers. Gradually fill the hole, packing the soil around the roots. Water thoroughly.

How should roses be fertilized?   A liberal dressing of a commercial rose fertilizer in early spring and again in June, with light applications of fertilizer, monthly, between April and August, will keep roses growing and blooming.

When should rosebushes be pruned?   In Southern California, roses try to be everblooming. This is not in the best interest of the plants. Water should be withheld after September, and the plants allowed to become dormant. Then, in December, a severe pruning is in order every other year. Reserve only 3 or 4 stout canes and reduce these to about ⅓ their length. Proper cutting of buds and dead blooms, leaving only about 3 eyes below the cut, will take care of most of the pruning in the intervening 2 years.

How should large-flowered climbers be pruned?   Climbers of this type differ from the hybrid teas in that wood of the previous season is required for bloom. They are best pruned after blooming. Old canes should be cut down low. The new canes may be shortened, and lateral growths restricted to 2 or 3 eyes. At this time, tying and training are best done.

What is the method of, and time for, pruning roses?   They are generally pruned by cutting off buds and dead blooms. If these are cut so that only 2 or 3 eyes are left on each cane, and all weak and crossing growths are removed, little more will be needed. Any heavier pruning that seems required should be done in December and January.

How should I care for roses in tubs on a patio?   Roses may be well grown in large tubs if feeding and watering are properly done. During the winter, cease feeding and reduce water. In the spring, a topdressing of fertilizer will be appreciated. Thereafter, feed monthly with a complete fertilizer. Because of the limited amount of soil in a tub, repotting with fresh soil every few years is a "must."

When are rose cuttings taken in California? Most roses are budded, for their own roots are weak. Understock roses are grown from hardwood cuttings inserted in the field in the winter. Greenwood cuttings may be rooted at almost anytime.

How many years before sapota and cherimoya bear fruit? Are 2 trees necessary for cross-pollinization? Seedling sapotas take 7 to 8 years; budded stock takes 4 to 5 years. Seedling cherimoyas bear in 4 or 5 years; budded stock takes 2 or 3 years. Two trees are not necessary in either case, but some growers recommend hand pollinization of cherimoyas for greater yield.

What is the proper culture for schizanthus and wallflower? Neither plant is difficult to grow. Seed is sown from July to September. There may be difficulty with seed during the hot months, so the later date may be more convenient. When a few inches high, the seedlings should be moved to the spot in the garden where they are to grow. Shade them for a few days, until they take hold. Neither seems too fussy about soil outdoors.

When are strawberries planted, and what is their care? Strawberries in California may be set in the fall. They must have a well-worked soil with good drainage and are planted on raised beds about 2 feet wide, with a shallow irrigation trench. They need copious water during the summer for they are shallow-rooting. They are generally left several years without replanting. A feeding of manure or a complete fertilizer in the spring is advisable. However, fruiting will be heavier if runners are rooted in pots so that a new row can be planted about every 3 years.

What are tangelos? Tangelos are fruits resulting from crossing the grapefruit and tangerine. The old name of grapefruits was pomelo, hence the name tangelo. They grow the same as oranges, requiring identical care, and produce delicious tangy fruits in the winter. Several varieties are on the market that have fruiting periods from November until early summer.

Can the tea plant (Camellia sinensis) be safely planted outdoors in Southern California? The true tea plant is frequently found in Southern California, making a very attractive shrub. In adobe soil, plant it a little above the soil level. In sandy soils, plenty of water is necessary. Plant it in full sun. Acid fertilizer is most appreciated in the spring.

What vegetables may be planted in January and February? Among the many vegetables planted in Southern California in the winter are cabbage, broccoli, spinach, kohlrabi, beets, parsley, peas, turnips, carrots, and onions. In some areas, more favored by good drainage and mild climate, squash (under Hotkaps) may be planted at this time.

How are violets seeded or planted, and do they do well in Southern California? Violets do very well in California. They want a light soil, high in humus, and some shade. Though they must be divided every few years, they will become permanent if cared for. Try the huge flower type, 'Royal Robe'.

I have violets planted around an oak, growing and blossoming freely, but the whole plant heaves out. Why? Violets in California have this habit, and undoubtedly to a greater degree when leaves falling on them force them to grow upward for light. They should be divided every few years and replanted firmly, for they will lose vigor if growing too much on the surface.

How should walnuts be watered? Walnuts are irrigated more or less frequently, depending on the soil. Sandy soil may require monthly irrigation during the growing season, while adobe would need only one watering. Some experts claim that irrigation about two weeks before harvest makes shucking easier. If trees are grafted on black walnut stock, overwatering encourages black root rot.

Colorado

Our springs are dry and late in Colorado. Can you give me a list of annuals that can be planted in the fall? Larkspur, California poppy, calendula, echium, bartonia; in short, all of the hardy annuals. Cover the seed bed with a winter mulch. Remove when seeds germinate in the spring.

We live northeast of Colorado Springs, altitude 7,500 feet; I cannot get annuals to grow more than 6 inches high. Can it be the soil or cool weather? Cosmos and morning-glories do well. Since these annuals thrive this high in other parts of your region, your trouble may be poor soil, alkaline soil, or perhaps late planting.

How do you take care of boysenberry bushes during the winter in Colorado? Remove the canes from their supports, lay them flat and cover with straw, cornstalks, or spruce branches. It is advisable to spray first with lime-sulfur, or aluminum sulfate, to make them less attractive to mice. Or place mouse poison inside drain tiles laid between the canes.

We irrigate our land in Colorado. I have a bank that I wish to cover with some drought-resistant ground cover; it will have to depend on rain for moisture. What shall I use? *Sedum stoloniferum* can "take it," making a year-round cover. Burlap helps to hold the new surface if the bank is steep.

What treatment should be given monkshood (aconitum)?   In any except subalpine regions in Colorado, aconitum would resent open sunshine and consequent dryness. Try changing to shade, or semishade, and deep, rich, peaty soil.

What can I do to raise pansies successfully in southern Colorado?   Sow seeds in a prepared seed bed early in September. In colder areas, plants will survive better in a cold frame. Keep moist and mulch when the ground begins to freeze. Next May, transplant to a permanent bed of good loam enriched with rotted manure and peat moss and in open sun. Keep seed pods picked.

What are the best, showiest, and easiest grown perennials for late-summer blooming in this climate?   *Anemone japonica,* anthemis, chrysanthemums, *Clematis heracleafolia,* eupatorium, helenium, *Heliopsis* 'Pitcherana', monarda, perennial asters, *Phlox paniculata, Physostegia virginiana,* ceratostigma, rudbeckia hybrids, *Salvia argentea, S. pratensis.*

What perennial, preferably a foliage plant, would make the best low-growing border for my garden in eastern Colorado?   *Cerastium tomentosum* (kept within bounds), *Festuca ovina glauca, Euphorbia myrsinites*—all 3 have silver-gray foliage. *Teucrium chamaedrys,* kept shorn, makes a neat, green, miniature hedge, suggestive of boxwood edging.

Hybrid tea roses bloom prolifically in this climate but are hard to keep from freezing during the winter months. How would you advise to mulch and protect for the winter?   Prune down to 6 or 8 inches in autumn, mound up soil or peat moss around each plant. Cover with a layer of any open material that will shade from the sun and permit air circulation, such as spruce or fir branches, or straw held down with wire. The plastic cones now available are unusually successful unless left on too late in the spring.

Will you suggest some hardy roses for high altitudes in Colorado?   *Rosa hugonis, R. rugosa* and its hybrids; 'Harison's Yellow'; 'Frühlingsgold'; hybrid perpetuals 'Frau Karl Druschki' and 'General Jacquemot'.

Can you give some information on spring versus fall planting of roses, shrubs, and trees in Denver, a mile above sea level?   In such regions of dry, sunny cold winters, the difficulties of watering and protecting newly planted woody material make spring planting preferable.

How can I grow sweet peas successfully in southern Colorado?   In autumn dig a trench 12 inches wide and 12 to 18 inches deep. In the bottom put a 6-inch layer of rich compost or manure. Fill with good, rich, friable loam. Early the following March, sow seed. Unless sweet peas have been grown in the soil before, be sure to inoculate the seed with a suitable legume culture available from most mail-order seed houses or garden centers.

Florida

When is the best time to transplant amaryllis? Root action commences in late September or early October. The bulbs should be lifted, divided, and reset, therefore, in the early autumn. Bone meal or another alkaline plant food is suggested for these bulbs.

We must move to southern Florida. Can you recommend a gardening book for that area? *Florida Gardening Month by Month,* by Nixon Smiley (University of Miami Press, Coral Gables, Florida).

What is the best type of soil for blackberries in Florida? A sandy loam soil that has a relatively high organic content is best for the bramble fruits. A heavy hammock type is ideal, particularly if there is a constant water table 2 or 3 feet below the surface. A slightly acid soil is considered best.

How are caladiums grown? Plant the tubers in a partly shaded position that is sheltered from strong winds. The soil should contain an abundance of humus and should be reasonably moist at all times. Feeding with liquid fertilizer during the season of active growth is very beneficial.

What is the correct culture for calla-lilies in northern Florida? Callas are tropical bulbous plants easily injured by frost. The roots are usually received in November, and they can be planted at once in a rich, acid, mucky mixture in large pots or urns. These containers may be plunged under trees and taken indoors when frost is forecast. They can be held in a dormant state until the danger of frost has passed in March, and then planted in a rich acid bed out-of-doors. South of Bradenton, callas are best left in the soil permanently.

What is frenching and bronzing of citrus fruits, and how is it cured? Frenching is the result of a zinc deficiency and is corrected by adding zinc sulfate to the sprays. Bronzing results when there is insufficient magnesium available to orange trees. Dolomite in judicious amounts will usually correct a bronzed condition. Epsom salts and a potassium-magnesium sulfate will also correct the deficiency.

What causes oranges to split open before they are ripe, and how is this prevented? It is usually thought to be caused by a deficiency of copper. Small amounts of copper sulfate (bluestone) will tend to ameliorate the condition.

What are the brown dots on the undersides of orange leaves? Round brown dots with reddish centers are Florida red scale. This pest can be controlled with an oil emulsion spray, used according to the directions on the package.

What are some of the best climbers for central Florida? Bougainvilleas in their several attractive colors; the very colorful flamevine; herald trumpet—a rampant tropical creeper; queen's-wreath, with its gorgeous purple blossoms; *Quisqualis indica* (Rangoon-creeper); the luxuriant coral-vine; the fast-growing skyflower; and the fragrant Confederate jasmine, and several other climbing jasmines, are among the most popular of Florida's many vines.

What about columbines for central Florida? Although columbines are native to extreme western Florida, they do not grow readily in the peninsula. They can be flowered, however, with good culture. Get plants from the North and set them in a partially shaded place in November, feeding them a balanced plant food every 2 or 3 weeks as they grow. They need an abundance of water and must not have too much root competition for water or nutrients.

When should dahlias be planted in southern Florida? For spring and summer bloom, plant the roots in January or February; for autumn bloom, arrange to have roots held in cold storage and delivered in late August or early September.

How may good dahlias be grown in central Florida? The roots are procured in February or March and are planted about 5 inches deep in garden beds that have been enriched with compost and a commercial fertilizer. Drive a stout stake by the stem end of the root and tie the plant every 8 inches or so as it grows. Feed liberally every 3 or 4 weeks. Dust with sulfur or malathion at the first signs of red spider.

How can I have dahlias in central Florida? Set the roots in good soil about 5 inches deep; water and feed liberally as the plants grow. These roots will be difficult to carry over in Florida, so it is suggested that you treat them as annuals, starting over each autumn. Don't overlook the small-flowered types from seed grown as annuals.

Can I increase my very beautiful flame-of-the-woods? Yes, use softwood tip cuttings in June or July and insert them in clean white sand in a new box. Place cheesecloth over the box; set in on the north side of the house and sprinkle daily with a fine spray. The cuttings should root in 4 or 5 weeks.

Will foxgloves grow in northern Florida?   Possibly in the extreme western end of the state, but they are certain to be a disappointment in most areas. Like many other perennials, they need a long, cold winter for inducing an unbroken dormancy.

How shall I fertilize, water, and care for a lawn of centipede grass?   Centipede grass is one of the best lawn materials for the light, sandy soils of Florida. An application of a lawn fertilizer in March, another in June or July, should suffice. Water the fertilizer in as soon as applied, and irrigate often enough to keep the grass leaves from curling and turning gray-green. Frequent mowing is necessary for a good centipede turf. During the growing season, the mower must be used at least once each week.

Will heliophila grow in northern Florida?   Yes, these South African annuals, commonly known as cape-stock, should do well if the seeds are sown in flats in January, the seedlings grown in a not too moist soil, and the plants set out in March.

What can I do to have irises from Kentucky bloom in Florida?   Nothing! Excepting in extreme western Florida, bearded irises are not successful. The light, sandy soils and lack of sustained low winter temperatures do not suit these favorites of temperate gardens. Why not use native southern species that do succeed so beautifully?

When should I fertilize my lawn?   Early in March, apply a lawn fertilizer; then again when the rains start in June, make a second application. In all parts of Florida except the extreme north, additional small monthly feedings in January and February help to keep the grass green through the colder months and build it up for its spurt of spring growth.

Can old-fashioned lilacs be raised as far south as Jacksonville?   No, the light, sandy acid soils and lack of a real dormant season do not suit these popular temperate garden plants and they are certain to be disappointing. Why plant lilacs in Florida when the lovely crape-myrtle (*Lagerstroemia*) is available in a wider range of color?

When should a mulberry tree be pruned to be sure of a good crop in Florida?   Mulberry trees should be pruned directly after they have finished fruiting in the spring.

What is the best time to plant nasturtiums in Florida?   Nasturtiums must be grown in autumn in order to mature blossoms before frost; or in spring, by sowing after the last frost for blooming before hot weather sets in and kills the plants.

When should my oleanders be cut back?   Just after flowering. If plants are to be kept from getting very large, root prune them at this time by driving a spade deep in a circle about 2 or 3 feet from the plant.

Is peat from local bogs good for us to use on our gardens? Local peat is excellent if it comes from an inland bog. Be very certain that you do not buy muck from a tidal marsh, however, as this saline material will kill or injure plants.

Can peonies be grown successfully in the central part of Florida? Peonies are a complete failure in peninsular Florida. The light, sandy soil and the lack of continuously cold winter to assure complete dormancy combine to defeat our best attempts to make southerners out of these temperate garden favorites.

What roses do best in southern Florida? If you can give them good loam, with enough humus in it to hold moisture, grow the old teas like 'Lady Hillington' and 'Marechal Niel' and the more enduring of the hybrid teas such as 'Radiance', 'Red Radiance', and 'Crimson Glory'. Among floribundas, most will do well for a time, but especially recommended are 'Fashion', 'Floradora', and 'Pinocchio'. If the heat and sandy soil is too much for these, you may want to purchase inexpensive plants from Texas yearly and grow them as annuals.

I want to use old-fashioned roses. Which ones will do best with the least care? The old French rose grows well. Among our most dependable old roses are 'Louis Philippe', 'Safrano', 'Duchesse de Brabant', 'Marie van Houtte', 'Minnie Francis', 'Belle of Portugal', and 'Mme. Lombard'. Plants of these varieties will thrive in your southern garden long after plants of cutting varieties have succumbed. You will have trouble finding them, though. (See Section 6 for information on Heritage Roses.)

When is the best time of year to set rosebushes? Roses planted in December and early January will have time to make good root growth before top growth is started by the warm days of early spring. The earliest possible planting is considered best for Florida.

How far back should roses be trimmed, and what time of the year is best? Bush roses should be pruned, in January or February, to 4 or 5 strong eyes on each of 4 or 5 canes. Make the pruning cuts about ¼ inch above a strong eye that points away from the center of the plant. Ramblers can be pruned at the same time, using a renewal system to remove all of the canes more than 1 or 2 years old, as blossoms are borne from spurs on 1-year canes. As large-flowered climbers bloom on 2-year-old wood, merely prune out dead canes and cut flowering stems back to 2 or 3 eyes. Train canes horizontally to encourage many flowering shoots.

Will Centaurea moschata (sweet sultan) grow in northern Florida? Yes, very excellent sweet sultans have been grown and sold in this area. Sow seeds in a flat in October. The seed will germinate better if stored in a refrigerator for 2 weeks before planting. Transplant seedlings to well-enriched beds in midwinter. Plants should blossom in April and May. Red spiders must be forestalled with sulfur dust or malathion during dry periods.

Will violas succeed here? Yes, these miniature pansies do very well if plants are bought from a northern specialist in November and planted at once to grow through the cool winter.

What is the culture for watsonia in northern Florida? Watsonia, like gladiolus, can be planted in February in northern Florida. Set the corms about 3 inches deep in beds that have been enriched with compost and a commercial plant food. The blossoms should be produced in April and May.

Will the willow oak grow in Florida? Yes, the willow oak (*Quercus phellos*) is native to northern Florida and will succeed as a fast-growing, desirable tree as far south as the central part of the peninsula. Unless the upright growth of the willow oak is wanted, the live oak (*Quercus virginiana*) is a superior tree. It is evergreen with a majestic spreading habit.

Will the weeping willow grow successfully in Florida? It will grow in heavy soils close to watercourses in northern Florida, but it will not grow as well as it does farther north, nor can it be considered nearly as beautiful here as in the temperate states.

Can you tell us about Florida lawns? As new home owners from the North, we were appalled when we faced southern grasses for the first time. True, the first look at St. Augustine lawns can be something of a shock! Coarser than either crabgrass or quackgrass, abhorred in the North, it does seem an improbable substitute for bluegrasses. Once the shock is over, you will learn to live with St. Augustine grass; yes, even to love its springy texture underfoot. Florida soils, particularly the sterile coastal sands, present still further problems, for which new techniques are needed if grasses are to survive.

What grass should I use on my lawn in central Florida? The first choice of an inexperienced lawn owner should be St. Augustine. It is coarse, aggressive, and invasive, and far from smooth in appearance, but it is green, survives, and has few enemies. It is salt-resistant (a major problem in coastal areas) and can be quickly established from sprigs (short lengths of cut stems). It requires less fertilizer than do Bermuda and zoysia, which do make lawns more closely resembling those of the North. Most important, it is quite shade-tolerant. Its one weakness is its lack of resistance to chinch bugs.

Is there any control for chinch bugs? Malathion doesn't touch them. Diazinon (trade name Spectracide) is a specific control. The variety 'Floratan' is resistant, and where chinch bugs attack year after year, it should be planted in place of common St. Augustine.

Is 'Bitter Blue' St. Augustine superior to common? When first introduced, it was a darker, richer green, had shorter internodes with finer leaves, and produced a smoother, more attractive sod. Since then it has become mixed with common. If you are buying 'Bitter Blue', be sure to examine it in the field first, checking against common. Even better is 'Floratine' (not 'Floratan'), but more expensive. It has the finest stems, with short internodes. To get the genuine, be sure that the 'Floratine' has a blue state certification tag.

I am told that I must feed my fine-leaved Bermuda lawn often. How often and how much? For superior growth, the fine-leaved Bermuda grasses need to be fed about a pound of actual nitrogen per 1,000 square feet for every month they are in active growth, which usually means from March through November. This can be reduced by using slow-acting fertilizers that contain nitrogen in the form of IBDU, ureaform, or sulfur-coated urea. These must, of course, contain other nutrients in addition to nitrogen. They can be applied quarterly and will feed for about 3 months from each application.

Friends are urging me to plant Bahia grass. They say it looks more like Kentucky bluegrass than any other Florida grass. Bahia is being oversold. While it is freer from pests and other ills than most grasses, it is severely attacked by mole crickets. It must be mowed high, 2½ to 3 inches, which destroys the illusion of a bluegrass lawn. At this height it seeds heavily and must be cut every week to look even reasonably neat. This mowing cannot be skipped at any time between the end of April and Thanksgiving. It is tough and takes a powerful mower to cut. It does not form a true sod and the soil beneath is exposed. In alkaline soils it must be treated regularly with a solution of ferrous ammonium sulfate if it is to hold a deep-green color. Bahia is not all bad. It is fairly tolerant of light shade and will grow on acid soil. On clay soil, which it prefers, it is one of the hardiest of the warm-season grasses.

My friends tell me that the only grass that will do well on my poor soil is centipede. What do you advise? Centipede is also called lazy man's grass because it can stand more neglect than any other. It requires very little feeding and will actually die out if overfed. It is low-growing: the stems hug the ground so closely that it needs mowing only once every other week. It is not salt-tolerant and is damaged both by nematodes and ground-pearl scale. If you need a low-maintenance turf, this is it, but it won't be a model lawn.

I have heard that Florida lawns can be kept green all winter by overseeding. What seed do I use for this purpose? Either Italian or common ryegrass is the usual grass used for overseeding. The newer fine-leaved ryegrasses are somewhat more vigorous but not superior in appearance. 'Highland' bent grass is fairly expensive, but the seed is so fine that it goes much farther and costs little more.

Is zoysia a good grass for Florida lawns? Common zoysia from seed is worthless. The finer 'Emerald' zoysia and *Zoysia tenuifolia* are excellent but demand heavy feeding and liberal irrigation. *Zoysia matrella* (Manila grass) is spectacular as a shade grass but difficult to maintain.

My lawn is being destroyed by mole crickets. How can I control them? Use baits containing Baygon, Dursban, or malathion placed on the lawn in June. Or spray with Baygon 70 per cent Wettable Powder, 1 or 2 ounces of solution to 1,000 square feet.

I am confused by catalog descriptions of citrus fruits. What are some good home-garden varieties? You may have to ask your Cooperative Extension Service office for sources, since the better home-garden varieties are not grown commercially to any extent. Oranges: 'King', 'Ponkan' ('Chinese Honey'); tangelos: 'Orlando', 'Minneola', 'Seminole', 'Temple'; grapefruit: 'Marsh Seedless'; lemon: 'Meyer'. There are no named varieties of kumquat, calamondin, or tangerine.

Please list some noncitrus fruits for Florida. Banana: 'Dwarf Cavendish', 'Lady Finger'; figs: 'Osborn's Prolific', 'Ronde Noire', 'White Genos', 'Celeste', 'Brunswick', 'Magnolia'; mango: 'Irwin', 'Fascell', 'Kent'. There are no named varieties, but the following fruits are delicious: papaya, Otaheite-gooseberry, Barbados-cherry, Natal-plum, Surinam-cherry, and sea-grape.

I have heard that apples can be grown in Florida, particularly a variety called 'Helm'. 'Helm' will fruit in Florida, but it is so poor that it isn't worth growing. See local garden centers for some of the warm-climate fruit varieties originated in Israel. To throw apple trees into dormancy so they will develop flower buds, you may have to defoliate them completely in mid-November, picking off every leaf by hand. The defoliants used for taking leaves off roses to put them into dormancy can also be used, but this is a tricky operation, better left to experts.

Georgia

What grows most satisfactorily in partial shade in this state other than azaleas and camellias?   Oakleaf hydrangea (*H. quercifolia*), St. Johnswort (*Hypericum*), heavenly-bamboo (*Nandina domestica*), stewartia, *Gordonia lasianthus,* and illicium are all excellent shrubs for the shady garden.

What is the best position and soil for amaryllis?   Amaryllis grown outdoors in the South does well in a sunny or lightly shaded position in a well-drained fertile soil that is neutral or very slightly acid.

What are the cultural needs of amaryllis?   Apply balanced fertilizer immediately after blooming; water well through dry periods during its growing season. In the fall, mulch with half-rotted leaves to which have been added some bone meal and dehydrated cow manure or compost.

The tops of my amaryllis are green all year. Some of the outer leaves turn yellow and soft, but they do not yellow like other bulbs. When should they be dug?   They should be dug in late fall. If the foliage has not completely died down (and this does not happen with all amaryllis), it can be artificially ripened off by drying in a sunny, airy place.

About 20 months ago, I planted some amaryllis seeds, the plants from which have been green ever since, without blooming. What time of year should they be given a rest period? How?   The best results are obtained if seeding amaryllis are grown on without rest until after they produce their first blooms. This is usually in from 18 to 36 months from the time of sowing. The giant-flowered hybrids may take up to 4 years to bloom.

My fancy-leaved caladium plants die down in the fall. What shall I do with them?   In November, lift them; cut off the few remaining leaves; pack the tubers in peat, vermiculite, dry sand, or sawdust, and store the container in a frost-free place until spring.

What causes the black scum on my cape-jasmine bush, and how can I prevent it?   This sooty mold on gardenia leaves follows the attacks of whitefly and can be corrected and prevented by occasional applications of an oil emulsion spray or malathion. One application in September, another 2 or 3 weeks later, and possibly a third during midwinter should prevent this condition. Your garden center will have oil sprays put up in small cans for your convenience.

I have read that daffodils of the North have longer stems than those of the South. What can I add to the soil to make my daffodils have longer stems? In all probability, the climate is responsible for the shorter daffodil stems, and even though your bulbs are adequately fed, there will be a tendency to shorter stems.

When do you plant dahlias in Georgia? In March and April. If the emerging tips are nipped by the latest spring frosts, no great damage will be done; but it is best to plan your planting so that there will be no frost damage.

When is the best time to transplant dogwoods, redbuds, and other trees from the woods? December through February, while the trees are dormant and without leaves. Remember that transplanting is a surgical operation and extreme care must be exercised to keep the roots covered and the trees protected from sun and wind during transport. Cut back moderately the lateral branches, plant at the same depth they formerly grew, and wrap the trunks with burlap or muslin as protection against sunscald and borers. Use trees under 8 feet in height rather than larger ones.

What is the best method of protecting gerbera plants from the cold? If gerbera plants are killed to the ground, you can cover the crowns with a light mulch of pine straw or oak leaves. If you are in the southern part of the state and wish to keep the plants from being killed on cold nights, cover with a heavy blanket of Spanish-moss, uncovering after the danger of severe cold has passed.

How are gerbera plants cared for? These South African daisies are not particular as to soil type, provided it is well fortified with plant food and plants have enough water. They will be benefited by a good mulch of oak leaves, compost, or similar organic material.

Should I use fertilizer when I plant my gladioli? A balanced commercial fertilizer can be scattered in the bottom of the 4-inch deep planting furrow and lightly cultivated in. Then set out the corms.

How can I grow gourds in a hot, dry location? If it is too hot and dry for gourds to thrive in your part of Georgia, get an early start with them and allow them to mature in midsummer. However, gourds should thrive in most sections of Georgia.

How are herbs grown in Georgia? Except for mint, herbs require a position in full sun on well-drained light soil for best flavor. It is believed that when grown in rich garden loam, herb flavor is less intense.

What herbs are best for middle and south Georgia? For fall planting: anise, chives, winter savory, sage, and dill. For spring planting:

sweet basil, summer savory, sweet fennel, coriander, thyme, and sweet marjoram.

What is the ivy that is so effectively used around the huge oaks in the Tallahassee and Thomasville area? This is the Algerian ivy (*Hedera canariensis*), a relative of the English ivy. It is considered one of the very best ground covers for spots where grass will not grow.

Can I make a good lawn in a wooded area? On the land, spread a layer of manure or compost, rotted oak leaves, together with some balanced lawn fertilizer. Spade or till this deeply; rake until level; plant as follows: In October or November, sow Italian ryegrass for a winter effect until warm weather, then plant sprigs of St. Augustine grass in rows about 12 inches apart. Always water well, as growing grass needs a great deal of moisture. St. Augustine grass goes dormant in the winter. It must be overseeded with Italian ryegrass in late fall if a green lawn in winter is wanted.

What is the best grass for a wooded lawn? Italian rye, in the winter, if there is partial protection from fallen pine needles. In southern Georgia, St. Augustine grass is excellent for shady locations.

Why do nandina berries drop? They will not drop if there has been good pollination at flowering time. If there is rain when the blossoms open, the pollen will be washed away, and there will be either no set or a poor one.

When is the proper time to plant nandina berries? How long does it take for them to come up? Nandina berries can be sown when they are red or as they begin to fall from the plant. Germination is slow and the plantlets will probably not appear until the following spring or summer.

What can I use in place of pansies during the heat of the summer? Torenia (wishbone-flower) is an excellent substitute for pansies to grow during summer months. Sow seeds in flats in April or May, and transplant to a garden when the pansies are pulled out.

Will peonies do well in this climate? Would you advise early, mid-season, or late varieties? None will succeed south of Atlanta. Use only tried early varieties in north Georgia.

How can we get perennial flower seed to come up in August and September when, in this area, it is so hot and dry? Germination will be poor at this season. Hold the seeds until later in the autumn for best results. Even better, sow in well-prepared soil, just before freezing weather, to germinate in March or April.

Will perennial poppies grow year after year in this locality? Possibly they will succeed in extreme north Georgia; from Macon southward, they are a failure.

Can roses be grown in the far South in sandy soil? The sandy soils, warm winters, and the prevalence of disease make rose growing difficult in the far South. Large wholesale nurseries in eastern Texas have lowered the price of roses in recent years and many successful gardeners grow roses frankly as annuals. The plants are bought in the fall, planted well in very rich beds, and forced for blooms during the following spring. In the summer, they are usually discarded as worthless.

When should climbing roses be pruned? From November to January in Georgia; a renewal system is used—old canes are cut low down, leaving this year's and last year's shoots only. Climbing roses flower from spurs that are borne on last year's canes. Old wood is not floriferous.

What is the name of the hardy red rose that grows so freely here? There is also a light blush pink that seems to thrive without any care. The red rose is 'Louis Philippe', sometimes called the "cracker rose." The light, shell pink is probably 'Marie van Houtte'. 'Safrano', 'Minnie Francis', and 'Duchesse de Brabant' are also old-fashioned roses that will grow for many years in southern gardens.

When is the best time to transplant the red spider-lily? This flower, *Nerine sarniensis* (often misnamed *Lycoris radiata*), is best transplanted in July or early August. It is also called the Guernsey-lily.

Will you give some suggestions as to the planting of shrubbery around small residences in the vicinity of Atlanta? Plants that are evergreen, slow-growing, hardy, and resistant to drought would include azalea, camellia, podocarpus, box, Japanese holly, Chinese holly, boxthorn, cotoneaster, pyracantha, jasmine, wax or glossy privet (*Ligustrum lucidum*), and abelia. These are all suitable for foundation planting but use them sparingly. Small houses will soon be overwhelmed by most of these plants unless they are used with restraint.

When shall I prune shrubs that were injured by frost? It is more tidy to cut the shrubs back as soon as the injured parts turn brown, repeating later if inspection shows that the injury extends farther than your first pruning.

Can you suggest pink- and blue-flowering shrubs and flowers for my town garden, and yellow, orange, and white for my country place? For the town garden: camellia, rose, azalea, deutzia, weigela—all pink; buddleia, plumbago, althaea, vitex—all blue. For the country: yellow—hypericum, *Galphimia glauca,* forsythia; orange—jasmine, basket of gold alyssum, *Rosa hugonis;* white—gardenia, philadelphus, camellia, rose, althaea, ligustrum, azalea.

Can tulip bulbs in the South be grown and increased for a number of years, as are narcissus? They are not satisfactory beyond one season except for certain varieties of tulips in sections of the upper South. In the lower South, tulips of certain varieties must be placed in cold storage for 2 months and planted in December. If held below 40° F. for longer than 2 months, they will root in the package.

How can I grow large tulips in north Georgia? In extreme north Georgia, use only varieties that are recommended; plant in well-enriched beds.

Will verbena act as a perennial in the lower South? Yes, plants can be grown from seed or cuttings. Old plants can be lifted, divided, and reset in the winter for spring bloom. Red spiders must be controlled in hot, dry weather with sulfur dust or malathion.

Hawaii

I am interested in growing orchids. How should I begin? Visit the Orchidarium Hawaii, 524 Manono Street, Hilo, a half-acre botanical garden devoted to orchids and their culture.

How do I obtain information on home gardening in Hawaii, which will be my future home? From the University of Hawaii, Honolulu, Hawaii 96822. There are also many botanical and public gardens to visit that feature plants native to the islands as well as tropical plants from other countries.

Idaho

What perennial daisies, other than white ones, would you suggest for Idaho (elevation about 3,500 feet)? You might try golden marguerite, *Anthemis tinctoria,* which can be grown from seed or plants and can be purchased from most mail-order nurseries. Any of the earlier Michaelmas daisies (hardy asters) should be suitable. *Aster* x *frikartii* is more like a daisy and very lovely. Hardy chrysanthemums are very satisfactory where the season is long enough. Choose varieties recommended for far north gardens.

What are the names of some hedges that will stay green all year in this climate? Probably none except your native evergreens. Spruce and juniper make lovely hedges and can be kept within bounds by clipping.

Can you give a list of low-growing (not to exceed 12 inches) perennial flowers that will provide bloom from early spring to late fall? They would be in sun, no shade.   *Anemone pulsatilla; Campanula carpatica, C. pusilla;* heuchera, various; *Phlox subulata; Gypsophila repens; Iberis semperflorens; Thymus serpyllum; Saponaria ocymoides; Penstemon crandallii, P. caespitosus, P. humulis;* alyssum; arabis; aubrieta; lewisia; antennaria; helianthemum; dianthus, various; sempervivum; *Veronica spuria; Melampodium cinereum; Malvastrum (Sphaeralcea) coccineum; Linum flavum* and *L. alpinum; Oenothera caespitosa, O. lavandulifolia,* and *O. missouriensis; Ceratostigma plumbaginoides;* iris, dwarf varieties; *Abronia fragrans; Physaria didymocarpa; Teucrium chamaedrys.*

What causes red raspberry blight in irrigated ground?   If the blight referred to is the yellowing of the leaves, it is usually caused by too wet subsoils, especially heavy or clay soils. Install underground drainage or plant in lighter, better-drained soils.

I live in an area having neutral to slightly alkaline soil, at an altitude of 4,250 feet. It is irrigated country. There are many plants that will not do well, either because of the short growing season or because of water around the roots. Can you name some shrubs, besides lilacs, bridalwreath, and snowballs, that might thrive?   The following shrubs are suggested for trial: highbush-cranberry (*Viburnum opulus*); *Spiraea* x *arguta,* or *S. thunbergii;* buffalo berry (*Shepherdia argentea*); Austrian copper rose. Trees: river birch (*Betula nigra*); weeping willow; soft maple or silver maple; and possibly sycamore. Evergreens: blue or Black Hills spruce; and possibly *Juniperus scopulorum* and *J. pfitzerana.*

What hardy roses would you suggest for Idaho?   In the Boise Valley and near Lewiston below 2,500 feet, the species like *R. hugonis, R. setigera, R. rugosa* and hybrids thrive without winter protection.

Can the trumpet vine be grown where there are zero winters?   If you mean *Bignonia capreolata,* the answer is no. If you mean *Campsis radicans,* yes. Both are called trumpet vine.

Illinois

What are the best 4 or 5 apple trees for the Midwest and for the small home garden?   The best way to choose apples is to try the fruit and see what you like. For summer: 'Lodi', 'Jerseymac', 'Yellow Transparent'. For fall: 'Jonamac', 'Macoun'. For winter: 'Golden Delicious', 'Jonathan', 'Spigold'.

Why don't I have any success with asters? Is it the climate here in north Illinois? No, your difficulty (if by aster you mean the so-called annual China-aster grown from seed) is probably due to disease, either aster wilt or aster yellows. The answer to wilt is to use wilt-resistant varieties. For yellows, spray the plants with malathion to kill the leafhoppers, which spread this disease.

What pruning is required on azaleas in the Midwest? Only enough to keep them shapely. Such pruning as is required should be done immediately after blooming. Careless use of the pruning shears can destroy bloom for 2 or 3 years and spoil the natural shape of the bush.

How can I control orange rust in my blackberries? Eliminate wild brambles from the locality; remove diseased plants in the patch, including roots, as soon as the disease appears in early spring; plant a resistant variety.

Can blueberries be raised successfully in northwestern Illinois? Yes, provided you acidify the soil properly. (See Blueberry.)

Can blueberries be successfully raised in eastern central Illinois? Yes, provided good culture and soil acidification receive careful attention.

What is a sweet cherry for central Illinois? 'Black Tartarian' is most universally successful, but it is necessary to have 2 or more trees, as they are self-sterile, and sour cherry pollen does not fertilize them. Plant a 'Napoleon' with it.

Will crape-myrtle live through the winter in the latitude of Chicago? No, even the so-called hardy type will winter-kill.

What is the proper care for wintering perennial foxglove? If possible, handle in cold frames, with the glass on, covered with mats to shut out winter sun. Lacking this, use umbrellalike coverings that allow the air to get in, but not water and sun. It is a tricky species to grow in Illinois.

What plants will provide the most cutting flowers to be grown in a small garden in Chicago? Among the annuals, perhaps more blooms can be cut from marigolds and zinnias than from any others in this class. Petunias are excellent because they provide low edgings in the garden picture yet yield satisfactory flowers for cutting too.

For people who do not like the ever-present foundation plantings of evergreens, what do you consider the best substitute for my locality, near Chicago? It would have to be something that will do at least reasonably well in a good deal of shade. A neat, healthy, clean shrub that will grow in shade is a problem, but *Euonymus alatus* 'Compactus' comes pretty close to filling the bill. With clean, dark-green foliage and striking autumn color, it is a highly desirable semiformal shrub and would make an attractive accent near the house.

I have a home on Lake Michigan, and have plenty of sand in front down to the lake; what would you suggest for a ground covering of character? If in sun, and if you incorporate plenty of leafmold or peat moss, this sounds like a place for the bearberry (*Arctostaphylos uva-ursi*).

Where can we secure information on the best table grapes that will grow in this locality? (Winnetka.) The New York Fruit Testing Association, Geneva, N.Y. 14456, or your local State Experiment Station, Urbana, Ill. 61801, will give you the information you want.

Which are the varieties of herbs most practical for growing in this latitude? How should the seed bed be prepared for best results in herb production? *Perennials:* sage, thyme, chives, mint. *Annuals:* sweet basil, sweet marjoram, and dill. These are the easiest to grow, but since taste is such a personal thing, the only criterion is, after all, what you like. (See Herb Gardens.)

How far north will Kerria japonica grow? Into southern Wisconsin.

I have trouble in growing perennial lupine. Is there any special treatment? Yes. They are legumes and must have the special inoculating bacteria to form the nodules they require in order to extract nitrogen from the air. Also, while they require calcium, they need more iron than most legumes. The trick is to keep them at a pH of about 5.9 to 6.8, where by juggling iron and calcium you can give them what they want.

What magnolias are suitable for northern climes? Only two magnolias are commonly grown in Illinois, the saucer magnolia (*M.* x *soulangeana*) and the star magnolia (*M. stellata*).

What pruning is required on magnolias in the Midwest? In the Midwest, the problem is to get them to make adequate growth, not to cut out any excess wood. Throw away the pruning shears and you'll have better luck. Only if branches are badly placed or broken should they be touched.

How far north will nectarines bear? While they will bear in Illinois, they are so subject to curculio damage that they are seldom successful there.

Can I be sure of a crop if I plant southern paper-shell pecans in Illinois? Not as a general rule. Even in southern Illinois, the 'Stuart', one of the hardiest southern varieties, seldom matures its kernels.

How far north will pecan nuts grow? Southern Illinois is about the northern limit of the pecan.

What is the best time to plant peonies in southern Illinois? Specialists in this area try to plant as close to September 15 as possible.

Is it necessary to mulch such perennials as delphinium, phlox, or carnation in this latitude? They are better for a mulch if it is not too dense and soggy. Think of a mulch for these plants as protecting the ground from winter sun, not as a blanket of insulation to shut out all cold. Make it airy but shady. Allow the breeze to blow through. Evergreen boughs are ideal.

Why can't we keep perennials during the winter? We cover them for the winter months. They were probably killed with loving kindness: a dense covering of leaves or other compact material will smother rather than protect plants. Use light, airy mulches, but apply *after* the ground freezes, not before. Remove early in the spring (about March 15 in the Chicago area) to avoid damaging spring growth.

I have a rhododendron in a 15-inch pot. Can this be planted in the garden and safely left outside all winter? I live in a suburb near Chicago. Probably not, but it depends on how hardy a species or variety it is. It would need protection from cold, wind, and sun during the winter, especially its first few winters after planting.

Should roses be planted in full sunshine or in partial shade? Some of the delicate pinks and the types of red that "blue" in sunshine are better for light shade at midday. But they should have at least five to six hours of full sun, preferably early in the day.

Can roses be hilled up 6 or 8 inches with soil before the ground has frozen and before their leaves have fallen? I always wait for leaves to fall and wood to ripen; then the ground freezes suddenly and I don't get them covered. Choosing the right time to cover roses is one of those things that makes gardening interesting (and confusing). The leaves must be off before they are covered, which means after a good sharp freeze, but usually there is a warm spell after such a freeze which allows for pulling the earth around the plant. If you have only a few plants, you might try the old trick of saving a few bushels of unfrozen earth in the cellar and applying this after the wood has ripened. For larger rose gardens, place mounds of hilling soil or compost near the beds and cover with burlap or tarpaulins during the first cold night to prevent freezing. Then hill up the plants the following day. Where cost is not a factor, plastic rose cones (in most garden catalogs) are excellent. Since they often save their cost in roses, they are worth considering.

What bush roses are best suited for the Chicago area? All hybrid perpetual roses are suited to Chicago; in fact, they are much more so than the more favored hybrid teas. With hybrid perpetuals, choose any that strike your fancy: they're all hardy. Perhaps the most satisfactory of the true shrub roses is *Rosa rugosa.* Above all, avoid the overpromoted *Rosa multiflora,* a weedy species recommended for hedges.

What climbing roses can be left on a fence or trellis all winter with little protection?   The old rambler types (which bloom on new wood) survive this sort of treatment, even though their condition horrifies the meticulous rosarian. The dead wood can be cut out after bloom. However, be prepared for the white mildew that attacks practically all roses of the rambler type.

How far north will spicebush grow?   The spicebush, *Lindera benzoin,* makes satisfactory growth as far north as southern Wisconsin.

Are there any strawberry varieties resistant to the red stele root-rot disease?   Yes, the 'Sparkle', 'Midway', and 'Red Chief' varieties are resistant. Check with your county extension agent for others.

How can I succeed in growing everbearing strawberries?   It is not easy to grow these fruits well, especially during the heat of summer. They require very fertile soil of good texture and a continuous supply of water throughout the season. The ground should be mulched lightly to keep the berries clean. A protective winter mulch is also necessary. (See Strawberry.)

Is it possible to transplant the sweet-gum tree in central Illinois? I have been unable to do so successfully.   Yes, but get a nursery-grown tree with fine, fibrous roots. Be sure you plant it in rich, deep land. It won't grow in dry soil.

Is the birch bothered with borers in central Illinois?   The birch borer makes this beautiful tree all but impossible to grow in central Illinois. By the time the pest is discovered, the damage is done, and there is no preventive treatment.

Can espalier fruit trees be grown in Illinois?   Yes, but do not expect too much from them. The training of fruit trees in special shapes was originated in Europe, so that they could be planted along stone walls where the heat would help ripen the fruit. In the Midwest, the problem is too much heat, not too little. Use espaliers for special ornamental effects, not where fruit in quantity is the object.

How late (in the fall) can fruit trees be planted in central Illinois?   Planting can go on all winter long provided good cultural practices are followed, but March or April should be equally satisfactory. It is a question of convenience and comfort, not of the thermometer, which ends the fall planting season.

What are the best fruit and nut trees for the average property in this region? The best sure-fire fruit trees for Illinois are apples, crab apples, and sour cherries. Native walnuts are about the only nut trees that are really reliable, and these must have light, loamy soil and good drainage.

Are there any wildflowers, which can be developed from seed, that can be grown in northern Illinois? Most wildflowers depend on seed for their continuation. Many are perennials and require as much care as other perennial seeds. Some possibilities are: *Aquilegia canadensis,* many violets, goldenrod, Allegheny foamflower, butterfly-weed, wild asters, Dutchman's-breeches, *Phlox divaricata,* and many others.

Will a tree wisteria grow in Chicago climate? Yes, provided its other requirements are met. It grows in almost any soil, but thrives best in a deep, rich loam that does not get too dry.

Indiana

Can you tell me how to grow delphinium in Indiana? Delphiniums come from cold regions and resent hot summers. To coax them into good behavior, give them a deeply prepared friable loam and under each plant put a 4-inch layer of peat moss mixed with rich compost. Spray weekly with Kelthane to control cyclamen mite. Cut flower stems off before they begin to seed. Grow the beautiful Pacific Hybrids as biennials. Sow seed from the current season's crop as soon as 50° F. readings begin in autumn. Keep fresh seed in a refrigerator until planting time.

What are the most desirable flowers to plant in a rock garden in northern Indiana? See Plants for Rock Gardens, Section 2.

Can Smyrna fig plants winter in the backyard in this section of Indiana? Definitely not; but figs can be grown in tubs and carried over in a cool cellar (between freezing and 40° F.) and set out again in early May. These will *not* be the Smyrna fig (which requires a special wasp for pollination) but the mission type, which can be pollinated by American insects.

Is there an American holly to use in climates such as Indiana in order to have enough berries to be attractive in the winter? You can't grow holly such as you see on Christmas cards. The deciduous species *Ilex verticillata* (black-alder or winterberry) is deciduous but bears bright-red holly berries on bare stems well into the winter.

Can pecans, English walnuts, and filberts be successfully grown? What types are best?   Only in the southern end of Indiana are pecans and English walnuts likely to succeed. Filberts can be grown in most of the state.

What kind of peach trees would be best for Indiana climates?   Practically any varieties in commerce are successful in your state.

What is the best time to plant roses in southern and northern Indiana? Should plants be 1, 2, or 3 years old?   Either late-fall or early-spring planting is satisfactory for roses of any age. Most roses sold commercially are 2 years old.

When is the best time to set out monthly blooming roses?   Either late-fall or early-spring planting should prove satisfactory. Which is better depends upon what kind of a winter or summer follows planting—something no one can foretell. However, planting in the spring does save overwinter losses and is preferred by most gardeners.

What kinds of plants, shrubs, or evergreens shall I place on the north and west side of my house?   Large shrubs of coarse texture are suitable near a big old structure; smaller, neater ones of fine texture are better for colonial or modern homes. Combine a few shrubs with ground covers rather than plant a solid line of shrubs.

What summer- and fall-blooming shrubs, especially evergreens, are particularly suitable for this locality? The soil is sandy loam.   There are practically no evergreen shrubs that would have good flowers during the summer and fall in this locality. Most evergreen shrubs like *Pieris japonica, Kalmia latifolia,* and hardy evergreen azaleas bloom in the spring.

When is the best time to put out strawberry plants in this locality?   Late March or early April, if you can get them into the ground.

Iowa

Has the bayberry, so common in coastal New England, ever been grown in midwestern gardens?   Yes, but not successfully. It requires acid soil and a moist, cool atmosphere—conditions that cannot easily be supplied in Iowa.

Can blueberries be grown successfully in central Iowa?   Yes, provided rules for cultivation and acidifying the soil are observed. (See Blueberry.)

Are flowering dogwoods hardy in south Iowa? Yes, although flower buds are usually killed in severe winters.

Is it possible to grow American holly (Ilex opaca) in northern Iowa? No, it is not winter-hardy in Iowa.

What could we plant on bare ground that would be lawn enough for our 15-month-old son to play on by June? It needn't be a permanent lawn. This is a question to make someone knowledgeable about lawns cringe, since the only answer is to recommend planting either timothy or oats. Both will cover the ground with a rough, haylike coating that can be mowed, but neither is really satisfactory. The only other possibility, perennial ryegrass, makes a very good temporary turf that lasts a couple of years.

Can I grow flowering magnolias here in Iowa? *Magnolia* x *soulangeana* and *M. stellata* do well on any rich, loamy soil well supplied with humus, but would probably need watering during summer droughts. Wrapping in burlap when small will protect buds from winterkilling, but when the plant attains tree size, you will have to be reconciled to losing bloom about every third spring.

Will nectarine trees survive southeast Iowa winters? No.

What nut trees are hardy as far north as central Iowa? Butternut, black walnut, and hickory. Central Iowa is the northern limit of all three.

Will the passion-flower (Passiflora) live out-of-doors in southeast Iowa? *Passiflora incarnata,* the passion-flower, will survive in Iowa, but it is not the exotic tropical beauty one might imagine from its name. The more showy species will not survive.

What kinds of peach and pear trees are most adaptable to Iowa? Among hardier peaches, there are 'Harbelle' from Canada and 'Reliance' from New Hampshire. Among pears are 'Maxine', 'Magness', and 'Moonglow'. Consult your county extension agent at the Cooperative Extension Service (under county government) for others.

What is a good low-growing perennial for the north side of a house? If you mean the dense shade north of a house, where no sunshine ever falls, no showy perennial will grow. If the shade is only moderately dense, with sunshine sifting through the foliage of trees, you might try *Phlox divaricata, Vinca minor,* dwarf irises, *Dicentra eximia,* dwarf columbines, *Campanula carpatica,* or various primroses.

Is there a red raspberry suited to this midwestern climate that will bear the first year? 'Latham' has been successful over a wide range of the Midwest, but should not be allowed to bear the first year, nor should any other variety be allowed to do so.

My black raspberries dried up on the plants this summer. The canes are weak and all pitted with gray spots. What can I do about this condition?   Your plants are infected with the common and serious disease known as anthracnose. Cut out the canes most badly infected; feed the plants with a straw-manure mulch or complete fertilizer in early spring; spray the canes carefully with either Bordeaux mixture or lime-sulfur at least twice a year, especially when the leaves are unfolding and just before the blooms open. Consult your Cooperative Extension Service for local recommendations.

Can roses and other shrubs be successfully planted in the fall in northern Iowa?   Yes, provided the normal precautions are taken. Fall planting is much preferred to late-spring planting, except for roses. But don't wait too long in the spring. Plant before apple trees are in bloom.

I understand that the large-flowered climbers should not be pruned. How should they be grown in northern Iowa? Must one take them down each fall?   This type does need pruning to keep in bounds and to cut out old, unproductive wood. But remember that the plants bloom on 2-year-old wood, and if all the old growth is cut away, you get no bloom. Protect in winter by laying them down and covering them with earth.

When is the best time to transplant strawberries in Iowa? I see some transplanted in the fall and some in the spring.   As early in the spring as the soil can be planted and worked is best. Only pot-grown plants have much chance to succeed if planted in late spring.

Should tritoma be stored for winter?   Yes, dig the clump with soil adhering to the roots and store in a cool (from 33° to 40° F.) cellar until late April.

Is vitex hardy in this part of Iowa? I have tried to grow it and it winter-kills.   It is not hardy outdoors without very heavy protection. Or it can be cut back and, taking up the clumps of roots, wintered in a cold frame.

Are Carpathian walnut trees hardy in Iowa?   No records are available, but they have survived severe weather in central Wisconsin.

Is the lovely low-growing yew suitable to our Iowa climate?   Practically all of the low-growing varieties of the Japanese yew are fully winter-hardy in your locality, provided drainage is good and suitable cultural practices are followed. Protect from harsh, drying winter winds.

Kansas

Should cherry trees be pruned each year to get larger fruit and better yield? If so, when? Cherry trees do not usually need or stand severe pruning. In early spring, remove diseased wood and broken branches and thin out crowding and crossing branches.

I have a good grapevine. How can I get more plants just like it? Most native grapes are propagated easily by cuttings. In early spring, cut several of the best 1-year-old canes into pieces about 15 inches long with 2 or more buds on each piece. Plant these in good soil, with at least 1 good bud above the ground. With good care, many of these cuttings will root and grow. The best plants may be reset in a permanent location the following spring.

We seeded a new lawn early this spring and have a good stand of grass. Should it be mowed or left to grow this year? It can be mowed, but not shorter than 2 inches. The final mowing height after midsummer will depend on variety (in bluegrasses). (See Lawns.)

Should grass clippings be raked off the lawn? It is not necessary unless the grass is exceptionally high. (See Lawns.)

We have been told that we should cut our grass high. How high is "high"? Leaving 2 to 3 inches is high-cut. Many bluegrass varieties can be mowed as short as 1 inch where this is desirable.

How can we raise good lupines? Lupines are cool-season plants that do well in acid soils and consequently cannot be expected to do well in your locality.

Why do monthly roses grow tall instead of bushy? Shade will draw up the plants somewhat. If the canes are very long and don't produce blooms, they are probably coming from the understock on which the monthly rose was budded. Canes of this kind should be cut out.

I have hybrid tea roses that I wish to transplant in the spring. When should this be done? Transplant as early as the soil can be worked. Prune the tops back, leaving only 3 or 4 inches. Take up a good ball of soil with each plant. (See Roses.)

A polyantha rose planted last spring did not have a bud on it all summer. What is the cause of its failing to bloom? Polyanthas normally bloom freely the first season. Possibly the polyantha top died and the understock on which it was budded came up and did not bloom. If the plant is producing long, straggly canes, it would be better to replace it.

What is the best winter protection for roses in western Kansas? Hill the soil up around the plants approximately 8 inches. Wait until the ground is frozen and then add straw or similar material several inches deep, so that all of the soil mounds and the level soil between plants are mulched.

How heavily shall I prune roses in the fall that were put out in the spring? Don't prune your roses in the fall. Wait until spring, and then prune out the wood that has been winter-killed. (See Roses.)

Kentucky

At what depth should freesia bulbs be planted? What month should they be planted? Freesias should be planted heavy end down, with the tips barely below the soil level. A good test for depth is to be able to feel the bulb tops without being able to see them. September is the best planting month for freesias. They must have a heavy (but airy) mulch during the winter. Even then they may not survive.

How can one get rid of Bermuda grass in this state? If it gets a start on either lawn or farmland, nothing else will grow. Where vegetables or flowers are planted, Bermuda grass must be constantly dug out until entirely eradicated. Several herbicides, used according to directions, will eradicate this. Consult your county extension agent.

How can I get pansies started in the winter? Pansies can be started in a cold frame or hotbed or in flats in the house during the winter. They cannot be successfully started from seeds outdoors after late summer or early fall. The plants themselves will be fairly hardy in your locality after becoming established, but winter-planted seeds outdoors would not germinate until the following spring.

Is it possible to have healthy perennial phlox plants in this vicinity, where we have very humid, hot summers? What soil conditions are suitable to them? The Ohio Valley has the above summer conditions, and freezing and thawing for 5 months in the winter. Perennial phlox can be grown in your area as successfully as anywhere else. They are entirely hardy and like good, rich soil. With established plantings, fertilizer may be put on the top of the ground during the winter. A mulch on the surface of the soil during the hot months of summer will keep the reflected heat from burning the lower foliage; watering should be done by laying the hose on the ground, soaking the soil but not sprinkling the leaves.

What is the proper culture for tritoma? Tritoma (*Kniphofia*) should go through the winter safely without extra protection. It is wise, however, to cut the foliage down after the first frost and cover the area with 6 or 8 inches of leafmold or other mulch. Tritomas are not particular as to soil, but an occasional fertilization will produce larger blooms. The usual method of propagation is from divisions of the old plants taken up in early fall and replanted promptly.

Louisiana

How can chrysanthemums be grown in northeastern Louisiana? Garden chrysanthemums are started from tip cuttings rooted in sand in April and set into beds of fertilized soil when they have become well rooted. If divisions of the old clumps are used, the plants can have a great deal of leafspot, and so cuttings are much to be preferred.

What is the proper time to trim crape-myrtle in northern Louisiana? When the leaves fall in the autumn. Crape-myrtle flowers on the current year's wood, so pruning must be done *before* growth starts, never after.

What are the best flowering evergreens to plant in the vicinity of New Orleans? Among the choicest evergreens for this area are the many beautiful varieties of azaleas and camellias, the last including the tea of commerce, a very beautiful flowering evergreen shrub. Others are illicium, banana-shrub, the poinsettia, and (in sheltered locations) the hibiscus.

What care and culture does gerbera require? If you can get fresh seeds, these will germinate well in about 2 weeks; if not, buy divisions of old plants, set them at the same depth at which they grew previously in beds that have been made rich by spading in compost. Use a mulch of oak leaves to cover the soil around the plants and apply a balanced plant food in January and June—watering well during all dry periods.

Should one take up gladiolus bulbs every year? Yes, it is by far the best practice to lift gladiolus corms every year, just after the foliage turns yellow. The tops are cut off, the mother corms are discarded, and the new corms are stored in shallow boxes in a cool, shaded place. (See Gladiolus.)

Should calla-lilies be left in the ground all winter? Mine did not bloom, but the leaves are still green. I planted them last February or March. In semitropical sections of Louisiana, calla-lilies can be left in the ground all year. The soil must be acid, mucky, retentive of moisture, and free from too much competition from the roots of large shrubs and trees.

When is the best time to move spider-lilies? White spider-lily (*Hymenocallis*), in early spring. Red spider-lily (*Lycoris*), July or early August.

Which roses thrive best in the Louisiana soil and climate? Many of the true tea roses, such as 'Safrano', 'Marie van Houtte', 'Minnie Francis', 'Duchesse de Brabant', and 'Louis Philippe' will survive for many years. It is best to grow the modern hybrid tea varieties as annuals, renewing a part of all of your rose bed each autumn.

How late can rosebushes be planted in central Louisiana? What is the best fertilizer to use? Early planting is recommended, and December to February is considered the best period. However, the latest possible date would be about April 1. Commercial rose mixtures are satisfactory.

What is the proper care for roses and the best time to plant in southern Louisiana? Roses should be set between December and February, the earlier the better, so that the root systems may become well established before the top starts to grow in the warm weather of spring. Have the beds fertilized in advance, plant at the same depth as they grew in the nursery, and water in well. Be sure that the plants never suffer from drought, and feed every 4 weeks during growing weather.

What is the best way to keep snapdragons during the winter in Louisiana? Young plants (less than 1 year old) should carry through the winter in the open ground without special preparation if the drainage and other conditions are normally good.

Michigan

Will chrysanthemums winter safely in northern Michigan, near Petoskey? Yes, with protection. A blanket of evergreen branches intermingled with leaves would be the best covering. Apply when the soil is slightly frozen. The soil should be well drained.

How late is it safe to plant crocus, hyacinth bulbs, and other early spring-blooming bulbs in southern Michigan? Crocus, scilla, and hyacinth bulbs can be planted safely as late as sound unshriveled bulbs are available, although earlier planting is preferable. Late-planted hyacinths will have to be mulched if they are to survive. Tulips, on the other hand, should not go in until about the middle of October. While most experts condemn late planting of narcissus, they can be planted as late as December 1 with good results by setting them 6 inches deep—over the *top* of the bulb. They bloom late, but with perfect flowers.

Can you suggest evergreens suitable for this climate? *Juniperus chinensis, J. pfitzerana, J. monosperma, J. scopulorum, J. horizontalis, J. sabina* 'Tamariscifolia'; *Picea pungens; Pinus aristata, P. mugo, P. nigra, P. ponderosa, P. strobus,* and *P. sylvestris; Taxus canadensis; Thuya; Tsuga; Abies lasiocarpa* and *A. concolor; Pseudotsuga menziesii; Rhododendron* in variety in southern Michigan.

Can you give me information on the raising of foxglove (Digitalis purpurea)? Plant seed in late May in a shaded cold frame. When fall rains start, put on the glass to protect from excess moisture. Cover plants with marsh hay or evergreen boughs after the first freeze and replace the glass. Transplant into a permanent situation (light shade and loose, loamy soil, with plenty of humus) toward the end of April or the first of May.

Can gum trees (Liquidambar styraciflua and Nyssa sylvatica) be grown in central or northern Michigan? *Nyssa sylvatica* (sour gum or black gum) is not considered hardy in central Michigan. It is difficult to transplant, unless nursery-grown stock is used. It likes low, damp soil with plenty of humus. It is hardly worth trying in this region. *Liquidambar* (sweet-gum) is hardy over most of the lower peninsula of Michigan, provided that conditions are right. This is the northern limit of its range. It must have deep, rich, moist soil and stand free from all shade. Neither species would attain full stature in Michigan.

Will you please give me, as nearly complete as possible, a list of herbs that will thrive in this vicinity? *Annual:* basil, borage, parsley, summer savory, anise, burnet, caraway, coriander, dill, and sweet marjoram. *Perennial:* balm, camomile, catnip, chives, horehound, lavender, mint, rue, sage, thyme, and yarrow.

Can Hibiscus rosa-sinensis be grown in Michigan? No, it is a tropical and will tolerate no frost whatever.

Will Ilex crenata be hardy in Grosse Pointe (Detroit), Michigan? The Japanese holly is not considered reliably hardy north of the Ohio River, though it sometimes survives a hundred miles north of there in well-sheltered spots. It is not a good bet for Michigan.

Can American holly (Ilex opaca) be grown in the northern states? No, it is not hardy in the North. It grows in protected spots in Massachusetts, but Michigan winters would be too hard on it.

Is there any shrub holly, 5 to 10 feet high, that is reliably hardy in

southern Michigan? The word "reliably" is the pinch. You probably mean an evergreen holly that is 100 per cent hardy and looks like the pictures on the Christmas cards. The answer to that is "No." There are three deciduous hollies, all of which have attractive winter berries: *Ilex glabra* (inkberry), *I. laevigata* (smooth winterberry), and *I. verticillata* (black-alder). The first species has black berries; the other two, red. All three need a humus-rich soil that retains moisture. Oregon holly-grape (*Mahonia aquifolium*) will give the foliage effect of true holly, but the fruit will be blue, not red.

Which are the best nut trees to plant in Michigan? Black walnut, hickory, and butternut. If you are near any of the Great Lakes, toward the southern part of the state, the hazels or filberts may do well for you.

Can 'Alberta' pears be raised successfully in lower Michigan? Do you mean the 'Elberta' peach? The southwestern corner of Michigan is one of the world's great peach sections. On the other hand, if the Canadian hybrid pears (like 'Tait-Dropmore' and 'Pioneer', or the Chinese sand pears grown in Canada) are meant, the answer is also "Yes." However, these pears are a compromise between hardiness and quality, and ought to be dropped from consideration for high-quality sorts that will do well in Michigan, such as 'Cayuga' or old favorites like 'Bartlett' and 'Seckel'.

Can perennial phlox be transplanted in the early spring in Michigan? Yes, this is the preferred time. Move as soon as the ground can be worked.

What plants are best for Michigan's climate? Only the hardier types. Investigate the large number of species and varieties being grown in the Nichols Arboretum of the University of Michigan, Ann Arbor, Michigan, and the Matthaei Botanical Gardens, also of the University of Michigan, Ann Arbor.

What low-growing rock-garden perennials are hardy in northern Michigan—30° to 40° F. below zero in the winter? *Hymenoxys acaulis; Androsace sarmentosa; Anemone blanda* and *A. quinquefolia; Aethionema,* various; *Callirhoe involucrata; Gypsophila repens; Campanula muralis; Hypericum reptans; Iberis sempervirens; Arenaria,* various; *Armeria laucheana; Aubrieta; Campanula pusilla; Dianthus alpinus; Heuchera sanguinea; Iris pumila; Linum alpinum; Aquilegia saximontana* and *A. alpina; Primula,* various; *Phlox subulata, P. bifida; Penstemon caespitosus, P. crandallii,* and *P. alpinus; Physaria didymocarpa; Saponaria ocymoides; Papaver alpinum; Veronica prostrata.*

Is it possible to grow rhododendrons successfully in Detroit, Michigan? Yes, but this is no tyro's job. Careful preparation of the soil is essential. Protection from winter sun and wind are particularly important. The best trick is to plant on the north side of a building or dense hedge, so that on June 21 the sun just touches the base of the stem. Then as the sun recedes to the south in the winter, the shade protection, such as burlap or wrapping in straw, will still be needed. Above all, don't neglect watering, even during the winter. And see that the soil remains acid. The following rhododendron species have been grown in the East Lansing area and are generally recommended for the Great Lakes region: *Rhododendron carolinianum; R. catawbiense; R. x laetevirens; R. maximum; R. micranthum; R. mucronulatum; R. racemosum; R. smirnowii; R. yakusimanum*. The following rhododendron hybrids are recommended: 'Boule de Neige'; 'Mrs. Charles S. Sargent'; 'Nova Zembla'; 'Pinnacle'; 'P.J.M.'; 'Ramapo'; 'Roseum Elegans'; 'The General'; 'Windbeam'.

When is the best time to set out hybrid tea roses in southeastern Michigan? There is no "best" time, since we cannot tell in advance what the weather will be. Plant as early as possible in the spring, or as late as possible in the fall. Many commercial growers and landscapers set out stocks during thaws in December and January. In fall planting, hilling up is necessary. Sometimes good pot-grown plants (7-inch to 8-inch pots) are available for late-spring and early-summer planting.

Is fall planting of hybrid tea roses considered safe in Michigan, in the area of Grand Rapids? If done *late* enough, fall planting is usually better than spring planting. Protection by hilling up the soil over the crowns of the plants is necessary.

Why can't roses in central Michigan be pruned in autumn? They can; but there is not much point in doing so, since the branches will have to be cut back to live buds in the spring, anyway, and the unpruned branches help hold snow in place, which forms a good mulch.

Is clematis hardy in northern Michigan? Most clematis are hardy, with proper culture.

What shrub or evergreen can you recommend for planting on the north side of a house where the soil is dry? Your native *Cornus sericea*, the red Osier dogwood, is a highly desirable and hardy shrub for just such a situation. Pfitzer's juniper is a desirable evergreen subject, but may need some watering to become established.

Minnesota

Will you please name several of the spring-flowering bulbs, other than tulips and narcissus, that we can grow here in southern Minnesota? Chionodoxa (glory-of-the-snow), crocus, galanthus (snowdrops), muscari (grape-hyacinth), ornithogalum (star-of-Bethlehem), scilla (squill).

How can I protect Canterbury bells for winter? Keep moisture out of the center of the rosette of leaves—this is where rot starts. They can be wintered satisfactorily in a cold frame. If this is not available, use a light straw mulch on the ground around the plants and under the leaves. Then place a thick layer of lightweight brush over the bed and cover this with straw or marsh hay. The brush is necessary to keep the straw from smothering the green leaves that remain all winter.

Will you give the name of a good cherry-plum tree that is suited to the climate in central Minnesota? The list of hardy varieties includes 'Oka', 'Sapa', and 'Sapalta'. The 'Compass' variety is an excellent pollinizer for the above.

I want to plant some currants. What is a good variety? There are several excellent varieties, including the old 'Perfection' and the newer 'Red Lake'. These are hardy in your state. In some localities, however, planting is restricted because of danger from the spread of the white pine blister rust. Consult your county extension agent at St. Paul.

We grow some dogwoods here, but not the beautiful large-flowering kind. Do you think that we could? The flowering dogwood of the South and East is not hardy in your area.

Our little evergreen trees don't look quite right, and we have been told that they have red spiders. Is there a cure? See Spider Mites.

When is the best time to prune evergreens like junipers and arborvitae? Wait until new growth is 3 to 4 inches long. Then snip off half the length of this new growth. This will avoid leaving dead stubs. Only Japanese yew retains live buds on wood older than one year. It can be cut back to old hardwood as late as July 15.

We have extremely cold winters here (over 30° below zero). I have never seen a forsythia this far north. Would one survive our buds are winter-killed when exposed to such low temperatures. **winters?** Some of the hardier forsythias may survive, but the flower

Can gladiolus bulbs be left in the ground if heavily mulched and well drained? I recently read an article where it was claimed that they were being successfully wintered that way, even here in Minnesota. Yes. Cover with a 12-inch mulch of compost or straw after the ground freezes. It is usually considered better and easier to dig, store, and replant the bulbs.

Is it necessary to give winter cover to grapevines here in southern Minnesota? Most of the standard grape varieties must be protected during the winter. The varieties 'Fredonia' and 'Beta' are usually winter-hardy if the wood is well matured before cold weather.

My arborvitae hedge is almost 7 feet tall, and I would like to have it just about 3 feet. Can it be cut back to that height? No. Evergreens like this should not be pruned back beyond the green, actively growing shoots. They do not renew themselves from old hardwood as deciduous shrubs do.

Even the hardiest privet hedges kill back here in the winter. What would you suggest for a clipped hedge about 6 feet tall? Consider *Cotoneaster acutifolia* or *Lonicera tatarica* and its varieties.

When and how is pansy seed sown? Sow the seed about August 1 in a seed bed well loosened up with leafmold or peat moss. When the seedlings are large enough, transplant to a cold frame, using a similar soil, where they are kept during the winter.

When should pansies be planted out in the garden? Pansies, if grown in a cold frame during the winter, will not be injured by the frosts and light freezing of early spring. Plant them in the garden as early as the soil can be worked.

Do you know the name of a good pear suited to the climate of central Minnesota? The University of Minnesota has originated several pear varieties. 'Parker' and 'Patten' are recommended. These 2 varieties planted together help, through cross-pollination, to ensure heavier crops.

We have read about mixing peat moss with soil to make it acid. There is a lot of peat moss near here. Could we use it? Not all peat moss is necessarily acid. The only way to be sure is to have it tested. It can be used as humus in your soil, however, whether acid or not. To acidify soil, add flowers of sulfur. (See Section 1.)

How deep should peonies be set? Cover the pink buds on root divisions about 2 inches, no deeper.

Will you give a list of hardy perennials for central Minnesota? Coreopsis, gaillardia, peonies, iris, delphinium, hosta, aquilegia, Shasta daisy, thalictrum, dictamnus, hardy asters, hemerocallis, hardy chrysanthemums, phlox, veronica.

What perennials would form a good backbone for a northern Minnesota garden where frost comes early and winterkilling is a problem? Coreopsis, gaillardia, peony, iris, delphinium, aquilegia, Shasta daisy, veronica.

Will black raspberries do well in this part of the country? Black raspberries are doubtfully hardy in the extreme north.

When is it best to plant roses—fall or spring? It is safer to plant roses in the early spring. If fall planted, they must be very well protected against severe winter temperatures.

What is the best way to protect a tree rose during the winter in Minnesota? Dig up the plant carefully so as not to injure roots. Lay it in a long trench and carefully work the soil around and over it. Cover with at least 6 inches of soil. After the ground freezes 1 or 2 inches, cover with several inches of straw or evergreen boughs.

How much of hybrid tea rose tops should you prune off in the fall? Don't prune in the fall. After they are uncovered in the spring, cut back to good, sound, live wood.

We have sandy soil and 40° below zero in the winter. Can I raise climbing roses? Yes, if they are given good winter protection. Take the canes off their support in the fall and tie them together to make one long bundle. Lay this bundle flat on the ground and completely cover with soil. Have 2 or 3 inches of soil over all the canes. Mulch over the soil with several inches of straw. Select such superhardy varieties as 'Viking Queen', 'White Dawn', and 'Blaze'.

What roses are best for northern Minnesota? Shrub roses like *Rosa hugonis, R. rugosa* and hybrids, and also the sub-zeros such as 'Queen O' The Lakes' and 'Arctic Flame'.

What causes climbing roses, after being uncovered in the spring, to die back to within 2 feet of the ground? The buds are alive, yet the canes die back. The canes are wrapped with marsh hay and waterproof paper. If there is a section near the base where canes are exposed or poorly protected, the canes will be killed from that point to their tips. Also canker, a fungus disease, may girdle the canes, producing similar results.

What fruit-bearing shrubs are hardy enough for our northern climate? Korean cherry, Juneberry, elderberry, American highbush-cranberry, and some of the flowering quinces are hardy, especially in favorable situations. Buffalo berry (*Shepherdia argentea*) produces fruit that many enjoy, but not everyone. It is particularly grown in western Minnesota.

Which of the cultivated varieties of walnut are hardy enough to be

planted in central Minnesota? The named varieties are not always winter-hardy in central Minnesota. Even in southern Minnesota, the standard varieties are recommended only for trial.

Mississippi

When is the best time to set out new chrysanthemum plants? Rooted cuttings of chrysanthemums should be set out in the garden in May or June. It is better to use cuttings than divisions from the old clumps, as in this way you will avoid carrying over infection of the leafspotting disease. Choose an overcast afternoon, water well, and shade for a day or two.

How can rain-lilies be made to bloom and thrive in the Delta section of Mississippi? These little flowers (*Zephyranthes*) of the West will usually succeed quite well in this state. With sufficient moisture, fertilizer, and freedom from severe competition, they should bloom profusely during the summer months.

How deep should gladiolus corms be planted? In light, sandy soils of the lower South, it is best to set gladiolus corms 3 to 4 inches deep. Thus, they will have better moisture and will not topple over when in bloom.

What grass is best suited for the Gulf Coast? There are several excellent lawn grasses for this area. For shade, under trees—St. Augustine. Poor soil, not much shade—centipede. Full sun, good soil—Bermuda. Good soil, lots of moisture—carpet grass or 'Meyer' zoysia, which must have plenty of water until well established but is then drought resistant (grows in sun or shade). (See also Florida.)

Could I trim a gardenia bush to shape? Would it bloom? When should it be cut? Prune, if necessary, just when growth begins in the spring, by thinning out crowded shoots and cutting back straggly branches.

Tell me why my white spider-lilies (Hymenocallis) will not bloom even though the foliage develops. They have been in the ground several years. Too much shade; lack of plant food (they are gross feeders and respond well to fertilizing); or lack of moisture during the growing season.

Will the loquat or "Oriental-plum" grow in the lower cotton belt? Yes, the loquat is a most ornamental evergreen tree, hardy in the Gulf Coast region. Ordinarily it bears large annual crops of delicious yellow fruits that are esteemed as fresh fruit and for pies, tarts, and conserves.

Can nandina be grown from cuttings? Attempts to grow nandina from cuttings will be disappointing, in spite of the best possible care. Propagate these shrubs by sowing ripened seeds in a flat. Care for them until the following summer, when germination should be complete.

When is the best time to plant roses on the Gulf Coast? Between December and February. Early planting is much to be preferred, as the root systems will then have time to become well established before top growth is forced out by the warm weather of spring.

What is the best soil for growing roses? A sandy loam or Delta soil that is fairly high in organic matter, retentive of moisture, and well fortified with readily available nutrients.

Is the old-fashioned moss rose obtainable? Where? You will find the moss rose listed by a few specialists in old roses. It is curious, rather than beautiful. Unless you are familiar with it, better see it in bloom before planting.

Missouri

I would like to know when to plant bulbs of Sprekelia formosissima, commonly known as Jacobean-lily, in Missouri—in early spring, or should I wait until May? What kind of soil and fertilization is needed? Plant after the danger of hard frosts has passed. It will thrive on a variety of soils but prefers a medium loam. The soil should be highly fertile; very old manure or compost and liberal supplies of superphosphate are good.

What annual can I plant that will bloom all summer in a north garden that gets sun in early morning and late afternoon? Annuals are notorious sun lovers. A few that will condescend to grow without full sunshine are balsam, impatiens, godetia, lobelia, nicotiana, *Centaurea imperialis* (sweet sultan), clarkia, *Cynoglossum amabile* (Chinese forget-me-not), petunia.

What care should I give perennial asters set out in the fall? A light mulch of straw, hay, or dry leaves during the winter is all that they need. Remove the mulch before growth starts early in the spring.

What azaleas will grow well in Jackson, Missouri? Consider the following: Knaphill and Exbury azaleas; Mollis azaleas; the flame azalea (*Rhododendron calendulaceum*); pinxterbloom azalea (*R. nudiflorum*);

snow azalea (*R. mucronatum*); varieties of *R. obtusum*, such as 'Amoenum' and 'Hinodegiri'.

What sweet cherries are hardy and satisfactory in the Midwest? Sweet cherries are not a reliable crop in the Midwest except in western Michigan. You might consider the variety 'Kansas Sweet', a red-fruited variety recommended for the Midwest. It should be planted with 'Montmorency' for cross-pollination. They lack hardiness, both as to heat and to cold.

What would be the best type of living Christmas tree for us? Colorado blue spruce or red-cedar.

How can one grow large chrysanthemums outdoors in Missouri? Most large-flowering commercial or greenhouse chrysanthemums do well outdoors in Missouri. Grow just 3 or 4 stems on each plant. Remove all side buds, letting only the top bud flower. Plenty of water, fertilizer, and cultural care are essential.

What shrubs and flowers would be good for a city garden in this state? Shrubs: *Cotoneaster divaricata* and *C. acutifolia; Deutzia* x *lemoinei; Kerria japonica; Philadelphus,* various; *Spiraea prunifolia; Viburnum carlesii.* Perennials: tulips; daffodils; ornithogalum; phlox, early varieties; Oriental poppy; dianthus; lupine; pyrethrum; linum; gaillardia; dictamnus; hybrid lilies; chrysanthemum; aster (Michaelmas daisy). Annuals: calendula; marigold; petunia; verbena; *Phlox drummondii;* gypsophila; larkspur; dimorphotheca; zinnia; calliopsis; *Mirabilis jalapa* (four-o'clock).

I have a Shasta daisy from Idaho. Its flowers there were very large, but mine are smaller. Does Missouri climate have something to do with it? Climate is not to blame. Shasta daisies need full sun, fertile loam soil, a good supply of water during the growing season, and a light mulch of straw or leaves during the winter.

Can we raise delphiniums in the Midwest successfully? Set out strong plants in the spring. A deep, fertile loam soil is required. Add a generous amount of ground limestone if the soil is acid. Full exposure to the sun and constant moisture at the roots during the growing season are essential. Cultivate frequently and provide good drainage to prevent winter injury. A light mulch of straw or hay during the winter may be beneficial. The striking Pacific Hybrids are best grown as biennials in your area, sowing fresh seed from the current year's bloom as soon as nighttime temperatures below 50° F. occur. Keep seed in the refrigerator if hot weather continues. A cold frame should be used during the winter.

What hardy ferns will succeed in Missouri, and how are they

grown? Ferns like a cool, shady exposure (northern). Any soil that contains a good supply of leafmold or peat moss, and constant moisture, will be satisfactory. Plant ferns in the fall before the ground freezes. Collect native species from your vicinity or purchase from a wildflower specialist.

What kind of herbs can we raise here? Anise, caraway, chervil, chives, coriander, dill, fennel, tarragon, lavender, sage, lemon balm, rosemary, spearmint, summer savory, sweet basil, thyme, sweet marjoram.

Can lavender be grown in Missouri? How is it cured (as used in sachet bags)? Yes, lavender can be grown in Missouri. Plants can be obtained from most nurseries. Hang small bunches of the flowers in a warm room or shed where they will dry quickly. They can be stripped from the flowering stems, put in sachet bags, etc., as soon as dry.

Is it possible to grow Magnolia grandiflora in the vicinity of St. Louis, Missouri? What soil does it prefer? Yes. Since St. Louis is about the northern limit for this tree, growth is slow and mature specimens are relatively small. A southern exposure with a north to northwest windbreak is most favorable. It grows best in a fertile clay loam soil. Flowers appear in July.

What culture is needed for hardy phlox in Missouri? Give full sun, a fertile loam soil containing a good supply of organic matter, adequate drainage to prevent winter injury, frequent cultivation, and irrigation during a dry growing season. Transplanting or dividing may be necessary after the plants have grown in one spot for 3 or 4 years.

What is the proper winter protection for rhododendrons and azaleas in Missouri? A 6- to 10-inch mulch of dry leaves, preferably oak leaves. Rhododendrons exposed to direct sun during the winter should have a burlap or lath screen to prevent the leaves from "burning" or turning brown.

Can tree roses be grown in central Missouri? Plant in the spring in fertile clay loam soil well supplied with humus. Cut back the top growth or "head" to 3 or 4 eyes, and tie the main stem firmly to a strong stake. Full sun and a constant supply of moisture are necessary. For winter protection, loosen the roots on one side, bend the plant over, cover the top with soil and a heavy straw mulch, first wrapping the main stem with burlap or paper. Uncover early in the spring before growth starts.

What is the best time to plant roses and when is the best time to prune? Set out roses in the fall if the plants are dormant; otherwise wait until early spring. Prune hybrid teas in early spring. Climbing roses are pruned after they flower. (See Roses.)

Why do my rosebushes grow so tall and have very few leaves? Any of the following might be the cause: too much shade; suckers from seedling stock at the base of the grafted plant; black spot, defoliating plants; excess nitrogen in the soil.

How much should a climbing 'Peace' rose be pruned each year (flowers are 5 inches in diameter—now 2 years old)? Also 'Blaze'? It depends on the type of trellis and the effect desired. For extensive coverage, remove only the dead wood and a few of the oldest canes each year. Drastic pruning results in few flowers until the plant gets reestablished. All large-flowered climbers bloom best on 2-year-old canes.

What flowers would be best for a shady garden, with some sun in the afternoon? Anchusa, balsam, impatiens, bleedingheart, spring-flowering bulbs, campanula, columbine, ferns, forget-me-not, fuchsia, eupatorium, godetia, day-lily, lobelia, mertensia, primroses, lily-of-the-valley, plantain-lily, tuberous-rooted begonia, thalictrum, tradescantia, vinca, violets.

Is it good or bad to cover strawberries with straw or leaves during the winter in Missouri? A straw mulch is recommended, especially for young plants just getting established. Leaves are all right if they are not permitted to remain excessively wet, pack down, and thus smother the plants.

How should Urceolina peruviana be cared for in order to have it bloom? This rare Andean bulb will probably not be hardy in Missouri. Grow it in a pot of light but rich soil in a sunny greenhouse or window. Rest it by keeping it quite dry after its leaves die away in the winter. Repot in the spring as growth begins.

Are there any large-flowered white or yellow violets that will grow well in a midwestern climate? *Viola blanda* (white), *Viola hastata* (yellow), and *Viola rotundifolia* (yellow). Violets need light shade, friable soil containing lots of leafmold or peat moss, and extra water during dry weather. Protect them with a light mulch of leaves or straw during the winter.

Montana

What are some good shade-tolerant flowers for the north of a house and under trees in this climate? *Brunnera macrophylla;* aconite; lily-of-the-valley; bleedingheart; hosta; mertensia; myosotis; primroses; *Phlox* *divaricata* and *P. carolina; Campanula carpatica* and *C. rotundifolia;* bloodroot; trollius; thalictrum; violet; *Epimedium grandiflorum.*

Our gladiolus bulbs seem to "run out." Is this because of the short season? Possibly the season is too short to mature the new corms. Rich, deeply prepared soil and sufficient moisture at the roots to keep them growing vigorously in an open sunny location, protected from the wind, should help to produce better corms.

What hedge is best suited to this climate? To form a neat shorn hedge, Amur River privet. For an informal taller hedge, Persian lilac, *Rosa hugonis, R. rubrifolia,* and Chinese elm.

Is the tree peony adapted to the northern Rocky Mountain region? Many tree peony varieties can be grown in Montana if altitude is not more than about 4,000 feet above sea level. They grow with coaxing, in Denver, Colorado, at 5,280 feet in altitude. Drying of the stems by winter wind and sun seems to be the difficulty.

Could you suggest perennials for a cold climate and a short growing season, at an elevation of 5,700 feet? Peony; iris; columbine; *Phlox subulata, P. divaricata, P. paniculata; Trollius europaeus; Mertensia virginica;* campanula; pyrethrum; *Papaver orientale, P. nudicaule;* primroses; delphinium; rudbeckia hybrids; *Centaurea macrocephala; Physostegia virginiana; Clematis integrifolia, C. recta, C. grandiflora; Monarda didyma.*

What can be done to control rust or blight in sweet peas? See Section 13. Where days are hot and nights are cool, do all watering as infrequently as practical, but always thoroughly and always before noon. Try the spring-flowering type.

Nebraska

Will you list some annuals that bloom most of the summer and can endure the heat and drought of Nebraska? Zinnia, marigold, petunia, portulaca, annual gaillardia, *Catharanthus roseus, Anchusa capensis,* annual phlox, scabiosa, cosmos.

Is boxwood out of the question in this locality? Boxwood is not hardy under your conditions.

Why did a hard November freeze kill Chinese elm and still not affect other trees in Nebraska? Most of the other shade trees used in your state go into a state of dormancy without the help of moderately cold weather in early fall. The Chinese elm apparently requires some cold weather to harden it off before it becomes dormant and is able to stand a hard freeze. The Siberian elm (*Ulmus pumila*) is a more reliable species. Chinese elms are semievergreen.

We have some evergreens planted against the front of our house. Do you advise mulching the ground there for winter? Yes, a loose mulch of peat moss mixed with compost, leafmold, or some similar material helps to conserve soil moisture and prevents too deep freezing. Since evergreens give off moisture even when the soil is frozen, it is important to water thoroughly before freezing occurs.

What annual herbs can be grown in Nebraska? Sweet basil is easily propagated from seed and very easy to grow. It makes a dense, bushy growth about 24 inches high. Sweet marjoram, dill, and lemon balm are propagated from seed and are also easily grown. (See Herbs.)

Will you name 3 perennial herbs that can be grown in Nebraska, and give their uses? Chives are onionlike plants having small stems that are cut several times during the year and used as flavoring or as a garnish. Sage is a commonly grown perennial herb. Its principal use is in the flavoring of sausage, in dressings for poultry or rabbit, and as sage tea. Lavender is a member of the mint family used as a natural perfume for silks and linens.

My tulips and narcissus do well, but my hyacinths always fail. Is there any special care they should have? Your experience appears to be typical. Hyacinths don't seem to be adapted to your area of the country.

I know that iris should be moved in the summer, but if it is necessary, can they be transplanted in early fall? Yes, though it is beyond the recommended planting season.

What lilies can we grow most easily here? Try the hybrids. (See Lily.)

What perennials can we grow that will stand heat and drought? Iris, perennial sweet pea, veronica, euphorbia, statice, gypsophila, hardy asters, liatris, physostegia, hemerocallis (day-lily).

When do you advise planting hybrid tea roses? Early spring is safer than fall planting in your area. If you plant early, just as soon as the ground can be worked in the spring, the plants will come along as rapidly as fall-planted stock.

Must I hill up the soil around hybrid tea roses for the winter? This makes good winter protection where temperatures drop low enough to freeze the ground deeply. After the ground freezes, add a mulch of some loose, light material.

On what date should I hill the soil around my hybrid tea

roses? About mid-October. It should be done just before the first hard freeze. If not done before the ground freezes, you will have trouble handling the soil.

What is the best kind of winter protection for roses in this state? Hill the plants 10 to 12 inches high. Fill the holes thus left with leaves and branches and cover the plants completely. Climbers should be hilled and branches laid down and covered completely with soil and mulch. Or use plastic rose cones available from mail-order nurseries and most garden centers. Be sure to uncover early but slowly in spring.

Will you tell me what to do after I uncover my hybrid tea roses? Hybrid tea roses should be pruned after they are uncovered in the spring. Cut back to good, sound, live wood. Ordinarily that leaves canes of 6 inches or less in length.

When is the best time to plant trees—spring or fall? Spring planting is safer than fall planting. Planting should be done very early to get the most good from spring moisture.

Nevada

Are there any azaleas hardy enough for this climate? Last winter the coldest was 16° below zero but temperatures sometimes go to 37° below zero. Azaleas require very acid soils and refuse to grow in soils that contain lime. Most western soils are filled with lime and for this reason azaleas will not thrive. It is doubtful if they would survive 37° below even if the soil were suitable.

When should one set out fruit trees? Plant in Nevada in early spring after severe cold is over but before the buds start to swell—the latter part of March or the first part of April, depending on the altitude.

Should rosebushes be trimmed back to 8 inches in the vicinity of Reno, Nevada? All roses except the shrub roses should be cut back to firm, healthy wood in early spring. Flowers come on the new growth and too much old wood will produce small and inferior flowers.

New Mexico

How long should dahlias be kept out of the ground before planting again? Only until climatic conditions permit replanting. They can be planted in the spring just before the last heavy frost is expected. Be ready to cover if an unusual late frost occurs.

What are the best bush fruits and when should they be planted? Raspberry, loganberry, boysenberry, strawberry, and grape. Plant in spring in the north; fall or spring in central and south New Mexico.

What are the best tree fruits to plant in this climate? In the higher-altitude regions of northern New Mexico: apple, crab, pear, plum, and cherry. Toward the south, and in lower altitudes: peach, apricot, cherry, pear, fig, persimmon.

What is the best lawn grass to plant in western New Mexico? In high-altitude regions of northern New Mexico: Kentucky bluegrass and varieties. Central and southern: Bermuda grass or zoysia.

Is there any grass that will stay green all year? In regions with sufficiently cool summers, yet not too extremely cold winters, Kentucky bluegrass keeps green all winter if well watered.

When would you make a lawn in New Mexico? March to June in the north; September to November in the south.

How can a lawn be kept in good growing condition? First, by providing a surface, at least 4 inches deep, of good loam containing adequate humus on which to seed or plant the grass. In the dry air of the Southwest, lawns keep in better growing condition when given a mulch in November of 50 per cent peat moss and 50 per cent compost or manure pulverized and raked in, followed by watering as needed to keep roots moist. 'Meyer' zoysia is drought-resistant when established. (See also the following questions.)

How often should grass be mowed here? A little, secluded, intimate lawn should be kept shorn more frequently and closely than is necessary for a large expanse. In general, lawns in New Mexico are better mown not too frequently or too closely, since the slightly longer grass helps provide shade and so prevents surface drying.

What fertilizer should I use for a lawn? Before seeding, apply a lawn fertilizer. If growth is not vigorous, give a second application in June. A feeding in September is probably the most important of the year. At this time old roots die off and new roots begin growth. Fertilize again during late winter to encourage growth.

How often should I water my lawn? In New Mexico, lawns need watering as frequently and as thoroughly, both summer and winter, as is necessary to keep the grass roots moist at all times. This is true of even the higher-altitude regions, except where snow covers the ground most of the winter.

When is the best time to plant roses in New Mexico?   Spring in the north; fall or early spring in the south.

What winter protection do roses need?   In the north, mound the plants up with soil or compost and peat moss; cover with spruce branches or cornstalks. In the center and south, no winter protection is necessary. No protection is necessary for shrub roses or polyantha-type roses anywhere below 7,000 feet altitude. Above that, they are hardly worth the necessary coddling.

When is winter protection necessary for roses?   Winter protection for hybrid teas and climbers can be applied after the surface inch or two of ground freezes.

What hybrid tea roses are continual bloomers here?   Almost all hybrid teas thrive and bloom where the altitude does not exceed 6,500 feet. Hybrid perpetuals do well in alkaline soil.

Will you name some shrub roses for northern New Mexico?   'Frühlingsgold', 'Harison's Yellow', *Rosa hugonis; R. setigera; R. rubrifolia; R. rugosa* and its hybrids.

What climbing roses are suitable for New Mexico?   Any and all climbers revel in the sun of southern New Mexico. Some that bloom most profusely are 'Silver Moon', 'Blaze', and all the climbing hybrid teas. In higher altitudes, the choice is more limited and climbers require protection from winter sun.

North and South Carolina

Will gardenias and camellias grow out-of-doors in this part of North Carolina?   Camellias should do very well for you, blooming profusely in March. Gardenias would remain alive but it is doubtful whether you would ever have any blooms. The gardenia will stand temperatures as low as 20° to 24°, but anything lower than this kills the plant back to the roots. Both must have wood at least a year old on which to bloom. Your best chance would be to grow them as tub or box plants, keeping them indoors and well watered during the more severe winter weather.

How often should camellias planted in boxes be watered during the winter months in a greenhouse? What are the best plans for building a greenhouse 12 × 20 feet especially for camellias?   Often enough to keep the soil always moist but never waterlogged. When water is applied, give enough to saturate the whole body of soil. Build the greenhouse where it receives full sunshine. Allow for ample ventilation both at the top and sides. Provide a heating system that keeps a deep-night temperature of 50° F.

Can I grow the double varieties of Camellia japonica outside in South Carolina? Yes.

Please give some hints on pruning or shearing evergreens. Also, what is the proper time? I live in western North Carolina. Evergreens are not pruned in the general sense of that word. They may be clipped or sheared during the growing season, beginning in spring. This should be done after new growth is 3 to 4 inches long. Then half of the new soft twig is snipped off. One exception to this is the Japanese yew and its varieties. It is the only evergreen that retains live but dormant buds on wood older than one year. Shear it at any time before mid-July. This encourages bushier, more compact growth, but any late-fall or winter shearing would increase the danger of winterkilling.

Can I grow grass in the shade? Ground covers are best in heavy shade. In light shade, plant a shady grass mixture recommended for your region.

What is the proper fertilizer to use on nandina to produce the maximum number of berries? Old rotted cow manure (if you have it) or rich compost and superphosphate. It needs a well-drained position and generous amounts of water in dry weather. (See the next question.)

Why doesn't my nandina have berries after having bloomed? Rainfall influences the production of berries. Cross-pollination from one plant to another is necessary. Plant in groups for this reason. There are chemical preparations that can be sprayed on the blossoms of nandina hollies and on many other plants. These usually produce heavier crops of fruits or berries. Try this on your nandina next spring.

Should I trim nandina plants? If so, when? Pruning is usually unnecessary. If, however, they are too large for the space you want them to occupy, the entire plant can be trimmed back; or the older, heavier shoots can be cut clear back to the ground. During the winter or very early spring, new shoots will appear from the roots.

Will pansy seeds planted December 1 bloom the following spring? If planted in a cold frame in October or in a hotbed the first of December, the plants will be large enough to set out in the open in early spring and will start to bloom almost immediately. Planted in the open ground the first of December, seeds will not germinate until spring, and would be several weeks coming into bloom. By planting both in a cold frame (for early bloom) and in the open (for late bloom), you can enjoy pansies over a longer period in the summer. Seed for October sowing should be held in the refrigerator for 2 weeks prior to sowing.

Do peonies in South Carolina require partial shade or full sun to best stand our hot summers? Peonies will stand partial shade in temperate gardens, but do well only in the extreme northwestern corner of South Carolina. They require a long, cold winter to induce complete and unbroken dormancy and are a disappointment in most parts of the cotton belt.

What hardy perennials can be depended upon for summer bloom in the mountain region of western North Carolina? You may almost take your choice from perennials listed in dealers' catalogs. Practically all well-known, and many unusual, perennials flourish in the western mountain section of your state. Pick the ones that appeal to you most, and plant them with full assurance that they will succeed for you there.

Will you please give information about the growing of all plants, especially roses, in this locality? Most articles are written for the states north of us or south of us, or the western part of the country. You live in a latitude where all annuals grow rapidly and where practically every variety of perennial plant will do well. Only the doubtfully hardy ones need any winter protection and your main handicap in growing hybrid tea roses would be the false springs and late freezes that occur almost every year. When roses go dormant in early winter, hill the soil up around them to a depth of about 6 inches, and do not give any other protection. Your area is ideal for growing climbing roses and floribundas. The same rules for fertilization and spraying apply there as in every other part of the country.

Are there any roses that will grow on a fairly windy shore (eastern exposure) in eastern North Carolina? The soil is well drained, with a good sand-humus mixture. You might not be able to succeed as well with hybrid tea roses as growers in other areas, but hardy climbers and floribundas adapt themselves perfectly to your locality, soil, and climatic conditions. *R. rugosa* and many of its hybrids like 'Max Graf' and 'Pink Grootendorst' are ideally suited to seashore conditions. A few of the more reliable hybrid tea roses are satisfactory if not given too much winter protection. This causes them to make premature growth in the spring, which frequently is killed back by late freezes.

Can you recommend quick-growing, medium-sized shade trees for lawns in this area? The fastest-growing are Siberian elm, box-elder (*Acer negundo*), and weeping willow, but they are not among the most desirable or longest lived. Tulip-poplar, sweet-gum, and your native maple grow fast enough and are among the best of the permanent shade trees for your locality. Native evergreens do well if moved when small.

What are the fruiting shrubs and trees, semitropical and otherwise, that would grow and fruit in eastern North Carolina? All kinds of barberries, cotoneaster, dogwood (both tree and bush forms), euonymus, hollies, honeysuckles, privets, and viburnums will give a varied display in fall and winter. Many shrub roses also bear attractively colored hips. The callicarpas have lilac and violet fruits; snowberries and coralberries bear profusely, as do the various types of Russian-olive, which have orange and silvery fruits. Among the trees, nothing is prettier than your native hawthorn, wild plum, magnolia, and mountain-ash. Several North Carolina nurseries list most hardy trees and shrubs.

When should I plant sweet peas in South Carolina? Sow the early-flowering or later kinds in November. Protect with litter—straw, rough compost, leaves—during severe spells. The early sorts should bloom in May; the late sorts, 2 or 3 weeks later.

North and South Dakota

How deep should I plant daffodils? Do they need any special winter protection? Cover bulbs with 5 or 6 inches of soil when planting. They can be protected with a loose mulch of straw or coarse hay. The mulch goes on after the ground is frozen.

When is the best time to sow Kentucky bluegrass seed? In early spring or in late summer.

How can one grow and winter lilies in North Dakota? Plant in the fall or early spring in well-drained soil. The top of the bulb should have about 8 inches of soil above it when planted. Mulch with 2 to 4 inches of straw after the ground freezes in the fall.

Where can hybrid nut seed or trees be obtained for trial in this locality (northern Great Plains)? Contact your State Experiment Station at Fargo, North Dakota, or the Experiment Station at Morden, Manitoba.

Can peonies be planted this spring or must we wait until fall? Fall is the better time to plant peonies, and you will be just as far ahead if planting is done then.

When is the best time to plant perennials in our cold country? Early spring. Good-sized clumps of the hardier sorts can be planted about the first of September, and if properly mulched they will winter well.

Will hybrid tea roses winter-kill in South Dakota? No tea or hybrid tea rose will winter successfully in South Dakota without being covered with a heavy mulch of earth. Some shrub roses like *R. hugonis*, *R. spinosissima*, *R. rugosa* and hybrids should winter without protection.

What is the best time to dig tulip bulbs in North Dakota? Two or 3 weeks after the foliage matures, dig the bulbs and leave the stems and foliage attached. Spread them out in shallow trays and store in a dry, cool place. The tops can be removed and the bulbs cleaned up in late summer.

How soon should tulips be replanted? They were dug in early summer. Replant these bulbs about October 1.

Ohio

What is the best type of soil for growing apples in central Ohio? What cover crop would you recommend while the trees are small? Central Ohio is largely a silty clay loam. Make sure that the soil is well drained. Sow soybeans in early June and plow under in September. Then sow ryegrass as a cover crop if the soil is not to be kept cultivated.

Can gerbera be wintered over in Sandusky, Ohio? How are the roots stored? If by "wintering over," outdoor culture is meant, this is theoretically possible, except that a mulch heavy enough to protect the plant will probably smother it. Gerbera plants can be lifted after a sharp frost has killed the leaves, with soil adhering to the roots, and stored in a cool place (above freezing, but it must not go above 40° F.) covered with damp sand or peat to retain moisture. Examine during the winter and sprinkle if needed. Plant out again in the spring when apples bloom.

Have you any suggestions for growing herbs for flavoring in Ohio? All of the annual and most of the perennial herbs can be grown in Ohio. In general, a rather poor sandy soil in full sunshine is their preference. (See Herbs.)

Will you please give me a list of some herbs that will grow here? *Annuals:* basil, chervil, coriander, caraway, dill, fennel, summer savory. *Perennials:* burnet, chives, hyssop, marjoram, mint, sage, sorrel, tarragon, winter savory.

What is the best rose collection to plant in this part of the country? All the hybrid teas can be grown in Ohio. Your State Experiment Station at Columbus is one of the best sources of information on roses anywhere.

What is the proper time to plant hardy shrubs and perennials in northern Ohio in the spring? Crape-myrtle, catalogs state, is hardy north of Virginia, with protection. What kind of protection is meant? Plant anytime before the leaf buds begin to open. "Protection" means some kind of burlap wrapping or screen, as of pine boughs, to protect them from winter winds. You will not find crape-myrtle as satisfactory as lilacs in Ohio.

How and when should I plant everbearing strawberries in central Ohio? Plant as early in the spring as the plants are available and the soil can be prepared. Avoid newly turned sod because of the danger of grub damage. Any good loam will grow strawberries; even light sandy soils, if fertilized.

Oklahoma

Can you give me pointers on how to grow the rose daphne (Daphne cneorum)? Daphne is propagated by cuttings and layers. *Daphne cneorum* seems to need a green finger. It will tolerate much sunshine, also partial shade; sometimes, but not always, it resents acid soil and likes a little lime, a friable soil, and a rock at its back.

How can I succeed with delphinium in Oklahoma? Delphiniums are cool-climate plants and dislike heat. Deeply prepared, friable, sandy loam is preferable. A layer of peat moss under their roots is also a good idea. Treat them as annuals or biennials.

What flowers, if any, can be grown as borders to shrubs in a shady lawn? Chiefly early flowers that do their growing before trees are in leaf: *Brunnera macrophylla;* bleedingheart; columbine; day-lily; daffodils; Oriental poppy; *Phlox divaricata; Ceratostigma plumbaginoides;* primroses; plantain-lily; *Trollius europaeus;* tulips; tuberous begonias; impatiens.

What flowers that are good honey producers will grow in an Oklahoma garden? Willow, linden, apple, plum, and pear trees. Crocus, nepeta, clover, Michaelmas daisy, and monarda (bee-balm).

Can you give a list of fruit trees, berries, and small fruits that do the best in this climate? Strawberry; boysenberry; dewberry; plums: Japanese varieties and 'Green Gage' ('Reine Claude'); cherry, early varieties; peach; apricot; apple; crab apple; and pear.

When shall I plant gladiolus in Oklahoma? First planting, between March 1 and 15. Successive plantings, every two weeks until mid-May.

Will you tell me how to get rid of Bermuda grass? Grasses are difficult to eradicate, since their narrow leaves do not succumb to most herbicides. An airtight covering of heavy building paper or black plastic is effective, as is persistent hoeing of grass blades as they appear. No plant survives long when smothered or sheared above the ground in its growing season. Consult your county extension agent concerning the use of dalapon (trade name, Dowpon) and other herbicides.

What would be the best grass for a lawn that will grow under trees and will stand dry weather?   A shady lawn mixture containing a high percentage of one of the fine-leaved fescues, if it is to be sprinkled or irrigated; otherwise, buffalo grass or carpet grass; or if too shady for this, a ground cover such as *Vinca minor*.

Our lawn is barren of Bermuda grass in the shade of trees and where their tiny roots come to the surface. Will you recommend a grass or ground vine that will overcome this and withstand the hot winds of Oklahoma?   *Vinca minor* is a presentable ground cover, tolerant of shade, heat, and some dryness.

How shall we care for peonies in the South?   Peonies do not like a hot climate. Give them deeply prepared rich soil with a layer of peat moss below their roots. Plant with the eyes 2½ inches below the surface of the ground. For larger blooms, remove all side flower buds. They must have a long dormancy induced by cold weather.

What perennials will do well in partial shade and in full shade?   If shade is caused by trees, enrich the soil and add leafmold or peat moss. Aconitum; anemones, several varieties; *Brunnera macrophylla**; columbine; bleedingheart; hosta*; lily-of-the-valley; *Mertensia virginica**; *Phlox divaricata;* primroses; *Vinca minor**; violets*; *Uvularia grandiflora**; most ferns.*

What perennials will give color from spring to frost?   Continuous bloom from spring until frost is possible from a succession of different varieties such as spring-flowering bulbs; mertensia; *Clematis davidiana;* peonies; irises; dictamnus; *Phlox divaricata, P. subulata, P. carolina,* and *P. paniculata; Campanula carpatica, C. persificifolia; Nepeta* x *faassenii;* eupatorium; monarda; chrysanthemum; Michaelmas daisies. However, if continuous bloom is really important, you will find annuals more satisfactory. There will be periods in any perennial planting without flowers. Buy bedding plants for earliest color; sow seed for mid-summer-on bloom.

What perennials will grow best on the north side of a house in Oklahoma?   Ferns, columbine, *Phlox divaricata, P. carolina, Trollius europaeus, Brunnera macrophylla,* primroses, campanula, bleedingheart.

Will you give some information on rose culture and protection in the

* These will grow in full shade.

Southwest? Roses in the Southwest need a deep, rich soil—a 6-inch layer of rotted manure, or compost and peat moss to keep their roots cool—and an open, sunny place with good air circulation. For winter protection, hill the soil up around them, and cover with spruce branches, straw, or any light covering that will protect them from winter sun. Or use the more reliable plastic rose cones if the cost is not a factor. They will save more roses, at least partially offsetting their higher cost.

When should roses be pruned back in the summer? How much pruning should they receive? As soon as the rush of summer bloom is over. A mulch of compost in midsummer encourages fall bloom. As soon as first fall buds form, feed a balanced fertilizer. Climbing roses and hybrid perpetuals bloom on 2-year-old wood. Leave all vigorous canes of last season's growth. Cut out at the ground all wood older than this.

Our new property is entirely without shade. What trees are the fastest-growing and make good shade? Siberian and Chinese elms will grow rapidly and provide shade. *Acer saccharinum* (the silver maple) is also a fast grower. Unless you are over 60, however, don't be too impatient. In a few years a pin oak will outgrow any of the less permanent trees.

Oregon

Can I grow camellias? Yes. (See Tender Shrubs.)

When should daffodil bulbs be planted in Portland? Throughout the fall months; the earlier, the better.

Should daffodils be lifted annually and the soil fertilized before planting? Lift only when the bulbs become overcrowded and the flowers begin to deteriorate—usually after being in the ground for 3 or 4 years or even more. Divide the bulbs after the foliage has browned; replant. The bulbs are rich feeders and should be fertilized annually.

Will you give a good list of hardy evergreens for 20° F. below zero; and the soil they require? Blue spruce, Norway spruce; Douglas-fir; concolor fir; Scots pine, ponderosa pine, Austrian pine, mugo pine; juniper, both upright and spreading; any of the American arborvitae. Deciduous: Western larch. They will grow in any good garden soil.

What annual herbs and perennial herbs are grown in Oregon? *Annuals:* summer savory, sweet marjoram, dill, chervil, pot-marigold, coriander, sweet basil. *Perennials:* chives, tarragon, sweet woodruff, lemon balm, curly mint, sweet cicely, wild marjoram, rosemary, winter savory, thyme.

Do perennial herbs require winter protection?   In the colder areas, some of them do. (See Herbs.)

I was presented with a double red hibiscus plant sent from Southern California. A local nursery advises that it is hardy in this climate. I planted it on the west side of my house to protect it from east winds, but it looks sick. What do you advise?   Herbaceous perennial species of hibiscus and the hardy shrub species (such as rose-of-Sharon) will grow outside in the Northwest, but not tropical shrub species. We cannot tell from your description which kind yours is. However, if it is ailing, chances are it is *Hibiscus rosa-sinensis,* which would not be hardy in Oregon.

Where, and how, shall I plant lilies-of-the-valley for good blooms? My plants thrive but have no blooms.   On the north side, where they get plenty of light and filtered sunshine part of the day. Lily-of-the-valley, once established, becomes quite rampant. They like a rich, woodsy soil containing a little well-rotted manure or rich compost. Try confining your plants within an area with boards to force blooms.

Will magnolias live in northern Oregon?   Deciduous magnolia can be grown. Some evergreen varieties succeed in milder parts, but are not recommended for colder areas.

Shall I plant nandina and Mexican-orange in the sun or shade? One source says in the sun and another says in the shade. I am perplexed.   Plant them in full sun in the Pacific Northwest. Neither plant is given a high rating for hardiness, so both should be placed in a protected situation.

How shall I care for oleander that is 6 years old? It buds each year but never blooms. Is it too cold here? I have it outdoors all year.   If the plant and buds do not suffer definite injury from frost, it is not too cold. Lack of sufficient light may cause a lack of bloom. Prune the previous year's shoots well back in the spring.

Shall I plant pernettya in the sun or shade?   In the Pacific Northwest, the plants do much better when planted in full sun.

How can I make pernettya have more berries?   Three or more plants must be grown together for cross-pollination; plants should be pruned annually, removing some of the old wood. Sometimes root pruning is necessary to prevent them from spreading and making too much sucker growth at the expense of fruiting.

When should roses be planted?   Plant in the fall or spring (former, preferably) in holes sufficiently wide and deep to accommodate the roots without crowding. Set budded plants with buds about 2 inches below the surface of the soil. Prune the roots at the time of planting. Shorten the canes of fall-planted bushes; prune in the spring. Prune spring-planted ones at the time of planting. If the soil is dry, water well. Surface dress with fertilizer after the plants have become established.

Should rosebushes be planted in full sun, or where they have some shade? A situation fully exposed to sun is best.

What makes Sagina subulata turn brown in spots? Air pockets that form under the "moss." Remove the brown part and substitute a healthy piece of the plant, first placing a little fresh soil and fertilizer in the hole. Sagina must be kept well pressed to the ground to avoid brown spots and needs renewal occasionally to keep it in good condition.

Will you suggest a few shrubs that will grow well at the coast in the briny atmosphere? *Hypericum* x *moseranum,* hydrangea, kerria, azalea, rhododendron, flowering quince, deutzia, weigela, symphoricarpus, *Ilex aquifolium, Jasminum nudiflorum,* kalmia, *Viburnum tinus*.

Can you suggest locations for planting some shrubs—deutzia, flowering quince, and pomegranate? In your state, growing conditions are so good that most shrubs are easy. Deutzias like well-drained soil with a generous supply of humus, in the sun or partial shade. The quince does well in any good soil in full sun. *Punica granatum* (pomegranate) needs deep, heavy soil, sun, and elbow room. Fertilize, if necessary, when planting by incorporating rotted dairy manure or rich compost in the soil below the roots.

How shall I treat my violets to make them bloom? They do best in good loamy soil containing a little old manure or rich compost, and leafmold. To encourage plenty of blooms, runners must be removed. After plants of good size have flowered, they should be lifted, divided, and replanted.

South Carolina (See page 1408)

South Dakota (See page 1411)

Tennessee

Will pink amaryllis grow outdoors in the climate of southern Tennessee? There are many so-called bulbous plants that belong to the amaryllis family. Those which are so frequently grown in pots are not reliable outdoor subjects. The best for your purpose is the one called "hardy-amaryllis," correctly known as *Lycoris squamigera*. The bulbs increase year after year in the open ground.

When should boxwood be pruned in Tennessee? It is not customary to prune established boxwoods unless special shaping is wanted. Sometimes the smaller ones will send out precocious shoots that are cut off to retain the symmetry of the bush. Where pruning or shearing is necessary, this should be done during the growing season. Fall or winter pruning increases the danger of winterkilling.

In Chattanooga, buddleias hold their green leaves all year. As they bloom on 1-year wood, where should they be cut back to make the most and the largest flowers? The old, heavy canes should be cut back to the ground in late fall or early winter. The strong younger shoots will bear larger blooms. If the entire plant is left undisturbed, you will have more blooms, but smaller ones.

If Canterbury bell seeds are planted in a seed bed during the latter part of winter, will they bloom that same summer? The Canterbury bell is a biennial plant and is best sown in early summer. Young plants can be transferred to the beds in early fall and given a light covering of leaves. These will bloom the following year. Seeds planted in late winter can be transplanted the following spring or fall for bloom the second year.

Will cape-jasmine stand the winters of this area (Johnson City) in Tennessee? The cape-jasmine or gardenia is not reliably hardy. It will stand 20° to 24° F. without damage. It blooms only on old wood, and if this is frozen back, there will be no blooms the next year, even though the roots remain alive and the plant continues to send out new growth. In your area it would be far better to grow gardenias as tub plants: outdoors in the spring, summer, and fall, and indoors during the cold winter months.

If dahlias are left in the ground during the winter, will the new shoots bloom and do as well as if the tubers had been taken up? Dahlias can be given extra covering and left in the open ground in your area. The clumps should be taken up in the spring, however, divided, and replanted; such divisions will bloom just as well as those taken up and stored. The only danger is an occasional extremely severe winter during which they might be frozen.

What winter protection should be given rose trees planted in the upper South, where temperatures go to zero? Only the grafted head of a tree rose is likely to be damaged by zero-degree weather. Dig up one side of the root, bend the plant down until the head touches the soil, and cover with mixed soil and leaves, pinning the mound down with a burlap sack. In the spring, this covering is taken off, the head pruned, and the soil packed around the roots to hold the tree upright again. In Tennessee, packing the standing tree in straw bound in by burlap would probably be sufficient protection.

Texas

Will Japanese anemone grow here? What location is best? What kind of soil is needed? A partially shaded situation, sheltered from strong, drying winds, is best. It requires a rich, moist soil, and a generous supply of water during dry periods.

Can I leave anemone corms in the ground after they bloom? Are they supposed to come up year after year? It is better to lift the bulbs and store them in peat moss or in dry sand until inspection shows that they are beginning to push for another season of growth.

Will you please give me some practical suggestions as to the means of winter storage of tender tubers and bulbs when basement or root-cellar facilities are not available? Tender bulbs can be lifted when the foliage turns brown or is frosted, and stored in containers of slightly moist peat, vermiculite, sand, bagasse, or rice hulls. The containers should be placed in a cool, shaded place. If they can be put in cold storage at about 50° F., they will keep very well.

When is the proper time to graft citrus fruit trees on trifoliate orange stock? When the bark will "slip" or separate easily from the wood; ordinarily after a good rain during May, June, or July.

Do you think columbine and bleedingheart can be grown in central Texas? With good care, columbine will succeed; and bleedingheart also, if the soil is slightly acid and a sheltered position is given.

Will you give the care for dahlias? Is late planting best for here? Set out tubers about 10 days before the average date of the latest spring frost. This will vary for different sections of the state, but March should be right for the warmer sections, April planting for sections farther north. Set roots about 5 inches deep in beds enriched with compost; tie plants to a stout stake as they grow; feed every 3 or 4 weeks with a balanced fertilizer. Dahlias must have plenty of water if you wish to cut an abundance of fine blooms.

Is it O.K. to leave dahlia bulbs in the ground until ready to plant in the spring, or should they be taken up in the fall after stalks die? Both systems work. If you have been successful in leaving them in the ground, well and good. But if too many clumps have been disappearing, lift and carefully store in peat, sand, or similar material in a cool, shady place. With either method, the clump should be divided into single roots, each with a bud or eye showing.

Can Shasta daisies be dug up in the spring to permit the soil's being turned over and limed? They can be lifted, divided, and reset in the spring, but autumn is much preferred, so the plants will have many well-established roots before warm weather.

Will dogwood grow in this state? Yes, with proper preparation. A neutral or slightly acid soil, a high amount of organic matter, and good drainage are essential. Water freely in periods of drought and wrap the trunks with burlap for the first season or two.

When is the best time to transplant dogwood? During early winter, when they are without leaves. Dig as much of the roots as you can, protect from the sun and wind, and set at the same level as they formerly grew. Wrap the trunks with cloth as a protection against sunscald and the entry of borers.

Will you list some of the best annual and perennial flowers for this section of the Gulf Coast? *Annuals and perennials treated as annuals, for winter:* sweet-alyssum, blanket flower, California poppy, calliopsis, carnation, delphinium, larkspur, lupine, pansy, petunia, phlox, poppy, statice, sweet pea. *Annuals, for summer:* cosmos, ageratum, marigold, morning-glory, nasturtium, portulaca, verbena, zinnia. *Perennials:* hemerocallis, Louisiana iris, blue sage, Stokes'-aster, violet, canna, chrysanthemum, four-o'clock, moraea, Shasta daisy, Transvaal daisy (gerbera), golden glow.

Which flowers are easily grown in the extreme South? (Gulf Coastal area.) Practically all annuals may be grown in the Gulf Coastal area if fitted into the season that suits their needs. Hardy annuals during the autumn and winter; heat lovers, like marigolds, cosmos, and zinnias, during the hot, humid summers. See seed catalogs.

What is the best time to plant flowers this far south? *Hardy annu-*

als: sweet-alyssum, calendula, calliopsis, carnation, pansy, petunia, statice, and sweet pea, in the fall in warmer sections. *Tender annuals for the summer:* cosmos, ageratum, torenia, portulaca, nasturtium, and zinnia, after the danger of frost has passed. Perennials should be divided in the winter or when they are through blooming rather than in the spring.

What is the correct time to plant seeds of annual flowers in Austin? When should I set out perennials? For the cool-weather group—such as calendula, snapdragon, and pansy—October through December. For the heat-tolerant group—such as marigold and zinnia—March to April. Perennials should be divided in the winter, December through February, or immediately after blooming.

Should leaves be left on perennial borders in our climate? Yes, but do not let them pack down heavily over the crowns of the plants. New leaves should be added as the mulch decomposes.

What are the best fruits for this climate? Oranges, grapefruit, peaches, pears, plums, bramble fruits, and figs.

How can I grow gardenias in Dallas? A slightly acid soil, rich in organic matter, a mulch of oak leaves, and facilities for watering during dry times are essential. An occasional watering with a solution of copperas will supply iron, and periodic spraying with an oil emulsion will control whitefly and sooty mold.

What is the best location for gladioli—partial shade or all sun? When is the best time to plant for this part of the country? Gladioli are sun-demanding; corms should always be set in full sun. The planting time should be gauged by the time of the latest killing frost for your area. Then plant about 2 or 3 weeks ahead of this date. Late February and early March for southern sections; 2 or 3 weeks later farther north in the state.

Is there a practical way to get rid of "nut" or coco grass? It is very difficult to eradicate once it gets beyond the hand-digging stage. However, there are herbicides available. Consult your local county extension agent for advice.

How can I kill Bermuda grass in my flower beds? There is no safe selective chemical for flower beds. Weed by hand.

When is the time to plant California privet hedge in central Texas? December to February. Cut the plants back heavily at planting time; set at the same level that the plants grew; water well at once.

What herbs would you suggest for Gulf Coast country, for growing on a commercial scale? Sage (*Salvia officinalis*) promises to be the best prospect for commercial production, following trials at the State Experiment Station in this area.

When should hibiscus be moved? December to February. If the plant is frosted in early winter, cut it back severely and move it to the selected site.

What variety of holly that will bear berries can best be grown here? What soil and treatment are required? The Chinese holly (*Ilex cornuta*), the Dahoon holly (*Ilex cassine*), American holly (*Ilex opaca*)—varieties of all of these species succeed in this locality.

My hydrangeas do not grow and bloom as they should. What kind of soil and fertilizer are best for them in southeast Texas? I used well-rotted leaves and animal manure. Are they too rich for them? Your soil sounds all right, provided it is not strongly alkaline. Sulfur and alum will acidify the soil; rotting leaves should help. Be sure not to prune after the wood is mature, as flower buds would be removed. Pinch or prune no later than July.

How can I make hydrangeas, planted outdoors in Texas, bloom? A soil not too alkaline, an abundance of organic matter, and water are essential. Severe competition from tree roots, winterkilling, or late pruning can cause failure to bloom, as the flower buds are formed before the plants go dormant in the fall.

How can I protect Dutch iris from the cold? When low temperatures are forecast, cover plants with evergreen boughs or some other light mulch until the danger from that particular cold snap has passed. Generally, the plants should be uncovered after 2 or 3 days. Newspapers or a single thickness of cloth is of no value.

Why do tall bearded irises refuse to bloom along the Gulf Coast? Our light, sandy soils and lack of a real and prolonged dormant season combine to rule out this popular perennial for the Gulf Coast. In some areas, 1 or 2 varieties seem to be pretty much at home, but not like the semitropical perennials that really succeed here. Try some of the Louisiana irises instead.

My yellow jasmine is a beautiful shrub, three years old, and has had only 1 small bloom on it. Can you tell me why? Jasmine requires plenty of sunshine. Possibly too much shade is the cause of your trouble.

Are lilacs and rhododendrons suitable for moist coastal areas? These temperate shrubs are sure to be disappointing to you here. They must have a complete dormant period (induced by long, unbroken cold) and a heavy, rich soil. Better stick to the beautiful semitropical flowering shrubs that succeed in your area. For example, try crape-myrtle (*Lagerstroemia*), which comes in a wider range of color than do lilacs.

What lilies will do well in semi-alkaline soil? Easter lilies, madonna lilies (*L. candidum*), *L. chalcedonicum*, *L. bulbiferum*, *L. martagon*, *L. x testaceum* and other European types should all succeed if your soil is not too basic (alkaline). Of course, the incorporating of acid organic materials will help in the culture of all of these and many of the modern hybrids.

Please advise if lycoris is adapted to this climate. What will make it bloom? *Lycoris squamigera* should flower in the northern section of Texas if the bulbs are properly fed and watered and do not suffer too much root competition. *Lycoris radiata* will probably succeed in the southern areas under conditions of good culture and freedom from too many roots.

Rice hulls make very light soil, but are they too rich for pansies? If so, what besides sand should be used? Mixed with sandy soil, rice hulls make a good compost for pansies.

How many species of passion-flower are there? Will any of these grow in Texas? There are about 400 species. The fruits and flowers are of many kinds; some few of the fruits are edible, most are not. *Passiflora caerulea* and *P. incarnata* should do well in gardens in southern Texas.

What is the best understock for peaches in the South, where root rot is prevalent in areas with high alkaline soil? Tennessee wild peaches are the most widely used understocks in all parts of Texas, but are not resistant to root rot.

Will peonies do well in central Texas in a black, waxy soil? If so, what varieties do best? No, peonies will not succeed in this climate. (See question on peonies in South Carolina, this section.)

What is the best time to divide and reset perennials in Austin? Autumn or winter; or immediately after flowering. In this way, the roots will be widespread and well established before spring growth commences.

What is the best time for planting perennials? Fall. Practically all herbaceous perennials can be lifted in late fall, or very early winter, and reset.

Should ranunculus bulbs remain in the ground year after year? It is better to lift them each year after the foliage has died down and store in a dry place.

Will you list some good rock-garden plants for use in this state? Probably the best groups are the true cacti and semitropical succulents that succeed out-of-doors in the South. The usual alpine rock-garden plants used in the North will be a disappointment to you in Texas.

What roses are best for southern gardens?   The teas do well if they have good care. Some old-fashioned roses, like 'Louis Philippe', 'Mme. Lombard', 'Minnie Francis', 'Duchesse de Brabant', and 'Safrano' will thrive long years after many choice cutting roses have succumbed to this climate. A few Texas nurseries specialize in these varieties for southern gardens. You can grow hybrid teas by treating them as annuals. They are produced by the millions commercially in Tyler, Texas.

What makes roses die so quickly here?   Black spot, dieback, crown gall, an excessively alkaline soil, lack of a distinct rest period—all contribute toward a short life for modern roses. In many southern gardens, hybrid teas are being grown as annuals.

Could I grow roses in a dry clay soil?   To do so successfully, it will be necessary to improve the soil by the addition of compost, rotted leaves, sand, and other materials. An abundance of water is essential, and frequent feeding during growing weather, with a balanced commercial fertilizer.

Will you tell me the proper time to set out new rosebushes in southern Texas?   Early planting is strongly recommended for the South, December to February being best by all odds.

Is fall or spring the best time to plant roses in west Texas?   Fall planting (or, more accurately, winter planting) is better by far. If the plants are set in December to February, roots can become established before top growth starts in the spring.

What is the cause of roses planted in either fall or spring growing and blooming all summer, apparently strong and healthy, then suddenly dying in the fall? The trouble starts with black patches on the stems, while 25 per cent of bushes are not affected. (Galveston.)   Patches on the canes are caused by the so-called dieback disease, for which no dependable control is known. Prune away diseased parts and mop the cuts with Bordeaux or sulfur paste. Black spots, followed by yellow areas on the leaves, are a manifestation of black spot, which can be controlled by a fungicide.

Will you please give some information as to the enemies of roses in the South and Southwest? Also, what kinds are best for this state?   The greatest trouble is black spot, a fungus disease that can be controlled by the frequent use of captan or maneb. In the Deep South, so-called dieback is a serious trouble for which no dependable control is yet known. Old-fashioned varieties in the tea group are most dependable.

What shrubs shall I plant in southwestern Texas, where there is a dry

climate, wind, and alkaline soil? It is best to use natives, and some of the best of these are *Leucophyllum frutescens; Tecoma stans; Diospyros texana; Rhus virens* and other species of sumacs; several species of *Acacia; Chilopsis linearis; Sophora secundiflora;* several species of salvia; *Clematis drummondii;* several species of juniper; several species of yucca and agave.

Can I have a list of flowering trees or shrubs for Houston? *Trees:* Magnolia, mimosa, huisache. *Shrubs:* crape-myrtle, pittosporum, photinia, privet, oleander, jasmine, forsythia, spiraea, weigela, pyracantha, camellia, azalea, and gardenia.

What are some of the best shrubs for foundation plantings? Azalea, camellia, podocarpus, euonymus, cotoneaster, pyracantha, Japanese box, Japanese holly, jasmine, abelia, feijoa, and hibiscus.

Utah

Can I have a list of rock-garden plants hardy in Utah? The following should be hardy in Utah, at altitudes below 6,000 feet: any of the sedums, pinks (*Dianthus*), dwarf phlox (*P. subulata*), bellflower (*Campanula carpatica*), saponaria, globeflower (*trollius*), coralbells (*Heuchera*), and violas. The last 3 should have partial shade.

Is there any fairly good climbing rose that will go through the winter without covering in a climate where the temperature occasionally goes from 10° to 15° F.? Try 'Blaze' and 'Dr. J. H. Nicolas'; a southern or eastern exposure is preferable. If its stems are trained horizontally, 'Climbing Peace' can be sensational. 'Queen of the Prairies', with large clusters of blush to rose, cupped, globular flowers, blooms late and only once each season but is very hardy. Ramblers would also probably survive without protection.

Do you have a list of flowering shrubs and trees that would grow in an altitude of 6,000 feet? Try French hybrid lilacs; they should do well at this altitude. Other good shrubs would be mock orange ('Virginal' or 'Galahad'); highbush-cranberry; wayfaring tree (*Viburnum lantana*); buffalo berry (*Shepherdia argentea*). *Small trees:* Colorado pink locust; hawthorn; or 'Hopa' flowering crab.

Washington

When and in what kind of soil and location should alstromeria be planted?   Plant tubers 5 to 6 inches deep in September or early October in a rich, well-drained soil, and in full sun or partial shade; place the little eyes up and the tubers down.

Does alstromeria require winter protection in the Pacific Northwest?   Alstromeria makes growth during the winter, and if the weather is cold, they should be mulched so that frosts do not freeze them down to the tubers, which are tender and will perish if once frozen.

What time should one take up dahlia tubers?   Lift as soon as early frosts have cut down the tops, usually in late October or early November.

Is there any secret to growing cutleaf weeping birch trees? Every season I notice a few die off here in Yakima. It's heartbreaking to grow one for 6 or 7 years and then see it wither and die.   The tree calls for no special culture. It likes a sandy loam soil. Being a shallow rooter, it must have plenty of moisture, particularly during dry periods. Leaf diseases and a birch borer are among its enemies. The borer is known to be somewhat prevalent in your area and could be responsible for the death of the trees. It is responsible for birches dying at the top, known as "stag heading."

When is the proper time to plant fruit trees in the Seattle, Washington, area?   December is the ideal time. Planting, however, may be carried on through January and February.

How do I trim boysenberry, loganberry, and grapes in Seattle?   Grapes—in February, cut back the previous year's growth to 2 or 3 eyes. Remove weak canes. Loganberry and boysenberry—cut back all the old wood to the ground as early as possible after the fruit has been picked. This gives new shoots, which produce the next crop, a better chance to develop. Thin these, leaving only the strong ones, and nip off the ends or tips.

I have heard of a plant called pearlwort, which is supposed to be a moss. Is it suitable to plant instead of grass?   This is *Sagina subulata,* a creeping perennial, evergreen, hardy, bearing little white flowers, and in habit of growth similar to moss; but it is *not* a moss. It is used as a ground cover, also for planting between steppingstones, and sometimes for making lawns. It's much inclined to get humpy and must be kept flat by rolling or tamping. If this is neglected, the humps turn brown. Grass makes a much superior lawn and requires only a little more care.

Is montbretia hardy in the Pacific Northwest? I lost mine last winter— the first time in 20 years. Montbretias are not always hardy, although in the milder parts of Washington they go through the average winter outside without being harmed. To be on the safe side, either mulch or lift and store them in frost-free quarters for the winter.

What are some nut trees that will grow in Spokane? The black walnut and hardy filbert. Others, such as butternut and English walnut, have been planted but do not survive for long.

Would a rhododendron be hardy in eastern Washington? Many fine rhododendrons may be grown in eastern Washington, provided that they are given an acid soil, good drainage, some shade, and protection from cold winds. The soil in this area is alkaline and must be replaced with one that is on the acid side and which is kept so by an occasional application of sulfur. Select only varieties of known hardiness.

What are a dozen or more good roses for a beginner in Washington? All the hybrid teas and floribundas do superbly well in your climate. Select varieties from the catalog of one of the famous West Coast rose breeders and growers. A few outstanding varieties of *hybrid teas* are: 'Mojave', orange; 'Helen Traubel', apricot-pink; 'Charlotte Armstrong', 'Chrysler Imperial', red. *Grandifloras:* 'Buccaneer', yellow; 'American Heritage', blend of yellows and reds; 'Queen Elizabeth', rose-pink; and 'Scarlet Knight', red. *Floribundas:* 'Circus', multicolored; 'Spartan', orange-red; 'Fashion', coral pink; 'Frensham', red.

In the Pacific Northwest, can roses be transplanted any time during the winter? Yes, but November and December are the preferred months.

Will a tamarix hedge grow well in a rainy climate? Yes. It grows very rapidly in the Pacific Northwest. It should be pruned annually.

What are some shrubs that will do well on a dry, hot hillside exposed to the south? Tolerance of widely varying conditions makes the following shrubs grow almost anywhere in the Temperate Zone: *Berberis thunbergii* and *B.* x *mentorensis; Cotoneaster acutifolius, C. divaricatus,* and *C. salicifolius; Amorpha fruticosa,* and *A. canescens; Holodiscus dumosus; Mahonia repens; Caragana arborescens; Colutea arborescens; Hypericum prolificum; Ceanothus fendleri; Lonicera; Potentilla fruticosa; Prunus besseyi* and *P. tomentosa; Rhus; Rosa spinosissima; Shepherdia argentea; Symphoricarpos orbiculatus; Philadelphus microphyllus; Jamesia americana; Prunus tenella.*

Will you suggest shrubs that will do well in moist shade? *Mahonia aquifolium* and *M. repens; Euonymus fortunei radicans; Cornus; Hydrangea; Rhodotypos scandens; Ribes; Rubus deliciosus; Symphoricarpos albus* and *S. orbiculatus; Viburnum lentago, V. carlesii,* and *V.* x *burkwoodii; Arctostaphylos uva-ursi; Physocarpus opulifolius; Ptelea trifoliata; Lonicera involucrata; Genista tinctoria; Amelanchier; Cotoneaster divaricatus, C. horizontalis, C. acutifolius,* and *C. franchetii.*

Wisconsin

How and when should chrysanthemums be given winter protection in Kenosha County, Wisconsin? Apply a light covering of dry leaves and top with evergreen branches when the soil is slightly frozen.

Are any varieties of azaleas or rhododendrons hardy as far north as Wisconsin? You might try 'P.J.M.' rhododendron and the Chinese azalea, *R. molle,* in protected parts of your garden.

Will bent grass thrive in north-central Wisconsin? Yes, provided you are willing to fuss with it. But for the home gardener, the less touchy, hardier grasses, such as bluegrass, are far more satisfactory.

Is the blue beech hardy in this midwestern climate? Yes. *Carpinus caroliniana* (blue beech or hornbeam) is native from Minnesota to Florida and is fully hardy. Plant it in rich, moist soil.

In this climate, what is the best time to plant seeds of Canterbury bells? Plant in late May to allow a full season's growth before the plants go through the winter. Carry over in the cold frame. Canterbury bells all belong to the species *Campanula medium,* and all varieties are equally hardy, but none is easy to grow.

Can I grow the large-flowered chrysanthemums in the garden? These chrysanthemums are neither hardy nor early enough for Wisconsin, but flowers of some of the University of Minnesota hybrids reach 3½ to 4 inches in diameter.

What is the proper method of planting and caring for Daphne cneorum in southeastern Wisconsin? *Daphne cneorum* likes a situation open to the sun but sheltered from winter winds. An opening in a planting of evergreens that faces south is ideal. Plant slightly deeper than the plant stood in the nursery, and fill up to the ground level with soil and leafmold or rich compost. A pH reaction of between 5.9 and 6.8 is satisfactory. Use balled and burlapped or container-grown stock and plant in the spring.

What fruits (cherries, plums, pears, grapes) are hardy in Wisconsin? All sour cherries are reasonably hardy, but where high winds prevail, better stick to the sand-cherry and plum hybrids, which, while not so high in quality, do make good jams and pies. Of the true plums, a series from the University of Minnesota is recommended. 'Superior' and 'Pipestone' are good. Add some cherry-plum hybrids, such as 'Sapalta', 'Compass', and 'Oka', for variety. The 'Beta' grape (a 'Concord'-wild-grape hybrid) is reliably hardy but should be used only if 'Concord' does not do well near you. 'Parker' and 'Patten' are good pears that can take it. Check with local nurseries to see if older, tested sorts are hardy in your neighborhood, since most of those mentioned above are recommended largely because they will not winter-kill, not for highest quality.

Is there an apricot that will withstand our winters? Two apricots from the University of Minnesota that have been developed for rugged climates are 'Moongold' and 'Sungold'. Plant one of each for cross-pollination.

What dwarf fruit trees will grow well in southeastern Wisconsin? Whatever standard varieties are hardy in your area. Dwarfness does not affect hardiness. Pears and apples, the two species most commonly dwarfed by grafting, should be 100 per cent hardy. However, don't overlook the possibility of growing full-sized varieties as semi-dwarfs, keeping them cut down to shrub forms. This is often more satisfactory for regions where apples do not do too well. Most apples in England are grown in bush form, by the way.

Can white or green grapes be raised in central Wisconsin? 'Minnesota 66' is a green grape that has gone through 40° F. below zero. Worth trying, but not too reliable, are the old green 'Niagara', yellowish 'Seneca', and early green 'Ontario'.

Can you tell me what grapes and nuts I can grow? The only grape that produces fair fruit and will survive your severe winter is the 'Concord'-wild-grape hybrid 'Beta'. You are about on the northern limit of black walnut, hickory, and butternut.

Will the shrub lantana thrive in Wisconsin's climate? What you mean by the shrub lantana is probably *Viburnum lantana,* the wayfaring tree, which is hardy at Lake Geneva and possibly north of that point; *Viburnum carlesii* is about the same for hardiness and is far superior in bloom and fragrance. *V. lantana* makes a splendid dense hedge. *Lantana camara,* the true lantana, is a tender shrub grown in the north under glass or as a bedding plant like heliotrope.

Are pansies hardy in Wisconsin?   Not in the sense that they can be left outdoors without protection and survive. In Wisconsin, they can be started in cold frames, wintered with the glass on, and set out in the spring.

When and how should pansies be started from seed?   Pansy seed does not germinate satisfactorily at temperatures above 65° F. This means late seeding (about August 20) in your area. Plant in a cold frame in well-drained soil, not too heavy, and not too rich in nitrogen. Potash (which promotes tougher growth) helps the plants to winter over. Wait until snow flies and cover lightly with pine or spruce boughs, or with marsh hay, and apply the sash to the frames. Remove the glass about April 1 and set the plants in a permanent position about May 1.

I have my rosebushes hilled up about 8 inches. Where and when should the tops be cut off?   You might as well wait until spring. The tops will have to be cut back to live wood anyway, and one cut is easier to make than two. Also, the tops help catch and hold snow—the natural cover for roses.

Should a climbing rose be taken down from its trellis each year and covered with leaves during the winter?   In Wisconsin, climbing roses should be laid down (a trellis hinged at the bottom so it can be dropped over without removing the canes is best) and covered. But do not cover with leaves; damp soil is much better. It keeps the canes moist and does not allow wind to blow off the covering.

Will you name the 12 best all-around varieties of hybrid tea roses for this area?   The reliable rose specialists and large American nursery concerns usually offer collections that are made up of roses satisfactory over a wide range of territory, beautiful in flower, and reasonable in price. You can do far worse than to trust to their expert judgment in this matter of variety. (See Roses.)

What kinds of shrubs with red berries are hardy for northern Wisconsin?   *Berberis thunbergii, Crataegus* (hawthorn); *Euonymus europaeus; Lonicera tatarica* (bush honeysuckle); 'Hopa' crab; *Prunus tomentosa; Rosa palustris; Sambucus microbotrys* (bunchberry elder); *Symphoricarpus orbiculatus; Viburnum lantana* (red to black berries); *V. opulus; V. trilobum.*

What perennials should I plant for a succession of bloom in Wisconsin for spring and summer?   Achillea; aconitum; delphinium; aquilegia; *Artemisia lactiflora;* asters; *Dicentra spectabilis; Centaurea macrocephala;* chrysanthemum, earliest varieties; iris; dictamnus; peony; erigeron; hemerocallis; linum; lupine; *Papaver orientale* and *P. nudicaule;*

physostegia; *Phlox subulata, P. divaricata,* and *P. paniculata; Trollius europaeus;* thalictrum.

When is tree planting most successful—spring or fall? Unless one has the gift of long-range forecasting, this cannot be answered categorically. For most trees, the best time to plant is as soon as possible, since waiting merely means delay in getting the tree established. But certainly fall planting (anytime after the leaves fall) is much preferred to the usual practice of waiting until the trees are in leaf in May before setting out. Exceptions are the thin-barked trees like sycamore and birches, and those with fleshy roots like magnolias, which do best when planted as early as practicable in the spring. Professionals, with the use of modern transplanting techniques and equipment, can move large specimens with huge balls of earth at any time of the year.

Can you suggest some reliable shrubs (flowering) for Wisconsin? *Amelanchier; Berberis thunbergii* and *B.* x *mentorensis; Buddleia alternifolia; Desmodium; Euonymus europaeus; Exochorda racemosa; Hypericum prolificum; Lonicera; Physocarpus opulifolius; Prunus tomentosa* and *P.* x *cistena; Rubus deliciosus; Sambucus; Spiraea; Syringa; Viburnum; Rosa rugosa; R. rubrifolia.*

Wyoming

Should I mulch my bleedingheart or in any way give it extra protection this winter? A mound of leafmold or coarse compost over its crown would be helpful but not absolutely necessary.

Please name some good perennials to grow in the different climates of the state of Wyoming. Variation in climate seems less a difficulty in Wyoming than the quality and condition of the soil. The following grow successfully where some protection from the wind is possible: basket of gold; *Centaurea macrocephala; Saponaria ocymoides;* pyrethrum; peony; iris; oenothera; nepeta; lupine; linum; hemerocallis; *Heliopsis* 'Pitcherana'; gypsophila; euphorbia; *Phlox subulata* and *P. paniculata;* chrysanthemum; delphinium; aster; hollyhock; *Clematis integrifolia* and *C. recta;* anchusa.

What climbing roses would you recommend for Wyoming? 'Blaze', 'Dr. J. H. Nicolas', and 'White Dawn' are extra-hardy varieties. Try also the continuous bloomer 'Golden Showers'. 'Viking Queen' is another toughie.

What roses do well in Wyoming?   Floribunda roses do excellently in Wyoming and require little or no winter care. Among the best of these are 'Frensham', red; 'Eutin', red; 'Circus', multicolored; 'Spartan', orange-red; and 'Fashion', coral-salmon.

16. Sources for Further Information

Books

AFRICAN-VIOLETS AND OTHER GESNERIADS

African-Violet Handbook for Judges and Exhibitors. Ruth G. Carey. R. G. Carey, Knoxville, Tenn.

African-Violets. M. J. Robey. Barnes.

African-Violets. Sunset Editors. Lane.

All About African Violets (Revised Edition). Montague Free and Charles Marden Fitch. Doubleday.

Helen Van Pelt Wilson's African-Violet Book. Helen Van Pelt Wilson. Hawthorn.

Miracle House Plants: The Gesneriad Family. Virginie and George A. Elbert. Crown.

ANNUALS

Annuals. Brooklyn Botanic Garden.

Annuals. James U. Crockett. Time-Life.

Picture Book of Annuals. Arno and Irene Nehrling. Hearthside.

Woman's Day Book of Annuals and Perennials. Jean Hersey. Simon & Schuster.

BEGONIAS

Begonias: The Complete Reference Guide. Ed and Mildred Thompson. Times Books.

Begonias as House Plants. Jack Kramer. Van Nostrand.

Begonias for Beginners. Elda Haring. Bookworm Pub.

Tuberous Begonia. Brian Langdon. International Publications Service.

BIRDS

Bird Feeders and Shelters You Can Make. Ted S. Pettit. Putnam.
New Handbook of Attracting Birds. Thomas P. McElroy. Knopf.
Songbirds in Your Garden. John K. Terres. Hawthorn.
Trees, Shrubs and Vines for Attracting Birds. Richard M. De Graaf and Gretchin M. Witman. University of Massachusetts Press.

BOTANY

Botany. Taylor Alexander et al. Western Pub.
Introductory Botany. Arthur Cronquist. Harper & Row.
Introductory Plant Science. Henry T. Northen. Wiley.
Manual of Cultivated Plants. Liberty H. Bailey. Macmillan.
Manual of Cultivated Trees and Shrubs Hardy in North America. Alfred Rehder. Macmillan.

BROMELIADS

Bromeliads. Victoria Padilla. Crown.
Bromeliads for Home, Garden and Greenhouse. Werner Rauh. Sterling.
Bromeliads: The Colorful House Plants. Jack Kramer. Van Nostrand.

BULBS

Bulbs. James U. Crockett. Time-Life.
Bulbs. Sunset Editors. Lane.
Bulbs for the Home Gardener. Bebe Miles. Grosset and Dunlap.
Complete Book of Bulbs (Revised Edition). F. F. Rockwell, Esther C. Grayson, and Marjorie J. Dietz. Lippincott.
Hardy Bulbs. Louise B. Wilder. Dover.
Hardy Garden Bulbs. Gertrude S. Wister. Dutton.

CACTI AND SUCCULENTS

Book of Cacti and Other Succulents. Claude Chidamian. Doubleday.
Cacti. John Borg. Sterling.
Cacti and Other Succulents. Jack Kramer. Harry N. Abrams.
Cacti and Succulents. Time-Life Books Editors. Time-Life.
Plant Jewels of the High Country: Sempervivums and Sedums. Helen E. Payne. Pine Cone Pubs., Medford, Oregon.

CHRYSANTHEMUMS

Chrysanthemums. J. F. Smith. Hippocrene.

Chrysanthemums: Year Round Growing. Barrie J. Machin and Nigel Scopes. Sterling.

Pocket Encyclopedia of Chrysanthemums in Colour. Stanley Gosling. Arco.

CITY, SHADE, AND SEASIDE GARDENS

City Gardener. P. Truex. Knopf.

Gardening by the Sea. Daniel J. Foley. Chilton.

Gardening in the City. Carla Wallach. Harcourt, Brace, Jovanovich.

Gardening in the Shade. Brooklyn Botanic Garden.

Shade Gardens. Oliver E. Allen. Time-Life.

Successful Gardening in the Shade. Helen Van Pelt Wilson. Doubleday.

The Terrace Gardener's Handbook. Linda Yang. Doubleday.

Your City Garden. Jack Kramer. Scribner's.

CONTAINER AND HANGING PLANTS

Container and Hanging Gardens. Staff of Ortho Books. Ortho.

Container Gardening Indoors & Out. Jack Kramer. Doubleday.

Container Gardening Outdoors. George Taloumis. Simon & Schuster.

Hanging Plants for Home, Terrace and Garden. John P. Baumgardt. Simon & Schuster.

Window Box and Container Gardening. Judith Berrisford. Transatlantic.

EVERGREENS

Conifers for Your Garden. Adrian Bloom. Scribner's.

Evergreens. James U. Crockett. Time-Life.

Handbook on Conifers. Brooklyn Botanic Garden.

FERNS

Ferns. Philip Perl. Time-Life.

Ferns to Know and Grow. Gordon Foster. Hawthorn.

Handbook on Ferns. Brooklyn Botanic Garden.

Home Gardener's Book of Ferns. John Mickel and Evelyn Fiore. Holt, Rinehart and Winston.

FLOWER ARRANGEMENT AND PRESERVATION

Complete Book of Flower Preservation. Geneal Condon. Prentice-Hall.

Complete Flower Arranger. Amalie A. Ascher. Simon & Schuster.

Decorating with Plants. Time-Life Editors. Time-Life.

Flower Arrangements for Special Occasions. Winifrede Morrison. Hippocrene.

Flower Growing for Flower Arrangement. Arno and Irene Nehrling. Dover.

Flowers, Space and Motion. Helen Van Pelt Wilson. Simon & Schuster.

Keeping the Plants You Pick. L. L. Foster. Crowell.

FLOWER SHOW MANAGEMENT

Handbook for Flower Shows. National Council of State Garden Clubs. St. Louis, Mo.

FLOWERS IN GENERAL

Color Dictionary of Flowers and Plants for Home and Garden. Roy Hay and Patrick M. Synge. Crown.

FRUITS (See also Vegetables.)

All About Growing Fruits and Berries. Staff of Ortho Books. Ortho.

Fruit Trees and Shrubs. Brooklyn Botanic Garden.

Fruits for the Home Garden. Ken & Pat Kraft. Morrow.

Green Thumb Book of Fruit and Vegetable Gardening. George Abraham. Prentice-Hall.

GARDEN CONSTRUCTION, FURNITURE, AND ACCESSORIES

Book of Garden Ornament. Peter Hunt, ed. Architectural Book Publishing Company.

Complete Book of Garden and Outdoor Lighting. Bernard Gladstone. Hearthside.

Fences and Gates. Sunset Editors. Lane.

Garden Art and Decoration. Sunset Editors. Lane.

Garden Construction. Ogden Tenner. Time-Life.

How to Build Fences, Gates and Walls. Stanley Schuler. Macmillan.

Walks, Walls and Patio Floors. Sunset Editors. Lane.

GENERAL GARDENING

America's Garden Book. James Bush-Brown. Scribner's.
Complete Guide to Successful Gardening. Marjorie J. Dietz, ed. Mayflower.
Complete Illustrated Book of Garden Magic. Roy E. Biles and Marjorie J. Dietz. Ferguson and Doubleday.
Encyclopedia of Gardening. Norman Taylor, ed. Houghton Mifflin.
Reader's Digest Illustrated Guide to Gardening. Carroll Calkins, ed. Reader's Digest.
Rockwells' Complete Guide to Successful Gardening. F. F. Rockwell and Esther C. Grayson. Doubleday.
Standard Cyclopedia of Horticulture. Liberty H. Bailey, ed. 3 volumes. Macmillan.
Wyman's Gardening Encyclopedia. Donald Wyman, ed. Macmillan.

GERANIUMS

Geraniums. H. G. Fogg. Branford.
Joy of Geraniums. Helen Van Pelt Wilson. Morrow.
Miniature Geraniums. Harold Bagusi. Branford.

GLADIOLUS (See Bulbs.)

How to Grow Gladiolus. N. A. Gladiolus Council. Peru, Ind.

GREENHOUSES

Commercial Flower Forcing. Alex Laurie and others. McGraw-Hill.
Complete Greenhouse Book. Peter Clegg and Derry Watkins. Garden Way.
Garden Rooms and Greenhouses. Jack Kramer. Harper & Row.
Gardening Under Glass. Jerome A. Eaton. Macmillan.
Greenhouse Gardening. Henry and Rebecca Northen. Wiley.
Greenhouse Gardening. Time-Life Editors. Time-Life.
Winter Flowers in Greenhouse and Sun-heated Pit. K. S. Taylor and E. W. Gregg. Scribner's.

GROUND COVERS

All About Ground Covers. Staff of Ortho Books. Ortho.
Ground Cover Plants. Donald Wyman. Macmillan.
Ground Covers for Easier Gardening. Daniel J. Foley. Dover.

GROWTH REGULATORS

Plant Growth Substances. Folke Skoog, ed. University of Wisconsin Press.

Plant Growth Substances in Agriculture. Robert J. Weaver. Freeman.

HERBS

Complete Book of Herbs and Spices. Sarah Garland. Viking.

Gardening with Herbs for Flavor and Fragrance. Helen M. Fox. Dover.

Herb Gardening At Its Best. Sal Gilbertie. Atheneum.

Herbs and Their Ornamental Uses. Brooklyn Botanic Garden.

Herbs for Every Garden. G. B. Foster. Dutton.

Herbs: How to Grow Them and How to Use Them. Helen N. Webster. Branford.

Herbs: Their Culture and Uses. Rosetta E. Clarkson. Macmillan.

Herbs to Grow Indoors. Adelma Grenier Simmons. Hawthorn.

HOUSE PLANTS AND INDOOR LIGHT GARDENING

After-Dinner Gardening Book. Richard W. Langer. Macmillan.

All About House Plants (Revised Edition). Montague Free and Marjorie J. Dietz. Doubleday.

Complete Book of Houseplants Under Lights. Charles Marden Fitch. Hawthorn.

Decorative Gardening in Containers. Elvin McDonald. Doubleday.

Exotic Plant Manual. Alfred B. Graf. Scribner's.

Flowering House Plants. James U. Crockett. Time-Life.

Foliage House Plants. James U. Crockett. Time-Life.

Gardening Under Lights. Time-Life Books Editors. Time-Life.

House Plant Decorating Book. Virginie F. and George A. Elbert. Dutton.

Indoor Light Gardening Book. George A. Elbert. Crown.

IRIS

Iris Book. Molly Price. Dover.

Irises. Harry Randall. Taplinger.

World of Irises. Bee Warburton. American Iris Society, 6518 Beachy Avenue, Wichita, Kansas.

LANDSCAPING AND DESIGN

Art of Home Landscaping. Garrett Eckbo. McGraw-Hill.

How to Plan and Plant Your Own Property. Alice R. Ireys. Morrow.

How to Plan Your Own Home Landscape. Nelva M. Weber. Bobbs-Merrill.

Landscape Gardening. James U. Crockett. Time-Life.

Landscaping and the Small Garden. Marjorie J. Dietz. Doubleday.

Patios, Terraces, Decks, and Roof Gardens. Alice Upham Smith. Hawthorn.

Your Private World: A Study of Intimate Gardens. Thomas Church. Chronicle Books.

LAWNS

Lawn Keeping. Robert W. Schery. Prentice-Hall.

Lawns and Ground Covers. James U. Crockett. Time-Life.

Lawns and Ground Covers. Sunset Editors. Lane.

ORCHIDS

All About Orchids. Charles Marden Fitch. Doubleday.

Home Orchid Growing. Rebecca T. Northen. Van Nostrand-Reinhold.

Miniature Orchids. R. T. Northen. Van Nostrand-Reinhold.

Orchids. Alice F. Skelsey. Time-Life.

Orchids and How to Grow Them. Gloria Jean Sessler. Prentice-Hall.

Orchids for Home and Garden. F. A. Fennell, Jr. Holt, Rinehart & Winston.

Orchids You Can Grow. Harry B. Logan. Hawthorn.

ORGANIC GARDENING

Basic Book of Organically-Grown Foods. Organic Gardening & Farming Magazine Editors. Rodale.

How to Have a Green Thumb Without an Aching Back. Ruth Stout. Exposition.

Organic Gardening Under Glass. George and Katy Abraham. Rodale.

Organic Gardening Without Poisons. Hamilton Tyler. Van Nostrand.

Organic Vegetable Gardening. Joseph A. Cocannouer. Arc Books.

Weeds: Guardians of the Soil. Joseph A. Cocannouer. Devin-Adair.

PERENNIALS

Better Homes & Gardens Perennials You Can Grow. Better Homes & Gardens Editors. Meredith.

Gardening with Perennials Month by Month. Joseph G. Hudak. Times Books.

Low Maintenance Perennials. Robert S. Hebb. Times Books.

Perennials. James U. Crockett. Time-Life.

Picture Book of Perennials. Arno and Irene Nehrling. Hearthside.

PESTS AND DISEASES

Diseases and Pests of Ornamental Plants. Pascal P. Pirone. Wiley.

Gardener's Bug Book. Cynthia Westcott. Doubleday.

Handbook on Garden Pests. Brooklyn Botanic Garden.

Pests and Diseases. Time-Life Editors. Time-Life.

Plant Disease Handbook. Cynthia Westcott. Van Nostrand-Reinhold.

PLANT BREEDING

Plant Breeding. Kenneth J. Frey, ed. Iowa State University Press.

Plant Breeding for Pest and Disease Resistance. Gordon E. Russell. Butterworths.

Principles of Plant Breeding. Robert W. Allard. Wiley.

PROPAGATION

Plant Propagation. John P. Mahlstede and E. S. Haber. Wiley.

Plant Propagation in Pictures (Revised Edition). Montague Free and Marjorie J. Dietz. Doubleday.

Plant Propagation Practices. James S. Wells. Macmillan.

Step-By-Step Guide to Plant Propagation. Philip M. Browse. Simon & Schuster.

PRUNING AND BONSAI

Bonsai. Sunset Editors. Lane.

Bonsai, Saikei and Bonkei. Robert L. Behme. Morrow.

How to Prune Almost Everything. John Philip Baumgardt. Morrow.

Japanese Art of Miniature Trees and Landscapes. Yuji Yashimura and Giovanna M. Halford. Tuttle.

Pruning Manual. Edwin F. Steffek. Little, Brown.

Pruning Manual, based on *Bailey's Pruning Manual*. E. P. Christopher. Macmillan.

Pruning Simplified. Lewis Hill. Rodale.

Step-by-Step Guide to Pruning. Christopher Brickell. Simon & Schuster.

Sunset Pruning Handbook. Sunset Editors. Lane.

REGIONAL GARDENING

Florida Gardening Month By Month. Nixon Smiley. University of Miami Press.

Flower Growing in the North: A Month-by-Month Guide. G. E. Luxton. University of Minnesota Press.

Gardening in the Upper Midwest. L. C. Snyder. University of Minnesota Press.

Gardening Round the Year. Margaret T. Wheatly. (Santa Barbara) Woodbridge Press.

Southern California Month-by-Month Flower Gardening Book. Margaret Redfield. Tarcher.

The Southern Garden. Ben Arthur Davis. Mockingbird Books.

Way to Beauty: Planting and Landscaping in the Rocky Mountains. George W. Kelly. Pruett.

RHODODENDRONS AND AZALEAS

Dwarf Rhododendrons. Peter A. Cox. Macmillan.

Rhododendrons and Their Relatives. Brooklyn Botanic Garden.

Rhododendrons in America. Ted Van Veen. Van Veen Nursery, Portland, Oregon.

Rhododendrons of the World. David G. Leach. Scribner's.

ROCK GARDENING

Rock Gardens. Brooklyn Botanic Garden.

Rock Gardens and Water Plants in Color. Francis B. Stark and Conrad B. Link. Doubleday.

ROSES

Anyone Can Grow Roses. Cynthia Westcott. Macmillan.

Complete Book of Miniature Roses. Charles Marden Fitch. Hawthorn.

Modern Roses VII. McFarland Company, Harrisburg, Pennsylvania.

Old Roses. Ethelyn E. Keays. E. M. Coleman.

Peter Malins' Rose Book. Peter Malins and M. M. Graff. Dodd Mead.

Rockwells' Complete Book of Roses. Frederick F. Rockwell and Esther C. Grayson. Doubleday.

Rose Lover's Guide. Roland Browne. Atheneum.

Roses. James U. Crockett. Time-Life.

SHRUBS (See also Trees.)

Dwarf Shrubs. Donald Wyman. Macmillan.

Flowering Shrubs. James U. Crockett. Time-Life.

Guide to Garden Shrubs and Trees. Norman Taylor. Houghton Mifflin.

Nursery Source Guide. Brooklyn Botanic Garden.

Shrub Identification Book. George W. Symonds. Morrow.

Shrubs and Vines for American Gardens. Donald Wyman. Macmillan.

SOILLESS GARDENING

Beginner's Guide to Hydroponics. J. S. Douglas. Drake.

Hydroponic Gardening. R. Bridwell. Woodbridge Press.

Hydroponics. Dudley Harris. David Charles.

The Indoor Water Gardener's How-to Handbook. Peter Loewer. Walker & Company.

SOILS AND FERTILIZERS

Our Soils and Their Management. Roy L. Donahue, et al. Interstate.

Soil Fertility and Fertilizers. Samuel Tisdale and Werner Nelson. Macmillan.

Soils: An Introduction to Soils and Plant Growth. R. L. Donahue, et al. Prentice-Hall.

Soils That Support Us. Charles E. Kellogg. Macmillan.

TERRARIUMS

Complete Book of Terrariums. Charles Marden Fitch. Hawthorn.

Fun with Terrarium Gardening. Virginia and George A. Elbert. Crown.

Gardens in Glass Containers. Robert C. Baur. Hearthside.

Gardens Under Glass. Jack Kramer. Simon & Schuster.

Terrarium Book. Charles Evans and Roberta Pliner. Random House.

Terrariums and Miniature Gardens. Sunset Editors. Lane.

TREES

Evergreen Garden Trees and Shrubs. Denis Hardwicke and Alan R. Toogood. Macmillan.

Flowering Trees. Brooklyn Botanic Garden.

The Gardener's Basic Book of Trees and Shrubs. Stanley Schuler. Simon & Schuster.

Tree Identification Book. George W. Symonds. Morrow.

Tree Maintenance. P. P. Pirone. Oxford University Press.

Trees. James U. Crockett. Time-Life.

Trees for American Gardens. Donald Wyman. Macmillan.

Trees for Architecture and the Landscape. Robert Zion. Van Nostrand-Reinhold.

TULIPS

Book of Tulips. Tom Lodewijk. Viking.

VEGETABLES AND FRUITS

Food-Lover's Garden. Angelo M. Pellegrini. Knopf.

Garden-to-Table Cookbook. James Beard, et al. McGraw-Hill.

Home Vegetable Garden. Brooklyn Botanic Garden.

New Vegetable and Fruit Garden Book. R. Milton Carleton. Regnery.

Vegetables and Fruits. James U. Crockett. Time-Life.

VINES

Shrubs and Vines for American Gardens. Donald Wyman. Macmillan.

Vines. Richard H. Cravens. Time-Life.

WATER GARDENING

Garden Pools, Fountains and Waterfalls. Sunset Editors. Lane.

Gardening With Water, Plantings and Stone. Carroll Calkins. Cornerstone.

Water Gardening Indoors and Out. Reginald Dutta. Crown.

WEEDS

Common Weeds of the United States. U.S.D.A. Research Service. Dover.

Weed Biology and Control. T. J. Muzik. McGraw-Hill.

Weeds. Alexander C. Martin. Western Publishing Company.

Weeds of Lawn and Garden. J. M. Fogg, Jr. University of Pennsylvania Press.

Wild Green Things in the City. Anne O. Dowden. Crowell.

WILDFLOWER PLANTS AND GARDENS

American Wildlife and Plants. Alexander C. Martin, et al. Dover.

Feasting Free on Wild Edibles. Bradford Angier. Stackpole.

Field Guide to Wildflowers. Roger T. Peterson and Margaret McKenny. Houghton Mifflin.

Growing Wild Flowers. Marie Sperka. Harper & Row.

Growing Woodland Plants. Clarence and Eleanor Birdseye. Dover.

Handbook of Wild Flower Cultivation. Kathryn S. Taylor and Stephen F. Hamblin. Macmillan.

Pioneering with Wild Flowers. George D. Aiken. Countryman.

Using Wayside Plants. Nelson Coon. Hearthside.

Wild Flower Gardening. Time-Life Books Editors. Time-Life.

Wildflowers: Perennials for Your Garden. Bebe Miles. Hawthorn.

State Agricultural Experiment Stations

The addresses of state agricultural experiment stations are given below. They, often in cooperation with the U. S. Department of Agriculture, the various state agricultural colleges, and the county Cooperative Extension Service, offer regional gardening advice and publish bulletins, leaflets, and reports that are free or available at small cost. Addresses of the Cooperative Extension Service will be found in your telephone book under the county government. There are Cooperative Extension Service offices in 3,150 county seats. Lists of bulletins and leaflets published exclusively by the U. S. Department of Agriculture can be obtained from the Superintendent of Documents, U. S. Government Printing Office, Washington, D.C. 20402.

Alabama: Auburn, 36830
Alaska: Fairbanks, 99701
Arizona: Tucson, 85721
Arkansas: Fayetteville, 72701
California: Davis, 95616; Parlier, 93648; Riverside, 92502
Colorado: Fort Collins, 80523
Connecticut: Storrs, 06268; New Haven, 06504; Windsor, 06095
Delaware: Newark, 19711
Florida: Gainesville, 32601

Georgia: Athens, 30602; Tifton (Coastal Plain Station), 31794; Experiment, 30212

Guam: Agaro, 96910

Hawaii: Honolulu, 96822

Idaho: Moscow, 83843

Illinois: Urbana, 61801

Indiana: Lafayette, 47907

Iowa: Ames, 50010

Kansas: Manhattan, 66506

Kentucky: Lexington, 40506

Louisiana: Baton Rouge, 70893; Calhoun, 71225

Maine: Orono, 04473; Monmouth, 04259; Presque Isle, 04769

Maryland: College Park, 20742

Massachusetts: Amherst, 01002

Michigan: East Lansing, 48823

Minnesota: St. Paul, 55108

Mississippi: State College, 39762; Poplarville, 39470

Missouri: Columbia, 65201

Montana: Bozeman, 59715

Nebraska: Lincoln, 68503

Nevada: Reno, 89507

New Hampshire: Durham, 03824

New Jersey: New Brunswick, 08903

New Mexico: Las Cruces, 88003

New York: Geneva, 14456; Ithaca, 14850; Highland, 12528

North Carolina: Raleigh, 27607

North Dakota: Fargo, 58102

Ohio: Columbus, 43210; Caldwell, 43724; Ripley, 45167

Oklahoma: Stillwater, 74074

Oregon: Corvallis, 97331

Pennsylvania: University Park, 16802

Puerto Rico: Rio Piedras, 00928

Rhode Island: Kingston, 02881

South Carolina: Clemson, 29631

South Dakota: Brookings, 57006

Tennessee: Knoxville, 37901

Texas: College Station, 77843; Lubbock, 79401

Utah: Logan, 84322

Vermont: Burlington, 05401

Virgin Islands: Kingshill. St. Croix, 00850

Virginia: Blacksburg, 24061

Washington: Pullman, 99163
West Virginia: Morgantown, 26506
Wisconsin: Madison, 53706
Wyoming: Laramie, 82071

Horticultural and Special Plant Societies

African Violet Society of America, Box 1326, Knoxville, Tenn. 37901
American Amaryllis Society Group (see American Plant Life Society)
American Begonia Society, 10692 Bolsa St., Garden Grove, Calif. 92643
American Bonsai Society, 1263 W. 6th St., Erie, Pa. 16505
American Boxwood Society, Box 85, Boyce, Va. 22620
American Camellia Society, Box 1217, Fort Valley, Ga. 31030
American Daffodil Society, Tyner, N.C. 27980
American Dahlia Society, 1649 Beech, Melrose Park, Pa. 19126
American Fern Society, George Mason University, Fairfax, Va. 22030
American Fuchsia Society, Hall of Flowers, 9th Ave. and Lincoln Way, San Francisco, Calif. 94122
American Gloxinia/Gesneriad Society, Box 312, Ayer, Mass. 01432
American Gourd Society, P.O. Box 274, Mt. Gilead, Ohio 43338
American Hemerocallis Society, Rte. 2, Box 360, De Queen, Ark. 71832
American Hibiscus Society, 206 N.E. 40th St., Pompano Beach, Fla. 33064
American Horticultural Society, Mount Vernon, Va. 22121
American Hosta Society, 980 Stanton Ave., Baldwin, N.Y. 11510
American Iris Society, 2315 Tower Grove Ave., St. Louis, Mo. 63110
American Ivy Society, National Center for American Horticulture, Mount Vernon, Va. 22121
American Magnolia Society, 14876 Pheasant Hill Ct., Chesterfield, Mo. 63017
American Orchid Society, 84 Sherman St., Cambridge, Mass. 02140
American Penstemon Society, Box 450, Briarcliff Manor, N.Y. 10510
American Peony Society, 250 Interlachen Rd., Hopkins, Minn. 55343
American Plant Life Society & The American Amaryllis Society Group, Box 150, La Jolla, Calif. 92038
American Primrose Society, G. Fenderson, Grout Hill, Acworth, N.H. 03607

American Rhododendron Society, 617 Fairway Dr., Aberdeen, Wash. 98520

American Rock Garden Society, Rte. 1, Box 282, Mena, Ark. 71953

American Rose Society, Box 30,000, Shreveport, La. 71130

Bamboo Society, 1101 San Leon Ct., Solana Beach, Calif. 92075

Bonsai Clubs International, Box 2098, Sunnyvale, Calif. 94087

Bromeliad Society, Box 41261, Los Angeles, Calif. 90041

Cactus and Succulent Society of America, 2288 Highland Vista Dr., Arcadia, Calif. 91006

California Horticultural Society, California Academy of Sciences, Golden Gate Park, San Francisco, Calif. 94118

Chicago Horticultural Society and Botanic Garden, 18 South Michigan Ave., Chicago, Ill. 60603

Cymbidium Society of America, 1250 Orchid Dr., Santa Barbara, Calif. 93111

Epiphyllum Society of America, P.O. Box 1395, Monrovia, Calif. 91016

Garden Club Federations:

There are three national federations of garden clubs: the Garden Club of America, the National Council of State Garden Clubs, and the Men's Garden Clubs of America. Each is listed here alphabetically, and names of member clubs may be obtained through their offices.

Garden Club of America, 598 Madison Ave., New York, N.Y. 10022

Herb Society of America, 300 Massachusetts Ave., Boston, Mass. 02115

Holly Society of America, 407 Fountain Hill Rd., Bel Air, Md. 21014

Horticultural Society of New York, 128 W. 58th St., New York, N.Y. 10019

Indoor Light Gardening Society of America, 423 Powell Dr., Bay Village, Ohio 44140

International Geranium Society, Dept. AHS, 6501 Yosemite Dr., Buena Park, Calif. 90620

International Lilac Society, Box 315, Rumford, Me. 04276

Marigold Society of America, Box 1776, Stillwell, Ind. 46351

Massachusetts Horticultural Society, 300 Massachusetts Ave., Boston, Mass. 02115

Men's Garden Clubs of America, 5560 Merle Hay Rd., Des Moines, Iowa 50323

National Chrysanthemum Society, B. L. Markham, 2612 Beverly Blvd., S.W., Roanoke, Va. 24015

National Council of State Garden Clubs, 4401 Magnolia Ave., St. Louis, Mo. 63110

National Fuchsia Society, 110 So. F. St., Oxnard, Calif. 93030

National Junior Horticultural Assoc., 384 Colonial Ave., Worthington, Ohio 43085

National Oleander Society, 5127 Avenue 01/2, Galveston, Tex. 77550

North American Gladiolus Council, 30 Highland Place, Peru, Ind. 46970

North American Lily Society, Box 40134, Indianapolis, Ind. 46351

Northern Nut Growers Assoc., 3100 Kane Rd., Aliquippa, Pa. 15001

Palm Society, 1320 S. Venetian Way, Miami, Fla. 33139

Pennsylvania Horticultural Society, 325 Walnut St., Philadelphia, Pa. 19106

Saintpaulia International, Box 549, Knoxville, Tenn. 37901

Southern California Horticultural Institute, P.O. Box 49798, Barrington Sta., Los Angeles, Calif. 90049

Botanical Gardens, Arboreta, and Public Gardens

Arboretum of the Barnes Foundation, 300 Latches Lane, Merion Station, Pa. 19066

Arnold Arboretum, The Arborway, Jamaica Plain, Mass. 02130

Arthur Hoyt Scott Horticultural Foundation, Swarthmore College, Swarthmore, Pa. 19081

Bayard Cutting Arboretum, P.O. Box 66, Montauk Highway, Oakdale, N.Y. 11769

Bellingrath Gardens, Theodore, Ala. 36582

Berkshire Garden Center, Stockbridge, Mass. 01262

Birmingham Botanical Garden, 2612 Lane Park Rd., Birmingham, Ala. 35223

Boerner Botanical Gardens, 5879 South 92nd St., Hales Corners, Wis. 53130

Bowman's Hill State Wildflower Preserve, Washington Crossing State Park, Rte. 32, River Rd., Washington Crossing, Pa. 18977

Boyce Thompson Southwestern Arboretum, P.O. Box AB, Superior, Ariz. 85273

Brookgreen Gardens, Murrels Inlet, S.C. 29576

Brooklyn Botanic Garden, 1000 Washington Ave., Brooklyn, N.Y. 11225

Callaway Gardens, Rte. 27, Pine Mountain, Ga. 31822

Cary Arboretum of the New York Botanical Garden, P.O. Box AB, Millbrook, N.Y. 12545

Colonial Williamsburg Foundation, Drawer C, Williamsburg, Va. 23185

Cornell Plantations, 100 Judd Falls Rd., Ithaca, N.Y. 14853

Dawes Arboretum, Rte. 5, Box 270, Newark, Ohio 43055

Denver Botanic Gardens, 909 York St., Denver, Col. 80206

Descanso Gardens, 1418 Descanso Dr., La Canada, Calif. 91011

Desert Botanical Garden, 1200 Galvin Parkway, P.O. Box 5415, Phoenix, Ariz. 85010

Duke Gardens Foundation, Rte. 206 South, Somerville, N.J. 08876

Dumbarton Oaks, 1703 32nd St., N.W., Washington, D.C. 20007

Fairchild Tropical Garden, 10901 Old Cutler Rd., Miami, Fla. 33156

Florida Cypress Gardens, P.O. Box 1, Cypress Gardens, Fla. 33880

Garfield Park Conservatory, 300 N. Central Park Blvd., Chicago, Ill. 60624

Hammond Museum Oriental Stroll Gardens, Deveau Rd., North Salem, N.Y. 10560

Hershey Rose Gardens and Arboretum, Hershey, Pa. 17033

Highland Park, 375 Westfall Rd., Rochester, N.Y. 14620

Holden Arboretum, 9500 Sperry Rd., Mentor, Ohio 44060

Huntington Botanical Gardens, 1151 Oxford Rd., San Marino, Calif. 91108

Longue Vue Gardens, 7 Bamboo Rd., New Orleans, La. 70124

Longwood Gardens, Kennett Square, Pa. 19348

Los Angeles State and County Arboretum, 301 N. Baldwin Ave., Arcadia, Calif. 91006

Magnolia Gardens, Rte. 4, Charleston, S.C. 29407

Marie Selby Botanical Gardens, 800 S. Palm Ave., Sarasota, Fla. 33577

Middleton Place, Rte. 4, Charleston, S.C. 29407

Missouri Botanical Garden, 2345 Tower Grove Ave., St. Louis, Mo. 63110

Morris Arboretum, 9414 Meadowbrook Ave., Philadelphia, Pa. 19118

Morton Arboretum, Rte. 53, Lisle, Ill. 60532

Mount Vernon Gardens, Mount Vernon, Va. 22121

New York Botanical Garden, Bronx Park, Bronx, N.Y. 10458

Norfolk Botanical Gardens, Airport Rd., Norfolk, Va. 23518

Old Westbury Gardens, P.O. Box 430, Old Westbury Rd., Old Westbury, N.Y. 11568

Pacific Tropical Botanical Garden, P.O. Box 340, Lawai, Kauai, Hawaii 96765

Phipps Conservatory, Schenley Park, Pittsburgh, Pa. 15213

Planting Fields Arboretum, P.O. Box 58, Planting Fields Rd., Oyster Bay, N.Y. 11771

Queens Botanical Garden, 43-50 Main St., Flushing, N.Y. 11355

Rancho Santa Ana Botanic Garden, 1500 N. College Ave., Claremont, Calif. 91711

Strybing Arboretum and Botanical Gardens, Golden Gate Park, San Francisco, Calif. 94122

Swiss Pines, Charlestown Rd., R.D. 1, P.O. Box 127, Malvern, Pa. 19355

U.S. National Arboretum, 24th & R Sts., N.E., Washington, D.C. 20002

University of Washington Arboretum, Seattle, Wash. 98195

Wave Hill, 675 W. 252 St., Bronx, N.Y. 10471

Winterthur Gardens, Rte. 52, Winterthur, Del. 19735

Some Sources for Plants and Seeds

ANNUALS (General)

Burpee Seed Co., Warminster, Pa. 18991; Clinton, Iowa 52732; Riverside, Calif. 92502

Henry Field Seed & Nursery Co., 407 Sycamore St., Shenandoah, Iowa 51602

Gurney Seed & Nursery Co., 2nd & Capitol, Yankton, S.D. 57079

Joseph Harris Co., Inc., Moreton Farm, Rochester, N.Y. 14624

Herbst Brothers, Seedsmen, Inc., 1000 N. Main St., Brewster, N.Y. 10509

J. W. Jung Seed Co., Randolph, Wis. 53956

Earl May Seed & Nursery Co., Shenandoah, Iowa 51603

Olds Seed Co., Box 7790, Madison, Wis. 53707

George W. Park Seed Co., Inc., Greenwood, S.C. 29647

R. H. Shumway, Rockford, Ill. 61101

Thompson & Morgan Inc., P.O. Box 100, Farmingdale, N.J. 07727

Otis S. Twilley Seed Co., Inc., P.O. Box 65, Trevose, Pa. 19047

World Seed Service, J. L. Hudson, Seedsman, Box 1058, Redwood City, Calif. 94064

ANNUALS (British Sources)

Samuel Dobie & Sons Ltd., Llangollen, North Wales, England
Suttons Seeds Ltd., Hele Rd., Torquay, Devon, TQ2 7Q5 England
Thompson & Morgan Ltd., London Rd., Ipswich, IP2, OBA, England

BULBS

Antonelli Brothers, 2545 Capitola Rd., Santa Cruz, Calif. 95062
Burpee Seed Co., Warminster, Pa. 18991; Clinton, Iowa 52732; Riverside, Calif. 92502
Connell's Dahlias, 10216 40th Ave. East, Tacoma, Wash. 98446
De Jager Bulbs, Inc., 188 Asbury St., South Hamilton, Mass. 01982
International Growers Exchange, Box 397-N, Farmington, Mich. 48024 (perennials)
John Messelaar Bulb Co., Box 269, Ipswich, Mass. 01938
Rex Bulb Farms, Box 774, Port Townsend, Wash. 98368
John Scheepers Inc., 63 Wall St., New York, N.Y. 10005
Van Bourgondien Brothers, 245 Farmingdale Rd., P.O. Box A, Babylon, N.Y. 11702
Wayside Gardens Co., Hodges, S.C. 29695
White Flower Farm, Litchfield, Conn. 06759

FRUITS

Alexander's Nurseries, 1225 Wareham St., Middleboro, Mass. 02346 (blueberries)
W. F. Allen Co., Berry Lane, P.O. Box 1577, Salisbury, Md. 21801 (strawberry, blueberry, raspberry, and blackberry plants, grapevines, asparagus)
Brittingham Plant Farms, Dept. 7, Salisbury, Md. 21801 (strawberries, blueberries, raspberries, grapes, blackberries)
Burpee Seed Co., Warminster, Pa. 18991; Clinton, Iowa 52732; Riverside, Calif. 92502 (general)
The Conner Co., Inc., P.O. Box 534, Augusta, Ark. 72006 (strawberries)
Farmer Seed & Nursery Co., 818 N.W. 4th St., Faribault, Minn. 55021 (general)
Henry Field Seed & Nursery Co., 407 Sycamore St., Shenandoah, Iowa 51602 (general)
Dean Foster Nurseries, Hartford, Mich. 49057 (general)
Gurney Seed & Nursery Co., 2nd & Capitol, Yankton, S.D. 57079 (general)

Inter-State Nurseries, 1423 E. St., Hamburg, Iowa 51644 (general)

Kelly Bros. Nurseries, Inc., Dansville, N.Y. 14437 (general)

Henry Leuthardt, Montauk Hwy., East Moriches, N.Y. 11940 (dwarf and semidwarf, espaliers)

J. E. Miller Nurseries, West Lake Rd., Canandaigua, N.Y. 14424 (general)

Rayner Bros., Inc., P.O. Box 1617, Salisbury, Md. 21801 (strawberries, blueberries, raspberries, grapes, asparagus roots)

Shasta Nursery, Inc., 165 Logan St., Watsonville, Calif. 95076 (strawberry plants)

Dave Wilson Nursery, Hughson, Calif. 95326 (dwarf, general)

HERBS

(Seeds are listed in most general seed catalogs. Plants may often be found in local garden centers. A few specialists are listed below.)

Comstock, Ferre and Co., Box 125, Wethersfield, Conn. 06109 (seeds)

Greene Herb Gardens, Greene, R.I. 02827 (enclose self-addressed, stamped envelope)

Merry Gardens, Camden, Me. 04843 (plants)

Nichols Garden Nursery, 1190 N. Pacific Hwy., Albany, Oreg. 97321

Tool Shed Herb Farm, Turkey Hill Rd., Salem Center, Purdy Station, N.Y. 10578

INDOOR PLANTS (House and Greenhouse)

Alberts & Merkel Bros., 2210 S. Federal Hwy., Boynton Beach, Fla. 33435 (orchids, bromeliads, foliage plants)

Arthur Eames Allgrove, Wilmington, Mass. 01887 (terrarium plants)

Antonelli Brothers, 2545 Capitola Rd., Santa Cruz, Calif. 95062 (tuberous begonias, dahlias, and others)

Buell's Greenhouses, P.O. Box 218DO, Weeks Rd., Eastford, Conn. 06242 (African-violets, gloxinias, gesneriads; also seeds)

Edelweiss Gardens, 54 Robb Allentown Rd., Robbinsville, N.J. 08691 (terrarium plants, orchids, ferns, begonias, and bromeliads)

Fennell Orchid Co., 26719 S.W. 157 Ave., Homestead, Fla. 33031 (orchids, bromeliads, ferns, rare tropical house plants, along with complete growing instructions)

Finck Floral Co., 9849 Kimker Lane, St. Louis, Mo. 63127 (orchids)

Fischer Greenhouses, Oak Ave., Linwood, N.J. 08221 (African-violets and related plants)

International Growers Exchange, Box 397-N, Farmington, Mich. 48024 (general)

Jones & Scully Inc., 2200 N.W. 33rd Ave., Miami, Fla. 33142 (orchids)

Kartuz Greenhouses, Inc., 1408 Sunset Dr., Vista, Calif. 92083 (gloxinias, African-violets, begonias)

Logee's Greenhouses, 55 North St., Danielson, Conn. 06239 (begonias, rare plants, geraniums, herbs)

Lyndon Lyon Greenhouses, Inc., Dolgeville, N.Y. 13329 (African-violets, miniature roses, and house plants)

Matsu Bonsai Nursery, Livingston Manor, N.Y. 12758 (bonsai plants, tools, and containers)

Rod McLellan Co., 1450 El Camino Real, South San Francisco, Calif. 94080 (orchids)

Merry Gardens, Camden, Me. 04843 (geraniums, ivy, fuchsia, and many others)

George W. Park Seed Co. Inc., Greenwood, S.C. 29647 (plants, seeds, lights, and materials)

John Scheepers Inc., 37 Wall St., New York, N.Y. 10005 (mostly bulbs)

The House Plant Corner Ltd., Box 617, Kennett Square, Pa. 19348

Ed and Mildred Thompson, P.O. Drawer PP, Southampton, N.Y. 11968 (begonias)

Tinari Greenhouses, 2325 Valley Rd., Box 190, Huntingdon Valley, Pa. 19006 (African-violets)

Volkmann Bros. Greenhouses, 2714 Minert St., Dallas, Tex. 75219 (African-violets)

Wayside Gardens Co., Hodges, S.C. 29695 (bulbs)

Wilson Bros. Floral Co. Inc., Roachdale, Ind. 46172 (geraniums and others)

PERENNIALS (General)

Bluestone Perennials, 7231 Middle Ridge, Madison, Ohio 44057

Burpee Seed Co., Warminster, Pa. 18991; Clinton, Iowa 52732; Riverside, Calif. 92502 (seeds)

Inter-State Nurseries, 1423 E. St., Hamburg, Iowa 51644

Lamb Nurseries, E. 101 Sharp Ave., Spokane, Wash. 99202

George W. Park Seed Co. Inc., Greenwood, S.C. 29647 (seeds)

Spring Hill Nurseries, Reservation Center, P.O. Box 1758, Peoria, Ill. 61656

Wayside Gardens Co., Hodges, S.C. 29695
White Flower Farm, Litchfield, Conn. 06759

PERENNIALS (Specialists)

Cooley's Gardens, P.O. Box 126, Silverton, Oreg. 97381 (iris)
Eden Road Iris Garden, P.O. Box 117, Wenatchee, Wash. 98801 (iris)
Far North Gardens, 15621 Auburndale Ave., Livonia, Mich. 48154 (primroses)
Huff's Garden Mums, Box 187, Burlington, Kan. 66839 (chrysanthemums)
Klehm Nursery, 2 E. Algonquin Rd., Arlington Heights, Ill. 60005 (peonies)
Melrose Gardens, 309 Best Road S., Stockton, Calif. 95205 (iris, daylilies, daffodils)
Oakhill Gardens, 1960 Cherry Knoll Rd., Dallas, Oreg. 97338 (sedums and sempervivums)
Savory's Greenhouses, 5300 Whiting Ave., Edina, Minn. 55435 (hosta)
Schreiner's Gardens, 3625 Quinaby Rd., N.E., Salem, Oreg. 97303 (iris)
Louis Smirnow & Son, 85 Linden Lane, Glen Head, P.O. Brookville, N.Y. 11545 (peonies)
Gilbert H. Wild & Son, Sarcoxie, Mo. 64862 (iris, peonies, day-lilies)

ROSES

Armstrong Nurseries Inc., 1239 S. Palmetto, Ontario, Calif. 91761
Inter-State Nurseries, 1423 E. St., Hamburg, Iowa 51644
Jackson & Perkins Co., Medford, Oreg. 97501
Roses of Yesterday & Today, 802 Brown's Valley Rd., Watsonville, Calif. 95076
Wyant Roses, Inc., 200 Johnny Cake Ridge, Mentor, Ohio 44060 (old and new)

TREES, SHRUBS, AND VINES (General)

Burgess Seed & Plant Co., Bloomington, Ill. 61701
Farmer Seed & Nursery Co., 818 N.W. 4th St., Faribault, Minn. 55021
Earl Ferris Nursery, 811 4th St., N.E., Hampton, Iowa 50441
Henry Field Seed & Nursery Co., 407 Sycamore St., Shenandoah, Iowa 51602
Girard Nurseries, P.O. Box 428, Geneva, Ohio 44041
Gurney Seed & Nursery Co., 2nd & Capitol, Yankton, S.D. 57079

H. G. Hastings Co., Box 4274, Atlanta, Ga. 30302
Inter-State Nurseries, 1423 E. St., Hamburg, Iowa 51644
Kelly Bros. Nurseries, Inc., Dansville, N.Y. 14437
Mellinger's, 2310 West South Range Rd., North Lima, Ohio 44452
Musser Forests, Inc., Box 340, Indiana, Pa. 15701
Wayside Gardens Co., Hodges, S.C. 29695
Western Maine Forest Nursery Co., Fryeburg, Me. 04037
White Flower Farm, Litchfield, Conn. 06759

TREES, SHRUBS, AND VINES (Specialists)

Alexander's Nurseries, 1225 Wareham St., Middleboro, Mass. 02346 (lilacs)

Armstrong Nurseries Inc., 1265 S. Palmetto, Ontario, Calif. 91761 (deciduous fruit and shade trees)

Baldsiefen Nursery, Box 88, Bellvale, N.Y. 10912 (rhododendrons and azaleas)

California Nursery Co., Box 2278, Fremont, Calif. 94536 (fruit and nut trees, grapevines)

D. S. George Nurseries, 2491 Penfield Rd., Fairport, N.Y. 14450 (clematis; mostly wholesale)

Nuccio's Nurseries, 3555 Chaney Trail, Altadena, Calif. 91001 (camellias and azaleas)

Orinda Nursery, Bridgeville, Del. 19933 (camellias and rhododendrons)

A. Shammarello & Son Nursery, 4508 Monticello Blvd., South Euclid, Ohio 44143 (rhododendrons and azaleas)

VEGETABLES

Burgess Seed & Plant Co., Bloomington, Ill. 61701
Burpee Seed Co., Warminster, Pa. 18991; Clinton, Iowa 52732; Riverside, Calif. 92502
Comstock, Ferre and Co., Box 125, Wethersfield, Conn. 06109
DeGiorgi Co., Inc., P.O. Box 413, Council Bluffs, Iowa 51502
Farmer Seed & Nursery Co., 818 N.W. 4th St., Faribault, Minn. 55021
Henry Field Seed & Nursery Co., 407 Sycamore St., Shenandoah, Iowa 51602
Gurney Seed & Nursery Co., 2nd & Capitol, Yankton, S.D. 57079
Joseph Harris Co. Inc., Moreton Farm, Rochester, N.Y. 14624
Johnny's Selected Seeds, Albion, Me. 04910
J. W. Jung Seed Co., Randolph, Wisc. 53956

Earl May Seed & Nursery Co., Shenandoah, Iowa 51603
Nichols Garden Nursery, 1198 Pacific, Albany, Oreg. 97321
Olds Seed Co., Box 7790, Madison, Wisc. 53707
George W. Park Seed Co. Inc., Greenwood, S.C. 29646
R. H. Shumway, Rockford, Ill. 61101
Stokes Seeds Inc., 737 Main St., Box 548, Buffalo, N.Y. 14240
Thompson & Morgan Inc., P.O. Box 100, Farmingdale, N.J. 07727

VEGETABLES (British Sources)

Samuel Dobie & Sons Ltd., Llangollen, North Wales, England
Suttons Seeds Ltd., Hele Rd., Torquay, Devon, TQ2 7Q5 England
Thompson & Morgan Ltd., London Rd., Ipswich, IP2, OBA, England

WATER-LILIES

Lilypons Water Gardens, 10000 Garden Rd., Lilypons, Md. 21717;
   839Q FM 1489, Brookshire, Texas 77423
Paradise Gardens, Bedford and May Sts., Whitman, Mass. 02382
Slocum Water Gardens, 1101 Cypress Gardens Rd., Winter Haven, Fla.
   33880
William Tricker Inc., Box 398, Saddle River, N.J. 07458; Box 7843,
   Independence, Ohio 44131
Van Ness Water Gardens, 2460 North Euclid, Upland, Calif. 91786

WILDFLOWERS

Gardens of The Blue Ridge, Box 10, Pineola, N.C. 28662
Putney Nursery, Putney, Vt. 05346
Siskiyou Rare Plants Nursery, 2825 Cummings Rd., Medford, Oreg.
   97501 (plants only, for alpine, rock, or woodland gardens)

Index

Phosphorus, 13, 49, 777; effect on plant growth, 47

Phosphorus deficiency, 49

Photinia, 1263

Photosynthesis, 14

pH scale, 10

Phyllophaga, 1174

Phylloxera, 904

Pick-a-back (*Tolmiea*), 1078–79

Picket fence, 107, 109

Pickles, 1298

Pie-plant, *see* Rhubarb

Pieris (*Andromeda*), 37, 39, 430–31, 1263

Pieris japonica, 431

Pinching, 242–43

Pinching back, 665

Pine, 37, 398, 407–9, 1231; pest control, 1263–65; soil around, 30; white, 408, 446, 1264

Pineapple (*Ananas*), 1078–79

Pineapple-guava (*F. sellowiana*), 1361

Pine bark, 115–16

Pine beetle, 1264

Pine mice, 467

Pine needles, 45, 53, 67; mulching with, 234

Pink dogwood, 343–44

Pink hawthorn, 206

Pink hydrangea, 373

Pink lady's-slipper (*C. acaule*), 181

Pinks, 167, 596, 597, 672

Pinkshell (*R. vaseyi*), 359

Pin oak, 14, 337

Pinxterbloom (*R. nudiflorum*), 358, 359

Pipsissewa (*C. umbellata*), 183

Pissard (or purpleleaf) plum, 350

Pistachio, 996

Pitcher plant (*S. purpurea*), 173, 182

Pit house, sun-heated, 274

Plane, *see* Sycamore

Planning and landscaping, 85–191; to attract birds, 184; banks, 104–5; bonsai, 185; books on, 1439; children's gardens, 183–84; container gardens, 185–87; design principles, 91–96; driveways, 111–13; entrances, 96–100; espaliers, 110–11; fences, gates, and walls, 106–10; foundation, 88–89, 96–100; fragrant gardens, 187; game areas, 128–30; garden features and accessories, 131–33; garden lighting, 121; herbs, 133–54; influences on, 85–86; lawns, 106; outdoors, 86–87; on paper, 87; paths and walks, 114–16; patio or terrace, 89–90, 116–21; pools and water gardens, 121–28; for privacy and comfort, 92; recreation areas, 90–91; rock gardens, 154–69; roof gardens, 187–89; screening, 100–1; shade, 102–4; sun deck, 90; sunken gardens, 189; surface drainage, 105–6; tool houses and utility areas, 130–31; trees and shrubs, 87–88, 101–2; wildflower gardens, 169–83; window-box, 190–91

Plantain, 743, 1334, 1337

Plant breeding, books on, 1440

Plant food, *see* Fertilizers; Manure

Plant injury, how to diagnose, 1140

Plant lice, *see* Aphids; Lice

Plant nutrition, *see* Nutrients

Plant room, compared to a greenhouse, 1021

Plant societies, list of, 1446–48

Plastic molded pools, 122–23

Plastic pots, 1012

Plowing, soil, 31–32

Plugs (biscuits of sod), 722

Plum, 38, 350, 943–44, 1265, 1311, 1325, 1326–27, 1429; age to plant, 908; European, 902; productive life of, 915; rootstocks, 904; seeds, 919; varieties of, 902

Plumbago (leadwort), 644–45

Plum curculio, 900, 1318, 1323